Find Public Records Fast

The Complete State, County, and Courthouse Locator

©1998 By Facts on Demand Press
4653 South Lakeshore Drive, Suite 3
Tempe, AZ 85282
(800) 929-3764
Fax (800) 929-4981
www.brbpub.com

Find Public Records Fast

The Complete State, County, and Courthouse Locator!

©1998 By Facts on Demand Press
4653 South Lakeshore Drive, Suite 3
Tempe, AZ 85282
(800) 929-3811

ISBN 1-889150-04-5

Edited by: Michael Sankey & Carl R. Ernst
Cover Design by Robin Fox & Associates

Cataloging-in-Publication Data

353   **Sankey, Michael L., 1949-**
SAN   Find public records fast : the complete state, county and courthouse locator /
       [edited by: Michael L Sankey & Carl R. Ernst]. - Rev. ed. Tempe, Ariz. : Facts
       on Demand Press, © 1998.
           528 p. ; 7 x 10 in.
           Summary: A national directory to over 11,500 major federal, state and
       county public record locations.
           ISBN 1-889150-04-5
           1. Public Records - United States - Directories I. Ernst, Carl. R. II. Title

                                                   353_dc20

Table of Contents

Introduction

Are you interested or involved in— 1
The Information Paper Trail 1
Privacy Issues are Hot 2

What Are Public Records Anyway?

How Do Public Records Help Me? 5
Defining Some Information Terms..6
Where Public Records are Maintained 7

Public Record & Public Information Categories

Descriptions of 23 Categories...7

Public Record Searching

How to Search 15
Fees, Charges, and Usage 16
Public Records Online..16

Searching for Court Records

First...Some Court Basics 18
Types of Litigation in Trial Courts..18
State Court Structure 19
Locating the Right County Court to Search 19
Locating the Right Documents 20
Federal Court Structure 20
How Federal Trial Courts Are Organized 21
Record Keeping in the Federal Courts 22

Nationwide Programs for Electronic Access 23
Regional Records Services Facilitys and the National Archives 24

Searching for Real Estate, UCC, and Other County Records

The County Rule 25
  The Exceptions 25
  The Personal Property Problem and the Fifth Exception 25
The County Rule State Specifics Table 26

Searching for State Public Records

A Word or Two about the Internet 28

State Profiles

Alabama—Wyoming 29

State Agency Public Record Restrictions Table

Eleven Categories Analyzed for Access 518

The Appeals and Regional Records Services Facility Locator 520

US Appeals Courts & Regional Records Services Facility Addresses & Phone Numbers 522

Introduction

Are you interested or involved in—

☑ **Finding a Missing Person?**   A missing relative, friend, classmate or perhaps someone who owes you money.

☑ **Locating Asset or Financial Information?**   Determining if someone or some entity is a good credit risk; if there are assets and if they are for real; if there are undisclosed liens.

☑ **Checking the Background of an Individual?**   Hiring an employee; evaluating a future business partner, client or professional; checking on a future spouse.

☑ **Checking the Background of a Business?**   Entering into a contract; going into a strategic alliance; investing in a company.

—Then you need this book!

 ## The Information Paper Trail

It's no secret that our society has become extremely dependent on information. Government and private industry require record keeping to regulate, license or hire. Individuals and entities create a **paper trail of information** that is a **history of daily life**. You could say that the trail starts with a birth certificate, a Social Security Number or articles of incorporation. There are many records—some accessible, some not—that create an identity.

We are going to examine these paper trails—where they exist, when they affect your life, and how you can use them to your benefit.

This is not a simple process. *Find Public Records Fast* is organized to help you work your way through the maze and mysteries of public records. It will probe public records in general, analyze the record types and categories, their applications and uses, and tell you how to search effectively. The state-by-state exploration of record locations that follow will lead you to where records are kept, access requirements, and searching hints. With the information contained in these pages, **you can use the facts and knowledge not only to access the information you need, but also to find your own paper trail!**

Privacy Issues Are Hot

Consider what has happened just in the 6 months prior to the printing of this book—

- The Federal Trade Commission (FTC) has made major changes in the Fair Credit Reporting Act effective 9/30/97.

- South Carolina and Oklahoma challenged (in federal court) the constitutionality of the Driver's Privacy Protection Act and WON.

- The FTC is conducting a "Computer Data Base Study" regarding privacy and the use of Social Security Numbers.

- 10 of the nations' largest providers of personal information formed the "Individual Reference Service Group (IRSG)" to establish a code of professional conduct and to police the industry, among other goals.

- The Personal Information Privacy Act was introduced in the US Senate.

The privacy issue has two distinct schools of thought doing battle on various playing fields, and is a book in itself. We are not going to address what should or should not be, but rather what is or is not. The pages in the following chapter do give a descriptive overview to what are public records, public information, and personal information.

 Editor's Note

 We do recommend reading the chapters in the front of this book. They will greatly help you in effectively finding the information you need *FAST*!

What Are Public Records Anyway?

 Public Records Unveiled

The words "Public Records" often convey a complex, almost mysterious source of information that is perceived as inaccessible, difficult to find and likely to be of interest only to private investigators and reporters. This view could not be further from the *truth*!

Indeed, the use of public records is one of the fundamental pillars of our democratic society.

Have you ever—

- ☑ applied for a job?
- ☑ purchased a home or a vehicle?
- ☑ applied for a credit card?
- ☑ looked into your "family tree?"
- ☑ or renewed your driver's license?

If so, **you** have become part of the "public record information food chain!"

Definition of public records

The strict **definition** of **public records** is—

"Those records maintained by government agencies that are open without restriction to public inspection, either by statute or by tradition."

If access to a record held by a government agency is restricted in some way, it is not a public record.

Adding to the mystique of government records is the accessibility paradox. For example, in some states a specific category of records is severely restricted and records are consequently are not public, while the very same category of records may be 100% open in other states. (Among these categories are criminal histories, vehicle ownership records and worker's compensation records.)

How Do Public Records Help Me?

Let's start with a few basic examples of benefits to public record searching.

For your family and friends	<ul><li>knowing your child's teacher is/is not a child molester;</li><li>assuring your spouse or ex-spouse is/is not hiding assets;</li><li>finding that a long lost friend is alive and well.</li></ul>
For your business	<ul><li>knowing a prospective employee is/is not lying on a resume;</li><li>finding out whether a possible business partner is who he says he is;</li><li>knowing a new client is not a deadbeat and will pay its bills.</li></ul>
For your community	<ul><li>knowing that a bus driver does/does not have a series of DUIs;</li><li>knowing that a public official is not a convicted felon;</li><li>knowing that 911 and the fire department know where you live.</li></ul>

Public records are meant to be used for the benefit of society. You are the public, whether you are a business owner, a reporter, an investigator, a father trying to check on your daughter's first date or riding a bus on a public transit system. You or someone in authority is entitled to review government information.

The goal of this book is to not only make you aware of how to use public records, but also to direct you to the correct source.

Defining Some Information Terms

Before reading further, let's define types of records held by government or by private industry. Of course, not all information about a company or individual is public. The boundaries between public and private information are not well understood, and are these boundaries undergoing intense scrutiny lately. Here is an introduction to the subject from a viewpoint of a professional record searcher.

Public Record	Public records are records of **incidents** or **actions** filed or recorded with a government agency for the purpose of notifying others about the matter - the "public." The **deed** to your house recorded at the county recorder's office is a public record—it is a legal requirement that you record it with the county recorder. Anyone requiring details about your property may review or copy the documents.
Public Information	Your **telephone listing** in the phone book is public information; that is, you freely furnished the information to ease the flow of commercial and private communications.
Personal Information	Any information about a person or business that the person or business might consider private and confidential in nature such as, your **social security number**, is personal information. Such information will remain private to a limited extent unless it is disclosed to some outside entity that could make it public. **Personal information may be found in either public records or in public information.**

Many people confuse these three categories, lump them into one, and wonder how "big brother" accumulated so much information about them. These distinctions are important. The fact is that **much of this information is given willingly**. There are two ways that personal information can enter the public domain—statutory and voluntary. In a **voluntary** transaction, you **share** personal information of your own free will. In a **statutory** transaction, you **disclose** personal information because the law requires you to.

The confusion of terms used today feeds the increasing conflict between privacy advocates and commercial interests. This, in turn, is driving legislation towards more and more **restrictions** on the **dissemination of personal information**—the same personal information which, in fact, is willingly shared by most people and companies in order to participate in our market economy.

Where Public Records are Maintained

There are two places you can find public records—

- at a government agency;
- within the database of a private company.

Government agencies keep or maintain records in a variety of ways. While many state agencies and highly populated county agencies are computerized, many still use microfiche, microfilm, and paper storage of files and indexes. Agencies that have converted to computer will not necessarily place complete file records on their system; they are more apt to include only an index, pointer or summary data to the files.

Private enterprises develop their databases in one of two ways: they buy the records in bulk from government agencies; or they send personnel to the agencies and compile this information by using a copy machine or keying into a laptop computer. The database is then available for internal use or for resale purposes. An example of such a company is *Superior Information Services* (800 848-0489). Superior maintains a very comprehensive database of civil judgments, tax liens, Uniform Commercial Code filings and bankruptcy data for the mid-Atlantic states.

Public Record & Public Information Categories

The following are the categories which fall into the definition of public records or public information. Although these categories are not necessarily the only ones in use, they are comprehensive enough so everyone can use a common vocabulary. There are, of course, more general ways to categorize this information, such as vehicle records and court records. However, those generalizations tend to mask important variations in how certain type of records are subjected to access restrictions.

In considering these summaries, keep the following points in mind:

- Very little of what you may perceive as government record information is truly open to the general public. Even the seemingly most harmless information is subject to restrictions somewhere in the US; and on the other hand even what you may think of as highly confidential information is likely public information somewhere.

- Just because your state or county has certain rules, regulations and practices regarding the accessibility and content of public records, this does not mean that any other state or county has the same rules.

Addresses & Telephone Numbers

—*Basic locator information about a person or organization.*

This is a category of information that may be obtained from both government and private sources. Even though you have an unlisted telephone number, anyone can still find you if you have listed your number on, for example, a voter registration card or magazine subscription form.

The most elementary of public information categories, addresses and telephone numbers are no longer considered unrestricted information by some people.

Bankruptcy

—*Case information about people and businesses that have filed for protection under the bankruptcy laws of the United States.*

Only federal courts handle bankruptcy cases. Some private companies compile databases with names and dates.

Many types of financial records maintained by government agencies are considered public records; bankruptcy records, unlike some other court records, are in this class of fully open court records.

Corporate & Trade Names

—Registration information about corporations and other business entities.

Each state maintains basic information about businesses which register with them for the purpose of making their business name public and protecting its uniqueness. As in most other categories, private companies will compile and offer such a database for resale.

The amount of information collected by government agencies varies widely from state to state. Much, but not all, of the information collected by government agencies during this process is open to public inspection. For example, annual reports are not available in some states, yet are available for a fee in others.

Credit Information

—Records derived from financial transactions of people or businesses.

Private companies maintain this information; government only regulates access.

Availability of certain credit information about individuals is restricted by law, such as the Fair Credit Reporting Act, at the federal level and by even more restrictive laws in many states. Credit information about businesses is not restricted by law and is fully open to anyone who requests (pays for) it.

Criminal Information

—Information about criminal activities, primarily originating from court records.

Criminal records can be found in state databases and at the local county courthouse. The federal database (NCIC) is not open to the public. Very few private companies purchase local records to create databases for resale.

This category of information has probably the most diverse treatment of all the categories of public record. All states maintain some type of central database of information about arrest and criminal court activity. 14 states consider this information open public record, while 10 states consider it closed. The remaining 28 states impose various types of restrictions on access to the information. In most states, criminal court information is openly accessible from the local court where the arraignments, preliminary hearings and trials took place. One open source of information about criminal activities is the newspaper, freely and openly accessible in any public library and searchable online through various services.

Driver & Vehicle

—Information about licensed drivers and registered motor vehicles of all types.

The states maintain records of drivers, vehicle registrations, and vehicle owners. Some private companies buy records from permitting states and offer commercial access to name, address and vehicle data.

Driver history, accident reports, and vehicle information, which traditionally have been open public record in most states, were the subject of recent federal legislation. The Drivers Privacy Protection Act (DPPA) requires each state to impose at least a minimum set of restrictions on access to that information.

Education & Employment

—Information about an individual's schooling, training, education, and jobs.

The learning institutions maintain their own records of attendance, completion and degree/certification granted. Employers will confirm certain information about former employees.

This is an example of private information that becomes public by voluntary disclosure. As part of your credit record, this information would be considered restricted. If, however, you disclose this information to Who's Who, or to a credit card company, it becomes public information.

Environmental

—Information about hazards to the environment.

There is little tradition and less law regarding how open or restricted information is at the state and local (recorder's office) levels.

Most information about hazardous materials, soil composition, and even OSHA inspection reports is in fact public record.

Legislation & Regulations

—Laws and regulations at all levels of government

The state legislative branches make this information available, although older records are harder to find. Some private companies market regulatory books and CD-ROMs.

This information is always open public record.

Licenses, Registrations & Permits

—Registration of individuals and businesses with government agencies related to specific professions, businesses, or activities.

Basic information about registrants, including address and status, is generally public record from state agencies and licensing boards. However, keep in mind some boards do not consider that their data should be open to the public.

There is significant variation in the extent of information that each state or local agency will disclose from a particular record.

Litigation & Civil Judgments

—Information about civil litigation in municipal, state or federal courts.

Actions under federal laws are found at US District Courts. Actions under state laws are found within the state court system at the county level. Municipalities also have courts. Litigation and judgment information is often collected by commercial database vendors.

The traditional general rule is that what goes on in a courtroom is public record. However, in fact, there are some types of court proceedings, such as juvenile cases, that are closed, and judges may close or seal any portion of any case record at their discretion.

Medical

—Information about an individual's medical status and history.

Medical records are summarized in various repositories which are accessible only to authorized insurance and other private company employees.

Medical information is neither public information nor closed record. Like credit information, it is not meant to be shared with anyone, unless you give authorization.

Military Service

—Information about individuals who are or were in military service.

Each branch maintains its own records. Much of this, such as years of service and rank, is open public record. However, some details in the file of an individual may be subject to restrictions on access—approval by the subject may be required.

Real Estate & Assessor

—Information about the ownership, transfer, value and mortgaging of real property.

The county (or parish) recorder's office is the source. However, many private companies purchase entire county records and create their own database for commercial purposes.

Traditionally, real estate records are public so that everyone can know who owns what property. Liens on real estate must be public record so a buyer knows all the facts.

SEC & Other Financial Data

—Information on publicly and privately held businesses.

The Securities and Exchange Commission is the public repository for information about publicly held companies, which are required to share their material facts with existing and prospective stockholders.

Private companies, on the other hand, are not subject to public scrutiny, so their financial information is public information only to the extent that the company itself decides to disclose information.

Social Security Numbers

—The most extensively used individual identifier in the US.

There is a persistent myth that a Social Security Number is private information. The truth is individuals gave up the privacy of that number by writing it on a voter registration form, using it a driver's license number, or any of a myriad of other voluntary disclosures made over the years. It is probable that one can find the Social Security Number of anyone (along with at least an approximate birth date) with ease.

Tax & Other Involuntary Liens

—Liens filed by the government and others against individuals and businesses without their consent.

Liens are filed, according to the state law, either at a state agency or county recorder's office. Some states require filing at both locations.

Mortgages and UCC liens are voluntary liens accepted by a borrower in order to obtain financing. Involuntary liens, on the other hand, are ones that arise by action of law against a person or business which owes a debt that would otherwise be unsecured. The federal and state governments file tax liens when there is a failure to pay income or withholding taxes. A contractor can file a mechanics lien to get first in line to receive payment for materials used on a job.

Tenant

—*History information about people who rent.*

This, like credit history, is another example of a combination of public and proprietary information collected by private businesses for the purpose of tracking an element of personal life important to an industry, in this case the housing rental industry.

These records are shared throughout the industry on a restricted basis according to disclosure rules set by the companies themselves.

Trademarks,
Patents,
&
Copyrights

—*Protection of intellectual property and proprietary ideas.*

The state agency controlling trademarks and service marks is generally at the same location as corporate records. The Lanham Act provides for a trademark registration system by the federal government. The federal government controls copyrights and patents. There are several private companies who maintain searchable databases of trademarks, service marks, and patents.

The filing for public review of trademarks and patents is designed to protect these assets from copying.

Uniform
Commercial
Code

—*Transactions that are secured by personal property.*

As with tax liens, UCC recordings are filed, according to the state law, either at the state or county level. Some states require dual filing. There are a number of private companies who have created their own databases for commercial resale.

UCC filings are to personal property what mortgages are to real property. They are in the category of financial records that must be fully open to public scrutiny so that other potential lenders are on notice about which assets of the borrower have been pledged.

Vital
Records

—*Birth, death, marriage and divorce information.*

Most states have developed central repositories for each of these four types of vital records. In some states divorce records are maintained at the county, but the state maintains a searchable index.

State regulations vary regarding which of these four types of records are public and which are subject to restrictions. States impose approval or use restrictions similar to those imposed by schools on access to transcript information.

Voter
Registration

—Information on the application to become a registered voter.

Voter registration applications are maintained on the local level. They are, generally, a public record accessible by anyone. This makes them an important source, for instance, of the real signature of a person or of an unlisted telephone number. At the state level, many states aggregate the local information into a central database.

Access to many of the state-held databases is restricted to non-commercial use. However, more than half the states have set no restrictions on the use of voter registration records, including information gathered that otherwise would be considered private, such as a Social Security Number or unlisted telephone number.

Worker's
Compensation
Records

—Work related injury claims and case history.

Each state has a board or commission responsible for these records.

Access to this information is generally restricted to those who have a direct interest in the case. Only nine states consider their workers compensation records to be open public record.

Remember the first rule of public record searching—

> "Just because records are maintained in a certain way in your state or county, do not assume that any other county or state does things the same way you are used to."

Editor's Note

There are any number of fine how to books found at book stores or libraries that offer hands-on advice and procedures on using public records/information. Two we find attractive for the price are—

Get the Facts on Anyone by Dennis King (Macmillan, ISBN 0-02-860026-6, $14.95) is a well-written, no-nonsense book. The title separates itself from the rest of pack because it is not filled tales of "cases" or with out-dated addresses and telephone numbers.

Naked in Cyberspace by Carole Lane (Pemberton Press, ISBN 0-910965-17-X, $29.95) is an excellent manual summarizing a multitude of sources of information available to the general public. Although the appendices were out of date when published, Pemberton has updates available on their web site.

Public Record Searching

How to Search

How you search depends on what information you have, what you are looking for, and the time frame you are dealing with. There are five ways you can access information from government agencies and courts as follows—

☎Telephone & Fax

While the amount of information released over the telephone access rules vary by agency or court, this is an inexpensive way to begin a search. Today's widespread computerization of records allows agency/court personnel access to more readily available data. This book contains the phone numbers for over 11,000 jurisdictions. A special automated telephone access system—VCIS—is available for searching US Bankruptcy Court records.

✉ Mail

Many courts and state agencies will conduct a search based upon a written request. Generally, you can call first to see if the agency has the record you are seeking and what the fee is. Always be sure to be specific in your written request and include a self-addressed stamped envelope for quicker service.

👤 In Person

If you are near the court or agency where you want to search, you can visit the location yourself. Personnel are usually available to assist you. Many courts now have public access computer terminals to view case information within their districts. You should take the opportunity to visit the nearest court or recorder's office for another reason: by seeing how the office is physically organized and by chatting with personnel, you will get a better feel for what is involved in searching a similar agency elsewhere. Rules for searching in the federal court system are fairly consistent when compared to the state level court systems.

💻 Online

You will find online access is more readily available at the federal courts and certain state agencies than at the local county court or recorder's office. Most federal courts have now computerized their operations making docket information available in two ways: (1) on-site public access terminals and (2) remote access through PACER. (Read about PACER on pages 23-24.)

$	**Provider** **or** **Retriever** **Firm**	Hiring a service company which knows the court(s) and state agency(s) is frequently the only way to access remote locations effectively. There are national companies that cover all courts, and local companies that cover courts in their geographic vicinity.

Whichever access method you decide to use, and before you undertake any of the above, you must gather as much information as you can and be prepared to be as specific as possible.

Fees, Charges, and Usage

Public records are not necessarily free of charge, certainly not if they are maintained by private industry. Remember, **public records are records of incidents or transactions**. These incidents can be civil or criminal court actions, recordings, filings or occurrences such as speeding tickets or accidents. **It costs money** (time, salaries, supplies, etc.) **to record and track these events**. Common charges found at the government level include copy fees (to make copies of the document), search fees (for clerical personnel to search for the record), and certification fees (to certify the document as being accurate and coming from the particular agency). Fees can vary from $.10 per page for copies to a $15.00 search fee for court personnel to do the actual look-up. Some government agencies will allow you to walk in and view records at no charge. Yet fewer will release information over the phone for no fee.

If a private enterprise is in the business of maintaining a public records database, it generally does so to offer these records for resale. Typical clients include financial institutions, the legal industry, the insurance industry, and pre-employment screening firms. Usually, records are sold via online or on a CD-ROM.

Also, there are many public record search firms—companies that will do a record search for a client for a fee. These companies do not warehouse the records, but search on demand for specific records at government agencies.

Private companies usually offer different price levels based on volume of usage, while government agencies have one price per category, regardless of the amount of requests. (One exception is when government agencies sell databases in bulk, in which case prices are on a "per thousand records" basis.)

Public Records Online

No, you are not going to find an abundance of public records on the Internet. The availability of online public records is not as widespread as one might think. According to studies performed by the *Public Record Research Library*, only **15% of public records can be found online**.

A key to purchasing public records online direct from a government agency is the **frequency of usage**. Many agencies require a minimum amount of requests per month or per session. Certainly, it does not make economic sense to spend a lot of money on programming and set-up fees if you are only going to order 5 records a month. You would be better off to do the search by more conventional methods (mail, visit in person) or hire a vendor. Going direct online to the source is not always the least expensive way to go!

There are approximately 165 private companies which offer online access to their proprietary database(s) of public record information. There is some overlap (competition), but there is, also, an enormous amount of sharing and wholesaling of data between vendors and resellers.

Recommended Online Resources	*Public Records Online* by **Facts on Demand Press** (800-929-3764), a complete and accurate national guide to all sources of online public records—including government agencies and private companies.
	The Sourcebook of Online Public Record Experts by **BRB Publications** (800-929-3764) profiles not only the private online and CD-ROM sources, but also gateways, distributors, and firms that one can hire for a special project or search.
	Fulltext Sources Online, by **Bibliodata** (617-444-1154), is an excellent source of periodicals, newspapers, newsletters, newswires, and TV/radio transcripts. The topics covered include science, technology, medicine, law, finance, business and much more. Editions are published twice a year.
	The Online 100, carried by **Pemberton Press** (800-248-8466), gives clear and concise descriptions of 100 of the most popular online text databases. The book provides in-depth profiles, including a full evaluation of strengths and weaknesses.
	An abundance of public information and/or full text materials such as newspaper articles and abstracts from are available from vendors such as DIALOG, Data Times, Newsnet, and LEXIS.

Searching for Court Records

First...Some Court Basics

Before you go trudging into a courthouse and demand to view a document, you should be armed with some court basics!

Whether the case is filed in federal, state, or municipal court, each case follows a similar process.

A **civil case** usually commences when plaintiffs file a complaint against defendants with a court. The defendants respond to the complaint with an answer. After this initial round, there may be literally hundreds of activities before the court issues a judgment. These activities can include revised complaints and their answers, motions of various kinds, discovery proceedings, including depositions, to establish the documentation and facts involved in the case. All of these activities are listed on a **docket sheet**.

Once a judgment is issued by the court, either party may appeal the ruling to an appellate division or court and, in the case of a money judgment, the winning side can usually file it as a judgment lien with the county recorder. The appellate division usually deals only with the legal issues and not with the facts of the case.

In **criminal cases**, the plaintiff is a government jurisdiction, which brings the action against the defendant under one of its statutes. In **bankruptcy cases**, there is neither defendant nor plaintiff; instead, the debtor files voluntarily for bankruptcy protection against creditors, or the creditor's file against the debtor in order to force it into involuntary bankruptcy.

Types of Litigation in Trial Courts

Criminal
: Criminal cases are categorized as *felonies* or *misdemeanors*. A general rule to distinguish these is that a felony usually may involve a jail term of one year or more, whereas a misdemeanor may only involve a money *fine*.

Civil
: Civil cases are categorized as *tort*, *contract*, and *real property* rights. Torts include *automobile accidents*, *medical malpractice*, and *product liability* cases. Actions for small money damages, typically under $3,000, are known as *small claims*.

Other
: Other types of cases that frequently are handled by separate courts or divisions of courts include *juvenile*, *probate* (wills and estates), and *domestic relations*.

State Court Structure

The secret to determining where a state court case is located is to understand how the court system is structured in each state. The general structure of all the states' court systems has four parts:

1. Appellate courts
2. Intermediate appellate courts
3. General jurisdiction courts
4. Limited jurisdiction courts

The two highest levels only hear cases on appeal from the trial courts. Opinions of these appellate courts are of interest primarily to attorneys who need legal precedents for new cases.

General jurisdiction courts usually handle a full range of civil and criminal litigation. Felonies and larger civil cases are usually handled by these courts.

Limited jurisdiction courts come in two varieties. First, many limited jurisdiction courts handle smaller civil claims (usually $10,000 or less), misdemeanors, and pretrial hearing for felonies. Second, some of these courts, sometimes called special jurisdiction courts, are limited to one type of litigation, such as the Court of Claims in New York, which only handles liability cases against the state.

Some states, like Iowa, have consolidated their general and limited jurisdiction court structure into one combined court system. In other states there is a further distinction between state-supported courts and municipal courts. In New York, for example, nearly 1,500 Justice Courts handle local ordinance and traffic violations, including DWI.

Nationwide generalizations cannot be made about where specific types of cases are handled in different states. Misdemeanors, probate, landlord/tenant, domestic relations, and juvenile cases may be handled at either or both the general and limited jurisdiction courts. In *Find Public Records Fast*, the types of cases handled by each court listed are specified to help you locate the right court to perform your search.

Locating the Right County Court to Search

The next step in determining the location of case records depends upon: (1) in which county is the subject located; (2) the specific court structure of that state; and (3) the types of cases to look for.   At the **state and municipal level**, the problem of locating the right court is complicated by these three variables that can be summarized in the phrase **overlapping jurisdiction.**

The three types of overlapping jurisdiction are described as follows—

Geographic   Two courts may have jurisdiction over the same area. For example, a municipal court may handle DWI cases within its city limits whereas the state court may handle cases in the rest of the county.

Choice of Court
: In some states, the plaintiff may decide which court to bring certain actions in.

Type of Case
: In some states judges may assign cases to different courts to balance workload.

Locating the Right Documents

When you are searching for information about a specific case, you should first obtain a copy of the **docket sheet**. The docket sheet contains the basics of the case: name of court, including location (division) and the judge assigned; case number and case name; names of all plaintiffs and defendants/debtors; names and addresses of attorneys; nature and cause of action. Information from cover sheets and from documents filed as a case goes forward is also recorded on the docket sheet. While docket sheets differ somewhat in format, the basic information contained on a docket sheet is consistent from court to court. Docket sheets are used in the state court systems and the federal court systems. Usually the items will be numbered so that you can easily order a copy of each document from the docket sheet.

Most courts are computerized, which means that the docket sheet data is entered into a computer system. Checking a computer index is the quickest way to find if case records exist. If you need copies of the case records, court personnel may make copies for you for a fee, or you may be able to make copies yourself if the court allows. Also, court personnel may certify the document for you for a fee.

Federal Court Structure

The Federal Court system includes three levels of courts, plus some special courts, described as follows—

Supreme Court of the United States
: *The Supreme Court of the United States is the court of last resort in the United States. It is located in Washington, DC, where it hears appeals from the United States Courts of Appeals and from the highest courts of each state.*

United States Court of Appeals
: *The United States Court of Appeals consists of thirteen appellate courts which hear appeals of verdicts from the courts of general jurisdiction. They are designated as follows:*

- The **Federal Circuit Court** of Appeals hears appeals from the US Claims Court and the US Court International Trade. It is located in Washington, DC.

- The **District of Columbia Circuit Court of Appeals** hears appeals from the district courts in Washington DC as well as from the Tax Court.

- 11 geographic **Courts of Appeals**— each of these appeal courts covers a designated number of states and territories. The chart on the page 522 lists the circuit numbers (1 through 11) and location of the Court of Appeals for each state.

United States District Courts

The United States District Courts are the courts of general jurisdiction, or trial courts, and are subdivided into two categories—

- The **District Courts** are courts of general jurisdiction, or trial courts, for federal matters, excluding bankruptcy. Essentially, this means they hear cases involving federal law and cases where there is diversity of citizenship. Both **civil** and **criminal** cases come before these courts.

- The **Bankruptcy Courts** generally follow the same geographic boundaries as the US District Courts. There is at least one bankruptcy court for each state; within a state there may be one or more judicial districts and within a judicial district there may be more than one location (division) where the courts hear cases. While civil lawsuits may be filed in either state or federal courts depending upon the applicable law, all bankruptcy actions are filed with the US Bankruptcy Courts.

Special Courts/ Separate Courts

The Special Courts/Separate Courts have been created to hear cases or appeals for certain areas of litigation demanding special expertise. Examples include the US Tax Court, the Court of International Trade and the US Claims Court.

How Federal Trial Courts Are Organized

At the federal level, all cases involve federal or US constitutional law or interstate commerce. The task of locating the right court is seemingly simplified by the nature of the federal system—

- All court locations are based upon the county of plaintiff's domicile.

- All civil and criminal cases go to the US District Courts.

- All bankruptcy cases go to the US Bankruptcy Courts.

However, a plaintiff or defendant may have cases in any of the 500 court locations, so it is really not all that simple to find them.

There is at least one District and one Bankruptcy Court in each state. In many states there is more than one court, often divided further into judicial districts—e.g., the State of New York comprises four judicial districts, the Northern, Southern, Eastern and Western.

Further, many judicial districts contain more than one court location (usually called a division). Note that although some districts call their divisions by general, geographic names—e.g., Northern Division of the Southern District—we call them by their city-location name so that you can find them more easily.

The Bankruptcy Courts generally follow the same judicial districting as the District Courts. If court locations differ, the usual variance is to have fewer Bankruptcy Court locations.

Record Keeping in The Federal Courts

Case Numbering

When a case is filed with a federal court, a case number is assigned. This is the primary indexing method. Therefore, in searching for case records, you will need to know or find the applicable case number. If you have the number in good form already, your search should be fast and reasonably inexpensive.

You should be aware that case numbering procedures are not consistent throughout the Federal Court system: one judicial district may assign numbers by district while another may assign numbers by location (division) within the judicial district or by judge. Remember that case numbers appearing in legal text citations may not be adequate for searching unless they appear in the proper form for the particular court.

All the basic civil case information that is entered onto docket sheets, and into computerized systems like PACER, starts with standard form JS-44, the Civil Cover Sheet, or the equivalent.

Docket Sheet

Information from cover sheets, and from documents filed as a case goes forward, is recorded on the docket sheet, which then contains the case history from initial filing to its current status. While docket sheets differ somewhat in format, the basic information contained on a docket sheet is consistent from court to court. As noted earlier in the state court section, all docket sheets contain:

- Name of court, including location (division) and the judge assigned;

- Case number and case name;

- Names of all plaintiffs and defendants/debtors;

- Names and addresses of attorneys for the plaintiff or debtor;

- Nature and cause (e.g., US civil statute) of action;

- Listing of documents filed in the case, including docket entry number, the date and a short description (e.g., 12-2-92, #1, Complaint).

Assignment of Cases

Traditionally, cases were assigned within a district by county. Although this is still true in most states, the introduction of computer systems to track dockets has led to a more flexible approach to case assignment, as is the case in Minnesota and Connecticut. Rather than blindly assigning all cases from a county to one judge, their districts are using random numbers and other logical methods to balance caseloads among their judges.

This trend may appear to confuse the case search process. Actually, the only problem that the searcher may face is to figure out where the case records themselves are located. Finding cases has become significantly easier with the wide availability of PACER from remote access, and on-site terminals in each court location with the same district-wide information base.

Computerization

All federal courts are computerized, which means that the docket sheet data is entered into a computer system. Within a judicial district, the courts may be linked together via a single computer system. For example, in the Northern District of New York, the four courts comprising the judicial district are linked via computer so you may search at any one of the four courts for case information existing anywhere in this judicial district.

However, in some judicial districts, such as the Central District of California, the courts are not linked together. In these cases, you must be very careful when determining, based upon the county of the subject, which court(s) to search.

Docket sheets from cases closed before computerization are generally not in the computer system. For pre-computer cases, most courts keep summary case information on microfilm, microfiche or index cards.

Case documents are never kept on computer. They are available only from the court where the case records are located. Hence, in the Northern District of New York a case being heard in Utica may be located on the computer terminal at any of the four court locations, but copies of specific documents may only be obtained in Utica.

Computerized Indexes are Available

Computerized courts generally index each case record by the names of some or all the parties to the case—the plaintiffs and defendants (debtors and creditors in Bankruptcy Court) as well as by case number. Therefore, when you search by name you will first receive a listing of all cases in which the name appears, both as plaintiff and defendant.

Nationwide Programs for Electronic Access

Numerous programs have been developed for electronic access to Federal Court records. In recent years the Administrative Office of the United States Courts in Washington, DC has developed three innovative public access programs: PACER, VCIS, and ABBS. The two most useful for searching, PACER and VCIS, are explained in more detail.

VCIS

Nearly all of the US Bankruptcy Court judicial districts provide **VCIS** (Voice Case Information System), for information regarding open bankruptcy cases. The telephone number is in the court's listing in this book.

You can search, at no charge, for either an individual or a business name by entering the letters on a touch-tone telephone set. Individual names are entered last name first with as much of the first name as you wish to include. For example, Carl R. Ernst could be entered as ERNSTC or ERNSTCARL. Do not enter the middle initial. Business names are entered as they are written, without blanks.

PACER

PACER is an acronym for **P**ublic **A**ccess to **C**ourt **E**lectronic **R**ecords. PACER allows any user with a personal computer to dial-in to a district or bankruptcy court computer and retrieve official electronic case information and court dockets. User fee is $.60 per minute. Each court controls its own computer system and case information database; therefore, there are some variations among jurisdictions as to the information offered. Be aware that the district courts and bankruptcy courts provide PACER in different formats.

All sign-up and technical support is handled at the PACER Service Center in San Antonio, Texas (800) 676-6856. You cannot sign up for all or multiple districts at once. In many judicial districts, when you sign up for PACER access, you will receive a PACER Primer that has been customized for each district. The primer contains a summary of how to access PACER, how to select cases, how to read case numbers and docket sheets, some searching tips, who to call for problem resolution, and district specific program variations.

Online Systems Other Than PACER

Before the ascendancy of PACER, some courts had developed their own electronic access systems. They have names like NIBS, JAMS and BANCAP. All but a few of these are now available for sign-up at the PACER Center in San Antonio.

Regional Records Services Facilities and the National Archives

After a federal case is closed, the documents are held by Federal Courts themselves for a number of years, then stored at a designated Regional Records Services Facility (RRSF). After 20 to 30 years, the records are then transferred from the RRSF to the regional archives offices of the National Archives and Records Administration (NARA). The length of time between a case being closed and its being moved to an RRSF varies widely by district. Each court has its own transfer cycle and determines access procedures to its case records, even after they have been sent to the RRSF.

When case records are sent to an RRSF, the boxes of records are assigned accession, location and box numbers. These numbers, which are called case locator information, **must be obtained from the originating court in order to retrieve documents from the RRSF.** Some courts will provide such information over the telephone, but others require a written request. This information is now available on PACER in certain judicial districts. The Regional Records Services Facility for each state is listed on pages 520-521.

For More Information...

Regarding federal court searching and in-depth profile of each court location housing records, we suggest that you refer to **BRB Publications' (800) 929-3811** *Federal Courts - US District and Bankruptcy.*

Searching for Real Estate, UCC, and Other County Records

The County Rule

The County Courts and Recording Offices section in each state chapter begins with detailed instructions and searching hints. Where to search for **recorded documents** usually isn't a difficult problem to overcome in everyday practice. In most states, these transactions are recorded at one designated recording office in the county where the property is located. We call this the "County Rule." It applies to types of public records such as real estate recordings, tax liens, **Uniform Commercial Code (UCC)** filings, vital records, and voter registration records. However, as with most government rules, there are a variety of exceptions which are summarized here.

THE EXCEPTIONS

The first four of the five categories of exceptions to the County Rule (or Parish Rule, if searching in Louisiana) are listed below (the details are discussed under "State Specifics")—

1. Special Recording Districts (AK, HI)

2. Multiple Recording Offices (AL, AR, IA, KY, ME, MA, MS, TN)

3. Independent Cities (MD, MO, NV, VA)

4. Recording at the Municipal Level (CT, RI, VT)

THE PERSONAL PROPERTY PROBLEM AND THE FIFTH EXCEPTION

The real estate recording system in the US is self-auditing to the extent that you generally cannot record a document in the wrong recording office. However, many documents are rejected for recording because they are submitted to the wrong recording office. There are a number of reasons why this occurs, one of which is the overlap of filing locations for real estate and UCC.

Finding the right location of a related UCC filing is a different and much more difficult problem from finding a real estate recording. In the majority of states, the usual place to file a UCC financing statement is at the Secretary of States office—these are called **central filing states**. In the **dual** and **local filing** states, the place to file, in addition to the central filing office, is **usually** at the same office where your real estate documents are recorded. However, there are some peculiar exceptions to this rule where place names become confusing, so we've added a fifth exemption, as follows:

5.   Identical Names—Different Place (CT, IL, MA, NE, NH, PA, RI, VT, VA)

The County Rule State Specifics Table

Each of these five categories of recording exceptions is summarized below by state.

AL	Four counties contain two separate recording offices. They are Barbour, Coffee, Jefferson, and St. Clair.
AK	The 23 Alaskan counties are called boroughs. However, real estate recording is done under a system that was established at the time of the Gold Rush (whenever that was) of **34 Recording Districts**. Some of the Districts are identical in geography to boroughs, such as the Aleutian Islands, but other boroughs and districts overlap. Therefore, you need to know which recording district any given town or city is located in.
AR	Ten counties contain two separate recording offices. They are Arkansas, Carroll, Clay, Craighead, Franklin, Logan, Mississippi, Prairie, Sebastian, and Yell.
CT	There is **no county recording** in this state. All recording is done at the city/town level. Lenders persist in attempting to record or file documents in Fairfield, Hartford, Litchfield, New Haven, New London, Tolland, and Windham related to property located in other cities/towns because each of these cities/towns bears the same name as a Connecticut county.
HI	All recording is done at one central office.
IL	Cook County has separate offices for real estate recording and UCC filing.
IA	Lee county has two recording offices.
KY	Kenton County has two recording offices. Jefferson County has a separate office for UCC filing.
LA	Louisiana counties are called **Parishes**. One parish, St. Martin, has two non-contiguous segments.
ME	Aroostock and Oxford counties have two separate recording offices.
MD	The City of Baltimore has its own separate recording office.
MA	Berkshire and Bristol counties each has three recording offices. Essex, Middlesex and Worcester counties each has two recording offices. Cities/towns bearing the same name as a county are Barnstable, Essex, Franklin, Hampden, Nantucket, Norfolk, Plymouth, and Worcester. UCC financing statements on personal property collateral are submitted to cities/towns, while real estate recording is handled by the counties.
MS	Ten counties contain two separate recording offices. They are Bolivar, Carroll, Chickasaw, Harrison, Hinds, Jasper, Jones, Panola, Tallahatchie, and Yalobusha.
MO	The City of St. Louis has its own recording office.
NE	Fifteen counties have separate offices for real estate recording and for UCC filing.
NH	Cities/towns bearing the same name as a county are Carroll, Grafton, Hillsborough, Merrimack, Strafford, and Sullivan. UCC financing statements on personal property collateral are submitted to cities/towns, while real estate recording is handled by the counties.

NV	Carson City has its own recording office.
PA	Each county has a separate recording office and prothonotary office. UCC financing statements on personal property are submitted to the prothonotary, and real estate documents are submitted to the recorder.
RI	There is **no county recording** in this state. All recording is done at the city/town level. Lenders persist in attempting to record or file documents in Bristol, Newport, and Providence related to property located in other cities/ towns because each of these cities/towns bears the same name as a Rhode Island county.
TN	Sullivan County has two separate recording offices.
VT	There is **no county recording** in this state. All recording is done at the city/town level. Lenders persist in attempting to record or file documents in Addison, Bennington, Chittenden, Essex, Franklin, Grand Isle, Orange, Rutland, Washington, Windham, and Windsor related to property located in other cities/towns because each of these cities/towns bears the same name as a Vermont county. Adding to the confusion, there are four place names in the state that refer to both a city and a town: Barre, Newport, Rutland, and St. Albans.
VA	There are 41 independent cities in Virginia. Twenty-seven have separate recording offices. The following 14 share their filing offices with the surrounding county:

INDEPENDENT CITY	*FILE-IN*
Bedford	Bedford County
Covington	Alleghany County
Emporia	Greenville County
Fairfax	Fairfax County
Falls Church	Arlington or Fairfax County
Franklin	Southhampton County
Galax	Carroll County
Harrisonburg	Rockingham County
Lexington	Rockbridge County
Manassas	Prince William County
Manassas Park	Prince William County
Norton	Wise County
Poquoson	York County
South Boston	Halifax County
Williamsburg	James City County

Searching for State Public Records

Each state chapter begins with a heading of the address and phone number of these offices: Governor, Attorney General, State Archives, and the State Legislation body. These are excellent starting points to answer questions about topics or agencies not covered in this book.

The summary page for each state is followed by a listing of the state agencies that maintain the records for the following 19 categories—

1.	Criminal Records	11.	Workers' Compensation Records
2.	Corporation Records	12.	Marriage Records
3.	Limited Partnership Records	13.	Divorce Records
4.	Limited Liability Company Records	14.	Birth Records
5.	Trademark, Trade Name	15.	Death Records
6.	Fictitious or Assumed Names	16.	Driver Records
7.	Uniform Commercial Code Filings	17.	Vehicle and Ownership Records
8.	Federal Tax Liens	18.	State Investigated Accident Reports
9.	State Tax Liens	19.	Hunting & Fishing Licenses
10.	Sales Tax Registrations		

For definitions and descriptions of these categories turn to pages 7-13. Profiles include the addresses, telephone and fax numbers, office hours, and the permissible access methods.

On pages 518-519, you will find the State Agency Public Record Restrictions Table. This is an excellent state-by-state access summary to 11 categories of records, indicating when signed authorizations of the subject are required.

A Word or Two about the Internet

We have included 4 or 5 state agency Internet sites in the front of each state chapter; sites we have logged into and summaries of what we found to be useful. Remember that the **Internet is constantly changing**. At any time, there are a number of states working on new sites. We do not view the Internet as a major source or method of obtaining public record information. As stated before, public records are records of incidents. It costs money to maintain the records in a mode that is easily accessible. In general, while a few states are beginning to use the Internet for access to corporation records and UCC filings, most do offer additional information about topics such as the Archives, Legislature, and Executive Branch.

In conclusion, there is no doubt that government is the largest source of information in the world. We are excited to be able to present, at your fingertips, the results of man-hours spent compiling documentation. With the acquired facts in this book, you are on your way to becoming an expert in *Finding Public Records Fast*!

Alabama

Capital: Montgomery (Montgomery County)	
Number of Counties: 67	**Population:** 4,252,982
County Court Locations:	**Federal Court Locations:**
•Circuit Courts: 17/40 Circuits	•District Courts: 10
•District Courts: 14/67 Districts	•Bankruptcy Courts: 6
•Combined Courts: 61	**State Agencies:** 19
Municipal Courts: 253	
•Probate Courts: 68	

State Agencies—Summary

General Help Numbers:

State Archives

State of Alabama	334-242-4435
Archives & History Department	Fax: 334-240-3433
Reference Room, PO Box 300100	8AM-5PM T-SA
Montgomery, AL 36130-0100	
Reference Librarian:	334-242-4435
Historical Society:	334-242-3182

Governor's Office

Governor's Office	334-242-7100
State Capitol, Suite 101	Fax: 334-242-4541
Montgomery, AL 36130-2751	7:30AM-5:30PM

Attorney General's Office

Attorney General's Office	334-242-7300
State House	Fax: 334-242-7458
11 S. Union Street	8AM-5PM
Montgomery, AL 36104	

State Legislation

Alabama Legislature	334-242-7826
State House	Fax: 334-242-8819
11 S Union St	8:30AM-4:30PM
Montgomery, AL 36130-4600	

An online access system, ALERT, provides access to bill status, voting history, statute retrieval and information about boards and commissions. The information is available 24 hours per day. There is a setup fee of $400.00 and five different monthly fee packages avail able. Monthly fees range from $100.00 to $200.00. Call Angela Hall at 334-242-7482 for more information.

Important State Internet Sites:

> **Webscape**
> File Edit View   Help

State of Alabama World Wide Web
www.state.al.us/

This site provides links to all of the state agencies and contains a name and address list of who's who.

The State Government Page
www.state.al.us/govern.html

This site links you to the Legislature, state agencies, education, and ALALINC information.

The Legislative Bills Page
www.state.al.us/97legis.html

Listed are only the bills introduced by the Governor.

Alabama State Legislature
www.state.al.us/legis.html

This site provides you with access to all of the members of the House of Representatives and the Senate. The history of the Legislature is found here.

UCC and Corporate Information
www.alalinc.net/alsecst/uniform.html

This site contains a downloadable UCC filing guide and information about corporation, limited partnership and more. Required forms are available for download.

State Agencies—Public Records

Criminal Records

Alabama Department of Public Safety, A.B.I., Identification Unit, PO Box 1511, Montgomery, AL 36192, Main Telephone: 334-242-4244, Fax: 334-265-2341, Hours: 8AM-5PM. Access by: mail, visit, PC.

Corporation Records
Limited Partnership Records
Trademarks/Servicemarks
Limited Liability Company Records

Secretary of State, Corporations Section, PO Box 5616, Montgomery, AL 36103-5616, Main Telephone: 334-242-5324, Fax: 334-240-3138, Hours: 8AM-5PM. Access by: mail, phone, visit, PC.

Uniform Commercial Code
Federal Tax Liens
State Tax Liens

UCC Division, Secretary of State, PO Box 5616, Montgomery, AL 36130-5616, Main Telephone: 334-242-5231, Hours: 8AM-5PM. Access by: mail, visit, PC.

Sales Tax Registrations

Alabama Department of Revenue, Sales, Use and Business Tax Division, 4303 Gordon Persons Bldg, 50 N Ripley St, Montgomery, AL 36104, Main Telephone: 334-242-1490, Fax 334-242-8916
Restricted access.

Birth Certificates

Center for Health Statistics, Vital Records Division, PO Box 5625, Montgomery, AL 36103-5625, Main Telephone: 334-206-5418, Hours: 8AM-5PM. Access by: mail, phone, visit.

Death Records

Center for Health Statistics, Vital Records Division, PO Box 5625, Montgomery, AL 36103-5625, Main Telephone: 334-613-5418, Alternate Telephone: 334-613-5417, Hours: 8AM-5PM. Access by: mail, phone, visit.

Marriage Certificates

Center for Health Statistics, Vital Records Division, PO Box 5625, Montgomery, AL 36103-5625, Main Telephone: 334-613-5418, Alternate Telephone: 334-613-5417, Hours: 8AM-5PM. Access by: mail, phone, visit.

Divorce Records

Center for Health Statistics, Vital Records Division, PO Box 5625, Montgomery, AL 36103-5625, Main Telephone: 334-613-5418, Alternate Telephone: 334-613-5417, Hours: 8AM-5PM. Access by: mail, phone, visit.

Workers' Compensation Records

Department of Industrial Relations, Disclosure Unit, 649 Monroe Street, Rm. 276, Montgomery, AL 36131, Main Telephone: 334-242-8980, Fax: 334-261-2304, Hours: 8AM-4:30PM. Access by: mail, visit.

Driver Records

Department of Public Safety, Central Records, Information Services, PO Box 1471, Montgomery, AL 36102-1471, Main Telephone: 334-242-4400, Fax: 334-242-4639, Hours: 8AM-5PM. Access by: mail, visit, PC. Ticket information must be secured at the local level.

Vehicle Ownership
Vehicle Identification

Motor Vehicle Division, Title Section, PO Box 327640, Montgomery, AL 36132-7640, Main Telephone: 334-242-9000, Fax: 334-242-0312, Hours: 8AM-5PM. Access by: mail, visit.

Accident Reports

Alabama Department of Public Safety, Accident Records, PO Box 1471, Montgomery, AL 36102-1471, Main Telephone: 334-242-4241, Hours: 8AM-5PM. Access by: mail, visit.

Hunting License Information
Fishing License Information

Records not available from state agency.

County Courts and Recording Offices

What You Need to Know...

<table>
<tr><td>

About the Courts

</td><td>

About the Recorder's Office

</td></tr>
</table>

About the Courts

Administration

Director of Courts	334-242-0300
300 Dexter Ave	Fax: 334-242-2099
Montgomery, AL 36104	8AM-5PM

Court Structure

The Circuit and District Courts generally have separate jurisdiction over case types as indicated in the charts. These courts are combined in all but eight larger counties. **Barbour, Coffee, Jefferson, St. Clair, Talladega**, and **Tallapoosa** Counties have two court locations within the county.

Jefferson County (Birmingham), **Madison** (Huntsville), **Marshall**, and **Tuscaloosa** Counties have separate criminal divisions for Circuit and/or District Courts. Misdemeanors committed with felonies are tried with the felony. The Circuit Courts are appeals courts for misdemeanors.

District Courts can receive guilty pleas in felony cases. All counties have separate probate courts. Probate court telephone numbers are generally included with the Circuit or District Court entry, although the court location may be different.

Searching Hints

In most counties Circuit and District courts are combined, although each index may be separate. Therefore, when you request a search of both courts, be sure to state that the search is to cover "both the Circuit and District Court records." Several offices do not perform searches. Some offices do not have public access computer terminals.

Online Access

Remote, on-line computer access is available through the **Remote Access** system of the State Judicial Information System **(SJIS).** Remote Access is designed to provide "off-site" users with a means to retrieve basic case information and to **allow a user access to any criminal, civil or traffic record in the state.** The system is available 24 hours per day.

To participate in Remote Access, a user must possess: a PC that is XT equivalent, a modem and modem software which allows VT-100 simulation ("Crosstalk" is recommended).

Call Mike Carroll or Cheryl Lenoir (334-242-0300 or 800-392-8077) for additional information.

About the Recorder's Office

Organization

67 counties, 71 filing offices. The recording officer is Judge of Probate. Four counties have two recording offices—Barbour, Coffee, Jefferson, and St. Clair. See the notes under each county regarding how to determine which office is appropriate to search. The entire state is in the Central Time Zone (CST).

UCC Records

Financing statements are filed at the state level, except for consumer goods, farm collateral and real estate related collateral, which are filed with the county Judge of Probate. Only one-third of counties will perform UCC searches. Use search request form UCC-11. Search fees vary from $5.00 to $11.00 per debtor name. Copies usually cost $1.00 per page.

Lien Records

Federal and state tax liens on personal property of businesses are filed with the Secretary of State. Other federal and state tax liens are filed with the county Judge of Probate. Counties do not perform tax lien searches although the liens are usually filed in the same index with UCC financing statements. Other liens include mechanics, judgment, lis pendens, hospital, and vendor.

Real Estate Records

Most counties do not perform real estate searches. Copy fees vary. Certification fees vary. Tax records are located at the Assessor's Office.

County Courts and Recording Offices

Autauga County

Real Estate Recording—Autauga County Judge of Probate, 134 North Court St., Suite 104, Prattville, AL 36067. 334-361-3731. Fax: 334-361-3740. 8:30AM-5PM (CST).

Felony, Misdemeanor, Civil, Eviction, Small Claims—Circuit & District Court, 134 N Court St, #114, Prattville, AL 36067-3049. 334-361-3737. 8AM-5PM (CST). Access by: Phone, mail, remote online, in person.

Probate—Probate Court, 134 N Court St, Suite 104, Prattville, AL 36067-3049. 334-361-3725. Fax: 334-361-3740. 8:30AM-5PM (CST). Access by: Mail, in person.

Baldwin County

Real Estate Recording—Baldwin County Judge of Probate, 1 Courthouse Square, Bay Minette, AL 36507. 334-937-0230. Fax: 334-580-2563. 8AM-4:30PM (CST).

Felony, Misdemeanor, Civil, Eviction, Small Claims—Circuit & District Court, PO Box 1149, Bay Minette, AL 36507. Civil: 334-937-0277. Criminal: 334-937-0280. Fax: 334-937-0280. 8AM-4:30PM (CST). Access by: Mail, remote online, in person.

Probate—Probate Court, PO Box 1258, Bay Minette, AL 36507. 334-937-9561. 8AM-4:30PM (CST). Access by: Phone, mail, in person.

Barbour County

Real Estate Recording—Barbour County Judge of Probate, Clayton Division, Court Square, Clayton, AL 36016. 334-775-8371. 8AM-4PM (CST).

Barbour County Judge of Probate, Eufaula Division, Broad St., Eufaula, AL 36027. 334-687-7637. Fax: 334-687-1579.

Felony, Misdemeanor, Civil, Eviction, Small Claims, Probate—Circuit & District Court-Clayton Division, PO Box 219, Clayton, AL 36016. 334-775-8366. Probate: 334-775-8371. Fax: 334-775-8366. 8AM-5PM (CST). Access by: Mail, remote online, in person.

Misdemeanor, Civil, Eviction, Small Claims, Probate—Circuit & District Court-Eufaula Division, 303 E Broad St, Rm 201, Eufaula, AL 36027. 334-687-1513. Probate: 334-687-7637. Fax: 334-687-1599. 8AM-4:30PM (CST). Access by: Remote online, in person.

Bibb County

Real Estate Recording—Bibb County Judge of Probate, Courthouse, Room 100, 455 Walnut St, Centerville, AL 35042. 205-926-3104. Fax: 205-926-3110. 8AM-5PM (CST).

Felony, Misdemeanor, Civil, Eviction, Small Claims, Probate—Circuit & District Court, Bibb County Courthouse, Centreville, AL 35042. 205-926-3103. Probate: 205-926-3108. Fax: 205-926-3110. 8AM-5PM (CST). Access by: Mail, remote online, in person.

Blount County

Real Estate Recording—Blount County Judge of Probate, 220 2nd Avenue East, Oneonta, AL 35121. 205-625-4180. 8AM-4PM M-W & F; 8AM-Noon Th & Sat (CST).

Felony, Misdemeanor, Civil, Eviction, Small Claims—Circuit & District Court, 220 2nd Ave East Room 208, Oneonta, AL 35121. 205-625-4153. 8AM-5PM (CST). Access by: Mail, remote online, in person.

Probate—Probate Court, PO Box 549, Oneonta, AL 35121. 205-625-4191. 8AM-4PM M,W,F 8AM-Noon Th,Sat (CST). Access by: Phone, mail, in person.

Bullock County

Real Estate Recording—Bullock County Judge of Probate, 217 North Prairie, Courthouse, Union Springs, AL 36089. 334-738-2250. Fax: 334-738-3839. 8AM-4:30PM (CST).

Felony, Misdemeanor, Civil, Eviction, Small Claims, Probate—Circuit & District Court, PO Box 230, Union Springs, AL 36089. 334-738-2280. Probate: 334-738-2250. Fax: 334-738-2282. 8AM-4:30PM (CST). Access by: Mail, remote online, in person.

Butler County

Real Estate Recording—Butler County Judge of Probate, 700 Court Square, Greenville, AL 36037. 334-382-3512. Fax: 334-382-5489. 8AM-4PM M,T,Th,F; 8AM-Noon W (CST).

Felony, Misdemeanor, Civil, Eviction, Small Claims, Probate—Circuit & District Court, PO Box 236, Greenville, AL 36037. 334-382-3521. Probate: 334-382-3512. 8AM-4PM (CST). Access by: Mail, remote online, in person.

Calhoun County

Real Estate Recording—Calhoun County Judge of Probate, 1702 Noble Street, Suite 102, Anniston, AL 36201. 205-236-8231. 8AM-4:30PM (CST).

Felony, Civil Actions Over $10,000—Circuit Court, 25 W 11th St, Anniston, AL 36201. 205-231-1750. Fax: 205-231-1826. (CST). Access by: Remote online, in person.

Misdemeanor, Civil Actions Under $10,000, Eviction, Small Claims—District Court, 25 W 11th St, Box 9, Anniston, AL 36201. 205-231-1850. Fax: 205-231-1826. 8AM-4:30PM (CST). Access by: Mail, remote online, in person.

Probate—Probate Court, 1702 Noble St, #102, Anniston, AL 36201. 205-236-8231. (CST).

Chambers County

Real Estate Recording—Chambers County Judge of Probate, Courthouse, Lafayette, AL 36862. 334-864-4397. Fax: 334-864-4394. 8AM-4:30PM (CST).

Felony, Misdemeanor, Civil, Eviction, Small Claims, Probate—Circuit & District Court, Chambers County Courthouse, Lafayette, AL 36862. 334-864-4348. Probate: 334-864-4372. Fax: 334-864-4387. 8AM-4:30PM (CST). Access by: Mail, remote online, in person.

Cherokee County

Real Estate Recording—Cherokee County Judge of Probate, Main Street, Centre, AL 35960. 205-927-3363. Fax: 205-927-6949. 8AM-4PM M-F; 8AM-Noon Sat (CST).

Felony, Misdemeanor, Civil, Eviction, Small Claims—Circuit & District Court, Cherokee County Courthouse, Centre, AL 35960. 205-927-3340. 8AM-4:30PM (CST). Access by: Mail, remote online, in person.

Probate—Probate Court, Cherokee County Courthouse, Centre, AL 35960. 205-927-3363. Fax: 205-927-6949. 8AM-4PM M-F, 8AM-Noon Sat (CST). Access by: Mail, in person.

Chilton County

Real Estate Recording—Chilton County Judge of Probate, 500 2nd Avenue North, Clanton, AL 35045. 205-755-1555. Fax: 205-280-7204. 8AM-4PM (CST).

Felony, Misdemeanor, Civil, Eviction, Small Claims, Probate—Circuit & District Court, PO Box 1946, Clanton, AL 35046. 205-755-4275. Probate: 205-755-4275. 8AM-5PM (CST). Access by: Mail, remote online, in person.

Choctaw County

Real Estate Recording—Choctaw County Judge of Probate, 117 South Mulberry, Courthouse, Butler, AL 36904. 205-459-2417. Fax: 205-459-4666. 8AM-4:30PM (CST).

Felony, Misdemeanor, Civil, Eviction, Small Claims, Probate—Circuit & District Court, Choctaw County Courthouse, Ste 10, Butler, AL 36904. 205-459-2155. Probate: 205-459-2417. Fax: 205-459-4666. 8AM-4:30PM (CST). Access by: Mail, remote online, in person.

Clarke County

Real Estate Recording—Clarke County Judge of Probate, 117 Court Street, Courthouse, Grove Hill, AL 36451. 334-275-3251. Fax: 334-275-8517. 8AM-5PM (CST).

Felony, Misdemeanor, Civil, Eviction, Small Claims, Probate—Circuit & District Court, PO Box 921, Grove Hill, AL 36451. 334-275-3363. Probate: 334-275-3251. 8AM-5PM (CST). Access by: Mail, remote online, in person.

Clay County

Real Estate Recording—Clay County Judge of Probate, Courthouse Square, Ashland, AL 36251. 205-354-3006. Fax: 205-354-2197. 8AM-4:30PM (CST).

Felony, Misdemeanor, Civil, Eviction, Small Claims, Probate—Circuit & District Court, PO Box 816, Ashland, AL 36251. 205-354-7926. Fax: 205-354-2249. 8AM-4:30PM (CST). Access by: Mail, remote online, in person.

Cleburne County

Real Estate Recording—Cleburne County Judge of Probate, 406 Vickery Street, Heflin, AL 36264. 205-463-5655. Fax: 205-463-5542. 8AM-5PM (CST).

Felony, Misdemeanor, Civil, Eviction, Small Claims, Probate—Circuit & District Court, 120 Vickery St Room 202, Heflin, AL 36264. 205-463-2651. Probate: 205-463-5655. Fax: 205-463-2257. 8AM-4:30PM (CST). Access by: Phone, mail, remote online, in person.

Coffee County

Real Estate Recording—Coffee County Judge of Probate, Elba Division, 230-P North Court Avenue, Elba, AL 36323. 334-897-2211. Fax: 334-897-2028. 8AM-4:30PM (CST).

Coffee County Judge of Probate, Enterprise Division, 99 S. Edwards St., Suite 102, Enterprise, AL 36330. 334-347-2688. Fax: 334-347-2095.

Felony, Misdemeanor, Civil, Eviction, Small Claims, Probate—Circuit & District Court-Elba Division, PO Box 402, Elba, AL 36323. 334-897-2954. 8AM-4:30PM (CST). Access by: Mail, remote online, in person.

Felony, Misdemeanor, Civil, Eviction, Small Claims—Circuit & District Court-Enterprise Division, PO Box 1294, Enterprise, AL 36331. 334-347-2519. 8AM-4:30PM (CST). Access by: Mail, remote online, in person.

Probate—Enterprise Division-Probate, PO Box 1256, Enterprise, AL 36331. 334-347-2688. Fax: 334-347-2689. 8AM-4:30PM (CST). Access by: Phone, mail, in person.

Colbert County

Real Estate Recording—Colbert County Judge of Probate, Probate Judge, 201 Main St., Tuscumbia, AL 35674. 205-386-8546. Fax: 205-386-8547. 8AM-4:30PM (CST).

Felony, Civil Actions Over $10,000, Probate—Circuit Court, Colbert County Courthouse, Tuscumbia, AL 35674. 205-386-8512. Probate: 205-386-8542. 8AM-4:30PM (CST). Access by: Remote online, in person.

Misdemeanor, Civil Actions Under $10,000, Eviction, Small Claims—District Court, Colbert County Courthouse, Tuscumbia, AL 35674. 205-386-8518. 7:30AM-4:30PM (CST). Access by: Remote online, in person.

Conecuh County

Real Estate Recording—Conecuh County Judge of Probate, Jackson Street, Court Square, Evergreen, AL 36401. 334-578-1221. Fax: 334-578-7002. 8AM-4PM (CST).

Felony, Misdemeanor, Civil, Eviction, Small Claims, Probate—Circuit & District Court, PO Box 107, Evergreen, AL 36401. 334-578-2066. Probate: 334-578-1221. 8AM-4PM (CST). Access by: Mail, remote online, in person.

Coosa County

Real Estate Recording—Coosa County Judge of Probate, Highway 231 and 22, Courthouse, Rockford, AL 35136. 205-377-4919. Fax: 205-377-2524. 8AM-4PM (CST).

Felony, Misdemeanor, Civil, Eviction, Small Claims, Probate—Circuit & District Court, PO Box 98, Rockford, AL 35136. 205-377-4988. Probate: 205-377-4919. (CST). Access by: Remote online, in person.

Covington County

Real Estate Recording—Covington County Judge of Probate, Court Square, Andalusia, AL 36420. 334-222-3189. Fax: 334-222-3091. 8AM-5PM (CST).

Felony, Misdemeanor, Civil, Eviction, Small Claims, Probate—Circuit & District Court, Covington County Courthouse, Andalusia, AL 36420. 334-222-4213. Probate: 334-222-3189. 8AM-5PM (CST). Access by: Remote online, in person.

Crenshaw County

Real Estate Recording—Crenshaw County Judge of Probate, 301 Glenwood Avenue, Luverne, AL 36049. 334-335-6568. Fax: 334-335-3616. 8AM-4:30PM (CST).

Felony, Misdemeanor, Civil, Eviction, Small Claims, Probate—Circuit & District Court, PO Box 167, Luverne, AL 36049. 334-335-6575. Probate: 334-335-6568. 8AM-4:30PM (CST). Access by: Mail, remote online, in person.

Cullman County

Real Estate Recording—Cullman County Judge of Probate, 500 2nd Avenue SW, Courthouse, Cullman, AL 35055. 205-739-3530. Fax: 205-739-7003. 8AM-4:30PM (CST).

Felony, Civil Actions Over $10,000, Probate—Circuit Court, Cullman County Courthouse, Rm 303, Cullman, AL 35055. 205-739-3530. Probate: 205-739-3530 X235. 8AM-5PM (CST). Access by: Mail, remote online, in person.

Misdemeanor, Civil Actions Under $10,000, Eviction, Small Claims—District Court, Cullman County Courthouse, Rm 211, Cullman, AL 35055-4197. 205-739-3530. 8AM-4:30PM (CST). Access by: Mail, remote online, in person.

Dale County

Real Estate Recording—Dale County Judge of Probate, Courthouse, Ozark, AL 36360. 334-774-2754. Fax: 334-774-0468. 8AM-5PM (CST).

Felony, Misdemeanor, Civil, Eviction, Small Claims, Probate—Circuit & District Court, PO Box 1350, Ozark, AL 36361. 334-774-5003. Probate: 334-774-2754. 8AM-4:30PM (CST). Access by: Remote online, in person.

Dallas County

Real Estate Recording—Dallas County Judge of Probate, 105 Lauderdale Street, Selma, AL 36701. 334-874-2516. 8:30AM-4:30PM (CST).

Felony, Civil Actions Over $10,000, Probate—Circuit Court, PO Box 1158, Selma, AL 36702. 334-874-2523. Probate: 334-874-2500. 8AM-5PM (CST). Access by: Phone, mail, remote online, in person.

Misdemeanor, Civil Actions Under $10,000, Eviction, Small Claims—District Court, PO Box 1158, Selma, AL 36702. 334-874-2526. 8AM-5PM (CST). Access by: Phone, mail, remote online, in person.

De Kalb County

Real Estate Recording—De Kalb County Judge of Probate, 300 Grand South West, Courthouse, Suite 100, Fort Payne, AL 35967. 205-845-8510. Fax: 205-845-8514. 7:45AM-4:15PM (CST).

Felony, Misdemeanor, Civil, Eviction, Small Claims, Probate—Circuit & District Court, De Kalb County Courthouse, Rm 202, Fort Payne, AL 35967. 205-845-8525. Probate: 205-845-8510. 8AM-4PM (CST). Access by: Phone, mail, remote online, in person.

Elmore County

Real Estate Recording—Elmore County Judge of Probate, Commerce Street, Wetumpka, AL 36092. 334-567-1143. 8AM-4:30PM (CST).

Civil—Circuit & District Court-Civil Division, PO Box 320, Wetumpka, AL 36092. 334-567-1123. Probate: 334-567-1138. Fax: 334-567-5957. 8AM-4:30PM (CST). Access by: Remote online, in person.

Felony, Misdemeanor—Criminal Circuit Court, PO Box 320, 8935 US Hwy 233, Wetumpka, AL 36092. 334-567-1123. Fax: 334-567-5957. 8AM-4:30PM (CST). Access by: Remote online, in person.

Escambia County

Real Estate Recording—Escambia County Judge of Probate, 318 Belleville Avenue, Brewton, AL 36426. 334-867-0206. Fax: 334-867-0283. 8AM-4PM (CST).

Felony, Misdemeanor, Civil, Eviction, Small Claims, Probate—Circuit & District Court, PO Box 856, Brewton, AL 36427. 334-867-6261. Probate: 334-867-0201. Fax: 334-867-0275. 8AM-4PM (CST). Access by: Mail, remote online, in person.

Etowah County

Real Estate Recording—Etowah County Judge of Probate, 800 Forrest Avenue, Courthouse, Gadsden, AL 35901. 205-549-5341. Fax: 205-546-1149. 8AM-5PM (CST).

Felony, Misdemeanor, Civil, Eviction, Small Claims, Probate—Circuit & District Court, PO Box 798, Gadsden, AL 35999. 205-549-5437. Probate: 205-549-8135. 8AM-5PM (CST). Access by: Mail, remote online, in person.

Fayette County

Real Estate Recording—Fayette County Judge of Probate, 113 Temple Avenue North, Courthouse, Fayette, AL 35555. 205-932-4519. Fax: 205-932-7600. 8AM-4PM (CST).

Felony, Misdemeanor, Civil, Eviction, Small Claims, Probate—Circuit & District Court, PO Box 206, Fayette, AL 35555. 205-932-4617. Probate: 205-932-5916. 8AM-4:30PM (CST). Access by: Mail, remote online, in person.

Franklin County

Real Estate Recording—Franklin County Judge of Probate, 410 North Jackson Street, Russellville, AL 35653. 205-332-8801. 8AM-5PM; 8AM-Noon Sat (CST).

Felony, Misdemeanor, Civil, Eviction, Small Claims, Probate—Circuit & District Court, PO Box 160, Russellville, AL 35653. 205-332-8861. 8AM-4:30PM (CST). Access by: Mail, remote online, in person.

Geneva County

Real Estate Recording—Geneva County Judge of Probate, Commerce Street, Courthouse, Geneva, AL 36340. 334-684-9300. 8AM-5PM (CST).

Felony, Misdemeanor, Civil, Eviction, Small Claims, Probate—Circuit & District Court, PO Box 86, Geneva, AL 36340. 334-684-2494. Probate: 334-684-2276. 8AM-5PM (CST). Access by: Mail, remote online, in person.

Greene County

Real Estate Recording—Greene County Judge of Probate, 400 Morrow Ave., Greene County Courthouse, Eutaw, AL 35462. 205-372-3340. Fax: 205-372-0499. 8AM-4PM (CST).

Felony, Misdemeanor, Civil, Eviction, Small Claims, Probate—Circuit & District Court, PO Box 307, Eutaw, AL 35462. 205-372-3598. Probate: 205-372-3340. 8AM-4PM (CST). Access by: Mail, remote online, in person.

Hale County

Real Estate Recording—Hale County Judge of Probate, 1001 Main Street, Courthouse, Greensboro, AL 36744. 334-624-8740. Fax: 334-624-8725. 8AM-4PM (CST).

Felony, Misdemeanor, Civil, Eviction, Small Claims, Probate—Circuit & District Court, Hale County Courthouse, Rm 8, Greensboro, AL 36744. 334-624-4334. Probate: 334-624-7391. 8AM-5PM (CST). Access by: Mail, remote online, in person.

Henry County

Real Estate Recording—Henry County Judge of Probate, Suite A, 101 West Court Square, Abbeville, AL 36310. 334-585-3257. Fax: 334-585-3610. 8AM-4:30PM (CST).

Felony, Misdemeanor, Civil, Eviction, Small Claims, Probate—Circuit & District Court, 101 W Court St, Suite J, Abbeville, AL 36310-2135. 334-585-2753. Probate: 334-585-

3257. Fax: 334-585-5006. 8AM-4:30PM (CST). Access by: Mail, remote online, in person.

Houston County

Real Estate Recording—Houston County Judge of Probate, 462 North Oates, 2nd Floor, Dothan, AL 36303. 334-677-4723. 8AM-4:30PM (CST).

Felony, Misdemeanor, Civil, Eviction, Small Claims, Probate—Circuit & District Court, PO Drawer 6406, Dothan, AL 36302. 334-677-4800. Probate: 334-677-4719. 7:30AM-4:30PM (CST). Access by: Mail, remote online, in person.

Jackson County

Real Estate Recording—Jackson County Judge of Probate, Courthouse Square, Courthouse, Scottsboro, AL 35768. 205-574-9292. Fax: 205-574-9318. 8AM-4:30PM (CST).

Felony, Misdemeanor, Civil, Eviction, Small Claims, Probate—Circuit & District Court, PO Box 397, Scottsboro, AL 35768. 205-574-9320. Civil: 205-574-9325. Criminal: 205-574-9322. Probate: 205-574-9290. 8AM-4:30PM (CST). Access by: Mail, remote online, in person.

Jefferson County

Real Estate Recording—Jefferson County Judge of Probate, Bessemer Division, 1801 3rd Ave., Bessemer, AL 35020. 205-481-4100.

Jefferson County Judge of Probate, Birmingham Division, 716 North 21st Street, Courthouse, Birmingham, AL 35203. 205-325-5112. Fax: 205-325-1437. 8AM-4:45PM (CST).

Felony, Civil Actions Over $10,000—Bessemer Division-Circuit Court, Rm 606, Courthouse Annex, Bessemer, AL 35020. 205-481-4165. 8AM-5PM (CST). Access by: Remote online, in person.

Misdemeanor, Civil Actions Under $10,000, Eviction, Small Claims—Bessemer Division-District Court, Rm 506, Courthouse Annex, Bessemer, AL 35020. 205-481-4187. 8AM-5PM (CST). Access by: Mail, remote online, in person.

Civil Actions Over $10,000—Birmingham Division-Civil Circuit Court, 716 N 21st St, Rm 313, Birmingham, AL 35263. 205-325-5355. 8AM-5PM (CST). Access by: Phone, mail, remote online, in person.

Felony—Birmingham Division-Criminal Circuit Court, 801 N 21st St, Rm 506, Birmingham, AL 35263. 205-325-5285. 8AM-4:55PM (CST). Access by: Remote online, in person.

Civil Actions Under $10,000, Eviction, Small Claims—Birmingham Division-Civil District Court, 801 N 21st St, Rm 901, Birmingham, AL 35263. 205-325-5331. 8AM-5PM (CST). Access by: Phone, mail, remote online, in person.

Misdemeanor—Birmingham Division-Criminal District Court, 801 21st St, Rm 207, Birmingham, AL 35263. 205-325-5309. 8AM-5PM (CST). Access by: Phone, mail, remote online, in person.

Probate—Probate Court, 716 N 21st St, Birmingham, AL 35203. 205-325-5420. Fax: 205-325-4885. (CST). Access by: In person only.

Lamar County

Real Estate Recording—Lamar County Judge of Probate, N. Pond St, Vernon, AL 35592. 205-695-9119. Fax: 205-695-8522. 8AM-5PM M,T,Th,F; 8AM-Noon W,Sat (CST).

Felony, Misdemeanor, Civil, Eviction, Small Claims, Probate—Circuit & District Court, PO Box 434, Vernon, AL 35592. 205-695-7193. Probate: 205-695-9119. Fax: 205-695-7427. 8AM-5PM (CST). Access by: Mail, remote online, in person.

Lauderdale County

Real Estate Recording—Lauderdale County Judge of Probate, 200 South Court Street, Florence, AL 35630. 205-760-5800. 8AM-5PM (CST).

Felony, Civil Actions Over $10,000, Probate—Circuit Court, PO Box 795, Florence, AL 35631. 205-760-5710. Probate: 205-760-5800. 8AM-Noon, 1-5PM (CST). Access by: Remote online, in person.

Misdemeanor, Civil Actions Under $10,000, Eviction, Small Claims—District Court, PO Box 363, Florence, AL 35631. 205-760-5726. 8AM-Noon, 1-5PM (CST). Access by: Remote online, in person.

Lawrence County

Real Estate Recording—Lawrence County Judge of Probate, 14330 Court Street, Suite 102, Moulton, AL 35650. 205-974-2439. Fax: 205-974-3188. 8AM-4PM (CST).

Felony, Misdemeanor, Civil, Eviction, Small Claims, Probate—Circuit & District Court, PO Box 265, Moulton, AL 35650. 205-974-2432. Probate: 205-974-2439. 8AM-5PM (CST). Access by: Remote online, in person.

Lee County

Real Estate Recording—Lee County Judge of Probate, 215 South 9th, Opelika, AL 36803. 334-745-9761. 8:30AM-4:30PM (CST).

Felony, Misdemeanor, Civil, Eviction, Small Claims, Probate—Circuit & District Court, 215 S 9th St, Opelika, AL 36801. 334-749-7141. Probate: 334-745-9761. Fax: 334-749-5886. 8AM-5PM (CST). Access by: Phone, mail, remote online, in person.

Limestone County

Real Estate Recording—Limestone County Judge of Probate, Courthouse, 2nd Floor, Athens, AL 35611. 205-233-6427. Fax: 205-233-6474. 8AM-4:30PM (CST).

Felony, Misdemeanor, Civil, Eviction, Small Claims, Probate—Circuit & District Court, PO Box 964, Athens, AL 35611. 205-233-6406. Probate: 205-233-6427. 8AM-4:30PM (CST). Access by: Mail, remote online, in person.

Lowndes County

Real Estate Recording—Lowndes County Judge of Probate, Courthouse, Hayneville, AL 36040. 334-548-2365. Fax: 334-548-5101. 8AM-4:30PM (CST).

Felony, Misdemeanor, Civil, Eviction, Small Claims, Probate—Circuit & District Court, PO Box 876, Hayneville, AL 36040. 334-548-2252. Probate: 334-548-2365. 8AM-4:30PM (CST). Access by: Phone, mail, remote online, in person.

Macon County

Real Estate Recording—Macon County Judge of Probate, 101 E. Northside St., Suite 101, Tuskegee, AL 36083. 334-724-2611. Fax: 334-724-2512. 8:30AM-4:30PM (CST).

Felony, Misdemeanor, Civil, Eviction, Small Claims, Probate—Circuit & District Court, 101 E Northside Ste 300, Tuskegee, AL 36083. 334-724-2614. Probate: 334-724-2611. 8AM-4:30PM (CST). Access by: Mail, remote online, in person.

Madison County

Real Estate Recording—Madison County Judge of Probate, 100 Northside Square, Huntsville, AL 35801. 205-532-3341. Fax: 205-532-6977. 8:30AM-5PM (CST).

Civil Actions Over $10,000, Probate—Civil Circuit Court, 100 N Side Square, Courthouse, Huntsville, AL 35801. 205-532-3381. Probate: 205-532-3439. 8AM-5PM (CST). Access by: Remote online, in person.

Felony—Criminal Circuit Court, 100 N Side Square, Courthouse, Huntsville, AL 35801-4820. 205-532-3386. 8AM-5PM (CST). Access by: Remote online, in person.

Misdemeanor, Civil Actions Under $10,000, Eviction, Small Claims—District Court, 100 N Side Square, Rm 822 Courthouse, Huntsville, AL 35801. 205-532-3622. Civil: 205-532-3622. Criminal: 205-532-3373. Fax: 205-532-3768. 8AM-5PM (CST). Access by: Remote online, in person.

Marengo County

Real Estate Recording—Marengo County Judge of Probate, 101 East Coats Avenue, Courthouse, Linden, AL 36748. 334-295-2210. Fax: 334-295-2254. 8AM-4:30PM (CST).

Felony, Misdemeanor, Civil, Eviction, Small Claims, Probate—Circuit & District Court, PO Box 566, Linden, AL 36748. 334-295-2223. 8AM-4:30PM (CST). Access by: Mail, remote online, in person.

Marion County

Real Estate Recording—Marion County Judge of Probate, Military St, Hamilton, AL 35570. 205-921-2471. Fax: 205-921-5109. 8AM-Noon, 1-5PM (CST).

Felony, Misdemeanor, Civil, Eviction, Small Claims, Probate—Circuit & District Court, PO Box 1595, Hamilton, AL 35570. 205-921-7451. Probate: 205-921-2471. 8AM-5PM (CST). Access by: Mail, remote online, in person.

Marshall County

Real Estate Recording—Marshall County Judge of Probate, 425 Gunter Avenue, Guntersville, AL 35976. 205-571-7767. Fax: 205-571-7732. 8AM-4:30PM (CST).

Felony, Misdemeanor, Civil, Eviction, Small Claims—Circuit & District Court-Albertville Division, 200 W Main, Albertville, AL 35950. 205-878-4522. 8AM-4:30PM (CST). Access by: Mail, remote online, in person.

Civil Actions Over $10,000, Small Claims, Probate—Civil Circuit Court-Guntersville Division, 425 Gunter Ave, Guntersville, AL 35976. 205-571-7789. Probate: 205-571-7764. 8AM-4:30PM (CST). Access by: Mail, remote online, in person.

Felony—Criminal Circuit Court-Guntersville Division, 425 Gunter Ave, PO Box 248, Guntersville, AL 35976. 205-571-7791. 8AM-4:30PM (CST). Access by: Mail, remote online, in person.

Mobile County

Real Estate Recording—Mobile County Judge of Probate, 101 Government Street, Mobile, AL 36602. 334-690-8497. Fax: 334-690-4939. 8AM-5PM (CST).

Felony, Civil Actions Over $10,000—Circuit Court, PO Box 298, Mobile, AL 36601. 334-690-8786. 8AM-5PM (CST). Access by: Phone, mail, remote online, in person.

Misdemeanor, Civil Actions Under $10,000, Eviction, Small Claims, Probate—District Court, State of Alabama, Mobile County, 205 Government St, Mobile, AL 36644. 334-690-8520. Civil: 334-690-8517. Criminal: 334-690-8511. Probate: 334-690-8502. Fax: 334-690-4840. (CST). Access by: Phone, mail, remote online, in person.

Monroe County

Real Estate Recording—Monroe County Judge of Probate, South Alabama Avenue, Courthouse Square, Monroeville, AL 36460. 334-743-4107. 8AM-5PM M,T,W,F; 8AM-Noon Th (CST).

Felony, Misdemeanor, Civil, Eviction, Small Claims, Probate—Circuit & District Court, County Courthouse, Monroeville, AL 36460. 334-743-2283. Probate: 334-743-4107. 8AM-5PM (CST). Access by: Phone, mail, remote online, in person.

Montgomery County

Real Estate Recording—Montgomery County Judge of Probate, Room 206, 100 South Lawrence, Montgomery, AL 36104. 334-832-1237. 8AM-5PM (CST).

Felony, Civil Actions Over $10,000, Probate—Circuit Court, PO Box 1667, Montgomery, AL 36102-1667. 334-832-1260. Probate: 334-832-1237. 8AM-5PM (CST). Access by: Mail, remote online, in person.

Misdemeanor, Civil Actions Under $10,000, Eviction, Small Claims—District Court, PO Box 1667, Montgomery, AL 36102. 334-832-1350. 8AM-5PM (CST). Access by: Mail, remote online, in person.

Morgan County

Real Estate Recording—Morgan County Judge of Probate, 302 Lee Street, Decatur, AL 35601. 205-351-4680. 8:30AM-4:30PM (CST).

Felony, Civil Actions Over $10,000, Probate—Circuit Court, PO Box 668, Decatur, AL 35602. 205-351-4600. Probate: 205-351-4675. 8:30AM-4:30PM (CST). Access by: Remote online, in person.

Misdemeanor, Civil Actions Under $10,000, Eviction, Small Claims—District Court, PO Box 668, Decatur, AL 35602. 205-351-4640. 8:30AM-4:30PM (CST). Access by: Phone, mail, remote online, in person.

Perry County

Real Estate Recording—Perry County Judge of Probate, Washington Street, Courthouse, Marion, AL 36756. 334-683-2210. Fax: 334-683-2201. 8AM-4:30PM (CST).

Felony, Misdemeanor, Civil, Eviction, Small Claims, Probate—Circuit & District Court, PO Box 505, Marion, AL 36756. 334-683-6106. Probate: 334-683-2210. 8AM-4:30PM (CST). Access by: Mail, remote online, in person.

Pickens County

Real Estate Recording—Pickens County Judge of Probate, Court Square, Probate Building, Carrollton, AL 35447. 205-367-2010. Fax: 205-367-2025. 8AM-4PM (CST).

Felony, Misdemeanor, Civil, Eviction, Small Claims, Probate—Circuit & District Court, PO Box 418, Carrollton, AL 35447. 205-367-2050. 8AM-4:30PM (CST). Access by: Mail, remote online, in person.

Pike County

Real Estate Recording—Pike County Judge of Probate, Church Street, Courthouse, Troy, AL 36081. 334-566-1246. Fax: 334-566-0142. 8AM-5PM (CST).

Felony, Misdemeanor, Civil, Eviction, Small Claims, Probate—Circuit & District Court, PO Box 948, Troy, AL 36081. 334-566-4622. Probate: 334-357-4933. 8AM-5PM (CST). Access by: Mail, remote online, in person.

Randolph County

Real Estate Recording—Randolph County Judge of Probate, Main Street, Courthouse, Wedowee, AL 36278. 205-357-4933. 8AM-5PM (CST).

Felony, Misdemeanor, Civil, Eviction, Small Claims, Probate—Circuit & District Court, PO Box 328, Wedowee, AL 36278. 205-357-4551. Probate: 205-357-4933. 8AM-Noon, 1-5PM (CST). Access by: Remote online, in person.

Russell County

Real Estate Recording—Russell County Judge of Probate, 501 14th Street, Phenix City, AL 36867. 334-298-7979. 8:30AM-5PM (CST).

Felony, Misdemeanor, Civil, Eviction, Small Claims, Probate—Circuit & District Court, PO Box 518, Phenix City, AL 36868. 334-298-0516. Probate: 205-669-3710. 8:30AM-4:30PM (CST). Access by: Remote online, in person.

Shelby County

Real Estate Recording—Shelby County Judge of Probate, Main Street, Columbiana, AL 35051. 205-669-3720. Fax: 205-669-3714. 8AM-4:30PM (CST).

Felony, Misdemeanor, Civil, Eviction, Small Claims, Probate—Circuit & District Court, PO Box 1810, Columbiana, AL 35051. 205-669-3760. Probate: 205-669-7979. 8AM-4:30PM (CST). Access by: Remote online, in person.

St. Clair County

Real Estate Recording—St. Clair County Judge of Probate, Northern Congressional District, Administrative Building, 5th Avenue, Ashville, AL 35953. 205-594-2124. Fax: 205-594-2110. 8AM-5PM (CST).

St. Clair Judge of Probate, Southern Congressional District, Courthouse, 1815 Cogswell Ave., Pell City, AL 35125. 205-338-9449.

Felony, Misdemeanor, Civil, Eviction, Small Claims, Probate—Circuit & District Court-Ashville Division, PO Box 476, Ashville, AL 35953. 205-594-2184. Probate: 205-594-2120. 8AM-5PM (CST). Access by: Mail, remote online, in person.

Circuit & District Court-Pell City Division, Cogswell Ave, Pell City, AL 35125. 205-338-2511. Probate: 205-338-9449. 8AM-5PM (CST). Access by: Mail, remote online, in person.

Sumter County

Real Estate Recording—Sumter County Judge of Probate, Courthouse Square, Livingston, AL 35470. 205-652-7281. Fax: 205-652-6206. 8AM-4PM (CST).

Felony, Misdemeanor, Civil, Eviction, Small Claims, Probate—Circuit & District Court, PO Box 936, Livingston, AL 35470. 205-652-2291. Probate: 205-652-7281. 8AM-4PM (CST). Access by: Mail, remote online, in person.

Talladega County

Real Estate Recording—Talladega County Judge of Probate, Courthouse, Talladega, AL 35160. 205-362-4175. Fax: 205-761-2128. 8AM-5PM (CST).

Felony, Misdemeanor, Civil, Eviction, Small Claims—Circuit & District Court-Northern Division, PO Drawer B, Talladega, AL 35160-0755. 205-761-2102. 8AM-5PM (CST). Access by: Remote online, in person.

Misdemeanor, Civil Actions Under $10,000, Eviction, Small Claims—District Court-Southern Division, PO Box 183, Sylacauga, AL 35150. 205-245-4352. 7:30AM-4:30AM (CST). Access by: Mail, remote online, in person.

Probate—Probate Court, PO Box 755, Talladega, AL 35160. 205-362-4175. (CST).

Tallapoosa County

Real Estate Recording—Tallapoosa County Judge of Probate, Courthouse, Room 126, 125 N. Broadnax St., Dadeville, AL 36853. 205-825-4266. Fax: 205-825-1604. 8AM-5PM (CST).

Felony, Misdemeanor, Civil, Eviction, Small Claims—Circuit & District Court-Western Division, PO Box 189, Alexander City, AL 35010. 205-329-8123. 8AM-5PM (CST). Access by: Mail, remote online, in person.

Felony, Misdemeanor, Civil, Eviction, Small Claims, Probate—Circuit & District Court-Eastern Division, Tallapoosa County Courthouse, Dadeville, AL 36853. 205-825-1098. Probate: 205-825-4266. 8AM-5PM (CST). Access by: Mail, remote online, in person.

Tuscaloosa County

Real Estate Recording—Tuscaloosa County Judge of Probate, 714 Greensboro Avenue, Tuscaloosa, AL 35401. 205-349-3870. 8:30AM-5PM (CST).

Civil Actions Over $10,000, Probate—Civil Circuit Court, 714 Greensboro Ave, Tuscaloosa, AL 35401. 205-349-3870. Probate: 205-349-3870 X203. 8:30AM-5PM (CST). Access by: Remote online, in person.

Felony—Criminal Circuit Court, 714 Greensboro Ave, Tuscaloosa, AL 35401. 205-349-3870. 8AM-5PM (CST). Access by: Mail, remote online, in person.

Misdemeanor, Civil Actions Under $10,000, Eviction, Small Claims—District Court, PO Box 1687, Tuscaloosa, AL 35403. 205-349-3870. 8:30AM-5PM (CST). Access by: Phone, mail, remote online, in person.

Walker County

Real Estate Recording—Walker County Judge of Probate, 1803 3rd Ave. S.W., Courthouse Room 102, Jasper, AL 35502. 205-384-7282. 8AM-4PM (CST).

Felony, Misdemeanor, Civil, Eviction, Small Claims, Probate—Circuit & District Court, PO Box 749, Jasper, AL 35501. 205-384-7268. Probate: 205-384-7280. Fax: 205-384-7271. 8AM-4:30PM (CST). Access by: Remote online, in person.

Washington County

Real Estate Recording—Washington County Judge of Probate, 1 Court Street, Chatom, AL 36518. 334-847-2201. Fax: 334-847-3677. 8AM-4:30PM (CST).

Felony, Misdemeanor, Civil, Eviction, Small Claims, Probate—Circuit & District Court, PO Box 548, Chatom, AL 36518. 334-847-2239. 8AM-4:30PM (CST). Access by: Remote online, in person.

Wilcox County

Real Estate Recording—Wilcox County Judge of Probate, 100 Broad Street, Courthouse, Camden, AL 36726. 334-682-4883. Fax: 334-682-9484. 8-11:30AM,Noon-4:30PM (CST).

Felony, Misdemeanor, Civil, Eviction, Small Claims, Probate—Circuit & District Court, PO Box 656, Camden, AL 36726. 334-682-4126. Probate: 334-682-4883. 8AM-4:30PM (CST). Access by: Mail, remote online, in person.

Winston County

Real Estate Recording—Winston County Judge of Probate, Main Street, Courthouse, Double Springs, AL 35553. 205-489-5219. Fax: 205-489-5135. 8AM-4:30PM (8AM-Noon 1st Sat of every month) (CST).

Felony, Misdemeanor, Civil, Eviction, Small Claims, Probate—Circuit & District Court, PO Box 309, Double Springs, AL 35553. 205-489-5533. Probate: 205-489-5219. 8AM-4:30PM (CST). Access by: Mail, remote online, in person.

Federal Courts

US District Court
Middle District of Alabama

Dothan Division, US District Court c/o Montgomery Division, PO Box 711, Montgomery, AL 36101. 334-223-7308. Counties: Coffee, Dale, Geneva, Henry, Houston

Montgomery Division, US District Court Records Search, PO Box 711, Montgomery, AL 36101-0711. 334-223-7308. Counties: Autauga, Barbour, Bullock, Butler, Chilton, Coosa, Covington, Crenshaw, Elmore, Lowndes, Montgomery, Pike

Opelika Division, US District Court c/o Montgomery Division, PO Box 711, Montgomery, AL 36101. 334-223-7308. Counties: Chambers, Lee, Macon, Randolph, Russell, Tallapoosa

Northern District of Alabama

Birmingham Division, US District Court Room 140, US Courthouse, 1729 5th Ave N, Birmingham, AL 35203. 205-731-1700. Counties: Bibb, Blount, Calhoun, Clay, Cleburne, Greene, Jefferson, Pickens, Shelby, Sumter, Talladega, Tuscaloosa

Florence Division, US District Court 210 Seminary St, Florence, AL 35631. 205-760-5815. Counties: Colbert, Franklin, Lauderdale

Gadsden Division, US District Court c/o Birmingham Division, Room 140, US Courthouse, 1729 5th Ave N, Birmingham, AL 35203. 205-731-1700. Counties: Cherokee, De Kalb, Etowah, Marshall, St. Clair

Huntsville Division, US District Court Clerk's Office, US Post Office & Courthouse, 101 Holmes Ave NE, Huntsville, AL 35801. 205-534-6495. Counties: Cullman, Jackson, Lawrence, Limestone, Madison, Morgan

Jasper Division, US District Court c/o Birmingham Division, Room 140, US Courthouse, 1729 5th Ave N, Birmingham, AL 35203. 205-731-1700. Counties: Fayette, Lamar, Marion, Walker, Winston

Southern District of Alabama

Mobile Division, US District Court Clerk, 113 St Joseph St, Mobile, AL 36602. 334-690-2371. Counties: Baldwin, Choctaw, Clarke, Conecuh, Escambia, Mobile, Monroe, Washington

Selma Division, US District Court c/o Mobile Division, 113 St Joseph St, Mobile, AL 36602. 334-690-2371. Counties: Dallas, Hale, Marengo, Perry, Wilcox

US Bankruptcy Court
Middle District of Alabama

Montgomery Division, US Bankruptcy Court, PO Box 1248, Montgomery, AL 36102. 334-206-6300. Counties: Autauga, Barbour, Bullock, Butler, Chambers, Chilton, Coffee, Coosa, Covington, Crenshaw, Dale, Elmore, Geneva, Henry, Houston, Lee, Lowndes, Macon, Montgomery, Pike, Randolph, Russell, Tallapoosa

Northern District of Alabama

Anniston Division, US Bankruptcy Court, Room 103, 12th & Noble Sts, Anniston, AL 36201. 205-237-5631. Counties: Calhoun, Cherokee, Clay, Cleburne, De Kalb, Etowah, Marshall, St. Clair, Talladega

Birmingham Division, US Bankruptcy Court, Room 120, 1800 5th Ave N, Birmingham, AL 35203-2111. 205-731-1614. Counties: Blount, Jefferson, Shelby

Decatur Division, US Bankruptcy Court, PO Box 1289, Decatur, AL 35602. 205-353-2817. Counties: Colbert, Cullman, Franklin, Jackson, Lauderdale, Lawrence, Limestone, Madison, Morgan. The part of Winston County north of Double Springs is handled by this division.

Tuscaloosa Division, US Bankruptcy Court, PO Box 3226, Tuscaloosa, AL 35403. 205-752-0426. Counties: Bibb, Fayette, Greene, Lamar, Marion, Pickens, Sumter, Tuscaloosa, Walker, Winston. The part of Winston County north of Double Springs is handled by Decatur Division

Southern District of Alabama

Mobile Division, US Bankruptcy Court, Clerk, 201 St. Louis St, Mobile, AL 36602. 334-441-5391. Voice Case Information System: 334-441-5637. Counties: Baldwin, Choctaw, Clarke, Conecuh, Dallas, Escambia, Hale, Marengo, Mobile, Monroe, Perry, Washington, Wilcox

Alaska

Capital: Juneau (Juneau Borough)	
Number of Counties: 23	**Population:** 603,617
County Court Locations:	**Federal Court Locations:**
•Superior Courts: 0/4 Districts	•District Courts: 5
•District Courts: 3/4 Districts	•Bankruptcy Courts: 1
•Combined Courts: 15	**State Agencies:** 18
•Magistrate Courts: 32	

State Agencies—Summary

General Help Numbers:

State Archives

Department of Education	907-465-2270
Archives Division	Fax: 907-465-2465
141 Willoughby Ave	9AM-5PM
Juneau, AK 99801-1720	
Alternate Telephone:	907-465-2275

Governor's Office

Office of the Governor	907-465-3500
PO Box 110001	Fax: 907-465-3532
Juneau, AK 99811-0001	8AM-5PM

Attorney General's Office

Attorney General's Office	907-465-2133
Law Department	Fax: 907-465-2075
PO Box 110300	8AM-4:30PM
Juneau, AK 99811-0300	

State Legislation

Alaska State Legislature	907-465-4648
State Capitol	Fax: 907-465-2864
130 Seward St, Suite 313	8AM-5PM
Juneau, AK 99801-1182	

In addition to the Internet site listed on this page, a service called "Basis" is available free after a setup fee of $100.00 which allows access to all records. Call 907-465-2419 to obtain a copy of the handbook and to order the program.

Important State Internet Sites:

🌐 *Webscape*	
File Edit View	**Help**

State of Alaska World Wide Web

www.state.ak.us/

This home page includes links to an agency directory, what's new, visitor information, white pages and a search engine.

Legislative Information Page

www.legis.state.ak.us

This site provides legislative information such as the status of bills and legislation, the constitution, bills and resolutions dating back to 1983 and general legislative information.

Alaska Congressional Delegations

www.state.ak.us/local/akpages/LEGISLATURE/home.htm

This site contains links to the House and Senate, committees and other sites.

Alaska Unclaimed Property

www.revenue.state.ak.us/iea/property/index.htm

Name searches for unclaimed property can be done from this site.

State Agencies—Public Records

Criminal Records

Department of Public Safety, Records and Identification, 5700 E Tudor Rd, Anchorage, AK 99507, Main Telephone: 907-269-5765, Fax: 907-269-5091, Hours: 8AM-4:30PM. Access by: mail, visit. There are several "levels" or types of reports released, depending on the requester. If authorized, a requester may all request a national check by the FBI for an additional $24.00.

Corporation Records
Trademarks/Servicemarks
Fictitious Name
Assumed Name
Limited Partnership Records
Limited Liability Company Records

Department of Commerce, Division of Banking, Securities & Corporations, PO Box 110808, Juneau, AK 99811, Main Telephone: 907-465-2530, Fax: 907-465-3257, Hours: 8AM-5PM. Access by: mail, phone, visit, fax, PC.

Uniform Commercial Code
Federal Tax Liens
State Tax Liens

UCC Central File Systems Office, Department of Natural Resources, 3601 C St, Suite 1140A, Anchorage, AK 99503-5947, Main Telephone: 907-269-8899, Hours: 7:30AM-3:30PM. Access by: mail only.

Sales Tax Registrations

State does not impose sales tax.

Birth Certificates

Department of Health & Social Services, Bureau of Vital Statistics, PO Box 110675, Juneau, AK 99811-0675, Main Telephone: 907-465-3391, Hours: 8AM-4:50PM. Access by: mail, phone, visit.

Death Records

Department of Health & Social Services, Bureau of Vital Statistics, PO Box 110675, Juneau, AK 99811-0675, Main Telephone: 907-465-3392, Hours: 8AM-4:50PM. Access by: mail, phone, visit.

Marriage Certificates

Department of Health & Social Services, Bureau of Vital Statistics, PO Box 110675, Juneau, AK 99811-0675, Main Telephone: 907-465-3392, Hours: 8AM-4:50PM. Access by: mail, phone, visit.

Divorce Records

Department of Health & Social Services, Bureau of Vital Statistics, PO Box 110675, Juneau, AK 99811-0675, Main Telephone: 907-465-3392, Hours: 8AM-4:50PM. Access by: mail, phone, visit.

Workers' Compensation Records

Workers' Compensation, PO Box 25512, Juneau, AK 99802, Main Telephone: 907-465-2790, Fax: 907-465-2797, Hours: 8AM-4:30PM. Access by: mail, phone, fax, visit, PC. This agency is working on a web site.

Driver Records

Division of Motor Vehicles, Driver's Records, PO Box 20020, Juneau, AK 99802-0020, Main Telephone: 907-465-4335, Fax: 907-463-5860, Hours: 8AM-5PM. Access by: mail, visit, PC. Copies of tickets are only released, in writing, to the participant, legal representative, or insurance representative.

Vehicle Ownership
Vehicle Identification

Division of Motor Vehicles, Research, 2150 E Dowling Rd, Anchorage, AK 99507, Main Telephone: 907-269-5551, Hours: 8AM-5PM. Access by: mail, visit.

Accident Reports

Department of Public Safety, Driver Services, PO Box 20020, Juneau, AK 99802-0020, Main Telephone: 907-465-4335, Fax: 907-463-5860, Hours: 8AM-5PM. Access by: mail, visit.

Hunting License Information
Fishing License Information

Department of Fish & Game, Licensing Section, PO Box 25525, Juneau, AK 99802-5525, Main Telephone: 907-465-2376, Fax: 907-465-2440, Hours: 8AM-5PM. Access by: mail, phone, fax, visit.

County Courts and Recording Offices

What You Need to Know...

About the Courts	About the Recorder's Office

Administration

Office of Administrative Director	907-264-0547
303 K St	Fax: 907-264-0881
Anchorage, AK 99501	8AM-4:30PM

Court Structure

Alaska is not organized into counties, but rather into 15 boroughs (3 unified home rule municipalities which is combination borough and city and 12 boroughs) and 12 home rule cities. They do not directly coincide with the 4 Judicial Districts into which the judicial system is divided, that is, judicial boundaries cross borough boundaries. In keeping with the format of this Sourcebook, we have listed the courts by their borough or home rule cities. You should search through the city court location names to determine the correct court for your search. Probate is handled by the Superior Courts.

Searching Hints

Documents may not be filed by fax in **any** AK court location without prior authorization of a judge.

The fees established by court rules for Alaska courts are: Search Fee $15.00 per hour or fraction thereof, Certification Fee $5.00 per document and $2.00 per page after the first, Copy Fee $.25 per page.

Magistrate Courts vary widely in how records are maintained and in the hours of operation (some are open only a few hours per week)

Online Access

There is no internal or external on-line judicial computer system available.

Organization

23 boroughs, 34 filing offices. Recording is done by districts, which overlay the borough system. The recording officer is District Recorder. The entire state except the Aleutian Islands is in the Alaska Time Zone (AK).

UCC Records

Financing statements are filed at the state level, except for consumer goods, farm collateral and real estate related collateral, which are filed with the District Recorder. All districts will perform UCC searches at $5.00 per debtor name for information and $15.00 with copies. Use search request form UCC-11. Copies ordered separately usually cost $2.00 per financing statement.

Lien Records

All state and federal tax liens are filed with the District Recorder. Districts do not perform tax lien searches.

Real Estate Records

Districts do not perform real estate searches. Certification fees are usually $5.00 per document.

County Courts and Recording Offices

Aleutian Islands

Real Estate Recording—Aleutian Islands District Recorder, 3601 C Street, Suite 1140, Anchorage, AK 99503. 907-269-8899. 8AM-3:30PM (HT).

Misdemeanor, Civil Actions Under $5,000, Small Claims—(3rd Dist) Sand Point Magistrate Court, Box 89, Sand Point, AK 99661-0089. 907-264-0456. Fax: 907-383-5385. 10AM-3:30PM (HT). Access by: Mail, in person.

(3rd Dist) St Paul Island Magistrate Court, Box 170, St Paul Island, AK 99660-0170. 907-546-2300. Fax: 907-546-2489. 11AM-2:30PM T/11AM-5PM W-Sat (HT). Access by: Mail, in person.

(3rd Dist) Unalaska Magistrate Court, Box 245, Unalaska, AK 99685-0245. 907-581-1266. Fax: 907-581-2809. 8:30AM-4:30PM (HT). Access by: Mail, in person.

Anchorage Borough

Real Estate Recording—Anchorage District Recorder, 3601 C Street, Suite 1140, Anchorage, AK 99503. 907-269-8899. 8AM-3:30PM (AK).

Felony, Misdemeanor, Civil, Eviction, Small Claims, Probate—(3rd Dist) Superior & District Court, 825 West 4th, Anchorage, AK 99501-2083. 907-264-0493. Probate: 907-264-0435. Fax: 907-264-0873. 8AM-4:30PM. Access by: Phone, fax, mail, in person.

Barrow District

Real Estate Recording—Barrow District Recorder, 1648 S. Cushman St. #201, Fairbanks, AK 99701. 907-452-3521. 8:30AM-4PM (AK).

Bethel

Real Estate Recording—Bethel District Recorder, 204 Chief Eddie Hoffman Highway, City Office Building, Bethel, AK 99559. 907-543-3391. 9:15AM-Noon, 1-3:15PM (AK).

Felony, Misdemeanor, Civil, Eviction, Small Claims, Probate—(4th Dist) Superior & District Court, Box 130, Bethel, AK 99559-0130. 907-543-2298. Fax: 907-543-4419. 8AM-4:30PM (AK). Access by: Phone, mail, in person.

Misdemeanor, Civil Actions Under $5,000, Small Claims—(4th Dist) Aniak Magistrate Court, Box 147, Aniak, AK 99557-0147. 907-675-4325. Fax: 907-675-4278. 8AM-4:30PM (AK). Access by: Mail, in person.

(4th Dist) Quinhagak Magistrate Court, PO Box 109, Quinhagak, AK 99655-0109. 907-556-8015. Fax: 907-556-8247. (AK). Access by: Mail, in person.

Bristol Bay Borough

Real Estate Recording—Bristol Bay District Recorder, 3601 C Street, Suite 1140, Anchorage, AK 99503. 907-269-8899. 8AM-3:30PM (AK).

Misdemeanor, Civil Actions Under $5,000, Small Claims—(3rd Dist) Naknek Magistrate Court, Box 229, Naknek, AK 99633-0229. 907-246-6151. Fax: 907-246-7418. 8:30AM-4PM. Access by: Mail, in person.

Cape Nome District

Real Estate Recording—Cape Nome District Recorder, Front Street, 3rd Floor, Old Federal Building, Nome, AK 99762. 907-443-5178. 8AM-12:30PM (AK).

Chitina District

Real Estate Recording—Chitina District Recorder, Mile 115 Richardson Hwy, ATHNA Bldg., Glennallen, AK 99588. 907-822-3726. 8:30AM-4PM (AK).

Cordova District

Real Estate Recording—Cordova District Recorder, 3601 C Street, Suite 1140, Anchorage, AK 99503. 907-269-8899. 8AM-3:30PM (AK).

Denali

Misdemeanor, Civil Actions Under $5,000, Small Claims—(4th Dist) Healy Magistrate Court, Box 298, Healy, AK 99743-0298. 907-683-2213. Fax: 907-683-1383. 8AM-4:30PM (AK). Access by: Mail, in person.

Dillingham

Misdemeanor, Civil Actions Under $5,000, Small Claims—(3rd Dist) Dillingham Magistrate Court, Box 909, Dillingham, AK 99576-0909. 907-842-5215. Fax: 907-842-5746. 8AM-4:30PM (AK). Access by: Mail, in person.

Fairbanks District

Real Estate Recording—Fairbanks District Recorder, 1648 S. Cushman St. #201, Fairbanks, AK 99701. 907-452-3521. 8:30AM-4PM (AK).

Fairbanks North Star Borough

Real Estate Recording—The proper location for real estate recording in Alaska is based on Recording Districts, not Boroughs.

Felony, Misdemeanor, Civil, Eviction, Small Claims, Probate—(4th Dist) Superior & District Court, 604 Barnette St, Fairbanks, AK 99701. 907-452-9265. Fax: 907-452-9342. 8AM-4:30PM. Access by: Mail, in person.

Fort Gibbon District

Real Estate Recording—Fort Gibbon District Recorder, 1648 S. Cushman St. #201, Fairbanks, AK 99701. 907-452-3521. 8:30AM-4PM (AK).

Haines Borough

Real Estate Recording—Haines District Recorder, 400 Willoughby, 3rd Floor, Juneau, AK 99801. 907-465-3449. 8:30AM-4PM (AK).

Misdemeanor, Civil Actions Under $50,000, Small Claims—(1st Dist) District Court, Box 169, Haines, AK 99827. 907-766-2801. Fax: 907-766-3148. 8AM-4:30PM. Access by: Phone, mail, in person.

Homer District

Real Estate Recording—Homer District Recorder, 195 E. Bunnell Ave., Suite A, Homer, AK 99603. 907-235-8136. 8:30AM-11:30AM, 12:30-4PM (AK).

Iliamna District

Real Estate Recording—Iliamna District Recorder, 3601 C Street, Suite 1140, Anchorage, AK 99503. 907-269-8899. 8AM-3:30PM (AK).

Juneau Borough

Real Estate Recording—Juneau District Recorder, 400 Willoughby, 3rd Floor, Juneau, AK 99801. 907-465-3449. 8:30AM-4PM (AK).

Felony, Misdemeanor, Civil, Eviction, Small Claims, Probate—(1st Dist) Superior & District Court, Diamond Courthouse, Box 114100, Juneau, AK 99811-4100. 907-463-4700. Fax: 907-463-3788. 8AM-4:30PM. Access by: Mail, in person.

Kenai District

Real Estate Recording—Kenai District Recorder, 120 Trading Bay Road, Suite 230, Kenai, AK 99611. 907-283-3118. 8:30AM-4PM (AK).

Kenai Peninsula Borough

Real Estate Recording—The proper place for real estate recording is based on Recording Districts, not Boroughs.

Felony, Misdemeanor, Civil, Eviction, Small Claims, Probate—(3rd Dist) Superior & District Court, 125 Trading Bay Dr, Ste 100, Kenai, AK 99611. 907-283-3110. Fax: 907-293-8535. 8AM-4:30PM. Access by: Mail, in person.

Misdemeanor, Civil Actions Under $50,000, Small Claims—(3rd Dist) District Court, 3670 Lake St, Ste 400, Homer, AK 99603-7686. 907-235-8171. Fax: 907-235-4257. 8AM-4:30PM. Access by: Mail, in person.

Misdemeanor, Civil Actions Under $5,000, Small Claims—(3rd Dist) Seward Magistrate Court, Box 1929, Seward, AK 99664-1929. 907-224-3075. Fax: 907-227-7192. 8AM-4:30PM. Access by: Fax, mail, in person.

Ketchikan District

Real Estate Recording—Ketchikan District Recorder, 415 Main Street, Room 320, Ketchikan, AK 99901. 907-225-3142. 8:30AM-4PM (AK).

Ketchikan Gateway Borough

Real Estate Recording—The proper location for real estate recording in Alaska is based on Recording Districts, not Boroughs.

Felony, Misdemeanor, Civil, Eviction, Small Claims, Probate—(1st Dist) Superior & District Court, 415 Main, Rm 400, Ketchikan, AK 99901-6399. 907-225-3195. Fax: 907-225-7849. 8AM-4:30PM. Access by: Mail, in person.

Kobuk Borough

Real Estate Recording—The proper place for real estate recording is based on Recording Districts, not Boroughs.

Kodiak District

Real Estate Recording—Kodiak District Recorder, 204 Mission Road, Room 16, Kodiak, AK 99615. 907-486-9432. 8:30AM-Noon, 1-4PM (AK).

Kodiak Island Borough

Real Estate Recording—The proper place for real estate recording is based on Recording DIstricts, not Boroughs.

Felony, Misdemeanor, Civil, Eviction, Small Claims, Probate—(3rd Dist) Superior & District Court, 204 Mission Road, Rm 10, Kodiak, AK 99615-7312. 907-486-1600. Fax: 907-486-1660. 8AM-4:30PM M,T,Th,F; 9AM-4:30PM W. Access by: Mail, in person.

Kotzebue District

Real Estate Recording—Kotzebue District Recorder, 1648 S. Cushman St. #201, Fairbanks, AK 99701. 907-452-3521. 8:30AM-4PM (AK).

Kuskokwim District

Real Estate Recording—Kuskokwim District Recorder, 204 Chief Eddie Hoffman Highway, City Office Building, Bethel, AK 99559. 907-543-3391. 9:15AM-Noon, 1-3:15PM (AK).

Kvichak District

Real Estate Recording—Kvichak District Recorder, 3601 C Street, Suite 1140, Anchorage, AK 99503. 907-269-8899. 8AM-3:30PM (AK).

Manley Hot Springs District

Real Estate Recording—Manley Hot Springs District Recorder, 1648 S. Cushman St. #201, Fairbanks, AK 99701. 907-452-3521. 8:30AM-4PM (AK).

Matanuska-Susitna Borough

Real Estate Recording—The proper place for real estate recording in Alaska is based on Recording Districts, not Boroughs.

Felony, Misdemeanor, Civil, Eviction, Small Claims, Probate—(3rd Dist) Superior & District Court, 435 S Denali, Palmer, AK 99645-6437. 907-746-8109. Fax: 907-746-4151. 8AM-4:30PM. Access by: Mail, in person.

Mount McKinley District

Real Estate Recording—Mount McKinley District Recorder, 1648 S. Cushman St. #201, Fairbanks, AK 99701. 907-452-3521. 8:30AM-4PM (AK).

Nenana District

Real Estate Recording—Nenana District Recorder, 1648 S. Cushman St. #201, Fairbanks, AK 99701. 907-452-3521. 8:30AM-4PM (AK).

Nome Borough

Real Estate Recording—The proper place for real estate recording in Alaska is based on Recording Districts, not Boroughs.

Felony, Misdemeanor, Civil, Eviction, Small Claims, Probate—(2nd Dist) Superior & District Court, Box 1110, Nome, AK 99762-1110. 907-443-5216. Fax: 907-443-2192. 8AM-4:30PM (AK). Access by: Phone, fax, mail, in person.

Misdemeanor, Civil Actions Under $5,000, Small Claims—(2nd Dist) Gambell Magistrate Court, Box 48, Gambell, AK 99742-0048. 907-985-5133. Fax: 907-985-5133. 8AM-11:30AM (AK). Access by: Phone, fax, mail, in person.

(2nd Dist) Unalakleet Magistrate Court, Box 250, Unalakleet, AK 99684-0185. 907-624-3015. Fax: 907-624-3118. 8AM-1:30PM (AK). Access by: Mail, in person.

North Slope Borough

Real Estate Recording—The proper place for real estate recording in Alaska is based on Recording Districts, not Boroughs.

Felony, Misdemeanor, Civil, Eviction, Small Claims, Probate—(2nd Dist) Superior & District Court, Box 270, Barrow, AK 99723-0270. 907-852-4800. Fax: 907-852-4804. 8AM-4:30PM. Access by: Phone, mail, in person.

Northwest Arctic Borough

Real Estate Recording—The proper place for real estate recording in Alaska is based on Recording Districts, not Boroughs.

Felony, Misdemeanor, Civil, Eviction, Small Claims, Probate—(2nd Dist) Superior & District Court, Box 317, Kotzebue, AK 99752-0317. 907-442-3208. Fax: 907-442-3974. 8AM-4:30PM. Access by: Mail, in person.

Misdemeanor, Civil Actions Under $5,000, Small Claims—(2nd Dist) Ambler Magistrate Court, Box 86028, Ambler, AK 99786. 907-445-2137. Fax: 907-445-2136. 9AM-2PM. Access by: Mail, in person.

(2nd Dist) Kiana Magistrate Court, Box 170, Kiana, AK 99749-0170. 907-475-2167. Fax: 907-475-2169. 10AM-3PM M,W,F. Access by: Mail, in person.

Nulato District

Real Estate Recording—Nulato District Recorder, 1648 S. Cushman St. #201, Fairbanks, AK 99701. 907-452-3521. 8:30AM-4PM (AK).

Palmer District

Real Estate Recording—Palmer District Recorder, 836 South Colony Way, Palmer, AK 99645. 907-745-3080. 8:30AM-4PM (AK).

Petersburg District

Real Estate Recording—Petersburg District Recorder, 415 Main Street, Room 320, Ketchikan, AK 99901. 907-225-3142. 8:30AM-Noon, 1-4PM (AK).

Prince of Wales-Outer Ketchikan

Real Estate Recording—The proper place for real estate recording in Alaska is based on Recording Districts, not Boroughs.

Misdemeanor, Civil Actions Under $5,000, Small Claims—(1st Dist) Craig Magistrate Court, Box 646, Craig, AK 99921. 907-826-3316. Fax: 907-826-3904. 8AM-4:30PM (AK). Access by: Phone, mail, in person.

Rampart District

Real Estate Recording—Rampart District Recorder, 1648 S. Cushman St. #201, Fairbanks, AK 99701. 907-452-3521. 8:30AM-4PM (AK).

Seldovia District

Real Estate Recording—Seldovia District Recorder, 195 E. Bunnell Ave., Suite A, Homer, AK 99603. 907-235-8136. 8:30-11:30AM, 12:30-4PM (AK).

Seward District

Real Estate Recording—Seward District Recorder, 5th & Adams, Municipal Building Room 208, Seward, AK 99664. 907-224-3075. 8:30AM-4PM (AK).

Sitka Borough

Real Estate Recording—Sitka District Recorder, 210C Lake Street, Sitka, AK 99835. 907-747-3275. 8:30AM-Noon, 1-4PM M-Th (AK).

Felony, Misdemeanor, Civil, Eviction, Small Claims, Probate—(1st Dist) Superior & District Court, 304 Lake St, Rm 203, Sitka, AK 99835-7759. 907-747-3291. Fax: 907-747-6690. 8AM-4:30PM. Access by: Phone, fax, mail, in person.

Skagway District

Real Estate Recording—Skagway District Recorder, 400 Willoughby, 3rd Floor, Juneau, AK 99801. 907-269-8899. 8:30AM-4PM (AK).

Skagway-Hoonah-Angoon

Misdemeanor, Civil Actions Under $50,000, Small Claims—(1st Dist) District Court, Box 430, Hoonah, AK 99829-0430. 907-945-3668. Fax: 907-945-3637. 8AM-Noon, 1-4:30PM. Access by: Mail, in person.

Misdemeanor, Civil Actions Under $5,000, Small Claims—(1st Dist) Angoon Magistrate Court, Box 202, Angoon, AK 99820. 907-788-3229. Fax: 907-788-3108. 11AM-2PM. Access by: Mail, in person.

(1st Dist) Pelican Magistrate Court, Box 36, Pelican, AK 99832-0036. 907-735-2217. Fax: 907-735-2482. 8:30-5PM M-T, Closed 12-1, 10AM-12:30PM F. Access by: Mail, in person.

(1st Dist) Skagway Magistrate Court, Box 495, Skagway, AK 99840-0495. 907-983-2368. Fax: 907-983-3800. 9AM-Noon, 1-4:30PM M; 8AM-Noon, 1-4:30PM T-F. Access by: Mail, in person.

(1st Dist) Yakutat Magistrate Court, Box 426, Yakutat, AK 99689-0426. 907-784-3274. Fax: 907-784-3257. 8AM-Noon. Access by: Phone, fax, mail, in person.

Skagway-Yakutat-Angoon Borough

Real Estate Recording—The proper place for real estate recording in Alaska is based on Recording Districts, not Boroughs.

Southeast Fairbanks

Real Estate Recording—The proper place for real estate recording in Alaska is based on Recording Districts, not Boroughs.

Misdemeanor, Civil Actions Under $5,000, Small Claims—(4th Dist) Delta Junction Magistrate Court, Box 401, Delta Junction, AK 99737-0401. 907-895-4211. Fax: 907-895-4204. 8AM-Noon, 1-4:30PM (AK). Access by: Mail, in person.

(4th Dist) Tok Magistrate Court, Box 187, Tok, AK 99780-0187. 907-883-5171. Fax: 907-883-4367. 8AM-4:30PM (AK). Access by: Mail, in person.

Talkeetna District

Real Estate Recording—Talkeetna District Recorder, 836 South Colony Way, Palmer, AK 99645. 907-745-3080. 8:30AM-4PM (AK).

Valdez District

Real Estate Recording—Valdez District Recorder, 213 Meals Avenue, Courthouse, Valdez, AK 99686. 907-835-2266. 8:30AM-Noon, 1-4PM (AK).

Valdez-Cordova Borough

Real Estate Recording—The proper place for real estate recording in Alaska is based on Recording Districts, not Boroughs.

Felony, Misdemeanor, Civil, Eviction, Small Claims, Probate—(3rd Dist) Superior & District Court, Box 127, Valdez, AK 99686-0127. 907-835-2266. Fax: 907-835-3764. 8AM-4:30PM (AK). Access by: Fax, mail, in person.

Misdemeanor, Civil Actions Under $5,000, Small Claims—(3rd Dist) Cordova Magistrate Court, Box 898, Cordova, AK 99574-0898. 907-424-3378. Fax: 907-424-7581. 8AM-4:30PM (AK). Access by: Phone, fax, mail, in person.

(3rd Dist) Glennallen Magistrate Court, Box 86, Glennallen, AK 99588-0086. 907-822-3405. Fax: 907-822-3601. 8AM-4:30PM (AK). Access by: Mail, in person.

(3rd Dist) Whittier Magistrate Court, Box 729, Whittier, AK 99693-0729. 907-472-2356. Fax: 907-472-2456. (AK). Access by: Mail, in person.

Wade Hampton Borough

Real Estate Recording—The proper place for real estate recording in Alaska is based on Recording Districts, not Boroughs.

Misdemeanor, Civil Actions Under $5,000, Small Claims—(2nd Dist) Chevak Magistrate Court, Box 238, Chevak, AK 99563-0238. 907-858-7231. Fax: 907-858-7230. 9AM-3:30PM (AK). Access by: Mail, in person.

(2nd Dist) Emmonak Magistrate Court, Box 176, Emmonak, AK 99581-0176. 907-949-1748. Fax: 907-949-1535. 8AM-4:30PM (AK). Access by: Mail, in person.

(2nd Dist) St Mary's Magistrate Court, Box 183, St Mary's, AK 99658-0183. 907-438-2912. Fax: 907-438-2819. 8AM-4:30PM (AK). Access by: Phone, fax, mail, in person.

Wrangell District

Real Estate Recording—Wrangell District Recorder, 415 Main Street, Room 320, Ketchikan, AK 99901. 907-225-3142. 8:30AM-Noon, 1-4PM (AK).

Wrangell-Petersburg Borough

Real Estate Recording—The proper place for real estate recording in Alaska is based on Recording Districts, not Boroughs.

Felony, Misdemeanor, Civil, Eviction, Small Claims, Probate—(1st Dist) Superior & District Court, Box 1009, Petersburg, AK 99833-1009. 907-772-3824. Fax: 907-772-3018. 8AM-4:30PM (AK). Access by: Phone, fax, mail, in person.

(1st Dist) Superior & District Court, Box 869, Wrangell, AK 99929-0869. 907-874-2311. Fax: 907-874-3509. 8AM-4:30PM (AK). Access by: Fax, mail, in person.

Misdemeanor, Civil Actions Under $5,000, Small Claims—(1st Dist) Kake Magistrate Court, Box 100, Kake, AK 99830-0100. 907-785-3651. Fax: 907-785-3152. 8AM-Noon (AK). Access by: Mail, in person.

Yukon-Koyukuk Borough

Real Estate Recording—The proper place for real estate recording in Alaska is based on Recording Districts, not Boroughs.

Misdemeanor, Civil Actions Under $5,000, Small Claims—(4th Dist) Fort Yukon Magistrate Court, Box 211, Fort Yukon, AK 99740-0211. 907-662-2336. Fax: 907-662-2824. 9:30AM-3PM (AK). Access by: Mail, in person.

(4th Dist) Galena Magistrate Court, Box 167, Galena, AK 99741-0167. 907-656-1322. Fax: 907-656-1546. 8AM-4:30PM (AK). Access by: Mail, in person.

(4th Dist) McGrath Magistrate Court, Box 167, Galena, AK 99741-0167. 907-656-1322. Fax: 907-656-1546. (AK). Access by: Mail, in person.

(4th Dist) Nenana Magistrate Court, Box 449, Nenana, AK 99760-0449. 907-832-5430. Fax: 907-832-5841. 8:30AM-4PM (AK). Access by: Mail, in person.

(4th Dist) Tanana Magistrate Court, Box 449, Nenana, AK 99777. 907-366-7243. Fax: 907-832-5841. Th-F 2nd full week ea month (AK). Access by: Mail, in person.

Federal Courts

US District Court
District of Alaska

Anchorage Division, US District Court Box 4, 222 W 7th Ave, Anchorage, AK 99513-7564. 907-271-5568. Counties: Aleutian Islands-East, Aleutian Islands-West, Anchorage Borough, Bristol Bay Borough, Kenai Peninsula Borough, Kodiak Island Borough, Matanuska-Susitna Borough, Valdez-Cordova

Fairbanks Division, US District Court Room 332, 101 12th Ave, Fairbanks, AK 99701. 907-451-5791. Counties: Bethel, Fairbanks North Star Borough, North Slope Borough, Northwest Arctic Borough, Southeast Fairbanks, Wade Hampton, Yukon-Koyukuk

Juneau Division, US District Court PO Box 020349, Juneau, AK 99802-0349. 907-586-7458. Counties: Haines Borough, Juneau Borough, Prince of Wales-Outer Ketchikan, Sitka Borough, Skagway-Hoonah-Angoon, Wrangell-Petersburg

Ketchikan Division, US District Court 648 Mission St, Room 507, Ketchikan, AK 99901. 907-247-7576. Counties: Ketchikan Gateway Borough

Nome Division, US District Court Box 130, Nome, AK 99762. 907-443-5216. Counties: Nome

US Bankruptcy Court
District of Alaska

Anchorage Division, US Bankruptcy Court, Historic Courthouse, Suite 138, 605 W 4th Ave, Anchorage, AK 99501-2296. 907-271-2655. Voice Case Information System: 907-271-2658. Counties: All boroughs and districts in Alaska

Arizona

Capital: Phoenix (Maricopa County)	
Number of Counties: 15	**Population:** 4,217,940
County Court Locations:	**Federal Court Locations:**
•Superior Courts: 15/ 15 Counties	•District Courts: 3
•Justice of the Peace: 80/ 83 Precincts	•Bankruptcy Courts: 3
Municipal Courts: 85	**State Agencies:** 19

State Agencies—Summary

General Help Numbers:

State Archives

Library, Archives & Public Records Dept.	602-542-4159
1700 W Washington, Room 442	Fax: 602-542-4972
Phoenix, AZ 85007	8AM-5PM
Historical Society:	602-929-0292
Reference Librarian:	602-542-3710

Governor's Office

Governor's Office	602-542-4331
State Capitol, W Wing,	
1700 W Washington	Fax: 602-542-7602
Phoenix, AZ 85007	8AM-5PM

Attorney General's Office

Attorney General's Office	602-542-5025
1275 W Washington	Fax: 602-542-1275
Phoenix, AZ 85007	8AM-5PM
Alternate Telephone:	602-542-4266

State Legislation

Arizona Legislature	Rep - 602-542-4221
State Senate - Room 203	Sen . 602-542-3559
House of Rep. Room 111	Rep Fax: 602-542-4099
1700 W Washington	Sen Fax: 602-542-3429
Phoenix, AZ 85007	8AM-5PM

Important State Internet Sites:

⚙ Webscape	
File Edit View	**Help**

State of Arizona World Wide Web
www.state.az.us/

Links to major locations in the State Government, such as the Legislature, Governor's office and other sites.

Arizona Legislative Information System
www.azleg.state.az.us

Contains information on legislative members, bills (status & full text), committees, and the constitution.

State Agencies & Other Government Resources
www.azleg.state.az.us/othergvt.htm

Provides links to 19 state agencies and 20 other government resources.

Arizona Archives
www.lib.az.us/archives/archdiv.html

Provides information about the State archives division.

UCC Information
www.sosaz.com/ucc.htm

This site provides a link to UCC searching online.

Unclaimed Property
www.revenue.state.az.us/unclprop.htm

This site provides online searching for unclaimed property.

State Agencies—Public Records

Criminal Records

Department of Public Safety, Criminal History Records Unit, PO Box 6638, Phoenix, AZ 85005-6638, Main Telephone: 602-223-2223, Hours: 8AM-5PM. Access by: mail only.

Corporation Records
Limited Liability Company Records
Limited Partnerships

Corporation Commission, 1300 W Washington, Phoenix, AZ 85007, Main Telephone: 602-542-3026, Fax: 602-542-3414, Hours: 8AM-5PM. Access by: mail, phone, fax, visit, PC. Fictitious Name & Assumed Name records are found at the county level.

Trademarks/Servicemarks
Trade Names
Limited Partnership Records

Secretary of State, Trademarks/Tradenames/Limited Partnership Division, 1700 W Washington , 7th Floor, Phoenix, AZ 85007, Main Telephone: 602-542-6187, Fax: 602-542-7386, Hours: 8AM-5PM. Access by: mail, phone, visit.

Uniform Commercial Code
Federal Tax Liens
State Tax Liens

UCC Division, Secretary of State, State Capitol, West Wing, 7th Floor, Phoenix, AZ 85007, Main Telephone: 602-542-6178, Fax: 602-542-7386, Hours: 8AM - 5PM. Access by: mail, visit, PC.

Sales Tax Registrations

Revenue Department, Taxpayer Assistance, 1600 W Monroe, Phoenix, AZ 85007, Main Telephone: 602-542-4656, Fax: 602-542-4772, Hours: 8AM-5PM. Access by: mail, phone, visit.

Birth Certificates

Department of Health Services, Vital Records Section, PO Box 3887, Phoenix, AZ 85030, Main Telephone: 602-255-3260, Fax: 602-249-3040, Hours: 8AM-5PM (counter closes at 4:30 PM). Access by: mail, fax, visit.

Death Records

Department of Health Services, Vital Records Section, PO Box 3887, Phoenix, AZ 85030, Main Telephone: 602-255-3260, Fax: 602-249-3040, Hours: 8AM-5PM (counter closes at 4:30 PM). Access by: mail, fax, visit.

Marriage Certificates
Divorce Records

Records not available from state agency; search at the county court level.

Workers' Compensation Records

State Compensation Fund, 3031 N Second St, Phoenix, AZ 85012, Main Telephone: 602-631-2000, Fax: 602-631-2213, Hours: 8AM-5PM. Access by: mail, visit.

Driver Records

Motor Vehicle Division, Record Services Section, PO Box 2100, Mail Drop 539M, Phoenix, AZ 85001, Main Telephone: 602-255-8357, Hours: 8AM-5PM. Access by: mail, visit, PC. Arizona will suspend the license for unpaid out-of-state tickets.

Vehicle Ownership
Vehicle Identification

Motor Vehicle Division, Record Services Section, PO Box 2100, Mail Drop 504M, Phoenix, AZ 85001, Main Telephone: 602-255-8359, Hours: 8AM-5PM. Access by: mail, visit.

Accident Reports

Department of Public Safety, Accident Reports, PO Box 6638, Phoenix, AZ 85005, Main Telephone: 602-223-2236, Hours: 8AM-5PM. Access by: mail, visit.

Hunting License Information
Fishing License Information

Game & Fish Department, Information & Licensing Division, 2222 W Greenway Rd, Phoenix, AZ 85023-4399, Main Telephone: 602-942-3000, Fax: 602-789-3924, Hours: 8AM-5PM.
Access by: mail, visit. This agency will also release watercraft registration information within specific legal constraints.

County Courts and Recording Offices

What You Need to Know...

<table>
<tr><td>

About the Courts

Administration

Administrative Offices of the Courts	602-542-9301
Arizona Supreme Court Bldg	8AM-5PM
1501 W Washington	

Court Structure

The Superior, Justice and Municipal courts generally have separate jurisdiction over case types as indicated in the charts. Most courts will search their records by plaintiff or defendant. Estate cases are handled by Superior Court. Fees are the same as for civil and criminal case searching.

Searching Hints

Many offices do not perform searches due to personnel and/or budget constraints. As computerization of record offices increases across the state, more record offices are providing public access computer terminals.

Fees across all jurisdictions, as established by the Arizona Supreme Court and State Legislature, are as follows: Search — $11.50 per name, Certification — $11.50 per document plus copy fee, Copies — $1.25 per page.

Online Access

A system called **ACAP** (Arizona Court Automation Project) is in development and will be implemented in 75 courts in 1998. ACAP is, fundamentally, a case and cash management information processing system. When finally implemented it will provide all participating courts access to all records on the system. It will **not** be available initially through remote access nor will the public be able to view certain case records since adoption, juvenile, and sealed records are considered confidential.

The Maricopa and Pima county courts maintain their own systems, but will also, under current planning, be part of ACAP. These two counties provide remote access capability. For current ACAP information, you may call 602-542-9300.

</td><td>

About the Recorder's Office

Organization

15 counties, 16 filing offices. **The Navajo Nation is profiled here.** The recording officer is County Recorder. Recordings are usually placed in a Grantor/Grantee index. As of January 15, 1995 all county offices except Maricopa changed their telephone area code to 520. The entire state is in the Mountain Time Zone (MST).

UCC Records

Financing statements are filed at the state level, except for consumer goods, farm collateral, and real estate related collateral, which are filed with the County Recorder. All counties will perform UCC searches. Use search request form UCC-3. Search fees are generally $10.00 per debtor name. Copies usually cost $1.00 per page.

Lien Records

Federal and state tax liens on personal property of businesses are filed with the Secretary of State. Other federal and state tax liens are filed with the County Recorder. Counties do **not** perform tax lien searches. Other Liens include executions, judgments, and labor.

Real Estate Records

Counties do **not** perform real estate searches. Copy fees are usually $1.00 per page. Certification fees are usually $3.00 per document.

</td></tr>
</table>

County Courts and Recording Offices

Apache County

Real Estate Recording—Apache County Recorder, 75 West Cleveland, St. Johns, AZ 85936. 520-337-4364. Fax: 520-337-2003. 8AM-5PM (MST).

Felony, Civil Actions Over $5,000, Probate—Superior Court, PO Box 365, St John's, AZ 85936. 520-337-4364. Fax: 520-337-2771. 8AM-5PM (MST). Access by: Mail, in person.

Misdemeanor, Civil Actions Under $5,000, Eviction, Small Claims—Chinle Justice Court, PO Box 888, Chinle, AZ 86503. 520-674-5922. Fax: 520-674-5926. 8AM-5PM (MST). Access by: Phone, fax, mail, in person. Phone access is discouraged.

Puerco Justice Court, PO Box 336, Sanders, AZ 86512. 520-688-2954. Fax: 520-688-2244. 8AM-12PM, 1PM-5PM (MST). Access by: Phone, mail, in person.

Round Valley Justice Court, PO Box 1356, Springerville, AZ 85938. 520-333-4613. Fax: 520-333-5761. 8AM-12PM 1PM-5PM (MST). Access by: Phone, fax, mail, in person.

St John's Justice Court, PO Box 308, St John's, AZ 85936. 520-337-4364. Fax: 520-337-2427. 8AM-5PM (MST). Access by: Mail, in person.

Cochise County

Real Estate Recording—Cochise County Recorder, Cochise County Administrative Building, 4 Ledge Ave., Bisbee, AZ 85603. 520-432-9270. Fax: 520-432-9274. 8AM-5PM (MST).

Felony, Civil Actions Over $5,000, Probate—Superior Court, PO Box CK, Bisbee, AZ 85603. 520-432-9364. Fax: 520-432-4850. 8AM-5PM (MST). Access by: Phone, fax, mail, in person.

Misdemeanor, Civil Actions Under $5,000, Eviction, Small Claims—Benson Justice Court, PO Box 2167, Benson, AZ 85602. 520-586-2247. Fax: 520-586-9647. 8AM-5PM (MST). Access by: Fax, mail, in person.

Bisbee Justice Court, PO Box 1893, Bisbee, AZ 85603. 520-432-9542. Fax: 520-432-9594. 8AM-5PM (MST). Access by: Phone, fax, mail, in person.

Bowie Justice Court, PO Box 317, Bowie, AZ 85605. 520-847-2303. Fax: 520-847-2242. 8AM-5PM (MST). Access by: Phone, fax, mail, in person.

Douglas Justice Court, 661 G Ave, Douglas, AZ 85607. 520-364-3561. Fax: 520-364-3684. 8AM-5PM (MST). Access by: Fax, mail, in person.

Sierra Vista Justice Court, 4001 E Foothills Dr, Sierra Vista, AZ 85635. 520-452-4980. Fax: 520-452-4986. 8AM-5PM (MST). Access by: Fax, mail, in person.

Willcox Justice Court, 450 S Haskell, Willcox, AZ 85643. 520-384-2105. Fax: 520-384-4305. 8AM-5PM (MST). Access by: Fax, mail, in person.

Coconino County

Real Estate Recording—Coconino County Recorder, 100 E. Birch, Flagstaff, AZ 86001. 520-779-6585. Fax: 520-779-6739. 8AM-5PM (MST).

Felony, Civil Actions Over $5,000, Probate—Superior Court, 100 E Birch St, Flagstaff, AZ 86001. 520-779-6535. 8AM-5PM (MST). Access by: Mail, in person.

Misdemeanor, Civil Actions Under $5,000, Eviction, Small Claims—Flagstaff Justice Court, 100 E Birch Ave, Flagstaff, AZ 86001. 520-779-6806. 8AM-5PM (MST). Access by: Mail, in person.

Fredonia Justice Court, 100 N Main, Fredonia, AZ 86022. 520-643-7472. Fax: 520-643-7472. 8AM-5PM (MST). Access by: Mail, in person.

Page Justice Court, PO Box 1565, Page, AZ 86040. 520-645-8871. Fax: 520-645-1869. 8AM-5PM (MST). Access by: Mail, in person.

Williams Justice Court, 117 W Route 66 #180, Williams, AZ 86046. 520-635-2691. 8AM-5PM (MST). Access by: Mail, in person.

Gila County

Real Estate Recording—Gila County Recorder, 1400 East Ash Street, Globe, AZ 85501. 520-425-3231. Fax: 520-425-9270. 8AM-5PM (MST).

Felony, Civil Actions Over $5,000, Probate—Superior Court, 1400 E Ash, Globe, AZ 85501. 520-425-3231. 8AM-5PM (MST). Access by: Mail, in person.

Misdemeanor, Civil Actions Under $5,000, Eviction, Small Claims—Globe Justice Court, 1400 E Ash, Globe, AZ 85501. 520-425-3231. 8AM-5PM (MST). Access by: Phone, mail, in person.

Miami Justice Court, 506 Sullivan St, Miami, AZ 85539. 520-473-4461. 8AM-5PM (MST). Access by: Mail, in person.

Payson Justice Court, 714 S Beeline Hwy #103, Payson, AZ 85541. 520-474-5267. Fax: 520-474-6214. 8AM-5PM (MST). Access by: Phone, fax, mail, in person.

Pine Justice Court, PO Box 2169, Pine, AZ 85544. 520-476-3525. Fax: 520-476-3128. 8AM-5PM (MST). Access by: Mail, in person.

Hayden-Winkleman Justice Court, PO Box 680, Winkelman, AZ 85292. 520-356-7638. 8AM-5PM (MST). Access by: Mail, in person.

Graham County

Real Estate Recording—Graham County Recorder, 921 Thatcher Blvd., Safford, AZ 85546. 520-428-3560. Fax: 520-428-5951. 8AM-5PM (MST).

Felony, Civil Actions Over $5,000, Probate—Superior Court, 800 Main St, Safford, AZ 85546-3803. 520-428-3100. Fax: 520-428-0061. 8AM-5PM (MST). Access by: Phone, fax, mail, in person.

Misdemeanor, Civil Actions Under $5,000, Eviction, Small Claims—Pima Justice Court Precinct #2, PO Box 1159, 136 W Center St, Pima, AZ 85543. 520-485-2771. Fax: 520-485-9961. 8AM-5PM (MST). Access by: Fax, mail, in person.

Safford Justice Court, 523 10th Ave, Safford, AZ 85546. 520-428-1210. 8AM-5PM (MST). Access by: Mail, in person.

Greenlee County

Real Estate Recording—Greenlee County Recorder, 5th & Leonard, Clifton, AZ 85533. 520-865-2632. Fax: 520-865-4417. 8AM-5PM (MST).

Felony, Civil Actions Over $5,000, Probate—Superior Court, PO Box 1027, Clifton, AZ 85533. 520-865-4108. Fax: 520-865-4665. 8AM-5PM (MST). Access by: Phone, fax, mail, in person.

Misdemeanor, Civil Actions Under $5,000, Eviction, Small Claims—Justice Court Precinct #1, PO Box 517, Clifton, AZ 85533. 520-865-4312. Fax: 520-865-4417. 9AM-5PM (MST). Access by: Mail, in person.

Justice Court Precinct #2, PO Box 208, Duncan, AZ 85534. 520-359-2536. 9AM-5PM (MST). Access by: Mail, in person.

La Paz County

Real Estate Recording—La Paz County Recorder, Suite 201, 1112 Joshua Ave., Parker, AZ 85344. 520-669-6136. Fax: 520-669-5638. 8AM-5PM (MST).

Felony, Civil Actions Over $5,000, Probate—Superior Court, 1316 Kofa Ave, Suite 607, Parker, AZ 85344. 520-669-6131. Fax: 520-669-2186. 8AM-5PM (MST). Access by: Mail, in person.

Misdemeanor, Civil Actions Under $5,000, Eviction, Small Claims—Parker Justice Court, 1105 Arizona Ave, Parker, AZ 85344. 520-669-2504. Fax: 520-669-2915. 8AM-5PM (MST). Access by: Phone, fax, mail, in person.

Quartzsite Justice Court, PO Box 580, Quartzsite, AZ 85346. 520-927-6313. Fax: 520-927-4842. 8AM-5PM (MST). Access by: Phone, mail, in person.

Salome Justice Court, PO Box 661, Salome, AZ 85348. 520-859-3871. Fax: 520-859-3709. 8AM-5PM (MST). Access by: Mail, in person.

Maricopa County

Real Estate Recording—Maricopa County Recorder, 111 South 3rd Avenue, Phoenix, AZ 85003. 602-506-3535. Fax: 602-506-3069. 8AM-5PM (MST).

Felony, Civil Actions Over $5,000, Probate—Superior Court, 201 W Jefferson, Phoenix, AZ 85003. 602-506-3360. Fax: 602-506-7619. 8AM-5PM (MST). Access by: Phone, fax, mail, in person, online.

Misdemeanor, Civil Actions Under $5,000, Eviction, Small Claims—Buckeye Justice Court, 100 N Apache Rd, Buckeye, AZ 85326. 602-386-4289. Fax: 602-386-5796. 8AM-5PM (MST). Access by: Mail, in person.

Chandler Justice Court, 2051 W Warner Rd, Chandler, AZ 85224. 602-963-6691. Fax: 602-786-6210. 8AM-5PM (MST). Access by: Mail, in person.

Gila Bend Justice Court, PO Box 648, Gila Bend, AZ 85337. 520-683-2651. Fax: 520-683-6412. 8AM-5PM (MST). Access by: Phone, fax, mail, in person.

Glendale Justice Court, 6830 N 57th Dr, Glendale, AZ 85301. 602-939-9477. Fax: 602-842-2260. 8AM-5PM (MST). Access by: Mail, in person.

West Mesa Justice Court, 2050 W University Dr, Mesa, AZ 85201. 602-964-2958. Fax: 602-969-1098. 8AM-5PM (MST). Access by: Fax, mail, in person.

East Mesa Justice Court, 4811 E Julep #128, Mesa, AZ 85205. 602-985-0188. Fax: 602-396-6327. 7AM-5PM (MST). Access by: Mail, in person.

North Mesa Justice Court, 1837 S Mesa Dr #A-201, Mesa, AZ 85210. 602-926-9731. Fax: 602-926-7763. 8AM-5PM (MST). Access by: Phone, fax, mail, remote online, in person. Public terminal only available in main Phoenix court.

South Mesa/Gilbert Justice Court, 1837 S Mesa Dr #B103, Mesa, AZ 85210. 602-926-3051. Fax: 602-545-1638. 8AM-5PM (MST). Access by: Mail, in person.

Peoria Justice Court, 7420 W Cactus Rd, Peoria, AZ 85381. 602-979-3234. Fax: 602-979-1194. 8AM-5PM (MST). Access by: Phone, fax, mail, in person.

Central Phoenix Justice Court, 1 W Madison St, Phoenix, AZ 85003. 602-506-1168. Fax: 602-506-1948. 8AM-5PM (MST). Access by: Mail, in person.

East Phoenix Justice Court #1, 1 W Madison St #1, Phoenix, AZ 85003. 602-506-3577. Fax: 602-506-1840. 8AM-5PM (MST). Access by: Mail, in person.

West Phoenix Justice Court, 527 W McDowell, Phoenix, AZ 85003. 602-256-0292. Fax: 602-256-7959. 8AM-5PM (MST). Access by: Mail, in person.

East Phoenix Justice Court #2, 4109 N 12th St, Phoenix, AZ 85014. 602-266-3741. Fax: 602-277-9442. 8AM-5PM (MST). Access by: In person only.

Northeast Phoenix Justice Court, 10255 N 32nd St, Phoenix, AZ 85028. 602-506-3731. Fax: 602-953-2315. 8AM-5PM (MST). Access by: Phone, fax, mail, in person.

Northwest Phoenix Justice Court, 11601 N 19th Ave, Phoenix, AZ 85029. 602-395-0293. Fax: 602-678-4508. 8AM-5PM (MST). Access by: In person only.

Maryvale Justice Court, 4622 W Indian School Rd Bldg D, Phoenix, AZ 85031. 602-245-0432. Fax: 602-245-1216. 8AM-5PM (MST). Access by: Mail, in person.

South Phoenix Justice Court, 217 E Olympic Dr, Phoenix, AZ 85040. 602-243-0318. Fax: 602-243-6389. 8AM-5PM (MST). Access by: Mail, in person.

Scottsdale Justice Court, 3700 N 75th St, Scottsdale, AZ 85251. 602-947-7569. Fax: 602-946-4284. 8AM-5PM (MST). Access by: Phone, mail, in person.

Tempe Justice Court, 1845 E Broadway #8, Tempe, AZ 85282. 602-967-8856. Fax: 602-921-7413. 8AM-5PM (MST). Access by: Mail, in person.

Tolleson Justice Court, 9550 W Van Buren #6, Tolleson, AZ 85353. 602-936-1449. Fax: 602-936-4859. 8AM-5PM (MST). Access by: Mail, in person.

Wickenburg Justice Court, 155 N Tegner, Suite D, Wickenburg, AZ 85390. 520-684-2401. 8AM-5PM (MST). Access by: Mail, in person.

Mohave County

Real Estate Recording—Mohave County Recorder, 315 Oak Street, Kingman, AZ 86401. 520-753-0701. 8AM-5PM (MST).

Felony, Civil Actions Over $5,000, Probate—Superior Court, PO Box 7000, Kingman, AZ 86402-7000. 520-753-0713. Fax: 520-753-0781. 8AM-5PM (MST). Access by: Phone, fax, mail, in person.

Misdemeanor, Civil Actions Under $5,000, Eviction, Small Claims—Bullhead City Justice Court, 2225 Trane Rd, Bullhead City, AZ 86442. 520-758-0709. Fax: 520-758-2644. 8AM-5PM (MST). Access by: Phone, mail, in person.

Kingman Justice Court, PO Box 29, Kingman, AZ 86402-0029. 520-753-0710. Fax: 520-753-7840. 8AM-5PM (MST). Access by: Phone, fax, mail, in person.

Lake Havasu City Justice Court, 2001 College Dr Suite 148, Lake Havasu City, AZ 86403. 520-453-0705. Fax: 520-680-0193. 8AM-5PM (MST). Access by: Fax, mail, in person.

Moccasin Justice Court, HC65 PO 90, Moccasin, AZ 86022. 520-643-7104. Fax: 520-643-7104. 8AM-4PM (MST). Access by: Mail, in person.

Navajo County

Real Estate Recording—Navajo County Recorder, 100 East Carter Dr, Courthouse, Holbrook, AZ 86025. 520-524-4190. Fax: 520-524-4308. 8AM-5PM (MST).

Felony, Civil Actions Over $5,000, Probate—Superior Court, PO Box 668, Holbrook, AZ 86025. 520-524-4188. Fax: 520-524-4261. 8AM-5PM (MST). Access by: Fax, mail, in person.

Misdemeanor, Civil Actions Under $5,000, Eviction, Small Claims—Holbrook Justice Court, PO Box 668, Holbrook, AZ 86025. 520-524-4229. Fax: 520-524-4230. 8AM-5PM (MST). Access by: Mail, in person.

Kayenta Justice Court, Box 38, Kayenta, AZ 86033. 520-697-3522. Fax: 520-697-3528. 8AM-Noon,1-5PM (MST). Access by: Mail, in person.

Pinetop-Lakeside Justice Court, Box 2020, Lakeside, AZ 85929. 520-368-6200. Fax: 520-368-8674. 8AM-5PM (MST). Access by: Fax, mail, in person.

Show Low Justice Court, PO Box 3085, Show Low, AZ 85901. 520-537-2213. Fax: 520-537-3081. 8AM-5PM (MST). Access by: Mail, in person.

Snowflake Justice Court, 73 West First South St, Snowflake, AZ 85937. 520-536-4141. Fax: 520-536-3511. 8AM-5PM (MST). Access by: Phone, fax, mail, in person.

Winslow Justice Court, Box 808, Winslow, AZ 86047. 520-289-2942. Fax: 520-289-2197. 8AM-5PM (MST). Access by: Fax, mail, in person.

Navajo Nation

Real Estate Recording—Real estate transactions within the Navajo Nation are recorded in the usual way in the county where the land lies. There is no separate recording required.

Pima County

Real Estate Recording—Pima County Recorder, 115 North Church Avenue, Tucson, AZ 85701. 520-623-3177. Fax: 520-623-1785. 8AM-5PM (MST).

Felony, Civil Actions Over $5,000, Probate—Superior Court, 110 W Congress, Tucson, AZ 85701. 520-740-3200. Fax: 520-798-3531. 8AM-5PM (MST). Access by: Mail, in person, online.

Misdemeanor, Civil Actions Under $5,000, Eviction, Small Claims—Ajo Justice Court, 111 La Mina, Ajo, AZ 85321. 520-387-7684. 8AM-5PM (MST). Access by: Mail, in person.

Green Valley Justice Court, 601 N LaCanada, Green Valley, AZ 85614. 520-648-0658. Fax: 520-648-2235. 8AM-5PM (MST). Access by: Mail, in person.

Pima County Consolidated Justice Court, 115 Church Ave, Tucson, AZ 85701. 520-740-3515. Fax: 520-620-6299. 8AM-5PM (MST). Access by: Fax, mail, in person.

Pinal County

Real Estate Recording—Pinal County Recorder, 383 N Main St., Florence, AZ 85232. 520-868-7100. Fax: 520-868-7170. 8AM-5PM (MST).

Felony, Civil Actions Over $5,000, Probate—Superior Court, PO Box 2730, Florence, AZ 85232-2730. 520-868-6296. Fax: 520-868-6252. 8AM-5PM (MST). Access by: Phone, mail, in person.

Misdemeanor, Civil Actions Under $5,000, Eviction, Small Claims—Apache Junction Justice Court, 575 N Idaho, Apache Junction, AZ 85219. 602-982-2921. Fax: 602-982-9472. 8AM-NOON, 1PM-5PM (MST). Access by: Fax, mail, in person.

Casa Grande Justice Court, 820 E Cottonwood Lane, Bldg B, Casa Grande, AZ 85222. 520-836-5471. Fax: 520-836-1621. 8AM-5PM (MST). Access by: Mail, in person.

Eloy Justice Court, PO Box 586, Eloy, AZ 85231. 520-466-9221. Fax: 520-466-4473. 8AM-Noon, 1PM-5PM (MST). Access by: Mail, in person.

Florence Justice Court, PO Box 1818, Florence, AZ 85232. 520-868-6578. Fax: 520-868-6510. 8AM-5PM (MST). Access by: Mail, in person.

Mammoth Justice Court, PO Box 117, Mammoth, AZ 85618. 520-487-2262. Fax: 520-487-2585. 8AM-5PM (MST). Access by: Mail, in person.

Maricopa Justice Court, PO Box 201, Maricopa, AZ 85239. 520-568-2451. Fax: 520-568-2924. 8AM-4PM (MST). Access by: Mail, in person.

Oracle Justice Court, PO Box 3924, Oracle, AZ 85623. 520-896-9250. Fax: 520-896-2867. 8AM-5PM (MST). Access by: Mail, in person.

Superior/Kearny Justice Court, 60 E Main St, Superior, AZ 85273. 520-689-5871. Fax: 520-689-2369. 8AM-Noon, 1-5PM (MST). Access by: Mail, in person.

Santa Cruz County

Real Estate Recording—Santa Cruz County Recorder, 2150 N. Congress, County Complex, Nogales, AZ 85621. 520-761-7800. Fax: 520-761-7938. 8AM-5PM (MST).

Felony, Civil Actions Over $5,000, Probate—Superior Court, PO Box 1265, Nogales, AZ 85628. 520-761-7808. Fax: 520-761-7857. 8AM-5PM (MST). Access by: Phone, mail, in person.

Misdemeanor, Civil Actions Under $5,000, Eviction, Small Claims—Santa Cruz Justice Court, PO Box 1150, Nogales, AZ 85628. 520-761-7853. Fax: 520-761-7929. 8AM-5PM (MST). Access by: Phone, fax, mail, in person.

East Santa Cruz County Justice Court-Precinct #2, PO Box 100, Patagonia, AZ 85624. 520-455-9302. Fax: 520-455-5517. 8:30AM-5PM (MST). Access by: Mail, in person.

Yavapai County

Real Estate Recording—Yavapai County Recorder, 1015 Fair St, Room 228, Prescott, AZ 86301. 520-771-3244. Fax: 520-778-4469. 8AM-5PM (MST).

Felony, Civil Actions Over $5,000, Probate—Superior Court, Yavapai County Courthouse, Prescott, AZ 86301. 520-771-3313. Fax: 520-771-3111. 8AM-5PM (MST). Access by: Fax, mail, in person.

Misdemeanor, Civil Actions Under $5,000, Eviction, Small Claims—Bagdad Justice Court, PO Box 243, Bagdad, AZ 86321. 520-633-2141. Fax: 520-633-2054. 8AM-1PM M,W,TH,F 8AM-5PM T (MST). Access by: Mail, in person.

Verde Valley Justice Court, 260 W Hwy Suite 101, Camp Verde, AZ 86322. 520-567-3353. Fax: 520-639-8188. 8AM-5PM (MST). Access by: Mail, in person.

Mayer Justice Court, PO Box 245, Mayer, AZ 86333. 520-771-3355. 8AM-5PM (MST). Access by: Mail, in person.

Prescott Justice Court, Yavapai County Courthouse, Prescott, AZ 86301. 520-771-3300. Fax: 520-771-3302. 8AM-5PM (MST). Access by: Mail, in person.

Seligman Justice Court, PO Box 56, Seligman, AZ 86337-0056. 520-422-3281. Fax: 520-422-3282. 8AM-5PM (MST). Access by: Phone, fax, mail, in person.

Bagdad-Yarnell Justice Court, PO Box 65, Yarnell, AZ 85362. 520-427-3318. Fax: 520-771-3362. 8AM-Noon, 1-5PM (MST). Access by: Mail, in person.

Yuma County

Real Estate Recording—Yuma County Recorder, 198 S. Main St, Yuma, AZ 85364. 520-329-2061. 8AM-5PM (MST).

Felony, Civil Actions Over $5,000, Probate—Superior Court, 168 S 2nd Ave, Yuma, AZ 85364. 520-329-2164. Fax: 520-329-2007. 8AM-5PM (MST). Access by: Fax, mail, in person.

Misdemeanor, Civil Actions Under $5,000, Eviction, Small Claims—Somerton Justice Court, PO Box 458, Somerton, AZ 85350. 520-627-2722. Fax: 520-627-1076. 8AM-5PM (MST). Access by: Phone, fax, mail, in person.

Wellton Justice Court, PO Box 384, Wellton, AZ 85356. 520-785-3321. Fax: 520-785-4933. 8AM-5PM (MST). Access by: Phone, fax, mail, in person.

Yuma Justice Court, 168 S 2nd Ave, Yuma, AZ 85364. 520-329-2180. Fax: 520-329-2005. 7:30AM-5:30PM (MST). Access by: Phone, mail, in person.. Access by: Phone, mail, in person.

Federal Courts

US District Court
District of Arizona

Phoenix Division, US District Court Room 1400, 230 N 1st Ave, Phoenix, AZ 85025-0093. 602-514-7101. Counties: Gila, La Paz, Maricopa, Pinal, Yuma

Prescott Division, US District Court c/o Phoenix Division, Room 1400, 230 N 1st Ave, Phoenix, AZ 85025-0093. 602-514-7101. Counties: Apache, Coconino, Mohave, Navajo, Yavapai

Tucson Division, US District Court Room 202, 44 E Broadway Blvd, Tucson, AZ 85701-1711. 520-620-7200. Counties: Cochise, Graham, Greelee, Pima, Santa Cruz. The Globe Division was closed effective January 1994, and all case records for that division are now found here

US Bankruptcy Court
District of Arizona

Phoenix Division, US Bankruptcy Court, PO Box 34151, Phoenix, AZ 85067-4151. 602-640-5800. Voice Case Information System: 602-640-5820. Counties: Apache, Coconino, Maricopa, Mohave, Navajo, Yavapai

Tucson Division, US Bankruptcy Court, Suite 8112, 110 S Church Ave, Tucson, AZ 85701-1608. 520-620-7500. Voice Case Information System: 520-620-7475. Counties: Cochise, Gila, Graham, Greenlee, Pima, Pinal, Santa Cruz

Yuma Division, US Bankruptcy Court, Suite D, 325 W 19th St, Yuma, AZ 85364. 520-783-2288. Counties: La Paz, Yuma

Arkansas

Capital: Little Rock (Pulaski County)	
Number of Counties: 75	**Population:** 2,483,769
County Court Locations:	**Federal Court Locations:**
•Circuit Courts: 1/24 Circuits	•District Courts: 11
•Combined Courts: 49	•Bankruptcy Courts: 2
•Circuit/Chancery Courts: 35	**State Agencies:** 20
•Municipal Courts: 77	
Common Pleas: 4	City Courts: 94
Justice of the Peace Courts: 55	Police Courts: 5

State Agencies—Summary

General Help Numbers:

State Archives

Arkansas History Commission	501-682-6900
State Archives	8AM-4:30PM
One Capitol Mall	
Little Rock, AR 72201	
Reference Librarian:	501-682-6900

Governor's Office

Governor's Office	501-682-2345
State Capitol, Room 250	Fax: 501-682-1382
Little Rock, AR 72201	8AM-5PM

Attorney General's Office

Attorney General's Office	501-682-2007
200 Catlett-Prien Bldg,	
323 Center St	Fax: 501-682-8084
Little Rock, AR 72201-2610	8AM-5PM

State Legislation

Arkansas Secretary of State	501-682-1010
State Capitol	Fax: 501-682-3408
Room 256 (2nd Floor)	8AM-5PM
Little Rock, AR 72201	

Important State Internet Sites:

❖ Webscape	
File Edit View	Help

State of Arkansas World Wide Web

www.state.ar.us/

Links to the Governor and State Legislature. It also has an extensive index about the State of Arkansas.

The Governor's Office

www.state.ar.us/governor/governor.html

Includes information about the Governor's press releases, biography, staff and enables you to send e-mail to the Governor.

The Government Relations Home Page

www.uark.edu/~govinfo/index.html

Links to the Arkansas State Senate and House of Representatives. Legislative acts may be searched.

Arkansas Library Information

www.state.ar.us/html/ark_library.html

Links to both the Arkansas and Federal Governments, library and the Arkansas state library.

Unclaimed Property

www.intersurf.com/~naupa/ar.htm

Information about searching for unclaimed property is found here. The required search form is also located at this site.

State Agencies—Public Records

Criminal Records

Arkansas State Police, Identification Bureau, PO Box 5901, Little Rock, AR 72215, Main Telephone: 501-221-8233, Fax: 501-224-5006, Hours: 8AM-5PM. Access by: mail, visit.

Corporation Records
Fictitious Name
Limited Liability Company Records
Limited Partnerships

Secretary of State, Corporation Department-Aegon Bldg, 5th & Wood Lane, Rm 310, Little Rock, AR 72201-1094, Main Telephone: 501-682-3409, Fax: 501-682-3437, Hours: 8AM-4:30PM. Access by: mail, phone, visit.

Trademarks/Servicemarks

Secretary of State, Trademarks Section, State Capitol, Room 01, Little Rock, AR 72201, Main Telephone: 501-682-3405, Hours: 8AM-5PM. Access by: mail, phone, visit.

Uniform Commercial Code
Federal Tax Liens
State Tax Liens

UCC Division, Secretary of State, State Capitol Bldg, Room 25, Little Rock, AR 72201-1094, Main Telephone: 501-682-5078, Fax: 501-682-3500, Hours: 8AM-4:30PM. Access by: mail, phone, visit. For federal tax liens, this agency maintains records for corporations and partnerships only. The agency is in the process of preparing a computer storage program.

Sales Tax Registrations

Finance & Administration Department, Sales & Use Tax Office, PO Box 1272, Little Rock, AR 72203, Main Telephone: 501-682-7104, Fax 501-682-7900 Access by: mail, phone.

Birth Certificates

Arkansas Department of Health, Division of Vital Records, 4815 W Markham St, Slot 44, Little Rock, AR 72205, Main Telephone: 501-661-2134, Message Number: 501-661-2336, Fax: 501-663-2832, Hours: 8AM-4:30PM. Access by: mail, phone, fax, visit.

Death Records

Arkansas Department of Health, Division of Vital Records, 4815 W Markham St, Slot 44, Little Rock, AR 72205, Main Telephone: 501-661-2134, Message number: 501-661-2336, Fax: 501-663-2832, Hours: 8AM-4:30PM. Access by: mail, phone, visit.

Marriage Certificates

Arkansas Department of Health, Division of Vital Records, 4815 W Markham St, Slot 44, Little Rock, AR 72205, Main Telephone: 501-661-2134, Message Number: 501-661-2336, Fax: 501-663-2832, Hours: 8AM-4:30PM. Access by: mail, phone, visit.

Divorce Records

Arkansas Department of Health, Department of Vital Records, 4815 W Markham St, Slot 44, Little Rock, AR 72205, Main Telephone: 501-661-2134, Message Number: 501-661-2336, Fax: 501-663-2832, Hours: 8AM-4:30PM. Access by: mail, phone, visit.

Workers' Compensation Records

Workers Compensation Department, Justice Bldg-Capitol Grounds, 4th & Spring Streets, PO Box 950, Little Rock, AR 72203-0950, Main Telephone: 501-682-3930, Fax: 501-682-2777, Hours: 8AM-4:30PM. Access by: mail, visit.

Driver Records

Department of Driver Services, Driving Records Division, PO Box 1272, Room 127, Little Rock, AR 72203, Main Telephone: 501-682-7207, Fax: 501-682-2075, Hours: 8AM-4:30PM. Access by: mail, visit. Copies of tickets are not available from the state; they must be requested from the actual jurisdiction where the ticket was issued.

Vehicle Ownership
Vehicle Identification

Office of Motor Vehicles, MV Title Records, PO Box 1272, Room 106, Little Rock, AR 72203, Main Telephone: 501-682-4692, Hours: 8AM-4:30PM. Access by: mail, phone, visit.

Accident Reports

Arkansas State Police, Accident Records Section, PO Box 5901, Little Rock, AR 72215, Main Telephone: 501-221-8236, Hours: 8AM-5PM. Access by: mail, visit.

Hunting License Information
Fishing License Information

Game & Fish Commission, Two Natural Resource Dr, Little Rock, AR 72205, Main Telephone: 501-223-6341, Fax: 501-223-6425, Hours: 8AM-4:30PM. Access by: mail, visit. Lists maintained here include fish farmers, put & take pay lakes, shell buyers, commercial game breeders, commercial shooting resorts, fur dealers, and bull frog permits.

County Courts and Recording Offices

What You Need to Know...

About the Courts

Administration

Administrative Office of Courts	501-682-9400
625 Marshall Street, Justice Bldg	Fax: 501-682-9410
Little Rock, AR 72201-1078	8AM-5PM

Court Structure

County Courts are, fundamentally, administrative courts dealing with county fiscal issues. Probate is handled by the Chancery and Probate Courts or by the County Clerk in some counties.

Searching Hints

Most courts which allow written search requests **require** an SASE. Fees vary widely across jurisdictions as do prepayment requirements.

Online Access

There is a very limited **internal** on-line computer system at the Administrative Office of Courts.

About the Recorder's Office

Organization

75 counties, 85 filing offices. The recording officer is the Clerk of Circuit Court, who is Ex Officio Recorder. Ten counties have two recording offices—Arkansas, Carroll, Clay, Craighead, Franklin, Logan, Mississippi, Prairie, Sebastian, and Yell. The entire state is in the Central Time Zone (CST).

UCC Records

This is a dual filing state. Financing statements are filed at the state level and with the Circuit Clerk, except for consumer goods, farm and real estate related collateral, which are filed only with the Circuit Clerk. Most counties will perform UCC searches. Use search request form UCC-11. Search fees are usually $6.00 per debtor name. Copy fees vary.

Lien Records

Federal tax liens on personal property of businesses are filed with the Secretary of State. Other federal and all state tax liens are filed with the Circuit Clerk. Many counties will perform tax lien searches. Search fees are usually $6.00 per name. Other liens include mechanics, lis pendens, judgments, hospital, child support, and materialman.

Real Estate Records

Most counties do not perform real estate searches. Copy fees and certification fees vary.

County Courts and Recording Offices

Arkansas County

Real Estate Recording—Arkansas County Circuit Clerk, Southern District, 101 Court Square, De Witt, AR 72042. 870-946-4219. Fax: 870-946-1394. 8AM-Noon,1-5PM (CST).

Felony, Civil Actions Over $3,000, Probate—Circuit and Chancery Courts-Northern District, PO Box 719, Stuttgart, AR 72160. 870-673-2056. Fax: 870-673-3869. 8AM-5PM (CST). Access by: Fax, mail, in person. Search request must be in writing.

Arkansas County Circuit Clerk, Northern District, 302 South College, Stuttgart, AR 72160. 870-673-2056. Fax: 870-673-3869. 8AM-Noon,1-5PM (CST).

Circuit and Chancery Courts-Southern District, 101 Courthouse Sq, De Witt, AR 72042. 870-946-4219. Fax: 870-946-1394. 8AM-5PM (CST). Access by: Fax, mail, in person. Search request must be in writing.

Misdemeanor, Eviction, Small Claims—Municipal Court, PO Box 819, Stuttgart, AR 72160. 870-673-7951. Fax: 870-673-6522. 8AM-5PM (CST). Access by: Phone, mail, in person.

Ashley County

Real Estate Recording—Ashley County Circuit Clerk, Jefferson Street, Courthouse, Hamburg, AR 71646. 870-853-2030. Fax: 870-853-2005. 8AM-4:30PM (CST).

Felony, Civil Actions Over $3,000, Probate—Circuit and Chancery Courts, Ashley County Courthouse, Hamburg, AR 71646. 870-853-2005. 8AM-4:30PM (CST). Access by: In person only.

Misdemeanor, Eviction, Small Claims—Municipal Court, PO Box 558 City Hall, Hamburg, AR 71646. 870-853-8326. Fax: 870-853-8134. 7AM-4PM (CST). Access by: Phone, mail, in person.

Baxter County

Real Estate Recording—Baxter County Circuit Clerk, Courthouse Square, 1 East 7th Street, Mountain Home, AR 72653. 870-425-3475. Fax: 870-425-5105. 8AM-4:30PM (CST).

Felony, Civil Actions Over $3,000, Probate—Circuit and Chancery Courts, 1 E 7th St Courthouse Square, Mountain Home, AR 72653. 870-425-3475. Fax: 870-424-5105. 8AM-4:30PM (CST). Access by: Mail, in person.

Misdemeanor, Eviction, Small Claims—Municipal Court, 720 S Hickory, Mountain Home, AR 72653. 870-425-3140. Fax: 870-425-9290. 8AM-4:30PM (CST). Access by: Phone, fax, mail, in person.

Benton County

Real Estate Recording—Benton County Circuit Clerk, 215 East Central Street, Suite 6, Bentonville, AR 72712. 870-271-1017. Fax: 870-271-5719. 8AM-4:30PM (CST).

Felony, Civil Actions Over $3,000, Probate—Circuit and Chancery Courts, 102 NE "A" St, Bentonville, AR 72712. 870-271-1015. Fax: 870-271-1019. 8AM-4:30PM (CST). Access by: Phone, mail, in person.

Misdemeanor, Eviction, Small Claims—Municipal Court, 117 W Central, Bentonville, AR 72712. 870-271-3120. Fax: 870-271-3134. 8AM-4:30PM (CST). Access by: Phone, fax, mail, in person.

Boone County

Real Estate Recording—Boone County Circuit Clerk, Courthouse, Suite 200, 100 N. Main, Harrison, AR 72602. 870-741-5560. 8:30AM-4PM (CST).

Felony, Civil Actions Over $3,000, Probate—Circuit and Chancery Courts, 100 N Main St #200, Harrison, AR 72601. 870-741-5560. 8:30AM-4:00PM (CST). Access by: In person only.

Misdemeanor, Eviction, Small Claims—Municipal Court, PO Box 968, Harrison, AR 72602. 870-741-2788. Fax: 870-741-4329. 8:30AM-4PM (CST). Access by: In person only.

Bradley County

Real Estate Recording—Bradley County Circuit Clerk, 101 E. Cedar Street, Courthouse, Warren, AR 71671. 870-226-2272. Fax: 501-226-8401. 8AM-4:30PM (CST).

Felony, Civil Actions Over $3,000, Probate—Circuit and County Courts, Bradley County Courthouse - Records, 101 E Cedar, Warren, AR 71671. 870-226-2272. Fax: 870-226-8401. 8AM-4:30PM (CST). Access by: In person only.

Misdemeanor, Eviction, Small Claims—Municipal Court, PO Box 352, Warren, AR 71671. 870-226-2567. Fax: 870-226-2567. 8AM-5PM (CST). Access by: Phone, fax, mail, in person.

Calhoun County

Real Estate Recording—Calhoun County Circuit Clerk, Main Street, Courthouse, Hampton, AR 71744. 870-798-2517. Fax: 501-798-2428. 8AM-4:30 (CST).

Felony, Civil Actions Over $3,000, Probate—Circuit and County Courts, PO Box 626, Hampton, AR 71744. 870-798-2517. 8:30AM-4:30PM (CST). Access by: Phone, mail, in person.

Misdemeanor, Eviction, Small Claims—Municipal Court, PO Box 864, Hampton, AR 71744. 870-798-2165. 8AM-4:30PM (CST). Access by: Mail, in person.

Carroll County

Real Estate Recording—Carroll County Circuit Clerk, Eastern District, 210 West Church, Berryville, AR 72616. 870-423-2422. Fax: 870-423-3866. 8:30AM-4:30PM (CST).

Carroll County Circuit Clerk, Western District, 44 South Main, Courthouse, Eureka Springs, AR 72632. 501-253-8646. 8:30AM-4:30PM (CST).

Felony, Civil Actions Over $3,000, Probate—Circuit and Chancery Courts, Berryville Circuit Court, PO Box 71, Berryville, AR 72616. 870-423-2422. Fax: 870-423-3866. 8:30AM-4:30PM (CST). Access by: Phone, mail, in person.

Circuit and County Courts, 44 S Main, PO Box 109, Eureka Springs, AR 72632. 870-253-8646. 8:30AM-4:30PM (CST). Access by: Phone, mail, in person.

Misdemeanor, Eviction, Small Claims—Municipal Court, 103 S Springs, Berryville, AR 72616. 870-423-6247. Fax: 870-423-7069. 8:30AM-4:30PM (CST). Access by: Fax, mail, in person.

Municipal Court, Courthouse, 44 S Main, Eureka Springs, AR 72632. 870-253-8574. Fax: 870-253-6967. 8AM-5PM (CST). Access by: Mail, in person.

Chicot County

Real Estate Recording—Chicot County Circuit Clerk, Courthouse, 108 Main St., Lake Village, AR 71653. 870-265-8010. 8AM-4:30PM (CST).

Felony, Civil Actions Over $3,000, Probate—Circuit and Chancery Courts, County Courthouse, Lake Village, AR 71653. 870-265-8010. Fax: 870-265-5102. 8AM-4:30PM (CST). Access by: Phone, fax, mail, in person.

Misdemeanor, Eviction, Small Claims—Municipal Court, PO Box 832, Lake Village, AR 71653. 870-265-3283. 9AM-5PM (CST). Access by: Mail, in person.

Clark County

Real Estate Recording—Clark County Circuit Clerk, Courthouse Square, Arkadelphia, AR 71923. 870-246-4281. 8:30AM-4:30PM (CST).

Felony, Civil Actions Over $3,000, Probate—Circuit and Chancery Courts, PO Box 576, Arkadelphia, AR 71923. 870-246-4281. 8:30AM-4:30PM (CST). Access by: Mail, in person.

Misdemeanor, Eviction, Small Claims—Municipal Court, PO Box 449, Arkadelphia, AR 71923. 870-246-9552. 8:30AM-4:30PM (CST). Access by: Phone, mail, in person.

Clay County

Real Estate Recording—Clay County Circuit Clerk, Western District, 800 West Second Street, Corning, AR 72422. 870-857-3271. Fax: 870-857-3271. 8AM-Noon, 1PM-4:30PM (CST).

Clay County Circuit Clerk, Eastern District, Courthouse, Piggott, AR 72454. 501-598-2524. Fax: 501-598-2524. 8AM-Noon,1-4:30PM (CST).

Felony, Civil Actions Over $3,000, Probate—Corning Circuit and County Courts, Courthouse, Corning, AR 72422. 870-857-3271. Fax: 870-857-3271. 8AM-4:30PM (CST). Access by: Phone, fax, mail, in person.

Piggott Circuit and County Courts, PO Box 29, Piggott, AR 72454. 870-598-2524. Fax: 870-598-2524. 8AM-4:30PM (CST). Access by: Mail, in person.

Misdemeanor, Eviction, Small Claims—Municipal Court, 194 W Court, Piggott, AR 72454. 870-598-2265. Fax: 870-598-3897. 8AM-4:30PM (CST). Access by: Fax, mail, in person.

Cleburne County

Real Estate Recording—Cleburne County Circuit Clerk, 300 West Main Street, Heber Springs, AR 72543. 870-362-8149. Fax: 870-362-4650. 8:30AM-4:30PM (CST).

Felony, Civil Actions Over $3,000, Probate—Circuit and County Courts, PO Box 543, Heber Springs, AR 72543. 870-362-8149. Fax: 870-362-4650. 8:30AM-4:30PM (CST). Access by: Phone, mail, in person.

Misdemeanor, Eviction, Small Claims—Municipal Court, 102 E Main, Heber Springs, AR 72543. 870-362-6585. Fax: 870-362-4614. 8:30AM-4:30PM (CST). Access by: Phone, mail, in person.

Cleveland County

Real Estate Recording—Cleveland County Circuit Clerk, Courthouse, Corner of Main & Magnolia, Rison, AR 71665. 870-325-6521. Fax: 870-325-6144. 8AM-4:30PM (CST).

Felony, Civil Actions Over $3,000, Probate—Circuit and County Courts, PO Box 368, Rison, AR 71665. 870-325-6921. Fax: 870-325-6144. 8:00AM-4:30PM (CST). Access by: In person only.

Misdemeanor, Eviction, Small Claims—Rison Municipal Court, PO Box 405, City Hall, Rison, AR 71665. 870-325-7382. Fax: 870-325-6152. 8AM-4PM (CST). Access by: Phone, mail, in person.

Columbia County

Real Estate Recording—Columbia County Circuit Clerk, Courthouse, Magnolia, AR 71753. 501-235-3700. Fax: 870-235-3778. 8AM-4:30PM (CST).

Felony, Civil Actions Over $3,000, Probate—Circuit and County Courts, 1 Court Square Ste 6, PO Box 327, Magnolia, AR 71753-3595. 870-235-3700. Fax: 870-235-3786. 8AM-4:30PM (CST). Access by: Mail, in person.

Misdemeanor, Eviction, Small Claims—Magnolia Municipal Court, PO Box 1126, Magnolia, AR 71753. 870-234-7312. 8AM-5PM (CST). Access by: Mail, in person.

Conway County

Real Estate Recording—Conway County Circuit Clerk, 115 S. Moose Street, County Courthouse - Room 206, Morrilton, AR 72110. 501-354-9617. Fax: 501-354-9612. 8AM-5PM (CST).

Felony, Civil Actions Over $3,000, Probate—Circuit and Chancery Courts, Conway County Courthouse, Rm 206, Morrilton, AR 72110. 501-354-9617. Fax: 501-354-9612. 8AM-5PM (CST). Access by: Phone, mail, in person.

Misdemeanor, Eviction, Small Claims—Municipal Court, PO Box 127,Conway County Courthouse, Morrilton, AR 72110. 501-354-9615. Fax: 501-354-9601. 8AM-4:30PM (CST). Access by: Mail, in person.

Craighead County

Real Estate Recording—Craighead County Circuit Clerk, Western District, Main Street and Washington, Jonesboro, AR 72401. 870-933-4530. Fax: 870-933-4534. 8AM-5PM (CST).

Craighead County Circuit Clerk, Eastern District, 405 Court Street, Lake City, AR 72437. 870-237-4342. Fax: 870-237-8174. 8AM-Noon, 1-5PM (CST).

Felony, Civil Actions Over $3,000, Probate—Jonesboro Circuit and Chancery Courts, PO Box 120, Jonesboro, AR 72403. 870-933-4530. Fax: 870-933-4534. 8:00AM-5:00PM (CST). Access by: Fax, mail, in person.

Lake City Circuit and County Courts, PO Box 537, Lake City, AR 72437. 870-237-4342. 8AM-5PM (CST). Access by: Phone, mail, in person.

Misdemeanor, Eviction, Small Claims—Municipal Court, 410 W Washington, Jonesboro, AR 72401. 870-933-4509. Fax: 870-933-4582. 8AM-5PM (CST). Access by: Phone, mail, in person.

Crawford County

Real Estate Recording—Linda Howard, Circuit/Chancery Clerk, 300 Main, Courthouse Room 22, Van Buren, AR 72956. 501-474-1821. 8AM-5PM (CST).

Felony, Civil Actions Over $3,000, Probate—Circuit and Chancery Courts, County Courthouse, 300 Main St, Rm 22, Van Buren, AR 72956. 501-474-1821. Fax: 501-471-0622. 8AM-5PM (CST). Access by: Mail, in person.

Misdemeanor, Eviction, Small Claims—Municipal Court, 1003 Broadway, Van Buren, AR 72956. 501-474-1671. Fax: 501-471-5010. 8AM-5PM (CST). Access by: In person only.

Crittenden County

Real Estate Recording—Crittenden County Circuit Clerk, Jackson Street, Courthouse, Marion, AR 72364. 870-739-3248. Fax: 870-739-3287. 8AM-4:30PM (CST).

Felony, Civil Actions Over $3,000, Probate—Circuit and County Courts, PO Box 70, Marion, AR 72364. 870-739-3248. 8AM-4:30PM (CST). Access by: Mail, in person.

Misdemeanor, Eviction, Small Claims—Municipal Court, 100 Court St, West Memphis, AR 72301. 870-732-7560. Fax: 870-732-7538. 8AM-5PM (CST). Access by: Phone, mail, in person.

Cross County

Real Estate Recording—Cross County Circuit Clerk, 705 East Union, Room 9, Wynne, AR 72396. 870-238-5720. Fax: 870-238-5739. 8AM-4PM (CST).

Felony, Civil Actions Over $3,000, Probate—Circuit and County Courts, County Courthouse, Wynne, AR 72396. 870-238-5720. Fax: 870-238-5739. 8AM-4PM (CST). Access by: Mail, in person.

Misdemeanor, Eviction, Small Claims—Municipal Court, 205 Mississippi St, Wynne, AR 72396. 870-238-9171. Fax: 870-238-4055. 8AM-5PM M-Th; 8AM-4PM F (CST). Access by: Mail, in person.

Dallas County

Real Estate Recording—Dallas County Circuit Clerk, Courthouse, 206 West 3rd St, Fordyce, AR 71742. 870-352-2307. Fax: 870-352-7179. 8:30AM-4:30PM (CST).

Felony, Civil Actions Over $3,000, Probate—Circuit and County Courts, Dallas County Courthouse, Fordyce, AR 71742. 870-352-2307. Fax: 870-352-7179. 8:30AM-4:30PM (CST). Access by: Mail, in person.

Misdemeanor, Eviction, Small Claims—Municipal Court, Dallas County Courthouse, Fordyce, AR 71742. 870-352-2332. Fax: 870-352-3414. 8AM-4PM (CST). Access by: Phone, mail, in person.

Desha County

Real Estate Recording—Desha County Circuit Clerk, Robert Moore Drive, Arkansas City Courthouse, Arkansas City, AR 71630. 870-877-2411. Fax: 870-877-3407. 8AM-4PM (CST).

Felony, Civil Actions Over $3,000, Probate—Circuit and Chancery Courts, PO Box 309, Arkansas City, AR 71630. 870-877-2411. Fax: 870-877-2531. 8AM-4PM (CST). Access by: Mail, in person.

Misdemeanor, Eviction, Small Claims—Dumas Municipal Court, 149 E Waterman, Dumas, AR 71639-2226. 870-382-2121. Fax: 870-382-1106. 8AM-4:30PM (CST). Access by: Mail, in person.

Drew County

Real Estate Recording—Drew County Circuit Clerk, 210 South Main, Monticello, AR 71655. 870-460-6250. Fax: 870-460-6246. 8AM-5PM (CST).

Felony, Civil Actions Over $3,000, Probate—Circuit and County Courts, 210 S Main, Monticello, AR 71655. 870-460-6250. Fax: 870-460-6246. 8AM-4:30PM (CST). Access by: Phone, mail, in person.

Misdemeanor, Eviction, Small Claims—Municipal Court, PO Box 505, Monticello, AR 71655. 870-367-4420. Fax: 870-367-4405. 8:30AM-5PM (CST). Access by: Fax, mail, in person.

Faulkner County

Real Estate Recording—Faulkner County Circuit Clerk, 801 Locust Street, Courthouse, Conway, AR 72032. 501-450-4911. Fax: 501-450-4948. 8AM-4:30PM (CST).

Felony, Civil Actions Over $3,000, Probate—Circuit and Chancery Courts, PO Box, Conway, AR 72033. 501-450-4911. Fax: 501-450-4948. 8AM-4:30PM (CST). Access by: Phone, fax, mail, in person.

Misdemeanor, Eviction, Small Claims—Municipal Court, 1105 Prairie, Conway, AR 72032. 501-450-6112. Fax: 501-450-6184. 8AM-4:30AM (CST). Access by: Phone, mail, in person.

Franklin County

Real Estate Recording—Franklin County Circuit Clerk, Charleston District, 460 East Main Street, Charleston, AR 72933. 501-965-7332. 8AM-Noon, 12:30-4:30PM (CST).

Franklin County Circuit Clerk, Ozark District, 211 West Commercial, Ozark, AR 72949. 501-667-3818. Fax: 501-667-2234. 8AM-4:30PM (CST).

Felony, Civil Actions Over $3,000, Probate—Charleston Circuit and Chancery Courts, PO Box 387, Charleston, AR 72933. 501-965-7332. 8:00AM-4:30PM (CST). Access by: Mail, in person.

Ozark Circuit and Chancery Courts, PO Box 1112, 211 W Commercial, Ozark, AR 72949. 501-667-3818. Probate: 501-667-3607. Fax: 501-667-4247. 8AM-4:30PM (CST). Access by: Mail, in person.

Misdemeanor, Eviction, Small Claims—Municipal Court, PO Box 426, Charleston, AR 72933. 501-965-7455. Fax: 501-965-2231. 8AM-5PM (CST). Access by: Mail, in person.

Fulton County

Real Estate Recording—Fulton County Circuit Clerk, Court Square Courthouse, Salem, AR 72576. 870-895-3310. Fax: 870-895-4114. 8AM-4:30PM (CST).

Felony, Civil Actions Over $3,000, Probate—Circuit and Chancery Courts, PO Box 485, Salem, AR 72576. 870-895-3310. Fax: 870-865-3362. 8AM-4:30PM (CST). Access by: Phone, mail, in person.

Misdemeanor, Eviction, Small Claims—Municipal Court, PO Box 928, Salem, AR 72576. 870-895-4136. Fax: 870-895-4114. 8AM-4:30PM (CST). Access by: Phone, fax, mail, in person.

Garland County

Real Estate Recording—Garland County Circuit Clerk, Courthouse - Room 207, Quachita and Hawthorn Streets, Hot Springs, AR 71901. 501-622-3630. 8AM-5PM (CST).

Felony, Civil Actions Over $3,000, Probate—Circuit and Chancery Courts, Garland County Courthouse, 501 Ouachita Ave, Room 207, Hot Springs, AR 71901. 501-622-3630. Probate: 501-622-3610. Fax: 501-624-0665. 8AM-5PM (CST). Access by: Phone, mail, in person.

Misdemeanor, Eviction, Small Claims—Municipal Court, PO Box 700, Hot Springs, AR 71902. 501-321-6765. Fax: 501-321-6809. 8AM-5PM (CST). Access by: Phone, fax, mail, in person.

Grant County

Real Estate Recording—Grant County Circuit Clerk, Courthouse, 101 W. Center, Room 106, Sheridan, AR 72150. 870-942-2631. Fax: 870-942-3564. 8AM-4:30PM (CST).

Felony, Civil Actions Over $3,000, Probate—Circuit and County Courts, Grant County Courthouse, Sheridan, AR 72150. 870-942-2631. Fax: 870-942-2442. 8AM-4:30PM (CST). Access by: Mail, in person.

Misdemeanor, Eviction, Small Claims—Municipal Court, PO Box 603, Sheridan, AR 72150. 870-942-3464. 8AM-4:30PM (CST). Access by: Phone, mail, in person.

Greene County

Real Estate Recording—Greene County Circuit & Chancery Clerk, 320 W. Court St., Room 124, Paragould, AR 72450. 870-239-6330. Fax: 870-239-3550. 8:30AM-4:30PM (CST).

Felony, Civil Actions Over $3,000, Probate—Circuit and County Courts, PO Box 1028, Paragould, AR 72451. 870-239-6330. Fax: 870-239-3550. 8:30AM-4:30PM (CST). Access by: Fax, mail, in person.

Misdemeanor, Eviction, Small Claims—Municipal Court, 221 W Court, Paragould, AR 72450. 870-239-7507. Fax: 870-239-7506. 8AM-4:30PM (CST). Access by: Fax, mail, in person.

Hempstead County

Real Estate Recording—Hempstead County Circuit Clerk, Fourth & Washington Streets, Courthouse, Hope, AR 71801. 870-777-2384. Fax: 870-777-7827. 8AM-4PM (CST).

Felony, Civil Actions Over $3,000, Probate—Circuit and Chancery Courts, PO Box 1420, Hope, AR 71801. 870-777-2384. Fax: 870-777-7814. 8AM-4PM (CST). Access by: Mail, in person.

Misdemeanor, Eviction, Small Claims—Municipal Court, PO Box 1420, Hope, AR 71801. 870-777-2525. Fax: 870-777-7814. 8AM-4:30PM (CST). Access by: Mail, in person.

Hot Spring County

Real Estate Recording—Hot Spring County Circuit Clerk, 200 Locust Street, Courthouse, Malvern, AR 72104. 501-332-2281. 8AM-4:30PM (CST).

Felony, Civil Actions Over $3,000, Probate—Circuit and Chancery Courts, 200 Locust St, PO Box 1200, Malvern, AR 72104. 501-332-2281. 8:00AM-4:30PM (CST). Access by: Mail, in person.

Misdemeanor, Eviction, Small Claims—Municipal Court, 305 Locust, Rm 205, Malvern, AR 72104. 501-332-7604. Fax: 501-332-7607. 8AM-4:30PM (CST). Access by: In person only.

Howard County

Real Estate Recording—Howard County Circuit Clerk, 421 North Main Street, Room 7, Nashville, AR 71852. 870-845-7506. 8AM-4:30PM (CST).

Felony, Civil Actions Over $3,000, Probate—Circuit and County Courts, 421 N Main, Rm 7, Nashville, AR 71852. 870-845-7506. 8AM-4:30PM (CST). Access by: Phone, mail, in person.

Misdemeanor, Eviction, Small Claims—Municipal Court, 426 N Main, Suite #7, Nashville, AR 71852-2009. 870-845-7522. Fax: 870-845-3705. 8AM-4:30PM (CST). Access by: In person only.

Independence County

Real Estate Recording—Independence County Circuit Clerk, 192 Main Street, Batesville, AR 72501. 870-793-8865. Fax: 870-793-8888. 8AM-4:30PM (CST).

Felony, Civil Actions Over $3,000, Probate—Circuit and County Courts, Main and Broad St, Batesville, AR 72501.

870-793-8833. Fax: 870-793-8888. 8AM-4:30PM (CST). Access by: Phone, mail, in person.

Misdemeanor, Eviction, Small Claims—Municipal Court, 368 E Main, Batesville, AR 72501. 870-793-8817. Fax: 870-793-8875. 8AM-4:30PM (CST). Access by: Phone, mail, in person.

Izard County

Real Estate Recording—Izard County Circuit Clerk, Main and Lunen Streets, Courthouse, Melbourne, AR 72556. 870-368-4316. Fax: 870-368-5042. 8:30AM-4:30PM (CST).

Felony, Civil Actions Over $3,000, Probate—Circuit and County Courts, PO Box 95, Melbourne, AR 72556. 870-368-4316. Fax: 870-368-5042. 8:30AM-4:30PM (CST). Access by: Fax, mail, in person.

Misdemeanor, Eviction, Small Claims—Municipal Court, PO Box 337, Melbourne, AR 72556. 870-368-4390. Fax: 870-368-5042. 8:30AM-4:30PM (CST). Access by: Mail, in person.

Jackson County

Real Estate Recording—Jackson County Circuit Clerk, Courthouse, Main Street, Newport, AR 72112. 870-523-7423. (CST).

Felony, Civil Actions Over $3,000, Probate—Circuit and Chancery Courts, Jackson County Courthouse, 208 Main St, Newport, AR 72112. 870-523-7423. Fax: 870-523-7404. 8AM-4:30PM (CST). Access by: Mail, in person.

Misdemeanor, Eviction, Small Claims—Municipal Court, 615 3rd St, Newport, AR 72112. 870-523-9555. Fax: 870-523-4365. 8AM-4:30PM (CST). Access by: Phone, fax, mail, in person.

Jefferson County

Real Estate Recording—Jefferson County Circuit Clerk, Main & Barraque, Room 101, Pine Bluff, AR 71601. 870-541-5309. 8:30AM-5PM (CST).

Felony, Civil Actions Over $3,000, Probate—Circuit and Chancery Courts, PO Box 7433, Pine Bluff, AR 71611. 870-541-5307. 8:30PM-5PM (CST). Access by: In person only.

Misdemeanor, Eviction, Small Claims—Municipal Court, 200 E 8th, Pine Bluff, AR 71601. 870-543-1860. 8AM-5PM (CST). Access by: Mail, in person.

Johnson County

Real Estate Recording—Johnson County Circuit Clerk, Main Street, Courthouse, Clarksville, AR 72830. 501-754-2977. Fax: 501-754-4235. 8AM-4:30PM (CST).

Felony, Civil Actions Over $3,000, Probate—Circuit and County Courts, PO Box 217, Clarksville, AR 72830. 501-754-2977. 8AM-4:30PM (CST). Access by: Phone, mail, in person.

Misdemeanor, Eviction, Small Claims—Municipal Court, PO Box 581, Clarksville, AR 72830. 501-754-8533. Fax: 501-754-6014. 8AM-4PM (CST). Access by: Phone, mail, in person.

Lafayette County

Real Estate Recording—Lafayette County Circuit Clerk, Courthouse Square, Lewisville, AR 71845. 870-921-4878. 8AM-4:30PM (CST).

Felony, Civil Actions Over $3,000, Probate—Circuit and Chancery Courts, PO Box 986, Lewisville, AR 71845. 870-921-4878. 8AM-4:30PM (CST). Access by: In person only.

Misdemeanor, Eviction, Small Claims—Municipal Court, PO Box 307, Lewisville, AR 71845. 870-921-5555. Fax: 870-921-4256. 8AM-4:30PM (CST). Access by: Phone, mail, in person.

Lawrence County

Real Estate Recording—Lawrence County Circuit Clerk, Main Street, Walnut Ridge, AR 72476. 870-886-1112. Fax: 870-886-1117. 8AM-4:30PM (CST).

Felony, Civil Actions Over $3,000, Probate—Circuit and Chancery Courts, PO Box 581, Walnut Ridge, AR 72476.

870-886-1112. Fax: 870-886-1117. 8:00AM-4:30PM (CST). Access by: Phone, mail, in person.

Misdemeanor, Eviction, Small Claims—Municipal Court, 201 SW 2nd, Walnut Ridge, AR 72476. 870-886-3905. 8AM-4:30PM (CST). Access by: Phone, mail, in person.

Lee County

Real Estate Recording—Lee County Circuit Clerk, 15 East Chestnut Street, Courthouse, Marianna, AR 72360. 870-295-7710. Fax: 870-295-7766. 8:30AM-4:30PM (CST).

Felony, Civil Actions Over $3,000, Probate—Circuit and Chancery Courts, 15 E Chestnut, Marianna, AR 72360. 870-295-7710. Fax: 870-295-7766. 8:30AM-4:30PM (CST). Access by: Mail, in person.

Misdemeanor, Eviction, Small Claims—Municipal Court, 15 East Chestnut, Marianna, AR 72360. 870-295-3813. Fax: 870-295-9419. 8AM-Noon; 1-5PM (CST). Access by: Mail, in person.

Lincoln County

Real Estate Recording—Lincoln County Circuit Clerk, 300 South Drew St, Star City, AR 71667. 870-628-3154. Fax: 870-628-5546. 8AM-5PM (CST).

Felony, Civil Actions Over $3,000, Probate—Circuit and County Courts, Courthouse, 300 S Drew, Star City, AR 71667. 870-628-3154. Fax: 870-628-5546. 8AM-5PM (CST). Access by: Mail, in person.

Misdemeanor, Eviction, Small Claims—Municipal Court, 300 S Drew, Star City, AR 71667. 870-628-4904. Fax: 870-628-4385. 8AM-4:30PM (CST). Access by: Mail, in person.

Little River County

Real Estate Recording—Little River County Circuit Clerk, 351 North Second, Ashdown, AR 71822. 870-898-7211. Fax: 870-898-7207. 8:30AM-4:30PM (CST).

Felony, Civil Actions Over $3,000, Probate—Circuit and County Courts, PO Box 575, Ashdown, AR 71822. 870-898-7211. Fax: 870-898-7207. 8:30AM-4:30PM (CST). Access by: Phone, mail, in person.

Misdemeanor, Eviction, Small Claims—Municipal Court, 351 N 2nd St, Ashdown, AR 71822. 870-898-7230. 8:30AM-4:30PM (CST). Access by: In person only.

Logan County

Real Estate Recording—Logan County Circuit Clerk, Southern District, Courthouse, 366 N Broadway #2, Booneville, AR 72927. 501-675-2894. Fax: 501-675-5739. 8AM-Noon, 1-4:30PM (CST).

Logan County Circuit Clerk, Northern District, Courthouse, Paris, AR 72855. 501-963-2164. 8AM-Noon 1-4:30PM (CST).

Felony, Civil Actions Over $3,000, Probate—Circuit and Chancery Courts, Courthouse, Paris, AR 72855. 501-963-2164. Fax: 501-963-3304. 8AM-4:30PM (CST). Access by: Mail, in person.

Misdemeanor, Eviction, Small Claims—Municipal Court, Paris Courthouse, Paris, AR 72855. 501-963-3792. 8:30AM-4:30PM (CST). Access by: Phone, mail, in person.

Lonoke County

Real Estate Recording—Lonoke County Circuit Clerk, Courthouse, Lonoke, AR 72086. 501-676-2316. 8AM-4:30PM (CST).

Felony, Civil Actions Over $3,000, Probate—Circuit and Chancery Courts, PO Box 231 Attn: Circuit Clerk, Lonoke, AR 72086. 501-676-2316. 8AM-4:30PM (CST). Access by: Mail, in person.

Misdemeanor, Eviction, Small Claims—Municipal Court, 203 W Front, Lonoke, AR 72086. 501-676-3585. Fax: 501-676-2500. 8AM-4:30PM (CST). Access by: Mail, in person.

Madison County

Real Estate Recording—Madison County Circuit Clerk, Main Street, Courthouse, Huntsville, AR 72740. 501-738-2215. Fax: 501-738-1544. 8AM-4:30PM (CST).

Felony, Civil Actions Over $3,000, Probate—Circuit and Chancery Courts, PO Box 416, Huntsville, AR 72740. 501-738-2215. Fax: 501-738-1544. 8AM-4:30PM (CST). Access by: In person only.

Misdemeanor, Eviction, Small Claims—Municipal Court, PO Box 549, Huntsville, AR 72740. 501-738-2911. Fax: 501-738-6846. 8AM-4:30PM (CST). Access by: Phone, mail, in person.

Marion County

Real Estate Recording—Marion County Circuit Clerk, Hwy 62, Courthouse, Yellville, AR 72687. 870-449-6226. Fax: 870-449-4979. 8AM-4:30PM (CST).

Felony, Civil Actions Over $3,000, Probate—Circuit and County Courts, PO Box 385, Yellville, AR 72687. 870-449-6226. Fax: 870-449-4979. 8AM-4:30PM (CST). Access by: In person only.

Misdemeanor, Eviction, Small Claims—Municipal Court, PO Box 301, Yellville, AR 72687. 870-449-6030. 8AM-4:30PM (CST). Access by: In person only.

Miller County

Real Estate Recording—Miller County Circuit Clerk, County Courthouse-Suite 109, 412 Laurel St., Texarkana, AR 71854. 870-774-4501. 8AM-4:30PM (CST).

Felony, Civil Actions Over $3,000, Probate—Circuit and County Courts, 412 Laurel St Rm 109, Texarkana, AR 71854. 870-774-4501. Fax: 870-772-5293. 8AM-4:30PM (CST). Access by: Phone, mail, in person.

Misdemeanor, Eviction, Small Claims—Municipal Court, 400 Laurel Suite 101, Texarkana, AR 71854. 870-772-2780. Fax: 870-773-3595. 8AM-4:30PM (CST). Access by: Mail, in person.

Mississippi County

Real Estate Recording—Mississippi County Circuit Clerk, Chickasawba District, 2nd & Walnut Street, Blytheville, AR 72315. 870-762-2332. Fax: 870-763-0150. 9AM-4:30PM (CST).

Mississippi County Circuit Clerk, Osceola District, Courthouse, Osceola, AR 72370. 870-563-6471. Fax: 870-563-2543. 9AM-4:30PM (CST).

Felony, Civil Actions Over $3,000, Probate—Blytheville Circuit and Chancery Courts, PO Box 1496, Blytheville, AR 72316. 870-762-2332. Fax: 870-763-0150. 9AM-4:30PM (CST). Access by: Phone, fax, mail, in person.

Osceola Circuit and Chancery Courts, County Courthouse, Osceola, AR 72370. 870-563-6471. 9AM-4:30PM (CST). Access by: Phone, mail, in person.

Misdemeanor, Eviction, Small Claims—Blytheville Municipal Court, City Hall, 2nd & Walnut, Blytheville, AR 72315. 870-763-7513. Fax: 870-762-0443. 8AM-5PM (CST). Access by: Fax, mail, in person.

Osceola Municipal Court, City Hall, Osceola, AR 72370. 870-563-1303. Fax: 870-563-2543. 9AM-4:30PM (CST). Access by: Mail, in person.

Monroe County

Real Estate Recording—Monroe County Circuit Clerk, 123 Madison Street, Clarendon, AR 72029. 870-747-3615. Fax: 870-747-3710. 8AM-4:30PM (CST).

Felony, Civil Actions Over $3,000, Probate—Circuit and Chancery Courts, 123 Madison St, Courthouse, Clarendon, AR 72029. 870-747-3615. Fax: 870-747-3710. 8AM-4:30PM (CST). Access by: Mail, in person.

Misdemeanor, Eviction, Small Claims—Municipal Court, Courthouse, 123 Madision St, Clarendon, AR 72029. 870-747-5200. Fax: 870-747-3903. 8AM-5PM (CST). Access by: Mail, in person.

Montgomery County

Real Estate Recording—Montgomery County Circuit Clerk, 101 George Street, Mount Ida, AR 71957. 501-867-3521. Fax: 870-867-4354. 8AM-4:30PM (CST).

Felony, Civil Actions Over $3,000, Probate—Circuit and County Courts, PO Box 377, Courthouse, Mount Ida, AR 71957. 870-867-3521. Fax: 870-867-4354. 8AM-4:30PM (CST). Access by: Mail, in person.

Misdemeanor, Eviction, Small Claims—Municipal Court, PO Box 558, Mount Ida, AR 71957. 870-867-2221. Fax: 870-867-4354. 8AM-4:30PM M-Th, other days hours may vary (CST). Access by: Phone, fax, mail, in person.

Nevada County

Real Estate Recording—Nevada County Circuit Clerk, 215 East Second Street, Prescott, AR 71857. 870-887-2511. Fax: 870-887-5795. 8AM-5PM (CST).

Felony, Civil Actions Over $3,000, Probate—Circuit and Chancery Courts, PO Box 204, Prescott, AR 71857. 870-887-2511. Fax: 870-887-5795. 8AM-5PM (CST). Access by: Phone, fax, mail, in person.

Misdemeanor, Eviction, Small Claims—Municipal Court, PO Box 22, Prescott, AR 71857. 870-887-6016. Fax: 870-887-5795. 8AM-5PM (CST). Access by: Mail, in person.

Newton County

Real Estate Recording—Newton County Circuit Clerk, Courthouse Street, Jasper, AR 72641. 870-446-5125. Fax: 870-446-2106. 8AM-4:30PM (CST).

Felony, Civil Actions Over $3,000, Probate—Circuit and Chancery Courts, PO Box 410, Jasper, AR 72641. 870-446-5125. Fax: 870-446-2106. 8AM-4:30PM (CST). Access by: In person only.

Misdemeanor, Eviction, Small Claims—Municipal Court, PO Box 550, Jasper, AR 72641. 870-446-5335. Fax: 870-446-2234. 8AM-4:30PM (CST). Access by: In person only.

Ouachita County

Real Estate Recording—Ouachita County Circuit Clerk, 145 Jefferson Street, Camden, AR 71701. 870-837-2230. 8AM-4:30PM (CST).

Felony, Civil Actions Over $3,000, Probate—Circuit and Chancery Courts, PO Box 667, Camden, AR 71701. 870-837-2230. Probate: 870-837-2220. Fax: 870-837-2252. 8AM-4:30PM (CST). Access by: Mail, in person.

Misdemeanor, Eviction, Small Claims—Municipal Court, 213 Madison St, Camden, AR 71701. 870-836-0331. Fax: 870-836-3369. 8AM-4:30PM (CST). Access by: Mail, in person.

Perry County

Real Estate Recording—Perry County Circuit Clerk, Main Street, Courthouse Square, Perryville, AR 72126. 501-889-5126. Fax: 501-889-5759. 8AM-4:30PM (CST).

Felony, Civil Actions Over $3,000, Probate—Circuit and Chancery Courts, PO Box 358, Perryville, AR 72126. 501-889-5126. Fax: 501-889-2574. 8AM-4:30PM (CST). Access by: In person only.

Misdemeanor, Eviction, Small Claims—Municipal Court, PO Box 186, Perryville, AR 72126. 501-889-5296. Fax: 501-889-2574. 8AM-4:30PM (CST). Access by: Mail, in person.

Phillips County

Real Estate Recording—Phillips County Circuit Clerk, Courthouse, Suite 206, 620 Cherry St., Helena, AR 72342. 870-338-5515. Fax: 870-338-5513. 8AM-4:30PM (CST).

Felony, Civil Actions Over $3,000, Probate—Circuit and Chancery Courts, Courthouse, 620 Cherry St Suite 206, Helena, AR 72342. 870-338-5515. Fax: 870-338-5513. 8AM-4:30PM (CST). Access by: Mail, in person.

Misdemeanor, Eviction, Small Claims—Municipal Court, 226 Perry, Helena, AR 72342. 870-338-6439. Fax: 870-338-9832. 8AM-4:30PM (CST). Access by: Phone, fax, mail, in person.

Pike County

Real Estate Recording—Pike County Circuit Clerk, Courthouse Square, Murfreesboro, AR 71958. 870-285-2231. Fax: 870-285-3281. 8AM-4:30PM (CST).

Felony, Civil Actions Over $3,000, Probate—Circuit and Chancery Courts, PO Box 219, Murfreesboro, AR 71958. 870-285-2231. Fax: 870-285-3281. 8AM-4:30PM (CST). Access by: Fax, mail, in person.

Misdemeanor, Eviction, Small Claims—Municipal Court, PO Box 197, Murfreesboro, AR 71958. 870-285-3865. 8AM-4:30PM (CST). Access by: Fax, mail, in person.

Poinsett County

Real Estate Recording—Poinsett County Circuit Clerk, 401 Market Street, Courthouse, Harrisburg, AR 72432. 870-578-4420. Fax: 870-578-2441. 8:30AM-4:30PM (CST).

Felony, Civil Actions Over $3,000, Probate—Circuit and Chancery Courts, PO Box 46, Harrisburg, AR 72432. 870-578-4420. Fax: 870-578-2441. 8:30AM-4:30PM (CST). Access by: Mail, in person.

Misdemeanor, Eviction, Small Claims—Municipal Court, 202 East St, Harrisburg, AR 72432. 870-578-4110. 8AM-4:30PM (CST). Access by: Mail, in person.

Polk County

Real Estate Recording—Polk County Circuit Clerk, 507 Church, Courthouse, Mena, AR 71953. 501-394-8100. 8AM-4:30PM (CST).

Felony, Civil Actions Over $3,000, Probate—Circuit and Chancery Courts, 507 Church St, Mena, AR 71953. 501-394-8100. 8AM-4:30PM (CST). Access by: Mail, in person.

Misdemeanor, Eviction, Small Claims—Municipal Court, 507 Church St, Mena, AR 71953. 501-394-3271. Fax: 501-394-6199. 8AM-4:30PM (CST). Access by: In person only.

Pope County

Real Estate Recording—Pope County Circuit Clerk, 100 West Main, 3rd Floor, County Courthouse, Russellville, AR 72801. 501-968-7499. 8AM-5PM (CST).

Felony, Civil Actions Over $3,000, Probate—Circuit and Chancery Courts, 100 W Main, Russellville, AR 72801. 501-968-7499. 9AM-5PM (CST). Access by: In person only.

Misdemeanor, Eviction, Small Claims—Municipal Court, 205 S Commerce, Russellville, AR 72801. 501-968-1393. Fax: 501-968-8050. 8:30AM-5PM (CST). Access by: Mail, in person.

Prairie County

Real Estate Recording—Prairie County Circuit Clerk, Southern District, 200 Court Square, Corner of Prairie & Magnolia, De Valls Bluff, AR 72041. 870-998-2314. Fax: 870-998-2314. 8AM-Noon, 1-4:30PM (CST).

Prairie County Circuit Clerk, Northern District, 200 Court Square, Des Arc, AR 72040. 870-256-4434. Fax: 870-256-4434. 8AM-4:30PM (CST).

Felony, Civil Actions Over $3,000, Probate—Circuit and Chancery Courts-Southern District, PO Box 283, De Valls Bluff, AR 72041. 870-998-2314. Fax: 870-998-2314. 8AM-4:30PM (CST). Access by: Phone, mail, in person.

Circuit and County Courts-Northern District, PO Box 1011, Des Arc, AR 72040. 870-256-4434. Fax: 870-256-4434. 8AM-4:30PM (CST). Access by: Phone, mail, in person.

Misdemeanor, Eviction, Small Claims—Municipal Court, PO Box 389, Des Arc, AR 72040. 870-256-3011. 8AM-5PM (CST). Access by: Mail, in person.

Pulaski County

Real Estate Recording—Pulaski County Circuit Clerk, Room S216, 401 W. Markham St., Little Rock, AR 72201. 501-340-8433. Fax: 501-340-8420. 8:30AM-4:30PM (CST).

Felony, Civil Actions Over $3,000, Probate—Circuit and Chancery Courts, Courthouse, Rm 200, Little Rock, AR 72201. 501-340-8431. Fax: 501-340-8420. 8:30AM-4:30PM (CST). Access by: Mail, in person.

Misdemeanor, Eviction, Small Claims—Municipal Court, 3001 W Roosevelt, Little Rock, AR 72204. 501-340-6824. Fax: 501-340-6899. 8AM-4:30PM (CST). Access by: Fax, mail, in person.

Randolph County

Real Estate Recording—Randolph County Circuit Clerk, 107 W. Broadway, Pocahontas, AR 72455. 870-892-5522. Fax: 870-892-8674. 8AM-4:30PM (CST).

Felony, Civil Actions Over $3,000, Probate—Circuit and Chancery Courts, 107 West Broadway, Pocahontas, AR 72455. 870-892-5522. Fax: 870-892-8794. 8AM-4:30PM (CST). Access by: Phone, mail, in person.

Misdemeanor, Eviction, Small Claims—Municipal Court, 410 N Marr, PO Box 896, Pocahontas, AR 72455. 870-892-4033. Fax: 870-892-9043. 7:30AM-4:30PM (CST). Access by: Fax, mail, in person.

Saline County

Real Estate Recording—Saline County Circuit Clerk, 200 N. Main St., Courthouse, Benton, AR 72015. 501-776-5615. Fax: 501-776-5675. 8AM-4:30PM (CST).

Felony, Civil Actions Over $3,000, Probate—Circuit and Chancery Courts, PO Box 1560, Benton, AR 72018. 501-776-5615. Fax: 501-776-5675. 8AM-4:30PM (CST). Access by: In person only.

Misdemeanor, Eviction, Small Claims—Municipal Court, 1605 Edison Ave, Benton, AR 72015. 501-776-5975. Fax: 501-776-5696. 8AM-4:30PM (CST). Access by: Phone, fax, mail, in person.

Scott County

Real Estate Recording—Scott County Circuit Clerk, 100 W. First, Courthouse, Waldron, AR 72958. 501-637-2642. Fax: 501-637-4199. 8AM-4:30PM (CST).

Felony, Civil Actions Over $3,000, Probate—Circuit and Chancery Courts, PO Box 2165, Waldron, AR 72958. 870-637-2642. 8AM-4:30PM (CST). Access by: Mail, in person.

Misdemeanor, Eviction, Small Claims—Municipal Court, PO Box 977, Waldron, AR 72958. 870-637-2642. Fax: 870-637-4199. 8AM-4:30PM (CST). Access by: Mail, in person.

Searcy County

Real Estate Recording—Searcy County Circuit Clerk, Courthouse, Town Square, Marshall, AR 72650. 870-448-3807. 8AM-4:30PM (CST).

Felony, Civil Actions Over $3,000, Probate—Circuit and Chancery Courts, PO Box 813, Marshall, AR 72650. 870-448-3807. 8AM-4:30PM (CST). Access by: Mail, in person.

Misdemeanor, Eviction, Small Claims—Municipal Court, General Delivery, PO Box 837, Marshall, AR 72650. 870-448-5411. 9AM-5PM (CST). Access by: Phone, mail, in person.

Sebastian County

Real Estate Recording—Sebastian County Circuit Clerk, Fort Smith District, 35 S. 6th St., Courthouse - 2nd Floor, Fort Smith, AR 72901. 501-782-1046. Fax: 501-784-1580. 8AM-5PM (CST).

Sebastian County Circuit Clerk, Southern District, Town Square, Courthouse, Greenwood, AR 72936. 501-996-4175. Fax: 501-996-6885. 8AM-5PM (CST).

Felony, Civil Actions Over $3,000—Circuit Court-Greenwood Division, PO Box 310, County Courthouse, Greenwood, AR 72936. 501-996-4175. Fax: 501-996-6885. 8AM-4:30PM (CST). Access by: Mail, in person.

Felony, Civil Actions Over $3,000, Probate—Circuit Court, 35 S 6th St or PO Box 1179, Fort Smith, AR 72902. 501-782-1046. Fax: 501-784-1580. 8AM-4:30PM (CST). Access by: Mail, in person.

Misdemeanor, Eviction, Small Claims—Municipal Court, Courthouse, 35 S 6th St, Fort Smith, AR 72901. 501-784-2420. Fax: 501-784-2438. 8:30AM-5PM (CST). Access by: Mail, in person.

Sevier County

Real Estate Recording—Sevier County Circuit Clerk, 115 North 3rd Street, De Queen, AR 71832. 870-584-3055. Fax: 870-642-9638. 8AM-4:30PM (CST).

Felony, Civil Actions Over $3,000, Probate—Circuit Court, 115 N 3rd, Courthouse, De Queen, AR 71832. 870-584-3055. Fax: 870-642-9638. 8AM-4:30PM (CST). Access by: Mail, in person.

Misdemeanor, Eviction, Small Claims—Municipal Court, 115 N 3rd, De Queen, AR 71832. 870-584-7311. 8AM-4:30PM (CST). Access by: Phone, mail, in person.

Sharp County

Real Estate Recording—Sharp County Circuit Clerk, Highway 167 North, Courthouse, Ash Flat, AR 72513. 870-994-7361. Fax: 870-994-7712. 8AM-4PM (CST).

Felony, Civil Actions Over $3,000, Probate—Circuit and County Courts, PO Box 307, Ash Flat, AR 72513. 870-994-7361. Fax: 870-994-7712. 8AM-4PM (CST). Access by: Fax, mail, in person.

Misdemeanor, Eviction, Small Claims—Municipal Court, PO Box 2, Ash Flat, AR 72513. 870-994-2745. Fax: 870-994-7901. 8AM-4PM (CST). Access by: Mail, in person.

St. Francis County

Real Estate Recording—St. Francis County Circuit Clerk, 313 South Izard Street, Forrest City, AR 72335. 870-261-1715. Fax: 870-261-1784. 8AM-4:30PM (CST).

Felony, Civil Actions Over $3,000, Probate—Circuit and County Courts, PO Box 1775, Forrest City, AR 72335. 870-261-1715. 8AM-4:30PM (CST). Access by: Mail, in person.

Misdemeanor, Eviction, Small Claims—Municipal Court, 313 S Izard, Forrest City, AR 72335. 870-261-1410. Fax: 870-261-1411. 8AM-4:30PM (CST). Access by: Mail, in person.

Stone County

Real Estate Recording—Stone County Circuit Clerk, Courthouse, Mountain View, AR 72560. 870-269-3271. Fax: 870-269-2303. 8AM-4:30PM (CST).

Felony, Civil Actions Over $3,000, Probate—Circuit and Chancery Courts, PO Drawer 120, Mountain View, AR 72560. 870-269-3271. Fax: 870-269-2303. 8AM-4:30PM (CST). Access by: Phone, fax, mail, in person.

Misdemeanor, Eviction, Small Claims—Municipal Court, PO Box 1284, Mountain View, AR 72560. 870-269-3465. 8AM-4:30PM (CST). Access by: Phone, mail, in person.

Union County

Real Estate Recording—Union County Circuit Clerk, 101 North Washington, Courthouse - Room 201, El Dorado, AR 71730. 501-864-1940. 8:30AM-5PM (CST).

Felony, Civil Actions Over $3,000, Probate—Circuit and Chancery Courts, PO Box 1626, El Dorado, AR 71730. 870-864-1940. 8:30AM-5PM (CST). Access by: Mail, in person.

Misdemeanor, Eviction, Small Claims—Municipal Court, 101 N Washington, Suite 203, El Dorado, AR 71730. 870-864-1950. Fax: 870-864-1955. 8:30AM-5PM (CST). Access by: Fax, mail, in person.

Van Buren County

Real Estate Recording—Van Buren County Circuit Clerk, Courthouse, Main & Griggs, Clinton, AR 72031. 501-745-4140. Fax: 501-745-7400. 8AM-5PM (CST).

Felony, Civil Actions Over $3,000, Probate—Circuit and County Courts, Route 6 Box 254-9, Clinton, AR 72031. 501-745-4140. 8AM-5PM (CST). Access by: Mail, in person.

Misdemeanor, Eviction, Small Claims—Municipal Court, PO Box 368, Clinton, AR 72031. 501-745-8894. 9:30AM-4:30PM (CST). Access by: In person only.

Washington County

Real Estate Recording—Washington County Circuit Clerk, Courthouse, 280 N. College, Suite 302, Fayetteville, AR 72701. 501-444-1538. Fax: 501-444-1537. 8AM-4:30PM (CST).

Felony, Civil Actions Over $3,000, Probate—Circuit and Chancery Courts, 280 N College, Fayetteville, AR 72701. 501-444-1542. Fax: 501-444-1537. 8AM-4:30PM (CST). Access by: Fax, mail, in person.

Misdemeanor, Eviction, Small Claims—Municipal Court, 100B W Rock, Fayetteville, AR 72701. 501-587-3596. Fax: 501-444-3480. 8AM-5PM (CST). Access by: Phone, fax, mail, in person.

White County

Real Estate Recording—White County Circuit Clerk, White County Courthouse, Searcy, AR 72143. 501-279-6203. 8AM-4:30PM (CST).

Felony, Civil Actions Over $3,000, Probate—Circuit and Chancery Courts, 301 W Arch, Searcy, AR 72143. 501-279-6223. Probate: 501-279-6204. Fax: 501-279-6218. 8AM-4:30PM (CST). Access by: Phone, mail, in person.

Misdemeanor, Eviction, Small Claims—Municipal Court, 311 N Gumm, Searcy, AR 72143. 501-268-7622. 8:30AM-4:30PM (CST). Access by: Phone, mail, in person.

Woodruff County

Real Estate Recording—Woodruff County Circuit Clerk, 500 North Third Street, Augusta, AR 72006. 870-347-2391. 8AM-4PM (CST).

Felony, Civil Actions Over $3,000, Probate—Circuit and County Courts, PO Box 492, Augusta, AR 72006. 870-347-2391. Fax: 870-347-2915. 8AM-4PM (CST). Access by: Phone, mail, in person.

Misdemeanor, Eviction, Small Claims—Municipal Court, PO Box 381, Augusta, AR 72006. 870-347-2790. Fax: 870-347-2436. 8:30AM-5PM (CST). Access by: Fax, mail, in person.

Yell County

Real Estate Recording—Yell County Circuit Clerk, Danville District, East 5th & Main, Danville, AR 72833. 870-495-2414. Fax: 870-495-3495. 8AM-4PM (CST).

Yell County Circuit Clerk, Dardanelle District, Union Street, Courthouse, Dardanelle, AR 72834. 870-229-4404. Fax: 870-229-1130. 8AM-4PM (CST).

Felony, Civil Actions Over $3,000, Probate—Danville Circuit and County Courts, PO Box 219, Danville, AR 72833. 870-495-2414. Fax: 870-495-3495. 8AM-4PM (CST). Access by: Mail, in person.

Dardanelle Circuit and County Courts, County Courthouse, Dardanelle, AR 72834. 870-229-4404. 8AM-4PM (CST). Access by: Mail, in person.

Misdemeanor, Eviction, Small Claims—Municipal Court, Courthouse, Dardanelle, AR 72834. 870-229-1389. 8AM-4PM (CST). Access by: Mail, in person.

Federal Courts

US District Court
Eastern District of Arkansas

Batesville Division, US District Court c/o Little Rock Division, PO Box 869, Little Rock, AR 72201. 501-324-5351. Counties: Cleburne, Fulton, Independence, Izard, Jackson, Sharp, Stone

Helena Division, US District Court c/o Little Rock Division, PO Box 869, Little Rock, AR 72203. 501-324-5351. Counties: Cross, Lee, Monroe, Phillips, St. Francis, Woodruff

Jonesboro Division, US District Court PO Box 7080, Jonesboro, AR 72403. 501-972-4610. Counties: Clay, Craighead, Crittenden, Greene, Lawrence, Mississippi, Poinsett, Randolph

Little Rock Division, US District Court Room 402, 600 W Capitol, Little Rock, AR 72201. 501-324-5351. Counties: Conway, Faulkner, Lonoke, Perry, Pope, Prairie, Pulaski, Saline, Van Buren, White, Yell

Pine Bluff Division, US District Court PO Box 8307, Pine Bluff, AR 71611-8307. 870-536-1190. Counties: Arkansas, Chicot, Cleveland, Dallas, Desha, Drew, Grant, Jefferson, Lincoln

Western District of Arkansas

El Dorado Division, US District Court PO Box 1566, El Dorado, AR 71731. 870-862-1202. Fax: 870-863-4800. Counties: Ashley, Bradley, Calhoun, Columbia, Ouachita, Union

Fayetteville Division, US District Court PO Box 6420, Fayetteville, AR 72702. 501-521-6980. Counties: Benton, Madison, Washington

Fort Smith Division, US District Court PO Box 1523, Fort Smith, AR 72902. 501-783-6833. Fax: 501-783-6308. Counties: Crawford, Franklin, Johnson, Logan, Polk, Scott, Sebastian

Harrison Division, US District Court c/o Fayetteville Division, PO Box 6420, Fayetteville, AR 72702. 501-521-6980. Counties: Baxter, Boone, Carroll, Marion, Newton, Searcy

Hot Springs Division, US District Court PO Drawer I, Hot Springs, AR 71902. 501-623-6411. Counties: Clark, Garland, Hot Spring, Montgomery, Pike

Texarkana Division, US District Court PO Box 2746, Texarkana, AR 75504. 870-773-3381. Counties: Hempstead, Howard, Lafayette, Little River, Miller, Nevada, Sevier

US Bankruptcy Court
Eastern District of Arkansas

Little Rock Division, US Bankruptcy Court, PO Drawer 3777, Little Rock, AR 72203. 501-324-6357. Voice Case Information System: 501-324-5770. Counties: Same counties as included in Eastern District of US District Court. All bankruptcy cases in Arkansas prior to mid 1993 were heard here

Western District of Arkansas

Fayetteville Division, US Bankruptcy Court, PO Box 3097, Fayetteville, AR 72702-3097. 501-582-9800. Voice Case Information System: 501-324-5770. Counties: Same counties as included in the Western District of the US District Courts.

California

Capital: Sacramento (Sacramento County)	
Number of Counties: 58	**Population:** 31,589,153
County Court Locations:	**Federal Court Locations:**
•Superior Courts: 66	•District Courts: 7
•Municipal Courts: 223	•Bankruptcy Courts: 13
•Combined Courts: 10	**State Agencies:** 20

State Agencies—Summary

General Help Numbers:

State Archives

Secretary of State	916-653-7715
State Archives	Fax: 916-653-7134
1020 "Q" St, Sacramento, CA 95814	9:30AM-4PM
Reference Librarian:	916-653-7715
Historical Society:	415-357-1848

Governor's Office

Governor's Office	916-445-2841
State Capitol, 1st Floor	Fax: 916-445-4633
Sacramento, CA 95814	8:30AM-5PM

Attorney General's Office

Attorney General's Office	916-445-9555
Justice Department	Fax: 916-324-5205
PO Box 944255	8AM-5PM
Sacramento, CA 94244-2550	
Alternate Telephone:	916-324-5437

State Legislation

California State Legislature	
State Capitol	9AM-5PM
Room B-32 (Legislative Bill Room)	
Sacramento, CA 95814	
Current/Pending Bills:	916-445-2323
State Archives:	916-653-7715

Important State Internet Sites:

🐾 Webscape	
File Edit View	**Help**

State of California World Wide Web
www.state.ca.us/

Contains a welcome from the Governor, links to state information and services, agency indexes (all searchable), what's new and state Internet servers.

California Senate and Assembly Bills
www.sen.ca.gov/www/leginfo/SearchText.html

This site allows you to search the State Archives for all Senate and Assembly Bills.

Department of Motor Vehicles
www.dmv.ca.gov/

Offers information on office locations, business licensing, handbooks, information brochures, etc.

California Unclaimed Property
www.sco.ca.gov/

This is the site of the California Controller's Office which will lead you to information on unclaimed property.

Secretary of State
www.ss.ca.gov/

Links to the different agency divisions including UCC.

State Agencies—Public Records

Criminal Records
State Repository, Reporting Evaluation & Analysis Section, PO Box 903417, Sacramento, CA 94203-4170, Main Telephone: 916-227-3460, Hours: 8AM-5PM. Restricted access.

Corporation Records
Limited Liability Company Records
Secretary of State, Certification Division-Status Unit, 1500 11th Street, Sacramento, CA 95814, Main Telephone: 916-657-5448, Hours: 8AM-4:30PM. Access by: mail, phone, visit, PC. Fictitious names & assumed names are found at the county levels.

Trademarks/Servicemarks
Limited Partnership Records
Secretary of State, Trademark Unit, 923 12th St, Room 301, Sacramento, CA 95814, Main Telephone: 916-653-4984, Hours: 8AM-4:30PM. Access by: mail only. A counter (walk-in) service is not provided.

Uniform Commercial Code
Federal Tax Liens
State Tax Liens
UCC Division, Secretary of State, PO Box 942835, Sacramento, CA 94235-0001, Main Telephone: 916-653-3516, Hours: 8AM-5PM. Access by: mail, visit, PC.

Sales Tax Registrations
Board of Equalization, Sales & Use Tax Department, PO Box 942879, Sacramento, CA 94279-0040, Main Telephone: 916-324-2926, In California Only: 800-400-7115, Fax: 916-322-0187, Hours: 8AM-5PM. Access by: mail, phone, visit. Phone searching by area: Oakland, 510-286-1260; Sacramento, 916-324-2397; San Diego, 619-525-4532; San Jose, 408-277-1003; Santa Ana, 714-558-4296; Van Nuys, 818-901-5525.

Birth Certificates
State Department of Health Svcs, Office of Vital Records, PO Box 730241, Sacramento, CA 94244-0241, Main Telephone: 916-445-2684, Attendant: 916-445-1719, Fax: 800-858-5553, Hours: 8AM-4:30PM. Access by: mail, phone, visit.

Death Records
State Department of Health Svcs, Office of Vital Records, PO Box 730241, Sacramento, CA 94244-0241, Main Telephone: 916-445-2684, Fax: 800-858-5553, Hours: 8AM-4:30PM. Access by: mail, phone, visit.

Marriage Certificates
State Department of Health Svcs, Office of Vital Records, PO Box 730241, Sacramento, CA 94244-0241, Main Telephone: 916-445-2684, Fax: 800-858-5553, Hours: 8AM-4:30PM. Access by: mail, phone, visit.

Divorce Records
State Department of Health Svcs, Office of Vital Records, PO Box 730241, Sacramento, CA 94244-0241, Main Telephone: 916-445-2684, Fax: 800-858-5553, Hours: 8AM-4:30PM. Access by: mail, phone, visit.

Workers' Compensation Records
Division of Workers' Compensation, Information & Assistance Unit, PO Box 420603, San Francisco, CA 94142, Main Telephone: 415-975-0730, Fax: 415-975-0724, Hours: 8AM-5PM. Access by: mail, visit.

Driver Records
Department of Motor Vehicles, Information Services, PO Box 944247, Mail Station G199, Sacramento, CA 94244-2470, Main Telephone: 916-657-8098, Hours: 8AM-5PM. Access by: mail, phone, visit, PC. Non-commercial requesters are known as "casual requesters." These requests are held for 10 days while the state notifies the licensee who can then deny the release. If released, address is shielded. Copies of tickets are not available at the state level.

Vehicle Ownership
Vehicle Identification
Department of Motor Vehicle, Public Contact Unit, PO Box 944247,, Sacramento, CA 94244-2470, Main Telephone: 916-657-8098, Commercial Accounts: 916-657-7914, Hours: 8AM-5PM. Access by: mail, phone, visit, PC. There are two types of requesters: "casual requesters" and "requester account holders." For those businesses and entities who need to access on a regular basis, call (916) 657-5564.

Accident Reports
Records not available from state agency.

Hunting License Information
Fishing License Information
Department of Fish & Game, License & Revenue Branch, 3211 "S" St, Sacramento, CA 95816, Main Telephone: 916-227-2244, Fax: 916-227-2261, Hours: 8AM-5PM. Restricted access.

County Courts and Recording Offices

What You Need to Know...

| About the Courts | About the Recorder's Office |

Administration

Administration Office of Courts	415-396-9100
303 2nd St, S Tower	Fax: 415-396-9349
San Francisco, CA 94107	8AM-4PM

Court Structure

With the passage of Proposition 191, **effective 1-1-95**, all justice courts were eliminated; existing justice courts have been elevated to and unified within the municipal courts. Operations, judges, and **records** have become part of the municipal court system.

The courts are going through a continuing process of combining and consolidating Superior and Municipal Courts. This Sourcebook contains accurate information about court locations and practices as of late 1996, and individual court profiles contain information about planned future changes.

Municipal Courts may try minor felonies not included under our definition.

Searching Hints

If there is more than one court of a type within a county, where the case is tried and where the record is held depends on how a citation is written, where the infraction occurred, or where the filer whose to file the case.

Some courts—see Alameda County—now require signed releases from the subject in order to perform criminal searches, and will no longer allow the public to conduct such searches.

Personal checks are acceptable by state law.

Although some fees are set by statute, courts interpret them differently. For example, the search fee is supposed to be $5.00 per name per year searched, but many courts only charge $5.00 per name.

Online Access

There is **no** online computer access available, internal or external, except that some courts may allow access to their internal case management systems by county residents. The State Judicial Council is investigating the feasibility, cost, and coverage of such a system. Two percent of all fines, penalties, and forfeitures in criminal cases is being set aside in an automation fund to be used exclusively to pay for the automation of court record keeping and case management systems for criminal cases. However, activity is at the planning and pilot level as of this writing.

Organization

58 counties, 58 filing offices. The recording officer is County Recorder. Recordings are usually located in a Grantor/Grantee or General index. The entire state is in the Pacific Time Zone (PST).

UCC Records

Financing statements are filed at the state level, except for consumer goods, crops, and real estate related collateral, which are filed only with the County Recorder. All counties will perform UCC searches. Use search request form UCC-11. Search fees are usually $15.00 per debtor name. Copies usually cost $1.00 for the first page of a filing and then $.50 per page of attachments.

Lien Records

Federal and state tax liens on personal property of businesses are filed with the Secretary of State. Other federal and state tax liens are filed with the County Recorder. Some counties will perform tax lien searches. Fees vary. Other liens include judgment (Note—some judgments also filed at Secretary of State), child support, and mechanics.

Real Estate Records

Most counties do not perform real estate searches. Copy fees and certification fees vary.

County Courts and Recording Offices

Alameda County

Real Estate Recording—Alameda County Recorder, 1225 Fallon Street, Courthouse, Room 100, Oakland, CA 94612. 510-272-6365. Fax: 510-272-6382. 8:30AM-4:30PM (PST).

Civil Actions Over $25,000, Probate—Southern Superior Court-Hayward Branch, 24405 Amador St Rm 108, Hayward, CA 94544. 510-670-5060. Fax: 510-783-9456. 8:30AM-4:30PM (PST). Access by: Mail, in person.

Northern Superior Court-Civil, 1225 Fallon St Rm 109, Oakland, CA 94612. 510-272-6799. 8:30AM-4:30PM (PST). Access by: Mail, in person.

Eastern Superior Court-Civil, 5672 Stoneridge Dr 2nd Fl, Pleasanton, CA 94588. 510-551-6886. 8:30AM-Noon, 1-4:30PM (PST). Access by: Mail, in person.

Felony—Superior Court-Criminal, 1225 Fallon St Rm 107, Oakland, CA 94612. 510-272-6777. Fax: 510-272-0796. 8:30AM-5PM (PST). Access by: Mail, in person.

Misdemeanor, Civil Actions Under $25,000, Eviction, Small Claims—Alameda Municipal Court, 2233 Shoreline Dr (PO Box 1470), Alameda, CA 94501. 510-268-4209. Civil: 510-268-7479. Criminal: 510-268-7483. Fax: 510-268-7307. 8:30AM-4:30PM (PST). Access by: Mail, in person. Only seven year search available.

Civil Actions Under $25,000, Eviction, Small Claims—Berkeley-Albany Municipal Court-Civil Division, 2000 Center St, Room 202, Berkeley, CA 94704. 510-644-6423. 8:30AM-4:30PM (PST). Access by: Mail, in person.

Misdemeanor—Berkeley-Albany Municipal Court-Criminal Division, 2120 Martin Luther King Jr Way, Berkeley, CA 94704. 510-644-6917. 8:30AM-4:30PM (PST). Access by: Mail, in person.

Misdemeanor, Civil Actions Under $25,000, Eviction, Small Claims—Fremont-Newark-Union City Municipal Court, 39439 Paseo Padre Pky, Fremont, CA 94538. Civil: 510-795-2345. Criminal: 510-795-2300. Fax: 510-795-2349. 8:30AM-5PM (PST). Access by: Fax, mail, in person.

San Leandro-Hayward Municipal Court, 24405 Amador St, Hayward, CA 94544. Civil: 510-670-6432. Criminal: 510-670-6434. Fax: 510-670-5522. 8:30AM-4:30PM (PST). Access by: Mail, in person.

Oakland Piedmont Municipal Court, 661 Washington St, Oakland, CA 94607. Civil: 510-268-7724. Criminal: 510-268-4222. Fax: 510-268-7807. 8:30AM-4:30PM (PST). Access by: Mail, in person.

Livermore-Pleasanton-Dublin Municipal Court, PO Box 8076, 5672 Stoneridge Dr, Pleasanton, CA 94566-8678. Civil: 510-463-7948. Criminal: 510-463-7947. Fax: 510-847-0863. 9AM-4:30PM (PST). Access by: Mail, in person.

Alpine County

Real Estate Recording—Alpine County Treasurer-Tax-Collector-Recorder, Administration Building, 99 Water St., Markleeville, CA 96120. 530-694-2286. Fax: 530-694-2491. 9AM-Noon,1-4PM (PST).

Felony, Civil Actions Over $25,000, Probate—Superior Court, PO Box 276, Markleeville, CA 96120. 530-694-2113. Fax: 530-694-2119. 8AM-12PM 1PM-5PM (PST). Access by: Mail, in person.

Misdemeanor, Civil Actions Under $25,000, Eviction, Small Claims—Alpine Municipal Court, Main St Courthouse (Box 515), Markleeville, CA 96120. 530-694-2113. Fax: 530-694-2119. 8AM-5PM (PST). Access by: Mail, in person.

Amador County

Real Estate Recording—Amador County Recorder, 500 Argonaut Lane, Jackson, CA 95642. 209-223-6468. 8AM-5PM (PST).

Felony, Civil Actions Over $25,000, Probate—Superior Court, 108 Court St, Jackson, CA 95642. 209-223-6463. 8AM-5PM (PST). Access by: Mail, in person.

Misdemeanor, Civil Actions Under $25,000, Eviction, Small Claims—Municipal Court, 108 Court St, Jackson, CA 95642. 209-223-6355. Civil: 209-223-6322. Fax: 209-223-4532. 8AM-5PM (PST). Access by: Phone, fax, mail, in person.

Butte County

Real Estate Recording—Butte County Recorder, 25 County Center Drive, Oroville, CA 95965. 530-538-7691. Fax: 530-538-7975. 9AM-5PM; Recording hours: 9AM-4PM (PST).

Felony, Civil Actions Over $25,000, Probate—Butte County Consolidated Courts, One Court St, Oroville, CA 95965. 530-538-7551. Fax: 530-538-2112. 9AM-4PM M-TH; 8AM-4PM F (PST). Access by: Mail, in person.

Misdemeanor, Civil Actions Under $25,000, Eviction, Small Claims—North Butte County Municipal Court, 655 Oleander Ave, Chico, CA 95926. Civil: 530-891-2702. Criminal: 530-891-2703. 8AM-1PM M-Th; 8AM-Noon F (PST). Access by: Mail, in person.

Gridley Municipal Court, 239 Sycamore, Gridley, CA 95948. 530-846-5701. 9AM-Noon, 1-2PM T-TH (PST). Access by: Mail, in person.

South Butte County Municipal Court, 1931 Arlin Rhine Dr, Oroville, CA 95965. 530-538-7747. Fax: 530-538-2181. 8AM-2PM M-TH; 8AM-Noon F; (phone hours: 9AM-12PM M-TH) (PST). Access by: Mail, in person.

Paradise Branch-Municipal Court, 747 Elliot Rd, Paradise, CA 95969. 530-872-6347. 8AM-1PM M,T; 8AM-Noon W,F; 8:15AM-Noon, 1-5PM Th (PST). Access by: Mail, in person.

Calaveras County

Real Estate Recording—Calaveras County Recorder, Government Center, 891 Mountain Ranch Rd, San Andreas, CA 95249. 209-754-6372. 8AM-4PM (PST).

Felony, Civil Actions Over $25,000, Probate—Superior Court, 891 Mt Ranch Rd, San Andreas, CA 95249. 209-754-6310. Fax: 209-754-6561. 8AM-5PM (PST). Access by: Phone, mail, in person.

Misdemeanor, Civil Actions Under $25,000, Eviction, Small Claims—Municipal Court, 891 Mt Ranch Rd, San Andreas, CA 95249. 209-754-6336. Fax: 209-754-6689. 8AM-4PM (PST). Access by: Mail, in person.

Colusa County

Real Estate Recording—Colusa County Recorder, 546 Jay Street, Colusa, CA 95932. 530-458-0500. Fax: 530-458-0510. 8:30AM-5PM (PST).

Felony, Civil Actions Over $25,000, Probate—Colusa County Superior Court, 547 Market St, Colusa, CA 95932. 530-458-0507. Fax: 530-458-4242. 8:30AM-5PM (PST). Access by: Mail, in person.

Misdemeanor, Civil Actions Under $25,000, Eviction, Small Claims—Colusa Municipal Court, 532 Oak St, Colusa, CA 95932. 530-458-5149. Fax: 530-458-2904. 8:30AM-Noon, 1-5PM (PST). Access by: Mail, in person.

Contra Costa County

Real Estate Recording—Contra Costa County Recorder, 730 Las Juntas, Martinez, CA 94553. 510-646-2360. 8AM-4PM (PST).

Felony, Civil Actions Over $25,000, Probate—Superior Court, 725 Court St Rm 103, Martinez, CA 94553. Civil: 510-646-2951. Criminal: 510-646-2047. 8AM-4PM (PST). Access by: Mail, in person.

Civil Actions Under $25,000, Eviction, Small Claims—Mt Diablo Municipal Court-Civil Division, 2970 Willow Pass

Rd, Concord, CA 94519. 510-646-5410. Fax: 510-646-5488. 9AM-4PM (PST). Access by: Mail, in person.

Misdemeanor—Mt Diablo Municipal Court-Criminal Division, 1010 Ward St, Martinez, CA 94553. 510-646-5415. Fax: 510-646-1079. 9AM-4PM (PST). Access by: Mail, in person.

Misdemeanor, Civil Actions Under $25,000, Eviction, Small Claims—Delta Municipal Court, 45 Civic Ave (PO Box 431), Pittsburg, CA 94565-0431. 510-427-8173. Fax: 510-427-8155. 8AM-4:30PM (PST). Access by: Mail, in person. Visitor may search microfiche only.

Bay Municipal Court, 100 37th St Rm 185, Richmond, CA 94805. Civil: 510-374-3138. Criminal: 510-374-3156. 8AM-4PM (PST). Access by: Mail, in person.

Walnut Creek-Danville Municipal Court, 640 Ygnacio Valley Rd (PO Box 5128), Walnut Creek, CA 94596-1128. Civil: 510-646-6579. Criminal: 510-646-6572. 8:30AM-4:30PM (PST). Access by: Mail, in person.

Del Norte County

Real Estate Recording—Del Norte County Recorder, 457 F Street, Crescent City, CA 95531. 707-464-7216. 8AM-Noon,1-5PM (PST).

Felony, Civil Actions Over $25,000, Probate—Superior Court, 450 "H" St Rm 182, Crescent City, CA 95531. 707-464-7205. 8AM-Noon,1-5PM (PST). Access by: Phone, mail, in person.

Misdemeanor, Civil Actions Under $25,000, Eviction, Small Claims—Municipal Court, 450 H Street Rm 182, Crescent City, CA 95531. 707-464-7205. Fax: 707-465-4005. 8AM-Noon,1-5PM (PST). Access by: Mail, in person.

El Dorado County

Real Estate Recording—El Dorado County Recorder, 360 Fair Lane, Placerville, CA 95667. 530-621-5490. Fax: 530-621-2147. 8AM-5PM (No recordings after 4PM) (PST).

Felony, Civil Actions Over $25,000, Probate—Placerville Superior Court, 495 Main St, Placerville, CA 95667. 530-621-6426. Fax: 530-622-9774. 8AM-4PM (PST). Access by: Mail, in person.

South Lake Tahoe Superior Court, 1354 Johnson Blvd #2, South Lake Tahoe, CA 96150. 530-573-3075. 8AM-4PM (PST). Access by: Phone, mail, in person.

Misdemeanor—Cameron Park Branch Municipal Court, 3321 Cameron Park Dr, Cameron Park, CA 95682. 530-621-5867. Fax: 916-672-2413. 8AM-4PM (PST). Access by: Mail, in person.

Misdemeanor, Civil, Eviction, Small Claims—El Dorado Unified Court District, 2850 Fairlane Ct, Placerville, CA 95667. Civil: 530-621-7470. Criminal: 530-621-7464. 8AM-4PM (PST). Access by: Mail, in person. Address to Dept 7.

Misdemeanor, Civil Actions Under $25,000, Eviction—South Lake Tahoe Municipal Court, 1354 Johnson Blvd #1, South Lake Tahoe, CA 96150. 530-573-3045. Fax: 916-542-9102. 8AM-4PM (PST). Access by: Mail, in person.

Small Claims—South Lake Tahoe Municipal Court-Small Claims, 3368 Lake Tahoe Blvd, South Lake Tahoe, CA 96150. 530-573-3442. 8AM-4PM (PST). Access by: Mail, in person.

Fresno County

Real Estate Recording—Fresno County Recorder, 2281 Tulare St., Room 302 / Hall of Records, Fresno, CA 93721. 209-488-3471. Fax: 209-488-6774. 9AM-4PM (PST).

Felony, Civil Actions Over $25,000, Probate—Superior Court, 1100 Van Ness Ave Rm 401, Fresno, CA 93721. 209-488-3352. Fax: 209-488-1976. 8:30AM-4:30PM (PST). Access by: Mail, in person.

Misdemeanor, Civil Actions Under $25,000, Eviction, Small Claims—Caruthers Division-Central Valley Municipal Court, 2215 W Tahoe, Caruthers, CA 93609. 209-864-3160. 8AM-4PM (PST). Access by: Mail, in person. records are filed in Fowler Municipal Court.

Clovis Municipal Court, 1011 5th St, Clovis, CA 93612. 209-299-4964. Fax: 209-299-2595. 8AM-4PM (PST). Access by: Mail, in person.

Coalinga Division-Central Valley Municipal Court, 166 W Elm St, Coalinga, CA 93210. 209-935-2017. Fax: 209-935-5324. 8AM-Noon, 1-4PM (PST). Access by: Mail, in person.

Firebaugh Division-Central Valley Municipal Court, 1325 "O" St, Firebaugh, CA 93622. 209-659-2011. Fax: 209-659-6228. 8AM-4:30 M 8AM-4PM T-F (PST). Access by: Fax, mail, in person.

Fowler Division-Central Valley Municipal Court, PO Box 400, Fowler, CA 93625. 209-834-3215. Fax: 209-864-3160. 8AM-4PM (PST). Access by: Mail, in person.

Consolidated Fresno Municipal Court, 1100 Van Ness Ave Rm 200, Fresno, CA 93724. 209-488-3379. Civil: 209-488-3453. Criminal: 209-488-3388. 8AM-4PM (PST). Access by: Mail, in person.

Kerman Division-Central Valley Municipal Court, 719 S Madera Ave, Kerman, CA 93630. 209-846-7371. Fax: 209-846-5751. 8AM-4PM M-F (2-4 for phone calls) (PST). Access by: Phone, mail, in person.

Kingsburg Division-Central Valley Municipal Court, 1380 Draper St, Kingsburg, CA 93631. 209-897-2241. Fax: 209-897-1419. 8AM-Noon, 1-4PM (2-4PM for phone calls) (PST). Access by: Mail, in person.

Parlier Branch-Central Valley Municipal Court, 580 Tulare St, Parlier, CA 93648. 209-646-2815. Fax: 209-646-3222. 8AM-12PM, 1PM-4PM (PST). Access by: Mail, in person.

Reedley/Dunlap Division-Central Valley Municipal Court, 815 "G" St, Reedley, CA 93654. 209-638-3114. Fax: 209-637-1534. 8AM-Noon, 1-4PM (2-4 for phone calls) (PST). Access by: Mail, in person.

Riverdale Branch-Central Valley Municipal Court, 3563 Henson (PO Box 595), Riverdale, CA 93656. 209-867-3448. Fax: 209-867-4250. 8AM-4PM M-F (2-4 phone calls) (PST). Access by: Mail, in person.

Sanger Division-Central Valley Municipal Court, 619 "N" St, Sanger, CA 93657. 209-875-7158. Fax: 209-875-0002. 8AM-Noon, 1-4PM (PST). Access by: Mail, in person.

Selma Division-Central Valley Municipal Court, 2117 Selma St, Selma, CA 93662. 209-896-2123. Fax: 209-896-4465. 8AM-Noon, 1-4PM (PST). Access by: In person only.

Glenn County

Real Estate Recording—Glenn County Recorder, 526 West Sycamore Street, Willows, CA 95988. 530-934-6412. Fax: 530-934-6305. 8AM-5PM (PST).

Felony, Civil Actions Over $25,000, Probate—Superior Court, 526 W Sycamore (PO Box 391), Willows, CA 95988. 530-934-6407. Fax: 530-934-6406. 8AM-5PM (PST). Access by: Mail, in person.

Misdemeanor, Civil Actions Under $25,000, Eviction, Small Claims—Glenn County Consolidated Courts, 526 W Sycamore St, Willows, CA 95988. 530-865-1101. Fax: 530-865-1104. 8AM-Noon, 1-5PM M-F (window 9AM-Noon, 1-3PM) (PST). Access by: Mail, in person.

Willows Branch-Glenn County Municipal Court, 543 W Oak St, Willows, CA 95988. 530-934-6446. Fax: 530-934-6449. 9AM-12PM 1PM-3PM M-F (PST). Access by: Phone, mail, in person.

Humboldt County

Real Estate Recording—Humboldt County Recorder, 825 Fifth Street, Room 108, Eureka, CA 95501. 707-445-7593. Fax: 707-445-7324. 10AM-5PM (PST).

Felony, Civil, Probate—Humboldt Superior & Municipal Court, 421 I St, Eureka, CA 95501-1153. 707-445-7355. 8:30AM-12PM 1PM-4PM (PST). Access by: Mail, in person.

Misdemeanor, Civil Actions Under $25,000, Eviction, Small Claims—Eel River Municipal Court, 777 9th St, Fortuna, CA 95540. 707-725-5121. Fax: 707-725-2880. 8AM-5PM (PST). Access by: Mail, in person.

Garberville Branch-Municipal Court, 483 Conger St, Garberville, CA 95542. 707-923-2141. Fax: 707-923-3133. 8:30AM-5PM (PST). Access by: Mail, in person.

Klamath/Trinity Branch-Municipal Court, PO Box 698, Hoopa, CA 95546. 916-625-4204. 8:30AM-12PM 1PM-5PM M-TH (PST). Access by: Mail, in person.

Imperial County

Real Estate Recording—Imperial County Clerk/Recorder, 940 Main Street, Room 206, El Centro, CA 92243. 760-339-4272. 9AM-4:30PM (PST).

Felony, Civil Actions Over $25,000, Probate—Superior Court, 939 W Main St, El Centro, CA 92243. 760-339-4217. Fax: 760-352-3184. 8AM-4PM (PST). Access by: Mail, in person.

Misdemeanor, Civil Actions Under $25,000, Eviction, Small Claims—Brawley Branch-Municipal Court, 383 Main St, Brawley, CA 92227. 760-344-0710. Fax: 760-344-9231. 8AM-4PM (PST). Access by: Phone, mail, in person.

Calexico Branch-Municipal Court, 415 4th St, Calexico, CA 92231. 760-357-3726. Fax: 760-357-6571. 8AM-4PM (PST). Access by: Mail, in person.

El Centro Branch-Municipal Court, 939 W Main St, El Centro, CA 92243. 760-339-4256. Fax: 760-352-3184. 8AM-4PM (PST). Access by: Mail, in person.

Winterhaven Branch-Municipal Court, PO Box 1087, Winterhaven, CA 92283. 760-572-0354. Fax: 760-572-2683. 8AM-4PM (PST). Access by: Phone, fax, mail, in person.

Inyo County

Real Estate Recording—Inyo County Recorder, 168 North Edwards, Independence, CA 93526. 760-878-0222. Fax: 760-872-2712. 9-Noon,1-5PM (PST).

Felony, Civil Actions Over $25,000, Probate—Superior Court, 168 N Edwards St (PO Drawer F), Independence, CA 93526. 760-878-0218. 9AM-5PM (PST). Access by: Mail, in person.

Misdemeanor, Civil Actions Under $25,000, Eviction, Small Claims—Bishop Branch-Municipal Court, 301 W Line St, Bishop, CA 93514. 760-872-4971. 9AM-5PM (PST). Access by: Mail, in person.

Independence Branch-Municipal Court, 168 N Edwards St (PO Box 518), Independence, CA 93526. 760-878-0319. Fax: 760-872-1060. 9AM-12PM 1PM-5PM (PST). Access by: Mail, in person.

Kern County

Real Estate Recording—Kern County Recorder, 1655 Chester Avenue, Hall of Records, Bakersfield, CA 93301. 805-861-2181. Fax: 805-631-9443. 8AM-5PM; Recording 8AM-2PM; Copy Service 8AM-4PM (PST).

Felony, Civil Actions Over $25,000, Probate—Superior Court, 1415 Truxtun Ave, Bakersfield, CA 93301. 805-861-2621. Fax: 805-634-4999. 8AM-5PM (PST). Access by: Mail, in person.

Misdemeanor, Civil Actions Under $25,000, Eviction, Small Claims—Bakersfield Municipal Court, 1215 Truxtun Ave, Bakersfield, CA 93301. 805-861-3061. Fax: 805-861-2005. 8AM-5PM (PST). Access by: In person only.

Delano/McFarland Branch-North Kern Municipal Court, 1122 Jefferson Sty, Delano, CA 93215. 805-725-8797. Fax: 805-721-1237. 8AM-Noon, 1-4:30PM (PST). Access by: Phone, mail, in person.

River Branch-East Kern Municipal Court, 7046 Lake Isabella Blvd, Lake Isabella, CA 93240. 619-379-3635. Fax: 619-379-4544. 8AM-4PM M-TH 8AM-5PM F (PST). Access by: Phone, mail, in person.

Arvin/Lamont Branch-South Kern Municipal Court, 12022 Main St, Lamont, CA 93241. 805-845-3460. Fax: 805-845-9142. 8AM-4PM (PST). Access by: Mail, in person.

Mojave Branch-East Kern Municipal Court, 1773 Hwy 58, Mojave, CA 93501. 805-824-2437. Civil: 8AM-Noon, 1-4PM M-Th; 8AM-Noon, 1-5PM F. Criminal: 8AM-4 (PST). Access by: Mail, in person.

East Kern Municipal Court, 132 E Coso St, Ridgecrest, CA 93555. 619-375-1397. Fax: 619-375-2112. 8AM-4PM M-T, 8AM-5PM F (PST). Access by: Mail, in person.

Indian Wells Branch-East Kern Municipal Court, 132 E Coso St, Ridgecrest, CA 93555. 619-375-1397. 8AM-5PM; Civil 8AM-Noon, 1-5PM (PST). Access by: Mail, in person.

Shafter/Wasco Branch-North Kern Municipal Court, 325 Central Valley Hwy, Shafter, CA 93263. 805-746-3312. Fax: 805-746-0545. 8AM-12PM 1PM-4PM; Phone hours 8AM-Noon, 1-3PM (PST). Access by: Phone, fax, mail, in person.

Maricopa/Taft Branch-Kern Municipal Court, 311 Lincoln St (PO Bin RB), Taft, CA 93268. 805-763-2401. Fax: 805-763-2439. 8-11AM (Phone) (PST). Access by: Mail, in person.

Kings County

Real Estate Recording—Kings County Clerk Recorder, 1400 West Lacey Blvd., Hanford, CA 93230. 209-582-3211. Fax: 209-582-6639. 8AM-3PM (PST).

Felony, Civil Actions Over $25,000, Probate—Superior Court, 1400 W Lacey Blvd, Hanford, CA 93230. 209-582-3211. 8AM-5PM (PST). Access by: Phone, mail, in person.

Misdemeanor, Civil Actions Under $25,000, Eviction, Small Claims—Avenal Division Municipal Court, 501 E Kings St, Avenal, CA 93204. 209-386-5225. Fax: 209-386-9452. 8AM-5PM (PST). Access by: Phone, fax, mail, in person.

Corcoran Division-Municipal Court, 1000 Chittenden Ave, Corcoran, CA 93212. 209-992-5193. Fax: 209-992-5933. 8AM-5PM (PST). Access by: Mail, in person.

Hanford Division-Municipal Court, 1400 W Lacey Blvd, Hanford, CA 93230. Civil: 209-582-4370. Criminal: 209-582-4370. Fax: 209-584-0319. 8AM-5PM (PST). Access by: Mail, in person.

Lemoore Division-Municipal Court, 449 "C" St, Lemoore, CA 93245. 209-924-7757. Fax: 209-925-0319. 8AM-5PM (PST). Access by: Mail, in person.

Lake County

Real Estate Recording—Lake County Recorder, 255 North Forbes, Lakeport, CA 95453. 707-263-2293. Fax: 707-263-3703. 9AM-5PM M-Th; 9-11:30AM F (PST).

Felony, Civil Actions Over $25,000, Probate—Superior Court, 255 N Forbes St, Lakeport, CA 95453. 707-263-2374. Fax: 707-262-1327. Public hours 8:30AM-12:30PM (PST). Access by: Mail, in person.

Misdemeanor, Civil Actions Under $25,000, Eviction, Small Claims—South Lake Division-Municipal Court, PO Box 670, Clearlake, CA 95422. Civil: 707-994-8262. Criminal: 707-994-6598. Fax: 707-994-1625. 8AM-Noon, 1-4PM; Phone hours 8:30AM-12:30PM (PST). Access by: In person only.

North Lake Division-Municipal Court, 255 N Forbes St, Lakeport, CA 95453. 707-263-2285. Civil: 707-263-2285. Criminal: 707-263-2572. Fax: 707-262-1327. 8AM-Noon,1-4PM (PST). Access by: In person only.

Lassen County

Real Estate Recording—Lassen County Recorder, 220 S. Lassen Street, Courthouse, Susanville, CA 96130. 530-251-8234. Fax: 530-257-3480. Public Hours: 10AM-Noon, 1-3PM; Phone Hours: 8AM-Noon, 1-5PM (PST).

Felony, Civil Actions Over $25,000, Probate—Lassen County Consolidated Courts, 220 S Lassen St, Susanville, CA 96130. 530-251-8124. 9AM-12PM, 1-4PM; Phone hours 9AM-Noon (PST). Access by: Phone, mail, in person.

Misdemeanor, Civil Actions Under $25,000, Eviction, Small Claims—Lassen Consolidated Municipal Court, 220 S Lassen St, Susanville, CA 96130. 530-251-8205. 8AM-1PM (PST). Access by: Mail, in person.

Los Angeles County

Real Estate Recording—Los Angeles County Recorder, Registrar-Recorder/County Clerk, 12400 E. Imperial Highway, Room 1007, Norwalk, CA 90650. 310-462-2125. 8AM-5PM (PST).

Felony, Civil Actions Over $25,000, Probate—Superior Court, 210 W Temple St Rm M-6, Los Angeles, CA 90012.

213-974-5259. Fax: 213-617-1224. 8:30AM-4:30PM (PST). Access by: Mail, in person.

Civil Actions Under $25,000, Eviction, Small Claims—Valley Division-Municipal Court-Civil Division, 14400 Delano St, Van Nuys, CA 91401. 818-374-3060. 8:30AM-4:30PM (PST). Access by: Mail, in person.

Misdemeanor—Valley Division-Municipal Court-Criminal Division, 14400 Erwin St Mall 2nd Fl, Van Nuys, CA 91401. 818-374-2628. 8:30AM-4:30PM (PST). Access by: Phone, mail, in person.

Misdemeanor, Civil Actions Under $25,000, Eviction, Small Claims—Alhambra Municipal Court, 150 W Commonwealth Ave, Alhambra, CA 91801. Civil: 818-308-5307. Criminal: 818-308-5525. 8AM-4:30PM (PST). Access by: Mail, in person.

Los Cerritos Municipal Court, 10025 E Flower St, Bellflower, CA 90706. Civil: 310-804-8008. Criminal: 310-804-8015. 8AM-4:30PM (PST). Access by: Mail, in person.

Beverly Hills Municipal Court, 9355 Burton Way, Beverly Hills, CA 90210. 310-288-1227. Civil: 310-288-1369. Criminal: 310-288-1372. 8:30AM-4:30PM (PST). Access by: Phone, mail, in person. 900# telephone service to begin Sept 1997.

Burbank Municipal Court, 300 E Olive, P O Box 750, Burbank, CA 91502. Civil: 818-557-2461. Criminal: 818-557-3466. 8AM-4:30PM (PST). Access by: Mail, in person.

Calabasas Branch-Malibu Municipal Court, 5030 N Pkwy Calabasas, Calabasas, CA 91302. Civil: 818-222-1895. Criminal: 818-222-1896. Fax: 818-222-1176. 8AM-5PM (PST). Access by: Mail, in person.

Compton Municipal Court, 200 W Compton Blvd, Compton, CA 90220. 310-603-7101. Civil: 310-603-7105. Criminal: 310-603-7112. Fax: 310-763-4984. 8AM-4:30PM (PST). Access by: Mail, in person.

Culver Municipal Court, 4130 Overland Ave, Culver City, CA 90230. Civil: 310-202-3160. Criminal: 310-202-3158. Fax: 310-836-8345. 8:30AM-4:30PM (PST). Access by: Mail, in person.

Downey Municipal Court, 7500 E Imperial Hwy, Downey, CA 90242. Civil: 562-803-7052. Criminal: 562-803-7049. 8AM-4:30PM T-F 12PM-7:30PM M (PST). Access by: Mail, in person.

Rio Hondo Municipal Court, 11234 E Valley Blvd, El Monte, CA 91731. Civil: 818-575-4116. Criminal: 818-575-4121. Fax: 818-444-9029. 8:15AM-5:30PM M (Traffic Court Only) 8:15AM-4:30PM T-F (PST). Access by: Mail, in person.

Glendale Municipal Court, 600 E Broadway, Glendale, CA 91206. Civil: 818-500-3538. Criminal: 818-500-3541. 8:30AM-4:30PM (PST). Access by: Mail, in person.

Southeast Municipal Court, 6548 Miles Ave, Huntington Park, CA 90255. Civil: 213-586-6365. Criminal: 213-586-6365. Fax: 213-589-6769. 8:30AM-4:30PM (PST). Access by: Mail, in person.

Inglewood Municipal Court, 1 Regent St Rm 205, Inglewood, CA 90301. 310-419-5121. Civil: 310-419-5125. Criminal: 310-419-5128. Fax: 310-674-4862. 8AM-4:30PM (PST). Access by: Mail, in person.

Antelope Municipal Court, 1040 W Ave J (PO Box 1898 93539), Lancaster, CA 93534. 805-945-6335. Civil: 805-945-6351. Criminal: 805-945-6355. Fax: 805-949-8628. 8AM-4:30PM (PST). Access by: Mail, in person.

Long Beach Municipal Court, 415 W Ocean Blvd, Long Beach, CA 90801. 562-491-6201. Civil: 562-491-6234. Criminal: 562-491-6226. Fax: 562-437-0147. 8:30AM-10:30AM, 1:30-3:30PM; Phone Hours 9-11AM, 2:30-4PM (PST). Access by: Fax, mail, in person.

Misdemeanor, Eviction—Metropolitan Branch-Municipal Court, 1945 S Hill St Rm 101, Los Angeles, CA 90007. 213-744-4036. Criminal: 213-744-4022. Fax: 213-744-1879. 8AM-5PM M-W & F 8AM-7PM TH (PST). Access by: Phone, mail, in person.

Civil Actions Under $25,000, Eviction, Small Claims—Los Angeles Municipal Court-Civil, 110 N Grand Ave Rm 426, Los Angeles, CA 90012. 213-974-6135. Fax: 213-621-2701. 8:30AM-4:30PM (PST). Access by: Mail, in person.

Misdemeanor—Los Angeles Municipal Court-Criminal, 210 W Temple St Rm 5-111, Los Angeles, CA 90012. 213-974-6151. 8AM-4:30PM (PST). Access by: Phone, in person.

Misdemeanor, Civil Actions Under $25,000, Eviction, Small Claims—East Los Angeles Municipal Court, 214 S Fetterly Ave, Los Angeles, CA 90022. Civil: 213-780-2017. Criminal: 213-780-2025. 8AM-4:30PM (PST). Access by: Phone, mail, in person.

West Los Angeles Branch-Municipal Court, 1633 Purdue Ave, Los Angeles, CA 90025. 310-312-6547. Fax: 310-312-2902. 8AM-4:30PM (PST). Access by: Mail, in person.

Hollywood Branch-Municipal Court, 5925 Hollywood Blvd Rm 102, Los Angeles, CA 90028. 213-856-5751. Fax: 213-962-6157. 8:30AM-4:30PM (PST). Access by: Mail, in person.

Malibu Municipal Court, 23525 W Civic Center Way, Malibu, CA 90265. 310-317-1312. 8AM-4:30PM (PST). Access by: Mail, in person.

Santa Anita Municipal Court, 300 W Maple Ave, Monrovia, CA 91016. Civil: 818-301-4050. Criminal: 818-301-4051. Fax: 818-357-7825. 8AM-4:30PM (PST). Access by: Mail, in person.

Pasadena Municipal Court, 200 N Garfield Ave, Pasadena, CA 91101. Civil: 626-356-5449. Criminal: 626-356-5254. Fax: 626-577-1310. 8:30AM-4:30PM (PST). Access by: Mail, in person.

Pomona Municipal Court, 350 W Mission Blvd, Pomona, CA 91766. 909-620-3201. Civil: 909-620-3215. Criminal: 909-620-3219. Fax: 909-622-2305. 8AM-12PM 2PM-4PM M-F (civil) 8AM-5PM M-F (criminal) (PST). Access by: Mail, in person.

Civil Actions Under $25,000, Eviction, Small Claims—South Bay Municipal Court-Beach Cities Branch, 117 W Torrance Blvd, Redondo Beach, CA 90277-3638. 310-798-6875. Fax: 310-376-4051. 8:30AM-4:30PM (PST). Access by: Mail, in person.

Misdemeanor, Small Claims—San Fernando Branch-Municipal Court, 120 N Maclay, San Fernando, CA 91340. 818-898-2401. Fax: 818-837-7910. 8AM-4:30PM (PST). Access by: Mail, in person.

Misdemeanor, Civil Actions Under $25,000, Eviction, Small Claims—San Pedro Branch Court, 505 S Centre St Rm 202, San Pedro, CA 90731. Civil: 310-519-6015. Criminal: 310-519-6018. Fax: 310-519-6015. 8:30AM-4:30PM (civ, sm claims & criminal); 8AM-5PM (traffic) (PST). Access by: Mail, in person.

Santa Monica Municipal Court, 1725 Main St Rm 224, Santa Monica, CA 90401. Civil: 310-260-3706. Criminal: 310-260-3517. 8:30AM-4:30PM (PST). Access by: Mail, in person.

Southeast Judicial District-South Gate Municipal Court, 8640 California Ave, South Gate, CA 90280. Civil: 213-563-4018. Criminal: 213-563-4012. 8:30AM-4:30PM T-F; 10AM-7PM M traffic (PST). Access by: Mail, in person.

South Bay Municipal Court, 825 Maple Ave, Torrance, CA 90503-5058. Civil: 310-222-6500. Criminal: 310-222-6505. Fax: 310-222-7277. 8:30AM-4:30PM (PST). Access by: Mail, in person.

Newhall Municipal Court, 23747 W Valencia Blvd, Valencia, CA 91355. Civil: 805-253-7313. Criminal: 805-253-7384. Fax: 805-254-4107. 8:30AM-4:30PM (PST). Access by: Mail, in person.

Citrus Municipal Court, 1427 W Covina Pky, West Covina, CA 91790. Civil: 818-813-3236. Criminal: 818-813-3239. Fax: 818-338-7364. 8AM-4:30PM (PST). Access by: Mail, in person.

Whittier Municipal Court, 7339 S Painter Ave, Whittier, CA 90602. Civil: 310-907-3127. Criminal: 310-907-3113. 12PM-8PM M 8AM-5PM T-F (PST). Access by: Mail, in person.

Madera County

Real Estate Recording—Madera County Recorder, 209 West Yosemite, Madera, CA 93637. 209-675-7724. Fax: 209-673-3302. (PST).

Felony, Civil Actions Over $25,000, Probate—Superior Court, 209 W Yosemite Ave, Madera, CA 93637. 209-675-7721. Fax: 209-675-0701. 8AM-5PM (PST). Access by: Mail, in person.

Misdemeanor, Civil Actions Under $25,000, Eviction, Small Claims—Sierra Municipal Court, 40601 Road 274, Bass Lake, CA 93604. 209-642-3235. Fax: 209-642-3445. 8AM-5PM (PST). Access by: Mail, in person.

Chowchilla Municipal Court, 141 S 2nd St, Chowchilla, CA 93610. 209-665-4861. Fax: 209-665-3185. 8AM-5PM (PST). Access by: Fax, mail, in person.

Madera Municipal Court, 209 W Yosemite Ave, Madera, CA 93637. 209-675-7734. Fax: 209-675-7618. 8AM-5PM (PST). Access by: Fax, mail, in person.

Borden Municipal Court, 14241 Road 28, Madera, CA 93638. 209-675-7786. Fax: 209-673-0542. 8AM-5PM (PST). Access by: Mail, in person.

Marin County

Real Estate Recording—Marin County Recorder, 3501 Civic Center Dr., Room 234, San Rafael, CA 94903. 415-499-6092. 8AM-4PM Research & Copies; 8AM-3PM Recording (PST).

Felony, Civil Actions Over $25,000, Probate—Marin County Combined Courts, PO Box 4988, San Rafael, CA 94913. Civil: 415-499-6407. Criminal: 415-499-6225. 8:30AM-4PM (PST). Access by: Mail, in person.

Misdemeanor, Civil Actions Under $25,000, Eviction, Small Claims—San Rafael Municipal Court, 3501 Civic Center Dr (PO Box 4988), San Rafael, CA 94913-4988. Civil: 415-499-6217. Criminal: 415-499-6233. 8AM-4PM (PST). Access by: Mail, in person.

Mariposa County

Real Estate Recording—Mariposa County Recorder, 4982 10th Street, Mariposa, CA 95338. 209-966-5719. 8AM-5PM (Recording Hours 8AM-3:30PM) (PST).

Felony, Civil Actions Over $25,000, Probate—Superior Court, 5088 Bullion St (PO Box 28), Mariposa, CA 95338. 209-966-2005. Fax: 209-742-6860. 8AM-5PM (PST). Access by: Phone, mail, in person.

Misdemeanor, Civil Actions Under $25,000, Eviction, Small Claims—Mariposa Municipal Court, 5088 Bullion (PO Box 316), Mariposa, CA 95338. 209-966-2005. Fax: 209-742-6860. 8AM-5PM (PST). Access by: In person only.

Mendocino County

Real Estate Recording—Mendocino County Recorder, 501 Low Gap Rd. Room 1020, Ukiah, CA 95482. 707-463-4376. Fax: 707-463-4257. 8AM-5PM (PST).

Felony, Civil Actions Over $25,000, Probate—Superior Court, State & Perkins Sts (PO Box 996), Ukiah, CA 95482. 707-463-4664. Fax: 707-468-3459. 8AM-5PM M-F 9:15AM-5PM TH (PST). Access by: Mail, in person.

Misdemeanor, Civil Actions Under $25,000, Eviction, Small Claims—Anderson Municipal Court, 14400 Hwy 128 Veteran Bldg, PO Box 336, Boonville, CA 95415. 707-895-3329. 9AM-1PM 2PM-5PM M-F, Closed Monday in Summer (PST). Access by: Mail, in person.

Round Valley Municipal Court, 76270 Grange St (PO Box 25), Covelo, CA 95428. 707-983-6446. Fax: 707-983-6446. 8:30AM-5PM M-Th (PST). Access by: Mail, in person.

Mendocino County Municipal Court, Coastal Division Ten Mile Branch, 700 S Franklin St, Fort Bragg, CA 95437. 707-964-3192. Fax: 707-961-2611. 8AM-4PM; Phone hours 8AM-Noon, 2-4 PM (PST). Access by: Phone, fax, mail, in person.

Long Valley Municipal Court, PO Box 157, Leggett, CA 95585. 707-925-6460. Fax: 707-925-6225. 8AM-5PM M-F (closed every 2nd Monday of month) (PST). Access by: Mail, in person.

Arena Municipal Court, 24000 S Hwy 1 (PO Box 153), Point Arena, CA 95468. 707-882-2116. 9AM-Noon, 1-4PM (PST). Access by: Mail, in person.

Mendocino County Municipal Court, Perkins & State Sts Rm 112 (PO Box 337), Ukiah, CA 95482. 707-463-4486. Fax: 707-463-4655. 8AM-4PM (PST). Access by: Mail, in person.

Willits Branch-Municipal Court, 125 E Commercial St Rm 100, Willits, CA 95490. 707-459-7800. 8AM-4PM (PST). Access by: Mail, in person.

Merced County

Real Estate Recording—Merced County Recorder, 2222 M Street, Merced, CA 95340. 209-385-7627. 8AM-4:30PM (PST).

Felony, Civil Actions Over $25,000, Probate—Superior Court, 2222 "M" St, Merced, CA 95340. 209-385-7531. Fax: 209-725-9223. 8AM-4PM (PST). Access by: Mail, in person.

Misdemeanor, Civil Actions Under $25,000, Eviction, Small Claims—Dos Palos Branch-Municipal Court, 445 I St, Los Balos, CA 93635. 209-826-6500. Fax: 209-826-8108. 8AM-4PM (PST). Access by: Mail, in person.

Los Banos Branch-Municipal Court, 445 "I" St, Los Banos, CA 93635. 209-826-6500. 8AM-4PM (PST). Access by: Mail, in person.

A, B, C & D Divisions-Municipal Court, 670 W 22nd St, Merced, CA 95340. Civil: 209-385-7337. Criminal: 209-385-7335. Fax: 209-725-0323. 8AM-5PM M-F (civil/sc) 12PM-4PM M-F (criminal) (PST). Access by: Mail, in person.

Modoc County

Real Estate Recording—Modoc County Recorder, 204 Court Street, Alturas, CA 96101. 530-233-6205. Fax: 530-233-6666. 8:30AM-Noon, 1-5PM (PST).

Felony, Civil Actions Over $25,000, Probate—Superior Court, 205 S East St, Alturas, CA 96101. 530-233-6515. Fax: 530-233-6500. 8:30AM-Noon, 1-5PM (PST). Access by: Mail, in person.

Felony, Misdemeanor, Civil, Eviction, Small Claims, Probate—Modoc County Trial Courts, 205 S East St, Alturas, CA 96101. 530-233-6516. Fax: 530-233-6500. 8:30AM-Noon, 1-5PM (PST). Access by: Phone, fax, mail, in person.

Mono County

Real Estate Recording—Mono County Recorder, Annex 2, Bryant St., Bridgeport, CA 93517. 619-932-5240. Fax: 760-932-7035. 9AM-5PM (PST).

Felony, Civil Actions Over $25,000, Probate—Superior Court, PO Box 537, Bridgeport, CA 93517. 619-932-5239. 8:30AM-5PM (PST). Access by: Mail, in person.

Misdemeanor, Civil Actions Under $25,000, Eviction, Small Claims—Mammoth Municipal Court, PO Box 1037 Sierra Ctr Old Mammoth Rd, Mammoth Lakes, CA 93546. 619-924-5444. Fax: 619-924-5419. 9AM-5PM (PST). Access by: Mail, in person.

Mono Municipal Court, PO Box 1037, Mammoth Lakes, CA 93546. 619-932-5203. Fax: 619-932-5305. 9AM-5PM (PST). Access by: Mail, in person.

Monterey County

Real Estate Recording—Monterey County Recorder, 240 Church Street, Room 305, Salinas, CA 93902. 408-755-5041. Fax: 408-755-5064. 8AM-4PM (PST).

Felony, Civil Actions Over $25,000, Probate—Superior Court-Monterey Branch, 1200 Aguajito Rd, Monterey, CA 93940. 408-647-7730. 8AM-4PM (PST). Access by: Mail, in person.

Superior Court-Salinas Branch, 240 Church St Rm 318 PO Box 1819, Salinas, CA 93902. 408-755-5030. 8AM-4PM (PST). Access by: Mail, in person.

Misdemeanor, Civil Actions Under $25,000, Eviction, Small Claims—King City Division-Municipal Court, 250 Franciscan Way PO Box 647, King City, CA 93930. Civil: 408-385-8339. Criminal: 408-385-8338. 8AM-5PM (PST). Access by: Mail, in person.

Misdemeanor, Small Claims—Monterey Division-Municipal Court, 1200 Aguajito Rd PO Box 751, Monterey, CA 93940. Civil: 408-647-7730. Criminal: 408-647-7751. Fax: 408-647-7883. 8AM-4PM (PST). Access by: Mail, in person.

Misdemeanor, Civil Actions Under $25,000, Eviction, Small Claims—Salinas Division-Municipal Court, 240 Church St PO Box 1051, Salinas, CA 93902. Civil: 408-755-5332. Criminal: 408-755-5052. Fax: 408-755-5483. 8AM-4PM (PST). Access by: Mail, in person.

Napa County

Real Estate Recording—Napa County Recorder, 900 Coombs Street, Room 116, Napa, CA 94559. 707-253-4246. Fax: 707-253-4390. 8AM-3PM (PST).

Civil Actions Over $25,000, Probate—Superior Court, 825 Brown St Rm 125, Napa, CA 94559. 707-253-4481. Fax: 707-253-4229. 8AM-4:30PM (PST). Access by: Mail, in person.

Felony, Misdemeanor, Civil Actions Under $25,000, Eviction, Small Claims—Superior & Municipal Courts, 825 Brown St (PO Box 880), Napa, CA 94559. Civil: 707-253-4481. Criminal: 707-253-4573. Fax: 707-253-4229. 8AM-5PM (PST). Access by: Mail, in person.

Nevada County

Real Estate Recording—Nevada County Recorder, 950 Maidu Avenue, Nevada City, CA 95959. 530-265-1221. Fax: 530-265-1497. 9AM-4PM (PST).

Felony, Civil Actions Over $25,000, Probate—Superior Court, 201 Church St Suite 9, Nevada City, CA 95959-6126. 530-265-1293. 8AM-5PM (PST). Access by: Mail, in person.

Misdemeanor, Civil Actions Under $25,000, Eviction, Small Claims—Nevada City Division-Municipal Court, 201 Church St #7, PO Box 158, Nevada City, CA 95959. Civil: 530-265-1318. Criminal: 530-265-1311. Fax: 530-265-1779. 8AM-5PM (PST). Access by: Fax, mail, in person.

Misdemeanor, Civil, Eviction, Small Claims—Nevada County Courts, 10075 Levon Ave #301, Truckee, CA 96161. Civil: 530-582-7837. Criminal: 530-582-7836. Fax: 530-582-7875. 8AM-5PM (PST). Access by: In person only.

Orange County

Real Estate Recording—Orange County Clerk-Recorder, 12 Civic Center Plaza, Room 101, Santa Ana, CA 92701. 714-834-2500. Fax: 714-834-2675. 8AM-4:30PM (PST).

Civil Actions Over $25,000—Superior Court-Civil, 700 Civic Center Dr W, Santa Ana, CA 92702. 714-834-2208. 9AM-5PM (PST). Access by: Mail, in person.

Felony—Superior Court-Criminal Operations, 700 Civic Center Dr W (PO Box 22024), Santa Ana, CA 92702. 714-834-2266. 9AM-5PM (PST). Access by: Mail, in person.

Misdemeanor, Civil Actions Under $25,000, Eviction, Small Claims—North Orange County Municipal Court, 1275 N Berkeley Ave, PO Box 5000, Fullerton, CA 92835-0500. Civil: 714-773-4415. Criminal: 714-773-4561. 7:30AM-4:30PM (PST). Access by: Mail, in person.

Civil Actions Under $25,000, Eviction, Small Claims—South Orange County Municipal Court-Civil Division, 23141 Moulton Pkwy 2nd Fl, Laguna Hills, CA 92653-1208. 714-472-6964. 8AM-5PM (PST). Access by: Mail, in person.

Misdemeanor—South Orange County Municipal Court-Criminal Division, 30143 Crown Valley Parkway, Laguna Niguel, CA 92677. 714-249-5113. 8AM-5PM (PST). Access by: Mail, in person.

Misdemeanor, Civil Actions Under $25,000, Eviction, Small Claims—Harbor Municipal Court, 4601 Jamboree Road #104, Newport Beach, CA 92660-2595. Civil: 714-476-4765. 8AM-4:30PM M-W, F; 8:30AM-4:30PM Th; Phone hours 9AM-Noon (PST). Access by: Mail, in person.

Central Orange County Municipal Court, 700 Civic Ctr Dr W (PO Box 1138, 92702), Santa Ana, CA 92701. Civil: 714-834-5589. Criminal: 714-834-3580. Fax: 714-953-9032. 8AM-4PM (PST). Access by: Mail, in person.

West Orange Municipal Court, 8141 13th St, Westminster, CA 92683. Civil: 714-896-7191. Fax: 714-896-7219. 8AM-4:30PM (PST). Access by: Mail, in person.

Probate—Probate Court, 341 The City Dr, PO Box 14171, Orange, CA 92613. 714-935-6061. 9AM-5PM (PST). Access by: Mail, in person.

Placer County

Real Estate Recording—Placer County Recorder, 11960 Heritage Oaks Place, Suite 15, Auburn, CA 95603. 916-889-7983. Fax: 916-887-0737. 8AM-5PM (Recording Hours 9AM-4PM) (PST).

Felony, Civil Actions Over $25,000, Probate—Superior Court, 101 Maple St, Auburn, CA 95603. 916-889-6550. 8AM-3PM (PST). Access by: Mail, in person.

Misdemeanor, Civil Actions Under $25,000, Eviction, Small Claims—Auburn Municipal Court-Dept 1, 11546 "B" Ave, Auburn, CA 95603. 916-889-7407. Fax: 916-889-7409. 8AM-4PM (PST). Access by: Mail, in person.

Colfax Municipal Court-Dept 15, 10 Culver St, PO Box 735, Colfax, CA 95713. 916-346-8721. Fax: 916-346-8721. 8AM-4PM (PST). Access by: Mail, in person.

Foresthill Municipal Court-Dept 4, 24580 Main St (PO Box 267), Foresthill, CA 95631. 916-367-2302. 8:30AM-Noon,1-4PM Mondays only (PST). Access by: Mail, in person.

Lincoln Municipal Court-Dept 17, 453 G St, Lincoln, CA 95648. 916-645-8955. Fax: 916-652-8284. 8AM-Noon, 12:30-4PM M & F only (PST). Access by: Phone, mail, in person.

Loomis Municipal Court-Dept 4, 3877 Shawn Way (PO Box 44), Loomis, CA 95650. 916-652-7212. Fax: 916-652-8284. 8AM-4PM (PST). Access by: Mail, in person.

Roseville Municipal Court-TWH Search, 300 Taylor St, Roseville, CA 95678. 916-784-6401. Fax: 916-784-6484. 8AM-4PM (PST). Access by: Mail, in person.

Tahoe Division, Placer County Municipal Court, PO Box 5669, Tahoe City, CA 96145. 916-581-6337. Fax: 916-581-6344. 8AM-5PM (PST). Access by: Mail, in person.

Plumas County

Real Estate Recording—Plumas County Recorder, 520 Main Street, Quincy, CA 95971. 530-283-6218. Fax: 530-283-6415. 8AM-5PM (PST).

Felony, Civil Actions Over $25,000, Probate—Superior Court, 520 W Main St (PO Box 10207), Quincy, CA 95971. 530-283-6305. Fax: 530-283-6415. 8AM-5PM (PST). Access by: Phone, fax, mail, in person.

Misdemeanor, Civil Actions Under $25,000, Eviction, Small Claims—Municipal Court, 1st & Willow Way (PO Box 722), Chester, CA 96020. 530-258-2646. 9AM-1PM M-TH (PST). Access by: Mail, in person.

Small Claims—Municipal Court, 115 Hwy 89 (PO Box 706), Greenville, CA 95947. 530-284-7213. 9AM-3PM M,T,Th (PST). Access by: Mail, in person.

Misdemeanor, Civil Actions Under $25,000, Eviction, Small Claims—Municipal Court, 161 Nevada St (PO Box 1054), Portola, CA 96122. 530-832-4286. 9AM-3PM M & W (PST). Access by: Phone, mail, in person.

Municipal Court, PO Box 10628, Quincy, CA 95971. 530-283-6232. Fax: 530-283-6293. 8AM-5PM (PST). Access by: Mail, in person.

Riverside County

Real Estate Recording—Riverside County Recorder, 4080 Lemon Street, Room 102, Riverside, CA 92501. 909-275-1990. Fax: 909-275-1954. 8AM-4:30PM (Recording Hours 8AM-2PM) (PST).

Civil Actions Over $25,000, Probate—Superior Court-Civil Division, 4050 Main St, Riverside, CA 92501. 909-275-1431. Fax: 909-275-1751. 8AM-5PM (PST). Access by: Mail, in person.

Felony—Superior Court-Criminal Division, 4100 Main St, Riverside, CA 92501. 909-275-1433. 8AM-5PM (PST). Access by: Mail, in person.

Misdemeanor, Civil Actions Under $25,000, Eviction, Small Claims—Banning Department-Municipal Court, 155 E Hayes St, Banning, CA 92220. Civil: 909-922-7155. Criminal: 909-922-7145. Fax: 909-922-7160. 8AM-4PM (PST). Access by: Mail, in person.

Desert Division-Blythe Consolidated Courts, 260 N Spring St, Blythe, CA 92225. 619-921-7828. Fax: 619-921-7941. 7:30AM-5PM (PST). Access by: Phone, mail, remote online, in person.

Consolidated Courts-Corona Branch, 505 S Buena Vista Rm 201, Corona, CA 91720. Civil: 909-272-5620. Criminal: 909-272-5630. Fax: 909-272-5651. 8AM-5PM (PST). Access by: Fax, mail, in person.

Hemet Department-Municipal Court, 880 N State St, Hemet, CA 92543. 909-766-2321. Criminal: 909-766-2310. Fax: 909-766-2317. 7:30AM-4:30PM; Criminal, Civil/SC 8AM-Noon; (PST). Access by: Mail, in person.

Desert Division-Indio Consolidated Courts, 46200 Oasis St, Indio, CA 92201. Civil: 619-863-8208. Criminal: 619-863-8206. Fax: 619-863-8707. 7:30AM-5PM (PST). Access by: Phone, fax, mail, in person.

Civil Actions Under $25,000, Eviction, Small Claims—Three Lakes District-Lake Elsinore Branch-Municipal Court, 117 S Langstaff, Lake Elsinore, CA 92530. 909-245-3370. Fax: 909-245-3366. 7:30AM-Noon,1-4PM (PST). Access by: In person only.

Misdemeanor, Civil Actions Under $25,000, Eviction, Small Claims—Consolidated Courts-Moreno Valley Branch, 13800 Heacock Ave Ste D201, Moreno Valley, CA 92553-3338. 909-697-4504. Civil: 909-341-8876 (traff.) Fax: 909-697-4526. 7:30AM-5PM (PST). Access by: Phone, fax, mail, remote online, in person.

Misdemeanor—Desert Division-Palm Springs Consolidated Courts, 3255 Tahkuits Canyon Way, Palm Springs, CA 92262. 619-778-2315. Fax: 619-863-8114. 8AM-5PM (PST). Access by: Fax, mail, in person.

Misdemeanor, Civil Actions Under $25,000, Eviction, Small Claims—Three Lakes District-Perris Department-Municipal Court, 277 N "D" St., Perris, CA 92370. Civil: 909-940-6820. Criminal: 909-940-6840. Fax: 909-940-6810. 7:30AM-Noon,1-4PM (PST). Access by: Mail, in person.

Civil Actions Under $25,000, Eviction, Small Claims—Three Lakes District-Temecula Branch-Municipal Court, 41002 County Center Dr, Temecula, CA 92390. 909-694-5160. 7:30AM-Noon,1-4PM (PST). Access by: In person only.

Sacramento County

Real Estate Recording—Sacramento County Clerk and Recorder, 600 8th Street, Sacramento, CA 95814. 916-440-6334. 8AM-5PM (PST).

Felony, Misdemeanor, Civil, Evicitons, Small Claims, Probate—Sacramento Superior Court, 720 9th St Rm 611, Sacramento, CA 95814. 916-440-5522. Criminal: 916-440-8436/5744. Probate: 916-440-5621. Fax: 916-440-5620. 8:30AM-4:30PM (PST). Access by: Phone, mail, in person.

Misdemeanor, Civil Actions Under $25,000, Eviction, Small Claims—South Sacramento Municipal Court-Elk Grove Branch, 8978 Elk Grove Blvd, Elk Grove, CA 95624. 916-685-9825. Fax: 916-685-4689. 8:30AM-4:30PM (PST). Access by: Mail, in person.

South Sacramento Municipal Court-Galt Division, 380 Civic Dr, Galt, CA 95632. 209-745-1577. Fax: 209-745-6176. 8:30AM-4:30PM (PST). Access by: Mail, in person.

Sacramento Municipal Court, 720 9th St, Sacramento, CA 95814. 916-440-5476. 8:30AM-4:30PM (PST). Access by: Phone, mail, in person.

South Sacramento Municipal Court-Walnut Grove Branch, 14177 Market St, PO Box 371, Walnut Grove, CA 95690. 916-776-1416. Fax: 916-776-1624. 8:30AM-4:30PM (PST). Access by: Mail, in person.

San Benito County

Real Estate Recording—San Benito County Recorder, 440 Fifth Street, Room 206, Hollister, CA 95023. 408-636-

4046. Fax: 408-636-2939. 9:30AM-4PM Recording hours; 8AM-5PM Office hours (PST).

Felony, Civil Actions Over $25,000, Probate—Superior Court, Courthouse, 440 5th St Rm 206, Hollister, CA 95023. 408-637-3786. 8AM-5PM (PST). Access by: Mail, in person.

Misdemeanor, Civil Actions Under $25,000, Eviction, Small Claims—Municipal Court, 440 5th St Rm 105, Hollister, CA 95023. 408-637-3741. Fax: 408-636-2939. 8AM-4PM (PST). Access by: Mail, in person.

San Bernardino County

Real Estate Recording—San Bernardino County Recorder, 222 W. Hospitality Ln., 1st Floor, San Bernardino, CA 92415. 909-387-8306. Fax: 909-386-8940. 8AM-5PM (PST).

Felony, Misdemeanor, Civil, Eviction, Small Claims—North Desert-Superior/Municipal Court, 235 E Mountain View, Barstow, CA 92311. Civil: 760-256-4755. Criminal: 760-256-4785. 8AM-4PM (PST). Access by: Mail, in person.

Eastern Desert-Superior/Municipal Court, 6527 White Feather Rd PO Box 6602, Joshua Tree, CA 92252. 619-366-4107. Fax: 619-366-4156. 8AM-4PM (PST). Access by: Mail, in person.

Felony, Misdemeanor, Civil, Eviction, Small Claims, Probate—West District-Superior/Municipal Court, 8303 Haven Ave, Rancho Cucamonga, CA 91730. Civil: 909-885-5532. Criminal: 909-885-2584. Fax: 909-945-4154. 8AM-4PM (PST). Access by: Phone, fax, mail, in person.

Central District-Superior/Municipal Court, 351 N Arrowhead, San Bernardino, CA 92415. Civil: 909-387-3922. Criminal: 909-384-1888. Fax: 909-387-4428. 8AM-4PM (PST). Access by: Mail, in person.

Felony, Misdemeanor, Civil, Eviction, Small Claims—Desert District-Superior/Municipal Court, 14455 Civic Dr, Victorville, CA 92392. Civil: 619-243-8672. Criminal: 760-243-8631. Fax: 760-243-8790. 8AM-4PM (PST). Access by: Mail, in person. Only court allowed to search computer index.

Misdemeanor, Civil Actions Under $25,000, Eviction, Small Claims—Big Bear Municipal Court, PO Box 2806, Big Bear Lake, CA 92315. Fax: 909-866-0150. 8AM-4PM (PST). Access by: Mail, in person.

Chino Division-Municipal Court, 13260 Central Ave, Chino, CA 91710. 909-465-5266. Civil: 909-465-5266. Criminal: 909-465-5260. Fax: 909-465-5306. 8AM-4PM (PST). Access by: Mail, in person.

Valley Division-Municipal Court, 17780 Arrow Blvd, Fontana, CA 92335. Civil: 909-884-5766. Criminal: 909-884-2794. 8AM-4PM (PST). Access by: Mail, in person.

Needles-Calzona Municipal Court, 1111 Bailey Ave, Needles, CA 92363. 760-326-9248. 8AM-4PM (PST). Access by: Mail, in person.

East Division-Municipal Court, 216 Brookside Ave, Redlands, CA 92374. 909-798-8541. Civil: 909-798-8541. Criminal: 909-798-8542. Fax: 909-798-8588. 8AM-4PM (PST). Access by: Mail, in person.

Central Division-Municipal Court, 351 N Arrowhead, San Bernardino, CA 92415. 909-885-0139. Civil: 909-387-3922. Criminal: 909-384-1888. Fax: 909-387-4428. 8AM-4PM (PST). Access by: Mail, in person.

San Bernadino County Municipal Court-Mountains Div.-Twin Peaks Br, 26010 State Hwy 189, PO Box 394, Twin Peaks, CA 92391. 909-336-0620. Fax: 909-337-2101. 8AM-4PM (PST). Access by: Mail, in person.

San Diego County

Real Estate Recording—San Diego Recorder/County Clerk, 1600 Pacific Highway, Room 260, San Diego, CA 92101. 619-237-0502. Fax: 619-551-4155. 8AM-5PM (PST).

Felony, Civil Actions Over $25,000, Probate—Superior Court, PO Box 2724, San Diego, CA 92112-4104. 619-531-3151. 9AM-4:30PM (PST). Access by: Mail, in person.

Superior Court, Hall of Justice, PO Box 128, San Diego, CA 92112-4104. Civil: 619-531-3151. Criminal: 619-685-6220. 9AM-4:30PM (PST). Access by: Mail, in person.

South Bay Branch-Superior Court, 500-C 3rd Ave, Chula Vista, CA 91910. Civil: 619-691-4780. Criminal: 619-691-4738. Fax: 619-691-4969. 8AM-4:30PM M-F (civil) 7:30AM-4PM M-F (criminal) (PST). Access by: Phone, fax, mail, in person.

El Cajon Branch-Superior Court, 250 E Main St, El Cajon, CA 92020. 619-441-4622. 8AM-4:30PM (PST). Access by: Mail, in person.

North County Branch-Superior Court, 325 S Melrose Dr, Suite 100, Vista, CA 92083-6627. 760-940-4442. 9AM-4:30PM (PST). Access by: Mail, in person.

Misdemeanor, Civil Actions Under $25,000, Eviction, Small Claims—South Bay Municipal Court, 500C 3rd Ave, Chula Vista, CA 91910. Civil: 619-691-4639. Criminal: 619-691-4728. Fax: 619-691-4438. 8AM-4:30PM (PST). Access by: Mail, in person. In person search requires picture ID.

El Cajon Municipal Court, 250 E Main St, El Cajon, CA 92020. Civil: 619-441-4461. Criminal: 619-441-4342. Fax: 619-441-4725. 8AM-4PM M-F 8AM-6PM W (PST). Access by: Mail, in person.

Escondido Branch-Municipal Court, 600 E Valley Pky, Escondido, CA 92025. Civil: 760-740-4021. 8AM-4:30PM (PST). Access by: Mail, in person.

Ramona Branch-Municipal Court, 1428 Montecito Rd, Ramona, CA 92065. 619-441-4244. 8AM-4PM M,F; 8:30AM-12:30PM, 1:30-4PM (PST). Access by: Mail, in person.

San Diego Municipal Court, 1409 4th Ave (Civil), 220 W Broadway Rm 2005 (Criminal), San Diego, CA 92101. Civil: 619-687-2180. Criminal: 619-531-3040. 8:30AM-4:30PM (PST). Access by: Mail, in person.

San Marcos-Municipal Court, 338 Via Vera Cruz, San Marcos, CA 92069-2693. 760-940-2888. Fax: 760-940-2802. 8AM-4PM (PST). Access by: Mail, in person.

North County Municipal Court, 325 S Melrose Dr Ste 120, Vista, CA 92083. 619-940-4644. Fax: 619-940-4976. 8AM-3PM M & F, 8AM-4PM T-TH (PST). Access by: Mail, in person.

Misdemeanor—San Marcos/Criminal-North County Municipal Court, 325 S Melrose Dr #120, Vista, CA 92083. 760-940-2888. 8AM-3PM M & F 8AM-4PM T-TH (PST). Access by: In person only.

San Francisco County

Real Estate Recording—San Francisco County Clerk-Recorder, Room 100, 875 Stevenson, San Francisco, CA 94103. 415-554-4176. Fax: 415-554-4179. 8AM-4PM (PST).

Civil Actions Over $25,000, Probate—Superior Court-Civil Division, 633 Folsom St #210, San Francisco, CA 94107/94103. 415-554-4161. 8AM-4PM (PST). Access by: Mail, in person.

Felony—Superior Court-Criminal Division, 850 Bryant St #306, San Francisco, CA 94107/94103. 415-553-1159. Fax: 415-553-1661. 8AM-4PM (PST). Access by: Phone, fax, mail, in person.

Civil Actions Under $25,000, Eviction, Small Claims—Municipal Court-Civil Division, 633 Folsom St, San Francisco, CA 94103. 415-554-4686. 8AM-4:30PM (PST). Access by: Mail, in person.

Misdemeanor—Municipal Court-Criminal Division, 850 Bryant St Rm 201, San Francisco, CA 94103. 415-553-1665. Criminal: 415-553-9395. 8AM-4:30PM (PST). Access by: Mail, in person.

Civil Actions Under $25,000, Eviction, Small Claims—Municipal Court-Civil Division, 633 Folsom St Rm 205, San Francisco, CA 94107. 415-554-4532. 8AM-4:30PM (PST). Access by: Mail, in person.

San Joaquin County

Real Estate Recording—San Joaquin County Recorder-County Clerk, 24 South Hunter Street, Room 304, Stockton, CA 95202. 209-468-3939. Fax: 209-468-8040. 8AM-5PM (PST).

Felony, Civil Actions Over $25,000, Probate—Superior Court, 222 E Weber St Rm 303, Stockton, CA 95202. 209-468-2355. 8:15AM-4:30PM (PST). Access by: Mail, in person.

Misdemeanor, Civil Actions Under $25,000, Eviction, Small Claims—Lodi Municipal Court, 315 W Elm St (Civil), 230 W Elm St (Criminal), Lodi, CA 95240. 209-333-6753. Civil: 209-333-6755. Criminal: 209-333-6750. Fax: 209-368-3157. 8AM-4PM (PST). Access by: Mail, in person.

Manteca-Ripon-Escalon-Tracy (Eastern Dept) Municipal Court, 315 E Center St, Manteca, CA 95336. 209-239-9188. Civil: 209-239-9188. Criminal: 209-239-1316. 8AM-4PM (PST). Access by: Phone, mail, in person. Special request form required to view files.

Stockton Municipal Court, 222 E Weber Ave, Stockton, CA 95202. 209-468-2949. Civil: 209-468-2933. Criminal: 209-468-2935. Fax: 209-468-8575. 8AM-4PM M-F (office) 8AM-3PM M-F (phones) (PST). Access by: Mail, in person.

Tracy (Western Dept) Municipal Court, 475 E 10th St, Tracy, CA 95376. Civil: 209-831-5902. Criminal: 209-831-5900. Fax: 209-831-5919. 8AM-4PM (PST). Access by: Phone, mail, in person.

San Luis Obispo County

Real Estate Recording—San Luis Obispo County Recorder, 1144 Monterey St., Suite C, San Luis Obispo, CA 93408. 805-781-5080. 8AM-5PM (PST).

Felony, Civil Actions Over $25,000, Probate—Superior Court, Government Center Rm 385, San Luis Obispo, CA 93408. 805-781-5241. 8AM-5PM (PST). Access by: Phone, mail, in person.

Misdemeanor, Civil Actions Under $25,000, Eviction, Small Claims—Grover Beach Branch-Municipal Court, 214 S 16th St, Grover Beach, CA 93433-2299. Civil: 805-473-7077. Criminal: 805-473-7072. 9AM-4PM (PST). Access by: Mail, in person.

Paso Robles Branch-Municipal Court, 549 10th St, Paso Robles, CA 93446-2593. Civil: 805-237-3079. Criminal: 805-237-3080. 9AM-4PM (PST). Access by: Phone, mail, in person.

Municipal Court, 1050 Monterey St Rm 220, County Government Center, San Luis Obispo, CA 93408-2510. Civil: 805-781-5678. Criminal: 805-781-5670. 9AM-4PM (PST). Access by: Phone, mail, in person.

San Mateo County

Real Estate Recording—San Mateo County Recorder, 6th Floor, 401 Marshall St., Redwood City, CA 94063. 650-363-4713. Fax: 650-363-4843. 8AM-5PM (PST).

Felony, Civil Actions Over $25,000, Probate—San Mateo County Superior & Municipal Courts, 401 Marshall St, Redwood City, CA 94063. 650-363-4711. Fax: 650-363-4914. 8:30AM-4PM (PST). Access by: Mail, in person.

Misdemeanor, Small Claims—Southern Branch-Municipal Court, 750 Middlefield Rd, Redwood City, CA 94063. 650-363-4302. 8AM-4PM (PST). Access by: Mail, in person.

Civil Actions Under $25,000, Eviction, Small Claims—Central Branch-Municipal Court, 800 N Humboldt St, San Mateo, CA 94401. 650-573-2611. Fax: 650-342-5438. 8AM-4PM (PST). Access by: Mail, in person.

Misdemeanor, Small Claims—Northern Branch-Municipal Court, 1050 Mission Rd, South San Francisco, CA 94080. 650-877-5773. 8AM-4PM (PST). Access by: Mail, in person.

Santa Barbara County

Real Estate Recording—Santa Barbara County Recorder, 1100 Anacapa Street, Santa Barbara, CA 93101. 805-568-2250. Fax: 805-568-2266. 8AM-4:30PM (PST).

Felony, Civil Actions Over $25,000, Probate—Superior Court, Box 21107, Santa Barbara, CA 93121. 805-568-2237. Fax: 805-568-2219. 8AM-4:45PM (PST). Access by: Phone, mail, in person.

Misdemeanor, Civil Actions Under $25,000, Eviction, Small Claims—North Santa Barbara Municipal Court-Lompoc Division, 115 Civic Center Plz, Lompoc, CA 93436. 805-737-7790. Civil: 805-737-7793. Criminal: 805-737-7791. Fax: 805-737-7786. 8:30AM-4:55PM (PST). Access by: Mail, in person.

Santa Barbara Municipal Court, 118 E Figueroa St, Santa Barbara, CA 93101. Civil: 805-568-2740. Criminal: 805-568-2765. 7:45AM-4PM (PST). Access by: Mail, in person.

North Santa Barbara Municipal Court-Santa Maria Division, 312-M East Cook St, Santa Maria, CA 93454. Civil: 805-346-7566. Criminal: 805-346-7566. Fax: 805-346-7591. 7:30AM-4:30PM (PST). Access by: In person only.

North Santa Barbara County Municipal Court-Solvang Division, 1745 Mission Dr (PO Box 228), Solvang, CA 93464. 805-686-5040. Fax: 805-686-5079. 8AM-4PM (PST). Access by: Phone, mail, in person.

Santa Clara County

Real Estate Recording—Santa Clara County Recorder, County Government Center, East Wing, 70 West Hedding St., San Jose, CA 95110. 408-299-2481. Fax: 408-280-1768. 8AM-4:30PM (PST).

Felony, Civil Actions Over $25,000, Probate—Superior Court, 190 W Hedding St, San Jose, CA 95110. 408-299-2974. 9AM-4PM (PST). Access by: Mail, in person.

Civil Actions Under $25,000, Eviction, Small Claims—Santa Clara Facility-Municipal Court, 1095 Homestead Rd, Santa Clara, CA 95050. 408-249-2690. 8:30AM-4PM (PST). Access by: Mail, in person.

Misdemeanor—Palo Alto Facility-Municipal Court-Criminal Division, 270 Grant Ave, Palo Alto, CA 94306. 415-324-0373. 8:30AM-4PM (PST). Access by: Mail, in person.

San Jose Facility-Municipal Court, 200 W Hedding St, San Jose, CA 95110. 408-299-2281. 8:30AM-4PM (PST). Access by: Mail, in person.

Small Claims—Los Gatos Facility-Municipal Court, 14205 Capri Dr, Los Gatos, CA 95032. 408-866-8331. 8:30AM-4PM (PST). Access by:

Misdemeanor, Civil Actions Under $25,000, Eviction, Small Claims—South County Facility-Municipal Court, 12425 Monterey Hwy, San Martin, CA 95046-9590. Civil: 408-686-3522. Criminal: 408-686-3511. 8:30AM-4PM (PST). Access by: Mail, in person.

Misdemeanor, Eviction, Small Claims—Sunnyvale Facility-Municipal Court, 605 W El Camino Real, Sunnyvale, CA 94087. 408-739-1502. Criminal: 408-739-1503. 8:30AM-4PM (PST). Access by: Mail, in person.

Santa Cruz County

Real Estate Recording—Santa Cruz County Recorder, 701 Ocean Street, Room 230, Santa Cruz, CA 95060. 408-454-2800. Fax: 408-454-2445. 8AM-4PM (PST).

Felony, Misdemeanor, Civil, Probate—Superior & Municipal Courts, 701 Ocean St Rm 110, Santa Cruz, CA 95060. 408-454-2155. 8AM-4PM (PST). Access by: In person only.

Misdemeanor, Civil Actions Under $25,000, Eviction, Small Claims—Municipal Court-Dept A, 1430 Freedom Blvd, Watsonville, CA 95076. Civil: 408-763-8060. Criminal: 408-763-8060. 8AM-4PM (PST). Access by: Mail, in person.

Shasta County

Real Estate Recording—Shasta County Recorder, Courthouse, Room 102, Redding, CA 96001. 530-225-5671. Fax: 530-225-5673. 8AM-5PM (PST).

Felony, Civil Actions Over $25,000, Probate—Shasta County Superior Court, 1500 Court St, Redding, CA 96001. 530-225-5631. Fax: 530-225-5564. 8:30AM-Noon,1-4PM (PST). Access by: Mail, in person.

Misdemeanor, Civil Actions Under $25,000, Eviction, Small Claims—Anderson Branch-Municipal Court, 1925 W Howard St, Anderson, CA 96007. 530-365-2563. Fax: 530-225-5372. 8:30AM-Noon, 1-4PM (PST). Access by: Mail, in person.

Misdemeanor, Eviction, Small Claims—Burney Branch-Municipal Court, 20509 Shasta St, Burney, CA 96013. 530-335-3571. Fax: 530-225-5684. 8:30AM-Noon, 1-4PM (PST). Access by: Mail, in person.

Misdemeanor, Civil Actions Under $25,000, Eviction, Small Claims—Redding Branch-Municipal Court, 1500 Court St, Redding, CA 96001. Civil: 530-225-5703. Criminal: 530-225-5136. 8:30AM-Noon, 1-4PM (PST). Access by: Mail, in person.

Sierra County

Real Estate Recording—Sierra County Recorder, 100 Courthouse Square, Downieville, CA 95936. 530-289-3295. Fax: 530-289-3300. 9-Noon,1-4PM (PST).

Felony, Civil Actions Over $25,000, Probate—Superior Court, PO Box 95 Courthouse Square, Downieville, CA 95936. 530-289-3698. Fax: 530-289-3318. 8AM-Noon, 1-5PM (PST). Access by: Phone, fax, mail, in person.

Misdemeanor, Civil Actions Under $25,000, Eviction, Small Claims—Downieville Municipal Court, PO Box 401 Courthouse Square, Downieville, CA 95936. 530-289-3215. Fax: 530-289-0205. 8AM-5PM (PST). Access by: Fax, mail, in person.

Siskiyou County

Real Estate Recording—Siskiyou County Recorder, 311 Fourth Street, Yreka, CA 96097. 530-842-8065. Fax: 530-842-8077. 8AM-4PM (PST).

Felony, Civil Actions Over $25,000, Probate—Superior Court, 311 4th St PO Box 1026, Yreka, CA 96097. 530-842-8084. 8AM-5PM (PST). Access by: Phone, mail, in person.

Misdemeanor, Civil Actions Under $25,000, Eviction, Small Claims—Municipal Court-Dorris/Tulelake Branch, PO Box 828, Dorris, CA 96023. 530-397-3161. 8AM-5PM (PST). Access by: Phone, mail, in person.

Southeastern Municipal Court, PO Box 530, Weed, CA 96094. 916-938-2718. Civil: 916-938-3897. Criminal: 530-938-2483. 8AM-5PM (PST). Access by: Mail, in person.

Western Branch Municipal Court, 311 4th St Rm 5 PO Box 1034, Yreka, CA 96097. Civil: 530-842-8180. Criminal: 530-842-8182. Fax: 530-842-8178. 8AM-4PM (PST). Access by: Fax, in person.

Solano County

Real Estate Recording—Solano County Assessor/Recorder, 580 Texas Street, Old Courthouse, Fairfield, CA 94533. 707-421-6290. 8AM-4PM; 8AM-3:30PM Recording hours; Copies 8AM-3PM (PST).

Civil, Eviction, Probate—Solano County Courts-Civil, 600 Union Ave, Fairfield, CA 94533. 707-421-6479. Fax: 707-421-7817. 8AM-4PM (PST). Access by: Mail, in person.

Felony, Misdemeanor—Solano County Courts-Criminal, 530 Union Ave #200, Fairfield, CA 94533. 707-421-7440. Fax: 707-421-7439. 8:15AM-4PM (PST). Access by: Mail, in person.

Misdemeanor, Civil Actions Under $25,000, Eviction, Small Claims—Vallejo-Benicia Branch, 321 Tuolumne St, Vallejo, CA 94590. Civil: 707-553-5346. Criminal: 707-553-5341. Fax: 707-553-5661. 8AM-4PM (PST). Access by: Mail, in person.

Sonoma County

Real Estate Recording—Sonoma County Recorder, 585 Fiscal Drive, Room 103F, Santa Rosa, CA 95403. 707-527-2651. Fax: 707-527-3905. 8AM-4:30PM (PST).

Felony, Civil Actions Over $25,000, Probate—Superior Court, PO Box 11187, Santa Rosa, CA 95406. 707-527-1100. 8AM-4PM (PST). Access by: Phone, mail, in person. Misdemeanor records destroyed after 10 years.

Civil Actions Under $25,000, Eviction, Small Claims—Santa Rosa Municipal Court-Civil Division, 600 Administration Dr, Rm 100J, Santa Rosa, CA 95403. 707-527-1100. 8AM-4PM (PST). Access by: Mail, in person.

Misdemeanor—Santa Rosa Municipal Court-Criminal Division, 600 Administration Dr, Rm 102J, Santa Rosa, CA 95403. 707-527-1100. 8AM-4PM (PST). Access by: Mail, in person.

Stanislaus County

Real Estate Recording—Stanislaus County Recorder, 1021 "I" St., Modesto, CA 95354. 209-525-5260. Fax: 209-525-5207. 8AM-Noon,1-4PM (PST).

Felony, Civil Actions Over $25,000, Probate—Superior Court, 800 11th St Rm 222 PO Box 1098, Modesto, CA 95353. 209-525-6416. 8AM-Noon, 1-3PM (PST). Access by: Mail, in person.

Misdemeanor, Civil Actions Under $25,000, Eviction, Small Claims—Modesto Division-Municipal Court, 1100 "I" St PO Box 828, Modesto, CA 95353. 209-558-6000. 8AM-Noon, 1PM-3PM (PST). Access by: Mail, in person.

Turlock Division-Municipal Court, 300 Starr Ave, Turlock, CA 95380. 209-632-3942. Fax: 209-669-8009. 8AM-3PM M-TH (PST). Access by: Phone, fax, mail, in person.

Sutter County

Real Estate Recording—Sutter County Recorder, 433 Second Street, Yuba City, CA 95991. 530-822-7134. Fax: 530-822-7214. 8AM-5PM (PST).

Civil, Eviction, Small Claims, Probate—Consolidated Superior & Municipal Court-Civil Division, 463 2nd St, Yuba City, CA 95991. 530-822-7175. 8AM-5PM (PST). Access by: Fax, mail, in person.

Felony, Misdemeanor—Consolidated Superior & Municipal Court-Criminal Division, 446 2nd St, Yuba City, CA 95991. 530-822-7360. Fax: 530-822-7159. 8AM-5PM (PST). Access by: Fax, mail, in person.

Tehama County

Real Estate Recording—Tehama County Recorder, 633 Washington Street, Red Bluff, CA 96080. 530-527-3350. Fax: 530-529-0980. 8AM-3PM (PST).

Felony, Civil Actions Over $25,000, Probate—Superior Court, PO Box 310, Red Bluff, CA 96080. 530-527-6441. 9AM-4PM (PST). Access by: In person only.

Misdemeanor, Civil Actions Under $25,000, Eviction, Small Claims—Corning (Southern) Municipal Court, 720 Hoag St, Corning, CA 96021. 530-824-4601. Fax: 530-824-6457. 8AM-4PM (PST). Access by: Mail, in person.

Red Bluff (Northern) Municipal Court, 445 Pine St PO Box 1170, Red Bluff, CA 96080. 530-527-3563. Civil: 530-527-7364. Criminal: 530-527-7314. Fax: 530-527-4974. 8AM-4PM (PST). Access by: Mail, in person.

Trinity County

Real Estate Recording—Trinity County Recorder, 101 Court Street, Courthouse, Weaverville, CA 96093. 530-623-1215. Fax: 530-623-3762. 10AM-Noon, 1-4PM (PST).

Felony, Misdemeanor, Civil, Eviction, Small Claims, Probate—Consolidated Superior & Municipal Court, 101 Court St PO Box 1258, Weaverville, CA 96093. 530-623-1208. Fax: 530-623-3762. 9AM-4PM (PST). Access by: Mail, in person.

Tulare County

Real Estate Recording—Tulare County Recorder, County Civic Center, Room 203, Visalia, CA 93291. 209-733-6377. 8AM-5PM; (Recording hours 8AM-3PM) (PST).

Felony, Civil Actions Over $25,000, Probate—Superior Court, Courthouse Rm 201, Visalia, CA 93291. 209-733-6374. 8AM-5PM (PST). Access by: Mail, in person.

Misdemeanor, Civil Actions Under $25,000, Eviction, Small Claims—Dinuba Municipal Court, 920 S College,

Dinuba, CA 93618. 209-591-5815. 8AM-4PM (PST). Access by: Mail, in person.

Central Division (Exeter-Farmersville Branch) Municipal Court, 125 S "B" St, Exeter, CA 93221. 209-592-2177. Fax: 209-592-3374. 8AM-4PM (PST). Access by: Phone, mail, in person.

Porterville Municipal Court, 87 E Morton Ave, Porterville, CA 93257. 209-782-4710. Fax: 209-782-4805. 8AM-4PM (PST). Access by: Mail, in person.

Tulare/Pixley Division-Municipal Court, 425 E Kern St PO Box 1136, Tulare, CA 93275. 209-685-2556. Fax: 209-685-2663. 8AM-4PM (PST). Access by: Mail, in person.

Visalia Municipal Court, County Civic Center Rm 124, Visalia, CA 93291. Civil: 209-733-6198. Criminal: 209-733-6830. 8AM-4PM (PST). Access by: Mail, in person.

Tuolumne County

Real Estate Recording—Tuolumne County Recorder, 2 South Green Street, County Administration Center, Sonora, CA 95370. 209-533-5531. Fax: 209-533-5613. 8AM-4PM M-Th; 8AM-5PM F (PST).

Felony, Civil Actions Over $25,000, Probate—Superior Court, 2 S Green St, Sonora, CA 95370. 209-533-5555. Criminal: 209-533-5563. Fax: 209-533-5618. 8AM-4PM (PST). Access by: Mail, in person.

Misdemeanor, Civil Actions Under $25,000, Eviction, Small Claims—Tuolumne County Municipal Court, 60 N Washington St, Sonora, CA 95370. 209-533-5671. 8AM-3PM (PST). Access by: Mail, in person. Records destroyed after 10 years.

Ventura County

Real Estate Recording—Ventura County Recorder, 800 South Victoria Avenue, Ventura, CA 93009. 805-654-2292. Fax: 805-654-2392. 8AM-4PM (PST).

Felony, Misdemeanor, Civil, Eviction, Small Claims, Probate—East County Superior & Municipal Court, 3855 Blgd F, Alamo St, Ventura, CA 93006. 805-582-8080. 8AM-5PM (PST). Access by: Mail, in person.

Ventura County Superior & Municipal Courts, 800 S Victoria Ave PO Box 6489, Ventura, CA 93006. 805-662-6620. Fax: 805-650-4032. 8AM-5PM (PST). Access by: Mail, remote online, in person.

Yolo County

Real Estate Recording—Yolo County Recorder, 625 Court Street, Room 105, Woodland, CA 95695. 530-666-8130. Fax: 530-666-8109. 8AM-4PM (PST).

Felony, Misdemeanor, Civil, Eviction, Small Claims, Probate—Combined Superior & Municipal Court, 725 Court St, Woodland, CA 95695. Civil: 530-666-8170. Criminal: 530-666-8050. 8AM-Noon, 1-3PM (PST). Access by: Mail, in person.

Yuba County

Real Estate Recording—Yuba County Recorder, 935 14th Street, Marysville, CA 95901. 530-741-6547. Fax: 530-741-6285. 10AM-3PM (PST).

Felony, Civil Actions Over $25,000, Probate—Yuba County Superior Court, 215 5th St, Marysville, CA 95901. 530-741-6258. Fax: 530-634-7681. 8:30AM-4:30PM (PST). Access by: Mail, in person.

Misdemeanor, Civil Actions Under $25,000, Eviction, Small Claims—Marysville Municipal Court, 215 5th St, Marysville, CA 95901. 530-741-6351. 8:30AM-5PM (PST). Access by: Mail, in person.

Federal Courts

US District Court

Central District of California

Los Angeles (Western) Division, US District Court US Courthouse, 312 N Spring St, Room G-8, Los Angeles, CA 90012. 213-894-5261. Counties: Los Angeles, San Luis Obispo, Santa Barbara, Ventura

Riverside (Eastern) Division, US District Court US Courthouse, PO Box 13000, Riverside, CA 92502-3000. 909-276-6170. Counties: Riverside, San Bernardino

Santa Ana (Southern) Division, US District Court 751 W Santa Ana Blvd, Room 101, Santa Ana, CA 92701-4599. 714-836-2468. Counties: Orange

Eastern District of California

Fresno Division, US District Court US Courthouse, Room 5000, 1130 "O" St, Fresno, CA 93721-2201. 209-498-7483. Counties: Fresno, Inyo, Kern, Kings, Madera, Mariposa, Merced, Stanislaus, Tulare, Tuolumne

Sacramento Division, US District Court 2546 United States Courthouse, 650 Capitol Mall, Sacramento, CA 95814-4797. 916-498-5415. Counties: Alpine, Amador, Butte, Calaveras, Colusa, El Dorado, Glenn, Lassen, Modoc, Mono, Nevada, Placer, Plumas, Sacramento, San Joaquin, Shasta, Sierra, Siskiyou, Solano, Sutter, Tehama, Trinity, Yolo, Yuba

Northern District of California

San Jose Division, US District Court Room 2112, 280 S 1st St, San Jose, CA 95113. 408-535-5364. Counties: Alameda, Contra Costa, Del Norte, Humboldt, Lake, Marin, Mendocino, Monterey, Napa, San Benito, San Francisco, San Mateo, Santa Clara, Santa Cruz, Sonoma

Southern District of California

San Diego Division, US District Court Room 4290, 880 Front St, San Diego, CA 92101-8900. 619-557-5600. Counties: San Diego. Some cases from Yuma, AZ

US Bankruptcy Court

Central District of California

Los Angeles Division, US Bankruptcy Court, 300 N Los Angeles St, Los Angeles, CA 90012. 213-894-3118. Voice Case Information System: 213-894-4111. Counties: Los Angeles. Certain Los Angeles ZIP Codes are assigned to a new location, San Fernando Valley, as of early 1995

Riverside Division, US Bankruptcy Court, 3420 12th St, Riverside, CA 92501-3819. 909-774-1000. Voice Case Information System: 909-383-5552. Counties: Riverside, San Bernardino

San Fernando Valley Division, US Bankruptcy Court, 21041 Burbank Blvd, Woodland Hills, CA 91367. 818-587-2900. Voice Case Information System: 818-587-2936. Counties: Certain ZIP Codes in Los Angeles, Ventura and Kern counties: 90263, 90265, 90290, 91301-91311, 91313, 91316, 91320-91322, 91324-91328, 91330-91331, 91333-91335, 91337, 91340-91346, 91350-91362, 91364-91365, 91367, 91376, 91380-91386, 91392, 91400-91413, 91416, 91423, 91426, 91436, 91600-91610, 91614-91616, 91618, 93062-93063, 93065, 93093, 93243 (Kern), 93510, 93523 (Kern), 93532, 93534-93536, 93539, 93543-93544, 93550-93553, 93563.

Santa Ana Division, US Bankruptcy Court, 34 Civic Center Plaza, Room 506, Santa Ana, CA 92701. 714-836-2993. Voice Case Information System: 714-836-2278. Counties: Orange

Santa Barbara Division, US Bankruptcy Court, Room 101, 222 Carrillo St, Santa Barbara, CA 93101. 805-897-3870. Voice Case Information System: 805-899-7755. Counties: San Luis Obispo, Santa Barbara, Ventura. Certain Ventura ZIP Codes are assigned to the new office, San Fernando Valley

Eastern District of California

Fresno Division, US Bankruptcy Court, Room 2656, 1130 O Street, Fresno, CA 93721. 209-498-7217. Voice Case Information System: 916-498-5583. Counties: Fresno, Inyo, Kern, Kings, Madera, Mariposa, Merced, Tulare. Three Kern ZIP Codes, 93243 and 93523-24, are handled by San Fernando Valleyin the Central District

Modesto Division, US Bankruptcy Court, PO Box 5276, Modesto, CA 95352. 209-521-5160. Voice Case Information System: 916-498-5583. Counties: Calaveras, San Joaquin, Stanislaus, Tuolumne. The following ZIP Codes in San Joaquin County are handled by the Sacramento Division: 95220, 95227, 95234, 95237, 95240-95242, 95253, 95258, and 95686. Mariposa and Merced counties were transferred to the Fresno Division as of January 1, 1995

Sacramento Division, US Bankruptcy Court, 8308 US Courthouse, 650 Capitol Mall, Sacramento, CA 95814. 916-498-5525. Voice Case Information System: 916-498-5583. Counties: Alpine, Amador, Butte, Colusa, El Dorado, Glenn, Lassen, Modoc, Mono, Nevada, Placer, Plumas, Sacramento, Shasta, Sierra, Siskiyou, Solano, Sutter, Tehama, Trinity, Yolo, Yuba. This court also handles the following ZIP Codes in San Joaquin County: 95220, 95227, 95234, 95237, 95240-95242, 95253, 95258 and 95686

Northern District of California

Oakland Division, US Bankruptcy Court, PO Box 2070, Oakland, CA 94604. 510-879-3600. Voice Case Information System: 415-705-3160. Counties: Alameda, Contra Costa

San Francisco Division, US Bankruptcy Court, PO Box 7341, San Francisco, CA 94120-7341. 415-268-2300. Voice Case Information System: 415-705-3160. Counties: San Francisco, San Mateo

San Jose Division, US Bankruptcy Court, Room 3035, 280 S 1st St, San Jose, CA 95113-3099. 408-535-5118. Voice Case Information System: 415-705-3160. Counties: Monterey, San Benito, Santa Clara, Santa Cruz

Santa Rosa Division, US Bankruptcy Court, 99 South E St, Santa Rosa, CA 95404. 707-525-8539. Voice Case Information System: 415-705-3160. Counties: Del Norte, Humboldt, Lake, Marin, Mendocino, Napa, Sonoma

Southern District of California

San Diego Division, US Bankruptcy Court, Office of the Clerk, US Courthouse, 325 West "F" St., San Diego, CA 92101. 619-557-5620. Voice Case Information System: 619-557-6521. Counties: Imperial, San Diego

Colorado

Capital: Denver (Denver County)	
Number of Counties: 63	**Population:** 3,746,585
County Court Locations:	**Federal Court Locations:**
•District Courts: 14/22 Districts	•District Courts: 1
•County Courts: 16/63 Counties	•Bankruptcy Courts: 1
•Combined Courts: 49	**State Agencies:** 18
•Denver Probate Courts: 1	
•Municipal Courts: 206	
•Denver Juvenile Courts: 1	
•Water Courts: 7/7 Districts	

State Agencies—Summary

General Help Numbers:

State Archives

Colorado Information Tech Srvs	303-866-2055
Archives & Public Records	Fax: 303-866-2257
1313 Sherman St, Room 1B20	9AM-4:45PM
Denver, CO 80203	
Historical Society:	303-866-3682
Reference Librarian:	303-866-2358

Governor's Office

Governor's Office	303-866-2471
136 State Capitol Bldg	Fax: 303-866-2003
Denver, CO 80203-1792	8AM-5PM

Attorney General's Office

Attorney General's Office	303-866-3617
1525 Sherman St, 5th Floor	Fax: 303-866-5691
Denver, CO 80203	8AM-5PM

State Legislation

Colorado General Assembly	303-866-2045
State Capitol	8AM-4:30PM
200 E Colfax Ave	
Denver, CO 80203-1784	
Bill Data (during session):	303-866-3055
Archives:	
	303-866-2358

Important State Internet Sites:

> **Webscape**
> File   Edit   View   Help

State of Colorado World Wide Web
www.state.co.us/

Provides a directory of links leading to general information, current Colorado activities and current legislative information

Colorado Government
www.state.co.us/gov_dir/govmenu.html

This site provides access to all branches of state and local government, departments of government, and federal government

State Legislation
www.state.co.us/gov_dir/stateleg.html

Included with this site are the 1997 digest of bills, the final House and Senate bills, the latest House and Senate journals and the Colorado Revised Statutes.

UCC Information
www.state.co.us/gov_dir/sos/diracces.html#UCC

The new Central Indexing System may be accessed at www.cocis.com. See the entry for Uniform Commercial Code on the next page for more information.

State Agencies—Public Records

Criminal Records

Bureau of Investigation, State Repository, Identification Unit, 690 Kipling St, Suite 3000, Denver, CO 80215, Main Telephone: 303-239-4208, Fax: 303-239-0865, Hours: 8AM-4PM. Access by: mail, visit, PC.

Corporation Records
Trademarks/Servicemarks
Fictitious Name
Limited Liability Company Records
Assumed Name

Secretary of State, Corporation Division, 1560 Broadway, Suite 200, Denver, CO 80202, Main Telephone: 303-894-2251, Fax: 303-894-2242, Hours: 8:30AM-5PM. Access by: mail, phone, visit, fax, PC.

Uniform Commercial Code
Federal Tax Liens
State Tax Liens

UCC Division, Secretary of State, 1560 Broadway, Suite 200, Denver, CO 80202, Main Telephone: 303-894-2200, Fax: 303-894-2242, Hours: 8:30AM-5PM. Access by: mail, phone, fax, visit, PC. This office enters data and then passes to Central Indexing System, a designated contractor, for scanning. By mid 1998, the Central Indexing System will handle all record requests, including those made at the county level.

Sales Tax Registrations

Revenue Department, Taxpayers Services Office, 1375 Sherman St, Denver, CO 80261, Main Telephone: 303-232-2416, Fax 303-866-3211 Access by: mail, phone, visit.

Birth Certificates

Department of Public Health & Environment, Vital Records Section HSVR-A1, 4300 Cherry Creek Dr S, Denver, CO 80222-1530, Main Telephone: 303-756-4464, Ordering: 303-692-2224, Fax: 800-423-1108, Hours: 8:30AM-4:30PM. Access by: mail, phone, fax, visit. Certified copies for birth years 1964 to present can also be ordered at most county health departments.

Death Records

Department of Public Health & Environment, Vital Records Section HSVR-A1, 4300 Cherry Creek Dr S, Denver, CO 80222-1530, Main Telephone: 303-756-4464, Fax: 800-423-1108, Hours: 8:30AM-4:30PM. Access by: mail, phone, fax, visit.

Marriage Certificates
Divorce Records

Records not available from state agency.
Access by: mail, visit. Marriage and divorce records are found at county of issue. The State will verify marriage and divorce names, dates, and county only from 1900-1939 and 1975 to present (marriage) and 1968 to present (divorce). The 1900-1939 marriage index is by groom.

Workers' Compensation Records

Division of Workers Compensation, Customer Service, 1515 Arapahoe St, Tower 2, Ste 500, Denver, CO 80202, Main Telephone: 303-575-8700, Fax: 303-575-8882, Hours: 8AM-5PM. Access by: mail, phone, fax, visit. The agency will only release date of injury, part of body, employer, and workers' comp. case number.

Driver Records

Motor Vehicle Division, Driver Services, Denver, CO 80261-0016, Main Telephone: 303-205-5600, Fax: 303-205-5990, Hours: 8AM-5PM. Access by: mail, visit. Copies of tickets may be obtained from the address mentioned above at a fee of $2.20 per record. All requests must be submitted in writing and include the driver's name, DOB, and the specific ticket number.

Vehicle Ownership
Vehicle Identification

Department of Motor Vehicles, Driver Services, Denver, CO 80261-0016, Main Telephone: 303-623-9463, Hours: 8AM-5PM. Access by: mail, visit.

Accident Reports

Department of Motor Vehicles, Driver Services, Driver Services, Denver, CO 80261-0016, Main Telephone: 303-205-5613, Hours: 8AM-5PM. Access by: mail, visit.

Hunting License Information
Fishing License Information

Department of Natural Resources, Wildlife Division, 6060 Broadway, Denver, CO 80216, Main Telephone: 303-291-7380, Fishing Information: 303-291-7440, Fax: 303-294-0874, Hours: 8AM-5PM. Access by: mail, phone, visit.

County Courts and Recording Offices

What You Need to Know...

<table>
<tr><td>

About the Courts

Administration

State Court Administrator
1301 Pennsylvania St, Suite 300
Denver, CO 80203

303-861-1111
Fax: 303-837-2340
8AM-5PM

Court Structure

The District and County Courts have overlapping jurisdiction over civil cases involving less than $10,000. The District and County Courts are combined in 53 counties. Combined courts usually search both civil or criminal indexes for a single fee, except as indicated in the profiles. Denver is the only county with a separate Probate Court.

Searching Hints

Effective 1-1-95, **all state agencies in Colorado, including the courts,** require a self-addressed, stamped envelope (SASE) for return of information.

Financial data from criminal cases is **not released** in Colorado.

There are 7 Water Courts which are divisions of District Courts and co-located with them. The records are maintained by the Water Clerk and fees are similar to those for other court records. To retrieve a Water Court record, one must furnish the Case Number or the Legal Description (section, township, and range) or the Full Name of the respondent (note that the case number or legal description are preferred). The Water Courts are located in Weld, Pueblo, Alamosa, Montrose, Garfield, Routt, and La Platta counties; see the District Court discussion for those counties to determine the jurisdictional area for the court.

Online Access

There is currently no statewide online computer system available in Colorado.

</td><td>

About the Recorder's Office

Organization

63 counties, 63 filing offices. The recording officer is County Clerk and Recorder. The entire state is in the Mountain Time Zone (MST).

UCC Records

Financing statements are filed at the state level, except for consumer goods, farm and real estate related collateral, which are filed with the County Clerk and Recorder. All counties will perform UCC searches. Use search request form UCC-11. Search fees are usually $5.00 per debtor name for the first year and $2.00 for each additional year searched (or $13.00 for a five year search). Copies usually cost $1.25 per page.

Lien Records

Federal and some state tax liens on personal property are filed with the Secretary of State. Other federal and state tax liens are filed with the County Clerk and Recorder. Many counties will perform tax lien searches, usually at the same fees as UCC searches. Copies usually cost $1.25 per page. Other liens include judgments, motor vehicle, and mechanics.

Real Estate Records

Counties do **not** perform real estate searches. Copy fees are usually $1.25 per page and certification fees are usually $1.00 per document. Tax records are located in the Assessor's Office.

</td></tr>
</table>

County Courts and Recording Offices

Adams County

Real Estate Recording—Adams County Clerk and Recorder, 450 South 4th Avenue, Administrative Building, Brighton, CO 80601. 303-654-6020. Fax: 303-654-6011. 8AM-4:30PM (MST).

Felony, Civil Actions Over $10,000, Probate—17th District Court, 1931 E Bridge St, Brighton, CO 80601. 303-659-1161. Fax: 303-654-3216. 8AM-5PM (MST). Access by: Mail, in person.

Misdemeanor, Civil Actions Under $10,000, Eviction, Small Claims—County Court, 1931 E Bridge St, Brighton, CO 80601. 303-654-3300. 8AM-5PM (MST). Access by: Mail, in person.

Alamosa County

Real Estate Recording—Alamosa County Clerk and Recorder, 402 Edison Street, Alamosa, CO 81101. 719-589-6681. Fax: 719-589-6118. 8AM-4:30PM (MST).

Felony, Civil Actions Over $10,000, Probate—12th District Court, 702 4th St, Alamosa, CO 81101. 719-589-4996. Fax: 719-589-4998. 8AM-5PM (MST). Access by: Mail, in person.

Misdemeanor, Civil Actions Under $10,000, Eviction, Small Claims—Alamosa County Court, 702 4th St, Alamosa, CO 81101. 719-589-6213. 8AM-5PM (MST). Access by: Mail, in person.

Arapahoe County

Real Estate Recording—Arapahoe County Clerk and Recorder, 5334 South Prince Street, Littleton, CO 80166. 303-795-4520. Fax: 303-794-4625. 7AM-4:30PM (MST).

Felony, Civil Actions Over $10,000, Probate—18th District Court, 7325 S Potomac, Englewood, CO 80112. 303-649-6355. Fax: 303-792-6355. 8AM-5PM (MST). Access by: Mail, in person.

Misdemeanor, Civil Actions Under $10,000, Eviction, Small Claims—Arapahoe County Court Division B, 15400 E 14th Pl, Aurora, CO 80011. 303-363-8004. 8AM-5PM (MST). Access by: Mail, in person.

Littleton County Court Division A, 1790 W Littleton Blvd, Littleton, CO 80120-2060. 303-730-0358. Civil: 303-730-4592. Criminal: 303-798-4592. 8AM-4PM (MST). Access by: Mail, in person.

Archuleta County

Real Estate Recording—Archuleta County Clerk and Recorder, 449 San Juan Street, Pagosa Springs, CO 81147. 970-264-5633. Fax: 970-264-4896. 8AM-4PM (MST).

Felony, Misdemeanor, Civil, Eviction, Small Claims, Probate—6th District & County Courts, PO Box 148, Pagosa Springs, CO 81147. 970-264-2400. Fax: 970-264-2407. 8AM-5PM (MST). Access by: Mail, in person.

Baca County

Real Estate Recording—Baca County Clerk and Recorder, 741 Main Street, Courthouse, Springfield, CO 81073. 719-523-4372. Fax: 719-523-4882. 8:30AM-4:30PM (MST).

Felony, Misdemeanor, Civil, Eviction, Small Claims, Probate—Baca County District & County Courts, 741 Main St, Springfield, CO 81073. 719-523-4555. 8AM-5PM (MST). Access by: Mail, in person.

Bent County

Real Estate Recording—Bent County Clerk and Recorder, 725 Carson, Courthouse, Las Animas, CO 81054. 719-456-2009. Fax: 719-456-2223. 8AM-5PM (MST).

Felony, Misdemeanor, Civil, Eviction, Small Claims, Probate—16th District Court, Bent County Courthouse, Las Animas, CO 81054. 719-456-1353. Fax: 719-456-0040. 8AM-5PM (MST). Access by: Mail, in person.

Boulder County

Real Estate Recording—Boulder County Clerk and Recorder, 2020 13th Street, Courthouse - 2nd Floor, Boulder, CO 80302. 303-441-3515. 8AM-4:30PM (MST).

Felony, Misdemeanor, Civil, Eviction, Small Claims, Probate—20th District & County Courts, 6th & Canyon, PO Box 4249, Boulder, CO 80306. 303-441-3750. Fax: 303-441-4862. 8AM-5PM (MST). Access by: Mail, in person.

Chaffee County

Real Estate Recording—Chaffee County Clerk and Recorder, 104 Crestone Ave., Salida, CO 81201. 719-539-6913. Fax: 719-539-7442. 8AM-4PM Recording; 8AM-5PM Researching (MST).

Felony, Civil Actions Over $10,000, Probate—11th District Court, PO Box 279, Salida, CO 81201. 719-539-2561. Fax: 719-539-6281. 8AM-5PM (MST). Access by: Fax, mail, in person.

Misdemeanor, Civil Actions Under $10,000, Eviction, Small Claims—County Court, PO Box 279, Salida, CO 81201. 719-539-6031. Fax: 719-539-6281. 8AM-5PM (MST). Access by: Fax, mail, in person.

Cheyenne County

Real Estate Recording—Cheyenne County Clerk and Recorder, 51 South 1st Street, Cheyenne Wells, CO 80810. 719-767-5685. Fax: 719-767-5540. 8AM-4PM (MST).

Felony, Misdemeanor, Civil, Eviction, Small Claims, Probate—15th District & County Courts, PO Box 696, Cheyenne Wells, CO 80810. 719-767-5649. 8AM-4:30PM (MST). Access by: Mail, in person.

Clear Creek County

Real Estate Recording—Clear Creek County Clerk and Recorder, 405 Argentine, Courthouse, Georgetown, CO 80444. 303-569-3251. Fax: 303-569-0731. 8:30AM-4:30PM (MST).

Felony, Misdemeanor, Civil, Eviction, Small Claims, Probate—5th District & County Courts, PO Box 367, Georgetown, CO 80444. 303-569-3273. Fax: 303-569-3274. 8AM-5PM (MST). Access by: Mail, in person.

Conejos County

Real Estate Recording—Conejos County Clerk and Recorder, 6683 County Road 13, Conejos, CO 81129. 719-376-5422. Fax: 719-376-5661. 8AM-4:30PM (MST).

Felony, Misdemeanor, Civil, Eviction, Small Claims, Probate—12th District & County Courts, PO Box 128, Conejos, CO 81129. 719-376-5466. Fax: 719-376-5465. 8AM-4PM (MST). Access by: Mail, in person.

Costilla County

Real Estate Recording—Costilla County Clerk and Recorder, 354 Main Street, San Luis, CO 81152. 719-672-3301. Fax: 719-672-3962. (MST).

Felony, Misdemeanor, Civil, Eviction, Small Claims, Probate—12th District & County Courts, PO Box 301, San Luis, CO 81152. 719-672-3681. Fax: 719-672-3681. 8AM-Noon, 1-4PM (MST). Access by: Mail, in person.

Crowley County

Real Estate Recording—Crowley County Clerk and Recorder, 110 W. 6th St., Ordway, CO 81063. 719-267-4643. Fax: 719-267-4608. 8AM-4PM (MST).

Felony, Misdemeanor, Civil, Eviction, Small Claims, Probate—16th District & County Courts, 6th & Main, Ordway, CO 81063. 719-267-4468. Fax: 719-267-3753. 8AM-4:30PM (MST). Access by: Mail, in person.

Custer County

Real Estate Recording—Custer County Clerk and Recorder, 205 South 6th Street, Westcliffe, CO 81252. 719-783-2441. Fax: 719-783-2885. 8AM-4PM (MST).

Felony, Misdemeanor, Civil, Eviction, Small Claims, Probate—11th District & County Courts, PO Box 60, Westcliffe, CO 81252. 719-783-2274. Fax: 719-783-9782. 9AM-2PM (MST). Access by: Mail, in person.

Delta County

Real Estate Recording—Delta County Clerk and Recorder, 501 Palmer Street, Suite 211, Delta, CO 81416. 970-874-2150. Fax: 970-874-2161. 8:30AM-4:30PM (MST).

Felony, Misdemeanor, Civil, Eviction, Small Claims, Probate—7th District & County Courts, 501 Palmer St Rm 338, Delta, CO 81416. 970-874-4416. 8:30AM-4:30PM (MST). Access by: Mail, in person.

Denver County

Real Estate Recording—Denver County Clerk and Recorder, 1437 Bannock Street, # 200, Denver, CO 80202. 303-640-7290. Fax: 303-640-3628. 8AM-4:30PM (MST).

Felony, Civil Actions Over $10,000—2nd District Court, 1437 Bannock Rm 426, Denver, CO 80202. Civil: 303-575-2419. Criminal: 303-575-2876. 8AM-5PM (MST). Access by: Mail, in person.

Civil Actions Under $10,000, Eviction, Small Claims—County Court-Civil Division, 1515 Cleveland Pl 4th Floor, Denver, CO 80202. 303-640-5161. Fax: 303-640-4730. 8AM-5PM (MST). Access by: Mail, in person.

Misdemeanor—County Court-Criminal Division, 1437 Bannock St Room 111A, Denver, CO 80202. 303-640-5911. 8AM-5PM (MST). Access by: Mail, in person.

Probate—Probate Court, 1437 Bannock, Rm 230, Denver, CO 80202. 303-640-2327. 8AM-5PM (MST). Access by: In person only.

Dolores County

Real Estate Recording—Dolores County Clerk and Recorder, 409 North Main Street, Dove Creek, CO 81324. 970-677-2381. Fax: 970-677-2815. 8:30AM-4:30PM (MST).

Felony, Misdemeanor, Civil, Eviction, Small Claims, Probate—22nd District & County Courts, PO Box 511, Dove Creek, CO 81324. 970-677-2258. 8AM-5PM M; 8AM-3PM T,W (MST). Access by: Phone, mail, in person.

Douglas County

Real Estate Recording—Douglas County Clerk and Recorder, 301 Wilcox Street, Castle Rock, CO 80104. 303-660-7446. Fax: 303-688-3060. 8AM-4:30PM (MST).

Felony, Misdemeanor, Civil, Eviction, Small Claims, Probate—Douglas County Combined Court, PO Box 1690, Castle Rock, CO 80104-1690. 303-660-6800. 8AM-5PM (MST). Access by: Mail, in person.

Eagle County

Real Estate Recording—Eagle County Clerk and Recorder, 500 Broadway, Eagle, CO 81631. 970-328-8723. Fax: 970-328-8716. 8AM-5PM (MST).

Felony, Misdemeanor, Civil, Eviction, Small Claims, Probate—5th District & County Courts, PO Box 597, Eagle, CO 81631. 970-328-6373. Fax: 970-328-6328. 8AM-5PM (MST). Access by: In person only.

El Paso County

Real Estate Recording—El Paso County Clerk and Recorder, 200 South Cascade, Colorado Springs, CO 80903. 719-520-6200. Fax: 719-520-6230. 8:30AM-4:30PM (MST).

Felony, Civil Actions Over $10,000, Probate—4th District Court, 20 E Vermijo Rm 105, Colorado Springs, CO 80903. 719-630-2837. 8AM-5PM (MST). Access by: Mail, in person.

Misdemeanor, Civil Actions Under $10,000, Eviction, Small Claims—County Court, 20 E Vermijo, Rm 101, Colorado Springs, CO 80903. 719-448-7684. Fax: 719-448-7695. 8AM-5PM (MST). Access by: Mail, in person.

Elbert County

Real Estate Recording—Elbert County Clerk and Recorder, 215 Comanche Street, Kiowa, CO 80117. 303-621-3116. Fax: 303-621-2343. 8AM-4:30PM (MST).

Felony, Misdemeanor, Civil, Eviction, Small Claims, Probate—18th District & County Courts, PO Box 232, Kiowa, CO 80117. 303-621-2131. 8AM-5PM (MST). Access by: Phone, mail, in person.

Fremont County

Real Estate Recording—Fremont County Clerk and Recorder, 615 Macon Avenue, Room 100, Canon City, CO 81212. 719-275-1522. Fax: 719-275-1594. 8:30AM-4:30PM (MST).

Felony, Misdemeanor, Civil, Eviction, Small Claims, Probate—District & County Courts, 615 Macon Rm 204, Canon City, CO 81212. 719-275-7522. Fax: 719-275-2359. 8AM-4PM (MST). Access by: Mail, in person.

Garfield County

Real Estate Recording—Garfield County Clerk and Recorder, 109 8th Street, Suite 200, Glenwood Springs, CO 81601. 970-945-2377. Fax: 970-945-7785. 8:30AM-5PM (MST).

Felony, Misdemeanor, Civil, Eviction, Small Claims, Probate—9th District & County Courts, 109 8th St #104, Glenwood Springs, CO 81601. 970-945-5075. Fax: 970-945-8756. 8AM-5PM (MST). Access by: Mail, in person.

Misdemeanor, Civil Actions Under $10,000, Eviction, Small Claims—County Court-Rifle, 110 E 18th St, Rifle, CO 81650. 970-625-5100. Fax: 970-625-1125. 8AM-5PM (MST). Access by: Phone, fax, mail, in person.

Gilpin County

Real Estate Recording—Gilpin County Clerk and Recorder, 203 Eureka Street, Central City, CO 80427. 303-582-5321. Fax: 303-582-5440. 8AM-5PM (MST).

Felony, Misdemeanor, Civil, Eviction, Small Claims, Probate—1st District & County Courts, 2960 Dory Hill Rd #200, Golden, CO 80403-8768. 303-582-5323. Fax: 303-582-3112. 8AM-5PM (MST). Access by: Mail, in person.

Grand County

Real Estate Recording—Grand County Clerk and Recorder, 308 Byers Avenue, Hot Sulphur Springs, CO 80451. 970-725-3347. Fax: 970-725-0100. 8:30AM-5PM (MST).

Felony, Misdemeanor, Civil, Eviction, Small Claims, Probate—14th District & County Courts, PO Box 192, Hot Sulphur Springs, CO 80451. 970-725-3357. Fax: 970-725-3216. 8AM-5PM (MST). Access by: Mail, in person.

Gunnison County

Real Estate Recording—Gunnison County Clerk and Recorder, 200 East Virginia Avenue, Courthouse, Gunnison, CO 81230. 970-641-1516. Fax: 970-641-3061. 8AM-5PM (MST).

Felony, Misdemeanor, Civil, Eviction, Small Claims, Probate—7th District & County Courts, 200 E Virginia Ave, Gunnison, CO 81230. 970-641-3500. Fax: 970-641-6876. 8:30AM-4:30PM (MST). Access by: Mail, in person.

Hinsdale County

Real Estate Recording—Hinsdale County Clerk and Recorder, 317 Henson Street, Lake City, CO 81235. 970-944-2228. Fax: 970-944-2202. 7AM-5:30PM (MST).

Felony, Misdemeanor, Civil, Eviction, Small Claims, Probate—7th District & County Courts, PO Box 245, Lake City, CO 81235. 970-944-2227. Fax: 970-944-2289. 8:30-Noon MWF (Jun-Aug) 8:30-12:00 TF (Sept-May) (MST). Access by: Phone, fax, mail, in person.

Huerfano County

Real Estate Recording—Huerfano County Clerk and Recorder, 401 Main Street, Courthouse, Walsenburg, CO 81089. 719-738-2380. Fax: 719-738-3996. 8AM-4PM (MST).

Felony, Misdemeanor, Civil, Eviction, Small Claims, Probate—3rd District & County Courts, 401 Main St, Suite

304, Walsenburg, CO 81089. 719-738-1040. Fax: 719-738-3113. 8AM-4PM (MST). Access by: Mail, in person.

Jackson County

Real Estate Recording—Jackson County Clerk and Recorder, 396 LaFever Street, Walden, CO 80480. 970-723-4334. 8AM-5PM (MST).

Felony, Misdemeanor, Civil, Eviction, Small Claims, Probate—8th District & County Courts, PO Box 308, Walden, CO 80480. 970-723-4363. 9AM-1PM (MST). Access by: Mail, in person.

Jefferson County

Real Estate Recording—Jefferson County Clerk and Recorder, 100 Jefferson County Parkway, #2530, Golden, CO 80419. 303-271-8182. Fax: 303-271-8180. 7:30AM-5:30PM (MST).

Felony, Misdemeanor, Civil, Eviction, Small Claims, Probate—1st District & County Courts, 100 Jefferson County Parkway, Golden, CO 80401-6002. 303-271-6267. Fax: 303-271-6188. 8AM-5PM (MST). Access by: Mail, in person.

Kiowa County

Real Estate Recording—Kiowa County Clerk and Recorder, 1305 Goff Street, Eads, CO 81036. 719-438-5421. Fax: 719-438-5327. 8AM-4:30PM (MST).

Felony, Misdemeanor, Civil, Eviction, Small Claims, Probate—15th District & County Courts, PO Box 353, Eads, CO 81036. 719-438-5558. Fax: 719-438-5300. 8AM-5PM (MST). Access by: Phone, mail, in person.

Kit Carson County

Real Estate Recording—Kit Carson County Clerk and Recorder, 251 16th Street, Suite 203, Burlington, CO 80807. 719-346-8638. Fax: 719-346-7242. 8AM-4PM (MST).

Felony, Misdemeanor, Civil, Eviction, Small Claims, Probate—13th District & County Courts, PO Box 547, Burlington, CO 80807. 719-346-5524. 8:30AM-Noon, 1:30-5PM (MST). Access by: Mail, in person. Prefer mail search requests.

La Plata County

Real Estate Recording—La Plata County Clerk and Recorder, Courthouse, Room 134, 1060 E. 2nd Ave., Durango, CO 81301. 970-382-6281. Fax: 970-382-6299. 8AM-5PM (MST).

Felony, Civil Actions Over $10,000, Probate—6th District Court, PO Box 3340, Durango, CO 81302-3340. 970-247-2304. Fax: 970-247-4348. 8AM-4PM (MST). Access by: Mail, in person.

Misdemeanor, Civil Actions Under $10,000, Eviction, Small Claims—County Court, PO Box 759, Durango, CO 81302. 970-247-2004. Fax: 970-247-4348. 8AM-4PM (MST). Access by: Mail, in person.

Lake County

Real Estate Recording—Lake County Clerk and Recorder, 505 Harrison Avenue, Leadville, CO 80461. 719-486-4131. Fax: 719-486-3972. 9AM-5PM (MST).

Felony, Misdemeanor, Civil, Eviction, Small Claims, Probate—Lake County Combined Courts, PO Box 55, Leadville, CO 80461. 719-486-0535. 8AM-5PM (MST). Access by: Mail, in person.

Larimer County

Real Estate Recording—Larimer County Clerk and Recorder, 200 West Oak, Fort Collins, CO 80521. 970-498-7860. 7:30AM-4:30PM (MST).

Felony, Civil Actions Over $10,000, Probate—8th District Court, PO Box 2066, Ft Collins, CO 80522. 970-498-7918. Fax: 970-498-7940. 8AM-5PM (MST). Access by: Mail, in person. Signed release required for certain cases.

Misdemeanor, Civil Actions Under $10,000, Eviction, Small Claims—County Court, PO Box 800, Ft Collins, CO 80522. 970-498-7550. Fax: 970-498-7569. 8AM-5PM (MST). Access by: Mail, in person.

Las Animas County

Real Estate Recording—Las Animas County Clerk and Recorder, 200 Maple Street, Trinidad, CO 81082. 719-846-3314. Fax: 719-846-0333. 8AM-4PM (MST).

Felony, Misdemeanor, Civil, Eviction, Small Claims, Probate—3rd District & County Courts, 200 E 1st St Rm 304, Trinidad, CO 81082. 719-846-3316. Fax: 719-846-9367. 8AM-5PM (MST). Access by: Phone, fax, mail, in person.

Lincoln County

Real Estate Recording—Lincoln County Clerk and Recorder, 103 3rd Avenue, Hugo, CO 80821. 719-743-2444. Fax: 719-743-2838. 8AM-4PM (MST).

Felony, Misdemeanor, Civil, Eviction, Small Claims, Probate—18th District & County Courts, PO Box 128, Hugo, CO 80821. 719-743-2455. 8AM-4:30PM (MST). Access by: Phone, mail, in person.

Logan County

Real Estate Recording—Logan County Clerk and Recorder, 315 Main Street, Logan County Courthouse, Sterling, CO 80751. 970-522-1544. Fax: 970-522-4018. 8AM-5PM (MST).

Felony, Civil Actions Over $10,000, Probate—13th District Court, PO Box 71, Sterling, CO 80751. 970-522-6565. Fax: 970-522-6566. 8AM-4PM (MST). Access by: Mail, in person.

Misdemeanor, Civil Actions Under $10,000, Eviction, Small Claims—County Court, PO Box 1907, Sterling, CO 80751. 970-522-1572. Fax: 970-522-2875. 8AM-4PM (MST). Access by: Phone, mail, in person.

Mesa County

Real Estate Recording—Mesa County Clerk and Recorder, 544 Rood Avenue, Grand Junction, CO 81501. 970-244-1679. Fax: 970-244-1804. 8:30AM-4:30PM (MST).

Felony, Civil Actions Over $10,000, Probate—21st District Court, PO Box 20000, Grand Junction, CO 81502-5032. 970-257-3625. 8AM-5PM (MST). Access by: Mail, in person.

Misdemeanor, Civil Actions Under $10,000, Eviction, Small Claims—County Court, PO Box 20000, Grand Junction, CO 81502-5032. 970-243-1136. 8AM-5PM (MST). Access by: Phone, mail, in person.

Mineral County

Real Estate Recording—Mineral County Clerk and Recorder, 1201 N. Main St., Courthouse, Creede, CO 81130. 719-658-2440. Fax: 719-658-2764. 8AM-4PM (MST).

Felony, Misdemeanor, Civil, Eviction, Small Claims, Probate—12th District & County Courts, PO Box 337, Creede, CO 81130. 719-658-2575. Fax: 719-658-2575. 10AM-3PM (MST). Access by: Mail, in person.

Moffat County

Real Estate Recording—Moffat County Clerk and Recorder, 221 West Victory Way, Craig, CO 81625. 970-824-5484. Fax: 970-824-3995. 8AM-4PM (MST).

Felony, Misdemeanor, Civil, Eviction, Small Claims, Probate—14th District & County Courts, 221 W Victory Wy, Craig, CO 81625. 970-824-8254. 8AM-5PM (MST). Access by: Mail, in person.

Montezuma County

Real Estate Recording—Montezuma County Clerk and Recorder, 109 West Main Street, Room 108, Cortez, CO 81321. 970-565-3728. Fax: 970-564-0215. 8:30AM-4:30PM (MST).

Felony, Civil Actions Over $10,000, Probate—22nd District Court, 109 W Main St, Cortez, CO 81321. 970-565-1111. 8AM-5PM (MST). Access by: Mail, in person.

Misdemeanor, Civil Actions Under $10,000, Eviction, Small Claims—County Court, 601 N Mildred Rd, Cortez, CO 81321. 970-565-7580. Fax: 970-565-8798. 8AM-4:30PM (MST). Access by: Mail, in person.

Montrose County

Real Estate Recording—Montrose County Clerk and Recorder, 320 South First Street, Courthouse, Montrose, CO 81401. 970-249-3362. Fax: 970-249-0757. 8:30AM-4:30PM (MST).

Felony, Misdemeanor, Civil, Eviction, Small Claims, Probate—7th District & County Courts, PO Box 368, Montrose, CO 81402. 970-249-9676. Fax: 970-249-8546. 8:30AM-4:30PM (MST). Access by: Mail, in person.

Morgan County

Real Estate Recording—Morgan County Clerk and Recorder, 231 Ensign Street, Administration Building, Fort Morgan, CO 80701. 970-867-5616. Fax: 970-867-6485. 8AM-4PM (MST).

Felony, Civil Actions Over $10,000, Probate—13th District Court, PO Box 130, Ft Morgan, CO 80701. 970-867-8266. Fax: 970-867-7142. 8AM-4PM (MST). Access by: Fax, mail, in person.

Misdemeanor, Civil Actions Under $10,000, Eviction, Small Claims—County Court, PO Box 695, Ft Morgan, CO 80701. 970-867-8244. Fax: 970-867-7142. 8AM-4PM (MST). Access by: Mail, in person.

Otero County

Real Estate Recording—Otero County Clerk and Recorder, 3rd & Colorado, Courthouse, La Junta, CO 81050. 719-383-3020. Fax: 719-383-3090. 8AM-5PM (MST).

Felony, Civil Actions Over $10,000, Probate—16th District Court, Courthouse Rm 207, La Junta, CO 81050. 719-384-4951. Fax: 719-384-4991. 8AM-5PM (MST). Access by: Mail, in person.

Misdemeanor, Civil Actions Under $10,000, Eviction, Small Claims—County Court, Courthouse Rm 105, La Junta, CO 81050. 719-384-4721. Fax: 719-384-4991. 8AM-Noon, 1-5PM (MST). Access by: Mail, in person.

Ouray County

Real Estate Recording—Ouray County Clerk and Recorder, 541 Fourth Street, Ouray, CO 81427. 970-325-4961. Fax: 970-325-0452. 9AM-5PM (MST).

Felony, Misdemeanor, Civil, Eviction, Small Claims, Probate—7th District & County Courts, PO Box 643, Ouray, CO 81427. 970-325-4405. Fax: 970-325-7364. 8:30AM-4PM (MST). Access by: Fax, mail, in person.

Park County

Real Estate Recording—Park County Clerk and Recorder, 501 Main Street, Fairplay, CO 80440. 719-836-2771. Fax: 719-836-4348. 8AM-5PM (MST).

Felony, Misdemeanor, Civil, Eviction, Small Claims, Probate—Park County Combined Courts, PO Box 190, Fairplay, CO 80440. 719-836-2940. Fax: 719-836-2892. 8AM-4PM (MST). Access by: Mail, in person. Release needed for juvenile cases.

Phillips County

Real Estate Recording—Phillips County Clerk and Recorder, 221 South Interocean, Holyoke, CO 80734. 970-854-3131. Fax: 970-664-3811. 8AM-4:30PM (MST).

Felony, Misdemeanor, Civil, Eviction, Small Claims, Probate—13th District & County Courts, 221 S Interocean, Holyoke, CO 80734. 970-854-3279. Fax: 970-854-3179. 8AM-Noon,1-4PM (MST). Access by: Mail, in person.

Pitkin County

Real Estate Recording—Pitkin County Clerk and Recorder, 530 East Main St., #101, Aspen, CO 81611. 970-920-5180. Fax: 970-920-5196. 8:30AM-4:30PM (MST).

Felony, Misdemeanor, Civil, Eviction, Small Claims, Probate—9th District & County Courts, 506 E Main St, Ste 300, Aspen, CO 81611. 970-925-7635. Fax: 970-925-6349. 8AM-Noon, 1PM-5PM (MST). Access by: Mail, in person.

Prowers County

Real Estate Recording—Prowers County Clerk and Recorder, 301 South Main Street, Lamar, CO 81052. 719-336-4337. Fax: 719-336-2255. 8:30AM-4:30PM (MST).

Felony, Civil Actions Over $10,000, Probate—15th District Court, PO Box 1178, Lamar, CO 81052. 719-336-7424. Fax: 719-336-9757. 8AM-5PM (MST). Access by: Fax, mail, in person.

Misdemeanor, Civil Actions Under $10,000, Eviction, Small Claims—County Court, PO Box 525, Lamar, CO 81052. 719-336-7416. Fax: 719-336-9757. 8AM-5PM (MST). Access by: Mail, in person.

Pueblo County

Real Estate Recording—Pueblo County Clerk and Recorder, 215 West 10th Street, Pueblo, CO 81003. 719-583-6625. Fax: 719-583-6549. 8AM-4:30PM (MST).

Felony, Misdemeanor, Civil, Eviction, Small Claims, Probate—10th District & County Courts, 320 West 10th St, Pueblo, CO 81003. 719-583-7000. 8AM-5PM (District) 8AM-4PM (County) (MST). Access by: Mail, in person.

Rio Blanco County

Real Estate Recording—Rio Blanco County Clerk and Recorder, 555 Main Street, P.O. Box 1067, Meeker, CO 81641. 970-878-5068. 8AM-5PM (MST).

Felony, Misdemeanor, Civil, Eviction, Small Claims, Probate—9th District & County Courts, 555 Main St Rm 303, PO Box 1150, Meeker, CO 81641. 970-878-5622. 8AM-Noon, 1-5PM (MST). Access by: Phone, mail, in person.

Rio Grande County

Real Estate Recording—Rio Grande County Clerk and Recorder, Annex Building, 965 6th St., Del Norte, CO 81132. 719-657-3334. Fax: 719-657-2621. 8AM-4PM (MST).

Felony, Misdemeanor, Civil, Eviction, Small Claims, Probate—12th District & County Courts, 6th & Cherry, PO Box W, Del Norte, CO 81132. 719-657-3394. 8AM-Noon, 1-4PM (MST). Access by: Mail, in person.

Routt County

Real Estate Recording—Routt County Clerk and Recorder, 522 Lincoln Avenue, Steamboat Springs, CO 80487. 970-879-5556. Fax: 970-870-1329. 8:30AM-4:30PM (MST).

Felony, Misdemeanor, Civil, Eviction, Small Claims, Probate—Routt Combined Courts, PO Box 773117, Steamboat Springs, CO 80477. 970-879-5020. Fax: 970-879-3531. 8AM-5PM (MST). Access by: Mail, in person.

Saguache County

Real Estate Recording—Saguache County Clerk and Recorder, 501 4th St., Saguache, CO 81149. 719-655-2512. Fax: 719-655-2635. 8AM-4PM (MST).

Felony, Misdemeanor, Civil, Eviction, Small Claims, Probate—12th District & County Courts, PO Box 164, Saguache, CO 81149. 719-655-2522. Fax: 719-655-2522. 8AM-Noon, 1PM-5PM (MST). Access by: Mail, in person.

San Juan County

Real Estate Recording—San Juan County Clerk and Recorder, 15th & Green Street, Silverton, CO 81433. 970-387-5671. Fax: 970-387-5671. 9AM-5PM (MST).

Felony, Misdemeanor, Civil, Eviction, Small Claims, Probate—6th District & County Courts, PO Box 441, Silverton, CO 81433. 970-387-5790. 8AM-4PM T & TH, 8AM-Noon W (MST). Access by: Mail, in person.

San Miguel County

Real Estate Recording—San Miguel County Clerk and Recorder, 305 West Colorado Avenue, Telluride, CO 81435. 970-728-3954. 9AM-Noon,1-5PM (MST).

Felony, Misdemeanor, Civil, Eviction, Small Claims, Probate—7th District & County Courts, PO Box 919, Telluride, CO 81435. 970-728-3891. Fax: 970-728-6216. 9AM-Noon, 1:00PM-4:30PM (MST). Access by: Mail, in person.

Sedgwick County

Real Estate Recording—Sedgwick County Clerk and Recorder, 315 Cedar St., Courthouse, Julesburg, CO 80737. 970-474-3346. Fax: 970-474-0954. 8AM-4PM (MST).

Felony, Misdemeanor, Civil, Eviction, Small Claims, Probate—13th District & County Courts, Courthouse Square, Julesburg, CO 80737. 970-474-3627. Fax: 970-474-2749. 8AM-1PM (MST). Access by: Fax, mail, in person.

Summit County

Real Estate Recording—Summit County Clerk and Recorder, 208 East Lincoln, Breckenridge, CO 80424. 970-453-2561. Fax: 970-453-3535. 8AM-5PM (MST).

Felony, Misdemeanor, Civil, Eviction, Small Claims, Probate—5th District & County Courts, PO Box 185, Breckenridge, CO 80424. 970-453-2272. 8AM-5PM (MST). Access by: In person only.

Teller County

Real Estate Recording—Teller County Clerk and Recorder, 101 West Bennett Avenue, Cripple Creek, CO 80813. 719-689-2951. Fax: 719-689-3524. 8AM-4:30PM (MST).

Felony, Misdemeanor, Civil, Eviction, Small Claims, Probate—4th District & County Courts, PO Box 997, Cripple Creek, CO 80813. 719-689-2543. 8:30AM-4PM (MST). Access by: Mail, in person.

Washington County

Real Estate Recording—Washington County Clerk, 150 Ash, Courthouse, Akron, CO 80720. 970-345-6565. Fax: 970-345-6607. 8AM-4:30PM (MST).

Felony, Misdemeanor, Civil, Eviction, Small Claims, Probate—13th District & County Courts, PO Box 455, Akron, CO 80720. 970-345-2756. Fax: 970-345-2829. 8AM-Noon, 1PM-5PM (MST). Access by: Phone, mail, in person.

Weld County

Real Estate Recording—Weld County Clerk and Recorder, 1402 N. 17th Ave., Greeley, CO 80631. 970-353-3840. Fax: 970-353-1964. 8:30PM-4:30PM (MST).

Felony, Misdemeanor, Civil, Eviction, Small Claims, Probate—19th District & County Courts, PO Box C, Greeley, CO 80632. 970-351-7300. Fax: 970-356-4356. 8AM-5PM (MST). Access by: Mail, in person.

Yuma County

Real Estate Recording—Yuma County Clerk and Recorder, Third & Ash, Wray, CO 80758. 970-332-5809. 8:30AM-4:30PM (MST).

Felony, Misdemeanor, Civil, Eviction, Small Claims, Probate—13th District & County Courts, PO Box 347, Wray, CO 80758. 970-332-4118. Fax: 970-332-4119. 8AM-4PM (MST). Access by: Mail, in person.

Federal Courts

US District Court
District of Colorado

Denver Division, US District Court US Courthouse, Room C-145 (Civil) Room C-161 (Criminal), 1929 Stout St, Denver, CO 80294-3589. 303-844-3433. Counties: All counties in Colorado

US Bankruptcy Court
District of Colorado

Denver Division, US Bankruptcy Court, US Custom House, Room 114, 721 19th St, Denver, CO 80202-2508. 303-844-4045. Voice Case Information System: 303-844-0267. Counties: All counties in Colorado

Connecticut

Capital: Hartford (Hartford County)	
Number of Counties: 8	**Population:** 3,274,662
County Court Locations:	**Federal Court Locations:**
•Superior Courts: 18/21 Areas	•District Courts: 3
•Geographic Area Courts 19	•Bankruptcy Courts: 3
•Probate Courts: 129	**State Agencies:** 19

State Agencies—Summary

General Help Numbers:

State Archives

Connecticut State Library	860-566-5650
History & Genealogy Unit	Fax: 860-566-2133
231 Capitol Ave	9:30AM-5PM
Hartford, CT 06106	
Historical Society:	860-236-5621
Reference Librarian:	860-566-3690

Governor's Office

Governor's Office	860-566-4840
State Capitol,	
210 Capitol Ave, Room 202	Fax: 860-566-4677
Hartford, CT 06106	8AM-6PM

Attorney General's Office

Attorney General's Office	860-566-2026
55 Elm St	Fax: 860-566-1704
Hartford, CT 06106	8:30AM-4:30PM

State Legislation

Connecticut General Assembly	860-566-5736
State Library	Fax: 860-566-2133
231 Capitol Ave, Bill Room	8:30AM-4:30PM
Hartford, CT 06106	

Important State Internet Sites:

```
🕭 Webscape
File   Edit   View                                    Help
```

State of Connecticut World Wide Web

www.state.ct.us/

Includes links to many sites. Some of those sites are the Judicial, Legislative and Executive branches of government. A search engine is also located here.

The Governor's Office

www.state.ct.us/governor/govpag.htm

This page includes information about the Governor and his State of the State Address.

Connecticut Legislative Home Page

www.state.ct.us/ldp/

This is the site to search for legislation, browse different publications and to locate legislators e-mail addresses.

Department of Motor Vehicles

dmvct.org/dmvhompg.htm

This site provides links to many different motor vehicle information sites.

Unclaimed Property

www.state.ct.us/ott/ucp.htm

Locates unclaimed property such as, checking and savings accounts, payroll, wages, insurance, refunds and much more. Property is searchable by owner's name.

State Agencies—Public Records

Criminal Records
Department of Public Safety, Bureau of Identification, PO Box 2794, Middleton, CT 06759-9294, Main Telephone: 860-685-8480, Fax: 860-685-8361, Hours: 8AM-5PM. Access by: mail only. Records of inmates can be obtained from the Department of Corrections at 860-685-8361. There is no fee for a name search.

Corporation Records
Limited Partnership Records
Trademarks/Servicemarks
Limited Liability Company Records
Secretary of State, Commercial Recording Division, 30 Trinity St, Hartford, CT 06106, Main Telephone: 860-566-8570, Hours: 8:45AM-3PM. Access by: mail, phone, visit, PC. Assumed names are found at the county level.

Uniform Commercial Code
Federal Tax Liens
State Tax Liens
UCC Division, Secretary of State, PO Box 150470, Hartford, CT 06115-0470, Main Telephone: 860-566-4021, Hours: 8:45AM-3PM. Access by: mail, visit.

Sales Tax Registrations
Department of Revenue, Taxpayer Registration Division, 25 Sigourney St, Hartford, CT 06104, Main Telephone: 860-297-4880, Fax: 860-297-5714, Hours: 8:15AM-4:45PM. Access by: phone, visit.

Birth Certificates
Department of Public Health, Vital Records Section MS# 11VRS, PO Box 340308, Hartford, CT 06134-0308, Main Telephone: 860-509-7899, Alternate Telephone: 860-509-7897, Fax: 860-509-7964, Hours: 8:30AM-4:30PM M-F. Access by: mail, visit.

Death Records
Department of Public Health, Vital Records Section, PO Box 340308, Hartford, CT 06134-0308, Main Telephone: 860-509-7899, Hours: 9AM-4:30PM (Genealogical searches 9-12 F). Access by: mail, visit.

Marriage Certificates
Department of Public Health, Vital Records Section, PO Box 340308, Hartford, CT 06134-0308, Main Telephone: 860-509-7899, Hours: 9AM-4:30PM (Genealogical searches 9-12 F). Access by: mail, visit.

Divorce Records
Records not available from state agency.

Workers' Compensation Records
Workers Compensation Commission, 21 Oak Street, Hartford, CT 06106, Main Telephone: 860-493-1500, Hours: 8:30AM-4:30PM. Access by: mail, phone, visit. All files are kept at one of the eight district offices. This agency will forward the request to the proper district office.

Driver Records
Department of Motor Vehicles, Copy Records Section, 60 State St, Room 305, Wethersfield, CT 06109-1896, Main Telephone: 860-566-3720, Hours: 8:30AM-4:30PM T,W,F; 8:30AM-7:30PM TH; 8:30AM-12:30 S. Access by: mail, visit, PC. Copies of tickets may be obtained from the Superior Court Records Center, 111 Phoenix Ave, Enfield, 06082, 203-741-3714 for a fee of $1, or $3 for certified. Written requests must include name, DOB, date of disposition, document # and court.

Vehicle Ownership
Vehicle Identification
Department of Motor Vehicles, Copy Record Unit, 60 State St, Branch Operations, Wethersfield, CT 06109-1896, Main Telephone: 860-566-3720, Hours: 8:30AM-4:30PM T,W,F; 8:30AM-7:30 PM TH; 8:30AM-12:30 S. Access by: mail, visit, PC. With the passage of Public Act 94-206, the release of records to non-contract vendors has become very restrictive.

Accident Reports
Department of Public Safety, Reports and Records Section, PO Box 2794, Middletown, CT 06457, Main Telephone: 860-685-8250, Hours: 8:30AM-4:30PM. Access by: mail only.

Hunting License Information
Fishing License Information
Department of Environmental Protection, License Division, 79 Elm St, Hartford, CT 06106, Main Telephone: 860-424-3105, Hours: 9AM-3:30PM. Access by: mail, visit.

County Courts and Recording Offices

What You Need to Know...

<table>
<tr><th>About the Courts</th><th>About the Recorder's Office</th></tr>
</table>

About the Courts

Administration

Chief Court Administrator	860-566-4461
231 Capitol Ave	Fax: 860-566-3309
Hartford, CT 06106	9AM-5PM

Court Structure

The Superior Court is divided into four sessions; **civil, criminal, housing and family.** The Superior Court-Civil Session handles civil judgments over $2500 and evictions if there is not housing session. Geographical Area Courts handle civil actions under $2500 and small claims.

The Superior Court-Criminal Session handles felonies and the Geographical Area Court handles preliminary felonies, some minor felonies, and misdemeanors.

Searching Hints

There is a State Record Center, which serves as the repository for criminal and some civil records, in Enfield CT open 9AM-5PM M-F. **Case records are sent to the Record Center from 3 months to 5 years after disposition by the courts** and are maintained 10 years for misdemeanors and 20+ years for felonies. If a requester is certain that the record is at the Record Center, it is quicker to direct the request there rather than the original court of record. Only written requests are accepted. Search requirements include: Full defendant name, Docket Number, Disposition Date, and Court Action. Fee is $5.00 for each docket. Fee payee is Treasurer-State of Connecticut. Direct Requests to: Connecticut Record Center, 111 Phoenix Avenue, Enfield CT 06082, 860-741-3714.

Personal checks must have name and address printed on the check; if requesting in person, check must have same address as drivers' license.

Many clerks state that they will send an extract of a records without copying originals or certification at no charge.

Online Access

An on-line system called Civil/Family System, which provides direct access to Superior Court records, is available through **CATER**, the Connecticut Administrative Center. The user can access data concerning all civil and family cases statewide. The system is available from 8AM to 5PM Eastern Time Monday through Friday except on holidays. The fee is $30.00 per month network charge, $10.00 per use per month user authorization fee plus a per minute usage fee. For an information brochure or subscription information call the CT JIS Office at 860-566-8580. There is currently no on-line access to criminal records, but there is a central repository (see next section).

About the Recorder's Office

Organization

8 counties and 170 towns/cities. The recording officer is Town/City Clerk. **Counties have no administrative offices.** Be careful not to confuse searching in the following towns/cities as equivalent to a county-wide search : Fairfield, Hartford, Litchfield, New Haven, New London, Tolland, and Windham. The entire state is in the Eastern Time Zone (EST).

UCC Records

Financing statements are filed at the state level, except for real estate related collateral, which are filed only with the Town/City Clerk. Towns will **not** perform UCC searches. Copies usually cost $1.00 per page.

Lien Records

All federal and state tax liens on personal property are filed with the Secretary of State. Federal and state tax liens on real property are filed with the Town/City Clerk. Towns will **not** perform tax lien searches. Other liens include mechanics, judgments, lis pendens, municipal, welfare, carpenter, sewer & water, and city/town.

Real Estate Records

Towns do **not** perform real estate searches. Copy fees are usually $1.00 per page. Certification fees are usually $1.00 per document or per page.

County Courts and Recording Offices

Andover Town

Real Estate Recording—Andover Town Clerk, Town Office Building, 17 School Road, Andover, CT 06232. 860-742-0188. Fax: 860-742-7535. 8:30-12,1-4,5-7 M; 8:30-Noon,1-4PM T-Th;8:30-12:30PM F (EST).

Ansonia City

Real Estate Recording—Ansonia City Clerk, 253 Main Street, City Hall, Ansonia, CT 06401. 203-736-5980. 8:30AM-4:30PM (EST).

Ashford Town

Real Estate Recording—Ashford Town Clerk, 25 Pompey Hollow Road, Ashford, CT 06278. 860-429-7044. Fax: 860-429-6829. 8:30AM-3PM M-W & F; 7-8:30PM Wed (EST).

Avon Town

Real Estate Recording—Avon Town Clerk, 60 West Main Street, Avon, CT 06001. 860-677-2634. Fax: 860-677-8428. 8:30AM-4:30PM (Summer hours: 8AM-4:45PM M-Th; 8AM-12:30PM F) (EST).

Barkhamsted Town

Real Estate Recording—Barkhamsted Town Clerk, Route 318, 67 Ripley Hill Rd., Town Hall, Pleasant Valley, CT 06063. 860-379-8665. Fax: 860-379-9284. 9AM-4PM (F open until 1PM) (EST).

Beacon Falls Town

Real Estate Recording—Beacon Falls Town Clerk, 10 Maple Avenue, Beacon Falls, CT 06403. 203-729-8254. Fax: 203-720-1078. 9AM-Noon, 1-4PM (EST).

Berlin Town

Real Estate Recording—Berlin Town Clerk, 240 Kensington Road, Kensington, CT 06037. 860-828-7075. Fax: 860-828-8628. M-W, 8:30AM-4:30PM; Th 8:30AM-7PM; F 8:30AM-1PM (EST).

Bethany Town

Real Estate Recording—Bethany Town Clerk, 40 Peck Road, Bethany, CT 06524. 203-393-0820. Fax: 203-393-0821. 9:30AM-4:30PM (No copying or recording after 4PM) (EST).

Bethel Town

Real Estate Recording—Bethel Town Clerk, 1 School St., Bethel, CT 06801. 203-794-8505. Fax: 203-794-8588. 9AM-5PM M-W, F; 9AM-7PM Th (EST).

Bethlehem Town

Real Estate Recording—Bethlehem Town Clerk, 36 Main St. So., Bethlehem, CT 06751. 203-266-7510. Fax: 203-266-7677. 9AM-Noon T,W,Th,F,Sat (EST).

Bloomfield Town

Real Estate Recording—Bloomfield Town Clerk, 800 Bloomfield Avenue, Town Hall, Bloomfield, CT 06002. 860-769-3506. Fax: 860-769-3597. 9AM-5PM (EST).

Bolton Town

Real Estate Recording—Bolton Town Clerk, 222 Bolton Center Road, Bolton, CT 06043. 860-649-8066. Fax: 860-643-0021. 9AM-4PM M,W,Th; 9AM-5PM, 6-8PM T; 9AM-3PM F (EST).

Bozrah Town

Real Estate Recording—Bozrah Town Clerk, 1 River Road, Town Hall, Bozrah, CT 06334. 860-889-2689. Fax: 860-887-5449. 9AM-4PM T,W,Th; 9AM-Noon Sat (EST).

Branford Town

Real Estate Recording—Branford Town Clerk, 1019 Main Street, Town Hall, Branford, CT 06405. 203-488-6305. Fax: 203-481-5561. 9AM-4:30PM (9AM-4PM Recording hours) (EST).

Bridgeport Town

Real Estate Recording—Bridgeport Town Clerk, 45 Lyon Terrace, City Hall, Room 124, Bridgeport, CT 06604. 203-576-7207. 9AM-4:30PM; Recording until 4PM (EST).

Bridgewater Town

Real Estate Recording—Bridgewater Town Clerk, Main Street, Town Hall, Bridgewater, CT 06752. 860-354-5102. Fax: 860-350-5944. 8AM-Noon M,W,F; 8AM-5PM T (EST).

Bristol City

Real Estate Recording—Bristol City Clerk, 111 North Main Street, City Hall, Bristol, CT 06010. 860-584-7656. Fax: 860-584-3827. 8:30AM-5PM (EST).

Brookfield Town

Real Estate Recording—Brookfield Town Clerk, Pocono Road, Town Hall, Brookfield, CT 06804. 203-775-7313. 8:30AM-4:30PM (EST).

Brooklyn Town

Real Estate Recording—Brooklyn Town Clerk, 4 Wolf Den Road, Town Hall, Brooklyn, CT 06234. 860-774-9543. Fax: 860-779-3744. M-W 9AM-4:30PM; Th 9AM-6PM; F 9AM-1PM (EST).

Burlington Town

Real Estate Recording—Burlington Town Clerk, 200 Spielman Highway, Burlington, CT 06013. 860-673-2108. Fax: 860-675-9312. 8:30AM-4PM (EST).

Canaan Town

Real Estate Recording—Canaan Town Clerk, 107 Main Street, Town Hall, Canaan, CT 06031. 860-824-0707. Fax: 860-824-4506. 9AM-3PM (EST).

Canterbury Town

Real Estate Recording—Canterbury Town Clerk, 45 Westminster Road, Town Hall, P.O. Box 27, Canterbury, CT 06331. 860-546-9377. Fax: 860-546-7805. 9:30AM-4:30PM M-W; 9:30AM-7PM Th; 9:30AM-2PM F (EST).

Canton Town

Real Estate Recording—Canton Town Clerk, 4 Market Street, Collinsville, CT 06022. 860-693-7870. Fax: 860-693-7840. 8:30AM-4:30PM (EST).

Chaplin Town

Real Estate Recording—Chaplin Town Clerk, 495 Phoenixville Road, Town Hall, Chaplin, CT 06235. 860-455-9455. Fax: 860-455-0027. 9AM-3PM M,Th,F; 9AM-1PM, 7-9PM T; (EST).

Cheshire Town

Real Estate Recording—Cheshire Town Clerk, 84 South Main Street, Town Hall, Cheshire, CT 06410. 203-271-6601. 8:30AM-4PM (Recording until 3:30PM) (EST).

Chester Town

Real Estate Recording—Chester Town Clerk, 65 Main Street, Chester, CT 06412. 860-526-0006. Fax: 860-526-0014. 9AM-Noon, 1-4PM M,W,Th; 9AM-Noon, 1-7PM T; 9AM-Noon F (EST).

Clinton Town

Real Estate Recording—Clinton Town Clerk, 54 East Main Street, Clinton, CT 06413. 860-669-9101. 9AM-4PM (EST).

Colchester Town

Real Estate Recording—Colchester Town Clerk, 127 Norwich Avenue, Colchester, CT 06415. 860-537-7215. Fax:

860-537-0547. 8:30AM-4:30PM M-W & F; 8:30-7PM Th (EST).

Colebrook Town

Real Estate Recording—Colebrook Town Clerk, 558 Colebrook Road, Town Hall, Colebrook, CT 06021. 860-379-3359. Fax: 860-379-7215. (EST).

Columbia Town

Real Estate Recording—Columbia Town Clerk, 323 Jonathan Trumbull Hwy, Columbia, CT 06237. 860-228-3284. Fax: 860-228-1952. 8:30AM-3PM M-W; 9AM-7PM Th; 8AM-Noon (EST).

Cornwall Town

Real Estate Recording—Cornwall Town Clerk, 26 Pine St., Cornwall, CT 06753. 860-672-2709. 9AM-4PM M-Th (EST).

Coventry Town

Real Estate Recording—Coventry Town Clerk, 1712 Main Street, Coventry, CT 06238. 860-742-7966. Fax: 860-742-8911.

Cromwell Town

Real Estate Recording—Cromwell Town Clerk, 41 West Street, Cromwell, CT 06416. 860-632-3440. Fax: 860-635-5741. 8:30AM-4PM (EST).

Danbury City

Real Estate Recording—Danbury Town Clerk, 155 Deer Hill Avenue, City Hall, Danbury, CT 06810. 203-797-4531. 8:30AM-4:30PM (EST).

Darien Town

Real Estate Recording—Darien Town Clerk, 2 Renshaw Road, Darien, CT 06820. 203-656-7307. 8:30AM-4:30PM (EST).

Deep River Town

Real Estate Recording—Deep River Town Clerk, 174 Main Street, Town Hall, Deep River, CT 06417. 860-526-6024. Fax: 860-526-6023. 9AM-Noon,1-4PM (EST).

Derby City

Real Estate Recording—Derby Town Clerk, 35 Fifth Street, Derby, CT 06418. 203-736-1462. 9AM-5PM (EST).

Durham Town

Real Estate Recording—Durham Town Clerk, 30 Town House Road, Town Hall, Durham, CT 06422. 860-349-3452. Fax: 860-349-8391. 9AM-4:30PM (EST).

East Granby Town

Real Estate Recording—East Granby Town Clerk, 9 Center Street, Town Hall, East Granby, CT 06026. 860-653-6528. Fax: 860-653-4017. 8:30AM-Noon, 1-4PM M-Th; 8:30am-1PM F (EST).

East Haddam Town

Real Estate Recording—East Haddam Town Clerk, Goodspeed Plaza, Town Office Building. PO Box K, East Haddam, CT 06423. 860-873-5027. 9AM-Noon, 1-4PM M,T,W,Th; 9AM-Noon F (T open until 7PM) (EST).

East Hampton Town

Real Estate Recording—East Hampton Town Clerk, 20 East High Street, Town Hall, East Hampton, CT 06424. 860-267-2519. Fax: 860-267-1027. 8AM-4PM M,W,Th; 8AM-7:30PM T; 8:30AM-12:30PM F (EST).

East Hartford Town

Real Estate Recording—East Hartford Town Clerk, 740 Main Street, East Hartford, CT 06108. 860-291-7230. Fax: 860-289-0831. 8:30AM-4:30PM (EST).

East Haven Town

Real Estate Recording—East Haven Town Clerk, 250 Main Street, East Haven, CT 06512. 203-468-3201. Fax: 203-468-3372. 8:30AM-4:15PM (EST).

East Lyme Town

Real Estate Recording—East Lyme Town Clerk, 108 Pennsylvania Avenue, Niantic, CT 06357. 860-739-6931. Fax: 860-739-6930. 8:30AM-4:30PM (EST).

East Windsor Town

Real Estate Recording—East Windsor Town Clerk, 11 Rye Street, Town Hall, Broad Brook, CT 06016. 860-623-9467. 8:30-4:30PM M,T,W; 8:30AM-7:30PM Th; 8:30AM-12:30PM F (EST).

Eastford Town

Real Estate Recording—Eastford Town Clerk, 16 Westford Road, Eastford, CT 06242. 860-974-1885. Fax: 860-974-0624. 10AM-Noon, 1-4PM T,W (EST).

Easton Town

Real Estate Recording—Easton Town Clerk, 225 Center Road, Easton, CT 06612. 203-268-6291. Fax: 203-261-6080. 8:30AM-4:30PM (EST).

Ellington Town

Real Estate Recording—Ellington Town Clerk, 55 Main Street, PO Box 187, Ellington, CT 06029. 860-875-3190. Fax: 860-875-0788. 9AM-7PM M; 9AM-4:30PM T-F (EST).

Enfield Town

Real Estate Recording—Enfield Town Clerk, 820 Enfield Street, Enfield, CT 06082. 860-253-6440. Fax: 860-253-6310. 9AM-5PM (EST).

Essex Town

Real Estate Recording—Essex Town Clerk, 29 West Avenue, Essex, CT 06426. 860-767-4344. 9AM-4PM (EST).

Fairfield County

Real Estate Recording—There is no real estate recording at the county level in Connecticut. For real estate recording, you must determine the town or city where the property is located.

Felony, Civil Actions Over $2,500—Fairfield Superior Court, 1061 Main St Attn: criminal or civil, Bridgeport, CT 06604. 203-579-6527. 9AM-5PM (EST). Access by: Mail, in person.

Danbury Superior Court, 146 White St, Danbury, CT 06810. 203-797-4400. 9AM-1PM, 2:30-4PM (EST). Access by: Mail, in person.

Stamford-Norwalk Superior Court, 123 Hoyt St, Stamford, CT 06905. Civil: 203-965-5307. Criminal: 203-965-5208. 9AM-Noon, 1:30PM-4PM (EST). Access by: Phone, mail, in person.

Misdemeanor, Eviction, Small Claims—Geographical Area Court #2, 172 Golden Hill St, Bridgeport, CT 06604. 203-579-6560. 9AM-5PM (EST). Access by: In person only.

Geographical Area Court #3, 146 White St, Danbury, CT 06810. 203-797-4400. 9AM-5PM (EST). Access by: Mail, in person. In person search results returned by mail only.

Geographical Area Court #20, 17 Belden Ave, Norwalk, CT 06850. 203-846-3237. 9AM-5PM (EST). Access by: Mail, in person. In person search results mailed back.

Probate—Bethel Probate Court, Town Hall, 5 Library Place, Bethel, CT 06801. 203-794-8508. Fax: 203-794-8552. (EST). Access by:

Bridgeport Probate District, 202 State St McLevy Hall, Bridgeport, CT 06604. 203-333-4165. 9AM-4PM (EST). Access by: Mail, in person.

Brookfield Probate Court, PO Box 5192, Brookfield, CT 06804-5192. 203-775-3700. 8:30AM-1:30PM M-Thu, (And by appointment) (EST). Access by:

Danbury Probate Court, 155 Deer Hill Ave, Danbury, CT 06810. 203-797-4521. Fax: 203-796-1526. 8:30AM-4:30PM (EST). Access by: Mail, in person.

Darien Probate Court, Town Hall, 2 Renshaw Rd, Darien, CT 06820. 203-656-7342. Fax: 203-656-7385. 9AM-12:30PM, 1:30PM-4:30PM M-F, 9AM-12:30PM Fri July-Labor Day (EST). Access by:

Fairfield Probate Court, Independence Hall, Fairfield, CT 06430. 203-256-3041. Fax: 203-256-3080. 9AM-5PM M-F, 9AM-4:30PM (July-Aug) (EST). Access by:

Greenwich Probate Court, PO Box 2540, Greenwich, CT 06836. 203-622-7880. Fax: 203-662-6451. 9AM-4:30PM M-F, 9AM-12PM Fri (July-Aug) (EST). Access by:

New Canaan Probate Court, PO Box 326, 77 Main St, New Canaan, CT 06840. 203-972-7500. Fax: 203-966-5555. 8:30AM-1PM 2-4:30PM M-F, (8:30AM-Noon Fri July-Aug) (EST). Access by: Mail, in person.

New Fairfield Probate Court, Town Hall, New Fairfield, CT 06810. 203-746-8160. Fax: 203-746-1250. 9AM-12PM Wed-Thu (EST). Access by: In person only.

Newtown Probate Court, Edmond Town Hall, 45 Main St, Newtown, CT 06470. 203-270-4280. Fax: 203-270-4205. 8:30AM-Noon,1-4:30PM (EST). Access by: Mail.

Norwalk Probate Court, 125 East Ave, PO Box 2009, Norwalk, CT 06852-2009. 203-854-7737. Fax: 203-854-7817. 9AM-4:30PM M-F (And by appointment) (EST). Access by:

Redding Probate Court, PO Box 1125, Redding, CT 06875-1125. 203-938-2326. Fax: 203-938-8816. 9AM-1PM (EST). Access by: Mail, in person.

Ridgefield Probate Court, Town Hall, 400 Main St, Ridgefield, CT 06877. 203-431-2776. Fax: 203-431-2772. 9AM-5PM M-F, 9AM-12PM (July-Aug) (EST). Access by:

Shelton Probate Court, PO Box 127, 40 White St, Shelton, CT 06484. 203-924-8462. Fax: 203-924-8943. 9AM-Noon, 1-4:30PM (EST). Access by: Mail, in person.

Sherman Probate Court, Mallory Town Hall, Sherman, CT 06784. 860-355-1821. Fax: 860-355-6943. 9AM-Noon Tue (And by appointment) (EST). Access by: Mail, in person.

Stamford Probate Court, 888 Washington Blvd, 8th Floor, PO Box 10152, Stamford, CT 06904-2152. 203-323-2149. Fax: 203-964-1830. 9AM-4PM (EST). Access by:

Stratford Probate Court, Town Hall, 2725 Main St, Stratford, CT 06497. 203-385-4023. Fax: 203-375-6253. 9:30AM-4:30PM (EST). Access by:

Trumbull Probate Court, Town Hall, Trumbull, CT 06611. 203-452-5068. Fax: 203-452-5038. 9AM-4:30PM (EST). Access by: Mail, in person.

Westport Probate Court, Town Hall, 110 Myrtle Ave, Westport, CT 06880. 203-226-8311. Fax: 203-341-1153. 9AM-4:30PM (EST). Access by:

Fairfield Town

Real Estate Recording—Fairfield Town Clerk, 611 Old Post Road, Fairfield, CT 06430. 203-256-3090. Fax: 203-256-3114. 8:30AM-5PM (8:30AM-4:30PM Third M June-August) (EST).

Farmington Town

Real Estate Recording—Farmington Town Clerk, 1 Monteith Drive, Farmington, CT 06032. 860-673-8247. Fax: 860-675-7140. 8:30AM-4:30PM (EST).

Franklin Town

Real Estate Recording—Franklin Town Clerk, 7 Meeting House Hill Road, Town Hall, North Franklin, CT 06254. 860-642-7352. Fax: 860-642-6606. 9AM-4PM M-Th; 6PM-8PM T (EST).

Glastonbury Town

Real Estate Recording—Glastonbury Town Clerk, 2155 Main Street, Glastonbury, CT 06033. 860-652-7616. Fax: 860-652-7610. 8AM-4:30PM (EST).

Goshen Town

Real Estate Recording—Goshen Town Clerk, 42 North Street, Town Office Building, Goshen, CT 06756. 860-491-3647. Fax: 860-491-6028. 9AM-Noon,1-4PM (EST).

Granby Town

Real Estate Recording—Granby Town Clerk, 15 North Granby Road, Granby, CT 06035. 860-653-8949. 9AM-Noon,1-4PM (EST).

Greenwich Town

Real Estate Recording—Greenwich Town Clerk, 101 Field Point Road, Town Hall, Greenwich, CT 06836. 203-622-7897. 8AM-4PM (EST).

Griswold Town

Real Estate Recording—Griswold Town Clerk, 32 School Street, Jewett City, CT 06351. 860-376-7064. Fax: 860-376-7070. 8:30AM-4PM M,T,Th,F; 8:30AM-Noon W (EST).

Groton Town

Real Estate Recording—Groton Town Clerk, 45 Fort Hill Road, Groton, CT 06340. 860-441-6642. 8:30AM-4:30PM M-W & F; 9AM-4:30PM Th (EST).

Guilford Town

Real Estate Recording—Guilford Town Clerk, 31 Park Street, Town Hall, Guilford, CT 06437. 203-453-8001. 8:30AM-4:30PM (EST).

Haddam Town

Real Estate Recording—Haddam Town Clerk, 30 Field Park Drive, Town Hall, Haddam, CT 06438. 860-345-8531. Fax: 860-345-3730. 9AM-4PM M,T,W,; 9AM-7PM Th; 9AM-Noon F (EST).

Hamden Town

Real Estate Recording—Hamden Town Clerk, 2372 Whitney Avenue, Memorial Town Hall, Hamden, CT 06518. 203-287-2510. Fax: 203-287-2518. 9AM-4PM (EST).

Hampton Town

Real Estate Recording—Hampton Town Clerk, Town Office Building, 164 Main St., Hampton, CT 06247. 860-455-9132. Fax: 860-455-0517. 9AM-4PM T,Th; 9AM-Noon Sat (EST).

Hartford City

Real Estate Recording—Hartford City Clerk, 550 Main Street, Hartford, CT 06103. 860-543-8580. Fax: 860-722-8041. 8:30AM-4:30 PM (EST).

Hartford County

Real Estate Recording—There is no real estate recording at the county level in Connecticut. For recording, you must determine the town or city where the property is located.

Felony, Civil Actions Over $2,500—New Britain Superior Court, 177 Columbus Blvd, New Britain, CT 06051. Civil: 860-827-7133. Criminal: 860-827-7104. 9AM-5PM (EST). Access by: Mail, in person.

Misdemeanor, Eviction, Small Claims—Geographical Area Court #17, 131 N Main St, Bristol, CT 06010. 860-582-8111. 9AM-1PM, 2:30PM-4PM (EST). Access by: Phone, mail, in person.

Geographical Area Court #13, 111 Phoenix, Enfield, CT 06082. 860-741-3727. 9AM-1PM, 2:30PM-4PM (EST). Access by: Mail, in person.

Geographical Area Court #14, 101 LaFayette St, Hartford, CT 06106. 860-566-1630. 1PM-2:30PM (EST). Access by: Phone, mail, in person.

Geographical Area Court #12, 410 Center St, Manchester, CT 06040. 860-647-1091. 9AM-5PM (EST). Access by: Mail, in person. In person search results returned by mail only.

Geographical Area Court #15, 125 Columbus Blvd, New Britain, CT 06051. 860-827-7106. 8:30AM-1PM, 2:30PM-4PM (EST). Access by: Phone, mail, in person. Phone access is limited to the hours 2:30PM-4PM.

Geographical Area Court #16, 105 Raymond Rd, West Hartford, CT 06107. 860-236-4551. Civil: 860-236-5166. Criminal: 860-236-4551. Fax: 860-236-9311. 9AM-1PM, 2:30-4PM (EST). Access by: Mail, in person.

Civil Actions Over $2,500—Hartford Superior Court-Civil, 95 Washington St, Hartford, CT 06106. 860-548-2700. Fax: 860-548-2711. 9AM-5PM (EST). Access by: Mail, in person.

Felony—Hartford Superior Court-Criminal, 101 LaFayette St, Hartford, CT 06106. 860-566-1634. 9AM-5PM (EST). Access by: Mail, in person.

Probate—Avon Probate Court, 60 W Main St, Avon, CT 06001-0578. 860-677-2634. Fax: 860-677-8428. 9AM-Noon (EST). Access by: Mail, in person.

Bloomfield Probate Court, Town Hall, 800 Bloomfield Ave, Bloomfield, CT 06002. 860-769-3598. Fax: 860-243-8971. 9AM-1PM, 2AM-4:30PM (EST). Access by:

Suffield Probate Court, 83 Mountain Rd, PO Box 234, Brendan Heights, CT 06078. 860-668-3835. Fax: 860-668-3898. 8AM-12:30PM M & F, 8AM-3PM T-Th (EST). Access by: Mail, in person.

Bristol Probate Court, City Hall, 111 N Main St, Bristol, CT 06010. 860-584-7650. Fax: 860-584-3818. 9AM-5PM (EST). Access by:

Burlington Probate Court, Town Hall, Route 4, Burlington, CT 06013. 860-673-2108. 9AM-1PM Fri (EST). Access by:

Canton Probate Court, Town Hall, Main St, Collinsville, CT 06022. 860-693-8684. 8:30AM-1:30PM Tue-Fri (And by appointment) (EST). Access by:

East Granby Probate Court, PO Box 542, East Granby, CT 06026. 860-653-3434. Fax: 860-653-4017. 9AM-12PM Tue-Thu (And by appointment) (EST). Access by:

East Hartford Probate Court, Town Hall, 740 Main St, East Hartford, CT 06108. 860-291-7278. 9AM-4:30PM (EST). Access by:

Enfield Probate Court, 820 Enfield St, Enfield, CT 06082. 860-745-5065. Fax: 860-745-1550. 9AM-4:30PM (EST). Access by:

Farmington Probate Court, One Monteith, Farmington, CT 06032. 860-673-8250. Fax: 860-673-8262. 9AM-4PM (EST). Access by:

Glastonbury Probate Court, 2155 Main St, PO Box 6523, Glastonbury, CT 06033. 860-633-3723. Fax: 860-659-8292. 9AM-12:30PM 1:30PM-4:30PM M-Thu, 12AM-4:30PM Fri (EST). Access by: Mail, in person.

Granby Probate Court, 15 N Granby Rd, Town Hall, Granby, CT 06035. 860-653-8944. Fax: 860-653-4769. 9AM-12PM Tue, Wed, Fri (EST). Access by: Mail, in person.

Hartford Probate Court, 10 Prospect St, Hartford, CT 06103. 860-522-1813. Fax: 860-724-1503. 9AM-4PM (EST). Access by:

Manchester Probate Court, 66 Center St, Manchester, CT 06040. 860-647-3227. Fax: 860-647-3226. 8:30AM-12PM 1AM-4:30PM M-F, 6:30PM-8PM Thu (By appointment) (EST). Access by:

Marlborough Probate Court, PO Box 29, N Main St, Marlborough, CT 06447. 860-295-9574. Fax: 860-295-0317. By appointment (EST). Access by:

Berlin Probate Court, 177 Columbus Blvd, PO Box 400, New Britain, CT 06050-0400. 860-826-2696. Fax: 860-826-2695. 9AM-4PM (EST). Access by: Mail, in person.

Newington Probate Court, 66 Cedar Street, Newington, CT 06111. 860-665-1285. 9AM-4PM (EST). Access by:

Simsbury Probate Court, PO Box 495, 933 Hopmeadow St, Simsbury, CT 06070. 860-658-3200. Fax: 860-658-3206. 9AM-1PM, 2-4:30PM M-F (And by appointment) (EST). Access by:

East Windsor Probate Court, Town Hall, 1540 Sullivan Ave, South Windsor, CT 06074. 860-644-2511. Fax: 860-644-3781. 8AM-1PM M-Th, Noon-4:30PM Fri (And by appointment) (EST). Access by: Mail, in person.

Southington Probate Court, PO Box 165, Southington, CT 06489. 860-276-6253. Fax: 860-628-8669. 8:30AM-Noon, 1-4:30PM (EST). Access by: In person only.

West Hartford Probate Court, 50 S Main St, West Hartford, CT 06107. 860-523-3174. Fax: 860-236-8352. 8:30AM-4:30PM (EST). Access by:

Hartland Probate Court, PO Box 100, West Hartland, CT 06091. 860-653-9710. 10AM-1PM Mon-Fri (And by appointment) (EST). Access by: Mail, in person.

Windsor Locks Probate Court, Town Office Bldg, 50 Church St, Windsor Locks, CT 06096. 860-627-1450. Fax: 860-292-1121. 9AM-2PM Mon-Thu (EST). Access by:

Windsor Probate Court, PO Box 342, 275 Broad St, Windsor, CT 06095. 860-285-1975. Fax: 860-285-1909. 8:30AM-4:30PM M-Th; 8:30AM-Noon Fri (EST). Access by: Mail, in person.

Hartland Town

Real Estate Recording—Hartland Town Clerk, Town Office Building, 22 South Road, East Hartland, CT 06027. 860-653-3542. Fax: 860-653-7919. 1-4PM M,T,W (T open 7-8PM) (EST).

Harwinton Town

Real Estate Recording—Harwinton Town Clerk, 100 Bentley Drive, Town Hall, Harwinton, CT 06791. 860-485-9613. Fax: 860-485-0051. 8:30AM-4PM (EST).

Hebron Town

Real Estate Recording—Hebron Town Clerk, 15 Gilead Street, Hebron, CT 06248. 860-228-9406. Fax: 860-228-4859. 8AM-4PM M-W; 8AM-7PM Th; 8AM-12:30PM F (EST).

Kent Town

Real Estate Recording—Kent Town Clerk, 41 Kent Green Blvd., Town Hall, Kent, CT 06757. 860-927-3433. 9AM-Noon, 1-4PM (EST).

Killingly Town

Real Estate Recording—Killingly Town Clerk, 172 Main Street, Danielson, CT 06239. 860-779-5307. Fax: 860-779-5394. 8:30AM-4:30PM (EST).

Killingworth Town

Real Estate Recording—Killingworth Town Clerk, 323 Route 81, Killingworth, CT 06419. 860-663-1616. Fax: 860-663-3305. 9AM-Noon,1-4PM (EST).

Lebanon Town

Real Estate Recording—Lebanon Town Clerk, 579 Exeter Road, Town Hall, Lebanon, CT 06249. 860-642-7319. 9AM-4PM M,T,F; 9AM-7PM Th (EST).

Ledyard Town

Real Estate Recording—Ledyard Town Clerk, 741 Col. Ledyard Highway, Ledyard, CT 06339. 860-464-8740. Fax: 860-464-1126. 8:30AM-4:30PM (EST).

Lisbon Town

Real Estate Recording—Lisbon Town Clerk, 1 Newent Road, RD 2 Town Hall, Lisbon, CT 06351. 860-376-2708. Fax: 860-376-6545. 9AM-4PM M,T,Th; 9AM-8PM W; 9AM-2PM F; 9AM-Noon Sat (EST).

Litchfield County

Real Estate Recording—There is no real estate recording at the county level in Connecticut. For recording, you must determine the town or city in which the property is located.

Felony, Civil Actions Over $2,500—Litchfield Superior Court, PO Box 247, 15 West St, Litchfield, CT 06759. 860-567-0885. Fax: 860-567-4779. 9AM-1PM, 2:30-4PM (EST). Access by: Fax, mail, in person.

Misdemeanor, Eviction, Small Claims—Geographical Area Court #18, 80 Doyle Rd (PO Box 667), Bantam, CT 06750. 860-567-3942. 9AM-1PM; 2:30-4PM (EST). Access by: Mail, in person.

Probate—Canaan Probate Court, PO Box 905, Town Hall, Canaan, CT 06018-0905. 860-824-7114. Fax: 860-824-9922. 9AM-1PM M-F (And by appointment) (EST). Access by:

Cornwall Probate Court, PO Box 157, Town Office Bldg, Cornwall, CT 06753-0157. 860-672-2677. Fax: 860-672-4959. 9AM-12PM Tue-Thu (And by appointment) (EST). Access by: Mail, in person.

Harwinton Probate Court, Town Hall, 100 Bently Dr, Harwinton, CT 06791. 860-485-1403. Fax: 860-485-0051. 2AM-4PM Tue-Thu, Fri afternoon by appointment (EST). Access by:

Kent Probate Court, PO Box 185, Town Hall, Kent, CT 06757. 860-927-3729. Fax: 860-927-1313. 9AM-12PM Tue & Thu (And by appointment) (EST). Access by: Mail, in person.

Litchfield Probate Court, West St, PO Box 505, Litchfield, CT 06759. 860-567-8065. Fax: 860-567-7552. 9AM-1PM (EST). Access by: Mail, in person.

New Hartford Probate Court, PO Box 308, Town Hall, New Hartford, CT 06057. 860-379-3254. By appointment (EST). Access by:

New Milford Probate Court, 10 Main St, New Milford, CT 06776. 860-355-6029. Fax: 860-355-6002. 9AM-12PM 1PM-5PM M-F, 9AM-12PM Fri (July-Aug) (EST). Access by: Mail, in person.

Norfolk Probate Court, PO Box 648, Marple Ave, Norfolk, CT 06058. 860-542-5134. Fax: 860-542-5876. 9AM-12PM Tue & Thu (And by appointment) (EST). Access by:

Barkhamsted Probate Court, 67 Ripley Hill Rd, Pleasant Valley, CT 06063. 860-379-8665. Fax: 860-379-9284. 10AM-1PM M-W (And by appointment) (EST). Access by: Mail, in person.

Roxbury Probate Court, Town Hall, 29 North St, Roxbury, CT 06783. 860-354-1184. Fax: 860-355-4550. 9AM-3PM T-Th (EST). Access by: Mail, in person.

Salisbury Probate Court, PO Box 525, Town Hall, Salisbury, CT 06068. 860-435-5183. Fax: 860-435-5172. 9Am-12PM M-F (And by appointment) (EST). Access by:

Sharon Probate Court, PO Box 1177, Sharon, CT 06069. 860-364-5514. Fax: 860-364-5789. 3PM-5PM M-W & F (and by appointment) (EST). Access by: In person only.

Plymouth Probate Court, 80 Main St, Terryville, CT 06786. 860-585-4014. 9AM-1PM (EST). Access by:

Thomaston Probate Court, PO Box 136, Town Hall Bldg 158 Main St, Thomaston, CT 06787. 860-283-4874. Fax: 860-284-1013. 9AM-Noon M-F (And by appointment) (EST). Access by: Mail, in person.

Torrington Probate Court, Municipal Bldg, 140 Main St, Torrington, CT 06790. 860-871-3640. Fax: 860-871-3663. 12:30-4:30PM M; 9AM-Noon W & F; 5:30-8:30PM Th (EST). Access by:

Washington Probate Court, Town Hall, PO Box 295 Washington Depot, Washington Depot, CT 06794. 860-868-7974. Fax: 860-868-9685. 9AM-Noon, 1-3PM M,W,F (EST). Access by: Mail, in person.

Watertown Probate Court, 37 DeForest St, PO Box 7, Town Hall, Watertown, CT 06795. 860-945-5237. Fax: 860-596-7975. 9AM-Noon, 1-3PM (EST). Access by:

Winchester Probate Court, PO Box 625, 338 Main St, Winsted, CT 06098. 860-379-5576. Fax: 860-738-7053. 9AM-12PM 1PM-4PM (EST). Access by:

Woodbury Probate Court, PO Box 84, 281 Main St, South, Woodbury, CT 06798. 203-263-2417. Fax: 203-263-2748. 9AM-Noon, 1-4PM Thurs (EST). Access by: Mail, in person.

Litchfield Town

Real Estate Recording—Litchfield Town Clerk, 74 West Street, Town Office Building, Litchfield, CT 06759. 860-567-7561. 9AM-4:30PM (EST).

Lyme Town

Real Estate Recording—Lyme Town Clerk, 480 Hamburg Rd., Town Hall, Lyme, CT 06371. 860-434-7733. Fax: 860-434-2989. 9AM-4PM (EST).

Madison Town

Real Estate Recording—Madison Town Clerk, 8 Campus Dr., Madison, CT 06443. 203-245-5672. Fax: 203-245-5613. 8:30AM-4PM (EST).

Manchester Town

Real Estate Recording—Manchester Town Clerk, 41 Center Street, Manchester, CT 06040. 860-647-3037. 8:30AM-5PM (EST).

Mansfield Town

Real Estate Recording—Mansfield Town Clerk, 4 South Eagleville Road, Mansfield, CT 06268. 860-429-3302. 8:30AM-4:30PM (EST).

Marlborough Town

Real Estate Recording—Marlborough Town Clerk, 26 North Main Street, Marlborough, CT 06447. 860-295-6206. Fax: 860-295-0317. 8AM-4:30PM M-Th; 8AM-7PM T; 8AM-Noon F (EST).

Meriden City

Real Estate Recording—Meriden City Clerk, 142 East Main Street, Meriden, CT 06450. 203-630-4030. Fax: 203-630-4059. 9AM-7PM M; 9AM-5PM T-F (EST).

Middlebury Town

Real Estate Recording—Middlebury Town Clerk, Town Hall, 1212 Whittemore Rd., Middlebury, CT 06762. 203-758-2557. 9AM-Noon,1-5PM (EST).

Middlefield Town

Real Estate Recording—Middlefield Town Clerk, 393 Jackson Hill Road, Middlefield, CT 06455. 860-349-7116. Fax: 860-349-7115. 9AM-5PM M; 9AM-4PM T-Th; 9AM-3PM F (EST).

Middlesex County

Real Estate Recording—There is no real estate recording at the county level in Connecticut. You must determine the town or city where the property is located.

Civil—Middlesex Superior Court-Civil, 1 Court St, 2nd Floor, Middletown, CT 06457-3374. 860-343-6400. Fax: 860-343-6423. 9AM-1PM, 2:30-4PM; (EST). Access by: Mail, in person.

Felony—Middlesex Superior Court-Criminal, 1 Court St, 2nd Floor, Middletown, CT 06457. 860-344-3091. 9AM-5PM (EST). Access by: Mail, in person.

Probate—Saybrook Probate Court, PO Box 628, 65 Main St, Chester, CT 06412. 860-526-0007. Fax: 860-526-0014. 9AM-Noon, 1-4PM M-Th; 9AM-Noon F (EST). Access by:

Clinton Probate Court, 54 E Main St, Clinton, CT 06413-0130. 860-669-6447. Fax: 860-664-4469. 9AM-12PM, 1-4PM (EST). Access by: In person only.

Deep River Probate Court, Town Hall, 174 Main St, Deep River, CT 06417. 860-526-5266. 10AM-12PM, 2PM-4PM Tue & Thu (And by appointment) (EST). Access by:

East Haddam Probate Court, Godspeed Plaza, PO Box 217, East Haddam, CT 06423. 860-873-5028. Fax: 860-873-5025. 10AM-2PM M-F (And by appointment) (EST). Access by:

Essex Probate Court, Town Hall, 29 West Ave, Essex, CT 06426. 860-767-4347. Fax: 860-767-8509. 9AM-1PM M-F (And by appointment) (EST). Access by: Mail, in person.

Haddam Probate Court, 30 Field Park Dr, Haddam, CT 06438. 860-345-8531. Fax: 860-345-3730. 10AM-3PM Tue, Wed, Thu (EST). Access by:

Killingworth Probate Court, 323 Routew 81, Killingworth, CT 06419. 860-663-1276. Fax: 860-663-3305. 9AM-Noon Mon, Wed, Fri (And by appointment) (EST). Access by: Mail, in person.

Middletown Probate Court, 94 Court St, Middletown, CT 06457. 860-347-7424. 8:30AM-4:30PM M-F, 6PM-7:40PM Tue (Sept-May) (EST). Access by:

Old Saybrook Probate Court, PO Box 791, 302 Main St, Old Saybrook, CT 06475. 860-395-3128. Fax: 860-395-3125. 9AM-1PM or by appointment (EST). Access by:

Portland Probate Court, PO Box 71, 265 Main St, Portland, CT 06480. 860-342-6739. Fax: 860-342-0001. 9AM-12PM Mon-Fri, 7AM-8:40PM Thu (EST). Access by:

Westbrook Probate Court, PO Box G, Westbrook, CT 06498. 860-399-5661. 2-5:30PM (EST). Access by: Mail, in person.

Middletown City

Real Estate Recording—Middletown Town Clerk, 245 DeKoven Drive, Middletown, CT 06457. 860-344-3459. Fax: 860-344-3591. 8:30AM-4:30PM (EST).

Milford City

Real Estate Recording—Milford City Clerk, 70 West River Street, Milford, CT 06460. 203-783-3210. Fax: 203-876-9872. 8:30AM-5PM (EST).

Monroe Town

Real Estate Recording—Monroe Town Clerk, 7 Fan Hill Road, Monroe, CT 06468. 203-452-5417. Fax: 203-261-6197. 9AM-5PM (EST).

Montville Town

Real Estate Recording—Montville Town Clerk, 310 Norwich-New London Tpke., Town Hall, Uncasville, CT 06382. 860-848-1349. Fax: 860-848-4534. 9AM-5PM (EST).

Morris Town

Real Estate Recording—Morris Town Clerk, 3 East Street, Morris, CT 06763. 860-567-5387. Fax: 860-567-3678. 9AM-Noon, 1-4PM (EST).

Naugatuck Town

Real Estate Recording—Naugatuck Town Clerk, Town Hall, 229 Church Street, Naugatuck, CT 06770. 203-729-4571. Fax: 203-723-8157. 8:30AM-4PM (EST).

New Britain Town

Real Estate Recording—New Britain Town Clerk, 27 W. Main Street, New Britain, CT 06051. 860-826-3344. 8:15AM-3:45PM M-W & F; 8:15AM-6:45PM Th (EST).

New Canaan Town

Real Estate Recording—New Canaan Town Clerk, 77 Main Street, Town Hall, New Canaan, CT 06840. 203-972-2323. Fax: 203-966-0309. 8:30AM-4:30PM (EST).

New Fairfield Town

Real Estate Recording—New Fairfield Town Clerk, Route 39, Town Hall, New Fairfield, CT 06812. 203-746-8110. 8:30AM-5PM T-F; 8:30AM-Noon Sat (EST).

New Hartford Town

Real Estate Recording—New Hartford Town Clerk, 530 Main Street, Town Hall, New Hartford, CT 06057. 860-379-5037. Fax: 860-379-0940. 9AM-Noon, 12:40-4PM M,T,Th; 9AM-Noon, 1PM-6PM W; 9AM-Noon F (EST).

New Haven City

Real Estate Recording—New Haven City Clerk, 200 Orange Street, Room 202, New Haven, CT 06510. 203-946-8339. Fax: 203-946-6974. 9AM-5PM (EST).

New Haven County

Real Estate Recording—There is no real estate recording at the county level in Connecticut. You must determine the town or city in which the property is located.

Felony, Civil Actions Over $2,500—Ansonia-Milford Superior Court, 14 W River St (PO Box 210), Milford, CT 06460. 203-877-4293. 9AM-5PM (EST). Access by: Mail, in person.

New Haven Superior Court, 235 Church St, New Haven, CT 06510. 203-789-7908. Fax: 203-789-6424. 9AM-1PM, 2:30-4PM (EST). Access by: Fax, mail, in person.

Waterbury Superior Court, 300 Grand St, Waterbury, CT 06702. 203-596-4023. Fax: 203-596-4032. 9AM-5PM (EST). Access by: Fax, mail, in person.

Misdemeanor, Eviction, Small Claims—Geographical Area Court #5, 106 Elizabeth St, Derby, CT 06418. 203-735-7438. 9AM-1PM, 2:30PM-4PM (EST). Access by: Mail, in person.

Geographical Area Court #7, 54 W Main St, Meriden, CT 06450. 203-238-6130. Fax: 203-238-6322. 9AM-5PM (EST). Access by: Phone, mail, in person.

Geographical Area Court #22, 14 W River St, Milford, CT 06460. 203-874-0674. 1PM-2:30PM, 4PM-5PM (EST). Access by: Mail, in person.

Geographical Area Court #6, 121 Elm St, New Haven, CT 06510. 203-789-7461. Fax: 203-789-6455. 9AM-5PM (EST). Access by: Mail, in person. In person search results mailed back.

Geographical Area Court #4, 7 Kendrick Ave, Waterbury, CT 06702. Civil: 203-596-4050. Criminal: 203-596-4053. Fax: 203-596-4057. 9AM-5PM (EST). Access by: Phone, mail, in person.

Civil Actions Over $2,500—New Haven Superior Court-Meriden, 54 W Main St, Meriden, CT 06451. 203-238-6666. 9AM-1PM, 2:30-4PM (EST). Access by: Mail, in person.

Probate—Derby Probate Court, PO Box 253, 16 Westford Rd, Ansonia, CT 06401. 203-734-1277. Fax: 203-734-0922. 9AM-4PM (EST). Access by:

Bethany Probate Court, Town Hall, 40 Peck Rd, Bethany, CT 06524. 203-393-3774. Fax: 203-393-0821. 9:30AM-11:30PM Tue & Thu, Appointments between 9:30AM-8PM (EST). Access by:

Branford Probate Court, PO Box 638, 1019 Main St, Branford, CT 06405-0638. 203-488-0318. Fax: 203-481-5561. 9AM-12PM, 1AM-4:30PM (EST). Access by: Mail, in person.

Cheshire Probate Court, 84 S Main St, Cheshire, CT 06410-3193. Fax: 203-271-6664. 8:30AM-12:30PM, 1:30PM-4PM (EST). Access by: Mail, in person.

East Haven Probate Court, 250 Main St, East Haven, CT 06512. 203-468-3895. 9:30AM-1PM 2PM-3:30PM M, 9:30AM-1PM Tu-Wd, 9:30-1PM 2AM-4:30PM (EST). Access by:

Guilford Probate Court, Town Hall, Park St, Guilford, CT 06437. 203-453-8007. 9AM-Noon,1-4PM M,T,Th,F; 9AM-Noon W (EST). Access by: Mail, in person.

Madison Probate Court, PO Box 205, Town Hall, Madison, CT 06443. 203-245-5661. Fax: 203-245-5613. 9AM-3PM M-F (And by appointment) (EST). Access by:

Meriden Probate Court, City Hall, E Main St, Meriden, CT 06450. 203-235-4325. Fax: 203-630-4025. 8:30AM-12PM 1PM-4:30PM (EST). Access by: In person only.

Milford Probate Court, 70 W River St, PO Box 414, Parsons Office Complex, Milford, CT 06460. 203-783-3206. Fax: 203-876-1960. 9AM-5PM (EST). Access by: Mail, in person.

Naugatuck Probate Court, Town Hall, 229 Church St, Naugatuck, CT 06770. 203-729-4571. 9AM-4PM (EST). Access by: Mail, in person.

New Haven Probate Court, PO Box 905, 200 Orange St, 4th Floor, New Haven, CT 06504. 203-777-4880. Fax: 203-777-5962. 9AM-4PM (EST). Access by: Mail.

North Branford Probate Court, PO Box 214, 1599 Foxon Rd, North Branford, CT 06471. 203-481-0829. 9AM-12PM (EST). Access by:

North Haven Probate Court, 18 Church St, North Haven, CT 06473. 203-239-5321. Fax: 203-234-2130. 8:30AM-4:30PM M-Th (EST). Access by:

Orange Probate Court, 525 Orange Center Rd, Orange, CT 06477. 203-891-2160. Fax: 203-891-2161. 9AM-12PM (EST). Access by:

Oxford Probate Court, c/o Town Hall, 486 Oxford Rd, Oxford, CT 06478. 203-888-2543. Fax: 203-888-2136. 7AM-9PM Mon, 1PM-5PM Tue & Wed, 9AM-5PM 7PM-9PM Thu (EST). Access by: Mail, in person.

Southbury Probate Court, Townhall Annex, 421 Main St South, PO Box 674, Southbury, CT 06488. 203-262-0641. Fax: 203-264-9310. 9AM-4:30PM M-F (And by appointment) (EST). Access by: Mail, in person.

Wallingford Probate Court, 45 S Main St, Wallingford, CT 06492. 203-294-2100. Fax: 203-294-2073. 9AM-5PM (EST). Access by:

Waterbury Probate Court, 236 Grand St Chase Bldg, Waterbury, CT 06702. 203-755-1127. Fax: 203-597-0824. 9AM-4:45PM MTWF, 9AM-6PM Thu, 9AM-12PM Sat (EST). Access by:

West Haven Probate Court, PO Box 127, 355 Main St, West Haven, CT 06516. 203-937-3552. Fax: 203-937-3556. 9AM-Noon, 1-4PM; closed 2nd Th of the month (EST). Access by:

Woodbridge Probate Court, Town Hall, 11 Meetinghouse Ln, Woodbridge, CT 06525. 203-389-3410. Fax: 203-289-3480. 3-7PM M, 9AM-1PM W (EST). Access by:

New London City

Real Estate Recording—New London City Clerk, 181 State Street, New London, CT 06320. 860-447-5205. Fax: 860-447-7971. 8:30AM-4PM (EST).

New London County

Real Estate Recording—There is no real estate recording at the county level in Connecticut. You must determine the town or city where the property is located.

Felony, Civil Actions Over $2,500—New London Superior Court, 70 Huntington St, New London, CT 06320. 860-443-5363. 9AM-5PM (EST). Access by: Mail, in person.

Misdemeanor, Eviction, Small Claims—Geographical Area Court #10, 112 Broad St, New London, CT 06320. 860-443-8343. 1:00PM-2:30PM, 4PM-5PM (EST). Access by: Mail, in person.

Geographical Area Court #21, 1 Courthouse Sq, Norwich, CT 06360. 860-889-7338. 1:00PM-2:30PM, 4PM-5PM (EST). Access by: Mail, in person.

Civil Actions Over $2,500—Norwich Superior Court, 1 Courthouse Square, Norwich, CT 06360. 860-887-3515. Fax: 860-885-0509. 9AM-5PM (EST). Access by: Mail, in person.

Probate—Colchester Probate Court, Town Hall, 127 Norwich Ave, Colchester, CT 06415. 860-537-7290. Fax: 860-537-0547. 12:30AM-4:30PM MTTF, 9AM-1PM Wed (and by appointment) (EST). Access by: Mail, in person.

Bozrah Probate Court, 486 Fitchville Rd, Gilman, CT 06336-1000. 860-859-0852. By appointment only (EST). Access by:

Griswold Probate Court, Town Hall, 32 School St, Jewett City, CT 06351. 860-376-0216. Fax: 860-376-9747. 9AM-12PM Wed (And by appointment) (EST). Access by:

Lebanon Probate Court, Town Hall, 579 Exeter Rd, Lebanon, CT 06249. 860-642-7429. Fax: 860-642-7716. 10AM-12PM Tues & Fri (And by appointment) (EST). Access by:

Ledyard Probate Court, PO Box 28, Col Ledyard Hwy (Route 117), Ledyard, CT 06339. 860-464-8740. Fax: 860-464-1126. 9:30AM-12:30PM M-F (And by appointment) (EST). Access by: Mail, in person.

Lyme Probate Court, Town Hall, 480 Hamburg Rd, Lyme, CT 06371. 860-434-7733. Fax: 860-434-2989. 9AM-1PM M-F (And by appointment) (EST). Access by:

New London Probate Court, 181 Captain's Walk Municipal Bldg, PO Box 148, New London, CT 06320. 860-443-7121. Fax: 860-437-8155. 9AM-4PM (EST). Access by:

East Lyme Probate Court, PO Box 519, 108 Pennsylvania Ave, Niantic, CT 06357. 860-739-6931. Fax: 860-739-6930. 8:30AM-12:30PM (EST). Access by:

North Stonington Probate Court, PO Box 204, North Stonington, CT 06359. 860-535-8441. Fax: 860-535-8441. 9AM-Noon M & W; 1-4PM T,Th & F (EST). Access by:

Norwich Probate Court, PO Box 38, City Hall, Norwich, CT 06360. 860-887-2160. Fax: 860-887-2401. 9AM-4:30PM (EST). Access by: Mail, in person.

Old Lyme Probate Court, PO Box 273, 52 Lyme St, Old Lyme, CT 06371. 860-434-1406. Fax: 860-434-9283. 9AM-Noon, 1-4PM (EST). Access by: Mail, in person.

Salem Probate Court, 270 Hartford Rd, Salem, CT 06420-3809. 860-859-3873. Fax: 860-443-5160. By appointment (EST). Access by:

Stonington Probate Court, PO Box 312, 152 Elm St, Stonington, CT 06378. 860-535-5090. Fax: 860-535-0520. 9AM-Noon, 1-4PM (EST). Access by:

Montville Probate Court, 310 Norwich-New London Turnpike, Uncasville, CT 06382. 860-848-9847. Fax: 860-848-4534. 9AM-1PM MTTF, 9AM-6:30PM Wed (EST). Access by: Mail, in person.

New Milford Town

Real Estate Recording—New Milford Town Clerk, 18 Church Street, New Milford, CT 06776. 860-355-6020. Fax: 860-355-6002. 9AM-5PM (EST).

Newington Town

Real Estate Recording—Newington Town Clerk, 131 Cedar Street, Newington, CT 06111. 860-665-8545. 8:30AM-4:30PM (EST).

Newtown Town

Real Estate Recording—Newtown Town Clerk, 45 Main Street, Newtown, CT 06470. 203-270-4210. 8AM-4:30PM (EST).

Norfolk Town

Real Estate Recording—Norfolk Town Clerk, 19 Maple Avenue, Norfolk, CT 06058. 860-542-5679. 9AM-Noon, 1-4PM (EST).

North Branford Town

Real Estate Recording—North Branford Town Clerk, 1599 Foxon Road, North Branford, CT 06471. 203-315-6015. 8:30AM-4:30PM (EST).

North Canaan Town

Real Estate Recording—North Canaan Town Clerk, 100 Pease Street, Town Hall, North Canaan, CT 06018. 860-824-3138. Fax: 860-824-3139. 9:30AM-Noon, 1-4PM (EST).

North Haven Town

Real Estate Recording—North Haven Town Clerk, 18 Church Street, Town Hall, North Haven, CT 06473. 203-239-5321. 8:30AM-4:30PM (EST).

North Stonington Town

Real Estate Recording—North Stonington Town Clerk, 40 Main Street, North Stonington, CT 06359. 860-535-2877. Fax: 860-535-4554. 9AM-Noon; 12:30PM-4PM (EST).

Norwalk City

Real Estate Recording—Norwalk Town Clerk, 125 East Avenue, City Hall, Norwalk, CT 06851. 203-854-7746. 8:30AM-5PM (EST).

Norwich City

Real Estate Recording—Norwich City Clerk, 100 Broadway, City Hall, Room 214, Norwich, CT 06360. 860-823-3732. Fax: 860-823-3790. 8:30AM-4:30PM (EST).

Old Lyme Town

Real Estate Recording—Old Lyme Town Clerk, 52 Lyme Street, Town Hall, Old Lyme, CT 06371. 860-434-1655. Fax: 860-434-9283. 9AM-Noon, 1-4PM (EST).

Old Saybrook Town

Real Estate Recording—Old Saybrook Town Clerk, 302 Main Street, Old Saybrook, CT 06475. 860-395-3135. Fax: 860-395-5014. 8:30AM-4:30PM (EST).

Orange Town

Real Estate Recording—Orange Town Clerk, Town Hall, 617 Orange Center Rd., Orange, CT 06477. 203-891-2122. Fax: 203-891-2185. 8:30AM-4:30PM (EST).

Oxford Town

Real Estate Recording—Oxford Town Clerk, 486 Oxford Road, Oxford, CT 06478. 203-888-2543. 9AM-5PM M-Th; 7-9PM Mon & Th (EST).

Plainfield Town

Real Estate Recording—Plainfield Town Clerk, 8 Community Avenue, Town Hall, Plainfield, CT 06374. 860-564-4075. 8:30AM-4:30PM M,T,W,F; 8:30AM-6:30PM Th (EST).

Plainville Town

Real Estate Recording—Plainville Town Clerk, 1 Central Square, Municipal Center, Plainville, CT 06062. 860-793-0221. 8:30AM-4:30PM (EST).

Plymouth Town

Real Estate Recording—Plymouth Town Clerk, 80 Main Street, Town Hall, Terryville, CT 06786. 860-585-4039. Fax: 860-585-4015. 8:30-4:30PM (EST).

Pomfret Town

Real Estate Recording—Pomfret Town Clerk, 5 Haven Road, Pomfret Center, CT 06259. 860-974-0343. Fax: 860-974-3950. 9AM-4PM (EST).

Portland Town

Real Estate Recording—Portland Town Clerk, 265 Main Street, Portland, CT 06480. 860-342-6743. Fax: 860-342-0001. 9AM-4:30PM (EST).

Preston Town

Real Estate Recording—Preston Town Clerk, 389 Route 2, Town Hall, Preston, CT 06365. 860-887-9821. Fax: 860-885-1905. 9AM-Noon, 12:30PM-4:30PM T-F; Th until 7:30 (EST).

Prospect Town

Real Estate Recording—Prospect Town Clerk, 36 Center Street, Prospect, CT 06712. 203-758-4461. Fax: 203-758-4466. 9AM-4PM (EST).

Putnam Town

Real Estate Recording—Putnam Town Clerk, 126 Church Street, Putnam, CT 06260. 860-963-6807. Fax: 860-963-6814. 8:30AM-Noon,1-4:30PM (EST).

Redding Town

Real Estate Recording—Redding Town Clerk, Route 107, 100 Hill Rd., Town Office Building, Redding, CT 06875. 203-938-2377. Fax: 203-938-8816. 9AM-4:30PM (EST).

Ridgefield Town

Real Estate Recording—Ridgefield Town Clerk, 400 Main Street, Ridgefield, CT 06877. 203-431-2783. Fax: 203-431-2722. 9AM-5PM (EST).

Rocky Hill Town

Real Estate Recording—Rocky Hill Town Clerk, 699 Old Main Street, Rocky Hill, CT 06067. 860-258-2705. 8:30AM-4:30PM (EST).

Roxbury Town

Real Estate Recording—Roxbury Town Clerk, 29 North St., Roxbury, CT 06783. 860-354-3328. Fax: 860-355-4450. 9AM-Noon, 1-4PM T & Th; 9AM-Noon F (EST).

Salem Town

Real Estate Recording—Salem Town Clerk, Town Office Building, 270 Hartford Road, Salem, CT 06420. 860-859-3873. Fax: 860-859-1184. 8AM-4PM (EST).

Salisbury Town

Real Estate Recording—Salisbury Town Clerk, 27 Main Street, Town Hall, Salisbury, CT 06068. 860-435-5182. Fax: 860-435-5172. 9AM-4PM (EST).

Scotland Town

Real Estate Recording—Scotland Town Clerk, 9 Devotion Rd., Town Hall, Scotland, CT 06264. 860-423-9634. Fax: 860-423-3666. 9AM-3PM M,T,Th,; Noon-8PM F (EST).

Seymour Town

Real Estate Recording—Seymour Town Clerk, 1 First Street, Town Hall, Seymour, CT 06483. 203-888-0519. 9AM-5PM (No Recording after 4:15PM) (EST).

Sharon Town

Real Estate Recording—Sharon Town Clerk, 63 Main Street, Town Hall, Sharon, CT 06069. 860-364-5224. Fax: 860-364-5789. 9:00AM-Noon, 1PM-4PM (EST).

Shelton City

Real Estate Recording—Shelton City Clerk, 54 Hill Street, Shelton, CT 06484. 203-924-1555. Fax: 203-924-1721. 8AM-5:30PM (EST).

Sherman Town

Real Estate Recording—Sherman Town Clerk, 9 Route 39 North, Town Hall, Sherman, CT 06784. 860-354-5281. Fax: 860-350-5041. 9AM-Noon, 1-4PM T,W,Th,F; 9AM-Noon Sat (EST).

Simsbury Town

Real Estate Recording—Simsbury Town Clerk, 933 Hopmeadow Street, Simsbury, CT 06070. 860-658-3243. Fax: 860-658-3206. 8:30AM-4:30PM (EST).

Somers Town

Real Estate Recording—Somers Town Clerk, 600 Main Street, Somers, CT 06071. 860-763-8206. Fax: 860-763-0973. 8:30AM-4:30PM (EST).

South Windsor Town

Real Estate Recording—South Windsor Town Clerk, 1540 Sullivan Avenue, Town Hall, South Windsor, CT 06074. 860-644-2511. Fax: 860-644-3781. 8AM-4:30PM M-W & F; 8AM-7:30PM Th (EST).

Southbury Town

Real Estate Recording—Southbury Town Clerk, 501 Main Street South, Southbury, CT 06488. 203-262-0657. Fax: 203-264-9762. 8:30AM-4:30PM (EST).

Southington Town

Real Estate Recording—Southington Town Clerk, 75 Main Street, Town Office Building, Southington, CT 06489. 860-276-6211. Fax: 860-628-8669. 8:30AM-4:30PM (EST).

Sprague Town

Real Estate Recording—Sprague Town Clerk, 1 Main Street, Baltic, CT 06330. 860-822-3001. Fax: 860-822-3013. 8:30AM-4PM M-F (Th Open Until 6:30PM) (EST).

Stafford Town

Real Estate Recording—Stafford Town Clerk, Warren Memorial Town Hall, 1 Main St., Stafford Springs, CT 06076. 860-684-2532. 8:15AM-4PM M-W; 8:15AM-6:30PM Th; 8AM-Noon F (EST).

Stamford City

Real Estate Recording—Stamford City Clerk, 888 Washington Blvd, Stamford, CT 06901. 203-977-4054. 8:30AM-4:30PM (July,August 8AM-4PM) (EST).

Sterling Town

Real Estate Recording—Sterling Town Clerk, 1114 Plainfield Pike, Oneco, CT 06373. 860-564-2657. Fax: 860-564-1660. 8:30AM-3:30PM (EST).

Stonington Town

Real Estate Recording—Stonington Town Clerk, 152 Elm Street, Stonington, CT 06378. 860-535-5060. Fax: 860-535-1046. 8:30AM-4PM (EST).

Stratford Town

Real Estate Recording—Stratford Town Clerk, 2725 Main Street, Room 101, Stratford, CT 06497. 203-385-4020. Fax: 203-385-4108. 8AM-4:30PM (EST).

Suffield Town

Real Estate Recording—Suffield Town Clerk, 83 Mountain Road, Town Hall, Suffield, CT 06078. 860-668-3880. 8:30AM-4:30PM; Summer: 8AM-4:30PM M-Th; 8AM-1PM F (EST).

Thomaston Town

Real Estate Recording—Thomaston Town Clerk, 158 Main Street, Thomaston, CT 06787. 860-283-4141. 9AM-4:30PM (EST).

Thompson Town

Real Estate Recording—Thompson Town Clerk, 815 Riverside Drive, No. Grosvenor Dale, CT 06255. 860-923-9900. Fax: 860-923-3836. 9AM-5PM (EST).

Tolland County

Real Estate Recording—There is no real estate recording at the county level in Connecticut. You must determine the town or city where the property is located.

Felony—Tolland Superior Court-Criminal Branch, 20 Park St, Rockville, CT 06066. 860-870-3200. 9AM-5PM (EST). Access by: Mail, in person.

Civil Actions Over $2,500—Tolland Superior Court-Civil Branch, 69 Brooklyn St, Rockville, CT 06066. 860-875-6294. 9AM-5PM (EST). Access by: Mail, in person.

Misdemeanor—Geographical Area Court #19, PO Box 980, 20 Park St, Vernon, CT 06066-0980. 860-870-3200. 9AM-5PM (EST). Access by: Mail, in person.

Probate—Ashford Probate Court, Route 44, PO Box 61, Ashford, CT 06278. 860-429-4986. 1AM-3:30PM Thu (and by appointment) (EST). Access by:

Andover Probate Court, 222 Bolton Center Rd, Bolton, CT 06043. 860-649-8066. Fax: 860-643-0021. 9AM-4PM M & W; 9AM-3PM F (EST). Access by: Mail, in person.

Coventry Probate Court, Town Hall, 1712 Main St, Coventry, CT 06238. 860-742-6791. Fax: 860-742-5570. 9AM-Noon W,Th; 7:30PM-9PM Tue (EST). Access by: Mail, in person.

Hebron Probate Court, 15 Gilead Rd, Hebron, CT 06248. 860-228-9406. Fax: 860-228-4859. 10AM-4PM Mon & Wed, 8AM-12:30PM Fri (and by appointment July/Aug) (EST). Access by:

Ellington Probate Court, PO Box 268, 14 Park Place, Rockville, CT 06066. 860-872-0519. Fax: 860-871-9459. 9AM-4PM M-F (And by appointment) (EST). Access by:

Somers Probate Court, PO Box 308, 600 Main St, Somers, CT 06071. 860-763-8206. Fax: 860-763-0973. 9AM-1PM Tue & Thu (and by appointment) (EST). Access by:

Stafford Probate Court, PO Box 63, Main St, Stafford Springs, CT 06076. 860-684-3423. 9AM-Noon, 1-4:30PM M; 9AM-Noon Tue-Fri (EST). Access by:

Mansfield Probate Court, 4 South Eagleville Rd, Storrs, CT 06268. 860-429-3313. Fax: 860-429-6863. 2-5PM T,W; 3-5PM Th or by appointment (EST). Access by: Mail, in person.

Tolland Probate Court, Po Box 667, Tolland Green, Tolland, CT 06084. 860-871-3640. Fax: 860-871-3663. 12:30-4:30PM M; 9AM-Noon W & F; 5:30-8:30PM (EST). Access by:

Tolland Town

Real Estate Recording—Tolland Town Clerk, Hicks Memorial Municipal Center, 21 Tolland Green, Tolland, CT 06084. 860-871-3630. 9AM-4:30PM M,T,W,Th; 9AM-12:30PM F; (Th open 5:30-8:30PM) (EST).

Torrington City

Real Estate Recording—Torrington City Clerk, 140 Main Street, City Hall, Torrington, CT 06790. 860-489-2236. 8AM-4:30PM (EST).

Trumbull Town

Real Estate Recording—Trumbull Town Clerk, 5866 Main Street, Trumbull, CT 06611. 203-452-5035. Fax: 203-452-5038. 9AM-5PM (EST).

Union Town

Real Estate Recording—Union Town Clerk, 1024 Buckley Highway, Route 171, Union, CT 06076. 860-684-3770. Fax: 860-684-3770. 9AM-Noon T,Th; 9AM-Noon, 1-3PM W (EST).

Vernon Town

Real Estate Recording—Vernon Town Clerk, 14 Park Place, Rockville, CT 06066. 860-872-8591. 9AM-5PM (EST).

Voluntown Town

Real Estate Recording—Voluntown Town Clerk, Main Street, Town Hall, Voluntown, CT 06384. 860-376-4089. Fax: 860-376-3295. 9AM-2PM; 6-8PM T Evening (EST).

Wallingford Town

Real Estate Recording—Wallingford Town Clerk, 45 South Main Street, Municipal Building, Room 108, Wallingford, CT 06492. 203-294-2145. Fax: 203-294-2073. 9AM-5PM (EST).

Warren Town

Real Estate Recording—Warren Town Clerk, 7 Sackett Hill Road, Town Hall, Warren, CT 06754. 860-868-0090. Fax: 860-868-0090. 10AM-4PM W,Th; 10AM-Noon M,F (EST).

Washington Town

Real Estate Recording—Washington Town Clerk, Bryan Memorial Town Hall, Washington Depot, CT 06794. 860-868-2786. Fax: 860-868-3103. 9AM-4:45PM M,T,Th,F; 9AM-Noon W (EST).

Waterbury City

Real Estate Recording—Waterbury Town Clerk, 235 Grand Street, City Hall, Waterbury, CT 06702. 203-574-6806. Fax: 203-574-6887. 8:30AM-4:50PM (EST).

Waterford Town

Real Estate Recording—Waterford Town Clerk, 15 Rope Ferry Road, Waterford, CT 06385. 860-444-5831. Fax: 860-437-0352. 8AM-4PM (EST).

Watertown Town

Real Estate Recording—Watertown Town Clerk, 37 DeForest Street, Watertown, CT 06795. 860-945-5230. 9AM-5PM (EST).

West Hartford Town

Real Estate Recording—West Hartford Town Clerk, 50 South Main Street, Room 313 Town Hall Common, West Hartford, CT 06107. 860-523-3148. Fax: 860-523-3522. 8:30AM-4:30PM (EST).

West Haven City

Real Estate Recording—West Haven City Clerk, 355 Main Street, West Haven, CT 06516. 203-937-3535. 9AM-5PM (EST).

Westbrook Town

Real Estate Recording—Westbrook Town Clerk, 1163 Boston Post Road, Westbrook, CT 06498. 860-399-3044. Fax: 860-399-9568. 9AM-4PM M-W & F; 9AM-6:30PM Th (EST).

Weston Town

Real Estate Recording—Weston Town Clerk, 56 Norfield Road, Weston, CT 06883. 203-222-2616. Fax: 203-222-8871. 9AM-4:30PM (EST).

Westport Town

Real Estate Recording—Westport Town Clerk, 110 Myrtle Avenue, Westport, CT 06881. 203-341-1110. Fax: 203-341-1112. 8:30AM-4:30PM (EST).

Wethersfield Town

Real Estate Recording—Wethersfield Town Clerk, 505 Silas Deane Highway, Wethersfield, CT 06109. 860-721-2880. Fax: 860-721-2994. 8AM-4:30PM (EST).

Willington Town

Real Estate Recording—Willington Town Clerk-UCC Recorder, 40 Old Farms Road, Willington, CT 06279. 860-429-9965. Fax: 860-429-9778. 9AM-2PM (M open 6-8PM) (EST).

Wilton Town

Real Estate Recording—Wilton Town Clerk, 238 Danbury Road, Wilton, CT 06897. 203-834-9205. 8:30AM-4:30PM, Memorial Day to Labor Day; 9AM-5PM (EST).

Winchester Town

Real Estate Recording—Winchester Town Clerk, 338 Main Street, Town Hall, Winsted, CT 06098. 860-379-2713. Fax: 860-738-7053. 8AM-4PM (EST).

Windham County

Real Estate Recording—There is no real estate recording at the county level in Connecticut. You must determine the town or city where the property is located.

Felony, Civil Actions Over $2,500—Windham Superior Court, 155 Church St, Putnam, CT 06260. 860-928-7749. Fax: 860-928-7076. 9AM-5PM (EST). Access by: Phone, mail, in person.

Misdemeanor, Eviction, Small Claims—Geographical Area Court #11, 172 Main St (PO Box 688), Danielson, CT 06239. 860-774-8516. Fax: 860-774-1209. 9AM-1PM, 2:30-4PM (EST). Access by: Phone, mail, in person.

Probate—Brooklyn Probate Court, Town Hall, Route 6, PO Box 356, Brooklyn, CT 06234-0356. 860-774-5973. Fax: 860-779-3744. 11:30AM-4:30PM Tues, (And by appointment) (EST). Access by:

Canterbury Probate Court, 43 Maple Lane, Canterbury, CT 06331. 860-546-9605. Fax: 860-546-9693. 8AM-4:30PM Wed (And by appointment, evenings) (EST). Access by:

Chaplin Probate Court, Route 198, Chaplin, CT 06235. 860-455-0027. Fax: 860-455-0027. 7PM-9PM Tue (And by appointment) (EST). Access by:

Killingly Probate Court, 172 Main St, Danielson, CT 06239. 860-774-8601. Fax: 860-774-5811. 1AM-4:30PM (EST). Access by: Mail, in person.

Eastford Probate Court, PO Box 359, 16 Westford Rd, Eastford, CT 06242. 860-974-1885. Fax: 860-974-0624. 10AM-12PM Wed (And by appointment) (EST). Access by:

Hampton Probate Court, Town Hall, 164 Main St, Hampton, CT 06247. 860-455-9132. 9AM-12PM Thu (And by appointment) (EST). Access by:

Thompson Probate Court, 815 Riverside Dr, Town Hall, North Grosvendale, CT 06255. 860-923-2203. Fax: 860-923-3836. 9AM-Noon M-F (And by Appointment) (EST). Access by:

Sterling Probate Court, PO Box 157, Town Hall, Oneco, CT 06373. 860-564-8488. Fax: 860-564-1660. 8:30AM-3:30PM (EST). Access by:

Plainfield Probate Court, Town Hall, 8 Community Ave, Plainfield, CT 06374. 860-564-0019. Fax: 860-564-0612. 12:30-4:30PM M,Th; 8:30AM-12:30PM T,W,F (EST). Access by: Mail, in person.

Pomfret Probate Court, 5 Haven Rd, Pomfret Center, CT 06259. 860-974-0186. Fax: 860-974-3950. 10AM-4PM Tue-Thu (And by appointment) (EST). Access by:

Putnam Probate Court, 195 Providence Street, Putnam, CT 06260. 860-963-6868. Fax: 860-963-6814. 9AM-Noon (EST). Access by: Mail, in person.

Windham Probate Court, PO Box 34, 979 Main St, Willimantic, CT 06226. 860-465-3049. Fax: 860-465-3012. 9AM-1PM M-Th; 9AM-Noon F (EST). Access by: Mail.

Woodstock Probate Court, PO Box 123, Route 169, Woodstock, CT 06281. 860-928-2223. Fax: 860-963-7557. 3PM-6PM Wed, 1:30PM-4:30PM Thu (And by appointment) (EST). Access by: In person only.

Windham Town

Real Estate Recording—Windham Town Clerk, 979 Main Street, Willimantic, CT 06226. 860-465-3013. Fax: 860-465-3012. 8AM-5PM M-W; 8AM-7:30PM Th; 8AM-Noon F (EST).

Windsor Locks Town

Real Estate Recording—Windsor Locks Town Clerk, 50 Church Street, Town Office Building, Windsor Locks, CT 06096. 860-627-1441. 8:30AM-4:30PM (EST).

Windsor Town

Real Estate Recording—Windsor Town Clerk, 275 Broad Street, Windsor, CT 06095. 860-285-1900. Fax: 860-285-1909. 8AM-5PM (EST).

Wolcott Town

Real Estate Recording—Wolcott Town Clerk, 10 Kenea Avenue, Town Hall, Wolcott, CT 06716. 203-879-8100. 9AM-4:30PM (Recording until 4PM) (EST).

Woodbridge Town

Real Estate Recording—Woodbridge Town Clerk, 11 Meetinghouse Lane, Woodbridge, CT 06525. 203-389-3422. Fax: 203-389-3480. 8:30AM-4PM (EST).

Woodbury Town

Real Estate Recording—Woodbury Town Clerk, 275 Main Street South, Woodbury, CT 06798. 203-263-2144. Fax: 203-263-4755. 8:30AM-4:30PM (Summer Hours 8AM-4PM) (EST).

Woodstock Town

Real Estate Recording—Woodstock Town Clerk, Town Office Building, 415 Route 169, Woodstock, CT 06281. 860-928-6595. Fax: 860-963-7557. 8:30AM-4:30PM M,T,Th; 8:30AM-6PM W; 8:30AM-3PM F (EST).

Federal Courts

US District Court

District of Connecticut

Bridgeport Division, US District Court Office of the Clerk, Room 400, 915 Lafayette Blvd, Bridgeport, CT 06604. 203-579-5861. Counties: Fairfield (prior to 1993). Since 01/93, cases from any county may be assigned to any of the 3 divisions in the district, including New Haven.

Hartford Division, US District Court 450 Main St, Hartford, CT 06103. 860-240-3200. Counties: Hartford, Tolland, Windham (prior to 1993). Since 1993, cases from any county may be assigned to any of the three divisions in the district

New Haven Division, US District Court 141 Church St, New Haven, CT 06510. 203-773-2140. Counties: Litchfield, Middlesex, New Haven, New London (prior to 1993). Since 1993, cases from any county may be assigned to any of the three divisions in the district

US Bankruptcy Court

District of Connecticut

Bridgeport Division, US Bankruptcy Court, 915 Lafayette Blvd, Bridgeport, CT 06604. 203-579-5808. Voice Case Information System: 203-240-3345. Counties: Fairfield

Hartford Division, US Bankruptcy Court, 450 Main St, Hartford, CT 06103. 860-240-3675. Voice Case Information System: 203-240-3345. Counties: Hartford, Litchfield, Middlesex, Tolland, Windham

New Haven Division, US Bankruptcy Court, The Connecticut Financial Center, 157 Church St, 18th Floor, New Haven, CT 06510. 203-773-2009. Voice Case Information System: 203-240-3345. Counties: New Haven, New London

Delaware

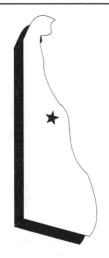

Capital: Dover (Kent County)	
Number of Counties: 3	**Population:** 717,197
County Court Locations:	**Federal Court Locations:**
•Superior Courts: 3	•District Courts: 1
•Chancery Courts: 3	•Bankruptcy Courts: 1
•Court of Common Pleas: 3	**State Agencies:** 19
•Justice of the Peace Courts: 18	
•Municipal Courts 1	
Alderman's Courts 9	
Family Courts 3	

State Agencies—Summary

General Help Numbers:

State Archives

Delaware Public Archives	302-739-5318
Hall of Records	Fax: 302-739-2578
Public Archives	8:30AM-4:15PM
Dover, DE 19903	
Historical Society:	302-655-7161

Governor's Office

Office of the Governor	302-577-3210
820 N. French St, Carvel State Bldg	Fax: 302-577-3118
Wilmington, DE 19801	9AM-5:30PM

Attorney General's Office

Attorney General's Office	302-577-3047
Carvel State Office Bldg	Fax: 302-577-3090
820 N French St, 7th floor	8:30AM-4:30PM
Wilmington, DE 19801	
Alternate Telephone:	302-577-3838

State Legislation

Delaware General Assembly	302-739-4114
Legislative Avenue	8AM-4:30PM
Room 29	
Dover, DE 19903	
Archives for old bills:	302-739-5318

Important State Internet Sites:

⟁ Webscape
File   Edit   View   Help

State of Delaware World Wide Web
www.state.de.us/

Key site for information about the state of Delaware. All locations are easily indexed and accessible from the home page. The topics listed are budget, business finance, camping, census information, chemical hazards, Delaware, education, elected officials, fishing, fraud, fraud and consumer protection.

Additional topics include the Governor, hunting, Internet help, legislative information, Lieutenant Governor, natural hazards, nuclear hazards, parks, phone directory, public defense, Representatives, schools, Senators, sight seeing, state police, tax forms, tax incentives, primary results, veterans information and victims guide.

Legislative Information
www.state.de.us

Bill tracking is available for the 138th and 139th General Assemblies, along with the daily agendas for the Senate and House.

State Agencies—Public Records

Criminal Records

Delaware State Police Headquarters, Criminal Records Section, PO Box 430, Dover, DE 19903-0430, Main Telephone: 302-739-5880, Fax: 302-739-5888, Hours: 8AM-4PM. Access by: mail, visit. This agency will only release records with dispositions for pre-employment requesters.

Corporation Records
Limited Partnership Records
Trademarks/Servicemarks
Limited Liability Company Records
Assumed Name

Secretary of State, Division of Corporations, PO Box 898, Dover, DE 19903, Main Telephone: 302-739-4279, Fax: 302-739-3812, Hours: 8AM-4:30PM. Access by: mail, phone, visit, PC.

Uniform Commercial Code
Federal Tax Liens
State Tax Liens

UCC Division, Secretary of State, PO Box 793, Dover, DE 19903, Main Telephone: 302-739-4279, Fax: 302-739-3813, Hours: 8:30AM-4:30PM. Access by: mail, visit.

Sales Tax Registrations

Finance Department, Revenue Division, PO Box 8911, Wilmington, DE 19899-8911, Main Telephone: 302-577-3321, Fax: 302-577-3689, Hours: 8AM-4PM M-F. Access by: mail, phone, fax, visit. This state has a gross receipts tax, not a sales tax per se. They will release the information found on the face of the certificate issued to the business.

Birth Certificates

Department of Health, Office of Vital Statistics, PO Box 637, Dover, DE 19903, Main Telephone: 302-739-4721, Hours: 8AM-4:30PM (Counter closes at 4:20 PM). Access by: mail, phone, visit.

Death Records

Department of Health, Office of Vital Statistics, PO Box 637, Dover, DE 19903, Main Telephone: 302-739-4721, Hours: 8AM-4:30PM. Access by: mail, phone, visit.

Marriage Certificates

Department of Health, Office of Vital Statistics, PO Box 637, Dover, DE 19903, Main Telephone: 302-739-4721, Hours: 8AM-4:30PM. Access by: mail, phone, visit.

Divorce Records

Records not available from state agency.

Workers' Compensation Records

Labor Department, Industrial Accident Board, 4425 N Market Street, Wilmington, DE 19802, Main Telephone: 302-761-8200, Fax: 302-761-6611, Hours: 8AM-4:30PM. Access by: mail, phone.

Driver Records

Division of Motor Vehicles, Driver Services, PO Box 698, Dover, DE 19903, Main Telephone: 302-739-4343, Fax: 302-739-2602, Hours: 8AM-4:30PM M-T-TH-F; 12:00PM-8PM W. Access by: mail, visit, PC. Delaware does not keep copies of tickets in a central repository for request purposes and suggests you go to the appropriate local jurisdiction.

Vehicle Ownership
Vehicle Identification

Division of Motor Vehicles, Correspondence Section, PO Box 698, Dover, DE 19903, Main Telephone: 302-739-3147, Fax: 302-739-2042, Hours: 8:30AM-4:30PM M-T-TH-F; 12-8PM W. Access by: mail, visit, PC.

Accident Reports

Delaware State Police Traffic Section, Accident Records, PO Box 430, Dover, DE 19903, Main Telephone: 302-739-5931, Fax: 302-739-5982, Hours: 8AM-4PM. Access by: mail, visit.

Hunting License Information
Fishing License Information

Natural Resources & Environmental Control Dept, Divsion of Fish & Wildlife, 80 Kings Hwy, Dover, DE 19901, Main Telephone: 302-739-5296, Fax: 302-739-6157, Hours: 8AM-4:30PM. Access by: mail, phone, fax, visit.[DS1]

County Courts and Recording Offices

What You Need to Know...

About the Courts

Administration

Administrative Office of the Courts	302-577-2480
PO Box 8911	Fax: 302-577-3139
Wilmington, DE 19899	8:30AM-4:30PM

Court Structure

The Superior Court and Court of Common Pleas handle the case types and limits indicated in the charts. The Superior Courts have jurisdiction over felonies and all drug offenses, the Court of Common Pleas and Municipal Court of Wilmington have jurisdiction over all misdemeanors except those involving drug offenses. (The Common Pleas courts handle some minor "felonies" as defined in state statutes.) Probate is handled by the Register of Wills within the Court of Chancery.

The Municipal Court of Wilmington may merge with the Court of Common Pleas in New Castle in the future.

Searching Hints

The civil case limit of the Justice of the Peace Courts is $15,000 and the limit of the Courts of Common Pleas is $50,000.

Criminal histories are available **with a signed release from the offender** at the State Bureau of Identification in Dover DE. For information on retrieval requirements call 302-739-5880.

Online Access

A prototype on-line system called **CLAD,** developed by Mead Data Central and the New Castle Superior Court is currently available in Delaware. It contains only toxic waste, asbestos, and class action cases; however, based on CLAD's success, Delaware may pursue on-line availability of other public records in conjunction with private information resource enterprises.

About the Recorder's Office

Organization

Delaware has 3 counties and 3 filing offices. The recording officer is the County Recorder.

UCC Records

Financing statements are filed at the state level, except for real estate related collateral, which is filed only with the County Recorder. All counties perform UCC searches.

Lien Records

Federal tax liens on personal property of businesses are filed with the Secretary of State. Other federal and all state tax liens on personal property are filed with the County Recorder.

Real Estate Records

Counties do **not** perform real estate searches, you must hire a retriever or access online through a private company.

County Courts and Recording Offices

Kent County

Real Estate Recording—Kent County Recorder of Deeds, County Administration Bldg., Room 218, 414 Federal St., Dover, DE 19901. 302-736-2060. Fax: 302-736-2200. 8:30AM-4:30PM (EST).

Civil, Probate—Chancery Court, 38 The Green, Dover, DE 19901. 302-736-2242. Probate: 302-736-2233. Fax: 302-736-2244. 8:30AM-4:30PM (EST). Access by: Mail, in person.

Felony, Misdemeanor, Civil Actions Over $50,000—Superior Court, Office of Prothonotary, 38 The Green, Dover, DE 19901. 302-739-3184. Fax: 302-739-6717. 8AM-5PM (EST). Access by: In person only.

Misdemeanor, Civil Actions Under $50,000—Court of Common Pleas, 38 The Green, Dover, DE 19901. 302-739-4618. Fax: 302-739-4501. 8:30AM-4:30PM (EST). Access by: In person only.

Civil Actions Under $15,000, Eviction, Small Claims—Dover Justice of the Peace, 516 W Loockerman St, Dover, DE 19904. 302-739-4316. 8AM-4PM (EST).

Misdemeanor—Dover Justice of the Peace, 516 W Loockerman, Dover, DE 19903. 302-739-4554. (EST). Access by: Phone, fax, in person.

Harrington Justice of the Peace, Rte 13 Box 3, Harrington, DE 19952. 302-398-8247. (EST). Access by: Mail, in person.

Smyrna Justice of the Peace, 100 Monrovia Ave, Smyrna, DE 19977. 302-653-7083. Fax: 302-653-2888. (EST). Access by: Phone, mail, in person.

New Castle County

Real Estate Recording—New Castle County Recorder of Deeds, 800 French Street, 4th Floor, Wilmington, DE 19801. 302-571-7550. Fax: 302-571-7708. 9AM-4:45PM (EST).

Civil, Probate—Chancery Court, 1020 N King St, Wilmington, DE 19801. 302-571-7540. Probate: 302-571-7545. Fax: 302-571-7751. 9AM-5PM (EST). Access by: Fax, mail, in person.

Felony, Misdemeanor, Civil Actions Over $50,000—Superior Court, County Courthouse, Prothonotary Office, Wilmington, DE 19801. 302-577-6470. Fax: 302-577-6487. 8:30AM-5PM (EST). Access by: Mail, in person.

Misdemeanor, Civil Actions Under $50,000—Court of Common Pleas, 1000 N King St, Wilmington, DE 19801-3348. 302-577-2430. Fax: 302-577-2193. 8:30AM-4:30PM (EST). Access by: Fax, mail, in person.

Civil Actions Under $15,000, Eviction, Small Claims—Wilmington Justice of the Peace, 820 N French St, 2nd Floor, Wilmington, DE 19801. 302-577-2550. Fax: 302-577-2562. 8AM-4PM (EST).

Wilmington Justice of the Peace, 212 Greenbank Rd, Wilmington, DE 19808. 302-995-8646. Fax: 302-995-8642. 8:30AM-4:30PM (EST).

Misdemeanor—New Castle Justice of the Peace, 61 Christiana Rd, New Castle, DE 19720. 302-323-4450. Fax: 302-323-4452. (EST). Access by: In person only.

Wilmington Justice of the Peace, 820 N French St, 2nd Floor, Wilmington, DE 19801. 302-577-2552. Fax: 302-577-2526. 8AM-4PM (EST). Access by: In person only.

Wilington Justice of the Peace, 210 Greenbank Rd, Wilmington, DE 19808. 302-995-8640. Fax: 302-995-8642. (EST). Access by: Fax, mail, in person.

Wilmington Justice of the Peace, 716 Philadelphia Pike, Wilmington, DE 19809. 302-764-4142. Fax: 302-762-6781. 8AM-4PM M; 8AM-Midnight T-F; 8AM-4PM Sat (EST). Access by: Fax, mail, in person.

Wilmington Justice of the Peace, 1301 E 12th St, Wilmington, DE 19809. 302-429-7740. 8AM-Midnight (EST). Access by: Phone, fax, mail, in person.

Wilmington Municipal Court, PO Box 8978, Wilmington, DE 19899. 302-571-4530. 9AM-5PM (EST). Access by: Mail, in person.

Sussex County

Real Estate Recording—Sussex County Recorder of Deeds, Administration Bldg., Lower Level, Georgetown, DE 19947. 302-855-7785. Fax: 302-855-7787. 8:30AM-4:30PM (EST).

Civil, Probate—Chancery Court, PO Box 424, Georgetown, DE 19947. 302-855-7842. Probate: 302-855-7875. 8:30AM-4:30PM (EST). Access by: Mail, in person.

Felony, Misdemeanor, Civil Actions—Superior Court, PO Box 756, Georgetown, DE 19947. 302-856-5740. Fax: 302-856-5739. 8AM-4:30PM (EST). Access by: In person only.

Misdemeanor, Civil Actions Under $50,000—Court of Common Pleas, PO Box 426, Georgetown, DE 19947. 302-856-5333. Fax: 302-856-5056. 8:30AM-4:30PM (EST). Access by: Phone, fax, mail, in person.

Civil Actions Under $15,000, Eviction, Small Claims—Georgetown Justice of the Peace, 17 Shortly Rd, Georgetown, DE 19947. 302-856-1447. Fax: 302-856-5923. 8AM-4PM (EST). Access by: Mail, in person.

Seaford Justice of the Peace Court #19, 408 Stein Highway, Seaford, DE 19973. 302-629-5433. 8AM-4PM (EST).

Misdemeanor—Georgetown Justice of the Peace, 17 Shortly Rd, Georgetown, DE 19947. 302-856-1445. (EST). Access by: In person only.

Lewes Justice of the Peace, Rt3 9 Box 175, Lewes, DE 19958. 302-645-6163. Fax: 302-645-8842. 8AM-4PM M-W, F,Sat; 8AM-Midnight Th (EST). Access by: Phone, in person.

Milford Justice of the Peace, 715 S DuPont Highway, Milford, DE 19963. 302-422-5922. (EST). Access by: In person only.

Millsboro Justice of the Peace, Pte 113 PO Box 192, 553 E DuPont Hwy, Millsboro, DE 19966. 302-934-7268. Fax: 302-934-1414. 8AM-4PM (EST). Access by: Phone, fax, mail, in person.

Seaford Justice of the Peace, 408 Stein Highway, Seaford, DE 19973. 302-628-2036. Fax: 302-528-2049. 8AM-4PM (EST). Access by: In person only.

Federal Courts

US District Court
District of Delaware

Wilmington Division, US District Court US Courthouse, Lock Box 18, 844 N King St, Wilmington, DE 19801. 302-573-6170. Counties: All counties in Delaware

US Bankruptcy Court
District of Delaware

Wilmington Division, US Bankruptcy Court, 824 Market St, 5th Floor, Marine Midland Plaza, Wilmington, DE 19801. 302-573-6174. Voice Case Information System: 302-573-6233. Counties: All counties in Delaware

District of Columbia

General Statistics	
Court Locations:	**Population:** 554,256
•Superior Courts: 2	**Federal Court Locations:**
•Probate/Tax: 1	•District Courts: 1
	•Bankruptcy Courts: 1
	District Agencies: 18

DC Agencies—Summary

General Help Numbers:

State Archives

Secretary of the District of Columbia Office	202-727-2052
Office of Archives/Public Records	Fax: 202-727-6076
1300 Naylor Ct NW	
Washington, DC 20001-4225	
Historical Society:	202-785-2068
Reference Librarian:	202-727-1199

Mayor's Office

Office of the Mayor	202-727-2980
One Judiciary Square,	
441 4th St NW	Fax: 202-727-2975
Washington, DC 20001	8:30AM-5:30PM

District Legislation

Council of the District of Columbia	202-724-8050
1350 Pennsylvania Ave, NW, Room 28	
Washington, DC 20004	

Important Internet Sites:

⬩ **Webscape**
File Edit View   Help

Welcome to the White House
www.whitehouse.gov/WH/Welcome.html

This site gives you information about the President, provides a tour and history of past Presidents, has a virtual library and allows you to browse some historical documents.

District of Columbia World Wide Web
www.capcityon-line.com

Very limited web site that is under construction.

Smithsonian Museum
www.si.edu

Learn all about the Smithsonian Museums, events, resources, tours and memberships.

Library of Congress
www.loc.gov/

From this site you can learn about House and Senate floor activities, bills, the Congressional Record, research historical documents, view Civil War photographs and much more.

U.S. Senators
www.senate.gov/

Provides a complete directory of U.S. Senators, e-mail addresses, voting records and committee assignments.

U.S. House of Representatives
www.house.gov/

Provides data about members, their committees, how to reach them and access to legislative information.

DC Agencies—Public Records

Criminal Records
Metropolitan Police Department, Identification and Records Section, 300 Indiana Ave NW, Rm 3055, Washington, DC 20001, Main Telephone: 202-727-4302, Superior Court: 202-879-1373, Hours: 8AM-5PM. Access by: mail, visit. The Superior Court, Criminal Division, is located at 500 Indiana NW, same zip. They do not charge a fee for a search and they will indicate over the phone if there is an existing record.

Corporation Records
Limited Partnership Records
Limited Liability Company Records
Department of Consumer & Regulatory Affairs, 614 H St, NW, Room 407, Washington, DC 20001, Main Telephone: 202-727-7283, Hours: 9AM-3PM. Access by: mail, phone, visit.

Uniform Commercial Code
Federal Tax Liens
State Tax Liens
UCC Recorder, District of Columbia Recorder of Deeds, 515 D Street NW, Room 203, Washington, DC 20001, Main Telephone: 202-727-5381, Hours: 8:15AM-4:45PM. Access by: mail, visit.

Sales Tax Registrations
Finance & Revenue Department, Sales Tax Audit, 441 4th St NW, Suite 550, Washington, DC 20001, Main Telephone: 202-727-6070, Fax: 202-727-9069, Hours: 8:30AM-5PM. Access by: mail, phone.

Birth Certificates
Department of Health, Vital Records Branch, 800 9th Street SW, #100, Washington, DC 20024, Main Telephone: 202-727-5314, Hours: 8:30AM-3:30PM. Access by: mail, visit.

Death Records
Department of Health, Vital Records Branch, 800 9th Street SW, #100, Washington, DC 20024, Main Telephone: 202-727-5314, Hours: 8:30AM-3:30PM. Access by: mail, visit.

Marriage Certificates
Superior Court House, Marriage Bureau, 500 Indiana Ave, NW, Room 4485, Washington, DC 20001, Main Telephone: 202-879-4840, Fax: 202-879-1280, Hours: 9AM-4PM. Access by: mail, visit.

Divorce Records
Superior Court House, Divorce Records, 500 Indiana Ave, NW, Room 4230, Washington, DC 20001, Main Telephone: 202-879-1421, Fax: 202-879-1572, Hours: 9AM-4PM. Access by: mail, visit.

Workers' Compensation Records
Office of Workers Compensation, PO Box 56098 3rd Floor, Washington, DC 20011, Main Telephone: 202-576-6265, Fax: 202-541-3595, Hours: 8AM-5PM. Access by: mail, phone, fax, visit.

Driver Records
Department of Motor Vehicles, Driver Records Division, 301 "C" St, NW, Washington, DC 20001, Main Telephone: 202-727-6761, Hours: 8:15AM-4PM M-T-TH-F; 8:15AM-7:00PM W. Access by: mail, visit, PC. Copies of tickets are available from the Bureau of Traffic Adjudication, Correspondence Unit, 65 "K" Street, NE, Washington 20002. The fee is $1.00 per ticket.

Vehicle Ownership
Vehicle Identification
Department of Motor Vehicles, Vehicle Control Division, 301 "C" St, NW, Room 1063, Washington, DC 20001, Main Telephone: 202-727-4768, Hours: 8:15AM-4PM M-T-TH-F; 8:15AM-7PM W. Access by: mail, visit.

Accident Reports
Insurance Operations Branch, Accident Report Section, 65 "K" St, NE, Room 2100, 2nd Floor, Washington, DC 20002, Main Telephone: 202-727-5986, Fax: 202-727-4601, Hours: 8:30AM-3PM. Access by: mail, visit.

Fishing License Information
Environmental Regulation Administration, Fisheries & Wildlife Management Branch, 2100 M L King, Jr Ave SE, Ste 203, Washington, DC 20020, Main Telephone: 202-404-1155, Fax: 202-404-1141, Hours: 8AM-5PM.
Restricted access.

DC Courts and Recording Offices

What You Need to Know...

About the Courts

Administration

Executive Office	202-879-1700
500 Indiana Ave NW, Room 1500	Fax: 202-879-4829
Washington, DC 20001	8:30AM-5PM

Court Structure

The Superior Court in DC is divided into 17 divisions, 4 of which are profiled in this Sourcebook: Criminal, Civil, Family, and Tax-Probate. The Superior Court - Civil lower limit changed to **$5,000** during 3rd Quarter 1994 and the Small Claims limit was raised to **$5,000**. Probate is handled by the Tax-Probate Division of the Superior Court.

Online Access

The Court of Appeals maintains a bulletin board system for various court notices, and can be dialed from computer at 202-626-8863.

About the Recorder's Office

Organization

The recording officer is the county recorder.

UCC Records

Financing statements are filed at the state level, except for real estate related collateral, which are filed only with the County Recorder. The recorder's office will perform UCC searches.

Lien Records

Federal tax liens on personal property of businesses are filed with the Secretary of State. Other federal and all state tax liens on personal property are filed with the County Recorder.

Real Estate Records

Counties do **not** perform real estate searches.

DC Courts and Recording Offices

District of Columbia

Real Estate Recording—District of Columbia Recorder of Deeds, 515 D Street NW, Room 203, Washington, DC 20001. 202-727-5374. 8:15AM-4:45PM (EST).

Civil Actions Over $5,000, Eviction—Superior Court-Civil Division, 500 Indiana Ave NW JM 170, Washington, DC 20001. 202-879-1133. 9AM-4PM (EST). Access by: Mail, in person.

Civil Actions Under $5,000, Eviction, Small Claims—Superior Court-Civil Division-Small Claims Branch, 500 Indiana Ave NW Room JM 260, Washington, DC 20001. 202-879-1120. 8:30AM-4PM (EST). Access by: Mail, in person.

Felony, Misdemeanor—Superior Court-Criminal Division, 500 Indiana Ave NW Room 4001, Washington, DC 20001. 202-879-1373. Fax: 202-638-5352. 9AM-4PM (EST). Access by: Phone, fax, mail, in person.

Probate—Superior Court-Tax/Probate Division, 500 Indiana Ave NW, Washington, DC 20001. 202-879-4800. Fax: 202-393-5849. 9AM-4PM (EST). Access by: Mail, in person.

Federal Courts

US District Court
District of Columbia

Division, US District Court US Courthouse, Clerk's Office, 333 Constitution Ave NW, Washington, DC 20001. 202-273-0555. Counties: District of Columbia

US Bankruptcy Court
District of Columbia

Division, US Bankruptcy Court, Court Clerk, Room 4400, 333 Constitution Ave NW, Washington, DC 20001. 202-273-0042. Voice Case Information System: 202-273-0048. Counties: District of Columbia

Florida

Capitol: Tallahassee (Leon County)	
Number of Counties: 67	**Population:** 14,165,570
County Court Locations:	**Federal Court Locations:**
•Circuit Courts: 10/20 Circuits	•District Courts: 14
•County Courts: 13	•Bankruptcy Courts: 8
•Combined Courts: 79	**State Agencies:** 20

State Agencies—Summary

General Help Numbers:

State Archives
Library & Information Services Division	904-487-2073
Archives & Records	Fax: 904-488-4894
R A Gray Bldg,	
500 S Bronough	8AM-5PM M-F; 9AM-3PM SA
Tallahassee, FL 32399-0250	
Reference Librarian:	904-487-2073
Historical Society:	407-407-690-1971

Governor's Office
Governor's Office	904-488-4441
The Capitol	Fax: 904-487-0801
Tallahassee, FL 32399-0001	8AM-5PM

Attorney General's Office
Attorney General's Office	904-488-2526
Legal Affairs Department	Fax: 904-488-5106
The Capitol, PL-01	8AM-5PM
Tallahassee, FL 32399-1050	
Alternate Telephone:	904-487-1963

State Legislation
Joint Legislative Mgmt Committee	904-488-4371
Legislative Information Division	8AM-5PM
111 W Madison St, Pepper Bldg, Rm 704	
Tallahassee, FL 32399	
Bill Information (FL callers):	800-342-1827

Full text of bills updated each day at 11PM is available at their web site, www.leg.state.fl.us.
There is also a Bill History Session service that updates activities in real time, but which does not contain the text. This service costs $500 per year. To sign up for it, contact Deloris Colston at 904-488-4371.

Important State Internet Sites:

Webscape
File   Edit   View   Help

State of Florida World Wide Web
www.state.fl.us/

Extensive web site with links to arts and culture, attractions, business, communities, education, environment, events, government and politics, health, legal system, news, public safety and science and technology.

Florida Access to Government
fcn.state.fl.us/fcn/3/access.html

A virtual card catalog of Florida Government and all state agencies.

Florida Unclaimed Property
www.dbf.state.fl.us/abanprop.html

Locates unclaimed property such as, checking and savings accounts, payroll, wages, insurance, refunds and much more. Property is searchable by owner's name.

Florida Department of Motor Vehicles
fcn.state.fl.us/hsmv/

At this site you have access to drivers license information, auto and boat registration, voter registration and links to many other DMV sites.

State Agencies—Public Records

Criminal Records

Florida Department of Law Enforcement, User Services Bureau, PO Box 1489, Tallahassee, FL 32302, Main Telephone: 904-488-6236, Fax: 904-488-1413, Hours: 8AM-5PM. Access by: mail, visit, PC.

Corporation Records
Limited Liability Company Records
Limited Partnership Records
Trademarks/Servicemarks
Assumed Name

Division of Corporations, Department of State, PO Box 6327, Tallahassee, FL 32314, Main Telephone: 904-488-9000, Hours: 8:30AM-4:30PM. Access by: visit, PC. They recommend use of a retriever service or to come in person.

Fictitious Names

Department of State, Fictitious Names Division, PO Box 6327, Tallahassee, FL 32314, Main Telephone: 904-487-6058, Hours: 8:30AM-4:30PM. Access by: mail, phone, visit, PC.

Uniform Commercial Code
Federal Tax Liens
State Tax Liens

UCC Division, Secretary of State, PO Box 5588, Tallahassee, FL 32314, Main Telephone: 904-487-6055, Fax: 904-487-6013, Hours: 8AM-4:30PM. Access by: mail, phone, visit, PC.

Sales Tax Registrations

Revenue Department, Tax Collection & Enforcement Division, 5050 W Tennessee St, Bldg F4, Tallahassee, FL 32399-0100, Main Telephone: 904-487-7000, Fax: 904-488-0024, Hours: 8AM-5PM. Access by: mail, phone, visit.

Birth Certificates

Department of Health, Office of Vital Statistics, PO Box 210, Jacksonville, FL 32231-0042, Main Telephone: 904-359-6911, Fax: 904-359-6993, Hours: 8AM-5PM. Access by: mail, phone, visit. The web site (sung.dms.state.fl.us/health/) includes general information and ordering instructions.

Death Records

Department of Health, Office of Vital Statistics, PO Box 210, Jacksonville, FL 32231-0042, Main Telephone: 904-359-6911, Fax: 904-359-6993, Hours: 8AM-5PM. Access by: mail, phone, visit. The web site contains general information, ordering instructions, and forms.

Marriage Certificates

Department of Health, Office of Vital Statistics, PO Box 210, Jacksonville, FL 32231-0042, Main Telephone: 904-359-6911, Fax: 904-359-6993, Hours: 8AM-5PM. Access by: mail, phone, visit. The web site contains general information, ordering instructions and order forms to download.

Divorce Records

Department of Health, Office of Vital Statistics, PO Box 210, Jacksonville, FL 32231-0042, Main Telephone: 904-359-6911, Fax: 904-359-6993, Hours: 8AM-5PM. Access by: mail, phone, visit. The web site provides general information and ordering instructions.

Workers' Compensation Records

Workers Compensation Division, Information Management Unit, Forrest Bldg, 2728 Centerview Dr, Ste 20, Tallahassee, FL 32399, Main Telephone: 904-488-3030, Hours: 7:30AM-5PM. Access by: mail, visit.

Driver Records

Department of Highway Safety & Motor Vehicles, Division of Drivers Licenses, PO Box 5775, Tallahassee, FL 32314-5775, Main Telephone: 850-487-4303, Fax: 850-487-7080, Hours: 8AM-4:30PM. Access by: mail, visit, PC. Copies of tickets may be obtained from the same address listed above. The fee is $.50 each or $1.00 for certified copies.

Vehicle Ownership
Vehicle Identification

Division of Motor Vehicles, Information Research Section, Neil Kirkman Bldg, A-126, Tallahassee, FL 32399, Main Telephone: 904-488-5665, Fax: 904-488-8983, Hours: 8AM-4:30PM. Access by: mail, visit. The state has outsourced on-line access to registration and ownership records through two vendors; TML Information Services 800-743-7891 and CompuServe 800-848-8199.

Accident Reports

Crash Records-Room A325, DHSMV, Neil Kirkman Bldg, 2900 Apalachee Prky, Tallahassee, FL 32399-0538, Main Telephone: 904-488-5017, Fax: 904-922-0488, Hours: 8AM-4:45PM. Access by: mail, visit.

Hunting License Information
Fishing License Information

Records not available from state agency.

County Courts and Recording Offices

What You Need to Know...

About the Courts

Administration

Office of Courts Administrator	904-922-5082
Supreme Court Bldg, 500 S Duval	8AM-5PM
Tallahassee, FL 32399-1900	

Court Structure

All but the largest counties have combined Circuit and County Courts.

Searching Hints

Most courts have one address and switchboard; however, the divisions within the court(s) are completely separate. Suggest that requesters address which court and which division, e.g., Circuit Civil, County Civil, etc., the request is directed to, even though some counties will automatically check both with one request.

Fees are set by statute and are as follows: Search Fee — $1.00 per name per year, Certification Fee — $1.00 per document plus copy fee, Copy Fee — $1.00 per certified page; $.15 per non-certified page.

Most Courts have **very lengthy** phone recording systems.

Online Access

There is a statewide, online computer system for **internal** use only; there is **no** external access available nor planned currently.

Some counties do offer their own online access to civil and criminal records.

About the Recorder's Office

Organization

67 counties, 67 filing offices. The recording officer is Clerk of the Circuit Court. All transactions are recorded in the "Official Record," a grantor/grantee index. A number of counties make their records available on-line. Some counties will search by type of transaction while others will return everything on the index. 57 counties are in the Eastern Time Zone (EST) and 10 are in the Central Time Zone (CST).

UCC Records

Financing statements are filed at the state level, except for farm and real estate related collateral. All but a few counties will perform UCC searches. Use search request form UCC-11. Search fees are usually $1.00 per debtor name per year searched and include all lien and real estate transactions on record. Copies usually cost $1.00 per page.

Lien Records

Federal tax liens on personal property of businesses are filed with the Secretary of State. All other federal and state tax liens on personal property are filed with the county Clerk of Circuit Court. Usually tax liens on personal property are filed in the same index with UCC financing statements and real estate transactions. Most counties will perform a tax lien as part of a UCC search. Copies usually cost $1.00 per page. Other liens include judgments, hospital, mechanics, sewer, and ambulance.

Real Estate Records

Any name searched in the "Official Records" will usually include all types of liens and property transfers for that name. Most counties will perform searches. In addition to the usual $1.00 per page copy fee, certification of documents usually cost $1.00 per document. Tax records are located at the Property Appraiser Office.

County Courts and Recording Offices

Alachua County
Real Estate Recording—Alachua County Clerk of the Circuit Court, 12 S.E. 1st St., County Administration Bldg.-Room 151, Gainesville, FL 32601. 352-374-3625. Fax: 352-491-4649. 8:30AM-5PM (EST).

Felony, Misdemeanor, Civil, Eviction, Small Claims, Probate—Circuit and County Courts, PO Box 600, Gainesville, FL 32602. 352-374-3611. Fax: 352-338-3201. 8:30AM-5PM (EST). Access by: Mail, remote online, in person.

Baker County
Real Estate Recording—Baker County Clerk of the Circuit Court, 339 East MacClenny Avenue, MacClenny, FL 32063. 904-259-3121. Fax: 904-259-4176. 8:30AM-5PM (EST).

Civil, Eviction, Small Claims, Probate—Circuit and County Courts-Civil, 339 E Macclenny Ave, Macclenny, FL 32063. 904-259-3121. 8:30AM-5PM (EST). Access by: Mail, in person.

Felony, Misdemeanor—Circuit and County Courts-Criminal, 339 E Macclenny Ave, Macclenny, FL 32063. 904-259-3121. Fax: 904-259-4176. 8:30AM-5PM (EST). Access by: Phone, mail, in person.

Bay County
Real Estate Recording—Bay County Clerk of the Circuit Court, 300 East 4th Street, Courthouse, Panama City, FL 32401. 850-747-5104. Fax: 850-747-5188. 8AM-4:30PM (CST).

Civil Actions Over $15,000, Probate—Circuit Court-Civil, PO Box 2269, Panama City, FL 32402. 904-763-9061. Fax: 904-747-5188. 8AM-5PM (CST). Access by: Phone, fax, mail, in person.

Civil Actions Under $15,000, Eviction, Small Claims—County Court-Civil, PO Box 2269, Panama City, FL 32402. 850-763-9061. Fax: 850-747-5188. 8AM-4:30PM (CST). Access by: Phone, fax, mail, in person.

Felony—Circuit Court-Criminal, PO Box 2269, Panama City, FL 32402. 850-747-5123. Fax: 850-747-5188. 8AM-4:30PM (CST). Access by: Fax, mail, in person.

Misdemeanor—County Court-Misdemeanor, PO Box 2269, Panama City, FL 32402. 850-747-5144. Fax: 850-747-5188. 8AM-4:30PM (CST). Access by: Phone, fax, mail, in person.

Bradford County
Real Estate Recording—Bradford County Clerk of the Circuit Court, 945 North Temple Avenue, Starke, FL 32091. 904-964-6280. Fax: 904-964-4454. 8AM-5PM (EST).

Felony, Civil Actions Over $15,000, Probate—Circuit Court, PO Drawer B, Starke, FL 32091. 904-964-6280. Fax: 904-964-4454. 8AM-5PM (EST). Access by: Phone, mail, in person.

Misdemeanor, Civil Actions Under $15,000, Eviction, Small Claims—County Court, PO Drawer B, Starke, FL 32091. 904-964-6280. Fax: 904-964-4454. 8AM-5PM (EST). Access by: Mail, in person.

Brevard County
Real Estate Recording—Brevard County Clerk of the Circuit Court, 700 South Park Ave., Building #2, Titusville, FL 32780. 407-264-5244. Fax: 407-264-5246. 8AM-5PM (EST).

Civil, Eviction, Small Claims, Probate—Circuit and County Courts-Civil, PO Box H, 700 S Park Ave, Titusville, FL 32780. 407-264-5245. Fax: 407-264-5246. 8AM-5PM (EST). Access by: Phone, fax, mail, remote online, in person.

Felony—Circuit Court-Felony, 700 Park Ave (PO Box H, 32781-0239), Titusville, FL 32780. 407-264-5350. Fax: 407-264-5395. 8AM-4:30PM (EST). Access by: Phone, fax, mail, remote online, in person. Contact Lori Raulerson for infor-

mation about remote access. This system is being converted to the Internet at www.clerk.co.brevard.fl.us..

Misdemeanor—County Court-Misdemeanor, 700 Park Ave (PO Box H, 32781-0239), Titusville, FL 32780. 407-264-5350. Fax: 407-264-5395. 8AM-4:30PM (EST). Access by: Phone, fax, mail, remote online, in person. Contact Lori Raulerson for information about remote access. This system is being converted to the Internet at www.clek.co.brevard.fl.us..

Broward County
Real Estate Recording—Broward County Board of County Commissioners, 115 South Andrews Avenue, Room 114, Fort Lauderdale, FL 33301. 954-357-7281. Fax: 954-357-7267. 8:30AM-4:30PM M,T,Th,F; 8:30AM-Noon W (EST).

Felony, Misdemeanor, Civil, Eviction, Small Claims, Probate—Circuit and County Courts, 201 SE 6th St, Ft Lauderdale, FL 33301. 954-831-5729. Criminal: 954-765-4573. Fax: 954-831-7166. 9AM-4PM (EST). Access by: Phone, mail, in person.

Calhoun County
Real Estate Recording—Calhoun County Clerk of the Circuit Court, 425 East Central Avenue, Room 130, Blountstown, FL 32424. 850-674-4545. Fax: 850-674-5553. 8AM-4PM (CST).

Felony, Misdemeanor, Civil, Eviction, Small Claims, Probate—Circuit and County Court, 425 E Central Ave, Blountstown, FL 32424. 850-674-4545. Fax: 850-674-5553. 8AM-4PM (CST). Access by: Phone, fax, mail, in person.

Charlotte County
Real Estate Recording—Charlotte County Clerk of the Circuit Court, 410 Taylor Rd., Punta Gorda, FL 33950. 941-637-2199. Fax: 941-637-2172. 8AM-5PM (EST).

Civil, Eviction, Small Claims, Probate (Separate)—Circuit and County Courts-Civil Division, PO Box 1687, Punta Gorda, FL 33951-1687. 941-637-2230. Probate: 941-637-2210/2174. Fax: 941-637-2159. 8AM-5PM (EST). Access by: Mail, in person.

Felony, Misdemeanor—Circuit and County Courts-Criminal Division, PO Box 1687, Punta Gorda, FL 33951-1687. 941-637-2115. Fax: 941-637-2159. 8AM-5PM (EST). Access by: Phone, mail, in person.

Citrus County
Real Estate Recording—Citrus County Clerk of the Circuit Court, 110 North Apopka Ave. Room 101, Inverness, FL 34450. 352-637-9468. Fax: 352-637-9477. 8AM-4:30PM (EST).

Felony, Civil Actions Over $15,000, Probate—Circuit Court, 110 N Apopka Rm 101, Inverness, FL 34450. 352-637-9400. Fax: 352-637-9413. 8AM-4:30PM (EST). Access by: Phone, fax, mail, in person.

Misdemeanor, Civil Actions Under $15,000, Eviction, Small Claims—County Court, 110 N Apopka, Inverness, FL 34450. 352-637-9400. Fax: 352-637-9413. 8AM-4:30PM (EST). Access by: Mail, in person.

Clay County
Real Estate Recording—Clay County Clerk of the Circuit Court, 825 North Orange Avenue, Green Cove Springs, FL 32043. 904-284-6300. Fax: 904-284-6390. 8:30AM-4:30PM (EST).

Felony, Civil Actions Over $15,000, Probate—Circuit Court, PO Box 698, Green Cove Springs, FL 32043. 904-284-6302. Fax: 904-284-6390. 8:30AM-4:30PM (EST). Access by: Mail, in person.

Misdemeanor, Civil Actions Under $15,000, Eviction, Small Claims—County Court, PO Box 698, Green Cove Springs, FL 32043. 904-284-6316. Fax: 904-284-6390.

8:30AM-4:30PM (EST). Access by: Mail, remote online, in person.

Collier County

Real Estate Recording—Collier County Clerk of the Circuit Court, 3301 Tamiami Trail East, Administration Bldg., 4th floor, Naples, FL 34112. 941-732-2606. Fax: 941-774-8408. 8AM-5PM (No recording after 4:30PM) (EST).

Felony, Civil Actions Over $15,000, Probate—Circuit Court, PO Box 413044, Naples, FL 33941. 941-732-2646. 8AM-5PM (EST). Access by: Mail, in person.

Misdemeanor, Civil Actions Under $15,000, Eviction, Small Claims—County Court, PO Box 413044, Naples, FL 33941. 941-732-2646. Fax: 941-774-8020. 8AM-5PM (EST). Access by: Mail, in person.

Columbia County

Real Estate Recording—Columbia County Clerk of the Circuit Court, 145 North Hernando Street, Lake City, FL 32055. 904-758-1342. Fax: 904-758-1337. 8AM-5PM (EST).

Felony, Misdemeanor, Civil, Eviction, Small Claims, Probate—Circuit and County Courts, PO Drawer 2069, Lake City, FL 32056. 904-758-1353. 8AM-5PM (EST). Access by: Mail, in person.

Dade County

Real Estate Recording—Dade County Clerk of the Circuit Court, 44 West Flager Street, 8th Floor, Miami, FL 33130. 305-275-1155. Fax: 305-372-7775. 8:30AM-4:30PM (EST).

Civil, Eviction, Small Claims, Probate—Circuit and County Courts-Civil, 73 W Flagler St, Miami, FL 33130. 305-275-1155. Fax: 305-375-5819. 8:30AM-4:30PM (EST). Access by: Phone, fax, mail, in person.

Felony, Misdemeanor—Circuit and County Courts-Criminal, 1351 NW 12th St, Miami, FL 33125. 305-547-4888. Fax: 305-545-2295. 8:30AM-4:30PM (EST). Access by: Fax, mail, in person.

De Soto County

Real Estate Recording—De Soto County Clerk of the Circuit Court, 115 East Oak Street, Arcadia, FL 33821. 941-993-4876. Fax: 941-993-4669. 8:30AM-4:30PM (EST).

Felony, Misdemeanor, Civil, Eviction, Small Claims, Probate—Circuit and County Courts, PO Box 591, Arcadia, FL 33821. 941-993-4876. Fax: 941-993-4669. 8AM-5PM (EST). Access by: Phone, fax, mail, in person.

Dixie County

Real Estate Recording—Dixie County Clerk of the Circuit Court, Corner Highway 351 & King Avenue, Courthouse, Cross City, FL 32628. 352-498-1200. Fax: 352-498-1201. 9AM-Noon,1-5PM (EST).

Felony, Misdemeanor, Civil, Eviction, Small Claims, Probate—Circuit and County Courts, PO Drawer 1206, Cross City, FL 32628-1206. 352-498-1200. Fax: 352-498-1201. 9AM-5PM (EST). Access by: Mail, in person.

Duval County

Real Estate Recording—Duval County Clerk of the Circuit Court, 330 East Bay Street, Courthouse, Jacksonville, FL 32202. 904-630-2043. Fax: 904-630-2959. 8AM-5PM (EST).

Civil, Eviction, Small Claims, Probate—Circuit and County Courts-Civil Division, 330 E Bay St, Jacksonville, FL 32202. 904-630-2039. Fax: 904-630-2959. 8AM-5PM (EST). Access by: Mail, in person.

Felony, Misdemeanor—Circuit and County Courts-Criminal Division, 330 E Bay St, Jacksonville, FL 32202. 904-630-2070. Fax: 904-630-7505. 8AM-5PM (EST). Access by: Mail, remote online, in person. Contact Mike O'Brien at 904-630-1140 for information about remote access. Costs include $100 setup, $30 per month and $.25 per minute. System available 24 hours per day at minimum 9600 baud. Records go back to 1992.

Escambia County

Real Estate Recording—Escambia Clerk of Circuit Court, 223 Palafox Place, Old Courthouse, Pensacola, FL 32501. 850-436-5700. Fax: 850-436-5120. 8AM-5PM (CST).

Civil, Eviction, Small Claims, Probate—Circuit and County Courts-Civil Division, 190 Governmental Center, Pensacola, FL 32501. 850-436-5260. Fax: 850-436-5610. 8AM-5PM (CST). Access by: Mail, in person.

Felony, Misdemeanor—Circuit and County Courts-Criminal Division, 190 Governmental Center, Pensacola, FL 32501. 850-436-5160. Fax: 850-436-5610. 8AM-5PM (CST). Access by: Fax, mail, in person.

Flagler County

Real Estate Recording—Flagler County Clerk of the Circuit Court, 200 East Moody Blvd., Courthouse 1st floor, Bunnell, FL 32010. 904-437-7442. (EST).

Felony, Misdemeanor, Civil, Eviction, Small Claims, Probate—Circuit and County Courts, PO Box 787, Bunnell, FL 32110. 904-437-7430. Fax: 904-437-7406. 8AM-5PM (EST). Access by: Phone, fax, mail, in person.

Franklin County

Real Estate Recording—Franklin County Clerk of the Circuit Court, 33 Market Street, Apalachicola, FL 32320. 850-653-8861. Fax: 850-653-2261. 8:30AM-4:30PM (EST).

Felony, Misdemeanor, Civil, Eviction, Small Claims, Probate—Circuit and County Courts, 33 Market St, Suite 203, Apalachicola, FL 32321. 850-653-8862. Fax: 850-653-2261. 8:30AM-4:30PM (EST). Access by: Mail, in person.

Gadsden County

Real Estate Recording—Gadsden County Clerk of the Circuit Court, 10 East Jefferson Street, Quincy, FL 32351. 850-875-8603. Fax: 850-875-8612. 8:30AM-5PM (EST).

Civil, Eviction, Small Claims, Probate—Circuit and County Courts-Civil Division, PO Box 1649, Quincy, FL 32353. 850-875-8621. Fax: 850-875-8612. 8:30AM-5PM (EST). Access by: Phone, fax, mail, in person.

Felony, Misdemeanor—Circuit and County Courts-Criminal Division, 112 South Adams St, Quincy, FL 32351. 850-875-8609. Fax: 850-875-7625. 8:30AM-5PM (EST). Access by: Mail, in person.

Gilchrist County

Real Estate Recording—Gilchrist County Clerk of the Circuit Court, Courthouse, 112 S. Main St., Trenton, FL 32693. 352-463-3170. Fax: 352-463-3166. 8:30AM-5PM (EST).

Felony, Misdemeanor, Civil, Eviction, Small Claims, Probate—Circuit and County Courts, 112 S Main St, Trenton, FL 32693. 352-463-3170. Fax: 352-463-3166. 8:30AM-5PM (EST). Access by: Phone, fax, mail, in person.

Glades County

Real Estate Recording—Glades County Clerk of the Circuit Court, Highway 27 and 5th Street, 500 Ave. J, Moore Haven, FL 33471. 941-946-0113. Fax: 941-946-0560. 8AM-5PM (EST).

Felony, Misdemeanor, Civil, Eviction, Small Claims, Probate—Circuit and County Courts, PO Box 10, Moore Haven, FL 33471. 941-946-0113. Fax: 941-946-0560. 8AM-5PM (EST). Access by: Mail, in person.

Gulf County

Real Estate Recording—Gulf County Clerk of the Circuit Court, 1000 5th Street, Port St. Joe, FL 32456. 850-229-6113. Fax: 850-229-6174. 9AM-5PM (CST).

Felony, Misdemeanor, Civil, Eviction, Small Claims, Probate—Circuit and County Courts, 1000 5th St, Port St Joe, FL 32456. 850-229-6112. Fax: 850-229-6174. 9AM-5PM (CST). Access by: Mail, in person.

Hamilton County

Real Estate Recording—Hamilton County Clerk of the Circuit Court, 207 NE 1st Street, Room 106, Jasper, FL

32052. 904-792-1288. Fax: 904-792-3524. 8:30AM-4:30PM (EST).

Felony, Misdemeanor, Civil, Eviction, Small Claims, Probate—Circuit and County Courts, 207 NE 1st St #106, Jasper, FL 32052. 904-792-1288. Fax: 904-792-3524. 8:30AM-4:30PM (EST). Access by: Phone, mail, in person.

Hardee County

Real Estate Recording—Hardee County Clerk of the Circuit Court, 417 West Main Street, Wauchula, FL 33873. 941-773-4174. Fax: 941-773-4422. 8:30AM-5PM; 8:30AM-3:15PM Recording hours (EST).

Felony, Misdemeanor, Civil, Eviction, Small Claims, Probate—Circuit and County Courts, PO Drawer 1749, Wauchula, FL 33873-1749. 941-773-4174. Fax: 941-773-4422. 8:30AM-5PM (EST). Access by: Mail, in person.

Hendry County

Real Estate Recording—Hendry County Clerk of the Circuit Court, Corner of Highway 80 and 29, Courthouse, La Belle, FL 33935. 941-675-5217. 8:30AM-5PM (EST).

Felony, Misdemeanor, Civil, Eviction, Small Claims, Probate—Circuit and County Courts, PO Box 1760, La-Belle, FL 33935-1760. 941-675-5217. Fax: 941-675-5238. 8:30AM-5PM (EST). Access by: Phone, mail, in person.

Hernando County

Real Estate Recording—Hernando County Clerk of the Circuit Court, 20 North Main, Room 215, Brooksville, FL 34601. 352-754-4201. Fax: 352-754-4243. 8AM-5PM (EST).

Felony, Misdemeanor, Civil, Eviction, Small Claims, Probate—Circuit and County Courts, 20 N Main St, Brooksville, FL 34601. 352-754-4201. Fax: 352-754-4239. 8:30AM-5PM (EST). Access by: Fax, mail, remote online, in person.

Highlands County

Real Estate Recording—Highlands County Clerk of the Circuit Court, 430 South Commerce Avenue, Sebring, FL 33870. 941-386-6590. 8:00AM-4:30PM (EST).

Felony, Misdemeanor, Civil, Eviction, Small Claims, Probate—Circuit and County Courts, 430 S Commerce Ave, Sebring, FL 33870. 941-385-2581. Fax: 941-386-6575. 8AM-4:30PM (EST). Access by: Mail, in person.

Hillsborough County

Real Estate Recording—Hillsborough County Clerk of the Circuit Court, 419 Pierce Street, Room 114-K, Tampa, FL 33602. 813-276-8100. Fax: 813-276-2114. 8AM-5PM (EST).

Felony, Misdemeanor, Civil, Eviction, Small Claims, Probate—Circuit and County Courts, 419 Pierce St, Tampa, FL 33602. 813-276-8100. Fax: 813-272-7707. 8AM-5PM (EST). Access by: Mail, in person.

Holmes County

Real Estate Recording—Holmes County Clerk of the Circuit Court, 201 North Oklahoma Street, Bonifay, FL 32425. 850-547-1102. Fax: 850-547-6630. 8AM-4PM (CST).

Felony, Misdemeanor, Civil, Eviction, Small Claims, Probate—Circuit and County Courts, PO Box 397, Bonifay, FL 32425. 904-547-1100. Fax: 850-547-6630. 8AM-4PM (CST). Access by: Mail, in person.

Indian River County

Real Estate Recording—Indian River County Clerk of the Circuit Court, 2000 16th Ave., Vero Beach, FL 32960. 561-770-5174. 8:30AM-5PM (EST).

Felony, Misdemeanor, Civil, Eviction, Small Claims, Probate—Circuit and County Courts, PO Box 1028, Vero Beach, FL 32961. 561-567-5185. Fax: 561-770-5008. 8:30AM-5PM (EST). Access by: Mail, in person.

Jackson County

Real Estate Recording—Jackson County Clerk of the Circuit Court, 4445 East Lafayette Street, Courthouse, Marianna, FL 32446. 850-482-9552. Fax: 850-482-7849. 8AM-4:30PM (CST).

Felony, Misdemeanor, Civil, Eviction, Small Claims, Probate—Circuit and County Courts, PO Box 510, Marianna, FL 32447. 850-482-9552. Fax: 850-482-7849. 8AM-4:30PM (CST). Access by: Fax, mail, in person.

Jefferson County

Real Estate Recording—Jefferson County Clerk of the Circuit Court, Courthouse, Room 10, Monticello, FL 32344. 850-342-0218. Fax: 850-342-0222. 8AM-5PM (EST).

Felony, Misdemeanor, Civil, Eviction, Small Claims, Probate—Circuit and County Courts, Jefferson County Courthouse, Rm 10, Monticello, FL 32344. 850-997-3596. Fax: 850-997-4855. 8AM-5PM (EST). Access by: Mail, remote online, in person. Contact Dale Boatwright for information about remote access..

Lafayette County

Real Estate Recording—Lafayette County Clerk of the Circuit Court, Main & Fletcher Streets, Courthouse, Mayo, FL 32066. 904-294-1600. Fax: 904-294-4231. 8AM-5PM (EST).

Felony, Misdemeanor, Civil, Eviction, Small Claims, Probate—Circuit and County Courts, PO Box 88, Mayo, FL 32066. 904-294-1600. Fax: 904-294-4231. 8AM-5PM (EST). Access by: Phone, fax, mail, in person.

Lake County

Real Estate Recording—Lake County Clerk of the Circuit Court, 550 West Main Street, Tavares, FL 32778. 352-742-4114. Fax: 352-742-4166. 8:30AM-5PM (Recording hours: 8:30AM-4:30PM) (EST).

Felony, Misdemeanor, Civil, Eviction, Small Claims, Probate—Circuit and County Courts, 550 W Main St or PO Box 7800, Tavares, FL 32778. 352-742-4100. Fax: 352-742-4166. 8:30AM-5PM (EST). Access by: Phone, fax, mail, in person.

Lee County

Real Estate Recording—Lee County Clerk of the Circuit Court, 2115 Second Street, Courthouse - 2nd Floor, Fort Myers, FL 33901. 941-335-2291. 7:45AM-5PM (EST).

Felony, Misdemeanor, Civil, Eviction, Small Claims, Probate—Circuit and County Courts, PO Box 2469, Ft Myers, FL 33902. 941-335-2283. 7:45AM-5PM (EST). Access by: Mail, in person.

Leon County

Real Estate Recording—Leon County Clerk of the Circuit Court, 301 South Monroe Street, Room 123, Tallahassee, FL 32301. 850-488-7538. Fax: 850-921-1310. 8:30AM-5PM (EST).

Felony, Misdemeanor, Civil, Eviction, Small Claims, Probate—Circuit and County Courts, PO Box 726, Tallahassee, FL 32302. 850-488-7534. Fax: 850-488-8863. 8:30AM-5PM (EST). Access by: Mail, in person.

Levy County

Real Estate Recording—Levy County Clerk of the Circuit Court, Courthouse, 355 N. Court St., Bronson, FL 32621. 904-486-5228. 8AM-5PM (EST).

Felony, Misdemeanor, Civil, Eviction, Small Claims, Probate—Circuit and County Courts, PO Box 610, Bronson, FL 32621. 904-486-5100. Fax: 904-486-5166. 8AM-5PM (EST). Access by: Mail, in person.

Liberty County

Real Estate Recording—Liberty County Clerk of the Circuit Court, Highway 20, Courthouse, Bristol, FL 32321. 850-643-2215. Fax: 850-643-2866. 8AM-5PM (EST).

Felony, Misdemeanor, Civil, Eviction, Small Claims, Probate—Circuit and County Courts, PO Box 399, Bristol, FL 32321. 850-643-2215. Fax: 850-643-2866. 8AM-5PM (EST). Access by: Mail, in person.

Madison County

Real Estate Recording—Madison County Clerk of the Circuit Court, Courthouse, 101 South Range Street, Room

108, Madison, FL 32340. 850-973-1500. Fax: 850-973-2059. 8AM-5PM (EST).

Felony, Misdemeanor, Civil, Eviction, Small Claims, Probate—Circuit and County Courts, PO Box 237, Madison, FL 32341. 850-973-1500. Fax: 850-973-2059. 8AM-5PM (EST). Access by: Phone, mail, in person.

Manatee County

Real Estate Recording—Manatee County Clerk of the Circuit Court, 1115 Manatee Avenue West, Bradenton, FL 34205. 941-741-4040. Fax: 941-741-4082. 8:30AM-5PM (EST).

Felony, Misdemeanor, Civil, Eviction, Small Claims, Probate—Circuit and County Courts, PO Box 1000, Bradenton, FL 34206. 941-749-1800. Fax: 941-741-4082. 8:30AM-5PM (EST). Access by: Phone, mail, remote online, in person.

Marion County

Real Estate Recording—Marion County Clerk of the Circuit Court, 110 N.W. First Avenue, Ocala, FL 34475. 352-620-3925. 8AM-5PM (EST).

Felony, Misdemeanor, Civil, Eviction, Small Claims, Probate—Circuit and County Courts, PO Box 1030, Ocala, FL 34478. 352-620-3904. Fax: 352-620-3300. 8AM-5PM (EST). Access by: Mail, in person.

Martin County

Real Estate Recording—Martin County Clerk of the Circuit Court, 100 E. Ocean Blvd, 3rd Floor, Stuart, FL 34994. 561-288-5551. Fax: 561-223-7929. 8AM-4:30PM (EST).

Felony, Misdemeanor, Civil, Eviction, Small Claims, Probate—Circuit and County Courts, PO Box 9016, Stuart, FL 34995. 407-288-5576. Fax: 407-288-5990. 8AM-5PM (EST). Access by: Phone, fax, mail, remote online, in person.

Monroe County

Real Estate Recording—Monroe County Clerk of the Circuit Court, 500 Whitehead Street, Courthouse, Key West, FL 33040. 305-292-3540. Fax: 305-295-3660. 8:30AM-5PM (EST).

Felony, Misdemeanor, Civil, Eviction, Small Claims, Probate—Circuit and County Courts, 500 Whitehead St, Key West, FL 33040. 305-294-4641. Civil: 305-292-3310. Criminal: 305-292-3390. Fax: 305-295-3623. 8:30AM-5PM (EST). Access by: Mail, in person.

Nassau County

Real Estate Recording—Nassau County Clerk of the Circuit Court, 416 Centre Street, Fernandina Beach, FL 32034. 904-321-5700. Fax: 904-321-5723. 9AM-5PM (Recording Hours: 9AM-4PM) (EST).

Felony, Misdemeanor, Civil, Eviction, Small Claims, Probate—Circuit and County Courts, PO Box 456, Fernandina Beach, FL 32035. 904-321-5700. Fax: 904-321-5723. 9AM-5PM (EST). Access by: Mail, in person.

Okaloosa County

Real Estate Recording—Okaloosa County Clerk of the Circuit Court, 101 East James Lee Blvd., Crestview, FL 32536. 904-689-5847. Fax: 904-689-5886. 8AM-5PM (CST).

Felony, Misdemeanor, Civil, Eviction, Small Claims, Probate—Circuit and County Courts, 1250 Eglin Pkwy, Shalimar, FL 32579. 904-651-7200. Fax: 904-651-7230. 8AM-5PM (CST). Access by: Mail, in person.

Okeechobee County

Real Estate Recording—Okeechobee County Clerk of the Circuit Court, 304 N.W. 2nd Street, Room 101, Okeechobee, FL 34972. 941-763-2131. 8:30AM-5PM (EST).

Felony, Misdemeanor, Civil, Eviction, Small Claims, Probate—Circuit and County Courts, 304 NW 2nd St Rm 101, Okeechobee, FL 34972. 941-763-2131. 7:30AM-5PM (EST). Access by: Mail, in person.

Orange County

Real Estate Recording—Orange County Comptroller, 390 N. Orange Ave., # 650A, Orlando, FL 32801. 407-836-5115. Fax: 407-836-5101. 8:30AM-4PM (EST).

Felony, Misdemeanor, Civil, Eviction, Small Claims, Probate—Circuit and County Courts, 37 N Orange Ave #550, Orlando, FL 32801. 407-836-2060. 8AM-5PM (EST). Access by: Mail, remote online, in person.

Misdemeanor, Civil Actions Under $15,000, Eviction, Small Claims—County Court-Apopka Branch, 1111 N Rock Springs Rd, Apopka, FL 32712. 407-889-4176. Fax: 407-836-2225. 8AM-5PM (EST). Access by: Mail, in person.

County Court #3, 475 W Story Rd, Ocoee, FL 34761. 407-656-3229. 8AM-5PM (EST). Access by: Mail, in person.

County Court-NE Orange Division, 450 N Lakemont Ave, Winter Park, FL 32792. 407-671-1116. 8AM-5PM (EST). Access by: Mail, in person.

Osceola County

Real Estate Recording—Osceola County Clerk of the Circuit Court, Room 231-C, Dept R, 17 S. Vernon Ave., Kissimmee, FL 34741. 407-847-1423. Fax: 407-847-0783. 8:30AM-5PM; 8:30AM-4PM Recording hours (EST).

Civil Actions Over $2,500—Circuit Court-Civil, 12 S Vernon Ave, Kissimmee, FL 34741. 407-847-1300. 8:30AM-5PM (EST). Access by: Mail, in person.

Eviction, Small Claims—County Court-Civil, 12 S Vernon Ave, Kissimmee, FL 34741. 407-847-1300. 8:30AM-5PM (EST). Access by: Mail, in person.

Felony, Misdemeanor—Circuit and County Courts-Criminal Division, 17 S Vernon Ave, Kissimmee, FL 34741. 407-847-1315. 8:30AM-5PM (EST). Access by: Mail, in person.

Palm Beach County

Real Estate Recording—Palm Beach County Clerk of the Circuit Court, 205 N. Dixie Highway, Room 4.2500, West Palm Beach, FL 33402. 407-355-2991. 8AM-5PM (EST).

Civil, Eviction, Small Claims, Probate—Circuit and County Courts-Civil Division, PO Box 667, West Palm Beach, FL 33402. 561-355-2986. Fax: 561-355-4643. 8AM-5PM (EST). Access by: Phone, mail, in person. same as civil.

Felony, Misdemeanor—Circuit and County Courts-Criminal Division, 205 North Dixie, Room 3.2400, West Palm Beach, FL 33401. 561-355-2519. Fax: 561-355-3802. 8AM-5PM (EST). Access by: Phone, fax, mail, remote online, in person. Contact Betty Jones at 407-355-6783 for information about remote access. Fees include $145 setup and $65 per month. Civil records available back to 1988.

Pasco County

Real Estate Recording—Pasco County Clerk of the Circuit Court, 38053 Live Oak Ave., Room 205, Dade City, FL 33523. 352-521-4469. 8:30AM-5PM (EST).

Civil, Eviction, Small Claims, Probate—Circuit and County Courts-Civil Division, 38053 Live Oak Ave, Dade City, FL 33525. 352-521-4482. 8:30AM-5PM (EST). Access by: Mail, in person.

Felony, Misdemeanor—Circuit and County Courts-Criminal Division, 38053 Live Oak Ave, Dade City, FL 33525. 352-521-4482. 8:30AM-5PM (EST). Access by: Mail, in person.

Pinellas County

Real Estate Recording—Pinellas County Clerk of the Circuit Court, 315 Court Street, Room 150, Clearwater, FL 33756. 813-464-3204. Fax: 813-464-4383. 8AM-5PM (EST).

Civil, Eviction, Small Claims, Probate—Circuit and County Courts-Civil Division, 315 Court St, Clearwater, FL 34616. 813-464-3267. Fax: 813-464-4070. 8AM-5PM (EST). Access by: Mail, in person.

Felony—Criminal Justice Center, Circuit Criminal Court Records, 14250 49th St N, Clearwater, FL 34622. 813-464-3267. Fax: 813-464-6233. 8AM-5PM (EST). Access by: Phone, mail, remote online, in person. Contact Marlin Maskeny at 813-464-3779 for information about remote access. The setup fee is $50 plus per minute access fees. Criminal index goes back to 1972. Available 24 hours per day at minimum 9600 baud.

Misdemeanor—County Court-Criminal Division, 14250 49th St N, Clearwater, FL 34622-2831. 813-464-6800. Fax: 813-464-6072. 8AM-5PM (EST). Access by: Mail, remote online, in person. Contact Marlin Maskeny at 813-464-3779 for information about remote access. Fees include $60 setup and per minute charge. Criminal index goes back to 1972.

Polk County

Real Estate Recording—Polk County Clerk of the Circuit Court, 255 N. Broadway, Bartow, FL 33830. 941-534-4516. Fax: 941-534-4089. 8:30AM-4:30PM (EST).

Civil Actions Over $15,000, Probate—Circuit Court-Civil Division, PO Box 9000 Drawer CC4, Bartow, FL 33831-9000. 941-534-4488. Probate: 941-534-4478. Fax: 941-534-4089. 8:30AM-4PM (EST). Access by: Phone, mail, online, in person.

Felony—Circuit and County Courts-Felony Division, PO Box 9000 Drawer CC9, Bartow, FL 33830. 941-534-4000. Fax: 941-534-4089. 8AM-5PM (EST). Access by: Phone, mail, online, in person.

Misdemeanor—Circuit and County Courts-Misdemeanor Division, PO Box 9000 Drawer CC10, Bartow, FL 33830. 941-534-4421. Fax: 941-534-4089. 8AM-5PM (EST). Access by: Phone, mail, in person.

Civil Actions Under $15,000, Eviction, Small Claims—County Court-Civil Division, PO Box 9000 Drawer CC12, Bartow, FL 33830-9000. 941-534-4556. Fax: 941-534-4089. 8:30AM-4:45PM (EST). Access by: Phone, mail, in person.

Putnam County

Real Estate Recording—Putnam County Clerk of the Circuit Court, 518 St. Johns Avenue, Bldg. 1-E, Palatka, FL 32177. 904-329-0256. Fax: 904-329-0889. 8:30AM-5PM (EST).

Civil, Eviction, Small Claims, Probate—Circuit and County Courts-Civil Division, PO Box 758, Palatka, FL 32178. 904-329-0361. Fax: 904-329-0888. 8:30AM-5PM (EST). Access by: Mail, in person.

Felony, Misdemeanor—Circuit and County Courts-Criminal Division, PO Box 758, Palatka, FL 32178. 904-329-0249. Fax: 904-329-0888. 8:30AM-5PM (EST). Access by: Phone, fax, mail, remote online, in person. Write Lonnie Thompson to register; include a check for $400 as a setup fee. The monthly charge is $40 plus $.05 per minute over 20 hours. Criminal records go back to 1972. System includes civil and real propert.

Santa Rosa County

Real Estate Recording—Santa Rosa County Clerk of the Circuit Court, Clerk of Courts Recording Dept, 6865 Caroline Street, Milton, FL 32570. 850-983-1031. Fax: 850-626-7248. 8AM-4:30PM (CST).

Civil, Eviction, Small Claims, Probate—Circuit and County Courts-Civil Division, PO Box 472, Milton, FL 32572. 850-623-0135. Fax: 850-626-7248. 8AM-4:30PM (CST). Access by: Fax, mail, in person.

Felony, Misdemeanor—Circuit and County Courts-Criminal Division, PO Box 472, Milton, FL 32572. 850-623-0135. Fax: 850-626-7248. 8AM-4:30PM (CST). Access by: Fax, mail, in person.

Sarasota County

Real Estate Recording—Sarasota County Clerk of the Circuit Court, 2000 Main Street, Sarasota, FL 34237. 941-951-5231. 8:30AM-5PM (EST).

Civil, Eviction, Small Claims, Probate—Circuit and County Courts-Civil Division, PO Box 3079, Sarasota, FL 34230. 941-951-5206. 8:30AM-5PM (EST). Access by: Mail, in person.

Felony, Misdemeanor—Circuit and County Courts-Criminal, PO Box 3079, Sarasota, FL 34230. 941-362-4066. 8:30AM-5PM (EST). Access by: Mail, in person.

Seminole County

Real Estate Recording—Seminole County Clerk of the Circuit Court, 301 N. Park Avenue, Room A-132, Sanford, FL 32771. 407-323-4330. 8AM-4:30PM (EST).

Civil, Eviction, Small Claims, Probate—Circuit and County Courts-Civil Division, PO Drawer C, Sanford, FL 32772-0659. 407-323-4330. Fax: 407-330-7193. 8AM-4:30PM (EST). Access by: Mail, in person.

Felony, Misdemeanor—Circuit and County Courts-Criminal Division, PO Drawer C, Sanford, FL 32771. 407-323-4330. 8AM-4:30PM (EST). Access by: Mail, in person.

St. Johns County

Real Estate Recording—St. Johns County Clerk of the Circuit Court, 4010 Lewis Speedway, St. Augustine, FL 32095. 904-823-2333. Fax: 904-823-2294. 8AM-5PM (No Recording after 4:15PM) (EST).

Civil, Eviction, Small Claims, Probate—Circuit and County Courts-Civil Division, PO Drawer 300, St Augustine, FL 32085-0300. 904-823-2333. Fax: 904-823-2294. 8AM-5PM (EST). Access by: Fax, mail, in person.

Felony, Misdemeanor—Circuit and County Courts-Criminal Division, PO Drawer 300, St Augustine, FL 32085-0300. 904-823-2333. Fax: 904-823-2294. 8AM-5PM (EST). Access by: Fax, mail, in person.

St. Lucie County

Real Estate Recording—St. Lucie County Clerk of the Circuit Court, 221 South Indian River Drive, Fort Pierce, FL 34950. 561-462-6928. Fax: 561-462-1283. 8AM-5PM (EST).

Civil, Eviction, Small Claims, Probate—Circuit and County Courts-Civil Division, PO Drawer 700, Ft Pierce, FL 34954. 561-462-2758. Fax: 561-462-1283. 8AM-5PM (EST). Access by: Mail, in person.

Felony, Misdemeanor—Circuit and County Courts-Criminal Division, PO Drawer 700, Ft Pierce, FL 34954. 561-462-6900. Fax: 561-462-6975. 8AM-5PM (EST). Access by: Fax, mail, in person.

Sumter County

Real Estate Recording—Sumter County Clerk of the Circuit Court, 209 North Florida Street, Room 106, Bushnell, FL 33513. 352-793-0215. Fax: 352-793-0218. 8:30AM-5PM (EST).

Civil, Eviction, Small Claims, Probate—Circuit and County Courts-Civil Division, 209 N Florida St, Bushnell, FL 33513. 352-793-0215. Fax: 352-793-0218. 8:30AM-5PM (EST). Access by: Mail, in person.

Felony, Misdemeanor—Circuit and County Courts-Criminal Division, 209 N Florida St, Bushnell, FL 33513. 352-793-0215. Fax: 352-793-0218. 8:30AM-5PM (EST). Access by: Mail, in person.

Suwannee County

Real Estate Recording—Suwannee County Clerk of the Circuit Court, 200 South Ohio Avenue, Live Oak, FL 32060. 904-364-3498. Fax: 904-362-2421. 8:30AM-5PM (EST).

Felony, Misdemeanor, Civil, Eviction, Small Claims, Probate—Circuit and County Courts, 200 S Ohio Ave, Live Oak, FL 32060. 904-364-3532. Fax: 904-362-2421. 8AM-5PM (EST). Access by: Mail, in person.

Taylor County

Real Estate Recording—Taylor County Clerk of the Circuit Court, 108 North Jefferson Street, Perry, FL 32348. 850-838-3506. Fax: 850-838-3549. 8AM-5PM (EST).

Felony, Misdemeanor, Civil, Eviction, Small Claims, Probate—Circuit and County Courts, PO Box 620, Perry, FL 32347. 850-838-3506. Fax: 850-838-3507. 8AM-5PM (EST). Access by: Phone, fax, mail, in person.

Union County

Real Estate Recording—Union County Clerk of the Circuit Court, State Road 100, Courthouse Room 103, Lake

Butler, FL 32054. 904-496-3711. Fax: 904-496-1535. 8AM-5PM (EST).

Felony, Misdemeanor, Civil, Eviction, Small Claims, Probate—Circuit and County Courts, Courthouse Rm 103, Lake Butler, FL 32054. 904-496-3711. 8AM-5PM (EST). Access by: Mail, in person.

Volusia County

Real Estate Recording—Volusia County Clerk of the Circuit Court, 235 W. New York Ave., De Land, FL 32720. 904-736-5912. Fax: 904-740-5104. 8AM-4:30PM (EST).

Civil, Eviction, Small Claims, Probate—Circuit and County Courts-Civil Division, PO Box 43, De Land, FL 32721. 904-736-5915. Fax: 904-822-5711. 8AM-4:30PM (EST). Access by: Mail, in person.

Felony, Misdemeanor—Circuit and County Courts-Criminal Division, PO Box 43, De Land, FL 32721-0043. 904-736-5915. Fax: 904-822-5711. 8AM-4:30PM (EST). Access by: Mail, in person.

Wakulla County

Real Estate Recording—Wakulla County Clerk of the Circuit Court, Wakulla County Court House, Highway 319, Crawfordville, FL 32327. 850-926-3331. Fax: 850-926-8326. 8AM-4PM (EST).

Felony, Misdemeanor, Civil, Eviction, Small Claims, Probate—Circuit and County Courts, PO Box 337, Crawfordville, FL 32326. 850-926-3331. Fax: 850-926-8326. 8AM-5PM (EST). Access by: Phone, fax, mail, in person.

Walton County

Real Estate Recording—Walton County Clerk of the Circuit Court, 571 US Highway 90 East, Courthouse, De Funiak Springs, FL 32433. 850-892-8115. Fax: 850-892-7551. 8AM-4PM (CST).

Felony, Misdemeanor, Civil, Eviction, Small Claims, Probate—Circuit and County Courts, PO Box 1260, De Funiak Springs, FL 32433. 850-892-8115. Fax: 850-892-7551. 8AM-4:30PM (CST). Access by: Fax, mail, in person.

Washington County

Real Estate Recording—Washington County Clerk of the Circuit Court, 1293 Jackson Avenue, Suite 101, Chipley, FL 32428. 850-638-6285. Fax: 850-638-6297. 8AM-4PM (CST).

Felony, Misdemeanor, Civil, Eviction, Small Claims, Probate—Circuit and County Courts, PO Box 647, Chipley, FL 32428-0647. 850-638-6285. Fax: 850-638-6297. 8AM-4PM (CST). Access by: Phone, fax, mail, in person.

Federal Courts

US District Court
Middle District of Florida

Fort Myers Division, US District Court 2301 First St, Fort Myers, FL 33901. 941-332-3937. Counties: Charlotte, Collier, De Soto, Glades, Hendry, Lee

Jacksonville Division, US District Court PO Box 53558, Jacksonville, FL 32201. 904-232-2854. Counties: Baker, Bradford, Clay, Columbia, Duval, Flagler, Hamilton, Nassau, Putnam, St. Johns, Suwannee, Union

Ocala Division, US District Court c/o Jacksonville Division, PO Box 53558, Jacksonville, FL 32201. 904-232-2854. Counties: Citrus, Lake, Marion, Sumter

Orlando Division, US District Court Room 218, 80 North Hughey Ave, Orlando, FL 32801. 407-648-6366. Counties: Brevard, Orange, Osceola, Seminole, Volusia

Tampa Division, US District Court Office of the Clerk, US Courthouse, Room B-100, 611 N Florida Ave, Tampa, FL 33602. 813-228-2105. Counties: Hardee, Hernando, Hillsborough, Manatee, Pasco, Pinellas, Polk, Sarasota

Northern District of Florida

Gainesville Division, US District Court 401 SE First Ave, Room 243, Gainesville, FL 32601. 352-380-2400. Counties: Alachua, Dixie, Gilchrist, Lafayette, Levy. Records for cases prior to July 1996 are maintained at the Tallahassee Division

Panama City Division, US District Court c/o Pensacola Division, 1 N Palafox St, #226, Pensacola, FL 32501. 904-435-8440. Counties: Bay, Calhoun, Gulf, Holmes, Jackson, Washington

Pensacola Division, US District Court US Courthouse, 1 N Palafox St #226, Pensacola, FL 32501. 850-435-8440. Counties: Escambia, Okaloosa, Santa Rosa, Walton

Tallahassee Division, US District Court Suite 122, 110 E Park Ave, Tallahassee, FL 32301. 850-942-8826. Counties: Franklin, Gadsden, Jefferson, Leon, Liberty, Madison, Taylor, Wakulla

Southern District of Florida

Fort Lauderdale Division, US District Court 299 E Broward Blvd, Room 108, Fort Lauderdale, FL 33301. 954-769-5400. Counties: Broward

Fort Pierce Division, US District Court 300 S. 6th Street, Fort Pierce, FL 34950. 561-595-9691. Counties: Highlands, Indian River, Martin, Okeechobee, St. Lucie

Key West Division, US District Court c/o Miami Division, Room 150, 301 N Miami Ave, Miami, FL 33128-7788. 305-536-4131. Counties: Monroe

Miami Division, US District Court Room 150, 301 N Miami Ave, Miami, FL 33128-7788. 305-536-4131. Counties: Dade

West Palm Beach Division, US District Court Room 402, 701 Clematis St, West Palm Beach, FL 33401. 561-803-3400. Counties: Palm Beach

US Bankruptcy Court
Middle District of Florida

Jacksonville Division, US Bankruptcy Court, PO Box 559, Jacksonville, FL 32201. 904-232-2852. Voice Case Information System: 904-232-1313. Counties: Baker, Bradford, Citrus, Clay, Columbia, Duval, Flagler, Hamilton, Marion, Nassau, Putnam, St. Johns, Sumter, Suwannee, Union, Volusia

Orlando Division, US Bankruptcy Court, Suite 950, 135 W Central Blvd, Orlando, FL 32801. 407-648-6364. Voice Case Information System: 407-648-6800. Counties: Brevard, Lake, Orange, Osceola, Seminole

Tampa Division, US Bankruptcy Court, Suite 200, 4921 Memorial Hwy, Tampa, FL 33624. 813-243-5162. Counties: Charlotte, Collier, De Soto, Glades, Hardee, Hendry, Hernando, Hillsborough, Lee, Manatee, Pasco, Pinellas, Polk, Sarasota

Northern District of Florida

Pensacola Division, US Bankruptcy Court, Suite 700, 220 W Garden St, Pensacola, FL 32501. 850-435-8475. Counties: Escambia, Okaloosa, Santa Rosa, Walton

Tallahassee Division, US Bankruptcy Court, Room 3120, 227 N Bronough St, Tallahassee, FL 32301-1378. 850-942-8933. Counties: Alachua, Bay, Calhoun, Dixie, Franklin, Gadsden, Gilchrist, Gulf, Holmes, Jackson, Jefferson, Lafayette, Leon, Levy, Liberty, Madison, Taylor, Wakulla, Washington

Southern District of Florida

Fort Lauderdale Division, US Bankruptcy Court, 299 E Broward Blvd, Room 310, Fort Lauderdale, FL 33301. 954-769-5700. Voice Case Information System: 305-536-5979. Counties: Any case in the Miami Division may be assigned here

Miami Division, US Bankruptcy Court, Room 1517, 51 SW 1st Ave, Miami, FL 33130. 305-536-5216. Voice Case Information System: 305-536-5979. Counties: Broward, Dade, Highlands, Indian River, Martin, Monroe, Okeechobee, Palm Beach, St. Lucie. Cases may also be assigned to Fort Lauderdale or to West Palm Beach

West Palm Beach Division, US Bankruptcy Court, Federal Bldg Room 202, 701 Clematis St, West Palm Beach, FL 33401. 561-655-6774. Voice Case Information System: 305-536-5979. Counties: Any case in the Miami Division may be assigned here

Georgia

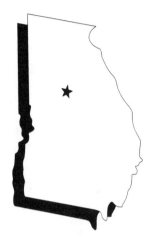

Capitol: Atlanta (Fulton County)	
Number of Counties: 159	**Population:** 7,200,882
County Court Locations:	**Federal Court Locations:**
•Superior Courts: 100/ 46 Circuits	•District Courts: 16
•State Courts: 16	•Bankruptcy Courts: 8
•Combined Courts: 43	**State Agencies:** 20
•Magistrate Courts: 145	
•Combined Superior/Magistrate Court: 17	Municipal Courts: 474
Civil Courts: 2	•Probate Courts: 153
County Recorder's Courts: 3	Juvenile Courts: 159

State Agencies—Summary

General Help Numbers:

State Archives

Secretary of State	404-656-2393
Archives & History Department	Fax: 404-651-9270
330 Capitol Ave SE	8 AM - 4:45 PM
Atlanta, GA 30334	
Reference Librarian:	404-656-2350

Governor's Office

Governor's Office	404-656-1776
203 State Capitol	Fax: 404-657-7332
Atlanta, GA 30334	8AM-4:30PM

Attorney General's Office

Attorney General's Office	404-656-3300
40 Capitol Square SW	Fax: 404-651-9148
Atlanta, GA 30334-1300	8:30AM-5PM
Alternate Telephone:	404-656-4585

State Legislation

General Assembly of Georgia	404-656-5040
State Capitol	8:30AM-4:30PM
Room 351	
Atlanta, GA 30334	
Archives:	
	404-656-2370

Important State Internet Sites:

> 🌐 **Webscape**
> **File Edit View**   **Help**

State of Georgia World Wide Web

www.state.ga.us/

Key site for information about the state of Georgia. Links to major locations in the Georgia State Government such as the Governor's office, the Senate and the House of Representatives and many other interesting sites.

The Georgia State Senate

www.ganet.org/homepages/senate/

From this site you can search for your Senator by name or district and look up Senate committees and their members. Site also links to legislative information.

The Georgia House of Representatives

www.state.ga.us/Legis/1997_98/house/index.htm

From this site you can search for your Congressperson by name or district and look up House committees and their members.

State Archives and Historical Records

www.state.ga.us/SOS/Archives/

This Georgia Department of Archives and History site includes hours of operation, programs and services, publications and links to related web sites.

State Agencies—Public Records

Criminal Records

Georgia Bureau of Investigations, Attn: GCIC, PO Box 370748, Decatur, GA 30037-0748, Main Telephone: 404-244-2601, Fax: 404-244-2878, Hours: 8AM-4PM. Access by: mail, visit. GCIC is the central repository of criminal records for the State. All data reported by local agencies is available. Certain misdemeanors and local ordinance violations are not maintained by GCIC.

Corporation Records
Limited Partnership Records
Limited Liability Company Records

Secretary of State, Corporation Division, 2 M L King Dr, Suite 315, W Tower, Atlanta, GA 30334-1530, Main Telephone: 404-656-2817, Filing Questions: 404-657-1375, Fax: 404-651-9059, Hours: 8AM-5PM. Access by: mail, phone, visit. Trade names, fictitious names and assumed names are found at the county level. DBA's are also found at the county level.

Trademarks/Servicemarks

Secretary of State, Trademark Division, 2 Martin Luther King, Room 315, W Tower, Atlanta, GA 30334, Main Telephone: 404-656-2861, Fax: 404-657-6380, Hours: 8AM-4:30PM. Access by: mail, phone, fax, visit.

Uniform Commercial Code
Federal Tax Liens
State Tax Liens

Superior Court Clerks' Cooperative Authority, Galleria 75 Office Park, 3200 Professional Parkway, Suite 260, Atlanta, GA 30339, Main Telephone: 770-988-8288, Fax: 770-984-2157, Hours: 9AM-5PM. Access by: mail, fax, PC. High volume, ongoing requesters can open a "search account" and receive expedited service.

Sales Tax Registrations

Sales & Use Tax Division, Taxpayer Services Unit, 270 Washington St SW, Atlanta, GA 30334, Main Telephone: 404-651-8651, Fax 404-651-9490 Access by: phone only.

Birth Certificates

Department of Human Resources, Vital Records Unit, 47 Trinity Ave, SW, Room 217-H, Atlanta, GA 30334, Main Telephone: 404-656-7456, Fax: 404-651-9427, Hours: 8AM-4PM. Access by: mail, phone, visit.

Death Records

Department of Human Resources, Vital Records Unit, 47 Trinity Ave, SW, Room 217-H, Atlanta, GA 30334, Main Telephone: 404-656-7456, Fax: 404-651-9427, Hours: 8AM-4PM. Access by: mail, phone, visit.

Marriage Certificates

Department of Human Resources, Vital Records Unit, 47 Trinity Ave, SW, Room 217-H, Atlanta, GA 30334, Main Telephone: 404-656-7456, Fax: 404-651-9427, Hours: 8AM-4PM. Access by: mail, phone, visit.

Divorce Records

Department of Human Resources, Vital Records Unit, 47 Trinity Ave, SW, Room 217-H, Atlanta, GA 30334, Main Telephone: 404-656-7456, Fax: 404-651-9427, Hours: 8-4.

Workers' Compensation Records

Workers Compensation Department, 270 Peachtree St, Atlanta, GA 30303-1299, Main Telephone: 404-656-3818, Fax: 404-657-6018, Hours: 8AM-4:30PM. Access by: mail only.

Driver Records

Department of Motor Vehicles, Driver's License Section, MVR Unit, PO Box 1456, Atlanta, GA 30371, Main Telephone: 404-624-7478, Hours: 8AM-3:30PM. Access by: mail, visit. Copies of tickets are not available from a central depository. It is recommended you go directly to the issuing court.

Vehicle Ownership
Vehicle Identification

Department of Revenue, Motor Vehicle Division - Research, PO Box 740381, Atlanta, GA 30374-0381, Main Telephone: 404-362-6500, Hours: 8AM-4:30PM. Access by: mail, visit.

Accident Reports

Department of Public Safety, Accident Reporting Section, PO Box 1456, Atlanta, GA 30371, Main Telephone: 404-624-7660, Fax: 404-624-7835, Hours: 8AM-3:30PM. Access by: mail, phone, visit.

Hunting License Information
Fishing License Information

Records not available from state agency.

County Courts and Recording Offices

What You Need to Know...

About the Courts

Administration

Administrative Office of the Courts	404-656-5171
244 Washington St SW, Suite 550	Fax: 404-651-6449
Atlanta, GA 30334	8AM-5PM

Court Structure

Depending upon the size of the county, the Superior Court is combined either with the State Court or the Magistrate Court.

The Magistrate Court has jurisdiction over one type of misdemeanor related to passing bad checks. This court also issues arrest warrants.

Online Access

There is no online access available locally or statewide.

About the Recorder's Office

Organization

159 counties, 159 filing offices. The recording officer is Clerk of Superior Court. All transactions are recorded in a "General Execution Docket." The entire state is in the Eastern Time Zone (EST).

UCC Records

Financing statements are filed only with the Clerk of Superior Court in each county. **A new system went into effect January 1, 1995**, merging all new UCC filings into a central statewide database, and which allows statewide searching for **new filings only** from any county office. However, filings prior to that date will remain at the county offices. Only a few counties will perform local UCC searches. Use search request form UCC-11 for local searches. Search fees vary from $2.50 to $25.00 per debtor name. Copies usually cost $.25 per page if you make it and $1.00 per page if the county makes it—latter fee is shown in this section.

Lien Records

All tax liens on personal property are filed with the county Clerk of Superior Court in a "General Execution Docket" (grantor/grantee) or "Lien Index." Most counties will **not** perform tax lien searches. Copy fees are the same as for UCC. Other liens include judgments, hospital, materialman, county tax, lis pendens, child support, labor, mechanics.

Real Estate Records

Most counties will **not** perform real estate searches. Copy fees are the same as for UCC. Certification fees are usually $2.00 per document—$1.00 for seal and $1.00 for stamp—plus $.50 per page.

County Courts and Recording Offices

Appling County

Real Estate Recording—Appling County Clerk of the Superior Court, Courthouse Square, Baxley, GA 31513. 912-367-8126. 8AM-5PM (EST).

Felony, Misdemeanor, Civil Actions Over $5,000—Superior & State Court, PO Box 269, Baxley, GA 31513. 912-367-8126. 8AM-5PM (EST). Access by: In person only.

Civil Actions Under $5,000, Eviction, Small Claims—Magistrate Court, Box 366, Baxley, GA 31513. 912-367-8116. Fax: 912-367-8126. 8:30AM-5PM (EST). Access by: In person only.

Probate—Probate Court, Courthouse Square, Baxley, GA 31513. 912-367-8114. 8:30AM-5PM (EST). Access by: Mail, in person.

Atkinson County

Real Estate Recording—Atkinson County Clerk of the Superior Court, Highway 441 South, Courthouse, Pearson, GA 31642. 912-422-3343. Fax: 912-422-3429. 8AM-Noon, 1-5PM (EST).

Felony, Misdemeanor, Civil Actions Over $5,000—Superior Court, PO Box 6, South Main, Courthouse Square, Pearson, GA 31642. 912-422-3343. Fax: 912-422-3429. 8AM-NOON, 1PM-5PM (EST). Access by: In person only.

Civil Actions Under $5,000, Eviction, Small Claims—Magistrate Court, PO Box 74, Pearson, GA 31642. 912-422-7158. Fax: 912-422-3429. 9AM-4:30PM (EST). Access by: In person only.

Probate—Probate Court, PO Box 855, Pearson, GA 31642. 912-422-3552. Fax: 912-422-3429. 8AM-5PM (EST).

Bacon County

Real Estate Recording—Bacon County Clerk of the Superior Court, 301 N. Pierce St., Alma, GA 31510. 912-632-4915. Fax: 912-632-6545. 9AM-5PM (EST).

Felony, Misdemeanor, Civil Actions Over $5,000—Superior Court, PO Box 376, Alma, GA 31510. 912-632-4915. 9AM-5PM (EST). Access by: Mail, in person.

Civil Actions Under $5,000, Eviction, Small Claims—Magistrate Court, Box 389, Alma, GA 31510. 912-632-5961. 9AM-5PM (EST). Access by: In person only.

Probate—Probate Court, PO Box 146, Alma, GA 31510. 912-632-7661. Fax: 912-632-2757. 9AM-5PM (EST).

Baker County

Real Estate Recording—Baker County Clerk of the Superior Court, Courthouse Way, Newton, GA 31770. 912-734-3004. 9AM-5PM (EST).

Felony, Misdemeanor, Civil Actions Over $5,000—Superior Court, PO Box 10, Governmental Bldg, Newton, GA 31770. 912-734-3004. 9AM-5PM (EST). Access by: In person only.

Civil Actions Under $5,000, Eviction, Small Claims—Magistrate Court, Box 548, Newton, GA 31770. 912-734-3007. 9AM-5PM (EST). Access by: In person only.

Probate—Probate Court, PO Box 548, Newton, GA 31770. 912-734-3007. Fax: 912-734-8822. 9AM-5PM M-W & F; 9AM-Noon Th (EST). Access by: In person only.

Baldwin County

Real Estate Recording—Baldwin County Clerk of the Superior Court, 121 N. Wilkinson Street, Suite 209, Milledgeville, GA 31061. 912-453-6327. 8:30AM-5PM (EST).

Felony, Misdemeanor, Civil Actions Over $5,000—Superior & State Court, PO Drawer 987, Milledgeville, GA 31061. 912-453-6324. Fax: 912-453-6320. 8:30AM-5PM (EST). Access by: In person only.

Civil Actions Under $5,000, Eviction, Small Claims—Magistrate Court, 201 W Hancock, Rm 30A, Milledgeville, GA 31061. 912-453-4446. Fax: 912-453-5656. 8:30AM-5PM (EST). Access by: In person only.

Probate—Probate Court, 201 W Hancock St, PO Box 964, Milledgeville, GA 31061. 912-453-4807. Fax: 912-453-5178. 8:30AM-5PM (EST).

Banks County

Real Estate Recording—Banks County Clerk of the Superior Court, Courthouse, Homer, GA 30547. 706-677-2320. 8:30AM-5PM (EST).

Felony, Misdemeanor, Civil Actions Over $5,000—Superior Court, PO Box 337, 144 Yorah Homer Road, Homer, GA 30547. 706-677-2320. Fax: 706-677-2337. 8:30AM-5PM (EST). Access by: In person only.

Civil Actions Under $5,000, Eviction, Small Claims—Magistrate Court, Box 364, Homer, GA 30547. 706-677-2320. Fax: 706-677-2337. 8:30AM-5PM (EST). Access by: In person only.

Probate—Probate Court, PO Box 7, Homer, GA 30547. 706-677-2320. Fax: 706-677-2337. 8:30AM-5PM (EST). Access by: Mail, in person.

Barrow County

Real Estate Recording—Barrow County Clerk of the Superior Court, 30 North Broad Street, Winder, GA 30680. 770-307-3035. 8AM-5PM (EST).

Felony, Misdemeanor, Civil Actions Over $5,000—Superior Court, PO Box 1280, Winder, GA 30680. 770-307-3035. Fax: 770-307-3033. 8:30AM-5PM (EST). Access by: In person only.

Civil Actions Under $5,000, Eviction, Small Claims—Magistrate Court, 30 N Broad St, Ste 331, Winder, GA 30680. 770-307-3050. 8AM-5PM (EST). Access by: In person only.

Probate—Probate Court, Barrow County Courthouse, 30 N Broad St, Winder, GA 30680. 770-307-3045. Fax: 770-867-4800. 8AM-5PM (EST).

Bartow County

Real Estate Recording—Bartow County Clerk of the Superior Court, 135 W. Cherokee Ave., Suite 233, Cartersville, GA 30120. 770-387-5025. Fax: 770-386-0846. 8AM-5PM (EST).

Felony, Misdemeanor, Civil Actions Over $5,000—Superior Court, 135 W Cherokee #233, Cartersville, GA 30120. 770-387-5025. Fax: 770-386-0846. 8:00AM-5PM (EST). Access by: Phone, mail, in person.

Civil Actions Under $5,000, Eviction, Small Claims—Magistrate Court, 135 W Cherokee #233, Cartersville, GA 30120-3101. 770-387-5070. Fax: 770-387-5073. 8AM-5PM (EST). Access by: In person only.

Probate—Probate Court, 135 W Cherokee #243A, Cartersville, GA 30120. 770-387-5075. Fax: 770-387-5074. 8AM-5PM (EST).

Ben Hill County

Real Estate Recording—Ben Hill County Clerk of the Superior Court, 401 E. Central Ave., Courthouse, Fitzgerald, GA 31750. 912-426-5135. Fax: 912-426-5106. 8:30AM-5PM (EST).

Felony, Misdemeanor, Civil Actions Over $5,000—Superior Court, PO Box 1104, 401 Central, Fitzgerald, GA 31750. 912-423-3736. Fax: 912-423-5715. 8:00AM-5PM (EST). Access by: Phone, mail, in person.

Civil Actions Under $5,000, Eviction, Small Claims—Magistrate Court, Box 1163, Fitzgerald, GA 31750. 912-423-5854. 8:30AM-5:30PM (EST). Access by: In person only.

Probate—Probate Court, PO Box 187, Fitzgerald, GA 31750. 912-423-2317. Fax: 912-423-5715. 9AM-5PM (EST).

Berrien County

Real Estate Recording—Berrien County Clerk of the Superior Court, 101 E. Marion Ave. #3, Nashville, GA 31639. 912-686-5506. 8AM-5PM (EST).

Felony, Misdemeanor, Civil Actions Over $5,000—Superior Court, 101 E Marion Ave, Ste 3, Nashville, GA 31639. 912-686-5506. 8AM-5PM (EST). Access by: Mail, in person.

Civil Actions Under $5,000, Eviction, Small Claims—Magistrate Court, 115 S Davis, Box 103, Nashville, GA 31639. 912-686-7019. Fax: 912-686-6328. 8:30AM-4:30PM (EST). Access by: In person only.

Probate—Probate Court, 101 E Marion Ave, Ste 1, Nashville, GA 31639. 912-686-5213. Fax: 912-686-9495. 7AM-5PM Sun-Sat (EST).

Bibb County

Real Estate Recording—Bibb County Clerk of the Superior Court, 275 Second Street, Suite 216, Macon, GA 31201. 912-749-6527. Fax: 912-749-6539. 8:30AM-5PM (EST).

Felony, Misdemeanor, Civil Actions Over $5,000—Superior Court, PO Box 1015, 601 Mulberry St Rm 216, Macon, GA 31202. 912-749-6527. 8:30AM-5PM (EST). Access by: In person only.

Misdemeanor, Civil Actions Over $5,000—State Court, PO Box 5086, Macon, GA 31213-7199. 912-749-6676. Fax: 912-748-6326. 8:30AM-5:30PM (EST). Access by: Mail, in person.

Civil Actions Under $25,000, Eviction, Small Claims—Civil & Magistrate Court, 601 Mulberry St, Macon, GA 31201. 912-749-6495. Fax: 912-749-6470. 8AM-5PM (EST). Access by: In person only.

Probate—Probate Court, PO Box 6518, Macon, GA 31202. 912-749-6494. Fax: 912-749-6686. 8AM-5PM (EST). Access by: Mail, in person.

Bleckley County

Real Estate Recording—Bleckley County Clerk of the Superior Court, Courthouse, Cochran, GA 31014. 912-934-3210. Fax: 912-934-3205. 8:30AM-5PM (EST).

Felony, Misdemeanor, Civil Actions Over $5,000—Superior Court, 306 SE 2nd St, Cochran, GA 31014. 912-934-3210. Fax: 912-934-3205. 8:30AM-5PM (EST). Access by: In person only.

Civil Actions Under $5,000, Eviction, Small Claims—Magistrate Court, 101 Eighth St, Cochran, GA 31014. 912-934-3202. Fax: 912-934-3226. 8:30AM-5PM (EST). Access by: In person only.

Probate—Probate Court, 306 SE Second St, Cochran, GA 31014. 912-934-3204. Fax: 912-934-3205. 8:30AM-5PM (EST).

Brantley County

Real Estate Recording—Brantley County Clerk of the Superior Court, Corner of Brantley & Highway 301, Nahunta, GA 31553. 912-462-5635. Fax: 912-462-5538. 8AM-5PM (EST).

Felony, Misdemeanor, Civil Actions Over $5,000—Superior Court, PO Box 1067, 117 Brantley St, Nahunta, GA 31553. 912-462-5635. Fax: 912-462-5073. 8AM-5PM (EST). Access by: Mail, in person.

Civil Actions Under $5,000, Eviction, Small Claims—Magistrate Court, PO Box 998, Nahunta, GA 31553. 912-462-6780. 8AM-4:30PM (EST). Access by: Phone, fax, mail, in person.

Probate—Probate Court, PO Box 207, Nahunta, GA 31553. 912-462-5192. Fax: 912-462-5538. 9AM-5PM (EST).

Brooks County

Real Estate Recording—Brooks County Clerk of the Superior Court, Screven Street, Courthouse, Quitman, GA 31643. 912-263-4747. Fax: 912-263-7559. 8:30AM-5PM (EST).

Felony, Misdemeanor, Civil Actions Over $5,000—Superior Court, PO Box 630, Quitman, GA 31643. 912-263-4747. Fax: 912-263-7559. 8:30AM-5PM (EST). Access by: In person only.

Civil Actions Under $5,000, Eviction, Small Claims—Magistrate Court, Box 387, Quitman, GA 31643. 912-263-9989. 8:30AM-5PM (EST). Access by: In person only.

Probate—Probate Court, PO Box 665, Quitman, GA 31643. 912-263-5567. 8:30AM-5PM (EST).

Bryan County

Real Estate Recording—Bryan County Clerk of the Superior Court, 401 South College Street, Pembroke, GA 31321. 912-653-4681. Fax: 912-653-4691. 8AM-5PM (EST).

Felony, Misdemeanor, Civil Actions Over $5,000—Superior & State Court, PO Drawer H, Pembroke, GA 31321. 912-653-4681. Fax: 912-653-4691. 8AM-5PM (EST). Access by: In person only.

Civil Actions Under $5,000, Eviction, Small Claims—Magistrate Court, Box 927, Pembroke, GA 31321. 912-653-4681. Fax: 912-653-4691. 8AM-5PM (EST). Access by: In person only.

Probate—Probate Court, PO Box 757, Pembroke, GA 31321. 912-653-4681. Fax: 912-653-4691. 8AM-5PM (EST).

Bulloch County

Real Estate Recording—Bulloch County Clerk of the Superior Court, North Main Street, Courthouse, Room 102, Statesboro, GA 30458. 912-764-9009. 8:30AM-5PM (EST).

Felony, Misdemeanor, Civil Actions Over $5,000—Superior & State Court, N Main St, Statesboro, GA 30458. 912-764-9009. 8:30AM-5PM (EST). Access by: Mail, in person.

Civil Actions Under $5,000, Eviction, Small Claims—Magistrate Court, Box 1004, Statesboro, GA 30458. 912-764-6458. Fax: 912-489-6731. 8AM-5PM (EST). Access by: In person only.

Probate—Probate Court, PO Box 1005, Statesboro, GA 30459. 912-489-8749. Fax: 912-764-8740. 8:30AM-5PM (EST). Access by: Mail, in person.

Burke County

Real Estate Recording—Burke County Clerk of the Superior Court, 111 East 6th St., Courthouse, Waynesboro, GA 30830. 706-554-2279. 9AM-5PM (EST).

Felony, Misdemeanor, Civil Actions Over $5,000—Superior & State Court, PO Box 803, Waynesboro, GA 30830. 706-554-2279. 9AM-5PM (EST). Access by: In person only.

Civil Actions Under $5,000, Eviction, Small Claims—Magistrate Court, Box 401, Waynesboro, GA 30830. 706-554-4281. 9AM-5PM (EST). Access by: In person only.

Probate—Probate Court, PO Box 322, Waynesboro, GA 30830. 706-554-3000. 9AM-5PM (EST).

Butts County

Real Estate Recording—Butts County Clerk of the Superior Court, 26 Third Street, Jackson, GA 30233. 770-775-8215. Fax: 770-775-8211. 8AM-5PM (EST).

Felony, Misdemeanor, Civil Actions Over $5,000—Superior Court, PO Box 320, 26 3rd St, Jackson, GA 30233. 770-775-8215. 8AM-5PM (EST). Access by: Phone, mail, in person.

Civil Actions Under $5,000, Eviction, Small Claims—Magistrate Court, Box 457, Jackson, GA 30233. 770-775-8220. Fax: 770-775-8211. 8AM-5PM (EST). Access by: Mail, in person.

Probate—Probate Court, PO Box 91, Jackson, GA 30233. 770-775-8204. Fax: 770-775-8211. 8AM-5PM (EST).

Calhoun County

Real Estate Recording—Calhoun County Clerk of the Superior Court, Courthouse Square, 111 School Street, Morgan, GA 31766. 912-849-2715. Fax: 912-849-0099. 8AM-5PM (EST).

Felony, Misdemeanor, Civil Actions Over $5,000—Superior Court, PO Box 69, Morgan, GA 31766. 912-849-

2715. Fax: 912-849-0099. 8AM-5PM (EST). Access by: Mail, in person.

Civil Actions Under $5,000, Eviction, Small Claims— Magistrate Court, Box 87, Morgan, GA 31766. 912-849-2115. Fax: 912-849-2072. 8AM-5PM (EST). Access by: Mail, in person.

Probate—Probate Court, PO Box 87, Morgan, GA 31766. 912-849-2115. (EST).

Camden County

Real Estate Recording—Camden County Clerk of the Superior Court, 200 East 4th St., Courthouse Square, Woodbine, GA 31569. 912-576-5601. 9AM-5PM (EST).

Felony, Misdemeanor, Civil Actions Over $5,000— Superior Court, PO Box 578, 200 E Courthouse Square, Woodbine, GA 31569. 912-576-5601. 9AM-5PM (EST). Access by: Mail, in person.

Civil Actions Under $5,000, Eviction, Small Claims— Magistrate Court, Box 386, Woodbine, GA 31569. 912-576-5601. Fax: 912-576-5647. 9AM-5PM (EST). Access by: In person only.

Probate—Probate Court, PO Box 818, Woodbine, GA 31569. 912-576-5601. Fax: 912-576-5484. 8AM-Noon, 1-5PM (EST). Access by: Mail, in person.

Candler County

Real Estate Recording—Candler County Clerk of the Superior Court, 355 South Broad Street, West, Courthouse, Metter, GA 30439. 912-685-5257. Fax: 912-685-2160. 8:30AM-5PM (EST).

Felony, Misdemeanor, Civil Actions Over $5,000— Superior & State Court, PO Draawer 830, Metter, GA 30439. 912-685-5257. 8:30AM-5PM (EST). Access by: In person only.

Civil Actions Under $5,000, Eviction, Small Claims— Magistrate Court, Box 683, Metter, GA 30439. 912-685-2888. 9AM-5PM (EST). Access by: Mail, in person.

Carroll County

Real Estate Recording—Carroll County Clerk of the Superior Court, 311 Newnan Street, Room 203, Carrollton, GA 30117. 770-830-5830. 8AM-5PM (EST).

Felony, Misdemeanor, Civil Actions Over $5,000— Superior & State Court, PO Box 1620, Carrollton, GA 30117. 770-830-5830. Fax: 770-830-5988. 8AM-5PM (EST). Access by: Mail, in person.

Civil Actions Under $5,000, Eviction, Small Claims— Magistrate Court, PO Box 338, Carrollton, GA 30117. 770-830-5874. Fax: 770-830-5851. 9AM-5PM (EST). Access by: Mail, in person.

Probate—Probate Court, PO Box 338, Rm 204, Carrollton, GA 30117. 770-830-5840. Fax: 770-830-5842. 8AM-5PM (EST). Access by: Mail, in person.

Catoosa County

Real Estate Recording—Catoosa County Clerk of the Superior Court, 875 Lafayette Street, Courthouse, Ringgold, GA 30736. 706-935-4231. 8:30AM-5PM (EST).

Felony, Misdemeanor, Civil, Eviction, Small Claims— Superior & Magistrate Court, 206 E Nashville St, Ringgold, GA 30736. 706-935-4231. 8:30AM-5PM (EST). Access by: In person only.

Probate—Probate Court, Courthouse, Ringgold, GA 30736. 706-935-3511. 9AM-5PM (EST). Access by: In person only.

Charlton County

Real Estate Recording—Charlton County Clerk of the Superior Court, Courthouse, Folkston, GA 31537. 912-496-2354. 8AM-5PM (EST).

Felony, Misdemeanor, Civil Actions Over $5,000— Superior Court, Courthouse, Folkston, GA 31537. 912-496-2354. 8AM-5PM (EST). Access by: Mail, in person.

Civil Actions Under $5,000, Eviction, Small Claims— Magistrate Court, 100 A County St, Folkston, GA 31537.

912-496-2617. Fax: 912-496-2560. 8AM-5PM (EST). Access by: In person only.

Probate—Probate Court, 100 S 3rd St, Folkston, GA 31537. 912-496-2230. 8AM-5PM (EST).

Chatham County

Real Estate Recording—Chatham County Clerk of the Superior Court, 133 Montgomery Street, Courthouse Rm. 304, Savannah, GA 31401. 912-652-7204. Fax: 912-652-7380. 8AM-5PM (EST).

Felony, Misdemeanor, Civil Actions Over $5,000— Superior Court, PO Box 10227, 133 Montgomery St, Savannah, GA 31412. 912-652-7209. 8AM-5PM (EST). Access by: Mail, in person.

Misdemeanor, Civil—State Court, County Courthouse 133 Montgomery St, Savannah, GA 31401. 912-652-7224. Fax: 912-652-7229. 8AM-5PM (EST). Access by: Mail, in person.

Civil Actions Under $5,000, Eviction, Small Claims— Magistrate Court, 133 Montgomery St Room 303, Savannah, GA 31401. 912-652-7188. Fax: 912-652-7550. 8AM-5PM (EST). Access by: Phone, mail, in person.

Probate—Probate Court, 133 Montgomery St, Savannah, GA 31401. 912-652-7367. Fax: 912-652-7262. 8AM-5PM (EST). Access by: Mail, in person.

Chattahoochee County

Real Estate Recording—Chattahoochee County Clerk of the Superior Court, Broad Street, Courthouse, Cusseta, GA 31805. 706-989-3424. Fax: 706-989-0396. 8AM-5PM (EST).

Felony, Misdemeanor, Civil, Eviction, Small Claims— Superior & Magistrate Court, PO Box 120, Cusseta, GA 31805. 706-989-3424. Fax: 706-989-2005. 8AM-5PM (EST). Access by: In person only.

Probate—Probate Court, PO Box 119, Cusseta, GA 31805. 706-989-3603. 8AM-Noon, 1-5PM (EST).

Chattooga County

Real Estate Recording—Chattooga County Clerk of the Superior Court, Commerce Street, Courthouse, Summerville, GA 30747. 706-857-0706. 8:30AM-5PM (EST).

Felony, Misdemeanor, Civil, Eviction, Small Claims— Superior & State Court, PO Box 159, Summerville, GA 30747. 706-857-0706. 8:30AM-5PM (EST). Access by: Mail, in person.

Probate—Probate Court, PO Box 467, Summerville, GA 30747. 706-857-0709. Fax: 706-857-0726. 8:30AM-Noon, 1-5PM (EST).

Cherokee County

Real Estate Recording—Cherokee County Clerk of the Superior Court, 90 North Street, Suite G-170, Canton, GA 30114. 770-479-0537. 8:30AM-5PM (EST).

Felony, Misdemeanor, Civil Actions Over $5,000— Superior & State Court, 990 North St, Ste G170, Canton, GA 30114. 770-479-0538. 8:30AM-5PM (EST). Access by: In person only.

Civil Actions Under $5,000, Eviction, Small Claims— Magistrate Court, PO Box 255, Canton, GA 30114. 770-479-8516. 8:30AM-5PM (EST). Access by: In person only.

Probate—Probate Court, 90 North St, Rm 340, Canton, GA 30114. 770-479-0541. Fax: 770-479-0567. (EST).

Clarke County

Real Estate Recording—Athens-Clarke County Clerk of the Superior Court, 325 East Washington Street, Room 100, Athens, GA 30601. 706-613-3195. Fax: 706-613-3189. 8AM-5PM (EST).

Felony, Misdemeanor, Civil Actions Over $5,000— Superior & State Court, PO Box 1805, Athens, GA 30603. 706-613-3190. 8AM-5PM (EST). Access by: In person only.

Civil Actions Under $5,000, Eviction, Small Claims— Magistrate Court, 325 E Washington St, Athens, GA 30601. 706-613-3313. Fax: 706-613-3314. 8AM-5PM (EST). Access by: Mail, in person.

Probate—Probate Court, 325 E Washington St, Rm 215, Athens, GA 30601. 706-613-3320. Fax: 706-613-3323. 8AM-5PM (EST).

Clay County

Real Estate Recording—Clay County Clerk of the Superior Court, 210 Washington Street, Courthouse, Fort Gaines, GA 31751. 912-768-2631. Fax: 912-768-3047. 8AM-4:30PM (EST).

Felony, Misdemeanor, Civil, Eviction, Small Claims—Superior & Magistrate Court, PO Box 550, Ft Gaines, GA 31751. 912-768-2631. Fax: 912-768-3443. 8AM-4:30PM (EST). Access by: In person only.

Probate—Probate Court, PO Box 448, Ft. Gaines, GA 31751. 912-768-2445. Fax: 912-768-2710. 8AM-4:30PM (EST).

Clayton County

Real Estate Recording—Clayton County Clerk of the Superior Court, 121 South McDonough Street, Room 202, Jonesboro, GA 30236. 770-477-3395. 8AM-5PM (EST).

Felony, Misdemeanor, Civil Actions Over $5,000—Superior Court, 121 S McDonough St, Jonesboro, GA 30236. 770-477-3405. 8AM-5PM (EST). Access by: In person only.

Misdemeanor—State Court, 121 S McDonough St, Jonesboro, GA 30236. 770-477-3389. 8AM-5PM (EST). Access by: In person only.

Civil Actions Under $5,000, Eviction, Small Claims—Magistrate Court, 121 S McDonaugh St, Jonesboro, GA 30236. 770-477-3443. 8AM-5PM (EST). Access by: In person only.

Probate—Probate Court, 121 S McDonough St, Annex 3, Jonesboro, GA 30236-3694. 770-477-3299. Fax: 770-477-3306. 8AM-5PM (EST). Access by: Mail, in person.

Clinch County

Real Estate Recording—Clinch County Clerk of the Superior Court, Courthouse, Homerville, GA 31634. 912-487-5854. Fax: 912-487-3083. 8AM-5PM (EST).

Felony, Misdemeanor, Civil Actions Over $5,000—Superior & State Court, PO Box 433, Homerville, GA 31634. 912-487-5854. Fax: 912-489-3083. 8AM-5PM (EST). Access by: Mail, in person.

Civil Actions Under $5,000, Eviction, Small Claims—Magistrate Court, 100 Court Square, Homerville, GA 31634. 912-487-2514. Fax: 912-487-2514. 9AM-5PM (EST). Access by: In person only.

Probate—Probate Court, PO Box 364, Homerville, GA 31634. 912-487-5523. Fax: 912-487-3083. 9AM-5PM (EST).

Cobb County

Real Estate Recording—Cobb County Clerk of the Superior Court, 10 East Park Square, Marietta, GA 30090. 770-528-1360. 8AM-5PM (EST).

Felony, Misdemeanor, Civil Over $5,000—Superior Court, PO Box 3370, Marietta, GA 30061. 770-528-1300. Fax: 770-528-1382. 8AM-5PM (EST). Access by: Phone, mail, in person.

Misdemeanor, Civil, Eviction—State Court-Civil & Criminal Divisions, 12 East Park Square, Marietta, GA 30090-9630. Civil: 770-528-1219. Criminal: 770-528-1245. Fax: 770-528-2668. 8AM-5PM (EST). Access by: Fax, mail, in person.

Civil Actions Under $5,000, Small Claims—Magistrate Court, 32 Waddell St, Marietta, GA 30090-9656. 770-528-8910. Fax: 770-528-8929. 8AM-5PM (EST). Access by: Mail, in person.

Probate—Probate Court of Cobb County, 32 Waddell St, Marietta, GA 30060. 770-528-1900. Fax: 770-528-1996. 8AM-4:30PM (EST).

Coffee County

Real Estate Recording—Coffee County Clerk of the Superior Court, Courthouse, 101 S. Peterson Ave., Douglas, GA 31533. 912-384-2865. 8:30AM-5PM (EST).

Felony, Misdemeanor, Civil Actions Over $5,000—Superior & State Court, 101 S Peterson Ave, Douglas, GA 31533. 912-384-2865. 8:30AM-5PM (EST). Access by: Mail, in person.

Civil Actions Under $5,000, Eviction, Small Claims—Magistrate Court, 101 S Peterson Ave, Douglas, GA 31533. 912-384-2983. 8AM-5PM (EST). Access by: In person only.

Probate—Probate Court, 109 S Peterson Ave, Douglas, GA 31533. 912-384-5213. Fax: 912-384-0291. 9AM-5PM (EST). Access by: Mail, in person.

Colquitt County

Real Estate Recording—Colquitt County Clerk of the Superior Court, 9 Main Street, Courthouse, Moultrie, GA 31776. 912-985-1324. 8AM-5PM (EST).

Felony, Misdemeanor, Civil Actions Over $5,000—Superior & State Court, PO Box 886, Moultrie, GA 31776. 912-985-1324. 8AM-5PM (EST). Access by: In person only.

Civil Actions Under $5,000, Eviction, Small Claims—Magistrate Court, PO Box 70, Moultrie, GA 31776. 912-891-7450. 8AM-5PM (EST). Access by: In person only.

Probate—Probate Court, 9 Main St, PO Box 264, Moultrie, GA 31768. 912-891-7415. Fax: 912-985-3054. (EST).

Columbia County

Real Estate Recording—Columbia County Clerk of the Superior Court, 1954 Appling Harlem Rd., Appling, GA 30802. 706-541-1139. Fax: 706-541-4013. 8AM-5PM (EST).

Felony, Misdemeanor, Civil Actions Over $5,000—Superior Court, PO Box 100, Appling, GA 30802. 706-541-1139. 8AM-5PM (EST). Access by: Phone, mail, in person.

Civil Actions Under $5,000, Eviction, Small Claims—Magistrate Court, PO Box 777, Evans, GA 30809. 706-868-3316. Fax: 706-868-3314. 8AM-5PM (EST). Access by: Phone, mail, in person.

Probate—Probate Court, Courthouse Annex, PO Box 58, Appling, GA 30802. 706-541-1254. Fax: 706-541-4001. 8AM-5PM (EST).

Cook County

Real Estate Recording—Cook County Clerk of the Superior Court, 212 North Hutchinson Avenue, Adel, GA 31620. 912-896-7717. 8:30AM-4:30PM (EST).

Felony, Misdemeanor, Civil Actions Over $5,000—Superior Court, 212 N Hutchinson Ave, Adel, GA 31620. 912-896-7717. Fax: 912-896-3977. 8:30AM-4:30PM (EST). Access by: Mail, in person.

Civil Actions Under $5,000, Eviction, Small Claims—Magistrate Court, 212 N Hutchinson Ave, Adel, GA 31620. 912-896-3151. Fax: 912-896-7629. 8:30AM-4:30PM (EST). Access by: Mail, in person.

Probate—Probate Court, 212 N Hutchinson Ave, Adel, GA 31620. 912-896-3941. 8:30AM-5PM (EST). Access by: Mail, in person.

Coweta County

Real Estate Recording—Coweta County Clerk of the Superior Court, Courthouse, Court Square, Newnan, GA 30263. 770-254-2690. 8:30AM-5PM (EST).

Felony, Misdemeanor, Civil Actions Over $5,000—Superior & State Court, PO Box 943, Newnan, GA 30264. 770-254-2690. Fax: 770-254-3700. 8:30AM-5PM (EST). Access by: Phone, mail, in person. Can only conduct felony searches from 1990 to present.

Civil Actions Under $5,000, Eviction, Small Claims—Magistrate Court, 22-34 E Broad St, Newnan, GA 30263. 770-254-2610. Fax: 770-254-2610. 8AM-5PM (EST). Access by: Mail, in person.

Probate—Probate Court, 22 E Broad St, Newnan, GA 30263. 770-254-2640. Fax: 770-254-2648. 8AM-5PM (EST). Access by: Mail, in person.

Crawford County

Real Estate Recording—Crawford County Clerk of the Superior Court, Courthouse, US Highway 80 & State

Highway 42, Knoxville, GA 31050. 912-836-3328. 9AM-5PM (EST).

Felony, Misdemeanor, Civil, Eviction, Small Claims— Superior & Magistrate Court, PO Box 1037, Roberta, GA 31058. 912-836-3328. 9AM-5PM (EST). Access by: Mail, in person.

Probate—Probate Court, PO Box 1028, Roberta, GA 31078. 912-836-3313. 8:30AM-4:30PM (EST). Access by: Mail, in person.

Crisp County

Real Estate Recording—Crisp County Clerk of the Superior Court, 210 7th Street South, Courthouse, Cordele, GA 31015. 912-276-2616. 8:30AM-5PM (EST).

Felony, Misdemeanor, Civil Actions Over $5,000— Superior & Juvenile Court, PO Box 747, Cordele, GA 31010-0747. 912-276-2616. 8:30AM-5PM (EST). Access by: Mail, in person.

Civil Under $5,000, Eviction, Small Claims—Magistrate Court, 210 S 7th St Room 102, Cordese, GA 31015. 912-276-2618. (EST).

Probate—Probate Court, 201 S 7th St, PO Box 26, Cordele, GA 31015. 912-276-2621. 9AM-5PM (EST).

Dade County

Real Estate Recording—Dade County Clerk of the Superior Court, Main Street-U.S. Highway 11, Courthouse Sq., Trenton, GA 30752. 706-657-4778. Fax: 706-657-8284. 8:30AM-5PM (EST).

Felony, Misdemeanor, Civil, Eviction, Small Claims— Superior Court, PO Box 417, Trenton, GA 30752. 706-657-4778. 8:30AM-5PM (EST). Access by: Mail, in person.

Probate—Probate Court, PO Box 605, Trenton, GA 30752. 706-657-4414. Fax: 706-657-5116. 8:30AM-5PM (EST). Access by: Mail, in person.

Dawson County

Real Estate Recording—Dawson County Clerk of the Superior Court, Courthouse, 25 Tucker Ave., Dawsonville, GA 30534. 706-265-2525. Fax: 706-265-2358. 8AM-5PM (EST).

Felony, Misdemeanor, Civil Actions Over $5,000— Superior Court, PO Box 222, Dawsonville, GA 30534. 706-265-2525. 8AM-5PM (EST). Access by: In person only.

Civil Actions Under $5,000, Eviction, Small Claims— Magistrate Court, PO Box 254, Dawsonville, GA 30534. 706-265-8000. 8:30AM-5PM (EST). Access by: In person only.

Probate—Probate Court, PO Box 252, Dawsonville, GA 30534. 706-265-2271. Fax: 706-265-2358. 8AM-5PM (EST).

De Kalb County

Real Estate Recording—De Kalb County Clerk of the Superior Court, 556 North McDonough Street, Courthouse, Room 208, Decatur, GA 30030. 404-371-2762. 8:30AM-5PM (EST).

Felony, Misdemeanor, Civil Actions Over $5,000— Superior Court, 556 N McDonough St, Decatur, GA 30030. Civil: 404-371-2028. Criminal: 404-371-2836. 8AM-5PM (EST). Access by: Mail, in person.

State Court, 556 N McDonough St, Decatur, GA 30030. 404-371-2261. Fax: 404-371-3064. 8:30AM-5PM (EST). Access by: In person only.

Civil Actions Under $5,000, Eviction, Small Claims— Magistrate Court, 556 N McDonough St, Decatur, GA 30030. 404-371-2268. Fax: 404-371-3064. 8:30AM-5PM (EST). Access by: In person only.

Probate—Probate Court, 556 N McDonough St, Rm 103, Decatur, GA 30030. 404-371-2601. Fax: 404-371-7055. 8:30AM-4PM (EST).

Decatur County

Real Estate Recording—Decatur County Clerk of the Superior Court, 112 West Water Street, Bainbridge, GA 31717. 912-248-3025. Fax: 912-248-3053. 9AM-5PM (EST).

Felony, Misdemeanor, Civil Actions Over $5,000— Superior & State Court, PO Box 336, Bainbridge, GA

31717. 912-248-3025. 9AM-5PM (EST). Access by: In person only.

Civil Actions Under $5,000, Eviction, Small Claims— Magistrate Court, 912 Spring Creek Rd Box #3, Bainbridge, GA 31717. 912-248-3014. 9AM-5PM (EST). Access by: Mail, in person.

Probate—Probate Court, 112 W Water, PO Box 234, Bainbridge, GA 31718. 912-248-3016. Fax: 912-246-2062. 9AM-5PM (EST). Access by: Mail.

Dodge County

Real Estate Recording—Dodge County Clerk of the Superior Court, Anson Avenue, Courthouse, Eastman, GA 31023. 912-374-2871. 9AM-Noon,1-5PM (EST).

Felony, Misdemeanor, Civil Actions Over $5,000— Superior Court, PO Drawer 4276, 407 Anson Ave, Eastman, GA 31023. 912-374-2871. 9AM-5PM (EST). Access by: Mail, in person.

Civil Actions Under $5,000, Eviction, Small Claims— Magistrate Court, Courthouse Square, Eastman, GA 31023. 912-374-7243. 8:30AM-4:30PM (EST). Access by: In person only.

Probate—Probate Court, PO Box 514, Eastman, GA 31023. 912-374-3775. Fax: 912-374-8124. 9AM-Noon, 1-5PM (EST). Access by: Mail, in person.

Dooly County

Real Estate Recording—Dooly County Clerk of the Superior Court, 104 Second Street, Room 12, Vienna, GA 31092. 912-268-4234. Fax: 912-268-6142. 8:30AM-5PM (EST).

Felony, Misdemeanor, Civil Actions Over $5,000— Superior Court, PO Box 326, Vienna, GA 31092-0326. 912-268-4234. Fax: 912-268-6142. 8:30AM-5PM (EST). Access by: Fax, mail, in person. Prefer to have public to perform searches.

Civil Actions Under $5,000, Eviction, Small Claims— Magistrate Court, W Union St, Courthouse Annex, Vienna, GA 31092. 912-268-4324. 8AM-12PM M,W 1PM-5PM F (EST). Access by: In person only.

Probate—Probate Court, 104 2nd St, Vienna, GA 31092. 912-268-4217. Fax: 912-268-6142. 8AM-5PM M,T,Th,F; 8:30AM-Noon W & Sat or by appointment (EST).

Dougherty County

Real Estate Recording—Dougherty County Clerk of the Superior Court, 225 Pine Avenue, Room 126, Albany, GA 31702. 912-431-2198. Fax: 912-431-2850. 8:30AM-5PM (EST).

Felony, Misdemeanor, Civil Actions Over $5,000— Superior & State Court, PO Box 1827, Albany, GA 31703. 912-431-2198. 8:30AM-5PM (EST). Access by: In person only.

Civil Actions Under $5,000, Eviction, Small Claims— Magistrate Court, 225 Pine Ave, Albany, GA 31703. 912-431-3216. Fax: 912-434-2692. 8:30AM-5PM (EST). Access by: In person only.

Probate—Probate Court, 225 Pine Ave, PO Box 1827, Albany, GA 31702. 912-431-2102. Fax: 912-434-2694. 8:30AM-5PM (EST).

Douglas County

Real Estate Recording—Douglas County Clerk of the Superior Court, 6754 Broad Street, Room 210, Douglasville, GA 30134. 770-920-7341. 8AM-5PM (EST).

Felony, Misdemeanor, Civil Actions Over $5,000— Superior Court, 6754 Broad St, Douglasville, GA 30134. 770-920-7252. 8AM-5PM (EST). Access by: In person only.

Civil Actions Under $5,000, Eviction, Small Claims— Magistrate Court, 6754 Broad St, Rm 202, Douglasville, GA 30134. 770-920-7215. 8AM-5PM (EST). Access by: In person only.

Probate—Probate Court, 6754 Broad St, Douglasville, GA 30134. 770-920-7249. Fax: 770-920-7381. 8AM-5PM (EST). Access by: Mail, in person.

Early County

Real Estate Recording—Early County Clerk of the Superior Court, Courthouse, Court Square, Blakely, GA 31723. 912-723-3033. Fax: 912-723-5246. 8AM-5PM (EST).

Felony, Misdemeanor, Civil Actions Over $5,000—Superior & State Court, PO Box 849, Blakely, GA 31723. 912-723-3033. Fax: 912-723-5246. 8AM-5PM (EST). Access by: In person only.

Civil Actions Under $5,000, Eviction, Small Claims—Magistrate Court, Courthouse Square, Blakely, GA 31723. 912-723-5492. 8AM-5PM (EST). Access by: In person only.

Probate—Probate Court, Early Courthouse Square, Rm 8, Blakely, GA 31723. 912-723-5492. Fax: 912-723-5246. 9AM-5PM (EST).

Echols County

Real Estate Recording—Echols County Clerk of the Superior Court, Courthouse, Highway 94 & Highway 129, Statenville, GA 31648. 912-559-5642. Fax: 912-559-5792. 8AM-Noon, 1-4:30PM (EST).

Felony, Misdemeanor, Civil Actions Over $5,000—Superior Court, PO Box 213, Statenville, GA 31648. 912-559-5642. Fax: 912-559-5792. 8AM-Noon, 1-4:30PM (EST). Access by: In person only.

Civil Actions Under $5,000, Eviction, Small Claims—Magistrate Court, HWY 94 & 129, Statenville, GA 31648. 912-559-7526. Fax: 912-559-5792. 8:30AM-4:30PM (EST). Access by: In person only.

Probate—Probate Court, PO Box 118, Statenville, GA 31648. 912-559-7526. Fax: 912-559-5792. 9AM-5PM (EST). Access by: Mail, in person.

Effingham County

Real Estate Recording—Effingham County Clerk of the Superior Court, 901 North Pine Street, Courthouse, Springfield, GA 31329. 912-754-6071. 8:30AM-5PM (EST).

Felony, Misdemeanor, Civil Actions Over $5,000—Superior & State Court, PO Box 387, Springfield, GA 31329. 912-754-6071. 8:30AM-5PM (EST). Access by: Mail, in person.

Civil Actions Under $5,000, Eviction, Small Claims—Magistrate Court, PO Box 387, Springfield, GA 31329. 912-754-6071. 8AM-5PM (EST). Access by: Mail, in person.

Probate—Probate Court, PO Box 387, Springfield, GA 31329. 912-754-6071. Fax: 912-754-3894. 8:30AM-5PM (EST). Access by: Mail, in person.

Elbert County

Real Estate Recording—Elbert County Clerk of the Superior Court, Courthouse, Oliver Street, Elberton, GA 30635. 706-283-2005. Fax: 706-283-2028. 8AM-5PM (EST).

Felony, Misdemeanor, Civil Actions Over $5,000—Superior & State Court, PO Box 619, Elberton, GA 30635. 706-283-2005. Fax: 706-283-2028. 8AM-5PM (EST). Access by: In person only.

Civil Actions Under $5,000, Eviction, Small Claims—Magistrate Court, PO Box 763, Elberton, GA 30635. 706-283-2027. 8AM-5PM (EST). Access by: Phone, mail, in person.

Probate—Probate Court, Elbert County Courthouse, Elberton, GA 30635. 706-283-2016. 8AM-5PM (EST). Access by: Mail, in person.

Emanuel County

Real Estate Recording—Emanuel County Clerk of the Superior Court, Court Street, Courthouse, Swainsboro, GA 30401. 912-237-8911. Fax: 912-237-2173. 9AM-5PM (EST).

Felony, Misdemeanor, Civil Actions Over $5,000—Superior & State Court, PO Box 627, Swainsboro, GA 30401. 912-237-8911. Fax: 912-237-2173. 8AM-5PM (EST). Access by: In person only.

Civil Actions Under $5,000, Eviction, Small Claims—Magistrate Court, 107 N Main St, Swainsboro, GA 30401. 912-237-7278. 8AM-4:30PM (EST). Access by: In person only.

Probate—Probate Court, Court St, PO Drawer 70, Swainsboro, GA 30401. 912-237-7091. Fax: 912-237-3651. 8AM-5PM (EST).

Evans County

Real Estate Recording—Evans County Clerk of the Superior Court, 123 W. Main Street, Courthouse, Claxton, GA 30417. 912-739-3868. Fax: 912-739-2327. 8AM-5PM (EST).

Felony, Misdemeanor, Civil Actions Over $5,000—Superior & State Court, PO Box 845, Claxton, GA 30417. 912-739-3868. 8AM-5PM (EST). Access by: In person only.

Civil Actions Under $5,000, Eviction, Small Claims—Magistrate Court, PO Box 637, Claxton, GA 30417. 912-739-3745. Fax: 912-739-3745. 8AM-5PM (EST). Access by: Phone, fax, mail, in person.

Probate—Probate Court, County Courthouse, PO Box 852, Claxton, GA 30417. 912-739-4080. Fax: 912-739-0111. 8AM-5PM (EST).

Fannin County

Real Estate Recording—Fannin County Clerk of the Superior Court, 420 West Main St., Courthouse, Blue Ridge, GA 30513. 706-632-2039. 9AM-5PM (EST).

Felony, Misdemeanor, Civil Actions Over $5,000—Superior Court, PO Box 1300, 420 W Main St, Blue Ridge, GA 30513. 706-632-2039. 9AM-5PM (EST). Access by: Phone, mail, in person.

Civil Actions Under $5,000, Eviction, Small Claims—Magistrate Court, PO Box 1658, Blue Ridge, GA 30513. 706-632-5558. Fax: 706-632-8236. 9AM-5PM (EST). Access by: In person only.

Probate—Probate Court, PO Box 245, Blue Ridge, GA 30513. 706-632-3011. Fax: 706-632-8236. 8AM-5PM (EST).

Fayette County

Real Estate Recording—Fayette County Clerk of the Superior Court, 145 Johnson Avenue, Fayetteville, GA 30214. 770-461-4703. 8AM-5PM (EST).

Felony, Misdemeanor, Civil Actions Over $5,000—Superior Court, PO Box 130, Fayetteville, GA 30214. 770-461-4703. 8AM-5PM (EST). Access by: In person only.

Civil Actions Under $5,000, Eviction, Small Claims—Magistrate Court, 145 Johnson Ave, Fayetteville, GA 30214. 770-461-2116. Fax: 770-719-2357. 8AM-5PM (EST). Access by: Mail, in person.

Probate—Probate Court, 145 Johnson Ave, Fayetteville, GA 30214. 770-461-9555. Fax: 770-460-8685. 8AM-5PM (EST).

Floyd County

Real Estate Recording—Floyd County Clerk of the Superior Court, 3 Government Plaza, Suite 101, Rome, GA 30162. 706-291-5159. Fax: 706-233-0035. 8AM-5PM (EST).

Felony, Misdemeanor, Civil Actions Over $5,000—Superior Court, PO Box 1110, #3 Government Plaza #101, Rome, GA 30163. 706-291-5190. Fax: 706-233-0035. 8AM-5PM (EST). Access by: Fax, mail, in person.

Civil Actions Under $5,000, Eviction, Small Claims—Magistrate Court, 401 Tribune St, Room 227, Rome, GA 30161. 706-291-5250. Fax: 706-291-5269. 9AM-5PM (EST). Access by: In person only.

Probate—Probate Court, #3 Government Plaza, Rome, GA 30162. 706-291-5136. Fax: 706-291-5189. 8AM-4:30PM (EST). Access by: Mail, in person.

Forsyth County

Real Estate Recording—Forsyth County Clerk of the Superior Court, 100 Courthouse Square, Cumming, GA 30130. 770-781-2120. 8:30AM-5PM (EST).

Felony, Misdemeanor, Civil, Eviction, Small Claims—Superior, State & Magistrate Court, 100 Courthouse Square, Rm 110, Cumming, GA 30130. 770-886-4865. 8:30AM-5PM (EST). Access by: Mail, in person.

Probate—Probate Court, County Courthouse, 100 Courthouse Sq, Rm 150, Cumming, GA 30130. 770-781-2140. 8:30AM-5PM (EST).

Franklin County

Real Estate Recording—Franklin County Clerk of the Superior Court, Courthouse Square, 9592 Lavonia Rd., Carnesville, GA 30521. 706-384-2514. Fax: 706-384-2185. 8AM-4:30PM M,T,Th,F; 8AM-Noon W & Sat (EST).

Felony, Misdemeanor, Civil Actions Over $5,000—Superior Court, PO Box 70, Carnesville, GA 30521. 706-384-2514. 8AM-5PM (EST). Access by: In person only.

Civil Actions Under $5,000, Eviction, Small Claims—Magistrate Court, PO Box 204, Carnesville, GA 30521. 706-384-7473. 8AM-5PM (EST). Access by: In person only.

Probate—Probate Court, PO Box 207, Carnesville, GA 30521. 706-384-2403. Fax: 706-384-2245. 8AM-4:30PM (EST).

Fulton County

Real Estate Recording—Fulton County Clerk of the Superior Court, 136 Pryor Street, Atlanta, GA 30303. 404-730-5371. Fax: 404-730-7993. 8:30AM-5PM (EST).

Felony, Misdemeanor, Civil Over $5,000, Eviction—Superior Court, 136 Pryor St SW, Rm 106, Atlanta, GA 30303. Civil: 404-730-4518. Criminal: 404-730-5242. Fax: 404-730-7993. 8:30AM-5PM (EST). Access by: Mail, in person.

Misdemeanor, Civil Actions Over $5,000—State Court, TG100 Justice Center Tower, 185 Central Ave SW, Atlanta, GA 30303. 404-730-5000. 8:30AM-5PM (EST). Access by: Mail, in person.

Civil Actions to $5,000, Eviction, Small Claims—Magistrate Court, 185 Central Ave SW, Rm TG700, Atlanta, GA 30303. 404-730-5078. Civil: 404-730-5045. Criminal: 404-730-4752. Fax: 404-730-5027. 8:30AM-5PM (EST). Access by: Mail, in person.

Probate—Probate Court, 136 Pryor St SW #C230, Atlanta, GA 30303. 404-730-4640. Fax: 404-730-8283. 8:30AM-5PM (EST). Access by: Mail, in person.

Gilmer County

Real Estate Recording—Gilmer County Clerk of the Superior Court, 1 West Side Square, Courthouse, Ellijay, GA 30540. 706-635-4462. Fax: 706-635-1462. 8:30AM-5PM (EST).

Felony, Misdemeanor, Civil Actions Over $5,000—Superior Court, #1 Westside Square, Ellijay, GA 30540. 706-635-4462. Fax: 706-635-1462. 8:30AM-5PM (EST). Access by: Mail, in person.

Civil Actions Under $5,000, Eviction, Small Claims—Magistrate Court, #1 Westside Square, Ellijay, GA 30540. 706-635-2515. 8:30AM-5PM (EST). Access by: In person only.

Probate—Probate Court, #1 Westside Square, Ellijay, GA 30540. 706-635-4763. Fax: 706-635-4761. 8:30AM-5PM (EST). Access by: Mail.

Glascock County

Real Estate Recording—Glascock County Clerk of the Superior Court, 62E Main Street, Courthouse, Gibson, GA 30810. 706-598-2084. 8AM-Noon,1-5PM (EST).

Felony, Misdemeanor, Civil Actions Over $5,000—Superior Court, PO Box 231, 62 E Main St, Gibson, GA 30810. 706-598-2084. Fax: 706-598-2577. 8AM-Noon, 1-5PM (EST). Access by: In person only.

Civil Actions Under $5,000, Eviction, Small Claims—Magistrate Court, PO Box 201, Gibson, GA 30810. 706-598-2013. 9AM-Noon W,Sat (EST). Access by: In person only.

Probate—Probate Court, Courthouse, Main St, PO Box 64, Gibson, GA 30810. 706-598-3241. 8AM-Noon, 1-5PM (EST).

Glynn County

Real Estate Recording—Glynn County Clerk of the Superior Court, 701 H Street, Brunswick, GA 31520. 912-267-5610. Fax: 912-267-5625. 8:30AM-5PM (EST).

Felony, Misdemeanor, Civil—Superior Court, PO Box 1355, Brunswick, GA 31521. 912-267-5610. Fax: 912-267-

5625. 8:30AM-5PM (EST). Access by: Phone, fax, mail, in person.

Misdemeanor, Civil Actions Over $5,000—State Court, PO Box 879, Brunswick, GA 31521. 912-267-5674. Fax: 912-261-3849. 9AM-5PM (EST). Access by: In person only.

Civil Actions Under $5,000, Eviction, Small Claims—Magistrate Court, 701 H St, Brunswick, GA 31521. 912-267-5650. Fax: 912-267-5677. 8:30AM-5PM (EST). Access by: In person only.

Probate—Probate Court, 701 H St, Brunswick, GA 31521. 912-267-5626. Fax: 912-267-5628. 8:30AM-5PM (EST). Access by: Mail, in person.

Gordon County

Real Estate Recording—Gordon County Clerk Court, 100 Wall Street, Courthouse, Calhoun, GA 30701. 706-629-9533. 9AM-5PM M,T,W,Th; 9AM-5:30PM F (EST).

Felony, Misdemeanor, Civil Actions Over $5,000—Superior Court, PO Box 367, Calhoun, GA 30703. 706-629-9533. Fax: 706-625-3310. 8:30AM-5PM (EST). Access by: Mail, in person.

Civil Actions Under $5,000, Eviction, Small Claims—Magistrate Court, 100 Wall St, Calhoun, GA 30703. 706-629-6818. 8:30AM-5PM (EST). Access by: In person only.

Probate—Probate Court, 100 Wall St, PO Box 669, Calhoun, GA 30703. 706-629-7314. Fax: 706-629-4698. 8:30AM-5PM (EST). Access by: Mail, in person.

Grady County

Real Estate Recording—Grady County Clerk of the Superior Court, 250 North Broad Street, Box 8, Cairo, GA 31728. 912-377-2912. 8:30AM-5PM (EST).

Felony, Misdemeanor, Civil Actions Over $5,000—Superior Court, 250 N Broad St, Box 8, Cairo, GA 31728. 912-377-2912. 8:30AM-5PM (EST). Access by: In person only.

Civil Actions Under $5,000, Eviction, Small Claims—Magistrate Court, 250 N Broad St, Cairo, GA 31728. 912-377-4132. Fax: 912-377-4127. 8:30AM-5PM (EST). Access by: Mail, in person.

Probate—Probate Court, Courthouse, 250 N Broad St, Cairo, GA 31728. 912-377-4621. Fax: 912-377-4127. 8:30AM-5PM (EST).

Greene County

Real Estate Recording—Greene County Clerk of the Superior Court, Courthouse, 113E North Main St., Greensboro, GA 30642. 706-453-3340. Fax: 704-453-7346. 7:30AM-5PM (EST).

Felony, Misdemeanor, Civil, Eviction, Small Claims—Superior & Magistrate Court, 113 E North Main St, Greensboro, GA 30642. 706-453-3340. 8AM-5PM (EST). Access by: Mail, in person.

Probate—Probate Court, 113C N Main St, Greensboro, GA 30642. 706-453-3346. Fax: 706-453-7649. 8:30AM-5PM (EST). Access by: Mail, in person.

Gwinnett County

Real Estate Recording—Gwinnett County Clerk of the Superior Court, 75 Langley Drive, Lawrenceville, GA 30245. 770-822-8100. 8AM-5PM (EST).

Felony, Misdemeanor, Civil, Eviction, Small Claims—Superior, State & Magistrate Court, PO Box 880, Lawrenceville, GA 30246-0880. 770-822-8100. 8AM-5PM (EST). Access by: In person only.

Probate—Probate Court, 75 Langley Dr, Lawrenceville, GA 30245. 770-822-8250. Fax: 770-822-8274. 8:30AM-4:30PM (EST). Access by: Mail, in person.

Habersham County

Real Estate Recording—Habersham County Clerk of the Superior Court, Highway 115, 555 Monroe St., Unit 35, Clarkesville, GA 30523. 706-754-2923. Fax: 706-754-8779. 8:30AM-5PM (EST).

Felony, Misdemeanor, Civil Actions Over $5,000—Superior & State Court, 555 Monroe St, Unit 35, Clarkesville, GA 30523. 706-754-2923. 8:30AM-5PM (EST). Access by: In person only.

Civil Actions Under $5,000, Eviction, Small Claims—Magistrate Court, PO Box 587, Clarkesville, GA 30523. 706-754-4871. Fax: 706-754-5093. 8AM-5PM (EST). Access by: In person only.

Probate—Probate Court, PO Box 615, Clarkesville, GA 30523. 706-754-2013. Fax: 706-754-5093. 8:30AM-5PM (EST).

Hall County

Real Estate Recording—Hall County Clerk of the Superior Court, 111 Spring Street, Courthouse, Gainesville, GA 30501. 770-531-7054. Fax: 770-536-0702. 8AM-5PM (EST).

Felony, Misdemeanor, Civil Actions Over $5,000—Superior & State Court, PO Box 1275, Gainesville, GA 30503. 770-531-7025. Fax: 770-531-7070. 8AM-5PM (EST). Access by: In person only.

Civil Actions Under $5,000, Eviction, Small Claims—Magistrate Court, PO Box 1435, Gainesville, GA 30503. 770-531-6912. Fax: 770-531-6917. 8AM-5PM (EST). Access by: In person only.

Probate—Probate Court, Hall County Courthouse, Rm 123, Gainesville, GA 30501. 770-531-6921. Fax: 770-531-4946. 8AM-5PM (EST). Access by: Mail, in person.

Hancock County

Real Estate Recording—Hancock County Clerk of the Superior Court, Courthouse Square, Sparta, GA 31087. 706-444-6644. Fax: 706-444-6221. 8AM-5PM M-W & F; 9AM-12 Th (EST).

Felony, Misdemeanor, Civil Actions Over $5,000—Superior Court, PO Box 451, Courthouse Square, Sparta, GA 31087. 706-444-6644. 8AM-5PM, 8AM-12PM Th (EST). Access by: Mail, in person.

Civil Actions Under $5,000, Eviction, Small Claims—Magistrate Court, 601 Courthouse Square, Sparta, GA 31087. 706-444-6234. 9AM-5PM (EST). Access by: In person only.

Probate—Probate Court, Courthouse Sq, Sparta, GA 31087. 706-444-5343. 8AM-5PM M-W & F; 8AM-Noon Th (EST).

Haralson County

Real Estate Recording—Haralson County Clerk of the Superior Court, 4485 State Highway 120 East, Buchanan, GA 30113. 770-646-2005. Fax: 770-646-2035. 8:30AM-5PM (EST).

Felony, Misdemeanor, Civil Actions Over $5,000—Superior Court, Drawer 849, 4485 Georgia Hwy 120, Buchanan, GA 30113. 770-646-2005. Fax: 770-646-2035. 8:30AM-5PM (EST). Access by: Mail, in person.

Civil Actions Under $5,000, Eviction, Small Claims—Magistrate Court, PO Box 1040, Buchanan, GA 30113. 770-646-2015. 8:30AM-5PM (EST). Access by: In person only.

Probate—Probate Court, PO Box 620, Buchanan, GA 30113. 770-646-2008. Fax: 770-646-3419. 8:30AM-5PM (EST). Access by: Mail, in person.

Harris County

Real Estate Recording—Harris County Clerk of the Superior Court, Courthouse, 102 College St., Highway 27, Hamilton, GA 31811. 706-628-5570. 8AM-5PM (EST).

Felony, Misdemeanor, Civil Actions Over $5,000—Superior Court, PO Box 528, Hamilton, GA 31811. 706-628-4944. 8AM-5PM (EST). Access by: In person only.

Civil Actions Under $5,000, Eviction, Small Claims—Magistrate Court, PO Box 347, Hamilton, GA 31811. 706-628-4977. Fax: 706-628-4223. 8AM-5PM (EST). Access by: In person only.

Probate—Probate Court, PO Box 569, Hamilton, GA 31811. 706-628-5038. Fax: 706-628-4223. 8AM-Noon, 1-5PM (EST). Access by: Mail, in person.

Hart County

Real Estate Recording—Hart County Clerk of the Superior Court, 185 West Franklin Street, Courthouse Annex, Rm 1, Hartwell, GA 30643. 706-376-7189. Fax: 706-376-1277. 8:30AM-5PM (EST).

Felony, Misdemeanor, Civil Actions Over $5,000—Superior Court, PO Box 386, Hartwell, GA 30643. 706-376-7189. Fax: 706-376-1277. 8:30AM-5PM (EST). Access by: In person only.

Civil Actions Under $5,000, Eviction, Small Claims—Magistrate Court, PO Box 698, Hartwell, GA 30643. 706-376-9872. Fax: 706-376-6821. 8:30AM-3PM (EST). Access by: In person only.

Probate—Probate Court, PO Box 1159, Hartwell, GA 30643. 706-376-2565. 8:30AM-5PM (EST).

Heard County

Real Estate Recording—Heard County Clerk of the Superior Court, Courthouse, 215 E. Court Sq., Franklin, GA 30217. 706-675-3301. Fax: 706-675-0819. (EST).

Felony, Misdemeanor, Civil Actions Over $5,000—Superior Court, PO Box 249, Franklin, GA 30217. 706-675-3301. 8AM-5PM (EST). Access by: Mail, in person.

Civil Actions Under $5,000, Eviction, Small Claims—Magistrate Court, PO Box 395, Franklin, GA 30217. 706-675-3002. Fax: 706-675-0819. 8:30AM-5PM (EST). Access by: Mail, in person.

Probate—Probate Court, PO Box 478, Franklin, GA 30217. 706-675-3353. Fax: 706-675-0819. 8:30AM-5PM (EST). Access by: Mail, in person.

Henry County

Real Estate Recording—Henry County Clerk of the Superior Court, Courthouse, #1 Courthouse Square, McDonough, GA 30253. 770-954-2121. 8AM-5PM (EST).

Felony, Misdemeanor, Civil Actions Over $5,000—Superior Court, One Courthouse Square, McDonough, GA 30253. 770-954-2121. 8AM-5PM (EST). Access by: In person only.

Civil Actions Under $5,000, Eviction, Small Claims—Magistrate Court, 30 Atlanta St, McDonough, GA 30253. 770-954-2111. Fax: 770-957-2116. 8AM-5PM (EST). Access by: In person only.

Probate—Probate Court, 20 Lawrenceville St, McDonough, GA 30253. 770-954-2303. Fax: 770-954-2308. 8AM-4:45PM (EST).

Houston County

Real Estate Recording—Houston County Clerk of the Superior Court, 800 Carroll Street, Perry, GA 31069. 912-987-2170. Fax: 912-987-3252. 8:30AM-5PM (EST).

Felony, Misdemeanor, Civil Actions Over $5,000—Superior Court, 800 Carroll St, Perry, GA 31069. 912-987-2170. Fax: 912-987-3252. 8:30AM-5PM (EST). Access by: Fax, mail, in person.

Misdemeanor, Civil Actions Over $5,000—State Court, 202 Carl Vinson Pkwy, Warner Robins, GA 31088. 912-542-2105. Fax: 912-542-2077. 8AM-5PM (EST). Access by: Phone, fax, mail, in person.

Civil Actions Under $5,000, Eviction, Small Claims—Magistrate Court, 732 Main St, Perry, GA 31069. 912-987-4695. Fax: 912-987-5313. 8AM-5PM (EST). Access by: Mail, in person.

Probate—Probate Court, PO Box 1801, Perry, GA 31069. 912-987-2770. Fax: 912-988-4511. 8AM-4PM (EST). Access by: Mail, in person.

Irwin County

Real Estate Recording—Irwin County Clerk of the Superior Court, Courthouse, 301 S. Irwin Avenue, Ocilla, GA 31774. 912-468-5356. 8AM-5PM (EST).

Felony, Misdemeanor, Civil Actions Over $5,000—Superior Court, PO Box 186, Ocilla, GA 31774. 912-468-5356. 8:30AM-5PM (EST). Access by: Phone, mail, in person.

Civil Actions Under $5,000, Eviction, Small Claims—Magistrate Court, 207 S Irwin Ave Suite 3, Ocilla, GA 31774. 912-468-7671. Fax: 912-468-9672. 8AM-5PM (EST). Access by: Mail.

Probate—Probate Court, 301 W 2nd St, PO Box 566, Ocilla, GA 31774. 912-468-5138. Fax: 912-468-7765. 8AM-5PM (EST). Access by: In person only.

Jackson County

Real Estate Recording—Jackson County Clerk of the Superior Court, Courthouse, 85 Washington Street, Jefferson, GA 30549. 706-367-6360. Fax: 706-367-2468. 8AM-5PM (EST).

Felony, Misdemeanor, Civil Actions Over $5,000—Superior & State Court, PO Box 7, Jefferson, GA 30549. 706-367-6360. Fax: 706-367-2468. 8AM-5PM (EST). Access by: In person only.

Civil Actions Under $5,000, Eviction, Small Claims—Magistrate Court, PO Box 332, Commerce, GA 30529. 706-335-6545. Fax: 706-335-5221. 8AM-5PM (EST). Access by: In person only.

Probate—Probate Court, 85 Washington St, Jefferson, GA 30549. 706-367-6367. Fax: 706-367-2468. 8:30AM-5PM (EST). Access by: Mail, in person.

Jasper County

Real Estate Recording—Jasper County Clerk of the Superior Court, Courthouse, Monticello, GA 31064. 706-468-4901. Fax: 706-468-4946. 8:30AM-Noon, 1-5PM (EST).

Felony, Misdemeanor, Civil Actions Over $5,000—Superior Court, County Courthouse, Monticello, GA 31064. 706-468-4901. Fax: 706-468-4946. 8:30AM-5PM (EST). Access by: In person only.

Civil Actions Under $5,000, Eviction, Small Claims—Magistrate Court, County Courthouse, 123 W Green St, Monticello, GA 31064. 706-468-4909. Fax: 706-468-4928. 8:30AM-4:30PM (EST). Access by: In person only.

Probate—Jasper County Probate Court, Jasper County Courthouse, Monticello, GA 31064. 706-468-4903. Fax: 706-468-4946. 8AM-4:30PM (EST). Access by: Mail, in person.

Jeff Davis County

Real Estate Recording—Jeff Davis County Clerk of the Superior Court, Jeff Davis Street, Courthouse Annex, Hazlehurst, GA 31539. 912-375-6615. Fax: 912-375-0378. 8AM-5PM (EST).

Felony, Misdemeanor, Civil Actions Over $5,000—Superior & State Court, PO Box 248, Hazlehurst, GA 31539. 912-375-6615. Fax: 912-375-0378. 8AM-5PM (EST). Access by: Fax, mail, in person.

Civil Actions Under $5,000, Eviction, Small Claims—Magistrate Court, PO Box 568, Hazlehurst, GA 31539. 912-375-6630. 8AM-5PM (EST). Access by: Mail, in person.

Probate—Probate Court, PO Box 13, Hazlehurst, GA 31539. 912-375-6626. Fax: 912-375-0378. 9AM-5PM (EST).

Jefferson County

Real Estate Recording—Jefferson County Clerk of the Superior Court, 202 E. Broad Street, Courthouse, Louisville, GA 30434. 912-625-7922. 9AM-5PM (EST).

Felony, Misdemeanor, Civil Actions Over $5,000—Superior & State Court, PO Box 151, Louisville, GA 30434. 912-625-7922. Fax: 912-625-4002. 9AM-5PM (EST). Access by: Mail, in person.

Civil Actions Under $5,000, Eviction, Small Claims—Magistrate Court, PO Box 749, Louisville, GA 30434. 912-625-8834. 8AM-5PM (EST). Access by: In person only.

Probate—Probate Court, 202 Broad St, PO Box 307, Louisville, GA 30434. 912-625-3258. Fax: 912-625-3258. 9AM-4:30PM (EST).

Jenkins County

Real Estate Recording—Jenkins County Clerk of the Superior Court, Harvey Street, Courthouse, Millen, GA 30442. 912-982-4683. Fax: 912-982-1274. 8:30AM-Noon, 1PM-5PM (EST).

Felony, Misdemeanor, Civil Actions Over $5,000—Superior & State Court, PO Box 659, Millen, GA 30442. 912-982-4683. Fax: 912-982-1274. 8:30AM-5PM (EST). Access by: In person only.

Civil Actions Under $5,000, Eviction, Small Claims—Magistrate Court, PO Box 659, Millen, GA 30442. 912-982-5580. 8:30AM-5PM (EST). Access by: In person only.

Probate—Probate Court, PO Box 904, Millen, GA 30442. 912-982-5581. Fax: 912-982-3233. 8:30AM-5PM (EST). Access by: Mail, in person.

Johnson County

Real Estate Recording—Johnson County Clerk of the Superior Court, Courthouse Square, Wrightsville, GA 31096. 912-864-3484. Fax: 912-864-1343. 9AM-5PM (EST).

Felony, Misdemeanor, Civil, Eviction, Small Claims—Superior & Magistrate Court, PO Box 321, Wrightsville, GA 31096. 912-864-3484. Fax: 912-864-1343. 9AM-5PM (EST). Access by: Mail, in person.

Probate—Probate Court, 301 S Marcus St, PO Box 264, Wrightsville, GA 31096. 912-864-3316. Fax: 912-864-0745. (EST).

Jones County

Real Estate Recording—Jones County Clerk of the Superior Court, Jefferson Street, Courthouse, Gray, GA 31032. 912-986-6671. 8:30AM-4:30PM (EST).

Felony, Misdemeanor, Civil Actions Over $5,000—Superior Court, PO Drawer 39, Courthouse Jefferson St, Gray, GA 31032. 912-986-6671. 8:30AM-4:30PM (EST). Access by: Mail, in person.

Civil Actions Under $5,000, Eviction, Small Claims—Magistrate Court, PO Box 88, Gray, GA 31032. 912-986-5113. Fax: 912-986-1715. 8:30AM-4:30PM (EST). Access by: In person only.

Probate—Probate Court, PO Box 1359, Gray, GA 31032. 912-986-6668. Fax: 912-986-1715. 8:30AM-4:30PM (EST).

Lamar County

Real Estate Recording—Lamar County Clerk of the Superior Court, 326 Thomaston Street, Courthouse, Barnesville, GA 30204. 770-358-5145. Fax: 770-358-5149. 8AM-5PM (EST).

Felony, Misdemeanor, Civil Actions Over $5,000—Superior Court, 326 Thomaston St, Barnesville, GA 30204. 770-358-5145. Fax: 770-358-5149. 8AM-5PM (EST). Access by: In person only.

Civil Actions Under $5,000, Eviction, Small Claims—Magistrate Court, 121 Roberta Dr, Barnesville, GA 30204. 770-358-5154. 8AM-5PM (EST). Access by: In person only.

Probate—Probate Court, 326 Thomaston St, Barnesville, GA 30204. 770-358-5155. Fax: 770-358-5149. 8AM-5PM (EST).

Lanier County

Real Estate Recording—Lanier County Clerk of the Superior Court, County Courthouse, 100 Main Street, Lakeland, GA 31635. 912-482-3594. Fax: 912-482-8333. 8AM-Noon,1-5PM (EST).

Felony, Misdemeanor, Civil Actions Over $5,000—Superior Court, County Courthouse, 100 Main St, Lakeland, GA 31635. 912-482-3594. Fax: 912-482-8333. 8AM-Noon, 1PM-5PM (EST). Access by: Mail, in person.

Civil Actions Under $5,000, Eviction, Small Claims—Magistrate Court, County Courthouse, Lakeland, GA 31635. 912-482-2207. Fax: 912-482-8358. 8AM-5PM (EST). Access by: Mail, in person.

Probate—Probate Court, County Courthouse, 100 Main St, Lakeland, GA 31635. 912-482-3668. Fax: 912-482-8333. 8AM-5PM (EST).

Laurens County

Real Estate Recording—Laurens County Clerk of the Superior Court, Courthouse Square, 101 N. Jefferson St., Dublin, GA 31021. 912-272-3210. 8:30AM-5:30PM (EST).

Felony, Misdemeanor, Civil, Eviction, Small Claims— Superior & Magistrate Court, PO Box 2028, Dublin, GA 31040. 912-272-3210. 8:30AM-5:30PM (EST). Access by: Mail, in person.

Probate—Probate Court, PO Box 2098, Dublin, GA 31040. 912-272-2566. Fax: 912-277-2932. 8:30AM-5:30PM (EST). Access by: Mail, in person.

Lee County

Real Estate Recording—Lee County Clerk of the Superior Court, 100 Leslie Highway, Leesburg, GA 31763. 912-759-6018. 8AM-5PM (EST).

Felony, Misdemeanor, Civil Actions Over $5,000— Superior Court, PO Box 597, Leesburg, GA 31763. 912-759-6018. 8AM-5PM (EST). Access by: Mail, in person.

Civil Actions Under $5,000, Eviction, Small Claims— Magistrate Court, PO Box 522, Leesburg, GA 31763. 912-759-6016. Fax: 912-759-6382. 8AM-5PM (EST). Access by: In person only.

Probate—Probate Court, 100 Leslie Hwy, PO Box 592, Leesburg, GA 31763. 912-759-6006. Fax: 912-759-6050. 8AM-5PM (EST).

Liberty County

Real Estate Recording—Liberty County Clerk of the Superior Court, Courthouse Square, Main St., Hinesville, GA 31313. 912-876-3625. Fax: 912-369-5463. 8AM-5PM (EST).

Felony, Misdemeanor, Civil Actions Over $5,000— Superior & State Court, PO Box 50, Hinesville, GA 31313-0050. 912-876-3625. 8AM-5PM (EST). Access by: Mail, in person.

Civil Actions Under $5,000, Eviction, Small Claims— Magistrate Court, PO Box 50, Hinesville, GA 31313. 912-876-2343. Fax: 912-369-5463. 8AM-5PM (EST). Access by: Mail, in person.

Probate—Probate Court, 112 N Main St, Courthouse Annex Rm 100, PO Box 28, Hinesville, GA 31313. 912-876-3635. Fax: 912-876-3589. 8AM-5PM (EST).

Lincoln County

Real Estate Recording—Lincoln County Clerk of the Superior Court, 210 Humphrey Street, Courthouse Room 103, Lincolnton, GA 30817. 706-359-4444. 9AM-Noon, 1PM-5PM (EST).

Felony, Misdemeanor, Civil Actions Over $5,000— Superior Court, PO Box 340, Lincolnton, GA 30817. 706-359-4444. 9AM-4:30PM (EST). Access by: In person only.

Civil Actions Under $5,000, Eviction, Small Claims— Magistrate Court, PO Box 205, Lincolnton, GA 30817. 706-359-4444. Fax: 706-359-4729. 9AM-4PM (EST). Access by: Mail, in person.

Probate—Probate Court, PO Box 340, Lincolnton, GA 30817. 706-359-4444. Fax: 706-359-4729. 9AM-5PM (EST).

Long County

Real Estate Recording—Long County Clerk of the Superior Court, Courthouse, MacDonald Street, Ludowici, GA 31316. 912-545-2123. 8:30AM-4:30PM (EST).

Felony, Misdemeanor, Civil Actions Over $5,000— Superior & State Court, PO Box 458, Ludowici, GA 31316. 912-545-2123. 8:30AM-4:30PM (EST). Access by: Mail, in person.

Civil Actions Under $5,000, Eviction, Small Claims— Magistrate Court, PO Box 87, Ludowici, GA 31316. 912-545-2315. 8:30AM-4:30PM (EST). Access by: Mail, in person.

Probate—Probate Court, McDonald St, PO Box 426, Ludowici, GA 31316. 912-545-2131. Fax: 912-545-2150. 8:30AM-4:30PM (EST). Access by: Mail, in person.

Lowndes County

Real Estate Recording—Lowndes County Clerk of the Superior Court, 108 E. Central Ave., Valdosta, GA 31601. 912-333-5125. Fax: 912-333-7637. 8AM-5PM (EST).

Felony, Misdemeanor, Civil Actions Over $5,000— Superior & State Court, PO Box 1349, Valdosta, GA 31603. 912-333-5101. 8AM-5PM (EST). Access by: In person only.

Civil Actions Under $5,000, Eviction, Small Claims— Magistrate Court, PO Box 1349, Valdosta, GA 31603. 912-333-5110. Fax: 912-333-7616. 9AM-5PM (EST). Access by: In person only.

Probate—Probate Court, PO Box 72, Valdosta, GA 31603. 912-333-5103. Fax: 912-333-7646. 8AM-5PM (EST).

Lumpkin County

Real Estate Recording—Lumpkin County Clerk of the Superior Court, 99 Courthouse Hill, Suite D, Dahlonega, GA 30533. 706-864-3736. Fax: 706-864-5298. 8AM-5PM (EST).

Felony, Misdemeanor, Civil, Eviction, Small Claims— Superior & Magistrate Court, 279 Courthouse Hill, Dahlonega, GA 30533-1142. 706-864-3736. Fax: 706-864-5298. 8AM-5PM (EST). Access by: In person only.

Probate—Probate Court, 99 Courthouse Hill St, Suite C, Dahlonega, GA 30533. 706-864-3847. Fax: 706-864-9271. 8:30AM-4:30PM (EST). Access by: Mail, in person.

Macon County

Real Estate Recording—Macon County Clerk of the Superior Court, 100 Sumter Street, Courthouse, Oglethorpe, GA 31068. 912-472-7661. 8:30AM-5PM (EST).

Felony, Misdemeanor, Civil Actions Over $5,000— Superior Court, PO Box 337, Oglethorpe, GA 31068. 912-472-7661. 8:30AM-5PM (EST). Access by: Mail, in person.

Civil Actions Under $5,000, Eviction, Small Claims— Magistrate Court, PO Box 605, Oglethorpe, GA 31068. 912-472-8509. 8:30AM-5PM (EST). Access by: Phone, mail, in person.

Probate—Probate Court, PO Box 216, Oglethorpe, GA 31068. 912-472-7685. 8AM-Noon, 1-5PM (EST).

Madison County

Real Estate Recording—Madison County Clerk of the Superior Court, Courthouse Square, Hwy 29, Danielsville, GA 30633. 706-795-3351. Fax: 706-795-5668. 8AM-5PM (EST).

Felony, Misdemeanor, Civil Actions Over $5,000— Superior Court, PO Box 247, Danielsville, GA 30633. 706-795-3351. Fax: 706-795-5668. 8AM-5PM (EST). Access by: In person only.

Civil Actions Under $5,000, Eviction, Small Claims— Magistrate Court, PO Box 6, Danielsville, GA 30633. 706-795-3351. Fax: 706-795-5668. 8AM-5PM (EST). Access by: In person only.

Probate—Probate Court, PO Box 207, Danielsville, GA 30633. 706-795-3354. Fax: 706-795-5668. 8AM-5PM (EST). Access by: Mail, in person.

Marion County

Real Estate Recording—Marion County Clerk of the Superior Court, Courthouse Square, Broad Street, Buena Vista, GA 31803. 912-649-7321. Fax: 912-649-2059. 9AM-5PM (EST).

Felony, Misdemeanor, Civil, Eviction, Small Claims— Superior & Magistrate Court, PO Box 41, Buena Vista, GA 31803. 912-649-7321. Fax: 912-649-2059. 8:30AM-5PM (EST). Access by: Mail, in person.

Probate—Probate Court, Courthouse Sq, PO Box 207, Buena Vista, GA 31803. 912-649-5542. Fax: 912-649-2059. 8:30AM-Noon, 1-5PM (EST). Access by: Mail, in person.

McDuffie County

Real Estate Recording—McDuffie County Clerk of the Superior Court, 337 Main Street, Courthouse, Thomson, GA 30824. 706-595-2134. Fax: 716-595-4710. 8AM-5PM (EST).

Felony, Misdemeanor, Civil Actions Over $5,000— Superior Court, PO Box 158, 337 Main St, Thomson, GA 30824. 706-595-2134. 9AM-5PM (EST). Access by: Mail, in person.

Civil Actions Under $5,000, Eviction, Small Claims—
Magistrate Court, PO Box 52, Thomson, GA 30824. 706-597-2618. Fax: 706-597-4710. 9AM-5PM (EST). Access by: Mail, in person.

Probate—Probate Court, PO Box 2028, Thomson, GA 30824. 706-595-2124. Fax: 706-595-4710. 8AM-5PM (EST).

McIntosh County

Real Estate Recording—McIntosh County Clerk of the Superior Court, Courthouse, 310 Northway, Darien, GA 31305. 912-437-6641. Fax: 912-437-6673. 8AM-4:30PM (EST).

Felony, Misdemeanor, Civil Actions Over $5,000—
Superior & State Court, PO Box 1661, Darien, GA 31305. 912-437-6641. Fax: 912-437-6673. 8AM-4:30PM (EST). Access by: Mail, in person.

Civil Actions Under $5,000, Eviction, Small Claims—
Magistrate Court, PO Box 459, Darien, GA 31305. 912-437-4888. Fax: 912-437-2768. 8AM-5PM (EST). Access by: In person only.

Probate—Probate Court, PO Box 453, Darien, GA 31305. 912-437-6636. Fax: 912-437-6635. 8AM-5PM (EST).

Meriwether County

Real Estate Recording—Meriwether County Clerk of the Superior Court, 100 Court Square, Meriwether County Courthouse, Greenville, GA 30222. 706-672-4416. Fax: 706-472-4900. 9AM-5PM (EST).

Felony, Misdemeanor, Civil Actions Over $5,000—
Superior Court, PO Box 160, Greenville, GA 30222. 706-672-4416. 9AM-5PM (EST). Access by: In person only.

Civil Actions Under $5,000, Eviction, Small Claims—
Magistrate Court, PO Box 702, Greenville, GA 30222. 706-672-1247. 9AM-4:30PM M,T,TH,F/9AM-11:30PM W (EST). Access by: In person only.

Probate—Probate Court, PO Box 608, Greenville, GA 30222. 706-672-4952. Fax: 706-672-1886. 8:30AM-5PM (EST). Access by: Mail, in person.

Miller County

Real Estate Recording—Miller County Clerk of the Superior Court, 155 First Street, Colquitt, GA 31737. 912-758-4102. Fax: 912-758-2229. 8AM-Noon,1-5PM (EST).

Felony, Misdemeanor, Civil Actions Over $5,000—
Superior & State Court, PO Box 66, Colquitt, GA 31737. 912-758-4102. 8AM-5PM (EST). Access by: In person only.

Civil Actions Under $5,000, Small Claims, Probate—
Magistrate & Probate Court, 155 S 1st St, Rm 1, Colquitt, GA 31737. 912-758-4110. Fax: 912-758-2229. 8AM-5PM (EST). Access by: In person only.

Probate—Probate Court, 155 S 1st St, Box 1, Colquitt, GA 31737. 912-758-4110. Fax: 912-758-2229. 8AM-Noon, 1-5PM (EST). Access by: Mail, in person.

Mitchell County

Real Estate Recording—Mitchell County Clerk of the Superior Court, Broad Street, Courthouse, Camilla, GA 31730. 912-336-2022. Fax: 912-336-2003. 8:30AM-5PM (EST).

Felony, Misdemeanor, Civil Actions Over $5,000—
Superior & State Court, PO Box 427, Camilla, GA 31730. 912-336-2022. 8:30AM-5PM (EST). Access by: In person only.

Civil Actions Under $5,000, Eviction, Small Claims—
Magistrate Court, PO Box 626, Camilla, GA 31730. 912-336-2077. Fax: 912-336-2077. 8:30AM-5PM (EST). Access by: In person only.

Probate—Probate Court, 11 Broad St, PO Box 229, Camilla, GA 31730. 912-336-2016. Fax: 912-336-2003. 8:30AM-5PM (EST).

Monroe County

Real Estate Recording—Monroe County Clerk of the Superior Court, 1 Courthouse Square, Forsyth, GA 31029. 912-994-7022. Fax: 912-994-7053. 8:30AM-4:30PM (EST).

Felony, Misdemeanor, Civil Actions Over $5,000—
Superior Court, PO Box 450, 1 Courthouse Square, Forsyth, GA 31029. 912-994-7022. Fax: 912-994-7053. 8:30AM-4:30PM (EST). Access by: Mail, in person.

Civil Actions Under $5,000, Eviction, Small Claims—
Magistrate Court, PO Box 974, Forsyth, GA 31029. 912-994-7018. Fax: 912-994-7284. 8:30AM-4:30PM, Closed 12PM-1:30PM (EST). Access by: In person only.

Probate—Monroe County Probate Court, Monroe County Courthouse, Rm 2, PO Box 187, Forsyth, GA 31029. 912-994-7036. Fax: 912-994-7054. 8:30AM-4:30PM (EST).

Montgomery County

Real Estate Recording—Montgomery County Clerk of the Superior Court, Highway 221 & 56, Courthouse, Mount Vernon, GA 30445. 912-583-4401. 9AM-5PM (EST).

Felony, Misdemeanor, Civil Actions Over $5,000—
Superior Court, PO Box 311, Mt Vernon, GA 30445. 912-583-4401. 8AM-5PM (EST). Access by: In person only.

Civil Actions Under $5,000, Eviction, Small Claims—
Magistrate Court, PO Box 174, Mt Vernon, GA 30445. 912-583-2170. Fax: 912-583-4915. 8:30AM-5PM (EST). Access by: In person only.

Probate—Probate Court, 400 Railroad Ave, PO Box 302, Mt Vernon, GA 30445. 912-583-2681. Fax: 912-583-4915. 9AM-5PM (EST). Access by: Mail.

Morgan County

Real Estate Recording—Morgan County Clerk of the Superior Court, 141 East Jefferson Street, Madison, GA 30650. 706-342-3605. (EST).

Felony, Misdemeanor, Civil Actions Over $5,000—
Superior Court, PO Box 130, 149 E Jefferson St, Madison, GA 30650. 706-342-3605. 8:30AM-5PM (EST). Access by: Mail, in person.

Civil Actions Under $5,000, Eviction, Small Claims—
Magistrate Court, Courthouse, Rm 105, Madison, GA 30650. 706-342-3088. Fax: 706-343-0000. 8AM-5PM (EST). Access by: In person only.

Probate—Probate Court, Morgan County Courthouse, Madison, GA 30650. 706-342-1373. Fax: 706-342-5085. 8AM-5PM (EST). Access by: Mail, in person.

Murray County

Real Estate Recording—Murray County Clerk of the Superior Court, 121 N 3rd Avenue, Courthouse, Chatsworth, GA 30705. 706-695-2932. 8:30AM-5PM (EST).

Felony, Misdemeanor, Civil Actions Over $5,000—
Superior Court, PO Box 1000, Chatsworth, GA 30705. 706-695-2932. 8:30AM-5PM (EST). Access by: Phone, mail, in person.

Civil Actions Under $5,000, Eviction, Small Claims—
Magistrate Court, 121 4th Ave, Chatsworth, GA 30705. 706-695-3021. Fax: 706-695-8721. 8AM-Noon, 1PM-5PM (EST). Access by: In person only.

Probate—Murray County Probate Court, 115 Fort St, Chatsworth, GA 30705. 706-695-3812. Fax: 706-517-1340. 8:30AM-5PM (EST).

Muscogee County

Real Estate Recording—Muscogee County Clerk of the Superior Court, 100 10th Street, Columbus, GA 31901. 706-653-4358. Fax: 706-653-4359. 8:30AM-5PM (EST).

Felony, Misdemeanor, Civil Actions Over $5,000—
Superior & State Court, PO Box 2145, Columbus, GA 31994. 706-571-5820. Fax: 706-571-4921. 8:30AM-5PM (EST). Access by: Mail, in person.

Civil Actions Under $5,000, Eviction, Small Claims—
Magistrate Court, Box 1563, Columbus, GA 31902. 706-571-4870. Fax: 706-571-2010. 8:30AM-5PM (EST). Access by: In person only.

Probate—Probate Court, 100 10th St, PO Box 1340, Columbus, GA 31993. 706-571-4847. 8:30AM-4PM (EST).

Newton County

Real Estate Recording—Newton County Clerk of the Superior Court, 1124 Clark Street, Covington, GA 30209. 404-784-2040. 8AM-5PM (EST).

Felony, Misdemeanor, Civil Actions Over $5,000—Superior Court, 1124 Clark St, Covington, GA 30209. 770-784-2035. 8AM-5PM (EST). Access by: In person only.

Civil Actions Under $5,000, Eviction, Small Claims—Magistrate Court, 1132 Usher St, Covington, GA 30209. 770-784-2050. 8AM-5PM (EST). Access by: In person only.

Probate—Probate Court, 1124 Clark St, Covington, GA 30209. 770-784-2045. Fax: 770-784-2145. 8AM-5PM (EST).

Oconee County

Real Estate Recording—Oconee County Clerk of the Superior Court, 23 N. Main Street, Watkinsville, GA 30677. 706-769-3940. Fax: 706-769-3948. 8:30AM-5PM (EST).

Felony, Misdemeanor, Civil, Eviction, Small Claims—Superior & Magistrate Courts, PO Box 113, Watkinsville, GA 30677. 706-769-3940. Fax: 706-769-3948. 8AM-5PM (EST). Access by: In person only.

Probate—Probate Court, PO Box 54, Watkinsville, GA 30677. 706-769-3936. Fax: 706-769-3934. 8AM-5PM (EST).

Oglethorpe County

Real Estate Recording—Oglethorpe County Clerk of the Superior Court, Main Street, Courthouse, Lexington, GA 30648. 706-743-5731. Fax: 706-743-5270. 8:30AM-5PM (EST).

Felony, Misdemeanor, Civil Actions Over $5,000—Superior Court, PO Box 68, Lexington, GA 30648. 706-743-5731. Fax: 706-743-5250. 8AM-5PM (EST). Access by: In person only.

Civil Actions Under $5,000, Eviction, Small Claims—Magistrate Court, Box 356, Lexington, GA 30648. 706-743-8321. Fax: 706-743-8321. 8AM-5PM (EST). Access by: In person only.

Probate—Probate Court, Main St Hwy 78, PO Box 70, Lexington, GA 30648. 706-743-5350. Fax: 706-743-5270. 8AM-Noon, 1-5PM (EST).

Paulding County

Real Estate Recording—Paulding County Clerk of the Superior Court, 11 Courthouse Sq., Room G-2, Dallas, GA 30132. 770-443-7527. 8AM-5PM (EST).

Felony, Misdemeanor, Civil Actions Over $5,000—Superior Court, 11 Courthouse Square, Rm G2, Dallas, GA 30132. 770-443-7529. 8AM-5PM (EST). Access by: In person only.

Civil Actions Under $5,000, Eviction, Small Claims—Magistrate Court, 11 Courthouse Square, Rm G2, Dallas, GA 30132. 770-443-7529. 8AM-5PM (EST). Access by: In person only.

Probate—Probate Court, 11 Courthouse Square, Rm G2, Dallas, GA 30132. 770-443-7529. 8AM-5PM (EST).

Peach County

Real Estate Recording—Peach County Clerk of the Superior Court, 205 West Church Street, Courthouse, Fort Valley, GA 31030. 912-825-5331. 8:30AM-5PM (EST).

Felony, Misdemeanor, Civil Actions Over $5,000—Superior Court, PO Box 389, Ft Valley, GA 31030. 912-825-5331. 8:30AM-5PM (EST). Access by: Mail, in person.

Civil Actions Under $5,000, Eviction, Small Claims—Magistrate Court, PO Box 853, Ft Valley, GA 31030. 912-825-2060. Fax: 912-825-1893. 8AM-5PM (EST). Access by: Mail, in person.

Probate—Probate Court, PO Box 327, Ft Valley, GA 31030. 912-825-2313. Fax: 912-825-2678. (EST).

Pickens County

Real Estate Recording—Pickens County Clerk of the Superior Court, 213 North Main Street, Courthouse Annex - Suite 102, Jasper, GA 30143. 706-692-2014. 8AM-5PM (EST).

Felony, Misdemeanor, Civil Actions Over $5,000—Superior Court, 52 N Main St Ste 102, Jasper, GA 30143. 706-692-2014. 8AM-5PM (EST). Access by: Mail, in person.

Civil Actions Under $5,000, Eviction, Small Claims—Magistrate Court, 50 N Main St, Jasper, GA 30143. 706-692-3556. Fax: 706-692-2850. 8AM-5PM (EST). Access by: Mail, in person.

Probate—Probate Court, 52 N Main St, Jasper, GA 30143. 706-692-3556. Fax: 706-692-2850. 8AM-Noon, 1-5PM (EST).

Pierce County

Real Estate Recording—Pierce County Clerk of the Superior Court, Courthouse, Highway 84, Blackshear, GA 31516. 912-449-2020. 9AM-5PM (EST).

Felony, Misdemeanor, Civil Actions Over $5,000—Superior Court, PO Box 588, Blackshear, GA 31516. 912-449-2020. 9AM-5PM (EST). Access by: In person only.

Misdemeanor, Civil Actions Over $5,000—State Court, PO Box 588, Blackshear, GA 31516. 912-449-2020. 9AM-5PM (EST). Access by: In person only.

Civil Actions Under $5,000, Eviction, Small Claims—Magistrate Court, 102 Hwy 84 W, Blackshear, GA 31516. 912-449-2027. Fax: 912-449-2024. 9AM-5PM (EST). Access by: Mail, in person.

Probate—Probate Court, PO Box 406, Blackshear, GA 31516. 912-449-2029. 9AM-5PM (EST).

Pike County

Real Estate Recording—Pike County Clerk of the Superior Court, Highway 18 & Highway 19, Courthouse Square, Zebulon, GA 30295. 770-567-2000. 8AM-5PM (EST).

Felony, Misdemeanor, Civil Actions Over $5,000—Superior Court, PO Box 10, Zebulon, GA 30295. 770-567-2000. 8AM-5PM (EST). Access by: In person only.

Civil Actions Under $5,000, Eviction, Small Claims—Magistrate Court, PO Box 466, Zebulon, GA 30295. 770-567-2004. Fax: 770-567-2032. 8AM-5PM (EST). Access by: In person only.

Probate—Probate Court, PO Box 324, Zebulon, GA 30295. 770-567-8734. Fax: 770-567-2006. 9AM-5PM (EST).

Polk County

Real Estate Recording—Polk County Clerk of the Superior Court, Pryor Street, Courthouse #1, Cedartown, GA 30125. 770-749-2114. Fax: 770-749-2117. 9AM-5PM (EST).

Felony, Misdemeanor, Civil Actions Over $5,000—Superior Court, PO Box 948, Cedartown, GA 30125. 770-749-2114. Fax: 770-749-2148. 9AM-5PM (EST). Access by: Mail, in person.

Civil Actions Under $5,000, Eviction, Small Claims—Magistrate Court, PO Box 948, Cedartown, GA 30125. 770-749-2114. Fax: 770-749-2117. 9AM-5PM (EST). Access by: In person only.

Probate—Polk County Probate Court, Polk County Courthouse, Cedartown, GA 30125. 770-749-2128. 9AM-5PM (EST).

Pulaski County

Real Estate Recording—Pulaski County Clerk of the Superior Court, Courthouse, 350 Commerce Street, Hawkinsville, GA 31036. 912-783-1911. Fax: 912-892-3308. 8AM-5PM (EST).

Felony, Misdemeanor, Civil Actions Over $5,000—Superior Court, PO Box 60, Hawkinsville, GA 31036. 912-783-1911. Fax: 912-892-3308. 8AM-5PM (EST). Access by: Mail, in person.

Civil Actions Under $5,000, Eviction, Small Claims—Magistrate Court, PO Box 667, Hawkinsville, GA 31036. 912-783-1357. Fax: 912-892-3308. 8AM-5PM (EST). Access by: In person only.

Probate—Probate Court, PO Box 156, Hawkinsville, GA 31036. 912-783-2061. Fax: 912-892-3308. 8AM-5PM (EST). Access by: Mail, in person.

Putnam County

Real Estate Recording—Putnam County Clerk of the Superior Court, Courthouse, 100 S. Jefferson St., Eatonton, GA 31024. 706-485-4501. Fax: 706-485-2515. 8AM-5PM (EST).

Felony, Misdemeanor, Civil Actions Over $5,000—Superior & State Court, County Courthouse, Eatonton, GA 31024. 706-485-4501. 8AM-5PM (EST). Access by: In person only.

Civil Actions Under $5,000, Eviction, Small Claims—Magistrate Court, 100 N Jefferson Ave, Eatonton, GA 31024. 706-485-4306. Fax: 706-485-2515. 8AM-5PM (EST). Access by: Mail, in person.

Probate—Putnam County Probate Court, County Courthouse, 100 S Jefferson St, Eatonton, GA 31024. 706-485-5476. Fax: 706-485-2515. 8AM-5PM (EST).

Quitman County

Real Estate Recording—Quitman County Clerk of the Superior Court, Main Street, Courthouse, Georgetown, GA 31754. 912-334-2578. Fax: 912-334-2151. 8AM-5PM (EST).

Felony, Misdemeanor, Civil Actions Over $5,000—Superior Court, PO Box 307, Georgetown, GA 31754. 912-334-2578. 8:30AM-5PM (EST). Access by: Mail, in person.

Civil Actions Under $5,000, Eviction, Small Claims—Magistrate Court, PO Box 7, Georgetown, GA 31754. 912-334-2224. Fax: 912-334-2151. 8:30AM-5PM (EST). Access by: In person only.

Probate—Probate Court, Courthouse Main St, PO Box 7, Georgetown, GA 31754. 912-334-2224. Fax: 912-334-2151. 8AM-5PM (EST). Access by: Mail, in person.

Rabun County

Real Estate Recording—Rabun County Clerk of the Superior Court, 25 Courthouse Square # 7, Clayton, GA 30525. 706-782-3615. Fax: 706-782-7588. 8:30AM-5PM (EST).

Felony, Misdemeanor, Civil Actions Over $5,000—Superior Court, PO Box 893, Clayton, GA 30525. 706-782-3615. Fax: 706-782-7588. 8:30AM-5PM (EST). Access by: Mail, in person.

Civil Actions Under $5,000, Eviction, Small Claims—Magistrate Court, PO Box 893, Clayton, GA 30525. 706-782-3615. 8:30AM-5PM (EST). Access by: Mail, in person.

Probate—Probate Court, 25 Courthouse Square, Box 15, Clayton, GA 30525. 706-782-3614. Fax: 706-782-7588. 8:30AM-Noon, 1-5PM (EST). Access by: Mail, in person.

Randolph County

Real Estate Recording—Randolph County Clerk of the Superior Court, 208 Court Street, Cuthbert, GA 31740. 912-732-2216. Fax: 912-732-5881. 8AM-5PM (EST).

Felony, Misdemeanor, Civil Actions Over $5,000—Superior Court, PO Box 98, Cuthbert, GA 31740. 912-732-2216. Fax: 912-732-5781. 8:30AM-5PM (EST). Access by: In person only.

Civil Actions Under $5,000, Eviction, Small Claims—Magistrate Court, PO Box 6, Cuthbert, GA 31740. 912-732-6182. Fax: 912-732-5781. 9AM-5PM (EST). Access by: Mail, in person.

Probate—Probate Court, Court St, PO Box 424, Cuthbert, GA 31740. 912-732-2671. Fax: 912-732-5781. 8AM-5PM (EST).

Richmond County

Real Estate Recording—Richmond County Clerk of the Superior Court, 530 Green Street, 5th Floor, Room 503, Augusta, GA 30911. 706-821-2467. Fax: 706-821-2448. 8:30AM-5PM (EST).

Felony, Misdemeanor, Civil Actions Over $5,000—Superior Court, PO Box 2046, Augusta, GA 90901. 706-821-2460. Fax: 706-821-2448. 8:30AM-5PM (EST). Access by: Phone, mail, in person.

Misdemeanor, Civil Actions Over $5,000—State Court, PO Box 2046, Augusta, GA 30911. 706-821-1233. 8:30AM-5PM (EST). Access by: In person only.

Civil Actions Under $45,000, Eviction, Small Claims—Magistrate & Civil Court, 530 Greene St, Rm 705, Augusta, GA 30911. 706-821-2370. Fax: 706-821-2557. 8:30AM-5PM (EST). Access by: In person only.

Probate—Probate Court, Municipal Bldg Rm 401, 530 Greene St, Augusta, GA 30911. 706-821-2434. Fax: 706-821-2442. 8:30AM-5PM (EST). Access by: Mail, in person.

Rockdale County

Real Estate Recording—Rockdale County Clerk of the Superior Court, 922 Court Street, Room 203, Conyers, GA 30207. 770-929-4069. Fax: 770-860-0381. 8AM-5PM (EST).

Felony, Misdemeanor, Civil Actions Over $5,000—Superior Court, PO Box 937, 922 Court St, Conyers, GA 30207. 770-929-4021. 8AM-5PM (EST). Access by: Phone, mail, in person.

Misdemeanor, Civil Actions Over $5,000—State Court, PO Box 938, Conyers, GA 30207. 770-929-4019. 8AM-4:45PM (EST). Access by: Mail, in person.

Civil Actions Under $5,000, Eviction, Small Claims—Magistrate Court, PO Box 289, Conyers, GA 30207. 770-929-4014. Fax: 770-785-2496. 8:30AM-4:30PM (EST). Access by: In person only.

Probate—Probate Court, 922 Court St, Rm 107, Conyers, GA 30207. 770-929-4058. Fax: 770-483-4376. 8:30AM-4:30PM (EST).

Schley County

Real Estate Recording—Schley County Clerk of the Superior Court, US Highway 19, Courthouse Square, Ellaville, GA 31806. 912-937-5581. Fax: 912-937-2609. 8AM-Noon, 1-5PM (EST).

Felony, Misdemeanor, Civil Actions Over $5,000—Superior Court, PO Box 7, US Hwy 19-Courthouse Square, Ellaville, GA 31806. 912-937-5581. Fax: 912-937-2609. 8AM-Noon, 1-5PM (EST). Access by: Mail, in person.

Civil Actions Under $5,000, Eviction, Small Claims—Magistrate Court, PO Box 7, Ellaville, GA 31806. 912-937-5581. Fax: 912-937-2609. 8AM-5PM (EST). Access by: In person only.

Probate—Probate Court, Hwy 19, PO Box 385, Ellaville, GA 31806. 912-937-2905. Fax: 912-937-2609. 8AM-Noon, 1-5PM (EST).

Screven County

Real Estate Recording—Screven County Clerk of the Superior Court, 216 Mims Road, Sylvania, GA 30467. 912-564-2614. Fax: 912-564-2622. 8:30AM-5PM (EST).

Felony, Misdemeanor, Civil Actions Over $5,000—Superior Court, PO Box 156, Sylvania, GA 30467. 912-564-2614. Fax: 912-564-2622. 8:30AM-5PM (EST). Access by: In person only.

Misdemeanor, Civil Actions Over $5,000—State Court, PO Box 156, Sylvania, GA 30467. 912-564-2614. Fax: 912-564-2622. 8:30AM-5PM (EST). Access by: In person only.

Civil Actions Under $5,000, Eviction, Small Claims—Magistrate Court, PO Box 64, Sylvania, GA 30467. 912-564-7375. 8:30AM-4:30PM (EST). Access by: In person only.

Probate—Probate Court, 216 Mims Rd, Sylvania, GA 30467. 912-564-2783. Fax: 912-564-2562. 8:30AM-5PM (EST).

Seminole County

Real Estate Recording—Seminole County Clerk of the Superior Court, Second Street, Courthouse, Donalsonville, GA 31745. 912-524-2525. Fax: 912-524-8528. 9AM-5PM (EST).

Felony, Misdemeanor, Civil Actions Over $5,000—Superior Court, PO Box 672, Main St, Donalsonville, GA 31745. 912-524-2525. Fax: 912-524-8528. 8AM-5PM (EST). Access by: Fax, mail, in person.

Civil Actions Under $5,000, Eviction, Small Claims—Magistrate Court, PO Box 672, Donalsonville, GA 31745.

·912-524-5256. Fax: 912-524-8528. 8AM-5PM (EST). Access by: Mail, in person.

Probate—Probate Court, Seminole County Courthouse, 2nd St, Donalsonville, GA 31745. 912-524-5256. Fax: 912-524-8528. 9AM-5PM (EST). Access by: Mail, in person.

Spalding County

Real Estate Recording—Spalding County Clerk of the Superior Court, 132 East Solomon Street, Griffin, GA 30223. 770-228-9900. 8AM-5PM (EST).

Felony, Misdemeanor, Civil Actions Over $5,000—Superior Court, PO Box 1046, Griffin, GA 30224. 770-228-9900. 8AM-5PM (EST). Access by: In person only.

Misdemeanor, Civil—State Court, PO Box 1046, Griffin, GA 30224. 770-467-4745. 8AM-5PM (EST). Access by: In person only.

Civil Actions Under $5,000, Eviction, Small Claims—Magistrate Court, 132 E Solomon, Griffin, GA 30224. 770-467-4321. Fax: 770-467-0081. 8AM-5PM (EST). Access by: In person only.

Probate—Probate Court, 132 E Solomon St, Griffin, GA 30224. 770-228-9900. 8AM-5PM (EST).

Stephens County

Real Estate Recording—Stephens County Clerk of the Superior Court, Stephens County Courthouse, 150 West Doyle St., Toccoa, GA 30577. 706-886-9496. 8AM-5PM (EST).

Felony, Misdemeanor, Civil Actions Over $5,000—Superior Court, 150 W Doyle St, Toccoa, GA 30577. 706-886-3598. 8AM-5PM (EST). Access by: Mail, in person.

Misdemeanor, Civil Actions Over $5,000—State Court, 150 W Doyle St, Toccoa, GA 30577. 706-886-3598. 8AM-5PM (EST). Access by: Mail, in person.

Civil Actions Under $5,000, Eviction, Small Claims—Magistrate Court, PO Box 1374, Courthouse Annex Room 303, Toccoa, GA 30577. 706-886-6205. Fax: 706-886-5569. 8AM-5PM (EST). Access by: Mail, in person.

Probate—Probate Court, County Courthouse, PO Box 456, Toccoa, GA 30577. 706-886-2828. (EST). Access by: Mail, in person.

Stewart County

Real Estate Recording—Stewart County Clerk of the Superior Court, Main Street, Courthouse, Lumpkin, GA 31815. 912-838-6220. 8AM-4:30PM (EST).

Felony, Misdemeanor, Civil Actions Over $5,000—Superior Court, PO Box 910, Main St, Lumpkin, GA 31815. 912-838-6220. 8AM-5PM (EST). Access by: In person only.

Civil Actions Under $5,000, Eviction, Small Claims—Magistrate Court, PO Box 713, Lumpkin, GA 31815. 912-838-4261. 8AM-5PM (EST). Access by: Mail, in person.

Probate—Probate Court, PO Box 876, Lumpkin, GA 31815. 912-838-4394. Fax: 912-838-4394. 8AM-Noon, 1-5PM (EST). Access by: Mail, in person.

Sumter County

Real Estate Recording—Sumter County Clerk of the Superior Court, Lamar Street, Courthouse, Americus, GA 31709. 912-924-5626. (EST).

Felony, Misdemeanor, Civil Actions Over $5,000—Superior Court, PO Box 333, Americus, GA 31709. 912-924-5626. 9AM-5PM (EST). Access by: Phone, mail, in person.

Misdemeanor, Civil Actions Over $5,000—State Court, PO Box 333, Americus, GA 31709. 912-924-5626. 9AM-5PM (EST). Access by: In person only.

Civil Actions Under $5,000, Eviction, Small Claims—Magistrate Court, PO Box 563, Americus, GA 31709. 912-924-6699. 9AM-5PM (EST). Access by: In person only.

Probate—Probate Court, Courthouse, Lamar St, PO Box 246, Americus, GA 31709. 912-924-7693. 9AM-5PM (EST).

Talbot County

Real Estate Recording—Talbot County Clerk of the Superior Court, Monroe Street, Courthouse Square #1, Talbotton, GA 31827. 706-665-3239. Fax: 706-665-8637. 9AM-5PM (EST).

Felony, Misdemeanor, Civil Actions Over $5,000—Superior Court, PO Box 325, Talbotton, GA 31827. 706-665-3239. Fax: 706-665-8199. 9AM-5PM (EST). Access by: In person only.

Civil Actions Under $5,000, Eviction, Small Claims—Magistrate Court, PO Box 157, Talbotton, GA 31827. 706-665-3598. Fax: 706-665-8199. 8AM-5PM (EST). Access by: In person only.

Probate—Probate Court, Hwy 80, PO Box 157, Talbotton, GA 31827. 706-665-8866. Fax: 706-665-8199. 8AM-5PM (EST). Access by: Mail, in person.

Taliaferro County

Real Estate Recording—Taliaferro County Clerk of the Superior Court, Monument Street, Courthouse, Crawfordville, GA 30631. 706-456-2123. 9AM-Noon, 1-5PM (EST).

Felony, Misdemeanor, Civil Actions Over $5,000—Superior Court, PO Box 182, Crawfordville, GA 30631. 706-456-2123. 9AM-5PM (EST). Access by: In person only.

Civil Actions Under $5,000, Eviction, Small Claims—Magistrate Court, PO Box 85, Crawfordville, GA 30631. 706-456-2253. Fax: 706-456-2904. 8AM-5PM (EST). Access by: In person only.

Probate—Probate Court, PO Box 85, Crawfordville, GA 30631. 706-456-2253. Fax: 706-456-2904. 8:30AM-4:30PM (EST).

Tattnall County

Real Estate Recording—Tattnall County Clerk of the Superior Court, 108 Brazell Street, Courthouse, Reidsville, GA 30453. 912-557-6716. Fax: 912-557-4556. 8AM-4:30PM (EST).

Felony, Misdemeanor, Civil Actions Over $5,000—Superior Court, PO Box 59, Reidsville, GA 30453. 912-557-6716. 8AM-4:30PM (EST). Access by: Phone, mail, in person.

Misdemeanor, Civil Actions Over $5,000—State Court, PO Box 59, Reidsville, GA 30453. 912-557-6716. Fax: 912-557-6723. 8AM-4:30PM (EST). Access by: Mail, in person.

Civil Actions Under $5,000, Eviction, Small Claims—Magistrate Court, PO Box 513, Reidsville, GA 30453. 912-557-4372. Fax: 912-557-3136. 8AM-4:30PM (EST). Access by: Mail, in person.

Probate—Probate Court, PO Box 710, Reidsville, GA 30453. 912-557-6719. Fax: 912-557-3976. 8:30AM-4:30PM (EST). Access by: In person only.

Taylor County

Real Estate Recording—Taylor County Clerk of the Superior Court, Courthouse Square, Butler, GA 31006. 912-862-5594. Fax: 912-862-5334. 8AM-5PM (EST).

Felony, Misdemeanor, Civil Actions Over $5,000—Superior Court, PO Box 248, Courthouse Square, Butler, GA 31006. 912-862-5594. Fax: 912-862-5334. 8AM-5PM (EST). Access by: In person only.

Civil Actions Under $5,000, Eviction, Small Claims—Magistrate Court, PO Box 536, Butler, GA 31006. 912-862-3357. Fax: 912-862-2871. 8AM-5PM (EST). Access by: In person only.

Probate—Probate Court, Courthouse Sq, PO Box 536, Butler, GA 31006. 912-862-3357. Fax: 912-862-2871. 8AM-5PM (EST). Access by: Mail, in person.

Telfair County

Real Estate Recording—Telfair County Clerk of the Superior Court, Courthouse, Oak Street, McRae, GA 31055. 912-868-6525. Fax: 912-868-7956. 8:30AM-4:30PM (EST).

Felony, Misdemeanor, Civil Actions Over $5,000—Superior Court, Courthouse, Oak St, McRae, GA 31055. 912-868-6525. Fax: 912-868-7956. 8:30AM-4:30PM (EST). Access by: Phone, fax, mail, in person.

Civil Actions Under $5,000, Eviction, Small Claims—Magistrate Court, County Courthouse, McRae, GA 31055.

912-868-6772. Fax: 912-868-7956. 8:30AM-4:30PM (EST). Access by: In person only.

Probate—Probate Court, Courthouse Square, McRae, GA 31055. 912-868-6038. Fax: 912-868-7956. 8:30AM-Noon, 1-4:30PM (EST).

Terrell County

Real Estate Recording—Terrell County Clerk of the Superior Court, 235 Lee Street, Courthouse, Dawson, GA 31742. 912-995-2631. 8:30AM-5PM (EST).

Felony, Misdemeanor, Civil Actions Over $5,000—Superior Court, PO Box 189, 335 E Lee, Dawson, GA 31742. 912-995-2631. 8:30AM-5PM (EST). Access by: Mail, in person.

Civil Actions Under $5,000, Eviction, Small Claims—Magistrate Court, PO Box 793, Dawson, GA 31742. 912-995-3757. 8:30AM-5PM (EST). Access by: Mail, in person.

Probate—Probate Court, PO Box 67, Dawson, GA 31742. 912-995-5515. (EST).

Thomas County

Real Estate Recording—Thomas County Clerk of the Superior Court, 225 North Broad Street, Courthouse, Thomasville, GA 31792. 912-225-4108. Fax: 912-225-4110. 8AM-5PM (EST).

Felony, Misdemeanor, Civil—Superior & State Court, PO Box 1995, Thomasville, GA 31799. 912-225-4108. Fax: 912-225-4108. 8AM-5PM (EST). Access by: In person only.

Civil Actions Under $5,000, Eviction, Small Claims—Magistrate Court, PO Box 879, Thomasville, GA 31799. 912-225-3330. Fax: 912-225-3342. 8AM-5PM (EST). Access by: Mail, in person.

Probate—Probate Court, (225 N Broad, 31792), PO Box 1582, Thomasville, GA 31799. 912-225-4116. Fax: 912-226-3430. 8AM-5PM (EST). Access by: Mail, in person.

Tift County

Real Estate Recording—Tift County Clerk of the Superior Court, Corner of Tift Avenue & 2nd Street, Courthouse, Tifton, GA 31794. 912-386-7810. Fax: 912-386-7807. 9AM-5PM (EST).

Felony, Misdemeanor, Civil Actions Over $5,000—Superior & State Court, PO Box 354, Tifton, GA 31793. 912-386-7810. 8AM-5PM (EST). Access by: In person only.

Civil Actions Under $5,000, Eviction, Small Claims—Magistrate Court, PO Box 214, Tifton, GA 31793. 912-386-7907. Fax: 912-386-7978. 8:30AM-5PM (EST). Access by: In person only.

Probate—Probate Court, PO Box 792, Tifton, GA 31793. 912-386-7913. Fax: 912-386-7955. 8AM-Noon, 1-5PM (EST).

Toombs County

Real Estate Recording—Toombs County Clerk of the Superior Court, 100 Courthouse Square, Lyons, GA 30436. 912-526-3501. Fax: 912-526-1004. 8:30AM-5PM (EST).

Felony, Misdemeanor, Civil Actions Over $5,000—Superior & State Court, PO Drawer 530, Lyons, GA 30436. 912-526-3501. Fax: 912-526-1004. 8:30AM-5PM (EST). Access by: In person only.

Civil Actions Under $5,000, Eviction, Small Claims—Magistrate Court, PO Box 184, Lyons, GA 30436. 912-526-8985. 8:30AM-5PM (EST). Access by: Mail, in person.

Probate—Probate Court, PO Box 1370, Lyons, GA 30436. 912-526-8696. Fax: 912-526-1004. 8:30AM-5PM (EST).

Towns County

Real Estate Recording—Towns County Clerk of the Superior Court, 48 River St., Courthouse, Suite E, Hiawassee, GA 30546. 706-896-2130. 8:30AM-4:30PM (EST).

Felony, Misdemeanor, Civil Actions Over $5,000—Superior Court, 48 River St Suite E, Hiawassee, GA 30546. 706-896-2130. 8:30AM-4:30PM (EST). Access by: Phone, mail, in person.

Civil Actions Under $5,000, Eviction, Small Claims, Probate—Magistrate Court, 48 River St, Hiawassee, GA 30546.

706-896-3467. Fax: 706-896-1772. 8:30AM-4:30PM (EST). Access by: Mail, in person.

Treutlen County

Real Estate Recording—Treutlen County Clerk of the Superior Court, 200 Georgia Ave., Soperton, GA 30457. 912-529-4215. 8AM-5PM (EST).

Felony, Misdemeanor, Civil Actions Over $5,000—Superior & State Court, PO Box 356, Soperton, GA 30457. 912-529-4215. 8AM-5PM (EST). Access by: Mail, in person.

Civil Actions Under $5,000, Eviction, Small Claims, Probate—Magistrate Court, 200 W Georgia Ave, Soperton, GA 30457. 912-529-3342. Fax: 912-529-6062. (EST). Access by: Mail, in person.

Troup County

Real Estate Recording—Troup County Clerk of the Superior Court, Courthouse, 118 Ridley Avenue, LaGrange, GA 30241. 706-883-1740. 8AM-5PM (EST).

Felony, Misdemeanor, Civil Actions Over $5,000—Superior & State Court, 118 Ridley Ave (PO Box 866, 30241), LaGrange, GA 30240. 706-883-1740. 8AM-5PM (EST). Access by: In person only.

Civil Actions Under $5,000, Eviction, Small Claims—Magistrate Court, 900 Dallis St, LaGrange, GA 30240. 706-883-1695. 8AM-5PM (EST). Access by: Mail, in person.

Probate—Probate Court, 900 Dallis St, LaGrange, GA 30240. 706-883-1690. Fax: 706-812-7933. 8AM-5PM (EST). Access by: Mail, in person.

Turner County

Real Estate Recording—Turner County Clerk of the Superior Court, 219 East College Avenue, Ashburn, GA 31714. 912-567-2011. Fax: 912-567-0450. 8AM-5PM (EST).

Felony, Misdemeanor, Civil Actions Over $5,000—Superior Court, PO Box 106, 219 E College Ave, Ashburn, GA 31714. 912-567-2011. Fax: 912-567-0450. 8AM-5PM (EST). Access by: Phone, mail, in person.

Civil Actions Under $5,000, Eviction, Small Claims—Magistrate Court, 219 E College Ave, Rm 2, Ashburn, GA 31714. 912-567-3155. 9AM-6PM M,T,Th/9AM-1PM F (EST). Access by: Mail.

Probate—Probate Court, 219 E College Ave, PO Box 2506, Ashburn, GA 31714. 912-567-2151. Fax: 912-567-0358. 8AM-5PM (EST). Access by: Mail, in person.

Twiggs County

Real Estate Recording—Twiggs County Clerk of the Superior Court, 109 E. Main St., Jeffersonville, GA 31044. 912-945-3350. Fax: 912-945-6751. 8AM-5PM (EST).

Felony, Misdemeanor, Civil Actions Over $5,000—Superior Court, PO Box 228, Jeffersonville, GA 31044. 912-945-3350. 8AM-5PM (EST). Access by: Phone, mail, in person.

Civil Actions Under $5,000, Eviction, Small Claims—Magistrate Court, PO Box 146, Jeffersonville, GA 31044. 912-945-3428. 9AM-5PM (EST). Access by: Mail, in person.

Probate—Probate Court, PO Box 307, Jeffersonville, GA 31044. 912-945-3390. Fax: 912-945-6070. 9AM-5PM (EST).

Union County

Real Estate Recording—Union County Clerk of the Superior Court, 114 Courthouse Street, Box 5, Blairsville, GA 30512. 706-745-2611. Fax: 706-745-3822. 8AM-5PM (EST).

Felony, Misdemeanor, Civil Actions Over $5,000—Superior Court, 114 Courthouse St, Box 5, Blairsville, GA 30512. 706-745-2611. Fax: 706-745-3822. 8AM-5PM (EST). Access by: Phone, fax, mail, in person.

Civil Actions Under $5,000, Eviction, Small Claims, Probate—Magistrate & Probate Court, 114 Courthouse St, Box 8, Blairsville, GA 30512. 706-745-2654. Fax: 706-745-1311. 8AM-4:30PM (EST). Access by: Mail, in person.

Upson County

Real Estate Recording—Upson County Clerk of the Superior Court, 116 W. Main Street, Courthouse Annex, Thomaston, GA 30286. 706-647-7835. Fax: 706-647-7030. 8AM-5PM (EST).

Felony, Misdemeanor, Civil Actions Over $5,000—Superior Court, PO Box 469, Thomaston, GA 30286. 706-647-7835. Fax: 706-647-7030. 8AM-5PM (EST). Access by: In person only.

Civil Actions Under $5,000, Eviction, Small Claims—Magistrate Court, PO Box 890, Thomaston, GA 30286. 706-647-6891. Fax: 706-647-1248. 8AM-5PM (EST). Access by: Mail, in person.

Probate—Probate Court, PO Box 906, Thomaston, GA 30286. 706-647-7015. 8AM-5PM (EST). Access by: Mail, in person.

Walker County

Real Estate Recording—Walker County Clerk of the Superior Court, South Duke Street, Courthouse, La Fayette, GA 30728. 706-638-1742. 8AM-5PM (EST).

Felony, Misdemeanor, Civil Actions Over $5,000—Superior & State Court, PO Box 448, LaFayette, GA 30728. 706-638-1772. 8AM-5PM (EST). Access by: In person only.

Civil Actions Under $5,000, Eviction, Small Claims—Magistrate Court, PO Box 854, LaFayette, GA 30728. 706-638-1217. Fax: 706-638-1218. 8AM-5PM (EST). Access by: Mail, in person.

Probate—Probate Court, PO Box 436, LaFayette, GA 30728. 706-638-2852. Fax: 706-638-2869. 8AM-5PM (EST). Access by: Mail, in person.

Walton County

Real Estate Recording—Walton County Clerk of the Superior Court, 116 S. Broad St. Judicial Bldg., Monroe, GA 30655. 770-267-1304. Fax: 770-267-1441. 8:30AM-5PM (EST).

Felony, Misdemeanor, Civil Actions Over $5,000—Superior Court, PO Box 745, Monroe, GA 30655. 770-267-1307. Fax: 770-267-1441. 8:30AM-5PM (EST). Access by: In person only.

Civil Actions Under $5,000, Eviction, Small Claims—Magistrate Court, PO Box 1188, Monroe, GA 30655. 770-267-1349. Fax: 770-267-1417. 8:30AM-5PM (EST). Access by: Mail, in person.

Probate—Probate Court, 111 E Spring St, PO Box 629, Monroe, GA 30655. 770-267-1345. Fax: 770-267-1417. 8:30AM-5PM (EST). Access by: Mail, in person.

Ware County

Real Estate Recording—Ware County Clerk of the Superior Court, 800 Church Street, Waycross, GA 31501. 912-287-4340. 9AM-5PM (EST).

Felony, Misdemeanor, Civil Actions Over $5,000—Superior & State Court, PO Box 776, Waycross, GA 31502. 912-287-4340. 9AM-5PM (EST). Access by: Mail, in person.

Civil Actions Under $5,000, Eviction, Small Claims—Magistrate Court, 201 State St, Rm 102, Waycross, GA 31501. Civil: 912-287-4373. Criminal: 912-287-4375. Fax: 912-287-4377. 9AM-5PM (EST). Access by: Mail, in person.

Probate—Probate Court, Courthouse, Rm 105, Waycross, GA 31501. 912-287-4315. Fax: 912-287-4301. 9AM-5PM (EST). Access by: Mail, in person.

Warren County

Real Estate Recording—Warren County Clerk of the Superior Court, 100 Main Street, Courthouse, Warrenton, GA 30828. 706-465-2262. (EST).

Felony, Misdemeanor, Civil Actions Over $5,000—Superior Court, PO Box 346, 100 Main St, Warrenton, GA 30828. 706-465-2262. Fax: 706-465-0290. 8AM-5PM (EST). Access by: Mail, in person.

Civil Actions Under $5,000, Eviction, Small Claims—Magistrate Court, PO Box 203, Warrenton, GA 30828. 706-465-3123. 8AM-5PM (EST). Access by: Mail, in person.

Probate—Probate Court, 100 E Main St, PO Box 364, Warrenton, GA 30828. 706-465-2227. 8AM-5PM (EST).

Washington County

Real Estate Recording—Washington County Clerk of the Superior Court, Courthouse, Sandersville, GA 31082. 912-552-3186. 9AM-5PM (EST).

Felony, Misdemeanor, Civil Actions Over $5,000—Superior & State Court, PO Box 231, Sandersville, GA 31082. 912-552-3186. 9AM-5PM (EST). Access by: In person only.

Civil Actions Under $5,000, Eviction, Small Claims—Magistrate Court, PO Box 1053, Sandersville, GA 31082. 912-552-3591. 9AM-5PM (EST). Access by: In person only.

Probate—Probate Court, 132 W Haynes St, PO Box 669, Sandersville, GA 31082. 912-552-3304. Fax: 912-552-7424. 9AM-Noon, 1-5PM (EST). Access by: Mail, in person.

Wayne County

Real Estate Recording—Wayne County Clerk of the Superior Court, 240 E. Walnut, Courthouse Square, Jesup, GA 31546. 912-427-5930. Fax: 912-427-5939. 8:30AM-5PM (EST).

Felony, Misdemeanor, Civil Actions Over $5,000—Superior & State Court, PO Box 918, Jesup, GA 31545. 912-427-5930. Fax: 912-427-5906. 8:30AM-5PM (EST). Access by: In person only.

Civil Actions Under $5,000, Eviction, Small Claims—Magistrate Court, PO Box 27, Jesup, GA 31545. 912-427-5960. Fax: 912-427-5906. 8:30AM-5PM (EST). Access by: In person only.

Probate—Probate Court, PO Box 1093, Jesup, GA 31598. 912-427-5940. Fax: 912-427-5944. (EST).

Webster County

Real Estate Recording—Webster County Clerk of the Superior Court, County Courthouse, U.S. Highway 280, Preston, GA 31824. 912-828-3525. 8AM-Noon, 12:30PM-4:30PM (EST).

Felony, Misdemeanor, Civil Actions Over $5,000—Superior Court, PO Box 117, Preston, GA 31824. 912-828-3525. 8AM-4:30PM (EST). Access by: Mail, in person.

Civil Actions Under $5,000, Eviction, Small Claims—Magistrate Court, PO Box 18, Preston, GA 31824. 912-828-5775. Fax: 912-828-8870. 8:30AM-4:30PM (EST). Access by: Fax, mail, in person.

Probate—Probate Court, Hwy 280, PO Box 135, Preston, GA 31824. 912-828-3615. 8AM-Noon, 12:30-4:30PM (EST).

Wheeler County

Real Estate Recording—Wheeler County Clerk of the Superior Court, 119 West Pearl St., Alamo, GA 30411. 912-568-7137. 8AM-4PM (EST).

Felony, Misdemeanor, Civil Actions Over $5,000—Superior Court, PO Box 38, Alamo, GA 30411. 912-568-7137. 8AM-4PM (EST). Access by: Mail, in person.

Civil Actions Under $5,000, Eviction, Small Claims, Probate—Magistrate & Probate Court, PO Box 477, Alamo, GA 30411. 912-568-7133. 8AM-4PM (EST). Access by: In person only.

White County

Real Estate Recording—White County Clerk of the Superior Court, 59 South Main Street, Courthouse, Suite B, Cleveland, GA 30528. 706-865-2613. Fax: 706-219-3239. 8:30AM-5PM (EST).

Felony, Misdemeanor, Civil Actions Over $5,000—Superior Court, 59 S Main St, Ste B, Cleveland, GA 30528. 706-865-2613. Fax: 706-865-7749. 8:30AM-5PM (EST). Access by: In person only.

Civil Actions Under $5,000, Eviction, Small Claims—Magistrate Court-Civil Division, 59 S Main St, Ste B, Cleveland, GA 30528. 706-865-2613. Fax: 706-865-7749. 8:30AM-5PM (EST).

Magistrate Court-Criminal Division, 59 S Main St, Ste D, Cleveland, GA 30528. 706-865-2613. Fax: 706-865-7738. 9AM-5PM (EST). Access by: Phone, fax, mail, in person.

Probate—Probate Court, 59 S Main St Ste H, Cleveland, GA 30528. 706-865-4141. Fax: 706-865-1324. 8:30AM-5PM (EST). Access by: Mail, in person.

Whitfield County

Real Estate Recording—Whitfield County Clerk of the Superior Court, 300 West Crawford Street, Courthouse, Dalton, GA 30722. 706-275-7450. Fax: 706-275-7456. 8AM-5PM (EST).

Felony, Misdemeanor, Civil Actions Over $5,000—Superior Court, PO Box 868, Dalton, GA 30722. 706-275-7450. Fax: 706-275-7456. 8AM-5PM (EST). Access by: In person only.

Civil Actions Under $5,000, Eviction, Small Claims—Magistrate Court, 210 Thorton Ave PO Box 386, Dalton, GA 30722-0386. 706-278-5052. Fax: 706-278-8810. 8AM-5PM (EST). Access by: In person only.

Probate—Probate Court, 301 Crawford St, Dalton, GA 30720. 706-275-7400. 8AM-5PM (EST). Access by: Mail, in person.

Wilcox County

Real Estate Recording—Wilcox County Clerk of the Superior Court, Courthouse, Abbeville, GA 31001. 912-467-2442. Fax: 912-467-2000. 9AM-5PM (EST).

Felony, Misdemeanor, Civil, Eviction, Small Claims—Superior & Magistrate Courts, 103 N Broad St, Abbeville, GA 31001. 912-467-2442. Fax: 912-467-2000. 9AM-5PM (EST). Access by: Mail, in person.

Probate—Probate Court, 103 N Broad St, Abbeville, GA 31001. 912-467-2220. Fax: 912-467-2000. 9AM-5PM (EST).

Wilkes County

Real Estate Recording—Wilkes County Superior Court Clerk, 23 East Court Street, Room 205, Washington, GA 30673. 706-678-2423. Fax: 706-678-2115. 9AM-5PM (EST).

Felony, Misdemeanor, Civil Actions Over $5,000—Superior Court, 23 E Court St, Rm 205, Washington, GA 30673. 706-678-2423. 9AM-5PM (EST). Access by: Mail, in person.

Civil Actions Under $5,000, Eviction, Small Claims—Magistrate Court, 23 E Court St, Rm 427, Washington, GA 30673. 706-678-1881. Fax: 706-678-1865. 8:30AM-5PM (EST). Access by: In person only.

Probate—Probate Court, 23 E Court St, Rm 422, Washington, GA 30673. 706-678-2523. Fax: 706-678-1865. 8:30AM-5PM (EST).

Wilkinson County

Real Estate Recording—Wilkinson County Clerk of the Superior Court, 100 Main Street, Courthouse, Irwinton, GA 31042. 912-946-2221. Fax: 912-946-3767. 8AM-5PM (EST).

Felony, Misdemeanor, Civil Actions Over $5,000—Superior Court, PO Box 250, Irwinton, GA 31042. 912-946-2221. Fax: 912-946-3767. 8AM-5PM (EST). Access by: In person only.

Civil Actions Under $5,000, Eviction, Small Claims, Probate—Magistrate Court, PO Box 201, Irwinton, GA 31042. 912-946-2222. Fax: 912-946-3767. 8AM-5PM (EST). Access by: In person only.

Worth County

Real Estate Recording—Worth County Clerk of the Superior Court, 201 North Main Street, Courthouse, Room 13, Sylvester, GA 31791. 912-776-8205. 8AM-5PM (EST).

Felony, Misdemeanor, Civil, Eviction, Small Claims—Superior, State & Magistrate Court, 201 N Main St, Rm 13, Sylvester, GA 31791. 912-776-8205. Fax: 912-776-8232. 8AM-5PM (EST). Access by: Mail, in person.

Probate—Probate Court, 201 N Main St, Rm 12, Sylvester, GA 31791. 912-776-8207. Fax: 912-776-8232. 8AM-5PM (EST).

Federal Courts

US District Court

Middle District of Georgia

Albany/Americus Division, US District Court PO Box 1906, Albany, GA 31702. 912-430-8432. Counties: Baker, Calhoun, Dougherty, Early, Lee, Miller, Mitchell, Schley, Sumter, Terrell, Turner, Webster, Worth

Athens Division, US District Court c/o Macon Division, PO Box 128, Macon, GA 31202. 912-752-3497. Counties: Clarke, Elbert, Franklin, Greene, Hart, Madison, Morgan, Oconee, Oglethorpe, Walton

Columbus Division, US District Court PO Box 124, Columbus, GA 31902. 706-649-7816. Counties: Chattahoochee, Clay, Harris, Marion, Muscogee, Quitman, Randolph, Stewart, Talbot, Taylor

Macon Division, US District Court PO Box 128, Macon, GA 31202-0128. 912-752-3497. Counties: Baldwin, Ben Hill, Bibb, Bleckley, Butts, Crawford, Crisp, Dooly, Hancock, Houston, Jasper, Jones, Lamar, Macon, Monroe, Peach, Pulaski, Putnam, Twiggs, Upson, Washington, Wilcox, Wilkinson

Thomasville Division, US District Court c/o Valdosta Division, PO Box 68, Valdosta, GA 31601. 912-242-3616. Counties: Brooks, Colquitt, Decatur, Grady, Seminole, Thomas

Valdosta Division, US District Court PO Box 68, Valdosta, GA 31603. 912-242-3616. Counties: Berrien, Clinch, Cook, Echols, Irwin, Lanier, Lowndes, Tift

Northern District of Georgia

Atlanta Division, US District Court 2211 US Courthouse, 75 Spring St SW, Atlanta, GA 30303-3361. 404-331-6496. Counties: Cherokee, Clayton, Cobb, De Kalb, Douglas, Fulton, Gwinnett, Henry, Newton, Rockdale

Gainesville Division, US District Court Room 201, Federal Bldg, 121 Spring St SE, Gainesville, GA 30501. 770-534-5954. Counties: Banks, Barrow, Dawson, Fannin, Forsyth, Gilmer, Habersham, Hall, Jackson, Lumpkin, Pickens, Rabun, Stephens, Towns, Union, White

Newnan Division, US District Court PO Box 939, Newnan, GA 30264. 770-253-8847. Counties: Carroll, Coweta, Fayette, Haralson, Heard, Meriwether, Pike, Spalding, Troup

Rome Division, US District Court PO Box 1186, Rome, GA 30162-1186. 706-291-5629. Counties: Bartow, Catoosa, Chattooga, Dade, Floyd, Gordon, Murray, Paulding, Polk, Walker, Whitfield

Southern District of Georgia

Augusta Division, US District Court PO Box 1130, Augusta, GA 30903. 706-722-2074. Counties: Burke, Columbia, Glascock, Jefferson, Lincoln, McDuffie, Richmond, Taliaferro, Warren, Wilkes

Brunswick Division, US District Court PO Box 1636, Brunswick, GA 31521. 912-265-1758. Counties: Appling, Camden, Glynn, Jeff Davis, Long, McIntosh, Wayne

Dublin Division, US District Court c/o Augusta Division, PO Box 1130, Augusta, GA 30903. 706-722-2074. Counties: Dodge, Johnson, Laurens, Montgomery, Telfair, Treutlen, Wheeler

Savannah Division, US District Court PO Box 8286, Savannah, GA 31412. 912-650-4020. Counties: Bryan, Chatham, Effingham, Liberty

Statesboro Division, US District Court c/o Savannah Division, PO Box 8286, Savannah, GA 31412. 912-650-4020. Counties: Bulloch, Candler, Emanuel, Evans, Jenkins, Screven, Tattnall, Toombs

Waycross Division, US District Court c/o Savannah Division, PO Box 8286, Savannah, GA 31412. 912-650-4020. Counties: Atkinson, Bacon, Brantley, Charlton, Coffee, Pierce, Ware

US Bankruptcy Court
Middle District of Georgia

Columbus Division, US Bankruptcy Court, PO Box 2147, Columbus, GA 31902. 706-649-7837. Voice Case Information System: 912-752-8183. Counties: Berrien, Brooks, Chattahoochee, Clay, Clinch, Colquitt, Cook, Decatur, Echols, Grady, Harris, Irwin, Lanier, Lowndes, Marion, Muscogee, Quitman, Randolph, Seminole, Stewart, Talbot, Taylor, Thomas, Tift

Macon Division, US Bankruptcy Court, PO Box 1957, Macon, GA 31202. 912-752-3506. Voice Case Information System: 912-752-8183. Counties: Baldwin, Baker, Ben Hill, Bibb, Bleckley, Butts, Calhoun, Clarke, Crawford, Crisp, Dooly, Dougherty, Early, Elbert, Franklin, Greene, Hancock, Hart, Houston, Jasper, Jones, Lamar, Lee, Macon, Madison, Miller, Mitchell, Monroe, Morgan, Oconee, Oglethorpe, Peach, Pulaski, Putnam, Schley, Sumter, Terrell, Turner, Twiggs, Upson, Walton, Washington, Webster, Wilcox, Wilkinson, Worth

Northern District of Georgia

Atlanta Division, US Bankruptcy Court, 1340 US Courthouse, 75 Spring St SW, Atlanta, GA 30303-3361. 404-331-6886. Voice Case Information System: 404-730-2866. Counties: Cherokee, Clayton, Cobb, De Kalb, Douglas, Fulton, Gwinnett, Henry, Newton, Rockdale

Gainesville Division, US Bankruptcy Court, 126 Washington St, Room 203-C, Gainesville, GA 30501. 770-536-0556. Voice Case Information System: 404-730-2866. Counties: Banks, Barrow, Dawson, Fannin, Forsyth, Gilmer, Habersham, Hall, Jackson, Lumpkin, Pickens, Rabun, Stephens, Towns, Union, White

Newnan Division, US Bankruptcy Court, Clerk, PO Box 2328, Newnan, GA 30264. 770-251-5583. Voice Case Information System: 404-730-2866. Counties: Carroll, Coweta, Fayette, Haralson, Heard, Meriwether, Pike, Spalding, Troup

Rome Division, US Bankruptcy Court, Clerk, 600 E 1st St, Rome, GA 30161-3187. 706-291-5639. Voice Case Information System: 404-730-2866. Counties: Bartow, Catoosa, Chattooga, Dade, Floyd, Gordon, Murray, Paulding, Polk, Walker, Whitfield

Southern District of Georgia

Augusta Division, US Bankruptcy Court, PO Box 1487, Augusta, GA 30903. 706-724-2421. Counties: Bulloch, Burke, Candler, Columbia, Dodge, Emanuel, Evans, Glascock, Jefferson, Jenkins, Johnson, Laurens, Lincoln, McDuffie, Montgomery, Richmond, Screven, Taliaferro, Tattnall, Telfair, Toombs, Treutlen, Warren, Wheeler, Wilkes

Savannah Division, US Bankruptcy Court, PO Box 8347, Savannah, GA 31412. 912-650-4100. Counties: Appling, Atkinson, Bacon, Brantley, Bryan, Camden, Charlton, Chatham, Coffee, Effingham, Glynn, Jeff Davis, Liberty, Long, McIntosh, Pierce, Ware, Wayne

Hawaii

Capitol: Honolulu (Honolulu County)	
Number of Counties: 4	**Population:** 1,186,815
County Court Locations:	**Federal Court Locations:**
•Circuit Courts: 4/4 Circuits	•District Courts: 1
•District Courts: 6/4 Circuits	•Bankruptcy Courts: 1
	State Agencies: 19

State Agencies—Summary

General Help Numbers:

State Archives

State Archives	808-586-0329
Iolani Palace Grounds	Fax: 808-586-0330
Honolulu, HI 96813	9AM-4PM
Historical Society:	808-537-6271

Governor's Office

Office of the Governor	808-586-0034
Leiopapa A Kamehameha Bldg	Fax: 808-586-0006
235 S Beretania St	7:30AM-5:30PM
Honolulu, HI 96813	

Attorney General's Office

Attorney General's Office	808-586-1500
425 Queen St	Fax: 808-586-1239
Honolulu, HI 96813	7:45AM-4:30PM
Alternate Telephone:	808-586-1282

State Legislation

Hawaii Legislature	808-587-0700
415 S Beretania St	Fax: 808-586-1239
Honolulu, HI 96813	7AM-6PM
Clerk's Office-Senate:	808-586-6720
Clerk's Office-House:	808-586-6400
State Library:	808-586-0690

To dial-in for current year bill information online, call 808-296-4636. There is no fee, the system is up 24 hours.

Important State Internet Sites:

> **◊ Webscape**
> File   Edit   View   Help

State of Hawaii World Wide Web

www.state.hi.us/

Key site for information about the state of Hawaii. Links to major locations in the Hawaii State Government such as the Governor's office, the Senate and the House of Representatives and many other departments in the state government. It also includes a message from the Governor.

The Governor's Office

gov.state.hi.us

This site includes information about the Governor, media releases and enables you to send e-mail to the Governor.

Legislative Reference Library

www.hawaii.gov/lrb/desk.html

This site provides links to 37 state legislative sites. Individual state sites provide directories of legislators and many provide information on current bills and resolutions.

Officials Directory

www.state.hi.us/lrb/dir/dirdoc.html

Complete directory of state, county and federal officials. It is also a link to all of the different government agencies.

State Agencies—Public Records

Criminal Records
Hawaii Criminal Justice Data Center, Liane Moriyama, Administrator, 465 S King St, Room 101, Honolulu, HI 96813, Main Telephone: 808-587-3106, Hours: 8AM-4PM. Access by: mail, visit.

Corporation Records
Fictitious Name
Limited Partnership Records
Assumed Name
Trademarks/Servicemarks
Business Registration Division, PO Box 40, Honolulu, HI 96810, Main Telephone: 808-586-2727, Fax: 808-586-2733, Hours: 7:45AM-4:30PM. Access by: mail, visit, PC.

Uniform Commercial Code
Federal Tax Liens
State Tax Liens
UCC Division, Bureau of Conveyances, PO Box 2867, Honolulu, HI 96803, Main Telephone: 808-587-0154, Fax: 808-587-0136, Hours: 7:45AM-4:30PM. Access by: mail, visit.

Sales Tax Registrations
State does not impose sales tax.

Birth Certificates
State Department of Health, Vital Records Section, PO Box 3378, Honolulu, HI 96801, Main Telephone: 808-586-4539, Alternate Number: 808-586-4542, Message Phone: 808-586-4533, Fax: 808-586-4606, Hours: 7:45AM-2:30PM. Access by: mail, visit.

Death Records
State Department of Health, Vital Records Section, PO Box 3378, Honolulu, HI 96801, Main Telephone: 808-586-4539, Alternate Number: 808-586-4542, Message Phone: 808-586-4533, Hours: 7:45AM-2:30PM. Access by: mail, visit.

Marriage Certificates
State Department of Health, Vital Records Section, PO Box 3378, Honolulu, HI 96801, Main Telephone: 808-586-4539, Alternate Number: 808-586-4542, Message Phone: 808-586-4533, Hours: 7:45AM-2:30PM. Access by: mail, visit.

Divorce Records
State Department of Health, Vital Records Section, PO Box 3378, Honolulu, HI 96801, Main Telephone: 808-586-4539, Alternate Number: 808-586-4542, Message Phone: 808-586-4533, Hours: 7:45AM-2:30PM. Access by: mail, visit.

Workers' Compensation Records
Labor & Industrial Relations, Disability Compensation Division, 830 Punchbowl St, Room 209, Honolulu, HI 96813, Main Telephone: 808-586-9151, Hours: 7:45AM-4:30PM. Access by: mail, visit.

Driver Records
Traffic Violations Bureau, Abstract Section, 1111 Alakea St, Honolulu, HI 96813, Main Telephone: 808-538-5530, Hours: 7:45AM-9:00PM. Access by: mail, visit. Copies of tickets are available only to the person cited for a fee $1.00 for first copy, $.50 each additional copy, at the address listed above.

Vehicle Ownership
Vehicle Identification
Restricted access.

Accident Reports
Restricted access.

Hunting License Information
Fishing License Information
Records not available from state agency.

County Courts and Recording Offices

What You Need to Know…

About the Courts

Administration

Administrative Director of Courts	808-539-4900
PO Box 2560	Fax: 808-539-4865
Honolulu, HI 96804	

Court Structure

There are 4 circuits in HI; #1, #2, #3, and #5; the 4th Circuit merged with the 3rd Circuit in 1943. Effective 7/1/94, minor traffic offense were decriminalized by ACT 214; thus, there are no records available for minor traffic offenses after that date.

The District Court handles some minor "felonies."

Online Access

Online computer access is not available.

About the Recorder's Office

Organization

All UCC financing statements, tax liens and real estate documents are filed centrally with the Bureau of Conveyances. The entire state is in the Hawaii Time Zone (HT).

County Courts and Recording Offices

Bureau of Conveyances

Real Estate Recording—Bureau of Conveyances, 1151 Punchbowl Street, Room 120, Honolulu, HI 96813. 808-587-0134. Fax: 808-587-0136. 7:45AM-4:30PM (HT).

Hawaii County

Real Estate Recording—There is no real estate recording at the county level in Hawaii. All documents should be submitted to the Bureau of Conveyances.

Felony, Misdemeanor, Civil Actions Over $5,000, Probate—3rd Circuit Court Legal Documents Section, PO Box 1007, Hilo, HI 96721-1007. 808-961-7404. Fax: 808-961-7416. 7:45AM-4:30PM (HT). Access by: Phone, mail, in person.

Misdemeanor, Civil Actions Under $20,000, Eviction, Small Claims—District Court, PO Box 4879, Hilo, HI 96720. 808-961-7470. Fax: 808-961-7447. 7:45AM-4:30PM (HT). Access by: Phone, fax, mail, in person.

Honolulu County

Real Estate Recording—There is no real estate recording at the county level in Hawaii. Submit all documents to the Bureau of Conveyances.

Felony, Civil Actions Over $5,000, Probate—1st Circuit Court, Legal Documents Branch, 777 Punchbowl St, Honolulu, HI 96813. 808-539-4300. Fax: 808-539-4314. 7:45AM-4:30PM (HT). Access by: Mail, in person.

Misdemeanor, Civil Actions Under $15,000, Eviction, Small Claims—District Court, 1111 Alakea St, 9th Fl Records, Honolulu, HI 96813. 808-538-5300. Fax: 808-538-5309. 7:45AM-4:30PM (HT). Access by: Fax, mail, in person.

Kalawao

Real Estate Recording—There is no real estate recording at the county level in Hawaii. Submit all documents to the Bureau of Conveyances.

Kauai County

Real Estate Recording—There is no real estate recording at the county level in Hawaii. Submit all documents to the Bureau of Conveyances.

Felony, Misdemeanor, Civil Actions Over $10,000, Probate—5th Circuit Court, 3059 Umi St Rm #101, Lihue, HI 96766. 808-246-3300. 7:45AM-4:30PM (HT). Access by: Mail, in person.

Misdemeanor, Civil Actions Under $20,000, Eviction, Small Claims—District Court, 3059 Umi St, Room 111, Lihue, HI 96766. 808-246-3300. Fax: 808-246-9204. 7:45AM-4:30PM (HT). Access by: Mail, in person.

Maui County

Real Estate Recording—There is no real estate recording at the county level in Hawaii. Submit all documents to the Bureau of Conveyances.

Felony, Misdemeanor, Civil Actions Over $5,000, Probate—2nd Circuit Court, 2145 Main St, Wailuku, HI 96793. 808-244-2929. Fax: 808-244-2932. 7:45AM-4:30PM (HT). Access by: Mail, in person.

Misdemeanor, Civil Actions Under $20,000, Eviction, Small Claims—Molokai District Court, PO Box 284, Kaunakakai, HI 96748. 808-533-5451. Fax: 808-553-3374. 7:45AM-4:30PM (HT). Access by: Mail, in person.

Lanai District Court, PO Box 70, Lanai City, HI 96763. 808-565-6447. 8AM-4:30PM (HT). Access by: Mail, in person.

Wailuku District Court, 2145 Main St, Ste 137, Wailuku, HI 96793. 808-244-2800. Fax: 808-244-2849. 7:45AM-4:30PM (HT). Access by: Fax, mail, in person.

Federal Courts

US District Court
District of Hawaii

Honolulu Division, US District Court Box 50129, Honolulu, HI 96850. 808-541-1300. Counties: Hawaii, Honolulu, Kalawao, Kauai, Maui

US Bankruptcy Court
District of Hawaii

Honolulu Division, US Bankruptcy Court, 1132 Bishop St #250-L, Honolulu, HI 96813. 808-541-1791. Counties: Hawaii, Honolulu, Kalawao, Kauai, Maui

Idaho

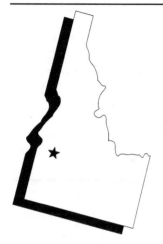

Capitol: Boise (Ada County)	
Number of Counties: 44	**Population:** 1,163,261
County Court Locations:	**Federal Court Locations:**
• District Courts: 0/7 Districts	•District Courts: 4
•Magistrates Courts: 3/ 7 Districts	•Bankruptcy Courts: 4
•Combined Courts: 44	**State Agencies:** 19

State Agencies—Summary

General Help Numbers:

State Archives

Idaho State Historical Society	208-334-3356
Historical Library & Archives	Fax: 208-334-2198
450 North 4th Street	9AM-5PM
Boise, ID 83702-6027	
Museum: 208-334-3356	

Governor's Office

Office of the Governor	208-334-2100
PO Box 83720	Fax: 208-334-2175
Boise, ID 83720-0034	8AM-6PM

Attorney General's Office

Attorney General's Office	208-334-2400
PO Box 83720	Fax: 208-334-2530
Boise, ID 83720-0010	8AM-5PM

State Legislation

Legislature Services Office	208-334-2475
Research and Legislation	Fax: 208-334-2125
PO Box 83720	8AM-5PM
Boise, ID 83720-0054	

Important State Internet Sites:

Webscape
File   Edit   View   Help

State of Idaho World Wide Web
www.state.id.us/

Links to major locations in the Idaho State Government such as the Governor's office, the Senate and the House of Representatives and other departments.

The Governor's Office
www.state.id.us/gov/govhmpg.htm

Contains the Governor's media releases and weekly schedule. You can also send e-mail to the Governor.

Current Legislation
www.state.id.us/search.html

Provides access to current legislation, a state agency directory, appellate opinions, Idaho statutes and constitution.

Idaho State Legislature
www.state.id.us/legislat/legislat.html

Contains information about the Senate and House of Representatives, such as its members, committees and rules. Links to 1996 and 1997 legislation.

Uniform Commercial Code
www.idsos.state.id.us/ucc/uccindex.htm

This site provides information about fees and enables you to download the required forms.

State Agencies—Public Records

Criminal Records

State Repository, Bureau of Criminal Identification, PO Box 700, Meridian, ID 83680-0700, Main Telephone: 208-884-7130, Fax: 208-884-7193, Hours: 8AM-5PM. Access by: mail, visit.

Corporation Records
Limited Partnerships
Trademarks/Servicemarks
Limited Liability Company Records
Fictitious Names
Trade Names

Secretary of State, Corporation Division, Statehouse, Room 203, Boise, ID 83720, Main Telephone: 208-334-2300, Fax: 208-334-2847, Hours: 8AM-5PM. Access by: mail, visit, PC. Effective 1/1/97, trade names, fictitious names and assumed names are found at this office. (Previously they have been filed at the county level.) All renewals must file with this office.

Uniform Commercial Code
Federal Tax Liens
State Tax Liens

UCC Division, Secretary of State, PO Box 83720, Boise, ID 83720-0080, Main Telephone: 208-334-3191, Fax: 208-334-2847, Hours: 8AM-5PM. Access by: mail, phone, visit, fax, PC.

Sales Tax Registrations

Revenue Operations Division, Records Management, PO Box 36, Boise, ID 83722, Main Telephone: 208-334-7660, Records Management: 208-334-7792, Fax: 208-334-7846, Hours: 8AM-5:30PM. Access by: mail, fax, phone.

Birth Certificates

State Department of Health & Welfare, Center for Vital Statistics & Health Policy, PO Box 83720, Boise, ID 83720-0036, Main Telephone: 208-334-5988, Fax: 208-389-9096, Hours: 8AM-5PM. Access by: mail, fax, visit.

Death Records

State Department of Health, Center for Vital Statistics & Health Policy, PO Box 83720, Boise, ID 83720-0036, Main Telephone: 208-334-5988, Fax: 208-389-9096, Hours: 8AM-5PM. Access by: mail, fax, visit.

Marriage Certificates

State Department of Health, Center for Vital Statistics & Health Policy, PO Box 83720, Boise, ID 83720-0036, Main Telephone: 208-334-5988, Fax: 208-389-9096, Hours: 8AM-5PM. Access by: mail, fax, visit.

Divorce Records

State Department of Health, Center for Vital Statistics & Health Policy, PO Box 83720, Boise, ID 83720-0036, Main Telephone: 208-334-5988, Fax: 208-389-9096, Hours: 8AM-5PM. Access by: mail, fax, visit. This agency only maintains certificates of divorce; copies of decrees are available through the court system.

Workers' Compensation Records

Industrial Commission of Idaho, Workers Compensation Division, 317 Main St, Statehouse Mall, Boise, ID 83720-0041, Main Telephone: 208-334-6000, Fax: 208-334-2321, Hours: 8AM-5PM. Access by: mail, fax, visit.

Driver Records

Idaho Transportation Department, Driver's Services, PO Box 34, Boise, ID 83731-0034, Main Telephone: 208-334-8736, Fax: 208-334-8739, Hours: 8:30AM-5PM. Access by: mail, visit, fax, PC. Records requested on individuals who have opted-out (under DPPA), are not accessible to private citizens. Copies of tickets are available from the address listed above for a $4.00 fee per record.

Vehicle Ownership
Vehicle Identification

Idaho Transportation Department, Vehicle Services, PO Box 34, Boise, ID 83731-0034, Main Telephone: 208-334-8773, Fax: 208-334-8542, Hours: 8:30AM-5PM. Access by: mail, visit, fax, PC.

Accident Reports

Idaho Transportation Department, Office of Highway Safety-Accident Records, PO Box 7129, Boise, ID 83707-1129, Main Telephone: 208-334-8100, Fax: 208-334-4430, Hours: 8AM-12:00PM; 1PM-5PM. Access by: mail, fax, phone, visit.

Hunting License Information
Fishing License Information

Fish & Game Department, Fish & Game Licenses Division, PO Box 25, Boise, ID 83707-0025, Main Telephone: 208-334-3717, Enforcement Office: 208-334-3736, Fax: 208-334-2114, Hours: 8AM-5PM. Access by: mail, visit. The license division says that if you want an individual name, you must call the Enforcement Office. This office will not release individual records with addresses, they will only confirm is there is a license issued.

County Courts and Recording Offices

What You Need to Know...

About the Courts

Administration

Administrative Director of the Courts 208-334-2246
451 W State St, Supreme Court Bldg Fax: 208-334-2146
Boise, ID 83720 9AM-5PM

Court Structure

Small claims are handled by the Magistrate Division of the District Court. Probate is handled by the Magistrate Division of the District Court.

Searching Hints

When submitting a search request to a combined court, specify to search both courts.

Many courts require a signed release for employment record searches.

The following fees are mandated statewide: Search Fee: none; Certification Fee: $1.00 per document plus copy fee; Copy Fee: $1.00 per page. Not all jurisdictions currently follow these guidelines.

Online Access

There is **no** statewide computer system offering external access. **ISTARS** is a statewide intra-court/intra-agency system run and managed by the State Supreme Court. All counties were on ISTARS by year end 1995. Many courts provide public access terminals

About the Recorder's Office

Organization

44 counties, 44 filing offices. The recording officer is County Recorder. Many counties utilize a grantor/grantee index containing all transactions recorded with them. 34 counties are in the Mountain Time Zone (MST), and 10 are in the Pacific Time Zone (PST).

UCC Records

Financing statements are filed at the state level except for real estate related filings. All counties will perform UCC searches. Use search request form UCC-4. Search fees are usually $6.00 per debtor name for a listing of filings and $12.00 per debtor name for a listing plus copies at no additional charge. Separately ordered copies usually cost $1.00 per page.

Lien Records

Federal tax liens on personal property of businesses are filed with the Secretary of State. Other federal and all state tax liens on personal property are filed with the County Recorder. Some counties will perform a combined tax lien search for $5.00 while others will **not** perform tax lien searches. Other liens include judgments, hospital, labor, mechanics.

Real Estate Records

Most counties will **not** perform real estate searches. Certification of copies usually costs $1.00 per document.

County Courts and Recording Offices

Ada County

Real Estate Recording—Ada County Clerk and Recorder, 650 Main Street, Boise, ID 83702. 208-364-2222. 8:30AM-4:30PM (MST).

Felony, Misdemeanor, Civil, Eviction, Small Claims, Probate—District & Magistrate Courts-I, 514 W. Jefferson St, Boise, ID 83702-5931. 208-364-2000. 8:30AM-5PM (MST). Access by: Mail, in person.

Misdemeanor—Magistrate Court II-Misdemeanor, 7180 Barrister, Boise, ID 83702. 208-364-2000. 8:30AM-5PM (MST). Access by: Mail, in person.

Adams County

Real Estate Recording—Adams County Clerk and Recorder, Michigan St., Council, ID 83612. 208-253-4561. Fax: 208-253-1141. 8AM-Noon, 1-5PM (MST).

Felony, Misdemeanor, Civil, Eviction, Small Claims, Probate—District & Magistrate Courts, PO Box 48, Council, ID 83612. 208-253-4561. Fax: 208-253-1141. 8AM-Noon, 1-5PM (MST). Access by: Fax, mail, in person.

Bannock County

Real Estate Recording—Bannock County Clerk and Recorder, 624 East Center, Courthouse, Room 211, Pocatello, ID 83201. 208-236-7340. Fax: 208-236-7345. 8AM-5PM (MST).

Felony, Misdemeanor, Civil, Eviction, Small Claims, Probate—District & Magistrate Courts, PO Box 4847, Pocatello, ID 83205. 208-236-7352. Fax: 208-236-7013. 8AM-5PM (MST). Access by: Fax, mail, in person.

Bear Lake County

Real Estate Recording—Bear Lake County Clerk and Recorder, 7th East Center, Paris, ID 83261. 208-945-2212. Fax: 208-945-2780. 8:30AM-5PM (MST).

Felony, Misdemeanor, Civil, Eviction, Small Claims, Probate—District & Magistrate Courts, PO Box 190, Paris, ID 83261. 208-945-2208. Fax: 208-945-2780. 8:30AM-5PM (MST). Access by: Fax, mail, in person.

Benewah County

Real Estate Recording—Benewah County Clerk and Recorder, 701 College, St. Maries, ID 83861. 208-245-3212. Fax: 208-245-3046. 9AM-5PM (PST).

Felony, Misdemeanor, Civil, Eviction, Small Claims, Probate—District & Magistrate Courts, Courthouse, St Maries, ID 83861. 208-245-3241. Fax: 208-245-3046. 9AM-5PM (PST). Access by: Fax, mail, in person.

Bingham County

Real Estate Recording—Bingham County Clerk and Recorder, 501 North Maple, Courthouse, Blackfoot, ID 83221. 208-785-5005. Fax: 208-785-5199. 8AM-5PM (MST).

Felony, Misdemeanor, Civil, Eviction, Small Claims, Probate—District & Magistrate Courts, PO Box 807 (Mag) PO Box 717 (Dist), Blackfoot, ID 83221. 208-785-5005. Fax: 208-785-8057. 8AM-Noon, 1-5PM (MST). Access by: Phone, fax, mail, in person.

Blaine County

Real Estate Recording—Blaine County Clerk and Recorder, Courthouse, 206 1st Ave. South, Hailey, ID 83333. 208-788-5505. Fax: 208-788-5501. 9AM-5PM (MST).

Felony, Misdemeanor, Civil, Eviction, Small Claims, Probate—District & Magistrate Courts, PO Box 1006, Hailey, ID 83333. 208-788-5525. Fax: 208-788-4759. 9AM-5PM (MST). Access by: Phone, fax, mail, in person.

Boise County

Real Estate Recording—Boise County Clerk and Recorder, 420 Main, Courthouse, Idaho City, ID 83631. 208-392-4431. Fax: 208-392-4473. 8AM-5PM (MST).

Felony, Misdemeanor, Civil, Eviction, Small Claims, Probate—District & Magistrate Courts, PO Box 126, Idaho City, ID 83631. 208-392-4452. Fax: 208-392-6712. 8AM-5PM (MST). Access by: Fax, mail, in person.

Bonner County

Real Estate Recording—Bonner County Clerk and Recorder, 215 South First, Sandpoint, ID 83864. 208-265-1432. Fax: 208-265-1447. 9AM-5PM (PST).

Felony, Misdemeanor, Civil, Eviction, Small Claims, Probate—District & Magistrate Courts, 215 S. First St, Sandpoint, ID 83864. 208-265-1432. Fax: 208-265-1447. 8AM-5PM (PST). Access by: Fax, mail, in person.

Bonneville County

Real Estate Recording—Bonneville County Clerk and Recorder, 605 North Capital, Idaho Falls, ID 83402. 208-529-1350. Fax: 208-529-1353. 8AM-5PM (MST).

Felony, Misdemeanor, Civil, Eviction, Small Claims, Probate—District & Magistrate Courts, 605 N. Capital, Idaho Falls, ID 83402. 208-529-1350. Fax: 208-529-1300. 8AM-5PM (MST). Access by: In person only.

Boundary County

Real Estate Recording—Boundary County Clerk and Recorder, 6452 Kootenai, Courthouse, Bonners Ferry, ID 83805. 208-267-2242. Fax: 208-267-7814. 9AM-5PM (PST).

Felony, Misdemeanor, Civil, Eviction, Small Claims, Probate—1st Judicial District Courts, Boundary County Courthouse, PO Box 419, Bonners Ferry, ID 83805. 208-267-5504. Fax: 208-267-7814. 9AM-5PM (PST). Access by: Phone, fax, mail, in person.

Butte County

Real Estate Recording—Butte County Clerk and Recorder, 248 West Grand, Courthouse, Arco, ID 83213. 208-527-3021. Fax: 208-527-3295. 9AM-5PM (MST).

Felony, Misdemeanor, Civil, Eviction, Small Claims, Probate—District & Magistrate Courts, PO Box 737, Arco, ID 83213. 208-527-3021. Fax: 208-527-3021. 9AM-5PM (MST). Access by: Phone, fax, mail, in person.

Camas County

Real Estate Recording—Camas County Clerk and Recorder, Corner of Soldier & Willow, Courthouse, Fairfield, ID 83327. 208-764-2242. Fax: 208-764-2349. 8:30AM-Noon, 1-5PM (MST).

Felony, Misdemeanor, Civil, Eviction, Small Claims, Probate—District & Magistrate Courts, PO Box 430, Fairfield, ID 83327. 208-764-2238. Fax: 208-764-2349. 8:30AM-Noon, 1-5PM (MST). Access by: Mail, in person.

Canyon County

Real Estate Recording—Canyon County Recorder, 1115 Albany Street, Caldwell, ID 83605. 208-454-7556. 8:30AM-5PM (MST).

Felony, Misdemeanor, Civil, Eviction, Small Claims, Probate—District & Magistrate Courts, 1115 Albany, Caldwell, ID 83605. Civil: 208-454-7570. Criminal: 208-454-7571. Fax: 208-454-7525. 8:30AM-5PM (MST). Access by: In person only.

Caribou County

Real Estate Recording—Caribou County Clerk and Recorder, 159 South Main, Soda Springs, ID 83276. 208-547-4324. Fax: 208-547-4759. 9AM-5PM (MST).

Felony, Misdemeanor, Civil, Eviction, Small Claims, Probate—District & Magistrate Courts, 159 S. Main, Soda Springs, ID 83276. 208-547-4342. Fax: 208-547-4759. 9AM-5PM (MST). Access by: Phone, fax, mail, in person.

Cassia County

Real Estate Recording—Cassia County Clerk and Recorder, 1459 Overland Avenue, Burley, ID 83318. 208-678-5240. Fax: 208-677-1003. 8:30AM-5PM (MST).

Felony, Misdemeanor, Civil, Eviction, Small Claims, Probate—District & Magistrate Courts, 1451 Overland, Burley, ID 83318. 208-678-7351. Fax: 208-677-1003. 8:30AM-5PM (MST). Access by: Fax, mail, in person.

Clark County

Real Estate Recording—Clark County Clerk and Recorder, 320 West Main, Courthouse, Dubois, ID 83423. 208-374-5304. Fax: 208-374-5609. 9AM-5PM (MST).

Felony, Misdemeanor, Civil, Eviction, Small Claims, Probate—District & Magistrate Courts, PO Box 205, DuBois, ID 83423. 208-374-5402. Fax: 208-374-5609. 9AM-5PM (MST). Access by: Fax, mail, in person.

Clearwater County

Real Estate Recording—Clearwater County Clerk and Recorder, 150 Michigan Avenue, Courthouse, Orofino, ID 83544. 208-476-5615. Fax: 208-476-3127. 8AM-5PM (PST).

Felony, Misdemeanor, Civil, Eviction, Small Claims, Probate—District & Magistrate Courts, PO Box 586, Orofino, ID 83544. 208-476-5596. Fax: 208-476-5159. 8AM-5PM (PST). Access by: Phone, fax, mail, in person.

Custer County

Real Estate Recording—Custer County Clerk and Recorder, Main Street, Courthouse, Challis, ID 83226. 208-879-2360. Fax: 208-879-5246. 9AM-5PM (MST).

Felony, Misdemeanor, Civil, Eviction, Small Claims, Probate—District & Magistrate Courts, PO Box 385, Challis, ID 83226. 208-879-2359. Fax: 208-879-5246. 8AM-5PM (MST). Access by: Phone, fax, mail, in person.

Elmore County

Real Estate Recording—Elmore County Clerk and Recorder, 150 South 4th East, Suite #3, Mountain Home, ID 83647. 208-587-2130. 9AM-5PM (MST).

Felony, Misdemeanor, Civil, Eviction, Small Claims, Probate—District & Magistrate Courts, 150 S 4th East, Ste 5, Mountain Home, ID 83647. 208-587-2133. Fax: 208-587-2159. 9AM-5PM (MST). Access by: Fax, mail, in person.

Franklin County

Real Estate Recording—Franklin County Clerk and Recorder, 39 West Oneida, Preston, ID 83263. 208-852-1090. Fax: 208-852-1094. 9AM-5PM (MST).

Felony, Misdemeanor, Civil, Eviction, Small Claims, Probate—District & Magistrate Courts, 39 West Oneida, Preston, ID 83263. 208-852-0877. Fax: 208-852-2926. 9AM-5PM (MST). Access by: Phone, mail, in person.

Fremont County

Real Estate Recording—Fremont County Clerk and Recorder, 151 West 1st N. Room 12, St. Anthony, ID 83445. 208-624-7332. Fax: 208-624-4607. 9AM-5PM (MST).

Felony, Misdemeanor, Civil, Eviction, Small Claims, Probate—District & Magistrate Courts, 151 W 1st North, St Anthony, ID 83445. 208-624-7401. Fax: 208-624-4607. 9AM-5PM (MST). Access by: Mail, in person.

Gem County

Real Estate Recording—Gem County Clerk and Recorder, 415 East Main, Emmett, ID 83617. 208-365-4561. Fax: 208-365-6172. 8AM-5PM (MST).

Felony, Misdemeanor, Civil, Eviction, Small Claims, Probate—District & Magistrate Courts, 415 East Main St, Emmett, ID 83617. 208-365-4561. Fax: 208-365-6172. 8AM-5PM (MST). Access by: Mail, in person.

Gooding County

Real Estate Recording—Gooding County Clerk and Recorder, 624 Main, Courthouse, Gooding, ID 83330. 208-934-4841. 9AM-5PM (MST).

Felony, Misdemeanor, Civil, Eviction, Small Claims, Probate—District & Magistrate Courts, PO Box 477, Gooding, ID 83330. 208-934-4261. Fax: 208-934-4408. 8AM-5PM (MST). Access by: In person only.

Idaho County

Real Estate Recording—Idaho County Clerk and Recorder, 320 W. Main, Room 5, Grangeville, ID 83530. 208-983-2751. Fax: 208-983-1428. 8:30AM-5PM (PST).

Felony, Misdemeanor, Civil, Eviction, Small Claims, Probate—District & Magistrate Courts, 320 West Main, Grangeville, ID 83530. 208-983-2776. Fax: 208-983-2376. 8:30AM-5PM (PST). Access by: Phone, fax, mail, in person.

Jefferson County

Real Estate Recording—Jefferson County Clerk and Recorder, 134 North Clark, Courthouse, Rigby, ID 83442. 208-745-7756. Fax: 208-745-6636. 9AM-5PM (MST).

Felony, Misdemeanor, Civil, Eviction, Small Claims, Probate—District & Magistrate Courts, PO Box 71, Rigby, ID 83442. 208-745-7736. Fax: 208-745-9212. 9AM-5PM (MST). Access by: Fax, mail, in person.

Jerome County

Real Estate Recording—Jerome County Clerk and Recorder, 300 North Lincoln, Courthouse, Room 301, Jerome, ID 83338. 208-324-8811. Fax: 208-324-2719. 8:30AM-5PM (MST).

Felony, Misdemeanor, Civil, Eviction, Small Claims, Probate—District & Magistrate Courts, 300 N Lincoln St, Jerome, ID 83338. 208-324-8811. Fax: 208-324-2719. 8:30AM-5PM (MST). Access by: Fax, mail, in person.

Kootenai County

Real Estate Recording—Kootenai County Clerk and Recorder, 501 Government Way, Coeur d'Alene, ID 83814. 208-769-4400. 9AM-5PM (PST).

Felony, Misdemeanor, Civil, Eviction, Small Claims, Probate—District Court, 324 West Garden Ave PO Box 9000, Coeur d'Alene, ID 83816-9000. Civil: 208-769-4430. Criminal: 208-769-4440. Fax: 208-664-0639. 9AM-5PM (PST). Access by: Fax, mail, in person.

Latah County

Real Estate Recording—Latah County Clerk and Recorder, Room 101, 5th and Van Buren, Moscow, ID 83843. 208-882-8580. Fax: 208-883-2280. 8AM-5PM (PST).

Felony, Misdemeanor, Civil, Eviction, Small Claims, Probate—District & Magistrate Courts, PO Box 8068, Moscow, ID 83843. 208-883-2255. Fax: 208-883-2259. 8:30AM-5PM M-W, 8AM-5PM TH,F (PST). Access by: Phone, fax, mail, in person.

Lemhi County

Real Estate Recording—Lemhi County Clerk and Recorder, 206 Courthouse Drive, Salmon, ID 83467. 208-756-2815. Fax: 208-756-8424. 9AM-5PM (MST).

Felony, Misdemeanor, Civil, Eviction, Small Claims, Probate—District & Magistrate Courts, 206 Courthouse Dr, Salmon, ID 83467. 208-756-2815. Fax: 208-756-8424. 9AM-5PM (MST). Access by: Fax, mail, in person.

Lewis County

Real Estate Recording—Lewis County Clerk and Recorder, 510 Oak, Courthouse, Nezperce, ID 83543. 208-937-2661. 9AM-5PM (PST).

Felony, Misdemeanor, Civil, Eviction, Small Claims, Probate—District & Magistrate Courts, 510 Oak St (PO Box 39), Nezperce, ID 83543. 208-937-2251. Fax: 208-937-2113. 9AM-5PM (PST). Access by: Phone, fax, mail, in person.

Lincoln County

Real Estate Recording—Lincoln County Clerk and Recorder, 111 West B Street, Courthouse, Shoshone, ID 83352. 208-886-7641. Fax: 208-886-2458. 8:30AM-5PM (MST).

Felony, Misdemeanor, Civil, Eviction, Small Claims, Probate—District & Magistrate Courts, Drawer A, Shoshone, ID 83352. 208-886-2173. Fax: 208-886-2458. 9AM-5PM (MST). Access by: Phone, fax, mail, in person.

Madison County

Real Estate Recording—Madison County Clerk and Recorder, 134 East Main, Courthouse Annex Bldg., Rexburg, ID 83440. 208-356-3662. Fax: 208-356-8396. 9AM-5PM (MST).

Felony, Misdemeanor, Civil, Eviction, Small Claims, Probate—District & Magistrate Courts, PO Box 389, Rexburg, ID 83440. 208-356-9383. Fax: 208-356-5425. 9AM-5PM (MST). Access by: Mail, in person.

Minidoka County

Real Estate Recording—Minidoka County Clerk and Recorder, 715 G Street, Courthouse, Rupert, ID 83350. 208-436-9511. Fax: 208-436-0737. 8:30AM-5PM (MST).

Felony, Misdemeanor, Civil, Eviction, Small Claims, Probate—District & Magistrate Courts, PO Box 474, Rupert, ID 83350. 208-436-9041. Fax: 208-436-5272. 8:30AM-5PM (MST). Access by: Phone, mail, in person.

Nez Perce County

Real Estate Recording—Nez Perce County Auditor and Recorder, 1230 Main Street, Room 100, Lewiston, ID 83501. 208-799-3020. Fax: 208-799-3070. 8AM-5PM (PST).

Felony, Misdemeanor, Civil, Eviction, Small Claims, Probate—District Courts, PO Box 896, Lewiston, ID 83501. 208-799-3040. Fax: 208-799-3058. 8AM-5PM (PST). Access by: Fax, mail, in person.

Oneida County

Real Estate Recording—Oneida County Clerk and Recorder, 10 Court Street, Malad, ID 83252. 208-766-4116. Fax: 208-766-4285. 9AM-5PM (MST).

Felony, Misdemeanor, Civil, Eviction, Small Claims, Probate—District & Magistrate Courts, 10 Court St, Malad City, ID 83252. 208-766-4285. Fax: 208-766-4285. 9AM-5PM (MST). Access by: Phone, fax, mail, in person.

Owyhee County

Real Estate Recording—Owyhee County Clerk and Recorder, Highway 78, Courthouse, Murphy, ID 83650. 208-495-2421. Fax: 208-495-1173. 8:30AM-5PM (MST).

Felony, Misdemeanor, Civil, Eviction, Small Claims, Probate—District & Magistrate Courts-I, Courthouse, Murphy, ID 83650. 208-495-2806. Fax: 208-495-1173. 8:30AM-5PM (MST). Access by: Fax, mail, in person. Signed release required for search of juvenile records.

Misdemeanor, Civil Actions Under $10,000, Eviction, Small Claims—Magistrate Court II, 31 W Wyoming Ave, Homedale, ID 83628-3402. 208-337-4540. Fax: 208-337-3035. 8:30AM-5PM (MST). Access by: Mail, in person.

Payette County

Real Estate Recording—Payette County Clerk and Recorder, 1130 3rd Avenue North, Courthouse, Payette, ID 83661. 208-642-6000. Fax: 208-642-6011. 9AM-5PM (MST).

Felony, Misdemeanor, Civil, Eviction, Small Claims, Probate—District & Magistrate Courts, 1130 3rd Ave N, Payette, ID 83661. 208-642-6000. Fax: 208-642-6011. 9AM-5PM (MST). Access by: Fax, mail, in person.

Power County

Real Estate Recording—Power County Clerk and Recorder, 543 Bannock, American Falls, ID 83211. 208-226-7611. Fax: 208-226-7612. 9AM-5PM (MST).

Felony, Misdemeanor, Civil, Eviction, Small Claims, Probate—District & Magistrate Courts, 543 Bannock Ave, American Falls, ID 83211. 208-226-7611. Fax: 208-226-7612. 9AM-5PM (MST). Access by: Phone, fax, mail, in person.

Shoshone County

Real Estate Recording—Shoshone County Clerk and Recorder, 700 Bank Street, Courthouse, Wallace, ID 83873. 208-752-1264. Fax: 208-753-2711. 9AM-5PM (PST).

Felony, Misdemeanor, Civil, Eviction, Small Claims, Probate—District & Magistrate Courts, 700 Bank St, Wallace, ID 83873. 208-752-1266. Fax: 208-753-0921. 9AM-5PM (PST). Access by: Phone, mail, in person.

Teton County

Real Estate Recording—Teton County Clerk and Recorder, 89 North Main, Courthouse, Driggs, ID 83422. 208-354-2905. Fax: 208-354-8410. 9AM-5PM (MST).

Felony, Misdemeanor, Civil, Eviction, Small Claims, Probate—District & Magistrate Courts, PO Box 756, Driggs, ID 83422. 208-354-2905. Fax: 208-354-8410. 9AM-5PM (MST). Access by: Phone, fax, mail, in person.

Twin Falls County

Real Estate Recording—Twin Falls County Clerk and Recorder, 425 Shoshone Street North, Twin Falls, ID 83301. 208-736-4004. Fax: 208-736-4182. 8AM-5PM (MST).

Felony, Misdemeanor, Civil, Eviction, Small Claims, Probate—District & Magistrate Courts, PO Box 126, Twin Falls, ID 83301. 208-736-4013. Fax: 208-736-4002. 8AM-5PM (MST). Access by: Phone, fax, mail, in person.

Valley County

Real Estate Recording—Valley County Clerk and Recorder, 219 North Main, Courthouse, Cascade, ID 83611. 208-382-4297. Fax: 208-382-4955. 9AM-5PM (MST).

Felony, Misdemeanor, Civil, Eviction, Small Claims, Probate—District & Magistrate Courts-I, PO Box 650, Cascade, ID 83611. 208-382-4150. Fax: 208-382-3098. 9AM-5PM (MST). Access by: Phone, fax, mail, in person.

Misdemeanor, Civil Actions Under $10,000, Eviction, Small Claims—Magistrate Court II, Valley County Courthouse Annex, 550 Deinhard Lane, McCall, ID 83638. 208-634-8102. Fax: 208-634-4040. 9AM-5PM (MST). Access by: Phone, fax, mail, in person.

Washington County

Real Estate Recording—Washington County Clerk and Recorder, 256 East Court Street, Weiser, ID 83672. 208-549-2092. Fax: 208-549-3925. 8:30AM-5PM (MST).

Felony, Misdemeanor, Civil, Eviction, Small Claims, Probate—District & Magistrate Courts, PO Box 670, Weiser, ID 83672. 208-549-2092. Fax: 208-549-3925. 8:30AM-5PM (MST). Access by: In person only.

Federal Courts

US District Court

District of Idaho

Boise Division, US District Court MSC 039, Federal Bldg, 550 W Fort St, Room 400, Boise, ID 83724. 208-334-1361. Counties: Ada, Adams, Blaine, Boise, Camas, Canyon, Cassia, Elmore, Gem, Gooding, Jerome, Lincoln, Minidoka, Owyhee, Payette, Twin Falls, Valley, Washington

Coeur d' Alene, Division, US District Court c/o Boise Division, Box 039, Federal Bldg, 550 W Fort St, Boise, ID 83724. 208-334-1361. Counties: Benewah, Bonner, Boundary, Kootenai, Shoshone

Moscow Division, US District Court c/o Boise Division, Box 039, Federal Bldg, 550 W Fort St, Boise, ID 83724. 208-334-1361. Counties: Clearwater, Latah, Lewis, Nez Perce

Pocatello Division, US District Court c/o Boise Division, Box 039, Federal Bldg, 550 W Fort St, Boise, ID

83724. 208-334-1361. Counties: Bannock, Bear Lake, Bingham, Bonneville, Butte, Caribou, Clark, Custer, Franklin, Fremont, Idaho, Jefferson, Lemhi, Madison, Oneida, Power, Teton

US Bankruptcy Court
District of Idaho

Boise Division, US Bankruptcy Court, MSC 042, US Courthouse, 550 W Fort St, Room 400, Boise, ID 83724. 208-334-1074. Voice Case Information System: 208-334-9386. Counties: Ada, Adams, Blaine, Boise, Camas, Canyon, Cassia, Elmore, Gem, Gooding, Jerome, Lincoln, Minidoka, Owyhee, Payette, Twin Falls, Valley, Washington

Coeur d' Alene Division, US Bankruptcy Court, 205 N 4th St, 2nd Floor, Coeur d'Alene, ID 83814. 208-664-4925. Voice Case Information System: 208-334-9386. Counties: Benewah, Bonner, Boundary, Kootenai, Shoshone

Moscow Division, US Bankruptcy Court, 220 E 5th St, Moscow, ID 83843. 208-882-7612. Voice Case Information System: 208-334-9386. Counties: Clearwater, Idaho, Latah, Lewis, Nez Perce

Pocatello Division, US Bankruptcy Court, 250 S 4th Ave, Room 263, Pocatello, ID 83201. 208-236-6912. Voice Case Information System: 208-334-9386. Counties: Bannock, Bear Lake, Bingham, Bonneville, Butte, Caribou, Clark, Custer, Franklin, Fremont, Jefferson, Lemhi, Madison, Oneida, Power, Teton

Illinois

Capitol: Springfield (Sangamon County)	
Number of Counties: 102	**Population:** 11,829,940
County Court Locations:	**Federal Court Locations:**
•Circuit Courts: 102/22Circuits	•District Courts: 8
•Cook County Smaller Civil: 1	•Bankruptcy Courts: 7
•Cook County Criminal: 2	**State Agencies:** 18

State Agencies—Summary

General Help Numbers:

State Archives

Secretary of State	217-782-4682
Archives Division	Fax: 217-524-3930
Norton Bldg, Capitol Complex	8AM-4:30PM
Springfield, IL 62756	
Reference Librarian:	217-782-4866
Historical Society:	217-782-4836

Governor's Office

Governor's Office	217-782-6830
222 S. College	Fax: 217-782-3560
Springfield, IL 62706	8:30AM-5PM

Attorney General's Office

Attorney General Office	217-782-1090
500 S 2nd St	Fax: 217-785-2551
Springfield, IL 62706	8:45AM-4:45PM

State Legislation

Illinois General Assembly	217-782-3944
State House	8AM-4:30PM
House (or Senate) Bills Division	
Springfield, IL 62706	
Index Div-Older Bills:	217-782-7017
House Bills:	217-782-5799
Senate Bills:	217-782-9778

The Legislative Information System is available by 2400 bps modem. The sign-up fee is $500, which includes 100 free minutes of access. Thereafter, time is billed at $1.00 per minute. The system is accessible from 8AM to 10PM when the legislature is in session and 8AM-5PM at other times. Contact Craig Garrett at 217-782-4083 to set up the account.

Important State Internet Sites:

> **Webscape**
> File   Edit   View   Help

State of Illinois World Wide Web
www.state.il.us/

Key site for information about the state of Illinois. Links to major locations in the Illinois State Government such as the Governor's office, the Senate and the House of Representatives, state agencies, education, tourism, libraries and museums.

The Governor's Office
www.state.il.us/gov/

This site includes information about the Governor, his media releases, speeches, initiatives and accomplishments and enables you to send e-mail to the Governor.

Illinois State Legislature
www.state.il.us/legis/default.htm

This site lists state legislators by name and district. A list of the members of the U.S House of Representatives is available.

Unclaimed Property
www.state.il.us/dfi/

This new web site provides you with the information needed to search for unclaimed property.

State Agencies—Public Records

Criminal Records

Illinois State Police, Bureau of Identification, 260 N Chicago St, Joliet, IL 60432-4075, Main Telephone: 815-740-2655, Fax: 815-740-5193, Hours: 8AM-4PM M-F. Access by: mail, visit, PC.

Corporation Records
Limited Partnership Records
Trade Names
Assumed Name
Limited Liability Company Records

Department of Business Services, Corporate Department, Howlett Bldg, 3rd Floor, Copy Section, Springfield, IL 62756, Main Telephone: 217-782-7880, Fax: 212-782-4528, Hours: 8AM-4:30PM. Access by: mail, phone, visit, PC.

Uniform Commercial Code
Federal Tax Liens
State Tax Liens

UCC Division, Secretary of State, 2nd & Edwards St, Howlett Bldg, Room 030, Springfield, IL 62756, Main Telephone: 217-782-7518, Hours: 8AM-4:30PM. Access by: mail, visit.

Sales Tax Registrations

Revenue Department, Taxpayer Services, 101 W Jefferson St, Springfield, IL 62794, Main Telephone: 800-732-8866, Fax: 217-782-4217, Hours: 8AM-5PM. Access by: mail, phone.

Birth Certificates

State Department of Health, Division of Vital Records, 605 W Jefferson St, Springfield, IL 62702-5097, Main Telephone: 217-782-6553, Fax: 217-785-3209, Hours: 8AM-5PM M-F. Access by: mail, phone, visit.

Death Records

State Department of Health, Division of Vital Records, 605 W Jefferson St, Springfield, IL 62702-5097, Main Telephone: 217-782-6553, Fax: 217-785-3209, Hours: 8AM-5PM. Access by: mail, phone, visit.

Marriage Certificates
Divorce Records

Records not available from state agency.

Workers' Compensation Records

Industrial Commission, 100 W Randolph, 8th Floor, Chicago, IL 60601, Main Telephone: 312-814-6611, Hours: 8AM-4:30PM. Access by: mail, phone, visit.

Driver Records

Driver Analysis Section, Drivers Services Department, 2701 S Dirksen Parkway, Springfield, IL 62723, Main Telephone: 217-782-2720, Hours: 8AM-4:30PM. Access by: mail, phone, visit. Copies of tickets can be obtained from the county of the incident for $1.00 or copies may be requested at the above address for a fee of $.50 per copy.

Vehicle Ownership
Vehicle Identification

Vehicle Services Department, Vehicle Record Inquiry, 408 Howlett Bldg, Springfield, IL 62756, Main Telephone: 217-782-6992, Fax: 217-524-0122, Hours: 8AM-4:30PM. Access by: mail, visit.

Accident Reports

Illinois State Police, Records Bureau, 500 Iles Park Place, Ste 200, Springfield, IL 62718, Main Telephone: 217-785-0612, Hours: 8AM-5PM. Access by: mail, phone, visit. If crash occurred on IL Tollway System, send $5 check or money order payable to: IL Toll Highway Authority, Attn: State Police District 15, One Authority Drive, Downers Grove, IL 60515.

Hunting License Information
Fishing License Information

Records not available from state agency.

County Courts and Recording Offices

What You Need to Know...

About the Courts	About the Recorder's Office

About the Courts

Administration

Administrative Office of Courts	312-793-3250
222 N. LaSalle, 13th Floor	Fax: 312-793-1335
Chicago, IL 60601	8AM-4PM

Court Structure

Illinois is divided into 22 judicial circuits; 3 are single county (Cook, Du Page (18th Circuit) and Will (12th Circuit). The other 19 consist of 2 or more contiguous counties. The Circuit Court in **Cook County** is divided as follows: civil cases over $30,000 and civil cases under $30,000. The Circuit Court in **Cook County** is divided into a criminal section and a misdemeanor section. The case indexes are maintained in one location. Felony and misdemeanor cases are heard at six locations within the county. All felony cases are maintained at one central location; however, misdemeanor case files are located at each of the hearing locations, as follows—

Felony Division, 2600 S. California, Chicago, IL 60608 (See court profile)
District 2, 5600 Old Orchard Rd., Skokie, IL 60077, 708-470-7200
District 3, 2121 Euclid Ave., Rolling Meadows, IL 60008, 708-818-3000
District 4, 1500 Maybrook Dr., Maywood, IL 60153, 708-865-5186
District 5, 10220 S. 76th Ave., Bridgeview, IL 60455, 708-974-6282
District 6, 16501 S. Kedzie, Markham, IL 60426, 708-210-4551
Probate is handled by the Circuit Court in all counties.

Searching Hints

The search fee is set by statute and has 3 levels based on the county population. The higher the population the larger the fee. In most courts, both civil and criminal data is on computer from the same starting date. In most courts, the search fee is charged on a **per name per year** basis.

Online Access.

Champaign County offers online access to criminal and civil records through their PASS program. **DuPage** County has indicated it is planning to replace the Civic Link program from Ameritech with a new online access program.

About the Recorder's Office

Organization

102 counties, 103 filing offices. **Cook County** has separate offices for UCC and real estate recording. The recording officer is Recorder of Deeds. Many counties utilize a grantor/grantee index containing all transactions. The entire state is in the Central Time Zone (CST).

UCC Records

Financing statements are filed at the state level except for consumer goods, farm related and real estate related filings. Most counties will perform UCC searches. Use search request form UCC-11. Search fees are usually $10.00 per debtor name/address combination. Copies usually cost $1.00 per page.

Lien Records

Federal tax liens on personal property of businesses are filed with the Secretary of State. Other federal and all state tax liens on personal property are filed with the County Recorder of Deeds. Some counties will perform tax lien searches for $5.00-$10.00 per name (state and federal are separate searches in many of these counties) and $1.00 per page of copy. Other liens include judgments, mechanics, contractor, medical, lis pendens, oil & gas, and mobile home.

Real Estate Records

Most counties will **not** perform real estate searches. Cost of certified copies varies widely, but many counties charge the same as the cost of recording the document. Tax records are usually located at the Treasurer's Office.

County Courts and Recording Offices

Adams County

Real Estate Recording—Adams County Recorder, 521 Vermont Street, Quincy, IL 62306. 217-223-6300. 8AM-4PM (CST).

Felony, Misdemeanor, Civil, Eviction, Small Claims, Probate—Circuit Court, 521 Vermont St, Quincy, IL 62301. 217-223-6300. Fax: 217-222-5534. 8AM-4:30PM (CST). Access by: Mail, in person.

Alexander County

Real Estate Recording—Alexander County Recorder, 2000 Washington Avenue, Cairo, IL 62914. 618-734-7000. Fax: 618-734-7002. 8AM-Noon, 1PM-4PM (CST).

Felony, Misdemeanor, Civil, Eviction, Small Claims, Probate—Circuit Court, 2000 Washington Ave, Cairo, IL 62914. 618-734-0107. Fax: 618-734-7003. 8AM-4PM (CST). Access by: Fax, mail, in person.

Bond County

Real Estate Recording—Bond County Recorder, 203 West College Avenue, Greenville, IL 62246. 618-664-0449. Fax: 618-664-9414. 8AM-4PM (CST).

Felony, Misdemeanor, Civil, Eviction, Small Claims, Probate—Circuit Court, 200 W College St, Greenville, IL 62246. 618-664-3208. Fax: 618-664-4676. 8AM-4PM (CST). Access by: Mail, in person.

Boone County

Real Estate Recording—Boone County Recorder, 601 North Main Street, Suite 202, Belvidere, IL 61008. 815-544-3103. Fax: 815-547-8701. 8:30AM-5PM (CST).

Felony, Misdemeanor, Civil, Eviction, Small Claims, Probate—Circuit Court, 601 N Main, Belvidere, IL 61008. 815-544-0371. 8:30AM-5PM (CST). Access by: Mail, in person.

Brown County

Real Estate Recording—Brown County Recorder, Courthouse - Room 4, #1 Court Street, Mount Sterling, IL 62353. 217-773-3421. Fax: 217-773-2233. 8:30AM-4:30PM (CST).

Felony, Misdemeanor, Civil, Eviction, Small Claims, Probate—Circuit Court, County Courthouse, Mt Sterling, IL 62353. 217-773-2713. 8:30AM-4:30PM (CST). Access by: Phone, mail, in person.

Bureau County

Real Estate Recording—Bureau County Recorder, 700 South Main St., Courthouse, Princeton, IL 61356. 815-875-3239. Fax: 815-872-0027. 8AM-4PM (CST).

Felony, Misdemeanor, Civil, Eviction, Small Claims, Probate—Circuit Court, 700 S Main, Princeton, IL 61356. 815-872-2001. Fax: 815-872-0027. 8AM-4PM (CST). Access by: Mail, in person.

Calhoun County

Real Estate Recording—Calhoun County Clerk and Recorder, County Road, Hardin, IL 62047. 618-576-2351. Fax: 618-576-9041. 8:30AM-4:30PM (CST).

Felony, Misdemeanor, Civil, Eviction, Small Claims, Probate—Circuit Court, PO Box 486, Hardin, IL 62047. 618-576-2451. 8:30AM-4:30PM (CST). Access by: Phone, mail, in person.

Carroll County

Real Estate Recording—Carroll County Recorder, 301 North Main, Mount Carroll, IL 61053. 815-244-0223. Fax: 815-244-3709. 8:30AM-4:30AM (CST).

Felony, Misdemeanor, Civil, Eviction, Small Claims, Probate—Circuit Court, 301 N Main St, PO Box 32, Mt Carroll, IL 61053. 815-244-0230. Fax: 815-244-3869. 8:30AM-4:30PM (CST). Access by: Mail, in person.

Cass County

Real Estate Recording—Cass County Recorder, Courthouse, Virginia, IL 62691. 217-452-7217. Fax: 217-452-7219. 8:30AM-4:30PM (CST).

Felony, Misdemeanor, Civil, Eviction, Small Claims, Probate—Circuit Court, PO Box 203, Virginia, IL 62691. 217-452-7225. 8:30AM-4:30PM (CST). Access by: Mail, in person.

Champaign County

Real Estate Recording—Champaign County Recorder, 1776 E. Washington, Urbana, IL 61802. 217-384-3774. Fax: 217-384-3896. 8AM-4:30PM (CST).

Felony, Misdemeanor, Civil, Eviction, Small Claims, Probate—Circuit Court, 101 E Main, Urbana, IL 61801. 217-384-3725. Fax: 217-384-3879. 8:30AM-4:30PM (CST). Access by: Mail, in person, online

Christian County

Real Estate Recording—Christian County Recorder, Courthouse on the Square, Taylorville, IL 62568. 217-824-4960. Fax: 217-824-5105. 8AM-4PM (CST).

Felony, Misdemeanor, Civil, Eviction, Small Claims, Probate—Circuit Court, PO Box 617, Taylorville, IL 62568. 217-824-4966. Fax: 217-824-5105. 8AM-4PM (CST). Access by: Phone, mail, in person.

Clark County

Real Estate Recording—Clark County Recorder, Courthouse, Marshall, IL 62441. 217-826-8311. 8AM-4PM (CST).

Felony, Misdemeanor, Civil, Eviction, Small Claims, Probate—Circuit Court, PO Box 187, Marshall, IL 62441. 217-826-2811. 8AM-4PM (CST). Access by: In person only.

Clay County

Real Estate Recording—Clay County Recorder, County Building Room 106, Louisville, IL 62858. 618-665-3626. Fax: 618-665-3626. 8AM-4PM (CST).

Felony, Misdemeanor, Civil, Eviction, Small Claims, Probate—Circuit Court, PO Box 100, Louisville, IL 62858. 618-665-3523. Fax: 618-665-4933. 8AM-4PM (CST). Access by: Fax, mail, in person.

Clinton County

Real Estate Recording—Clinton County Recorder, Courthouse, Carlyle, IL 62231. 618-594-2464. Fax: 618-594-8715. 8AM-4PM (CST).

Felony, Misdemeanor, Civil, Eviction, Small Claims, Probate—Circuit Court, County Courthouse, PO Box 407, Carlyle, IL 62231. 618-594-2415. 8AM-4PM (CST). Access by: Mail, in person.

Coles County

Real Estate Recording—Coles County Recorder, 7th & Monroe Street, Charleston, IL 61920. 217-348-7325. Fax: 217-348-7337. 8:30AM-4:30PM (CST).

Felony, Misdemeanor, Civil, Eviction, Small Claims, Probate—Circuit Court, PO Box 48, Charleston, IL 61920. 217-348-0516. 8:30AM-4:30PM (CST). Access by: Mail, in person.

Cook County

Real Estate Recording—Cook County Recorder, 118 North Clark St., Room 120, Chicago, IL 60602. 312-443-5134. Fax: 312-443-5063.

Civil Actions Over $30,000—Circuit Court-Civil, 50 W Washington Rm 601, Chicago, IL 60602. 312-443-5030. Civil: 312-443-5116. 9AM-5PM (CST). Access by: Phone, mail, in person.

Civil Actions Under $30,000, Eviction, Small Claims, Probate—Circuit Court-Civil, 50 W Washington, Chicago,

IL 60602. 312-443-5030. Fax: 312-443-4557. 8:30AM-4:30PM (CST). Access by: In person only.

Misdemeanor—Circuit Court-Criminal, 50 W Washington Rm 1006, Chicago, IL 60602. 312-443-4641. Fax: 312-443-4557. 9AM-5PM (CST). Access by: In person only.

Felony—Circuit Court-Criminal, 2650 S California Ave, Chicago, IL 60608. 312-890-3140. Fax: 312-890-4444. 9AM-5PM (CST). Access by: Mail, in person.

Crawford County

Real Estate Recording—Crawford County Recorder, Courthouse, 1 Courthouse Square, Robinson, IL 62454. 618-546-1212. Fax: 618-546-0140. 8AM-4PM (CST).

Felony, Misdemeanor, Civil, Eviction, Small Claims, Probate—Circuit Court, PO Box 655, Robinson, IL 62454-0655. 618-544-3512. Fax: 618-546-5826. 8AM-4PM (CST). Access by: Fax, mail, in person.

Cumberland County

Real Estate Recording—Cumberland County Recorder, 740 Courthouse Square, Toledo, IL 62468. 217-849-2631. Fax: 217-849-2968. 8AM-4PM (CST).

Felony, Misdemeanor, Civil, Eviction, Small Claims, Probate—Circuit Court, PO Box 145, Toledo, IL 62468. 217-849-3601. 8AM-4PM (CST). Access by: Phone, mail, in person.

De Kalb County

Real Estate Recording—De Kalb County Recorder, 110 East Sycamore Street, Sycamore, IL 60178. 815-895-7156. 8:30AM-4:30PM (CST).

Felony, Misdemeanor, Civil, Eviction, Small Claims, Probate—Circuit Court, 133 W State St, Sycamore, IL 60178. 815-895-7138. Fax: 815-895-7140. 8:30AM-4:30PM (CST). Access by: Mail, in person.

De Witt County

Real Estate Recording—De Witt County Recorder, 201 West Washington Street, Clinton, IL 61727. 217-935-2119. Fax: 217-935-4596. 8:30AM-4:30PM (CST).

Felony, Misdemeanor, Civil, Eviction, Small Claims, Probate—Circuit Court, 201 Washington St, Clinton, IL 61727. 217-935-2195. Fax: 217-935-3310. 8:30AM-4:30PM (CST). Access by: Mail, in person.

Douglas County

Real Estate Recording—Douglas County Recorder, 401 South Center, Second Floor, Tuscola, IL 61953. 217-253-4410. Fax: 217-253-2233. 8:30AM-4:30PM (CST).

Felony, Misdemeanor, Civil, Eviction, Small Claims, Probate—Circuit Court, PO Box 50, Tuscola, IL 61953. 217-253-2352. 8:30AM-4:30PM (CST). Access by: Mail, in person.

Du Page County

Real Estate Recording—Du Page County Recorder, 421 North County Farm Road, Wheaton, IL 60187. 630-682-7200. Fax: 630-682-7204. 8AM-4:30PM (CST).

Felony, Misdemeanor, Civil, Eviction, Small Claims, Probate—Circuit Court, PO Box 707, Wheaton, IL 60189-0707. Civil: 630-682-7100. Criminal: 630-682-7080. Fax: 630-682-7082. 8:30AM-4:30PM (CST). Access by: Phone, mail, remote online, in person.

Edgar County

Real Estate Recording—Edgar County Recorder, Courthouse - Room "J", 115 W. Court St., Paris, IL 61944. 217-465-4151. Fax: 217-463-3137. 8AM-4PM (CST).

Felony, Misdemeanor, Civil, Eviction, Small Claims, Probate—Circuit Court, County Courthouse, Paris, IL 61944. 217-465-4107. 8AM-4PM (CST). Access by: Mail, in person.

Edwards County

Real Estate Recording—Edwards County Recorder, 50 East Main Street, Courthouse, Albion, IL 62806. 618-445-2115. Fax: 618-445-3505. 8AM-4PM (CST).

Felony, Misdemeanor, Civil, Eviction, Small Claims, Probate—Circuit Court, County Courthouse, Albion, IL 62806. 618-445-2016. Fax: 618-445-2505. 8AM-4PM (CST). Access by: Mail, in person.

Effingham County

Real Estate Recording—Effingham County Clerk and Recorder, 101 North 4th Street, Suite 201, Effingham, IL 62401. 217-342-6535. Fax: 217-342-3577. 8AM-4PM (CST).

Felony, Misdemeanor, Civil, Eviction, Small Claims, Probate—Circuit Court, PO Box 586, Effingham, IL 62401. 217-342-4065. Fax: 217-342-6183. 8AM-4PM (CST). Access by: Mail, in person.

Fayette County

Real Estate Recording—Fayette County Recorder, 221 South 7th Street, Vandalia, IL 62471. 618-283-5000. Fax: 618-283-5004. 8AM-4PM (CST).

Felony, Misdemeanor, Civil, Eviction, Small Claims, Probate—Circuit Court, 221 S 7th St, Vandalia, IL 62471. 618-283-5009. 8AM-4PM (CST). Access by: Mail, in person.

Ford County

Real Estate Recording—Ford County Recorder, 200 West State Street, Room 101, Paxton, IL 60957. 217-379-2721. Fax: 217-379-3258. 8:30AM-4:30PM (CST).

Felony, Misdemeanor, Civil, Eviction, Small Claims, Probate—Circuit Court, 200 W State St, Paxton, IL 60957. 217-379-2641. Fax: 217-379-3258. 8:30AM-4:30PM (CST). Access by: Mail, in person.

Franklin County

Real Estate Recording—Franklin County Clerk & Recorder, Courthouse, Benton, IL 62812. 618-438-3221. Fax: 618-439-4119. 8AM-4PM (CST).

Felony, Misdemeanor, Civil, Eviction, Small Claims, Probate—Circuit Court, County Courthouse, Benton, IL 62812. 618-439-2011. 8AM-4PM (CST). Access by: Mail, in person.

Fulton County

Real Estate Recording—Fulton County Recorder, 100 North Main, Lewistown, IL 61542. 309-547-3041. 8AM-4PM (CST).

Felony, Misdemeanor, Civil, Eviction, Small Claims, Probate—Circuit Court, 100 N Main, Lewistown, IL 61542. 309-547-3041. Fax: 309-547-3674. 8AM-4PM (CST). Access by: Mail, in person.

Gallatin County

Real Estate Recording—Gallatin County Recorder, West Lincoln Blvd, Shawneetown, IL 62984. 618-269-3025. Fax: 618-269-4324. 8AM-4PM (CST).

Felony, Misdemeanor, Civil, Eviction, Small Claims, Probate—Circuit Court, County Courthouse, Shawneetown, IL 62984. 618-269-3140. Fax: 618-269-4324. 8AM-4PM (CST). Access by: Mail, in person.

Greene County

Real Estate Recording—Greene County Recorder, 519 North Main Street, Courthouse, Carrollton, IL 62016. 217-942-5443. 8AM-4PM (CST).

Felony, Misdemeanor, Civil, Eviction, Small Claims, Probate—Circuit Court, 519 N Main, County Courthouse, Carrollton, IL 62016. 217-942-3421. Fax: 217-942-6211. 8AM-4PM (CST). Access by: Phone, fax, mail, in person. No felonies by phone. Include signed release with felony search requests.

Grundy County

Real Estate Recording—Grundy County Recorder, 111 East Washington Street, Morris, IL 60450. 815-941-3224. Fax: 815-942-2220. 8AM-4:30PM (CST).

Felony, Misdemeanor, Civil, Eviction, Small Claims, Probate—Circuit Court, PO Box 707, Morris, IL 60450. 815-941-3256. Fax: 815-942-2222. 8AM-4:30PM (CST). Access by: Mail, in person.

Hamilton County

Real Estate Recording—Hamilton County Recorder, Courthouse, Room 2, Mcleansboro, IL 62859. 618-643-2721. 8AM-4:30PM (CST).

Felony, Misdemeanor, Civil, Eviction, Small Claims, Probate—Circuit Court, County Courthouse, McLeansboro, IL 62859. 618-643-3224. Fax: 618-643-3455. 8AM-4:30PM (CST). Access by: Mail, in person.

Hancock County

Real Estate Recording—Hancock County Recorder, 500 Blk Main Street, Courthouse, 2nd Floor, Carthage, IL 62321. 217-357-3911. 8AM-4PM (CST).

Felony, Misdemeanor, Civil, Eviction, Small Claims, Probate—Circuit Court, PO Box 189, Carthage, IL 62321. 217-357-2616. 8AM-4PM (CST). Access by: Mail, in person.

Hardin County

Real Estate Recording—Hardin County Recorder, Courthouse, Elizabethtown, IL 62931. 618-287-2251. Fax: 618-287-7833. 8AM-4PM (CST).

Felony, Misdemeanor, Civil, Eviction, Small Claims, Probate—Circuit Court, County Courthouse, Elizabethtown, IL 62931. 618-287-2735. Fax: 618-287-7833. 8AM-4PM (CST). Access by: Mail, in person. ·

Henderson County

Real Estate Recording—Henderson County Recorder, 4th & Warren Streets, Oquawka, IL 61469. 309-867-2911. Fax: 309-867-2033. 8AM-4PM (CST).

Felony, Misdemeanor, Civil, Eviction, Small Claims, Probate—Circuit Court, County Courthouse, PO Box 546, Oquawka, IL 61469. 309-867-3121. Fax: 309-867-3207. 8AM-4PM (CST). Access by: Phone, mail, in person.

Henry County

Real Estate Recording—Henry County Recorder, 100 South Main, Cambridge, IL 61238. 309-937-2426. Fax: 309-937-2796. 8AM-4PM (CST).

Felony, Misdemeanor, Civil, Eviction, Small Claims, Probate—Circuit Court, Henry County Courthouse, PO Box 9, Cambridge, IL 61238. 309-937-5192. 8AM-4PM (CST). Access by: Mail, in person.

Iroquois County

Real Estate Recording—Iroquois County Recorder, 1001 East Grant Street, Watseka, IL 60970. 815-432-6962. Fax: 815-432-6984. 8:30AM-4:30PM (CST).

Felony, Misdemeanor, Civil, Eviction, Small Claims, Probate—Circuit Court, 550 S 10th St, Watseka, IL 60970. 815-432-6950. Fax: 815-432-6953. 8AM-4PM (CST). Access by: Fax, mail, in person.

Jackson County

Real Estate Recording—Jackson County Recorder, The Courthouse, 10th & Walnut, Murphysboro, IL 62966. 618-687-7360. 8AM-4PM (CST).

Felony, Misdemeanor, Civil, Eviction, Small Claims, Probate—Circuit Court, County Courthouse, PO Box 730, Murphysboro, IL 62966. 618-687-7300. 8AM-4PM (CST). Access by: Mail, in person.

Jasper County

Real Estate Recording—Jasper County Recorder, 100 West Jourdan, Newton, IL 62448. 618-783-3124. Fax: 618-783-4137. 8AM-4:30PM (CST).

Felony, Misdemeanor, Civil, Eviction, Small Claims, Probate—Circuit Court, 100 W Jourdan St, Newton, IL 62448. 618-783-2524. 8AM-4:30PM (CST). Access by: Mail, in person.

Jefferson County

Real Estate Recording—Jefferson County Recorder, Courthouse, 100 S. 10th St., Room 105, Mount Vernon, IL 62864. 618-244-8020. 8AM-5PM (CST).

Felony, Misdemeanor, Civil, Eviction, Small Claims, Probate—Circuit Court, PO Box 1266, Mt Vernon, IL 62864. 618-244-8008. Fax: 618-244-8029. 8AM-5PM (CST). Access by: Phone, mail, in person.

Jersey County

Real Estate Recording—Jersey County Recorder, 201 West Pearl Street, Courthouse, Jerseyville, IL 62052. 618-498-5571. Fax: 618-498-6128. 8:30AM-4:30PM (CST).

Felony, Misdemeanor, Civil, Eviction, Small Claims, Probate—Circuit Court, 201 W Pearl St, Jerseyville, IL 62052. 618-498-5571. Fax: 618-498-6128. 8:30AM-4:30PM (CST). Access by: Phone, mail, in person.

Jo Daviess County

Real Estate Recording—Jo Daviess County Recorder, 330 North Bench Street, Galena, IL 61036. 815-777-9694. Fax: 815-777-3688. 8AM-4PM (CST).

Felony, Misdemeanor, Civil, Eviction, Small Claims, Probate—Circuit Court, 330 N Bench St, Galena, IL 61036. 815-777-2295. Fax: 815-777-3688. 8AM-4PM (CST). Access by: Mail, in person.

Johnson County

Real Estate Recording—Johnson County Recorder, Courthouse Square, Vienna, IL 62995. 618-658-3611. Fax: 618-658-2908. 8AM-Noon,1-4PM (CST).

Felony, Misdemeanor, Civil, Eviction, Small Claims, Probate—Circuit Court, PO Box 517, Vienna, IL 62995. 618-658-4751. Fax: 618-658-2908. 8AM-4PM (CST). Access by: Mail, in person.

Kane County

Real Estate Recording—Kane County Recorder, 719 South Batavia Avenue, Bldg C, Geneva, IL 60134. 630-232-5935. Fax: 630-232-5945. 8:30AM-4:30PM (CST).

Felony, Misdemeanor, Civil, Eviction, Small Claims, Probate—Circuit Court, PO Box 112, Geneva, IL 60134. Civil: 630-208-3323. Criminal: 630-208-3319. Fax: 630-208-2172. 8:30AM-4:30PM (CST). Access by: Phone, mail, in person.

Kankakee County

Real Estate Recording—Kankakee County Recorder, 189 East Court Street, Kankakee, IL 60901. 815-937-2980. Fax: 815-937-3657. 8:30AM-4:30PM (CST).

Felony, Misdemeanor, Civil, Eviction, Small Claims, Probate—Circuit Court, 450 E Court St, County Courthouse, Kankakee, IL 60901. 815-937-2905. Fax: 815-939-8830. 8:30AM-4:30PM (CST). Access by: Mail, in person.

Kendall County

Real Estate Recording—Kendall County Recorder, 111 West Fox Street, Yorkville, IL 60560. 630-553-4112. Fax: 630-553-4119. 8AM-4:30PM (CST).

Felony, Misdemeanor, Civil, Eviction, Small Claims, Probate—Circuit Court, PO Drawer M, Yorkville, IL 60560. 630-553-4183. 8AM-4:30PM (CST). Access by: Mail, in person. Court planning to offer online access. Call 1-800-1100 for more information.

Knox County

Real Estate Recording—Knox County Recorder, County Court House, Galesburg, IL 61401. 309-345-3818. Fax: 309-343-7002. 8:30AM-4:30PM (CST).

Felony, Misdemeanor, Civil, Eviction, Small Claims, Probate—Circuit Court, County Courthouse, Galesburg, IL 61401. 309-345-3817. 8:30AM-4:30PM (CST). Access by: Phone, mail, in person.

La Salle County

Real Estate Recording—La Salle County Recorder, 707 Etna Road, Government Center Room 269, Ottawa, IL 61350. 815-434-8226. 8AM-4:30PM (CST).

Felony, Misdemeanor, Civil, Eviction, Small Claims, Probate—Circuit Court, PO Box 617, Ottawa, IL 61350-0617. 815-434-8671. Fax: 815-433-9198. 8AM-4:30PM (CST). Access by: In person only.

Lake County

Real Estate Recording—Lake County Recorder, 18 North County Street, Courthouse - 2nd Floor, Waukegan, IL 60085. 847-360-6673. Fax: 847-625-7200. 8:30AM-5PM (CST).

Felony, Misdemeanor, Civil, Eviction, Small Claims, Probate—Circuit Court, 18 N County St, Waukegan, IL 60085. 708-360-6794. 8:30-5PM (CST). Access by: Mail, in person.

Lawrence County

Real Estate Recording—Lawrence County Recorder, Courthouse, Lawrenceville, IL 62439. 618-943-5126. Fax: 618-943-5205. 9AM-5PM (CST).

Felony, Misdemeanor, Civil, Eviction, Small Claims, Probate—Circuit Court, County Courthouse, Lawrenceville, IL 62439. 618-943-2815. Fax: 618-943-5205. 9AM-5PM (CST). Access by: Mail, in person.

Lee County

Real Estate Recording—Lee County Recorder, 112 E. Second St., Dixon, IL 61021. 815-288-3309. Fax: 815-288-6492. 8:30AM-4:30PM (CST).

Felony, Misdemeanor, Civil, Eviction, Small Claims, Probate—Circuit Court, PO Box 325, Dixon, IL 61021. 815-284-5234. 8:30AM-4:30PM (CST). Access by: Mail, in person.

Livingston County

Real Estate Recording—Livingston County Recorder, 112 West Madison, Courthouse, Pontiac, IL 61764. 815-844-2006. Fax: 815-842-1844. 8AM-4:30PM (CST).

Felony, Misdemeanor, Civil, Eviction, Small Claims, Probate—112 W Madison St, Pontiac, IL 61764. 815-844-5166. 8AM-4:30PM (CST). Access by: Mail, in person. Signed release required for juvenile cases.

Logan County

Real Estate Recording—Logan County Recorder, Courthouse, 601 Broadway Room 20, Lincoln, IL 62656. 217-732-4148. Fax: 217-732-6064. 8:30AM-4:30PM (CST).

Felony, Misdemeanor, Civil, Eviction, Small Claims, Probate—Circuit Court, County Courthouse, Lincoln, IL 62656. 217-735-2376. 8:30AM-4:30PM (CST). Access by: Mail, in person.

Macon County

Real Estate Recording—Macon County Recorder, 141 S. Main St., Room 201, Decatur, IL 62523. 217-424-1359. Fax: 217-428-2908. 8:30AM-4:30PM (CST).

Felony, Misdemeanor, Civil, Eviction, Small Claims, Probate—Circuit Court, 253 E Wood St, Decatur, IL 62523. 217-424-1454. Fax: 217-424-1350. 8AM-4:30PM (CST). Access by: Phone, mail, in person.

Macoupin County

Real Estate Recording—Macoupin County Recorder, Courthouse, Carlinville, IL 62626. 217-854-3214. Fax: 217-854-8461. 8:30AM-4:30PM (CST).

Felony, Misdemeanor, Civil, Eviction, Small Claims, Probate—Circuit Court, PO Box 197, Carlinville, IL 62626. 217-854-3211. Fax: 217-854-8461. 8:30AM-4:30PM (CST). Access by: Mail, in person.

Madison County

Real Estate Recording—Madison County Recorder, 157 North Main, Suite 221, Madison County Administration Bldg., Edwardsville, IL 62025. 618-692-6200. Fax: 618-692-9843. 8AM-5PM (CST).

Felony, Misdemeanor, Civil, Eviction, Small Claims, Probate—Circuit Court, 155 N Main St, Edwardsville, IL 62025. 618-692-6240. Fax: 618-692-0676. 8AM-5PM (CST). Access by: Mail, in person.

Marion County

Real Estate Recording—Marion County Recorder, Marion County Courthouse, 100 E. Main St., Room 201, Salem, IL 62881. 618-548-3400. Fax: 618-548-2226. 8AM-4PM (CST).

Felony, Misdemeanor, Civil, Eviction, Small Claims, Probate—Circuit Court, PO Box 130, Salem, IL 62881. 618-548-3856. 8AM-4PM (CST). Access by: Mail, in person.

Marshall County

Real Estate Recording—Marshall County Recorder, 122 North Prairie, Lacon, IL 61540. 309-246-6325. Fax: 309-246-3667. 8:30AM-4:30PM (CST).

Felony, Misdemeanor, Civil, Eviction, Small Claims, Probate—Circuit Court, 122 N Prairie-Box 98, Lacon, IL 61540. 309-246-6435. Fax: 309-246-3667. 8:30AM-Noon, 1-4:30PM (CST). Access by: Mail, in person.

Mason County

Real Estate Recording—Mason County Recorder, 100 North Broadway, Havana, IL 62644. 309-543-6661. Fax: 309-543-2085. 8AM-4PM (CST).

Felony, Misdemeanor, Civil, Eviction, Small Claims, Probate—Circuit Court, 125 N Plum, Havana, IL 62644. 309-543-6619. Fax: 309-543-2085. 8AM-4PM (CST). Access by: Mail, in person.

Massac County

Real Estate Recording—Massac County Recorder, Courthouse, Room 2-A, Superman Square, Metropolis, IL 62960. 618-524-5213. Fax: 618-524-4230. 8AM-4PM (CST).

Felony, Misdemeanor, Civil, Eviction, Small Claims, Probate—Circuit Court, PO Box 152, Metropolis, IL 62960. 618-524-9359. Fax: 618-524-4850. 8AM-Noon, 1-4PM (CST). Access by: Mail, in person.

McDonough County

Real Estate Recording—McDonough County Recorder, 1 Courthouse Square, Macomb, IL 61455. 309-833-2474. Fax: 309-836-3013. 8AM-4PM (CST).

Felony, Misdemeanor, Civil, Eviction, Small Claims, Probate—Circuit Court, County Courthouse, PO Box 348, Macomb, IL 61455. 309-837-4889. Fax: 309-836-3013. 8AM-4PM (CST). Access by: Phone, fax, mail, in person.

McHenry County

Real Estate Recording—McHenry County Recorder, 2200 North Seminary Avenue, Room A280, Woodstock, IL 60098. 815-334-4110. Fax: 815-338-9612. 8AM-4:30PM (CST).

Felony, Misdemeanor, Civil, Eviction, Small Claims, Probate—Circuit Court, 2200 N Seminary Ave, Woodstock, IL 60098. 815-338-2098. Fax: 815-338-8583. 8AM-4:30PM (CST). Access by: Phone, mail, in person.

McLean County

Real Estate Recording—McLean County Recorder, 104 West Front Street, Room 708, Bloomington, IL 61701. 309-888-5170. Fax: 309-888-5209. 8AM-4:30PM (CST).

Felony, Misdemeanor, Civil, Eviction, Small Claims, Probate—Circuit Court, PO Box 2420, Bloomington, IL 61702-2420. Civil: 309-888-5341. Criminal: 309-888-5320. 8:30AM-4:30PM (CST). Access by: Mail, in person.

Menard County

Real Estate Recording—Menard County Recorder, Seventh Street, Courthouse, Petersburg, IL 62675. 217-632-2415. Fax: 217-632-4124. 8:30AM-4:30PM (CST).

Felony, Misdemeanor, Civil, Eviction, Small Claims, Probate—Circuit Court, PO Box 466, Petersburg, IL 62675. 217-632-2615. 8:30AM-4:30PM (CST). Access by: Mail, in person.

Mercer County

Real Estate Recording—Mercer County Recorder, 100 S.E. 3rd Street, 2nd Floor, Aledo, IL 61231. 309-582-7021. Fax: 309-582-7022. 8AM-4PM (CST).

Felony, Misdemeanor, Civil, Eviction, Small Claims, Probate—Circuit Court, PO Box 175, Aledo, IL 61231. 309-582-7122. Fax: 309-582-3028. 8AM-4PM (CST). Access by: Phone, mail, in person.

Monroe County

Real Estate Recording—Monroe County Recorder, 100 South Main, Courthouse, Waterloo, IL 62298. 618-939-8681. Fax: 618-939-5132. 8AM-4:30PM (CST).

Felony, Misdemeanor, Civil, Eviction, Small Claims, Probate—Circuit Court, 100 S Main St, Waterloo, IL 62298. 618-939-8681. Fax: 618-939-5132. 8AM-4:30PM (CST). Access by: Phone, mail, in person.

Montgomery County

Real Estate Recording—Montgomery County Recorder, Courthouse, Hillsboro, IL 62049. 217-532-9532. 8AM-4PM (CST).

Felony, Misdemeanor, Civil, Eviction, Small Claims, Probate—Circuit Court, PO Box C, Hillsboro, IL 62049. 217-532-9546. 8AM-4PM (CST). Access by: Mail, in person.

Morgan County

Real Estate Recording—Morgan County Recorder, 300 West State Street, Courthouse, Jacksonville, IL 62650. 217-243-8581. 8:30AM-4:30PM (CST).

Felony, Misdemeanor, Civil, Eviction, Small Claims, Probate—Circuit Court, 300 W State St, Jacksonville, IL 62650. 217-243-5419. Fax: 217-243-2009. 8:30AM-4:30PM (CST). Access by: Mail, in person.

Moultrie County

Real Estate Recording—Moultrie County Recorder, Courthouse, Sullivan, IL 61951. 217-728-4389. Fax: 217-728-8178. 8:30AM-4:30PM (CST).

Felony, Misdemeanor, Civil, Eviction, Small Claims, Probate—Circuit Court, County Courthouse, Sullivan, IL 61951. 217-728-4622. 8:30AM-4:30PM (CST). Access by: Mail, in person.

Ogle County

Real Estate Recording—Ogle County Recorder, Fourth & Washington Streets, Oregon, IL 61061. 815-732-3201. 8:30AM-4:30PM (CST).

Felony, Misdemeanor, Civil, Eviction, Small Claims, Probate—Circuit Court, PO Box 337, Oregon, IL 61061. 815-732-3201. 8:30AM-4:30PM (CST). Access by: Mail, in person.

Peoria County

Real Estate Recording—Peoria County Recorder, County Courthouse - Room G04, 324 Main Street, Peoria, IL 61602. 309-672-6090. 9AM-5PM (CST).

Felony, Misdemeanor, Civil, Eviction, Small Claims, Probate—Circuit Court, 324 Main St, Peoria, IL 61602. 309-672-6953. Fax: 309-672-6079. 9AM-5PM (CST). Access by: Phone, mail, in person.

Perry County

Real Estate Recording—Perry County Recorder, Rt 1 Box 63, Pinckneyville, IL 62274. 618-357-5116. 8AM-4PM (CST).

Felony, Misdemeanor, Civil, Eviction, Small Claims, Probate—Circuit Court, PO Box 219, Pinckneyville, IL 62274. 618-357-6726. 8AM-4PM (CST). Access by: Mail, in person.

Piatt County

Real Estate Recording—Piatt County Recorder, 101 West Washington, Courthouse, Room 101, Monticello, IL 61856. 217-762-9487. Fax: 217-762-7563. 8:30AM-4:30PM (CST).

Felony, Misdemeanor, Civil, Eviction, Small Claims, Probate—Circuit Court, PO Box 288, Monticello, IL 61856. 217-762-4966. Fax: 217-762-8394. 8:30AM-4:30PM (CST). Access by: Phone, fax, mail, in person.

Pike County

Real Estate Recording—Pike County Recorder, Courthouse, 100 E. Washington St., Pittsfield, IL 62363. 217-285-6812. 8:30AM-4PM (CST).

Felony, Misdemeanor, Civil, Eviction, Small Claims, Probate—Circuit Court, Pike County Courthouse, Pittsfield, IL 62363. 217-285-6612. Fax: 217-285-4726. 8:30AM-4:30PM (CST). Access by: Mail, in person.

Pope County

Real Estate Recording—Pope County Recorder, Courthouse, Golconda, IL 62938. 618-683-4466. 8AM-Noon, 1-4PM (CST).

Felony, Misdemeanor, Civil, Eviction, Small Claims, Probate—Circuit Court, County Courthouse, Golconda, IL 62938. 618-683-3941. Fax: 618-683-2211. 8AM-4PM (CST). Access by: Phone, mail, in person.

Pulaski County

Real Estate Recording—Pulaski County Recorder, Corner of 2nd & High, Courthouse, Mound City, IL 62963. 618-748-9360. 8AM-Noon, 1-4PM (CST).

Felony, Misdemeanor, Civil, Eviction, Small Claims, Probate—Circuit Court, PO Box 88, Mound City, IL 62963. 618-748-9300. Fax: 618-748-9338. 8AM-4PM (CST). Access by: Mail, in person.

Putnam County

Real Estate Recording—Putnam County Recorder, Courthouse, 120 North 4th Street, Hennepin, IL 61327. 815-925-7129. Fax: 815-925-7549. 8AM-Noon, 1-4:30PM (CST).

Felony, Misdemeanor, Civil, Eviction, Small Claims, Probate—Circuit Court, 120 N 4th St, Hennepin, IL 61327. 815-925-7016. Fax: 815-925-7549. 8AM-12PM-1PM-4:30PM (CST). Access by: Mail, in person.

Randolph County

Real Estate Recording—Randolph County Recorder, 1 Taylor Street, Courthouse, Chester, IL 62233. 618-826-5000. Fax: 618-826-3750. 8AM-4:30PM (CST).

Felony, Misdemeanor, Civil, Eviction, Small Claims, Probate—Circuit Court, County Courthouse, Chester, IL 62233. 618-826-5000. 8AM-4PM (CST). Access by: Mail, in person.

Richland County

Real Estate Recording—Richland County Recorder, 103 West Main, Courthouse, Olney, IL 62450. 618-392-3111. Fax: 618-393-4005. 8AM-4PM (CST).

Felony, Misdemeanor, Civil, Eviction, Small Claims, Probate—Circuit Court, 103 W Main #21, Olney, IL 62450. 618-392-2151. Fax: 618-395-8445. 8AM-4PM (CST). Access by: Mail, in person.

Rock Island County

Real Estate Recording—Rock Island County Recorder, 210 15th Street, Rock Island, IL 61201. 309-786-4451. 8AM-5PM (CST).

Felony, Misdemeanor, Civil, Eviction, Small Claims, Probate—Circuit Court, 210 15th St, PO Box 5230, Rock Island, IL 61204-5230. 309-786-4451. Fax: 309-786-3029. 8AM-4:30PM (CST). Access by: Fax, mail, in person.

Saline County

Real Estate Recording—Saline County Recorder, 10 E. Poplar, Harrisburg, IL 62946. 618-253-8197. 8AM-4PM (CST).

Felony, Misdemeanor, Civil, Eviction, Small Claims, Probate—Circuit Court, County Courthouse, Harrisburg, IL 62946. 618-253-5096. Fax: 618-252-8438. 8AM-4PM (CST). Access by: Mail, in person.

Sangamon County

Real Estate Recording—Sangamon County Recorder, 200 S. 9th St., Room 211, Springfield, IL 62701. 217-535-3150. Fax: 217-535-3159. 8:30AM-5PM (CST).

Felony, Misdemeanor, Civil, Eviction, Small Claims, Probate—Circuit Court, 200 S Ninth St Rm 405, Springfield, IL 62701. 217-753-6674. Fax: 217-753-6665. 8:30AM-4:30PM (CST). Access by: Fax, mail, in person.

Schuyler County

Real Estate Recording—Schuyler County Recorder, Courthouse, 102 S. Congress, Rushville, IL 62681. 217-322-4734. Fax: 217-322-6164. 8AM-4PM (CST).

Felony, Misdemeanor, Civil, Eviction, Small Claims, Probate—Circuit Court, PO Box 80, Rushville, IL 62681. 217-322-4633. Fax: 217-322-6164. 8AM-4PM (CST). Access by: Mail, in person.

Scott County

Real Estate Recording—Scott County Recorder, Courthouse, Winchester, IL 62694. 217-742-3178. Fax: 217-742-5853. 8AM-4PM (CST).

Felony, Misdemeanor, Civil, Eviction, Small Claims, Probate—Circuit Court, 35 E Market St, Winchester, IL 62694. 217-742-5217. Fax: 217-742-5853. 8AM-Noon, 1-4PM (CST). Access by: Mail, in person.

Shelby County

Real Estate Recording—Shelby County Recorder, Courthouse, Shelbyville, IL 62565. 217-774-4421. Fax: 217-774-2690. 8AM-4PM (CST).

Felony, Misdemeanor, Civil, Eviction, Small Claims, Probate—Circuit Court, County Courthouse, Shelbyville, IL 62565. 217-774-4212. Fax: 217-774-2690. 8AM-4PM (CST). Access by: Phone, mail, in person.

St. Clair County

Real Estate Recording—St. Clair County Recorder, #10 Public Square, County Building, Belleville, IL 62222. 618-277-6600. 8:30AM-5PM (CST).

Felony, Misdemeanor, Civil, Eviction, Small Claims, Probate—Circuit Court, 10 Public Square, Belleville, IL 62220-1623. 618-227-6600. Fax: 618-277-6832. 9AM-4PM (CST). Access by: Mail, in person.

Stark County

Real Estate Recording—Stark County Recorder, 130 West Main, Toulon, IL 61483. 309-286-5911. Fax: 309-286-6091. 8AM-Noon, 12:30-4:30PM (CST).

Felony, Misdemeanor, Civil, Eviction, Small Claims, Probate—Circuit Court, 130 E Main St, Toulon, IL 61483. 309-286-5941. 8AM-4:30PM (CST). Access by: Mail, in person.

Stephenson County

Real Estate Recording—Stephenson County Recorder, 15 North Galena Avenue, Freeport, IL 61032. 815-235-8385. 8:30AM-4:30PM (CST).

Felony, Misdemeanor, Civil, Eviction, Small Claims, Probate—Circuit Court, 15 N Galena Ave, Freeport, IL 61032. 815-235-8266. 8:30AM-4:30PM (CST). Access by: Mail, in person.

Tazewell County

Real Estate Recording—Tazewell County Recorder, Arcade Bldg., 13 S. Capitol St., Pekin, IL 61554. 309-477-2210. 9AM-5PM (CST).

Felony, Misdemeanor, Civil, Eviction, Small Claims, Probate—Circuit Court, Courthouse, 4th & Court Sts, Pekin, IL 61554. 309-477-2214. 9AM-5PM (CST). Access by: Mail, in person.

Union County

Real Estate Recording—Union County Recorder, 311 West Market, Jonesboro, IL 62952. 618-833-5711. Fax: 618-833-8712. 8AM-4PM (CST).

Felony, Misdemeanor, Civil, Eviction, Small Claims, Probate—Circuit Court, PO Box 360, Jonesboro, IL 62952. 618-833-5913. Fax: 618-833-5223. 8AM-Noon,1-4PM (CST). Access by: Mail, in person.

Vermilion County

Real Estate Recording—Vermilion County Recorder, 6 North Vermilion Street, Danville, IL 61832. 217-431-2604. Fax: 217-431-7460. 8AM-4:30PM (CST).

Felony, Misdemeanor, Civil, Eviction, Small Claims, Probate—Circuit Court, 7 N Vermilion, Danville, IL 61832. 217-431-2534. 8:30AM-4:30PM (CST). Access by: Phone, mail, in person.

Wabash County

Real Estate Recording—Wabash County Recorder, 401 Market Street, Mount Carmel, IL 62863. 618-262-4561. 8AM-5PM (CST).

Felony, Misdemeanor, Civil, Eviction, Small Claims, Probate—Circuit Court, PO Box 1057, Mt Carmel, IL 62863. 618-262-5362. Fax: 618-263-4441. 8AM-4PM (CST). Access by: Mail, in person.

Warren County

Real Estate Recording—Warren County Recorder, Courthouse, 100 W. Broadway, Monmouth, IL 61462. 309-734-8592. Fax: 309-734-7406. 8AM-4:30PM (CST).

Felony, Misdemeanor, Civil, Eviction, Small Claims, Probate—Circuit Court, 100 W Broadway, Monmouth, IL 61462. 309-734-5179. 8AM-4:30PM (CST). Access by: Mail, in person.

Washington County

Real Estate Recording—Washington County Recorder, County Courthouse, 101 E. St. Louis Street, Nashville, IL 62263. 618-327-4800. Fax: 618-372-3378. 8AM-4PM (CST).

Felony, Misdemeanor, Civil, Eviction, Small Claims, Probate—Circuit Court, 101 E St Louis St, Nashville, IL 62263. 618-327-3383. 8AM-4PM (CST). Access by: Mail, in person.

Wayne County

Real Estate Recording—Wayne County Recorder, 301 East Main, Fairfield, IL 62837. 618-842-5182. Fax: 618-842-2556. 8AM-4:30PM (CST).

Felony, Misdemeanor, Civil, Eviction, Small Claims, Probate—Circuit Court, County Courthouse, Fairfield, IL 62837. 618-842-7684. Fax: 618-842-2556. 8AM-4:30PM (CST). Access by: Mail, in person.

White County

Real Estate Recording—White County Recorder, 301 East Main Street, Courthouse, Carmi, IL 62821. 618-382-7211. 8AM-4PM (CST).

Felony, Misdemeanor, Civil, Eviction, Small Claims, Probate—Circuit Court, PO Box 310, County Courthouse, Carmi, IL 62821. 618-382-2321. Fax: 618-382-2322. 8AM-4PM (CST). Access by: Mail, in person.

Whiteside County

Real Estate Recording—Whiteside County Recorder, 200 East Knox, Morrison, IL 61270. 815-772-5192. 8:30AM-4:30PM (CST).

Felony, Misdemeanor, Civil, Eviction, Small Claims, Probate—Circuit Court, 200 E Knox St, Morrison, IL 61270-2698. 815-772-5188. 8:30AM-4:30PM (CST). Access by: Phone, mail, in person.

Will County

Real Estate Recording—Will County Recorder, 302 N. Chicago Street, Joliet, IL 60432. 815-740-4637. Fax: 815-740-4697. 8:30AM-4:30PM (CST).

Felony, Misdemeanor, Civil, Eviction, Small Claims, Probate—Circuit Court, 14 W Jefferson St, Joliet, IL 60432. 815-727-8592. Fax: 815-727-8896. 8:30AM-4:30PM (CST). Access by: Mail, in person.

Williamson County

Real Estate Recording—Williamson County Recorder, 200 West Jefferson, Marion, IL 62959. 618-997-1301. Fax: 618-993-2071. 8AM-4PM (CST).

Felony, Misdemeanor, Civil, Eviction, Small Claims, Probate—Circuit Court, 200 W Jefferson St, Marion, IL 62959. 618-997-1301. 8AM-4:30PM (CST). Access by: Mail, in person.

Winnebago County

Real Estate Recording—Winnebago County Recorder, 404 Elm St., Rockford, IL 61101. 815-987-3100. Fax: 815-961-3261. 8AM-5PM (CST).

Felony, Misdemeanor, Civil, Eviction, Small Claims, Probate—Circuit Court, 400 W State St, Rockford, IL 61101. 815-987-2510. Fax: 815-987-3012. 8AM-5PM (CST). Access by: Phone, mail, remote online, in person.

Woodford County

Real Estate Recording—Woodford County Recorder, 115 North Main, Courthouse, Eureka, IL 61530. 309-467-2822. 8AM-5PM (CST).

Felony, Misdemeanor, Civil, Eviction, Small Claims, Probate—Circuit Court, County Courthouse, Eureka, IL 61530. 309-467-3312. 8AM-5PM (CST). Access by: Phone, mail, in person.

Federal Courts

US District Court

Central District of Illinois

Peoria Division, US District Court US District Clerk's Office, 305 Federal Bldg, 100 NE Monroe St, Peoria, IL 61602. 309-671-7117. Counties: Bureau, Fulton, Hancock, Knox, Livingston, McDonough, McLean, Marshall, Peoria, Putnam, Stark, Tazewell, Woodford

Rock Island Division, US District Court US District Clerk's Office, Room 40, Post Office Bldg, 211 19th St, Rock Island, IL 61201. 309-793-5778. Counties: Henderson, Henry, Mercer, Rock Island, Warren

Springfield Division, US District Court Clerk, 151 US Courthouse, 600 E Monroe, Springfield, IL 62701. 217-492-4020. Counties: Adams, Brown, Cass, Christian, De Witt, Greene, Logan, Macoupin, Mason, Menard, Montgomery, Morgan, Pike, Sangamon, Schuyler, Scott, Shelby

Urbana Division, US District Court, Room 218, 201 S Vine, Urbana, IL 61801. 217-373-5830. Counties: Champaign, Coles, Douglas, Edgar, Ford, Iroquois, Kankakee, Macon, Moultrie, Piatt, Vermilion

Northern District of Illinois

Chicago (Eastern) Division, US District Court 20th Floor, 219 S Dearborn St, Chicago, IL 60604. 312-435-5698. Counties: Cook, Du Page, Grundy, Kane, Kendall, Lake, La Salle, Will

Rockford Division, US District Court Room 211, 211 S Court St, Rockford, IL 61101. 815-987-4355. Counties: Boone, Carroll, De Kalb, Jo Daviess, Lee, McHenry, Ogle, Stephenson, Whiteside, Winnebago

Southern District of Illinois

Benton Division, US District Court 301 W Main St, Benton, IL 62812. 618-438-0671. Counties: Alexander, Clark, Clay, Crawford, Cumberland, Edwards, Effingham, Franklin, Gallatin, Hamilton, Hardin, Jackson, Jasper, Jefferson, Johnson, Lawrence, Massac, Perry, Pope, Pulaski, Richland, Saline, Union, Wabash, Wayne, White, Williamson. Cases may also be allocated to the Benton Division

East St Louis Division, US District Court PO Box 249, East St Louis, IL 62202. 618-482-9371. Counties: Bond, Calhoun, Clinton, Fayette, Jersey, Madison, Marion, Monroe, Randolph, St. Clair, Washington. Cases for these counties may also be allocated to the Benton Division

US Bankruptcy Court

Central District of Illinois

Danville Division, US Bankruptcy Court, 201 N Vermilion, Danville, IL 61834-4733. 217-431-4820. Voice Case Information System: 217-492-4550. Counties: Champaign, Coles, Douglas, Edgar, Ford, Iroquois, Kankakee, Moultrie, Piatt, Vermilion

Peoria Division, US Bankruptcy Court, 131 Federal Bldg, 100 NE Monroe, Peoria, IL 61602. 309-671-7035. Voice Case Information System: 217-492-4550. Counties: Bureau, Fulton, Hancock, Henderson, Henry, Knox, Livingston, Marshall, McDonough, Mercer, Peoria, Putnam, Rock Island, Stark, Tazewell, Warren, Woodford

Springfield Division, US Bankruptcy Court, 226 US Courthouse, Springfield, IL 62701-4551. 217-492-4551. Voice Case Information System: 217-492-4550. Counties: Adams, Brown, Cass, Christian, De Witt, Greene, Logan, Macon, Macoupin, Mason, McLean, Menard, Montgomery, Morgan, Pike, Sangamon, Schuyler, Scott, Shelby

Northern District of Illinois

Chicago (Eastern) Division, US Bankruptcy Court, 219 S Dearborn St, Chicago, IL 60604-1802. 312-435-5587. Voice Case Information System: 312-408-5089. Counties: Cook, Du Page, Grundy, Kane, Kendall, La Salle, Lake, Will

Rockford Division, US Bankruptcy Court, Room 110, 211 S Court St, Rockford, IL 61101. 815-987-4350. Voice Case Information System: 815-987-4487. Counties: Boone, Carroll, De Kalb, Jo Daviess, Lee, McHenry, Ogle, Stephenson, Whiteside, Winnebago

Southern District of Illinois

Benton Division, US Bankruptcy Court, 301 W Main, Benton, IL 62812. 618-435-2200. Voice Case Information System: 618-482-9365. Counties: Alexander, Edwards, Franklin, Gallatin, Hamilton, Hardin, Jackson, Jefferson, Johnson, Massac, Perry, Pope, Pulaski, Randolph, Saline, Union, Wabash, Washington, Wayne, White, Williamson

East St Louis Division, US Bankruptcy Court, PO Box 309, East St Louis, IL 62202-0309. 618-482-9400. Voice Case Information System: 618-482-9365. Counties: Bond, Calhoun, Clark, Clay, Clinton, Crawford, Cumberland, Effingham, Fayette, Jasper, Jersey, Lawrence, Madison, Marion, Monroe, Richland, St. Clair

Indiana

Capitol: Indianapolis (Marion County)	
Number of Counties: 92	**Population:** 5,803,471
County Court Locations:	**Federal Court Locations:**
•Circuit Courts: 20	•District Courts: 8
•Circuit/Superior Courts: 67	•Bankruptcy Courts: 8
•Circuit/County Courts: 6	**State Agencies:** 20
•Municipal Courts: 1	
City Courts: 48	
Small Claims: 9	
Town Courts: 24	
Probate Court: 1	

State Agencies—Summary

General Help Numbers:

State Archives

Indiana State Archives	317-232-3660
Commission on Public Records	Fax: 317-232-1085
140 N Senate Ave, Rm 117	8AM-4:30PM
Indianapolis, IN 46204	
Historical Society:	317-232-1879
Reference Librarian:	317-232-3660

Governor's Office

Governor's Office	317-232-4567
206 State House	Fax: 317-232-3443
Indianapolis, IN 46204	8AM-5PM

Attorney General's Office

Attorney General's Office	317-232-6201
219 State House	Fax: 317-232-7979
Indianapolis, IN 46204	8:15AM-4:45PM

State Legislation

Legislative Services Agency	317-232-9856
State House	8:15AM-4:45PM
200 W Washington, Room 302	
Indianapolis, IN 46204-2789	

Important State Internet Sites:

> 🌐 **Webscape**
> **File Edit View**   **Help**

State of Indiana World Wide Web
www.state.in.us/

Key site for information about the state of Indiana. It links to the Indiana State Government, weather, press releases and a search for information site.

Indiana General Assembly
www.ai.org/legislative/

This site list bills introduced by the current legislature, lists all of the legislators and links to their respective home pages. Maps of the Senate, House and Congressional districts are also available.

Unclaimed Property
www.state.in.us/cgi-bin/hoosieradvocate/UCP/ucp.cgi

Locates unclaimed property, such as checking and savings accounts, payroll, wages, insurance, refunds and much more. Property is searchable by owner's name.

State Archives and Historical Records
www.ai.org/acin/icpr/index.html

Linked to this site are the state archives and historical records. There is an extensive table of contents that links to many sites, and there is a records retention schedule database to search through.

State Agencies—Public Records

Criminal Records
Indiana State Police, Central Records, IGCN - 100 N Senate Ave Room 302, Indianapolis, IN 46204-2259, Main Telephone: 317-232-8266, Hours: 8AM-4:30PM. Access by: mail, visit.

Corporation Records
Limited Partnerships
Fictitious Name
Assumed Name
Limited Liability Company Records
Corporation Division, Secretary of State, 302 W Washington St, Room E018, Indianapolis, IN 46204, Main Telephone: 317-232-6576, Fax: 317-233-3387, Hours: 8AM-5:30PM M-F. Access by: mail, phone, visit.

Trademarks/Servicemarks
Secretary of State, Trademark Division, 302 W Washington St, IGC-East, Room E111, Indianapolis, IN 46204, Main Telephone: 317-232-6540, Fax: 317-233-3675, Hours: 8:45AM-4:45PM. Access by: mail, phone, fax, visit. These records are considered public and are available with no restrictions.

Uniform Commercial Code
Federal Tax Liens
State Tax Liens
UCC Division, Secretary of State, 302 West Washington St, Room E-018, Indianapolis, IN 46204, Main Telephone: 317-233-3984, Fax: 317-233-3387, Hours: 8AM-5:30PM. Access by: mail, fax, visit.

Sales Tax Registrations
Revenue Department, Taxpayer Services, Government Center, 100 N Senate Ave, Room N248, Indianapolis, IN 46204, Main Telephone: 317-233-4015, Fax: 317-232-2103, Hours: 8:15AM-4:45PM. Access by: mail, phone.

Birth Certificates
State Department of Health, Vital Records Office, PO Box 7125, Indianapolis, IN 46206-7125, Main Telephone: 317-383-6100, Automated ordering: 317-233-2700, Fax: 317-233-7210, Hours: 8:15AM-4:45PM. Access by: mail, phone, fax, visit.

Death Records
State Department of Health, Vital Records Office, PO Box 7125, Indianapolis, IN 46206-7125, Main Telephone: 317-383-6100, Message Phone: 317-633-6276, Fax: 317-233-7210, Hours: 8:15AM-4:45PM. Access by: mail, phone, fax, visit.

Marriage Certificates
State Department of Health, Vital Records Office, PO Box 7125, Indianapolis, IN 46206-7125, Main Telephone: 317-383-6100, Fax: 317-233-7210, Hours: 8:15AM-4:45PM. Access by: mail only. Marriage records are found at county of issue, but the above department will check their index to verify marriage. Index is from 1958 on. The state tells us that the index can also be found at the Indiana State Library.

Divorce Records
Records not available from state agency.

Workers' Compensation Records
Workers Compensation Board, 402 W Washington St, Room W196, Indianapolis, IN 46204-2753, Main Telephone: 317-232-3808, Hours: 8AM-4:30PM. Access by: mail only.

Driver Records
Bureau of Motor Vehicles, Driver Records, Indiana Government Center North, Room N405, Indianapolis, IN 46204, Main Telephone: 317-233-6000, Hours: 8:15AM-4:30PM. Access by: mail, visit, PC. Copies of tickets are available at the address listed above for a fee of $8.00 per ticket.

Vehicle Ownership
Vehicle Identification
Bureau of Motor Vehicles, Vehicle Records, 100 N Senate Ave, Room N404, Indianapolis, IN 46204, Main Telephone: 317-233-2513, Hours: 8:15AM-4:45PM. Access by: mail, visit, PC. Indiana law provides that all records of the department, unless opted out or declared confidential and except personal identifiers, are open for inspection and readily available to the public.

Accident Reports
State Police Department, Vehicle Crash Records Sections, Room N301, Indiana Government Center, Indianapolis, IN 46204, Main Telephone: 317-232-8286, Hours: 8AM-4PM. Access by: mail, phone, visit. The only reports released are those of the officers. Indiana operator report forms are not released.

Hunting License Information
Fishing License Information
Records not available from state agency.

County Courts and Recording Offices

What You Need to Know...

About the Courts

Administration

State Court Administrator   317-232-2542
323 State House
Indianapolis, IN 46204

Court Structure

Note that Small Claims in Marion County are heard at the **township** and records are maintained at that level. The phone number for the township offices are indicated in Marion County.

Searching Hints

The Circuit Court Clerk/County Clerk in every county is a common individual and is responsible for keeping **all** county judicial records. However, it is recommended that, when requesting a record, the request indicate which court heard the case (Circuit, Superior, or county).

Many courts are no longer performing searches, especially criminal searches, based on a 7/8/96 statement by the State Board of Accounts.

Certification and copy fees are set by statute as $1.00 per document plus copy fee for certification and $1.00 per page for copies.

Online Access

There is **no** online access computer system, internal or external, available, except for Indianapolis courts.

About the Recorder's Office

Organization

92 counties, 92 filing offices. The recording officer is County Recorder (Circuit Clerk for state tax liens on personal property). Many counties utilize a "Miscellaneous Index" for tax and other liens. 81 counties are in the Eastern Time Zone (EST), and 11 are in the Central Time Zone (CST).

UCC Records

Financing statements are filed at the state level except for consumer goods, farm related and real estate related filings. All counties will perform UCC searches. Use search request form UCC-11. Search fees are usually $1.00 per debtor name. Copies usually cost $.50 per page. Most counties also charge $.50 for each financing statement reported on a search.

Lien Records

All federal tax liens on personal property are filed with the **County Recorder**. State tax liens on personal property are filed with the **Circuit Clerk**, who is in a different office from the Recorder. Refer to *The Sourcebook of County Court Records* for information about Indiana Circuit Courts. Most counties will **not** perform tax lien searches. Other liens include judgments, mechanics, hospital, sewer, utility, and innkeeper.

Real Estate Records

Most counties will **not** perform real estate searches. Copies usually cost $1.00 per page, and certification usually costs $5.00 per document.

County Courts and Recording Offices

Adams County

Real Estate Recording—Adams County Recorder, Adams County Service Complex, 313 W. Jefferson, Room 240, Decatur, IN 46733. 219-724-2600. Fax: 219-724-2815. 8AM-4:30PM (EST).

Felony, Misdemeanor, Civil, Eviction, Small Claims, Probate—Circuit & Superior Court, 2nd St Courthouse, Decatur, IN 46733. 219-724-2600. Fax: 219-724-3848. 8AM-4:30PM (EST). Access by: In person only.

Allen County

Real Estate Recording—Allen County Recorder, 1 East Main Street, City County Building Room 206, Fort Wayne, IN 46802. 219-449-7165. 8AM-4:30PM (EST).

Felony, Misdemeanor, Civil, Eviction, Small Claims, Probate—Circuit & Superior Court, 715 S. Calhoun St. Rm 200 Courthouse, Ft Wayne, IN 46802. 219-449-7245. 8AM-4:30PM (EST). Access by: Mail, in person.

Bartholomew County

Real Estate Recording—Bartholomew County Recorder, 440 3rd Street, Suite 203, Columbus, IN 47201. 812-379-1520. 8AM-5PM (EST).

Felony, Misdemeanor, Civil, Eviction, Small Claims, Probate—Circuit & Superior Court, Box 924, Columbus, IN 47202-0924. 812-379-1600. Fax: 812-379-1675. 8AM-5PM (EST). Access by: Phone, fax, mail, in person.

Benton County

Real Estate Recording—Benton County Recorder, 706 East 5th Street, Suite 24, Fowler, IN 47944. 317-884-1630. Fax: 317-884-2013. 8:30AM-Noon, 1-4PM (EST).

Felony, Misdemeanor, Civil, Eviction, Small Claims, Probate—Circuit Court, 706 E 5th St, Suite 23, Fowler, IN 47944-1556. 317-884-0930. Fax: 317-884-2013. 8:30AM-4PM (EST). Access by: Phone, mail, in person.

Blackford County

Real Estate Recording—Blackford County Recorder, 110 West Washington Street, Courthouse, Hartford City, IN 47348. 317-348-2207. Fax: 317-348-7213. 8AM-4PM (EST).

Felony, Misdemeanor, Civil, Eviction, Small Claims, Probate—Circuit & County Court, 110 W Washington St, Hartford City, IN 47348. 317-348-1130. 8AM-4PM (EST). Access by: Mail, in person.

Boone County

Real Estate Recording—Boone County Recorder, 202 Courthouse Square, Lebanon, IN 46052. 317-482-3070. 8AM-4PM (EST).

Felony, Misdemeanor, Civil, Eviction, Small Claims, Probate—Circuit & Superior Court I & II, Rm 212, Courthouse Sq, Lebanon, IN 46052. 317-482-3510. 7AM-4PM (EST). Access by: Mail, in person.

Brown County

Real Estate Recording—Brown County Recorder, Corner of Gould St. & Locust Lane, County Office Bldg., Nashville, IN 47448. 812-988-5462. Fax: 812-988-5520. 8AM-4PM (EST).

Felony, Misdemeanor, Civil, Eviction, Small Claims, Probate—Circuit Court, Box 85, Nashville, IN 47448. 812-988-5510. Fax: 812-988-5562. 8AM-4PM (EST). Access by: Phone, fax, mail, in person.

Carroll County

Real Estate Recording—Carroll County Recorder, Court House, 101 West Main St,, Delphi, IN 46923. 317-564-2124. Fax: 317-564-2576. 8AM-5PM M,T,Th,F; 8AM-Noon W (EST).

Felony, Misdemeanor, Civil, Eviction, Small Claims, Probate—Circuit & Superior Court, Courthouse, 101 W Main, Delphi, IN 46923. 317-564-4485. Fax: 317-564-6907. 8AM-5PM M,T,Th,F; 8AM-Noon W (EST). Access by: Mail, in person.

Cass County

Real Estate Recording—Cass County Recorder, 200 Court Park, Logansport, IN 46947. 219-753-7810. 8AM-4PM; F 8AM-5PM (EST).

Felony, Misdemeanor, Civil, Eviction, Small Claims, Probate—Circuit & Superior Court, 200 Court Park, Logansport, IN 46947. 219-753-7870. 8AM-4PM (EST). Access by: Mail, in person.

Clark County

Real Estate Recording—Clark County Recorder, 501 East Court Avenue, Jeffersonville, IN 47130. 812-285-6236. 8AM-5PM (EST).

Felony, Misdemeanor, Civil, Eviction, Small Claims, Probate—Circuit, Superior, & County Court, 501 E Court, Jeffersonville, IN 47130. 812-285-6244. 8:30AM-4:30PM M-F, 8:30-Noon S (EST). Access by: Mail, in person.

Clay County

Real Estate Recording—Clay County Recorder, Courthouse, 609 E National Ave., Brazil, IN 47834. 812-448-9005. Fax: 812-442-0425. 8AM-4PM (EST).

Felony, Misdemeanor, Civil, Eviction, Small Claims, Probate—Circuit & Superior Court, Box 33, Brazil, IN 47834. 812-448-8727. 8AM-4PM (EST). Access by: Mail, in person.

Clinton County

Real Estate Recording—Clinton County Recorder, 270 Courthouse Square, Frankfort, IN 46041. 317-659-6320. Fax: 317-659-6391. 8AM-4PM M,T,W; 8AM-Noon Th; 8AM-6PM F (EST).

Felony, Misdemeanor, Civil, Eviction, Small Claims, Probate—Circuit & Superior Court, 265 Courthouse Square, Frankfort, IN 46041. 317-659-6335. 8AM-4PM M-W,8AM-Noon Th,8AM-6PM F (EST). Access by: Mail, in person.

Crawford County

Real Estate Recording—Crawford County Recorder, Courthouse, PO Box 214, English, IN 47118. 812-338-2615. Fax: 812-338-2507. 8AM-4PM M & F; 8AM-6PM T & Th; Closed W (EST).

Felony, Misdemeanor, Civil, Eviction, Small Claims, Probate—Circuit Court, Box 375, English, IN 47118. 812-338-2565. Fax: 812-338-2507. 8AM-4PM (EST). Access by: Fax, mail, in person.

Daviess County

Real Estate Recording—Daviess County Recorder, 200 East Walnut Street, Courthouse, Washington, IN 47501. 812-254-8675. Fax: 812-254-8697. 8AM-4PM (EST).

Felony, Misdemeanor, Civil, Eviction, Small Claims, Probate—Circuit & Superior Court, PO Box 739, Washington, IN 47501. 812-254-8664. Fax: 812-254-8698. 8AM-4PM (EST). Access by: Mail, in person.

DeKalb County

Real Estate Recording—DeKalb County Recorder, Courthouse, 1st Floor, 100 S. Main St., Auburn, IN 46706. 219-925-2112. Fax: 219-925-5126. 8:30AM-4:30PM (EST).

Felony, Misdemeanor, Civil, Eviction, Small Claims, Probate—Circuit & Superior Court, PO Box 230, Auburn, IN 46706. 219-925-0912. Fax: 219-925-5126. 8:30AM-4:30PM (EST). Access by: In person only.

Dearborn County

Real Estate Recording—Dearborn County Recorder, 215 B West High Street, Lawrenceburg, IN 47025. 812-537-1040. 8:30AM-4:30PM (EST).

Felony, Misdemeanor, Civil, Eviction, Small Claims, Probate—Circuit & County Court, Courthouse, Lawrenceburg, IN 47025. 812-537-8867. Fax: 812-537-4295. 8:30AM-4:30PM (EST). Access by: In person only.

Decatur County

Real Estate Recording—Decatur County Recorder, 150 Courthouse Square, Suite 2, Greensburg, IN 47240. 812-663-4681. Fax: 812-663-2242. 8AM-4PM (F open until 5PM) (EST).

Felony, Misdemeanor, Civil, Eviction, Small Claims, Probate—Circuit & Superior Court, 150 Courthouse Square, Ste 1, Greensburg, IN 47240. 812-663-8223. Fax: 812-663-7957. 8AM-4PM, 8AM-5PM F (EST). Access by: Mail, in person.

Delaware County

Real Estate Recording—Delaware County Recorder, 100 West Main Street, Room 209, Muncie, IN 47305. 317-747-7804. 8:30AM-4:30PM (EST).

Felony, Misdemeanor, Civil, Eviction, Small Claims, Probate—Circuit & Superior Court, Box 1089, Muncie, IN 47308. 317-747-7726. Fax: 317-747-7768. 8:30AM-4:30PM (EST). Access by: Phone, fax, mail, in person.

Dubois County

Real Estate Recording—Dubois County Recorder, Room 101, 1 Courthouse Square, Jasper, IN 47546. 812-481-7067. Fax: 812-481-7044. 8AM-4PM (EST).

Felony, Misdemeanor, Civil, Eviction, Small Claims, Probate—Circuit & Superior Court, 1 Courthouse Square, Jasper, IN 47546. 812-481-7070. Fax: 812-481-7044. 8AM-4PM (EST). Access by: In person only.

Elkhart County

Real Estate Recording—Elkhart County Recorder, 117 North 2nd Street, Room 205, Goshen, IN 46526. 219-535-6756. 8AM-4PM; F 8AM-5PM (EST).

Felony, Misdemeanor, Civil, Eviction, Small Claims, Probate—Circuit, Superior & County Court, Courthouse, 101 N. Main St, Goshen, IN 46526. 219-534-3541. Fax: 219-535-6471. 8AM-4PM M-Th, 8AM-5PM F (EST). Access by: In person only.

Fayette County

Real Estate Recording—Fayette County Recorder, 401 Central Avenue, Connersville, IN 47331. 317-825-3051. Fax: 317-827-4936. 8:30AM-4PM (8:30AM-5PM F) (EST).

Felony, Misdemeanor, Civil, Eviction, Small Claims, Probate—Circuit & Superior Court, Box 607, Connersville, IN 47331-0607. 317-825-1813. 8:30AM-4PM M-Th, 8:30AM-5PM F (EST). Access by: In person only.

Floyd County

Real Estate Recording—Floyd County Recorder, 311 West 1st Street, New Albany, IN 47150. 812-948-5430. 8AM-4PM (EST).

Felony, Misdemeanor, Civil, Eviction, Small Claims, Probate—Circuit, Superior, & County Court, Box 1056, City County Bldg, New Albany, IN 47150. 812-948-5414. Fax: 812-948-4711. 8AM-4PM (EST). Access by: Mail, in person.

Fountain County

Real Estate Recording—Fountain County Recorder, 301 4th Street, Covington, IN 47932. 317-793-2431. Fax: 317-793-5002. 8AM-4PM (EST).

Felony, Misdemeanor, Civil, Eviction, Small Claims, Probate—Circuit Court, Box 183, Covington, IN 47932. 317-793-2192. Fax: 317-793-5002. 8AM-4PM (EST). Access by: Mail, in person.

Franklin County

Real Estate Recording—Franklin County Recorder, 459 Main Street, Brookville, IN 47012. 765-647-5131. 8:30AM-4PM (EST).

Felony, Misdemeanor, Civil, Eviction, Small Claims, Probate—Circuit Court, 459 Main, Brookville, IN 47012. 317-647-5111. Fax: 317-647-3224. 8:30AM-4PM (EST). Access by: In person only.

Fulton County

Real Estate Recording—Fulton County Recorder, 815 Main Street, Rochester, IN 46975. 219-223-2914. 8AM-4PM (F 8AM-5PM) (EST).

Felony, Misdemeanor, Civil, Eviction, Small Claims, Probate—Circuit Court, 815 Main St, PO Box 524, Rochester, IN 46975. 219-223-2911. Fax: 219-223-8304. 8AM-4PM M-TH, 8AM-5PM F (EST). Access by: Mail, in person.

Gibson County

Real Estate Recording—Gibson County Recorder, 101 North Main, Courthouse, Princeton, IN 47670. 812-385-3332. 8AM-4PM (CST).

Felony, Misdemeanor, Civil, Eviction, Small Claims, Probate—Circuit & Superior Court, Courthouse, Princeton, IN 47670. 812-386-8401. Fax: 812-386-5025. 8AM-4PM (CST). Access by: In person only.

Grant County

Real Estate Recording—Grant County Recorder, 401 South Adams Street, Marion, IN 46953. 317-668-8871. 8AM-4PM (EST).

Felony, Misdemeanor, Civil, Eviction, Small Claims, Probate—Circuit & Superior Court, Courthouse 101 E 4th St, Marion, IN 46952. 317-668-8121. Fax: 317-668-6541. 8AM-4PM (EST). Access by: Fax, mail, in person.

Greene County

Real Estate Recording—Greene County Recorder, Courthouse, Room 109, Bloomfield, IN 47424. 812-384-2020. Fax: 812-384-2044. 8AM-4PM (EST).

Felony, Misdemeanor, Civil, Eviction, Small Claims, Probate—Circuit & Superior Court, PO Box 229, Bloomfield, IN 47424. 812-384-8532. Fax: 812-384-8458. 8AM-4PM (EST). Access by: In person only.

Hamilton County

Real Estate Recording—Hamilton County Recorder, Courthouse, 33 N. 9th St, Suite 309, Noblesville, IN 46060. 317-776-9688. 8AM-4:30PM (EST).

Felony, Misdemeanor, Civil, Eviction, Small Claims, Probate—Circuit & Superior Court, Hamilton Courthouse Square, Suite 106, Noblesville, IN 46060-2233. 317-776-9629. Fax: 317-776-9727. 8AM-4:30PM (EST). Access by: In person only.

Hancock County

Real Estate Recording—Hancock County Recorder, 9 East Main Street, Courthouse, Room 204, Greenfield, IN 46140. 317-462-1142. 8AM-4PM (EST).

Felony, Misdemeanor, Civil, Eviction, Small Claims, Probate—Circuit & Superior Court, 9 E Main St, Rm 201, Greenfield, IN 46140. 317-462-1109. 8AM-4PM (EST). Access by: Phone, mail, in person.

Harrison County

Real Estate Recording—Harrison County Recorder, 300 Capitol Avenue, Courthouse, Room 204, Corydon, IN 47112. 812-738-3788. Fax: 812-738-1153. 8AM-4PM M,T,Th,F; 8AM-Noon W & Sat (EST).

Felony, Misdemeanor, Civil, Eviction, Small Claims, Probate—Circuit & Superior Court, 300 N Capitol, Corydon, IN 47112. 812-738-4289. 8AM-4PM MT,ThF; 8AM-Noon W,S (EST). Access by: In person only.

Hendricks County

Real Estate Recording—Hendricks County Recorder, Courthouse, Danville, IN 46122. 317-745-9224. 8AM-4PM (EST).

Felony, Misdemeanor, Civil, Eviction, Small Claims, Probate—Circuit & Superior Court, PO Box 599, Danville, IN 46122. 317-745-9231. Fax: 317-745-9306. 8AM-4PM (EST). Access by: In person only.

Henry County

Real Estate Recording—Henry County Recorder, Courthouse, 216 S. 12th St., New Castle, IN 47362. 317-529-4304. Fax: 317-521-7017. 8AM-4PM (F 8AM-5PM) (EST).

Felony, Misdemeanor, Civil, Eviction, Small Claims, Probate—Circuit & Superior Court, PO Box B, New Castle, IN 47362. 317-529-6401. 8AM-4PM (EST). Access by: Mail, in person.

Howard County

Real Estate Recording—Howard County Recorder, Courthouse, Room 202, 117 N. Main St., Kokomo, IN 46901. 317-456-2210. Fax: 317-456-2259. 8AM-4PM (EST).

Felony, Misdemeanor, Civil, Eviction, Small Claims, Probate—Circuit & Superior Court, PO Box 9004, Kokomo, IN 46904. 317-456-2204. Fax: 317-456-2267. 8AM-4PM (EST). Access by: Mail, in person.

Huntington County

Real Estate Recording—Huntington County Recorder, 201 N. Jefferson St., Room 101, Huntington, IN 46750. 219-358-4848. Fax: 219-358-4823. 8AM-4:30PM (EST).

Felony, Misdemeanor, Civil, Eviction, Small Claims, Probate—Circuit & Superior Court, Courthouse, Rm 201, Huntington, IN 46750. 219-358-4817. 8AM-4:40PM (EST). Access by: In person only.

Jackson County

Real Estate Recording—Jackson County Recorder, 101 S. Main - Main Floor, Brownstown, IN 47220. 812-358-6113. 8AM-4PM (EST).

Felony, Misdemeanor, Civil, Eviction, Small Claims, Probate—Circuit & Superior Court, PO Box 122, Brownstown, IN 47220. 812-358-6116. 8AM-4PM (EST). Access by: Mail, in person.

Jasper County

Real Estate Recording—Jasper County Recorder, 115 W Washington, Rensselaer, IN 47978. 219-866-4923. Fax: 219-866-4940. 8AM-4PM (CST).

Felony, Misdemeanor, Civil, Probate—Superior Court I, 115 W Washington St, Rensselaer, IN 47978. 219-866-4913. 8AM-4PM (CST). Access by: Mail, in person.

Felony, Misdemeanor, Civil, Eviction, Small Claims, Probate—Superior Court II, 105 1/2 W Kellner Blvd, Rensselaer, IN 47978. 219-866-4913. 8AM-4PM (CST). Access by: Mail, in person.

Jay County

Real Estate Recording—Jay County Recorder, 120 West Main Street, Portland, IN 47371. 219-726-4572. 9AM-4PM (EST).

Felony, Misdemeanor, Civil, Eviction, Small Claims, Probate—Circuit & Superior Court, Courthouse, Portland, IN 47371. 219-726-4951. 8:30AM-4:30PM (EST). Access by: Mail, in person.

Jefferson County

Real Estate Recording—Jefferson County Recorder, Courthouse - Room 104, 300 E. Main St., Madison, IN 47250. 812-265-8903. 8AM-4PM (EST).

Felony, Misdemeanor, Civil, Eviction, Small Claims, Probate—Circuit & Superior Court, Courthouse 300E Main St, Madison, IN 47250. 812-265-8923. Fax: 812-265-8950. 8AM-4PM (EST). Access by: Mail, in person.

Jennings County

Real Estate Recording—Jennings County Recorder, Courthouse, Vernon, IN 47282. 812-346-3152. Fax: 812-346-4605. 8AM-4PM (EST).

Felony, Misdemeanor, Civil, Eviction, Small Claims, Probate—Circuit Court, Courthouse, Vernon, IN 47282. 812-346-5977. 8AM-4PM (EST). Access by: Mail, in person.

Johnson County

Real Estate Recording—Johnson County Recorder, 86 West Court Street, Franklin, IN 46131. 317-736-3718. Fax: 317-736-8066. 8AM-4:30PM (EST).

Felony, Misdemeanor, Civil, Eviction, Small Claims, Probate—Circuit & Superior Court, Courthouse, PO Box 368, Franklin, IN 46131. 317-736-3708. Fax: 317-736-3749. 8AM-4:30PM (EST). Access by: Phone, fax, mail, in person.

Knox County

Real Estate Recording—Knox County Recorder, Courthouse, Vincennes, IN 47591. 812-885-2508. Fax: 812-886-2414. 8AM-4PM (EST).

Felony, Misdemeanor, Civil, Eviction, Small Claims, Probate—Circuit & Superior Court, 101 N 7th St, Vincennes, IN 47591. 812-885-2521. 8AM-4PM (EST). Access by: Mail, in person.

Kosciusko County

Real Estate Recording—Kosciusko County Recorder, 100 West Center Street, Courthouse Room 14, Warsaw, IN 46580. 219-372-2360. 8AM-4PM (F open until 6PM) (EST).

Felony, Misdemeanor, Civil, Eviction, Small Claims, Probate—Circuit, Superior, & County Court, 121 N Lake, Warsaw, IN 46580. 219-272-2331. 8AM-4PM (EST). Access by: Mail, in person.

La Porte County

Real Estate Recording—La Porte County Recorder, 813 Lincolnway, La Porte, IN 46350. 219-326-6808. 8:30AM-5PM (Recording hours 8:30AM-4PM) (CST).

Felony, Misdemeanor, Civil, Eviction, Small Claims, Probate—Circuit & Superior Court, Lincolnway, La Porte, IN 46350. 219-326-6808. 8:30AM-5PM (CST). Access by: In person only.

LaGrange County

Real Estate Recording—LaGrange County Recorder, 114 West Michigan Street, County Office Building PO Box 214, LaGrange, IN 46761. 219-463-7807. 8AM-4PM M-Th; 8AM-5PM F (EST).

Felony, Misdemeanor, Civil, Eviction, Small Claims, Probate—Circuit & Superior Court, 105 N Detroit St, Courthouse, LaGrange, IN 46761. 219-463-3442. 8AM-4PM M-TH, 8AM-5PM F (EST). Access by: Phone, mail, in person.

Lake County

Real Estate Recording—Lake County Recorder, 2293 N Main Street, Crown Point, IN 46307. 219-755-3730. Fax: 219-755-3257. 8:30AM-4:30PM (CST).

Felony, Misdemeanor, Civil, Eviction, Small Claims, Probate—Circuit & Superior Court, 2293 N Main St, Courthouse, Crown Point, IN 46307. 219-755-3000. 8:30AM-4:20PM (CST). Access by: Mail, in person.

Lawrence County

Real Estate Recording—Lawrence County Recorder, Courthouse, Room 21, Bedford, IN 47421. 812-275-3245. Fax: 812-275-4138. 8:30AM-4:30PM (EST).

Felony, Misdemeanor, Civil, Eviction, Small Claims, Probate—Circuit, Superior, & County Court, 31 Courthouse, Bedford, IN 47421. 812-275-7543. Fax: 812-277-2024. 8:30AM-4:30PM (EST). Access by: In person only.

Madison County

Real Estate Recording—Madison County Recorder, 16 East 9th Street, Anderson, IN 46016. 765-641-9618. 8AM-4PM (EST).

Felony, Misdemeanor, Civil, Eviction, Small Claims, Probate—Circuit, Superior, & County Court, 16 E 9th, Box 5, Anderson, IN 46016. 317-641-9443. Fax: 317-640-4203. 8AM-4PM (EST). Access by: Mail, in person.

Marion County

Real Estate Recording—Marion County Recorder, 200 E. Washington, Suite 721, Indianapolis, IN 46204. 317-327-4020. Fax: 317-327-3942. 8AM-4:30PM (EST).

Felony, Misdemeanor, Civil, Eviction, Small Claims, Probate—Circuit & Superior Court, 200 E Washington St, Indianapolis, IN 46204. 317-327-4600. Civil: 317-327-4724. Criminal: 317-327-4733. 8AM-4:30PM (EST). Access by: Mail, in person, online.

Marshall County

Real Estate Recording—Marshall County Recorder, 112 West Jefferson Street, Room 201, Plymouth, IN 46563. 219-935-8515. 8AM-4PM (EST).

Felony, Misdemeanor, Civil, Eviction, Small Claims, Probate—Circuit & Superior Court, 211 W Madison St, Plymouth, IN 46563. 219-936-8922. Fax: 219-936-8893. 8AM-4PM M,W-F, 8AM-6PM T (EST). Access by: Mail, in person.

Martin County

Real Estate Recording—Martin County Recorder, Capital Street, Courthouse, Shoals, IN 47581. 812-247-2420. Fax: 812-247-2756. 8AM-4PM (EST).

Felony, Misdemeanor, Civil, Eviction, Small Claims, Probate—Circuit Court, PO Box 120, Shoals, IN 47581. 812-247-3651. Fax: 812-247-3901. 8AM-4PM (EST). Access by: Mail, in person.

Miami County

Real Estate Recording—Miami County Recorder, Courthouse, Peru, IN 46970. 317-472-3901. Fax: 317-472-2756. 8AM-4PM (EST).

Felony, Misdemeanor, Civil, Eviction, Small Claims, Probate—Circuit & Superior Court, PO Box 184, Peru, IN 46970. 317-472-3901. Fax: 317-472-1412. 8AM-4PM (EST). Access by: Fax, mail, in person.

Monroe County

Real Estate Recording—Monroe County Recorder, Courthouse, Room 122, Bloomington, IN 47404. 812-349-2520. 8AM-4PM (EST).

Felony, Misdemeanor, Civil, Eviction, Small Claims, Probate—Circuit Court, PO Box 547, Bloomington, IN 47402. 812-349-2600. 8AM-4PM (EST). Access by: Mail, in person.

Montgomery County

Real Estate Recording—Montgomery County Recorder, 100 East Main Street, Crawfordsville, IN 47933. 317-364-6415. Fax: 317-364-6404. 8AM-4PM (EST).

Felony, Misdemeanor, Civil, Eviction, Small Claims, Probate—Circuit, Superior, & County Court, PO Box 768, Crawfordsville, IN 47933. 317-364-6430. Fax: 317-364-6434. 8:30AM-4:30PM (EST). Access by: Phone, mail, in person.

Morgan County

Real Estate Recording—Morgan County Recorder, 180 S. Main, Suite 125, Martinsville, IN 46151. 317-342-1077. 8AM-4PM (8AM-5PM F) (EST).

Felony, Misdemeanor, Civil, Eviction, Small Claims, Probate—Circuit, Superior, & County Court, PO Box 1556, Martinsville, IN 46151. 317-342-1025. Fax: 317-342-1111. 8AM-4PM M-Th, 8AM-5PM F (EST). Access by: In person only.

Newton County

Real Estate Recording—Newton County Recorder, 201 N. 3rd St., Courthouse - Room 104, Kentland, IN 47951. 219-474-6081. 8AM-4PM (CST).

Felony, Misdemeanor, Civil, Eviction, Small Claims, Probate—Circuit & Superior Court, PO Box 49, Kentland, IN 47951. 219-474-6081. 8AM-4PM (CST). Access by: Mail, in person.

Noble County

Real Estate Recording—Noble County Recorder, 101 North Orange Street, Albion, IN 46701. 219-636-2672. Fax: 219-636-7877. 8AM-4PM (EST).

Felony, Misdemeanor, Civil, Eviction, Small Claims, Probate—Circuit, Superior, & County Court, 101 N Orange St, Albion, IN 46701. 219-636-2736. Fax: 219-636-3053. 8AM-4PM (EST). Access by: Fax, mail, in person.

Ohio County

Real Estate Recording—Ohio County Recorder, Main Street, Courthouse, Rising Sun, IN 47040. 812-438-3369. Fax: 812-438-4590. 9AM-4PM M,T,Th,F; 9AM-12 Sat; Closed W (EST).

Felony, Misdemeanor, Civil, Eviction, Small Claims, Probate—Circuit & Superior Court, PO Box 185, Rising Sun, IN 47040. 812-438-2610. Fax: 812-438-4590. 9AM-4PM M,T,Th,F 9AM-Noon S (EST). Access by: Phone, fax, mail, in person.

Orange County

Real Estate Recording—Orange County Recorder, 205 East Main Street, Courthouse, Paoli, IN 47454. 812-723-3600. 8AM-4PM (EST).

Felony, Misdemeanor, Civil, Eviction, Small Claims, Probate—Circuit & County Court, Courthouse, Court St, Paoli, IN 47454. 812-723-2649. 8AM-4PM (EST). Access by: Mail, in person.

Owen County

Real Estate Recording—Owen County Recorder, Courthouse, Spencer, IN 47460. 812-829-5014. Fax: 812-829-5034. 8AM-4PM (EST).

Felony, Misdemeanor, Civil, Eviction, Small Claims, Probate—Circuit Court, PO Box 146, Courthouse, Spencer, IN 47460. 812-829-5015. Fax: 812-829-5052. 8AM-4PM (EST). Access by: In person only.

Parke County

Real Estate Recording—Parke County Recorder, 116 W. High St., Room 102, Rockville, IN 47872. 317-569-3419. Fax: 317-569-4037. 8AM-4PM (EST).

Felony, Misdemeanor, Civil, Eviction, Small Claims, Probate—Circuit Court, 116 W High St, Rm 204, Rockville, IN 47872. 317-569-5132. 8AM-4PM (EST). Access by: In person only.

Perry County

Real Estate Recording—Perry County Recorder, 2219 Payne St., Room W2, Tell City, IN 47586. 812-547-4261. 8AM-4PM (EST).

Felony, Misdemeanor, Civil, Eviction, Small Claims, Probate—Circuit Court, 2219 Payne St, Courthouse, Tell City, IN 47586. 812-547-3741. 8AM-4PM (EST). Access by: Phone, mail, in person.

Pike County

Real Estate Recording—Pike County Recorder, Main Street, Courthouse, Petersburg, IN 47567. 812-354-6747. Fax: 812-354-3500. 8AM-4PM (EST).

Felony, Misdemeanor, Civil, Eviction, Small Claims, Probate—Circuit Court, 801 Main St. Courthouse, Petersburg, IN 47567-1298. 812-354-6025. Fax: 812-354-3552. 8AM-4PM (EST). Access by: Mail, in person.

Porter County

Real Estate Recording—Porter County Recorder, 155 Indiana Ave, Suite 210, Valparaiso, IN 46383. 219-465-3465. Fax: 219-465-3592. 8:30AM-4:30PM (CST).

Misdemeanor, Civil, Small Claims, Probate—Superior Court, 3560 Willow Creek Dr, Portage, IN 46368. 219-759-2501. (CST). Access by: Mail, in person.

Felony, Misdemeanor, Civil, Eviction, Small Claims, Probate—Circuit Court, Records Division, Courthouse Suite 217, 16 E Lincolnway, Valparaiso, IN 46383-5659.

219-465-3453. Fax: 219-465-3592. 8:30AM-4:30PM (CST). Access by: Mail, in person.

Posey County

Real Estate Recording—Posey County Recorder, Courthouse, Mount Vernon, IN 47620. 812-838-1314. Fax: 812-838-8563. 8AM-4PM (CST).

Felony, Misdemeanor, Civil, Eviction, Small Claims, Probate—Circuit & County Court, 300 Main St, Mount Vernon, IN 47620-1897. 812-838-1306. Fax: 812-838-1344. 8AM-4PM (CST). Access by: Mail, in person.

Pulaski County

Real Estate Recording—Pulaski County Recorder, Courthouse - Room 220, 112 E. Main St., Winamac, IN 46996. 219-946-3844. 8AM-4PM (EST).

Felony, Misdemeanor, Civil, Eviction, Small Claims, Probate—Circuit & Superior Court, Courthouse, Winamac, IN 46996. 219-946-3313. Fax: 219-946-4953. 8AM-4PM (EST). Access by: In person only.

Putnam County

Real Estate Recording—Putnam County Recorder, Courthouse Square, Room 25, Greencastle, IN 46135. 317-653-5613. 8AM-4PM (EST).

Felony, Misdemeanor, Civil, Eviction, Small Claims, Probate—Circuit & County Court, PO Box 546, Greencastle, IN 46135. 317-653-2648. 8AM-4PM (EST). Access by: In person only.

Randolph County

Real Estate Recording—Randolph County Recorder, Courthouse, Room 101, Winchester, IN 47394. 765-584-7300. 8AM-4PM (EST).

Felony, Misdemeanor, Civil, Eviction, Small Claims, Probate—Circuit & Superior Court, PO Box 230 Courthouse, Winchester, IN 47394-0230. 317-584-7070. Fax: 317-584-2958. 8AM-4PM (EST). Access by: Fax, mail, in person.

Ripley County

Real Estate Recording—Ripley County Recorder, Courthouse, 115 N. Main St., Versailles, IN 47042. 812-689-5808. 8AM-4PM (EST).

Felony, Misdemeanor, Civil, Eviction, Small Claims, Probate—Circuit Court, PO BOX 177, Versailles, IN 47042. 812-689-6115. 8AM-4PM (EST). Access by: Mail, in person.

Rush County

Real Estate Recording—Rush County Recorder, Courthouse, Room 8, Rushville, IN 46173. 317-932-2388. 8AM-4PM (EST).

Felony, Misdemeanor, Civil, Eviction, Small Claims, Probate—Circuit & County Court, PO Box 429, Rushville, IN 46173. 317-932-2086. Fax: 317-932-2357. 8AM-4PM (EST). Access by: In person only.

Scott County

Real Estate Recording—Scott County Recorder, 75 North 1st Street, Scottsburg, IN 47170. 812-752-8442. Fax: 812-752-7914. 8:30AM-4:30PM (EST).

Felony, Misdemeanor, Civil, Eviction, Small Claims, Probate—Circuit & Superior Court, 1 E. McClain Ave, Scottsburg, IN 47170. 812-752-8420. Fax: 812-752-5459. 8:30AM-4:30PM (EST). Access by: Mail, in person.

Shelby County

Real Estate Recording—Shelby County Recorder, 407 South Harrison, Courthouse, Shelbyville, IN 46176. 317-392-6370. Fax: 317-392-6393. 8AM-4PM (EST).

Felony, Misdemeanor, Civil, Eviction, Small Claims, Probate—Circuit & Superior Court, PO Box 198, Shelbyville, IN 46176. 317-392-6320. 8AM-4PM (EST). Access by: In person only.

Spencer County

Real Estate Recording—Spencer County Recorder, Courthouse, Rockport, IN 47635. 812-649-6013. Fax: 812-649-6005. 8AM-4PM (CST).

Felony, Misdemeanor, Civil, Eviction, Small Claims, Probate—Circuit Court, PO Box 12, Rockport, IN 47635. 812-649-6027. Fax: 812-649-6030. 8AM-4PM (CST). Access by: In person only.

St. Joseph County

Real Estate Recording—St. Joseph County Recorder, 227 West Jefferson, Room 321, South Bend, IN 46601. 219-235-9525. 8AM-4:30PM (EST).

Felony, Misdemeanor, Civil, Eviction, Small Claims, Probate—Circuit & Superior Court, 101 South Main St, South Bend, IN 46601. 219-235-9635. Fax: 219-235-9838. 8AM-4:30PM (EST). Access by: In person only.

Starke County

Real Estate Recording—Starke County Recorder, Courthouse, 53 E. Mound, Knox, IN 46534. 219-772-9110. Fax: 219-772-9119. 8:30AM-4PM (CST).

Felony, Misdemeanor, Civil, Eviction, Small Claims, Probate—Circuit Court, Courthouse, Knox, IN 46534. 219-772-9128. 8:30AM-4PM (CST). Access by: In person only.

Steuben County

Real Estate Recording—Steuben County Recorder, 317 S. Wayne St., Suite 2F, Angola, IN 46703. 219-668-1000. 8AM-4:30PM (EST).

Felony, Misdemeanor, Civil, Eviction, Small Claims, Probate—Circuit & Superior Court, Courthouse, 55 S. Public Square, Angola, IN 46703. 219-665-2361. 8AM-4:30PM (EST). Access by: In person only.

Sullivan County

Real Estate Recording—Sullivan County Recorder, Room 205, 100 Court House Square, Sullivan, IN 47882. 812-268-4844. Fax: 812-268-0521. 8AM-4PM (EST).

Felony, Misdemeanor, Civil, Eviction, Small Claims, Probate—Circuit & Superior Court, Courthouse, 3rd Fl, Sullivan, IN 47882. 812-268-4657. 8AM-4PM (EST). Access by: In person only.

Switzerland County

Real Estate Recording—Switzerland County Recorder, Courthouse, Vevay, IN 47043. 812-427-2544. 8AM-3:30PM (EST).

Felony, Misdemeanor, Civil, Eviction, Small Claims, Probate—Circuit & Superior Court, Courthouse, Vevay, IN 47043. 812-427-3175. Fax: 812-427-2017. 8:30-3:30PM M-W & F (EST). Access by: Mail, in person.

Tippecanoe County

Real Estate Recording—Tippecanoe County Recorder, 20 North 3rd Street, Lafayette, IN 47901. 765-423-9353. Fax: 765-423-9196. 8AM-4:30PM (EST).

Felony, Misdemeanor, Civil, Eviction, Small Claims, Probate—Circuit, Superior, & County Court, PO Box 1665, Lafayette, IN 47902. 317-423-9326. Fax: 317-423-9194. 8AM-4:30PM (EST). Access by: In person only.

Tipton County

Real Estate Recording—Tipton County Recorder, Courthouse, 101 E. Jefferson St., Tipton, IN 46072. 317-675-4614. (EST).

Felony, Misdemeanor, Civil, Eviction, Small Claims, Probate—Circuit Court, Tipton County Courthouse, Tipton, IN 46072. 317-675-2795. Fax: 317-675-7797. 8AM-4PM M-Th, 8AM-5PM F (EST). Access by: In person only.

Union County

Real Estate Recording—Union County Recorder, 26 West Union Street, Box 106, Liberty, IN 47353. 317-458-5434. 8AM-4PM (EST).

Felony, Misdemeanor, Civil, Eviction, Small Claims, Probate—Circuit Court, 26 W Union St, Liberty, IN 47353. 317-458-6121. Fax: 317-458-5263. 8AM-4PM (EST). Access by: Mail, in person.

Vanderburgh County

Real Estate Recording—Vanderburgh County Recorder, 231 City-County Admin. Building, 1 NW Martin Luther King, Jr. Blvd., Evansville, IN 47708. 812-435-5215. 8AM-4:30PM (CST).

Felony, Misdemeanor, Civil, Eviction, Small Claims, Probate—Circuit & Superior Court, PO Box 3356, Evansville, IN 47732-3356. 812-435-5160. Fax: 812-435-5849. 8AM-4:30PM (CST). Access by: In person only.

Vermillion County

Real Estate Recording—Vermillion County Recorder, Courthouse, Room 202, Newport, IN 47966. 317-492-5003. 8AM-4PM (EST).

Felony, Misdemeanor, Civil, Eviction, Small Claims, Probate—Circuit Court, PO Box 8, Newport, IN 47966. 317-492-3500. 8AM-4PM (EST). Access by: In person only.

Vigo County

Real Estate Recording—Vigo County Recorder, 201 Cherry Street, Terre Haute, IN 47807. 812-462-3301. 8AM-4PM (EST).

Felony, Misdemeanor, Civil, Eviction, Small Claims, Probate—Circuit, Superior, & County Court, 2nd Fl, Courthouse, PO Box 8449, Terre Haute, IN 47807-8449. 812-462-3211. Fax: 812-640-4203. 8AM-4PM (EST). Access by: In person only.

Wabash County

Real Estate Recording—Wabash County Recorder, Courthouse, One West Hill St., Wabash, IN 46992. 219-563-0661. 8AM-4PM (EST).

Felony, Misdemeanor, Civil, Eviction, Small Claims, Probate—Circuit & Superior Court, One West Hill St, Wabash, IN 46992. 219-563-0661. Fax: 219-563-3451. 8AM-4PM (EST). Access by: Fax, mail, in person.

Warren County

Real Estate Recording—Warren County Recorder, 125 N. Monroe, Courthouse - Suite 10, Williamsport, IN 47993. 317-762-3174. Fax: 317-762-7222. 8AM-4PM (EST).

Felony, Misdemeanor, Civil, Eviction, Small Claims, Probate—Circuit Court, Ste 11, 125 N Monroe, Williamsport, IN 47993. 317-762-3510. Fax: 317-762-7222. 8AM-4PM (EST). Access by: Fax, mail, in person.

Warrick County

Real Estate Recording—Warrick County Recorder, 107 W Locust St., Suite 204, Boonville, IN 47601. 812-897-6165. Fax: 812-897-6167. 8AM-4PM (CST).

Felony, Misdemeanor, Civil, Eviction, Small Claims, Probate—Circuit & Superior Court, 107 W Locust, Rm 201, Boonville, IN 47601. 812-897-6160. 8AM-4PM (CST). Access by: Phone, mail, in person.

Washington County

Real Estate Recording—Washington County Recorder, Courthouse, Salem, IN 47167. 812-883-4001. 8:30AM-4PM (F 8:30AM-6PM) (EST).

Felony, Misdemeanor, Civil, Eviction, Small Claims, Probate—Circuit & Superior Court, Courthouse, Salem, IN 47167. 812-883-1634. Fax: 812-883-1933. 8:30AM-4PM M-Th, 8:30AM-6PM F (EST). Access by: Phone, mail, in person.

Wayne County

Real Estate Recording—Wayne County Recorder, 401 East Main Street, County Administration Building, Richmond, IN 47374. 317-973-9235. Fax: 317-973-9321. 8:30AM-5PM M; 8:30AM-4:30 PM T-F (EST).

Felony, Misdemeanor, Civil, Eviction, Small Claims, Probate—Circuit & Superior Court, PO Box 1172, Richmond, IN 47375. 317-973-9200. Fax: 317-973-9250. (EST). Access by: Mail, in person.

Wells County

Real Estate Recording—Wells County Recorder, Courthouse - Suite 203, 102 W. Market St., Bluffton, IN 46714. 219-824-6507. 8AM-4:30PM (EST).

Felony, Misdemeanor, Civil, Eviction, Small Claims, Probate—Circuit & Superior Court, 102 West Market, Rm 201, Bluffton, IN 46714. 219-824-6479. 8AM-4:30PM (EST). Access by: In person only.

White County

Real Estate Recording—White County Recorder, Corner of Main & Broadway, Courthouse, Monticello, IN 47960. 219-583-5912. 8AM-4PM (EST).

Felony, Misdemeanor, Civil, Eviction, Small Claims, Probate—Circuit & Superior Court, PO Box 350, Monticello, IN 47960. 219-583-7032. 8AM-4PM (EST). Access by: In person only.

Whitley County

Real Estate Recording—Whitley County Recorder, Courthouse, 2nd Floor - Room 18, Columbia City, IN 46725. 219-248-3106. Fax: 219-248-3137. 8AM-4PM (8AM-6PM F) (EST).

Felony, Misdemeanor, Civil, Eviction, Small Claims, Probate—Circuit & Superior Court, 101 W Van Buren, Rm 10, Columbia City, IN 46725. 219-248-3102. Fax: 219-248-3137. 8AM-4PM (EST). Access by: In person only.

Federal Courts

US District Court
Northern District of Indiana

Fort Wayne Division, US District Court Room 1108, Federal Bldg, 1300 S Harrison St, Fort Wayne, IN 46802. 219-424-7360. Counties: Adams, Allen, Blackford, DeKalb, Grant, Huntington, Jay, Lagrange, Noble, Steuben, Wells, Whitley

Hammond Division, US District Court Room 101, 507 State St, Hammond, IN 46320. 219-937-5235. Counties: Lake, Porter

Lafayette Division, US District Court PO Box 1498, Lafayette, IN 47902. 765-742-0512. Counties: Benton, Carroll, Jasper, Newton, Tippecanoe, Warren, White

South Bend Division, US District Court Room 102, 204 S Main, South Bend, IN 46601. 219-246-8000. Counties: Cass, Elkhart, Fulton, Kosciusko, La Porte, Marshall, Miami, Pulaski, St. Joseph, Starke, Wabash

Southern District of Indiana

Evansville Division, US District Court 304 Federal Bldg, 101 NW Martin Luther King Blvd, Evansville, IN 47708. 812-465-6426. Counties: Daviess, Dubois, Gibson, Martin, Perry, Pike, Posey, Spencer, Vanderburgh, Warrick

Indianapolis Division, US District Court Clerk, Room 105, 46 E Ohio St, Indianapolis, IN 46204. 317-226-6670. Counties: Bartholomew, Boone, Brown, Clinton, Decatur, Delaware, Fayette, Fountain, Franklin, Hamilton, Hancock, Hendricks, Henry, Howard, Johnson, Madison, Marion, Monroe, Montgomery, Morgan, Randolph, Rush, Shelby, Tipton, Union, Wayne

New Albany Division, US District Court Room 210, 121 W Spring St, New Albany, IN 47150. 812-948-5238. Counties: Clark, Crawford, Dearborn, Floyd, Harrison, Jackson, Jefferson, Jennings, Lawrence, Ohio, Orange, Ripley, Scott, Switzerland, Washington

Terre Haute Division, US District Court 207 Federal Bldg, Terre Haute, IN 47808. 812-234-9484. Counties: Clay, Greene, Knox, Owen, Parke, Putnam, Sullivan, Vermillion, Vigo

US Bankruptcy Court

Northern District of Indiana

Fort Wayne Division, US Bankruptcy Court, PO Box 2547, Fort Wayne, IN 46801-2547. 219-420-5100. Voice Case Information System: 219-236-8814. Counties: Adams, Allen, Blackford, DeKalb, Grant, Huntington, Jay, Lagrange, Noble, Steuben, Wells, Whitley

Hammond Division at Gary, US Bankruptcy Court, 221 Federal Bldg, 610 Connecticut St, Gary, IN 46402-2595. 219-881-3335. Voice Case Information System: 219-236-8814. Counties: Lake, Porter

Hammond at Lafayette Division, US Bankruptcy Court, c/o Fort Wayne Division, 1300 S Harrison St, Fort Wayne, IN 46802. 219-420-5100. Voice Case Information System: 219-236-8814. Counties: Benton, Carroll, Jasper, Newton, Tippecanoe, Warren, White

South Bend Division, US Bankruptcy Court, Room 224, US Courthouse, PO Box 7003, South Bend, IN 46634-7003. 219-236-8247. Voice Case Information System: 219-236-8814. Counties: Cass, Elkhart, Fulton, Kosciusko, La Porte, Marshall, Miami, Pulaski, St. Joseph, Starke, Wabash

Southern District of Indiana

Evansville Division, US Bankruptcy Court, 352 Federal Building, 101 NW Martin Luther King Blvd, Evansville, IN 47708. 812-465-6440. Counties: Daviess, Dubois, Gibson, Martin, Perry, Pike, Posey, Spencer, Vanderburgh, Warrick

Indianapolis Division, US Bankruptcy Court, 123 US Courthouse, 46 E Ohio St, Indianapolis, IN 46204. 317-226-6710. Counties: Bartholomew, Boone, Brown, Clinton, Decatur, Delaware, Fayette, Fountain, Franklin, Hamilton, Hancock, Hendricks, Henry, Howard, Johnson, Madison, Marion, Monroe, Montgomery, Morgan, Randolph, Rush, Shelby, Tipton, Union, Wayne

New Albany Division, US Bankruptcy Court, 102 Federal Bldg, 121 W Spring St, New Albany, IN 47150. 812-948-5254. Counties: Clark, Crawford, Dearborn, Floyd, Harrison, Jackson, Jefferson, Jennings, Lawrence, Ohio, Orange, Ripley, Scott, Switzerland, Washington

Terre Haute Division, US Bankruptcy Court, 207 Federal Bldg, 30 N 7th St, Terre Haute, IN 47808. 812-238-1550. Counties: Clay, Greene, Knox, Owen, Parke, Putnam, Sullivan, Vermillion, Vigo

Iowa

Capitol: Des Moines (Polk County)	
Number of Counties: 99	**Population:** 2,841,764
County Court Locations:	**Federal Court Locations:**
•District Courts: 100/8 Districts	•District Courts: 7
	•Bankruptcy Courts: 2
	State Agencies: 19

State Agencies—Summary

General Help Numbers:

State Archives

State Historical Society of Iowa	515-281-6200
Library/Archives	Fax: 515-282-0502
600 E. Locust, Capitol Complex	9AM-4:30PM TU-SA
Des Moines, IA 50319	
Iowa City Main Number:	319-335-3916

Governor's Office

Office of the Governor	515-281-5211
State Capitol Bldg	Fax: 515-281-6611
Des Moines, IA 50319	8AM-4PM

Attorney General's Office

Attorney General's Office	515-281-5164
Hoover Bldg, 2nd Floor	Fax: 515-281-4209
Des Moines, IA 50319	8AM-4:30PM
Alternate Telephone:	515-281-8373

State Legislation

Iowa General Assembly	515-281-5129
Legislative Information Office	8AM-4:30PM
State Capitol	
Des Moines, IA 50319	

Important State Internet Sites:

> **Webscape**
> File   Edit   View   Help

State of Iowa World Wide Web

www.state.ia.us/

Provided at this state site is access to the Governor's welcome, business, tourism, education, government jobs, Iowa profiles and other Iowa Internet links.

Iowa State Government

www.state.ia.us/government/index.html

Access to all branches of state and local government can be found at this site, along with two different search engines. One engine is alphabetical while the other is by function.

State Library of Iowa

www.silo.lib.ia.us/

This is a very thorough library site. It includes a catalog of services, Iowa libraries online, ask a librarian and a site index.

Unclaimed Property

www.state.ia.us/government/treasurer

This site includes the telephone numbers to call in order to begin your search for unclaimed property.

Legislation

www2.legis.state.ia.us/Legislation.html

You can track all current bills and amendments at this site. A legislative search engine is also located here.

State Agencies—Public Records

Criminal Records

Division of Criminal Investigations, Bureau of Identification, Wallace State Office Bldg, Des Moines, IA 50319, Main Telephone: 515-281-5138, Alternate Telephone: 515-281-7996, Fax: 515-281-7991, Hours: 8AM-4:30PM. Access by: mail, fax, visit. Iowa law requires employers to pay the fee for potential employees' record checks.

Corporation Records
Limited Liability Company Records
Fictitious Name
Limited Partnership Records
Assumed Name
Trademarks/Servicemarks

Secretary of State, Corporation Division, 2nd Floor, Hoover Bldg, Des Moines, IA 50319, Main Telephone: 515-281-5204, Fax: 515-242-5953, Hours: 8AM-4:30PM. Access by: mail, phone, fax, visit, PC.

Uniform Commercial Code
Federal Tax Liens
State Tax Liens

UCC Division, Secretary of State, Hoover Bldg, East 14th & Walnut, Des Moines, IA 50319, Main Telephone: 515-281-5204, Fax: 515-242-6556, Hours: 8AM-4:30PM. Access by: mail, phone, visit, fax, PC.

Sales Tax Registrations

Revenue & Finance Department, Taxpayer Services Division, Hoover Bldg, Des Moines, IA 50319-0457, Main Telephone: 515-281-3114, Fax: 515-242-6040, Hours: 8AM-4PM. Access by: mail, phone, fax, visit.

Birth Certificates

Iowa Department of Public Health, Bureau of Vital Records, 321 E 12th St, 4th Floor, Lucas Bldg, Des Moines, IA 50319-0075, Main Telephone: 515-281-4944, Message Recording: 515-281-5871, Hours: 8AM-4:15PM. Access by: mail, visit. All vital records are open for inspection at the county level, usually for a $10.00 fee.

Death Records

Iowa Department of Public Health, Vital Records, 321 E 12th St, 4th Floor, Lucas Bldg, Des Moines, IA 50319-0075, Main Telephone: 515-281-4944, Message Recording: 515-281-5871, Hours: 8AM-4:15PM. Access by: mail, visit.

Marriage Certificates

Iowa Department of Public Health, Vital Records, 321 E 12th St, 4th Floor, Lucas Bldg, Des Moines, IA 50319-0075, Main Telephone: 515-281-4944, Message Recording: 515-281-5871, Hours: 8AM-4:15PM. Access by: mail, visit.

Divorce Records

Records not available from state agency.

Workers' Compensation Records

Iowa Work Force Development, Division of Industrial Services, 1000 E Grand Ave, Des Moines, IA 50319, Main Telephone: 515-281-5934, Fax: 515-281-6501, Hours: 8AM-4:30PM. Access by: mail, phone, fax, visit. Regular, ongoing requesters may apply for charge accounts.

Driver Records

Department of Transportation, Driver Service Records Section, PO Box 9204, Des Moines, IA 50306-9204, Main Telephone: 515-244-9124, Fax: 515-237-3152, Hours: 8AM-4:30PM. Access by: mail, visit. Copies of tickets can be requested from the same address as listed above at $.50 per copy.

Vehicle Ownership
Vehicle Identification

Department of Transportation, Office of Vehicle Services, PO Box 9278, Des Moines, IA 50306-9278, Main Telephone: 515-237-3148, Alternate Telephone: 515-237-3049, Fax: 515-237-3118, Hours: 8AM-4:30PM. Access by: mail, phone, fax, visit. Vehicle lien information is not maintained by this department.

Accident Reports

Department of Transportation, Office of Driver Services, Park Fair Mall, 100 Euclid, Des Moines, IA 50313, Main Telephone: 515-237-3070, Fax: 515-237-3152, Hours: 8AM-4:30PM. Access by: mail, visit.

Hunting License Information
Fishing License Information

Department of Natural Resources, Wallace Building, E 9th & Grand Ave, 4th Floor, Des Moines, IA 50319-0034, Main Telephone: 515-281-8145, Hours: 8AM-4:30PM. Access by: mail, phone, visit.

County Courts and Recording Offices

What You Need to Know...

About the Courts

About the Recorder's Office

Administration

State Court Administrator	515-281-5241
State Capitol	Fax: 515-242-6164
Des Moines, IA 50319	

Court Structure

The Small Claims limit is increased $4000.

Beginning July 1997, court records are being moved to the County Recorder's office in each county. There is no scheduled completion date for this conversion

Searching Hints

In most courts, the Certification Fee is $10.00 plus copy fee, and the copy fee is $.50 per page. Many courts do **not** do searches and recommend either in person searches or use of a retriever.

Courts which accept written search requests **do require** an SASE. Credit cards are **not** accepted statewide.

Online Access

There is a statewide on-line computer system called the Iowa Court Information System (**ICIS**), which is for internal use **only**. There is **no** public access system.

Organization

99 counties, 100 filing offices. The recording officer is County Recorder. Many counties utilize a grantor/grantee index containing all transactions recorded with them. **Lee County has two filing offices.** The entire state is in the Central Time Zone (CST).

UCC Records

Financing statements are filed at the state level, except for consumer goods and real estate related filings. All counties will perform UCC searches. Use search request form UCC-11. Search fees are usually $5.00 per debtor name ($6.00 if the standard UCC-11 form is **not** used). Copies usually cost $1.00 per page.

Lien Records

Federal tax liens on personal property of businesses are filed with the Secretary of State. Other federal and all state tax liens on personal property are filed with the County Recorder. County search practices vary widely, but most provide some sort of tax lien search for $6.00 per name. Other liens include home improvement, and job service

Real Estate Records

Most counties are hesitant to perform real estate searches, but some will provide a listing from the grantor/grantee index with the understanding that it is **not** certified in the sense that a title search is. Certification of copies usually costs $2.00 per document.

County Courts and Recording Offices

Adair County

Real Estate Recording—Adair County Recorder, Courthouse, 400 Public Square, Greenfield, IA 50849. 515-743-2411. Fax: 515-743-2565. 8AM-4:30PM (CST).

Felony, Misdemeanor, Civil, Eviction, Small Claims, Probate—5th District Court, PO Box L, Greenfield, IA 50849. 515-743-2445. Fax: 515-743-2974. 8AM-4:30PM (CST). Access by: In person only.

Adams County

Real Estate Recording—Adams County Recorder, 500 9th St., Corning, IA 50841. 515-322-3744. Fax: 515-322-3744. 8:30AM-4:30PM (CST).

Felony, Misdemeanor, Civil, Eviction, Small Claims, Probate—5th District Court, Courthouse, PO Box 484, Corning, IA 50841. 515-322-4711. Fax: 515-322-4523. 8AM-4:30PM (CST). Access by: Mail, in person.

Allamakee County

Real Estate Recording—Allamakee County Recorder, 110 Allamakee Street, Courthouse, Waukon, IA 52172. 319-568-2364. Fax: 319-568-4720. 8AM-4PM (CST).

Felony, Misdemeanor, Civil, Eviction, Small Claims, Probate—1st District Court, PO Box 248, Waukon, IA 52172. 319-568-6351. 8AM-4:30PM (CST). Access by: In person only.

Appanoose County

Real Estate Recording—Appanoose County Recorder, Courthouse, Centerville, IA 52544. 515-856-6103. Fax: 515-437-4850. (CST).

Felony, Misdemeanor, Civil, Eviction, Small Claims, Probate—8th District Court, PO Box 400, Centerville, IA 52544. 515-856-6101. Fax: 515-856-2282. 8AM-4:30PM (CST). Access by: In person only.

Audubon County

Real Estate Recording—Audubon County Recorder of Deeds, 318 Leroy St. #7, Audubon, IA 50025. 712-563-2119. Fax: 712-563-3730. 8AM-4:30PM (CST).

Felony, Misdemeanor, Civil, Eviction, Small Claims, Probate—4th District Court, 318 Leroy St #6, Audubon, IA 50025. 712-563-4275. Fax: 712-563-4276. 8AM-4:30PM (CST). Access by: Mail, in person.

Benton County

Real Estate Recording—Benton County Recorder, Courthouse, Vinton, IA 52349. 319-472-3309. 8AM-4:30PM (CST).

Felony, Misdemeanor, Civil, Eviction, Small Claims, Probate—6th District Court, PO Box 719, Vinton, IA 52349. 319-472-2766. 8AM-4:30PM (CST). Access by: In person only.

Black Hawk County

Real Estate Recording—Black Hawk County Recorder, 316 East 5th Street, Courthouse, Room 208, Waterloo, IA 50703. 319-291-2472. Fax: 319-291-2635. 8AM-5PM (CST).

Felony, Misdemeanor, Civil, Eviction, Small Claims, Probate—1st District Court, 316 E 5th St, Waterloo, IA 50703. 319-291-2612. 8AM-4:30PM (CST). Access by: In person only.

Boone County

Real Estate Recording—Boone County Recorder, 201 State Street, Boone, IA 50036. 515-433-0514. Fax: 515-432-8102. 8AM-4:30PM (CST).

Felony, Misdemeanor, Civil, Eviction, Small Claims, Probate—2nd District Court, 201 State St, Boone, IA 50036. 515-433-0561. 8AM-4:30PM (CST). Access by: In person only.

Bremer County

Real Estate Recording—Bremer County Recorder, Courthouse, 415 E. Bremer Ave., Waverly, IA 50677. 319-352-0401. Fax: 319-352-0518. 8AM-4:30PM (CST).

Felony, Misdemeanor, Civil, Eviction, Small Claims, Probate—2nd District Court, PO Box 328, Waverly, IA 50677. 319-352-5661. Fax: 319-352-0290. 8AM-4:30PM (CST). Access by: In person only.

Buchanan County

Real Estate Recording—Buchanan County Recorder, 210 5th Avenue NE, Independence, IA 50644. 319-334-4259. Fax: 319-334-7453. 8AM-4:30PM (CST).

Felony, Misdemeanor, Civil, Eviction, Small Claims, Probate—1st District Court, PO Box 259, Independence, IA 50644. 319-334-2196. Fax: 319-334-7455. 8AM-4:30PM (CST). Access by: Phone, mail, in person.

Buena Vista County

Real Estate Recording—Buena Vista County Recorder, Courthouse Square, Storm Lake, IA 50588. 712-749-2539. Fax: 712-749-2544. 8AM-4:30PM (CST).

Felony, Misdemeanor, Civil, Eviction, Small Claims, Probate—3rd District Court, PO Box 1186, Storm Lake, IA 50588. 712-749-2546. Fax: 712-749-2700. 8AM-4:30PM (CST). Access by: In person only.

Butler County

Real Estate Recording—Butler County Recorder, 428 6th Street, Allison, IA 50602. 319-267-2735. Fax: 319-267-2628. 8AM-4PM (CST).

Felony, Misdemeanor, Civil, Eviction, Small Claims, Probate—2nd District Court, PO Box 307, Allison, IA 50602. 319-267-2487. Fax: 319-267-2487. 8AM-4:30PM (CST). Access by: In person only.

Calhoun County

Real Estate Recording—Calhoun County Recorder, Courthouse, Rockwell City, IA 50579. 712-297-8121. 8:30AM-4:30PM (CST).

Felony, Misdemeanor, Civil, Eviction, Small Claims, Probate—2nd District Court, Box 273, Rockwell City, IA 50579. 712-297-8122. Fax: 712-297-8101. 8AM-4:30PM (CST). Access by: In person only.

Carroll County

Real Estate Recording—Carroll County Recorder of Deeds, 6th & Main, Courthouse, Carroll, IA 51401. 712-792-3328. Fax: 712-792-9493. 8AM-4:30PM (CST).

Felony, Misdemeanor, Civil, Eviction, Small Claims, Probate—2nd District Court, PO Box 867, Carroll, IA 51401. 712-792-4327. Fax: 712-792-4328. 8AM-4:30PM (CST). Access by: In person only.

Cass County

Real Estate Recording—Cass County Recorder, 5 West 7th, Atlantic, IA 50022. 712-243-1692. Fax: 712-243-5503. 8AM-4:30PM (CST).

Felony, Misdemeanor, Civil, Eviction, Small Claims, Probate—4th District Court, 5 W 7th St, Courthouse, Atlantic, IA 50022. 712-243-2105. 8AM-4:30PM (CST). Access by: In person only.

Cedar County

Real Estate Recording—Cedar County Recorder, 400 Cedar Street, Courthouse, Tipton, IA 52772. 319-886-2230. Fax: 319-886-2095. 8AM-4PM (CST).

Felony, Misdemeanor, Civil, Eviction, Small Claims, Probate—7th District Court, PO Box 111, Tipton, IA 52772. 319-886-2101. 8AM-4:30PM (CST). Access by: Mail, in person.

Cerro Gordo County

Real Estate Recording—Cerro Gordo County Recorder of Deeds, 220 North Washington, Mason City, IA 50401. 515-421-3056. Fax: 515-421-3138. 8AM-4:30PM (CST).

Felony, Misdemeanor, Civil, Eviction, Small Claims, Probate—2nd District Court, 220 W Washington, Mason City, IA 50401. 515-424-6431. 8AM-4:30PM (CST). Access by: In person only.

Cherokee County

Real Estate Recording—Cherokee County Recorder of Deeds, 520 West Main, Cherokee, IA 51012. 712-225-6735. Fax: 712-225-3228. 8AM-4:30PM (CST).

Felony, Misdemeanor, Civil, Eviction, Small Claims, Probate—3rd District Court, Courthouse Drawer F, Cherokee, IA 51012. 712-225-6744. 8AM-4:30PM (CST). Access by: In person only.

Chickasaw County

Real Estate Recording—Chickasaw County Recorder, Courthouse, 8 E. Prospect, New Hampton, IA 50659. 515-394-2336. 8:30AM-4:30PM (CST).

Felony, Misdemeanor, Civil, Eviction, Small Claims, Probate—1st District Court, County Courthouse, New Hampton, IA 50659. 515-394-2106. Fax: 515-394-5106. 8AM-4:30PM (CST). Access by: In person only.

Clarke County

Real Estate Recording—Clarke County Recorder, Courthouse, Osceola, IA 50213. 515-342-3313. Fax: 515-342-3893. 8:30AM-4:30PM (CST).

Felony, Misdemeanor, Civil, Eviction, Small Claims, Probate—5th District Court, Clarke County Courthouse, Osceola, IA 50213. 515-342-6096. Fax: 515-342-2463. 8AM-4:30PM (CST). Access by: Mail, in person.

Clay County

Real Estate Recording—Clay County Recorder of Deeds, Administration Building, 300 W. 4th St, #3, Spencer, IA 51301. 712-262-1081. Fax: 712-262-5793. 8AM-4:30PM (CST).

Felony, Misdemeanor, Civil, Eviction, Small Claims, Probate—3rd District Court, Courthouse 215 W 4th St, Spencer, IA 51301. 712-262-4335. 8AM-4:30PM (CST). Access by: In person only.

Clayton County

Real Estate Recording—Clayton County Recorder, High Street, Elkader, IA 52043. 319-245-2710. Fax: 319-245-2353. 8AM-4:30PM (CST).

Felony, Misdemeanor, Civil, Eviction, Small Claims, Probate—1st District Court, PO Box 418, Clayton County Courthouse, Elkader, IA 52043. 319-245-2204. Fax: 319-245-2825. 8AM-4:30PM (CST). Access by: In person only.

Clinton County

Real Estate Recording—Clinton County Recorder of Deeds, Courthouse, 614 N. 2nd St., Clinton, IA 52732. 319-243-6210. 8AM-4:30PM (CST).

Felony, Misdemeanor, Civil, Eviction, Small Claims, Probate—7th District Court, Courthouse (PO Box 2957), Clinton, IA 52733. 319-243-6210. Fax: 319-243-3655. 8AM-4:30PM (CST). Access by: In person only.

Crawford County

Real Estate Recording—Crawford County Recorder, 12th & Broadway, Denison, IA 51442. 712-263-3643. Fax: 712-263-8382. 8AM-4:30PM (CST).

Felony, Misdemeanor, Civil, Eviction, Small Claims, Probate—3rd District Court, PO Box 546, Denison, IA 51442. 712-263-2242. Fax: 712-263-5753. 8AM-4:30PM (CST). Access by: In person only.

Dallas County

Real Estate Recording—Dallas County Recorder, 801 Court Street, Room 203, Adel, IA 50003. 515-993-5804. Fax: 515-933-5790. 8AM-4:30PM (CST).

Felony, Misdemeanor, Civil, Eviction, Small Claims, Probate—5th District Court, 801 Court St, Adel, IA 50003. 515-993-5816. Fax: 515-993-4752. 8AM-4:30PM (CST). Access by: In person only.

Davis County

Real Estate Recording—Davis County Recorder, Courthouse, Bloomfield, IA 52537. 515-664-2321. Fax: 515-664-3317. 8AM-4PM (CST).

Felony, Misdemeanor, Civil, Eviction, Small Claims, Probate—8th District Court, Davis County Courthouse, Bloomfield, IA 52537. 515-664-2011. Fax: 515-664-2041. 8AM-4:30PM (CST). Access by: In person only.

Decatur County

Real Estate Recording—Decatur County Recorder, 207 North Main Street, Leon, IA 50144. 515-446-4322. Fax: 515-446-4322. 8AM-4:30PM (CST).

Felony, Misdemeanor, Civil, Eviction, Small Claims, Probate—5th District Court, 207 N Main St, Leon, IA 50144. 515-446-4331. Fax: 515-446-7159. 8AM-4:30PM (CST). Access by: Phone, fax, mail, in person.

Delaware County

Real Estate Recording—Delaware County Recorder, Courthouse, 301 East Main, Manchester, IA 52057. 319-927-4665. Fax: 319-927-6423. 8AM-4:30PM (CST).

Felony, Misdemeanor, Civil, Eviction, Small Claims, Probate—1st District Court, PO Box 527, Manchester, IA 52057. 319-927-4942. Fax: 319-927-3074. 8AM-4:30PM (CST). Access by: In person only.

Des Moines County

Real Estate Recording—Des Moines County Recorder, 513 North Main Street, Burlington, IA 52601. 319-753-8221. Fax: 319-753-8721. 8AM-4:30PM (CST).

Felony, Misdemeanor, Civil, Eviction, Small Claims, Probate—8th District Court, PO Box 158, Burlington, IA 52601. 319-753-8262. Fax: 319-753-8253. 8AM-3:30PM (CST). Access by: In person only.

Dickinson County

Real Estate Recording—Dickinson County Recorder, Corner of Hill and 18th Streets, Courthouse, Spirit Lake, IA 51360. 712-336-1495. Fax: 712-336-2677. 8AM-4:30PM (CST).

Felony, Misdemeanor, Civil, Eviction, Small Claims, Probate—3rd District Court, PO Drawer O N, Spirit Lake, IA 51360. 712-336-1138. Fax: 712-336-4005. 8AM-4:30PM (CST). Access by: In person only.

Dubuque County

Real Estate Recording—Dubuque County Recorder, 7th & Central, Courthouse, Dubuque, IA 52001. 319-589-4434. Fax: 319-589-4484. 8:30AM-5PM (CST).

Felony, Misdemeanor, Civil, Eviction, Small Claims, Probate—1st District Court, 720 Central, Dubuque, IA 52001. 319-589-4418. 8AM-4:30PM (CST). Access by: In person only.

Emmet County

Real Estate Recording—Emmet County Recorder, 609 1st Avenue North, Estherville, IA 51334. 712-362-4115. Fax: 712-362-7454. 8AM-4:30PM (CST).

Felony, Misdemeanor, Civil, Eviction, Small Claims, Probate—3rd District Court, Emmet County, Estherville, IA 51334. 712-362-3325. 8AM-4:30PM (CST). Access by: In person only.

Fayette County

Real Estate Recording—Fayette County Recorder, Courthouse, 114 N. Vine St., West Union, IA 52175. 319-422-3687. Fax: 319-422-9201. 8AM-4:30PM (CST).

Felony, Misdemeanor, Civil, Eviction, Small Claims, Probate—Fayette County District Court, PO Box 458, West Union, IA 52175. 319-422-6061. 8AM-4:30PM (CST). Access by: Mail, in person.

Floyd County

Real Estate Recording—Floyd County Recorder, Courthouse, 101 S. Main, Charles City, IA 50616. 515-257-6154. Fax: 515-228-6458. 8AM-4:30PM (CST).

Felony, Misdemeanor, Civil, Eviction, Small Claims, Probate—2nd District Court, 101 S Main St, Charles City, IA 50616. 515-257-6122. Fax: 515-257-6125. 8AM-4:30PM (CST). Access by: In person only.

Franklin County

Real Estate Recording—Franklin County Recorder, Courthouse, Hampton, IA 50441. 515-456-5675. Fax: 515-456-5748. 8AM-4PM (CST).

Felony, Misdemeanor, Civil, Eviction, Small Claims, Probate—2nd District Court, PO Box 28, Hampton, IA 50441. 515-456-5626. Fax: 515-456-5628. 8AM-4:30PM (CST). Access by: In person only.

Fremont County

Real Estate Recording—Fremont County Recorder, Courthouse, Sidney, IA 51652. 712-374-2315. Fax: 712-374-2826. 8AM-4:30PM (CST).

Felony, Misdemeanor, Civil, Eviction, Small Claims, Probate—4th District Court, PO Box 549, Sidney, IA 51652. 712-374-2232. Fax: 712-374-3330. 8AM-4:30PM (CST). Access by: Mail, in person.

Greene County

Real Estate Recording—Greene County Recorder, Courthouse, 114 N. Chestnut, Jefferson, IA 50129. 515-386-3716. Fax: 515-386-2216. 8AM-4:30PM (CST).

Felony, Misdemeanor, Civil, Eviction, Small Claims, Probate—2nd District Court, Greene County Courthouse, 114 N Chestnut, Jefferson, IA 50129. 515-386-2516. 8AM-4:30PM (CST). Access by: In person only.

Grundy County

Real Estate Recording—Grundy County Recorder, 706 G Avenue, Grundy Center, IA 50638. 319-824-3234. 8AM-4:30PM (CST).

Felony, Misdemeanor, Civil, Eviction, Small Claims, Probate—1st District Court, Grundy County Courthouse, 706 Gave, Grundy Center, IA 50638. 319-824-5229. Fax: 319-824-3447. 8AM-4:30PM (CST). Access by: In person only.

Guthrie County

Real Estate Recording—Guthrie County Recorder, 200 North 5th, Courthouse, Guthrie Center, IA 50115. 515-747-3412. (CST).

Felony, Misdemeanor, Civil, Eviction, Small Claims, Probate—5th District Court, Courthouse, Guthrie Center, IA 50115. 515-747-3415. 8AM-4:30PM (CST). Access by: In person only.

Hamilton County

Real Estate Recording—Hamilton County Recorder, 2300 Superior Street, Webster City, IA 50595. 515-832-9535. Fax: 515-833-9525. 8AM-4PM (CST).

Felony, Misdemeanor, Civil, Eviction, Small Claims, Probate—2nd District Court, Courthouse PO Box 845, Webster City, IA 50595. 515-832-9600. 8AM-4:30PM (CST). Access by: In person only.

Hancock County

Real Estate Recording—Hancock County Recorder, 855 State Street, Garner, IA 50438. 515-923-2464. Fax: 515-923-3912. 8AM-4PM (CST).

Felony, Misdemeanor, Civil, Eviction, Small Claims, Probate—2nd District Court, 855 State St, Garner, IA 50438. 515-923-2532. Fax: 515-923-3521. 8AM-4:30PM (CST). Access by: In person only.

Hardin County

Real Estate Recording—Hardin County Recorder, Courthouse, 1215 Edgington Ave., Eldora, IA 50627. 515-858-3461. Fax: 515-858-3468. 8AM-4:30PM (CST).

Felony, Misdemeanor, Civil, Eviction, Small Claims, Probate—2nd District Court, Courthouse, PO Box 495, Eldora, IA 50627. 515-858-2328. Fax: 515-858-2320. 8AM-4:30PM (CST). Access by: In person only.

Harrison County

Real Estate Recording—Harrison County Recorder, Courthouse, Logan, IA 51546. 712-644-2545. Fax: 712-644-2643. 8AM-4:30PM (CST).

Felony, Misdemeanor, Civil, Eviction, Small Claims, Probate—District Court, Court House, Logan, IA 51546. 712-644-2665. 8AM-4:30PM (CST). Access by: In person only.

Henry County

Real Estate Recording—Henry County Recorder, Washington and Main Streets, Courthouse, Mount Pleasant, IA 52641. 319-385-0765. Fax: 319-385-0778. 8AM-4:30PM (CST).

Felony, Misdemeanor, Civil, Eviction, Small Claims, Probate—8th District Court, PO Box 176, Mount Pleasant, IA 52641. 319-385-2632. Fax: 319-385-4144. 8AM-4:30PM (CST). Access by: In person only.

Howard County

Real Estate Recording—Howard County Recorder, Court House, Cresco, IA 52136. 319-547-3621. Fax: 319-547-2629. 8AM-4:30PM (CST).

Felony, Misdemeanor, Civil, Eviction, Small Claims, Probate—1st District Court, Courthouse, Cresco, IA 52136. 319-547-2661. 8AM-4:30PM (CST). Access by: Mail, in person.

Humboldt County

Real Estate Recording—Humboldt County Recorder, 203 Main Street, Court House, Dakota City, IA 50529. 515-332-3693. Fax: 515-332-1738. 8AM-4:30PM (CST).

Felony, Misdemeanor, Civil, Eviction, Small Claims, Probate—2nd District Court, Courthouse, Dakota City, IA 50529. 515-332-1806. Fax: 515-332-7100. 8AM-4:30PM (CST). Access by: In person only.

Ida County

Real Estate Recording—Ida County Recorder, 401 Moorehead, Courthouse, Ida Grove, IA 51445. 712-364-2220. Fax: 712-364-2746. 8AM-4:30PM (CST).

Felony, Misdemeanor, Civil, Eviction, Small Claims, Probate—3rd District Court, Courthouse, 401 Moorehead St, Ida Grove, IA 51445. 712-364-2628. Fax: 712-364-2699. 8AM-4:30PM (CST). Access by: In person only.

Iowa County

Real Estate Recording—Iowa County Recorder, 901 Court Ave., Marengo, IA 52301. 319-642-3622. Fax: 319-642-7637. 8AM-4:30PM (CST).

Felony, Misdemeanor, Civil, Eviction, Small Claims, Probate—6th District Court, PO Box 266, Marengo, IA 52301. 319-642-3914. 8AM-4:30PM (CST). Access by: Mail, in person.

Jackson County

Real Estate Recording—Jackson County Recorder, 201 West Platt, Maquoketa, IA 52060. 319-652-2504. Fax: 319-652-6975. 8:30AM-4:30PM (CST).

Felony, Misdemeanor, Civil, Eviction, Small Claims, Probate—7th District Court, 201 West Platt, Maquoketa, IA 52060. 319-652-4946. Fax: 319-652-2708. 8AM-4:30PM (CST). Access by: In person only.

Jasper County

Real Estate Recording—Jasper County Recorder, Courthouse, Room 205, Newton, IA 50208. 515-792-5442. Fax: 515-791-3680. 8AM-5PM (CST).

Felony, Misdemeanor, Civil, Eviction, Small Claims, Probate—5th District Court, PO Box 666, Newton, IA 50208. 515-792-3255. Fax: 515-792-2818. 8AM-4:30PM (CST). Access by: Mail, in person.

Jefferson County

Real Estate Recording—Jefferson County Recorder, 51 West Briggs, Fairfield, IA 52556. 515-472-4331. Fax: 515-472-6695. 8AM-4:30PM (CST).

Felony, Misdemeanor, Civil, Eviction, Small Claims, Probate—8th District Court, PO Box 984, Fairfield, IA 52556. 515-472-3454. Fax: 515-472-9472. 8AM-4:30PM (CST). Access by: In person only.

Johnson County

Real Estate Recording—Johnson County Recorder, 913 S. Dubuque Street, Suite 202, Iowa City, IA 52240. 319-356-6093. Fax: 319-356-6086. 8AM-4PM (CST).

Felony, Misdemeanor, Civil, Eviction, Small Claims, Probate—6th District Court, PO Box 2510, Iowa City, IA 52244. 319-356-6060. Fax: 319-339-6153. 8AM-4:30PM (CST). Access by: Phone, mail, in person.

Jones County

Real Estate Recording—Jones County Recorder, Courthouse, Room 116, 500 W. Main, Anamosa, IA 52205. 319-462-2477. Fax: 319-462-5802. 8AM-4PM (CST).

Felony, Misdemeanor, Civil, Eviction, Small Claims, Probate—6th District Court, PO Box 19, Anamosa, IA 52205. 319-462-4341. 8AM-4:30PM (CST). Access by: Phone, mail, in person.

Keokuk County

Real Estate Recording—Keokuk County Recorder, Courthouse, Sigourney, IA 52591. 515-622-2540. Fax: 515-622-2286. 8AM-4:30PM (CST).

Felony, Misdemeanor, Civil, Eviction, Small Claims, Probate—8th District Court, Courthouse, Sigourney, IA 52591. 515-622-2210. Fax: 515-622-2171. 8AM-4:30PM (CST). Access by: Mail, in person.

Kossuth County

Real Estate Recording—Kossuth County Recorder, 114 West State, Algona, IA 50511. 515-295-5660. Fax: 515-295-9304. 8AM-4PM (CST).

Felony, Misdemeanor, Civil, Eviction, Small Claims, Probate—3rd District Court, Kossuth County Courthouse, 114 W State St, Algona, IA 50511. 515-295-3240. 8AM-4PM (CST). Access by: In person only.

Lee County

Real Estate Recording—Lee County Recorder, Northern District, 933 Avenue H, Fort Madison, IA 52627. 319-372-4662. Fax: 319-372-7033. 8:30AM-4:30PM (CST).

Lee County Recorder, Southern District, 25 North 7th, Keokuk, IA 52632. 319-524-1126. Fax: 319-524-1544. 8:30AM-4:30PM (CST).

Felony, Misdemeanor, Civil, Eviction, Small Claims, Probate—8th District Court, PO Box 1443, Ft Madison, IA 52627. 319-372-3523. 8AM-4:30PM (CST). Access by: In person only.

Linn County

Real Estate Recording—Linn County Recorder, 930 First Street S.W., Cedar Rapids, IA 52404. 319-398-3441. Fax: 319-362-5329.

Felony, Misdemeanor, Civil, Eviction, Small Claims, Probate—District Court, PO Box 1468, Cedar Rapids, IA 52406-1468. 319-398-3411. Fax: 319-398-3964. 8AM-4:30PM (CST). Access by: Mail, in person.

Louisa County

Real Estate Recording—Louisa County Recorder, 117 South Main Street, Wapello, IA 52653. 319-523-5361. Fax: 319-523-3713. 8AM-4:30PM (CST).

Felony, Misdemeanor, Civil, Eviction, Small Claims, Probate—8th District Court, PO Box 268, Wapello, IA 52653. 319-523-4541. Fax: 319-523-4542. 8AM-4:30PM (CST). Access by: Fax, mail, in person.

Lucas County

Real Estate Recording—Lucas County Recorder, Courthouse, Chariton, IA 50049. 515-774-2413. Fax: 515-774-2993. 8AM-4PM (CST).

Felony, Misdemeanor, Civil, Eviction, Small Claims, Probate—5th District Court, Courthouse, Chariton, IA 50049. 515-774-4421. Fax: 515-774-8669. 8AM-4:30PM (CST). Access by: Mail, in person.

Lyon County

Real Estate Recording—Lyon County Recorder, 206 Second Avenue, Courthouse, Rock Rapids, IA 51246. 712-472-2381. 8AM-4:30PM (CST).

Felony, Misdemeanor, Civil, Eviction, Small Claims, Probate—3rd District Court, Courthouse, Rock Rapids, IA 51246. 712-472-2623. Fax: 712-472-2422. 8AM-4:30PM (CST). Access by: In person only.

Madison County

Real Estate Recording—Madison County Recorder, North John Wayne Drive, Courthouse, Winterset, IA 50273. 515-462-3771. Fax: 515-462-2506. 8AM-4:30PM; 9AM-Noon Last Sat of the month (CST).

Felony, Misdemeanor, Civil, Eviction, Small Claims, Probate—5th District Court, PO Box 152, Winterset, IA 50273. 515-462-4451. Fax: 515-462-9125. 8AM-4:30PM (CST). Access by: In person only.

Mahaska County

Real Estate Recording—Mahaska County Recorder, Courthouse, Oskaloosa, IA 52577. 515-673-8187. 8AM-4:30PM (CST).

Felony, Misdemeanor, Civil, Eviction, Small Claims, Probate—8th District Court, Courthouse, Oskaloosa, IA 52577. 515-673-7786. 8AM-4:30PM (CST). Access by: In person only.

Marion County

Real Estate Recording—Marion County Recorder, 214 E. Main St., Knoxville, IA 50138. 515-828-2211. Fax: 515-842-3593. 8AM-4:30PM (CST).

Felony, Misdemeanor, Civil, Eviction, Small Claims, Probate—5th District Court, PO Box 497, Knoxville, IA 50138. 515-828-2207. Fax: 515-828-7580. 8AM-4:30PM (CST). Access by: In person only.

Marshall County

Real Estate Recording—Marshall County Recorder, Courthouse, 3rd Floor, 1 East Main St., Marshalltown, IA 50158. 515-754-6355. Fax: 515-754-6321. 8AM-4:30PM (CST).

Felony, Misdemeanor, Civil, Eviction, Small Claims, Probate—2nd District Court, Courthouse, Marshalltown, IA 50158. 515-754-6373. Fax: 515-754-6376. 8AM-4:30PM (CST). Access by: In person only.

Mills County

Real Estate Recording—Mills County Recorder, Courthouse, 418 Sharp St., Glenwood, IA 51534. 712-527-9315. 8AM-4:30PM (CST).

Felony, Misdemeanor, Civil, Eviction, Small Claims, Probate—4th District Court, 418 Sharp St, Courthouse, Glenwood, IA 51534. 712-527-4880. Fax: 712-527-4936. 8AM-4:30PM (CST). Access by: Mail, in person.

Mitchell County

Real Estate Recording—Mitchell County Recorder, 508 State Street, Osage, IA 50461. 515-732-5861. 8AM-4:30PM (CST).

Felony, Misdemeanor, Civil, Eviction, Small Claims, Probate—2nd District Court, 508 State St, Osage, IA 50461. 515-732-3726. Fax: 515-732-3728. 8AM-4:30PM (CST). Access by: Phone, mail, in person.

Monona County

Real Estate Recording—Monona County Recorder, 610 Iowa Avenue, Onawa, IA 51040. 712-423-2575. Fax: 712-423-3034. 8AM-4:30PM (CST).

Felony, Misdemeanor, Civil, Eviction, Small Claims, Probate—3rd District Court, PO Box 14, Onawa, IA 51040. 712-423-2491. 8AM-4:30PM (CST). Access by: In person only.

Monroe County

Real Estate Recording—Monroe County Recorder, Courthouse, 10 Benton Ave. East, Albia, IA 52531. 515-932-5164. Fax: 515-932-2863. 8AM-4PM (CST).

Felony, Misdemeanor, Civil, Eviction, Small Claims, Probate—8th District Court, Courthouse, 10 Benton Ave E, Albia, IA 52531. 515-932-5212. Fax: 515-932-3245. 8AM-4:30PM (CST). Access by: In person only.

Montgomery County

Real Estate Recording—Montgomery County Recorder, Courthouse, Red Oak, IA 51566. 712-623-4363. Fax: 712-623-2346. 8AM-4:30PM (CST).

Felony, Misdemeanor, Civil, Eviction, Small Claims, Probate—4th District Court, Courthouse, Red Oak, IA 51566. 712-623-4986. 8AM-4:30PM (CST). Access by: In person only.

Muscatine County

Real Estate Recording—Muscatine County Recorder, 401 East 3rd Street, Courthouse, Muscatine, IA 52761. 319-263-7741. Fax: 319-263-7248. 8AM-4:30PM (CST).

Felony, Misdemeanor, Civil, Eviction, Small Claims, Probate—7th District Court, PO Box 327, Courthouse, Muscatine, IA 52761. 319-263-6511. Fax: 319-264-3622. 8AM-4:30PM (CST). Access by: In person only.

O'Brien County

Real Estate Recording—O'Brien County Recorder, Courthouse, Primghar, IA 51245. 712-757-3045. Fax: 712-757-3046. 8AM-4:30PM (CST).

Felony, Misdemeanor, Civil, Eviction, Small Claims, Probate—3rd District Court, Courthouse Criminal Records, Primghar, IA 51245. 712-757-3255. Fax: 712-757-2965. 8AM-4:30PM (CST). Access by: In person only.

Osceola County

Real Estate Recording—Osceola County Recorder, Courthouse, 300 7th Street, Sibley, IA 51249. 712-754-3345. Fax: 712-754-2872. 8AM-4:30PM (CST).

Felony, Misdemeanor, Civil, Eviction, Small Claims, Probate—3rd District Court, Courthouse Criminal Records, Sibley, IA 51249. 712-754-3595. Fax: 712-754-2486. 8AM-4:30PM (CST). Access by: In person only.

Page County

Real Estate Recording—Page County Recorder, 112 E. Main St., Courthouse, Clarinda, IA 51632. 712-542-3130. Fax: 712-542-5019. 8AM-4:30PM (CST).

Felony, Misdemeanor, Civil, Eviction, Small Claims, Probate—4th District Court, 112 E Main Box 263, Clarinda, IA 51632. 712-542-3214. 8AM-4:30PM (CST). Access by: In person only.

Palo Alto County

Real Estate Recording—Palo Alto County Recorder, 1010 Broadway, Emmetsburg, IA 50536. 712-852-3701. Fax: 712-852-3643. 8AM-4PM (CST).

Felony, Misdemeanor, Civil, Eviction, Small Claims, Probate—3rd District Court, PO Box 387, Emmetsburg, IA 50536. 712-852-3603. 8AM-4:30PM (CST). Access by: In person only.

Plymouth County

Real Estate Recording—Plymouth County Recorder, Courthouse, 3rd Ave & 2nd Street SE, Le Mars, IA 51031. 712-546-4020. 8AM-5PM (CST).

Felony, Misdemeanor, Civil, Eviction, Small Claims, Probate—3rd District Court, Courthouse 215-4th Ave SE, Le Mars, IA 51031. 712-546-4215. 8AM-4:30PM (CST). Access by: In person only.

Pocahontas County

Real Estate Recording—Pocahontas County Recorder, 99 Court Square, Pocahontas, IA 50574. 712-335-4404. Fax: 712-335-4300. 8AM-4PM (CST).

Felony, Misdemeanor, Civil, Eviction, Small Claims, Probate—2nd District Court, Courthouse, Pocahontas, IA 50574. 712-335-4208. Fax: 712-335-4608. 8AM-4:30PM (CST). Access by: In person only.

Polk County

Real Estate Recording—Polk County Recorder, 111 Court Avenue, Rooom 250, County Administration Building, Des Moines, IA 50309. 515-286-3160. Fax: 515-286-3608. 8AM-4:30PM (CST).

Felony, Misdemeanor, Civil, Eviction, Small Claims, Probate—District Court, 5th & Mulberry Rm 201, Des Moines, IA 50309. 515-286-3772. Fax: 515-286-3172. 8AM-4:30PM (CST). Access by: In person only.

Pottawattamie County

Real Estate Recording—Pottawattamie County Recorder, 227 South Sixth Street, Council Bluffs, IA 51501. 712-328-5612. Fax: 712-328-4738. 8AM-4PM (CST).

Felony, Misdemeanor, Civil, Eviction, Small Claims, Probate—4th District Court, 227 S 6th St, Council Bluffs, IA 51501. 712-328-5604. 9AM-4:30PM (CST). Access by: In person only.

Poweshiek County

Real Estate Recording—Poweshiek County Recorder, 302 East Main Street, Montezuma, IA 50171. 515-623-5434. Fax: 515-623-5120. 8AM-4PM (CST).

Felony, Misdemeanor, Civil, Eviction, Small Claims, Probate—8th District Court, PO Box 218, Montezuma, IA 50171. 515-623-5644. Fax: 515-623-5320. 8AM-4:30PM (CST). Access by: In person only.

Ringgold County

Real Estate Recording—Ringgold County Recorder, Courthouse, Mount Ayr, IA 50854. 515-464-3231. Fax: 515-464-2568. 8AM-4PM (CST).

Felony, Misdemeanor, Civil, Eviction, Small Claims, Probate—5th District Court, 109 W Madison (PO Box 523), Mount Ayr, IA 50854. 515-464-3234. Fax: 515-464-2478. 8AM-4:30PM (CST). Access by: In person only.

Sac County

Real Estate Recording—Sac County Recorder, 100 NW State St., Sac City, IA 50583. 712-662-7789. Fax: 712-662-7129. 8AM-4:30PM (CST).

Felony, Misdemeanor, Civil, Eviction, Small Claims, Probate—2nd District Court, PO Box 368, Sac City, IA 50583. 712-662-7791. 8AM-4:30PM (CST). Access by: In person only.

Scott County

Real Estate Recording—Scott County Recorder, 416 West 4th Street, Davenport, IA 52801. 319-326-8621. Fax: 319-322-1269. 8AM-4:30PM (CST).

Felony, Misdemeanor, Civil, Eviction, Small Claims, Probate—7th District Court, 416 W 4th St, Davenport, IA 52801. 319-326-8784. 8AM-4:30PM (CST). Access by: In person only.

Shelby County

Real Estate Recording—Shelby County Recorder, 612 Court Street, Room 201, Harlan, IA 51537. 712-755-5640. Fax: 712-755-2519. 8AM-4:30PM (CST).

Felony, Misdemeanor, Civil, Eviction, Small Claims, Probate—4th District Court, PO Box 431, Harlan, IA 51537. 712-755-5543. Fax: 712-755-2667. 8AM-4:30PM (CST). Access by: Mail, in person.

Sioux County

Real Estate Recording—Sioux County Recorder, 210 Central Avenue SW, Courthouse, Orange City, IA 51041. 712-737-2229. Fax: 712-737-2537. 8AM-4:30PM (CST).

Felony, Misdemeanor, Civil, Eviction, Small Claims, Probate—3rd District Court, PO Box 47, Courthouse, Orange City, IA 51041. 712-737-2286. Fax: 712-737-8908. 8AM-4:30PM (CST). Access by: In person only.

Story County

Real Estate Recording—Story County Recorder, 900 6th Street, Courthouse, Nevada, IA 50201. 515-382-7230. Fax: 515-382-7326. 8AM-5PM (No recording after 4:30PM) (CST).

Felony, Misdemeanor, Civil, Eviction, Small Claims, Probate—2nd District Court, PO Box 408, Nevada, IA 50201. 515-382-6581. 8AM-4:30PM (CST). Access by: In person only.

Tama County

Real Estate Recording—Tama County Recorder, High Street, Toledo, IA 52342. 515-484-3320. 8AM-4:30PM (CST).

Felony, Misdemeanor, Civil, Eviction, Small Claims, Probate—6th District Court, PO Box 306, Toledo, IA 52342. 515-484-3721. 8AM-4:30PM (CST). Access by: Mail, in person.

Taylor County

Real Estate Recording—Taylor County Recorder, 405 Jefferson St., Courthouse, Bedford, IA 50833. 712-523-2275. Fax: 712-523-2274. (CST).

Felony, Misdemeanor, Civil, Eviction, Small Claims, Probate—5th District Court, Courthouse, Bedford, IA 50833. 712-523-2095. Fax: 712-523-2936. 8AM-4:30PM (CST). Access by: In person only.

Union County

Real Estate Recording—Union County Recorder, 301 North Pine Street, Creston, IA 50801. 515-782-7616. Fax: 515-782-8404. 8:30AM-4:30PM (CST).

Felony, Misdemeanor, Civil, Eviction, Small Claims, Probate—5th District Court, Courthouse, Creston, IA 50801. 515-782-7315. Fax: 515-782-8241. 8AM-4:30PM (CST). Access by: In person only.

Van Buren County

Real Estate Recording—Van Buren County Recorder, Dodge and Fourth Street, Keosauqua, IA 52565. 319-293-3240. Fax: 319-293-3828. 8AM-4:30PM (CST).

Felony, Misdemeanor, Civil, Eviction, Small Claims, Probate—8th District Court, Courthouse Criminal Records, Keosauqua, IA 52565. 319-293-3108. 8AM-4:30PM (CST). Access by: In person only.

Wapello County

Real Estate Recording—Wapello County Recorder, 101 West 4th Street, Ottumwa, IA 52501. 515-683-0045. Fax: 515-683-0019. 8AM-4:30PM (CST).

Felony, Misdemeanor, Civil, Eviction, Small Claims, Probate—8th District Court, 101 W 4th, Ottumwa, IA 52501. 515-683-0060. 8AM-4:30PM (CST). Access by: In person only.

Warren County

Real Estate Recording—Warren County Recorder, Courthouse, Town Square, Indianola, IA 50125. 515-961-1089. 8AM-4:30PM (CST).

Felony, Misdemeanor, Civil, Eviction, Small Claims, Probate—5th District Court, PO Box 379, Indianola, IA 50125. 515-961-1033. Fax: 515-961-1071. 8AM-4:30PM (CST). Access by: Mail, in person.

Washington County

Real Estate Recording—Washington County Recorder, 224 West Main St., Washington, IA 52353. 319-653-7727. 8AM-4:30PM (CST).

Felony, Misdemeanor, Civil, Eviction, Small Claims, Probate—8th District Court, PO Box 391, Washington, IA 52353. 319-653-7741. Fax: 319-653-7787. 8AM-4:30PM (CST). Access by: In person only.

Wayne County

Real Estate Recording—Wayne County Recorder, Junction of Highway 2 and 14, Courthouse, Corydon, IA 50060. 515-872-1676. Fax: 515-872-2843. 8AM-4PM (CST).

Felony, Misdemeanor, Civil, Eviction, Small Claims, Probate—5th District Court, PO Box 424, Corydon, IA 50060. 515-872-2264. Fax: 515-872-2431. 8AM-4:30PM (CST). Access by: Phone, mail, in person.

Webster County

Real Estate Recording—Webster County Recorder, 701 Central Avenue, Courthouse, Fort Dodge, IA 50501. 515-576-2401. Fax: 515-574-3722. 8AM-4:30PM (CST).

Felony, Misdemeanor, Civil, Eviction, Small Claims, Probate—2nd District Court, 701 Central Ave, Courthouse, Ft Dodge, IA 50501. 515-576-7115. 8AM-4:30PM (CST). Access by: In person only.

Winnebago County

Real Estate Recording—Winnebago County Recorder, 126 South Clark Street, Courthouse, Forest City, IA 50436. 515-582-2094. Fax: 515-582-2891. 8AM-4:30PM (CST).

Felony, Misdemeanor, Civil, Eviction, Small Claims, Probate—2nd District Court, 126 W Clark, Box 468, Forest City, IA 50436. 515-582-4520. Fax: 515-582-2615. 8AM-4:30PM (CST). Access by: In person only.

Winneshiek County

Real Estate Recording—Winneshiek County Recorder, 201 West Main Street, Decorah, IA 52101. 319-382-3486. Fax: 319-387-4083. 8AM-4PM (CST).

Felony, Misdemeanor, Civil, Eviction, Small Claims, Probate—1st District Court, 201 W Main St, Decorah, IA 52101. 319-382-2469. Fax: 319-382-0603. 8AM-4:30PM (CST). Access by: In person only.

Woodbury County

Real Estate Recording—Woodbury County Recorder, 7th & Douglas Street, Courthouse Room 106, Sioux City, IA 51101. 712-279-6528. Fax: 712-252-4921. 8AM-4:30PM (CST).

Felony, Civil, Eviction, Probate—3rd District Court, 620 Douglas St, Sioux City, IA 51101. 712-279-6616. 7:30AM-4:30PM (CST). Access by: In person only.

Misdemeanor, Civil, Eviction, Small Claims—3rd District Court, 407 7th St, Sioux City, IA 51101. 712-279-6624. 8AM-4:30PM (CST). Access by: In person only.

Worth County

Real Estate Recording—Worth County Recorder, 1000 Central Avenue, Northwood, IA 50459. 515-324-2734. Fax: 515-324-2316. 8AM-4PM (CST).

Felony, Misdemeanor, Civil, Eviction, Small Claims, Probate—2nd District Court, PO Box 172, Courthouse, Northwood, IA 50459. 515-324-2840. Fax: 515-324-2360. 8AM-4:30PM (CST). Access by: In person only.

Wright County

Real Estate Recording—Wright County Recorder, 115 North Main, Courthouse, Clarion, IA 50525. 515-532-3204. 8AM-4PM (CST).

Felony, Misdemeanor, Civil, Eviction, Small Claims, Probate—2nd District Court, PO Box 306, Clarion, IA 50525. 515-532-3113. Fax: 515-532-2343. 8AM-4:30PM (CST). Access by: In person only.

Federal Courts

US District Court
Northern District of Iowa

Cedar Rapids Division, US District Court Clerk, Federal Bldg, US Courthouse, PO Box 74710, Cedar Rapids, IA 52407. 319-364-2447. Counties: Benton, Cedar, Cerro Gordo, Grundy, Hardin, Iowa, Jones, Linn, Tama

Dubuque Division, US District Court c/o Cedar Rapids Division, PO Box 74890, Cedar Rapids, IA 52407. 319-286-2300. Counties: Allamakee, Black Hawk, Bremer, Buchanan, Chickasaw, Clayton, Delaware, Dubuque, Fayette, Floyd, Howard, Jackson, Mitchell, Winneshiek

Ft Dodge Division, US District Court c/o Sioux City, Room 301, Federal Bldg, 320 6th St, Sioux City, IA 51101. 712-252-3336. Counties: Butler, Calhoun, Carroll, Emmet, Franklin, Hamilton, Hancock, Humboldt, Kossuth, Palo Alto, Pocahontas, Webster, Winnebago, Worth, Wright

Sioux City Division, US District Court Room 301, Federal Bldg, 320 6th St, Sioux City, IA 51101. 712-233-3900. Counties: Buena Vista, Cherokee, Clay, Crawford, Dickinson, Ida, Lyon, Monona, O'Brien, Osceola, Plymouth, Sac, Sioux, Woodbury

Southern District of Iowa

Council Bluffs Division, US District Court PO Box 307, Council Bluffs, IA 51502. 712-328-0283. Counties: Adair, Adams, Audubon, Cass, Clarke, Clinton, Decatur, Fremont, Harrison, Lucas, Mills, Montgomery, Page, Pottawattamie, Ringgold, Shelby, Taylor, Union, Wayne

Davenport Division, US District Court PO Box 256, Davenport, IA 52805. 319-322-3223. Counties: Henry, Johnson, Lee, Louisa, Muscatine, Scott, Van Buren, Washington

Des Moines Division, US District Court PO Box 9344, Des Moines, IA 50306-9344. 515-284-6248. Counties: Appanoose, Boone, Dallas, Davis, Des Moines, Greene, Guthrie, Jasper, Jefferson, Keokuk, Madison, Mahaska, Marion, Marshall, Monroe, Polk, Poweshiek, Story, Wapello, Warren

US Bankruptcy Court
Northern District of Iowa

Cedar Rapids Division, US Bankruptcy Court, PO Box 74890, Cedar Rapids, IA 52407-4890. 319-286-2200. Voice Case Information System: 800-249-9859. Counties: Allamakee, Benton, Black Hawk, Bremer, Buchanan, Buena Vista, Butler, Calhoun, Carroll, Cedar, Cerro Gordo, Cherokee, Chickasaw, Clay, Clayton, Crawford, Delaware, Dickinson, Dubuque, Emmet, Fayette, Floyd, Franklin, Grundy, Hamilton, Hancock, Hardin, Howard, Humboldt, Ida, Iowa, Jackson, Jones, Kossuth, Linn, Lyon, Mitchell, Monona, O'Brien, Osceola, Palo Alto, Plymouth, Pocahontas, Sac, Sioux, Tama, Webster, Winnebago, Winneshiek, Woodbury, Worth, Wright

Southern District of Iowa

Des Moines Division, US Bankruptcy Court, PO Box 9264, Des Moines, IA 50306-9264. 515-284-6230. Voice Case Information System: 515-284-6427. Counties: Adair, Adams, Appanoose, Audubon, Boone, Cass, Clarke, Clinton, Dallas, Davis, Decatur, Des Moines, Fremont, Greene, Guthrie, Harrison, Henry, Jasper, Jefferson, Johnson, Keokuk, Lee, Louisa, Lucas, Madison, Mahaska, Marion, Marshall, Mills, Monroe, Montgomery, Muscatine, Page, Polk, Pottawattamie, Poweshiek, Ringgold, Scott, Shelby, Story, Taylor, Union, Van Buren, Wapello, Warren, Washington, Wayne

Kansas

Capitol: Topeka (Shawnee County)	
Number of Counties: 105	**Population:** 2,565,328
County Court Locations:	**Federal Court Locations:**
•District Courts: 109/ 31 Districts	•District Courts: 3
	•Bankruptcy Courts: 3
Municipal Courts: 350	**State Agencies:** 19

State Agencies—Summary

General Help Numbers:

State Archives

Historical Society	913-272-8681
Archives Department	Fax: 913-272-8682
6425 SW 6th Ave	9AM-4:30PM M-SA
Topeka, KS 66615	

Governor's Office

Governor's Office	913-296-3232
State Capitol Bldg, Room 212S	Fax: 913-296-7973
Topeka, KS 66612-1590	8AM-5:30PM

Attorney General's Office

Attorney General's Office	913-296-2215
Kansas Judicial Center, 2nd Floor	Fax: 913-296-6296
Topeka, KS 66612-1597	8AM-5PM

State Legislation

Kansas State Library	913-296-2149
Capitol Bldg	Fax: 913-296-6650
3rd Floor, North Wing	8AM-5PM
Topeka, KS 66612	

Important State Internet Sites:

Webscape
File Edit View   Help

State of Kansas World Wide Web

www.state.ks.us/

This home page includes links to many sites. Some of those sites are the Governor, the government, professional services, education, libraries, and the Information Network of Kansas.

UCC Information

www.state.ks.us/public/sos/iemain.html

Information is provided about the availability of UCC information. You must subscribe to the Information Network of Kansas system to obtain access to this UCC information. There is a fee associated with this service.

Kansas State Government

www.state.ks.us/public/legislative/

This site provides full access to state elected officials and the full text of bills from the current legislature.

Unclaimed Property

www.treasurer.state.ks.us/upsearch.htm

This page provides you with all the information necessary to search for unclaimed property, such as checking and savings accounts, payroll, wages, insurance, refunds and much more.

State Historical Society

history.cc.ukans.edu/heritage/kshs/
kshs1.html

This is the site of the Kansas Historical Society and the heritage archives.

State Agencies—Public Records

Criminal Records

Kansas Bureau of Investigation, Criminal Justice Records Division, 1620 SW Tyler, Attn: NCJRC, Topeka, KS 66612-1837, Main Telephone: 913-296-8200, Fax: 913-296-6781, Hours: 8AM-5PM. Access by: mail only. Non-criminal justice agencies, organizations, individuals and commercial companies are entitled to receive recorded conviction information. Arrests with no convictions are not shown, unless the arrest is 12 months old and there is no disposition.

Corporation Records
Limited Partnerships
Limited Liability Company Records

Secretary of State, Corporation Division, 300 SW 10th St, 2nd Floor, Topeka, KS 66612-1594, Main Telephone: 913-296-4564, Fax: 913-296-4570, Hours: 8AM-5PM. Access by: mail, phone, fax, visit, PC.

Trademarks/Servicemarks

Secretary of State, Trademarks/Servicemarks Division, 300 SW 10th Ave, 2nd floor, Topeka, KS 66612, Main Telephone: 913-296-4564, Fax: 913-296-4570, Hours: 8AM-5PM. Access by: mail, phone, fax, visit.

Uniform Commercial Code
Federal Tax Liens
State Tax Liens

UCC Division, Secretary of State, State Capitol, 300 W Tenth, 2nd Floor, Topeka, KS 66612-1594, Main Telephone: 913-296-3650, Fax: 913-296-3659, Hours: 8AM-5PM. Access by: mail, phone, fax, visit, PC.

Sales Tax Registrations

Kansas Department of Revenue, Taxation Assistance, Docking State Office Bldg, 915 SW Harrison, Topeka, KS 66612-1588, Main Telephone: 913-296-0222, Fax: 913-296-2073, Hours: 7AM-5PM.
Restricted access; records are considered confidential and not open to public in general.

Birth Certificates

Kansas State Department of Health & Environment, Office of Vital Statistics, 900 SW Jackson, Landon State Office Bldg, Topeka, KS 66612-2221, Main Telephone: 913-296-1400, Fax: 913-357-4332, Hours: 9AM-4PM. Access by: mail, phone, fax, visit. Please note that vital records are not considered public records in this state and are open only to family members or their represetnatives.

Death Records

Kansas State Department of Health & Environment, Office of Vital Statistics, 900 SW Jackson, Landon State Office Bldg, Topeka, KS 66612-2221, Main Telephone: 913-296-1400, Fax: 913-357-4332, Hours: 9AM-4PM. Access by: mail, phone, fax, visit.

Marriage Certificates

Kansas State Department of Health & Environment, Office of Vital Statistics, 900 SW Jackson, Landon State Office Bldg, Topeka, KS 66612-2221, Main Telephone: 913-296-1400, Fax: 913-357-4332, Hours: 9AM-4PM. Access by: mail, phone, fax, visit.

Divorce Records

Kansas State Department of Health & Environment, Office of Vital Statistics, 900 SW Jackson, Landon State Office Bldg, Topeka, KS 66612-2221, Main Telephone: 913-296-1400, Fax: 913-357-4332, Hours: 9AM-4PM. Access by: mail, phone, fax, visit

Workers' Compensation Records

Human Resources Department, Workers Compensation Division, 800 SW Jackson, Suite 600, Topeka, KS 66612-1227, Main Telephone: 913-296-3441, Claims Advisor: 800-332-0353, Fax: 913-296-0839, Hours: 8AM-5PM. Access by: mail, phone, fax, visit, PC.

Driver Records
Accident Reports

Department of Revenue, Driver Control Bureau, PO Box 12021, Topeka, KS 66612-2021, Main Telephone: 913-296-3671, Hours: 8AM-4:45PM. Access by: mail, visit, PC.

Vehicle Ownership
Vehicle Identification

Division of Vehicles, Title and Registration Bureau, 915 Harrison, Topeka, KS 66612, Main Telephone: 913-296-3621, Fax: 913-296-3852, Hours: 7:30AM-4:45PM. Access by: mail, visit, PC.

Hunting License Information

Wildlife & Parks Department, Operations Office, Fish & Wildlife, 512 SE 25th Ave, Pratt, KS 67124-8174, Main Telephone: 316-672-5911, Fax: 316-672-6020, Hours: 8AM-5PM. Access by: mail, visit.

County Courts and Recording Offices

What You Need to Know...

About the Courts

Administration

Judicial Administrator	913-296-4873
Kansas Judicial Center,	
301 W 10th St	Fax: 913-296-7076

Court Structure

If an individual in Municipal Court wants a jury trial, it must be filed de novo in a District Court.

Searching Hints

Five counties—Cowley, Crawford, Labette, Montgomery and Neosho have two hearing locations, but only one record center, which is the location included in this Sourcebook.

The court search fee is usually $10.80 per hour. The certification fee is $1.00 per document plus copy fee and the copy fee is $.25 per page.

Many of the courts **not** do searches, and will refer any criminal request to the Kansas Bureau of Investigation.

Online Access

Online computer access is available for District Court Records in 4 counties—Johnson, Sedgewick, Shawnee, and Wyandotte through the Information Network of Kansas (**INK**) Services. There is also a wide range of other state information available through INK. To access INK, a user needs a PC and a Hayes compatible telephone modem (9600 or 2400 baud rate). There is a $50.00 annual subscription fee and a $.40 per minute connect time charge plus additional "per search" fees for Drivers License, Title, Registration, Lien, and UCC searches. Access to INK is through a toll-free number and the first 60 seconds of each log on are free. For additional information or a registration packet, call 800-4-KANSAS (800-452-6727).

About the Recorder's Office

Organization

105 counties, 105 filing offices. The recording officer is Register of Deeds. Many counties utilize a "Miscellaneous Index" for tax and other liens, separate from real estate records. 100 counties are in the Central Time Zone (CST) and 5 are in the Mountain Time Zone (MST).

UCC Records

Financing statements are filed at the state level except for consumer goods and real estate related filings. All counties will perform UCC searches. Use search request form UCC-3. Search fees are usually $8.00 per debtor name. Copies usually cost $1.00 per page.

Lien Records

Federal tax liens on personal property of businesses are filed with the Secretary of State. Other federal tax liens and all state tax liens on personal property are filed with the county Register of Deeds. Most counties automatically include tax liens on personal property with a UCC search. Tax liens on personal property may usually be searched separately for $8.00 per name. Other liens include mechanics, harvesters, lis pendens, and threshers.

Real Estate Records

Most counties will **not** perform real estate searches, although some will do as an accommodation with the understanding that they are **not** "certified." Some counties will also do a search based upon legal description to determine owner. Copy fees vary, and certification fees are usually $1.00 per document. Tax records are located at the Appraiser's Office.

County Courts and Recording Offices

Allen County

Real Estate Recording—Allen County Register of Deeds, 1 North Washington, Courthouse, Iola, KS 66749. 316-365-1412. Fax: 316-365-1414. 8AM-5PM (CST).

Felony, Misdemeanor, Civil, Eviction, Small Claims, Probate—District Court, PO Box 630, Iola, KS 66749. 316-365-1425. Fax: 316-365-1429. 8AM-5PM (CST). Access by: In person only.

Anderson County

Real Estate Recording—Anderson County Register of Deeds, Courthouse, 100 E. 4th Street, Garnett, KS 66032. 785-448-5620. Fax: 785-448-5621. 8AM-5PM (CST).

Felony, Misdemeanor, Civil, Eviction, Small Claims, Probate—District Court, PO Box 305, Garnett, KS 66032. 785-448-6886. Fax: 785-448-3230. 8AM-5PM (CST). Access by: In person only.

Atchison County

Real Estate Recording—Atchison County Register of Deeds, 423 North 5th St., Courthouse, Atchison, KS 66002. 913-367-2568. Fax: 913-367-0227. 8:30AM-5PM (CST).

Felony, Misdemeanor, Civil, Eviction, Small Claims, Probate—District Court, PO Box 408, Atchison, KS 66002. 913-367-7400. Fax: 913-367-1171. 8AM-5PM (CST). Access by: Mail, in person.

Barber County

Real Estate Recording—Barber County Register of Deeds, 120 East Washington Street, Courthouse, Medicine Lodge, KS 67104. 316-886-3981. Fax: 316-886-5045. 8:30AM-5PM (CST).

Felony, Misdemeanor, Civil, Eviction, Small Claims, Probate—District Court, 118 E Washington, Medicine Lodge, KS 67104. 316-886-5639. Fax: 316-886-5854. 8AM-Noon,1-5PM (CST). Access by: Fax, mail, in person.

Barton County

Real Estate Recording—Barton County Register of Deeds, 1400 Main Street, Courthouse, Great Bend, KS 67530. 316-793-1849. Fax: 316-793-1807. 8AM-5PM (CST).

Felony, Misdemeanor, Civil, Eviction, Small Claims, Probate—District Court, 1400 N Main, Rm 306, Great Bend, KS 67530. 316-793-1856. Fax: 316-793-1860. 8:30AM-5PM (CST). Access by: Fax, mail, in person.

Bourbon County

Real Estate Recording—Bourbon County Register of Deeds, 210 South National, Fort Scott, KS 66701. 316-223-3800. Fax: 316-223-5241. 8:30AM-4:30PM (CST).

Felony, Misdemeanor, Civil, Eviction, Small Claims, Probate—District Court, PO Box 868, Ft Scott, KS 66701. 316-223-0780. Fax: 316-223-5303. 8:30AM-4:30PM (CST). Access by: Fax, mail, in person.

Brown County

Real Estate Recording—Brown County Register of Deeds, Courthouse, 601 Oregon, Hiawatha, KS 66434. 785-742-3741. Fax: 785-742-3255. 8AM-5PM (CST).

Felony, Misdemeanor, Civil, Eviction, Small Claims, Probate—District Court, PO Box 417, Hiawatha, KS 66434. 785-742-7481. Fax: 785-742-3506. 8AM-5PM (CST). Access by: Phone, fax, mail, in person.

Butler County

Real Estate Recording—Butler County Register of Deeds, 205 West Central, Courthouse, Suite 104, El Dorado, KS 67042. 316-322-4113. Fax: 316-321-1011. 8AM-5PM (CST).

Felony, Misdemeanor, Civil, Eviction, Small Claims, Probate—District Court, PO Box 1367, El Dorado, KS 67042. 316-321-1200. Fax: 316-321-9486. 8:30AM-5PM (CST). Access by: In person only.

Chase County

Real Estate Recording—Chase County Register of Deeds, Courthouse Plaza, Cottonwood Falls, KS 66845. 316-273-6398. Fax: 316-273-6617. 8AM-5PM (CST).

Felony, Misdemeanor, Civil, Eviction, Small Claims, Probate—District Court, PO Box 207, Cottonwood Falls, KS 66845. 316-273-6319. Fax: 316-273-6890. 8:30AM-5PM (CST). Access by: In person only.

Chautauqua County

Real Estate Recording—Chautauqua County Register of Deeds, 215 North Chautauqua, Courthouse, Sedan, KS 67361. 316-725-5830. Fax: 316-725-3256. 8AM-Noon,1-4PM (CST).

Felony, Misdemeanor, Civil, Eviction, Small Claims, Probate—District Court, 215 N Chautauqua, Sedan, KS 67361. 316-725-5870. Fax: 316-725-3027. 8AM-5PM (CST). Access by: Mail, in person.

Cherokee County

Real Estate Recording—Cherokee County Register of Deeds, 110 West Maple, Room 121, Courthouse, Columbus, KS 66725. 316-429-3777. Fax: 316-429-1042. 9AM-5PM (CST).

Felony, Misdemeanor, Civil, Eviction, Small Claims, Probate—District Court, PO Box 189, Columbus, KS 66725. 316-429-3880. Fax: 316-429-1130. 8:30AM-5PM (CST). Access by: In person only.

Cheyenne County

Real Estate Recording—Cheyenne County Register of Deeds, 212 East Washington, St. Francis, KS 67756. 785-332-8820. Fax: 785-332-8825. 8AM-Noon,1-5PM (CST).

Felony, Misdemeanor, Civil, Eviction, Small Claims, Probate—District Court, PO Box 646, St Francis, KS 67756. 785-332-8850. Fax: 785-332-8851. 8AM-Noon,1-5PM (CST). Access by: In person only.

Clark County

Real Estate Recording—Clark County Register of Deeds, Courthouse, 913 Highland, Ashland, KS 67831. 316-635-2812. Fax: 316-635-2393. 8:30AM-Noon, 1PM-4:30PM (CST).

Felony, Misdemeanor, Civil, Eviction, Small Claims, Probate—District Court, PO Box 790, Ashland, KS 67831. 316-635-2753. Fax: 316-635-2155. 8AM-5PM (CST). Access by: Mail, in person.

Clay County

Real Estate Recording—Clay County Register of Deeds, Courthouse Square, Clay Center, KS 67432. 785-632-3811. Fax: 785-632-2651. 8AM-5PM (CST).

Felony, Misdemeanor, Civil, Eviction, Small Claims, Probate—District Court, PO Box 203, Clay Center, KS 67432. 785-632-3443. Fax: 785-632-2651. 8AM-5PM (CST). Access by: In person only.

Cloud County

Real Estate Recording—Cloud County Register of Deeds, 811 Washington Street, Concordia, KS 66901. 785-243-8121. Fax: 785-243-8123. 8AM-4:30PM (CST).

Felony, Misdemeanor, Civil, Eviction, Small Claims, Probate—District Court, 811 Washington, Concordia, KS 66901. 785-243-8124. Fax: 785-243-8188. 8:30AM-5PM (CST). Access by: Mail, in person.

Coffey County

Real Estate Recording—Coffey County Register of Deeds, Courthouse, Room 205, 110 S. 6th St., Burlington, KS 66839. 316-364-2423. 8AM-5PM (CST).

Felony, Misdemeanor, Civil, Eviction, Small Claims, Probate—District Court, PO Box 330, Burlington, KS 66839. 316-364-8628. Fax: 316-364-8535. 8AM-5PM (CST). Access by: Mail, in person.

Comanche County

Real Estate Recording—Comanche County Register of Deeds, 201 South New York, Courthouse, Coldwater, KS 67029. 316-582-2152. Fax: 316-582-2390. 9AM-Noon,1-5PM (CST).

Felony, Misdemeanor, Civil, Eviction, Small Claims, Probate—District Court, PO Box 722, Coldwater, KS 67029. 316-582-2182. Fax: 316-582-2603. 8:30AM-5PM (CST). Access by: Fax, mail, in person.

Cowley County

Real Estate Recording—Cowley County Register of Deeds, 311 East 9th, Courthouse, Winfield, KS 67156. 316-221-5461. 8AM-Noon,1-5PM (CST).

Felony, Misdemeanor, Civil, Eviction, Small Claims, Probate—Arkansas City District Court, PO Box 1152, Arkansas City, KS 67005. 316-441-4520. Fax: 316-442-7213. 8AM-Noon,1-4PM (CST). Access by: Mail, in person.

Winfield District Court, PO Box 472, Winfield, KS 67156. 316-221-5470. Fax: 316-221-1097. 8AM-Noon,1-4PM (CST). Access by: Mail, in person.

Crawford County

Real Estate Recording—Crawford County Register of Deeds, Courthouse, 2nd Floor, Girard, KS 66743. 316-724-8218. Fax: 316-724-8823. 8:30AM-4:30PM (CST).

Felony, Misdemeanor, Civil, Eviction, Small Claims, Probate—Girard District Court, PO Box 69, Girard, KS 66743. 316-724-6211. Fax: 316-724-4987. 8:30AM-4:30PM (CST). Access by: Fax, mail, in person.

Decatur County

Real Estate Recording—Decatur County Register of Deeds, 194 South Penn, Courthouse, Oberlin, KS 67749. 785-475-8105. Fax: 785-475-8150. 8AM-Noon,1-5PM (CST).

Felony, Misdemeanor, Civil, Eviction, Small Claims, Probate—District Court, PO Box 89, Oberlin, KS 67749. 785-475-8107. Fax: 785-475-8170. 8AM-5PM (CST). Access by: In person only.

Dickinson County

Real Estate Recording—Dickinson County Register of Deeds, First & Buckeye, Courthouse, Abilene, KS 67410. 785-263-3073. Fax: 785-263-1512. 8AM-5PM (CST).

Felony, Misdemeanor, Civil, Eviction, Small Claims, Probate—District Court, PO Box 127, Abilene, KS 67410. 785-263-3142. Fax: 785-263-4407. 8AM-5PM (CST). Access by: Mail, in person.

Doniphan County

Real Estate Recording—Doniphan County Register of Deeds, Courthouse, Main St., Troy, KS 66087. 785-985-3932. Fax: 785-985-3723. 8AM-5PM (CST).

Felony, Misdemeanor, Civil, Eviction, Small Claims, Probate—District Court, PO Box 295, Troy, KS 66087. 785-985-3582. Fax: 785-985-2402. 8AM-5PM (CST). Access by: Phone, mail, in person.

Douglas County

Real Estate Recording—Douglas County Register of Deeds, 1100 Massachusetts, Courthouse, Lawrence, KS 66044. 913-832-5282. Fax: 913-841-4036. 8AM-5PM (CST).

Felony, Misdemeanor, Civil, Eviction, Small Claims, Probate—District Court, 111 E 11th St Rm 144, Lawrence, KS 66044-2966. 913-841-7700. Fax: 913-832-5174. 9AM-5PM (CST). Access by: Phone, fax, mail, in person. Fax for emergency only.

Edwards County

Real Estate Recording—Edwards County Register of Deeds, 312 Massachusetts, Courthouse, Kinsley, KS 67547. 316-659-3131. Fax: 316-659-2583. 8AM-5PM (CST).

Felony, Misdemeanor, Civil, Eviction, Small Claims, Probate—District Court, PO Box 232, Kinsley, KS 67547. 316-659-2442. Fax: 316-659-2998. 8AM-5PM (CST). Access by: Mail, in person.

Elk County

Real Estate Recording—Elk County Register of Deeds, Court House, 127 N. Pine, Howard, KS 67349. 316-374-2472. Fax: 316-374-2771. 8AM-4:30PM (CST).

Felony, Misdemeanor, Civil, Eviction, Small Claims, Probate—District Court, PO Box 306, Howard, KS 67349. 316-374-2370. Fax: 316-374-2555. 8AM-4:30PM (CST). Access by: In person only.

Ellis County

Real Estate Recording—Ellis County Register of Deeds, 1204 Fort Street, Hays, KS 67601. 785-628-9450. Fax: 785-628-9451. 8AM-5PM (CST).

Felony, Misdemeanor, Civil, Eviction, Small Claims, Probate—District Court, PO Box 8, Hays, KS 67601. 785-628-9415. Fax: 785-628-8415. 8:30AM-4:30PM (CST). Access by: In person only.

Ellsworth County

Real Estate Recording—Ellsworth County Register of Deeds, 210 N. Kansas, Courthouse, Ellsworth, KS 67439. 913-472-3022. Fax: 913-472-4912. 8AM-Noon,1-5PM (CST).

Felony, Misdemeanor, Civil, Eviction, Small Claims, Probate—District Court, 210 N Kansas, Ellsworth, KS 67439-3118. 913-472-3832. Fax: 913-472-5712. 8AM-5PM (CST). Access by: Phone, fax, mail, in person.

Finney County

Real Estate Recording—Finney County Register of Deeds, 425 North Eighth Street, Courthouse, Garden City, KS 67846. 316-272-3520. Fax: 316-272-3624. 8AM-5PM (CST).

Felony, Misdemeanor, Civil, Eviction, Small Claims, Probate—District Court, PO Box 798, Garden City, KS 67846. Civil: 316-272-3534. Criminal: 316-272-3552. Fax: 316-272-3611. 8AM-4:30PM (CST). Access by: In person only.

Ford County

Real Estate Recording—Ford County Register of Deeds, 100 Gunsmoke, Ford County Government Center, Dodge City, KS 67801. 316-227-4565. Fax: 316-227-4699. 9AM-5PM (CST).

Felony, Misdemeanor, Civil, Eviction, Small Claims, Probate—District Court, 101 W Spruce, Dodge City, KS 67801. Civil: 316-227-4610. Criminal: 316-227-4608. 9AM-5PM (CST). Access by: Mail, in person.

Franklin County

Real Estate Recording—Franklin County Register of Deeds, 315 South Main, Courthouse, Room 103, Ottawa, KS 66067. 913-229-3440. Fax: 913-229-3419. 8AM-4:30PM (CST).

Felony, Misdemeanor, Civil, Eviction, Small Claims, Probate—District Court, PO Box 637, Ottawa, KS 66067. 913-242-6000. Fax: 913-242-5970. 8AM-5PM (CST). Access by: Mail, in person.

Geary County

Real Estate Recording—Geary County Register of Deeds, 139 East 8th, County Office Building, Junction City, KS 66441. 785-238-5531. Fax: 785-238-5419. 8:30AM-5PM (CST).

Felony, Misdemeanor, Civil, Eviction, Small Claims, Probate—District Court, PO Box 1147, Junction City, KS 66441. 785-762-5221. Fax: 785-762-4420. 8:30AM-4:30PM (CST). Access by: Mail, in person.

Gove County

Real Estate Recording—Gove County Register of Deeds, 520 Washington Street, Courthouse, Gove, KS 67736. 785-938-4465. Fax: 785-938-4486. 8AM-Noon, 1PM-5PM (CST).

Felony, Misdemeanor, Civil, Eviction, Small Claims, Probate—District Court, PO Box 97, Gove, KS 67736. 785-938-2310. Fax: 785-938-2312. 8AM-Noon, 1-5PM (CST). Access by: Fax, mail, in person.

Graham County

Real Estate Recording—Graham County Register of Deeds, 410 North Pomeroy, Hill City, KS 67642. 785-674-2551. 8:30AM-5PM (CST).

Felony, Misdemeanor, Civil, Eviction, Small Claims, Probate—District Court, 410 N Pomeroy, Hill City, KS 67642. 785-674-3458. Fax: 785-674-5463. 8AM-5PM (CST). Access by: In person only.

Grant County

Real Estate Recording—Grant County Register of Deeds, 108 South Glenn, Courthouse, Ulysses, KS 67880. 316-356-1538. Fax: 316-356-5379. 9AM-5PM (CST).

Felony, Misdemeanor, Civil, Eviction, Small Claims, Probate—District Court, 108 S Glenn, Ulysses, KS 67880. 316-356-1526. Fax: 316-356-2131. 8:30AM-5PM (CST). Access by: In person only.

Gray County

Real Estate Recording—Gray County Register of Deeds, 300 South Main, Courthouse, Cimarron, KS 67835. 316-855-3835. Fax: 316-855-3107. 8AM-5PM (CST).

Felony, Misdemeanor, Civil, Eviction, Small Claims, Probate—District Court, PO Box 487, Cimarron, KS 67835. 316-855-3812. Fax: 316-855-7037. 8:30AM-5PM (CST). Access by: In person only.

Greeley County

Real Estate Recording—Greeley County Register of Deeds, 616 Second Street, Courthouse, Tribune, KS 67879. 316-376-4275. Fax: 316-376-2294. 9AM-5PM (MST).

Felony, Misdemeanor, Civil, Eviction, Small Claims, Probate—District Court, PO Box 516, Tribune, KS 67879. 316-376-4292. 9AM-Noon, 1-5PM (MST). Access by: In person only.

Greenwood County

Real Estate Recording—Greenwood County Register of Deeds, Courthouse, 311 N. Main, Eureka, KS 67045. 316-583-8162. Fax: 316-583-8124. 8AM-5PM (CST).

Felony, Misdemeanor, Civil, Eviction, Small Claims, Probate—District Court, 311 N Main, Eureka, KS 67045. 316-583-8153. Fax: 316-583-6818. 8AM-5PM (CST). Access by: Mail, in person.

Hamilton County

Real Estate Recording—Hamilton County Register of Deeds, 219 North Main, Courthouse, Syracuse, KS 67878. 316-384-6925. Fax: 316-384-5853. 8AM-Noon, 12:30-4:30PM (MST).

Felony, Misdemeanor, Civil, Eviction, Small Claims, Probate—District Court, PO Box 745, Syracuse, KS 67878. 316-384-5159. Fax: 316-384-7806. 8AM-5PM (MST). Access by: In person only.

Harper County

Real Estate Recording—Harper County Register of Deeds, Courthouse, 201 North Jennings, Anthony, KS 67003. 316-842-5336. Fax: 316-842-3455. 8AM-Noon,1-5PM (CST).

Felony, Misdemeanor, Civil, Eviction, Small Claims, Probate—District Court, PO Box 467, Anthony, KS 67003. 316-842-3721. Fax: 316-842-5937. 8:30AM-5PM (CST). Access by: In person only.

Harvey County

Real Estate Recording—Harvey County Register of Deeds, 8th & Main, Courthouse, Newton, KS 67114. 316-284-6950. 8AM-5PM (CST).

Felony, Misdemeanor, Civil, Eviction, Small Claims, Probate—District Court, PO Box 665, Newton, KS 67114-0665. 316-284-6890. Civil: 316-284-6894. Criminal: 316-284-6895. Fax: 316-283-4601. 8AM-5PM (CST). Access by: In person only. Call KBI for thorough search.

Haskell County

Real Estate Recording—Haskell County Register of Deeds, 300 S. Inman, Courthouse, Sublette, KS 67877. 316-675-8343. 9AM-Noon,1-5PM (CST).

Felony, Misdemeanor, Civil, Eviction, Small Claims, Probate—District Court, PO Box 146, Sublette, KS 67877. 316-675-2671. Fax: 316-675-8599. 8AM-5PM (CST). Access by: In person only.

Hodgeman County

Real Estate Recording—Hodgeman County Register of Deeds, Main Street, Courthouse, Jetmore, KS 67854. 316-357-8536. (CST).

Felony, Misdemeanor, Civil, Eviction, Small Claims, Probate—District Court, PO Box 187, Jetmore, KS 67854. 316-357-6522. Fax: 316-357-6216. 8:30AM-5PM (CST). Access by: In person only.

Jackson County

Real Estate Recording—Jackson County Register of Deeds, Kogers, 415 New York, Holton, KS 66436. 785-364-3591. Fax: 785-364-3420. 8AM-4:30PM (CST).

Felony, Misdemeanor, Civil, Eviction, Small Claims, Probate—District Court, PO Box 1026, Holton, KS 66436. 785-364-2191. Fax: 785-364-3804. 8AM-4:30PM (CST). Access by: In person only.

Jefferson County

Real Estate Recording—Jefferson County Register of Deeds, 310 Jefferson Street, Courthouse, Oskaloosa, KS 66066. 913-863-2243. Fax: 913-863-3135. 8AM-6:30PM M; 8AM-4PM T-F (CST).

Felony, Misdemeanor, Civil, Eviction, Small Claims, Probate—District Court, PO Box 327, Oskaloosa, KS 66066. 913-863-2461. Fax: 913-863-2369. 8AM-4:30PM (CST). Access by: Fax, mail, in person.

Jewell County

Real Estate Recording—Jewell County Register of Deeds, 307 North Commercial Street, Courthouse, Mankato, KS 66956. 785-378-4070. Fax: 785-378-4075. 8:30AM-Noon, 1-4:30PM (CST).

Felony, Misdemeanor, Civil, Eviction, Small Claims, Probate—District Court, 307 N Commercial, Mankato, KS 66956. 785-378-4030. Fax: 785-378-4035. 8AM-5PM (CST). Access by: Phone, fax, mail, in person.

Johnson County

Real Estate Recording—Johnson County Register of Deeds, 111 South Cherry St., Suite 1300, Johnson County Administration Bldg., Olathe, KS 66061. 913-764-8484. Fax: 913-782-6523. 8AM-5PM (CST).

Felony, Misdemeanor, Civil, Eviction, Small Claims, Probate—District Court, 100 N Kansas, Olathe, KS 66061. 913-782-5000. Fax: 913-791-5826. 8:30AM-5PM (CST). Access by: Fax, mail, in person, online.

Kearny County

Real Estate Recording—Kearny County Register of Deeds, 304 North Main, Courthouse, Lakin, KS 67860. 316-355-6241. Fax: 316-355-7382. 8AM-5PM (MST).

Felony, Misdemeanor, Civil, Eviction, Small Claims, Probate—District Court, PO Box 64, Lakin, KS 67860. 316-355-6481. Fax: 316-355-7462. 8AM-Noon,1-5PM (CST). Access by: Mail, in person.

Kingman County

Real Estate Recording—Kingman County Register of Deeds, 130 North Spruce, Kingman, KS 67068. 316-532-3211. Fax: 316-532-2037. 8AM-Noon,1-5PM (CST).

Felony, Misdemeanor, Civil, Eviction, Small Claims, Probate—District Court, PO Box 495, Kingman, KS 67068. 316-532-5151. Fax: 316-532-2952. 8AM-Noon, 1-5PM (CST). Access by: Mail, in person.

Kiowa County

Real Estate Recording—Kiowa County Register of Deeds, 211 East Florida, Greensburg, KS 67054. 316-723-2441. Fax: 316-723-3302. 8:30AM-Noon, 1-5PM (CST).

Felony, Misdemeanor, Civil, Eviction, Small Claims, Probate—District Court, 211 E Florida, Greensburg, KS 67054. 316-723-3317. Fax: 316-723-2970. 8AM-5PM (CST). Access by: Fax, mail, in person.

Labette County

Real Estate Recording—Labette County Register of Deeds, Courthouse, 521 Merchant, Oswego, KS 67356. 316-795-4931. 8:30AM-5PM (CST).

Felony, Misdemeanor, Civil, Eviction, Small Claims, Probate—District Court, Courthouse, 201 S Central, Parsons, KS (67357), Oswego, KS 67356. 316-795-4533. Fax: 316-795-3056. 8AM-5PM (CST). Access by: In person only.

District Court, 201 South Central, Parsons, KS 67357. 316-795-4533. Fax: 316-421-3056. 8AM-5PM (CST). Access by: In person only.

Lane County

Real Estate Recording—Lane County Register of Deeds, 144 South Lane, Courthouse, Dighton, KS 67839. 316-397-2803. Fax: 316-397-5937. 8AM-Noon,1-5PM (CST).

Felony, Misdemeanor, Civil, Eviction, Small Claims, Probate—District Court, PO Box 188, Dighton, KS 67839. 316-397-2805. Fax: 316-397-5526. 8AM-5PM (CST). Access by: In person only.

Leavenworth County

Real Estate Recording—Leavenworth County Register of Deeds, 300 Walnut, Room 103, Courthouse, Leavenworth, KS 66048. 913-684-0424. Fax: 913-684-0406. 8AM-5PM (CST).

Felony, Misdemeanor, Civil, Eviction, Small Claims, Probate—District Court, 4th & Walnut, Leavenworth, KS 66048. 913-684-0713. Fax: 913-684-0492. 8:30AM-5PM (CST). Access by: Mail, in person.

Lincoln County

Real Estate Recording—Lincoln County Register of Deeds, 216 East Lincoln, Lincoln, KS 67455. 913-524-4657. Fax: 913-524-5008. 8AM-Noon,1-5PM (CST).

Felony, Misdemeanor, Civil, Eviction, Small Claims, Probate—District Court, 216 E Lincoln Ave, Lincoln, KS 67455. 913-524-4057. Fax: 913-524-3204. 8:30AM-5PM (CST). Access by: Fax, mail, in person.

Linn County

Real Estate Recording—Linn County Register of Deeds, Courthouse, 315 Main Street, Mound City, KS 66056. 913-795-2226. Fax: 913-795-2889. 8AM-Noon, 12:30-4:30PM (CST).

Felony, Misdemeanor, Civil, Eviction, Small Claims, Probate—District Court, PO Box 350, Mound City, KS 66056-0350. 913-795-2660. Fax: 913-795-2004. 8AM-5PM (CST). Access by: In person only.

Logan County

Real Estate Recording—Logan County Register of Deeds, 710 West 2nd Street, Courthouse, Oakley, KS 67748. 785-672-4224. Fax: 785-672-3517. 8AM-Noon,1-5PM (CST).

Felony, Misdemeanor, Civil, Eviction, Small Claims, Probate—District Court, 710 W 2nd St, Oakley, KS 67748. 785-672-3654. Fax: 785-672-3517. 8:30AM-Noon, 1-5PM (CST). Access by: Fax, mail, in person.

Lyon County

Real Estate Recording—Lyon County Register of Deeds, 402 Commercial Street, Emporia, KS 66801. 316-341-3241. Fax: 316-342-2652. 8AM-5PM (CST).

Felony, Misdemeanor, Civil, Eviction, Small Claims, Probate—District Court, 402 Commercial St, Emporia, KS 66801. 316-342-4950. Fax: 316-342-8005. 8AM-4PM (CST). Access by: In person only.

Marion County

Real Estate Recording—Marion County Register of Deeds, Courthouse Square, Marion, KS 66861. 316-382-2151. Fax: 316-382-3420. 8:30AM-5PM (CST).

Felony, Misdemeanor, Civil, Eviction, Small Claims, Probate—District Court, PO Box 298, Marion, KS 66861. 316-382-2104. Fax: 316-382-2259. 8:30AM-5PM (CST). Access by: Mail, in person.

Marshall County

Real Estate Recording—Marshall County Register of Deeds, 1201 Broadway, Courthouse, Marysville, KS 66508. 785-562-3226. Fax: 785-562-5685. 8:30AM-5PM (CST).

Felony, Misdemeanor, Civil, Eviction, Small Claims, Probate—District Court, PO Box 86, Marysville, KS 66508. 785-562-5301. Fax: 785-562-2458. 8:30AM-5PM (CST). Access by: Fax, mail, in person.

McPherson County

Real Estate Recording—McPherson County Register of Deeds, 119 North Maple, Courthouse, McPherson, KS 67460. 316-241-5050. Fax: 316-241-1372. 8AM-5PM (CST).

Felony, Misdemeanor, Civil, Eviction, Small Claims, Probate—District Court, PO Box 1106, McPherson, KS 67460. 316-241-3422. Fax: 316-241-1372. 8AM-5PM (CST). Access by: Fax, mail, in person.

Meade County

Real Estate Recording—Meade County Register of Deeds, 200 North Fowler, Courthouse, Meade, KS 67864. 316-873-8705. Fax: 316-873-8713. 8AM-5PM (CST).

Felony, Misdemeanor, Civil, Eviction, Small Claims, Probate—District Court, PO Box 623, Meade, KS 67864. 316-873-8750. Fax: 316-873-8759. 8AM-5PM (CST). Access by: Mail, in person.

Miami County

Real Estate Recording—Miami County Register of Deeds, 120 South Pearl, Courthouse, Paola, KS 66071. 913-294-3716. Fax: 913-294-9515. 8AM-4:30PM (CST).

Felony, Misdemeanor, Civil, Eviction, Small Claims, Probate—District Court, PO Box 187, Paola, KS 66071. 913-294-3326. Fax: 913-294-2535. 8AM-4:30PM (CST). Access by: Mail, in person.

Mitchell County

Real Estate Recording—Mitchell County Register of Deeds, 111 South Hersey, Courthouse, Beloit, KS 67420. 785-738-3854. Fax: 785-738-5844. 8:30AM-5PM (CST).

Felony, Misdemeanor, Civil, Eviction, Small Claims, Probate—District Court, 115 S Hersey, Beloit, KS 67420. 785-738-3753. Fax: 785-738-4101. 8AM-5PM (CST). Access by: Mail, in person.

Montgomery County

Real Estate Recording—Montgomery County Register of Deeds, 5th & Main, Courthouse, Independence, KS 67301. 316-331-2180. Fax: 316-331-2619. 8:30AM-5PM (CST).

Felony, Misdemeanor, Civil, Eviction, Small Claims, Probate—Coffeyville District Court, PO Box 409, Coffeyville, KS 67337. 316-251-1060. Fax: 316-251-2734. 8AM-5PM (CST). Access by: Fax, mail, in person.

Independence District Court, PO Box 768, Independence, KS 67301. 316-331-2550. Fax: 316-331-6120. 8:30AM-4PM (CST). Access by: Fax, mail, in person.

Morris County

Real Estate Recording—Morris County Register of Deeds, Courthouse, Council Grove, KS 66846. 316-767-5614. Fax: 316-767-6861. 8AM-5PM (CST).

Felony, Misdemeanor, Civil, Eviction, Small Claims, Probate—District Court, County Courthouse, Council Grove, KS 66846. 316-767-6838. Fax: 316-767-6488. 8:30AM-5PM (CST). Access by: Fax, mail, in person.

Morton County

Real Estate Recording—Morton County Register of Deeds, 1025 Morton, Courthouse, Elkhart, KS 67950. 316-697-2561. Fax: 316-697-4386. 9AM-5PM (CST).

Felony, Misdemeanor, Civil, Eviction, Small Claims, Probate—District Court, PO Box 825, Elkhart, KS 67950. 316-697-2563. Fax: 316-697-4289. 8AM-Noon, 1-5PM (CST). Access by: In person only.

Nemaha County

Real Estate Recording—Nemaha County Register of Deeds, 607 Nemaha, Courthouse, Seneca, KS 66538. 785-336-2120. Fax: 785-336-3373. 8AM-4:30PM (CST).

Felony, Misdemeanor, Civil, Eviction, Small Claims, Probate—District Court, PO Box 213, Seneca, KS 66538. 785-336-2146. Fax: 785-336-6450. 8AM-5PM (CST). Access by: Phone, mail, in person.

Neosho County

Real Estate Recording—Neosho County Register of Deeds, 100 Main, Courthouse, Erie, KS 66733. 316-244-3858. Fax: 316-244-3860. 8AM-4:30PM (CST).

Felony, Misdemeanor, Civil, Eviction, Small Claims, Probate—Chanute District Court, 102 S Lincoln, PO Box 889, Chanute, KS 66720. 316-431-5700. Fax: 316-431-5710. (CST). Access by: In person only.

Erie District Court, Neosho County Courthouse, PO Box 19, Erie, KS 66733. 316-244-3831. Fax: 316-244-3830. 8AM-4:30PM (CST). Access by: In person only.

Ness County

Real Estate Recording—Ness County Register of Deeds, 202 West Sycamore, Courthouse, Ness City, KS 67560. 913-798-3127. Fax: 913-798-3829. 8AM-Noon, 1PM-5PM (CST).

Felony, Misdemeanor, Civil, Eviction, Small Claims, Probate—District Court, PO Box 445, Ness City, KS 67560. 913-798-3693. Fax: 913-798-3348. 8AM-5PM (CST). Access by: In person only.

Norton County

Real Estate Recording—Norton County Register of Deeds, Courthouse, Norton, KS 67654. 785-877-5765. Fax: 785-877-5703. 8AM-Noon, 1-5PM (CST).

Felony, Misdemeanor, Civil, Eviction, Small Claims, Probate—District Court, PO Box 70, Norton, KS 67654. 785-877-5720. Fax: 785-877-5722. 8AM-5PM (CST). Access by: In person only.

Osage County

Real Estate Recording—Osage County Register of Deeds, Courthouse, Lyndon, KS 66451. 785-828-4523. Fax: 785-828-4749. 8AM-5PM (CST).

Felony, Misdemeanor, Civil, Eviction, Small Claims, Probate—District Court, PO Box 549, Lyndon, KS 66451. 785-828-4713. Fax: 785-828-4704. 8AM-Noon,1-5PM (CST). Access by: Mail, in person.

Osborne County

Real Estate Recording—Osborne County Register of Deeds, Courthouse, 423 W. Main, Osborne, KS 67473. 785-346-2452. Fax: 785-346-5992. 8:30AM-Noon, 1-5PM (CST).

Felony, Misdemeanor, Civil, Eviction, Small Claims, Probate—District Court, 423 W Main, Osborne, KS 67473. 785-346-5911. Fax: 785-246-5992. 8:30AM-5PM (CST). Access by: Fax, in person.

Ottawa County

Real Estate Recording—Ottawa County Register of Deeds, Courthouse - Suite 220, 307 N. Concord, Minneapolis, KS 67467. 785-392-2078. 8AM-Noon,1-5PM (CST).

Felony, Misdemeanor, Civil, Eviction, Small Claims, Probate—District Court, 307 N Concord, Minneapolis, KS 67467. 785-392-2917. 8:30AM-5PM (CST). Access by: Mail, in person.

Pawnee County

Real Estate Recording—Pawnee County Register of Deeds, Courthouse, 2nd Floor, 715 Broadway St., Larned, KS 67550. 316-285-3276. Fax: 316-285-3802. 8:30AM-5PM (CST).

Felony, Misdemeanor, Civil, Eviction, Small Claims, Probate—District Court, PO Box 270, Larned, KS 67550. 316-285-6937. Fax: 316-285-3665. 8AM-5PM (CST). Access by: In person only.

Phillips County

Real Estate Recording—Phillips County Register of Deeds, Courthouse, 301 State St., Phillipsburg, KS 67661. 785-543-6875. 8AM-5PM (CST).

Felony, Misdemeanor, Civil, Eviction, Small Claims, Probate—District Court, PO Box 564, Phillipsburg, KS 67661. 785-543-6830. Fax: 785-543-6832. 8AM-5PM (CST). Access by: In person only.

Pottawatomie County

Real Estate Recording—Pottawatomie County Register of Deeds, 207 N. 1st, Westmoreland, KS 66549. 785-457-3471. Fax: 785-457-3577. 8:30AM-4:40PM (CST).

Felony, Misdemeanor, Civil, Eviction, Small Claims, Probate—District Court, PO Box 129, Westmoreland, KS 66549. 785-457-3392. Fax: 785-457-2107. 8:30AM-4:30PM (CST). Access by: Fax, mail, in person.

Pratt County

Real Estate Recording—Pratt County Register of Deeds, 3rd & Ninnescah, Courthouse, Pratt, KS 67124. 316-672-4140. 8AM-Noon,1-5PM (CST).

Felony, Misdemeanor, Civil, Eviction, Small Claims, Probate—District Court, PO Box 984, Pratt, KS 67124. 316-672-4100. Fax: 316-672-2902. 8AM-Noon, 1-5PM (CST). Access by: Mail, in person.

Rawlins County

Real Estate Recording—Rawlins County Register of Deeds, 607 Main, Courthouse, Atwood, KS 67730. 785-626-3172. Fax: 785-626-9481. 9AM-Noon,1-5PM (CST).

Felony, Misdemeanor, Civil, Eviction, Small Claims, Probate—District Court, PO Box 257, Atwood, KS 67730. 785-626-3465. Fax: 785-626-3350. 9AM-5PM (CST). Access by: Fax, mail, in person.

Reno County

Real Estate Recording—Reno County Register of Deeds, 206 West First, Hutchinson, KS 67501. 316-694-2942. Fax: 316-694-2944. 8AM-5PM (CST).

Felony, Misdemeanor, Civil, Eviction, Small Claims, Probate—District Court, 206 W 1st, Hutchinson, KS 67501. 316-694-2956. Fax: 316-694-2958. 8AM-Noon,1-5PM (CST). Access by: Mail, in person.

Republic County

Real Estate Recording—Republic County Register of Deeds, Courthouse, Belleville, KS 66935. 913-527-5691. Fax: 913-527-2659. 8AM-5PM (CST).

Felony, Misdemeanor, Civil, Eviction, Small Claims, Probate—District Court, PO Box 8, Belleville, KS 66935. 913-527-5691. Fax: 913-527-2714. 8:30AM-5PM (CST). Access by: Mail, in person.

Rice County

Real Estate Recording—Rice County Register of Deeds, 101 West Commercial, Lyons, KS 67554. 316-257-2931. Fax: 316-257-3039. 8:30AM-5PM (CST).

Felony, Misdemeanor, Civil, Eviction, Small Claims, Probate—District Court, 101 W Commercial, Lyons, KS 67554. 316-257-2383. Fax: 316-257-3826. 8:30AM-5PM (CST). Access by: Fax, mail, in person.

Riley County

Real Estate Recording—Riley County Register of Deeds, 110 Courthouse Plaza, Manhattan, KS 66502. 785-537-6340. Fax: 785-537-6331. 8AM-5PM (CST).

Felony, Misdemeanor, Civil, Eviction, Small Claims, Probate—District Court, PO Box 158, Manhattan, KS 66505-0158. 785-537-6364. 8:30AM-5PM (CST). Access by: In person only.

Rooks County

Real Estate Recording—Rooks County Register of Deeds, 115 North Walnut St., Stockton, KS 67669. 785-425-6291. 8AM-Noon,1-5PM (CST).

Felony, Misdemeanor, Civil, Eviction, Small Claims, Probate—District Court, 115 N Walnut, Stockton, KS 67669. 785-425-6718. Fax: 785-425-6568. 8AM-5PM (CST). Access by: Mail, in person.

Rush County

Real Estate Recording—Rush County Register of Deeds, 715 Elm, Courthouse, La Crosse, KS 67548. 913-222-3312. Fax: 913-222-3559. 8:30AM-Noon, 1-5PM (CST).

Felony, Misdemeanor, Civil, Eviction, Small Claims, Probate—District Court, PO Box 387, La Crosse, KS 67548. 913-222-2718. Fax: 913-222-2748. 8AM-5PM (CST). Access by: In person only.

Russell County

Real Estate Recording—Russell County Register of Deeds, 4th & Main, Courthouse, Russell, KS 67665. 785-483-4612. Fax: 785-483-5725. 8:30AM-5PM (CST).

Felony, Misdemeanor, Civil, Eviction, Small Claims, Probate—District Court, PO Box 876, Russell, KS 67665. 785-483-5641. Fax: 785-483-2448. 8AM-5PM (CST). Access by: Fax, mail, in person.

Saline County

Real Estate Recording—Saline County Register of Deeds, 300 West Ash, City County Building, Room 212, Salina, KS 67401. 785-826-6570. Fax: 785-826-6629. 8AM-5PM (CST).

Felony, Misdemeanor, Civil, Eviction, Small Claims, Probate—District Court, PO Box 1756, Salina, KS 67402-1756. 785-826-6617. Fax: 785-826-7319. 8:30AM-4PM (CST). Access by: Mail, in person.

Scott County

Real Estate Recording—Scott County Register of Deeds, Courthouse, 303 Court St., Scott City, KS 67871. 316-872-3155. Fax: 316-872-7145. 8AM-5PM (CST).

Felony, Misdemeanor, Civil, Eviction, Small Claims, Probate—District Court, 303 Court, Scott City, KS 67871. 316-872-7208. 8AM-Noon, 1-5PM (CST). Access by: Mail, in person.

Sedgwick County

Real Estate Recording—Sedgwick County Register of Deeds, 525 North Main, 4th Floor/ room 415, Wichita, KS 67203. 316-383-7511. Fax: 316-383-8066. 8AM-5PM (CST). Marriage records index on line.

Felony, Misdemeanor, Civil, Eviction, Small Claims, Probate—District Court, 525 N Main, Wichita, KS 67203. Civil: 316-383-7302. Criminal: 316-383-7311. Fax: 316-383-7560. 8AM-5PM (CST). Access by: Phone, mail, online, in person.

Seward County

Real Estate Recording—Seward County Register of Deeds, 415 North Washington, Courthouse, Suite 105, Liberal, KS 67901. 316-626-3220. Fax: 316-626-5031. 8AM-5PM (CST).

Felony, Misdemeanor, Civil, Eviction, Small Claims, Probate—District Court, 415 N Washington, Liberal, KS 67901. 316-626-3238. Fax: 316-626-3302. 8:30AM-5PM (CST). Access by: Fax, mail, in person.

Shawnee County

Real Estate Recording—Shawnee County Register of Deeds, 200 East 7th Street, Suite 108, Topeka, KS 66603. 785-233-8200. Fax: 785-291-4912. 8AM-4:30PM (CST).

Felony, Misdemeanor, Civil, Eviction, Small Claims, Probate—District Court, 200 E 7th Rm 209, Topeka, KS

66603. 785-233-8200. Fax: 785-291-4911. 8:30AM-5PM (CST). Access by: Fax, mail, in person, online.

Sheridan County

Real Estate Recording—Sheridan County Register of Deeds, 925 9th Street, Courthouse, Hoxie, KS 67740. 785-675-3741. Fax: 785-675-3050. 8AM-Noon,1-5PM (CST).

Felony, Misdemeanor, Civil, Eviction, Small Claims, Probate—District Court, PO Box 753, Hoxie, KS 67740. 785-675-3451. Fax: 785-675-2256. 8:30AM-5PM (CST). Access by: Phone, fax, mail, in person.

Sherman County

Real Estate Recording—Sherman County Register of Deeds, 813 Broadway, Room 104, Goodland, KS 67735. 785-899-4845. Fax: 785-899-4848. 8AM-Noon,1-5PM (MST).

Felony, Misdemeanor, Civil, Eviction, Small Claims, Probate—District Court, 813 Broadway Rm 201, Goodland, KS 67735. 785-899-4850. Fax: 785-899-4858. 8:30AM-5PM (MST). Access by: Fax, mail, in person.

Smith County

Real Estate Recording—Smith County Register of Deeds, 218 South Grant, Smith Center, KS 66967. 913-282-5160. Fax: 913-282-6257. 8AM-Noon,1-5PM (CST).

Felony, Misdemeanor, Civil, Eviction, Small Claims, Probate—District Court, PO Box 273, Smith Center, KS 66967. 913-282-5140. Fax: 913-282-5145. 8:30AM-5PM (CST). Access by: Mail, in person.

Stafford County

Real Estate Recording—Stafford County Register of Deeds, 209 North Broadway, Stafford County Courthouse, St. John, KS 67576. 316-549-3505. 8AM-Noon,1-5PM (CST).

Felony, Misdemeanor, Civil, Eviction, Small Claims, Probate—District Court, PO Box 365, St John, KS 67576. 316-549-3295. 8:30AM-5PM (CST). Access by: Fax, mail, in person.

Stanton County

Real Estate Recording—Stanton County Register of Deeds, 201 North Main, Courthouse, Johnson, KS 67855. 316-492-2190. Fax: 316-492-2688. 8:30AM-Noon, 1-5PM (CST).

Felony, Misdemeanor, Civil, Eviction, Small Claims, Probate—District Court, PO Box 913, Johnson, KS 67855. 316-492-2180. Fax: 316-492-6410. 8AM-5PM (CST). Access by: Phone, fax, mail, in person.

Stevens County

Real Estate Recording—Stevens County Register of Deeds, 200 East 6th, Hugoton, KS 67951. 316-544-2630. Fax: 316-544-4081. 9AM-5PM (CST).

Felony, Misdemeanor, Civil, Eviction, Small Claims, Probate—District Court, 200 E 6th, Hugoton, KS 67951. 316-544-2484. Fax: 316-544-2528. 8:30AM-5PM (CST). Access by: Fax, mail, in person.

Sumner County

Real Estate Recording—Sumner County Register of Deeds, 500 Block North Washington, Wellington, KS 67152. 316-326-2041. Fax: 316-326-8172. 8AM-5PM (CST).

Felony, Misdemeanor, Civil, Eviction, Small Claims, Probate—District Court, PO Box 399, Sumner County Courthouse, Wellington, KS 67152. 316-326-5936. Fax: 316-326-5365. 8AM-12PM, 1PM-5PM (CST). Access by: Mail, in person.

Thomas County

Real Estate Recording—Thomas County Register of Deeds, 300 North Court, Colby, KS 67701. 785-462-4535. Fax: 785-462-4512. 8AM-Noon, 1PM-5PM (CST).

Felony, Misdemeanor, Civil, Eviction, Small Claims, Probate—District Court, PO Box 805, Colby, KS 67701. 785-462-4540. Fax: 785-462-2291. 8:30AM-5PM (CST). Access by: Fax, mail, in person.

Trego County

Real Estate Recording—Trego County Register of Deeds, 216 Main, WaKeeney, KS 67672. 913-743-6622. Fax: 913-743-2461. 8:30AM-5PM (CST).

Felony, Misdemeanor, Civil, Eviction, Small Claims, Probate—District Court, 216 N Main, Wakeeney, KS 67672. 913-743-2148. Fax: 913-743-2726. 8:30AM-5PM (CST). Access by: Mail, in person.

Wabaunsee County

Real Estate Recording—Wabaunsee County Register of Deeds, 215 Kansas Avenue, Courthouse, Alma, KS 66401. 785-765-3822. Fax: 785-765-3992. 8AM-4:30PM (CST).

Felony, Misdemeanor, Civil, Eviction, Small Claims, Probate—District Court, Courthouse, Alma, KS 66401. 785-765-2406. Fax: 785-765-2487. 8:30AM-5PM (CST). Access by: Fax, mail, in person.

Wallace County

Real Estate Recording—Wallace County Register of Deeds, 313 North Main, Courthouse, Sharon Springs, KS 67758. 785-852-4283. Fax: 785-852-4783. 8AM-12, 1PM-5PM (MST).

Felony, Misdemeanor, Civil, Eviction, Small Claims, Probate—District Court, PO Box 8, Sharon Springs, KS 67758. 785-852-4289. Fax: 785-852-4271. 8AM-Noon,1-5PM (MST). Access by: In person only.

Washington County

Real Estate Recording—Washington County Register of Deeds, 214 C Street, Courthouse, Washington, KS 66968. 785-325-2286. Fax: 785-325-2830. 8AM-5PM (CST).

Felony, Misdemeanor, Civil, Eviction, Small Claims, Probate—District Court, Courthouse , 214 C Street, Washington, KS 66968. 785-325-2381. Fax: 785-325-2557. 8AM-Noon,1-5PM (CST). Access by: Mail, in person.

Wichita County

Real Estate Recording—Wichita County Register of Deeds, Courthouse, 206 S. 4th, Leoti, KS 67861. 316-375-2733. Fax: 316-375-4350. 8AM-Noon,1-5PM (CST).

Felony, Misdemeanor, Civil, Eviction, Small Claims, Probate—District Court, 206 S 4th St, PO Box 968, Leoti, KS 67861. 316-375-4454. Fax: 316-375-2999. 8:30AM-5PM (CST). Access by: In person only.

Wilson County

Real Estate Recording—Wilson County Register of Deeds, Courthouse, Room 106, Fredonia, KS 66736. 316-378-3662. Fax: 316-378-3841. 8:30AM-5PM (CST).

Felony, Misdemeanor, Civil, Eviction, Small Claims, Probate—District Court, PO Box 246, Fredonia, KS 66736. 316-378-4533. Fax: 316-378-4531. 8:30AM-5PM (CST). Access by: Fax, mail, in person.

Woodson County

Real Estate Recording—Woodson County Register of Deeds, 105 W. Rutledge, Room 101, Yates Center, KS 66783. 316-625-8635. Fax: 316-625-8670. 8AM-Noon,1-5PM (CST).

Felony, Misdemeanor, Civil, Eviction, Small Claims, Probate—District Court, PO Box 228, Yates Center, KS 66783. 316-625-8610. Fax: 316-625-8674. 8AM-Noon,1-5PM (CST). Access by: In person only.

Wyandotte County

Real Estate Recording—Wyandotte County Register of Deeds, Courthouse, 710 N. 7th St., Kansas City, KS 66101. 913-573-2841. Fax: 913-321-3075. 8:30AM-5PM (CST).

Felony, Misdemeanor, Civil, Eviction, Small Claims, Probate—District Court, 710 N 7th St, Kansas City, KS 66101. 913-573-2901. Civil: 913-573-2901. Criminal: 913-573-2905. Fax: 913-573-4134. 8AM-5PM (CST). Access by: Phone, mail, in person, online.

Federal Courts

US District Court
District of Kansas

Kansas City Division, US District Court Clerk, 500 State Ave, Kansas City, KS 66101. 913-551-6719. Counties: Atchison, Bourbon, Brown, Cherokee, Crawford, Doniphan, Johnson, Labette, Leavenworth, Linn, Marshall, Miami, Nemaha, Wyandotte

Topeka Division, US District Court Clerk, US District Court, Room 490, 444 SE Quincy, Topeka, KS 66683. 785-295-2610. Counties: Allen, Anderson, Chase, Clay, Cloud, Coffey, Dickinson, Douglas, Franklin, Geary, Jackson, Jewell, Lincoln, Lyon, Marion, Mitchell, Morris, Neosho, Osage, Ottawa, Pottawatomie, Republic, Riley, Saline, Shawnee, Wabaunsee, Washington, Wilson, Woodson

Wichita Division, US District Court Clerk, 204 US Courthouse, 401 N Market, Wichita, KS 67202-2096. 316-269-6491. Counties: Barber, Barton, Butler, Chautauqua, Cheyenne, Clark, Comanche, Cowley, Decatur, Edwards, Elk, Ellis, Ellsworth, Finney, Ford, Gove, Graham, Grant, Gray, Greeley, Greenwood, Hamilton, Harper, Harvey, Haskell, Hodgeman, Jefferson, Kearny, Kingman, Kiowa, Lane, Logan, Mcpherson, Meade, Montgomery, Morton, Ness, Norton, Osborne, Pawnee, Phillips, Pratt, Rawlins, Reno, Rice, Rooks, Rush, Russell, Scott, Sedgwick, Seward, Sheridan, Smith, Stafford, Stanton, Stevens, Sumner, Thomas, Trego, Wallace, Wichita

US Bankruptcy Court
District of Kansas

Kansas City Division, US Bankruptcy Court, 500 State Ave, Room 161, Kansas City, KS 66101. 913-551-6732. Voice Case Information System: 316-269-6668. Counties: Atchison, Bourbon, Brown, Cherokee, Comanche, Crawford, Doniphan, Johnson, Labette, Leavenworth, Linn, Marshall, Miami, Nemaha, Wyandotte

Topeka Division, US Bankruptcy Court, 240 Federal Bldg, 444 SE Quincy, Topeka, KS 66683. 785-295-2750. Voice Case Information System: 316-269-6668. Counties: Allen, Anderson, Chase, Clay, Cloud, Coffey, Dickinson, Douglas, Franklin, Geary, Jackson, Jewell, Lincoln, Lyon, Marion, Mitchell, Morris, Neosho, Osage, Ottawa, Pottawatomie, Republic, Riley, Saline, Shawnee, Wabaunsee, Washington, Wilson, Woodson

Wichita Division, US Bankruptcy Court, 167 US Courthouse, 401 N Market, Wichita, KS 67202. 316-269-6486. Voice Case Information System: 316-269-6668. Counties: Barber, Barton, Butler, Chautauqua, Cheyenne, Clark, Cowley, Decatur, Edwards, Elk, Ellis, Ellsworth, Finney, Ford, Gove, Graham, Grant, Gray, Greeley, Greenwood, Hamilton, Harper, Harvey, Haskell, Hodgeman, Jefferson, Kearny, Kingman, Kiowa, Lane, Logan, Mcpherson, Meade, Montgomery, Morton, Ness, Norton, Osborne, Pawnee, Phillips, Pratt, Rawlins, Reno, Rice, Rooks, Rush, Russell, Scott, Sedgwick, Seward, Sheridan, Smith, Stafford, Stanton, Stevens, Sumner, Thomas, Trego, Wallace, Wichita

Kentucky

Capitol: Frankfort (Franklin County)	
Number of Counties: 120	**Population:** 3,860,219
County Court Locations:	**Federal Court Locations:**
•Circuit Courts: 19/56 Circuits	•District Courts: 10
•District Courts: 19/59 Districts	•Bankruptcy Courts: 2
•Combined Courts: 102	**State Agencies:** 20

State Agencies—Summary

General Help Numbers:

State Archives

Libraries & Archives Department	502-564-8300
PO Box 537	Fax: 502-564-5773
Frankfort, KY 40602-0537	8AM-4PM T-SA
Historical Society:	502-564-3016

Governor's Office

Governor's Office	502-564-2611
700 Capitol Ave, Room 100	Fax: 502-564-2517
Frankfort, KY 40601	7:30AM-5PM

Attorney General's Office

Attorney General's Office	502-564-4002
PO Box 2000, 116 State Capitol	Fax: 502-564-8310
Frankfort, KY 40601	8AM-5PM
Alternate Telephone:	502-573-7600

State Legislation

Kentucky General Assembly	502-372-7181
Legislative Research Commission	Fax: 502-223-5094
700 Capitol Ave, Room 300	8AM-4:30PM
Frankfort, KY 40601	
Bill Room::	502-564-8100

Important State Internet Sites:

> **Webscape**
> File   Edit   View   Help

State of Kentucky World Wide Web
www.state.ky.us/

Provides links to State Government, a virtual tour, what's new, Kentucky parks and a search engine.

State Government Information
www.state.ky.us/govtinfo.htm

Provides links to some of the state cabinets and agencies of State Government.

Library and Archive Reference Service
www.kdla.state.ky.us/

Archive search information is available at this site. There are no online searches at this time, they are all done on site.

State Legislature Information
www.lrc.state.ky.us/

This page provides links to House and Senate members, the text of bills for 1997, and the Kentucky Constitution and Revised Statutes.

UCC Information
www.sos.state.ky.us/admin/legal/ucc.htm

Information is provided about the UCC search process.

State Agencies—Public Records

Criminal Records

Kentucky State Police, Records Section, 1250 Louisville Rd, Frankfort, KY 40601, Main Telephone: 502-227-8713, Fax: 502-227-8734, Hours: 8AM-4PM. Access by: mail, visit. Fee is $4.00. Please note that all Kentucky courts at the local level will not do criminal searches and refer all requesters to the Administrative Office of Courts in Frankfurt (502-573-2350). They will do record checks for $10.00 per name. Records go back to 1988.

Corporation Records
Limited Partnerships
Assumed Name
Limited Liability Company Records

Secretary of State, Corporate Records, PO Box 718, Frankfort, KY 40602-0718, Main Telephone: 502-564-7330, Fax: 502-564-4075, Hours: 8AM-4PM. Access by: mail, phone, visit, PC.

Trademarks/Servicemarks

Secretary of State, Legal Department, 700 Capitol Ave, Room 79, Frankfort, KY 40601, Main Telephone: 502-564-7330, Hours: 8AM-4:30PM. Access by: mail, visit.

Uniform Commercial Code
Federal Tax Liens
State Tax Liens

UCC Division, Secretary of State, PO Box 718, Frankfort, KY 40602-0718, Main Telephone: 502-564-2848, Fax: 502-564-4075, Hours: 8AM-4:30PM. Restricted access. Office will not conduct searches for public, but does provides a terminal for your use.

Sales Tax Registrations

Revenue Cabinet, Tax Compliance Department, Sales Tax Section, Station 53, PO Box 181, Frankfort, KY 40602-0181, Main Telephone: 502-564-5170, Fax: 502-564-2041, Hours: 8AM-4:30PM. Access by: mail, phone, visit.

Birth Certificates

Department for Public Health, Office of Vital Records, 275 E Main St - IE-A, Frankfort, KY 40621-0001, Main Telephone: 502-564-4212, Fax: 502-227-0032, Hours: 8AM-4PM. Access by: mail, phone, visit.

Death Records

Department for Human Resources, Office of Vital Records, 275 E Main St - IE-A, Frankfort, KY 40621-0001, Main Telephone: 502-564-4212, Fax: 502-227-0032, Hours: 8AM-3PM. Access by: mail, phone, visit.

Marriage Certificates

Department for Human Resources, Office of Vital Records, 275 E Main St - IE-A, Frankfort, KY 40621-0001, Main Telephone: 502-564-4212, Fax: 502-227-0032, Hours: 8AM-3PM. Access by: mail, phone, visit.

Divorce Records

Department for Human Resources, Office of Vital Records, 275 E Main St - IE-A, Frankfort, KY 40621-0001, Main Telephone: 502-564-4212, Fax: 502-227-0032, Hours: 8AM-3PM. Access by: mail, phone, visit.

Workers' Compensation Records

Kentucky Department of Workers' Claims, Perimeter Park West, 1270 Louisville Rd, Bldg C, Frankfort, KY 40601, Main Telephone: 502-564-5550, Fax: 502-564-5732, Hours: 8AM-4:30PM. Access by: mail, phone, fax, visit.

Driver Records

Division of Driver's Licensing, State Office Bldg, MVRS, 501 High Street, 2nd Floor, Frankfort, KY 40622, Main Telephone: 502-564-6800, Fax: 502-564-5787, Hours: 8AM-4:30PM. Access by: mail, visit, PC. Requests for copies of tickets must be submitted in writing to; Cabinets Record Custodian, Department of Administrative Services, State Office Building, Frankfort 40622. There is a $.10 fee per document.

Vehicle Ownership
Vehicle Identification

Department of Motor Vehicles, Division of Motor Vehicle Licensing, State Office Bldg, 3rd Floor, Frankfort, KY 40622, Main Telephone: 502-564-4076, Fax: 502-564-1686, Hours: 8AM-4:30PM. Access by: mail, visit, PC.

Accident Reports

Department of State Police, Records Section, 1250 Louisville Rd, Frankfort, KY 40601, Main Telephone: 502-227-8700, Fax: 502-227-8734, Hours: 7:30AM-4:30PM. Access by: mail only.

Hunting License Information
Fishing License Information

Fish & Wildlife Resources Dept, Division of Administrative Srvs, 1 Game Farm Road, Frankfort, KY 40601, Main Telephone: 502-564-4224, Fax: 502-564-6508, Hours 8AM-4:30PM.
Access by: mail, visit. A database has been created, starting in 1996. Records are not released without written request and for good reason. Records are not available for commercial mail lists. Older records are archived in boxes. Record retrieval extremely difficult.

County Courts and Recording Offices

What You Need to Know...

About the Courts

Administration

Administrative Office of Courts	502-573-2350
100 Mill Creek Park	Fax: 502-695-1759
Frankfort, KY 40601	8AM-4PM

Court Structure

Many courts refer requests for criminal searches to the Administrative Office of Courts (AOC) due to lack of personnel at the court level. AOC maintains the records on an **internal** system called COURTNET which contains information on opening, closing, proceedings, disposition, and parties to include individual defendant. Felony convictions are available back to 1978, and Misdemeanors back five years. The required Release Form is available from the AOC at the number shown above. A check or money order for the Search Fee of $10.00 per requested individual is payable to the **State Treasurer of Kentucky,** and an SASE must accompany the request.

Probate is handled by the Circuit Court if contested and by the District Court if uncontested.

Searching Hints

Until 1978, county judges handled all cases; therefore, in many cases District and Circuit Court records go back only to 1978. Records prior to that time are archived.

Online Access

There is a statewide online computer system called SUSTAIN available for **internal** judicial/state agency use only.

About the Recorder's Office

Organization

120 counties, 122 filing offices. The recording officer is County Clerk. **Jefferson and Kenton Counties each has two filing offices.** See the notes under each county for how to determine which office is appropriate to search. 80 counties are in the Eastern Time Zone (EST) and 40 are in the Central Time Zone (CST).

UCC Records

Financing statements are filed with the County Clerk, except for non-resident debtors, which are filed at the state level. Many counties will **not** perform UCC searches. Use search request form UCC-11. Search fees and copy fees vary widely.

Lien Records

All federal and state tax liens on personal property are filed with the County Clerk, often in an "Encumbrance Book." Most counties will **not** perform tax lien searches. Other liens include judgments, motor vehicle, mechanics, lis pendens, and bail bonds.

Real Estate Records

Most counties will **not** perform real estate searches. Copy fees vary. The usual certification fee increased to $5.00 per document. Tax records are maintained by the Property Valuation Administrator, designated "Assessor" in this section.

County Courts and Recording Offices

Adair County

Real Estate Recording—Adair County Clerk, 424 Public Square, Columbia, KY 42728. 502-384-2801. Fax: 502-384-4805. 7:30AM-4PM (CST).

Felony, Misdemeanor, Civil, Eviction, Small Claims, Probate—Circuit and District Court, 500 Public Square, Columbia, KY 42728. 502-384-2626. Fax: 502-384-4299. 8AM-4PM (CST). Access by: Mail, in person.

Allen County

Real Estate Recording—Allen County Clerk, West Main Street, Scottsville, KY 42164. 502-237-3706. Fax: 502-237-9155. 8:30AM-4:30PM, 8:30AM-2PM Sat (CST).

Felony, Misdemeanor, Civil, Eviction, Small Claims, Probate—Circuit and District Court, Box 477, Scottsville, KY 42164. 502-237-3561. 8AM-3:30PM (CST). Access by: In person only.

Anderson County

Real Estate Recording—Anderson County Clerk, 151 South Main, Lawrenceburg, KY 40342. 502-839-3041. Fax: 502-839-3043. 8:30AM-5PM M-Th; 8:30AM-6PM F (EST).

Felony, Civil Actions Over $4,000—Circuit Court, Courthouse 151 S Main St, Lawrenceburg, KY 40342. 502-839-3508. 8:30AM-5PM (EST). Access by: In person only.

Misdemeanor, Civil Actions Under $4,000, Eviction, Small Claims, Probate—District Court, 151 S Main, Lawrenceburg, KY 40342. 502-839-5445. 8:30AM-5PM M-TH, 8:30AM-6PM F (EST). Access by: In person only.

Ballard County

Real Estate Recording—Ballard County Clerk, Court Street, Courthouse, Wickliffe, KY 42087. 502-335-5168. Fax: 502-335-3081. 8AM-4PM; 8AM-5:30PM F (CST).

Felony, Misdemeanor, Civil, Eviction, Small Claims, Probate—Circuit and District Court, Box 265, Wickliffe, KY 42087. 502-335-5123. Fax: 502-335-3849. 8AM-4PM (CST). Access by: Mail, in person.

Barren County

Real Estate Recording—Barren County Clerk, Courthouse, 103 Courthouse Square, Glasgow, KY 42141. 502-651-5200. Fax: 502-651-1083. 8AM-4:30AM (CST).

Felony, Misdemeanor, Civil, Eviction, Small Claims, Probate—Circuit and District Court, PO Box 1359, Glasgow, KY 42141-1359. 502-651-3763. Fax: 502-651-6203. 8AM-4:30PM (CST). Access by: Mail, in person.

Misdemeanor, Civil Actions Under $4,000, Eviction, Small Claims, Probate—District Court, PO Box 1359, Glasgow, KY 42142-1359. Civil: 502-651-9830. Criminal: 502-651-3763. Fax: 502-651-6203. 8AM-4:30PM (CST). Access by: Mail, in person.

Bath County

Real Estate Recording—Bath County Clerk, Courthouse, Main St., Owingsville, KY 40360. 606-674-2613. Fax: 606-674-2613. 8AM-4PM; 8AM-Noon Sat (EST).

Felony, Misdemeanor, Civil, Eviction, Small Claims, Probate—Circuit and District Court, Box 558, Owingsville, KY 40360. 606-674-2186. Fax: 606-674-3996. 8AM-4PM (EST). Access by: Mail, in person.

Bell County

Real Estate Recording—Bell County Clerk, Courthouse Square, Pineville, KY 40977. 606-337-6143. Fax: 606-337-5415. 8AM-4PM M-F; 8AM-Noon Sat (EST).

Felony, Misdemeanor, Civil, Eviction, Small Claims, Probate—Circuit and District Court, Box 306, Pineville, KY 40977. 606-337-2942. Fax: 606-337-8850. 8:30AM-4PM (EST). Access by: In person only.

Boone County

Real Estate Recording—Boone County Clerk, 2950 East Washington Square, Burlington, KY 41005. 606-334-2206. Fax: 606-334-2193. 8:30AM-4:30PM (EST).

Felony, Misdemeanor, Civil, Eviction, Small Claims, Probate—Circuit and District Court, Box 480, Burlington, KY 41005. 606-334-2149. Fax: 606-586-9413. 8:30AM-5:30PM (EST). Access by: In person only.

Bourbon County

Real Estate Recording—Bourbon County Clerk, Main Street, Courthouse, Paris, KY 40361. 606-987-2142. Fax: 606-987-5660. 8:30AM-4:30PM M-Th; 8:30AM-6PM F (EST).

Felony, Misdemeanor, Civil, Eviction, Small Claims, Probate—Circuit and District Court, Box 740, Paris, KY 40361. 606-987-2624. 8:30AM-4PM M-TH, 8:30AM-6PM F (EST). Access by: In person only.

Boyd County

Real Estate Recording—Boyd County Clerk, 2800 Louisa Street, Courthouse, Catlettsburg, KY 41129. 606-739-5116. Fax: 606-739-6357. 8:30AM-4PM Main Office (9AM-4:30PM & 9AM-Noon Sat Branch Office) (EST).

Felony, Misdemeanor, Civil, Eviction, Small Claims, Probate—Circuit and District Court, Box 694, Catlettsburg, KY 41129-0694. 606-739-4131. Fax: 606-739-5793. 8:30AM-4PM (EST). Access by: Mail, in person.

Boyle County

Real Estate Recording—Boyle County Clerk, 321 W. Main St., Room 123, Danville, KY 40422. 606-238-1112. Fax: 606-238-1114. 8:30AM-4PM M-Th; 8:30AM-5PM F (EST).

Felony, Civil Actions Over $4,000—Circuit Court, Courthouse, Main St, Danville, KY 40422. 606-236-7442. Fax: 606-238-1114. 8AM-5PM (EST). Access by: Phone, mail, in person.

Misdemeanor, Civil Actions Under $4,000, Eviction, Small Claims, Probate—District Court, Courthouse 3rd Fl, Danville, KY 40422. 606-239-7362. Fax: 606-236-9807. 8AM-4:30PM (EST). Access by: In person only.

Bracken County

Real Estate Recording—Bracken County Clerk, Courthouse, Brooksville, KY 41004. 606-735-2952. Fax: 606-735-2925. 9AM-4PM M,T,Th,F; 9AM-Noon W,Sat (EST).

Felony, Misdemeanor, Civil, Eviction, Small Claims, Probate—Circuit and District Court, Box 132 Courthouse, Brooksville, KY 41004. 606-735-3328. 9AM-4PM M,T,TH,F, 9AM-Noon W & Sat (EST). Access by: In person only.

Breathitt County

Real Estate Recording—Breathitt County Clerk, 1137 Main Street, Jackson, KY 41339. 606-666-3810. Fax: 606-666-3807. 8AM-4PM M,T,Th,F; 8AM-Noon W,Sat (EST).

Felony, Misdemeanor, Civil, Eviction, Small Claims, Probate—Circuit and District Court, 1137 Main St, Jackson, KY 41339. 606-666-5768. Fax: 606-666-4893. 8AM-4PM M,T,TH,F, 8AM-Noon W, 9AM-Noon Sat (EST). Access by: Phone, mail, in person.

Breckinridge County

Real Estate Recording—Breckinridge County Clerk, Main St., Hardinsburg, KY 40143. 502-756-6166. Fax: 502-756-1569. 8AM-4PM, 8AM-Noon Sat (CST).

Felony, Misdemeanor, Civil, Eviction, Small Claims, Probate—Circuit and District Court, Box 111, Hardinsburg, KY 40143. 502-756-2239. Fax: 502-756-1129. 8AM-4PM (CST). Access by: Phone, mail, in person.

Bullitt County

Real Estate Recording—Bullitt County Clerk, Courthouse Annex, 149 N. Walnut St., Shepherdsville, KY 40165. 502-543-2513. Fax: 502-543-9121. 8AM-4PM M,T,W,F; 8AM-6PM Th (EST).

Felony, Misdemeanor, Civil, Eviction, Small Claims, Probate—Circuit and District Court, Box 275, Shephardsville, KY 40165. 502-543-7104. Fax: 502-543-7158. 8AM-4PM (EST). Access by: Fax, mail, in person.

Butler County

Real Estate Recording—Butler County Clerk, Courthouse, Morgantown, KY 42261. 502-526-5676. Fax: 502-526-2658. 8AM-4PM (CST).

Felony, Misdemeanor, Civil, Eviction, Small Claims, Probate—Circuit and District Court, Box 625, Morgantown, KY 42261. 502-526-5631. 8AM-4PM M-F, 8AM-12PM SAT (CST). Access by: Mail, in person.

Caldwell County

Real Estate Recording—Caldwell County Clerk, 100 East Market Street, Courthouse - Room 3, Princeton, KY 42445. 502-365-6754. Fax: 502-365-7447. 8AM-4PM (CST).

Felony, Misdemeanor, Civil, Eviction, Small Claims, Probate—Circuit and District Court, 105 West Court Sq, Princeton, KY 42445. 502-365-6884. Fax: 502-365-6884. 8AM-4PM (CST). Access by: In person only.

Calloway County

Real Estate Recording—Calloway County Clerk, 101 South 5th Street, Murray, KY 42071. 502-753-3923. Fax: 502-759-9611. 8AM-4:30PM (CST).

Felony, Misdemeanor, Civil, Eviction, Small Claims, Probate—Circuit and District Court, 201 S 4th St Miller Annex, Murray, KY 42071. 502-753-2714. 8AM-4:30PM (CST). Access by: Mail, in person.

Campbell County

Real Estate Recording—Campbell County Clerk, 4th and York Streets, Courthouse, Newport, KY 41071. 606-292-3845. Fax: 606-292-0615. 8:30AM-4PM (EST).

Felony, Civil Actions Over $4,000—Circuit Court, 330 York St Rm 8, Newport, KY 41071. 606-292-6314. 8:30AM-4PM (EST). Access by: In person only.

Misdemeanor, Civil Actions Under $4,000, Eviction, Small Claims, Probate—District Court, 600 Columbia St, Newport, KY 41071. 606-292-6305. Fax: 606-292-6593. 8:30AM-4PM (EST). Access by: In person only.

Carlisle County

Real Estate Recording—Carlisle County Clerk, West Court Street, Bardwell, KY 42023. 502-628-3233. Fax: 502-628-0191. 8:30AM-4PM (CST).

Felony, Misdemeanor, Civil, Eviction, Small Claims, Probate—Circuit and District Court, Box 337, Bardwell, KY 42023. 502-628-5425. Fax: 502-628-3392. 8AM-4PM (CST). Access by: Phone, mail, in person.

Carroll County

Real Estate Recording—Carroll County Clerk, 440 Main Street, Court House, Carrollton, KY 41008. 502-732-7005. Fax: 502-732-7007. 8:30AM-4:30PM M,T,Th,F; 8:30AM-Noon W,Sat (EST).

Felony, Misdemeanor, Civil, Eviction, Small Claims, Probate—Circuit and District Court, 802 Clay St, Carrollton, KY 41008. 502-732-4305. 8:30AM-4:30PM (EST). Access by: Phone, mail, in person.

Carter County

Real Estate Recording—Carter County Clerk, 300 W. Main St., Room 232, Grayson, KY 41143. 606-474-5188. Fax: 606-474-5180. 8:30AM-4PM; 8:30AM-Noon Sat (EST).

Felony, Civil Actions Over $4,000—Circuit Court, 300 Courthouse, Rm 308 Grayson, KY 41143. 606-474-5191. Fax: 606-474-8826. 8:30AM-4PM M-F, 9AM-Noon SAT (EST). Access by: Mail, in person.

Misdemeanor, Civil Actions Under $4,000, Eviction, Small Claims, Probate—District Court, Courthouse Rm 203, Grayson, KY 41143. 606-474-6572. Fax: 606-474-8826. 8:30AM-4PM (EST). Access by: In person only.

Casey County

Real Estate Recording—Casey County Clerk, Courthouse, Liberty, KY 42539. 606-787-6471. Fax: 606-787-9155. 8AM-4:30PM; 8AM-Noon Sat (EST).

Felony, Misdemeanor, Civil, Eviction, Small Claims, Probate—Circuit and District Court, Box 147, Liberty, KY 42539. 606-787-6510. 8AM-4:30PM M-W, 8AM-4PM TH, 8AM-12PM SAT (EST). Access by: Phone, mail, in person.

Christian County

Real Estate Recording—Christian County Clerk, 511 South Main, Hopkinsville, KY 42240. 502-887-4105. 8AM-4:30PM (CST).

Felony, Misdemeanor, Civil, Eviction, Small Claims, Probate—Circuit and District Court, Box 635, Hopkinsville, KY 42241. 502-889-6539. Fax: 502-889-6564. 8AM-4:30PM (CST). Access by: Mail, in person.

Clark County

Real Estate Recording—Clark County Clerk, 34 South Main Street, Winchester, KY 40391. 606-745-0280. Fax: 606-745-4251. 8AM-5PM M; 8AM-4PM T-F (EST).

Felony, Civil Actions Over $4,000—Circuit Court, Box 715, Winchester, KY 40391. 606-737-7264. 8AM-4:30PM (EST). Access by: In person only.

Misdemeanor, Civil Actions Under $4,000, Eviction, Small Claims—District Court, PO Box 687, Winchester, KY 40392-0687. 606-737-7264. 8AM-4PM (EST). Access by: Mail, in person.

Clay County

Real Estate Recording—Clay County Clerk, 316 Main Street, Suite 143, Manchester, KY 40962. 606-598-2544. Fax: 606-598-7199. 8AM-4PM; 8AM-Noon Sat (EST).

Felony, Misdemeanor, Civil, Eviction, Small Claims, Probate—Circuit and District Court, Box 463, Manchester, KY 40962. 606-598-3663. Fax: 606-598-4047. 8AM-4PM (EST). Access by: In person only.

Clinton County

Real Estate Recording—Clinton County Clerk, 212 Washington Street, Courthouse, Albany, KY 42602. 606-387-5943. Fax: 606-387-5258. 8AM-4:30PM; 8AM-Noon Sat (CST).

Felony, Misdemeanor, Civil, Eviction, Small Claims, Probate—Circuit and District Court, Courthouse 2nd Fl, Albany, KY 42602. 606-387-6424. Fax: 606-387-8154. 8AM-4PM M-F, 8AM-12PM SAT (CST). Access by: Mail, in person.

Crittenden County

Real Estate Recording—Crittenden County Clerk, 107 South Main, Courthouse, Suite 203, Marion, KY 42064. 502-965-3403. Fax: 502-965-3447. 8AM-4:30PM M,T,Th,F; 8AM-Noon W,Sat (CST).

Felony, Misdemeanor, Civil, Eviction, Small Claims, Probate—Circuit and District Court, 107 S Main, Marion, KY 42064. 502-965-4200. 8AM-4:30PM (CST). Access by: Mail, in person.

Cumberland County

Real Estate Recording—Cumberland County Clerk, Courthouse - Public Square, Room 6, Burkesville, KY 42717. 502-864-3726. Fax: 502-864-5884. 8AM-4:30PM; 8AM-Noon Sat (CST).

Felony, Misdemeanor, Civil, Eviction, Small Claims, Probate—Circuit and District Court, Box 395, Burkesville, KY 42717. 502-864-2611. 8AM-4PM (CST). Access by: Mail, in person.

Daviess County

Real Estate Recording—Daviess County Clerk, 212 St. Ann Street, Owensboro, KY 42303. 502-685-8434. Fax: 502-686-7111. 8AM-4PM M-Th; 8AM-6PM F (CST).

Felony, Misdemeanor, Civil, Eviction, Small Claims, Probate—Circuit and District Court, Box 277, Owensboro, KY 42302. 502-686-3222. 8AM-4PM (CST). Access by: In person only.

Edmonson County

Real Estate Recording—Edmonson County Clerk, Main Street, Community Center, Brownsville, KY 42210. 502-597-2624. 8AM-5PM M,T,W,F; 8AM-Noon Sat (CST).

Felony, Misdemeanor, Civil, Eviction, Small Claims, Probate—Circuit and District Court, Box 130, Brownsville, KY 42210. 502-597-2584. Fax: 502-597-2884. 8AM-5PM M-W,F, 8AM-Noon Sat (CST). Access by: In person only.

Elliott County

Real Estate Recording—Elliott County Clerk, Main Street, Courthouse, Sandy Hook, KY 41171. 606-738-5421. Fax: 606-738-4462. 8AM-4PM; 9AM-Noon Sat (EST).

Felony, Misdemeanor, Civil, Eviction, Small Claims, Probate—Circuit and District Court, Box 788, Sandy Hook, KY 41171. 606-738-5238. Fax: 606-738-6962. 8AM-4PM M-F, 9AM-12PM SAT (EST). Access by: Phone, mail, in person.

Estill County

Real Estate Recording—Estill County Clerk, Courthouse, Irvine, KY 40336. 606-723-5156. Fax: 606-723-5108. 8AM-4PM M,T,Th,F; 8AM-Noon W,Sat (EST).

Felony, Misdemeanor, Civil, Eviction, Small Claims, Probate—Circuit and District Court, Courthouse 2nd Fl, Irvine, KY 40336. 606-723-3970. Fax: 606-723-1158. 8AM-4PM (EST). Access by: Phone, fax, mail, in person.

Fayette County

Real Estate Recording—Fayette County Clerk, 162 Main St, Room 132, Lexington, KY 40507. 606-253-3344. 8AM-4:30PM (EST).

Felony, Civil Actions Over $4,000—Circuit Court-Criminal and Civil Divisions, 215 W Main (Civil-Rm 200), Lexington, KY 40507. Civil: 606-246-2141. Criminal: 606-246-2224. 8:30AM-4:30PM (EST). Access by: Mail, in person.

Misdemeanor, Civil Actions Under $4,000, Eviction, Small Claims, Probate—District Court-Criminal and Civil, 140 N ML King Blvd (Criminal), 136 N ML King Blvd (Civil), Lexington, KY 40507. Civil: 606-246-2240. Criminal: 606-246-2228. 8AM-4PM (EST). Access by: Mail, in person.

Fleming County

Real Estate Recording—Fleming County Clerk, Court Square, Flemingsburg, KY 41041. 606-845-8461. Fax: 606-845-0212. 8:30AM-4:30PM M-F; 8:30AM-Noon Sat (EST).

Felony, Misdemeanor, Civil, Eviction, Small Claims, Probate—Circuit and District Court, Courthouse 100 Court Square, Flemingsburg, KY 41041. 606-845-7011. Fax: 606-849-2400. 8AM-4:30PM M-F; 8:30AM-Noon Sat (EST). Access by: Phone, fax, mail, in person.

Floyd County

Real Estate Recording—Floyd County Clerk, 3rd Avenue, Courthouse, Room 1, Prestonsburg, KY 41653. 606-886-3816. Fax: 606-886-8089. 8AM-4:30PM M,T,W,Th; 8AM-6PM F;9AM-Noon Sat (EST).

Felony, Civil Actions Over $4,000—Circuit Court, Box 109, Prestonsburg, KY 41653. 606-886-3090. Fax: 606-886-9075. 8AM-4PM (EST). Access by: Mail, in person.

Misdemeanor, Small Claims—District Court, Box 109, Prestonsburg, KY 41653. 606-886-9114. 8AM-4PM (EST). Access by: Phone, mail, in person.

Franklin County

Real Estate Recording—Franklin County Clerk, 315 W. Main Street, Courthouse Annex, Frankfort, KY 40601. 502-875-8710. Fax: 502-875-8718. 8AM-4:30PM (EST).

Felony, Civil Actions Over $4,000—Circuit Court, Box 678, Frankfort, KY 40602. 502-564-8380. Fax: 502-564-8188. 8AM-4:30PM (EST). Access by: Fax, mail, in person.

Misdemeanor, Civil Actions Under $4,000, Eviction, Small Claims, Probate—District Court, Box 678, Frankfort, KY 40601. 502-564-7013. Fax: 502-564-8188. 8AM-4:30PM (EST). Access by: Mail, in person.

Fulton County

Real Estate Recording—Fulton County Clerk, Wellington Street, Johnson Annex, Hickman, KY 42050. 502-236-2061. Fax: 502-236-3373. 8AM-4PM (CST).

Felony, Misdemeanor, Civil, Eviction, Small Claims, Probate—Circuit and District Court, Box 198, Hickman, KY 42050. 502-236-3944. Fax: 502-236-3729. 8:30AM-4PM (CST). Access by: In person only.

Gallatin County

Real Estate Recording—Gallatin County Clerk, Franklin & Washington, Warsaw, KY 41095. 606-567-5411. Fax: 606-567-5444. 8AM-4:30PM M,T,Th,F; 8AM-Noon Sat (EST).

Felony, Civil Actions Over $4,000—Circuit Court, Box 256, Warsaw, KY 41095. 606-567-5241. 8AM-4:30PM (EST). Access by: Phone, mail, in person.

Misdemeanor, Civil Actions Under $4,000, Eviction, Small Claims, Probate—District Court, Box 256, Warsaw, KY 41095. 606-567-2388. 8AM-4:30PM M,T,TH,F & SAT (EST). Access by: In person only.

Garrard County

Real Estate Recording—Garrard County Clerk, Courthouse Building, Lancaster, KY 40444. 606-792-3071. Fax: 606-792-2010. 8AM-4PM M,T,Th,F; 8AM-Noon W,Sat (EST).

Felony, Misdemeanor, Civil, Eviction, Small Claims, Probate—Circuit and District Court, 7 Public Square, Courthouse Annex, Lancaster, KY 40444. 606-792-6032. Fax: 606-792-6414. 8AM-4PM M,T,TH,F, 8AM-12PM SAT (EST). Access by: Mail, in person.

Grant County

Real Estate Recording—Grant County Clerk, Courthouse Basement, Room 15, 101 N. Main St., Williamstown, KY 41097. 606-824-3321. Fax: 606-824-3367. 8:30AM-4PM M-F; 8:30AM-Noon Sat (EST).

Felony, Misdemeanor, Civil, Eviction, Small Claims, Probate—Circuit and District Court, Courthouse 101 N Main, Williamstown, KY 41097. 606-824-4467. 8AM-4PM (EST). Access by: In person only.

Graves County

Real Estate Recording—Graves County Clerk, Courthouse, Mayfield, KY 42066. 502-247-1676. Fax: 502-247-1274. 8AM-4:30PM M-Th; 8AM-6PM F (CST).

Felony, Misdemeanor, Civil, Eviction, Small Claims, Probate—Circuit and District Court, Courthouse 100 E Broadway, Mayfield, KY 42066. 502-247-1733. Fax: 502-247-8221. 8AM-4:30PM (CST). Access by: Phone, mail, in person.

Grayson County

Real Estate Recording—Grayson County Clerk, 10 Public Square, Leitchfield, KY 42754. 502-259-5295. Fax: 502-259-9264. 8AM-4PM M,T,W,F; 8AM-Noon Th,Sat (CST).

Felony, Misdemeanor, Civil, Eviction, Small Claims, Probate—Circuit and District Court, 125 E White Oak, Leitchfield, KY 42754. 502-259-3040. Fax: 502-259-9866. 8AM-4PM M-F, 8AM-Noon Sat (CST). Access by: Mail, in person.

Green County

Real Estate Recording—Green County Clerk, 203 West Court Street, Greensburg, KY 42743. 502-932-5386. Fax: 502-932-3635. 8AM-4PM M-W,F; 8AM-2PM Sat (Closed Th) (EST).

Felony, Misdemeanor, Civil, Eviction, Small Claims, Probate—Circuit and District Court, 203 W Court St, Greensburg, KY 42743. 502-932-5631. Fax: 502-932-3635. 8AM-4PM M-W, F; 8AM-12:30PM SAT (EST). Access by: Mail, in person.

Greenup County

Real Estate Recording—Greenup County Clerk, Main Street, Courthouse, Greenup, KY 41144. 606-473-7396. Fax: 606-473-5354. 9AM-4:30PM M,T,W,F; 9AM-Noon Th,Sat (EST).

Felony, Misdemeanor, Civil, Eviction, Small Claims, Probate—Circuit and District Court, Courthouse Annex, Greenup, KY 41144. 606-473-9869. Fax: 606-473-7308. 9AM-4:30PM M-F (EST). Access by: Mail, in person.

Hancock County

Real Estate Recording—Hancock County Clerk, 225 Main & Cross St., Courthouse, Hawesville, KY 42348. 502-927-6117. Fax: 502-927-8639. 8AM-4PM M-W,F; 8AM-5:30PM Th (CST).

Felony, Misdemeanor, Civil, Eviction, Small Claims, Probate—Circuit and District Court, Courthouse, Hawesville, KY 42348. 502-927-8144. Fax: 502-927-8629. 8AM-4PM M,T,W,F, 8AM-5:30PM TH (CST). Access by: Mail, in person.

Hardin County

Real Estate Recording—Hardin County Clerk, 14 Public Square, Elizabethtown, KY 42701. 502-765-2171. Fax: 502-769-2682. 8:30AM-4:30PM (EST).

Felony, Misdemeanor, Civil, Eviction, Small Claims, Probate—Circuit and District Court, Courthouse 100 Public Square, Elizabethtown, KY 42701. 502-766-5000. Fax: 502-769-6505. 8AM-4:30PM; Radcliff District Court 8AM-4PM (EST). Access by: In person only.

Harlan County

Real Estate Recording—Harlan County Clerk, 210 E. Central St., Suite 205, Harlan, KY 40831. 606-573-3636. Fax: 606-573-0064. 8:30AM-4:30PM M-W & F; 8:30AM-6PM Th (EST).

Felony, Misdemeanor, Civil, Eviction, Small Claims, Probate—Circuit and District Court, Box 190, Harlan, KY 40831. 606-573-2680. 8AM-4:30PM (EST). Access by: In person only.

Harrison County

Real Estate Recording—Harrison County Clerk, 190 West Pike Street, Cynthiana, KY 41031. 606-234-7130. Fax: 606-234-8049. 9AM-4:30PM; 9AM-Noon Sat (EST).

Felony, Misdemeanor, Civil, Eviction, Small Claims, Probate—Circuit and District Court, Courthouse Box 10, Cynthiana, KY 41031. 606-234-1914. 8:30AM-4:30PM M-F, 9AM-12PM Sat (EST). Access by: Mail, in person.

Hart County

Real Estate Recording—Hart County Clerk, Main Street, Courthouse, Munfordville, KY 42765. 502-524-2751. Fax: 502-524-0458. 8AM-4PM (8AM-Noon Sat) (CST).

Felony, Misdemeanor, Civil, Eviction, Small Claims, Probate—Circuit and District Court, Box 548, Munfordville, KY 42765. 502-524-5181. 8AM-4PM M-F,8AM-12PM S (CST). Access by: In person only.

Henderson County

Real Estate Recording—Henderson County Clerk, Corner of Main & First, Courthouse, Henderson, KY 42420. 502-826-3906. Fax: 502-826-9677. 8AM-4:30PM M-Th; 8AM-6PM F (CST).

Felony, Civil Actions Over $4,000—Circuit and District Court, PO Box 675, Henderson, KY 42420. 502-826-2405.

Fax: 502-827-5932. 8AM-6PM M; 8AM-4:30PM T-F (CST). Access by: In person only.

Henry County

Real Estate Recording—Henry County Clerk, Courthouse, 30 N. Main, Ste A, New Castle, KY 40050. 502-845-5705. Fax: 502-845-5708. 8AM-4PM (EST).

Felony, Misdemeanor, Civil, Eviction, Small Claims, Probate—Circuit and District Court, PO Box 359, New Castle, KY 40050. 502-845-7551. 8AM-4:30PM M-F (EST). Access by: In person only.

Hickman County

Real Estate Recording—Hickman County Clerk, Courthouse, 110 E. Clay, Clinton, KY 42031. 502-653-2131. Fax: 502-653-4248. 8:30AM-4PM (CST).

Felony, Misdemeanor, Civil, Eviction, Small Claims, Probate—Circuit and District Court, 100 Clay St, Clinton, KY 42031. 502-653-3901. 8AM-4PM (CST). Access by: In person only.

Hopkins County

Real Estate Recording—Hopkins County Clerk, Corner of Main and Center Streets, Courthouse - Room 14, Madisonville, KY 42431. 502-825-5001. Fax: 502-825-5009. 8AM-4PM (CST).

Felony, Misdemeanor, Civil, Eviction, Small Claims, Probate—Circuit and District Court, Courthouse 30 S Main St, Madisonville, KY 42431. 502-824-7502. Fax: 502-824-7051. 8AM-4PM (CST). Access by: In person only.

Jackson County

Real Estate Recording—Jackson County Clerk, Main Street, Courthouse, McKee, KY 40447. 606-287-7800. Fax: 606-287-3277. 8AM-4PM; 8AM-Noon Sat (EST).

Felony, Civil Actions Over $4,000—Circuit Court, PO Box 84, McKee, KY 40447. 606-287-7783. Fax: 606-287-3277. 8AM-4PM M-F 8AM-Noon Sat (EST). Access by: Fax, mail, in person.

Misdemeanor, Civil Actions Under $4,000, Eviction, Small Claims, Probate—District Court, PO Box 84, McKee, KY 40447. 606-287-8651. Fax: 606-287-3277. 8AM-4PM M-F 8AM-12PM SAT (EST). Access by: Mail, in person.

Jefferson County

Felony, Misdemeanor, Civil, Eviction, Small Claims, Probate—Circuit and District Court, Hall of Justice 600 W Jefferson St, Louisville, KY 40202. 502-595-3064. Fax: 502-595-4629. 24 HOURS MON-SUN (EST). Access by: Mail, in person.

Jefferson County Recorder

Real Estate Recording—P.O. Box 35396, 527 West Jefferson, Louisville, KY 40202. 502-574-5785.

Jessamine County

Real Estate Recording—Jessamine County Clerk, 101 North Main Street, Nicholasville, KY 40356. 606-885-4161. Fax: 606-885-5837. 8AM-5PM M; 8AM-4PM T,W,F; 8AM-Noon Th; 9am-Noon Sat (EST).

Felony, Civil Actions Over $4,000—Circuit Court, 101 N Main St, Nicholasville, KY 40356. 606-885-4531. 8AM-5PM M 8AM-4:30PM T & W 8AM-12PM TH 8AM-4PM F (EST). Access by: In person only.

Misdemeanor, Civil Actions Under $4,000, Eviction, Small Claims, Probate—District Court, 101 N Main St, Nicholasville, KY 40356. 606-887-1005. 8AM-5PM M 8AM-4:30 T & W 8AM-12PM TH 8AM-4PM F (EST). Access by: Mail, in person.

Johnson County

Real Estate Recording—Johnson County Clerk, Courthouse, Court St., Paintsville, KY 41240. 606-789-2557. Fax: 606-789-2559. 8AM-5PM M-Th; 8AM-7PM F; 8:30AM-Noon Sat (EST).

Felony, Misdemeanor, Civil, Eviction, Small Claims, Probate—Circuit and District Court, Box 1405, Paintsville, KY 41240. 606-789-5181. Fax: 606-789-5611. 8AM-4:30PM;

830AM-Noon Sat Driver's license only (EST). Access by: In person only. Court will not conduct searches. Contact AOC for statewide search..

Kenton County

Real Estate Recording—Kenton County Clerk, 1st District, 3rd & Court Streets, Room 102, Covington, KY 41012. 606-491-0702. Fax: 606-491-4515. 8:30AM-4PM M-Th; 8:30AM-6PM F (EST).

Kenton County Clerk, 2nd District, 5272 Madison, Independence, KY 41051. 606-356-9272. Fax: 606-356-9278. 9AM-4PM M,T,Th,F; 9AM-6PM W (EST).

Felony, Civil Actions Over $4,000—Circuit Court, Box 669, Covington, KY 41012. 606-292-6521. Fax: 606-292-6611. 8AM-4:30PM (EST). Access by: Mail, in person.

Misdemeanor, Civil Actions Under $4,000, Eviction, Small Claims, Probate—District Court, PO Box 669, City Bldg Rm 408, Covington, KY 41012. 606-292-6523. Fax: 606-292-6611. 8AM-4:30PM (EST). Access by: Mail, in person.

Knott County

Real Estate Recording—Knott County Clerk, Main Street, Courthouse, Hindman, KY 41822. 606-785-5651. Fax: 606-785-0996. 8AM-4PM M,T,W,Th; 8AM-6PM F; 8AM-Noon Sat (EST).

Felony, Misdemeanor, Civil, Eviction, Small Claims, Probate—Circuit and District Court, Box 515, Hindman, KY 41822. 606-785-5021. 8AM-4PM (EST). Access by: Mail, in person.

Knox County

Real Estate Recording—Knox County Clerk, 401 Court Square, Suite 102, Barbourville, KY 40906. 606-546-3568. Fax: 606-546-3589. 8:30AM-4PM (EST).

Felony, Misdemeanor, Civil, Eviction, Small Claims, Probate—Circuit and District Court, PO Box 760, Barbourville, KY 40906. 606-546-3075. Fax: 606-546-7949. 8AM-4PM (EST). Access by: In person only.

Larue County

Real Estate Recording—Larue County Clerk, 209 W. High St., Hodgenville, KY 42748. 502-358-3544. Fax: 502-358-4528. 8AM-4:30PM M,T,Th,F; 8AM-Noon W,Sat (EST).

Felony, Misdemeanor, Civil, Eviction, Small Claims, Probate—Circuit and District Court, Courthouse Annex, Hodgenville, KY 42748. 502-358-9569. Fax: 502-358-3731. 8AM-4PM (EST). Access by: Mail, in person.

Laurel County

Real Estate Recording—Laurel County Clerk, 101 South Main, Courthouse, London, KY 40741. 606-864-5158. Fax: 606-864-7369. 8AM-4:30PM; 8:30AM-Noon Sat (EST).

Felony, Misdemeanor, Civil, Eviction, Small Claims, Probate—Circuit and District Court, Box 1798, London, KY 40743-1798. 606-864-2863. Fax: 606-864-8264. 8AM-4PM (EST). Access by: Mail, in person.

Lawrence County

Real Estate Recording—Lawrence County Clerk, 122 South Main Cross Street, Louisa, KY 41230. 606-638-4108. Fax: 606-638-0638. 8:30AM-4PM; 8:30AM-Noon Sat (EST).

Felony, Misdemeanor, Civil, Eviction, Small Claims, Probate—Circuit and District Court, Courthouse PO Box 212, Louisa, KY 41230. 606-638-4215. Fax: 606-638-3556. 8:30AM-4:30PM M-F 8:30AM-12PM SAT (EST). Access by: Mail, in person.

Lee County

Real Estate Recording—Lee County Clerk, Main Street, Courthouse - Room 11, Beattyville, KY 41311. 606-464-4115. Fax: 606-464-4102. 8AM-4PM (EST).

Felony, Misdemeanor, Civil, Eviction, Small Claims, Probate—Circuit and District Court, Box E, Beattyville, KY 41311. 606-464-8400. Fax: 606-464-0144. 8AM-4PM M-F 8:30AM-11:30 SAT (EST). Access by: In person only.

Leslie County

Real Estate Recording—Leslie County Clerk, Main Street, Courthouse, Hyden, KY 41749. 606-672-2193. Fax: 606-672-4264. 8AM-5PM; 8AM-Noon Sat (EST).

Felony, Misdemeanor, Civil, Eviction, Small Claims, Probate—Circuit and District Court, Box 1750, Hyden, KY 41749. 606-672-2505. Fax: 606-672-5128. 8AM-5PM M; 8AM-4PM T-F; 8AM-Noon Sat (EST). Access by: Mail, in person. by mail through Frankfort only.

Letcher County

Real Estate Recording—Letcher County Clerk, Old Mtn Comp Building, Main Street, Whitesburg, KY 41858. 606-633-2432. Fax: 606-632-9282. 8:30AM-4PM; 8:30AM-Noon Sat (EST).

Felony, Misdemeanor, Civil, Eviction, Small Claims, Probate—Circuit and District Court, 101 W Main St, Whitesburg, KY 41858. 606-633-7559. Fax: 606-633-5864. 8:30AM-4PM M-F 8:30AM-12PM 1st Sat of month (EST). Access by: Mail, in person.

Lewis County

Real Estate Recording—Lewis County Clerk, 514 Second Street, Courthouse, 2nd Floor, Vanceburg, KY 41179. 606-796-3062. Fax: 606-796-6511. 8:30AM-4:30PM M,T,Th,F; 9AM-1PM W; 8:30AM-12:30PM Sat (EST).

Felony, Misdemeanor, Civil, Eviction, Small Claims, Probate—Circuit and District Court, PO Box 70, Vanceburg, KY 41179. 606-796-3053. Fax: 606-796-3030. 8AM-4:30PM M,T,Th,F 8:30-Noon W,Sat (EST). Access by: Mail, in person.

Lincoln County

Real Estate Recording—Lincoln County Clerk, 102 East Main, Courthouse, Stanford, KY 40484. 606-365-4570. Fax: 606-365-4572. 8AM-4PM M-F; 9AM-Noon Sat (EST).

Felony, Misdemeanor, Civil, Eviction, Small Claims, Probate—Circuit and District Court, 102 E Main, Stanford, KY 40484. 606-365-2535. Fax: 606-365-3389. 8AM-4PM M-TH 8AM-5:30PM F (EST). Access by: Mail, in person.

Livingston County

Real Estate Recording—Livingston County Clerk, Court Street, Courthouse, Smithland, KY 42081. 502-928-2162. Fax: 502-928-4612. 8AM-4PM; 8AM-6PM M (CST).

Felony, Misdemeanor, Civil, Eviction, Small Claims, Probate—Circuit and District Court, PO Box 160, Smithland, KY 42081. 502-928-2172. 8AM-6PM M 8AM-4PM T-F (CST). Access by: In person only.

Logan County

Real Estate Recording—Logan County Clerk, 229 W. 3rd St., Russellville, KY 42276. 502-726-6061. Fax: 502-726-4355. 8:30AM-4:30PM M-Th; 8AM-5PM F (CST).

Felony, Civil Actions Over $4,000—Circuit Court, Box 420, Russellville, KY 42276-0420. 502-726-2424. Fax: 502-726-7893. 8AM-4:30PM M-TH; 8AM-5PM F (CST). Access by: In person only.

Misdemeanor, Civil Actions Under $4,000, Eviction, Small Claims, Probate—District Court, Box 420, Russellville, KY 42276. 502-726-3107. Fax: 502-726-7893. 8AM-4:30PM (CST). Access by: In person only.

Lyon County

Real Estate Recording—Lyon County Clerk, Dale Avenue, Courthouse, Eddyville, KY 42038. 502-388-2331. Fax: 502-388-0634. 8:30AM-4PM (EST).

Felony, Misdemeanor, Civil, Eviction, Small Claims, Probate—Circuit and District Court, Box 565, Eddyville, KY 42038. 502-388-7231. 8AM-4PM (EST). Access by: In person only.

Madison County

Real Estate Recording—Madison County Clerk, 101 W. Main Street, County Court House, Richmond, KY 40475. 606-624-4704. Fax: 606-623-3071. 8AM-4PM; 8AM-6PM M (EST).

Felony, Civil Actions Over $4,000—Circuit Court, PO Box 813, Richmond, KY 40476-0813. 606-624-4793. 8AM-4PM (EST). Access by: Phone, in person.

Misdemeanor, Civil Actions Under $4,000, Eviction, Small Claims, Probate—District Court, Courthouse Annex, 101 N 1st St, Richmond, KY 40475. 606-624-4720. Fax: 606-624-4746. 8AM-4PM (EST). Access by: In person only.

Magoffin County

Real Estate Recording—Magoffin County Clerk, Courthouse, Salyersville, KY 41465. 606-349-2216. Fax: 606-349-2328. 8:30AM-4PM; 8:30AM-Noon Sat (EST).

Felony, Misdemeanor, Civil, Eviction, Small Claims, Probate—Circuit and District Court, Box 147, Salyersville, KY 41465. 606-349-2215. Fax: 606-349-2209. 8AM-4PM (EST). Access by: Fax, mail, in person.

Marion County

Real Estate Recording—Marion County Clerk, 120 W. Main Street, Suite 3, Courthouse, Lebanon, KY 40033. 502-692-2651. Fax: 502-692-9811. 8:30AM-4:30PM; 8:30AM-Noon Sat (EST).

Felony, Misdemeanor, Civil, Eviction, Small Claims, Probate—Circuit and District Court, 120 W Main St, Lebanon, KY 40033. 502-692-2681. 8:30AM-4:30PM M-F 8:30AM-12PM SAT (EST). Access by: In person only.

Marshall County

Real Estate Recording—Marshall County Clerk, Courthouse, 1101 Main St., Benton, KY 42025. 502-527-4740. Fax: 502-527-4738. 8AM-5PM M; 8AM-4:30PM T-F (CST).

Felony, Misdemeanor, Civil, Eviction, Small Claims, Probate—Circuit and District Court, 1101 Main St, Benton, KY 42025. 502-527-3883. Fax: 502-527-5865. 8AM-4:30PM (CST). Access by: Phone, fax, mail, in person.

Martin County

Real Estate Recording—Martin County Clerk, Main Street, Courthouse, Inez, KY 41224. 606-298-2810. Fax: 606-298-0143. 8AM-5PM; 8AM-Noon Sat (EST).

Felony, Misdemeanor, Civil, Eviction, Small Claims, Probate—Circuit and District Court, Box 430, Inez, KY 41224. 606-298-3508. Fax: 606-298-4202. 8AM-4:30PM M-TH, 8AM-5:30PM F, 9AM-12PM SAT (EST). Access by: In person only.

Mason County

Real Estate Recording—Mason County Clerk, West Third Street, Courthouse, Maysville, KY 41056. 606-564-3341. Fax: 606-564-8979. 9AM-5PM; 9AM-Noon Sat (EST).

Felony, Civil Actions Over $4,000—Circuit Court, 27 W 3rd, Maysville, KY 41056. 606-564-4340. Fax: 606-564-0932. 8:30AM-5PM (EST). Access by: In person only.

Misdemeanor, Civil Actions Under $4,000, Eviction, Small Claims, Probate—District Court, 221 Court St, Maysville, KY 41056. 606-564-4011. Fax: 606-564-0932. 8:30AM-4:30PM (EST). Access by: In person only.

McCracken County

Real Estate Recording—McCracken County Clerk, 7th Street between Washington & Clark, Courthouse, Paducah, KY 42002. 502-444-4700. Fax: 502-444-4704. 8:30AM-4:30PM (M open until 5:30PM) (CST).

Felony, Civil Actions Over $4,000—Circuit Court, Box 1455, Paducah, KY 42002-1455. 502-575-7280. 8:30AM-5:30PM M, 8:30AM-4:30PM T-F (CST). Access by: Mail, in person.

Misdemeanor, Civil Actions Under $4,000, Eviction, Small Claims, Probate—District Court, Box 1436, Paducah, KY 42001. 502-444-8270. Fax: 502-444-8029. 8:30AM-4:30PM (CST). Access by: Mail, in person.

McCreary County

Real Estate Recording—McCreary County Clerk, Main Street, Courthouse, Whitley City, KY 42653. 606-376-2411. Fax: 606-376-3898. 8:30AM-4:30PM M-F; 9AM-Noon Sat (EST).

Felony, Misdemeanor, Civil, Eviction, Small Claims, Probate—Circuit and District Court, Box 40, Whitley City, KY 42653. 606-376-5041. Fax: 606-376-8844. 8AM-4:30PM (EST). Access by: Mail, in person.

McLean County

Real Estate Recording—McLean County Clerk, 210 Main Street, Courthouse, Calhoun, KY 42327. 502-273-3082. Fax: 502-273-5084. 8AM-4:30PM; 9AM-Noon Sat (CST).

Felony, Misdemeanor, Civil, Eviction, Small Claims, Probate—Circuit and District Court, Box 145, Calhoun, KY 42327. 502-273-3966. Fax: 502-273-3791. 8AM-4:30PM M-F; 9AM-Noon Sat (CST). Access by: Mail, in person.

Meade County

Real Estate Recording—Meade County Clerk, 516 Fairway Drive, Brandenburg, KY 40108. 502-422-2152. Fax: 502-422-2158. 8AM-4:30PM; 9AM-Noon Sat (EST).

Felony, Misdemeanor, Civil, Eviction, Small Claims, Probate—Circuit and District Court, Courthouse, Brandenburg, KY 40108. 502-422-4961. Fax: 502-422-2147. 8AM-4:30AM (EST). Access by: In person only.

Menifee County

Real Estate Recording—Menifee County Clerk, Main Street, Courthouse, Frenchburg, KY 40322. 606-768-3512. Fax: 606-768-2144. 8:30AM-4PM M,T,W,F; 8:30-11:30AM Th,Sat (EST).

Felony, Misdemeanor, Civil, Eviction, Small Claims, Probate—Circuit and District Court, Box 172, Frenchburg, KY 40322. 606-768-2461. Fax: 606-768-2462. 8:30AM-4PM (EST). Access by: Fax, mail, in person.

Mercer County

Real Estate Recording—Mercer County Clerk, 235 S. Main Street, Courthouse Annex, Harrodsburg, KY 40330. 606-734-6313. Fax: 606-734-6309. 8AM-4:30PM (EST).

Felony, Misdemeanor, Civil, Eviction, Small Claims, Probate—Circuit and District Court, Courthouse, 224 Main St S, Harrodsburg, KY 40330-1696. 606-734-6306. Fax: 606-734-9159. 8AM-4:30PM (EST). Access by: In person only.

Metcalfe County

Real Estate Recording—Metcalfe County Clerk, 100 E. Stockton St., Suite 1, Edmonton, KY 42129. 502-432-4821. Fax: 502-432-5176. 8AM-4PM (CST).

Felony, Misdemeanor, Civil, Eviction, Small Claims, Probate—Circuit and District Court, Box 485, Edmonton, KY 42129. 502-432-3663. Fax: 502-432-4437. 8AM-4PM (CST). Access by: Mail, in person.

Monroe County

Real Estate Recording—Monroe County Clerk, Main Street, Courthouse, Tompkinsville, KY 42167. 502-487-5471. Fax: 502-487-5976. 8AM-5PM M-F; 8AM-Noon Sat (CST).

Felony, Misdemeanor, Civil, Eviction, Small Claims, Probate—Circuit and District Court, Box 245, Tompkinsville, KY 42167. 502-487-5480. Fax: 502-487-0068. 8AM-5PM (CST). Access by: Phone, mail, in person.

Montgomery County

Real Estate Recording—Montgomery County Clerk, Court Street, Mount Sterling, KY 40353. 606-498-8700. Fax: 606-498-8729. 8:30AM-4PM; 8:30-6PM F (EST).

Felony, Misdemeanor, Civil, Eviction, Small Claims, Probate—Circuit and District Court, Courthouse One Court St, Mt Sterling, KY 40353. 606-498-5966. Fax: 606-498-9341. 8:30AM-4PM (EST). Access by: Mail, in person.

Morgan County

Real Estate Recording—Morgan County Clerk, 505 Prestonsburg Street, West Liberty, KY 41472. 606-743-3949. Fax: 606-743-2111. 8AM-4PM; 8AM-Noon Sat (EST).

Felony, Misdemeanor, Civil, Eviction, Small Claims, Probate—Circuit and District Court, Box 85, West Liberty,

KY 41472. 606-743-3763. Fax: 606-743-2633. 8AM-4PM (EST). Access by: Mail, in person.

Muhlenberg County

Real Estate Recording—Muhlenberg County Clerk, Courthouse, Greenville, KY 42345. 502-338-1441. Fax: 502-338-1774. 8AM-4PM; 8AM-6PM F (CST).

Felony, Civil Actions Over $4,000—Circuit Court, Box 776, Greenville, KY 42345. 502-338-4850. Fax: 502-338-7482. 8AM-4PM (CST). Access by: Mail, in person. Request to Frankfort, KY. Request form available.

Misdemeanor, Civil Actions Under $4,000, Eviction, Small Claims, Probate—District Court, Box 274, Greenville, KY 42345. 502-338-0995. Fax: 502-338-7482. 8AM-4PM (CST). Access by: In person only.

Nelson County

Real Estate Recording—Nelson County Clerk, 113 E. Stephen Foster Ave., Bardstown, KY 40004. 502-348-1830. Fax: 502-348-1822. 8:30AM-4:30PM M-F; 8AM-Noon Sat (EST).

Felony, Misdemeanor, Civil, Eviction, Small Claims, Probate—Circuit and District Court, Box 845, Bardstown, KY 40004. 502-348-3648. 8:30AM-4:30PM (EST). Access by: Mail, in person.

Nicholas County

Real Estate Recording—Nicholas County Clerk, Main Street, Courthouse, Carlisle, KY 40311. 606-289-3730. Fax: 606-289-3705. 8AM-4:30PM; 8-11:30AM Sat (EST).

Felony, Misdemeanor, Civil, Eviction, Small Claims, Probate—Circuit and District Court, PO Box 109, Carlisle, KY 40311. 606-289-2336. Fax: 606-289-6141. 8:30AM-4:30PM M-F, 9AM-noon SAT (EST). Access by: Phone, mail, in person.

Ohio County

Real Estate Recording—Ohio County Clerk, 301 South Main Street, Old Courthouse, Hartford, KY 42347. 502-298-4422. Fax: 502-298-4425. 8AM-4:30PM M-Th; 8AM-6PM F; 8AM-Noon Sat (CST).

Felony, Misdemeanor, Civil, Eviction, Small Claims, Probate—Circuit and District Court, Community Center, Hartford, KY 42347. 502-298-3671. Fax: 502-298-9565. 8:30AM-4:30PM (CST). Access by: In person only.

Oldham County

Real Estate Recording—Oldham County Clerk, 100 West Jefferson Street, Courthouse, LaGrange, KY 40031. 502-222-9311. Fax: 502-222-3208. 8:30AM-4PM M-W,F; 8:30AM-6PM Th (EST).

Felony, Misdemeanor, Civil, Eviction, Small Claims, Probate—Circuit and District Court, 105 E Jefferson, La Grange, KY 40031. 502-222-9837. Fax: 502-222-3047. 8AM-4PM (EST). Access by: In person only.

Owen County

Real Estate Recording—Owen County Clerk, Courthouse, Madison St., Owenton, KY 40359. 502-484-2213. Fax: 502-484-1002. 8AM-Noon, 1-4PM M,T,Th,F; 8AM-3PM Sat (EST).

Felony, Misdemeanor, Civil, Eviction, Small Claims, Probate—Circuit and District Court, Box 473, Owenton, KY 40359. 502-484-2232. Fax: 502-484-0625. 8AM-4PM (EST). Access by: Phone, mail, in person.

Owsley County

Real Estate Recording—Owsley County Clerk, Courthouse, Main St., Booneville, KY 41314. 606-593-5735. Fax: 606-593-5737. 8AM-4PM; 8AM-12 Sat (EST).

Felony, Misdemeanor, Civil, Eviction, Small Claims, Probate—Circuit and District Court, Box 146, Booneville, KY 41314. 606-593-6226. Fax: 606-593-6343. 8AM-4PM M-F, 8AM-Noon Sat (EST). Access by: In person only.

Pendleton County

Real Estate Recording—Pendleton County Clerk, Main Street, Courthouse Square, Falmouth, KY 41040. 606-654-3380. 8:30AM-4PM M-F; 8:30AM-Noon Sat (EST).

Felony, Misdemeanor, Civil, Eviction, Small Claims, Probate—Circuit and District Court, Courthouse Square, Falmouth, KY 41040. 606-654-3347. 8AM-4PM (EST). Access by: Mail, in person.

Perry County

Real Estate Recording—Perry County Clerk, Main Street, Courthouse, Hazard, KY 41701. 606-436-4614. Fax: 606-439-0557. 8AM-4PM (EST).

Felony, Civil Actions Over $4,000—Circuit Court, Box 7743, Hazard, KY 41701. 606-435-6000. 8AM-4PM (EST). Access by: Phone, mail, in person.

Misdemeanor, Civil Actions Under $4,000, Eviction, Small Claims, Probate—District Court, Box 7743, Hazard, KY 41702. 606-435-6002. 8AM-4PM (EST). Access by: Mail, in person.

Pike County

Real Estate Recording—Pike County Clerk, 320 Main Street, Pikeville, KY 41501. 606-432-6240. Fax: 606-432-6222. 8:30AM-4:30PM M,T,W.Th; 8:30AM-6PM F; 8:30AM-Noon Sat (EST).

Felony, Misdemeanor, Civil, Eviction, Small Claims, Probate—Circuit and District Court, 89 Div St, Hall of Justice, Pikeville, KY 41501. 606-433-7557. Fax: 606-433-1363. 8AM-4:30PM (EST). Access by: In person only.

Powell County

Real Estate Recording—Powell County Clerk, 130 Washington Street, Courthouse, Stanton, KY 40380. 606-663-6444. Fax: 606-663-6406. 9AM-4PM M-W; 9AM-Noon Th; 9AM-4PM F; 9AM-Noon Sat (EST).

Felony, Misdemeanor, Civil, Eviction, Small Claims, Probate—Circuit and District Court, Box 578, Stanton, KY 40380. 606-663-4141. Fax: 606-663-2710. 8AM-4PM M-F, 8AM-noon TH and SAT (EST). Access by: Mail, in person.

Pulaski County

Real Estate Recording—Pulaski County Clerk, Main Street, Somerset, KY 42501. 606-679-3652. Fax: 606-678-0073. 8AM-4:30PM (EST).

Felony, Misdemeanor, Civil, Eviction, Small Claims, Probate—Circuit and District Court, Box 664, Somerset, KY 42501. 606-677-4029. Fax: 606-677-4002. 8AM-4:30PM M-F, 8AM-Noon Sat (EST). Access by: In person only.

Robertson County

Real Estate Recording—Robertson County Clerk, Courthouse, Mount Olivet, KY 41064. 606-724-5212. 8:30-Noon, 1-4PM M,T,Th,F; 8:30AM-Noon W, Sat (EST).

Felony, Misdemeanor, Civil, Eviction, Small Claims, Probate—Circuit and District Court, Box 63, Mt Olivet, KY 41064. 606-724-5993. Fax: 606-724-5721. 8:30AM-4:30PM (EST). Access by: Phone, mail, in person.

Rockcastle County

Real Estate Recording—Rockcastle County Clerk, Courthouse, Mount Vernon, KY 40456. 606-256-2831. Fax: 606-256-4302. 8:30-4PM; 8;30-Noon Sat (EST).

Felony, Misdemeanor, Civil, Eviction, Small Claims, Probate—Circuit and District Court, Box 750, Mt Vernon, KY 40456. 606-256-2581. 8AM-4PM M-F 8AM-6PM TH 8:30AM-12PM SAT (EST). Access by: Mail, in person.

Rowan County

Real Estate Recording—Rowan County Clerk, Courthouse - 2nd Floor, 627 E. Main Street, Morehead, KY 40351. 606-784-5212. Fax: 606-784-2923. 8:30-4:30PM; 9AM-Noon Sat (EST).

Felony, Misdemeanor, Civil, Eviction, Small Claims, Probate—Circuit and District Court, 627 E Main, Morehead, KY 40351-1398. 606-784-4574. Fax: 606-784-1899.

8:30AM-4:30PM M-F 8:30AM-12PM SAT (EST). Access by: Mail, in person.

Russell County

Real Estate Recording—Russell County Clerk, Courthouse, Jamestown, KY 42629. 502-343-2125. Fax: 502-343-4700. 8AM-4PM; 8AM-Noon Sat (CST).

Felony, Misdemeanor, Civil, Eviction, Small Claims, Probate—Circuit and District Court, 410 Monument Square, Suite 203, Jamestown, KY 42629. 502-343-2185. Fax: 502-343-5808. 8AM-4:30PM M-F 8AM-Noon Sat (CST). Access by: In person only.

Scott County

Real Estate Recording—Scott County Clerk, Courthouse, 101 E. Main St., Georgetown, KY 40324. 502-863-7875. Fax: 502-863-7898. 8:30AM-4:30PM M-Th; 8:30AM-6PM F (EST).

Felony, Misdemeanor, Civil, Eviction, Small Claims, Probate—Circuit and District Court, 119 N Hamilton, Georgetown, KY 40324. 502-863-0474. 8AM-4:30PM (EST). Access by: Mail, in person.

Shelby County

Real Estate Recording—Shelby County Clerk, 501 Main Street, Shelbyville, KY 40065. 502-633-4410. Fax: 502-633-7887. 8:30AM-4:30PM; 8:30AM-Noon Sat (EST).

Felony, Misdemeanor, Civil, Eviction, Small Claims, Probate—Circuit and District Court, 501 Main St, Shelbyville, KY 40065. 502-633-1289. 8:30AM-4:30PM (EST). Access by: Phone, mail, in person.

Simpson County

Real Estate Recording—Simpson County Clerk, County Annex Building, 103 West Cedar Street, Franklin, KY 42134. 502-586-8161. Fax: 502-586-6464. 8AM-4PM (CST).

Felony, Misdemeanor, Civil, Eviction, Small Claims, Probate—Circuit and District Court, Box 261, Franklin, KY 42135-0261. 502-586-8910. Fax: 502-586-0265. 8AM-4PM (CST). Access by: Mail, in person.

Spencer County

Real Estate Recording—Spencer County Clerk, Courthouse, 2 W. Main Street, Taylorsville, KY 40071. 502-477-3215. Fax: 502-477-3216. 8AM-4:30PM M-F; 8AM-Noon Sat (EST).

Felony, Misdemeanor, Civil, Eviction, Small Claims, Probate—Circuit and District Court, Box 282, Taylorsville, KY 40071. 502-477-3220. Fax: 502-477-9368. 7:45AM-4PM (EST). Access by: In person only.

Taylor County

Real Estate Recording—Taylor County Clerk, 203 North Court Street, Suite # 5, Campbellsville, KY 42718. 502-465-6677. Fax: 502-789-1144. 8AM-4:30PM M-Th; 8AM-5PM F (EST).

Felony, Misdemeanor, Civil, Eviction, Small Claims, Probate—Circuit and District Court, 203 N Court Courthouse, Campbellsville, KY 42718. 502-465-6686. Fax: 502-789-4356. 8AM-4:30PM (EST). Access by: In person only.

Todd County

Real Estate Recording—Todd County Clerk, Washington Street, Courthouse, Elkton, KY 42220. 502-265-2363. Fax: 502-265-2588. 8AM-4:30PM (CST).

Felony, Misdemeanor, Civil, Eviction, Small Claims, Probate—Circuit and District Court, Box 337, Elkton, KY 42220. 502-265-5631. Fax: 502-265-2122. 8AM-4:30PM (CST). Access by: Fax, mail, in person.

Trigg County

Real Estate Recording—Trigg County Clerk, Main Street, Courthouse, Cadiz, KY 42211. 502-522-6661. Fax: 502-522-6662. 8AM-4PM M-Th; 8AM-5PM F (CST).

Felony, Misdemeanor, Civil, Eviction, Small Claims, Probate—Circuit and District Court, Box 673, Cadiz, KY 42211. 502-522-6270. 8AM-4PM M-F 9AM-11:30AM 1st SAT of each month (CST). Access by: In person only.

Trimble County

Real Estate Recording—Trimble County Clerk, Courthouse, Bedford, KY 40006. 502-255-7174. Fax: 502-255-7045. 8:30AM-4:30PM M,T,Th,F; 8:30AM-Noon Sat (EST).

Felony, Misdemeanor, Civil, Eviction, Small Claims, Probate—Circuit and District Court, Box 248, Bedford, KY 40006. 502-255-3213. Fax: 502-255-4953. 8AM-4:30PM M,T,Th,F 8AM-Noon Sat (EST). Access by: Mail, in person.

Union County

Real Estate Recording—Union County Clerk, Main & Morgan Streets, Courthouse, Morganfield, KY 42437. 502-389-1334. Fax: 502-389-9135. 8AM-4PM (CST).

Felony, Misdemeanor, Civil, Eviction, Small Claims, Probate—Circuit and District Court, Box 59, Morganfield, KY 42437. 502-389-1811. Fax: 502-389-9887. 8AM-4PM (No searches performed on Thursday) (CST). Access by: Mail, in person.

Warren County

Real Estate Recording—Warren County Clerk, 429 East 10th Street, Bowling Green, KY 42101. 502-842-9416. Fax: 502-843-5319. 8:30AM-4:30PM (CST).

Felony, Misdemeanor, Civil, Eviction, Small Claims, Probate—Circuit and District Court, Box 2170, Bowling Green, KY 42102. 502-746-7400. Fax: 502-842-9316. 8:30AM-4:30PM (CST). Access by: In person only.

Washington County

Real Estate Recording—Washington County Clerk, Cross Main Annex Building, Springfield, KY 40069. 606-336-5425. Fax: 606-336-5408. 9AM-4:30PM; 9AM-Noon Sat (EST).

Felony, Misdemeanor, Civil, Eviction, Small Claims, Probate—Circuit and District Court, PO Box 346, Springfield, KY 40069. 606-336-3761. Fax: 606-336-9824. 8:30AM-4:30PM (EST). Access by: Mail, in person.

Wayne County

Real Estate Recording—Wayne County Clerk, 109 N. Main St., Monticello, KY 42633. 606-348-6661. Fax: 606-348-8303. 8AM-4:30PM; 8AM-Noon Sat (CST).

Felony, Misdemeanor, Civil, Eviction, Small Claims, Probate—Circuit and District Court, Box 816, Monticello, KY 42633. 606-348-5841. Fax: 606-348-4225. 8AM-4:30PM M-F 8AM-12PM SAT (CST). Access by: Mail, in person.

Webster County

Real Estate Recording—Webster County Clerk, Main Street, Courthouse, Dixon, KY 42409. 502-639-7006. Fax: 502-639-7009. 8AM-4PM M; 8AM-4PM T-F (CST).

Felony, Misdemeanor, Civil, Eviction, Small Claims, Probate—Circuit and District Court, Box 217, Dixon, KY 42409. 502-639-9160. Fax: 502-639-6757. 8AM-4PM (CST). Access by: Mail, in person.

Whitley County

Real Estate Recording—Whitley County Clerk, Main Street, Courthouse, Room 2, Williamsburg, KY 40769. 606-549-6002. Fax: 606-549-2790. 8:30AM-4PM; 8:30AM-Noon Sat (EST).

Felony, Misdemeanor, Civil, Eviction, Small Claims, Probate—Corbin Circuit and District Court, 805 S Main St, Corbin, KY 40701. 606-523-1085. Fax: 606-523-2049. 8AM-4PM (EST). Access by: In person only.

Williamsburg Circuit and District Court, Box 329, Williamsburg, KY 40769. 606-549-5162. 8AM-4PM (EST). Access by: In person only.

Wolfe County

Real Estate Recording—Wolfe County Clerk, Courthouse, 1st Floor, 10 Court St., Campton, KY 41301. 606-668-3515. Fax: 606-668-3367. 8AM-4PM M,T,Th,F; 8AM-12 W & Sat (EST).

Felony, Misdemeanor, Civil, Eviction, Small Claims, Probate—Circuit and District Court, Box 296, Campton,

KY 41301. 606-668-3736. Fax: 606-668-3198. 8:30AM-4:30PM (EST). Access by: Mail, in person.

Woodford County

Real Estate Recording—Woodford County Clerk, Courthouse - Room 120, 103 S. Main St., Versailles, KY 40383.

606-873-3421. Fax: 606-873-6985. 8AM-4PM M,T,W,Th; 8AM-6PM F (EST).

Felony, Misdemeanor, Civil, Eviction, Small Claims, Probate—Circuit and District Court, 103 S Main St Rm 102, Versailles, KY 40383. 606-873-3711. 8AM-4PM M-TH 8AM-6PM F (EST). Access by: In person only.

Federal Courts

US District Court
Eastern District of Kentucky

Ashland Division, US District Court Suite 336, 1405 Greenup Ave, Ashland, KY 41101. 606-329-2465. Counties: Boyd, Carter, Elliott, Greenup, Lawrence, Lewis, Morgan, Rowan

Covington Division, US District Court Clerk, PO Box 1073, Covington, KY 41012. 606-655-3810. Counties: Boone, Bracken, Campbell, Gallatin, Grant, Kenton, Mason, Pendleton, Robertson

Frankfort Division, US District Court Room 313, 330 W Broadway, Frankfort, KY 40601. 502-223-5225. Counties: Anderson, Carroll, Franklin, Henry, Owen, Shelby, Trimble

Lexington Division, US District Court PO Drawer 3074, Lexington, KY 40596-3074. 606-233-2503. Counties: Bath, Bourbon, Boyle, Clark, Estill, Fayette, Fleming, Garrard, Harrison, Jessamine, Lee, Lincoln, Madison, Menifee, Mercer, Montgomery, Nicholas, Powell, Scott, Wolfe, Woodford. Lee and Wolfe Counties were part of the Pikeville Division before 10/31/92

London Division, US District Court PO Box 5121, London, KY 40745-5121. 606-864-5137. Counties: Bell, Clay, Harlan, Jackson, Knox, Laurel, Leslie, McCreary, Owsley, Perry, Pulaski, Rockcastle, Wayne, Whitley

Pikeville Division, US District Court Office of the Clerk, 203 Federal Bldg, 102 Main St, Pikeville, KY 41501-1144. 606-437-6160. Counties: Breathitt, Floyd, Johnson, Knott, Letcher, Magoffin, Martin, Pike. Lee and Wolfe Counties were part of this division until 10/31/92, when they were moved to the Lexington Division

Western District of Kentucky

Bowling Green Division, US District Court US District Court, 241 E Main St, Room 120, Bowling Green, KY 42101-2175. 502-781-1110. Counties: Adair, Allen, Barren, Butler, Casey, Clinton, Cumberland, Edmonson, Green, Hart, Logan, Metcalfe, Monroe, Russell, Simpson, Taylor, Todd, Warren

Louisville Division, US District Court Clerk, US District Court, 450 US Courthouse, 601 W Broadway, Louisville, KY 40202. 502-582-5156. Counties: Breckinridge, Bullitt, Hardin, Jefferson, Larue, Marion, Meade, Nelson, Oldham, Spencer, Washington

Owensboro Division, US District Court Federal Bldg, Room 126, 423 Frederica St, Owensboro, KY 42301. 502-683-0221. Counties: Daviess, Grayson, Hancock, Henderson, Hopkins, McLean, Muhlenberg, Ohio, Union, Webster

Paducah Division, US District Court Room 322, 501 Broadway, Paducah, KY 42001. 502-443-1337. Counties: Ballard, Caldwell, Calloway, Carlisle, Christian, Crittenden, Fulton, Graves, Hickman, Livingston, Lyon, McCracken, Marshall, Trigg

US Bankruptcy Court
Eastern District of Kentucky

Lexington Division, US Bankruptcy Court, PO Box 1111, Lexington, KY 40588. 606-233-2608. Voice Case Information System: 606-233-2657. Counties: Anderson, Bath, Bell, Boone, Bourbon, Boyd, Boyle, Bracken, Breathitt, Campbell, Carroll, Carter, Clark, Clay, Elliott, Estill, Fayette, Fleming, Floyd, Franklin, Gallatin, Garrard, Grant, Greenup, Harlan, Harrison, Henry, Jackson, Jessamine, Johnson, Kenton, Knott, Knox, Laurel, Lawrence, Lee, Leslie, Letcher, Lewis, Lincoln, Madison, Magoffin, Martin, Mason, McCreary, Menifee, Mercer, Montgomery, Morgan, Nicholas, Owen, Owsley, Pendleton, Perry, Pike, Powell, Pulaski, Robertson,

Rockcastle, Rowan, Scott, Shelby, Trimble, Wayne, Whitley, Wolfe, Woodford

Western District of Kentucky

Louisville Division, US Bankruptcy Court, 546 US Courthouse, 601 W Broadway, Louisville, KY 40202. 502-582-5145. Voice Case Information System: 502-625-7391. Counties: Adair, Allen, Ballard, Barren, Breckinridge, Bullitt, Butler, Caldwell, Calloway, Carlisle, Casey, Christian, Clinton, Crittenden, Cumberland, Daviess, Edmonson, Fulton, Graves, Grayson, Green, Hancock, Hardin, Hart, Henderson, Hickman, Hopkins, Jefferson, Larue, Livingston, Logan, Lyon, Marion, Marshall, McCracken, McLean, Meade, Metcalfe, Monroe, Muhlenberg, Nelson, Ohio, Oldham, Russell, Simpson, Spencer, Taylor, Todd, Trigg, Union, Warren, Washington, Webster

Louisiana

Capitol: Baton Rouge (East Baton Rouge Parish)	
Number of Parishes: 64	**Population:** 4,342,334
County Court Locations:	**Federal Court Locations:**
District Courts: 65/42 Districts	•District Courts: 7
New Orleans City Court: 1	•Bankruptcy Courts: 7
Ctiy & Parish Courts: 52	**State Agencies:** 18
Justice of the Peace Courts: 390	
Mayors Courts: 250	
Family Court: 1	
Juvenile Courts: 4	

State Agencies—Summary

General Help Numbers:

State Archives

Secretary of State   504-922-1206
Div of Archives Records & History   Fax: 504-902-0433
3851 Essen Lane   8AM-4:30PM, 9-5 SA 1-5 SU
Baton Rouge, LA 70809
Alternate Telephone: 504-922-1200
Reference Librarian: 504-922-1207

Governor's Office

Office of the Governor   504-342-7015
PO Box 94004   Fax: 504-342-7099
Baton Rouge, LA 70804-9004   8AM-4:30PM

Attorney General's Office

Attorney General's Office   504-342-7013
Justice Department   Fax: 504-342-7335
PO Box 94005   8:30AM-5PM
Baton Rouge, LA 70804-9005

State Legislation

Louisiana House (Senate) Representative 504-342-2456
State Capitol, 2nd Floor   8AM-5PM
PO Box 44486
Baton Rouge, LA 70804
General Information: 800-256-3793

Important State Internet Sites:

♦ Webscape	
File Edit View	**Help**

State of Louisiana World Wide Web

www.state.la.us/

This home page includes links to all of the government sites in the State, along with links to tourism, education, job listings and a Louisiana profile.

The Governor's Office

www. state.la.us/gov/gov.htm

This limited site includes a mission statement from the Governor and his address.

State Legislature Information

www.house.state.la.us/
www.senate.state.la.us/sen/senate.htm

These pages provide links to House and Senate members and how to contact them.

Unclaimed Property

www.rev.state.la.us/uncprop.htm

Online searching is available for unclaimed property at this site.

State Agencies—Public Records

Criminal Records

State Police, Bureau of Criminal Identification, 265 S Foster, Baton Rouge, LA 70806, Main Telephone: 504-925-6095, Fax: 504-925-7005, Hours: 8AM-5PM. Access by: mail, visit. Records are available for employment screening purposes only if the employment falls under a state statute requiring a criminal record check.

Corporation Records
Limited Partnership Records
Limited Liability Company Records
Trademarks/Servicemarks

Commercial Division, Corporation Department, PO Box 94125, Baton Rouge, LA 70804-4125, Main Telephone: 504-925-4704, Fax: 504-925-4726, Hours: 8AM-4:30PM. Access by: mail, phone, visit, PC. Fictitious Names and Assumed Names are found at the parish level.

Uniform Commercial Code
Federal Tax Liens
State Tax Liens

Secretary of State, UCC Records, PO Box 94125, Baton Rouge, LA 70804-9125, Main Telephone: 800-256-3758, Fax: 504-342-0316, Hours: 8AM-4:30PM. Access by: mail, PC. Access to UCC information is offered via online by the state. The statewide index of UCC filings is available in each parish office. All tax liens and financial statements are filed at the parish level. IRS liens show up on UCC records.

Sales Tax Registrations

Revenue and Tax Department, Sales Tax Director, PO Box 201, Baton Rouge, LA 70821-0201, Main Telephone: 504-925-7356, Fax: 504-925-3860, Hours: 8AM-4:30PM.
Restricted access.

Birth Certificates

Vital Records Registry, PO Box 60630, New Orleans, LA 70160, Main Telephone: 504-568-5152, For adoptions: 504-568-5167, Fax: 504-568-5391, Hours: 8AM-4PM. Access by: mail, fax, visit. Some certificates (all types of vital records) contain information at the bottom of the document which is confidential and is not released to anyone. This information was used for statistical purposes and varies depending on legislative actions.

Death Records

Vital Records Registry, PO Box 60630, New Orleans, LA 70160, Main Telephone: 504-568-5152, Corrections: 504-568-5273, Fax: 504-568-5391, Hours: 8AM-4PM. Access by: mail, fax, visit.

Marriage Certificates
Divorce Records

Records not available from state agency.

Workers' Compensation Records

Department of Labor, Office of Workers' Compensation, PO Box 94040, Baton Rouge, LA 70804-9040, Main Telephone: 504-342-7555, Fax: 504-342-7582, Hours: 7:45AM-4:15PM. Access by: mail, fax, visit.

Driver Records

Dept of Public Safety and Corrections, Office of Motor Vehicles, PO Box 64886, Baton Rouge, LA 70896, Main Telephone: 504-925-6009, Alternate Telephone: 504-922-2814, Hours: 8AM-4PM T-S. Access by: mail, visit, PC. Copies of tickets may be obtained from the address listed above. The fee is $5.00 per copy.

Vehicle Ownership
Vehicle Identification

Department of Public Safety & Corrections, Office of Motor Vehicles, PO Box 64884, Baton Rouge, LA 70896, Main Telephone: 504-925-6146, Fax: 504-925-3979, Hours: 8AM-4PM T-S. Access by: mail, visit, PC.

Accident Reports

Louisiana State Police, Accident Records, PO Box 66614, Baton Rouge, LA 70896, Main Telephone: 504-925-6156, Fax: 504-925-1898, Hours: 8AM-4:30PM. Access by: mail, visit.

Hunting License Information
Fishing License Information

Wildlife & Fisheries Department, Licenses Division, PO Box 98000, Baton Rouge, LA 70898-9000, Main Telephone: 504-765-2881, Fax: 504-765-2892, Hours: 8AM-4:30PM. Access by: mail, visit. Their central database is of commercial licensees and recreational lifetime licensees. Regular recreational licenses are held by the vendors then shipped here, but not databased.

Parish Courts and Recording Offices

What You Need to Know...

About the Courts

Administration

Judicial Administrator   504-568-5747
Judicial Council of the Supreme Court 8:30AM-4:30PM
301 Loyola Ave, Room 109
New Orleans, LA 70112

Court Structure

There is a District Court Clerk in each Parish who hold all the records for the Parish. Each Parish has its own clerk and courthouse.

Online Access

There is no online computer system available. There is planning in process on the Case Management Information System (**CMIS**); however, neither firm procedures, access criteria, nor dates have been established.

About the Recorder's Office

Organization

64 parishes (**not counties**), 64 filing offices. The recording officer is the Clerk of Court. Many parishes include tax and other non-UCC liens in their mortgage records. The entire state is in the Central Time Zone (CST).

UCC Records

Financing statements are filed with the Clerk of Court in any parish in the state and are entered onto a **statewide computerized database** of UCC financing statements available for searching at any parish office. All parishes perform UCC searches for $15.00 per debtor name. Use search request form UCC-11. Copies fees are $.50-1.00 per page.

Lien Records

All federal and state tax liens are filed with the Clerk of Court. Parishes usually file tax liens on personal property in their UCC or mortgage records, and most will perform tax lien searches for varying fees. Some parishes will automatically include tax liens on personal property in a mortgage certificate search. Other liens include judgments, labor, material, and hospital.

Real Estate Records

Most parishes will perform a mortgage search. Some will provide a record owner search. Copy and certification fees vary widely.

Parish Courts and Recording Offices

Acadia Parish

Real Estate Recording—Acadia Parish Clerk of Court, Parkerson Avenue, Court Circle, Crowley, LA 70526. 318-788-8881. Fax: 318-788-1048. 8:30AM-4:30PM (CST).

Felony, Misdemeanor, Civil, Probate—15th District Court, PO Box 922, Crowley, LA 70527. 318-788-8881. Fax: 318-788-1042. 8:30AM-4:30PM. Access by: Phone, mail, in person.

Allen Parish

Real Estate Recording—Allen Parish Clerk of Court, Main Street, Courthouse Square, Oberlin, LA 70655. 318-639-4351. Fax: 318-639-2030. 8AM-4:30PM (CST).

Felony, Misdemeanor, Civil, Probate—33rd District Court, PO Box 248, Oberlin, LA 70655. 318-639-4351. Fax: 318-639-2030. 8AM-4:30PM. Access by: Mail, in person.

Ascension Parish

Real Estate Recording—Ascension Parish Clerk of Court, 300 Houmas Street, Donaldsonville, LA 70346. 504-473-9866. Fax: 504-473-8641. 8:30AM-4:30PM (CST).

Felony, Misdemeanor, Civil, Probate—23rd District Court, PO Box 192, Donaldsonville, LA 70346. 504-473-9866. Fax: 504-473-8641. 8:30AM-4:30PM. Access by: Fax, mail, in person.

Assumption Parish

Real Estate Recording—Assumption Parish Clerk of Court, 4809 Highway 1, Courthouse, Napoleonville, LA 70390. 504-369-6653. Fax: 504-369-2032. 8:30AM-4:30PM (CST).

Felony, Misdemeanor, Civil, Probate—23rd District Court, PO Box 249, Napoleonville, LA 70390. 504-369-6653. Fax: 504-369-2032. 8:30AM-4:30PM. Access by: Fax, mail, in person.

Avoyelles Parish

Real Estate Recording—Avoyelles Parish Clerk of Court, East Mark Street, Marksville, LA 71351. 318-253-7523. Fax: 318-253-4614. 8:30AM-4:30PM (CST).

Felony, Misdemeanor, Civil, Probate—12th District Court, PO Box 196, Marksville, LA 71351. 318-253-7523. 8:15AM-4:30PM. Access by: Mail, in person.

Beauregard Parish

Real Estate Recording—Beauregard Parish Clerk of Court, 201 West First Street, Courthouse, De Ridder, LA 70634. 318-463-8595. Fax: 318-462-3916. 8AM-4:30PM (CST).

Felony, Misdemeanor, Civil, Probate—36th District Court, PO Box 100, DeRidder, LA 70634. 318-463-8595. Fax: 318-462-3916. 8AM-4:30PM. Access by: Mail, in person.

Bienville Parish

Real Estate Recording—Bienville Parish Clerk of Court, 601 Locust Street, Room 100, Arcadia, LA 71001. 318-263-2123. Fax: 318-263-7426. 8:30AM-4:30PM (CST).

Felony, Misdemeanor, Civil, Probate—2nd District Court, 601 Locust St., Rm. 100, Arcadia, LA 71001. 318-263-2123. Fax: 318-263-7405. 8:30AM-4:30PM. Access by: Mail, in person.

Bossier Parish

Real Estate Recording—Bossier Parish Clerk of Court, 200 Burt Blvd, Benton, LA 71006. 318-965-2336. 8:30AM-4PM (CST).

Felony, Misdemeanor, Civil, Probate—26th District Court, PO Box 369, Benton, LA 71006. 318-965-2336. Fax: 318-965-2713. 8:30AM-4:30PM. Access by: Mail, in person.

Caddo Parish

Real Estate Recording—Caddo Parish Clerk of Court, 501 Texas Street, Room 103, Shreveport, LA 71101. 318-226-6783. Fax: 318-227-9080. 8:30AM-5PM (CST).

Felony, Misdemeanor, Civil, Probate—1st District Court, 50 Texas St, Rm 103, Shreveport, LA 71101-5408. 318-226-6780. Fax: 318-227-9080. 8:30AM-5PM. Access by: Mail, in person.

Calcasieu Parish

Real Estate Recording—Calcasieu Parish Clerk of Court, 1000 Ryan Street, Lake Charles, LA 70601. 318-437-3550. Fax: 318-437-3350. 8:30AM-4:30PM (CST).

Felony, Misdemeanor, Civil, Probate—14th District Court, PO Box 1030, Lake Charles, LA 70602. 318-437-3550. Fax: 318-437-3350. 8:30AM-4:30PM. Access by: Mail, in person.

Caldwell Parish

Real Estate Recording—Caldwell Parish Clerk of Court, Main Street, Courthouse, Columbia, LA 71418. 318-649-2272. 8AM-4:30PM (CST).

Felony, Misdemeanor, Civil, Probate—37th District Court, PO Box 1327, Columbia, LA 71418. 318-649-2272. Fax: 318-649-2037. 8AM-4:30PM. Access by: Mail, in person.

Cameron Parish

Real Estate Recording—Cameron Parish Clerk of Court, 119 Smith Circle, Room 21, Cameron, LA 70631. 318-775-5316. Fax: 318-775-7172. 8:30AM-4:30PM (CST).

Felony, Misdemeanor, Civil, Probate—38th District Court, PO Box 549, Cameron, LA 70631. 318-775-5316. Fax: 318-775-7172. 8:30AM-4:30PM. Access by: Fax, mail, in person.

Catahoula Parish

Real Estate Recording—Catahoula Parish Clerk of Court, Courthouse Square, Harrisonburg, LA 71340. 318-744-5497. 8:30AM-4:30PM (CST).

Felony, Misdemeanor, Civil, Probate—7th District Court, PO Box 198, Harrisonburg, LA 71340. 318-744-5222. 8AM-4:30PM. Access by: Mail, in person.

Claiborne Parish

Real Estate Recording—Claiborne Parish Clerk of Court, 512 East Main Street, Homer, LA 71040. 318-927-9601. Fax: 318-927-2345. 8:30AM-4:30PM (CST).

Felony, Misdemeanor, Civil, Probate—2nd District Court, PO Box 330, Homer, LA 71040. 318-927-9601. Fax: 318-927-2345. 8:30AM-4:30PM. Access by: Mail, in person.

Concordia Parish

Real Estate Recording—Concordia Parish Clerk of Court, Courthouse, P.O. Box 790, Vidalia, LA 71373. 318-336-4204. 8:30AM-4:30PM (CST).

Felony, Misdemeanor, Civil, Probate—7th District Court, PO Box 790, Vidalia, LA 71373. 318-336-4204. Fax: 318-336-8217. 8:30AM-4:30PM. Access by: Mail, in person.

De Soto Parish

Real Estate Recording—De Soto Parish Clerk of Court, Texas Street, Courthouse Square, Mansfield, LA 71052. 318-872-3110. Fax: 318-872-4202. 8AM-4:30PM (CST).

Felony, Misdemeanor, Civil, Probate—11th District Court, PO Box 1206, Mansfield, LA 71052. 318-872-3110. Fax: 318-872-4202. 8AM-4:30PM. Access by: Mail, in person.

East Baton Rouge Parish

Real Estate Recording—East Baton Rouge Parish Clerk of Court, 222 St. Louis Street, Baton Rouge, LA 70821. 504-389-3985. Fax: 504-389-3392. 7:30AM-5:30PM (CST).

Felony, Misdemeanor, Civil, Probate—19th District Court, PO Box 1991, Baton Rouge, LA 70821. 504-389-3950. Fax: 504-389-3392. 7:30AM-5:30PM. Access by: Fax, mail, in person.

East Carroll Parish

Real Estate Recording—East Carroll Parish Clerk of Court, 400 First Street, Lake Providence, LA 71254. 318-559-2399. 8:30AM-4:30PM (CST).

Felony, Misdemeanor, Civil, Probate—6th District Court, 400 1st St, Lake Providence, LA 71254. 318-559-2399. 8:30AM-4:30PM. Access by: Mail, in person.

East Feliciana Parish

Real Estate Recording—East Feliciana Parish Clerk of Court, 12220 St. Helena Street, Courthouse Square, Clinton, LA 70722. 504-683-5145. Fax: 504-683-3556. 8AM-4:30PM (CST).

Felony, Misdemeanor, Civil, Probate—20th District Court, PO Box 595, Clinton, LA 70722. 504-683-5145. Fax: 504-683-3556. 8AM-4:30PM. Access by: Fax, mail, in person.

Evangeline Parish

Real Estate Recording—Evangeline Parish Clerk of Court, 200 Court Street, Courthouse Bldg., Ville Platte, LA 70586. 318-363-5671. 8AM-4:30PM (CST).

Felony, Misdemeanor, Civil, Probate—13th District Court, PO Drawer 347, Ville Platte, LA 70586. 318-363-5671. 8AM-4:30PM. Access by: Mail, in person.

Franklin Parish

Real Estate Recording—Franklin Parish Clerk of Court, 6550 Main Street, Courthouse, Winnsboro, LA 71295. 318-435-5133. Fax: 318-435-5134. 8:30AM-4:30PM (CST).

Felony, Misdemeanor, Civil, Probate—5th District Court, PO Box 431, Winnsboro, LA 71295. 318-435-5133. Fax: 318-435-5134. 8:30AM-4:30PM. Access by: Mail, in person.

Grant Parish

Real Estate Recording—Grant Parish Clerk of Court, 200 Main Street, Colfax, LA 71417. 318-627-3246. 8:30AM-4:30PM (CST).

Felony, Misdemeanor, Civil, Probate—35th District Court, PO Box 263, Colfax, LA 71417. 318-627-3246. 8:30AM-4:30PM. Access by: Phone, mail, in person.

Iberia Parish

Real Estate Recording—Iberia Parish Clerk of Court, 300 Block of Iberia Street, New Iberia, LA 70560. 318-365-7282. Fax: 318-365-0737. 8:30AM-4:30PM (CST).

Felony, Misdemeanor, Civil, Probate—16th District Court, PO Drawer 12010, New Iberia, LA 70562-2010. 318-365-7282. Fax: 318-365-0737. 8:30AM-4:30PM. Access by: Phone, fax, mail, in person.

Iberville Parish

Real Estate Recording—Iberville Parish Clerk of Court, 58050 Meriam Street, Plaquemine, LA 70764. 504-687-5160. Fax: 504-687-5260. 8:30AM-4:30PM (CST).

Felony, Misdemeanor, Civil, Probate—18th District Court, PO Box 423, Plaquemine, LA 70764. 504-687-5160. Fax: 504-687-5260. 8:30AM-5:00PM. Access by: Fax, mail, in person.

Jackson Parish

Real Estate Recording—Jackson Parish Clerk of Court, 500 East Court Avenue, Jonesboro, LA 71251. 318-259-2424. 8:30AM-4:30PM (CST).

Felony, Misdemeanor, Civil, Probate—2nd District Court, PO Drawer 730, Jonesboro, LA 71251. 318-259-2424. 8:30AM-4:30PM. Access by: Phone, mail, in person.

Jefferson Davis Parish

Real Estate Recording—Jefferson Davis Parish Clerk of Court, 300 State Street, Jennings, LA 70546. 318-824-1160. 8:30AM-4:30PM (CST).

Felony, Misdemeanor, Civil, Probate—31st District Court, PO Box 799, Jennings, LA 70546. 318-824-1160. Fax: 318-824-1354. 8:30AM-4:30PM. Access by: Mail, in person.

Jefferson Parish

Real Estate Recording—Jefferson Parish Clerk of Court, Clerk of Court/Mtg & Conv. Office, Gretna Courthouse Main Bldg. 3rd floor, Gretna, LA 70053. 504-364-2943. Fax: 504-364-2942. 7:30AM-4:30PM (CST).

Felony, Misdemeanor, Civil, Probate—24th District Court, PO Box 10, Gretna, LA 70053. 504-364-2992. Fax: 504-364-3797. 8:30AM-4:30PM. Access by: Fax, mail, in person.

La Salle Parish

Real Estate Recording—La Salle Parish Clerk of Court, Courthouse Street, Jena, LA 71342. 318-992-2158. Fax: 318-992-2157. 8:30AM-4:30PM (CST).

Felony, Misdemeanor, Civil, Probate—28th District Court, PO Drawer 1372, Jena, LA 71342. 318-992-2158. Fax: 318-992-2157. 8:30AM-4:30PM. Access by: Phone, mail, in person.

Lafayette Parish

Real Estate Recording—Lafayette Parish Clerk of Court, 800 South Buchanan Street, Lafayette, LA 70501. 318-233-0150. Fax: 318-269-6392. 8:30AM-4:30PM (CST).

Felony, Misdemeanor, Civil, Probate—15th District Court, PO Box 2009, Lafayette, LA 70502. 318-233-0150. Fax: 318-269-6392. 8:30AM-4:30PM. Access by: Phone, mail, remote online, in person. Remote system index goes back to 1986.

Lafourche Parish

Real Estate Recording—Lafourche Parish Clerk of Court, 309 West Third, Thibodaux, LA 70301. 504-447-4841. Fax: 504-447-5800. 8:30AM-4:30PM (CST).

Felony, Misdemeanor, Civil, Probate—17th District Court, PO Box 818, Thibodaux, LA 70302. 504-447-4841. Fax: 504-447-5800. 8:30AM-4:30PM. Access by: Fax, mail, in person.

Lincoln Parish

Real Estate Recording—Lincoln Parish Clerk of Court, 100 Texas Avenue, Courthouse - Room 103, Ruston, LA 71270. 318-251-5130. Fax: 318-255-6004. 8:30AM-4:30PM (CST).

Felony, Misdemeanor, Civil, Probate—3rd District Court, PO Box 924, Ruston, LA 71273-0924. 318-251-5130. Fax: 318-255-6004. 8:30AM-4:30PM. Access by: Mail, in person.

Livingston Parish

Real Estate Recording—Livingston Parish Clerk of Court, 20180 Iowa Street, Livingston, LA 70754. 504-686-2216. Fax: 504-686-1867. 8AM-4:30PM (CST).

Felony, Misdemeanor, Civil, Probate—21st District Court, PO Box 1150, Livingston, LA 70754. 504-686-2216. 8:00AM-4:30PM. Access by: Mail, in person.

Madison Parish

Real Estate Recording—Madison Parish Clerk of Court, 100 North Cedar, Courthouse, Tallulah, LA 71282. 318-574-0655. Fax: 318-574-3961. 8:30AM-4:30PM (CST).

Felony, Misdemeanor, Civil, Probate—6th District Court, 100 N Cedar, Tallulah, LA 71282. 318-574-0655. Fax: 318-574-0656. 8:30AM-4:30PM. Access by: Phone, mail, in person.

Morehouse Parish

Real Estate Recording—Morehouse Parish Clerk of Court, 100 East Madison Ave., Courthouse Building, Bastrop, LA 71220. 318-281-3343. Fax: 318-281-3775. 8:30AM-4:30PM (CST).

Felony, Misdemeanor, Civil, Probate—4th District Court, Courthouse, 100 East Madison, Bastrop, LA 71220-3893. 318-281-3343. Fax: 318-281-3775. 8:30AM-4:30PM. Access by: Mail, in person.

Natchitoches Parish

Real Estate Recording—Natchitoches Parish Clerk of Court, 200 Church Street, New Courthouse Building-Room 104, Natchitoches, LA 71457. 318-352-8152. Fax: 318-352-9321. 8:30AM-4:30PM (CST).

Felony, Misdemeanor, Civil, Probate—10th District Court, PO Box 476, Natchitoches, LA 71458. 318-352-8152. Fax: 318-352-9432. 8:15AM-4:30PM. Access by: Mail, in person.

Orleans Parish

Real Estate Recording—Orleans Parish Recorder of Mortgages, 421 Loyola Avenue, B-1, Civil Court Building, New Orleans, LA 70112. 504-592-9176. Fax: 504-592-9192. 9AM-4PM (CST).

Civil, Probate—Civil District Court, 421 Loyola Ave, Rm 402, New Orleans, LA 70112. 504-592-9100. Fax: 504-592-9128. 8AM-5PM. Access by: Phone, mail, in person.

Civil Actions Under $20,000, Small Claims—New Orleans City Court, 421 Loyola Ave, Rm 201, New Orleans, LA 70112. 504-592-9155. Fax: 504-592-9281. 8:30AM-4PM. Access by: Mail, in person.

Felony, Misdemeanor—4th District Court-Criminal Division, 2700 Tulane Ave, Rm 115, New Orleans, LA 70119. 504-827-3520. Fax: 504-827-3385. 8:15AM-3:30PM. Access by: Mail, in person.

Ouachita Parish

Real Estate Recording—Ouachita Parish Clerk of Court, 300 St. John, Suite 104, Monroe, LA 71201. 318-327-1444. Fax: 318-327-1462. 8:30AM-5PM (CST).

Felony, Misdemeanor, Civil, Probate—4th District Court, PO Box 1862, Monroe, LA 71210-1862. 318-327-1444. Fax: 318-327-1462. 8:30AM-5PM. Access by: Fax, mail, in person.

Plaquemines Parish

Real Estate Recording—Plaquemines Parish Clerk of Court, 18039 Hwy 15, Courthouse, Pointe a la Hache, LA 70082. 504-333-4377. Fax: 504-333-9202. 8:30AM-4:30PM (CST).

Felony, Misdemeanor, Civil, Probate—25th District Court, PO Box 129, Pointe A La Hache, LA 70082. 504-333-4377. Fax: 504-392-6690. 8:30AM-4:30PM. Access by: In person only.

Pointe Coupee Parish

Real Estate Recording—Pointe Coupee Parish Clerk of Court, 201 East Main, New Roads, LA 70760. 504-638-9596. Fax: 504-638-9590. 8:30AM-4:30PM (CST).

Felony, Misdemeanor, Civil, Probate—18th District Court, PO Box 86, New Roads, LA 70760. 504-638-9596. 8:30AM-4:30PM. Access by: In person only.

Rapides Parish

Real Estate Recording—Rapides Parish Clerk of Court, 701 Murray St., Alexandria, LA 71301. 318-473-8153. Fax: 318-473-4667. 8:30AM-4:30PM (CST).

Felony, Misdemeanor, Civil, Probate—9th District Court, PO Box 952, Alexandria, LA 71309. 318-473-8153. Fax: 318-473-4667. 8:30AM-4:30PM. Access by: Mail, in person.

Red River Parish

Real Estate Recording—Red River Parish Clerk of Court, 615 Carroll Street, Coushatta, LA 71019. 318-932-6741. 8:30AM-4:30PM (CST).

Felony, Misdemeanor, Civil, Probate—39th District Court, PO Box 485, Coushatta, LA 71019. 318-932-6741. 8:30AM-4:30PM. Access by: Mail, in person.

Richland Parish

Real Estate Recording—Richland Parish Clerk of Court, 100 Julia Street, Courthouse, Rayville, LA 71269. 318-728-4171. 8:30AM-4:30PM (CST).

Felony, Misdemeanor, Civil, Probate—5th District Court, PO Box 119, Rayville, LA 71269. 318-728-4171. 8:30AM-4:30PM. Access by: Mail, in person.

Sabine Parish

Real Estate Recording—Sabine Parish Clerk of Court, 400 S Capital Room 102, Many, LA 71449. 318-256-6223. Fax: 318-256-9037. 8AM-4:30PM (CST).

Felony, Misdemeanor, Civil, Probate—11th District Court, PO Box 419, Many, LA 71449. 318-256-6223. Fax: 318-256-9037. 8AM-4:30PM. Access by: Fax, mail, in person.

St. Bernard Parish

Real Estate Recording—St. Bernard Parish Clerk of Court, 1100 West St. Bernard Highway, Chalmette, LA 70043. 504-271-3434. 8:30AM-4:30PM (CST).

Felony, Misdemeanor, Civil, Probate—34th District Court, PO Box 1746, Chalmette, LA 70044. 504-271-3434. 8:30AM-4:30PM. Access by: Mail, in person.

St. Charles Parish

Real Estate Recording—St. Charles Parish Clerk of Court, 15045 River Road, Courthouse, Hahnville, LA 70057. 504-783-6632. 8:30AM-4:30PM (CST).

Felony, Misdemeanor, Civil, Probate—29th District Court, PO Box 424, Hahnville, LA 70057. 504-783-6632. Fax: 504-783-2005. 8:30AM-4:30PM. Access by: Mail, in person.

St. Helena Parish

Real Estate Recording—St. Helena Parish Clerk of Court, Courthouse Square, Highway 10, P.O. Box 308, Greensburg, LA 70441. 504-222-4514. 8:30AM-4:30PM (CST).

Felony, Misdemeanor, Civil, Probate—21st District Court, PO Box 308, Greensburg, LA 70441. 504-222-4514. 8:30AM-4:30PM. Access by: Mail, in person.

St. James Parish

Real Estate Recording—St. James Parish Clerk of Court, 5800 LA Highway 644, Courthouse, Convent, LA 70723. 504-562-2270. Fax: 504-562-2383. 8AM-4:30PM (CST).

Felony, Misdemeanor, Civil, Probate—23rd District Court, PO Box 63, Convent, LA 70723. 504-562-7496. Fax: 504-562-2383. 8AM-4:30PM. Access by: Mail, in person.

St. John the Baptist Parish

Real Estate Recording—St. John the Baptist Parish Clerk of Court, East 3rd Street & River Road, Edgard, LA 70049. 504-497-3331. 8:30AM-4:30PM (CST).

Felony, Misdemeanor, Civil, Probate—40th District Court, PO Box 280, Edgard, LA 70049. 504-497-3331. 8:30AM-4:30PM. Access by: Mail, in person.

St. Landry Parish

Real Estate Recording—St. Landry Parish Clerk of Court, Bellevue & Court Street, Opelousas, LA 70570. 318-942-5606. Fax: 318-948-7265. 8AM-4:30PM (CST).

Felony, Misdemeanor, Civil, Probate—27th District Court, PO Box 750, Opelousas, LA 70570. 318-942-5606. Fax: 318-948-7265. 8AM-4:30PM. Access by: Mail, in person.

St. Martin Parish

Real Estate Recording—St. Martin Parish Clerk of Court, 415 S. Main Street, Courthouse, St. Martinville, LA 70582. 318-394-2210. Fax: 318-394-7772. 8:30AM-4:30PM (CST).

Felony, Misdemeanor, Civil, Probate—16th District Court, PO Box 308, St. Martinville, LA 70582. 318-394-2210. Fax: 318-394-7772. 8:30AM-4:30PM. Access by: Fax, mail, in person.

St. Mary Parish

Real Estate Recording—St. Mary Parish Clerk of Court, 500 Main Street, Courthouse, Franklin, LA 70538. 318-828-4100. Fax: 318-828-2509. 8:30AM-4:30PM (CST).

Felony, Misdemeanor, Civil, Probate—16th District Court, PO Box 1231, Franklin, LA 70538. 318-828-4100. Fax: 318-828-2509. 8:30AM-4:30PM. Access by: In person only.

St. Tammany Parish

Real Estate Recording—St. Tammany Parish Clerk of Court, 510 East Boston Street, Covington, LA 70433. 504-898-2430. 8:30AM-4:30PM (CST).

Felony, Misdemeanor, Civil, Probate—22nd District Court, PO Box 1090, Covington, LA 70434. 504-898-2430. 8:30AM-4:30PM. Access by: Mail, in person.

Tangipahoa Parish

Real Estate Recording—Tangipahoa Parish Clerk of Court, Mulberry & Bay Street, Amite, LA 70422. 504-549-1611. Fax: 504-748-6503. 8:30AM-4:30PM (CST).

Felony, Misdemeanor, Civil, Probate—21st District Court, PO Box 667, Amite, LA 70422. 504-748-4146. Fax: 504-748-6503. 8:30AM-4:30PM. Access by: Fax, mail, in person.

Tensas Parish

Real Estate Recording—Tensas Parish Clerk of Court, Hancock Street, Courthouse, St. Joseph, LA 71366. 318-766-3921. (CST).

Felony, Misdemeanor, Civil, Probate—6th District Court, PO Box 78, St. Joseph, LA 71366. 318-766-3921. 8AM-4:30PM. Access by: In person only.

Terrebonne Parish

Real Estate Recording—Terrebonne Parish Clerk of Court, 7856 Main Street, Old Courthouse Building, Houma, LA 70360. 504-868-5660. 8:30AM-4:30PM (CST).

Felony, Misdemeanor, Civil, Probate—32nd District Court, PO Box 1569, Houma, LA 70361. 504-868-5660. 8:30AM-4:30PM. Access by: Mail, in person.

Union Parish

Real Estate Recording—Union Parish Clerk of Court, Courthouse, Farmerville, LA 71241. 318-368-3055. 8:30AM-4:30PM (CST).

Felony, Misdemeanor, Civil, Probate—3rd District Court, Courthouse Bldg, Farmerville, LA 71241. 318-368-3055. Fax: 318-368-2487. 8:30AM-4:30PM. Access by: Mail, in person.

Vermilion Parish

Real Estate Recording—Vermilion Parish Clerk of Court, South State Street, Courthouse, Abbeville, LA 70510. 318-898-1992. Fax: 318-898-0404. 8:30AM-4:30PM (CST).

Felony, Misdemeanor, Civil, Probate—15th District Court, PO Box 790, Abbeville, LA 70511-0790. 318-898-1992. Fax: 318-898-0404. 8:30AM-4:30PM. Access by: Phone, fax, mail, in person.

Vernon Parish

Real Estate Recording—Vernon Parish Clerk of Court, 201 South Third Street, Leesville, LA 71446. 318-238-1384. Fax: 318-238-9902. 8AM-4:30PM (CST).

Felony, Misdemeanor, Civil, Probate—30th District Court, PO Box 40, Leesville, LA 71496. 318-238-1384. Fax: 318-238-9902. 8AM-4:30PM. Access by: Mail, in person.

Washington Parish

Real Estate Recording—Washington Parish Clerk of Court, Corner of Washington & Main, Franklinton, LA 70438. 504-839-4663. 8AM-4:30PM (CST).

Felony, Misdemeanor, Civil, Probate—22nd District Court, PO Box 607, Franklinton, LA 70438. 504-839-4661. 8AM-4:30PM. Access by: Mail, in person.

Webster Parish

Real Estate Recording—Webster Parish Clerk of Court, 410 Main Street, Courthouse, Minden, LA 71058. 318-371-0366. Fax: 318-371-0226. 8:30AM-4:30PM (CST).

Felony, Misdemeanor, Civil, Probate—26th District Court, PO Box 370, Minden, LA 71058. 318-371-0366. Fax: 318-371-0226. 8:30AM-4:30PM. Access by: Fax, mail, in person.

West Baton Rouge Parish

Real Estate Recording—West Baton Rouge Parish Clerk of Court, 850 8th Street, Port Allen, LA 70767. 504-383-0378. Fax: 504-383-3694. 8:30AM-4:30PM (CST).

Felony, Misdemeanor, Civil, Probate—18th District Court, PO Box 107, Port Allen, LA 70767. 504-383-0378. 8:30AM-4:30PM. Access by: Mail, in person.

West Carroll Parish

Real Estate Recording—West Carroll Parish Clerk of Court, Main Street, Courthouse, Oak Grove, LA 71263. 318-428-3281. 8:30AM-4:30PM (CST).

Felony, Misdemeanor, Civil, Probate—5th District Court, PO Box 1078, Oak Grove, LA 71263. 318-428-3281. 8:30AM-4:30PM. Access by: Mail, in person.

West Feliciana Parish

Real Estate Recording—West Feliciana Parish Clerk of Court, Corner of Ferdinand & Prosperity, Courthouse, St. Francisville, LA 70775. 504-635-3794. Fax: 504-635-3770. 8:30AM-4:30PM (CST).

Felony, Misdemeanor, Civil, Probate—20th District Court, PO Box 1843, St Francisville, LA 70775. 504-635-3794. 8AM-4:30PM. Access by: Mail, in person.

Winn Parish

Real Estate Recording—Winn Parish Clerk of Court, Courthouse, Room 103, 100 Main St., Winnfield, LA 71483. 318-628-3515. Fax: 318-628-2753. 8AM-4:30PM (CST).

Felony, Misdemeanor, Civil, Probate—8th District Court, 100 Main St, Winnfield, LA 71483. 318-628-3515. 8AM-4:30PM. Access by: Mail, in person.

Federal Courts

US District Court

Eastern District of Louisiana

New Orleans Division, US District Court Clerk, Room 151, 500 Camp St, New Orleans, LA 70130. 504-589-7650. Counties: Assumption Parish, Jefferson Parish, Lafourche Parish, Orleans Parish, Plaquemines Parish, St. Bernard Parish, St. Charles Parish, St. James Parish, St. John the Baptist Parish, St. Tammany Parish, Tangipahoa Parish, Terrebonne Parish, Washington Parish

Middle District of Louisiana

Baton Rouge Division, US District Court PO Box 2630, Baton Rouge, LA 70821-2630. 504-389-3500. Counties: Ascension Parish, East Baton Rouge Parish, East Feliciana Parish, Iberville Parish, Livingston Parish, Pointe Coupee Parish, St. Helena Parish, West Baton Rouge Parish, West Feliciana Parish

Western District of Louisiana

Alexandria Division, US District Court PO Box 1269, Alexandria, LA 71309. 318-473-7415. Counties: Avoyelles

Parish, Catahoula Parish, Concordia Parish, Grant Parish, La Salle Parish, Natchitoches Parish, Rapides Parish, Vernon Parish, Winn Parish

Lafayette Division, US District Court Room 113, Federal Bldg, 705 Jefferson St, Lafayette, LA 70501. 318-262-6613. Counties: Acadia Parish, Evangeline Parish, Iberia Parish, Lafayette Parish, St. Landry Parish, St. Martin Parish, St. Mary Parish, Vermilion Parish

Lake Charles Division, US District Court 611 Broad St, Suite 188, Lake Charles, LA 70601. 318-437-3870. Counties: Allen Parish, Beauregard Parish, Calcasieu Parish, Cameron Parish, Jefferson Davis Parish

Monroe Division, US District Court PO Drawer 3087, Monroe, LA 71210. 318-322-6740. Counties: Caldwell Parish, East Carroll Parish, Franklin Parish, Jackson Parish, Lincoln Parish, Madison Parish, Morehouse Parish, Ouachita Parish, Richland Parish, Tensas Parish, Union Parish, West Carroll Parish

Shreveport Division, US District Court, US Court House, Suite 1167, 300 Fannin St, Shreveport, LA 71101-3083. 318-676-4273. Counties: Bienville Parish, Bossier Parish, Caddo Parish, Claiborne Parish, De Soto Parish, Red River Parish, Sabine Parish, Webster Parish

US Bankruptcy Court
Eastern District of Louisiana

New Orleans Division, US Bankruptcy Court, Hale Boggs Federal Building, 501 Magazine St #601, New Orleans, LA 70130. 504-589-7878. Voice Case Information System: 504-589-3951. Counties: Assumption Parish, Jefferson Parish, Lafourche Parish, Orleans Parish, Plaquemines Parish, St. Bernard Parish, St. Charles Parish, St. James Parish, St. John the Baptist Parish, St. Tammany Parish, Tangipahoa Parish, Terrebonne Parish, Washington Parish

Middle District of Louisiana

Baton Rouge Division, US Bankruptcy Court, Room 119, 707 Florida St, Baton Rouge, LA 70801. 504-389-0211.

Voice Case Information System: 504-382-2175. Counties: Ascension Parish, East Baton Rouge Parish, East Feliciana Parish, Iberville Parish, Livingston Parish, Pointe Coupee Parish, St. Helena Parish, West Baton Rouge Parish, West Feliciana Parish

Western District of Louisiana

Alexandria Division, US Bankruptcy Court, Hemenway Bldg, 300 Jackson St, Alexandria, LA 71301. 318-445-1890. Voice Case Information System: 318-676-4234. Counties: Avoyelles Parish, Catahoula Parish, Concordia Parish, Grant Parish, La Salle Parish, Natchitoches Parish, Rapides Parish, Vernon Parish, Winn Parish

Lafayette-Opelousas Division, US Bankruptcy Court, PO Box J, Opelousas, LA 70571-1909. 318-948-3451. Voice Case Information System: 318-676-4234. Counties: Acadia Parish, Evangeline Parish, Iberia Parish, Lafayette Parish, St. Landry Parish, St. Martin Parish, St. Mary Parish, Vermilion Parish

Lake Charles Division, US Bankruptcy Court, c/o Lafayette-Opelousas Division, PO Box J, Opelousas, LA 70571-1909. 318-948-3451. Voice Case Information System: 318-676-4234. Counties: Allen Parish, Beauregard Parish, Calcasieu Parish, Cameron Parish, Jefferson Davis Parish

Monroe Division, US Bankruptcy Court, c/o Shreveport Division, Suite 2201, 300 Fannin St, Shreveport, LA 71101. 318-676-4267. Voice Case Information System: 318-676-4234. Counties: Caldwell Parish, East Carroll Parish, Franklin Parish, Jackson Parish, Lincoln Parish, Madison Parish, Morehouse Parish, Ouachita Parish, Richland Parish, Tensas Parish, Union Parish, West Carroll Parish

Shreveport Division, US Bankruptcy Court, Suite 2201, 300 Fannin St, Shreveport, LA 71101-3089. 318-676-4267. Voice Case Information System: 318-676-4234. Counties: Bienville Parish, Bossier Parish, Caddo Parish, Claiborne Parish, De Soto Parish, Red River Parish, Sabine Parish, Webster Parish

Maine

Capitol: Augusta (Kennebec County)	
Number of Counties: 16	**Population:** 1,271,382
County Court Locations:	**Federal Court Locations:**
•Superior Courts: 18/ 16 Counties	•District Courts: 2
•District Courts: 32/13 Districts	•Bankruptcy Courts: 2
•Probate Courts: 16	**State Agencies:** 19

State Agencies—Summary

General Help Numbers:

State Archives

State Archives	207-287-5790
Cultural Bldg, Station 84	Fax: 207-287-5624
Augusta, ME 04333-0084	8:30AM-4PM
Reference Room:	207-287-5795
Historical Society:	207-287-2132

Governor's Office

Governor's Office	207-287-3531
1 State House Station, Room 236	Fax: 207-287-1034
Augusta, ME 04333	8AM-5PM

Attorney General's Office

Attorney General's Office	207-626-8800
6 State House Station	Fax: 207-287-3145
Augusta, ME 04333	8AM-5PM

State Legislation

Maine Legislature	207-287-1692
2 State House Station	8AM-5PM
Legislative Document Room, 3rd Floor	
Augusta, ME 04333-0002	
Document Room:	207-287-1408

Important State Internet Sites:

```
Webscape
File  Edit  View                    Help
```

State of Maine World Wide Web

www.state.me.us/

This home page includes links to many sites. Some of those sites are the Governor, state agencies, members of the State Legislature, Federal Legislators, the Office of Policy and Legal Analysis and a search engine, just to name a few.

The Governor's Office

www.state.me.us/governor/govhome.htm

This site includes information about the Governor, the State of the State address, legislative initiatives, and enables you to send e-mail to the Governor.

Division of Drivers Licensing

www.state.me.us/sos/bmv/bmv.htm

This site has a great deal of information about the Drivers Licensing and Control Division. Phone and fax numbers are provided for the different sections of the department.

Maine State Archives

www.state.me.us/sos/arc/general/admin/ mawww001.htm

Home page for the State of Maine Archives. A marriage database is available from this site.

Policy and Legal Analysis

www.state.me.us/legis/#billaw

This site links to legislative reports, bill summaries, joint standing committees and legislative studies. This site also links to the House and Senate.

State Agencies—Public Records

Criminal Records

Maine State Police, State Bureau of Identification, 36 Hospital St, Augusta, ME 04330, Main Telephone: 207-624-7009, Hours: 8AM-5PM. Access by: mail, visit. Normal turnaround time is 2 to 3 days, unless there is data on the record. Then the turnaround time can take up to 8 weeks.

Corporation Records
Limited Partnerships
Trademarks/Servicemarks
Assumed Name
Limited Liability Company Records

Secretary of State, Reports & Information Division, State House Station 101, Augusta, ME 04333-0101, Main Telephone: 207-287-4190, Fax: 207-287-5874, Hours: 8AM-5PM. Access by: mail, phone, visit.

Uniform Commercial Code
Federal Tax Liens
State Tax Liens

UCC Filing Section, Secretary of State, 101 State House Station, Augusta, ME 04333-0101, Main Telephone: 207-287-4177, Fax: 207-287-5874, Hours: 8AM-5PM. Access by: mail, phone, fax, visit.

Sales Tax Registrations

Taxation Bureau, Sales Tax Division, State House Station 24, Augusta, ME 04333, Main Telephone: 207-287-2336, Fax: 207-287-4028, Hours: 8AM-4PM. Access by: mail, phone, visit.

Birth Certificates

Maine Department of Human Services, Vital Records, 11 State House Station, Augusta, ME 04333-0011, Main Telephone: 207-287-3181, Message Phone: 207-287-3184, Fax: 207-287-1907, Hours: 8AM-5PM. Access by: mail, fax, visit.

Death Records

Maine Department of Human Services, Vital Records, 11 State House Station, Augusta, ME 04333-0011, Main Telephone: 207-287-3181, Message Phone: 207-287-3184, Fax: 207-287-1907, Hours: 8AM-4PM. Access by: mail, fax, visit.

Marriage Certificates

Maine Department of Human Services, Vital Records, 11 State House Station, Augusta, ME 04333-0011, Main Telephone: 207-287-3181, Message Phone: 207-287-3184, Fax: 207-287-1907, Hours: 8AM-4PM. Access by: mail, fax, visit.

Divorce Records

Maine Department of Human Services, Vital Records, 11 State House Station, Augusta, ME 04333-0011, Main Telephone: 207-287-3181, Message Phone: 207-287-3184, Fax: 207-287-1907, Hours: 8AM-4PM. Access by: mail, fax, visit.

Workers' Compensation Records

Workers Compensation Board, 27 State House Station, Augusta, ME 04333-0027, Main Telephone: 207-287-3751, Fax: 207-287-7198, Hours: 7:30AM-5PM. Access by: mail, phone, visit.

Driver Records

Bureau of Motor Vehicles, Driver License & Control, State House Station 29, Augusta, ME 04333, Main Telephone: 207-287-9005, Fax: 207-287-2592, Hours: 8AM-5PM. Access by: mail, visit, fax, PC.

Vehicle Ownership
Vehicle Identification

Department of Motor Vehicles, Registration Section, 29 State House Station, Augusta, ME 04333-0029, Main Telephone: 207-287-3556, Fax: 207-287-5219, Hours: 8AM-5PM M-T,TH-F; 8AM-4PM W. Access by: mail, phone, fax, visit, PC.

Accident Reports

Maine State Police, Traffic Section, 242 State St, Station 20, Augusta, ME 04333, Main Telephone: 207-624-8944, Fax: 207-624-8945, Hours: 7:30AM-4PM M-F. Access by: mail, fax, visit.

Hunting License Information
Fishing License Information

Inland Fisheries & Wildlife Department, Licensing Division, 41 State House Station, Augusta, ME 04333, Main Telephone: 207-287-5209, Fax: 602-287-8094, Hours: 8AM-5PM. Access by: mail, phone, fax, visit. The state is in the process of computerizing license data. Licenses are issued by Town Clerks and approved businesses and forwarded monthly to this department.

County Courts and Recording Offices

What You Need to Know...

About the Courts

Administration

State Court Administrator 207-822-0792
PO Box 4820 Fax: 207-822-0781
Portland, ME 04112

Court Structure

Circuit courts may accept civil cases involving less than $30,000 money claims. District courts handle some minor "felonies."

Probate Courts are now part of the county court system, not the state system. Even though the Probate Court may be housed with other state courts, it is on a different phone system and calls may not be transferred.

Searching Hints

Most courts will refer written requests for criminal searches to the Maine State Police.

The Judicial Branch has set standard fees for many services but individual court fees vary.

Online Access

Online computer access is not currently available. Development of a statewide judicial computer system is in process and will be available statewide sometime in the future. The system will be initially for judicial and law enforcement agencies and will **not** include public access in the near term.

About the Recorder's Office

Organization

16 counties, 17 filing offices. The recording officer is County Register of Deeds. Counties maintain a general index of all transactions recorded. **Aroostock County has two filing offices.** There are no county assessors; each town has its own. The entire state is in the Eastern Time Zone (EST).

UCC Records

Financing statements are filed both at the state level, except for real estate related filings, which are filed only with the Register of Deeds. Counties do **not** perform UCC searches. Copy fees are usually $1.00 per page.

Lien Records

All tax liens on personal property are filed with the Secretary of State. All tax liens on real property are filed with the Register of Deeds. Other liens include municipal, bail bond, and mechanics.

Real Estate Records

Counties do **not** usually perform real estate searches, but some will look up a name informally. Copy and certification fees vary widely. Assessor and tax records are located at the town/city level.

County Courts and Recording Offices

Androscoggin County

Real Estate Recording—Androscoggin County Register of Deeds, 2 Turner Street, Courthouse, Auburn, ME 04210. 207-782-0191. Fax: 207-784-3163. 8AM-5PM (EST).

Felony, Misdemeanor, Civil Actions Over $30,000—Androscoggin Superior Court, PO Box 3660, Auburn, ME 04212-3660. 207-783-5450. 8AM-4:30PM (EST). Access by: In person only.

Misdemeanor, Civil Actions Under $30,000, Eviction, Small Claims—Lewiston District Court-South #8, PO Box 1345, 84 Park St, Lewiston, ME 04243. Civil: 207-783-5403. Criminal: 207-783-5401. 8AM-4PM (EST). Access by: Mail, in person.

District Court North Androscoggin District 11, 2 Main St, Livermore Falls, ME 04254. 207-897-3800. 8AM-4PM T-Th (EST). Access by: Mail, in person.

Waterville District Court-District 7, 18 Colby St, PO Box 397, Waterville, ME 04903. 207-873-2103. 8AM-4PM (EST). Access by: Mail, in person.

Probate—Probate Court, 2 Turner St, Auburn, ME 04210. 207-782-0281. Fax: 207-782-5361. 8:30AM-5PM (EST). Access by: Mail, in person.

Aroostook County

Real Estate Recording—Northern Aroostook County Register of Deeds, Northern District, 13 Hall St., Fort Kent, ME 04743. 207-834-3925. Fax: 207-834-3138. 8AM-4:30PM (EST).

Aroostook County Register of Deeds, Southern District, 26 Court St., Suite 102, Houlton, ME 04730. 207-532-1500. 8AM-4:30PM (EST).

Felony, Misdemeanor, Civil Actions Over $30,000—Caribou Superior Court, 240 Sweden St, Caribou, ME 04736. 207-498-8125. 8AM-4PM (EST). Access by: Mail, in person.

Houlton Superior Court, PO Box 787, Houlton, ME 04730. 207-532-6563. 8AM-4PM (EST). Access by: In person only.

Misdemeanor, Civil Actions Under $30,000, Eviction, Small Claims—Caribou District Court-East #1, 240 Sweden St, Caribou, ME 04736. 207-493-3144. 8AM-4PM (EST). Access by: In person only.

Fort Kent District Court-District 1, Division of Western Aroostook, PO Box 473, Fort Kent, ME 04743. 207-834-5003. 8AM-4PM T-F (EST). Access by: Phone, mail, in person.

Houlton District Court-South #2, PO Box 457, Houlton, ME 04730. 207-532-2147. 8AM-4PM (EST). Access by: Phone, mail, in person.

Madawaska District Court-West, PO Box 127, 123 E Main St, Madawaska, ME 04756. 207-728-4700. 8AM-4PM M,T,F (EST). Access by: Phone, mail, in person.

District Court, PO Box 794 (27 Riverside Dr), Presque Isle, ME 04769. 207-764-2055. 8AM-4PM (EST). Access by: Mail, in person.

Probate—Probate Court, 26 Court St #103, Houlton, ME 04730. 207-532-1502. 8AM-4:30PM (EST). Access by: Mail, in person.

Cumberland County

Real Estate Recording—Cumberland County Register of Deeds, 142 Federal Street, Portland, ME 04101. 207-871-8389. Fax: 207-772-4162. 8:30AM-4:30PM (EST).

Civil Actions Over $30,000—Superior Court-Civil, PO Box 287-DTS, Portland, ME 04112. 207-822-4105. 8AM-4:30PM (EST). Access by: Mail, in person.

Felony, Misdemeanor—Superior Court-Criminal, PO Box 287, Portland, ME 04112. 207-822-4113. 8AM-4:30PM (EST). Access by: Phone, mail, in person.

Civil Actions Under $30,000, Eviction, Small Claims—Portland District Court-South #9-Civil, PO Box 412, 142 Federal St, Portland, ME 04112. 207-822-4200. 8AM-4:30PM (EST). Access by: Mail, in person.

Misdemeanor—Portland District Court-South #9-Criminal, PO Box 412, Portland, ME 04112. 207-822-4205. 8AM-4:30PM (EST). Access by: Mail, in person.

Misdemeanor, Civil Actions Under $30,000, Eviction, Small Claims—Bath District Court-East #6, RR 1, Box 310, Bath, ME 04530. 207-442-0200. 8AM-4PM (EST). Access by: In person only.

Bridgton District Court-North #9, 2 Chase Common, Bridgton, ME 04009. 207-647-3535. 8AM-4PM (EST). Access by: In person only.

Probate—Probate Court, 142 Federal St, Portland, ME 04101-4196. 207-871-8382. 8:30AM-4:30PM (EST). Access by: Mail, in person.

Franklin County

Real Estate Recording—Franklin County Register of Deeds, 38 Main Street, Courthouse, Farmington, ME 04938. 207-778-5889. Fax: 207-778-5899. 8:30AM-4PM (EST).

Felony, Misdemeanor, Civil Actions Over $30,000—Superior Court, 38 Main St, Farmington, ME 04938. 207-778-3346. 8AM-4PM (EST). Access by: In person only.

Misdemeanor, Civil Actions Under $30,000, Eviction, Small Claims—District Court #12, 25 Main St, Farmington, ME 04938. 207-778-5177. 8AM-4PM (EST). Access by: Mail, in person.

Probate—Probate Court, County Courthouse, 38 Main St, Farmington, ME 04938. 207-778-5888. Fax: 207-778-5899. 8:30AM-4PM (EST).

Hancock County

Real Estate Recording—Hancock County Register of Deeds, 60 State Street, Ellsworth, ME 04605. 207-667-8353. Fax: 207-667-1410. 8:30AM-4PM (EST).

Felony, Misdemeanor, Civil Actions Over $30,000—Superior Court, 60 State St, Ellsworth, ME 04605-1926. 207-667-7176. 8AM-4PM (EST). Access by: In person only.

Misdemeanor, Civil Actions Under $30,000, Eviction, Small Claims—Bar Harbor District Court-South #5, 93 Cottage St, Bar Harbor, ME 04609. 207-288-3082. 8AM-4PM (EST). Access by: Mail, in person.

Ellsworth District Court-Central #5, 60 State St, Ellsworth, ME 04605. 207-667-7141. 8AM-4PM (EST). Access by: Mail, in person.

Probate—Probate Court, 60 State St, Ellsworth, ME 04605. 207-667-8434. 8:30AM-4PM (EST). Access by: Mail, in person.

Kennebec County

Real Estate Recording—Kennebec County Register of Deeds, 1 Weston Court, Augusta, ME 04330. 207-622-0431. Fax: 207-622-1598. 8:30AM-4PM (EST).

Felony, Misdemeanor, Civil Actions Over $30,000—Superior Court, 95 State St, Clerk of Court, Augusta, ME 04330. 207-622-9357. 8AM-4PM (EST). Access by: In person only.

Misdemeanor, Civil Actions Under $30,000, Eviction, Small Claims—Maine District Court District 7, Division of Southern Kennebec, 145 State St, Augusta, ME 04330-7495. 207-287-8075. 8AM-4PM (EST). Access by: Phone, mail, in person.

Probate—Probate Court, 95 State St, Augusta, ME 04330. 207-622-7558. Fax: 207-621-1639. 8:30AM-4PM (EST). Access by: Mail, in person.

Knox County

Real Estate Recording—Knox County Register of Deeds, 62 Union Street, Rockland, ME 04841. 207-594-0422. Fax: 207-594-0446. 8AM-4PM (EST).

Felony, Misdemeanor, Civil Actions Over $30,000—Superior Court, PO Box 1024, Rockland, ME 04841. 207-594-2576. 8AM-4PM (EST). Access by: In person only.

Misdemeanor, Civil Actions Under $30,000, Eviction, Small Claims—District Court #6, PO Box 544, 62 Union St, Rockland, ME 04841. 207-596-2240. 8AM-4PM (EST). Access by: Phone, mail, in person.

Probate—Probate Court, 62 Union St, Rockland, ME 04841. 207-594-0427. Fax: 207-594-0443. 9AM-4PM (EST). Access by: Mail, in person.

Lincoln County

Real Estate Recording—Lincoln County Register of Deeds, High Street, Courthouse, Wiscasset, ME 04578. 207-882-7515. Fax: 207-882-4061. 8AM-4PM (EST).

Felony, Misdemeanor, Civil Actions Over $30,000—Superior Court, High St, Wiscasset, ME 04578. 207-882-7517. 8AM-4PM (EST). Access by: In person only.

Misdemeanor, Civil Actions Under $30,000, Eviction, Small Claims—District Court #6, High St, PO Box 249, Wiscasset, ME 04578. 207-882-6363. 8AM-4PM (EST). Access by: Mail, in person.

Probate—Probate Court, High St, PO Box 249, Wiscasset, ME 04578. 207-882-7392. Fax: 207-882-4061. 8AM-4PM (EST). Access by: Mail, in person.

Oxford County

Real Estate Recording—Oxford County Register of Deeds, West, 12 Portland St., Fryeburg, ME 04037. 207-935-2565. Fax: 207-935-4183.

Oxford County Register of Deeds, 126 Western Avenue, South Paris, ME 04281. 207-743-6211. Fax: 207-743-2656. 8AM-4PM (EST).

Felony, Misdemeanor, Civil Actions Over $30,000—Superior Court, Courthouse, 26 Western Ave, PO Box 179, South Paris, ME 04281-0179. 207-743-8936. Fax: 207-743-7346. 8AM-4PM (EST). Access by: Mail, in person.

Misdemeanor, Civil Actions Under $30,000, Eviction, Small Claims—Rumford District Court-North #11, Municipal Bldg, Congress St, Rumford, ME 04276. 207-364-7171. 8AM-4PM (EST). Access by: Mail, in person.

South Paris District Court-South #11, 26 Western Ave, South Paris, ME 04281. 207-743-8942. 8AM-4PM (EST). Access by: Mail, in person.

Probate—Probate Court, 26 Western Ave, PO Box 179, South Paris, ME 04281. 207-743-6671. Fax: 207-743-7346. 8AM-4PM (EST). Access by: Mail, in person.

Penobscot County

Real Estate Recording—Penobscot County Register of Deeds, 97 Hammond Street, Bangor, ME 04401. 207-942-8797. Fax: 207-945-4920. 8AM-4:30PM (EST).

Felony, Misdemeanor, Civil Actions Over $30,000—Superior Court, 97 Hammond St, Bangor, ME 04401. 207-947-0751. 8AM-4:30PM (EST). Access by: In person only.

Misdemeanor, Civil Actions Under $30,000, Eviction, Small Claims—Bangor District Court, 73 Hammond St, Bangor, ME 04401. 207-941-3040. 8AM-4PM (EST). Access by: Mail, in person.

Central District Court-Central #13, 66 Maine St, Lincoln, ME 04457. 207-794-8512. 8AM-4PM (EST). Access by: In person only.

Millinocket District Court-North #13, 207 Penobscot Ave, Millinocket, ME 04462. 207-723-4786. 8AM-4PM (EST). Access by: In person only.

Newport District Court-West #3, 16 Water St, Newport, ME 04953. 207-368-5778. 8AM-4PM (EST). Access by: Mail, in person.

Probate—Probate Court, 97 Hammond St, Bangor, ME 04401-4996. 207-942-8769. Fax: 207-941-8499. 8AM-4:30PM (EST). Access by: Mail, in person.

Piscataquis County

Real Estate Recording—Piscataquis County Register of Deeds, 51 East Main Street, Dover-Foxcroft, ME 04426. 207-564-2411. Fax: 207-564-7708. 8:30AM-4PM (EST).

Felony, Misdemeanor, Civil Actions Over $30,000—Superior Court, 51 E Main St, Dover-Foxcroft, ME 04426. 207-564-8419. 8AM-4PM (EST). Access by: Mail, in person.

Misdemeanor, Civil Actions Under $30,000, Eviction, Small Claims—District Court #13, 59 E Main St, Dover-Foxcroft, ME 04426. 207-564-2240. 8AM-4PM (EST). Access by: Mail, in person.

Probate—Probate Court, 51 E Main St, Dover-Foxcroft, ME 04426. 207-564-2431. Fax: 207-564-7708. 8:30AM-4PM (EST). Access by: Mail, in person.

Sagadahoc County

Real Estate Recording—Sagadahoc County Register of Deeds, 752 High Street, Bath, ME 04530. 207-443-8214. 9AM-4:30PM (EST).

Felony, Misdemeanor, Civil Actions Over $30,000—Superior Court, 752 High St, PO Box 246, Bath, ME 04530. 207-443-9733. 8AM-4:30PM (EST). Access by: In person only.

Misdemeanor, Civil Actions Under $30,000, Eviction, Small Claims—District Court #6, RR 1, Box 310, New Meadows Rd, Bath, ME 04530. 207-442-0200. 8AM-4PM (EST). Access by: In person only. Search requests are referred to central state repository.

Probate—Probate Court, 752 High St, PO Box 246, Bath, ME 04530. 207-443-8218. 9AM-Noon, 1-4:30PM (EST). Access by: In person only.

Somerset County

Real Estate Recording—Somerset County Register of Deeds, Corner of Court & High Street, Skowhegan, ME 04976. 207-474-3421. Fax: 207-474-3421. 8:30AM-4:30PM (EST).

Felony, Misdemeanor, Civil Actions Over $30,000—Superior Court, PO Box 725, Skowhegan, ME 04976. 207-474-5161. 8AM-4PM (EST). Access by: Mail, in person.

Misdemeanor, Civil Actions Under $30,000, Eviction, Small Claims—District Court #12, PO Box 525, 88 Water St, Skowhegan, ME 04976. 207-474-9518. 8AM-4PM (EST). Access by: Mail, in person.

Probate—Probate Court, Court St, Skowhegan, ME 04976. 207-474-3322. 8:30AM-4:30PM (EST). Access by: Mail, in person.

Waldo County

Real Estate Recording—Waldo County Register of Deeds, 137 Church Street, Belfast, ME 04915. 207-338-1710. Fax: 207-338-6360. 8AM-4PM (EST).

Felony, Misdemeanor, Civil Actions Over $30,000—Superior Court, 137 Church St, PO Box 188, Belfast, ME 04915. 207-338-1940. Fax: 207-338-1086. 8AM-4PM (EST). Access by: Mail, in person.

Misdemeanor, Civil Actions Under $30,000, Eviction, Small Claims—District Court #5, PO Box 382, 103 Church St, Belfast, ME 04915. 207-338-3107. 8AM-4PM (EST). Access by: Mail, in person.

Probate—Probate Court, 172 High St, PO Box 323, Belfast, ME 04915. 207-338-2780. Fax: 207-338-6360. 9AM-4PM (EST). Access by: Mail, in person.

Washington County

Real Estate Recording—Washington County Register of Deeds, 47 Court Street, Machias, ME 04654. 207-255-6512. 8AM-5PM (EST).

Felony, Misdemeanor, Civil Actions Over $30,000—Superior Court, Clerk of Court, PO Box 526, Machias, ME 04654. 207-255-3326. 8AM-4PM (EST). Access by: Mail, in person.

Misdemeanor, Civil Actions Under $30,000, Eviction, Small Claims—Calais District Court-North #4, 88 South St,

Calais, ME 04619. 207-454-2055. 8AM-4PM (EST). Access by: In person only.

Maine District Court-Division 4-Southern Washington, 47 Court St, PO Box 297, Machias, ME 04654. 207-255-3044. 8AM-4PM (EST). Access by: Mail, in person.

Probate—Probate Court, PO Box 297, Machias, ME 04654. 207-255-6591. 8AM-4PM (EST).

York County

Real Estate Recording—York County Register of Deeds, Court Street, Courthouse, Alfred, ME 04002. 207-324-1576. Fax: 207-324-2886. 8:30AM-4:30PM (EST).

Felony, Misdemeanor, Civil Actions Over $30,000—Superior Court, Clerk of Court, PO Box 160, Alfred, ME 04002. 207-324-5122. 8AM-4:30PM (EST). Access by: In person only.

Misdemeanor, Civil Actions Under $30,000, Eviction, Small Claims—Biddeford District Court-East #10, 35 Washington St, Biddeford, ME 04005. 207-283-1147. 8AM-4PM (EST). Access by: Mail, in person.

Springvale District Court-West #10, PO Box 95, Butler St, Springvale, ME 04083. 207-324-6737. 7:30AM-4PM (EST). Access by: In person only.

York District Court-South #10, PO Box 776, Chase's Pond Rd, York, ME 03909. 207-363-1230. 8AM-4PM (EST). Access by: In person only.

Probate—Probate Court, PO Box 399, Alfred, ME 04002. 207-324-1577. Fax: 207-324-0163. 8:30AM-4:30PM (EST). Access by: Mail, in person.

Federal Courts

US District Court
District of Maine

Bangor Division, US District Court Clerk, PO Box 1007, Bangor, ME 04402-1007. 207-945-0575. Counties: Aroostook, Franklin, Hancock, Kennebec, Penobscot, Piscataquis, Somerset, Waldo, Washington

Portland Division, US District Court Clerk, 156 Federal St, Portland, ME 04101. 207-780-3356. Counties: Androscoggin, Cumberland, Knox, Lincoln, Oxford, Sagadahoc, York

US Bankruptcy Court
District of Maine

Bangor Division, US Bankruptcy Court, PO Box 1109, Bangor, ME 04402-1109. 207-945-0348. Voice Case Information System: 207-780-3755. Counties: Aroostook, Franklin, Hancock, Kennebec, Knox, Lincoln, Penobscot, Piscataquis, Somerset, Waldo, Washington

Portland Division, US Bankruptcy Court, 537 Congress St, Portland, ME 04101. 207-780-3482. Voice Case Information System: 207-780-3755. Counties: Androscoggin, Cumberland, Oxford, Sagadahoc, York

Maryland

Capitol: Annapolis (Anne Arundel County)	
Number of Counties: 23	**Population:** 5,042,438
County Court Locations:	**Federal Court Locations:**
•Circuit Courts: 25/8 Circuits	•District Courts: 2
•District Courts: 26/12 Districts	•Bankruptcy Courts: 2
•Orphan's Courts: 24	**State Agencies:** 20

State Agencies—Summary

General Help Numbers:

State Archives

State Archives	410-974-3914
Hall of Records	Fax: 410-974-3895
350 Rowe Blvd	8AM-4:30PM TU-FR; 8:30-4:30 SA
Annapolis, MD 21401	
Reference Librarian:	410-974-3915
Historical Society:	410-685-3750

Governor's Office

Office of the Governor	410-974-3901
State House	Fax: 410-974-3275
Annapolis, MD 21401	7AM-5PM

Attorney General's Office

Attorney General's Office	410-576-6300
200 St Paul Place, 16th Floor	Fax: 410-576-7003
Baltimore, MD 21202	9AM-5PM

State Legislation

Maryland General Assembly	410-841-3810
Dept of Legislative Reference-Lib Div	Fax: 410-841-3850
90 State Circle	8AM-5PM
Annapolis, MD 21401	
Alternate Telephone:	410-841-3000

Important State Internet Sites:

Webscape
File   Edit   View   **Help**

State of Maryland World Wide Web
www.mec.state.md.us/

Links to major locations in the Maryland State Government, state libraries, government & law and many other interesting links.

Uniform Commercial Code
www.sos.state.md.us/sos/other/html/ucc.html

This page provides the contact for UCC searching and links to the Department of Assessment and Taxation.

Maryland General Assembly
mlis.state.md.us/

This site provides links to bill information and status, bill indexes and profiles and helps you locate and contact the elected officials. Bills can be searched by their number.

Archive Reference Service
www.mdarchives.state.md.us/

Home page for the state archives. Located in the archives are such records as county probate, land & court, colonial, state, county and municipal records. There are also maps, photographs and newspapers.

Unclaimed Property
www.comp.state.md.us/unclaim.htm

This page provides you with all the information necessary to search for unclaimed property, such as checking and savings accounts, payroll, wages, insurance, refunds and much more.

State Agencies—Public Records

Criminal Records

Criminal Justice Information System, Public Safety & Correctional Records, 6776 Reisterstown Rd, Rm 200, Pikeville, MD 21208-3899, Main Telephone: 410-764-4501, Fax: 410-974-2169, Hours: 8AM-5PM. Access by: mail, PC. All requesters must first write to this office and receive a "petition number." Employers and investigative firms are eligible to apply for this "petition number."

Corporation Records
Limited Partnerships
Trade Names
Limited Liability Company Records
Fictitious Name

Department of Assessments and Taxation, Corporations Division, 301 W Preston St, Room 809, Baltimore, MD 21201, Main Telephone: 410-767-1340, Charter Information: 410-767-1330, Fax: 410-767-7097, Hours: 8AM-4:30PM. Access by: mail, phone, fax, visit, PC.

Trademarks/Servicemarks

Secretary of State, Trademarks Division, 16 Francis Street, Annapolis, MD 21401, Main Telephone: 410-974-5531, Fax: 410-974-5527, Hours: 9AM-5PM. Access by: mail, phone, visit.

Uniform Commercial Code
Federal Tax Liens
State Tax Liens

UCC Division, Department of Assessments & Taxation, 301 West Preston St, Baltimore, MD 21201, Main Telephone: 410-767-1340, Fax: 410-333-7097, Hours: 8AM-4:30PM. Access by: PC only.

Sales Tax Registrations

Taxpayer Services, Revenue Administration Division, 301 W Preston St, Baltimore, MD 21201, Main Telephone: 410-767-1313, Fax: 410-767-1571, Hours: 8AM-5PM. Access by: mail, phone.

Birth Certificates

Department of Health, Division of Vital Records, 4201 Patterson Ave, 1st Floor, Baltimore, MD 21215, Main Telephone: 410-764-3038, Message Phone: 410-767-5988, General Info: 410-764-2452, Fax: 410-358-7381, Hours: 8AM-4:30PM M-F; 3rd Saturday of each month. Access by: mail, phone, visit.

Death Records

Department of Health, Division of Vital Records, 4201 Patterson Ave, 1st Floor, Baltimore, MD 21215, Main Telephone: 410-764-3038, Message Phone: 410-767-5988, Fax: 410-358-7381, Hours: 8AM-4:30PM M-F; 3rd Saturday of each month. Access by: mail, phone, visit.

Marriage Certificates

Department of Health, Division of Vital Records, 4201 Patterson Ave, 1st Floor, Baltimore, MD 21215, Main Telephone: 410-764-3038, Message Phone: 410-225-5988, Fax: 410-358-7381, Hours: 8AM-4:45PM M-F; 3rd Saturday of each month. Access by: mail, phone, visit.

Divorce Records

Department of Health, Division of Vital Records, 4201 Patterson Ave, 1st Floor, Baltimore, MD 21215, Main Telephone: 410-764-3038, Message Phone: 410-225-5988, Fax: 410-358-7381, Hours: 8AM-4:45PM M-F; 3rd Saturday of each month. Access by: mail, phone, visit.

Workers' Compensation Records

Workers Compensation Commission, Six N Liberty St, Baltimore, MD 21201, Main Telephone: 410-767-0900, Fax: 410-333-8122, Hours: 8AM-4:30PM. Access by: mail, phone, visit, PC.

Driver Records

Department of Motor Vehicles, Motor Vehicle Administration, 6601 Ritchie Hwy, NE, Counter 212, Glen Burnie, MD 21062, Main Telephone: 410-787-7758, Hours: 8:15AM-4:30PM. Access by: mail, visit, PC. Copies of tickets can be obtained from the MD District Court/MATS, 1750 Forest Dr, Annapolis, 21401. There is no charge for ticket copies, but a self addressed stamped envelope is advised.

Vehicle Ownership
Vehicle Identification

Department of Motor Vehicles, Vehicle Registration Division, Room 206, 6601 Ritchie Hwy, NE, Glen Burnie, MD 21062, Main Telephone: 410-768-7250, Fax: 410-768-7163, Hours: 8:15AM-4:30PM. Access by: mail, visit, PC.

Accident Reports

Maryland State Police, Central Records Division, 1711 Belmont Ave, Baltimore, MD 21244, Main Telephone: 410-298-3390, Fax: 410-298-3198, Hours: 8:15AM-4:30PM. Access by: mail, visit. This agency does not have reports for the City of Baltimore. Call 410-396-2359 for those reports.

Hunting License Information
Fishing License Information

Department of Natural Resources, Licensing & Registration Service, 580 Taylor Ave, Annapolis, MD 21401, Main Telephone: 410-260-8200, Fax: 410-260-8217, Hours: 8AM-4:30PM.

They have a central database on paper, organized by vendor who sold the general license. However, the state makes available a list or tape of their commercial fishing licenses.

County Courts and Recording Offices

What You Need to Know...

About the Courts

Administration

Administrative Office of the Courts	410-974-2141
Court of Appeals Bldg	Fax: 410-974-2169
361 Rowe Blvd	
Annapolis, MD 21401	

Court Structure

Certain categories of minor felonies are handled by the District Court.

The Circuit Court handles probate in Montgomery and Harford counties. In other counties, probate is handled by the Register of Wills and is a county, **not** a court, function.

Online Access

There is an online computer system called the Judicial Information System (**JIS**). JIS provides access to civil and criminal case information from: All District Courts; Anne Arundel and Carroll County Circuit Courts; and Baltimore City Court.

Inquiry may be made to: the District Court traffic system for case information data, calendar information data, court schedule data, or officer schedule data; the District Court criminal system for case information data or calendar caseload data; the District Court civil system for case information data, attorney name and address data; the land records system for land and plat records. The one-time fee for JIS access is $50.00, which must be included with the application and there is a charge of $.50 per minute for access time. For additional information or to receive a registration packet, write or call Judicial Information Systems, Security Administrator, 2661 Riva Rd., Suite 900, Annapolis, MD 21401, 410-841-1031.

About the Recorder's Office

Organization

23 counties and **one independent city**, 24 filing offices. The recording officer is Clerk of the Circuit Court. **Baltimore City has a recording office separate from the county of Baltimore.** See the City/County Locator section at the end of this chapter for ZIP Codes that include both the city and the county. The entire state is in the Eastern Time Zone (EST).

UCC Records

This is a **dual filing state** until July 1995. As of July 1995, **all new** UCC filings are submitted only to the central filing office. Financing statements are usually filed both at the state level and with the Clerk of Circuit Court, except for consumer goods, farm related and real estate related filings, which will still be filed with the Clerk after June 1995. Only one county performs UCC searches. Copy fees vary.

Lien Records

All tax liens are filed with the county Clerk of Circuit Court. Counties will **not** perform searches. Other liens include judgments, mechanics, county, hospital, and condominium.

Real Estate Records

Counties will **not** perform real estate searches. Copies usually cost $.50 per page, and certification fees $5.00 per document.

County Courts and Recording Offices

Allegany County

Real Estate Recording—Allegany County Clerk of the Circuit Court, 30 Washington Street, Cumberland, MD 21502. 301-777-5922. Fax: 301-777-2100. 8AM-4:30PM (EST).

Felony, Misdemeanor, Civil Actions Over $20,000—4th Judicial Circuit Court, 30 Washington St, PO Box 359, Cumberland, MD 21502. 301-777-5922. Fax: 301-777-2100. 8:30AM-4:30PM (EST). Access by: In person only.

Misdemeanor, Civil Actions Under $20,000, Eviction, Small Claims—District Court, 3 Pershing St, 2nd Floor, Cumberland, MD 21502. 301-777-2105. 8:30AM-4:30PM (EST). Access by: Mail, remote online, in person.

Probate—Register of Wills, Courthouse Washington St, Cumberland, MD 21502. 301-724-3760. 8AM-4:30PM (EST). Access by: Mail, in person.

Anne Arundel County

Real Estate Recording—Anne Arundel County Clerk of the Circuit Court, 7 Church Circle Street, Room 101, Annapolis, MD 21401. 410-222-1425. 8:30AM-4:30PM (EST).

Felony, Misdemeanor, Civil Actions Over $20,000—5th Judicial Circuit Court, Box 71, Annapolis, MD 21404. 410-222-1397. 8:30AM-4:30PM (EST). Access by: Phone, mail, remote online, in person.

Misdemeanor, Civil Actions Under $20,000, Eviction, Small Claims—District Court, 580 Taylor Ave, Annapolis, MD 21401. 410-974-2678. 8:30AM-4:30PM (EST). Access by: Mail, remote online, in person.

Probate—Register of Wills, 44 Calvert St (PO Box 2368), Annapolis, MD 21404-2368. 410-222-1430. Fax: 410-222-1467. 8:30AM-4PM (EST). Access by: In person only.

Baltimore City

Real Estate Recording—Circuit Court for Baltimore City, 100 North Calvert Street, Room 610, Baltimore, MD 21202. 410-333-3760. 8AM-4:30PM (EST).

Civil Actions Over $20,000—8th Judicial Circuit Court-Civil Division, 111 N Calvert, Rm 462, Baltimore, MD 21202. 410-333-3722. 8:30AM-4:30PM. Access by: Phone, mail, in person.

Felony, Misdemeanor—8th Judicial Circuit Court-Criminal Division, 110 N Calvert Rm 200, Baltimore, MD 21202. 410-333-3750. 8:30AM-4:30PM. Access by: Remote online, in person. Case index available through JIS. See state introduction.

Civil Actions Under $20,000, Eviction, Small Claims—District Court-Civil Division, 501 E Fayette St, Baltimore, MD 21202. 410-333-4664. 8:30AM-4:30PM. Access by: Mail.

Misdemeanor—District Court-Criminal Division, 1400 E North Ave, Baltimore, MD 21213. 410-554-4227. 8AM-4:30PM. Access by: Mail, remote online, in person. Online access available through SJIS. See state introduction.

Probate—Register of Wills, Courthouse East, 111 N Calvert St, Rm 352, Baltimore, MD 21202. 410-752-5131. Fax: 410-752-3494. 8AM-4:30PM. Access by: Mail, in person.

Baltimore County

Real Estate Recording—Baltimore County Clerk of the Circuit Court, Land Records, County Courts Building, Baltimore, MD 21204. 410-887-2658. Fax: 410-887-3062. 8AM-4:30PM (EST).

Felony, Misdemeanor, Civil Actions Over $20,000—3rd Judicial Circuit Court, 401 Bosley Ave, 2nd Floor, Towson, MD 21204. 410-887-2601. 8:30AM-4:30PM (EST). Access by: In person only.

Misdemeanor, Civil Actions Under $20,000, Eviction, Small Claims—District Court, 120 E Chesapeake Ave, Towson, MD 21286-5307. 410-321-3300. Civil: 410-321-3332. Criminal: 410-321-3322. 8:30AM-4:30PM (EST). Access by: Mail, remote online, in person.

Probate

Probate—Register of Wills, 401 Bosley Ave, Towson, MD 21204. 410-887-6685. Fax: 410-583-2517. 8AM-4:30PM (EST). Access by: Mail, in person.

Calvert County

Real Estate Recording—Calvert County Clerk of the Circuit Court, 175 Main Street, Courthouse, Prince Frederick, MD 20678. 410-535-1660. 8:30AM-4:30PM (EST).

Felony, Misdemeanor, Civil Actions Over $20,000—7th Judicial Circuit Court, 175 Main St Courthouse, Prince Frederick, MD 20678. 410-535-1600. 8:30AM-4:30PM (EST). Access by: Phone, mail, in person.

Misdemeanor, Civil Actions Under $20,000, Eviction, Small Claims—District Court, 200 Duke St Rm 2200, Prince Frederick, MD 20678. 410-535-8801. 8:30AM-4:30PM (EST). Access by: Mail, remote online, in person.

Probate—Register of Wills, 175 Main St Courthouse, Prince Frederick, MD 20678. 410-535-1600. Fax: 410-535-1787. 8:30AM-4:30PM (EST). Access by: Phone, mail, in person.

Caroline County

Real Estate Recording—Caroline County Clerk of the Circuit Court, Market Street, Courthouse, Denton, MD 21629. 410-479-1811. Fax: 410-479-1142. 8:30AM-4:30PM (EST).

Felony, Misdemeanor, Civil Actions Over $20,000—2nd Judicial Circuit Court, Box 458, Denton, MD 21629. 410-479-1811. Fax: 410-479-1142. 8:30AM-4:30PM (EST). Access by: In person only.

Misdemeanor, Civil Actions Under $20,000, Eviction, Small Claims—District Court, 207 S 3rd St, Denton, MD 21629. 410-479-5800. Fax: 410-479-5808. 8AM-4:30PM (EST). Access by: Remote online, in person.

Probate—Register of Wills, Carolyne County Courthouse, 109 Market St, Rm 108, PO Box 416, Denton, MD 21629. 410-479-0717. Fax: 410-479-4983. 8AM-4:30PM (EST). Access by: Mail, in person.

Carroll County

Real Estate Recording—Carroll County Clerk of the Circuit Court, 55 North Court Street, Room G8, Westminster, MD 21157. 410-857-2023. Fax: 410-876-0822. 8:30AM-4:30PM (EST).

Felony, Misdemeanor, Civil Actions Over $20,000—5th Judicial Circuit Court, Box 190, Westminster, MD 21158-0190. 410-876-1213. Fax: 410-876-0822. 8:30AM-4:30PM (EST). Access by: Remote online, in person.

Misdemeanor, Civil Actions Under $20,000, Eviction, Small Claims—District Court, 55 N Court St, Westminster, MD 21157. 410-848-2146. 8:30AM-4:30PM (EST). Access by: Remote online, in person.

Probate—Register of Wills, 55 N Court St, Rm 104, Westminster, MD 21157. 410-848-2586. 8:30AM-4:30PM (EST).

Cecil County

Real Estate Recording—Cecil County Clerk of the Circuit Court, 129 East Main St., Room 108, Elkton, MD 21921. 410-996-5375. 8:30AM-4:30PM (EST).

Felony, Misdemeanor, Civil Actions Over $20,000—2nd Judicial Circuit Court, 129 E Main St, Rm 108, Elkton, MD 21921. 410-996-5373. Fax: 410-392-6032. 8:30AM-4:30PM (EST). Access by: In person only.

Misdemeanor, Civil Actions Under $20,000, Eviction, Small Claims—District Court, 170 E Main St, Elkton, MD 21921. 410-996-0700. (EST). Access by: Remote online, in person.

Probate—Register of Wills, County Courthouse, Rm 307, Elkton, MD 21921. 410-996-5330. 8:30AM-4:30PM (EST). Access by: Phone, mail, in person.

Charles County

Real Estate Recording—Charles County Clerk of the Circuit Court, 200 Charles Street, Courthouse, La Plata, MD 20646. 301-932-3235. 8:30AM-4:30PM (EST).

Felony, Misdemeanor, Civil Actions Over $20,000—Circuit Court for Charles County, Box 970, La Plata, MD 20646. 301-932-3201. 8:30AM-4:30PM (EST). Access by: In person only.

Misdemeanor, Civil Actions Under $20,000, Eviction, Small Claims—District Court, PO Box 3070, La Plata, MD 20646. Civil: 301-932-3290. Criminal: 301-932-3295. 8:30AM-4:30PM (EST). Access by: Remote online, in person.

Probate—Register of Wills, Courthouse, Box 3080, La Plata, MD 20646. 301-932-3345. Fax: 301-932-3349. 8:30AM-4:30PM (EST). Access by: Phone, mail, in person.

Dorchester County

Real Estate Recording—Dorchester County Clerk of the Circuit Court, 206 High Street, Cambridge, MD 21613. 410-228-0481. 8:30AM-4:30PM (EST).

Felony, Misdemeanor, Civil Actions Over $20,000—1st Judicial Circuit Court, Box 150, Cambridge, MD 21613. 410-228-0481. 8:30AM-4:30PM (EST). Access by: In person only.

Misdemeanor, Civil Actions Under $20,000, Eviction, Small Claims—District Court, Box 547, Cambridge, MD 21613. 410-221-2580. 8:30AM-4:30PM (EST). Access by: Remote online, in person.

Probate—Register of Wills, Box 263, Cambridge, MD 21613. 410-228-4181. 8AM-4:30PM; Public hours 8:30AM-4:30PM (EST). Access by: Phone, mail, in person.

Frederick County

Real Estate Recording—Frederick County Clerk of the Circuit Court, 100 West Patrick Street, Frederick, MD 21701. 301-694-1964. Fax: 301-846-2245. 8:30AM-4:30PM (EST).

Felony, Misdemeanor, Civil Actions Over $20,000—6th Judicial Circuit Court, 100 W Patrick St, Frederick, MD 21701. 301-694-1972. 8AM-4:30PM (EST). Access by: In person only.

Misdemeanor, Civil Actions Under $20,000, Eviction, Small Claims—District Court, 100 W Patrick St, Frederick, MD 21701. 301-694-2000. 8:30AM-4:30PM (EST). Access by: Phone, mail, remote online, in person.

Probate—Register of Wills, 100 W Patrick St, Frederick, MD 21701. 301-663-3722. Fax: 301-846-0744. 8AM-4:30PM (EST). Access by: Phone, mail, in person.

Garrett County

Real Estate Recording—Garrett County Clerk of the Circuit Court, 203 South Fourth St., Room 109, Oakland, MD 21550. 301-334-1937. Fax: 301-334-5017. 8:30AM-4:30PM (EST).

Felony, Misdemeanor, Civil Actions Over $20,000—4th Judicial Circuit Court, PO Box 447, Oakland, MD 21550. 301-334-1937. Fax: 301-334-5017. 8:30AM-4:30PM (EST). Access by: Mail, in person.

Misdemeanor, Civil Actions Under $20,000, Eviction, Small Claims—District Court, 205 S 3rd St, Oakland, MD 21550. 301-334-8164. 8:30AM-4:30PM (EST). Access by: Mail, remote online, in person.

Probate—Register of Wills, 313 E Alder St, Room 103, Oakland, MD 21550. 301-334-1999. 8AM-4:30PM (EST). Access by: Mail, in person.

Harford County

Real Estate Recording—Harford County Clerk of the Circuit Court, 20 West Courtland Street, Bel Air, MD 21014. 410-638-3244. 8:30AM-4PM (EST).

Felony, Misdemeanor, Civil Actions Over $20,000—3rd Judicial Circuit, 20 W Courtland St, Bel Air, MD 21014. 410-638-3426. 8:30AM-4:30PM (EST). Access by: Phone, mail, in person.

Misdemeanor, Civil Actions Under $20,000, Eviction, Small Claims—District Court, 2 S Bond St, Bel Air, MD 21014. 410-838-2300. 8:30AM-4:30PM (EST). Access by: Phone, mail, remote online, in person.

Probate—Register of Wills, 20 W Courtland St, Room 304, Bel Air, MD 21014. 410-638-3275. Fax: 410-893-3177. 8:30AM-4:30PM (EST). Access by: In person only.

Howard County

Real Estate Recording—Howard County Clerk of the Circuit Court, 8360 Court Avenue, Ellicott City, MD 21043. 410-313-2111. 8:30AM-4:30PM (EST).

Felony, Misdemeanor, Civil Actions Over $20,000—5th Judicial Circuit Court, 8360 Court Ave, Ellicott City, MD 21043. 410-313-2111. 8:30AM-4:30PM (EST). Access by: In person only.

Misdemeanor, Civil Actions Under $20,000, Eviction, Small Claims—District Court, 3451 Courthouse Dr, Ellicott City, MD 21043. Civil: 410-461-0213. Criminal: 410-461-0208. 8:30AM-4:30PM (EST). Access by: Mail, remote online, in person.

Probate—Register of Wills, 8360 Court Ave, Ellicott City, MD 21043. 410-313-2133. Fax: 410-313-3409. 8:30AM-4:30PM (EST). Access by: In person only.

Kent County

Real Estate Recording—Kent County Clerk of the Circuit Court, Courthouse, 103 N. Cross St., Chestertown, MD 21620. 410-778-7460. 8:30AM-4:30PM (EST).

Felony, Misdemeanor, Civil Actions Over $20,000—2nd Judicial Circuit Court, 103 N Cross St Courthouse, Chestertown, MD 21620. 410-778-7460. 8:30AM-4:30PM (EST). Access by: In person only.

Misdemeanor, Civil Actions Under $20,000, Eviction, Small Claims—District Court, 103 N Cross St, Chestertown, MD 21620. 410-778-1830. Fax: 410-778-3474. 8:30AM-4:30PM (EST). Access by: Remote online, in person.

Probate—Register of Wills, 103 N Cross St, Chestertown, MD 21620. 410-778-7466. Fax: 410-778-7482. 8AM-4:30PM (EST). Access by: Mail, in person.

Montgomery County

Real Estate Recording—Montgomery County Clerk of the Circuit Court, 50 Maryland Ave., County Courthouse, Rockville, MD 20850. 301-217-7116. 8:30AM-4:30PM (EST).

Felony, Misdemeanor, Civil Actions Over $20,000—6th Judicial Circuit Court, 50 Maryland Ave, Rockville, MD 20850. 301-217-7202. 8:30AM-4:30PM (EST). Access by: In person only.

Misdemeanor, Civil Actions Under $20,000, Eviction, Small Claims—Rockville District Court, 27 Courthouse Square, Rockville, MD 20850. Civil: 301-279-1500. Criminal: 301-279-1565. 8:30AM-4:30PM (EST). Access by: Mail, remote online, in person.

District Court, 8665 Georgia Ave, Silver Spring, MD 20910. 301-608-0660. 8:30AM-4:30PM (EST). Access by: Mail, remote online, in person.

Probate—Register of Wills, 50 Courthouse, Rockville, MD 20850. 301-217-7150. Fax: 301-217-7306. 8:30AM-4:30PM (EST). Access by: Mail, in person.

Prince George's County

Real Estate Recording—Prince George's County Clerk of the Circuit Court, 14735 Main Street, Upper Marlboro, MD 20772. 301-952-3352. (EST).

Felony, Misdemeanor, Civil Actions Over $20,000—7th Judicial Circuit Court, 14735 Main St, Upper Marlboro, MD 20772. Civil: 301-952-3318. Criminal: 301-952-3344. 8:30AM-4:30PM (EST). Access by: Mail, remote online, in person. Remote access to be available through Civic Link. Call 1-800-307-1100 for information.

Misdemeanor, Civil Actions Under $20,000, Eviction, Small Claims—District Court, 14735 Main St, Rm 173B, Upper Marlboro, MD 20772. 301-952-4080. 8:30AM-4:30PM (EST). Access by: Mail, remote online, in person.

Probate—Register of Wills, 14735 Main St #306D, Upper Marlboro, MD 20772. 301-952-3250. Fax: 301-952-4489. 8:30AM-4:30PM (EST). Access by: Mail, in person.

Queen Anne's County

Real Estate Recording—Queen Anne's County Clerk of the Circuit Court, 100 Courthouse Square, Centreville, MD 21617. 410-758-1773. 8:30AM-4:30PM (EST).

Felony, Misdemeanor, Civil Actions Over $20,000—2nd Judicial Circuit Court, Courthouse, Centreville, MD 21617. 410-758-1773. 8:30AM-4:30PM (EST). Access by: In person only.

Misdemeanor, Civil Actions Under $20,000, Eviction, Small Claims—District Court, 120 Broadway, Centreville, MD 21617. 410-758-5200. 8:30AM-4:30PM (EST). Access by: Remote online, in person.

Probate—Register of Wills, Liberty Bldg, 107 N Liberty St #220, Centreville, MD 21617. 410-758-0585. Fax: 410-758-4408. 8AM-4:30PM (EST). Access by: Mail, in person.

Somerset County

Real Estate Recording—Somerset County Clerk of the Circuit Court, 30512 Prince William Street, Princess Anne, MD 21853. 410-651-1555. Fax: 410-651-1048. 8:30AM-4:30PM (EST).

Felony, Misdemeanor, Civil Actions Over $20,000—1st Judicial Circuit Court, Box 99, Princess Anne, MD 21853. 410-651-1555. Fax: 410-651-1048. 8AM-4:30PM (EST). Access by: In person only.

Misdemeanor, Civil Actions Under $20,000, Eviction, Small Claims—District Court, 11559 Somerset Ave, Princess Anne, MD 21853. 410-651-2713. 8:30AM-4:30PM (EST). Access by: Remote online, in person.

Probate—Register of Wills, 30512 Prince William St, Princess Anne, MD 21853. 410-651-1696. 8:30AM-4:30PM (EST). Access by: Mail, in person.

St. Mary's County

Real Estate Recording—St. Mary's County Clerk of the Circuit Court, 1 Courthouse Drive, Leonardtown, MD 20650. 301-475-4567. 8:30AM-4:30PM (EST).

Felony, Misdemeanor, Civil Actions Over $20,000—7th Judicial Circuit Court, Box 676, Leonardtown, MD 20650. 301-475-5621. 8:30AM-4:30PM (EST). Access by: In person only.

Misdemeanor, Civil Actions Under $20,000, Eviction, Small Claims—District Court, Carter State Office Bldg, 23110 Leonard Hall Dr, Leonardtown, MD 20650. 301-475-4530. Fax: 301-475-4535. 8:30AM-4:30PM (EST). Access by: Remote online, in person.

Probate—Register of Wills, PO Box 602, Leonardtown, MD 20650. 301-475-5566. Fax: 301-475-4968. 8:30AM-4:30PM (EST). Access by: Mail, in person.

Talbot County

Real Estate Recording—Talbot County Clerk of the Circuit Court, 11 N. Washington Street, Courthouse, Easton, MD 21601. 410-822-2611. Fax: 410-820-8168. 8:30AM-4:30PM (EST).

Felony, Misdemeanor, Civil Actions Over $20,000—2nd Judicial Circuit Court, Box 723, Easton, MD 21601. 410-822-2611. Fax: 410-820-8168. 8AM-4:30PM (EST). Access by: In person only.

Misdemeanor, Civil Actions Under $20,000, Eviction, Small Claims—District Court, South Wing, Easton, MD 21601. 410-822-2750. Fax: 410-822-1607. 8AM-4:30PM (EST). Access by: Remote online, in person.

Probate—Register of Wills, PO Box 816, Easton, MD 21601. 410-822-2470. Fax: 410-822-5452. 8AM-4:30PM (EST). Access by: Mail, in person.

Washington County

Real Estate Recording—Washington County Clerk of the Circuit Court, 95 West Washington Street, Suite 212, Hagerstown, MD 21740. 301-733-8660. Fax: 301-791-1151. 8:30AM-4:30PM (EST).

Felony, Misdemeanor, Civil Actions Over $20,000—Washington County Circuit Court, Box 229, Hagerstown, MD 21741. 301-733-8660. Fax: 301-791-1151. 8:30AM-4:30PM (EST). Access by: In person only.

Misdemeanor, Civil Actions Under $20,000, Eviction, Small Claims—District Court, 35 W Washington St, Hagerstown, MD 21740. 301-791-4740. 8:30AM-4:30PM (EST). Access by: Remote online, in person.

Probate—Register of Wills, 95 W Washington, Hagerstown, MD 21740. 301-739-3612. Fax: 301-733-8636. 8:30AM-4:30PM (EST). Access by: Mail, in person.

Wicomico County

Real Estate Recording—Wicomico County Clerk of the Circuit Court, 101 North Division St., Courthouse Room 105, Salisbury, MD 21801. 410-543-6551. 8:30AM-4:30PM (EST).

Felony, Misdemeanor, Civil Actions Over $20,000—1st Judicial Circuit Court, PO Box 198, Salisbury, MD 21803-0198. 410-543-6551. Fax: 410-548-5150. 8:30AM-4:30PM (EST). Access by: In person only.

Misdemeanor, Civil Actions Under $20,000, Eviction, Small Claims—District Court, 201 Baptist St, Salisbury, MD 21801. 410-543-6600. 8:30AM-4:30PM (EST). Access by: Remote online, in person.

Probate—Register of Wills, PO Box 787, Salisbury, MD 21803-0787. 410-543-6635. Fax: 410-334-3440. 8:30AM-4:30PM (EST). Access by: Mail, in person.

Worcester County

Real Estate Recording—Worcester County Clerk of the Circuit Court, 1 West Market St., Courthouse Room 104, Snow Hill, MD 21863. 410-632-1221. 8:30AM-4:30PM (EST).

Felony, Misdemeanor, Civil Actions Over $20,000—1st Judicial Circuit Court, Box 40, Snow Hill, MD 21863. Civil: 410-632-1222. Criminal: 410-632-1235. 8:30AM-4:30PM (EST). Access by: In person only.

Misdemeanor, Civil Actions Under $20,000, Eviction, Small Claims—District Court, 301 Commerce St, Snow Hill, MD 21863. 410-632-2525. 8:30AM-4:30PM (EST). Access by: Remote online, in person.

Probate—Register of Wills, Courthouse, Room 102, One W Market St, Snow Hill, MD 21863-1074. 410-632-1529. Fax: 410-632-5600. 8AM-4:30PM (EST). Access by: Mail, in person.

Federal Courts

US District Court
District of Maryland

Baltimore Division, US District Court Clerk, Room 404, 101 W Lombard, 4th Floor, Baltimore, MD 21201. 410-962-2600. Counties: Allegany, Anne Arundel, Baltimore, City of Baltimore, Caroline, Carroll, Cecil, Dorchester, Frederick, Garrett, Harford, Howard, Kent, Queen Anne's, Somerset, Talbot, Washington, Wicomico, Worcester

Greenbelt Division, US District Court Clerk, Room 240, 6500 Cherrywood Lane, Greenbelt, MD 20770. 301-344-0660. Counties: Calvert, Charles, Montgomery, Prince George's, St. Mary's

US Bankruptcy Court
District of Maryland

Baltimore Division, US Bankruptcy Court, 8515 US Courthouse, 101 W Lombard St, Baltimore, MD 21201. 410-

962-2688. Voice Case Information System: 410-962-0733. Counties: Anne Arundel, Baltimore, City of Baltimore, Caroline, Carroll, Cecil, Dorchester, Harford, Howard, Kent, Queen Anne's, Somerset, Talbot, Wicomico, Worcester

Rockville Division, US Bankruptcy Court, 6500 Cherrywood Ln, #300, Greenbelt, MD 20770. 301-344-8018. Voice Case Information System: 410-962-0733. Counties: Allegany, Calvert, Charles, Frederick, Garrett, Montgomery, Prince George's, St. Mary's, Washington

Massachusetts

Capitol: Boston (Suffolk County)	
Number of Counties: 14	**Population:** 6,073,550
County Court Locations:	**Federal Court Locations:**
• Superior Courts: 20 14 Counties	•District Courts: 3
•District Courts: 68/68 Geographic Divisions	•Bankruptcy Courts: 2
•Boston Municipal Court: 1	**State Agencies:** 20
Housing Courts: 7	
•Probate & Family Courts: 15/ 14 Counties	
Juvenile Courts: 7	
Land Courts: 1	

State Agencies—Summary

General Help Numbers:

State Archives

Massachusetts Archives at Columbia Point

	617-727-2816
Archives Division	Fax: 617-727-8429
220 Morrissey Blvd	9AM-5PM M-F; 9-3 SA
Boston, MA 02125	
Historical Society:	617-727-8470
Public Records Bureau:	617-727-2832
Public Records Bureau	FAX: 617-727-5914

Governor's Office

Governor's Office	617-727-3600
State House, Room 360	Fax: 617-727-9725
Boston, MA 02133	7:30AM-5:30PM

Attorney General's Office

Attorney General's Office	617-727-2200
One Ashburton Place, Room 2010	Fax: 617-727-5768
Boston, MA 02108	9AM-5PM

State Legislation

Massachusetts General Court	617-722-2860
State House	9AM-5PM
Beacon St, Room 428 (Document Room)	
Boston, MA 02133	

Important State Internet Sites:

Webscape
File   Edit   View   Help

State of Massachusetts World Wide Web

www.state.ma.us/

Links include: Massachusetts Government, reference shelf, forums, government on demand, and help.

Archive Reference Service

www.magnet.state.ma.us/sec/arc

Links to the Massachusetts Archives, where records of long term value are stored.

Direct Access

www.state.ma.us/sec/cor/coridirec/direcidx.htm

Explains how to obtain information on over four hundred thousand business and non-profit organizations as well as UCC filing information. There is an annual fee and a per minute charge to use this service.

UCC Information

www.state.ma.us/sec/cor/corucc/uccinf.htm

Includes information about UCC filing and searching.

Unclaimed Property

www.state.ma.us/cgi-bin/treasury/abp-mail.cgi

Online searching is available at this site.

State Agencies—Public Records

Criminal Records

Criminal History Systems Board, 200 Arlington Street, #2200, Chelsea, MA 02150, Main Telephone: 617-660-4600, Hours: 9AM-5PM. Access by: mail only. Records are only available for: conviction of crimes punishable by a sentence of 5 years or more; convicted of any crime and incarcerated; at the time of request is incarcerated, on parole or probation; released from incarceration within last 2 years.

Corporation Records
Trademarks/Servicemarks

Secretary of the Commonwealth, Corporation Division, One Ashburton Pl, 17th Floor, Boston, MA 02108, Main Telephone: 617-727-9640, Records: 617-727-2850, Trademarks: 617-727-8329, Forms request line: 617-727-9440, Fax: 617-742-4538, Hours: 8:45AM-5PM. Access by: mail, phone, visit, PC.

Uniform Commercial Code
Federal Tax Liens
State Tax Liens

UCC Division, Secretary of the Commonwealth, One Ashburton Pl, Room 1711, Boston, MA 02108, Main Telephone: 617-727-2860, Hours: 8:45AM-5PM. Access by: mail, phone, fax, visit, PC.

Sales Tax Registrations

Revenue Department, Taxpayer Assistance Office, 200 Arlington Street, 4th fl, Chelsea, MA 02150, Main Telephone: 617-887-6100, Access by: mail, phone. There are actually 6 offices in the state that will allow walk-in researchers. Be aware that the office in Chelsea will not let you in the building.

Birth Certificates

Registry of Vital Records and Statistics, 470 Atlantic Ave 2nd Floor, Boston, MA 02210-2224, Main Telephone: 617-753-8600, Fax: 617-753-8696, Hours: 8:45AM-4:45PM. Access by: mail, phone, fax, visit.

Death Records

Registry of Vital Records and Statistics, 470 Atlantic Ave 2nd Floor, Boston, MA 02210-2224, Main Telephone: 617-753-8600, Fax: 617-753-8696, Hours: 8:45AM-4:45PM. Access by: mail, phone, fax, visit.

Marriage Certificates

Registry of Vital Records and Statistics, 470 Atlantic Ave 2nd Floor, Boston, MA 02210-2224, Main Telephone: 617-753-8600, Fax: 617-753-8696, Hours: 8:45AM-4:45PM. Access by: mail, phone, fax, visit.

Divorce Records

Records not available from state agency.

Workers' Compensation Records

Keeper of Records, Department of Industrial Accidents, 600 Washington St, 7th Floor, Boston, MA 02111, Main Telephone: 617-727-4900, Hours: 8 AM - 4 PM. Access by: mail, visit.

Driver Records-Registry

Registry of Motor Vehicles, Box 199100, Boston, MA 02119-9100, Main Telephone: 617-351-4500, Hours: 8AM-4:30PM M-T-W-F; 8AM-7PM TH. Access by: mail, phone, visit. The driving records provided by the Registry are for employment or general business use. The same database of driver record histories is used by both the Registry and the Merit Rating Board.

Driver Records-Insurance

Merit Rating Board, Massachusetts Motor Vehicle Insurance, 1135 Tremont St, 6th Floor, Boston, MA 02120-2103, Main Telephone: 617-267-3636, Fax: 617-351-9660, Hours: 8:45AM-5:00PM. Access by: mail, visit. The Merit Rating Board processes driving records for the insurance industry in accordance with state statutes.

Vehicle Ownership
Vehicle Identification

Registry of Motor Vehicles, Customer Assistance-Mail List Dept., 1135 Tremont St, Boston, MA 02120, Main Telephone: 617-351-4500, Fax: 617-351-9524, Hours: 8AM-4:30PM M-T-W-F; 8AM-7PM TH. Access by: mail, visit, PC.

Accident Reports

Accident Records Section, Registry of Motor Vehicles, PO Box 199100, Roxbury, MA 02119-9100, Main Telephone: 617-351-9434, Fax: 617-351-9401, Hours: 8:45AM-5PM. Access by: mail, fax, visit. Accident reports may also be obtained from the local police department in the investigating jurisdiction. Normal fee is $1.00 per page.

Hunting License Information
Fishing License Information

Division of Fisheries & Wildlife, 100 Cambridge St, Room 1902, Boston, MA 02202, Main Telephone: 617-727-3151, Hours: 8:45AM-5PM. Access by: visit only.

County Courts and Recording Offices

What You Need to Know...

About the Courts

Administration

Chief Justice for Admin & Mgmt 617-742-8575.
2 Center Plaza, Room 540 Fax: 617-742-0968
Boston, MA 02108,

Court Structure

The various court sections are called "Departments." The small claims limit is $2,000.

While Superior and District courts have concurrent jurisdiction in civil cases, the practice is to assign cases **less than $25,000** to the District Court and those over $25,000 to Superior Court.

The District and Boston Municipal Courts have jurisdction over certain minor felonies in addition to misdemeanors.

There are more than 20 Probate and Family Court locations in MA, one per county plus 2 each in Plymouth and Bristol, a Middlesex satellite in Cambridge, and a satellite in Lawrence.

Online Access

There is no on-line access computer system, internal or external.

About the Recorder's Office

Organization

14 counties, 312 towns, and 39 cities; 365 filing offices. Each town/city profile indicates the county in which the town/city is located. Filing locations vary depending upon the type of document, as noted below. **Berkshire and Bristol Counties have three different filing offices; Essex, Middlesex and Worcester Counties each have two separate filing offices. Be careful to distinguish the following names that are identical for both a town/city and a county—** Barnstable, Essex, Franklin, Hampden, Nantucket, Norfolk, Plymouth and Worcester. Recording officers are Town/City Clerk (UCC), County Register of Deeds (real estate), and Clerk of US District Court (federal tax liens). The entire state is in the Eastern Time Zone (EST).

UCC Records

This is a **dual filing state**. Financing statements are usually filed both with the Town/City clerk and at the state level, except for real estate related collateral, which is recorded at the county Register of Deeds. All but twenty filing offices perform searches. Use search request form UCC-11. Search fees are usually $10.00 per debtor name. Copies fees vary widely.

Lien Records

Federal tax liens on personal property were filed with the Town/City Clerks **prior to 1970**. Since that time, **federal tax liens on personal property are filed with the US District Court in Boston as well as with the towns/cities**. Following is how to search the central index for federal tax liens—

> Address: US District Court (617-223-9152)
> Post Office & Courthouse Bldg.
> Boston, MA 02109

The federal tax liens are indexed here on a computer system. Searches are available by mail or in person. Do **not** use the telephone. The court suggests including the Social Security number and/or address of individual names in your search request in order to narrow the results. A mail search costs $15.00 and will take about two weeks. Copies are included. Make your check payable to Clerk, US District Court. You can do the search yourself at no charge on their public computer terminal. State tax liens on personal property are filed with the Town/City Clerk or Tax Collector. All tax liens against real estate are filed with the county Register of Deeds. Some towns file state tax liens on personal property with the UCC index and include tax liens on personal property automatically with a UCC search. Others will perform a separate state tax lien search, usually for a fee of $10.00 plus $1.00 per page of copies. Other liens include medical, town/city tax, and child support.

Real Estate Records

Real estate records are located at the county level. Each town/city profile indicates the county in which the town/city is located. Counties will **not** perform searches. Copy fee with certification is usually $.75 per page. Each town also has Assessor/Tax Collector/Treasurer offices from which real estate ownership and tax information is available.

County Courts and Recording Offices

Barnstable County

Real Estate Recording—Barnstable County Register of Deeds, 3195 Main Street, Route 6A, Barnstable, MA 02630. 508-362-2511. Fax: 508-362-5065. 8AM-4PM (EST).

Felony, Civil Actions Over $25,000—Superior Court, 3195 Main St, PO Box 425, Barnstable, MA 02630. 508-362-2511. 8AM-4:30PM (EST). Access by: Mail, in person.

Felony, Misdemeanor, Civil, Eviction, Small Claims—Barnstable Division District Court, Route 6A, PO Box 427, Barnstable, MA 02630. 508-362-2511. 8:30AM-4:30PM (EST). Access by: Phone, mail, in person.

Orleans Division District Court, 237 Rock Harbor Rd, Orleans, MA 02653. 508-255-4700. 8:30AM-4:30PM (EST). Access by: Phone, mail, in person.

Probate—Probate and Family Court, PO Box 346, Barnstable, MA 02630. 508-362-2511. Fax: 508-362-3662. 8:30AM-4:30PM (EST). Access by: Mail, in person.

Berkshire County

Real Estate Recording—Berkshire County Register of Deeds, Northern District, 65 Park Street, Adams, MA 01220. 413-743-0035. Fax: 413-743-1003. 8:30AM-4:30PM (EST).

Berkshire County Register of Deeds, Southern District, 334 Main Street, Great Barrington, MA 01230. 413-528-0146. Fax: 413-528-6878. 8:30AM-4:30PM; Recording hours 8:30AM-4PM (EST).

Berkshire County Register of Deeds (Middle District), Middle District, 44 Bank Row, Pittsfield, MA 01201. 413-443-7438. Fax: 413-448-6025. 8:30AM-4:30PM (No Recording after 3:59PM) (EST).

Felony, Civil Actions Over $25,000—Superior Court, 76 East St, Pittsfield, MA 01201. 413-499-7487. Fax: 413-442-9190. 8:30AM-4:30PM (EST). Access by: Mail, in person.

Felony, Misdemeanor, Civil, Eviction, Small Claims—North Berkshire Division District Court #30, 65 Park St, Adams, MA 01220. 413-743-0021. Fax: 413-743-4848. 8AM-4:30PM (EST). Access by: Mail, in person.

South Berkshire Division District Court, 9 Gilmore Ave, Great Barrington, MA 01230. 413-528-3520. Fax: 413-528-0757. 8:30AM-4:30PM (EST). Access by: Phone, mail, in person.

North Berkshire Division District Court #20, City Hall, North Adams, MA 01247. 413-663-5339. Fax: 413-664-7209. 8:30AM-4:30PM (EST). Access by: Phone, mail, in person.

Pittsfield Division District Court, 24 Wendell Ave, Pittsfield, MA 01201. 413-442-5468. Fax: 413-499-7327. 8:30AM-4:30PM (EST). Access by: Phone, mail, in person.

Probate—Probate and Family Court, 44 Bank Row, Pittsfield, MA 01201. 413-442-6941. Fax: 413-443-3430. 8:30AM-4PM (EST). Access by: Phone, fax, mail, in person.

Bristol County

Real Estate Recording—Bristol County Register of Deeds (Fall River District), Fall River District, 441 North Main Street, Fall River, MA 02720. 508-673-1651. Fax: 508-673-7633. 8:30AM-5PM (EST).

Bristol County Register of Deeds, Southern District, 25 North 6th Street, New Bedford, MA 02740. 508-993-2605. Fax: 508-997-4250. 8:30AM-5PM (EST).

Bristol County Register of Deeds, Northern District, 11 Court Street, Taunton, MA 02780. 508-822-0502. Fax: 508-880-4975. 8:30AM-5PM (EST).

Felony, Civil Actions Over $25,000—Superior Court-Taunton, 9 Court St, Taunton, MA 02780. 508-823-6588. 8AM-4:30PM (EST). Access by: Mail, in person.

Felony, Misdemeanor, Civil, Eviction, Small Claims—Attleboro Division District Court, Courthouse, 88 N Main St, Attleboro, MA 02703. 508-222-5900. Fax: 508-223-3916. 9AM-4:30PM (EST). Access by: Phone, mail, in person.

Fall River Division District Court, 45 Rock St, Fall River, MA 02720. 508-679-8161. Fax: 508-675-5477. 8AM-4:30PM (EST). Access by: In person only.

New Bedford Division District Court, 75 N 6th St, New Bedford, MA 02740. 508-999-9700. 8:30AM-4PM (EST). Access by: Mail, in person.

Taunton Division District Court, 15 Court St, Taunton, MA 02780. 508-824-4032. 8AM-4:30PM (EST). Access by: Phone, mail, in person.

Probate—New Bedford Probate and Family Court, 505 Pleasant St, New Bedford, MA 02740. 508-999-5249. Fax: 508-991-7421. 8AM-4:30PM (EST). Access by: Mail, in person.

Taunton Probate and Family Court, 11 Court St, Taunton, MA 02780. 508-824-4004. Fax: 508-822-9837. 8AM-4:30PM (EST). Access by: Mail, in person.

Dukes County

Real Estate Recording—Dukes County Register of Deeds, Main Street, Courthouse, Edgartown, MA 02539. 508-627-4025. Fax: 508-627-7821. 8:30AM-4:30PM (EST).

Felony, Civil Actions Over $25,000—Superior Court, PO Box 1267, Edgartown, MA 02539. 508-627-4668. Fax: 508-627-7571. 8AM-4PM (EST). Access by: Mail, in person.

Felony, Misdemeanor, Civil, Eviction, Small Claims—Edgartown District Court, Courthouse, 81 Main St, Edgartown, MA 02539-1284. 508-627-3751. 8:30AM-4:30PM (EST). Access by: Phone, mail, in person.

Probate—Probate and Family Court, PO Box 237, Edgartown, MA 02539. 508-627-4703. Fax: 508-627-7664. 8:30AM-4:30PM (EST). Access by: Mail, in person.

Essex County

Real Estate Recording—Essex County Register of Deeds, Northern District, 381 Common Street, Lawrence, MA 01840. 978-683-2745. Fax: 978-688-4679. 8AM-4:30PM (recording until 4PM.) (EST).

Essex County Register of Deeds, Southern District, 36 Federal Street, Salem, MA 01970. 978-741-0201. Fax: 978-744-5865. 8AM-4PM (EST).

Civil Actions Over $25,000—Superior Court-Lawrence, 43 Appleton Way, Lawrence, MA 01840. 978-687-7463. 8AM-4:30PM (EST). Access by: Mail, in person.

Felony, Civil Actions Over $25,000—Superior Court-Newburyport, 145 High St, Newburyport, MA 01950. 978-462-4474. 8AM-4:30PM (EST). Access by: Mail, in person.

Superior Court-Salem, 32 Federal St, Salem, MA 01970. 978-741-0200. Civil: 978-744-5500 X223. Criminal: 978-744-5500 X344. Fax: 978-741-0691. 8:00AM-4:30PM (EST). Access by: Phone, mail, in person.

Felony, Misdemeanor, Civil, Eviction, Small Claims—Haverhill Division District Court, PO Box 1389, Haverhill, MA 01831. 978-373-4151. Fax: 978-521-6886. 8:30AM-4:30PM (EST). Access by: Phone, fax, mail, in person.

Ipswich Division District Court, 30 South Main St, PO Box 246, Ipswich, MA 01938. 978-356-2681. 8:30AM-4:30PM (EST). Access by: Phone, fax, mail, in person.

Lawrence Division District Court, 381 Common St, Lawrence, MA 01840. 978-687-7184. Civil: 978-689-2810. 8AM-4:30PM (EST). Access by: Mail, in person.

Lynn Division District Court, 580 Essex St, Lynn, MA 01901. 617-598-5200. 8:00AM-4:30PM (EST). Access by: Phone, mail, in person.

Newburyport Division District Court, 188 State St, Newburyport, MA 01950. 978-462-2652. 8:30AM-4:30PM (EST). Access by: Phone, mail, in person.

Peabody Division District Court, PO Box 666, Peabody, MA 01960. 978-532-3100. 8:30AM-4:30PM (EST). Access by: Phone, mail, in person.

Salem Division District Court, 65 Washington St, Salem, MA 01970. 978-744-1167. 8:30AM-4:30PM (EST). Access by: Phone, mail, in person.

Probate—Probate and Family Court, 36 Federal St, Salem, MA 01970. 978-744-1020. 8:00AM-4:30PM (EST). Access by: Mail, in person.

Franklin County

Real Estate Recording—Franklin County Register of Deeds, 425 Main Street, Court House, Greenfield, MA 01301. 413-772-0239. Fax: 413-774-7150. 8:30AM-4:30PM (Recording until 4PM) (EST).

Felony, Civil Actions Over $25,000—Superior Court, PO Box 1573, Greenfield, MA 01302. 413-774-5535. Fax: 413-774-4770. 8:30AM-4:30PM (EST). Access by: Phone, mail, in person.

Felony, Misdemeanor, Civil, Eviction, Small Claims—Greenfield District Court, 425 Main St, Greenfield, MA 01301. 413-774-5533. Fax: 413-774-5328. 8:30AM-4:30PM (EST). Access by: Phone, fax, mail, in person.

Orange Division District Court, One Court Square, Orange, MA 01364. 508-544-8277. Fax: 508-544-5204. 8:30AM-4:30PM (EST). Access by: Phone, mail, in person.

Probate—Probate and Family Court, 425 Main St, (PO Box 590, 01302), Greenfield, MA 01301. 413-774-7011. Fax: 413-774-3829. 8AM-4:30PM (EST). Access by: Mail, in person.

Hampden County

Real Estate Recording—Hampden County Register of Deeds, 50 State Street, Hall of Justice, Springfield, MA 01103. 413-748-8622. Fax: 413-731-8190. 8:30AM-4:30PM; 9AM-4PM(Recording) (EST).

Felony, Civil Actions Over $25,000—Superior Court, 50 State St, PO Box 559, Springfield, MA 01102-0559. 413-748-8600. Fax: 413-737-1611. 8AM-4:30PM (EST). Access by: Mail, in person.

Felony, Misdemeanor, Civil, Eviction, Small Claims—Chicopee Division District Court, 30 Church St, Chicopee, MA 01020. 413-598-0099. 8AM-4PM (EST). Access by: Phone, mail, in person.

Holyoke Division District Court, 20 Court Sq, Holyoke, MA 01041-5075. 413-538-9710. 8:30AM-4:30PM (EST). Access by: Phone, mail, in person.

Palmer Division District Court, 234 Sykes St, Palmer, MA 01069. 413-283-8916. 8:30AM-4:30PM (EST). Access by: Phone, mail, in person.

Springfield Division District Court, 50 State St, Springfield, MA 01103. Civil: 413-748-8659. Criminal: 413-748-7982. Fax: 413-747-4841. 8:00AM-4:30PM (EST). Access by: Phone, mail, in person.

Westfield Division District Court, 27 Washington St, Westfield, MA 01085. 413-568-8946. 8AM-4PM (EST). Access by: Mail, in person.

Probate—Probate and Family Court, 50 State St, Springfield, MA 01103-0559. 413-748-8600. Fax: 413-781-5605. 8AM-4:25PM (EST). Access by: Phone, mail, in person.

Hampshire County

Real Estate Recording—Hampshire County Register of Deeds, 33 King Street, Hall of Records, Northampton, MA 01060. 413-584-3637. Fax: 413-584-4136. 8:30AM-4:30PM (Recording ends at 4PM) (EST).

Felony, Civil Actions Over $25,000—Superior Court, PO Box 1119, Northampton, MA 01061. 413-584-5810. Fax: 413-586-8217. 9AM-4PM (EST). Access by: Mail, in person.

Felony, Misdemeanor, Civil, Eviction, Small Claims—Northampton District Court, Courthouse, 15 Gothic St, Northampton, MA 01060. 413-584-7400. Criminal: 413-584-7400. Fax: 413-586-1980. 8:30AM-4:30PM (EST). Access by: Fax, mail, in person.

Ware Division District Court, PO Box 300, Ware, MA 01082. 413-967-3301. Fax: 413-967-7986. 8AM-4:30PM (EST). Access by: Phone, mail, in person.

Probate—Probate and Family Court, 33 King St, Northampton, MA 01060. 413-586-8500. Fax: 413-584-1132. 9AM-4:30PM (EST). Access by: Mail, in person.

Middlesex County

Real Estate Recording—Middlesex County Register of Deeds, Southern District, 208 Cambridge Street, East Cambridge, MA 02141. 617-494-4500. 8AM-4PM (EST).

Middlesex County Register of Deeds, Northern District, 360 Gorham Street, Lowell, MA 01852. 978-458-8474. Fax: 978-458-7765. 8:30AM-4:30PM (EST).

Felony, Civil Actions Over $25,000—Superior Court-East Cambridge, 40 Thorndike St, East Cambridge, MA 02141. 617-494-4010. 8:30AM-4:30PM (EST). Access by: Mail, in person.

Superior Court-Lowell, 360 Gorham St, Lowell, MA 01852. 978-453-0201. 8:30AM-4:30PM (EST). Access by: Mail, in person.

Felony, Misdemeanor, Civil, Eviction, Small Claims—Ayer Division District Court, 25 E Main St, Ayer, MA 01432. 978-772-2100. 8:30AM-4:30PM (EST). Access by: Phone, mail, in person.

Concord Division District Court, 305 Walden St, Concord, MA 01742. 978-369-0500. 8:30AM-4:30PM (EST). Access by: Mail, in person.

Cambridge Division District Court, PO Box 338, East Cambridge, MA 02141. 617-494-4310. Probate: 617-494-5233. 8:30AM-4:30PM (EST). Access by: In person only.

Framingham Division District Court, 600 Concord St, Framingham, MA 01701. 508-875-7461. 8:30AM-4:30PM (EST). Access by: Mail, in person.

Lowell Division District Court, 41 Hurd St, Lowell, MA 01852. 978-459-4101. 8:30AM-4:30PM (EST). Access by: Phone, mail, in person.

Malden Division District Court, 89 Summer, Malden, MA 02148. 617-322-7500. Fax: 617-322-1604. 8:30AM-4:30PM (EST). Access by: Phone, mail, in person.

Marlborough Division District Court, 45 Williams St, Marlborough, MA 01752. 508-485-3700. 8:30AM-4:30PM (EST). Access by: Phone, mail, in person.

Natick Division District Court, 117 E Central, Natick, MA 01760. 508-653-4332. 8:30AM-4:30PM (EST). Access by: Phone, mail, in person.

Somerville Division District Court, 175 Fellsway, Somerville, MA 02145. 617-666-8000. 8:30AM-4:30PM (EST). Access by: Phone, mail, in person.

Waltham Division District Court, 38 Linden St, Waltham, MA 02154. 617-894-4500. 8:30AM-4:30PM (EST). Access by: In person only.

Newton Division District Court, 1309 Washington, West Newton, MA 02165. 617-244-3600. Fax: 617-965-7584. 8:30AM-4:30PM (EST). Access by: In person only.

Woburn Division District Court, 30 Pleasant St, Woburn, MA 01801. 617-935-4000. 8:30AM-4:30PM (EST). Access by: Mail, in person.

Probate—Probate and Family Court, 208 Cambridge St. PO Box 410480, East Cambridge, MA 02141-0005. 617-494-4530. Fax: 617-225-0781. 8:00AM-4:00PM (EST). Access by: Mail, in person.

Nantucket County

Real Estate Recording—Nantucket Register of Deeds, 16 Broad Street, Nantucket, MA 02554. 508-228-7250. Fax: 508-325-5331. 8AM-4PM; Recording Hours: 8AM-Noon, 1-3:45PM (EST).

Felony, Civil Actions Over $25,000—Superior Court, PO Box 967, Nantucket, MA 02554. 508-228-2559. Fax: 508-228-3725. 8:30AM-4PM (EST). Access by: Phone, fax, mail, in person.

Felony, Misdemeanor, Civil, Eviction, Small Claims—Nantucket Division District Court, Broad Street, Nantucket, MA 02554. 508-228-0460. (EST). Access by: In person only.

Probate—Probate and Family Court, PO Box 1116, Nantucket, MA 02554. 508-228-2669. Fax: 508-228-3662. 8:30AM-4PM (EST). Access by: Phone, mail, in person.

Norfolk County

Real Estate Recording—Norfolk County Register of Deeds, 649 High Street, Dedham, MA 02026. 781-461-6122. Fax: 781-326-4742. 8:30AM-4:45PM (EST).

Felony, Civil Actions Over $25,000—Superior Court, 650 High St, Dedham, MA 02026. 781-326-1600. Civil: 781-326-3871. Criminal: 781-320-9726. Fax: 781-326-3871. 8:30AM-4:30PM (EST). Access by: Fax, mail, in person. After faxing call back later that day for information.

Felony, Misdemeanor, Civil, Eviction, Small Claims—Brookline Division District Court, 360 Washington St, Brookline, MA 02146. 617-232-4660. 8:30AM-4:30PM (EST). Access by: Mail, in person.

Dedham Division District Court, 631 High St, Dedham, MA 02026. 781-329-4777. 8:15AM-4:30PM (EST). Access by: In person only.

Quincy Division District Court, One Dennis Ryan Parkway, Quincy, MA 02169. 617-471-1650. 8:30AM-4:30PM (EST). Access by: Phone, mail, in person.

Stoughton Division District Court, 1288 Central St, Stoughton, MA 02072. 781-344-2131. 8:30AM-4:30PM (EST). Access by: In person only.

Wrentham Division District Court, PO Box 248, Wrentham, MA 02093. 508-384-3106. Fax: 508-384-5052. 8:30AM-4:30PM (EST). Access by: In person only.

Probate—Probate and Family Court, 649 High St, PO Box 269, Dedham, MA 02027. 781-326-7200. Fax: 781-326-5575. 8AM-4:30PM (EST). Access by: Phone, mail, in person.

Plymouth County

Real Estate Recording—Plymouth County Register of Deeds, 7 Russell Street, Plymouth, MA 02360. 508-830-9200. Fax: 508-830-9280. 8:15AM-4:30PM (Recording 9AM-4PM) (EST).

Felony, Civil Actions Over $25,000—Superior Court-Brockton, 72 Belmont St, Brockton, MA 02401. 508-583-8250. 8:30AM-4:30PM (EST). Access by: Mail, in person.

Superior Court-Plymouth, Court St, Plymouth, MA 02360. 508-747-6911. 8:30AM-4:30PM (EST). Access by: Phone, mail, in person.

Felony, Misdemeanor, Civil, Eviction, Small Claims—Brockton Division District Court, 155 West Elm St, Brockton, MA 02401. 508-587-8000. 8:30AM-4:30PM (EST). Access by: In person only.

Hingham Division District Court, 28 George Washington Blvd, Hingham, MA 02043. 617-749-7000. 8:30AM-4:30PM (EST). Access by: In person only.

Plymouth Division District Court, Courthouse, South Russell St, Plymouth, MA 02360. 508-747-0500. 8:30AM-4:30PM (EST). Access by: Mail, in person.

Wareham Division District Court, 2200 Cranberry Hwy, Junction Routes 28 & 58, West Wareham, MA 02576. 508-295-8300. Fax: 508-291-6376. 8:30AM-4:30PM (EST). Access by: Phone, mail, in person.

Probate—Probate and Family Court, 11 Russell, PO Box 3640, Plymouth, MA 02360. 508-747-6204. 8:30AM-4PM (EST). Access by: Mail, in person.

Suffolk County

Real Estate Recording—Suffolk County Register of Deeds, 1 Pemberton Square, The Old Courthouse, Boston, MA 02108. 617-725-8575. Fax: 617-720-4163. 9AM-4:30PM (EST).

Civil—Superior Court-Civil, Old Courthouse Bldg Rm 117, Boston, MA 02108. 617-725-8235. 8:30AM-5PM (EST). Access by: Mail, in person.

Felony—Superior Court-Criminal, New Courthouse, 712 Pemberton, Boston, MA 02108. 617-725-8160. Fax: 617-227-8834. 8:30AM-4:30PM (EST). Access by: Phone, mail, in person.

Misdemeanor, Civil, Small Claims—Suffolk County Courthouse Boston Municipal Court, Government Center, Boston, MA 02108. 617-725-8000. Civil: 617-725-8404. 8:30AM-4:30PM (EST). Access by: Mail, in person.

Felony, Misdemeanor, Civil, Eviction, Small Claims—Brighton Division District Court Department, 52 Academy Hill Rd, Brighton, MA 02135. 617-782-6521. Fax: 617-254-2127. 8:30AM-4:30PM (EST). Access by: Phone, mail, in person.

Chelsea Division District Court, 121 3rd St, Cambridge, MA 02141-1710. 617-252-0960. Fax: 617-621-9743. 8:30AM-4:30PM (EST). Access by: Phone, mail, in person.

Charleston Division District Court, 3 City Square, Charleston, MA 02129. 617-242-5400. Fax: 617-242-1677. 8:30AM-4:30PM (EST). Access by: Phone, fax, mail, in person.

Dorchester Division District Court, 450 Washington St, Dorchester, MA 02124. 617-288-9500. 8:30AM-4:30PM (EST). Access by: Mail, in person.

Misdemeanor, Civil Actions Under $25,000, Eviction, Small Claims—East Boston Division District Court, 37 Meridian St, East Boston, MA 02128. 617-569-7550. Fax: 617-561-4988. 8:30AM-4:30PM (EST). Access by: Mail, in person.

Felony, Misdemeanor, Civil, Eviction, Small Claims—West Roxbury Division District Court, Courthouse, 445 Arborway, Jamaica Plain, MA 02130. 617-522-4710. 8:30AM-4:30PM (EST). Access by: Phone, mail, in person.

Roxbury Division District Court, 85 Warren St, Roxbury, MA 02119. 617-427-7000. 8:30AM-5:30PM (EST). Access by: Phone, mail, in person.

South Boston Division District Court, 535 East Broadway, South Boston, MA 02127. 617-268-9292. Fax: 617-268-7321. 8:30AM-4:30PM (EST). Access by: Phone, mail, in person.

Probate—Probate and Family Court, Old Courthouse Bldg, Rm 120, Boston, MA 02108-1706. 617-725-8300. 8:30AM-4:30PM (EST). Access by: Mail, in person.

Worcester County

Real Estate Recording—Register of Deeds, Northern District, Courthouse, 84 Elm St., Fitchburg, MA 01420. 978-342-2637. Fax: 978-345-2865. 8:30AM-4:30PM; Recording Hours 8:30AM-4PM (EST).

Worcester County Register of Deeds (Worcester District), Worcester District, 2 Main Street, Courthouse, Worcester, MA 01608. 508-798-7713. Fax: 508-798-7746.

Felony, Civil Actions Over $25,000—Superior Court, 2 Main St Rm 21, Worcester, MA 01608. 508-756-2441. 8:30AM-4:30PM (EST). Access by: Mail, in person.

Felony, Misdemeanor, Civil, Eviction, Small Claims—Clinton Division District Court, Routes 62 & 70, Boylston St, PO Box 30, Clinton, MA 01510-0030. 978-368-7811. Fax: 978-368-7827. 8:30AM-4:30PM (EST). Access by: In person only.

Dudley Division District Court, PO Box 100, Dudley, MA 01571. 508-943-7123. Fax: 508-949-0015. 8AM-4:30PM (EST). Access by: Phone, mail, in person.

Spencer Division District Court, 544 E Main St, East Brookfield, MA 01515-1701. 508-885-6305. Fax: 508-885-7623. 8:30AM-4:30PM (EST). Access by: Phone, mail, in person.

Fitchburg District Court, 100 Elm St, Fitchburg, MA 01420. 978-345-2111. 8:30AM-4:30PM (EST). Access by: In person only.

Trial Court of the Commonwealth-Gardner Division, 108 Matthews St, PO Box 40, Gardner, MA 01440-0040. 978-632-2373. Fax: 978-630-3902. 8:30AM-4:30PM (EST). Access by: Phone, fax, mail, in person.

Leominster Division District Court, 25 School St, Leominster, MA 01453. 978-537-3722. Fax: 978-537-3970. 8:30AM-4:30PM (EST). Access by: Phone, mail, in person.

Milford Division District Court, PO Box 370, Milford, MA 01757. 508-473-1260. 8:30AM-4:30PM (EST). Access by: Mail, in person.

Uxbridge Division District Court, PO Box 580, Uxbridge, MA 01569. 508-278-2454. Fax: 508-278-2929. 8:30AM-4:30PM (EST). Access by: Phone, mail, in person.

Westborough Division District Court, 175 Milk St, Westborough, MA 01581. 508-366-8266. Fax: 508-366-8268. 8AM-4:30PM (EST). Access by: Mail, in person.

Winchendon Division District Court, PO Box 309, Winchendon, MA 01475. 978-297-0156. Fax: 978-297-0161. 8:30AM-4:30PM (EST). Access by: Phone, mail, in person.

Worcester Division District Court, 50 Harvard St., Worcester, MA 01608. 508-757-8350. Fax: 508-797-0716. 8AM-4:30PM (EST). Access by: Mail, in person.

Probate—Probate and Family Court, 2 Main St, Worcester, MA 01608. 508-770-0825. Fax: 508-752-6138. 8AM-4:30PM (EST). Access by: Mail, in person.

Federal Courts

US District Court

District of Massachusetts

Boston Division, US District Court Post Office & Courthouse Bldg, 90 Devonshire St, Room 707, Boston, MA 02109. 617-223-9152. Counties: Barnstable, Bristol, Dukes, Essex, Middlesex, Nantucket, Norfolk, Plymouth, Suffolk

Springfield Division, US District Court 1550 Main St, Springfield, MA 01103. 413-785-0214. Counties: Berkshire, Franklin, Hampden, Hampshire

Worcester Division, US District Court Room 502, 595 Main St, Worcester, MA 01608. 508-793-0552. Counties: Worcester

US Bankruptcy Court

District of Massachusetts

Boston Division, US Bankruptcy Court, Room 1101, 10 Causeway, Boston, MA 02222-1074. 617-565-6051. Voice Case Information System: 617-565-6025. Counties: Barnstable, Bristol, Dukes, Essex (except towns assigned to Worcester Division), Nantucket, Norfolk (except towns assigned to Worcester Division), Plymouth, Suffolk, and the following towns in Middlesex: Arlington, Belmont, Burlington, Everett, Lexington, Malden, Medford, Melrose, Newton, North Reading, Reading, Stoneham, Wakefield, Waltham, Watertown, Wilmington, Winchester and Woburn

Worcester Division, US Bankruptcy Court, 595 Main St, Worcester, MA 01608. 508-793-0518. Voice Case Information System: 617-565-6025. Counties: Berkshire, Franklin, Hampden, Hampshire, Middlesex (except the towns assigned to the Boston Division), Worcester and the following towns: in Essex-Andover, Haverhill, Lawrence, Methuen and North Andover; in Norfolk-Bellingham, Franklin, Medway, Millis and Norfolk

Michigan

Capitol: Lansing (Ingham County)	
Number of Counties: 83	**Population:** 9,549,353
County Court Locations:	**Federal Court Locations:**
•Circuit Courts: 83/57 Circuits	•District Courts: 9
•District Courts: 150/ 101 Districts	•Bankruptcy Courts: 5
•Recorder's Court of Detroit: 1	**State Agencies:** 20
Municipal Courts: 5	
•Probate Courts: 82	

State Agencies—Summary

General Help Numbers:

State Archives

State Archives of Michigan	517-373-1408
Historical Center	Fax: 517-241-1658
717 W Allegan	10AM-4PM
Lansing, MI 48918-1837	

Governor's Office

Governor's Office	517-373-3400
PO Box 30013	Fax: 517-335-6863
Lansing, MI 48909	7:30AM-5:30PM

Attorney General's Office

Attorney General's Office	517-373-1110
PO Box 30212, Law Bldg	Fax: 517-373-4916
Lansing, MI 48909	8AM-5PM

State Legislation

Michigan Legislature Document Room	517-373-0169
State Capitol	8:30AM-5PM
PO Box 30036	
Lansing, MI 48909	

Important State Internet Sites:

Webscape
File   Edit   View   Help

State of Michigan World Wide Web
www.migov.state.mi.us/

Links to state government officials and agencies.

The Governor's Office
www.migov.state.mi.us/migov.html

Includes information about the Governor's accomplishments, speeches, biography, and enables you to send e-mail to the Governor.

State Legislature Information
http://MichiganLegislature.org
www.migov.state.mi.us/legislature.html

These sites contain links to access the state House and Senate sites where you find their members, e-mail links and other government links. Bill text is also available.

Archive Reference Service
www.sos.state.mi.us/history/archive/archive.html

Contains information on the state archives, which has records back to 1797 and holds state and local government papers, private papers, photographs, and more.

Michigan Information Center
mic1.dmb.state.mi.us/michome/mic.html-ssi

Links to information about demographic, geographic, economic and educational data and the Michigan State data center program.

State Agencies—Public Records

Criminal Records

Michigan State Police, Applicant Ident. Team, Central Records Division, General Bldg, 7150 Harris Dr, Lansing, MI 48913, Main Telephone: 517-322-1955, Hours: 8AM-5PM. Access by: mail, visit. Searches done with or without fingerprints. Non-profit agencies/organizations may use Federal Form 501C3 in lieu of payment.

Corporation Records
Limited Liability Company Records
Fictitious Name
Limited Partnership Records
Assumed Name

Department of Consumer & Industrial Srvs, Corporation Division, PO Box 30054, Lansing, MI 48909-7554, Main Telephone: 517-334-6302, To order copies: 900-555-0031, Fax for orders: 517-334-7145, Information Unit: 517-334-7561, Fax: 517-334-7145, Hours: 8AM-5PM. Access by: mail, phone, fax, visit. Forms, policies, and procedures may be viewed at their web site.

Trademarks/Servicemarks

Department of Consumer & Industry Srvs, Securities Division, PO Box 30054, Lansing, MI 48909-7554, Main Telephone: 517-334-6200, Hours: 8AM-5PM. Access by: visit only. This agency will not perform record checks (unless you are applying for a mark). They suggest several outside firms to hire or come-in yourself.

Uniform Commercial Code
Federal Tax Liens
State Tax Liens

UCC Section, Department of State, PO Box 30197, Lansing, MI 48909-7697, Main Telephone: 517-322-1144, Fax: 517-322-5434, Hours: 8AM-5PM. Access by: mail, phone, visit.

Sales Tax Registrations

Revenue Bureau, Sales, Use, Withholding Tax Division, PO Box 15128, Lansing, MI 48901, Main Telephone: 517-373-2746, Fax 517-335-1135 Access by: mail, phone, visit.

Birth Certificates

Department of Community Health, Office of the State Registrar, PO Box 30195, Lansing, MI 48909, Main Telephone: 517-335-8656, Certification Unit: 517-335-8666, 800-361-6374, Hours: 8AM-5PM. Access by: mail, phone, visit.

Death Records

Department of Health, Office of the State Registrar, PO Box 30195, Lansing, MI 48909, Main Telephone: 517-335-8656, Hours: 8AM-5PM. Access by: mail, phone, visit.

Marriage Certificates

Department of Health, Office of the State Registrar, PO Box 30195, Lansing, MI 48909, Main Telephone: 517-335-8656, Hours: 8AM-5PM. Access by: mail, phone, visit.

Divorce Records

Department of Health, Office of the State Registrar, PO Box 30195, Lansing, MI 48909, Main Telephone: 517-335-8656, Hours: 8AM-5PM. Access by: mail, phone, visit.

Workers' Compensation Records

Department of Consumer & Industry Services, Workers Disability Compensation Division, 7150 Harris Dr, Lansing, MI 48909, Main Telephone: 517-322-1884, Fax: 517-322-1808, Hours: 8AM-5PM. Access by: mail only. In person requests are discouraged due to confidentiality of records and records may not be on site. Injured employee may review their own records, but should call first and make arrangements.

Driver Records

Department of State Police, Record Look-up Unit, 7064 Crowner Dr, Lansing, MI 48918, Main Telephone: 517-322-1624, Fax: 517-322-1181, Hours: 8AM-4:45PM. Access by: mail, phone, fax, visit, PC. Copies of tickets may be purchased at the same address for a fee of $6.55 per copy.

Vehicle Ownership
Vehicle Identification

Department of State Police, Record Look-up Unit, 7064 Crowner Dr, Lansing, MI 48918, Main Telephone: 517-322-1624, Fax: 517-322-1181, Hours: 8AM-4:45PM. Access by: mail, phone, fax, visit, PC.

Accident Reports

Department of State Police, Central Records Division/Freedom of Information, 7150 Harris Dr, Lansing, MI 48913, Main Telephone: 517-322-5509, Fax: 517-323-5350, Hours: 8AM-5PM. Access by: mail, visit.

Hunting License Information
Fishing License Information

Records not available from state agency.

County Courts and Recording Offices

What You Need to Know...

About the Courts

Administration

State Court Administrator   517-373-0130
309 N Washington Sq
Lansing, MI 48909

Court Structure

District Courts and Municipal Courts have jurisdiction over certain minor felonies.

There is a Court of Claims in Lansing which is a function of the 30th Circuit Court with jurisdiction over claims against the state of Michigan. Probate is handled by the Probate Courts, each of which, also, has a Juvenile Division and the associated records.

The Recorder's Court of Detroit was abolished as of October 1, 1997

Searching Hints

Some courts will not conduct criminal searches, but refer requests to the State Police.

Note that costs and searches requirements and procedures vary widely because each jurisdiction may create its own administrative orders.

Online Access

There is a wide range of online computerization of the judicial system from none to "fairly complete." There is **no** statewide network **nor** is there any external, public access.

About the Recorder's Office

Organization

83 counties, 83 filing offices. The recording officer is County Register of Deeds. 79 counties are in the Eastern Time Zone (EST) and 4 are in the Central Time Zone (CST).

UCC Records

Financing statements are filed at the state level except for consumer goods, farm related and real estate related filings. All counties will perform UCC searches. Use search request form UCC-11. Search fees are usually $3.00 per debtor name if federal tax identification number or Social Security number are given, or $6.00 without the number. Copies usually cost $1.00 per page.

Lien Records

Federal and state tax liens on personal property of businesses are filed with the Secretary of State. Other federal and state tax liens are filed with the Register of Deeds. Most counties search each tax lien index separately. Some charge one fee to search both, while others charge a separate fee for each one. When combining a UCC and tax lien search, total fee is usually $9.00 for all three searches. Some counties require tax identification number as well as name to do a search. Copy fees are usually $1.00 per page. Other liens include construction, and lis pendens.

Real Estate Records

Some counties will perform real estate searches. Copies usually cost $1.00 per page. and certification fees vary. Ownership records are located at the Equalization Office, designated "Assessor" in this section. Tax records are located at the Treasurer's Office.

County Courts and Recording Offices

Alcona County

Real Estate Recording—Alcona County Register of Deeds, 5th Street, Courthouse, Harrisville, MI 48740. 517-724-6802. Fax: 517-724-5684. 9AM-5PM (EST).

Felony, Civil Actions Over $10,000—26th Circuit Court, PO Box 308, Harrisville, MI 48740. 517-724-6807. Fax: 517-724-5684. 8AM-Noon, 1-4:30PM (EST). Access by: Phone, mail, in person.

Misdemeanor, Civil Actions Under $10,000, Eviction, Small Claims—82nd District Court, PO Box 385, Harrisville, MI 48740. 517-724-5313. Fax: 517-724-5397. 8:30AM-4:30PM (EST). Access by: Phone, fax, mail, in person.

Probate—Probate Court, PO Box 328, Harrisville, MI 48740. 517-724-6880. Fax: 517-724-6397. 8:30AM-4:30PM (EST). Access by: Mail, in person.

Alger County

Real Estate Recording—Alger County Register of Deeds, 101 Court Street, Munising, MI 49862. 906-387-2076. Fax: 906-387-2156. 8AM-4PM (EST).

Felony, Civil Actions Over $10,000—11th Circuit Court, 101 Court St, PO Box 538, Munising, MI 49862. 906-387-2076. Fax: 906-387-2156. 8AM-4PM (EST). Access by: Phone, fax, mail, in person.

Misdemeanor, Civil Actions Under $10,000, Eviction, Small Claims—93rd District Court, PO Box 186, Munising, MI 49862. 906-387-3879. Fax: 906-387-3289. 8AM-4PM (EST). Access by: Phone, fax, mail, in person.

Probate—Alger County Probate Court, 101 Court St, Munising, MI 49862. 906-387-2080. Fax: 906-387-2200. 8AM-Noon, 1-4PM (EST).

Allegan County

Real Estate Recording—Allegan County Register of Deeds, 113 Chestnut Street, County Court House, Allegan, MI 49010. 616-673-0380. Fax: 616-673-0298. 8AM-5PM (EST).

Felony, Civil Actions Over $10,000—48th Circuit Court, 113 Chestnut St, Allegan, MI 49010. 616-673-0300. Fax: 616-673-0298. 8AM-5PM (EST). Access by: Mail, in person.

Misdemeanor, Civil Actions Under $10,000, Eviction, Small Claims—57th District Court, 113 Chesnut St, Allegan, MI 49010. 616-673-0400. 8AM-5PM (EST). Access by: Mail, in person.

Probate—Probate Court, 113 Chesnut St, Allegan, MI 49010. 616-673-0250. Fax: 616-673-2200. 8AM-5PM (EST). Access by: Mail, in person.

Alpena County

Real Estate Recording—Alpena County Register of Deeds, 720 West Chisholm Street, Courthouse, Alpena, MI 49707. 517-356-3887. Fax: 517-356-6559. 8:30AM-4:30PM (EST).

Felony, Civil Actions Over $10,000—26th Circuit Court, 720 West Chisholm, Alpena, MI 49707. 517-356-0115. Fax: 517-356-6559. 8:30AM-4:30PM (EST). Access by: Mail, in person.

Misdemeanor, Civil Actions Under $10,000, Eviction, Small Claims—88th District Court, 719 West Chisholm, Alpena, MI 49707. 517-354-3330. Fax: 517-356-9522. 8:30AM-4:30PM (EST). Access by: Mail, in person.

Probate—Probate Court, 719 West Chisholm, Alpena, MI 49707. 517-354-8785. Fax: 517-356-3665. 8:30AM-4:30PM (EST). Access by: Mail, in person.

Antrim County

Real Estate Recording—Antrim County Register of Deeds, 205 East Cayuga Street, Bellaire, MI 49615. 616-533-6683. Fax: 616-533-6935. 8:30AM-5PM (EST).

Felony, Civil Actions Over $10,000—13th Circuit Court, PO Box 520, Bellaire, MI 49615. 616-533-8607. Fax: 616-533-6935. 8:30AM-5PM (EST). Access by: Phone, fax, mail, in person.

Misdemeanor, Civil Actions Under $10,000, Eviction, Small Claims—87th District Court, PO Box 597, Bellaire, MI 49615. 616-533-6441. Fax: 616-533-6322. 8AM-4:30PM (EST). Access by: Fax, mail, in person.

Probate—Probate Court, PO Box 130, Bellaire, MI 49615. 616-533-6681. Fax: 616-533-6600. 8:30AM-4:30PM (EST).

Arenac County

Real Estate Recording—Arenac County Register of Deeds, 120 Grove Street, Standish, MI 48658. 517-846-9201. 8:30AM-5PM (EST).

Felony, Civil Actions Over $10,000—34th Circuit Court, 120 N Grove St, PO Box 747, Standish, MI 48658. 517-846-4626. Fax: 517-846-6757. 8:30AM-5PM (EST). Access by: Mail, in person.

Misdemeanor, Civil Actions Under $10,000, Eviction, Small Claims—81st District Court, PO Box 129, Standish, MI 48658. 517-846-9538. Fax: 517-846-2008. 8:30AM-5PM (EST). Access by: Phone, fax, mail, in person.

Probate—Probate Court, 120 N Grove, PO Box 666, Standish, MI 48658. 517-846-6941. 9AM-5PM (EST).

Baraga County

Real Estate Recording—Baraga County Register of Deeds, Courthouse, 16 N. 3rd St., L'Anse, MI 49946. 906-524-6183. Fax: 906-524-6186. 8:30AM-Noon, 1-4:30PM (EST).

Felony, Civil Actions Over $10,000—12th Circuit Court, 16 North 3rd St, L'Anse, MI 49946. 906-524-6183. Fax: 906-524-6432. 8:30AM-4:30PM (EST). Access by: Phone, fax, mail, in person.

Misdemeanor, Civil Actions Under $10,000, Eviction, Small Claims—97th District Court, 16 North 3rd St, L'Anse, MI 49946. 906-524-6109. Fax: 906-524-6186. 8:30AM-Noon,1-4:30PM (EST). Access by: Mail, in person.

Probate—Probate Court, County Courthouse, 16 N 3rd St, L'Anse, MI 49946. 906-524-6390. Fax: 906-524-6186. 8:30AM-Noon, 1-4:30PM (EST). Access by: Mail, in person.

Barry County

Real Estate Recording—Barry County Register of Deeds, 220 West State Street, Courthouse, Hastings, MI 49058. 616-948-4824. Fax: 616-948-4820. 8AM-5PM (EST).

Felony, Civil Actions Over $10,000—5th Circuit Court, 220 West State St, Hastings, MI 49058. 616-948-4810. Fax: 616-945-0209. 8AM-5PM (EST). Access by: Fax, mail, in person.

Misdemeanor, Civil Actions Under $10,000, Eviction, Small Claims—56th & 1st District Court, 220 West Court St, Suite 202, Hastings, MI 49058. 616-948-4835. Fax: 616-948-3314. 8AM-5PM (EST). Access by: Phone, fax, mail, in person.

Probate—Probate Court, 220 West Court St., Suite 301, Hastings, MI 49058. 616-948-4842. Fax: 616-948-3322. 9AM-Noon, 1-5PM (EST). Access by: Mail, in person.

Bay County

Real Estate Recording—Bay County Register of Deeds, 515 Center Avenue, Bay City, MI 48708. 517-895-4228. Fax: 517-895-4296. 8AM-5PM (June-September 7:30AM-4PM) (EST).

Felony, Civil Actions Over $10,000—18th Circuit Court, 515 Center Ave, Bay City, MI 48708. 517-895-4280. Fax: 517-895-4284. 8AM-5PM Winter; 7:30AM-4PM Summer (EST). Access by: Phone, fax, mail, in person.

Misdemeanor, Civil Actions Under $10,000, Eviction, Small Claims—74th District Court, 515 Center Ave., Bay City, MI 48708. 517-895-4203. Fax: 517-895-4233. 8AM-5PM (EST). Access by: Fax, mail, in person.

Probate—Probate Court, 515 Center Ave., Bay City, MI 48708. 517-895-4205. Fax: 517-895-4194. 8AM-5PM; Summer hours 7:30AM-4PM (EST). Access by: Mail, in person.

Benzie County

Real Estate Recording—Benzie County Register of Deeds, 448 Court Place, Beulah, MI 49617. 616-882-0016. Fax: 616-882-4844. 8AM-Noon, 1-5PM (EST).

Felony, Civil Actions Over $10,000—19th Circuit Court, PO Box 398, Beulah, MI 49617. 616-882-9671. Fax: 616-882-5941. 8AM-5PM (EST). Access by: Phone, fax, mail, in person.

Misdemeanor, Civil Actions Under $10,000, Eviction, Small Claims—85th District Court, PO Box 398, Beulah, MI 49617. 800-759-5175. Fax: 616-882-0022. 9AM-5PM (EST). Access by: Mail, in person.

Probate—Probate Court, PO Box 398, Beulah, MI 49617. 616-882-9675. Fax: 616-882-5987. 8:30AM-Noon, 1-5PM (EST). Access by: Mail, in person.

Berrien County

Real Estate Recording—Berrien County Register of Deeds, 811 Port Street, Courthouse Room 106, St. Joseph, MI 49085. 616-983-7111. Fax: 616-982-8659. 8:30AM-5PM (EST).

Felony, Civil Actions Over $10,000—2nd Circuit Court, 811 Port St, St Joseph, MI 49085. 616-983-7111. Fax: 616-982-8647. 8:30AM-4PM (EST). Access by: Mail, in person.

Misdemeanor, Civil Actions Under $10,000, Eviction, Small Claims—5th District Court, Attn: Records, 811 Port St, St Joseph, MI 49085. 616-983-7111. Fax: 616-982-8643. 8:30AM-4PM (EST). Access by: Mail, in person.

Probate—Probate Court, 811 Port St., St Joseph, MI 49085. 616-983-7111. Fax: 616-982-8644. 8:30AM-5PM (EST).

Branch County

Real Estate Recording—Branch County Register of Deeds, 31 Division Street, Coldwater, MI 49036. 517-279-8411. 9AM-12, 1-5PM (EST).

Felony, Civil Actions Over $10,000—15th Circuit Court, 31 Division St, Coldwater, MI 49036. 517-279-8411. Fax: 517-278-5627. 9AM-5PM (EST). Access by: Mail, in person.

Misdemeanor, Civil Actions Under $10,000, Eviction, Small Claims—3A District Court, 31 Division St., Coldwater, MI 49036. 517-279-8411. Fax: 517-278-4130. 8AM-5PM (EST). Access by: Mail, in person.

Probate—Probate Court, 31 Division St., Coldwater, MI 49036. 517-279-8411. Fax: 517-278-4130. 9AM-Noon, 1-5PM (EST). Access by: Mail, in person.

Calhoun County

Real Estate Recording—Calhoun County Register of Deeds, 315 West Green Street, Marshall, MI 49068. 616-781-0730. 8AM-5PM (EST).

Felony, Civil Actions Over $10,000—37th Circuit Court, 161 East Michigan, Battle Creek, MI 49017-4066. 616-969-6518. 8:30AM-4PM (EST). Access by: Mail, in person.

Misdemeanor, Civil Actions Under $10,000, Eviction, Small Claims—10th District Court, 161 E Michigan Ave, Battle Creek, MI 49014. 616-969-6666. Fax: 616-969-6663. 8:30AM-4PM (EST). Access by: Fax, mail, in person.

10th District Court-Marshall Branch, 315 West Arlen, Marshall, MI 49068. 616-969-6678. Fax: 616-969-6663. 8:30AM-4PM (EST). Access by: Mail, in person.

Probate—Probate Court, Justice Center, 161 E Michigan Ave, Battle Creek, MI 49014. 616-969-6795. Fax: 616-969-6797. 8AM-5PM (EST).

Cass County

Real Estate Recording—Cass County Register of Deeds, 120 North Broadway, Suite 123, Cassopolis, MI 49031. 616-445-4464. Fax: 616-445-8978. 8AM-5PM (EST).

Felony, Civil Actions Over $10,000—43rd Circuit Court, 120 North Broadway, Cassopolis, MI 49031-1398. 616-445-4416. Fax: 616-445-8978. 8AM-5PM (EST). Access by: Fax, mail, in person.

Misdemeanor, Civil Actions Under $10,000, Eviction, Small Claims—4th District Court, 110 North Broadway, Cassopolis, MI 49031. 616-445-4424. Fax: 616-445-8978. 8AM-5PM (EST). Access by: Phone, mail, in person.

Probate—Probate Court, 110 North Broadway, Rm 202, Cassopolis, MI 49031. 616-445-4454. Fax: 616-445-4453. 8AM-Noon, 1-5PM (EST). Access by: Mail, in person.

Charlevoix County

Real Estate Recording—Charlevoix County Register of Deeds, 301 State Street, County Building, Charlevoix, MI 49720. 616-547-7204. Fax: 616-547-7246. 9AM-5PM (EST).

Felony, Civil Actions Over $10,000—33rd Circuit Court, 203 Antrim St, Charlevoix, MI 49720. 616-547-7200. Fax: 616-547-7217. 9AM-5PM (EST). Access by: Mail, in person.

Misdemeanor, Civil Actions Under $10,000, Eviction, Small Claims—90th District Court, 301 State St, Court Bldg, Charlevoix, MI 49720. 616-547-7227. Fax: 616-547-7253. 9AM-5PM (EST). Access by: Mail, in person.

Probate—Probate Court, 301 State St, County Bldg, Charlevoix, MI 49720. 616-547-7214. Fax: 616-547-7256. 9AM-5PM (EST).

Cheboygan County

Real Estate Recording—Cheboygan County Register of Deeds, 870 South Main Street, Cheboygan, MI 49721. 616-627-8866. 9AM-5PM (EST).

Felony, Civil Actions Over $10,000—53rd District Court, PO Box 70, Cheboygan, MI 49721. 616-627-8808. 9AM-5PM (EST). Access by: Phone, mail, in person.

Misdemeanor, Civil Actions Under $10,000, Eviction, Small Claims—89th District Court, PO Box 70, Cheboygan, MI 49721. 616-627-8853. Fax: 616-627-8444. 8:30AM-4PM (EST). Access by: Phone, mail, in person.

Probate—Probate Court, PO Box 70, Cheboygan, MI 49721. 616-627-8823. Fax: 616-627-8868. 9AM-5PM (EST).

Chippewa County

Real Estate Recording—Chippewa County Register of Deeds, Courthouse, 319 Court St., Sault Ste. Marie, MI 49783. 906-635-6312. Fax: 906-635-6325. 8AM-5PM (EST).

Felony, Civil Actions Over $10,000—50th Circuit Court, 319 Court St, Sault Ste Marie, MI 49783. 906-635-6300. Fax: 906-635-6851. 8:30AM-5PM (EST). Access by: Mail, in person.

Misdemeanor, Civil Actions Under $10,000, Eviction, Small Claims—91st District Court, 325 Court St, Sault Ste Marie, MI 49783. 906-635-6320. Fax: 906-635-6336. 8AM-4:30PM (EST). Access by: Mail, in person.

Probate—Probate Court, 319 Court St., Sault Ste Marie, MI 49783. 906-635-6314. Fax: 906-635-6852. 9AM-Noon, 1-5PM (EST). Access by: Mail, in person.

Clare County

Real Estate Recording—Clare County Register of Deeds, 225 West Main, Harrison, MI 48625. 517-539-7131. Fax: 517-539-6616. 8AM-4:30PM (EST).

Felony, Civil Actions Over $10,000—55th Circuit Court, 225 West Main St, PO Box 438, Harrison, MI 48625. 517-539-7131. Fax: 517-539-6616. 8AM-4:30PM (EST). Access by: Mail, in person.

Misdemeanor, Civil Actions Under $10,000, Eviction, Small Claims—80th District Court, 225 W. Main St, Harrison, MI 48625. 517-539-7173. Fax: 517-539-6616. 8AM-4:30PM (EST). Access by: Mail, in person.

Probate—Probate Court, 225 W. Main St., PO Box 96, Harrison, MI 48625. 517-539-7109. 8AM-4:30PM (EST). Access by: Phone, mail, in person.

Clinton County

Real Estate Recording—Clinton County Register of Deeds, 100 East State Street, St. Johns, MI 48879. 517-224-5270. Fax: 517-224-5254. 8AM-5PM (EST).

Felony, Civil Actions Over $10,000—29th Circuit Court, PO Box 69, St Johns, MI 48879-0069. 517-224-5140. Fax: 517-224-5254. 8AM-5PM (EST). Access by: Fax, mail, in person.

Misdemeanor, Civil Actions Under $10,000, Eviction, Small Claims—65th District Court, 409 South Whittemore St., St Johns, MI 48879. 517-224-5150. Fax: 517-224-5154. 8AM-5PM (EST). Access by: Mail, in person.

Probate—Probate Court, 100 E. State St., St Johns, MI 48879. 517-224-5190. Fax: 517-224-5254. 8AM-Noon, 1-5PM (EST). Access by: Mail, in person.

Crawford County

Real Estate Recording—Crawford County Register of Deeds, 200 West Michigan, Grayling, MI 49738. 517-348-2841. Fax: 517-348-7582. 8:30AM-4:30PM (EST).

Felony, Civil Actions Over $10,000—46th Circuit Court, 200 West Michigan Ave, Grayling, MI 49738. 517-348-2841. Fax: 517-348-7582. 8:30AM-4:30PM (EST). Access by: Mail, in person.

Misdemeanor, Civil Actions Under $10,000, Eviction, Small Claims—83rd District Court, 200 West Michigan Ave., Grayling, MI 49738. 517-348-2841. Fax: 517-348-7582. 8:30AM-4:30PM (EST). Access by: Mail, in person.

Probate—Probate Court, 200 West Michigan Ave., Grayling, MI 49738. 517-348-2841. Fax: 517-348-7582. 8:30AM-4:30PM (EST). Access by: Mail, in person.

Delta County

Real Estate Recording—Delta County Register of Deeds, 310 Ludington Street, Suite 104, Escanaba, MI 49829. 906-789-5116. Fax: 906-789-5196. 8AM-4PM (EST).

Felony, Civil Actions Over $10,000—47th Circuit Court, 310 Ludington St, Escanaba, MI 49829. 906-789-5105. Fax: 906-789-5196. 8AM-4PM (EST). Access by: Mail, in person.

Misdemeanor, Civil Actions Under $10,000, Eviction, Small Claims—94th District Court, 310 Ludington St., Escanaba, MI 49829. 906-789-5106. Fax: 906-789-5196. 8AM-4PM (EST). Access by: Mail, in person.

Probate—Probate Court, 310 Ludington St., Escanaba, MI 49829. 906-789-5112. Fax: 906-789-5140. 8AM-Noon, 1-4PM (EST). Access by: Mail, in person.

Dickinson County

Real Estate Recording—Dickinson County Register of Deeds, 700 Stephenson Avenue, Courthouse, Iron Mountain, MI 49801. 906-774-0955. Fax: 906-774-4660. 8AM-Noon, 1-4:30PM (CST).

Felony, Civil Actions Over $10,000—41st Circuit Court, PO Box 609, Iron Mountain, MI 49801. 906-774-0988. Fax: 906-774-4660. 8AM-4:30PM (CST). Access by: Mail, in person.

Misdemeanor, Civil Actions Under $10,000, Eviction, Small Claims—95 B District Court, County Courthouse, Iron Mountain, MI 49801. 906-774-0506. Fax: 906-774-3686. 8AM-4:30PM (CST). Access by: Mail, in person.

Probate—Probate Court, PO Box 609, Iron Mountain, MI 49801. 906-774-1555. Fax: 906-774-3686. 8AM-4:30PM (CST). Access by: Mail, in person.

Eaton County

Real Estate Recording—Eaton County Register of Deeds, 1045 Independence Blvd., Charlotte, MI 48813. 517-543-7500. Fax: 517-543-7377. 8AM-5PM (EST).

Felony, Civil Actions Over $10,000—56th Circuit Court, 1045 Independence Blvd, Charlotte, MI 48813. 517-543-7500. Fax: 517-543-4475. 8AM-5PM (EST). Access by: Phone, fax, mail, in person.

Civil Actions Under $10,000, Eviction, Small Claims—56th District Court-Civil Division, 1045 Independence Blvd, Charlotte, MI 48813. 517-543-7500. 8AM-5PM (EST). Access by: Mail, in person.

Misdemeanor—56th District Court-Criminal, 1045 Independence Blvd, Charlotte, MI 48813. 517-543-7500. Fax: 517-543-7377. 8AM-5PM (EST). Access by: Mail, in person.

Emmet County

Real Estate Recording—Emmet County Register of Deeds, 200 Division, Petoskey, MI 49770. 616-348-1761. Fax: 616-348-0633. 8:30AM-5PM (EST).

Felony, Civil Actions Over $10,000—57th Circuit Court, 200 Division St, Petoskey, MI 49770. 616-348-1744. Fax: 616-348-0633. 8AM-5PM (EST). Access by: Mail, in person.

Misdemeanor, Civil Actions Under $10,000, Eviction, Small Claims—90th District Court, 200 Division St., Petoskey, MI 49770. 616-348-1750. Fax: 616-348-0633. 8:30AM-5PM (EST). Access by: Mail, in person.

Probate—Probate Court, 200 Division St., Petoskey, MI 49770. 616-348-1707. Fax: 616-348-0672. 8AM-5PM (EST). Access by: Mail, in person.

Genesee County

Real Estate Recording—Genesee County Register of Deeds, 1101 Beach Street, Administration Building, Flint, MI 48502. 810-257-3060. Fax: 810-768-7965. 8AM-5PM (EST).

Felony, Civil Actions Over $10,000—7th Circuit Court, 900 South Saginaw, Flint, MI 48502. 810-257-3220. 8AM-5PM (EST). Access by: Mail, in person.

Misdemeanor, Civil Actions Under $10,000, Eviction, Small Claims—67th District Court, 630 South Saginaw, Flint, MI 48502. 810-257-3170. 8AM-4PM (EST). Access by: Mail, in person.

Probate—Probate Court, 919 Beach St, Flint, MI 48502. 810-257-3528. Fax: 810-257-3299. 8AM-4PM (EST).

Gladwin County

Real Estate Recording—Gladwin County Register of Deeds, 401 West Cedar Ave., Gladwin, MI 48624. 517-426-7551. 8:30AM-4:30PM (EST).

Felony, Civil Actions Over $10,000—55th Circuit Court, 401 West Cedar, Gladwin, MI 48624. 517-426-7351. 8:30AM-4:30PM (EST). Access by: Mail, in person.

Misdemeanor, Civil Actions Under $10,000, Eviction, Small Claims—80th District Court, 401 West Cedar, Gladwin, MI 48624. 517-426-9207. Fax: 517-426-4281. 8:30AM-4:30PM (EST). Access by: Mail, in person.

Probate—Probate Court, 401 West Cedar, Gladwin, MI 48624. 517-426-7451. Fax: 517-426-4281. 8:30AM-4:30PM (EST). Access by: Mail, in person.

Gogebic County

Real Estate Recording—Gogebic County Register of Deeds, Courthouse, 200 N. Moore St., Bessemer, MI 49911. 906-667-0381. Fax: 906-663-4660. 8:30AM-4:30PM (CST).

Felony, Civil Actions Over $10,000—32nd Circuit Court, 200 North Moore St, Bessemer, MI 49911. 906-663-4518. Fax: 906-663-4660. 8:30AM-4:30PM (CST). Access by: Mail, in person.

Misdemeanor, Civil Actions Under $10,000, Eviction, Small Claims—98th District Court, 200 North Moore St, Bessemer, MI 49911. 906-663-4611. Fax: 906-663-4660. 8:30AM-4PM (CST). Access by: Mail, in person.

Probate—Probate Court, 200 North Moore St., Bessemer, MI 49911. 906-667-0421. Fax: 906-663-4660. 8:30AM-Noon, 1-4:30PM (CST). Access by: Mail, in person.

Grand Traverse County

Real Estate Recording—Grand Traverse County Register of Deeds, 400 Boardman Avenue, Traverse City, MI 49684. 616-922-4753. 8AM-5PM (Vault closes at 4:30PM) (EST).

Felony, Civil Actions Over $10,000—13th Circuit Court, 328 Washington St, Traverse City, MI 49684. 616-922-4710. 8AM-5PM (EST). Access by: Phone, mail, in person.

Misdemeanor, Civil Actions Under $10,000, Eviction, Small Claims—86th District Court, 328 Washington St., Traverse City, MI 49684. 616-922-4580. Fax: 616-922-4454. 8AM-5PM (EST). Access by: Phone, mail, in person. 616-922-4578.

Probate—Probate Court, 400 Boardmen, Traverse City, MI 49684. 616-922-4640. Fax: 616-922-4636. 8AM-5PM (EST). Access by: Mail, in person.

Gratiot County

Real Estate Recording—Gratiot County Register of Deeds, 214 East Center Street, Ithaca, MI 48847. 517-875-5217. 8:30AM-5PM (EST).

Felony, Civil Actions Over $10,000—29th Circuit Court, 214 East Center St, Ithaca, MI 48847. 517-875-5215. 8:30AM-5PM (EST). Access by: Mail, in person.

Misdemeanor, Civil Actions Under $10,000, Eviction, Small Claims—65-1 District Court, 245 East Newark St, Ithaca, MI 48847. 517-875-5240. Fax: 517-875-5290. 8:30AM-5PM (EST). Access by: In person only.

Probate—Probate Court, PO Box 217, Ithaca, MI 48847. 517-875-5231. Fax: 517-875-3322. 8:30AM-5PM (EST).

Hillsdale County

Real Estate Recording—Hillsdale County Register of Deeds, Courthouse, Hillsdale, MI 49242. 517-437-2231. Fax: 517-437-0829. 8:30AM-5PM (EST).

Felony, Civil Actions Over $10,000—1st Circuit Court, 29 North Howell, Hillsdale, MI 49242. 517-437-3391. 8:30AM-5PM (EST). Access by: Mail, in person.

Misdemeanor, Civil Actions Under $10,000, Eviction, Small Claims—2nd District Court, 49 North Howell, Hillsdale, MI 49242. 517-437-7329. 8AM-4:30PM; 8AM-5PM Traffic (EST). Access by: Phone, mail, in person.

Probate—Probate Court, 29 North Howell, Hillsdale, MI 49242. 517-437-4643. 8:30AM-Noon, 1-5PM (EST).

Houghton County

Real Estate Recording—Houghton County Register of Deeds, 401 East Houghton Avenue, Houghton, MI 49931. 906-482-1311. Fax: 906-482-7238. 8AM-4:30PM (EST).

Felony, Civil Actions Over $10,000—12th Circuit Court, 401 East Houghton Ave, Houghton, MI 49931. 906-482-5420. 8AM-4:30PM (EST). Access by: Mail, in person.

Misdemeanor, Civil Actions Under $10,000, Eviction, Small Claims—97th District Court, 401 East Houghton Ave., Houghton, MI 49931. 906-482-4980. Fax: 906-482-7238. 8AM-4:30PM (EST). Access by: Fax, mail, in person.

Probate—Probate Court, 401 East Houghton Ave., Houghton, MI 49931. 906-482-3120. Fax: 906-487-5964. 8AM-4:30PM (EST). Access by: Mail, in person.

Huron County

Real Estate Recording—Huron County Register of Deeds, 250 East Huron Avenue, Bad Axe, MI 48413. 517-269-9941. 8:30AM-5PM (EST).

Felony, Civil Actions Over $10,000—52nd Circuit Court, 250 East Huron Ave, Bad Axe, MI 48413. 517-269-9942. Fax: 517-269-6152. 8:30AM-5PM (EST). Access by: Phone, mail, in person.

Misdemeanor, Civil Actions Under $10,000, Eviction, Small Claims—73rd District Court, 250 East Huron Ave., Bad Axe, MI 48413. 517-269-9987. Fax: 517-269-7221. 8:30AM-5PM (EST). Access by: Mail, in person.

Probate—Probate Court, 250 East Huron Ave., Bad Axe, MI 48413. 517-269-9944. Fax: 517-269-9644. 8:30AM-Noon, 1-5PM (EST). Access by: Mail, in person.

Ingham County

Real Estate Recording—Ingham County Register of Deeds, Jefferson St., Courthouse Square, Mason, MI 48854. 517-676-7216. Fax: 517-676-7287. 8AM-5PM (EST).

Felony, Civil Actions Over $10,000—30th Circuit Court, 333 South Capital Ave, Ste C, Lansing, MI 48933. 517-483-6500. Fax: 517-483-6501. 9AM-Noon, 1-5PM M,T,TH,F, 8AM-Noon, 1-5PM W (EST). Access by: Phone, mail, in person.

Misdemeanor, Civil Actions Under $10,000, Eviction, Small Claims—54 B District Court, 101 Linden, East Lansing, MI 48823. Civil: 517-351-1730. Criminal: 517-336-8630. Fax: 517-351-3371. 8:00AM-4:30PM (EST). Access by: Mail, in person.

54 A District Court, 124 West Michigan Ave, Lansing, MI 48933. 517-483-4333. 8AM-4:35PM (EST). Access by: In person only.

55th District Court, 700 Buhl, Mason, MI 48854. 517-676-8400. 8:30AM-4:30PM (EST). Access by: Mail, in person.

Probate—Lansing Probate Court, 303 West Kalamazoo, Lansing, MI 48933. 517-483-6105. Fax: 517-483-6150. 8AM-Noon, 1-5PM (EST). Access by: Phone, mail, in person.

Ingham County Probate Court, PO Box 176, Mason, MI 48854. 517-676-7276. Fax: 517-676-7344. 8AM-Noon, 1-5PM (EST).

Ionia County

Real Estate Recording—Ionia County Register of Deeds, 100 Main Street, Courthouse, Ionia, MI 48846. 616-527-5320. Fax: 616-527-5380. 8:30AM-Noon, 1-5PM (EST).

Felony, Civil Actions Over $10,000—8th Circuit Court, 100 Main, Ionia, MI 48846. 616-527-5322. Fax: 616-527-5380. 8:30AM-5PM (EST). Access by: Phone, fax, mail, in person.

Misdemeanor, Civil Actions Under $10,000, Eviction, Small Claims—64 A District Court, 101 West Main, Ionia, MI 48846. 616-527-5346. Fax: 616-527-5343. 8AM-5:30PM (EST). Access by: Fax, mail, in person.

Probate—Probate Court, 100 Main, Ionia, MI 48846. 616-527-5326. Fax: 616-527-5321. 8:30AM-Noon, 1-5PM (EST). Access by: Mail, in person.

Iosco County

Real Estate Recording—Iosco County Register of Deeds, 422 West Lake Street, Tawas City, MI 48763. 517-362-2021. Fax: 517-362-3494. 9AM-5PM (EST).

Felony, Civil Actions Over $10,000—23rd Circuit Court, PO Box 838, Tawas City, MI 48764. 517-362-3497. Fax: 517-362-1421. 9AM-5PM (EST). Access by: Phone, mail, in person.

Misdemeanor, Civil Actions Under $10,000, Eviction, Small Claims—81st District Court, PO Box 388, Tawas City, MI 48764. 517-362-4441. Fax: 517-362-3494. 8AM-5PM (EST). Access by: Mail, in person.

Probate—Probate Court, PO Box 421, Tawas City, MI 48764. 517-362-3991. Fax: 517-362-1459. 8AM-5PM (EST). Access by: Mail, in person.

Iron County

Real Estate Recording—Iron County Register of Deeds, 2 South Sixth Street, Courthouse Annex, Suite 11, Crystal Falls, MI 49920. 906-875-3321. Fax: 906-875-4626. 8AM-Noon, 12:30-4PM (CST).

Felony, Civil Actions Over $10,000—41st Circuit Court, 2 South 6th St, Crystal Falls, MI 49920. 906-875-3221. Fax: 906-875-3670. 8AM-4PM (CST). Access by: Fax, mail, in person.

Misdemeanor, Civil Actions Under $10,000, Eviction, Small Claims—95 B District Court, 2 South 6th St., Crystal Falls, MI 49920. 906-875-6658. 8AM-4PM (CST). Access by: Mail, in person.

Probate—Probate Court, 2 South 6th St., Crystal Falls, MI 49920. 906-875-3121. Fax: 906-875-6775. 8AM-Noon, 12:30-4PM (CST). Access by: Mail, in person.

Isabella County

Real Estate Recording—Isabella County Register of Deeds, 200 North Main Street, Mt. Pleasant, MI 48858. 517-772-0911. Fax: 517-773-7431. 8AM-4:30PM (EST).

Felony, Civil Actions Over $10,000—21st Circuit Court, 200 North Main St, Mount Pleasant, MI 48858. 517-772-0911. 8AM-4:30PM (EST). Access by: Mail, in person.

Misdemeanor, Civil Actions Under $10,000, Eviction, Small Claims—76th District Court, 200 North Main St., Mount Pleasant, MI 48858. 517-772-0911. Fax: 517-773-2419. 8AM-4:30PM (EST). Access by: Mail, in person.

Probate—Probate Court, 200 N Main St, Mount Pleasant, MI 48858. 517-772-0911. Fax: 517-773-2419. 8AM-4:30PM (EST). Access by: Mail, in person.

Jackson County

Real Estate Recording—Jackson County Register of Deeds, 120 West Michigan Avenue, 11th Floor, Jackson, MI 49201. 517-788-4350. Fax: 517-788-4686. 8AM-5PM (EST).

Felony, Civil Actions Over $10,000—4th Circuit Court, 312 South Jackson St, Jackson, MI 49201. 517-788-4268. 8AM-5PM (EST). Access by: Phone, mail, in person.

Misdemeanor, Civil Actions Under $10,000, Eviction, Small Claims—12th District Court, 312 South Jackson St., Jackson, MI 49201. 517-788-4260. Fax: 517-788-4262. 7AM-6PM (EST). Access by: Fax, mail, in person.

Probate—Probate Court, 120 West Michigan Ave, Jackson, MI 49201. 517-788-4290. 8AM-Noon, 1-4:30PM (EST).

Kalamazoo County

Real Estate Recording—Kalamazoo County Register of Deeds, 201 West Kalamazoo Avenue, Kalamazoo, MI 49007. 616-383-8970. 8AM-4:30PM (EST).

Felony, Civil Actions Over $10,000—9th Circuit Court, 227 West Michigan St, Kalamazoo, MI 49007. 616-384-8250. 9AM-4PM (EST). Access by: Mail, in person.

Misdemeanor, Civil Actions Under $10,000, Eviction, Small Claims—8th District Court, 227 West Michigan St., Kalamazoo, MI 49007. 616-384-8171. Fax: 616-384-8047. 8:30AM-4PM (EST). Access by: Fax, mail, in person.

9th District Court Division 1, 416 S. Rose, Kalamazoo, MI 49007. 616-337-8379. Fax: 616-337-8936. 8AM-4:15PM (EST). Access by: Mail, in person.

9th District Court Division 2, 7810 Shaver Rd., Portage, MI 49002. 616-329-4590. Fax: 616-329-4519. 8AM-4:30PM (EST). Access by: Mail, in person.

Probate—Probate Court, 227 West Michigan Ave., Kalamazoo, MI 49007. 616-383-8666. Fax: 616-383-8685. 9AM-Noon, 1-5PM M; 8AM-Noon, 1-5PM T-F (EST). Access by: Mail, in person.

Kalkaska County

Real Estate Recording—Kalkaska County Register of Deeds, 605 North Birch Street, Kalkaska, MI 49646. 616-258-3315. Fax: 616-258-3318. 9AM-5PM (EST).

Felony, Civil Actions Over $10,000—46th Circuit Court, PO Box 10, Kalkaska, MI 49646. 616-258-3300. 9AM-5PM (EST). Access by: Mail, in person.

Misdemeanor, Civil Actions Under $10,000, Eviction, Small Claims—87th District Court, PO Box 780, Kalkaska, MI 49684. 616-258-9031. Fax: 616-258-2424. 8AM-4:30PM (EST). Access by: Phone, mail, in person.

Probate—Probate Court, 605 North Birch, PO Box 780, Kalkaska, MI 49646. 616-258-3330. Fax: 616-258-3329. 9AM-Noon, 1-5PM (EST). Access by: Mail.

Kent County

Real Estate Recording—Kent County Register of Deeds, 300 Monroe Avenue NW, Grand Rapids, MI 49503. 616-336-3558. 8AM-5PM (EST).

Felony, Civil Actions Over $10,000—17th Circuit Court, 333 Monroe Ave NW, Grand Rapids, MI 49503. 616-336-3679. Fax: 616-336-3349. 8AM-5PM (EST). Access by: Mail, in person.

Misdemeanor, Civil Actions Under $10,000, Eviction, Small Claims—61st District Court-Grand Rapids, 333 Monroe Ave NW, Grand Rapids, MI 49503. Civil: 616-456-3370. Criminal: 616-456-3370. Fax: 616-456-3311. 7:45AM-4:45PM (EST). Access by: Mail, in person.

59th District Court-Grandville & Walker, 3181 Wilson Ave SW, Grandville, MI 49418. 616-538-9660. Fax: 616-538-5144. 8:30AM-Noon,1-5PM (EST). Access by: Mail, in person.

62 B District Court-Kentwood, PO Box 8848, Kentwood, MI 49518. 616-698-9310. Fax: 616-698-8199. 8AM-5PM (EST). Access by: Mail, in person.

63rd District Court-1st Division, 105 Maple St, Rockford, MI 49341. 616-866-1576. Fax: 616-866-3080. 8AM-5PM (EST). Access by: Mail, in person.

62 A District Court-Wyoming, 2650 De Hoop Ave SW, Wyoming, MI 49509. 616-530-7385. Fax: 616-249-3419. 8AM-5PM (EST). Access by: Mail, in person.

Probate—Probate Court, 320 Ottawa NW, Grand Rapids, MI 49503. 616-336-3630. Fax: 616-336-3574. 8:30AM-5PM (EST).

Keweenaw County

Real Estate Recording—Keweenaw County Register of Deeds, 4th Street, Courthouse, Eagle River, MI 49924. 906-337-2229. Fax: 906-337-2795. 9AM-4PM (EST).

Felony, Civil Actions Over $10,000—12th Circuit Court, HCI Box 607, Eagle River, MI 49924. 906-337-2229. Fax: 906-337-2795. 9AM-4PM (EST). Access by: Mail, in person.

Misdemeanor, Civil Actions Under $10,000, Eviction, Small Claims—97th District Court, HCI Box 607, Eagle River, MI 49924. 906-337-2229. Fax: 906-337-2795. 9AM-4PM (EST). Access by: Mail, in person.

Probate—Probate Court, H-C 1, PO Box 607, Eagle River, MI 49924. 906-337-1927. Fax: 906-337-2795. 9AM-4PM (EST).

Lake County

Real Estate Recording—Lake County Register of Deeds, 800 Tenth Street, Courthouse, Baldwin, MI 49304. 616-745-4641. Fax: 616-745-2241. 8:30AM-Noon, 1-5PM (EST).

Felony, Civil Actions Over $10,000—51st Circuit Court, PO Drawer B, Baldwin, MI 49304. 616-745-4641. 8:30AM-5PM (EST). Access by: Mail, in person.

Misdemeanor, Civil Actions Under $10,000, Eviction, Small Claims—78th District Court, PO Box 73, Baldwin, MI 49304. 616-745-2738. Fax: 616-745-2739. 8AM-5PM (EST). Access by: Mail, in person.

Probate—Lake County Trial Court, PO Box 1330, Baldwin, MI 49304. 616-745-4614. Fax: 616-745-1330. 8:30AM-5PM (EST). Access by: Mail, in person.

Lapeer County

Real Estate Recording—Lapeer County Register of Deeds, 279 North Court Street, Lapeer, MI 48446. 810-667-0211. 8AM-5PM (EST).

Felony, Civil Actions Over $10,000—40th Circuit Court, 255 Clay St, Lapeer, MI 48446. 810-667-0358. 8AM-5PM (EST). Access by: Mail, in person.

Misdemeanor, Civil Actions Under $10,000, Eviction, Small Claims—71 A District Court, 255 Clay St., Lapeer, MI 48446. 810-667-0300. Fax: 810-667-0297. 8AM-5PM (EST). Access by: Fax, mail, in person.

Probate—Probate Court, 255 Clay St., Lapeer, MI 48446. 810-667-0261. Fax: 810-667-0390. 8AM-5PM (EST). Access by: Mail, in person.

Leelanau County

Real Estate Recording—Leelanau County Register of Deeds, 301 S. Cedar, Leland, MI 49654. 616-256-9682. Fax: 616-256-7850. 9AM-5PM (EST).

Felony, Civil Actions Over $10,000—13th Circuit Court, PO Box 467, Leland, MI 49654. 616-256-9824. Fax: 616-256-7850. 9AM-5PM (EST). Access by: Mail, in person.

Misdemeanor, Civil Actions Under $10,000, Eviction, Small Claims—86th District Court, PO Box 486, Leland, MI 49654. 616-256-9931. Fax: 616-256-7850. 8AM-4PM (EST). Access by: Phone, fax, mail, in person.

Probate—Probate Court/Juvenile Division, PO Box 595, Leland, MI 49654. 616-256-9803. Fax: 616-256-9845. 9AM-5PM (EST). Access by: Mail, in person.

Lenawee County

Real Estate Recording—Lenawee County Register of Deeds, 301 N. Main St., Adrian, MI 49221. 517-264-4538. Fax: 517-264-4770. 8AM-4:30PM (EST).

Felony, Civil Actions Over $10,000—39th Circuit Court, 425 North Main St, Adrian, MI 49221. 517-264-4597. 8AM-4:30PM (EST). Access by: Mail, in person.

Misdemeanor, Civil Actions Under $10,000, Eviction, Small Claims—2nd District Court, 425 North Main St., Adrian, MI 49221. 517-263-8831. Fax: 517-264-4780. 8AM-4:30PM (EST). Access by: Fax, mail, in person.

Probate—Probate Court, 425 North Main St., Adrian, MI 49221. 517-264-4614. Fax: 517-264-4616. 8AM-4:30PM (EST). Access by: Mail, in person.

Livingston County

Real Estate Recording—Livingston County Register of Deeds, Courthouse, Howell, MI 48843. 517-546-0270. Fax: 517-546-5966. 8AM-5PM (EST).

Felony, Civil Actions Over $10,000—44th Circuit Court, 210 South Highlander Way, Howell, MI 48843. 517-546-9816. 8AM-5PM (EST). Access by: Mail, in person.

Misdemeanor, Civil Actions Under $10,000, Eviction, Small Claims—53 B District Court, 224 N First, Brighton, MI 48116. Civil: 810-229-6615. Criminal: 810-229-6615. Fax: 810-229-1770. 8AM-4:45PM (EST). Access by: Fax, mail, in person.

53 A District Court, 300 South Highlander Way, Howell, MI 48843. 517-548-1000. Fax: 517-548-9445. 8AM-4:45PM (EST). Access by: Mail, in person.

Probate—Probate Court, 200 East Grand River, Howell, MI 48843. 517-546-3750. Fax: 517-546-3731. 8AM-5PM (EST).

Luce County

Real Estate Recording—Luce County Register of Deeds, County Government Building, Newberry, MI 49868. 906-293-5521. Fax: 906-293-3581. 8AM-4PM (EST).

Felony, Civil Actions Over $10,000—11th Circuit Court, East Court St, Newberry, MI 49868. 906-293-5521. Fax: 906-293-3581. 8AM-4PM (EST). Access by: Mail, in person.

Misdemeanor, Civil Actions Under $10,000, Eviction, Small Claims—92nd District Court, 407 W Harrie, Newberry, MI 49868. 906-293-5531. Fax: 906-293-3581. 8AM-4PM (EST). Access by: Phone, mail, in person.

Probate—Probate Court, 407 W. Harrie, Newberry, MI 49868. 906-293-5601. Fax: 906-293-3581. 8AM-Noon, 1-4PM (EST). Access by: Mail, in person.

Mackinac County

Real Estate Recording—Mackinac County Register of Deeds, 100 Marley Street, Saint Ignace, MI 49781. 906-643-7306. Fax: 906-643-7302. 8:30AM-4:30PM (EST).

Felony, Civil Actions Over $10,000—50th Circuit Court, 100 Marley, St Ignace, MI 49781. 906-643-7300. Fax: 906-643-7302. 8:30AM-4:30PM (EST). Access by: Mail, in person.

Misdemeanor, Civil Actions Under $10,000, Eviction, Small Claims—92nd District Court, 100 Marley, St Ignace, MI 49781. 906-643-7321. Fax: 906-643-7302. 8:30AM-4:30PM (EST). Access by: Mail, in person.

Probate—Probate Court, 100 Marley, St Ignace, MI 49781. 906-643-7303. Fax: 906-643-7302. 8:30AM-Noon, 1-4:30PM (EST). Access by: Mail, in person.

Macomb County

Real Estate Recording—Macomb County Register of Deeds, 10 North Main, Mt. Clemens, MI 48043. 810-469-5342. Fax: 810-469-5130. 8:30AM-5PM (EST).

Felony, Civil Actions Over $10,000—16th Circuit Court, 40 N Main St, Mount Clemens, MI 48043. 810-469-5208. 8AM-4:30PM (EST). Access by: Mail, in person.

Misdemeanor, Civil Actions Under $10,000, Eviction, Small Claims—41 B District Court-Clinton, TWP, 40700 Romeo Plank Rd, Clinton Township, MI 48038. 810-286-8010. Fax: 810-228-2555. 8:30AM-4:30PM (EST). Access by: Mail, in person.

42nd District Court Division 2 (Lenox, Chesterfield), 36540 Green St, New Baltimore, MI 48047. Civil: 810-725-9266. Criminal: 810-725-9520. Fax: 810-469-5516. 8:30AM-5PM (EST). Access by: Mail, in person.

42nd District Court Division 1, 14713 Thirty-three Mile Rd., Romeo, MI 48065. 810-752-9679. Fax: 810-469-5515. 8:30AM-5:00PM (EST). Access by: Mail, in person.

39th District Court-Roseville and Frasier, 29733 Gratiot Ave, Roseville, MI 48066. 810-773-2010. Fax: 810-774-3310. 8AM-4:30PM (EST). Access by: Mail, in person.

41 A District Court-Shelby, 51660 Van Dyke, Shelby Township, MI 48316. 810-739-7325. Fax: 810-726-4555. 8AM-4:30PM (EST). Access by: Mail, in person.

40th District Court-St. Clair Shores, 27701 Jefferson, St. Clair Shores, MI 48081. 810-445-5281. Civil: 810-445-5282. Criminal: 810-445-5288. Fax: 810-445-4003. 8:30AM-5PM (EST). Access by: Mail, in person.

41 A District Court-Sterling Heights, 40555 Utica Rd, Sterling Heights, MI 48311. 810-977-6123. 8AM-4:30PM (EST). Access by: Mail, in person.

37th District Court-Warren and Center Line, 8300 Common Rd., Warren, MI 48093. 810-574-4928. Fax: 810-547-4932. 8:30AM-4:30PM (EST). Access by: Mail, in person.

Civil Actions Under $10,000, Eviction, Small Claims—41 B District Court-Mt Clemens, 1 Crocker Blvd, Mount Clemens, MI 48043. 810-469-6870. Fax: 810-469-5037. 8AM-4:30PM (EST). Access by: Mail, in person.

Probate—Probate Court, 21850 Dumham, Mount Clemens, MI 48043. 810-469-5290. 8:30AM-5PM (EST). Access by: Mail, in person.

Manistee County

Real Estate Recording—Manistee County Register of Deeds, 415 Third Street, Courthouse, Manistee, MI 49660. 616-723-2146. 8:30AM-12, 1-5PM (EST).

Felony, Civil Actions Over $10,000—19th Circuit Court, 415 3rd St, Manistee, MI 49660. 616-723-3331. Fax: 616-723-1492. 8:30AM-Noon, 1-5PM (EST). Access by: Mail, in person.

Misdemeanor, Civil Actions Under $10,000, Eviction, Small Claims—85th District Court, 415 3rd St, Manistee, MI 49660. 616-723-5010. Fax: 616-723-1491. 8:30AM-5PM (EST). Access by: In person only.

Probate—Probate Court, 415 3rd St, Manistee, MI 49660. 616-723-3261. Fax: 616-723-1492. 8:30AM-Noon, 1-5PM (EST).

Marquette County

Real Estate Recording—Marquette County Register of Deeds, 234 West Baraga Avenue, Courthouse, Marquette, MI 49855. 906-228-1528. Fax: 906-228-1625. 8AM-5PM (EST).

Felony, Civil Actions Over $10,000—25th Circuit Court, 234 W Baraga, Marquette, MI 49855. 906-228-1525. Fax: 906-228-1500. 8AM-5PM (EST). Access by: Mail, in person.

Misdemeanor, Civil Actions Under $10,000, Eviction, Small Claims—96th District Court, County Courthouse, Marquette, MI 49855. 906-228-1550. Fax: 906-228-8500. 8:30AM-5PM (EST). Access by: Fax, mail, in person.

Probate—Probate Court, 234 W Baraga, Marquette, MI 49855. 906-228-1514. Fax: 906-228-1500. 8AM-5PM (EST). Access by: Mail, in person.

Mason County

Real Estate Recording—Mason County Register of Deeds, 300 E. Ludington Avenue, Courthouse, Ludington, MI 49431. 616-843-4466. Fax: 616-843-1972. 9AM-5PM (EST).

Felony, Civil Actions Over $10,000—51st Circuit Court, 304 E Ludington Ave, Ludington, MI 49431. 616-845-1445. 9AM-5PM (EST). Access by: Phone, mail, in person.

Misdemeanor, Civil Actions Under $10,000, Eviction, Small Claims—79th District Court, County Court, Ludington, MI 49431. 616-843-4130. Fax: 616-845-7779. 8AM-5PM (EST). Access by: Fax, mail, in person.

Probate—Probate Court, PO Box 186, Ludington, MI 49431. 616-843-8666. Fax: 616-843-1972. 9AM-Noon, 1-5PM (EST).

Mecosta County

Real Estate Recording—Mecosta County Register of Deeds, 400 Elm Street, Big Rapids, MI 49307. 616-592-0148. 8:30AM-5PM (EST).

Felony, Civil Actions Over $10,000—49th Circuit Court, 400 Elm, Big Rapids, MI 49307. 616-592-0783. Fax: 616-592-0193. 8:30AM-5PM (EST). Access by: Mail, in person.

Misdemeanor, Civil Actions Under $10,000, Eviction, Small Claims—77th District Court, 400 Elm, Big Rapids, MI 49307. 616-592-0799. Fax: 616-796-2180. 8:30AM-4:30PM (EST). Access by: Fax, mail, in person. Signed release required for employment screening.

Probate—Probate Court, PO Box 820, Big Rapids, MI 49307. 616-592-0135. Fax: 616-592-0100. 8:30AM-5PM (EST).

Menominee County

Real Estate Recording—Menominee County Register of Deeds, Courthouse, 839 10th Ave., Menominee, MI 49858. 906-863-2822. 8AM-4:30PM (CST).

Felony, Civil Actions Over $10,000—41st Circuit Court, 839 10th Ave, Menominee, MI 49858. 906-863-9968. Fax: 906-863-8839. 8AM-4:30PM (CST). Access by: Fax, mail, in person.

Misdemeanor, Civil Actions Under $10,000, Eviction, Small Claims—95th District Court, 839 10th Ave, Menominee, MI 49858. 906-863-8532. Fax: 906-863-8839. 8AM-4:30PM (CST). Access by: Phone, fax, mail, in person.

Probate—Probate Court, 839 10th Ave., Menominee, MI 49858. 906-863-2634. Fax: 906-863-8839. 8AM-4:30PM (CST). Access by: Mail, in person.

Midland County

Real Estate Recording—Midland County Register of Deeds, 220 West Ellsworth Street, County Services Building, Midland, MI 48640. 517-832-6820. Fax: 517-832-6608. 8AM-5PM (EST).

Felony, Civil Actions Over $10,000—42nd Circuit Court, Courthouse, 301 W Main St, Midland, MI 48640. 517-832-6735. Fax: 517-832-6610. 8AM-5PM (EST). Access by: Mail, in person.

Civil Actions Under $10,000, Eviction, Small Claims—75th District Court-Civil Division, 301 W Main St, Midland, MI 48640. 517-832-6701. 8:00AM-5:00PM (EST). Access by: Mail, in person.

Misdemeanor—75th District Court-Criminal Division, 301 W Main St, Midland, MI 48640. 517-832-6702. 8:30AM-4:30PM (EST). Access by: Mail, in person.

Probate—Probate Court, 301 W Main St, Midland, MI 48640. 517-832-6880. Fax: 517-832-6607. 8AM-5PM (EST). Access by: Mail, in person.

Missaukee County

Real Estate Recording—Missaukee County Register of Deeds, 111 S. Canal St., Lake City, MI 49651. 616-839-4967. Fax: 616-839-3684. 9AM-5PM (EST).

Felony, Civil Actions Over $10,000—28th Circuit Court, PO Box 800, Lake City, MI 49651. 616-839-4967. Fax: 616-839-3684. 9AM-5PM (EST). Access by: Phone, fax, mail, in person.

Misdemeanor, Civil Actions Under $10,000, Eviction, Small Claims—84th District Court, PO Box 800, Lake City, MI 49651. 616-839-4590. 9AM-5PM (EST). Access by: Mail, in person.

Probate—Probate Court, PO Box 800, Lake City, MI 49651. 616-839-2266. Fax: 616-839-3684. 9AM-Noon, 1-5PM (EST). Access by: Mail, in person.

Monroe County

Real Estate Recording—Monroe County Register of Deeds, 106 East First Street, Monroe, MI 48161. 313-243-7046. 8:30AM-5PM (EST).

Felony, Civil Actions Over $10,000—38th Circuit Court, 106 E 1st St, Monroe, MI 48161. 313-243-7081. Fax: 313-243-7107. 8:30AM-4:30PM (EST). Access by: Mail, in person.

Misdemeanor, Civil Actions Under $10,000, Eviction, Small Claims—1st District Court, 106 E 1st St, Monroe, MI 48161. 313-243-7030. Fax: 313-243-7401. 8:30AM-4:45PM (EST). Access by: Mail, in person.

Probate—Probate Court, 106 E 1st St, Monroe, MI 48161. 313-243-7018. 8AM-Noon, 1-5PM (EST).

Montcalm County

Real Estate Recording—Montcalm County Register of Deeds, 211 West Main Street, Courthouse, Stanton, MI 48888. 517-831-7337. Fax: 517-831-7320. 8AM-Noon, 1-5PM (EST).

Felony, Civil Actions Over $10,000—8th Circuit Court, PO Box 368, Stanton, MI 48888. 517-831-7341. Fax: 517-831-7474. 8AM-5PM (EST). Access by: Mail, in person.

Misdemeanor, Civil Actions Under $10,000, Eviction, Small Claims—64 B District Court, PO Box 608, Stanton, MI 48888. 517-831-5226. Fax: 517-831-4747. 8AM-5PM (EST). Access by: Mail, in person.

Probate—Probate Court, PO Box 368, Stanton, MI 48888. 517-831-5226. Fax: 517-831-7314. 8AM-5PM (EST).

Montmorency County

Real Estate Recording—Montmorency County Register of Deeds, 12265 M-32, Courthouse, Atlanta, MI 49709. 517-785-3374. Fax: 517-785-2825. 8:30AM-Noon, 1-4:30PM (EST).

Felony, Civil Actions Over $10,000—26th Circuit Court, PO Box 415, Atlanta, MI 49709. 517-785-4794. Fax: 517-785-2266. 8:30AM-Noon,1-4:30PM (EST). Access by: Phone, fax, mail, in person.

Misdemeanor, Civil Actions Under $10,000, Eviction, Small Claims—88th District Court, 12265 M-32, County Courthouse, PO Box 415, Atlanta, MI 49709. 517-785-3122. Fax: 517-785-2376. 8:30AM-4:30PM (EST). Access by: Mail, in person.

Probate—Probate Court, PO Box 415, Atlanta, MI 49709. 517-785-4403. (EST). Access by: Mail, in person.

Muskegon County

Real Estate Recording—Muskegon County Register of Deeds, County Building, Muskegon, MI 49442. 616-724-6271. Fax: 616-724-6842. 8AM-5PM; Recording hours: 8AM-4:30PM (EST).

Felony, Civil Actions Over $10,000—14th Circuit Court, 990 Terrace, 6th Floor, Muskegon, MI 49442. 616-724-6447. Fax: 616-724-6695. 8AM-5PM (EST). Access by: Mail, in person.

Misdemeanor, Civil Actions Under $10,000, Eviction, Small Claims—60th District Court, 990 Terrace, 1st Floor, Muskegon, MI 49442. 616-724-6250. Fax: 616-722-7003. 8:30AM-4:45PM (EST). Access by: Mail, in person.

Probate—Probate Court, 990 Terrace St, 5th Floor, Muskegon, MI 49442. 616-724-6241. Fax: 616-724-6232. 8AM-5PM (EST).

Newaygo County

Real Estate Recording—Newaygo County Register of Deeds, 1087 Newell Street, County Administration Building, White Cloud, MI 49349. 616-689-7246. Fax: 616-689-7205. 8AM-5PM (EST).

Felony, Civil Actions Over $10,000—27th Circuit Court, PO Box 885, White Cloud, MI 49349-0885. 616-689-7269. Fax: 616-689-2120. 8AM-5PM (EST). Access by: Fax, mail, in person.

Misdemeanor, Civil Actions Under $10,000, Eviction, Small Claims—78th District Court, 1092 Newell St, White Cloud, MI 49349. 616-689-7257. Fax: 616-689-7258. 8AM-5PM (EST). Access by: Fax, mail, in person.

Probate—Probate Court, 1092 Newell, White Cloud, MI 49349. 616-689-7270. Fax: 616-689-7276. 8AM-Noon, 1-5PM (EST). Access by: Mail, in person.

Oakland County

Real Estate Recording—Oakland County Register of Deeds, 1200 North Telegraph Road, Dept 480, Pontiac, MI 48341. 248-858-0605. 8:30AM-5PM (EST).

Felony, Civil Actions Over $10,000—6th Circuit Court, 1200 N Telegraph Rd, Pontiac, MI 48341. 248-858-0581. 8:30AM-4:30PM (EST). Access by: Mail, in person.

Misdemeanor, Civil Actions Under $10,000, Eviction, Small Claims—45 A District Court-Berkley, 3338 Coolidge, Berkley, MI 48072. 248-544-3300. Fax: 248-546-2416. 8:30AM-4:30PM (EST). Access by: Mail, in person.

48th District Court, 4280 Telegraph Rd, Bloomfield Hills, MI 48302. 248-647-1141. Fax: 248-647-8955. 8:30AM-4:30PM (EST). Access by: Mail, in person.

52nd District Court-Division 2, 5850 Lorac, PO Box 169, Clarkston, MI 48347-0169. Civil: 248-625-4994. Criminal: 248-625-4888. Fax: 248-625-5602. 8:30AM-4:30PM (EST). Access by: Phone, fax, mail, in person.

47th District Court-Farmington, Farmington Hills, 32795 W Ten Mile Rd, Farmington, MI 48336. 248-477-5630. Fax: 248-477-2441. 8:30AM-4:30PM (EST). Access by: Mail, in person.

43rd District Court, 43 E Nine Mile Rd, Hazel Park, MI 48030. 248-547-3034. Fax: 248-546-4088. 8:30AM-5PM (EST). Access by: Mail, in person.

45 B District Court, 13600 Oak Park Blvd, Oak Park, MI 48237. 248-542-7042. Fax: 248-691-7158. 9AM-4:45PM (EST). Access by: Mail, in person.

52nd District Court-Division 3, 135 Barclay Circle, Rochester Hills, MI 48307. Civil: 248-853-5553 X302. Criminal: 248-853-5553 X300. Fax: 248-853-3277. 8:15AM-4:45PM (EST). Access by: Mail, in person. Ext 300.

44th District Court-Royal Oak, 211 Williams St, Royal Oak, MI 48068. 248-546-7780. Fax: 248-546-6366. 8AM-4:30PM (EST). Access by: Mail, in person.

46th District Court, 26000 Evergreen Rd, Southfield, MI 48076. 248-354-9506. Fax: 248-354-5315. 8AM-5PM (EST). Access by: Mail, in person.

52nd District Court-Division 4 (Troy, Clawson), 500 W Big Beaver Rd, Troy, MI 48084. 248-528-0400. Fax: 248-528-3588. 8:30AM-4:45PM (EST). Access by: Mail, in person.

52nd District Court-Division 1, 48150 Grand River, Walled Lake, MI 48374. Civil: 248-305-6080. Criminal: 248-305-6460. (EST). Access by: Mail, in person.

51st District Court-Waterford, 5100 Civic Center Dr, Waterford, MI 48329. 248-674-4655. 8:30AM-4:45PM (EST). Access by: Mail, in person.

Civil Actions Under $10,000, Eviction, Small Claims—50th District Court-Pontiac Civil Division, 70 N Saganaw, Pontiac, MI 48342. 248-857-8090. Fax: 248-857-6028. 8:30AM-5PM (EST). Access by: Mail, in person.

Misdemeanor—50th District Court-Pontiac Criminal Division, 70 N Saganaw, Pontiac, MI 48342. 248-857-8027. Fax: 248-857-6028. 8:30AM-5PM (EST). Access by: Mail, in person.

Probate—Probate Court, 1200 N Telegraph Rd, Pontiac, MI 48341. 248-858-0260. Fax: 248-452-2016. 8:30AM-5PM (EST). Access by: Mail, in person.

Oceana County

Real Estate Recording—Oceana County Register of Deeds, 100 State Street, Courthouse, Hart, MI 49420. 616-873-4158. 9AM-5PM (EST).

Felony, Civil Actions Over $10,000—27th Circuit Court, PO Box 189, Hart, MI 49420. 616-873-3977. 9AM-Noon,1-5PM (EST). Access by: Mail, in person.

Misdemeanor, Civil Actions Under $10,000, Eviction, Small Claims—79th District Court, PO Box 167, Hart, MI 49420. 616-873-4530. Fax: 616-873-4177. 8AM-5PM (EST). Access by: In person only.

Probate—Probate Court, PO Box 129, Hart, MI 49420. 616-873-3666. Fax: 616-873-4177. 9AM-Noon, 1-5PM (EST). Access by: Mail, in person.

Ogemaw County

Real Estate Recording—Ogemaw County Register of Deeds, 806 West Houghton Ave, Room 104, West Branch, MI 48661. 517-345-0728. 8:30AM-4:30PM (EST).

Felony, Civil Actions Over $10,000—34th Circuit Court, 806 W Houghton, West Branch, MI 48661. 517-345-0215. Fax: 517-345-4939. 8:30AM-4:30PM (EST). Access by: Phone, fax, mail, in person.

Misdemeanor, Civil Actions Under $10,000, Eviction, Small Claims—82nd District Court, PO Box 365, West Branch, MI 48661. 517-345-5040. Fax: 517-345-5910. 8:30AM-4:30PM (EST). Access by: Fax, mail, in person.

Probate—Probate Court, County Courthouse, Rm 203, West Branch, MI 48661. 517-345-0145. Fax: 517-345-5901. 8:30AM-Noon, 1-4:30PM (EST). Access by: Mail, in person.

Ontonagon County

Real Estate Recording—Ontonagon County Register of Deeds, 725 Greenland Road, Ontonagon, MI 49953. 906-884-4255. Fax: 906-884-2916. 8:30AM-4:30PM (EST).

Felony, Civil Actions Over $10,000—32nd Circuit Court, 725 Greenland Rd, Ontonagon, MI 49953. 906-884-4255. 8:30AM-4:30PM (EST). Access by: Mail, in person.

Misdemeanor, Civil Actions Under $10,000, Eviction, Small Claims—98th District Court, 725 Greenland Rd, Ontonagon, MI 49953. 906-884-2865. Fax: 906-884-2916. 8:30AM-4:30PM (EST). Access by: Mail, in person.

Probate—Probate Court, 725 Greenland Rd, Ontonagon, MI 49953. 906-884-4117. Fax: 906-884-2916. 8:30AM-4:30PM (EST).

Osceola County

Real Estate Recording—Osceola County Register of Deeds, 301 West Upton Ave., Reed City, MI 49677. 616-832-6113. 9AM-5PM (EST).

Felony, Civil Actions Over $10,000—49th Circuit Court, 301 W Upton, Osceola, MI 49677. 616-832-6102. Fax: 616-832-6149. 9AM-5PM (EST). Access by: Phone, fax, mail, in person.

Misdemeanor, Civil Actions Under $10,000, Eviction, Small Claims—77th District Court, 410 W Upton, Osceola, MI 49677. 616-832-6155. Fax: 616-832-9190. 8:30AM-4:30PM (EST). Access by: Fax, mail, in person.

Probate—Probate Court, 410 W Upton, Osceola, MI 49677. 616-832-6124. Fax: 616-832-9190. 8:30AM-Noon, 1-4:30PM (EST). Access by: In person only.

Oscoda County

Real Estate Recording—Oscoda County Register of Deeds, 310 Morenci Street, Courthouse, Mio, MI 48647. 517-826-1116. Fax: 517-826-3657. 10AM-4PM (EST).

Felony, Civil Actions Over $10,000—23rd Circuit Court, PO Box 399, Mio, MI 48647. 517-826-3241. Fax: 517-826-3657. 8:30AM-4:30PM (EST). Access by: Mail, in person.

Misdemeanor, Civil Actions Under $10,000, Eviction, Small Claims—82nd District Court, PO Box 365, West Branch, MI 48661. 517-345-5040. 8:30AM-4:30PM (EST). Access by: Mail, in person.

Probate—Probate Court, PO Box 399, Mio, MI 48647. 517-826-1100. (EST).

Otsego County

Real Estate Recording—Otsego County Register of Deeds, 225 West Main St., Room 108, Gaylord, MI 49735. 517-732-6484. Fax: 517-732-1562. 8AM-Noon, 1-4:30PM (EST).

Felony, Civil Actions Over $10,000—46th Circuit Court, 225 Main St, Gaylord, MI 49735. 517-732-6484. 8AM-4:30PM (EST). Access by: Phone, mail, in person.

Misdemeanor, Civil Actions Under $10,000, Eviction, Small Claims—87th District Court, PO Box 1218, Gaylord, MI 49735. 517-732-6486. Fax: 517-732-5130. 8AM-4:30PM (EST). Access by: Mail, in person.

Probate—Probate Court, 225 Main St, Gaylord, MI 49735. 517-732-6489. Fax: 517-732-1877. 8AM-Noon, 1-4:30PM (EST). Access by: In person only.

Ottawa County

Real Estate Recording—Ottawa County Register of Deeds, 414 Washington Avenue, Room 305, Grand Haven, MI 49417. 616-846-8240. Fax: 616-846-8131. 8AM-5PM (EST).

Felony, Civil Actions Over $10,000—20th Circuit Court, 414 Washington Ave, Grand Haven, MI 49417. 616-846-8310. Fax: 616-846-8138. 8AM-5PM (EST). Access by: Fax, mail, in person.

Misdemeanor, Civil Actions Under $10,000, Eviction, Small Claims—58th District Court-Grand Haven, 414 Washington Ave, Grand Haven, MI 49417. 616-846-8280. Fax: 616-392-5013. 8AM-5PM (EST). Access by: Mail, in person.

58th District Court-Holland, 57 W 8th St, Holland, MI 49423. 616-392-6991. Fax: 616-392-5013. 8AM-5PM (EST). Access by: Mail, in person.

58th District Court-Hudsonville, 3100 Port Sheldon, Hudsonville, MI 49426. 616-662-3100. Fax: 616-669-2950. 8AM-5PM (EST). Access by: In person only.

Probate—Probate Court, 12120 Fillmore St, West Olive, MI 49460. 616-786-4110. Fax: 616-786-4154. 8AM-5PM (EST). Access by: Mail, in person.

Presque Isle County

Real Estate Recording—Presque Isle County Register of Deeds, 151 East Huron Street, Rogers City, MI 49779. 517-734-2676. Fax: 517-734-7834. 9AM-5PM (EST).

Felony, Civil Actions Over $10,000—26th Circuit Court, PO Box 110, Rogers City, MI 49779. 517-734-3288. Fax: 517-734-7635. 9AM-5PM (EST). Access by: Phone, fax, mail, in person.

Misdemeanor, Civil Actions Under $10,000, Eviction, Small Claims—89th District Court, PO Box 110, Rogers City, MI 49779. 517-734-2411. Fax: 517-734-3400. 8:30AM-4:30PM (EST). Access by: Mail, in person.

Probate—Probate Court, PO Box 110, Rogers City, MI 49779. 517-734-3268. Fax: 517-734-7635. 9AM-Noon, 1-5PM (EST).

Roscommon County

Real Estate Recording—Roscommon County Register of Deeds, 500 Lake Street, Roscommon, MI 48653. 517-275-5931. Fax: 517-275-8640. 8:30AM-4:30PM (EST).

Felony, Civil Actions Over $10,000—34th Circuit Court, PO Box 98, Roscommon, MI 48653. 517-275-5923. Fax: 517-275-8640. 8:30AM-4:30PM (EST). Access by: Mail, in person.

Misdemeanor, Civil Actions Under $10,000, Eviction, Small Claims—83rd District Court, PO Box 189, Roscommon, MI 48653. 517-275-5312. Fax: 517-275-5675. 8:30AM-4:30PM (EST). Access by: Phone, fax, mail, in person.

Probate—Probate Court, PO Box 607, Roscommon, MI 48653. 517-275-5221. Fax: 517-275-8537. 8:30AM-4:30PM (EST). Access by: Mail, in person.

Saginaw County

Real Estate Recording—Saginaw County Register of Deeds, 111 South Michigan Avenue, Saginaw, MI 48602. 517-790-5270. Fax: 517-790-5278. 8AM-5PM (EST).

Felony, Civil Actions Over $10,000—10th Circuit Court, 111 S Michigan Ave, Saginaw, MI 48602. 517-790-5247. Fax: 517-793-8180. 8AM-5:00PM (EST). Access by: Mail, in person.

Civil Actions Under $10,000, Eviction, Small Claims—70th District Court-Civil Division, 111 S Michigan Ave, Saginaw, MI 48602. 517-790-5380. Fax: 517-790-5589. 8AM-4:45PM (EST). Access by: Mail, in person.

Misdemeanor—70th District Court-Criminal Division, 111 S Michigan Ave, Saginaw, MI 48602. 517-790-5385. Fax: 517-790-5589. 8AM-4:45PM (EST). Access by: Fax, mail, in person.

Probate—Probate Court, 111 S Michigan St, Saginaw, MI 48602. 517-790-5320. Fax: 517-790-5328. 8AM-5PM (EST). Access by: Mail, in person.

Sanilac County

Real Estate Recording—Sanilac County Register of Deeds, 60 West Sanilac, Sandusky, MI 48471. 810-648-2313. 8AM-Noon, 1-4:30PM (EST).

Felony, Civil Actions Over $10,000—24th Circuit Court, 60 W Sanilac, Sandusky, MI 48471. 810-648-3212. Fax: 810-648-5479. 8AM-4:30PM (EST). Access by: Mail, in person.

Misdemeanor, Civil Actions Under $10,000, Eviction, Small Claims—73rd District Court, 60 W Sanilac, Sandusky, MI 48471. 810-648-3250. 8AM-4:30PM (EST). Access by: Mail, in person.

Probate—Probate Court, 60 W Sanilac, Po Box 128, Sandusky, MI 48471. 810-648-3221. Fax: 810-648-2900. 8AM-Noon, 1-4:30PM (EST).

Schoolcraft County

Real Estate Recording—Schoolcraft County Register of Deeds, 300 Walnut Street, Room 164, Manistique, MI 49854. 906-341-3618. Fax: 906-341-5680. 8AM-4PM (EST).

Felony, Civil Actions Over $10,000—11th Circuit Court, 300 Walnut St, Rm 164, Manistique, MI 49854. 906-341-3618. 8AM-4PM (EST). Access by: Phone, mail, in person.

Misdemeanor, Civil Actions Under $10,000, Eviction, Small Claims—93rd District Court, 300 Walnut St, Rm 135, Manistique, MI 49854. 906-341-3630. Fax: 906-341-8006. 8AM-4PM (EST). Access by: Fax, mail, in person.

Probate—Probate Court, 300 Walnut St, Manistique, MI 49854. 906-341-2633. 8AM-Noon, 1-4PM (EST).

Shiawassee County

Real Estate Recording—Shiawassee County Register of Deeds, 208 North Shiawassee, Courthouse, Corunna, MI 48817. 517-743-2216. Fax: 517-743-2241. 8AM-5PM (EST).

Felony, Civil Actions Over $10,000—35th Circuit Court, 200 N Shiawassee St, Corunna, MI 48817. 517-743-2302. Fax: 517-743-2241. 8AM-5PM (EST). Access by: Phone, mail, in person.

Misdemeanor, Civil Actions Under $10,000, Eviction, Small Claims—66th District Court, 110 E Mack St, Corunna, MI 48817. 517-743-2244. 8AM-5PM (EST). Access by: Phone, mail, in person.

Probate—Probate Court, 110 E Mack St, Corunna, MI 48817. 517-743-2211. Fax: 517-743-2349. 8AM-5PM (EST).

St. Clair County

Real Estate Recording—St. Clair County Register of Deeds, 201 McMorran Blvd., Room 116, Port Huron, MI 48060. 810-985-2275. Fax: 810-985-4297. 8AM-4:30PM (EST).

Felony, Civil Actions Over $10,000—31st Circuit Court, 201 McMorran Blvd, Port Huron, MI 48060. 810-985-2200. Fax: 810-985-2050. 8AM-4:30PM (EST). Access by: Mail, in person.

Misdemeanor, Civil Actions Under $10,000, Eviction, Small Claims—72nd District Court, 201 McMorran Rd, Port Huron, MI 48060. 810-985-2072. Civil: 810-985-2077. Criminal: 810-985-2077. 8AM-4:30PM (EST). Access by: Mail, in person.

Probate—Probate Court, 201 McMorran Blvd Rm 216, Port Huron, MI 48060. 810-985-2066. Fax: 810-985-2179. 8AM-4:30PM (EST). Access by: Mail, in person.

St. Joseph County

Real Estate Recording—St. Joseph County Register of Deeds, 650 E. Main St., Centreville, MI 49032. 616-467-5553. Fax: 616-467-5600. 9AM-5PM (EST).

Felony, Civil Actions Over $10,000—45th Circuit Court, PO Box 189, Centreville, MI 49032. 616-467-5602. Fax: 616-467-5628. 9AM-5PM (EST). Access by: Mail, in person.

Misdemeanor, Civil Actions Under $10,000, Eviction, Small Claims—3-B District Court, PO Box 67, Centreville,

MI 49032. 616-467-5513. (EST). Access by: Fax, mail, in person. Signed release required for some searches.

Probate—Probate Court, PO Box 190, Centreville, MI 49032. 616-467-5538. Fax: 616-467-5628. 8AM-5PM (EST). Access by: Mail, in person.

Tuscola County

Real Estate Recording—Tuscola County Register of Deeds, 440 North State Street, Caro, MI 48723. 517-672-3840. Fax: 517-672-4266. 8AM-Noon, 1-4:30PM (EST).

Felony, Civil Actions Over $10,000—54th Circuit Court, 440 N State St, Caro, MI 48723. 517-673-5999. Fax: 517-672-4266. 8AM-3:30PM (EST). Access by: Mail, in person.

Misdemeanor, Civil Actions Under $10,000, Eviction, Small Claims—71 B District Court, 440 N State St., Caro, MI 48723. 517-673-5999. Fax: 517-673-0451. 8AM-4:30PM (EST). Access by: Phone, mail, in person.

Probate—Probate Court, 440 N State St, Caro, MI 48723. 517-672-3850. Fax: 517-672-4266. 8AM-Noon, 1-4:30PM (EST). Access by: Mail, in person.

Van Buren County

Real Estate Recording—Van Buren County Register of Deeds, 212 Paw Paw Street, Paw Paw, MI 49079. 616-657-8242. Fax: 616-657-7573. 8:30AM-5PM (EST).

Felony, Civil Actions Over $10,000—36th Circuit Court, 212 Paw Paw St, Paw Paw, MI 49079. 616-657-8218. 8:30AM-5:00PM (EST). Access by: Mail, in person.

Misdemeanor, Civil Actions Under $10,000, Eviction, Small Claims—7th District Court, 212 Paw Paw St, Paw Paw, MI 49079. 616-657-8222. Fax: 616-657-7573. 9AM-4:30PM (EST). Access by: Mail, in person.

7th District Court-West Division, 1007 E Wells, PO Box 311, South Haven, MI 49090. 616-637-5258. Fax: 616-637-9169. 8:30AM-4:30PM (EST). Access by: Mail, in person.

Probate—Probate Court, 212 Paw Paw St, Paw Paw, MI 49079. 616-657-8225. Fax: 616-657-7573. 8:30AM-5PM (EST).

Washtenaw County

Real Estate Recording—Washtenaw County Register of Deeds, 101 East Huron, Courthouse, Ann Arbor, MI 48107. 313-994-2517. 8:30AM-5PM (EST).

Felony, Civil Actions Over $10,000—22nd Circuit Court, PO Box 8645, Ann Arbor, MI 48107-8645. 313-994-2507. 8:30AM-4:30PM (EST). Access by: Phone, mail, in person.

Misdemeanor, Civil Actions Under $10,000, Eviction, Small Claims—14th District Court A-1, 4133 Washtenaw, Ann Arbor, MI 48107-8645. 313-971-6050. Fax: 313-971-5018. 8AM-4:30PM (EST). Access by: Mail, in person.

14th District Court A-3, 122 S Main St, Chelsea, MI 48118. 313-475-8606. Fax: 313-475-0460. 8AM-4:30PM (EST). Access by: Mail, in person.

14th District Court A-4, 7605 N Maple St, Saline, MI 48176. 313-475-8606. Fax: 313-475-0460. 8AM-4:30PM M-F (Office), 8AM-3:30PM M-F (Phone) (EST). Access by: Mail, in person.

14th District Court A-2, 415 W Michigan Ave, Ypsilanti, MI 48197. 313-484-6690. Fax: 313-484-6697. 8AM-4:30PM (EST). Access by: Mail, in person.

Civil Actions Under $10,000, Eviction, Small Claims—14th District Court-B-Civil Division, 7200 S Huron River Dr, Ypsilanti, MI 48197. 313-483-5300. Fax: 313-483-3630. 8AM-5PM (EST). Access by: Mail, in person.

Misdemeanor—14th District Court-B-Criminal Division, 7200 S Huron River Dr, Ypsilanti, MI 48197. 313-483-1333. Fax: 313-483-3630. 8AM-5PM (EST). Access by: Mail, in person.

Civil Actions Under $10,000, Eviction, Small Claims—15th District Court-Civil Division, 101 E Huron, Box 8650, Ann Arbor, MI 48107. 313-994-2749. Fax: 313-994-2617. 8AM-4:30PM (EST). Access by: In person only.

Misdemeanor—15th District Court-Criminal Division, 101 E Huron, Box 8650, Ann Arbor, MI 48107-8650. Civil: 313-994-2749. Criminal: 313-994-2745. Fax: 313-994-2617. 8AM-4:30PM (EST). Access by: In person only.

Probate—Probate Court, PO Box 8645, Ann Arbor, MI 48107. 313-994-2474. Fax: 313-996-3033. 8:30AM-5PM (EST).

Wayne County

Real Estate Recording—Wayne County Register of Deeds, 400 Monroe, Room 620, Detroit, MI 48226. 313-224-5850. Fax: 313-224-5884. 8AM-4:30PM (EST).

Civil Actions Over $10,000—3rd Circuit Court, 201 County Building, 2 Woodward, Detroit, MI 48226. 313-224-5509. 8AM-4:30PM (EST). Access by: Phone, mail, in person.

Felony—Frank Murphy Hall of Justice, 1441 St Antoine, Detroit, MI 48226. 313-224-2500. Fax: 313-224-2786. 8AM-4:30PM (EST). Access by: Mail, in person.

Civil Actions Under $10,000, Eviction, Small Claims—36th District Court-Civil (Detroit), 421 Madison Ave, Detroit, MI 48226. 313-965-5972. Fax: 313-965-4059. 8AM-4:30PM (EST). Access by: In person only.

Misdemeanor, Civil Actions Under $10,000, Eviction, Small Claims—24th District Court-Allen Park & Melvindale, 6515 Roosivelt, Allen Park, MI 48101-2524. 313-928-0535. Fax: 313-928-1860. 8:30AM-4:30PM (EST). Access by: Fax, mail, in person.

20th District Court, 6045 Fenton, Dearborn Heights, MI 48127. 313-277-7480. Fax: 313-277-7141. 9AM-5PM (EST). Access by: Mail, in person.

19th District Court, 16077 Michigan Ave, Dearborn, MI 48126. Civil: 313-943-2062. Criminal: 313-943-2056. Fax: 313-943-3071. 8AM-4:30PM (EST). Access by: Fax, mail, in person.

26-2 District Court, 3869 W Jefferson, Ecorse, MI 48229. 313-386-7900. Fax: 313-386-4316. 9AM-4PM (EST). Access by: Mail, in person.

21st District Court, 6000 North Middlebelt Rd, Garden City, MI 48135. 313-525-8805. Fax: 313-421-4797. 8:30AM-4:30PM (EST). Access by: Mail, in person.

31st District Court, 3401 Evaline Ave, Hamtramck, MI 48212. 313-876-7710. Fax: 313-876-7724. 8AM-4PM (EST). Access by: Mail, in person.

32 A District Court, 19617 Harper Ave, Harper Woods, MI 48225. 313-343-2590. Fax: 313-343-2594. 8:30AM-4:30PM (EST). Access by: Phone, fax, mail, in person.

30th District Court, 28 Gerard Ave, Highland Park, MI 48203. 313-252-0300. Fax: 313-865-1115. 8AM-4:30PM (EST). Access by: Mail, in person.

22nd District Court, 27331 S River Park Dr, Inkster, MI 48141. 313-277-8200. Fax: 313-277-8221. 8:30AM-4:30PM (EST). Access by: Mail, in person.

25th District Court, 1475 Cleophus, Lincoln Park, MI 48146. Civil: 313-382-9317. Criminal: 313-382-8600. Fax: 313-382-9361. 9AM-4:30PM (EST). Access by: Mail, in person.

16th District Court, 15140 Farmington Rd, Livonia, MI 48154. 313-466-2500. Civil: X3541. Criminal: X3452. 8:30AM-4:30PM (EST). Access by: In person only. General searches are not performed.

35th District Court, 660 Plymouth Rd, Plymouth, MI 48170. 313-459-4740. Fax: 313-454-9303. 8:30AM-4:25PM (EST). Access by: Mail, in person.

17th District Court, 15111 Beech-Daly Rd, Redford, MI 48239. 313-538-8244. Fax: 313-538-3468. 8:30AM-4:15PM (EST). Access by: Mail, in person.

26-1 District Court, 10600 W Jefferson, River Rouge, MI 48218. 313-842-7819. Fax: 313-842-5923. 8:30AM-4:30PM (EST). Access by: Fax, mail, in person.

27-2 District Court, 14100 Civic Park Dr, Riverview, MI 48192. 313-281-4204. 8:30AM-4:30PM (EST). Access by: Mail, in person.

34th District Court, 11131 S Wayne Rd, Romulus, MI 48174. 313-941-4462. 8:30AM-4:30PM (EST). Access by: Mail, in person.

28th District Court, 14720 Reaume Parkway, Southgate, MI 48195. 313-246-1360. Fax: 313-246-1405. 8:30AM-4:30PM (EST). Access by: Fax, mail, in person.

23rd District Court, 23511 Goddard Rd, Taylor, MI 48180. 313-374-1328. Fax: 313-374-1303. 8:30AM-4:45PM (EST). Access by: Mail, in person.

29th District Court, 34808 Sims Ave, Wayne, MI 48184. 313-722-5220. Fax: 313-722-7003. 8AM-4:30PM (EST). Access by: Mail, in person.

18th District Court, 36675 Ford Rd, Westland, MI 48185. 313-595-8720. Fax: 313-595-0160. 8:30AM-4PM M,F; 8:30AM-5:30PM T,W; 8:30AM-6PM Th (EST). Access by: Mail, in person.

33rd District Court, 19000 Van Horn Rd, Woodhaven, MI 48183. 313-671-0201. Fax: 313-671-0307. 8:45AM-4:30PM (EST). Access by: Fax, mail, in person.

27-1 District Court, 2015 Biddle Ave, Wyandotte, MI 48192. 313-246-4475. Fax: 313-246-4503. 8:30AM-4:30PM (EST). Access by: Mail, in person.

Wexford County

Real Estate Recording—Wexford County Register of Deeds, 437 East Division Street, Cadillac, MI 49601. 616-779-9455. Fax: 616-779-0292. 8:30AM-5PM (EST).

Felony, Civil Actions Over $10,000—28th Circuit Court, PO Box 490, Cadillac, MI 49601. 616-779-9450. 8:30AM-5PM (EST). Access by: Phone, mail, in person.

Misdemeanor, Civil Actions Under $10,000, Eviction, Small Claims—84th District Court, 501 S Garfield, Cadillac, MI 49601. 616-779-9515. Fax: 616-779-9485. 8:30AM-5PM (EST). Access by: Mail, in person.

Probate—Probate Court, 503 S Garfield, Cadillac, MI 49601. 616-779-9510. Fax: 616-779-9485. 8:30AM-5PM (EST).

Federal Courts

US District Court

Eastern District of Michigan

Ann Arbor Division, US District Court PO Box 8199, Ann Arbor, MI 48107. 313-741-2380. Counties: Jackson, Lenawee, Monroe, Oakland, Washtenaw. Cases may be assigned to the Detroit, Flint or Port Huron Divisions. Case files are maintained where the case is assigned

Bay City Division, US District Court PO Box 913, Bay City, MI 48707. 517-894-8800. Counties: Alcona, Alpena, Arenac, Bay, Cheboygan, Clare, Crawford, Gladwin, Gratiot, Huron, Iosco, Isabella, Midland, Montmorency, Ogemaw, Oscoda, Otsego, Presque Isle, Roscommon, Saginaw, Tuscola

Detroit Division, US District Court 564 Theodore Levin US Courthouse, 231 W Lafayette Blvd, Detroit, MI 48226. 313-234-5050. Counties: Macomb, St. Clair, Sanilac, Wayne. All civil cases from Flint and some cases from Ann Arbor and Port Huron may also be assigned here. Case files are kept where the case is assigned.

Flint Division, US District Court Clerk, Federal Bldg, Room 140, 600 Church St, Flint, MI 48502. 810-257-3170. Counties: Genesee, Lapeer, Livingston, Shiawassee. This office handles criminal only for these counties; civil cases go to Detroit office.

Port Huron Division, US District Court c/o Detroit Division, 564 Theodore Levin US Courthouse, 231 W Lafayette, Detroit, MI 48226. 313-234-5050. Counties: Cases are assigned out of the Detroit Division

Western District of Michigan

Grand Rapids Division, US District Court 452 Federal Bldg, 110 Michigan St NW, Grand Rapids, MI 49503. 616-456-2381. Counties: Antrim, Barry, Benzie, Charlevoix, Emmet, Grand Traverse, Ionia, Kalkaska, Kent, Lake, Leelanau, Manistee, Mason, Mecosta, Missaukee, Montcalm, Muskegon, Newaygo, Oceana, Osceola, Ottawa, Wexford. The Lansing and Kalamazoo Divisions also handle cases from these counties

Kalamazoo Division, US District Court B-35 Federal Bldg, 410 W Michigan Ave, Kalamazoo, MI 49007. 616-349-2922. Counties: Allegan, Berrien, Calhoun, Cass, Kalamazoo, St. Joseph, Van Buren. Kalamazoo and Lansing also handle cases from the counties in the Grand Rapids Division

Lansing Division, US District Court 113 Federal Bldg, 315 W Allegan, Lansing, MI 48933. 517-377-1559. Counties: Branch, Clinton, Eaton, Hillsdale, Ingham. Lansing and Kalamazoo also handle cases from the counties in the Grand Rapids Division

Marquette-Northern Division, US District Court PO Box 698, Marquette, MI 49855. 906-226-2021. Counties: Alger, Baraga, Chippewa, Delta, Dickinson, Gogebic, Houghton, Iron, Keweenaw, Luce, Mackinac, Marquette, Menominee, Ontonagon, Schoolcraft

US Bankruptcy Court

Eastern District of Michigan

Bay City Division, US Bankruptcy Court, PO Box X911, Bay City, MI 48707. 517-894-7796. Voice Case Information System: 313-961-4940. Counties: Alcona, Alpena, Arenac, Bay, Cheboygan, Clare, Crawford, Gladwin, Gratiot, Huron, Iosco, Isabella, Midland, Montmorency, Ogemaw, Oscoda, Otsego, Presque Isle, Roscommon, Saginaw, Tuscola

Detroit Division, US Bankruptcy Court, 211 W Fort St, 21st Floor, Detroit, MI 48226. 313-234-0065. Voice Case Information System: 313-961-4940. Counties: Jackson, Lenawee, Macomb, Monroe, Oakland, Sanilac, St. Clair, Washtenaw, Wayne

Flint Division, US Bankruptcy Court, 226 W 2nd St, Flint, MI 48502. 810-235-4126. Voice Case Information System: 313-961-4940. Counties: Genesee, Lapeer, Livingston, Shiawassee

Western District of Michigan

Grand Rapids Division, US Bankruptcy Court, PO Box 3310, Grand Rapids, MI 49501. 616-456-2693. Voice Case Information System: 616-456-2075. Counties: Allegan, Antrim, Barry, Benzie, Berrien, Branch, Calhoun, Cass, Charlevoix, Clinton, Eaton, Emmet, Grand Traverse, Hillsdale, Ingham, Ionia, Kalamazoo, Kalkaska, Kent, Lake, Leelanau, Manistee, Mason, Mecosta, Missaukee, Montcalm, Muskegon, Newaygo, Oceana, Osceola, Ottawa, St. Joseph, Van Buren, Wexford

Marquette Division, US Bankruptcy Court, PO Box 909, Marquette, MI 49855. 906-226-2117. Voice Case Information System: 616-456-2075. Counties: Alger, Baraga, Chippewa, Delta, Dickinson, Gogebic, Houghton, Iron, Keweenaw, Luce, Mackinac, Marquette, Menominee, Ontonagon, Schoolcraft

Minnesota

Capitol: St. Paul (Ramsey County)	
Number of Counties: 87	**Population:** 4,609,548
County Court Locations:	**Federal Court Locations:**
•District Courts: 97/10 Districts	•District Courts: 3
	•Bankruptcy Courts: 4
	State Agencies: 18

State Agencies—Summary

General Help Numbers:

State Archives

Historical Society	612-296-6126
Division of Libraries & Archives	Fax: 612-297-7436
345 Kellogg Blvd, W	9AM-5PM M-SA
St Paul, MN 55102-1906	
Reference Librarian:	612-296-6143

Governor's Office

Governor's Office	612-296-3391
130 Capitol Bldg,	
75 Constitution Ave	Fax: 612-296-2089
St Paul, MN 55155	7:30AM-5PM

Attorney General's Office

Attorney General's Office	612-296-6196
102 State Capitol	Fax: 612-297-4193
St Paul, MN 55155	8AM-5PM

State Legislation

Minnesota Legislature	612-296-2887
State Capitol	8AM-5PM
House-Room 211, Senate-Room 231	
St Paul, MN 55155	
House Bill Status:	612-296-6646
House Bill Copies:	612-296-2314
See right hand column for address of Internet site.	

Important State Internet Sites:

Webscape
File   Edit   View   Help

State of Minnesota World Wide Web
www.state.mn.us/

Very limited home page with access to 2 other sites where more information can be found.

The Governor's Office
www.governor.state.mn.us

Includes information about the Governor's press releases and enables you to send e-mail to the Governor.

State Legislature Information
www.leg.state.mn.us/

Links to access the state House and Senate sites where you find their members, e-mail links and other government links.

UCC Information
www.sos.state.mn.us/ucc.html

Includes complete information about UCC filing and searching.

Legislation and Bills
www.leg.state.mn.us/leg/legis.htm

Contains information about bills in Minnesota.

Motor Vehicle and Drivers License Site
www.dps.state.mn.us/dvs/dvs.html

Links to information about driver's licenses, vehicle registration and salvage vehicles.

State Agencies—Public Records

Criminal Records

Bureau of Criminal Apprehension, Records & Identification, 1246 University Ave, St Paul, MN 55104, Main Telephone: 612-642-0670, Hours: 8:15AM-4PM. Access by: mail, visit.

Corporation Records
Limited Liability Company Records
Assumed Name
Trademarks/Servicemarks
Limited Partnerships

Business Records Services, Secretary of State, 180 State Office Bldg, 100 Constitution Ave, St Paul, MN 55155-1299, Main Telephone: 612-296-2803, Fax: 612-215-0683, Hours: 8AM-4:30PM. Access by: mail, phone, visit, PC.

Uniform Commercial Code
Federal Tax Liens
State Tax Liens

UCC Division, Secretary of State, 180 State Office Bldg, St Paul, MN 55155-1299, Main Telephone: 612-296-2434, Fax: 612-297-9102, Hours: 8 AM - 4:30 PM. Access by: mail, visit, PC.

Sales Tax Registrations

Minnesota Department of Revenue, Sales & Use Tax Division, 10 River Park Plaza, MS:6330, St Paul, MN 55146-6330, Main Telephone: 612-296-6181, Fax: 612-296-1938, Hours: 7:30AM-5PM M-F. Access by: mail, phone, visit.

Birth Certificates

Minnesota Department of Health, Birth & Death Records, PO Box 9441, Minneapolis, MN 55440, Main Telephone: 612-623-5120, Alternate Telephone: 612-623-5121, Hours: 8AM-4PM. Access by: mail, phone, visit.

Death Records

Minnesota Department of Health, Section of Vital Records, PO Box 9441, Minneapolis, MN 55440, Main Telephone: 612-623-5120, Alternate Telephone: 612-623-5121, Hours: 8AM-4PM. Access by: mail, phone, visit.

Marriage Certificates
Divorce Records

Records not available from state agency.

Workers' Compensation Records

Labor & Industry Department, Workers Compensation Division - Records Section, 443 Lafayette Rd -IP4, St Paul, MN 55155, Main Telephone: 612-296-6845, Fax: 612-215-0080, Hours: 8AM-4:30PM. Access by: mail, visit.

Driver Records

Driver & Vehicle Services, Records Section, 445 Minnesota St, St Paul, MN 55101, Main Telephone: 612-296-6911, Hours: 8AM-4:30PM. Access by: mail, visit, PC. Copies of tickets can be requested from the same address. The fee is $4.50 per page (up to three tickets). Motor vehicle records are available; include license plate number or owner's full name and date of birth with request.

Vehicle Ownership
Vehicle Identification

Driver & Vehicle Services, Records Section, 445 Minnesota St, St Paul, MN 55101, Main Telephone: 612-296-6911, Hours: 8AM-4:30PM. Access by: mail, visit, PC.

Accident Reports

Driver & Vehicle Services, Accident Records, 445 Minnesota St, Suite 181, St Paul, MN 55101-5181, Main Telephone: 612-296-2060, Fax: 612-282-2360, Hours: 8AM-4:30PM. Access by: mail, fax, phone, visit.

Hunting License Information
Fishing License Information

Fish & Wildlife Division, License Information Bureau, 500 Lafayette Rd, St Paul, MN 55155-4040, Main Telephone: 612-296-6157, Hours: 8AM-4:30PM. Access by: mail, phone, visit.

County Courts and Recording Offices

What You Need to Know...

About the Courts	About the Recorder's Office

Administration

State Court Administrator	612-296-2474
135 Minnesota Judicial Center	Fax: 612-297-5636
25 Constitution Ave	
St Paul, MN 55155	

Searching Hints

There are statewide certification and copy fees, as follows: Certification Fee: $10.00 per document, Copy Fee: $5.00 **per document** (not per page).

An **exact** name is required to search, e.g., a request for "Robert Smith" will not result in finding "Bob Smith." The requester must request **both** names and pay 2 search and copy fees.

If a search is permitted by "plaintiff or defendant," most jurisdictions stated that a case is indexed by **only** the first plaintiff or defendant and a second or third party would **not** be sufficient to search.

Most courts take personal checks; exceptions are noted.

Online Access

There is no direct access online computer system available. There is a plan to have some criminal information available on-line from St Paul through the Criminal Access System of the Bureau of Criminal Apprehension (BCA). Additional information is available from BCA by calling 612-642-0610.

Organization

87 counties, 87 filing offices. The recording officer is County Recorder. The entire state is in the Central Time Zone (CST).

UCC Records

Financing statements are filed at the state level except for consumer goods, farm related and real estate related filings. Counties enter all non-real estate filings into a central statewide database which can be accessed from any county office. All counties will perform UCC searches. Use search request form UCC-11. Search fees are usually $15.00 per debtor name if the standard UCC-12 request form is used, or $20.00 if a nonstandard form is used. A UCC search can include tax liens. The search fee usually includes 10 listings or copies. Additional copies usually cost $1.00 per page.

Lien Records

Federal and state tax liens on personal property of businesses are filed with the Secretary of State. Other federal and state tax liens are filed with the County Recorder. A special search form UCC-12 is used for separate tax lien searches. Some counties search each tax lien index separately. Some charge one $15.00 fee to search both indexes, but others charge a separate fee for each index searched. Search and copy fees vary widely. Other liens include mechanics, hospital, judgment, and attorneys.

Real Estate Records

Some counties will perform real estate searches, especially short questions over the telephone. Copies fees vary, but do not apply to certified copies. Certification fees are usually $1.00 per page with a minimum of $5.00.

County Courts and Recording Offices

Aitkin County

Real Estate Recording—Aitkin County Recorder, 209 Second Street NW, Aitkin, MN 56431. 218-927-7336. 8AM-4PM (CST).

Felony, Misdemeanor, Civil, Eviction, Small Claims, Probate—9th Judicial District Court, 209 Second St NW, Aitkin, MN 56431. 218-927-7350. Fax: 218-927-4535. 8AM-4:30PM (CST). Access by: Mail, in person.

Anoka County

Real Estate Recording—Anoka County Recorder, 2100 3rd Ave., Anoka, MN 55303. 612-323-5400. Fax: 612-323-5421. 8AM-4:30PM (CST).

Felony, Misdemeanor, Civil, Eviction, Small Claims, Probate—10th Judicial District Court, 325 E Main St, Anoka, MN 55303. 612-442-7475. Criminal: 612-422-7385. Fax: 612-442-6919. 8AM-4:30PM (CST). Access by: Mail, in person.

Becker County

Real Estate Recording—Becker County Recorder, 915 Lake Avenue, Detroit Lakes, MN 56501. 218-846-7304. Fax: 218-846-7323. 8AM-4:30PM (CST).

Felony, Misdemeanor, Civil, Eviction, Small Claims, Probate—7th Judicial District Court, PO Box 787, Detroit Lakes, MN 56502. 218-846-7305. Fax: 218-847-7620. 8AM-4:30PM (CST). Access by: Phone, fax, mail, in person.

Beltrami County

Real Estate Recording—Beltrami County Recorder, 619 Beltrami Ave. NW, Courthouse, Bemidji, MN 56601. 218-759-4170. Fax: 218-759-4527. 8AM-4:30PM (CST).

Felony, Misdemeanor, Civil, Eviction, Small Claims, Probate—District Court, 619 Beltrami Ave NW, PO Box 108, Bemidji, MN 56601. 218-759-4531. Fax: 218-759-4209. 8AM-4:30PM (CST). Access by: Mail, in person.

Benton County

Real Estate Recording—Benton County Recorder's Office, 531 Dewey Street, Foley, MN 56329. 612-968-6254. 8AM-4:30PM (CST).

Felony, Misdemeanor, Civil, Eviction, Small Claims, Probate—7th Judicial District Court, 531 Dewey St, Foley, MN 56329. 612-968-6254. Fax: 612-968-6634. 8AM-4:30PM (CST). Access by: Mail, in person.

Big Stone County

Real Estate Recording—Big Stone County Recorder, Courthouse, 20 SE 2nd St., Ortonville, MN 56278. 612-839-2308. Fax: 612-839-2308. (CST).

Felony, Misdemeanor, Civil, Eviction, Small Claims, Probate—8th Judicial District Court, 20 SE 2nd St, Ortonville, MN 56278. 612-839-2536. Fax: 612-839-2537. 8AM-4:30PM (CST). Access by: In person only.

Blue Earth County

Real Estate Recording—Blue Earth County Recorder, 204 South 5th Street, Mankato, MN 56001. 507-389-8222. Fax: 507-389-8344. 8AM-5PM (CST).

Felony, Misdemeanor, Civil, Eviction, Small Claims, Probate—5th Judicial District Court, 204 S 5th St (PO Box 0347), Mankato, MN 56002-0347. 507-389-8310. Fax: 507-389-8437. 8AM-5PM (CST). Access by: Fax, mail, in person.

Brown County

Real Estate Recording—Brown County Recorder, 14 South State Street, New Ulm, MN 56073. 507-233-6653. Fax: 507-359-1430. 8AM-5PM (CST).

Felony, Misdemeanor, Civil, Eviction, Small Claims, Probate—5th Judicial District Court, PO Box 248, New Ulm, MN 56073-0248. 507-359-7900. Fax: 507-359-9562. 8AM-5PM (CST). Access by: Mail, in person.

Carlton County

Real Estate Recording—Carlton County Recorder, Courthouse, 301 Walnut St., Carlton, MN 55718. 218-384-9122. Fax: 218-384-9157. 8AM-4PM (CST).

Felony, Misdemeanor, Civil, Eviction, Small Claims, Probate—6th Judicial District Court, PO Box 190, Carlton, MN 55718. 218-384-4281. Fax: 218-384-9182. 8AM-4PM (CST). Access by: In person only.

Carver County

Real Estate Recording—Carver County Recorder, Carver County Govt Center, Admin Bldg, 600 East Fourth St, Chaska, MN 55318. 612-361-1930. Fax: 612-361-1931. 8AM-4:30PM (CST).

Felony, Misdemeanor, Civil, Eviction, Small Claims, Probate—1st Judicial District Court, 600 E 4th St, Chaska, MN 55318. 612-361-1420. Fax: 612-361-1491. 8AM-4:30PM (CST). Access by: Phone, in person.

Cass County

Real Estate Recording—Cass County Recorder, Courthouse, Highway 371, Walker, MN 56484. 218-547-7381. Fax: 218-547-2440. 8AM-4:30PM (CST).

Felony, Misdemeanor, Civil, Eviction, Small Claims, Probate—9th Judicial District Court, 300 Minnesota Ave, PO Box 3000, Walker, MN 56484. 218-547-7200. Fax: 218-547-1904. 8AM-4:30PM (CST). Access by: Mail, in person.

Chippewa County

Real Estate Recording—Chippewa County Recorder, 629 No. 11th St., Montevideo, MN 56265. 320-269-9431. Fax: 320-269-7168. 8AM-4:30PM (CST).

Felony, Misdemeanor, Civil, Eviction, Small Claims, Probate—8th Judicial District Court, 11th St and Hwy 7, Montevideo, MN 56265. 320-269-7774. Fax: 320-269-7733. 8AM-4:30PM (CST). Access by: Mail, in person.

Chisago County

Real Estate Recording—Chisago County Recorder, Government Center, Room/Box 277, 313 N. Main St., Center City, MN 55012. 612-257-1300. Fax: 612-257-0454. 8AM-4:30PM (CST).

Felony, Misdemeanor, Civil, Eviction, Small Claims, Probate—10th Judicial District Court, 313 N Main St, Rm 358, Center City, MN 55012. 612-257-1300. Fax: 612-257-0359. 8AM-4:30PM (CST). Access by: Mail, in person.

Clay County

Real Estate Recording—Clay County Recorder, 807 North 11th Street, Courthouse, Moorhead, MN 56560. 218-299-5031. Fax: 218-299-7500. 8AM-4:30PM (CST).

Felony, Misdemeanor, Civil, Eviction, Small Claims, Probate—7th Judicial District Court, PO Box 280, Moorhead, MN 56561. 218-299-5043. Fax: 218-299-7307. 8AM-4:30PM (CST). Access by: In person only. Court no longer performs searches as of July 1, 1997.

Clearwater County

Real Estate Recording—Clearwater County Recorder, 213 Main Avenue North, Bagley, MN 56621. 218-694-6129. Fax: 218-694-6244. 8AM-4:30PM (CST).

Felony, Misdemeanor, Civil, Eviction, Small Claims, Probate—9th Judicial District Court, 213 Main Ave North, Bagley, MN 56621. 218-694-6177. Fax: 218-694-6213. 8AM-4:30PM (CST). Access by: Mail, in person.

Cook County

Real Estate Recording—Cook County Recorder, Courthouse, 411 W. 2nd St., Grand Marais, MN 55604. 218-387-2282. Fax: 218-387-2610. 8AM-4PM (CST).

Felony, Misdemeanor, Civil, Eviction, Small Claims, Probate—6th Judicial District Court, Po Box 1150, Grand

Marais, MN 55604-1150. 218-387-2282. Fax: 218-387-2610. 8AM-4PM (CST). Access by: Mail, in person.

Cottonwood County

Real Estate Recording—Cottonwood County Recorder, 900 Third Avenue, Courthouse Room 6, Windom, MN 56101. 507-831-1458. Fax: 507-831-3675. 8AM-4:30PM (CST).

Felony, Misdemeanor, Civil, Eviction, Small Claims, Probate—5th Judicial District Court, PO Box 97, Windom, MN 56101. 507-831-1356. Fax: 507-831-1425. 8AM-4:30PM (CST). Access by: Mail, in person.

Crow Wing County

Real Estate Recording—Crow Wing County Recorder, 326 Laurel Street, Courthouse, Brainerd, MN 56401. 218-828-3965. 8AM-5PM (CST).

Felony, Misdemeanor, Civil, Eviction, Small Claims, Probate—326 Laurel St, Brainerd, MN 56401. 218-828-3959. Fax: 218-828-2905. 8AM-5PM (CST). Access by: Mail, in person.

Dakota County

Real Estate Recording—Dakota County Recorder, 1590 West Highway 55, Government Center, Hastings, MN 55033. 612-438-4355. Fax: 612-438-8176. 8AM-4:30PM (CST).

Felony, Misdemeanor, Civil, Eviction, Small Claims—1st Judicial District Court-Apple Valley, 14955 Galaxie Ave, Apple Valley, MN 55124. 612-891-7256. Fax: 612-891-7260. 8AM-4:30PM (CST). Access by: In person only.

Felony, Misdemeanor, Civil, Eviction, Small Claims, Probate—District Court, Judicial Center, 1560 Hwy 55, Hastings, MN 55033. 612-438-8100. Fax: 612-438-8162. 8AM-4:30PM (CST). Access by: In person only.

1st Judicial District Court-South St Paul, 125 3rd Ave North, South St Paul, MN 55075. 612-451-1791. Fax: 612-451-3526. 8AM-4:30PM (CST). Access by: In person only.

Dodge County

Real Estate Recording—Dodge County Recorder, Courthouse, 22 6th St. East, Mantorville, MN 55955. 507-635-6250. Fax: 507-635-6265. 8AM-4:30PM (CST).

Felony, Misdemeanor, Civil, Eviction, Small Claims, Probate—3rd Judicial District Court, PO Box 96, Mantorville, MN 55955. 507-635-6260. Fax: 507-635-6271. 8AM-4:30PM (CST). Access by: In person only. Effective July 1, 1997, this court will no longer conduct criminal record searches..

Douglas County

Real Estate Recording—Douglas County Recorder, 305 8th Avenue West, Courthouse, Alexandria, MN 56308. 612-762-3877. 8AM-4:30PM (CST).

Felony, Misdemeanor, Civil, Eviction, Small Claims, Probate—7th Judicial District Court, 305 8th Ave West, Alexandria, MN 56308. 612-762-2381. Fax: 612-762-8863. 8AM-4:30PM (CST). Access by: Mail, in person.

Faribault County

Real Estate Recording—Faribault County Recorder, 415 North Main Street, Blue Earth, MN 56013. 507-526-6252. Fax: 507-526-6227. 8:30AM-5PM (CST).

Felony, Misdemeanor, Civil, Eviction, Small Claims, Probate—5th Judicial District Court, PO Box 130, Blue Earth, MN 56013. 507-526-6273. Fax: 507-526-3054. 8:30AM-5PM (CST). Access by: Phone, fax, mail, in person.

Fillmore County

Real Estate Recording—Fillmore County Recorder, Courthouse, Preston, MN 55965. 507-765-3852. Fax: 507-765-4571. 8AM-4:30PM (CST).

Felony, Misdemeanor, Civil, Eviction, Small Claims, Probate—3rd Judicial District Court, 101 Fillmore St, PO Box 436, Preston, MN 55965. 507-765-4483. Fax: 507-765-4571. 8AM-4:30PM (CST). Access by: In person only. Effec-

tive July 1, 1997, this court will no longer conduct criminal record searches..

Freeborn County

Real Estate Recording—Freeborn County Recorder, 411 South Broadway, Court House, Albert Lea, MN 56007. 507-377-5130. Fax: 507-377-5260. 8AM-5PM (CST).

Felony, Misdemeanor, Civil, Eviction, Small Claims, Probate—3rd Judicial District Court, 411 S Broadway, Albert Lea, MN 56007. 507-377-5153. Fax: 507-377-5262. 8AM-5PM (CST). Access by: In person only. Effective July 1, 1997, this court will no longer conduct criminal record searches..

Goodhue County

Real Estate Recording—Goodhue County Recorder, 5th & West Avenue, Courthouse, Red Wing, MN 55066. 612-385-3149. Fax: 612-385-3039. 8AM-4:30PM (CST).

Felony, Misdemeanor, Civil, Eviction, Small Claims, Probate—1st Judicial District Court, PO Box 408, Rm 310, Red Wing, MN 55066. 612-385-3051. Fax: 612-385-3065. 8AM-4:30PM (CST). Access by: In person only.

Grant County

Real Estate Recording—Grant County Recorder, 10th Second Street NE, Courthouse, Elbow Lake, MN 56531. 218-685-4133. (CST).

Felony, Misdemeanor, Civil, Eviction, Small Claims, Probate—8th Judicial District Court, 10 2nd St NE, Elbow Lake, MN 56531. 218-685-4825. 8AM-4PM (CST). Access by: Mail, in person.

Hennepin County

Real Estate Recording—Hennepin County Recorder, 300 South 6th Street, 8-A Government Center, Minneapolis, MN 55487. 612-348-3066. 8AM-4:30PM (UCC); 8AM-5PM (Real Estate) (CST).

Felony, Misdemeanor, Civil, Probate—4th Judicial District Court-Division 1, 1153 C Government Center, 300 S 6th St, Minneapolis, MN 55487. 612-348-2611. Civil: 612-348-3170. Criminal: 612-348-2612. Fax: 612-348-6099. 8AM-4:30PM (CST). Access by: Fax, mail, in person.

Misdemeanor, Eviction, Small Claims—4th Judicial District Court-Division 2 Brookdale Area, 6125 Shingle Creek Pkwy, Brooklyn Center, MN 55430. 612-569-3700. Fax: 612-569-3697. 7:45AM-4:30PM (CST). Access by: Mail, in person.

4th Judicial District Court-Division 4 Southdale Area, 7009 York Ave South, Edina, MN 55435. 612-830-4905. Fax: 612-830-4993. 8AM-4:30PM (CST). Access by: Mail, in person.

4th Judicial District Court-Division 3 Ridgedale Area, 12601 Ridgedale Dr, Minnetonka, MN 55305. 612-541-8500. Fax: 612-541-6297. 8AM-4:30PM (CST). Access by: Mail, in person.

Houston County

Real Estate Recording—Houston County Recorder, 304 South Marshall Street, Caledonia, MN 55921. 507-724-5813. Fax: 507-724-2647. 8:30AM-5PM (CST).

Felony, Misdemeanor, Civil, Eviction, Small Claims, Probate—3rd Judicial District Court, 304 S Marshall, Caledonia, MN 55921. 507-724-5806. Fax: 507-724-5550. 8:30AM-5PM (CST). Access by: In person only. Effective July 1, 1997, this court will no longer conduct criminal record searches..

Hubbard County

Real Estate Recording—Hubbard County Recorder, Courthouse, Park Rapids, MN 56470. 218-732-3552. 8AM-4:30PM (CST).

Felony, Misdemeanor, Civil, Eviction, Small Claims, Probate—9th Judicial District Court, 301 Court St, Park Rapids, MN 56470. 218-732-3573. Fax: 218-732-0137. 8AM-4:30PM (CST). Access by: Mail, in person.

Isanti County

Real Estate Recording—Isanti County Recorder, Courthouse, Cambridge, MN 55008. 612-689-1191. 8AM-4:30PM (CST).

Felony, Misdemeanor, Civil, Eviction, Small Claims, Probate—10th Judicial District Court, 555 18th Ave SW, Cambridge, MN 55008-9386. 612-689-2292. Fax: 612-689-8340. 8AM-4:30PM (CST). Access by: Mail, in person.

Itasca County

Real Estate Recording—Itasca County Recorder, 123 NE 4th Street, Grand Rapids, MN 55744. 218-327-2856. Fax: 218-327-0689. 8AM-4:30PM (CST).

Felony, Misdemeanor, Civil, Eviction, Small Claims, Probate—9th Judicial District Court, 123 4th St NE, Grand Rapids, MN 55744-2600. 218-327-2870. Fax: 218-327-2897. 8:30AM-4PM (CST). Access by: Mail, in person.

Jackson County

Real Estate Recording—Jackson County Recorder, Courthouse, Jackson, MN 56143. 507-847-2580. Fax: 507-847-4718. 8:30AM-4:30PM (CST).

Felony, Misdemeanor, Civil, Eviction, Small Claims, Probate—5th Judicial District Court, PO Box G, Jackson, MN 56143. 507-847-4400. Fax: 507-847-5433. 8:30AM-4:30PM (CST). Access by: Fax, mail, in person.

Kanabec County

Real Estate Recording—Kanabec County Recorder, 18 North Vine Street, Mora, MN 55051. 320-679-0417. Fax: 320-679-9994. 8AM-4PM (CST).

Felony, Misdemeanor, Civil, Eviction, Small Claims, Probate—10th Judicial District Court, 18 North Vine, Mora, MN 55051. 320-679-1022. Fax: 320-679-9994. 8AM-4PM (CST). Access by: Mail, in person.

Kandiyohi County

Real Estate Recording—Kandiyohi County Recorder, 505 West Becker, Willmar, MN 56201. 320-231-6223. Fax: 320-231-6525. 8AM-4:30PM (CST).

Felony, Misdemeanor, Civil, Eviction, Small Claims, Probate—8th Judicial District Court, PO Box 1337, Willmar, MN 56201. 320-231-6206. Fax: 320-231-6276. 8AM-4:30PM (CST). Access by: Mail, in person.

Kittson County

Real Estate Recording—Kittson County Recorder, Courthouse, Hallock, MN 56728. 218-843-2842. Fax: 218-843-2020. 8:30AM-4:30PM (CST).

Felony, Misdemeanor, Civil, Eviction, Small Claims, Probate—9th Judicial District Court, PO Box 39, Hallock, MN 56728. 218-843-3632. Fax: 218-843-3634. 8:30AM-4:30PM (CST). Access by: Fax, mail, in person.

Koochiching County

Real Estate Recording—Koochiching County Recorder, Courthouse, International Falls, MN 56649. 218-283-6290. Fax: 218-283-6262. 8AM-5PM (CST).

Felony, Misdemeanor, Civil, Eviction, Small Claims, Probate—715 4th St, Court House, International Falls, MN 56649. 218-283-6261. Fax: 218-283-6262. 8AM-5PM (CST). Access by: Fax, mail, in person.

Lac qui Parle County

Real Estate Recording—Lac qui Parle County Recorder, 600 6th Street, Courthouse, Madison, MN 56256. 320-598-3724. 8:30AM-4:30PM (CST).

Felony, Misdemeanor, Civil, Eviction, Small Claims, Probate—8th Judicial District Court, PO Box 36, Madison, MN 56256. 320-598-3536. Fax: 320-598-3915. 8:30AM-4:30PM (CST). Access by: Fax, mail, in person.

Lake County

Real Estate Recording—Lake County Recorder, 601 Third Avenue, Two Harbors, MN 55616. 218-834-8347. Fax: 218-834-8365. 8AM-4:30PM (CST).

Felony, Misdemeanor, Civil, Eviction, Small Claims, Probate—6th Judicial District Court, 601 3rd Ave, Two Harbors, MN 55616. 218-834-8330. Fax: 218-834-8397. 8AM-4:30PM (CST). Access by: Fax, mail, in person.

Lake of the Woods County

Real Estate Recording—Lake of the Woods County Recorder, 206 Southeast Eighth Avenue, Baudette, MN 56623. 218-634-1902. Fax: 218-634-2509. 7:30AM-4PM (CST).

Felony, Misdemeanor, Civil, Eviction, Small Claims, Probate—9th Judicial District Court, PO Box 808, Baudette, MN 56623. 218-634-1451. Fax: 218-634-9444. 7:30AM-4PM (CST). Access by: Fax, mail, in person.

Le Sueur County

Real Estate Recording—Le Sueur County Recorder, 88 South Park Avenue, Courthouse, Le Center, MN 56057. 507-357-2251. Fax: 507-357-6375. 8AM-4:30PM (CST).

Felony, Misdemeanor, Civil, Eviction, Small Claims, Probate—1st Judicial District Court, 88 S Park Ave, Le Center, MN 56057. 507-357-2251. Fax: 507-357-6375. 8AM-4:30PM (CST). Access by: Mail, in person.

Lincoln County

Real Estate Recording—Lincoln County Recorder, 319 North Rebecca, Ivanhoe, MN 56142. 507-694-1360. Fax: 507-694-1198. 8:30AM-4:30PM (CST).

Felony, Misdemeanor, Civil, Eviction, Small Claims, Probate—5th Judicial District Court, PO Box 15, Ivanhoe, MN 56142-0015. 507-694-1355. Fax: 507-694-1717. 8:30AM-Noon,1-4:30PM (CST). Access by: Fax, mail, in person.

Lyon County

Real Estate Recording—Lyon County Recorder, 607 West Main Street, Marshall, MN 56258. 507-537-6722. Fax: 507-537-6091. 8:30AM-4:30PM (CST).

Felony, Misdemeanor, Civil, Eviction, Small Claims, Probate—5th Judicial District Court, 607 W Main, Marshall, MN 56258. 507-537-6734. Fax: 507-537-6150. 8:30AM-4:30PM (CST). Access by: Mail, in person.

Mahnomen County

Real Estate Recording—Mahnomen County Recorder, Courthouse, 311 N. Main, Mahnomen, MN 56557. 218-935-5528. Fax: 218-935-5946. 8AM-4:30PM M-T (CST).

Felony, Misdemeanor, Civil, Eviction, Small Claims, Probate—9th Judicial District Court, PO Box 459, Mahnomen, MN 56557. 218-935-2251. Fax: 218-935-2851. 8AM-4:30PM (CST). Access by: Mail, in person.

Marshall County

Real Estate Recording—Marshall County Recorder, 208 East Colvin, Warren, MN 56762. 218-745-4801. Fax: 218-745-4343. 8AM-4:30PM (CST).

Felony, Misdemeanor, Civil, Eviction, Small Claims, Probate—9th Judicial District Court, 208 E Colvin, Warren, MN 56762. 218-745-4921. Fax: 218-745-4343. 8AM-4:30PM (CST). Access by: Mail, in person.

Martin County

Real Estate Recording—Martin County Recorder, 201 Lake Avenue, Courthouse, Fairmont, MN 56031. 507-238-3213. Fax: 507-238-3259. 8:30AM-4:30PM (CST).

Felony, Misdemeanor, Civil, Eviction, Small Claims, Probate—5th Judicial District Court, 201 Lake Ave, Rm 304, Fairmont, MN 56031. 507-238-3214. Fax: 507-238-1913. 8:30AM-4:30PM (CST). Access by: Mail, in person.

McLeod County

Real Estate Recording—McLeod County Recorder, 2391 N. Hennepin Ave., North Complex, Glencoe, MN 55336. 320-864-5551. Fax: 320-864-1295. 8AM-4:30PM (CST).

Felony, Misdemeanor, Civil, Eviction, Small Claims, Probate—1st Judicial District Court, 830 E 11th, Glencoe, MN 55336. 320-864-5551. 8AM-4:30PM (CST). Access by: Mail, in person.

Meeker County

Real Estate Recording—Meeker County Recorder, 325 North Sibley Avenue, Courthouse, Litchfield, MN 55355. 320-693-5440. Fax: 320-693-5444. 8AM-4:30PM (CST).

Felony, Misdemeanor, Civil, Eviction, Small Claims, Probate—8th Judicial District Court, 325 N Sibley, Litchfield, MN 55355. 320-693-5230. Fax: 320-693-5254. 8AM-4:30PM (CST). Access by: Mail, in person.

Mille Lacs County

Real Estate Recording—Mille Lacs County Recorder, 635 2nd Street S.E., Milaca, MN 56353. 612-983-8309. 8AM-4:30PM (CST).

Felony, Misdemeanor, Civil, Eviction, Small Claims, Probate—7th Judicial District Court, Courthouse, Milaca, MN 56353. 612-983-8313. Fax: 612-983-8384. 8AM-4:30PM (CST). Access by: Mail, in person.

Morrison County

Real Estate Recording—Morrison County Recorder, Administration Building, 213 SE 1st Ave., Little Falls, MN 56345. 320-632-0145. Fax: 320-632-0141. 8AM-4:30PM (CST).

Felony, Misdemeanor, Civil, Eviction, Small Claims, Probate—7th Judicial District Court, 213 SE 1st Ave, Little Falls, MN 56345. 320-632-0325. Fax: 320-632-0340. 8AM-4:30PM (CST). Access by: In person only.

Mower County

Real Estate Recording—Mower County Recorder, 201 First Street NE, Austin, MN 55912. 507-437-9446. 8AM-5PM (CST).

Felony, Misdemeanor, Civil, Eviction, Small Claims, Probate—3rd Judicial District Court, 201 1st St NE, Austin, MN 55912. 507-437-9465. Fax: 507-437-9471. 8AM-5PM (CST). Access by: In person only. Effective July 1, 1997, this court will no longer conduct criminal record searches..

Murray County

Real Estate Recording—Murray County Recorder, 28th & Broadway Avenue, Slayton, MN 56172. 507-836-6148. Fax: 507-836-6019. 8:30AM-Noon, 1-5PM (CST).

Felony, Misdemeanor, Civil, Eviction, Small Claims, Probate—5th Judicial District Court, PO Box 57, Slayton, MN 56172-0057. 507-836-6163. Fax: 507-836-6019. 8AM-5PM (CST). Access by: Fax, mail, in person.

Nicollet County

Real Estate Recording—Nicollet County Recorder, 501 South Minnesota Avenue, St. Peter, MN 56082. 507-931-6800. Fax: 507-931-9220. 8AM-5PM (CST).

Felony, Misdemeanor, Civil, Eviction, Small Claims, Probate—District Court-Branch, PO Box 2055, North Mankato, MN 56002-2055. 507-625-4141. Fax: 507-345-1273. 8AM-5PM (CST). Access by: Fax, mail, in person.

5th Judicial District Court, PO Box 496, St Peter, MN 56082. 507-931-6800. Fax: 507-931-4278. 8AM-5PM (CST). Access by: Mail, in person.

Nobles County

Real Estate Recording—Nobles County Recorder, 315 10th Street, Nobles County Government Center, Worthington, MN 56187. 507-372-8236. Fax: 507-372-8223. 8AM-5PM (CST).

Felony, Misdemeanor, Civil, Eviction, Small Claims, Probate—5th Judicial District Court, PO Box 547, Worthington, MN 56187. 507-372-8263. Fax: 507-372-4994. 8AM-5PM (CST). Access by: Fax, mail, in person.

Norman County

Real Estate Recording—Norman County Recorder, 16 East 3rd Avenue, Ada, MN 56510. 218-784-4422. Fax: 218-784-3110. 8:30AM-4:30PM (CST).

Felony, Misdemeanor, Civil, Eviction, Small Claims, Probate—9th Judicial District Court, PO Box 272, Ada, MN 56510-0146. 218-784-7131. Fax: 218-784-3110. 8:30AM-4:30PM (CST). Access by: Mail, in person.

Olmsted County

Real Estate Recording—Olmsted County Recorder, 151 4th St. SE, Rochester, MN 55904. 507-285-8194. Fax: 507-287-7186. 8AM-5PM (CST).

Felony, Misdemeanor, Civil, Eviction, Small Claims, Probate—Olmsted County District Court, 151 4th St SE, Rochester, MN 55904. 507-285-8210. Fax: 507-285-8996. 8AM-5PM (CST). Access by: In person only. Effective July 1, 1997, this court will no longer conduct criminal record searches..

Otter Tail County

Real Estate Recording—Otter Tail County Recorder, Junius Avenue, Courthouse, Fergus Falls, MN 56537. 218-739-2271. 8AM-5PM (CST).

Felony, Misdemeanor, Civil, Eviction, Small Claims, Probate—Otter Tail County District Court, PO Box 417, Fergus Falls, MN 56538-0417. 218-739-2271. Fax: 218-739-4983. 8AM-5PM (CST). Access by: Mail, in person.

Pennington County

Real Estate Recording—Pennington County Recorder, 1st & Main Street, Courthouse, Thief River Falls, MN 56701. 218-681-2522. Fax: 218-681-1235. 8AM-4:30PM (CST).

Felony, Misdemeanor, Civil, Eviction, Small Claims, Probate—9th Judicial District Court, PO Box 619, Thief River Falls, MN 56701. 218-681-2407. 8AM-4:30PM (CST). Access by: Mail, in person.

Pine County

Real Estate Recording—Pine County Recorder, Courthouse, 315 Sixth St., Suite 3, Pine City, MN 55063. 320-629-6781. Fax: 320-629-7319. 8AM-4:30PM (CST).

Felony, Misdemeanor, Civil, Eviction, Small Claims, Probate—10th Judicial District Court, 315 6th St, Pine City, MN 55063. 320-629-6781. 8AM-4:30PM (CST). Access by: Mail, in person.

Pipestone County

Real Estate Recording—Pipestone County Recorder, 416 S. Hiawatha Ave., Pipestone, MN 56164. 507-825-4646. Fax: 507-825-4465. 8AM-4:30PM (CST).

Felony, Misdemeanor, Civil, Eviction, Small Claims, Probate—5th Judicial District Court, 416 S Hiawatha Ave (PO Box 337), Pipestone, MN 56164. 507-825-4550. Fax: 507-825-3256. 8:30AM-4:30PM (CST). Access by: Mail, in person.

Polk County

Real Estate Recording—Polk County Recorder, 612 Broadway, Courthouse, Suite 213, Crookston, MN 56716. 218-281-3464. Fax: 218-281-2204. 8AM-4:30PM (CST).

Felony, Misdemeanor, Civil, Eviction, Small Claims, Probate—9th Judicial District Court, Court Administrator, 612 N Broadway #301, Crookston, MN 56716. 218-281-2332. Fax: 218-281-2204. 8AM-4:30PM (CST). Access by: Mail, in person.

Pope County

Real Estate Recording—Pope County Recorder, 130 East Minnesota, Glenwood, MN 56334. 612-634-5723. Fax: 612-634-3087. 8AM-4:30PM (CST).

Felony, Misdemeanor, Civil, Eviction, Small Claims, Probate—8th Judicial District Court, 130 E Minnesota Ave (PO Box 195), Glenwood, MN 56334. 612-634-5222. 8AM-4:30PM (CST). Access by: Mail, in person.

Ramsey County

Real Estate Recording—Ramsey County Recorder, 50 West Kellogg Blvd., Suite 812 RCGC-W, St. Paul, MN 55102. 612-266-2060. 8AM-4:30PM (CST).

Misdemeanor—2nd Judicial District Court-Maplewood Area, 2785 White Bear Ave, Maplewood, MN 55109. 612-

777-9111. Fax: 612-777-3970. 8AM-4:30PM (CST). Access by: Phone, fax, mail, in person.

2nd Judicial District Court-New Brighton Area, 803 5th Ave NW, New Brighton, MN 55112. 612-636-7101. Fax: 612-635-0722. 8AM-4:30PM (CST). Access by: Fax, mail, in person.

Felony, Misdemeanor, Civil, Probate—2nd Judicial District Court, 15 W Kellogg, St Paul, MN 55101. Civil: 612-266-8266. Criminal: 612-266-8180. Fax: 612-266-8278. 8AM-4:30PM (CST). Access by: Mail, in person.

Red Lake County

Real Estate Recording—Red Lake County Recorder, 124 Main Avenue North, Red Lake Falls, MN 56750. 218-253-2997. Fax: 218-253-2656. 9AM-5PM (CST).

Felony, Misdemeanor, Civil, Eviction, Small Claims, Probate—9th Judicial District Court, PO Box 339, Red Lake Falls, MN 56750. 218-253-4281. Fax: 218-253-4287. 9AM-5PM (CST). Access by: Mail, in person.

Redwood County

Real Estate Recording—Redwood County Recorder, Courthouse Square, Main Floor, Redwood Falls, MN 56283. 507-637-4032. Fax: 507-637-4064. 8AM-4:30PM (CST).

Felony, Misdemeanor, Civil, Eviction, Small Claims, Probate—5th Judicial District Court, PO Box 130, Redwood Falls, MN 56283. 507-637-8327. Fax: 507-637-2611. 8AM-4:30PM (CST). Access by: Mail, in person.

Renville County

Real Estate Recording—Renville County Recorder, 500 East DePue, Olivia, MN 56277. 320-523-1000. Fax: 079-523-1172. 8AM-4:30PM (CST).

Felony, Misdemeanor, Civil, Eviction, Small Claims, Probate—8th Judicial District Court, 500 E DePue Ave, Olivia, MN 56277. 320-523-2080. Fax: 320-523-2084. 8AM-4:30PM (CST).

Rice County

Real Estate Recording—Rice County Recorder, 218 NW 3rd Street, Courthouse, Faribault, MN 55021. 507-332-6114. Fax: 507-332-5999. 8AM-4:30PM (CST).

Felony, Misdemeanor, Civil, Eviction, Small Claims, Probate—3rd Judicial District Court, 218 NW 3rd St, Faribault, MN 55021. 507-332-6107. 8AM-4:30PM (CST). Access by: In person only. Effective July 1, 1997, this court will no longer conduct criminal record searches..

Rock County

Real Estate Recording—Rock County Recorder, 204 East Brown, Luverne, MN 56156. 507-283-9177. Fax: 507-283-9178. 8AM-5PM (CST).

Felony, Misdemeanor, Civil, Eviction, Small Claims, Probate—5th Judicial District Court, PO Box 745, Luverne, MN 56156. 507-283-9501. Fax: 507-283-9504. 8AM-5PM (CST). Access by: Fax, mail, in person.

Roseau County

Real Estate Recording—Roseau County Recorder, 606 5th Ave. SW, Room 170, Roseau, MN 56751. 218-463-2061. 8AM-4:30PM (CST).

Felony, Misdemeanor, Civil, Eviction, Small Claims, Probate—9th Judicial District Court, 606 5th Ave SW Rm 20, Roseau, MN 56751. 218-463-2541. Fax: 218-463-1889. 8AM-4:30PM (CST). Access by: Mail, in person.

Scott County

Real Estate Recording—Scott County Recorder, 428 South Holmes Street, Shakopee, MN 55379. 612-496-8143. Fax: 612-496-8138. 8AM-4:30PM (CST).

Felony, Misdemeanor, Civil, Eviction, Small Claims, Probate—1st Judicial District Court, 428 S Holmes, Rm 212, Shakopee, MN 55379. 612-496-8200. Fax: 612-496-8211. 8AM-4:30PM (CST). Access by: Mail, in person.

Sherburne County

Real Estate Recording—Sherburne County Recorder, 13880 Highway 10, Elk River, MN 55330. 612-241-2915. Fax: 612-241-2995. 8AM-5PM (CST).

Felony, Misdemeanor, Civil, Eviction, Small Claims, Probate—10th Judicial District Court, Sherburne County Government Center, 13880 Hwy #10, Elkriver, MN 55330-4608. 612-241-2800. Fax: 612-241-2816. 8AM-5PM (CST). Access by: Mail, in person.

Sibley County

Real Estate Recording—Sibley County Recorder, 400 Court Street, Room 26, Gaylord, MN 55334. 507-237-5526. Fax: 507-237-5142. 8AM-5PM (CST).

Felony, Misdemeanor, Civil, Eviction, Small Claims, Probate—1st Judicial District Court, PO Box 867, Gaylord, MN 55334. 507-237-2427. Fax: 507-237-5142. 8AM-5PM (CST). Access by: Mail, in person.

St. Louis County

Real Estate Recording—St. Louis County Recorder, 100 North 5th Avenue West, Room 101, Duluth, MN 55802. 218-726-2677. Fax: 218-725-5052. 8AM-4:30PM (CST).

Felony, Misdemeanor, Civil, Eviction, Small Claims, Probate—6th Judicial District Court, 100 N 5th Ave W, Rm 320, Duluth, MN 55802-1294. 218-726-2442. Fax: 218-726-2473. 8AM-4:30PM (CST). Access by: In person only.

6th Judicial District Court-Hibbing Branch, 1810 12th Ave East, Hibbing, MN 55746. 218-262-0100. Fax: 218-262-0219. 8AM-4:30PM (CST). Access by: Mail, in person.

6th Judicial District Court-Virginia Branch, 300 S 5th Ave, Virginia, MN 55792. 218-749-7106. Fax: 218-749-7109. 8AM-4:30PM, closed at lunch (CST). Access by: Mail, in person.

Stearns County

Real Estate Recording—Stearns County Recorder, 705 Courthouse Square, Administration Center, Room 131, St. Cloud, MN 56303. 320-656-3855. Fax: 320-656-3916. 8AM-4:30PM (CST).

Felony, Misdemeanor, Civil, Eviction, Small Claims, Probate—7th Judicial District Court, PO Box 1168, St Cloud, MN 56302. 320-656-3620. Fax: 320-656-3626. 8AM-4:30PM (CST). Access by: Mail, in person.

Steele County

Real Estate Recording—Steele County Recorder, 111 East Main, Courthouse, Owatonna, MN 55060. 507-451-8040. Fax: 507-451-6803. 8AM-5PM (CST).

Felony, Misdemeanor, Civil, Eviction, Small Claims, Probate—3rd Judicial District Court, PO Box 487, Owatonna, MN 55060. 507-451-8040. Fax: 507-451-6803. 8AM-5PM (CST). Access by: In person only. Effective July 1, 1997, this court will no longer conduct criminal record searches..

Stevens County

Real Estate Recording—Stevens County Recorder, 5th & Colorado, Morris, MN 56267. 612-589-7414. Fax: 612-589-2036. 8:30AM-4:30PM (Summer Hours 8AM-4PM) (CST).

Felony, Misdemeanor, Civil, Eviction, Small Claims, Probate—8th Judicial District Court, PO Box 530, Morris, MN 56267. 320-589-7289. Fax: 320-589-7288. 8AM-4:30PM (8AM-4PM Summer hours) (CST). Access by: In person only.

Swift County

Real Estate Recording—Swift County Recorder, 301 14th Street North, Benson, MN 56215. 612-843-3377. Fax: 612-843-2299. 8AM-4:30PM (CST).

Felony, Misdemeanor, Civil, Eviction, Small Claims, Probate—8th Judicial District Court, PO Box 110, Benson, MN 56215. 612-843-2744. Fax: 612-843-4124. 8AM-4:30PM (CST). Access by: In person only.

Todd County

Real Estate Recording—Todd County Recorder, 215 First Avenue South, Long Prairie, MN 56347. 612-732-4428. Fax: 612-732-4001. 8AM-4:30PM (CST).

Felony, Misdemeanor, Civil, Eviction, Small Claims, Probate—7th Judicial District Court, 221 1st Ave South, Long Prairie, MN 56347. 612-732-4460. Fax: 612-732-2506. 8AM-4:30PM (CST). Access by: Mail, in person.

Traverse County

Real Estate Recording—Traverse County Recorder, Courthouse, 702 2nd Ave. North, Wheaton, MN 56296. 612-563-4622. 8AM-4:30PM (CST).

Felony, Misdemeanor, Civil, Eviction, Small Claims, Probate—8th Judicial District Court, 702 2nd Ave N (PO Box 867), Wheaton, MN 56296. 612-563-4343. Fax: 612-563-4311. 8AM-Noon, 12:30-4:30PM (CST). Access by: Fax, mail, in person.

Wabasha County

Real Estate Recording—Wabasha County Recorder, 625 Jefferson Avenue, Wabasha, MN 55981. 612-565-3623. Fax: 612-565-2774. 8AM-4PM (CST).

Felony, Misdemeanor, Civil, Eviction, Small Claims, Probate—3rd Judicial District Court, 625 Jefferson Ave, Wabasha, MN 55981. 612-565-3579. Fax: 612-565-2774. 8AM-4PM (CST). Access by: In person only. Effective July 1, 1997, this court will no longer conduct criminal record searches..

Wadena County

Real Estate Recording—Wadena County Recorder, 415 South Jefferson, Courthouse, Wadena, MN 56482. 218-631-2362. Fax: 218-631-2428. 8AM-4:30PM (CST).

Felony, Misdemeanor, Civil, Eviction, Small Claims, Probate—7th Judicial District Court, County Courthouse, 415 South Jefferson St, Wadena, MN 56482. 218-631-2895. Fax: 218-631-2895. 8AM-4:30PM (CST). Access by: In person only.

Waseca County

Real Estate Recording—Waseca County Recorder, 307 North State Street, Waseca, MN 56093. 507-835-0670. Fax: 507-835-0633. 8AM-4:30PM (CST).

Felony, Misdemeanor, Civil, Eviction, Small Claims, Probate—3rd Judicial District Court, 307 N State St, Waseca, MN 56093. 507-835-0540. Fax: 507-835-0633. 8AM-4:30PM (CST). Access by: In person only. Effective July 1, 1997, this court will no longer conduct criminal record searches..

Washington County

Real Estate Recording—Washington County Recorder, 14900 North 61st Street, P.O. Box 6, Stillwater, MN 55082. 612-430-6755. Fax: 612-430-6753. 8AM-4:30PM (CST).

Felony, Misdemeanor, Civil, Eviction, Small Claims, Probate—10th Judicial District Court, 14900 61st St North, PO Box 3802, Stillwater, MN 55082-3802. 612-439-3220. Fax: 612-430-6360. 8AM-4:30PM (CST). Access by: Mail, in person.

Watonwan County

Real Estate Recording—Watonwan County Recorder, Courthouse, St. James, MN 56081. 507-375-1216. 8:30AM-Noon, 1-5PM (CST).

Felony, Misdemeanor, Civil, Eviction, Small Claims, Probate—5th Judicial District Court, PO Box 518, St James, MN 56081. 507-375-1236. Fax: 507-375-5010. 8:30AM-5PM (CST). Access by: Fax, mail, in person.

Wilkin County

Real Estate Recording—Wilkin County Recorder, 300 South 5th Street, Courthouse, Breckenridge, MN 56520. 218-643-4012. Fax: 218-643-2230. 8AM-4:30PM (CST).

Felony, Misdemeanor, Civil, Eviction, Small Claims, Probate—8th Judicial District Court, PO Box 219, Breckenridge, MN 56520. 218-643-4972. Fax: 218-643-5733. 8AM-4:30PM (CST). Access by: Mail, in person.

Winona County

Real Estate Recording—Winona County Recorder, 171 West 3rd Street, Winona, MN 55987. 507-457-6340. Fax: 507-457-6469. 8AM-5PM (CST).

Felony, Misdemeanor, Civil, Eviction, Small Claims, Probate—3rd Judicial District Court, 171 West 3rd St, Winona, MN 55987. 507-457-6375. Fax: 507-457-6392. 8AM-5PM (CST). Access by: In person only. Effective July 1, 1997, this court will no longer conduct criminal record searches..

Wright County

Real Estate Recording—Wright County Recorder, 10 2nd Street NW, Room 210, Buffalo, MN 55313. 612-682-7360. 8AM-4:30PM (CST).

Felony, Misdemeanor, Civil, Eviction, Small Claims, Probate—10th Judicial District Court, 10 NW 2nd St, Room 201, Buffalo, MN 55313-1192. 612-682-7539. Fax: 612-682-7300. 8AM-4:30PM (CST). Access by: Mail, in person.

Yellow Medicine County

Real Estate Recording—Yellow Medicine County Recorder, 415 9th Avenue, Courthouse, Granite Falls, MN 56241. 320-564-2529. Fax: 320-564-4165. 8AM-4PM (CST).

Felony, Misdemeanor, Civil, Eviction, Small Claims, Probate—8th Judicial District Court, 415 9th Ave, Granite Falls, MN 56241. 320-564-3325. Fax: 320-564-4435. 8AM-4PM (CST). Access by: In person only.

Federal Courts

US District Court
District of Minnesota

Duluth Division, US District Court Clerk, 417 Federal Bldg, Duluth, MN 55802. 218-720-5250. Counties: Aitkin, *Becker, *Beltrami, Benton, *Big Stone, Carlton, Cass, *Clay, *Clearwater, Cook, Crow Wing, *Douglas, *Grant, *Hubbard, Itasca, Kanabec, *Kittson, Koochiching, Lake, *Lake of the Woods, *Mahnomen, *Marshall, Mille Lacs, Morrison, *Norman, *Otter Tail, *Pennington, Pine, *Polk, *Pope, *Red Lake, *Roseau, *Stearns, *Stevens, St. Louis, *Todd, *Traverse, *Wadena, *Wilkin. As of March 1, 1995, cases from the counties marked with an asterisk (*) are heard here. Previously cases for these counties were allocated between St. Paul and Minneapolis

Minneapolis Division, US District Court Clerk, Room 202, 300 S 4th St, Minneapolis, MN 55415. 612-664-5000. Counties: All counties not covered by the Duluth Division. Cases are allocated between Minneapolis and St Paul

St Paul Division, US District Court 708 Federal Bldg, 316 N Robert, St Paul, MN 55101. 612-290-3212. Counties: All counties not covered by the Duluth Division. Cases are allocated between Minneapolis and St Paul

US Bankruptcy Court
District of Minnesota

Duluth Division, US Bankruptcy Court, 416 US Courthouse, 515 W 1st St, Duluth, MN 55802. 218-720-5253. Voice Case Information System: 612-290-4070. Counties:

Aitkin, Benton, Carlton, Cass, Cook, Crow Wing, Itasca, Kanabec, Koochiching, Lake, Mille Lacs, Morrison, Pine, St. Louis. A petition commencing Chapter 11 or 12 proceedings may be filed in any of the four divisions, but may be assigned to another division

Fergus Falls Division, US Bankruptcy Court, 204 US Courthouse, 118 S Mill St, Fergus Falls, MN 56537. 218-739-4671. Voice Case Information System: 612-290-4070. Counties: Becker, Beltrami, Big Stone, Clay, Clearwater, Douglas, Grant, Hubbard, Kittson, Lake of the Woods, Mahnomen, Marshall, Norman, Otter Tail, Pennington, Polk, Pope, Red Lake, Roseau, Stearns, Stevens, Todd, Traverse, Wadena, Wilkin. A petition commencing Chapter 11 or 12 proceedings may be filed initially in any of the four divisions, but may be assigned to another division

Minneapolis Division, US Bankruptcy Court, 301 US Courthouse, 300 S 4th St, Minneapolis, MN 55415. 612-664-5200. Voice Case Information System: 612-290-4070. Coun-

ties: Anoka, Carver, Chippewa, Hennepin, Isanti, Kandiyohi, McLeod, Meeker, Renville, Sherburne, Swift, Wright. Initial petitions for Chapter 11 or 12 may be filed at any of the four divisions, but may be assigned to a judge in another division

St Paul Division, US Bankruptcy Court, 200 Federal Bldg, 316 N Robert St, St Paul, MN 55101. 612-290-3184. Voice Case Information System: 612-290-4070. Counties: Blue Earth, Brown, Chisago, Cottonwood, Dakota, Dodge, Faribault, Fillmore, Freeborn, Goodhue, Houston, Jackson, Lac qui Parle, Le Sueur, Lincoln, Lyon, Martin, Mower, Murray, Nicollet, Nobles, Olmsted, Pipestone, Ramsey, Redwood, Rice, Rock, Scott, Sibley, Steele, Wabasha, Waseca, Washington, Watonwan, Winona, Yellow Medicine. Cases from Benton, Kanabec Mille Lacs, Morrison, and Pine may also be heard here. A petition commencing Chapter 11 or 12 proceedings may be filed initially with any of the four divisions, but may be assigned to another division

Mississippi

Capitol: Jackson (Hinds County)	
Number of Counties: 82	**Population:** 2,697,243
County Court Locations:	**Federal Court Locations:**
•Circuit Courts: 70/22 Districts	•District Courts: 9
•County Courts: 3/19 Counties	•Bankruptcy Courts: 3
•Combined Courts: 20	**State Agencies:** 19
•Chancery Courts: 91/ 20 Districts	
•Justice Courts: 88	
Municipal Courts: 168	
Family Courts: 1	

State Agencies—Summary

General Help Numbers:

State Archives

Archives & History Department	601-359-6850
Archives & Library Division	Fax: 601-359-6905
PO Box 571	9AM-5PM TU-F; 8-1 SA
Jackson, MS 39205-0571	
Historical Society:	601-359-6850
Reference Librarian:	601-359-6876

Governor's Office

Governor's Office	601-359-3150
PO Box 139	Fax: 601-359-3741
Jackson, MS 39205	8AM-5PM
Alternate Telephone:	800-832-6123

Attorney General's Office

Attorney General's Office	601-359-3680
PO Box 220	Fax: 601-359-3796
Jackson, MS 39205	8AM-5PM
Alternate Telephone:	601-359-3692

State Legislation

Mississippi Legislature	601-359-3770
Documents	8AM-5PM
PO Box 1018	
Jackson, MS 39215	
Senate:	601-359-3229
House:	601-359-3358

Important State Internet Sites:

State of Mississippi World Wide Web

www.state.ms.us/

This site provides limited access to state government sites.

U.S. House and Senate Information

207.168.215.81

This site lists the MS members of the U.S. Congress, their addresses, phone numbers, their committees and you can send them e-mail from this site.

Uniform Commercial Code

www.sos.state.ms.us/

Listed under the Business Services section is the information needed to get started on UCC Searching. Forms are available online.

Legislature and Bill Status

www.ls.state.ms.us/

This site gives access to the State Senate and House as well as the bill tracking information.

State Agencies—Public Records

Criminal Records
Records not available from state agency.

Corporation Records
Limited Partnership Records
Limited Liability Company Records
Trademarks/Servicemarks
Corporation Commission, Secretary of State, PO Box 136, Jackson, MS 39205, Main Telephone: 601-359-1627, Alternate Telephone: 800-256-3494, Fax: 601-359-1607, Hours: 8AM-5PM. Access by: mail, phone, fax, visit, PC.

Uniform Commercial Code
Federal Tax Liens
State Tax Liens
UCC Division, Secretary of State, PO Box 136, Jackson, MS 39205, Main Telephone: 601-359-1621, Alternate Telephone: 601-359-1350, Fax: 601-359-1607, Hours: 8AM-5PM. Access by: mail, phone, visit, PC.

Sales Tax Registrations
Revenue Bureau, Sales Tax Division, PO Box 22828, Jackson, MS 39225-2828, Main Telephone: 601-359-1133, Fax: 601-359-2680, Hours: 8AM-5PM. Access by: mail, phone, visit.

Birth Certificates
State Department of Health, Vital Statistics & Records, PO Box 1700, Jackson, MS 39215-1700, Main Telephone: 601-960-7981, Fax: 601-352-0013, Hours: 7:30AM-5PM. Access by: mail, fax, phone, visit.

Death Records
State Department of Health, Vital Statistics, PO Box 1700, Jackson, MS 39215-1700, Main Telephone: 601-960-7981, Fax: 601-352-0013, Hours: 7:30AM-5PM. Access by: mail, phone, visit.

Marriage Certificates
State Department of Health, Vital Statistics, PO Box 1700, Jackson, MS 39215-1700, Main Telephone: 601-960-7981, Fax: 601-352-0013, Hours: 7:30AM-5PM. Access by: mail, phone, visit.

Divorce Records
State Department of Health, Vital Statistics, PO Box 1700, Jackson, MS 39215-1700, Main Telephone: 601-960-7981, Fax: 601-352-0013, Hours: 7:30AM-5PM. Access by: mail, visit. The state maintains a state-wide index and can refer to book and page number in county records. Requests for copies must be made to the county of record.

Workers' Compensation Records
Workers Compensation Commission, PO Box 5300, Jackson, MS 39296-5300, Main Telephone: 601-987-4200, Hours: 8AM-5PM. Access by: mail, visit. The state does not provide electronic access, but has sold the database to a third party who does provide online retrieval and the agency refers all calls to them. Call (601) 853-4636 for details.

Driver Records
Department of Public Safety, Driver Records, PO Box 958, Jackson, MS 39205, Main Telephone: 601-987-1274, Hours: 8AM-5PM. Access by: mail, visit. Copies of tickets may be obtained from the same address for a fee of $5.00 per record. A pre-addressed, stamped envelope is advised.

Vehicle Ownership
Vehicle Identification
Mississippi State Tax Commission, Registration Department, PO Box 1140, Jackson, MS 39215, Main Telephone: 601-923-7143, Fax: 601-923-7133, Fax: 601-923-7134, Hours: 8AM-5PM. Access by: mail, visit. Please note that title information (liens, histories) requests are processed by a different section than registration information. If mailing requests, use PO Box 1033 for the Title Department.

Accident Reports
Safety Responsibility, Accident Records, PO Box 958, Jackson, MS 39205, Main Telephone: 601-987-1260, Hours: 8AM-5PM. Access by: mail only. The above address is for Highway Patrol accident investigations only. Reports require authorization from person involved. You must go to the agency that did the investigation for reports not found with the Highway Patrol.

Hunting License Information
Fishing License Information
Department of Wildlife, Fisheries & Parks, 2906 N State St, 3rd Floor, Jackson, MS 39205, Main Telephone: 601-364-2031, Data Processing Div: 601-364-2057, Fax: 601-364-2125, Hours: 8AM-5PM. Access by: mail, phone, visit.

County Courts and Recording Offices

What You Need to Know...

About the Courts

Administration

Court Administrator	601-359-3697
Supreme Court, Box 117	Fax: 601-359-2443
Jackson, MS 39205	

Court Structure

A Court of Appeals will be in place effective 1-1-95.

Justice Courts were first created in 1984; thus, Justice Courts have records back only to 1984. Prior to 1984, records were kept separately by each judge and the location today is, often, unknown. Probate is handled by the Chancery Courts as are property matters.

Searching Hints

A number of counties have two Circuit Court Districts. A search of either court in such a county will include the index from the other court.

Full Name is a search requirement for all courts and DOB and SSN are very helpful to differentiate between like-named individuals.

A large portion of the state will change to a 228 area code. This is scheduled for completion by 9/98.

Online Access

A pilot program for a statewide online computer system is in process; however, it is not expected to be implemented within the next year or so. This system is intended for internal use only.

About the Recorder's Office

Organization

82 counties, 92 filing offices. The recording officers are Chancery Clerk and Clerk of Circuit Court (state tax liens). **Ten counties have two separate recording offices**—Bolivar, Carroll, Chickasaw, Craighead, Harrison, Hinds, Jasper, Jones, Panola, Tallahatchie, and Yalobusha. See the notes under each county for how to determine which office is appropriate to search. The entire state is in the Central Time Zone (CST).

UCC Records

This is a **dual filing state**. Financing statements are filed both at the state level and with the Chancery Clerk, except for consumer goods, farm related and real estate related filings, which are filed only with the Chancery Clerk. All but one county will perform UCC searches. Use search request form UCC-11. Search fees are usually $5.00 per debtor name. Copies fees vary from $.25 to $2.00 per page.

Lien Records

Federal tax liens on personal property of businesses are filed with the Secretary of State. Federal tax liens on personal property of individuals are filed with the county Chancery Clerk. **State tax liens on personal property are filed with the county Clerk of Circuit Court.** Refer to *The Sourcebook of County Court Records* for information about Mississippi Circuit Courts. State tax liens on real property are filed with the Chancery Clerk. Most Chancery Clerk offices will perform a federal tax lien search for a fee of $5.00 per name. Copy fees vary. Other liens include mechanics, lis pendens, judgment (Circuit Court), and construction.

Real Estate Records

A few counties will perform real estate searches. Copies usually cost $.50 per page and certification fees $1.00 per document. The Assessor maintains tax records.

County Courts and Recording Offices

Adams County

Real Estate Recording—Adams County Clerk of the Chancery Court, 1 Courthouse Square, Natchez, MS 39120. 601-446-6684. Fax: 601-445-7913. 8AM-5PM (CST).

Felony, Misdemeanor, Civil—Circuit and County Court, PO Box 1224, Natchez, MS 39121. 601-446-6326. 8AM-5PM (CST). Access by: Mail, in person.

Misdemeanor, Civil Actions Under $2,500, Eviction, Small Claims—Justice Court, PO Box 1048, Natchez, MS 39121. 601-446-6326. 8AM-5PM (CST). Access by: Mail, in person.

Probate—Chancery Court, PO Box 1006, Natchez, MS 39121. 601-446-6684. Fax: 601-445-7913. 8AM-5PM (CST). Access by: Mail, in person.

Alcorn County

Real Estate Recording—Alcorn County Clerk of the Chancery Court, 501 Waldron Street, Corinth, MS 38835. 601-286-7700. Fax: 601-286-7706. 8AM-5PM (CST).

Felony, Civil Actions Over $2,500—Circuit Court, PO Box 430 Attn: Circuit Clerk, Corinth, MS 38834. 601-286-7740. Fax: 601-286-5713. 8AM-5PM (CST). Access by: Mail, in person.

Misdemeanor, Civil Actions Under $2,500, Eviction, Small Claims—Justice Court, PO Box 226, Corinth, MS 38834. 601-286-7776. 8AM-5PM (CST). Access by: In person only.

Probate—Chancery Court, PO Box 69, Corinth, MS 38835-0069. 601-286-7702. Fax: 601-286-7706. (CST).

Amite County

Real Estate Recording—Amite County Clerk of the Chancery Court, 243 West Main Street, Liberty, MS 39645. 601-657-8022. Fax: 601-657-8288. 8AM-5PM (CST).

Felony, Civil Actions Over $2,500—Circuit Court, PO Box 312, Liberty, MS 39645. 601-657-8932. Fax: 601-657-8288. 8AM-5PM (CST). Access by: Fax, mail, in person.

Misdemeanor, Civil Actions Under $2,500, Eviction, Small Claims—Justice Court, PO Box 362, Liberty, MS 39645. 601-657-4527. 8AM-5PM (CST). Access by: Mail, in person.

Probate—Chancery Court, PO Box 680, Liberty, MS 39645. 601-657-8022. Fax: 601-657-8288. 8AM-5PM (CST).

Attala County

Real Estate Recording—Attala County Clerk of the Chancery Court, West Washington Street, Chancery Court Building, Kosciusko, MS 39090. 601-289-2921. Fax: 601-289-7662. 8AM-5PM (CST).

Felony, Civil Actions Over $2,500—Circuit Court, Courthouse, Kosciusko, MS 39090. 601-289-1471. Fax: 601-289-7666. 8AM-5PM (CST). Access by: Phone, fax, mail, in person.

Misdemeanor, Civil Actions Under $2,500, Eviction, Small Claims—Justice Court, Courthouse, Kosciusko, MS 39090. 601-289-7272. 8AM-5PM (CST). Access by: Mail, in person.

Probate—Chancery Court, 230 W. Washington, Kosciusko, MS 39090. 601-289-2921. Fax: 601-289-7662. 8AM-5PM (CST).

Benton County

Real Estate Recording—Benton County Clerk of the Chancery Court, Main Street, Courthouse, Ashland, MS 38603. 601-224-6300. Fax: 601-224-6303. 8AM-5PM (CST).

Felony, Civil Actions Over $2,500—Circuit Court, PO Box 262, Ashland, MS 38603. 601-224-6310. Fax: 601-224-6303. 8AM-5PM (CST). Access by: Mail, in person.

Misdemeanor, Civil Actions Under $2,500, Eviction, Small Claims—Justice Court, PO Box 152, Ashland, MS 38603. 601-224-6320. Fax: 601-224-6303. 8AM-5PM (CST). Access by: Mail, in person.

Probate—Chancery Court, PO Box 218, Ashland, MS 38603. 601-224-6300. Fax: 601-224-6303. 8AM-5PM (CST). Access by: Mail.

Bolivar County

Real Estate Recording—Bolivar County Clerk of the Chancery Court, 2nd District, Court Street, Courthouse, Cleveland, MS 38732. 601-843-2071. Fax: 601-846-2940. 8AM-5PM (CST).

Bolivar County Clerk of the Chancery Court, 1st District, 801 Main Street, Courthouse, Rosedale, MS 38769. 601-759-3762. Fax: 601-759-3467. 8AM-Noon,1-5PM (CST).

Felony, Misdemeanor, Civil—Circuit and County Court-2nd District, PO Box 670, Cleveland, MS 38732. 601-843-2061. Fax: 601-843-5880. 8:00AM-5:00PM (CST). Access by: Mail, in person.

Circuit and County Court-1st District, PO Box 205, Rosedale, MS 38769. 601-759-6521. 8AM-5PM (CST). Access by: Mail, in person.

Misdemeanor, Civil Actions Under $2,500, Eviction, Small Claims—Justice Court, PO Box 1507, Cleveland, MS 38732. 601-843-4008. 8:00AM-5:00PM (CST). Access by: Mail, in person.

Probate—Cleveland Chancery Court, PO Box 789, Cleveland, MS 38732. 601-843-2071. Fax: 601-846-5880. 8AM-5PM (CST). Access by: Mail, in person.

Rosedale Chancery Court, PO Box 238, Rosedale, MS 38769. 601-759-3762. Fax: 601-759-3467. 8AM-Noon, 1-5PM (CST).

Calhoun County

Real Estate Recording—Calhoun County Clerk of the Chancery Court, Courthouse Square, Pittsboro, MS 38951. 601-983-3117. Fax: 601-983-3128. 8AM-5PM (CST).

Felony, Civil Actions Over $2,500—Circuit Court, PO Box 25, Pittsboro, MS 38951. 601-983-3101. Fax: 601-983-3128. 8AM-5PM (CST). Access by: Mail, in person.

Misdemeanor, Civil Actions Under $2,500, Eviction, Small Claims—Justice Court, PO Box 7, Pittsboro, MS 38951. 601-983-3134. 8AM-5PM (CST). Access by: In person only.

Probate—Chancery Court, PO Box 8, Pittsboro, MS 38951. 601-983-3117. Fax: 601-983-3128. 8AM-5PM (CST).

Carroll County

Real Estate Recording—Carroll County Clerk of the Chancery Court, 1st District, Courthouse, Carrollton, MS 38917. 601-237-9274. 8AM-Noon, 1-5PM (CST).

Carroll County Clerk of the Chancery Court, 2nd District, 101 Highway 51, Courthouse, Vaiden, MS 39176. 601-464-5476. Fax: 601-464-7745. 8AM-5PM (CST).

Felony, Civil Actions Over $2,500—Circuit Court, PO Box 6, Vaiden, MS 39176. 601-464-5476. 8:00AM-5:00PM (CST). Access by: Mail, in person.

Misdemeanor, Civil Actions Under $2,500, Eviction, Small Claims—Justice Court, PO Box 10, Carrollton, MS 38917. 601-237-9285. 8AM-4PM (CST). Access by: Mail, in person.

Probate—Chancery Court, PO Box 60, Carrollton, MS 38917. 601-237-9274. 8AM-5PM (CST).

Chickasaw County

Real Estate Recording—Chickasaw County Clerk of the Chancery Court, 1st District, Courthouse, Houston, MS 38851. 601-456-2513. Fax: 601-456-5295. 8AM-5PM (CST).

Chickasaw County Clerk of the Chancery Court, 2nd District, 234 Main Street, Room 201, Okolona, MS 38860. 601-447-2092. Fax: 601-447-5024. 8AM-Noon,1-5PM (CST).

Felony, Civil Actions Over $2,500—Circuit Court-1st District, 1 Pinson Sq, Rm 2, Houston, MS 38851. 601-456-2331. Fax: 601-456-5295. 8AM-5PM (CST). Access by: Fax, mail, in person.

Circuit Court-2nd District, Courthouse, Okolona, MS 38860. 601-447-2838. Fax: 601-447-5024. 8AM-5PM (CST). Access by: Fax, mail, in person.

Misdemeanor, Civil Actions Under $2,500, Eviction, Small Claims—Justice Court, Courthouse, Houston, MS 38851. 601-447-3402. Fax: 601-456-5295. 8AM-5PM (CST). Access by: Mail, in person.

Probate—Chancery Court, Courthouse Bldg, 101 N Jefferson St, Houston, MS 38851. 601-456-2513. Fax: 601-456-5295. (CST).

Chancery Court, 234 W Main, Rm 201, Okolona, MS 38860-1438. 601-447-2090. Fax: 601-447-5024. (CST).

Choctaw County

Real Estate Recording—Choctaw County Clerk of the Chancery Court, Quinn Street, Ackerman, MS 39735. 601-285-6329. Fax: 601-285-3444. 8AM-Noon,1-5PM (CST).

Felony, Civil Actions Over $2,500—Circuit Court, PO Box 34, Ackerman, MS 39735. 601-285-6245. Fax: 601-285-3444. 8AM-5PM (CST). Access by: Phone, mail, in person.

Misdemeanor, Civil Actions Under $2,500, Eviction, Small Claims—Justice Court, PO Box 357, Ackerman, MS 39735. 601-285-3599. Fax: 601-285-3444. 8AM-5PM (CST). Access by: In person only.

Probate—Chancery Court, PO Box 250, Ackerman, MS 39735. 601-285-6329. Fax: 601-285-3444. 8AM-5PM (CST).

Claiborne County

Real Estate Recording—Claiborne County Clerk of the Chancery Court, 410 Main Street, Port Gibson, MS 39150. 601-437-4992. Fax: 601-437-4430. 8AM-5PM (CST).

Felony, Civil Actions Over $2,500—Circuit Court, PO Box 549, Port Gibson, MS 39150. 601-437-5841. 8AM-5PM (CST). Access by: Mail, in person.

Misdemeanor, Civil Actions Under $2,500, Eviction, Small Claims—Justice Court, PO Box 497, Port Gibson, MS 39150. 601-437-4478. 8AM-5PM (CST). Access by: Mail, in person.

Probate—Chancery Court, PO Box 449, Port Gibson, MS 39150. 601-437-4992. Fax: 601-437-4430. 8AM-5PM (CST).

Clarke County

Real Estate Recording—Clarke County Clerk of the Chancery Court, Archusa Street, Courthouse, Quitman, MS 39355. 601-776-2126. 8AM-5PM (CST).

Felony, Civil Actions Over $2,500—Circuit Court, PO Box 216, Quitman, MS 39355. 601-776-3111. Fax: 601-776-1001. 8AM-5PM (CST). Access by: Fax, mail, in person.

Misdemeanor, Civil Actions Under $2,500, Eviction, Small Claims—Justice Court, PO Box 4, Quitman, MS 39355. 601-776-5371. 8AM-5PM (CST). Access by: Mail, in person.

Probate—Chancery Court, PO Box 689, Quitman, MS 39355. 601-776-2126. 8AM-5PM (CST).

Clay County

Real Estate Recording—Clay County Clerk of the Chancery Court, 205 Court Street, West Point, MS 39773. 601-494-3124. 8AM-5PM (CST).

Felony, Civil Actions Over $2,500—Circuit Court, PO Box 364, West Point, MS 39773. 601-494-3384. 8AM-5PM (CST). Access by: Mail, in person.

Misdemeanor, Civil Actions Under $2,500, Eviction, Small Claims—Justice Court, PO Box 674, West Point, MS 39773. 601-494-6141. Fax: 601-494-4034. 8AM-5PM (CST). Access by: Mail, in person.

Probate—Chancery Court, PO Box 815, West Point, MS 39773. 601-494-3124. 8AM-5PM (CST). Access by: Mail, in person.

Coahoma County

Real Estate Recording—Coahoma County Clerk of the Chancery Court, 115 First Street, Clarksdale, MS 38614. 601-624-3000. Fax: 601-624-3029. 8AM-5PM (CST).

Felony, Misdemeanor, Civil—Circuit and County Court, PO Box 849, Clarksdale, MS 38614. 601-624-3014. Fax: 601-624-3075. 8AM-5PM (CST). Access by: Mail, in person.

Misdemeanor, Civil Actions Under $2,500, Eviction, Small Claims—Justice Court, 144 Ritch, Clarksdale, MS 38614. 601-624-3060. 8AM-5PM (CST). Access by: Mail, in person.

Probate—Chancery Court, PO Box 98, Clarksdale, MS 38614. 601-624-3000. Fax: 601-624-3029. 8AM-5PM (CST).

Copiah County

Real Estate Recording—Copiah County Clerk of the Chancery Court, 100 Caldwell Drive, Courthouse Square, Hazlehurst, MS 39083. 601-894-3021. Fax: 601-894-3026. 8AM-5PM (CST).

Felony, Civil Actions Over $2,500—Circuit Court, PO Box 467, Hazlehurst, MS 39083. 601-894-1241. Fax: 601-894-3026. 8AM-5PM (CST). Access by: Fax, mail, in person.

Misdemeanor, Civil Actions Under $2,500, Eviction, Small Claims—Justice Court, PO Box 798, Hazlehurst, MS 39083. 601-894-2163. Fax: 601-894-1676. 8:00AM-5:00PM (CST). Access by: Mail, in person.

Probate—Chancery Court, PO Box 507, Hazlehurst, MS 39083. 601-894-3021. Fax: 601-894-3026. 8AM-5PM (CST).

Covington County

Real Estate Recording—Covington County Clerk of the Chancery Court, 101 S. Elm St., Collins, MS 39428. 601-765-4242. Fax: 601-765-1052. 8AM-5PM (CST).

Felony, Civil Actions Over $2,500—Circuit Court, PO Box 667, Collins, MS 39428. 601-765-6506. Fax: 601-765-1052. 8AM-5PM (CST). Access by: Fax, mail, in person.

Misdemeanor, Civil Actions Under $2,500, Eviction, Small Claims—Justice Court, PO Box 665, Collins, MS 39428. 601-765-6581. 8AM-5PM (CST). Access by: Mail, in person.

Probate—Chancery Court, PO Box 1679, Collins, MS 39428. 601-765-4242. Fax: 601-765-1052. 8AM-5PM (CST).

De Soto County

Real Estate Recording—De Soto County Clerk of the Chancery Court, 2535 Highway 51 South, Courthouse, Hernando, MS 38632. 601-429-1361. 8AM-5PM (CST).

Felony, Misdemeanor, Civil—Circuit and County Court, 2535 Hwy 51 South, Hernando, MS 38632. 601-429-1325. 8AM-5PM (CST). Access by: Mail, in person.

Misdemeanor, Civil Actions Under $2,500, Eviction, Small Claims—Justice Court, 891 E. Rasco, Southaven, MS 38671. 601-393-5810. Fax: 601-393-5859. 8AM-5PM (CST). Access by: Mail, in person.

Probate—Chancery Court, 2535 Hwy 51 South, Hernando, MS 38632. 601-429-1318. Fax: 601-429-1311. 8AM-5PM (CST).

Forrest County

Real Estate Recording—Forrest County Clerk of the Chancery Court, 641 Main Street, Chancery Court Building, Hattiesburg, MS 39401. 601-545-6014. Fax: 601-545-6095. 8AM-5PM (CST).

Felony, Misdemeanor, Civil—Circuit and County Court, PO Box 992, Hattiesburg, MS 39403. 601-582-3213. Fax: 601-545-6093. 8AM-5PM (CST). Access by: Mail, in person.

Misdemeanor, Civil Actions Under $2,500, Eviction, Small Claims—Justice Court, 316 Forrest St, Hattiesburg, MS 39401. 601-544-3136. 8AM-5PM (CST). Access by: Mail, in person.

Probate—Chancery Court, PO Box 951, Hattiesburg, MS 39403. 601-545-6014. 8AM-5PM (CST).

Franklin County

Real Estate Recording—Franklin County Clerk of the Chancery Court, 101 Main Street, Courthouse, Meadville, MS 39653. 601-384-2330. Fax: 601-384-5864. 8AM-5PM (CST).

Felony, Civil Actions Over $2,500—Circuit Court, PO Box 267, Meadville, MS 39653. 601-384-2320. Fax: 601-384-5864. 8AM-5PM (CST). Access by: Mail, in person.

Misdemeanor, Civil Actions Under $2,500, Eviction, Small Claims—Justice Court, PO Box 365, Meadville, MS 39653. 601-384-2002. 8AM-5PM (CST). Access by: Mail, in person.

Probate—Chancery Court, PO Box 297, Meadville, MS 39653. 601-384-2330. Fax: 601-384-5864. 8AM-5PM (CST).

George County

Real Estate Recording—George County Clerk of the Chancery Court, Court House Square, Lucedale, MS 39452. 601-947-4801. 8AM-5PM; 9AM-Noon Sat (CST).

Felony, Civil Actions Over $2,500—Circuit Court, 355 Cox St, Suite C, Lucedale, MS 39452. 601-947-4881. Fax: 601-947-8804. 8AM-5PM M-F, 9AM-12PM Sat (CST). Access by: Fax, mail, in person.

Misdemeanor, Civil Actions Under $2,500, Eviction, Small Claims—Justice Court, 200 Cox St, Lucedale, MS 39452. 601-947-4834. 8AM-5PM (CST). Access by: Mail, in person.

Probate—Chancery Court, 200 Courthouse Square, Lucedale, MS 39452. 601-947-4801. Fax: 601-947-4812. 8AM-5PM (CST).

Greene County

Real Estate Recording—Greene County Clerk of the Chancery Court, Courthouse, Main St., Leakesville, MS 39451. 601-394-2377. (CST).

Felony, Civil Actions Over $2,500—Circuit Court, PO Box 310, Leakesville, MS 39451. 601-394-2379. Fax: 601-394-2334. 8AM-5PM M-F (CST). Access by: Fax, mail, in person.

Misdemeanor, Civil Actions Under $2,500, Eviction, Small Claims—Justice Court, PO Box 547, Leakesville, MS 39451. 601-394-2347. 8AM-5PM (CST). Access by: Mail, in person.

Probate—Chancery Court, PO Box 610, Leakesville, MS 39451. 601-394-2377. 8AM-5PM (CST).

Grenada County

Real Estate Recording—Grenada County Clerk of the Chancery Court, 59 Green Street, Courthouse, Grenada, MS 38901. 601-226-1821. Fax: 601-226-0427. 8AM-5PM (CST).

Felony, Civil Actions Over $2,500—Circuit Court, 59 Green St, Ste #8, Grenada, MS 38901. 601-226-1941. Fax: 601-226-0427. 8AM-5PM (CST). Access by: In person only.

Misdemeanor, Civil Actions Under $2,500, Eviction, Small Claims—Justice Court, 16 First St, Grenada, MS 38901. 601-226-3331. 8AM-5PM (CST). Access by: Mail, in person.

Probate—Chancery Court, PO Box 1208, Grenada, MS 38902. 601-226-1821. Fax: 601-226-0427. 8AM-5PM (CST).

Hancock County

Real Estate Recording—Hancock County Clerk of the Chancery Court, Chancery Clerk's Office, 152 Main St, Bay Saint Louis, MS 39520. 228-467-5404. Fax: 228-466-5994. 8AM-5PM (CST).

Felony, Civil Actions Over $2,500—Circuit Court, PO Box 249 Bay St., Bay St. Louis, MS 39520. 228-467-5265. Fax: 228-467-2779. 8AM-5PM (CST). Access by: Mail, in person.

Misdemeanor, Civil Actions Under $2,500, Eviction, Small Claims—Justice Court, PO Box 147, Bay St, Bay St. Louis, MS 39520. 228-467-5573. 8AM-5PM (CST). Access by: Mail, in person.

Probate—Chancery Court, PO Box 429 Bay St., Bay St. Louis, MS 39520. 228-467-5404. Fax: 228-466-5994. 8AM-5PM (CST).

Harrison County

Real Estate Recording—Harrison County Chancery Clerk, 2nd District, 730 Washington Loop, Biloxi, MS 39530. 228-435-8220. Fax: 228-435-8292. 8AM-5PM (CST).

Harrison County Clerk of the Chancery Court, 1st District, 1801 23rd Avenue, Gulfport, MS 39501. 228-865-4195. Fax: 228-868-1480. 8AM-5PM (CST).

Felony, Civil Actions Over $50,000—Circuit Court-2nd District, PO Box 235, Biloxi, MS 39533. 228-435-8258. Fax: 228-435-8277. 8AM-5PM (CST). Access by: Fax, mail, in person.

Circuit Court-1st District, PO Box 998, Gulfport, MS 39502. 228-865-4147. Fax: 228-865-4099. 8AM-5PM (CST). Access by: Mail, in person.

Misdemeanor, Civil Actions Under $50,000—County Court-2nd District, PO Box 235, Biloxi, MS 39533. 228-435-8231. Fax: 228-435-8277. 8AM-5PM (CST). Access by: Fax, mail, in person.

County Court-1st District, PO Box 998, Gulfport, MS 39502. 228-865-4097. 8AM-5PM (CST). Access by: Mail, in person.

Misdemeanor, Civil Actions Under $2,500, Eviction, Small Claims—Justice Court, PO Box 1754, Gulfport, MS 39502. Civil: 228-865-4193. Criminal: 228-865-4214. Fax: 228-865-4216. 8AM-5PM (CST). Access by: Mail, in person.

Probate—Biloxi Chancery Court, PO Box 544, Biloxi, MS 39533. 228-435-8224. Fax: 228-435-8251. 8AM-Noon, 1-5PM (CST).

Gulfport Chancery Court, PO Drawer CC, Gulfport, MS 39502. 228-865-4092. Fax: 228-865-1646. 8AM-Noon, 1-5PM (CST). Access by: In person only.

Hinds County

Real Estate Recording—Hinds County Clerk of the Chancery Court, 1st District, 316 South President Street, Jackson, MS 39201. 601-968-6516. Fax: 601-973-5535. 8AM-5PM (CST).

Hinds County Clerk of the Chancery Court, 2nd District, Main Street, Courthouse Annex, Raymond, MS 39154. 601-857-8055. 8AM-5PM (CST).

Felony, Misdemeanor, Civil—Circuit and County Court-1st District, PO Box 327, Jackson, MS 39205. 601-968-6628. 8AM-5PM (CST). Access by: Mail, in person.

Circuit and County Court-2nd District, PO Box 33, Raymond, MS 39154. 601-968-6653. 8AM-Noon, 1-5PM (CST). Access by: Mail, in person.

Misdemeanor, Civil Actions Under $2,500, Eviction, Small Claims—Justice Court, 407 E Pascagoula, 3rd floor, Jackson, MS 39207. 601-968-6781. Fax: 601-973-5532. 8AM-NOON, 1PM-5PM (CST). Access by: Mail, in person.

Probate—Jackson Chancery Court, PO Box 686, Jackson, MS 39205. 601-968-6540. Fax: 601-873-5554. 8AM-5PM (CST).

Raymond Chancery Court, PO Box 88, Raymond, MS 39154. 601-857-8055. Fax: 601-857-4953. 8AM-5PM (CST). Access by: Mail, in person.

Holmes County

Real Estate Recording—Holmes County Clerk of the Chancery Court, Courthouse, Lexington, MS 39095. 601-834-2508. 8AM-Noon,1-5PM (CST).

Felony, Civil Actions Over $2,500—Circuit Court, PO Box 718, Lexington, MS 39095. 601-834-2476. Fax: 601-834-2869. 8AM-5PM (CST). Access by: Fax, mail, in person.

Misdemeanor, Civil Actions Under $2,500, Eviction, Small Claims—Justice Court, PO Drawer D, Lexington, MS 39095. 601-834-4565. 8AM-NOON, 1PM-5PM (CST). Access by: Mail, in person.

Probate—Chancery Court, PO Box 239, Lexington, MS 39095. 601-834-2508. Fax: 601-834-3020. 8AM-Noon,1-5PM (CST). Access by: Mail, in person.

Humphreys County

Real Estate Recording—Humphreys County Clerk of the Chancery Court, 102 Castleman, Courthouse, Belzoni, MS

39038. 601-247-1740. Fax: 601-247-0101. 8AM-Noon, 1-5PM (CST).

Felony, Civil Actions Over $2,500—Circuit Court, PO Box 696, Belzoni, MS 39038. 601-247-3065. Fax: 601-247-3906. 8AM-5PM (CST). Access by: Phone, fax, mail, in person.

Misdemeanor, Civil Actions Under $2,500, Eviction, Small Claims—Justice Court, 102 Castleman St, Belzoni, MS 39038. 601-247-4337. Fax: 601-247-1095. 8AM-NOON, 1PM-5PM (CST). Access by: Mail, in person.

Probate—Chancery Court, PO Box 547, Belzoni, MS 39038. 601-247-1740. Fax: 601-247-1010. 8AM-Noon, 1-5PM (CST).

Issaquena County

Real Estate Recording—Issaquena County Clerk of the Chancery Court, 129 Court Street, Mayersville, MS 39113. 601-873-2761. Fax: 601-873-2061. 8AM-Noon,1-5PM (CST).

Felony, Civil Actions Over $2,500—Circuit Court, PO Box 27, Mayersville, MS 39113. 601-873-2761. 8AM-5PM (CST). Access by: In person only.

Misdemeanor, Civil Actions Under $2,500, Eviction, Small Claims—Justice Court, PO Box 27, Mayersville, MS 39113. 601-873-2761. 8AM-NOON, 1PM-5PM (CST). Access by: Mail, in person.

Probate—Chancery Court, PO Box 27, Mayersville, MS 39113. 601-873-2761. Fax: 601-873-2061. 8AM-5PM (CST).

Itawamba County

Real Estate Recording—Itawamba County Clerk of the Chancery Court, 201 West Main Street, Fulton, MS 38843. 601-862-3421. Fax: 601-862-4006. 8AM-5PM; 8AM-Noon Sat (CST).

Felony, Civil Actions Over $2,500—Circuit Court, 201 W Main, Fulton, MS 38843. 601-862-3511. Fax: 601-862-4006. 8AM-5PM (CST). Access by: Phone, fax, mail, in person.

Misdemeanor, Civil Actions Under $2,500, Eviction, Small Claims—Justice Court, 201 W Main, Fulton, MS 38843. 601-862-4315. Fax: 601-862-5805. 8AM-NOON, 1PM-5PM (CST). Access by: Mail, in person.

Probate—Chancery Court, 201 W Main, Fulton, MS 38843. 601-862-3421. Fax: 601-862-4006. 8AM-5PM M-F; 8AM-Noon Sat (CST). Access by: In person only.

Jackson County

Real Estate Recording—Jackson County Chancery Clerk, 1710A Market Street, Pascagoula, MS 39567. 228-769-3131. 8AM-5PM (CST).

Felony, Civil Actions Over $2,500—Circuit Court, PO Box 998, Pascagoula, MS 39568-0998. 228-769-3025. Fax: 228-769-3180. 8AM-5PM (CST). Access by: Fax, mail, in person.

Misdemeanor, Civil Actions Under $50,000—County Court, PO Box 998, Pascagoula, MS 39568. 228-769-3181. 8AM-5PM (CST). Access by: Mail, in person.

Misdemeanor, Civil Actions Under $2,500, Eviction, Small Claims—Justice Court, 5343 Jefferson St, Moss Point, MS 39563. 228-769-3080. Fax: 228-769-3364. (CST). Access by: Mail, in person.

Probate—Chancery Court, PO Box 998, Pascagoula, MS 39568. 228-769-3131. Fax: 228-769-3397. 8AM-5PM (CST). Access by: Mail, in person.

Jasper County

Real Estate Recording—Jasper County Clerk of the Chancery Court, 2nd District, Court Street, Bay Springs, MS 39422. 601-764-3026. Fax: 601-764-3468. 8AM-5PM (CST).

Jasper County Clerk of the Chancery Court, 1st District, Courthouse, Highway 503, Paulding, MS 39348. 601-727-4941. Fax: 601-727-4475. 8AM-5PM (CST).

Felony, Civil Actions Over $2,500—Circuit Court-2nd District, PO Box 447, Bay Springs, MS 39422. 601-764-2245. Fax: 601-764-3078. 8AM-5PM (CST). Access by: Mail, in person.

Circuit Court-1st District, PO Box 485, Paulding, MS 39348. 601-727-4941. 8AM-5PM (CST). Access by: Fax, mail, in person.

Misdemeanor, Civil Actions Under $2,500, Eviction, Small Claims—Justice Court, PO Box 1054, Bay Springs, MS 39422. 601-764-2065. Fax: 601-764-3402. 8AM-NOON, 1PM-5PM (CST). Access by: Mail, in person.

Probate—Bay Springs Chancery Court, PO Box 1047, Bay Springs, MS 39422. 601-764-3368. Fax: 601-764-3026. 8AM-5PM (CST).

Paulding Chancery Court, PO Box 494, Paulding, MS 39348. 601-727-4941. Fax: 601-727-4475. 8AM-5PM (CST).

Jefferson County

Real Estate Recording—Jefferson County Clerk of the Chancery Court, 307 Main, Fayette, MS 39069. 601-786-3021. Fax: 601-786-6009. 8AM-5PM (CST).

Felony, Civil Actions Over $2,500—Circuit Court, PO Box 305, Fayette, MS 39069. 601-786-3422. Fax: 601-786-6000. 8:00AM-5:00PM (CST). Access by: Mail, in person.

Misdemeanor, Civil Actions Under $2,500, Eviction, Small Claims—Justice Court, PO Box 1047, Fayette, MS 39069. 601-786-8594. Fax: 601-786-6000. 8AM-5PM (CST). Access by: Phone, fax, mail, in person.

Probate—Chancery Court, PO Box 145, Fayette, MS 39069. 601-786-3021. Fax: 601-786-6009. 8AM-5PM (CST).

Jefferson Davis County

Real Estate Recording—Jefferson Davis County Clerk of the Chancery Court, 1025 3rd St., Prentiss, MS 39474. 601-792-4204. Fax: 601-792-2894. 8AM-5PM (CST).

Felony, Civil Actions Over $2,500—Circuit Court, PO Box 1082, Prentiss, MS 39474. 601-792-4231. Fax: 601-792-2849. 8AM-5PM (CST). Access by: Fax, mail, in person.

Misdemeanor, Civil Actions Under $2,500, Eviction, Small Claims—Justice Court, PO Drawer 1407, Prentiss, MS 39474. 601-792-5129. 8AM-NOON, 1PM-5PM (CST). Access by: Mail, in person.

Probate—Chancery Court, PO Box 1137, Prentiss, MS 39474. 601-792-4231. Fax: 601-792-2894. 8AM-5PM (CST). Access by: Mail.

Jones County

Real Estate Recording—Jones County Clerk of the Chancery Court, 1st District, Court Street, Jones County Courthouse, Ellisville, MS 39437. 601-477-3307. (CST).

Jones County Clerk of the Chancery Court, 2nd District, 415 North 5th Avenue, Laurel, MS 39441. 601-428-0527. Fax: 601-428-3602. 8AM-5PM (CST).

Felony, Misdemeanor, Civil—Circuit and County Court-1st District, 101 N. Court St, Ellisville, MS 39437. 601-477-8538. 8AM-5PM (CST). Access by: Mail, in person.

Circuit and County Court-2nd District, PO Box 1336, Laurel, MS 39441. 601-425-2556. 8AM-5PM (CST). Access by: Mail, in person.

Misdemeanor, Civil Actions Under $2,500, Eviction, Small Claims—Justice Court, PO Box 1997, Laurel, MS 39441. 601-428-3137. Fax: 601-428-0526. 8AM-NOON, 1PM-5PM (CST). Access by: Fax, mail, in person.

Probate—Ellisville Chancery Court, 101 N. Court St., Ellisville, MS 39437. 601-477-3307. 8AM-Noon, 1-5PM (CST).

Laurel Chancery Court, PO Box 1468, Laurel, MS 39441. 601-428-0527. Fax: 601-428-3602. 8AM-5PM (CST). Access by: Mail.

Kemper County

Real Estate Recording—Kemper County Clerk of the Chancery Court, Courthouse Square, De Kalb, MS 39328. 601-743-2460. Fax: 601-743-2789. 8AM-5PM (CST).

Felony, Civil Actions Over $2,500—Circuit Court, PO Box 130, De Kalb, MS 39328. 601-743-2224. Fax: 601-743-2789. 8AM-5PM (CST). Access by: Mail, in person.

Misdemeanor, Civil Actions Under $2,500, Eviction, Small Claims—Justice Court, PO Box 661, De Kalb, MS 39328. 601-743-2793. Fax: 601-743-2789. 8AM-5PM (CST). Access by: Mail, in person.

Probate—Chancery Court, PO Box 188, De Kalb, MS 39328. 601-743-2460. Fax: 601-743-2789. 8AM-5PM (CST).

Lafayette County

Real Estate Recording—Lafayette County Clerk of the Chancery Court, Courthouse, Oxford, MS 38655. 601-234-2131. (CST).

Felony, Civil Actions Over $2,500—Circuit Court, LaFayette County Courthouse, Oxford, MS 38655. 601-234-4951. Fax: 601-236-0238. 8AM-5PM (CST). Access by: Mail, in person.

Misdemeanor, Civil Actions Under $2,500, Eviction, Small Claims—Justice Court, 1219 Monroe, Oxford, MS 38655. 601-234-1545. Fax: 601-238-7990. 8AM-5PM (CST). Access by: Mail, in person.

Probate—Chancery Court, PO Box 1240, Oxford, MS 38655. 601-234-2131. Fax: 601-234-5402. 8AM-5PM (CST).

Lamar County

Real Estate Recording—Lamar County Clerk of the Chancery Court, 203 Main Street, Purvis, MS 39475. 601-794-8504. Fax: 601-794-1049. 8AM-5PM (CST).

Felony, Civil Actions Over $2,500—Circuit Court, PO Box 369, Purvis, MS 39475. 601-794-8504. Fax: 601-794-1049. 8AM-5PM (CST). Access by: Mail, in person.

Misdemeanor, Civil Actions Under $2,500, Eviction, Small Claims—Justice Court, PO Box 1010, Purvis, MS 39475. 601-794-2950. Fax: 601-794-0149. 8AM-5PM (CST). Access by: Mail, in person.

Probate—Chancery Court, PO Box 247, Purvis, MS 39475. 601-794-8504. Fax: 601-794-1049. 8AM-5PM (CST).

Lauderdale County

Real Estate Recording—Lauderdale County Clerk of the Chancery Court, 500 Constitution Avenue, Room 105, Meridian, MS 39301. 601-482-9701. 8AM-5PM (CST).

Felony, Civil—Circuit and County Court, PO Box 1005, Meridian, MS 39302. 601-482-9738. Fax: 601-484-3970. 8AM-5PM (CST). Access by: Mail, in person.

Misdemeanor, Civil Actions Under $2,500, Eviction, Small Claims—Justice Court, PO Box 5126, Meridian, MS 39302. 601-482-9879. Fax: 601-482-9813. 8AM-5PM (CST). Access by: Mail, in person.

Probate—Chancery Court, PO Box 1587, Meridian, MS 39302. 601-482-9720. Fax: 601-486-4920. 8AM-Noon, 1-5PM (CST).

Lawrence County

Real Estate Recording—Lawrence County Clerk of the Chancery Court, Courthouse Square, Monticello, MS 39654. 601-587-7162. Fax: 601-587-3003. (CST).

Felony, Civil Actions Over $2,500—Circuit Court, PO Box 1249, Monticello, MS 39654. 601-587-4791. Fax: 601-587-3003. 8AM-5PM (CST). Access by: Phone, fax, mail, in person.

Misdemeanor, Civil Actions Under $2,500, Eviction, Small Claims—Justice Court, PO Box 903, Monticello, MS 39654. 601-587-7183. Fax: 601-587-3003. 8AM-5PM (CST). Access by: Fax, mail, in person.

Probate—Chancery Court, 821 Broad St, Courthouse Sq, PO Box 821, Monticello, MS 39654. 601-587-7162. Fax: 601-587-0750. 8AM-5PM (CST).

Leake County

Real Estate Recording—Leake County Clerk of the Chancery Court, Courthouse, Court Square, Carthage, MS 39051. 601-267-7371. Fax: 601-267-6132. 8AM-5PM (CST).

Felony, Civil Actions Over $2,500—Circuit Court, PO Box 67, Carthage, MS 39051. 601-267-8357. Fax: 601-267-6132. 8AM-5PM (CST). Access by: Mail, in person.

Misdemeanor, Civil Actions Under $2,500, Eviction, Small Claims—Justice Court, PO Box 69, Carthage, MS 39051. 601-267-5677. 8:00AM-5:00PM (CST). Access by: Mail, in person.

Probate—Chancery Court, PO Box 72, Carthage, MS 39051. 601-267-7371. Fax: 601-267-6137. 8AM-5PM (CST).

Lee County

Real Estate Recording—Lee County Clerk of the Chancery Court, 200 Jefferson Street, Tupelo, MS 38801. 601-841-9100. Fax: 601-680-6091. 8AM-5PM (CST).

Felony, Civil—Circuit and County Court, Circuit Court-PO Box 762, County Court - PO Box 736, Tupelo, MS 38802. 601-841-9022. Fax: 601-680-6079. 8AM-5PM (CST). Access by: Mail, in person.

Misdemeanor, Civil Actions Under $2,500, Eviction, Small Claims—Justice Court, PO Box 108, Tupelo, MS 38802. 601-841-9014. Fax: 601-680-6021. 8AM-5PM (CST). Access by: Mail, in person.

Probate—Chancery Court, PO Box 1785, Tupelo, MS 38801. 601-841-9100. Fax: 601-680-6091. 8AM-5PM (CST).

Leflore County

Real Estate Recording—Leflore County Clerk of the Chancery Court, 310 West Market, Courthouse, Greenwood, MS 38930. 601-455-7912. Fax: 601-455-7965. 8AM-5PM (CST).

Felony, Civil—Circuit and County Court, PO Box 1953, Greenwood, MS 38930. 601-453-1041. (CST). Access by: Mail, in person.

Misdemeanor, Civil Actions Under $2,500, Eviction, Small Claims—Justice Court, PO Box 8056, Greenwood, MS 38930. 601-453-1605. 8AM-5PM (CST). Access by: In person only.

Probate—Chancery Court, PO Box 1468, Greenwood, MS 38930. 601-453-1041. Fax: 601-455-7959. 8AM-5PM (CST). Access by: Mail, in person.

Lincoln County

Real Estate Recording—Lincoln County Clerk of the Chancery Court, 300 South First Street, Brookhaven, MS 39601. 601-835-3416. 8AM-5PM (CST).

Felony, Civil Actions Over $2,500—Circuit Court, PO Box 357, Brookhaven, MS 39601. 601-835-3435. 8AM-5PM (CST). Access by: Mail, in person.

Misdemeanor, Civil Actions Under $2,500, Eviction, Small Claims—Justice Court, PO Box 767, Brookhaven, MS 39601. 601-835-3474. 8:00AM-5:00PM (CST). Access by: Mail, in person.

Probate—Chancery Court, PO Box 555, Brookhaven, MS 39601. 601-835-3412. Fax: 601-835-3423. 8AM-5PM (CST). Access by: Mail, in person.

Lowndes County

Real Estate Recording—Lowndes County Clerk of the Chancery Court, 515 2nd Avenue North, Courthouse, Columbus, MS 39703. 601-329-5807. 8AM-5PM (CST).

Felony, Civil—Circuit and County Court, PO Box 31, Columbus, MS 39703. 601-329-5900. 8AM-5PM (CST). Access by: Mail, in person.

Misdemeanor, Civil Actions Under $2,500, Eviction, Small Claims—Justice Court, 11 Airline Rd, Columbus, MS 39702. 601-329-5929. Fax: 601-245-4619. 8AM-5PM (CST). Access by: Mail, in person.

Probate—Chancery Court, PO Box 684, Columbus, MS 39703. 601-329-5800. 8AM-5PM (CST).

Madison County

Real Estate Recording—Madison County Clerk, 146 W. Center Street, Courtyard Square, Canton, MS 39046. 601-859-1177. 8AM-5PM (CST).

Felony, Civil—Circuit and County Court, PO Box 1626, Canton, MS 39046. 601-859-4365. 8AM-5PM (CST). Access by: Mail, in person.

Misdemeanor, Civil Actions Under $2,500, Eviction, Small Claims—Justice Court, 175 N Union, Canton, MS 39046. 601-859-6337. Fax: 601-859-5878. 8AM-5PM (CST). Access by: Mail, in person.

Probate—Chancery Court, PO Box 404, Canton, MS 39046. 601-859-1177. Fax: 601-859-5875. 8AM-5PM (CST).

Marion County

Real Estate Recording—Marion County Clerk of the Chancery Court, 250 Broad Street, Suite 2, Columbia, MS 39429. 601-736-2691. Fax: 601-736-1232. 8AM-5PM (CST).

Felony, Civil Actions Over $2,500—Circuit Court, 250 Broad St, Suite 1, Columbia, MS 39429. 601-736-8246. 8:00AM-5:00PM (CST). Access by: Mail, in person.

Misdemeanor, Civil Actions Under $2,500, Eviction, Small Claims—Justice Court, 500 Courthouse Square, Columbia, MS 39429. 601-736-7572. Fax: 601-736-2580. 8AM-5PM (CST). Access by: Mail, in person.

Probate—Chancery Court, 250 Broad St, Suite 2, Columbia, MS 39429. 601-736-2691. Fax: 601-736-1232. 8AM-5PM (CST).

Marshall County

Real Estate Recording—Marshall County Clerk of the Chancery Court, Court Square, Holly Springs, MS 38635. 601-252-4431. Fax: 601-252-0004. 8AM-5PM (CST).

Felony, Civil Actions Over $2,500—Circuit Court, PO Box 459, Holly Springs, MS 38635. 601-252-3434. 8:00AM-5:00PM (CST). Access by: Mail, in person.

Misdemeanor, Civil Actions Under $2,500, Eviction, Small Claims—Justice Court-North and South Districts, PO Box 867, Holly Springs, MS 38635. 601-252-3585. 8AM-5PM (CST). Access by: Mail, in person.

Probate—Chancery Court, PO Box 219, Holly Springs, MS 38635. 601-252-4431. Fax: 601-252-0004. 8AM-5PM (CST).

Monroe County

Real Estate Recording—Monroe County Clerk of the Chancery Court, 201 West Commerce Street, Aberdeen, MS 39730. 601-369-8143. Fax: 601-369-7928. 8AM-5PM (CST).

Felony, Civil Actions Over $2,500—Circuit Court, PO Box 843, Aberdeen, MS 39730. 601-369-8695. Fax: 601-369-3684. 8AM-5PM (CST). Access by: In person only.

Misdemeanor, Civil Actions Under $2,500, Eviction, Small Claims—Justice Court-District 2, PO Box F, Aberdeen, MS 39730. 601-369-4971. 8AM-5PM (CST). Access by: Mail, in person.

Justice Court-District 1 & 3, 101 9th St, Amory, MS 38821. 601-256-8493. Fax: 601-256-7876. (CST). Access by: In person only.

Probate—Chancery Court, PO Box 578, Aberdeen, MS 39730. 601-369-8143. Fax: 601-369-7928. 8AM-5PM (CST).

Montgomery County

Real Estate Recording—Montgomery County Clerk of the Chancery Court, 614 Summit Street, Courthouse, Winona, MS 38967. 601-283-2333. Fax: 601-283-2233. 8AM-5PM (CST).

Felony, Civil Actions Over $2,500—Circuit Court, PO Box 765, Winona, MS 38967. 601-283-4161. 8AM-5PM (CST). Access by: Mail, in person.

Misdemeanor, Civil Actions Under $2,500, Eviction, Small Claims—Justice Court, PO Box 229, Winona, MS 38967. 601-283-2290. Fax: 601-283-2233. 8AM-5PM (CST). Access by: Mail, in person.

Probate—Chancery Court, PO Box 71, Winona, MS 38967. 601-283-2333. Fax: 601-283-2233. 8AM-5PM (CST).

Neshoba County

Real Estate Recording—Neshoba County Clerk of the Chancery Court, 401 Beacon Street, Suite 107, Philadelphia, MS 39350. 601-656-3590. 8AM-5PM (CST).

Felony, Civil Actions Over $2,500—Circuit Court, 401 E Beacon St Suite 110, Philadelphia, MS 39350. 601-656-4781. 8AM-5PM (CST). Access by: Mail, in person.

Misdemeanor, Civil Actions Under $2,500, Eviction, Small Claims—Justice Court, 401 E Beacon St, Philadelphia, MS 39350. 601-656-5361. (CST). Access by: In person only.

Probate—Chancery Court, 401 Beacon St Suite 107, Philadelphia, MS 39350. 601-656-3581. 8AM-5PM (CST). Access by: In person only.

Newton County

Real Estate Recording—Newton County Clerk of the Chancery Court, 92 West Broad St., Courthouse, Decatur, MS 39327. 601-635-2367. Fax: 601-635-3210. 8AM-5PM (CST).

Felony, Civil Actions Over $2,500—Circuit Court, PO Box 447, Decatur, MS 39327. 601-635-2368. Fax: 601-635-3210. 8AM-5PM (CST). Access by: Phone, mail, in person.

Misdemeanor, Civil Actions Under $2,500, Eviction, Small Claims—Justice Court, PO Box 69, Decatur, MS 39327. 601-635-2740. 8AM-5PM (CST). Access by: Mail, in person.

Probate—Chancery Clerk's Office, PO Box 68, Decatur, MS 39327. 601-635-2367. 8AM-5PM (CST).

Noxubee County

Real Estate Recording—Noxubee County Clerk of the Chancery Court, 505 South Jefferson, Macon, MS 39341. 601-726-4243. Fax: 601-726-2272. 8AM-5PM (CST).

Felony, Civil Actions Over $2,500—Circuit Court, PO Box 431, Macon, MS 39341. 601-726-5737. Fax: 601-726-2938. 8AM-5PM (CST). Access by: Mail, in person.

Misdemeanor, Civil Actions Under $2,500, Eviction, Small Claims—Justice Court-North & South Districts, 507 S Jefferson, Macon, MS 39341. 601-726-5834. Fax: 601-726-2938. 8AM-5PM (CST). Access by: Mail, in person.

Probate—Chancery Court, PO Box 147, Macon, MS 39341. 601-726-4243. Fax: 601-726-2938. 8AM-5PM (CST).

Oktibbeha County

Real Estate Recording—Oktibbeha County Clerk of the Chancery Court, 101 East Main, Courthouse, Starkville, MS 39759. 601-323-5834. 8AM-5PM (CST).

Felony, Civil Actions Over $2,500—Circuit Court, Courthouse, Starkville, MS 39759. 601-323-1356. 8AM-5PM (CST). Access by: Mail, in person.

Misdemeanor, Civil Actions Under $2,500, Eviction, Small Claims—Justice Court-Districts 1-3, 104 Felix Long Dr, Starkville, MS 39759. 601-324-3032. 8AM-5PM (CST). Access by: Mail, in person.

Probate—Chancery Court, Courthouse, 101 E Main, Starkville, MS 39759. 601-323-5834. 8AM-5PM (CST).

Panola County

Real Estate Recording—Panola County Clerk of the Chancery Court, 2nd District, 151 Public Square, Batesville, MS 38606. 601-563-6205. Fax: 601-563-8237. 8AM-5PM (CST).

Panola County Clerk of the Chancery Court, 1st District, 215 Pocahontas Street, Sardis, MS 38666. 601-487-2070. Fax: 601-487-3595. 8AM-5PM (CST).

Felony, Civil Actions Over $2,500—Circuit Court-2nd District, PO Box 346, Batesville, MS 38606. 601-487-2073. Fax: 601-487-8233. 8AM-5PM (CST). Access by: Phone, fax, mail, in person.

Circuit Court-1st District, PO Box 130, Sardis, MS 38666. 601-487-2073. 8AM-5PM (CST). Access by: Mail, in person.

Misdemeanor, Civil Actions Under $2,500, Eviction, Small Claims—Justice Court, PO Box 249, Sardis, MS 38666. 601-487-2080. 8AM-5PM (CST). Access by: Mail, in person.

Probate—Panola County Chancellor Clerk, 151 Public Square, Batesville, MS 38606. 601-563-6205. Fax: 601-563-8313. 8AM-5PM (CST).

Sardis Chancery Court, PO Box 130, Sardis, MS 38666. 601-487-2070. Fax: 601-487-3595. 8AM-Noon, 1-5PM (CST).

Pearl River County

Real Estate Recording—Pearl River County Clerk of the Chancery Court, 200 South Main Street, Poplarville, MS 39470. 601-795-2237. Fax: 601-795-3024. 8AM-5PM (CST).

Felony, Civil Actions Over $2,500—Circuit Court, Courthouse, Poplarville, MS 39470. 601-795-4911. Fax: 601-795-3084. 8AM-5PM (CST). Access by: Mail, in person.

Misdemeanor, Civil Actions Under $2,500, Eviction, Small Claims—Justice Court-Northern, Southeastern, and Southwestern Districts, 204 Julia St, Poplarville, MS 39470. 601-795-8018. Fax: 601-795-3063. 8AM-5PM (CST). Access by: Mail, in person.

Probate—Chancery Court, PO Box 431, Poplarville, MS 39470. 601-795-4911. Fax: 601-795-3024. 8AM-5PM (CST).

Perry County

Real Estate Recording—Perry County Clerk of the Chancery Court, Main Street, New Augusta, MS 39462. 601-964-8398. Fax: 601-964-8265. 8AM-5PM (CST).

Felony, Civil Actions Over $2,500—Circuit Court, PO Box 198, New Augusta, MS 39462. 601-964-8663. Fax: 601-964-8265. 8AM-5PM (CST). Access by: Mail, in person.

Misdemeanor, Civil Actions Under $2,500, Eviction, Small Claims—Justice Court, PO Box 455, New Augusta, MS 39462. 601-964-8366. 8AM-5PM (CST). Access by: Mail, in person.

Justice Court-District 1, 5091 Hwy 29, Petal, MS 39465. 601-544-3136. 8AM-5PM (CST). Access by: Mail, in person.

Probate—Chancery Court, PO Box 198, New Augusta, MS 39462. 601-964-8398. Fax: 601-964-8265. 8AM-5PM (CST). Access by: Mail, in person.

Pike County

Real Estate Recording—Pike County Clerk of the Chancery Court, East Bay, Magnolia, MS 39652. 601-783-3362. Fax: 601-783-2001. 8AM-5PM (CST).

Felony, Misdemeanor, Civil—Circuit and County Court, PO Drawer 31, Magnolia, MS 39652. 601-783-2581. Fax: 601-783-4101. 8:00AM-5:00PM (CST). Access by: Mail, in person.

Misdemeanor, Civil Actions Under $2,500, Eviction, Small Claims—Justice Court-Divisions 1-3, PO Box 509, Magnolia, MS 39652. 601-783-5333. Fax: 601-783-4181. 8AM-5PM (CST). Access by: In person only.

Probate—Chancery Court, PO Box 309, Magnolia, MS 39652. 601-783-3362. Fax: 601-783-4101. 8AM-5PM (CST).

Pontotoc County

Real Estate Recording—Pontotoc County Clerk of the Chancery Court, Courthouse, 11 E. Washington St., Pontotoc, MS 38863. 601-489-3900. 8AM-5PM (CST).

Felony, Civil Actions Over $2,500—Circuit Court, PO Box 428, Pontotoc, MS 38863. 601-489-3908. 8AM-5PM (CST). Access by: Mail, in person.

Misdemeanor, Civil Actions Under $2,500, Eviction, Small Claims—Justice Court-East & West Districts, PO Box 582, Pontotoc, MS 38863. 601-489-3920. 8AM-5PM (CST). Access by: Mail, in person.

Probate—Chancery Court, 12 Washington, PO Box 209, Pontotoc, MS 38863. 601-489-3900. 8AM-5PM (CST). Access by: Mail, in person.

Prentiss County

Real Estate Recording—Prentiss County Clerk of the Chancery Court, 100 North Main Street, Booneville, MS 38829. 601-728-8151. Fax: 601-728-2007. 8AM-5PM (CST).

Felony, Civil Actions Over $2,500—Circuit Court, 101 N Main St, Booneville, MS 38829. 601-728-4611. Fax: 601-728-2006. 8AM-5PM (CST). Access by: Mail, in person.

Misdemeanor, Civil Actions Under $2,500, Eviction, Small Claims—Justice Court-Northern & Southern Districts, 1904 E Chambers Dr, Booneville, MS 38829. 601-728-8696. (CST). Access by: In person only.

Probate—Chancery Court, PO Box 477, Booneville, MS 38829. 601-728-8151. Fax: 601-728-2007. 8AM-5PM (CST).

Quitman County

Real Estate Recording—Quitman County Clerk of the Chancery Court, Chestnut Street, Courthouse, Marks, MS 38646. 601-326-2661. Fax: 601-326-8004. 8AM-5PM (CST).

Felony, Civil Actions Over $2,500—Circuit Court, Courthouse, Marks, MS 38646. 601-326-8003. Fax: 601-326-8004. 8AM-5PM (CST). Access by: Phone, fax, mail, in person.

Misdemeanor, Civil Actions Under $2,500, Eviction, Small Claims—Justice Court-Districts 1 & 2, PO Box 100, Marks, MS 38646. 601-326-2104. Fax: 601-326-2330. 8AM-5PM (CST). Access by: Fax, mail, in person.

Probate—Chancery Court, Courthouse, Marks, MS 38646. 601-326-2661. Fax: 601-326-8004. 8AM-Noon, 1-5PM (CST).

Rankin County

Real Estate Recording—Rankin County Chancery Clerk, Suite D, 211 East Government St., Brandon, MS 39042. 601-825-1469. Fax: 601-824-7116. 8AM-5PM (CST).

Felony, Misdemeanor, Civil—Circuit and County Court, PO Drawer 1599, Brandon, MS 39043. 601-825-1466. 8AM-5PM (CST). Access by: Mail, in person.

Misdemeanor, Civil Actions Under $2,500, Eviction, Small Claims—Justice Court-Districts 1-4, 110 Paul Truitt Lane, Pearl, MS 39208. 601-939-1885. Fax: 601-939-2320. 8AM-5PM (CST). Access by: Mail, in person.

Probate—Chancery Court, 203 Town Sq, PO Box 700, Brandon, MS 39042. 601-825-1649. Fax: 601-824-2450. 8AM-5PM (CST). Access by: In person only.

Scott County

Real Estate Recording—Scott County Clerk of the Chancery Court, 100 Main Street, Forest, MS 39074. 601-469-1922. Fax: 601-469-5180. 8AM-5PM (CST).

Felony, Civil Actions Over $2,500—Circuit Court, PO Box 371, Forest, MS 39074. 601-469-3601. 8AM-5PM (CST). Access by: Mail, in person.

Misdemeanor, Civil Actions Under $2,500, Eviction, Small Claims—Justice Court, PO Box 371, Forest, MS 39074. 601-469-4555. 8AM-5PM (CST). Access by: Mail, in person.

Probate—Chancery Court, 100 Main St, PO Box 630, Forest, MS 39074. 601-469-1922. Fax: 601-469-5180. 8AM-5PM (CST). Access by: Mail, in person.

Sharkey County

Real Estate Recording—Sharkey County Clerk of the Chancery Court, 400 Locust St.are, Rolling Fork, MS 39159. 601-873-2755. Fax: 601-873-6045. 8AM-Noon,1-5PM (CST).

Felony, Civil Actions Over $2,500—Circuit Court, PO Box 218, Rolling Fork, MS 39159. 601-873-2766. Fax: 601-873-6045. 8AM-Noon, 1-5PM (CST). Access by: Mail, in person.

Misdemeanor, Civil Actions Under $2,500, Eviction, Small Claims—Justice Court, PO Box 218, Rolling Fork, MS 39159. 601-873-6140. 8AM-5PM (CST). Access by: Mail, in person.

Probate—Chancery Court, 400 Locust St, PO Box 218, Rolling Fork, MS 39159. 601-873-2755. Fax: 601-873-6045. 8AM-Noon,1-5PM (CST). Access by: Mail, in person.

Simpson County

Real Estate Recording—Simpson County Clerk of the Chancery Court, 109 Pine Avenue, Mendenhall, MS 39114. 601-847-2626. Fax: 601-847-7004. 8AM-5PM (CST).

Felony, Civil Actions Over $2,500—Circuit Court, PO Box 307, Mendenhall, MS 39114. 601-847-2474. Fax: 601-847-4011. 8AM-5PM (CST). Access by: Mail, in person.

Misdemeanor, Civil Actions Under $2,500, Eviction, Small Claims—Justice Court, 159 Court Ave, Mendenhall, MS 39114. 601-847-5848. 8AM-5PM (CST). Access by: Mail, in person.

Probate—Chancery Court, Chancery Building, PO Box 367, Mendenhall, MS 39114. 601-847-2626. 8AM-5PM (CST).

Smith County

Real Estate Recording—Smith County Clerk of the Chancery Court, Courthouse, 123 Main St., Raleigh, MS 39153. 601-782-9811. Fax: 601-782-4002. 8AM-5PM (CST).

Felony, Civil Actions Over $2,500—Circuit Court, PO Box 517, Raleigh, MS 39153. 601-782-4751. Fax: 601-782-9481. 8AM-5PM (CST). Access by: Mail, in person.

Misdemeanor, Civil Actions Under $2,500, Eviction, Small Claims—Justice Court, PO Box 171, Raleigh, MS 39153. 601-782-4334. 8AM-5PM (CST). Access by: Mail, in person.

Probate—Chancery Court, 123 Nine St, PO Box 39, Raleigh, MS 39153. 601-782-9811. 8AM-Noon, 1-5PM (CST).

Stone County

Real Estate Recording—Stone County Clerk of the Chancery Court, 323 Cavers Avenue, Wiggins, MS 39577. 601-928-5266. Fax: 601-928-5248. 8AM-5PM (CST).

Felony, Civil Actions Over $2,500—Circuit Court, Courthouse, 323 Cavers Ave, Wiggins, MS 39577. 601-928-5246. Fax: 601-928-5248. 8AM-5PM (CST). Access by: Fax, mail, in person.

Misdemeanor, Civil Actions Under $2,500, Eviction, Small Claims—Justice Court-West District, 720 Project Road, Perkinston, MS 39573. 601-928-4415. 8AM-5PM (CST). Access by: Mail, in person.

Justice Court, 231 3rd Street, Wiggins, MS 39577. 601-928-4415. Fax: 601-928-5248. 8AM-5PM (CST). Access by: Mail, in person.

Probate—Chancery Court, 323 E Cavers, PO Drawer 7, Wiggins, MS 39577. 601-928-5266. Fax: 601-928-5248. 8AM-5PM (CST). Access by: Mail, in person.

Sunflower County

Real Estate Recording—Sunflower County Clerk of the Chancery Court, 100 Court Street, Indianola, MS 38751. 601-887-4703. Fax: 601-887-7054. 8AM-5PM (CST).

Felony, Civil Actions Over $2,500—Circuit Court, PO Box 576, Indianola, MS 38751. 601-887-1252. Fax: 601-887-7077. 8AM-5PM (CST). Access by: Mail, in person.

Misdemeanor, Civil Actions Under $2,500, Eviction, Small Claims—Justice Court-Southern District, PO Box 487, Indianola, MS 38751. 601-887-6921. 8AM-5PM (CST). Access by: Mail, in person.

Justice Court-Northern District, PO Box 52, Ruleville, MS 38771. 601-756-2835. 8AM-NOON, 1PM-5PM (CST). Access by: Mail, in person.

Probate—Chancery Court, 200 Main St, PO Box 988, Indianola, MS 38751. 601-887-4703. Fax: 601-887-7054. 8AM-5PM (CST). Access by: Mail, in person.

Tallahatchie County

Real Estate Recording—Tallahatchie County Clerk of the Chancery Court, 1st District, Courthouse, Charleston, MS 38921. 601-647-5551. 8AM-Noon,1-5PM (CST).

Tallahatchie County Clerk of the Chancery Court, 2nd District, Main Street, Courthouse, Sumner, MS 38957. 601-375-8731. Fax: 601-375-7252. 8AM-5PM (CST).

Felony, Civil Actions Over $2,500—Charleston Circuit Court, PO Box 86, Charleston, MS 38921. 601-647-8758. Fax: 601-647-8490. 8AM-5PM (CST). Access by: Phone, mail, in person.

Misdemeanor, Civil Actions Under $2,500, Eviction, Small Claims—Justice Court, PO Box 96, Sumner, MS 38957. 601-375-8515. Fax: 601-375-7252. 8AM-5PM (CST). Access by: Mail, in person.

Probate—Chancery Court, #1 Main St, PO Drawer H, Charleston, MS 38921. 601-647-5551. Fax: 601-647-8490. 8AM-5PM (CST).

Chancery Court, PO Box 180, Sumner, MS 38957. 601-375-8731. Fax: 601-375-7252. 8AM-Noon, 1-5PM (CST).

Tate County

Real Estate Recording—Tate County Clerk of the Chancery Court, 201 Ward Street, Senatobia, MS 38668. 601-562-5661. Fax: 601-562-7486. 8AM-5PM (CST).

Felony, Civil Actions Over $2,500—Circuit Court, 201 Ward St, Senatobia, MS 38668. 601-562-5211. Fax: 601-562-7486. 8AM-5PM (CST). Access by: Mail, in person.

Misdemeanor, Civil Actions Under $2,500, Eviction, Small Claims—Justice Court, Justice Court, 201 Ward, Senatobia, MS 38668. 601-562-7626. 8AM-5PM (CST). Access by: Mail, in person.

Probate—Chancery Court, 201 Ward St, Senatobia, MS 38668. 601-562-5661. Fax: 601-562-7486. 8AM-5PM (CST).

Tippah County

Real Estate Recording—Tippah County Clerk of the Chancery Court, Courthouse, Ripley, MS 38663. 601-837-7374. Fax: 601-837-1030. 8AM-5PM (CST).

Felony, Civil Actions Over $2,500—Circuit Court, Courthouse, Ripley, MS 38663. 601-837-7370. Fax: 601-837-1030. 8AM-5PM (CST). Access by: Phone, mail, in person.

Misdemeanor, Civil Actions Under $2,500, Eviction, Small Claims—Justice Court, Justice Court, 205-B Spring Ave, Ripley, MS 38663. 601-837-8842. 8AM-5PM (CST). Access by: Mail, in person.

Probate—Chancery Court, PO Box 99, Ripley, MS 38663. 601-837-7374. Fax: 601-837-1030. 8AM-5PM (CST).

Tishomingo County

Real Estate Recording—Tishomingo County Clerk of the Chancery Court, 1008 Battleground Dr., Courthouse, Iuka, MS 38852. 601-423-7010. Fax: 601-423-7005. 8AM-5PM (CST).

Felony, Civil Actions Over $2,500—Circuit Court, 1008 Battleground Dr, Iuka, MS 38852. 601-423-7026. 8AM-5PM (CST). Access by: Phone, mail, in person.

Misdemeanor, Civil Actions Under $2,500, Eviction, Small Claims—Justice Court-Northern & Southern Districts, 1008 Battleground Drive, Iuka, MS 38852. 601-423-7033. 8AM-5PM (CST). Access by: Mail, in person.

Probate—Chancery Court, 1008 Battleground Dr, Iuka, MS 38852. 601-423-7010. Fax: 601-423-7005. 8AM-5PM (CST).

Tunica County

Real Estate Recording—Tunica County Clerk of the Chancery Court, Courthouse, Tunica, MS 38676. 601-363-2451. 8AM-Noon, 1-5PM (CST).

Felony, Civil Actions Over $2,500—Circuit Court, PO Box 184, Tunica, MS 38676. 601-363-2842. 8AM-5PM (CST). Access by: Mail, in person.

Misdemeanor, Civil Actions Under $2,500, Eviction, Small Claims—Justice Court-Southern District, Rt 2, Box 1950, Dundee, MS 38626. 601-363-2178. 8AM-5PM (CST). Access by: Mail, in person.

Justice Court-Northern District, PO Box 876, Tunica, MS 38676. 601-363-2178. (CST). Access by: Mail, in person.

Probate—Chancery Court, PO Box 217, Tunica, MS 38676. 601-363-2451. Fax: 601-357-5934. 8AM-Noon, 1-5PM (CST).

Union County

Real Estate Recording—Union County Clerk of the Chancery Court, Courthouse, New Albany, MS 38652. 601-534-1900. Fax: 601-534-1907. (CST).

Felony, Civil Actions Over $2,500—Circuit Court, PO Box 298, New Albany, MS 38652. 601-534-1910. Fax: 601-534-1961. 8AM-5PM (CST). Access by: Fax, mail, in person.

Misdemeanor, Civil Actions Under $2,500, Eviction, Small Claims—Justice Court-East & West Posts, PO Box 27, New Albany, MS 38652. 601-534-1951. Fax: 601-534-1907. 8AM-5PM (CST). Access by: Mail, in person.

Probate—Chancery Court, PO Box 847, New Albany, MS 38652. 601-534-1900. Fax: 601-534-1907. 8AM-5PM (CST).

Walthall County

Real Estate Recording—Walthall County Clerk of the Chancery Court, 200 Ball Avenue, Tylertown, MS 39667. 601-876-3553. Fax: 601-876-6688. 8AM-5PM (CST).

Felony, Civil Actions Over $2,500—Circuit Court, 200 Ball Ave, Tylertown, MS 39667. 601-876-5677. Fax: 601-876-6688. 8AM-5PM (CST). Access by: Mail, in person.

Misdemeanor, Civil Actions Under $2,500, Eviction, Small Claims—Justice Court-Districts 1 & 2, PO Box 507, Tylertown, MS 39667. 601-876-2311. 8AM-5PM (CST). Access by: Mail, in person.

Probate—Chancery Court, 200 Ball Ave, Tylertown, MS 39667. 601-876-3553. Fax: 601-876-7788. 8AM-5PM (CST).

Warren County

Real Estate Recording—Warren County Clerk of the Chancery Court, 1009 Cherry Street, Vicksburg, MS 39180. 601-636-4415. Fax: 601-634-4815. 8AM-5PM (CST).

Felony, Misdemeanor, Civil—Circuit and County Court, PO Box 351, Vicksburg, MS 39181. 601-636-3961. 8AM-5PM (CST). Access by: Mail, in person.

Misdemeanor, Civil Actions Under $2,500, Eviction, Small Claims—Justice Court-Northern, Central, and Southern Districts, PO Box 1598, Vicksburg, MS 39181. 601-634-6402. 8AM-5PM (CST). Access by: Mail, in person.

Probate—Chancery Court, PO Box 351, Vicksburg, MS 39181. 601-636-4415. Fax: 601-634-4815. (CST).

Washington County

Real Estate Recording—Washington County Clerk of the Chancery Court, 900 Washington Avenue, Greenville, MS 38701. 601-332-1595. Fax: 601-332-4452. 8AM-5PM (CST).

Felony, Misdemeanor, Civil—Circuit and County Court, PO Box 1276, Greenville, MS 38702. 601-378-2747. 8AM-5PM (CST). Access by: Mail, in person.

Misdemeanor, Civil Actions Under $2,500, Eviction, Small Claims—Justice Court-Districts 1-3, 905 W Alexander, Greenville, MS 38701. 601-332-0633. 8AM-5PM (CST). Access by: Mail, in person.

Probate—Chancery Court, PO Box 309, Greenville, MS 38702. 601-332-1595. Fax: 601-334-2725. 8AM-5PM (CST).

Wayne County

Real Estate Recording—Wayne County Chancery Clerk, Wayne Co. Courthouse, 609 Azalea Dr., Waynesboro, MS 39367. 601-735-2873. Fax: 601-735-6248. 8AM-5PM (CST).

Felony, Civil Actions Over $2,500—Circuit Court, PO Box 428, Waynesboro, MS 39367. 601-735-1171. 8:00AM-5:00PM (CST). Access by: Mail, in person.

Misdemeanor, Civil Actions Under $2,500, Eviction, Small Claims—Justice Court-Posts 1 & 2, Courthouse, Waynesboro, MS 39367. 601-735-3118. Fax: 601-735-6266. (CST). Access by: Phone, fax, mail, in person.

Probate—Chancery Court, Courthouse, 609 Azalea Dr, Waynesboro, MS 39367. 601-735-2873. Fax: 601-735-6248. 8AM-5PM (CST).

Webster County

Real Estate Recording—Webster County Clerk of the Chancery Court, Highway 9 North, Courthouse, Walthall, MS 39771. 601-258-4131. Fax: 601-258-6657. 8AM-5PM (CST).

Felony, Civil Actions Over $2,500—Circuit Court, PO Box 308, Walthall, MS 39771. 601-258-6287. Fax: 601-258-6657. 8AM-5PM (CST). Access by: Fax, mail, in person.

Misdemeanor, Civil Actions Under $2,500, Eviction, Small Claims—Justice Court-Districts 1 & 2, 114 Hwy 9 N, Eupora, MS 39744. 601-258-2590. 8AM-5PM (CST). Access by: Mail, in person.

Probate—Chancery Court, PO Box 398, Walthall, MS 39771. 601-258-4131. Fax: 601-258-6657. 8AM-5PM (CST).

Wilkinson County

Real Estate Recording—Wilkinson County Clerk of the Chancery Court, 525 Main Street, Woodville, MS 39669. 601-888-4381. Fax: 601-888-6776. 8AM-5PM (CST).

Felony, Civil Actions Over $2,500—Circuit Court, PO Box 327, Woodville, MS 39669. 601-888-6697. 8:00AM-5:00PM (CST). Access by: Mail, in person.

Misdemeanor, Civil Actions Under $2,500, Eviction, Small Claims—Justice Court-East & West Districts, PO Box 40, Woodville, MS 39669. 601-888-3538. Fax: 601-888-6776. 8AM-5PM (CST). Access by: Mail, in person.

Probate—Chancery Court, PO Box 516, Woodville, MS 39669. 601-888-4381. Fax: 601-888-6776. 8AM-5PM (CST).

Winston County

Real Estate Recording—Winston County Clerk of the Chancery Court, South Court Street, Louisville, MS 39339. 601-773-3631. Fax: 601-773-8831. 8AM-5PM (CST).

Felony, Civil Actions Over $2,500—Circuit Court, PO Drawer 785, Louisville, MS 39339. 601-773-3581. Fax: 601-773-8825. 8AM-5PM (CST). Access by: Phone, fax, mail, in person.

Misdemeanor, Civil Actions Under $2,500, Eviction, Small Claims—Justice Court, PO Box 337, Louisville, MS 39339. 601-773-6016. 8AM-5PM (CST). Access by: Mail, in person.

Probate—Chancery Court, PO Drawer 69, Louisville, MS 39339. 601-773-3631. Fax: 601-773-8825. 8AM-5PM (CST).

Yalobusha County

Real Estate Recording—Yalobusha County Clerk of the Chancery Court, 1st District, Courthouse, Coffeeville, MS 38922. 601-675-2716. Fax: 601-675-8187. 8AM-12, 1-5PM (CST).

Yalobusha County Clerk of the Chancery Court, 2nd District, Blackmur Drive, Courthouse, Water Valley, MS 38965. 601-473-2091. Fax: 601-473-5020. 8AM-Noon,1-5PM (CST).

Felony, Civil Actions Over $2,500—Coffeeville Circuit Court, PO Box 260, Coffeeville, MS 38922. 601-675-8187. Fax: 601-675-8004. 8AM-5PM (CST). Access by: Phone, fax, mail, in person.

Water Valley Circuit Court, PO Box 431, Water Valley, MS 38965. 601-473-1341. Fax: 601-473-5020. 8AM-5PM (CST). Access by: Mail, in person.

Misdemeanor, Civil Actions Under $2,500, Eviction, Small Claims—Justice Court-District 1, Rt. 3, Box 237, Coffeeville, MS 38922. 601-675-8115. 8AM-5PM (CST). Access by: Mail, in person.

Justice Court-Division 2, PO Box 272, Water Valley, MS 38965. 601-473-4502. 8AM-5PM (CST). Access by: Mail, in person.

Probate—Chancery Court, PO Box 260, Coffeeville, MS 38922. 601-675-2716. Fax: 601-675-8004. 8AM-Noon, 1-5PM (CST).

Chancery Court, PO Box 664, Water Valley, MS 38965. 601-473-2091. Fax: 601-473-5020. 8AM-5PM (CST).

Yazoo County

Real Estate Recording—Yazoo County Clerk of the Chancery Court, 211 East Broadway, Yazoo City, MS 39194. 601-746-2661. 8AM-5PM (CST).

Felony, Misdemeanor, Civil—Circuit and County Court, PO Box 108, Yazoo City, MS 39194. 601-746-1872. 8:00AM-5:00PM (CST). Access by: Mail, in person.

Misdemeanor, Civil Actions Under $2,500, Eviction, Small Claims—Justice Court-Northern & Southern Districts, PO Box 798, Yazoo City, MS 39194. 601-746-8181. 8AM-5PM (CST). Access by: Mail, in person.

Probate—Chancery Court, PO Box 68, Yazoo City, MS 39194. 601-746-2661. 8AM-5PM (CST).

Federal Courts

US District Court

Northern District of Mississippi

Aberdeen-Eastern Division, US District Court PO Box 704, Aberdeen, MS 39730. 601-369-4952. Counties: Alcorn, Attala, Chickasaw, Choctaw, Clay, Itawamba, Lee, Lowndes, Monroe, Oktibbeha, Prentiss, Tishomingo, Winston

Clarksdale/Delta Division, US District Court c/o Oxford-Northern Division, PO Box 727, Oxford, MS 38655. 601-234-1971. Counties: Bolivar, Coahoma, De Soto, Panola, Quitman, Tallahatchie, Tate, Tunica

Greenville Division, US District Court PO Box 190, Greenville, MS 38702. 601-335-1651. Counties: Carroll, Humphreys, Leflore, Sunflower, Washington

Oxford-Northern Division, US District Court PO Box 727, Oxford, MS 38655. 601-234-1971. Counties: Benton, Calhoun, Grenada, Lafayette, Marshall, Montgomery, Pontotoc, Tippah, Union, Webster, Yalobusha

Southern District of Mississippi

Biloxi Division, US District Court Room 243, 725 Washington Loop, Biloxi, MS 39530. 228-432-8623. Counties: George, Hancock, Harrison, Jackson, Pearl River, Stone

Hattiesburg Division, US District Court Suite 200, 701 Main St, Hattiesburg, MS 39401. 601-583-2433. Counties: Covington, Forrest, Greene, Jefferson Davis, Jones, Lamar, Lawrence, Marion, Perry, Walthall

Jackson Division, US District Court Suite 316, 245 E Capitol St, Jackson, MS 39201. 601-965-4439. Counties: Amite, Copiah, Franklin, Hinds, Holmes, Leake, Lincoln, Madison, Pike, Rankin, Scott, Simpson, Smith

Meridian Division, US District Court c/o Jackson Division, Suite 316, 245 E Capiton St, Jackson, MS 39201. 601-695-4439. Counties: Clarke, Jasper, Kemper, Lauderdale, Neshoba, Newton, Noxubee, Wayne

Vicksburg Division, US District Court c/o Jackson Division, Suite 316, 245 E Capitol St, Jackson, MS 39201. 601-965-4439. Counties: Adams, Claiborne, Issaquena, Jefferson, Sharkey, Warren, Wilkinson, Yazoo

US Bankruptcy Court

Northern District of Mississippi

Aberdeen Division, US Bankruptcy Court, PO Drawer 867, Aberdeen, MS 39730-0867. 601-369-2596. Voice Case Information System: 601-369-8147. Counties: Alcorn, Attala, Benton, Bolivar, Calhoun, Carroll, Chickasaw, Choctaw, Clay, Coahoma, De Soto, Grenada, Humphreys, Itawamba, Lafayette, Lee, Leflore, Lowndes, Monroe, Montgomery, Oktibbeha, Panola, Pontotoc, Prentiss, Quitman, Sunflower, Tallahatchie, Tate, Tippah, Tishomingo, Tunica, Union, Washington, Webster, Winston, Yalobusha

Southern District of Mississippi

Biloxi Division, US Bankruptcy Court, Room 117, 725 Washington Loop, Biloxi, MS 39530. 228-432-5542. Voice Case Information System: 601-435-2905. Counties: Clarke, Covington, Forrest, George, Greene, Hancock, Harrison, Jackson, Jasper, Jefferson Davis, Jones, Kemper, Lamar, Lauderdale, Lawrence, Marion, Neshoba, Newton, Noxubee, Pearl River, Perry, Stone, Walthall, Wayne

Jackson Division, US Bankruptcy Court, PO Drawer 2448, Jackson, MS 39225-2448. 228-965-5301. Voice Case Information System: 228-965-6106. Counties: Adams, Amite, Claiborne, Copiah, Franklin, Hinds, Holmes, Issaquena, Jefferson, Leake, Lincoln, Madison, Pike, Rankin, Scott, Sharkey, Simpson, Smith, Warren, Wilkinson, Yazoo

Missouri

Capitol: Jefferson City (Cole County)	
Number of Counties: 114	**Population:** 5,323,523
County Court Locations:	**Federal Court Locations:**
•Circuit Courts: 115/45 Circuits	•District Courts: 8
•Associate Circuit Courts: 114/ 45 Circuits	•Bankruptcy Courts: 2
•Combined Courts: 7	**State Agencies:** 18
•Probate Courts: 5	
Municipal Courts: 406	

State Agencies—Summary

General Help Numbers:

State Archives

Secretary of State	573-751-3280
Archives Division	Fax: 573-526-7333
PO Box 778	8AM-5PM M-F; 8:30-3:30 SA
Jefferson City, MO 65102-0778	
Alternate Telephone:	573-751-4717
Reference Librarian:	573-751-3280
Historical Society:	573-882-7083

Governor's Office

Office of the Governor	573-751-3222
PO Box 720	Fax: 573-751-1495
Jefferson City, MO 65102	8AM-5PM

Attorney General's Office

Attorney General's Office	573-751-3321
PO Box 899	Fax: 573-751-0774
Jefferson City, MO 65102	8AM-5PM

State Legislation

Legislative Library	573-751-4633
117A State Capitol	
Jefferson City, MO 65101	

Important State Internet Sites:

```
Webscape
File  Edit  View                                Help
```

State of Missouri World Wide Web
www.state.mo.us/
www.ecodev.state.mo.us/

This home page links to the executive, judicial and legislative branches of state government as well as the executive departments.

The Governor's Office
www.state.mo.us/gov/index.htm

This site includes information about the Governor, his State of the State address, his press releases, speeches, biography, bills signed and vetoed and enables you to send e-mail to the Governor.

Missouri General Assembly
www.moga.state.mo.us/

This site links to the members of the House and Senate, bill tracking, legislative committees, the Revised Statues and Constitution of Missouri.

House and Senate Bills
www.house.state.mo.us/bills97/HOMESRCH.htm

Online searches can be done from this site by bill number, sponsor or keyword.

Uniform Commercial Code
mosl.sos.state.mo.us/bus-ser/sosucc.html

Limited information is provided here about UCC searches.

State Agencies—Public Records

Criminal Records

Missouri State Highway Patrol, Criminal Record & Identification Division, PO Box 568, Jefferson City, MO 65102-0568, Main Telephone: 573-526-6153, Fax: 573-751-9382, Hours: 8AM-5PM. Access by: mail, visit.

Corporation Records
Fictitious Name
Limited Partnership Records
Assumed Name
Trademarks/Servicemarks
Limited Liability Company Records

Secretary of State, Corporation Services, PO Box 778, Jefferson City, MO 65102, Main Telephone: 573-751-4153, Hours: 8AM-5PM. Access by: mail, visit.

Uniform Commercial Code
Federal Tax Liens
State Tax Liens

UCC Division, Secretary of State, PO Box 1159, Jefferson City, MO 65102, Main Telephone: 573-751-2360, Fax: 573-751-5841, Hours: 8AM-5PM. Access by: mail, phone, visit.

Sales Tax Registrations

Department of Revenue, Tax Administration Bureau, PO Box 3300, Jefferson City, MO 65105-3300, Main Telephone: 573-751-5860, Fax: 573-751-3696, Hours: 7:45AM-4:45PM. Access by: mail, fax, phone, visit.

Birth Certificates

Department of Health, Bureau of Vital Records, PO Box 570, Jefferson City, MO 65102-0570, Main Telephone: 573-751-6387, Message Number: 573-751-6400, Hours: 8AM-5PM M-F. Access by: mail, phone, visit.

Death Records

Department of Health, Bureau of Vital Records, PO Box 570, Jefferson City, MO 65102-0570, Main Telephone: 573-751-6370, Message Number: 573-751-6400, Hours: 8AM-5PM M-F. Access by: mail, phone, visit.

Marriage Certificates
Divorce Records

Department of Health, Bureau of Vital Records, PO Box 570, Jefferson City, MO 65102-0570, Main Telephone: 573-751-6382, Message Number: 573-751-6400, Hours: 8AM-5PM, M-F. Access by: mail, visit. Actual marriage and divorce records are found at county of issue. This agency will issue a certificate of statement only.

Workers' Compensation Records

Labor & Industrial Relations Department, Workers Compensation Division, PO Box 58, Jefferson City, MO 65102, Main Telephone: 573-751-4231, Fax: 573-751-2012, Hours: 8AM-4:30PM. Access by: mail, visit.

Driver Records

Department of Revenue, Driver License Bureau, PO Box 200, Jefferson City, MO 65105-0200, Main Telephone: 573-751-4300, Fax: 573-526-4769, Hours: 7:45AM-4:45PM. Access by: mail, phone, fax, visit, PC. Copies of tickets are available from the same address. Requests must be in writing, include the name, DOB, license number, and specific violation information. The cost is $1.50 per ticket.

Vehicle Ownership
Vehicle Identification

Department of Revenue, Division of Motor Vehicles, PO Box 100, Jefferson City, MO 65105-0100, Main Telephone: 573-526-3669, Title Verification Number: 573-526-1234, Fax: 573-751-7060, Hours: 7:45AM-4:45PM. Access by: mail, phone, fax, visit.

Accident Reports

Missouri Highway Patrol, Traffic Division, PO Box 568, Jefferson City, MO 65102-0568, Main Telephone: 573-526-6113, Fax: 573-751-9914, Hours: 8AM-5PM. Access by: mail, visit.

Hunting License Information
Fishing License Information

Conservation Department, Fiscal Services, PO Box 180, Jefferson City, MO 65102-0180, Main Telephone: 573-751-4115, Fax: 573-751-4865, Hours: 8AM-Noon; 1PM-5PM. Access by: visit only.

County Courts and Recording Offices

What You Need to Know...

About the Courts

Administration

Court Administrator	573-751-4377
2112 Industrial Drive	Fax: 573-751-5540
Jefferson City, MO 65109	

Online Access

There is limited, online **internal** computer access available on systems called MOCIS and ACMS; however, there is **no** external access. There is legal permission to expand coverage using a $7.00 per case fee to be collected, but, to date, no implementation plans for the near term.

About the Recorder's Office

Organization

114 counties and **one independent city**, 115 filing offices. The recording officer is Recorder of Deeds. The **City of St. Louis** has its own recording office. See the City/County Locator section at the end of this chapter for ZIP Codes that cover both the city and county of St. Louis. The entire state is in the Central Time Zone (CST).

UCC Records

This is a **dual filing state**. Financing statements are filed both at the state level and with the Recorder of Deeds, except for consumer goods, farm related and real estate related filings, which are filed only with the Recorder. All but one county will perform UCC searches. Use search request form UCC-11. Search fees are usually $8.00 per debtor name without copies and $16.00 with copies. Copies usually cost $.50 per page.

Lien Records

All federal and state tax liens are filed with the county Recorder of Deeds. They are usually indexed together. Some counties will perform tax lien searches. Search and copy fees vary widely. Other liens include mechanics, judgments, and child support.

Real Estate Records

A few counties will perform real estate searches. Copy and certification fees vary.

County Courts and Recording Offices

Adair County

Real Estate Recording—Adair County Recorder of Deeds, Courthouse, 2nd Floor, 106 W. Washington St., Kirksville, MO 63501. 660-665-3890. Fax: 660-785-3212. 8:30AM-Noon, 1-4:30PM (CST).

Felony, Misdemeanor, Civil Actions Over $45,000—Circuit Court, PO Box 690, Kirksville, MO 63501. 660-665-2552. Fax: 660-665-3420. 8AM-5PM (CST). Access by: Fax, mail, in person.

Misdemeanor, Civil Actions Under $45,000, Eviction, Small Claims, Probate—Associate Circuit Court, Courthouse, Kirksville, MO 63501. 660-665-3877. Fax: 660-785-3222. 8AM-5PM (CST). Access by: Phone, fax, mail, in person. Signed release required for closed cases.

Andrew County

Real Estate Recording—Andrew County Recorder of Deeds, Courthouse, Savannah, MO 64485. 660-324-4221. Fax: 660-324-5667. 8AM-5PM (CST).

Felony, Misdemeanor, Civil Actions Over $45,000—Circuit Court, PO Box 208 Division I, Savannah, MO 64485. 660-324-4221. Fax: 660-324-5667. 8AM-5PM (CST). Access by: Phone, fax, mail, in person.

Misdemeanor, Civil Actions Under $45,000, Eviction, Small Claims, Probate—Associate Circuit Court, PO Box 49, Savannah, MO 64485. 660-324-3921. Fax: 660-324-5667. 8AM-5PM (CST). Access by: Mail, in person.

Atchison County

Real Estate Recording—Atchison County Recorder of Deeds, Courthouse, 400 Washington St., Rock Port, MO 64482. 660-744-2707. Fax: 660-744-5705. 8AM-Noon, 1-4:30PM (CST).

Felony, Misdemeanor, Civil Actions Over $45,000—Circuit Court, PO Box 280, Rock Port, MO 64482. 660-744-2707. Fax: 660-744-5705. 8:30AM-4:30PM (CST). Access by: Mail, in person.

Misdemeanor, Civil Actions Under $45,000, Eviction, Small Claims, Probate—Associate Division, PO Box 187, Rock Port, MO 64482. 660-744-2700. Fax: 660-744-5705. 8AM-4:30PM (CST). Access by: Fax, mail, in person.

Audrain County

Real Estate Recording—Audrain County Recorder of Deeds, Room 105, Audrain County Courthouse, 101 N. Jefferson, Mexico, MO 65265. 573-473-5830. Fax: 573-581-2380. 8AM-5PM (CST).

Felony, Misdemeanor, Civil Actions Over $45,000—Circuit Court, Courthouse, 101 N Jefferson, Mexico, MO 65265. 573-473-5840. Fax: 573-581-3237. 8AM-5PM (CST). Access by: In person only.

Misdemeanor, Civil Actions Under $45,000, Eviction, Small Claims, Probate—Associate Circuit Court, Courthouse, 101 N Jefferson, Rm 205, Mexico, MO 65265. 573-473-5850. Probate: 573-473-5854. Fax: 573-581-3237. 8AM-5PM (CST). Access by: Mail, in person.

Barry County

Real Estate Recording—Barry County Recorder of Deeds, Courthouse, Cassville, MO 65625. 417-847-2914. 8AM-4PM (CST).

Felony, Misdemeanor, Civil Actions Over $45,000—Circuit Court, Barry County Courthouse, 700 Main, Ste1, Cassville, MO 65625. 417-847-2361. 8AM-4PM (CST). Access by: Mail, in person.

Misdemeanor, Civil Actions Under $45,000, Eviction, Small Claims, Probate—Associate Circuit Court, Barry County Courthouse, Cassville, MO 65625. 417-847-2127. 7:30AM-4:00PM (CST). Access by: Mail, in person.

Barton County

Real Estate Recording—Barton County Recorder of Deeds, Courthouse, 1004 Gulf Street, Lamar, MO 64759. 417-682-2110. 8:30AM-Noon, 12:30-4:30PM (CST).

Felony, Misdemeanor, Civil Actions Over $45,000—Circuit Court, Courthouse, Lamar, MO 64759. 417-682-2444. Fax: 417-682-2960. 8AM-4:30PM (CST). Access by: Mail, in person.

Misdemeanor, Civil Actions Under $45,000, Eviction, Small Claims, Probate—1007 Broadway, Lamar, MO 64759. 417-682-5754. Fax: 417-682-2960. 8AM-4:30PM (CST). Access by: In person only.

Bates County

Real Estate Recording—Bates County Recorder of Deeds, Courthouse, 1 N. Delaware, Butler, MO 64730. 660-679-3611. 8:30AM-4:30PM (CST).

Felony, Misdemeanor, Civil Actions Over $45,000—Circuit Court, Bates County Courthouse, Butler, MO 64730. 660-679-5171. Fax: 660-679-4446. 8AM-4:30PM (CST). Access by: Mail, in person.

Misdemeanor, Civil Actions Under $45,000, Eviction, Small Claims, Probate—Associate Circuit Court, Courthouse, Butler, MO 64730. 660-679-3311. 8:30AM-4PM (CST). Access by: Mail, in person.

Benton County

Real Estate Recording—Benton County Recorder of Deeds, Van Buren Street, Courthouse, Warsaw, MO 65355. 660-438-5732. Fax: 660-438-5755. 8:30AM-Noon, 1-4:30PM (CST).

Felony, Misdemeanor, Civil Actions Over $25,000—Circuit Court, PO Box 37, Warsaw, MO 65355. 660-438-7712. Fax: 660-438-5755. 8AM-5PM (CST). Access by: In person only.

Misdemeanor, Civil Actions Under $25,000, Eviction, Small Claims, Probate—Associate Circuit Court, PO Box 666, Warsaw, MO 65355. 660-438-6231. 8:00AM-4:30PM (CST). Access by: In person only.

Bollinger County

Real Estate Recording—Bollinger County Recorder of Deeds, Courthouse, Marble Hill, MO 63764. 573-238-2710.

Fax: 573-238-2773. 8AM-4PM M,T,Th,F; 8AM-6PM W; 8Am-Noon 1st&last Sat (CST).

Felony, Misdemeanor, Civil Actions Over $25,000—Circuit Court, PO Box 949, Marble Hill, MO 63764. 573-238-2710. 8AM-4PM (CST). Access by: In person only.

Misdemeanor, Civil Actions Under $45,000, Eviction, Small Claims, Probate—Associate Circuit Court, PO Box 1040, Marble Hill, MO 63764-1040. 573-238-2730. Fax: 573-238-4511. 8AM-4PM (CST). Access by: In person only.

Boone County

Real Estate Recording—Boone County Recorder of Deeds, Boone County Gov't Center, 801 E. Walnut, Rm 132, Columbia, MO 65201. 573-886-4245. Fax: 573-886-4359. 8AM-5PM (CST).

Felony, Misdemeanor, Civil, Eviction, Small Claims, Probate—Circuit & Associate Circuit Courts, 701 E Walnut, Columbia, MO 65201. 314-886-4000. Fax: 314-886-4044. 8:00AM-5:00AM (CST). Access by: Fax, mail, in person.

Buchanan County

Real Estate Recording—Buchanan County Recorder of Deeds, 411 Jules Streets, Courthouse, St. Joseph, MO 64501. 816-271-1437. 8AM-4:30PM (CST).

Felony, Misdemeanor, Civil, Eviction, Small Claims—Circuit Court, 411 Jules St, St Joseph, MO 64501. 816-271-1462. Fax: 816-271-1538. 8AM-5PM (CST). Access by: In person only.

Probate—Buchanan County Courthouse, 411 Jules St, Rm 333, St Joseph, MO 64501. 816-271-1477. Fax: 816-271-1538. 8AM-5PM (CST).

Butler County

Real Estate Recording—Butler County Recorder of Deeds, 100 N. Main Street, Courthouse, Poplar Bluff, MO 63901. 573-686-8086. 8AM-4PM (CST).

Felony, Misdemeanor, Civil Actions Over $45,000—Circuit Court, Courthouse, Poplar Bluff, MO 63901. 573-686-8082. Fax: 573-688-8094. 7:30AM-4PM (CST). Access by: Mail, in person.

Misdemeanor, Civil Actions Under $45,000, Eviction, Small Claims, Probate—Associate Circuit Court, Courthouse, Poplar Bluff, MO 63901. 573-686-8087. Fax: 573-686-8093. 7:30AM-4:00PM (CST). Access by: Fax, mail, in person.

Caldwell County

Real Estate Recording—Caldwell County Recorder of Deeds, Courthouse, 49 E. Main St., Kingston, MO 64650. 660-586-2581. Fax: 660-586-2705. 8:30AM-4:30PM (CST).

Felony, Misdemeanor, Civil Actions Over $45,000—Circuit Court, PO Box 86, Kingston, MO 64650. 660-586-2581. Fax: 660-586-2705. 8:30AM-4:30PM (CST). Access by: Phone, mail, in person.

Misdemeanor, Civil Actions Under $45,000, Eviction, Small Claims, Probate—Associate Circuit Court, PO Box 5, Kingston, MO 64650. 660-586-2771. Fax: 660-586-2333. 8:00AM-4:30MM (CST). Access by: Mail, in person.

Callaway County

Real Estate Recording—Callaway County Recorder of Deeds, 10 East 5th Street, Fulton, MO 65251. 573-642-0787. 8AM-5PM (CST).

Felony, Misdemeanor, Civil Actions Over $45,000—Circuit Court, Courthouse, Fulton, MO 65251. 314-642-0780. Fax: 314-642-0700. 8AM-5PM (CST). Access by: Fax, mail, in person.

Misdemeanor, Civil Actions Under $45,000, Eviction, Small Claims, Probate—Associate Circuit Court, Courthouse, Fulton, MO 65251. 573-642-0777. Fax: 573-642-0700. 8AM-5PM (CST). Access by: Mail, in person.

Camden County

Real Estate Recording—Camden County Recorder of Deeds, 1 Court Circle, Camdenton, MO 65020. 573-346-4440. Fax: 573-236-5422. 8:30AM-4:30PM (CST).

Felony, Misdemeanor, Civil Actions Over $25,000—Circuit Court, PO Box 930, Camdenton, MO 65020. 573-346-4440. Fax: 573-346-5422. 8:30AM-4:30PM (CST). Access by: Mail, in person.

Civil Actions Under $25,000, Eviction, Small Claims, Probate—Associate Circuit Court-Civil Division, PO Box 19, Camdenton, MO 65020. 573-346-4440. 8AM-5PM (CST). Access by: In person only.

Misdemeanor—Associate Circuit Court-Criminal Division, PO Box 19, Camdenton, MO 65020. 573-346-4440. 8:00AM-5:00PM (CST). Access by: Mail, in person.

Cape Girardeau County

Real Estate Recording—Cape Girardeau County Recorder of Deeds, #1 Barton Square, Jackson, MO 63755. 573-243-8123. Fax: 573-243-8124. 8AM-4:30PM (CST).

Civil—Circuit & Associate Circuit Court-Civil Division, 44 N Lorimier, Cape Girardeau, MO 63701. 573-335-8253. Fax: 573-335-3809. 8AM-5PM (CST). Access by: Mail, in person.

Felony, Misdemeanor—Circuit Court-Criminal Division, 101 Court St, Jackson, MO 63755. 573-243-8446. Criminal: 573-243-1755(felony). Fax: 573-243-0787. 8AM-4:30PM (CST). Access by: Mail, in person.

Carroll County

Real Estate Recording—Carroll County Recorder of Deeds, Courthouse, Carrollton, MO 64633. 660-542-1466. Fax: 660-542-1444. 8:30AM-Noon, 1-4:30PM (CST).

Felony, Misdemeanor, Civil Actions Over $45,000—Circuit Court, PO Box 245, Carrollton, MO 64633. 660-542-1466. Fax: 660-542-1444. 8:30AM-4:30PM (CST). Access by: In person only.

Misdemeanor, Civil Actions Under $45,000, Eviction, Small Claims, Probate—Associate Circuit Court, Courthouse, Carrollton, MO 64633. 660-542-1818. Fax: 660-542-1444. 8:30AM-4:30PM (CST). Access by: Mail, in person.

Carter County

Real Estate Recording—Carter County Recorder of Deeds, 105 Main Street, Van Buren, MO 63965. 314-323-4513. Fax: 314-323-8577. 8AM-4PM (CST).

Felony, Misdemeanor, Civil Actions Over $45,000—Circuit Court, PO Box 578, Van Buren, MO 63965. 573-323-4513. Fax: 573-323-8577. 8AM-4PM (CST). Access by: Phone, mail, in person.

Misdemeanor, Civil Actions Under $45,000, Eviction, Small Claims, Probate—Associate Circuit Court, PO Box 328, Van Buren, MO 63965. 573-323-4344. Fax: 573-323-4344. 8:00AM-4:00PM (CST). Access by: Phone, fax, mail, in person.

Cass County

Real Estate Recording—Cass County Recorder of Deeds, 102 East Wall Street, County Court House, Harrisonville, MO 64701. 660-380-1510. Fax: 660-380-5136. 8AM-4:30PM (CST).

Felony, Misdemeanor, Civil Actions Over $45,000—Circuit Court, 100 E Wall, Harrisonville, MO 64701. 660-380-5100. Fax: 660-380-5798. 8AM-4:30PM (CST). Access by: In person only.

Misdemeanor, Civil Actions Under $45,000, Eviction, Small Claims, Probate—Associate Circuit Court, PO Box 384, Harrisonville, MO 64701. 660-380-1496. Civil: 660-380-1494. Criminal: 660-380-1495. Fax: 660-380-5023. 8AM-4:30PM (CST). Access by: In person only.

Cedar County

Real Estate Recording—Cedar County Recorder of Deeds, Courthouse, Stockton, MO 65785. 417-276-3213. 8AM-Noon, 1-4PM (CST).

Felony, Misdemeanor, Civil Actions Over $45,000—Circuit Court, PO Box 665, Stockton, MO 65785. 417-276-3213. Fax: 417-276-5001. 8:00AM-4:00PM (CST). Access by: In person only.

Misdemeanor, Civil Actions Under $45,000, Eviction, Small Claims, Probate—Associate Circuit Court, PO Box G,

Stockton, MO 65785. 417-276-4213. Fax: 417-276-5001. 8AM-4PM (CST). Access by: Mail, in person.

Chariton County

Real Estate Recording—Chariton County Recorder of Deeds, Highway 24 West, Courthouse, Keytesville, MO 65261. 660-288-3602. Fax: 660-288-3602. 8:30AM-Noon, 1-4:30PM (CST).

Felony, Misdemeanor, Civil Actions Over $25,000—Circuit Court, PO Box 112, Keytesville, MO 65261. 660-288-3602. Fax: 660-288-3602. 8:30AM-4:30PM (CST). Access by: Mail, in person.

Misdemeanor, Civil Actions Under $25,000, Eviction, Small Claims, Probate—Associate Circuit Court, 306 South Cherry, Keytesville, MO 65261. 660-288-3271. Fax: 660-288-3602. 8AM-4:30PM (CST). Access by: Phone, mail, in person.

Christian County

Real Estate Recording—Christian County Recorder of Deeds, Church Street, North Side Square, Room 100, Ozark, MO 65721. 417-581-6372. Fax: 417-581-0391. 8AM-4:30PM (CST).

Felony, Misdemeanor, Civil Actions Over $45,000—Circuit Court, PO Box 278, Ozark, MO 65721. 417-581-6372. Fax: 417-581-0391. 8AM-4PM (CST). Access by: Mail, in person.

Misdemeanor, Civil Actions Under $45,000, Eviction, Small Claims, Probate—Associate Circuit Court, PO Box 175 (criminal), PO Box 296 (cvil), Ozark, MO 65721. Civil: 417-581-4523. Criminal: 417-581-2425. Fax: 417-581-0391. 8AM-4PM (CST). Access by: Phone, mail, in person.

Clark County

Real Estate Recording—Clark County Recorder of Deeds, 111 East Court, Courthouse, Kahoka, MO 63445. 660-727-3292. Fax: 660-727-1088. 8AM-Noon,1-4PM (CST).

Felony, Misdemeanor, Civil Actions Over $45,000—Circuit Court, 111 E Court, Kahoka, MO 63445. 660-727-3292. Fax: 660-727-1088. 8AM-4PM (CST). Access by: Mail, in person.

Misdemeanor, Civil Actions Under $45,000, Eviction, Small Claims, Probate—Associate Circuit Court, 113 W Court, Kahoka, MO 63445. 660-727-3628. 8AM-4PM (CST). Access by: Mail, in person.

Clay County

Real Estate Recording—Clay County Recorder of Deeds, Courthouse Square, Administration Bldg., Liberty, MO 64068. 816-792-7641. 8AM-4PM (CST).

Felony, Misdemeanor, Civil Actions Over $45,000—Circuit Court, PO Box 218, Liberty, MO 64068. 816-792-7707. Fax: 816-792-7778. 8AM-5PM (CST). Access by: In person only.

Misdemeanor, Civil Actions Under $45,000, Eviction, Small Claims, Probate—Associate Circuit Court, PO Box 218, Liberty, MO 64068. 816-792-7706. Fax: 816-792-7778. 8AM-5PM (CST). Access by: Phone, mail, in person.

Clinton County

Real Estate Recording—Clinton County Recorder of Deeds, 207 North Street, Plattsburg, MO 64477. 816-539-3719. Fax: 816-539-3893. 8AM-Noon, 1-5PM (CST).

Felony, Misdemeanor, Civil Actions Over $45,000—Circuit Court, PO Box 275, Plattsburg, MO 64477. 816-539-3731. Fax: 816-539-3893. 8AM-5PM (CST). Access by: In person only.

Misdemeanor, Civil Actions Under $45,000, Eviction, Small Claims, Probate—Associate Circuit Court, PO Box 383, Plattsburg, MO 64477. 816-539-3755. Fax: 816-539-3893. 8AM-4:30PM (CST). Access by: Fax, mail, in person.

Cole County

Real Estate Recording—Cole County Recorder of Deeds, 311 East High, Jefferson City, MO 65101. 573-634-9115. 8AM-4:30PM (CST).

Felony, Misdemeanor, Civil Actions Over $45,000—
Circuit Court, PO Box 1156, Jefferson City, MO 65102-1156. 573-634-9151. Fax: 573-635-0796. 7AM-4:30PM (CST). Access by: In person only.

Misdemeanor, Civil Actions Under $45,000, Eviction, Small Claims, Probate—Associate Circuit Court, PO Box 503, Jefferson City, MO 65102. 573-634-9171. 8AM-4:30PM (CST). Access by: Mail, in person.

Cooper County

Real Estate Recording—Cooper County Recorder of Deeds, 200 Main Street, Courthouse - Room 26, Boonville, MO 65233. 660-882-2232. Fax: 660-882-2043. 8:30AM-5PM (CST).

Felony, Misdemeanor, Civil Actions Over $45,000—
Circuit Court, 200 Main St, Rm 26, Boonville, MO 65233. 660-882-2232. Fax: 660-882-2043. 8:30AM-5:00PM (CST). Access by: Mail, in person.

Misdemeanor, Civil Actions Under $25,000, Eviction, Small Claims, Pr—Associate Circuit Court, 200 Main, Rm 31, Boonville, MO 65233. 660-882-5604. Fax: 660-882-2043. 8:30AM-5PM (CST). Access by: Mail, in person.

Crawford County

Real Estate Recording—Crawford County Recorder of Deeds, Main Street, Steelville, MO 65565. 573-775-5048. Fax: 573-775-3365. 8AM-4:30PM (CST).

Felony, Misdemeanor, Civil Actions Over $45,000—
Circuit Court, PO Box 177, Steelville, MO 65565. 314-775-2866. Fax: 314-775-2452. 8AM-5PM (CST). Access by: Mail, in person.

Misdemeanor, Civil Actions Under $45,000, Eviction, Small Claims, Probate—Associate Circuit Court, PO Box B.C., Steelville, MO 65565. 314-775-2149. Fax: 314-775-4010. 8AM-5PM (CST). Access by: Mail, in person.

Dade County

Real Estate Recording—Dade County Recorder of Deeds, Courthouse, Greenfield, MO 65661. 417-637-2271. Fax: 417-637-5055. 8AM-4PM (CST).

Felony, Misdemeanor, Civil Actions Over $45,000—
Circuit Court, Courthouse, Greenfield, MO 65661. 417-637-2271. Fax: 417-637-5055. 8AM-4PM (CST). Access by: Mail, in person.

Misdemeanor, Civil Actions Under $45,000, Eviction, Small Claims, Probate—Associate Circuit Court, Courthouse, Greenfield, MO 65661. 417-637-2741. Fax: 417-637-5055. 8AM-4PM (CST). Access by: In person only.

Dallas County

Real Estate Recording—Dallas County Recorder of Deeds, Courthouse, Buffalo, MO 65622. 417-345-2242. Fax: 417-345-5539. 8AM-Noon,1-4PM (CST).

Felony, Misdemeanor, Civil Actions Over $45,000—
Circuit Court, PO Box 373, Buffalo, MO 65622. 417-345-2243. Fax: 417-345-5539. 8AM-4PM (CST). Access by: Fax, mail, in person.

Misdemeanor, Civil Actions Under $45,000, Eviction, Small Claims, Probate—Associate Circuit Court, PO Box 1150, Buffalo, MO 65622. 417-345-7641. Fax: 417-345-5358. 8:00AM-4:00PM (CST). Access by: Mail, in person.

Daviess County

Real Estate Recording—Daviess County Recorder of Deeds, Courthouse, 2nd Floor, Gallatin, MO 64640. 660-663-2932. Fax: 660-663-3376. 8AM-Noon, 1-4:30PM (CST).

Felony, Misdemeanor, Civil Actions Over $45,000—
Circuit Court, PO Box 337, Gallatin, MO 64640. 660-663-2932. Fax: 660-663-3376. 8AM-4:30PM (CST). Access by: Phone, fax, mail, in person.

Misdemeanor, Civil Actions Under $45,000, Eviction, Small Claims, Probate—Associate Circuit Court, Courthouse, Gallatin, MO 64640. 660-663-2532. Fax: 660-663-3376. 8AM-4:30PM (CST). Access by: Mail, in person.

De Kalb County

Real Estate Recording—De Kalb County Recorder of Deeds, Main Street & Highway 33, Courthouse, Maysville, MO 64469. 660-449-2602. Fax: 660-449-2440. 8:30AM-Noon, 1-4:30PM (CST).

Felony, Civil Actions Over $45,000—Circuit Court, PO Box 248, Maysville, MO 64469. 660-449-2602. Fax: 660-449-2440. 8:30AM-4:30PM (CST). Access by: In person only.

Misdemeanor, Civil Actions Under $45,000, Eviction, Small Claims, Probate—Associate Circuit Court, PO Box 512, Maysville, MO 64469. 660-449-5400. Fax: 660-449-2440. 8:30AM-4:30PM (CST). Access by: Mail, in person.

Dent County

Real Estate Recording—Dent County Recorder of Deeds, 112 East 5th Street, Salem, MO 65560. 573-729-3931. Fax: 573-729-9414. 8AM-4:30PM (CST).

Felony, Misdemeanor, Civil Actions Over $45,000—
Circuit Court, 112 E 5th St, Salem, MO 65560. 573-729-3931. Fax: 573-729-9414. 8AM-4:30PM (CST). Access by: Mail, in person.

Misdemeanor, Civil Actions Under $25,000, Eviction, Small Claims, Probate—Associate Circuit Court, 112 E 5th St, Salem, MO 65560. 573-729-3134. Fax: 573-729-5146. 8:00AM-4:30PM (CST). Access by: Mail, in person.

Douglas County

Real Estate Recording—Douglas County Recorder of Deeds, 203 Southeast 2nd Avenue, Ava, MO 65608. 417-683-4713. 8AM-4:30PM (CST).

Felony, Misdemeanor, Civil Actions Over $45,000—
Circuit Court, PO Box 655, Ava, MO 65608. 417-683-4713. Fax: 417-683-3100. 8AM-4:30PM (CST). Access by: Phone, mail, in person.

Misdemeanor, Civil Actions Under $45,000, Eviction, Small Claims, Probate—Associate Circuit Court, PO Box 276, Ava, MO 65608. 417-683-2114. Fax: 417-683-3121. 8AM-5PM (CST). Access by: Phone, mail, in person.

Dunklin County

Real Estate Recording—Dunklin County Recorder of Deeds, Courthouse Square, Room 204, Kennett, MO 63857. 314-888-3468. 8:30AM-Noon, 1-4:30PM (CST).

Felony, Misdemeanor, Civil Actions Over $45,000—
Circuit Court Division I, PO Box 567, Kennett, MO 63857. 314-888-2456. Fax: 314-888-6677. 8:30AM-4:30PM (CST). Access by: Phone, fax, mail, in person.

Misdemeanor, Civil Actions Under $45,000, Eviction, Small Claims, Probate—Associate Circuit Court, Courthouse Rm 103, Kennett, MO 63857. 314-888-3378. 8:30AM-4:30PM (CST). Access by: Mail, in person.

Franklin County

Real Estate Recording—Franklin County Recorder of Deeds, 300 East Main St., Room 101, Union, MO 63084. 314-583-6367. 8AM-4:30PM (CST).

Felony, Misdemeanor, Civil Actions Over $45,000—
Circuit Court, PO Box 272, Union, MO 63084. 314-583-6300. 8AM-4:30PM (CST). Access by: Mail, in person.

Misdemeanor, Civil Actions Under $45,000, Eviction, Small Claims, Probate—Associate Circuit Court, PO Box 526, Union, MO 63084. 314-583-6326. 8AM-4:30PM (CST). Access by: Mail, in person.

Gasconade County

Real Estate Recording—Gasconade County Recorder of Deeds, 119 E.1st St., Room 6, Hermann, MO 65041. 573-486-2632. Fax: 573-486-3693. 8AM-4:30PM (CST).

Felony, Misdemeanor, Civil Actions Over $45,000—
Circuit Court, 119 E 1st St, Rm 6, Hermann, MO 65041-1182. 573-486-2632. Fax: 573-486-3693. 8AM-4:30PM (CST). Access by: Phone, fax, mail, in person.

Misdemeanor, Civil Actions Under $45,000, Eviction, Small Claims, Probate—Associate Circuit Court, PO Box 228, Hermann, MO 65041. 573-486-2321. Fax: 573-486-

3693. 8:00AM-4:30PM (CST). Access by: Phone, mail, in person.

Gentry County

Real Estate Recording—Gentry County Recorder of Deeds, PO Box 27, Albany, 64402. 660-726-3618. Fax: 660-726-4102. 8AM-4:30PM (CST).

Felony, Misdemeanor, Civil Actions Over $45,000—Circuit Court, PO Box 27, Albany, MO 64402. 660-726-3618. Fax: 660-726-4102. 8AM-4:30PM (CST). Access by: Mail, in person.

Misdemeanor, Civil Actions Under $45,000, Eviction, Small Claims, Probate—Associate Circuit Court, 200 W Clay St, Albany, MO 64402. 660-726-3411. Fax: 660-726-4102. 8AM-4:30PM (CST). Access by: In person only.

Greene County

Real Estate Recording—Greene County Recorder of Deeds, 940 Boonville, Springfield, MO 65802. 417-868-4068. Fax: 417-868-4050. 8AM-4:30PM (CST).

Felony, Misdemeanor, Civil Actions Over $45,000—Circuit Court, 1010 Boomville, Springfield, MO 65802. 417-868-4074. 7:30AM-5:30AM (CST). Access by: Mail, in person.

Misdemeanor, Civil Actions Under $45,000, Eviction, Small Claims, Probate—Associate Circuit Court, 1010 N Boonville, Springfield, MO 65802. 417-868-4110. 7:30AM-5:30PM (CST). Access by: Mail, in person.

Grundy County

Real Estate Recording—Grundy County Recorder of Deeds, Courthouse, 700 Main St., Trenton, MO 64683. 660-359-5409. 8:30AM-4:30PM (CST).

Felony, Misdemeanor, Civil Actions Over $45,000—Circuit Court, Courthouse, Trenton, MO 64683. 660-359-6605. Fax: 660-359-3761. 8:30AM-4:30PM (CST). Access by: Mail, in person.

Misdemeanor, Civil Actions Under $45,000, Eviction, Small Claims, Probate—Associate Circuit Court, PO Box 26, Trenton, MO 64683. 660-359-6606. 8:30AM-4:30PM (CST). Access by: Mail, in person.

Harrison County

Real Estate Recording—Harrison County Recorder of Deeds, 1515 Main Street, Courthouse, Bethany, MO 64424. 660-425-6425. Fax: 660-425-3772. 8AM-Noon, 1-4:30PM (CST).

Felony, Misdemeanor, Civil Actions Over $45,000—Circuit Court, PO Box 525, Bethany, MO 64424. 660-425-6425. Fax: 660-425-3772. 8AM-4:30PM (CST). Access by: Mail, in person.

Misdemeanor, Civil Actions Under $45,000, Eviction, Small Claims, Probate—Associate Circuit Court, Box 525, Bethany, MO 64424. 660-425-6432. Fax: 660-425-3772. 8AM-5PM (CST). Access by: Mail, in person.

Henry County

Real Estate Recording—Henry County Recorder of Deeds, 100 W. Franklin #4, Courthouse, Clinton, MO 64735. 660-885-6963. 8:30AM-4:30PM (CST).

Felony, Misdemeanor, Civil Actions Over $45,000—Circuit Court, 100 W Franklin Rm 12, Clinton, MO 64735. 660-885-6963. Fax: 660-885-8247. 8AM-4:30PM (CST). Access by: Mail, in person.

Misdemeanor, Civil Actions Under $45,000, Eviction, Small Claims, Probate—Associate Circuit Court, Courthouse, Clinton, MO 64735. 660-885-6963. Fax: 660-885-8456. 8:00AM-4:30PM (CST). Access by: Mail, in person.

Hickory County

Real Estate Recording—Hickory County Recorder of Deeds, Courthouse, On the Square, Hermitage, MO 65668. 417-745-6421. Fax: 417-745-6670. 8AM-Noon, 12:30-4:30PM (CST).

Felony, Misdemeanor, Civil Actions Over $45,000—Circuit Court, PO Box 101, Hermitage, MO 65668. 417-745-

6421. Fax: 417-745-6670. 8AM-4:30PM (CST). Access by: Mail, in person.

Misdemeanor, Civil Actions Under $45,000, Eviction, Small Claims, Probate—Associate Circuit Court, PO Box 75, Hermitage, MO 65668. 417-745-6822. Fax: 417-745-6670. 8:00AM-4:30PM (CST). Access by: Mail, in person.

Holt County

Real Estate Recording—Holt County Recorder of Deeds, 100 West Nodaway, Courthouse, Oregon, MO 64473. 660-446-3301. 8:30AM-Noon, 1-4:30PM (CST).

Felony, Misdemeanor, Civil Actions Over $45,000—Circuit Court, PO Box 318, Oregon, MO 64473. 660-446-3301. Fax: 660-446-3328. 8AM-4:30PM (CST). Access by: Phone, mail, in person.

Misdemeanor, Civil Actions Under $45,000, Eviction, Small Claims, Probate—Associate Circuit Court, PO Box 173, Oregon, MO 64473. 660-446-3380. 8:30AM-4:30PM (CST). Access by: Mail, in person.

Howard County

Real Estate Recording—Howard County Recorder of Deeds, 1 Courthouse Square, Fayette, MO 65248. 660-248-2194. Fax: 660-248-1075. 8:30AM-4:30PM (CST).

Felony, Misdemeanor, Civil Actions Over $45,000—Circuit Court, 1 Courthouse Square, Fayette, MO 65248. 660-248-2194. Fax: 660-248-1075. 8:30AM-4:30PM (CST). Access by: In person only.

Misdemeanor, Civil Actions Under $45,000, Eviction, Small Claims, Probate—Associate Circuit Court, PO Box 370, Fayette, MO 65248. 660-248-3326. Fax: 660-248-1075. 8:30AM-4:30PM (CST). Access by: Phone, mail, in person.

Howell County

Real Estate Recording—Howell County Recorder of Deeds, Courthouse, West Plains, MO 65775. 417-256-3750. 8AM-5PM (CST).

Felony, Misdemeanor, Civil Actions Over $45,000—Circuit Court, PO Box 1011, West Plains, MO 65775. 417-256-3741. Fax: 417-256-4650. 8AM-5PM (CST). Access by: Mail, in person.

Misdemeanor, Civil Actions Under $45,000, Eviction, Small Claims, Probate—Associate Circuit Court, 222 Courthouse, West Plains, MO 65775. 417-256-4050. Fax: 417-256-5826. 8:00AM-4:30PM (CST). Access by: Mail, in person.

Iron County

Real Estate Recording—Iron County Recorder of Deeds, 250 South Main, Ironton, MO 63650. 573-546-2811. Fax: 573-546-2166. 8AM-5PM (CST).

Felony, Civil Actions Over $45,000—Circuit Court, PO Box 24, Ironton, MO 63650. 573-546-2811. 8AM-4PM (CST). Access by: In person only.

Misdemeanor, Civil Actions Under $45,000, Eviction, Small Claims, Probate—Associate Circuit Court, PO Box 325, Ironton, MO 63650. 314-546-2511. Fax: 314-546-6006. 9AM-4PM (CST). Access by: Mail, in person.

Jackson County

Real Estate Recording—Jackson County Recorder of Deeds, Independence, 308 West Kansas, Independence, MO 64050. 816-881-4482. Fax: 816-254-9560.

Jackson County Recorder of Deeds, Kansas City, 415 East 12th Street, Room 104, Kansas City, MO 64106. 816-881-3198. Fax: 816-881-3719. 8AM-5PM (CST).

Civil, Eviction, Small Claims, Probate—Independence Circuit Court-Civil Annex, 308 W Kansas, Independence, MO 64050. 816-881-4497. 8AM-5PM (CST).

Circuit Court-Civil Division, 415 E 12th, Kansas City, MO 64106. 816-881-3926. 8AM-5PM (CST). Access by: In person only.

Felony, Misdemeanor—Circuit Court-Criminal Division, 1315 Locust, Kansas City, MO 64106. 816-881-4350. Fax: 816-881-3420. 8AM-5PM (CST). Access by: Fax, mail, in person.

Jasper County

Real Estate Recording—Jasper County Recorder of Deeds, 3rd & Main, Room 207, Carthage, MO 64836. 417-358-0431. 8:30AM-4:30PM (CST).

Felony, Misdemeanor, Civil Actions Over $45,000—Circuit Court, Courthouse, Rm 303, Carthage, MO 64836. 417-358-0441. Fax: 417-358-0461. 8:00AM-5:00PM (CST). Access by: Fax, mail, in person.

Misdemeanor, Civil Actions Under $45,000, Eviction, Small Claims, Probate—Associate Circuit Court, Courthouse Rm 304, Carthage, MO 64836. 417-358-0450. Fax: 417-358-0460. 8:30AM-4:30PM (CST). Access by: Fax, mail, in person.

Jefferson County

Real Estate Recording—Jefferson County Recorder of Deeds, 2nd & Maple, Courthouse, Hillsboro, MO 63050. 314-789-5414. 8:30AM-4:30PM (CST).

Civil Actions Over $25,000—Circuit Court-Civil Division, PO Box 100, Hillsboro, MO 63050. 314-789-5446. Fax: 314-789-3804. 8:00AM-4:30PM (CST). Access by: Phone, fax, mail, in person.

Felony, Misdemeanor—Circuit Court-Criminal Division, PO Box 100, Hillsboro, MO 63050. 314-789-5370. Fax: 314-789-3804. 8AM-4:30PM (CST). Access by: Phone, fax, mail, in person.

Civil Under $25,000, Eviction, Small Claims, Probate—Associate Circuit Court, PO Box 100, Hillsboro, MO 63050. 314-789-5362. Probate: 314-789-5450. Fax: 314-789-3804. 8:00AM-4:30PM (CST). Access by: Fax, mail, in person.

Johnson County

Real Estate Recording—Johnson County Recorder of Deeds, North Holden Street, Courthouse, Warrensburg, MO 64093. 660-747-6811. 8:30AM-4:30PM (CST).

Felony, Civil Actions Over $45,000—Circuit Court, Courthouse, PO Box 436, Warrensburg, MO 64093. 660-747-6331. Fax: 660-747-7927. 8AM-4:30PM (CST). Access by: Mail, in person.

Misdemeanor, Civil Actions Under $45,000, Eviction, Small Claims, Probate—Associate Circuit Court, Johnson County Courthouse, Warrensburg, MO 64093. 660-747-2227. 8AM-4:30PM (CST). Access by: Mail, in person.

Knox County

Real Estate Recording—Knox County Recorder of Deeds, Courthouse, Edina, MO 63537. 660-397-2305. Fax: 660-397-3331. 8:30AM-4PM (CST).

Felony, Misdemeanor, Civil Actions Over $45,000—Circuit Court, PO Box 116, Edina, MO 63537. 660-397-2305. Fax: 660-397-3331. 8:30AM-4PM (CST). Access by: Mail, in person.

Misdemeanor, Civil Actions Under $45,000, Eviction, Small Claims, Probate—Associate Circuit Court, PO Box 126, Edina, MO 63537. 660-397-3146. Fax: 660-397-3331. 8:30AM-4PM (CST). Access by: Mail, in person.

Laclede County

Real Estate Recording—Laclede County Recorder of Deeds, 200 North Adams, Room 105, Courthouse, Lebanon, MO 65536. 417-532-4011. Fax: 417-588-9288. 8AM-4PM (CST).

Felony, Misdemeanor, Civil Actions Over $45,000—Circuit Court, 200 N Adams St, Lebanon, MO 65536. 417-532-2471. 8:00AM-4:00PM (CST). Access by: Mail, in person.

Misdemeanor, Civil Actions Under $45,000, Eviction, Small Claims, Probate—Associate Circuit Court, 200 N Adams St, Lebanon, MO 65536. 417-532-9196. 8AM-4:30PM (CST). Access by: Phone, mail, in person.

Lafayette County

Real Estate Recording—Lafayette County Recorder of Deeds, 11th & Main, Lexington, MO 64067. 660-259-6178. Fax: 660-259-2918. 8:30AM-4:30PM (CST).

Felony, Misdemeanor, Civil Actions Over $45,000—Circuit Court, PO Box 340, Lexington, MO 64067. 660-259-6101. Fax: 660-259-2918. 8:00AM-5:00PM (CST). Access by: Mail, in person.

Misdemeanor, Civil Actions Under $45,000, Eviction, Small Claims, Probate—Associate Circuit Court-Division III, PO Box 236, Lexington, MO 64067. 660-259-6151. Fax: 660-259-2884. 8AM-4:30PM (CST). Access by: Mail, in person.

Lawrence County

Real Estate Recording—Lawrence County Recorder of Deeds, Courthouse on the Square, Mount Vernon, MO 65712. 417-466-2670. Fax: 417-466-4995. 9AM-Noon, 1-5PM (CST).

Felony, Misdemeanor, Civil Actions Over $45,000—Circuit Court, PO Box 488, Mt Vernon, MO 65712. 417-466-2471. 8AM-5PM (CST). Access by: Mail, in person.

Misdemeanor, Civil Actions Under $45,000, Eviction, Small Claims, Probate—Associate Circuit Court, PO Box 390, Mt Vernon, MO 65712. 417-466-2463. 8:30AM-5:00PM (CST). Access by: Mail, in person.

Lewis County

Real Estate Recording—Lewis County Recorder of Deeds, Courthouse, 1 Courthouse Square, Monticello, MO 63457. 573-767-5440. Fax: 573-767-5378. 8AM-Noon,1-4PM (CST).

Felony, Misdemeanor, Civil Actions Over $45,000—Circuit Court, PO Box 97, Monticello, MO 63457. 573-767-5440. Fax: 573-767-5378. 8AM-Noon,1-4PM (CST). Access by: In person only.

Misdemeanor, Civil Actions Under $45,000, Eviction, Small Claims, Probate—Associate Circuit Court, PO Box 36, Monticello, MO 63457. 573-767-5352. Fax: 573-767-5412. 8AM-4:30PM (CST). Access by: Phone, mail, in person.

Lincoln County

Real Estate Recording—Lincoln County Recorder of Deeds, 201 Main Street, Troy, MO 63379. 314-528-7122. Fax: 314-528-2665. 8AM-4:30PM (CST).

Felony, Misdemeanor, Civil Actions Over $45,000—Circuit Court, 201 Main St, Troy, MO 63379. 314-528-4418. 8:00AM-4:30PM (CST). Access by: In person only.

Misdemeanor, Civil Actions Under $45,000, Eviction, Small Claims, Probate—Associate Circuit Court, 201 Main St, Troy, MO 63379. 314-528-4521. 8AM-4:30PM (CST). Access by: Phone, in person.

Linn County

Real Estate Recording—Linn County Recorder of Deeds, Courthouse, PO Box 151, Linneus, MO 64653. 660-895-5216. 9AM-Noon, 1-4:30PM (CST).

Felony, Misdemeanor, Civil Actions Over $45,000—Linneus Circuit Court, PO Box 84, Linneus, MO 64653. 660-895-5212. Fax: 660-895-5533. 8AM-5PM (CST). Access by: Phone, mail, in person.

Linn County Circuit Court, PO Box 84, Linneus, MO 64653-0084. 660-895-5212. Fax: 660-895-5277. 8AM-Noon,1-5PM (CST). Access by: Mail, in person.

Misdemeanor, Civil Actions Under $45,000, Eviction, Small Claims, Probate—Associate Circuit Court, Box 93, Linneus, MO 64653. 660-895-5419. Fax: 660-895-5533. 8:30AM-4:00PM (CST). Access by: Phone, mail, in person.

Livingston County

Real Estate Recording—Livingston County Recorder of Deeds, Courthouse, Suite 6, 700 Webster St., Chillicothe, MO 64601. 660-646-0166. 8:30AM-Noon, 1-4:30PM (CST).

Felony, Misdemeanor, Civil Actions Over $45,000—Circuit Court, 700 Webster St, Chillicothe, MO 64601. 660-646-1718. Fax: 660-646-2734. 8:30AM-4:30PM (CST). Access by: Mail, in person.

Misdemeanor, Civil Actions Under $25,000, Eviction, Small Claims, Probate—Associate Circuit Court, Livingston County Courthouse, Suite 8, Chillicothe, MO 64601. 660-

646-3103. Fax: 660-646-8014. Public hours: 8:30AM-4:30PM; Office hours: 8AM-5PM (CST). Access by: Phone, fax, mail, in person. Signed release required for closed records.

Macon County

Real Estate Recording—Macon County Recorder of Deeds, 101 E. Washington, Bldg #2, Macon, MO 63552. 660-385-2732. Fax: 660-385-7203. 8:30AM-4PM (CST).

Felony, Misdemeanor, Civil Actions Over $45,000—Circuit Court, PO Box 382, Macon, MO 63552. 660-385-4631. Fax: 660-385-7203. 8:30AM-4PM (CST). Access by: Fax, mail, in person.

Misdemeanor, Civil Actions Under $45,000, Eviction, Small Claims, Probate—Associate Circuit Court, PO Box 491, Macon, MO 63552. 660-385-3531. 8AM-4:30PM (CST). Access by: Mail, in person.

Madison County

Real Estate Recording—Madison County Recorder of Deeds, Courthouse, Courtsquare, Fredericktown, MO 63645. 573-783-2102. Fax: 573-783-2715. 8AM-5PM (CST).

Felony, Misdemeanor, Civil Actions Over $45,000—Circuit Court, PO Box 470, Fredericktown, MO 63645-0470. 573-783-2102. Fax: 573-783-2715. 8:00AM-5:00PM (CST). Access by: In person only.

Misdemeanor, Civil Actions Under $45,000, Eviction, Small Claims, Probate—Associate Circuit Court, PO Box 521, Fredericktown, MO 63645. 573-783-3105. Fax: 573-783-5920. 8AM-5PM (CST). Access by: Phone, fax, mail, in person.

Maries County

Real Estate Recording—Maries County Recorder of Deeds, 4th & Main, Courthouse, Vienna, MO 65582. 573-422-3338. Fax: 573-422-3100. 8AM-4:30PM (CST).

Felony, Misdemeanor, Civil Actions Over $45,000—Circuit Court, PO Box 213, Vienna, MO 65582. 573-422-3338. Fax: 573-422-3100. 8AM-4PM (CST). Access by: Mail, in person.

Misdemeanor, Civil Actions Under $45,000, Eviction, Small Claims, Probate—Associate Circuit Court, PO Box 140, Vienna, MO 65582. 573-422-3303. Fax: 573-422-3100. 8AM-4PM (CST). Access by: Mail, in person.

Marion County

Real Estate Recording—Marion County Recorder of Deeds, 100 South Main, Palmyra, MO 63461. 573-769-2550. Fax: 573-769-6012. 8:30AM-5PM (CST).

Felony, Misdemeanor, Civil Actions Over $45,000—Circuit Court (Twps of Miller and Mason only), 906 Broadway, Rm 6, Hannibal, MO 63401. 573-221-0198. 8AM-5PM (CST). Access by: Mail, in person.

Circuit Court, PO Box 392, Palmyra, MO 63461. 573-769-2550. Fax: 573-769-4312. 8:00AM-5:00PM (CST). Access by: Mail, in person.

Misdemeanor, Civil Actions Under $45,000, Eviction, Small Claims, Probate—Hannibal Associate Circuit Court, 906 Broadway, Hannibal, MO 63401. 573-221-0288. 8AM-5PM (CST). Access by: Mail, in person.

Palmyra Associate Circuit Court, PO Box 449, Palmyra, MO 63461. 573-769-2318. Fax: 573-769-2558. 8AM-5PM (CST). Access by: Mail, in person.

McDonald County

Real Estate Recording—McDonald County Recorder of Deeds, Highway W, Courthouse, Pineville, MO 64856. 417-223-7523. Fax: 417-223-4125. 8AM-4PM (CST).

Felony, Misdemeanor, Civil Actions Over $45,000—Circuit Court, PO Box 157, Pineville, MO 64856. 417-223-7515. Fax: 417-223-4124. 8AM-4:30PM (CST). Access by: In person only.

Misdemeanor, Civil Actions Under $45,000, Eviction, Small Claims, Probate—Associate Circuit Court, PO Box 674, Pineville, MO 64856. 417-223-7511. Fax: 417-223-4125. 8:00AM-4:30PM (CST). Access by: In person only.

Mercer County

Real Estate Recording—Mercer County Recorder of Deeds, Courthouse, Princeton, MO 64673. 660-748-4335. Fax: 660-748-3180. 8:30AM-Noon, 1-4:30PM (CST).

Felony, Misdemeanor, Civil Actions Over $45,000—Circuit Court, Courthouse, Princeton, MO 64673. 660-748-4335. Fax: 660-748-3180. 8:30AM-4:30PM (CST). Access by: Mail, in person.

Misdemeanor, Civil Actions Under $45,000, Eviction, Small Claims, Probate—Associate Circuit Court, Courthouse, Princeton, MO 64673. 660-748-4232. Fax: 660-748-3180. 8:30AM-4:30PM (CST). Access by: Mail, in person.

Miller County

Real Estate Recording—Miller County Recorder of Deeds, Main Street, Courthouse, Tuscumbia, MO 65082. 573-369-2911. Fax: 573-369-2910. 8AM-4:30PM (CST).

Felony, Misdemeanor, Civil Actions Over $45,000—Circuit Court, PO Box 11, Tuscumbia, MO 65082. 573-369-2303. Fax: 573-369-2910. 8:0AM-4:30PM (CST). Access by: Phone, fax, mail, in person.

Misdemeanor, Civil Actions Under $45,000, Eviction, Small Claims, Probate—Charleston Associate Circuit Court, PO Box 369, Charleston, MO 63834. 573-683-6228. Fax: 573-683-3904. 8AM-4:30PM (CST). Access by: Phone, fax, mail, in person.

Tuscumbia Associate Circuit Court, Miller County Courthouse Annex, Tuscumbia, MO 65082. 573-369-2330. 8AM-4PM (CST). Access by: Mail, in person.

Mississippi County

Real Estate Recording—Mississippi County Recorder of Deeds, 313 E. Main treet, Courthouse, East Prairie, MO 63845. 573-683-2146. Fax: 573-649-2284. 8:30AM-4:30PM (CST).

Felony, Misdemeanor, Civil Actions Over $45,000—Circuit Court, PO Box 369, Charleston, MO 63834. 573-683-2104. Fax: 573-683-3904. 8:30AM-4:30PM (CST). Access by: Phone, fax, mail, in person.

Misdemeanor, Civil Actions Under $45,000, Eviction, Small Claims, Probate—Associate Circuit Court, PO Box 369, Charleston, MO 63834. 573-683-6228. Fax: 573-683-3904. 8:00AM-4:30PM (CST). Access by: Phone, fax, mail, in person.

Moniteau County

Real Estate Recording—Moniteau County Recorder of Deeds, 200 East Main Street, California, MO 65018. 314-796-2071. 8AM-4:30PM (CST).

Felony, Misdemeanor, Civil Actions Over $45,000—Circuit Court, 200 E Main, California, MO 65018. 573-796-2071. 8AM-4:30PM (CST). Access by: In person only.

Misdemeanor, Civil Actions Under $45,000, Eviction, Small Claims, Probate—Associate Circuit Court, 200 E Main, California, MO 65018. 573-796-2814. 8AM-5PM (CST). Access by: Phone, mail, in person.

Monroe County

Real Estate Recording—Monroe County Recorder of Deeds, 300 Main Street, Courthouse, Paris, MO 65275. 660-327-5204. Fax: 660-327-5781. 8AM-4:30PM (CST).

Felony, Misdemeanor, Civil Actions Over $45,000—Circuit Court, PO Box 227, Paris, MO 65275. 660-327-5204. Fax: 660-327-5781. 8AM-4:30PM (CST). Access by: Fax, mail, in person.

Misdemeanor, Civil Actions Under $45,000, Eviction, Small Claims, Probate—Associate Circuit Court, County Courthouse, 300 N Main, Paris, MO 65275. 660-327-5220. Fax: 660-327-5781. 8AM-4:30PM (CST). Access by: Mail, in person.

Montgomery County

Real Estate Recording—Montgomery County Recorder of Deeds, 211 East 3rd Street, Montgomery City, MO 63361. 573-564-3157. Fax: 573-564-3914. 8AM-4:30PM (CST).

Felony, Misdemeanor, Civil Actions Over $45,000—Circuit Court, 211 E 3rd, Montgomery City, MO 63361. 573-564-3341. Fax: 573-564-3914. 8AM-4:30PM (CST). Access by: In person only.

Misdemeanor, Civil Actions Under $45,000, Eviction, Small Claims, Probate—Associate Circuit Court, 211 E 3rd St, Montgomery City, MO 63361. 573-564-3348. 8:00AM-4:30PM (CST). Access by: In person only.

Morgan County

Real Estate Recording—Morgan County Recorder of Deeds, 100 Newton Street, Courthouse, Versailles, MO 65084. 573-378-4029. Fax: 573-378-5790. 8:30AM-Noon, 1-4:30PM (CST).

Felony, Misdemeanor, Civil Actions Over $45,000—Circuit Court, 100 E Newton, Versailles, MO 65084. 573-378-4413. Fax: 573-378-5790. 8:30AM-4:30PM (CST). Access by: Phone, mail, in person.

Misdemeanor, Civil Actions Under $45,000, Eviction, Small Claims, Probate—Associate Circuit Court, 102 N Monroe, Versailles, MO 65084. 573-378-4235. Fax: 573-378-4066. 8:30AM-5PM (CST). Access by: Phone, mail, in person. Signed release required for some searches.

New Madrid County

Real Estate Recording—New Madrid County Recorder of Deeds, 450 Main Street, New Madrid, MO 63869. 573-748-5146. 8AM-12, 1-4:30PM (CST).

Felony, Misdemeanor, Civil Actions Over $45,000—Circuit Court, County Courthouse, New Madrid, MO 63869. 573-748-2228. 8:00AM-5:00PM (CST). Access by: Mail, in person.

Misdemeanor, Civil Actions Under $45,000, Eviction, Small Claims, Probate—Associate Circuit Court, County Courthouse, New Madrid, MO 63869. 573-748-5556. 8AM-5PM (CST). Access by: Phone, mail, in person.

Newton County

Real Estate Recording—Newton County Recorder of Deeds, Wood & Main Streets, Neosho, MO 64850. 417-451-8224. Fax: 417-451-8298. 8:30AM-5PM (CST).

Felony, Misdemeanor, Civil Actions Over $45,000—Circuit Court, PO Box 130, Neosho, MO 64850. 417-451-8257. Fax: 417-451-8298. 8:30AM-5:00PM (CST). Access by: Phone, fax, mail, in person.

Misdemeanor, Civil Actions Under $45,000, Eviction, Small Claims, Probate—Associate Circuit Court, PO Box 170, Neosho, MO 64850. 417-451-8212. 8:00AM-5:00PM (CST). Access by: Phone, mail, in person.

Nodaway County

Real Estate Recording—Nodaway County Recorder of Deeds, Courthouse Square, Maryville, MO 64468. 660-582-5711. Fax: 660-582-5499. 8:30AM-Noon, 1-4:30PM (CST).

Felony, Misdemeanor, Civil Actions Over $45,000—Circuit Court, PO Box 218, Maryville, MO 64468. 660-582-5431. Fax: 660-582-5499. 8AM-4:30PM (CST). Access by: Mail, in person.

Misdemeanor, Civil Actions Under $45,000, Eviction, Small Claims, Probate—Associate Circuit Court, Courthouse Annex, 303 N Market, Maryville, MO 64468. 660-582-2531. 8AM-4:30PM (CST). Access by: Phone, mail, in person.

Oregon County

Real Estate Recording—Oregon County Recorder of Deeds, Courthouse, Alton, MO 65606. 417-778-7460. Fax: 417-778-6641. 8AM-4PM (CST).

Felony, Misdemeanor, Civil Actions Over $45,000—Circuit Court, PO Box 406, Alton, MO 65606. 417-778-7460. Fax: 417-778-6641. 8AM-5PM (CST). Access by: Phone, fax, mail, in person.

Misdemeanor, Civil Actions Under $45,000, Eviction, Small Claims, Probate—Associate Circuit Court, PO Box 211, Alton, MO 65606. 417-778-7461. Fax: 417-778-6641. 8:00AM-4:00PM (CST). Access by: Mail, in person.

Osage County

Real Estate Recording—Osage County Recorder of Deeds, Main Street, Courthouse, Linn, MO 65051. 573-897-3114. 8AM-4:30PM (CST).

Felony, Misdemeanor, Civil Actions Over $45,000—Circuit Court, PO Box 825, Linn, MO 65051. 573-897-3114. 8AM-4:30PM (CST). Access by: Phone, mail, in person.

Misdemeanor, Civil Actions Under $45,000, Eviction, Small Claims, Probate—Associate Circuit Court, PO Box 470, Linn, MO 65051. 573-897-2136. Fax: 573-897-2285. 8AM-4:30PM (CST). Access by: Phone, mail, in person.

Ozark County

Real Estate Recording—Ozark County Recorder of Deeds, Courthouse, Gainesville, MO 65655. 417-679-4232. Fax: 417-679-4554. 8AM-Noon,1-5PM (CST).

Felony, Misdemeanor, Civil Actions Over $45,000—Circuit Court, PO Box 36, Gainesville, MO 65655. 417-679-4232. Fax: 417-679-4554. 8AM-4:30PM (CST). Access by: Mail, in person.

Misdemeanor, Civil Actions Under $45,000, Eviction, Small Claims, Probate—Associate Circuit Court, PO Box 278, Gainesville, MO 65655. 417-679-4611. Fax: 417-679-4611. 8AM-4:30PM (CST). Access by: Fax, mail, in person.

Pemiscot County

Real Estate Recording—Pemiscot County Recorder of Deeds, Courthouse, 610 Ward Ave., Caruthersville, MO 63830. 573-333-2204. 8:30AM-4:30PM (CST).

Felony, Misdemeanor, Civil Actions Over $45,000—Circuit Court, County Courthouse, Caruthersville, MO 63830. 573-333-0182. 7:30AM-4:30PM (CST). Access by: In person only.

Misdemeanor, Civil Actions Under $45,000, Eviction, Small Claims, Probate—Associate Circuit Court, County Courthouse, PO Drawer 228, Caruthersville, MO 63830. 573-333-2784. 7:30AM-4:30PM (CST). Access by: Mail, in person.

Perry County

Real Estate Recording—Perry County Recorder of Deeds, 15 West Ste. Marie Street, Suite 1, Perryville, MO 63775. 573-547-1611. (CST).

Felony, Misdemeanor, Civil Actions Over $45,000—Circuit Court, 15 W Saint Maries St, Perryville, MO 63775-1399. 573-547-6581. Fax: 573-547-2637. 8AM-5PM (CST). Access by: In person only.

Misdemeanor, Civil Actions Under $25,000, Eviction, Small Claims, Probate—Associate Circuit Court, 15 W Saint Maries, Suite 3, Perryville, MO 63775-1399. 573-547-7861. Fax: 573-547-2637. 8AM-5PM (CST). Access by: Mail, in person.

Pettis County

Real Estate Recording—Pettis County Recorder of Deeds, 415 South Ohio, Sedalia, MO 65301. 660-826-1136. Fax: 660-827-8637. 9AM-4:30PM (CST).

Felony, Misdemeanor, Civil Actions Over $45,000—Circuit Court, PO Box 804, Sedalia, MO 65302-0804. 660-826-0617. Fax: 660-827-8637. 8AM-5PM (CST). Access by: Fax, mail, in person.

Misdemeanor, Civil Actions Under $45,000, Eviction, Small Claims—Associate Circuit Court, 415 S Ohio, Sedalia, MO 65301. 660-826-4699. Fax: 660-827-8637. 8:30AM-5:00PM (CST). Access by: Fax, mail, in person.

Probate—Probate Court, 415 S. Ohio, Sedalia, MO 65301. 660-826-0368. Fax: 660-827-8637. 8:30AM-4:30PM (CST).

Phelps County

Real Estate Recording—Phelps County Recorder of Deeds, Courthouse, 200 N. Main, Rolla, MO 65401. 573-364-1891. Fax: 573-364-1419. 7:30AM-5PM (CST).

Felony, Misdemeanor, Civil Actions Over $45,000—Circuit Court, 200 N Main St, Rolla, MO 65401. 573-364-1891. Fax: 573-364-1419. 8AM-5PM (CST). Access by: Fax, mail, in person.

Misdemeanor, Civil Actions Under $45,000, Eviction, Small Claims—Associate Circuit Court, 200 N Main, Rolla, MO 65401. 573-364-1891. Fax: 573-364-1419. 8AM-5PM (CST). Access by: Fax, mail, in person.

Probate—Phelps County Courthouse, 200 N Main, PO Box 1550, Rolla, MO 65401. 573-364-1891. 8AM-Noon, 1-5PM (CST). Access by: Mail, in person.

Pike County

Real Estate Recording—Pike County Recorder of Deeds, 115 West Main Street, Bowling Green, MO 63334. 573-324-5567. 9AM-Noon, 1-4:30PM (CST).

Felony, Misdemeanor, Civil Actions Over $45,000—Circuit Court, 115 W Main, Bowling Green, MO 63334. 573-324-3112. 8AM-4:30PM (CST). Access by: Mail, in person.

Misdemeanor, Civil Actions Under $45,000, Eviction, Small Claims, Probate—Associate Circuit Court, 115 W Main, Bowling Green, MO 63334. 573-324-5582. Fax: 573-324-6297. 8AM-4:30PM (CST). Access by: Mail, in person.

Platte County

Real Estate Recording—Platte County Recorder of Deeds, 409 Third Street, Box 70, Platte City, MO 64079. 816-858-3322. Fax: 816-858-2379. 8AM-5PM (CST).

Felony, Misdemeanor, Civil Actions Over $45,000—Circuit Court, 328 Main St, Box 5CH, Platte City, MO 64079. 816-858-2232. Fax: 816-858-3392. 8AM-5PM (CST). Access by: Mail, in person.

Misdemeanor, Civil Actions Under $45,000, Eviction, Small Claims—Associate Circuit Court, 328 Main St, Box 5CH, Platte City, MO 64079. 816-858-2232. Fax: 816-858-3392. 8:00AM-5:00PM (CST). Access by: Mail, in person.

Probate—Probate Court, 328 Main St, Box 95CH, Platte City, MO 64079. 816-858-2232. Fax: 816-858-3392. 8AM-5PM (CST). Access by: Mail, in person.

Polk County

Real Estate Recording—Polk County Recorder of Deeds, 102 E. Broadway, Courthouse, Bolivar, MO 65613. 417-326-4924. Fax: 417-326-4194. 8AM-5PM (CST).

Felony, Misdemeanor, Civil Actions Over $45,000—Circuit Court, 102 E Broadway, Rm 14, Bolivar, MO 65613. 417-326-4912. Fax: 417-326-4194. 8AM-5PM (CST). Access by: Fax, mail, in person.

Misdemeanor, Civil Actions Under $45,000, Eviction, Small Claims, Probate—Associate Circuit Court, Courthouse, Rm 7, Bolivar, MO 65613. 417-326-4921. Fax: 417-326-5238. 8:00AM-5:00PM (CST). Access by: Mail, in person.

Pulaski County

Real Estate Recording—Pulaski County Recorder of Deeds, 301 Historic Route 66, Courthouse Suite 202, Waynesville, MO 65583. 573-774-6609. Fax: 573-774-6967. 8AM-4:30PM (CST).

Felony, Misdemeanor, Civil, Eviction, Small Claims—Circuit & Associate Circuit Courts, 301 Historic Rt 66 E, Suite 202, Waynesville, MO 65583. 573-774-6609. Fax: 573-774-6967. 8AM-4:30PM (CST). Access by: Mail, in person.

Probate—Probate Court, 301 Historic 66 East, Suite 306, Waynesville, MO 65583. 573-774-6609. Fax: 573-774-6967. (CST).

Putnam County

Real Estate Recording—Putnam County Recorder of Deeds, Courthouse - Room 202, 1601 W. Main, Unionville, MO 63565. 660-947-2071. Fax: 660-947-2320. 9AM-Noon,1-5PM (CST).

Felony, Misdemeanor, Civil Actions Over $45,000—Circuit Court, Courthouse Rm 202, Unionville, MO 63565. 660-947-2071. Fax: 660-947-2320. 9:00AM-5:00PM (CST). Access by: Mail, in person.

Misdemeanor, Civil Actions Under $45,000, Eviction, Small Claims, Probate—Associate Circuit Court, Courthouse Rm 101, Unionville, MO 63565. 660-947-2117. Fax: 660-947-3700. 9AM-5PM (CST). Access by: Mail, in person.

Ralls County

Real Estate Recording—Ralls County Recorder of Deeds, Main Street, Courthouse, New London, MO 63459. 573-985-5631. 8:30AM-Noon, 1-4:30PM (CST).

Felony, Misdemeanor, Civil Actions Over $45,000—Circuit Court, PO Box 444, New London, MO 63459. 573-985-5631. 8:30AM-4:30PM (CST). Access by: Mail, in person.

Misdemeanor, Civil Actions Under $45,000, Eviction, Small Claims, Probate—Associate Circuit Court, PO Box 466, New London, MO 63459. 573-985-5641. Fax: 573-985-3446. 8:30AM-4:30PM (CST). Access by: Phone, mail, in person.

Randolph County

Real Estate Recording—Randolph County Recorder of Deeds, 110 S. Main St., Courthouse, Huntsville, MO 65259. 660-277-4718. Fax: 660-277-3246. 8AM-4PM (CST).

Felony, Misdemeanor, Civil Actions Over $45,000—Circuit Court, 223 N Williams, Moberly, MO 65270. 660-263-4474. Fax: 660-263-5966. 8AM-4:30PM (CST). Access by: Phone, fax, mail, in person.

Misdemeanor, Civil Actions Under $45,000, Eviction, Small Claims, Probate—Associate Circuit Court, 223 N Williams, Moberly, MO 65270. 660-263-4450. Fax: 660-263-1007. 8AM-4:30PM (CST). Access by: Mail, in person.

Ray County

Real Estate Recording—Ray County Recorder of Deeds, Courthouse, 2nd Floor, Richmond, MO 64085. 660-776-4500. 8AM-Noon, 1-4PM (CST).

Felony, Misdemeanor, Civil Actions Over $45,000—Circuit Court, PO Box 594, Richmond, MO 64085. 660-776-3377. Fax: 660-776-6016. 8AM-4PM (CST). Access by: Phone, mail, in person.

Misdemeanor, Civil Actions Under $45,000, Eviction, Small Claims, Probate—Associate Circuit Court, Courthouse, Richmond, MO 64085. 660-776-2335. Fax: 660-470-2064. 8AM-4PM (CST). Access by: Fax, mail, in person.

Reynolds County

Real Estate Recording—Reynolds County Recorder of Deeds, Courthouse, Centerville, MO 63633. 573-648-2494. Fax: 573-648-2296. 8AM-4PM (CST).

Felony, Misdemeanor, Civil Actions Over $45,000—Circuit Court, PO Box 76, Centerville, MO 63633. 573-648-2494. Fax: 573-648-2296. 8AM-4PM (CST). Access by: In person only.

Misdemeanor, Civil Actions Under $45,000, Eviction, Small Claims, Probate—Associate Circuit Court, PO Box 39, Centerville, MO 63633. 573-648-2494. Fax: 573-648-2296. 8AM-4PM (CST). Access by: Phone, mail, in person.

Ripley County

Real Estate Recording—Ripley County Recorder of Deeds, 100 Courthouse Square, Suite 3, Doniphan, MO 63935. 573-996-2818. Fax: 573-966-5014. 8AM-4PM (CST).

Felony, Misdemeanor, Civil Actions Over $25,000—Circuit Court, Courthouse, Doniphan, MO 63935. 573-996-2818. Fax: 573-996-5014. 8AM-4PM (CST). Access by: Fax, mail, in person.

Misdemeanor, Civil Actions Under $25,000, Eviction, Small Claims, Probate—Associate Circuit Court, 100 Court Sq, Courthouse, Doniphan, MO 63935. 573-996-2013. Fax: 573-996-5014. 8AM-4PM (CST). Access by: Phone, mail, in person.

Saline County

Real Estate Recording—Saline County Recorder of Deeds, Courthouse, Room 206, Marshall, MO 65340. 660-886-2677. Fax: 660-886-2603. 8:30AM-Noon, 1-5PM (CST).

Felony, Misdemeanor, Civil Actions Over $45,000—Circuit Court, PO Box 597, Marshall, MO 65340. 660-886-2300. 8:00AM-5:00PM (CST). Access by: Mail, in person.

Misdemeanor, Civil Actions Under $45,000, Eviction, Small Claims, Probate—Associate Circuit Court, PO Box

751, Marshall, MO 65340. 660-886-6988. 8:00AM-5:00PM (CST). Access by: Phone, mail, in person.

Schuyler County

Real Estate Recording—Schuyler County Recorder of Deeds, Courthouse, Highway 136 East, Lancaster, MO 63548. 660-457-3784. Fax: 660-457-3016. 8AM-Noon,1-4PM (CST).

Felony, Misdemeanor, Civil Actions Over $45,000—Circuit Court, PO Box 186, Lancaster, MO 63548. 660-457-3784. Fax: 660-457-3016. 9AM-4PM (CST). Access by: Mail, in person.

Misdemeanor, Civil Actions Under $45,000, Eviction, Small Claims, Probate—Associate Circuit Court, Box 158, Lancaster, MO 63548. 660-457-3755. Fax: 660-457-3016. 8:15AM-4PM (CST). Access by: Mail, in person.

Scotland County

Real Estate Recording—Scotland County Recorder of Deeds, 117 South Market St., Room 106, Memphis, MO 63555. 660-465-8605. Fax: 660-465-7005. 9AM-Noon,1-4PM (CST).

Felony, Misdemeanor, Civil Actions Over $45,000—Circuit Court, Courthouse, Rm 106, Memphis, MO 63555. 660-465-8605. Fax: 660-465-7005. 9AM-4PM (CST). Access by: Mail, in person.

Misdemeanor, Civil Actions Under $45,000, Eviction, Small Claims, Probate—Associate Circuit Court, Courthouse, Rm 102, Memphis, MO 63555. 660-465-2404. 8AM-4:30PM (CST). Access by: Phone, mail, in person.

Scott County

Real Estate Recording—Scott County Recorder of Deeds, Courthouse, Highway 61, Benton, MO 63736. 573-545-3551. 8:30AM-5PM (CST).

Felony, Misdemeanor, Civil Actions Over $45,000—Circuit Court, PO Box 277, Benton, MO 63736. 573-545-3596. Fax: 573-545-3597. 8:30AM-5PM (CST). Access by: Fax, mail, in person.

Misdemeanor, Civil Actions Under $45,000, Eviction, Small Claims, Probate—Associate Circuit Court, PO Box 249, Benton, MO 63736. 573-545-3576. Fax: 573-545-4231. 8:30AM-5:00PM (CST). Access by: Phone, mail, in person.

Shannon County

Real Estate Recording—Shannon County Recorder of Deeds, Courthouse, Eminence, MO 65466. 573-226-3315. Fax: 573-226-5321. 8AM-Noon, 12:30-4:30PM (CST).

Felony, Misdemeanor, Civil Actions Over $45,000—Circuit Court, PO Box 148, Eminence, MO 65466. 573-226-3315. Fax: 573-226-5321. 8AM-4:30PM (CST). Access by: Mail, in person.

Misdemeanor, Civil Actions Under $45,000, Eviction, Small Claims, Probate—Associate Circuit Court, PO Box AB, Eminence, MO 65466. 573-226-5515. Fax: 573-226-5321. 8AM-4:30PM (CST). Access by: Mail, in person.

Shelby County

Real Estate Recording—Shelby County Recorder of Deeds, Courthouse, Shelbyville, MO 63469. 573-633-2151. Fax: 573-633-2493. 8AM-4:30PM (CST).

Felony, Misdemeanor, Civil Actions Over $45,000—Circuit Court, PO Box 176, Shelbyville, MO 63469. 573-633-2151. 8:00AM-4:30PM (CST). Access by: Mail, in person.

Misdemeanor, Civil Actions Under $45,000, Eviction, Small Claims, Probate—Associate Circuit Court, PO Box 206, Shelbyville, MO 63469. 573-633-2151. Fax: 573-633-2493. 8:00AM-4:00PM (CST). Access by: Phone, mail, in person.

St. Charles County

Real Estate Recording—St. Charles County Recorder of Deeds, 201 North 2nd, Room 338, St. Charles, MO 63301. 314-949-7505. Fax: 314-949-7512. 8:30AM-5PM (CST).

Felony, Misdemeanor, Civil Actions Over $45,000—Circuit Court, 300 N 2nd St, St. Charles, MO 63301. 314-949-3080. Fax: 314-949-7390. 8:30AM-5:00PM (CST). Access by: Mail, in person.

Misdemeanor, Civil Actions Under $45,000, Eviction, Small Claims, Probate—Associate Circuit Court, 300 N 2nd, St Charles, MO 63301. 314-949-3080. 8:30AM-5:00PM (CST). Access by: Mail, in person.

St. Clair County

Real Estate Recording—St. Clair County Recorder of Deeds, Courthouse Square, Osceola, MO 64776. 417-646-2226. Fax: 417-646-2401. 8AM-4:30PM (CST).

Felony, Misdemeanor, Civil, Eviction, Small Claims, Probate—Circuit & Associate Circuit Courts, PO Box 334, Osceola, MO 64776. 417-646-2226. Fax: 417-646-2401. 8:00AM-4:30PM (CST). Access by: Mail, in person.

St. Francois County

Real Estate Recording—St. Francois County Recorder of Deeds, Courthouse, Farmington, MO 63640. 573-756-2323. 8AM-4PM (CST).

Felony, Misdemeanor, Civil Actions Over $25,000—Circuit Court, 1 N Washington, 3rd Floor, Farmington, MO 63640. 573-756-4551. Fax: 573-756-3733. 8AM-5PM (CST). Access by: Fax, mail, in person.

Misdemeanor, Civil Actions Under $45,000, Eviction, Small Claims, Probate—Associate Circuit Court, County Courthouse, 2nd Fl, Farmington, MO 63640. 573-756-5755. Fax: 573-756-8173. 8AM-5PM (CST). Access by: In person only.

St. Louis City

Real Estate Recording—St. Louis City Recorder, Tucker & Market Streets, City Hall Room 126, St. Louis, MO 63103. 314-622-3259. Fax: 314-622-4175. 9AM-5PM (CST).

Civil, Eviction, Small Claims, Probate—Circuit & Associate Circuit Courts, 10 N Tucker, Civil Courts Bldg, St Louis, MO 63101. 314-622-4367. Fax: 314-622-4537. 8:00AM-5:00PM. Access by: Mail, in person.

Felony, Misdemeanor—City of St Louis Circuit Court, 1320 Market, St Louis, MO 63103. 314-622-4582. Fax: 314-622-3202. 8AM-5PM. Access by: Mail, in person.

St. Louis County

Real Estate Recording—St. Louis County Recorder of Deeds, 41 S. Central Avenue, Clayton, MO 63105. 314-889-2183. Fax: 314-889-3864. 8AM-5PM (CST).

Felony, Misdemeanor, Civil—Circuit Court of St. Louis County, 7900 Carondolet, Clayton, MO 63105-1766. 314-889-3029. Fax: 314-854-8739. 8AM-5PM (CST). Access by: Phone, fax, mail, in person.

Civil Actions Under $45,000, Eviction, Small Claims, Probate—Associate Circuit-Civil Division, 7900 Carondolet, Clayton, MO 63105. 314-889-3090. Probate: 314-889-2629. Fax: 314-889-2689. 8AM-5PM (CST). Access by: In person only.

Misdemeanor—Associate Circuit Court-Criminal Division, 7900 Carondolet, Clayton, MO 63105. 314-889-2675. Fax: 314-889-2689. (CST). Access by: Mail, in person.

Ste. Genevieve County

Real Estate Recording—Ste. Genevieve County Recorder of Deeds, 3rd Street, Court House, Ste. Genevieve, MO 63670. 573-883-2706. Fax: 573-883-9636. 8AM-4:30PM (CST).

Felony, Misdemeanor, Civil Actions Over $45,000—Circuit Court, 55 S 3rd, Rm 23, Ste Genevieve, MO 63670. 573-883-2705. Fax: 573-883-9351. 8AM-5PM (CST). Access by: In person only.

Misdemeanor, Civil Actions Under $45,000, Eviction, Small Claims, Probate—Associate Circuit Court, 3rd and Market, Ste Genevieve, MO 63670. 573-883-2265. Fax: 573-883-9351. 8AM-5PM (CST). Access by: In person only.

Stoddard County

Real Estate Recording—Stoddard County Recorder of Deeds, Courthouse Square, Prairie St., Bloomfield, MO

63825. 573-568-3444. Fax: 573-568-2194. 8:30AM-4:30PM (CST).

Felony, Misdemeanor, Civil Actions Over $45,000— Circuit Court, PO Box 30, Bloomfield, MO 63825. 573-568-4640. Fax: 573-568-2271. 8:30AM-4:30PM (CST). Access by: Fax, mail, in person.

Civil Actions Under $45,000, Eviction, Small Claims, Probate—Associate Circuit Court, PO Box 339, Bloomfield, MO 63825. 573-568-2181. (CST).

Misdemeanor—Associate Circuit Court-Criminal Division, PO Box 218, Bloomfield, MO 63825. 573-568-4671. Fax: 573-568-2299. 8:30AM-4:30PM (CST). Access by: In person only.

Stone County

Real Estate Recording—Stone County Recorder of Deeds, Courthouse Square, Galena, MO 65656. 417-357-6362. Fax: 417-357-8131. 8AM-4PM (CST).

Felony, Misdemeanor, Civil Actions Over $25,000— Circuit Court, PO Box 18, Galena, MO 65656. 417-357-6114. Fax: 417-357-6163. 7:30AM-4PM (CST). Access by: Phone, fax, mail, in person.

Misdemeanor, Civil Actions Under $25,000, Eviction, Small Claims, Probate—Circuit Court-Division II, PO Box 186, Galena, MO 65656. 417-357-6511. Fax: 417-357-6163. 7:30AM-4PM (CST). Access by: Fax, mail, in person.

Sullivan County

Real Estate Recording—Sullivan County Recorder of Deeds, Courthouse, Milan, MO 63556. 660-265-3630. Fax: 660-265-4711. 9AM-Noon, 1-4:30PM (CST).

Felony, Misdemeanor, Civil Actions Over $45,000— Circuit Court, Courthouse, Milan, MO 63556-1358. 660-265-4717. Fax: 660-265-4711. 9:00AM-4:30PM (CST). Access by: Fax, mail, in person.

Misdemeanor, Civil Actions Under $45,000, Eviction, Small Claims, Probate—Associate Circuit Court, Courthouse, Milan, MO 63556. 660-265-3303. Fax: 660-265-4711. 9:00AM-4:30PM (CST). Access by: Mail, in person.

Taney County

Real Estate Recording—Taney County Recorder of Deeds, Main & David, Courthouse, Forsyth, MO 65653. 417-546-7234. 8AM-5PM (CST).

Felony, Misdemeanor, Civil Actions Over $45,000— Circuit Court, PO Box 335, Forsyth, MO 65653. 417-546-6132. Fax: 417-546-6133. 8AM-5PM (CST). Access by: Mail, in person.

Misdemeanor, Civil Actions Under $45,000, Eviction, Small Claims, Probate—Associate Circuit Court, PO Box 129, Forsyth, MO 65653. 417-546-7212. Fax: 417-546-4513. 8AM-5PM (CST). Access by: Mail, in person.

Texas County

Real Estate Recording—Texas County Recorder of Deeds, 210 North Grand, P.O. Box 237, Houston, MO 65483. 417-967-3742. Fax: 417-967-4220. 8AM-5PM (CST).

Felony, Misdemeanor, Civil Actions Over $45,000— Circuit Court, 210 N Grand, Houston, MO 65483. 417-967-3742. Fax: 417-967-4220. 8AM-5PM (CST). Access by: Fax, mail, in person.

Misdemeanor, Civil Actions Under $45,000, Eviction, Small Claims, Probate—Associate Circuit Court, County Courthouse, Houston, MO 65483. 417-967-3663. Fax: 417-967-2100. 8AM-5PM (CST). Access by: Phone, fax, mail, in person.

Vernon County

Real Estate Recording—Vernon County Recorder of Deeds, Courthouse, Nevada, MO 64772. 417-448-2520. 8:30AM-Noon, 1-4:30PM (CST).

Felony, Misdemeanor, Civil Actions Over $45,000— Circuit Court, Courthouse, 3rd Fl, Nevada, MO 64772. 417-448-2525. Fax: 417-448-2512. 8AM-4:30PM (CST). Access by: Fax, mail, in person.

Misdemeanor, Civil Actions Under $45,000, Eviction, Small Claims, Probate—Associate Circuit Court, County Courthouse, Rm 9, Nevada, MO 64772. 417-448-2550. Fax: 417-448-2512. 8:30AM-4:30PM (CST). Access by: Mail, in person.

Warren County

Real Estate Recording—Warren County Recorder of Deeds, 104 West Boone's Lick Rd., Warrenton, MO 63383. 314-456-3363. 8AM-4:30PM (CST).

Felony, Misdemeanor, Civil Actions Over $45,000— Circuit Court, 104 W Main, Warrenton, MO 63383. 314-456-3363. Fax: 314-456-2422. 8AM-4:30PM (CST). Access by: In person only.

Misdemeanor, Civil Actions Under $25,000, Eviction, Small Claims, Pr—Associate Circuit Court, Warren County Courthouse, Warrenton, MO 63383. 314-456-3375. Fax: 314-456-2422. 8:30AM-4:30PM (CST). Access by: Phone, fax, mail, in person.

Washington County

Real Estate Recording—Washington County Recorder of Deeds, 102 North Missouri Street, Potosi, MO 63664. 573-438-4171. Fax: 573-438-7900. 8AM-5PM (CST).

Felony, Misdemeanor, Civil Actions Over $45,000— Circuit Court, PO Box 216, Potosi, MO 63664. 573-438-4171. Fax: 573-438-7900. 8AM-5PM (CST). Access by: Mail, in person.

Misdemeanor, Civil Actions Under $45,000, Eviction, Small Claims, Probate—Associate Circuit Court, 102 N Missouri St, Potosi, MO 63664. 573-438-3691. Fax: 573-438-7900. 8AM-5PM (CST). Access by: Mail, in person.

Wayne County

Real Estate Recording—Wayne County Recorder of Deeds, 106 Walnut, Courthouse, Greenville, MO 63944. 573-224-3221. Fax: 573-224-3225. 8:30AM-Noon, 1-4:30PM (CST).

Felony, Misdemeanor, Civil Actions Over $45,000— Circuit Court, PO Box 187A, Greenville, MO 63944. 573-224-3221. Fax: 573-224-3225. 8:30AM-4:30PM (CST). Access by: Mail, in person.

Misdemeanor, Civil Actions Under $45,000, Eviction, Small Claims, Probate—Associate Circuit Court, PO Box 188, Greenville, MO 63944. 573-224-3221. Fax: 573-224-3225. 8:30AM-4:30PM (CST). Access by: Phone, fax, mail, in person.

Webster County

Real Estate Recording—Webster County Recorder of Deeds, Courthouse, Marshfield, MO 65706. 417-468-2173. Fax: 417-468-3786. 8AM-4PM (CST).

Felony, Misdemeanor, Civil Actions Over $45,000— Circuit Court, PO Box 529, Marshfield, MO 65706. 417-859-2006. Fax: 417-468-3786. 8AM-5PM (CST). Access by: Fax, mail, in person.

Misdemeanor, Civil Actions Under $45,000, Eviction, Small Claims, Probate—Associate Circuit Court, Courthouse, Marshfield, MO 65706. 417-859-2041. Fax: 417-468-3786. 8AM-4:30PM (CST). Access by: In person only.

Worth County

Real Estate Recording—Worth County Recorder of Deeds, Courthouse on the Square, Grant City, MO 64456. 660-564-2210. Fax: 660-564-2432. 8:30AM-Noon, 1-4:30PM (CST).

Felony, Misdemeanor, Civil Actions Over $45,000— Circuit Court, PO Box H, Grant City, MO 64456. 660-564-2210. Fax: 660-564-2432. 8:30AM-4:30PM (CST). Access by: Mail, in person.

Misdemeanor, Civil Actions Under $45,000, Eviction, Small Claims, Probate—Associate Circuit Court, PO Box 428, Grant City, MO 64456. 660-564-2152. Fax: 660-564-2432. 9AM-4:30PM (CST). Access by: In person only.

Wright County

Real Estate Recording—Wright County Recorder of Deeds, Courthouse, Hartville, MO 65667. 417-741-7322. Fax: 417-741-7504. 8AM-4:30PM (CST).

Felony, Misdemeanor, Civil Actions Over $45,000—Circuit Court, PO Box 39, Hartville, MO 65667. 417-741-

7121. Fax: 417-741-7504. 8AM-4:30PM (CST). Access by: Mail, in person.

Misdemeanor, Civil Actions Under $45,000, Eviction, Small Claims, Probate—Associate Circuit Court, PO Box 58, Hartville, MO 65667. 417-741-6450. Fax: 417-741-6780. 8AM-4:30PM (CST). Access by: Phone, fax, mail, in person.

Federal Courts

US District Court
Eastern District of Missouri

Cape Girardeau Division, US District Court 339 Broadway, Cape Girardeau, MO 63701. 573-335-8538. Counties: Bollinger, Butler, Cape Girardeau, Carter, Dunklin, Madison, Mississippi, New Madrid, Pemiscot, Perry, Reynolds, Ripley, Scott, Shannon, Stoddard, Wayne

Hannibal Division, US District Court c/o St Louis Division, Room 260, 1114 Market St, St Louis, MO 63101. 314-539-2315. Counties: Adair, Audrain, Chariton, Clark, Knox, Lewis, Linn, Macon, Marion, Monroe, Montgomery, Pike, Ralls, Randolph, Schuyler, Scotland, Shelby

St Louis Division, US District Court Room 260, 1114 Market St, St Louis, MO 63101. 314-539-2315. Counties: Crawford, Dent, Franklin, Gasconade, Iron, Jefferson, Lincoln, Maries, Phelps, St. Charles, Ste. Genevieve, St. Francois, St. Louis, Warren, Washington, City of St. Louis

Western District of Missouri

Jefferson City-Central Division, US District Court 131 W High St, Jefferson City, MO 65101. 573-636-4015. Counties: Benton, Boone, Callaway, Camden, Cole, Cooper, Hickory, Howard, Miller, Moniteau, Morgan, Osage, Pettis

Joplin-Southwestern Division, US District Court c/o Kansas City Division, 201 US Courthouse, 811 Grand Ave, Kansas City, MO 64106. 816-426-2811. Counties: Barry, Barton, Jasper, Lawrence, McDonald, Newton, Stone, Vernon

Kansas City-Western Division, US District Court Clerk of Court, 201 US Courthouse, 811 Grand Ave, Kansas City, MO 64106. 816-426-2811. Counties: Bates, Carroll, Cass, Clay, Henry, Jackson, Johnson, Lafayette, Ray, St. Clair, Saline

Springfield-Southern Division, US District Court 222 N John Q Hammons Pkwy, Suite 1400, Springfield, MO 65806. 417-865-3869. Counties: Cedar, Christian, Dade,

Dallas, Douglas, Greene, Howell, Laclede, Oregon, Ozark, Polk, Pulaski, Taney, Texas, Webster, Wright

St Joseph Division, US District Court PO Box 387, 201 S 8th St, St Joseph, MO 64501. 816-279-2428. Counties: Andrew, Atchison, Buchanan, Caldwell, Clinton, Daviess, De Kalb, Gentry, Grundy, Harrison, Holt, Livingston, Mercer, Nodaway, Platte, Putnam, Sullivan, Worth

US Bankruptcy Court
Eastern District of Missouri

St Louis Division, US Bankruptcy Court, 1 Metropolitan Square, 7th Floor, St Louis, MO 63102-2734. 314-425-4222. Voice Case Information System: 314-425-4054. Counties: Adair, Audrain, Bollinger, Butler, Cape Girardeau, Carter, Chariton, Clark, Crawford, Dent, Dunklin, Franklin, Gasconade, Iron, Jefferson, Knox, Lewis, Lincoln, Linn, Macon, Madison, Maries, Marion, Mississippi, Monroe, Montgomery, New Madrid, Pemiscot, Perry, Phelps, Pike, Ralls, Randolph, Reynolds, Ripley, Schuyler, Scotland, Scott, Shannon, Shelby, St. Charles, St. Francois, St. Louis, St.Louis City, Ste. Genevieve, Stoddard, Warren, Washington, Wayne

Western District of Missouri

Kansas City-Western Division, US Bankruptcy Court, Room 913, 811 Grand Ave, Kansas City, MO 64106. 816-426-3321. Voice Case Information System: 816-842-7985. Counties: Andrew, Atchison, Barry, Barton, Bates, Benton, Boone, Buchanan, Caldwell, Callaway, Camden, Carroll, Cass, Cedar, Christian, Clay, Clinton, Cole, Cooper, Dade, Dallas, Daviess, De Kalb, Douglas, Gentry, Greene, Grundy, Harrison, Henry, Hickory, Holt, Howard, Howell, Jackson, Jasper, Johnson, Laclede, Lafayette, Lawrence, Livingston, McDonald, Mercer, Miller, Moniteau, Morgan, Newton, Nodaway, Oregon, Osage, Ozark, Pettis, Platte, Polk, Pulaski, Putnam, Ray, Saline, St. Clair, Sullivan, Taney, Texas, Vernon, Webster, Worth, Wright

Montana

Capitol: Helena (Lewis and Clark County)	
Number of Counties: 56	**Population:** 870,281
County Court Locations:	**Federal Court Locations:**
•District Courts: 56/21 Districts	•District Courts: 5
•Justice of the Peace Courts: 66/ 56 Counties	•Bankruptcy Courts: 1
City Courts: 83	**State Agencies:** 18
Municipal Courts: 1	
Water Courts: 4 Divisions	
Workers Compensation Courts: 1	

State Agencies—Summary

General Help Numbers:

State Archives

Historical Society	406-444-4774
Library/Archives Division	Fax: 406-444-2696
225 N Roberts St	8AM-5PM
Helena, MT 59620	
Historical Library:	406-444-2681

Governor's Office

Governor's Office	406-444-3111
State Capitol	Fax: 406-444-5529
Helena, MT 59620-0801	8AM-5PM

Attorney General's Office

Attorney General's Office	406-444-2026
PO Box 201401	Fax: 406-444-3549
Helena, MT 59620	8AM-5PM

State Legislation

State Legislature of Montana	406-444-3064
State Capitol	Fax: 406-444-3036
Room 138	8AM-5PM
Helena, MT 59620-1706	

In addition to the Internet site noted in the right hand column, there is a BBS available containing additional information about bills. The BBS requires special software which can be obtained by calling 406-444-1626.

Important State Internet Sites:

Webscape
File   Edit   View   Help

State of Montana World Wide Web
www.mt.gov/

Links to such sites as education, government, travel conditions, employment and what's new.

The Governor's Office
www.mt.gov/governor/governor.htm

Includes information about the Governor..

Montana Legislative Branch
www.mt.gov/leg/branch/branch.htm

Links to the Legislature and its members. 1997 & 1995 session bills which can be searched online and the Montana Code (contains the state constitution). This site offers bill downloading into a WP51 format.

Secretary of State's Office
www.mt.gov/sos.index.htm

A helpful site to review services and filing cost fees for all Secretary of State documents.

Law Library
161.7.121.6/

This is an excellent legal reference site which includes an online card catalogue, Montana legal information and law related links.

State Agencies—Public Records

Criminal Records

Department of Justice, Criminal History Records Program, 303 N Roberts, Room 374, Helena, MT 59620-1418, Main Telephone: 406-444-3625, Fax: 406-444-0689, Hours: 8AM-5PM. Access by: mail, visit.

Corporation Records
Limited Liability Company Records
Fictitious Name
Limited Partnerships
Assumed Name
Trademarks/Servicemarks

Business Services Bureau, Secretary of State, PO Box 202801, Helena, MT 59620-2801, Main Telephone: 406-444-3665, Fax: 406-444-3976, Hours: 8AM-5PM. Access by: mail, phone, fax, visit.

Uniform Commercial Code
Federal Tax Liens
State Tax Liens

Business Services Bureau, Secretary of State, PO Box 202801, Helena, MT 59620-2801, Main Telephone: 406-444-3665, Fax: 406-444-3976, Hours: 8AM-5PM. Access by: mail, fax, visit, PC.

Sales Tax Registrations

State does not impose sales tax.

Birth Certificates

Montana Department of Health, Vital Records, PO Box 4120, Helena, MT 59604, Main Telephone: 406-444-4228, Hours: 8AM-5PM. Access by: mail, phone, visit.

Death Records

Montana Department of Health, Vital Records, PO Box 4120, Helena, MT 59604, Main Telephone: 406-444-4228, Hours: 8AM-5PM. Access by: mail, phone, visit.

Marriage Certificates
Divorce Records

Records not available from state agency.

Workers' Compensation Records

State Compensation Fund, PO Box 4759, Helena, MT 59604-4759, Main Telephone: 406-444-6485, Hours: 8AM-5PM. Access by: mail, phone, visit.

Driver Records

Motor Vehicle Division, PO Box 201430, Helena, MT 59620-1430, Main Telephone: 406-444-4590, Fax: 406-444-1631, Hours: 8AM-5PM. Access by: mail, fax, visit. Copies of tickets are available from the same address; requests must be in writing.

Vehicle Ownership
Vehicle Identification

Department of Justice, Title and Registration Bureau, 1032 Buckskin Drive, Deer Lodge, MT 59722, Main Telephone: 406-846-6000, Fax: 406-846-1448, Hours: 8AM-5PM. Access by: mail, fax, phone, visit. Lien information is also released.

Accident Reports

Montana Highway Patrol, Accident Records, 2550 Prospect Ave, Helena, MT 59620-1419, Main Telephone: 406-444-3278, Fax: 406-444-4169, Hours: 8AM-5PM. Access by: mail, phone, visit.

Hunting License Information
Fishing License Information

Fish, Wildlife & Parks Department, Department of Fish & Wildlife, PO Box 200701, Helena, MT 59620-0701, Main Telephone: 406-444-3133, Fax: 406-444-4952, Hours: 8AM-5PM. Access by: mail only. Addresses are released.

County Courts and Recording Offices

What You Need to Know...

About the Courts

Administration

Court Administrator   406-444-2621
215 N Sanders, Justice Bldg, Room 315
Helena, MT 59620-3002

Court Structure

Many Justices of the Peace maintain case record indexes on their **personal** PC which does speed the retrieval process.

Online Access

There is no statewide internal or external online computer system available. Those courts with a computer system use it for internal purposes only.

About the Recorder's Office

Organization

56 counties, 56 filing offices. The recording officer is County Clerk and Recorder (Clerk of District Court for state tax liens). Yellowstone National Park is considered a county, but is not included as a filing location. The entire state is in the Mountain Time Zone (MST).

UCC Records

Financing statements are filed at the state level, except for consumer goods and real estate related collateral. All counties will perform UCC searches. Use search request form UCC-11. Search fees are usually $7.00 per debtor name. Copy fees vary.

Lien Records

Federal tax liens on personal property of businesses are filed with the Secretary of State. Other federal tax liens are filed with the county Clerk and Recorder. State tax liens are filed with the Clerk of District Court. Usually tax liens on personal property filed with the Clerk and Recorder are in the same index with UCC financing statements. Most counties will perform tax lien searches, some as part of a UCC search and others for a separate fee, usually $7.00 per name. Copy fees vary. Other liens include mechanics, thresherman, judgment, lis pendens, construction, and logger.

Real Estate Records

Some counties will perform real estate searches. Search and copy fees vary. Certification usually costs $2.00 per document.

County Courts and Recording Offices

Beaverhead County

Real Estate Recording—Beaverhead County Clerk and Recorder, 2 South Pacific, Dillon, MT 59725. 406-683-2642. Fax: 406-683-5776. 8AM-5PM (MST).

Felony, Civil Actions Over $5,000, Eviction, Probate—District Court, Beaverhead County Courthouse, 2 S Pacific St, Dillon, MT 59725. 406-683-5831. Fax: 406-683-5776. 8AM-5PM (MST). Access by: Fax, mail, in person.

Misdemeanor, Civil Actions Under $5,000, Eviction, Small Claims—Dillon Justice Court, 2 S Pacific, Cluster #16, Dillon, MT 59725. 406-683-2383. Fax: 406-683-5776. 8AM-Noon (MST). Access by: Mail, in person.

Beaverhead County Justice Court, PO Box 107, Lima, MT 59739. 406-276-3205. 4-6PM (MST). Access by: Mail, in person.

Big Horn County

Real Estate Recording—Big Horn County Clerk and Recorder, 121 West 3rd Street, Hardin, MT 59034. 406-665-1506. Fax: 406-665-1608. 8AM-5PM (MST).

Felony, Civil Actions Over $5,000, Eviction, Probate—District Court, 121 West 3rd St #221, Hardin, MT 59034. 406-665-1504. Fax: 406-665-1608. 8AM-5PM (MST). Access by: Phone, fax, mail, in person. Signed release required for confidential information.

Misdemeanor, Civil Actions Under $5,000, Eviction, Small Claims—Justice Court, PO Box H, Hardin, MT 59034. 406-665-2275. Fax: 406-665-1608. 8AM-5PM (MST). Access by: Fax, mail, in person.

Blaine County

Real Estate Recording—Blaine County Clerk and Recorder, 400 Ohio Street, Chinook, MT 59523. 406-357-3240. Fax: 406-357-2199. 8AM-5PM (MST).

Felony, Civil Actions Over $5,000, Eviction, Probate—District Court, PO Box 969, Chinook, MT 59523. 406-357-3230. Fax: 406-357-2199. 8AM-5PM (MST). Access by: Fax, mail, in person.

Misdemeanor, Civil Actions Under $5,000, Eviction, Small Claims—Chinook Justice Court, PO Box 1266, Chinook, MT 59523. 406-357-2335. 8AM-Noon (MST). Access by: Mail, in person.

Harlem Justice Court, PO Box 354, Harlem, MT 59526. 406-353-4971. Fax: 406-353-2361. 9AM-11AM (MST). Access by: Mail, in person.

Broadwater County

Real Estate Recording—Broadwater County Clerk and Recorder, 515 Broadway, Townsend, MT 59644. 406-266-3443. Fax: 406-266-3674. 8AM-Noon, 1-5PM (MST).

Felony, Civil Actions Over $5,000, Eviction, Probate—District Court, 515 Broadway, Townsend, MT 59644. 406-266-3418. Fax: 406-266-5354. 8AM-Noon, 1-5PM (MST). Access by: Phone, mail, in person.

Misdemeanor, Civil Actions Under $5,000, Eviction, Small Claims—Justice Court, 515 Broadway, Townsend, MT 59644. 406-266-3145. Fax: 406-266-5354. 8AM-5PM (MST). Access by: Mail, in person.

Carbon County

Real Estate Recording—Carbon County Clerk and Recorder, Courthouse, Red Lodge, MT 59068. 406-446-1220. Fax: 406-446-2640. 8AM-5PM (MST).

Felony, Civil Actions Over $5,000, Eviction, Probate—District Court, PO Box 948, Red Lodge, MT 59068. 406-446-1225. Fax: 406-446-2640. 8AM-5PM (MST). Access by: Mail, in person.

Misdemeanor, Civil Actions Under $5,000, Eviction, Small Claims—Joliet Justice Court, PO Box, Joliet, MT 59041. 406-662-3826. (MST). Access by: Mail, in person.

Carbon County Justice Court, Box 2, Red Lodge, MT 59068. 406-446-1440. Fax: 406-446-2640. 8AM-5PM (MST). Access by: Mail, in person.

Carter County

Real Estate Recording—Carter County Clerk and Recorder, Courthouse, 101 Park Street, Ekalaka, MT 59324. 406-775-8749. 8AM-Noon, 1-5PM (MST).

Felony, Civil Actions Over $5,000, Eviction, Probate—District Court, PO Box 322, Ekalaka, MT 59324. 406-775-8714. Fax: 406-775-8714. 8AM-5PM (MST). Access by: Fax, mail, in person.

Misdemeanor, Civil Actions Under $5,000, Eviction, Small Claims—Justice Court, HC 50 Box 10, Alzada, MT 59311. 406-775-8749. Fax: 406-775-8750. 1-5PM 1st&3rd Th; 9:30AM-2:30PM 2nd & 4th Th (MST). Access by: Mail, in person.

Cascade County

Real Estate Recording—Cascade County Clerk and Recorder, 415 2nd Ave North, Great Falls, MT 59401. 406-454-6800. Fax: 406-454-6802. 8AM-5PM (MST).

Felony, Civil Actions Over $5,000, Eviction, Probate—District Court, County Courthouse, Great Falls, MT 59403. 406-454-6780. 8AM-5PM (MST). Access by: Phone, mail, in person.

Misdemeanor, Civil Actions Under $5,000, Eviction, Small Claims—Cascade Justice Court, Cascade County Courthouse, Great Falls, MT 59401. 406-454-6870. 8AM-5PM (MST). Access by: Mail, in person.

Chouteau County

Real Estate Recording—Chouteau County Clerk and Recorder, 1308 Franklin, Fort Benton, MT 59442. 406-622-5151. Fax: 406-622-3631. 8AM-5PM (MST).

Felony, Civil Actions Over $5,000, Eviction, Probate—District Court, PO Box 459, Ft Benton, MT 59442. 406-622-5024. Fax: 406-622-3631. 8AM-5PM (MST). Access by: Fax, mail, in person.

Misdemeanor, Civil Actions Under $5,000, Eviction, Small Claims—Big Sandy Justice Court, PO Box 234, Big Sandy, MT 59520. 406-378-2203. 1-5PM Th (MST). Access by: Mail, in person.

Ft Benton Justice Court, PO Box 459, Ft Benton, MT 59442. 406-622-5502. Fax: 406-622-3815. 8AM-5PM M,W; 8AM-4PM, 7:30PM-9PM T (MST). Access by: Phone, mail, in person.

Custer County

Real Estate Recording—Custer County Clerk and Recorder, 1010 Main Street, Miles City, MT 59301. 406-233-3343. Fax: 406-233-3452. 8AM-5PM (MST).

Felony, Civil Actions Over $5,000, Eviction, Probate—District Court, 1010 Main, Miles City, MT 59301-3418. 406-233-3326. Fax: 406-233-3450. 8AM-5PM (MST). Access by: Mail, in person.

Misdemeanor, Civil Actions Under $5,000, Eviction, Small Claims—Justice Court, 1010 Main St, Miles City, MT 59301-3418. 406-232-7800. Fax: 406-232-7803. 8AM-Noon,1-5PM (MST). Access by: Mail, in person.

Daniels County

Real Estate Recording—Daniels County Clerk and Recorder, 213 Main Street, Scobey, MT 59263. 406-487-5561. 8AM-5PM (MST).

Felony, Civil Actions Over $5,000, Eviction, Probate—District Court, PO Box 67, Scobey, MT 59263. 406-487-2651. 8AM-5PM (MST). Access by: Phone, mail, in person.

Misdemeanor, Civil Actions Under $5,000, Eviction, Small Claims—Justice Court, PO Box 838, Scobey, MT 59263. 406-487-5432. 8AM-5PM (MST). Access by: Mail, in person.

Dawson County

Real Estate Recording—Dawson County Clerk and Recorder, 207 West Bell, Glendive, MT 59330. 406-365-3058. 8AM-5PM (MST).

Felony, Civil Actions Over $5,000, Eviction, Probate—District Court, 207 W Bell, Glendive, MT 59330. 406-365-3967. Fax: 406-365-2022. 8AM-5PM (MST). Access by: Mail, in person.

Misdemeanor, Civil Actions Under $5,000, Eviction, Small Claims—Justice Court, 207 W Bell, Glendive, MT 59330. 406-365-5425. Fax: 406-365-2022. 8AM-5PM (MST). Access by: Mail, in person.

Deer Lodge County

Real Estate Recording—Deer Lodge County Clerk and Recorder, 800 South Main St., Courthouse, Anaconda, MT 59711. 406-563-8421. Fax: 406-563-8428. 8AM-5PM (MST).

Felony, Civil Actions Over $5,000, Eviction, Probate—District Court, 800 S Main, Anaconda, MT 59711. 406-563-4040. Fax: 406-563-4001. 8AM-5PM (MST). Access by: Phone, fax, mail, in person.

Misdemeanor, Civil Actions Under $5,000, Eviction, Small Claims—Justice Court, 800 S Main, Anaconda, MT 59711. 406-563-4025. Fax: 406-563-4028. 8AM-5PM (MST). Access by: Phone, fax, mail, in person.

Fallon County

Real Estate Recording—Fallon County Clerk and Recorder, 10 West Fallon Avenue, Baker, MT 59313. 406-778-2883. Fax: 406-778-3431. 8AM-5PM (MST).

Felony, Civil Actions Over $5,000, Eviction, Probate—District Court, PO Box 1521, Baker, MT 59313. 406-778-2883. Fax: 406-778-2815. 8AM-5PM (MST). Access by: Mail, in person.

Misdemeanor, Civil Actions Under $5,000, Eviction, Small Claims—Justice Court, Box 846, Baker, MT 59313. 406-778-2883. 11:30AM-4:30PM M-W (MST). Access by: Phone, mail, in person.

Fergus County

Real Estate Recording—Fergus County Clerk and Recorder, 712 West Main, Lewistown, MT 59457. 406-538-5242. Fax: 406-538-9023. 8AM-5PM (MST).

Felony, Civil Actions Over $5,000, Eviction, Probate—District Court, PO Box 1074, Lewistown, MT 59457. 406-538-5026. Fax: 406-538-6076. 8AM-5PM (MST). Access by: Mail, in person.

Misdemeanor, Civil Actions Under $5,000, Eviction, Small Claims—Justice Court, 121 8th Ave South, Lewistown, MT 59457. 406-538-5418. 9AM-4PM (MST). Access by: Mail, in person.

Flathead County

Real Estate Recording—Flathead County Clerk and Recorder, 800 South Main, Courthouse, Kalispell, MT 59901. 406-758-5532. Fax: 406-758-5865. 8AM-5PM (MST).

Felony, Civil Actions Over $5,000, Eviction, Probate—District Court, 800 S Main, Kalispell, MT 59901. 406-758-5660. 8AM-5PM (MST). Access by: Phone, mail, in person.

Misdemeanor, Civil Actions Under $5,000, Eviction, Small Claims—Justice Court, 800 S Main St, Kalispell, MT 59901. 406-758-5660. 8AM-5PM (MST). Access by: Mail, in person.

Gallatin County

Real Estate Recording—Gallatin County Clerk and Recorder, 311 West Main, Room 204, Bozeman, MT 59715. 406-582-3050. 8AM-5PM (MST).

Felony, Civil Actions Over $5,000, Eviction, Probate—District Court, 615 S 16th, Rm 203, Bozeman, MT 59715. 406-582-2165. Fax: 406-582-2167. 8AM-5PM (MST). Access by: Mail, in person.

Misdemeanor, Civil Actions Under $5,000, Eviction, Small Claims—Belgrade Justice and City Court, 88 N Broadway, Belgrade, MT 59714. 406-388-4262. Fax: 406-388-4996. 8AM-5PM (MST). Access by: Mail, in person.

Bozeman Justice Court, 615 S 16th St, Bozeman, MT 59715. 406-582-2191. Fax: 406-582-2176. 8AM-5PM (MST). Access by: Mail, in person.

Garfield County

Real Estate Recording—Garfield County Clerk and Recorder, Courthouse, Jordan, MT 59337. 406-557-2760. Fax: 406-557-2625. 8AM-5PM (MST).

Felony, Civil Actions Over $5,000, Eviction, Probate—District Court, PO Box 8, Jordan, MT 59337. 406-557-6254. Fax: 406-557-2625. 8AM-5PM (MST). Access by: Phone, mail, in person.

Misdemeanor, Civil Actions Under $5,000, Eviction, Small Claims—Justice Court, PO Box 482, Jordan, MT 59337. 406-557-2733. Fax: 406-557-2625. 8AM-5PM W (MST). Access by: In person only.

Glacier County

Real Estate Recording—Glacier County Clerk and Recorder, 512 East Main, Cut Bank, MT 59427. 406-873-5063. Fax: 406-873-2125. 8AM-5PM (MST).

Felony, Civil, Eviction, Probate—District Court, 512 E Main St, Cut Bank, MT 59427. 406-873-5063. Fax: 406-873-5627. 8AM-5PM (MST). Access by: Fax, mail, in person. Written request required.

Misdemeanor, Civil Actions Under $5,000, Eviction, Small Claims—Justice Court, 512 E Main St, Cut Bank, MT 59427. 406-873-5063. Fax: 406-873-4218. 8AM-Noon, 1-5PM (MST). Access by: Mail, in person.

Golden Valley County

Real Estate Recording—Golden Valley County Clerk and Recorder, 107 Kemp, Ryegate, MT 59074. 406-568-2231. 8AM-5PM (MST).

Felony, Civil Actions Over $5,000, Eviction, Probate—District Court, PO Box 10, Ryegate, MT 59074. 406-568-2231. 8AM-5PM (MST). Access by: Mail, in person.

Misdemeanor, Civil Actions Under $5,000, Eviction, Small Claims—Justice Court, PO Box 10, Ryegate, MT 59074. 406-568-2231. Fax: 406-568-2598. 8AM-5PM Tues (MST). Access by: Mail, in person.

Granite County

Real Estate Recording—Granite County Clerk and Recorder, 220 North Sansome, Philipsburg, MT 59858. 406-859-3771. Fax: 406-859-3817. 8AM-Noon,1-5PM (MST).

Felony, Civil Actions Over $5,000, Eviction, Probate—District Court, PO Box J, Philipsburg, MT 59858. 406-859-3712. Fax: 406-859-3817. 8AM-Noon, 1-5PM (MST). Access by: Phone, fax, mail, in person.

Misdemeanor, Civil Actions Under $5,000, Eviction, Small Claims—Drummond Justice Court, PO Box 159, Drummond, MT 59832. 406-288-3446. Fax: 406-288-3050. 8AM-4PM MWF (MST). Access by: Mail, in person.

Philipsburg Justice Court, PO Box 356, Philipsburg, MT 59858. 406-859-3712. Fax: 406-859-3817. 11AM-Noon, 1-5PM MWF (MST). Access by: Mail, in person.

Hill County

Real Estate Recording—Hill County Clerk and Recorder, 315 4th Street, Courthouse, Havre, MT 59501. 406-265-5481. Fax: 406-265-2445. 8AM-5PM (MST).

Felony, Civil Actions Over $5,000, Eviction, Probate—District Court, County Courthouse, Havre, MT 59501. 406-265-5481. Fax: 406-265-1273. 8AM-5PM (MST). Access by: Phone, mail, in person.

Misdemeanor, Civil Actions Under $5,000, Eviction, Small Claims—Justice Court, County Courthouse, Havre, MT 59501. 406-265-5481. Fax: 406-265-5487. 8AM-5PM (MST). Access by: Mail, in person.

Jefferson County

Real Estate Recording—Jefferson County Clerk and Recorder, Corner Centennial & Washington, Boulder, MT 59632. 406-225-4020. Fax: 406-225-4149. 8AM-5PM (MST).

Felony, Civil Actions Over $5,000, Eviction, Probate—District Court, PO Box H, Boulder, MT 59632. 406-225-

4251. Fax: 406-225-3275. 8AM-Noon, 1-5PM (MST). Access by: Mail, in person.

Misdemeanor, Civil Actions Under $5,000, Eviction, Small Claims—Justice Court, PO Box H, Boulder, MT 59632. 406-225-4251. 8AM-4PM (MST). Access by: Mail, in person.

Judith Basin County

Real Estate Recording—Judith Basin County Clerk and Recorder, Courthouse, Stanford, MT 59479. 406-566-2277. Fax: 406-566-2211. 8AM-5PM (MST).

Felony, Civil Actions Over $5,000, Eviction, Probate—District Court, PO Box 307, Stanford, MT 59479. 406-566-2277. Fax: 406-566-2211. 8AM-5PM (MST). Access by: Phone, mail, in person.

Misdemeanor, Civil Actions Under $5,000, Eviction, Small Claims—Hobson Justice Court, PO Box 276, Hobson, MT 59452. 406-423-5503. 4PM-9PM (MST). Access by: Mail, in person.

Stanford Justice Court, PO Box 339, Stanford, MT 59479. 406-566-2277. 9AM-Noon MWF (MST). Access by: Mail, in person.

Lake County

Real Estate Recording—Lake County Clerk and Recorder, 106 4th Avenue East, Polson, MT 59860. 406-883-7210. Fax: 406-883-7283. 8AM-5PM (MST).

Felony, Civil Actions Over $5,000, Probate—District Court, 106 4th Ave E, Polson, MT 59860. 406-883-7254. Fax: 406-883-7343. 8AM-5PM (MST). Access by: Phone, fax, mail, in person.

Misdemeanor, Civil Actions Under $5,000, Eviction, Small Claims—Justice Court, 106 4th Ave E, Polson, MT 59860. 406-883-7258. Fax: 406-883-7283. 8AM-5PM (MST). Access by: Mail, in person.

Lewis and Clark County

Real Estate Recording—Lewis and Clark County Clerk and Recorder, 316 North Park Avenue, Helena, MT 59601. 406-447-8337. 8AM-5PM (MST).

Felony, Civil Actions Over $5,000, Eviction, Probate—District Court, 228 Broadway, PO Box 158 (59624), Helena, MT 59601. 406-447-8216. Fax: 406-447-8275. 8AM-5PM (MST). Access by: Fax, mail, in person.

Misdemeanor, Civil Actions Under $5,000, Eviction, Small Claims—Justice Court, 228 Broadway, Helena, MT 59601. 406-447-8202. Fax: 406-447-8275. 8AM-Noon, 1-5PM (MST). Access by: Mail, in person.

Liberty County

Real Estate Recording—Liberty County Clerk and Recorder, 101 First Street East, Chester, MT 59522. 406-759-5365. Fax: 406-759-5395. 8AM-5PM (MST).

Felony, Civil Actions Over $5,000, Eviction, Probate—District Court, PO Box 549, Chester, MT 59522. 406-759-5615. Fax: 406-759-5395. 8AM-5PM (MST). Access by: Phone, mail, in person.

Misdemeanor, Civil Actions Under $5,000, Eviction, Small Claims—Justice Court, PO Box 170, Chester, MT 59522. 406-759-5172. Fax: 406-759-5395. 9AM-5PM T (MST). Access by: Mail, in person.

Lincoln County

Real Estate Recording—Lincoln County Clerk and Recorder, 512 California Avenue, Libby, MT 59923. 406-293-7781. Fax: 406-293-8577. 8AM-5PM (MST).

Felony, Civil Actions Over $5,000, Eviction, Probate—District Court, 512 California Ave, Libby, MT 59923. 406-293-7781. Fax: 406-293-9816. 8AM-5PM (MST). Access by: Fax, mail, in person.

Misdemeanor, Civil Actions Under $5,000, Eviction, Small Claims—Eureka Justice Court #2, PO Box 403, Eureka, MT 59917. 406-296-2622. Fax: 406-296-2767. 8AM-Noon, 1-5PM (MST). Access by: Mail, in person.

Libby Justice Court #1, 418 Mineral Ave, Libby, MT 59923. 406-293-7781. Fax: 406-293-5640. 8AM-5PM (MST). Access by: Mail, in person.

Madison County

Real Estate Recording—Madison County Clerk and Recorder, 110 West Wallace, Virginia City, MT 59755. 406-843-5392. 8AM-Noon,1-5PM (MST).

Felony, Civil Actions Over $5,000, Eviction, Probate—District Court, PO Box 185, Virginia City, MT 59755. 406-843-4230. Fax: 406-843-5517. 8AM-5PM (MST). Access by: Fax, mail, in person.

Misdemeanor, Civil Actions Under $5,000, Eviction, Small Claims—Justice Court, PO Box 277, Virginia City, MT 59755. 406-843-5392. Fax: 406-843-5517. 8AM-5PM (MST). Access by: Phone, mail, in person.

McCone County

Real Estate Recording—McCone County Clerk and Recorder, 206 Second Avenue, Circle, MT 59215. 406-485-3505. Fax: 406-485-2689. 8AM-5PM (MST).

Felony, Civil Actions Over $5,000, Eviction, Probate—District Court, PO Box 199, Circle, MT 59215. 406-485-3410. Fax: 406-485-2689. 8AM-5PM (MST). Access by: Mail, in person.

Misdemeanor, Civil Actions Under $5,000, Eviction, Small Claims—Justice Court, PO Box 192, Circle, MT 59215. 406-485-3548. 2-5PM Wed (MST). Access by: Mail, in person.

Meagher County

Real Estate Recording—Meagher County Clerk and Recorder, 15 West Main, White Sulphur Springs, MT 59645. 406-547-3612. Fax: 406-547-3388. 8AM-Noon,1-5PM (MST).

Felony, Civil Actions Over $5,000, Eviction, Probate—District Court, PO Box 443, White Sulphur Springs, MT 59645. 406-547-3941. Fax: 406-547-3388. 8AM-5PM (MST). Access by: Phone, mail, in person.

Misdemeanor, Civil Actions Under $5,000, Eviction, Small Claims—Justice Court, PO Box 698, White Sulphur Springs, MT 59645. 406-547-3954. Fax: 406-547-3388. 8AM-5PM M-Th (MST). Access by: Mail, in person.

Mineral County

Real Estate Recording—Mineral County Clerk and Recorder, 300 River Street, Superior, MT 59872. 406-822-3520. Fax: 406-822-3579. 8AM-5PM (MST).

Felony, Civil Actions Over $5,000, Probate—District Court, PO Box 129, Superior, MT 59872. 406-822-3538. Fax: 406-822-3579. 8AM-Noon,1-5PM (MST). Access by: Phone, fax, mail, in person.

Misdemeanor, Civil Actions Under $5,000, Eviction, Small Claims—Justice Court, PO Box 658, Superior, MT 59872. 406-822-3550. Fax: 406-822-3599. 8AM-5PM (MST). Access by: Fax, mail, in person.

Missoula County

Real Estate Recording—Missoula County Clerk and Recorder, 200 West Broadway, Missoula, MT 59802. 406-523-4752. Fax: 406-721-4043. 8AM-5PM (MST).

Felony, Civil Actions Over $5,000, Eviction, Probate—District Court, 200 W Broadway, Missoula, MT 59802. 406-523-4780. Fax: 406-523-4899. 8AM-5PM (MST). Access by: Fax, mail, in person.

Misdemeanor, Civil Actions Under $5,000, Eviction, Small Claims—Justice Court, Dept 1, 200 W Broadway, Missoula, MT 59802. 406-721-5700. Fax: 406-721-4043. 8AM-5PM (MST). Access by: Mail, in person.

Musselshell County

Real Estate Recording—Musselshell County Clerk and Recorder, 506 Main Street, Courthouse, Roundup, MT 59072. 406-323-1104. Fax: 406-323-3303. 8AM-5PM (MST).

Felony, Civil Actions Over $5,000, Eviction, Probate—District Court, PO Box 357, Roundup, MT 59072. 406-323-1413. Fax: 406-323-1710. 8AM-5PM (MST). Access by: Phone, fax, mail, in person.

Misdemeanor, Civil Actions Under $5,000, Eviction, Small Claims—Justice Court, PO Box 656, Roundup, MT 59072. 406-323-1078. 9AM-Noon (MST). Access by: Mail, in person.

Park County

Real Estate Recording—Park County Clerk and Recorder, 414 East Callendar, Livingston, MT 59047. 406-222-4110. Fax: 406-222-4199. 8AM-5PM (MST).

Felony, Civil Actions Over $5,000, Eviction, Probate—District Court, PO Box 437, Livingston, MT 59047. 406-222-4125. Fax: 406-222-4128. 8AM-5PM (MST). Access by: Phone, mail, in person.

Misdemeanor, Civil Actions Under $5,000, Eviction, Small Claims—Justice Court, 414 E Callendar, Livingston, MT 59047. 406-222-4169. Fax: 406-222-4128. 8AM-Noon, 1-5PM (MST). Access by: Phone, fax, mail, in person.

Petroleum County

Real Estate Recording—Petroleum County Clerk and Recorder, 201 East Main, Winnett, MT 59087. 406-429-5311. Fax: 406-429-6328. 8AM-5PM (MST).

Felony, Civil Actions Over $5,000, Eviction, Probate—District Court, PO Box 226, Winnett, MT 59087. 406-429-5311. Fax: 406-429-6328. 8AM-5PM (MST). Access by: Phone, mail, in person.

Misdemeanor, Civil Actions Under $5,000, Eviction, Small Claims—Justice Court, PO Box 223, Winnett, MT 59087. 406-429-5311. Fax: 406-429-6328. 9AM-Noon Th (MST). Access by: Mail, in person.

Phillips County

Real Estate Recording—Phillips County Clerk and Recorder, 314 Second Avenue West, Malta, MT 59538. 406-654-2423. Fax: 406-654-2429. 8AM-5PM (MST).

Felony, Civil Actions Over $5,000, Eviction, Probate—District Court, PO Box I, Malta, MT 59538. 406-654-1023. 8AM-5PM (MST). Access by: Mail, in person.

Misdemeanor, Civil Actions Under $5,000, Eviction, Small Claims—Justice Court, PO Box 1396, Malta, MT 59538. 406-654-1118. Fax: 406-654-1213. 10AM-4PM (MST). Access by: Mail, in person.

Pondera County

Real Estate Recording—Pondera County Clerk and Recorder, 20 4th Avenue S.W., Conrad, MT 59425. 406-278-4000. Fax: 406-278-4070. 8AM-5PM (MST).

Felony, Civil Actions Over $5,000, Eviction, Probate—District Court, 20 Fourth Ave SW, Conrad, MT 59425. 406-278-4026. Fax: 406-278-4070. 8AM-5PM (MST). Access by: Fax, mail, in person.

Misdemeanor, Civil Actions Under $5,000, Eviction, Small Claims—Justice Court, 20 Fourth Ave SW, Conrad, MT 59425. 406-278-4030. Fax: 406-278-4070. 9AM-4PM (MST). Access by: Mail, in person.

Powder River County

Real Estate Recording—Powder River County Clerk and Recorder, Courthouse Square, Broadus, MT 59317. 406-436-2361. 8AM-5PM (MST).

Felony, Civil Actions Over $5,000, Eviction, Probate—District Court, PO Box 239, Broadus, MT 59317. 406-436-2320. Fax: 406-436-2325. 8AM-Noon, 1-5PM (MST). Access by: Fax, mail, in person.

Misdemeanor, Civil Actions Under $5,000, Eviction, Small Claims—Justice Court, PO Box 488, Broadus, MT 59317. 406-436-2503. Fax: 406-436-2866. 9AM-3:30PM M-Th (MST). Access by: Mail, in person.

Powell County

Real Estate Recording—Powell County Clerk and Recorder, 409 Missouri Avenue, Deer Lodge, MT 59722. 406-846-3680. 8AM-5PM (MST).

Felony, Civil Actions Over $5,000, Eviction, Probate—District Court, 409 Missouri Ave, Deer Lodge, MT 59722. 406-846-3680. Fax: 406-846-2742. 8AM-5PM (MST). Access by: Mail, in person.

Misdemeanor, Civil Actions Under $5,000, Eviction, Small Claims—Justice Court, 409 Missouri, Deer Lodge, MT 59722. 406-846-3680. 8AM-5PM (MST). Access by: Mail, in person.

Prairie County

Real Estate Recording—Prairie County Clerk and Recorder, Courthouse, Terry, MT 59349. 406-637-5575. Fax: 406-637-5576. 8AM-5PM (MST).

Felony, Civil Actions Over $5,000, Eviction, Probate—District Court, PO Box 125, Terry, MT 59349. 406-637-5575. 8AM-5PM (MST). Access by: Mail, in person.

Misdemeanor, Civil Actions Under $5,000, Eviction, Small Claims—Justice Court, PO Box 446, Terry, MT 59349. 406-637-2124. 1-5PM (MST). Access by: Mail, in person.

Ravalli County

Real Estate Recording—Ravalli County Clerk and Recorder, 205 Bedford, Courthouse, Hamilton, MT 59840. 406-363-1833. Fax: 406-363-1880. 8AM-5PM (MST).

Felony, Civil Actions Over $5,000, Probate—District Court, Ravalli County Courthouse, PO Box 5014, Hamilton, MT 59840. 406-375-6214. Fax: 406-375-6327. 8AM-5PM (MST). Access by: Fax, mail, in person.

Misdemeanor, Civil Actions Under $5,000, Eviction, Small Claims—Justice Court, Courthouse Box 5023, Hamilton, MT 59840. 406-375-6252. Fax: 406-363-1880. 8AM-5PM (MST). Access by: Phone, mail, in person.

Richland County

Real Estate Recording—Richland County Clerk and Recorder, 201 West Main Street, Sidney, MT 59270. 406-482-1708. Fax: 406-482-3731. 8AM-5PM (MST).

Felony, Civil Actions Over $5,000, Eviction, Probate—District Court, 201 W Main, Sidney, MT 59270. 406-482-1709. Fax: 406-482-3731. 8AM-5PM (MST). Access by: Phone, mail, in person.

Misdemeanor, Civil Actions Under $5,000, Eviction, Small Claims—Justice Court, 123 W Main, Sidney, MT 59270. 406-482-2815. Fax: 406-482-4766. 8AM-5PM (MST). Access by: Fax, mail, in person.

Roosevelt County

Real Estate Recording—Roosevelt County Clerk and Recorder, 400 Second Avenue South, Wolf Point, MT 59201. 406-653-1590. Fax: 406-653-3100. 8AM-5PM (MST).

Felony, Civil Actions Over $5,000, Eviction, Probate—District Court, County Courthouse, Wolf Point, MT 59201. 406-653-1590. Fax: 406-653-3100. 8AM-5PM (MST). Access by: Fax, mail, in person.

Misdemeanor, Civil Actions Under $5,000, Eviction, Small Claims—Culbertson Justice Court Post #2, PO Box 421, Culbertson, MT 59218. 406-787-6607. Fax: 406-787-6193. 9AM-3PM M-Th (MST). Access by: Mail, in person.

Wolf Point Justice Court Post #1, County Courthouse, Wolf Point, MT 59201. 406-653-1590. Fax: 406-653-3100. 8-11:30AM, 12:30-5PM (MST). Access by: Fax, mail, in person.

Rosebud County

Real Estate Recording—Rosebud County Clerk and Recorder, 1200 Main Street, Forsyth, MT 59327. 406-356-7318. Fax: 406-356-7551. 8AM-5PM (MST).

Felony, Civil Actions Over $5,000, Eviction, Probate—District Court, PO Box 48, Forsyth, MT 59327. 406-356-7322. Fax: 406-356-7551. 8AM-5PM (MST). Access by: Mail, in person.

Misdemeanor, Civil Actions Under $5,000, Eviction, Small Claims—Justice Court, PO Box 575, Colstrip, MT 59323. 406-748-2934. 8AM-5PM (MST). Access by: Mail, in person.

Forsyth Justice Court #1, PO Box 504, Forsyth, MT 59327. 406-356-2638. 8AM-5PM (MST). Access by: Mail, in person.

Sanders County

Real Estate Recording—Sanders County Clerk and Recorder, Courthouse, 1111 Main St., Thompson Falls, MT 59873. 406-827-4392. Fax: 406-827-4388. 8AM-5PM (MST).

Felony, Civil Actions Over $5,000, Eviction, Probate—District Court, PO Box 519, Thompson Falls, MT 59873. 406-827-4316. Fax: 406-827-4388. 8AM-5PM (MST). Access by: Fax, mail, in person.

Misdemeanor, Civil Actions Under $5,000, Eviction, Small Claims—Justice Court, PO Box 519, Thompson Falls, MT 59873. 406-827-4318. Fax: 406-827-4388. 8AM-5PM (MST). Access by: Fax, mail, in person.

Sheridan County

Real Estate Recording—Sheridan County Clerk and Recorder, 100 West Laurel Avenue, Plentywood, MT 59254. 406-765-2310. Fax: 406-765-2609. 8AM-5PM (MST).

Felony, Civil Actions Over $5,000, Eviction, Probate—District Court, 100 W Laurel, Plentywood, MT 59254. 406-765-2310. Fax: 406-765-2602. 8AM-Noon, 1-5PM (MST). Access by: Phone, mail, in person.

Misdemeanor, Civil Actions Under $5,000, Eviction, Small Claims—Justice Court, 100 W Laurel, Plentywood, MT 59254. 406-765-2310. Fax: 406-765-2129. 8AM-5PM (MST). Access by: Fax, mail, in person.

Silver Bow County

Real Estate Recording—Silver Bow County Clerk and Recorder, 155 West Granite, Butte, MT 59701. 406-723-8262. Fax: 406-782-6637. 8AM-5PM (MST).

Felony, Civil Actions Over $5,000, Eviction, Probate—District Court, 155 W Granite St, Butte, MT 59701. 406-723-8262. Fax: 406-723-1280. 8AM-5PM (MST). Access by: Fax, mail, in person.

Misdemeanor, Civil Actions Under $5,000, Eviction, Small Claims—Justice Court #1 & #2, 155 W Granite St, Butte, MT 59701. 406-723-8262. 8AM-5PM (MST). Access by: Mail, in person.

Stillwater County

Real Estate Recording—Stillwater County Clerk and Recorder, 400 Third Avenue North, Columbus, MT 59019. 406-322-4546. Fax: 406-322-4698. 8AM-5PM (MST).

Felony, Civil Actions Over $5,000, Eviction, Probate—District Court, PO Box 367, Columbus, MT 59019. 406-322-5332. Fax: 406-322-4698. 8AM-5PM (MST). Access by: Phone, mail, in person.

Misdemeanor, Civil Actions Under $5,000, Eviction, Small Claims—Justice Court, PO Box 77, Columbus, MT 59019. 406-322-4577. Fax: 406-322-4698. 8AM-5PM (MST). Access by: Phone, fax, mail, in person.

Sweet Grass County

Real Estate Recording—Sweet Grass County Clerk and Recorder, Courthouse, 200 W. 1st Ave., Big Timber, MT 59011. 406-932-5152. Fax: 406-932-4777. 8AM-5PM (MST).

Felony, Civil Actions Over $5,000, Eviction, Probate—District Court, PO Box 698, Big Timber, MT 59011. 406-932-5154. Fax: 406-932-4777. 8AM-Noon, 1-5PM (MST). Access by: Phone, mail, in person.

Misdemeanor, Civil Actions Under $5,000, Eviction, Small Claims—Justice Court, PO Box 1432, Big Timber, MT 59011. 406-932-5150. Fax: 406-932-4777. 8AM-5PM (MST). Access by: Fax, mail, in person.

Teton County

Real Estate Recording—Teton County Clerk and Recorder, Courthouse, Choteau, MT 59422. 406-466-2693. Fax: 406-466-2138. 8AM-5PM (MST).

Felony, Civil Actions Over $5,000, Eviction, Probate—District Court, PO Box 487, Choteau, MT 59422. 406-466-2909. Fax: 406-466-2138. 8AM-5PM (MST). Access by: Phone, mail, in person.

Misdemeanor, Civil Actions Under $5,000, Eviction, Small Claims—Justice Court, PO Box 337, Choteau, MT 59422. 406-466-5611. Fax: 406-466-2138. 1-5PM (MST). Access by: Mail, in person.

Toole County

Real Estate Recording—Toole County Clerk and Recorder, 226 1st Street South, Shelby, MT 59474. 406-434-2232. Fax: 406-434-2467. 8AM-5PM (MST).

Felony, Civil Actions Over $5,000, Eviction, Probate—District Court, PO Box 850, Shelby, MT 59474. 406-434-2271. Fax: 406-434-7225. 8AM-Noon, 1-5PM (MST). Access by: Phone, mail, in person.

Misdemeanor, Civil Actions Under $5,000, Eviction, Small Claims—Justice Court, PO Box 738, Shelby, MT 59474. 406-434-2651. 10AM-4PM (MST). Access by: Mail, in person.

Treasure County

Real Estate Recording—Treasure County Clerk and Recorder, 307 Rapelje Ave., Hysham, MT 59038. 406-342-5547. Fax: 406-342-5212. 8AM-Noon,1-5PM (MST).

Felony, Civil Actions Over $5,000, Eviction, Probate—District Court, PO Box 392, Hysham, MT 59038. 406-342-5547. Fax: 406-342-5445. 8AM-5PM (MST). Access by: Phone, fax, mail, in person.

Misdemeanor, Civil Actions Under $5,000, Eviction, Small Claims—Justice Court, PO Box 267, Hysham, MT 59038. 406-342-5532. 9AM-Noon (MST). Access by: Mail, in person.

Valley County

Real Estate Recording—Valley County Clerk and Recorder, 501 Court Square, Box 2, Glasgow, MT 59230. 406-228-8221. Fax: 406-228-9047. 8AM-5PM (MST).

Felony, Civil Actions Over $5,000, Eviction, Probate—District Court, 501 Court Sq #6, Glasgow, MT 59230. 406-228-8221. Fax: 406-228-4601. 8AM-5PM (MST). Access by: Phone, fax, mail, in person.

Misdemeanor, Civil Actions Under $5,000, Eviction, Small Claims—Justice Court, 501 Court Sq #10, Glasgow, MT 59230. 406-228-8221. Fax: 406-228-4601. 8AM-5PM (MST). Access by: Phone, mail, in person.

Wheatland County

Real Estate Recording—Wheatland County Clerk and Recorder, Courthouse, Harlowton, MT 59036. 406-632-4891. Fax: 406-632-5654. 8AM-5PM (MST).

Felony, Civil Actions Over $5,000, Eviction, Probate—District Court, Box 227, Harlowton, MT 59036. 406-632-4893. 8AM-5PM (MST). Access by: Phone, mail, in person.

Misdemeanor, Civil Actions Under $5,000, Eviction, Small Claims—Justice Court, PO Box 524, Harlowton, MT 59036. 406-632-4821. Fax: 406-632-5654. 10AM-1PM T,Th (MST). Access by: Phone, mail, in person.

Wibaux County

Real Estate Recording—Wibaux County Clerk and Recorder, 200 South Wibaux Street, Wibaux, MT 59353. 406-795-2481. Fax: 406-795-2625. 8AM-5PM (MST).

Felony, Civil Actions Over $5,000, Eviction, Probate—District Court, PO Box 292, Wibaux, MT 59353. 406-795-2484. Fax: 406-795-2625. 8AM-5PM, Closed 12-1 (MST). Access by: Phone, mail, in person.

Misdemeanor, Civil Actions Under $5,000, Eviction, Small Claims—Justice Court, PO Box 445, Wibaux, MT 59353. 406-795-2484. 8AM-Noon M,F; 1PM-5PM W (MST). Access by: Mail, in person.

Yellowstone County

Real Estate Recording—Yellowstone County Clerk and Recorder, 217 North 27th, Room 401, Billings, MT 59101. 406-256-2785. Fax: 406-256-2736. 8AM-5PM (MST).

Felony, Civil Actions Over $5,000, Eviction, Probate—District Court, PO Box 35030, Billings, MT 59107. 406-256-2860. Fax: 406-256-2995. 8AM-5PM (MST). Access by: Mail, in person.

Misdemeanor, Civil Actions Under $5,000, Eviction, Small Claims—Justice Court, PO Box 35032, Billings, MT

59107. 406-256-2895. Fax: 406-256-2898. 8AM-5PM (MST).   Access by: Mail, in person.

Federal Courts

US District Court
District of Montana

Billings Division, US District Court Clerk, Room 5405, Federal Bldg, 316 N 26th St, Billings, MT 59101. 406-247-7000. Counties: Big Horn, Carbon, Carter, Custer, Daniels, Dawson, Fallon, Garfield, Golden Valley, McCone, Musselshell, Park, Petroleum, Phillips, Powder River, Prairie, Richland, Roosevelt, Rosebud, Sheridan, Stillwater, Sweet Grass, Treasure, Valley, Wheatland, Wibaux, Yellowstone, Yellowstone National Park

Butte Division, US District Court Room 273, Federal Bldg, Butte, MT 59701. 406-782-0432. Counties: Beaverhead, Deer Lodge, Gallatin, Madison, Silver Bow

Great Falls Division, US District Court Clerk, PO Box 2186, Great Falls, MT 59403. 406-727-1922. Counties: Blaine, Cascade, Chouteau, Fergus, Glacier, Hill, Judith Basin, Liberty, Pondera, Teton, Toole

Helena Division, US District Court Federal Bldg, Drawer 10015, Helena, MT 59626. 406-441-1355. Counties: Broadwater, Jefferson, Lewis and Clark, Meagher, Powell

Missoula Division, US District Court Russell Smith Courthouse, PO Box 8537, Missoula, MT 59807. 406-542-7260. Counties: Flathead, Granite, Lake, Lincoln, Mineral, Missoula, Ravalli, Sanders

US Bankruptcy Court
District of Montana

Butte Division, US Bankruptcy Court, PO Box 689, Butte, MT 59703. 406-782-3354. Voice Case Information System: 406-782-1060. Counties: All counties in Montana

Nebraska

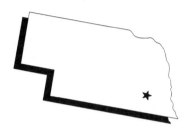

Capitol: Lincoln (Lancaster County)	
Number of Counties: 93	**Population:** 1,637,112
County Court Locations:	**Federal Court Locations:**
•District Courts: 92/12 Districts	•District Courts: 3
•County Courts: 93/12 Districts	•Bankruptcy Courts: 3
•Combined Courts: 1	**State Agencies:** 19
Juvenile Courts: 3/3 Counties	
Workers' Compensation Courts: 1	

State Agencies—Summary

General Help Numbers:

State Archives

Historical Society	402-471-3270
Archives	Fax: 402-471-3100
PO Box 82554 9:30AM-4:30PM M-F; 8-5 SA, 1:30-5 SU	
Lincoln, NE 68501-2554	
Alternate Telephone:	402-471-4784
Reference Librarian:	402-471-4784

Governor's Office

Governor's Office	402-471-2244
PO Box 94848	Fax: 402-471-6031
Lincoln, NE 68509-4848	8AM-5PM

Attorney General's Office

Attorney General's Office	402-471-2682
PO Box 98920	Fax: 402-471-3297
Lincoln, NE 68509-8920	8AM-5PM

State Legislation

Clerk of Legislature Office	402-471-2271
PO Box 94604	Fax: 402-471-2126
Lincoln, NE 68509-4604	

Important State Internet Sites:

> **Webscape**
> File   Edit   View   Help

State of Nebraska World Wide Web
www.state.ne.us/

This home page includes a welcome from the Governor and links to information about the Governor, the legislature, state agencies and other sites.

The Governor's Office
www.state.ne.us/gov/gov.html

This site includes information about the Governor's State of the State address, press releases, speeches, a biography and his weekly schedule.

The Nebraska Unicameral
unicam1.lcs.state.ne.us

Located at this page are the links to the Senators of the Unicameral, the Nebraska Statues and a link to the Senator and Committee Priority Bills.

Legislative Documents
unicam2.lcs.state.ne.us/legdocs/billdocs.htm

You can view introduced bills and resolutions and related documents. Slip laws are also viewable.

Corporation and UCC Records
www.nol.org/home/SOS/services.htm

Corporation and UCC searches are available online by subscribing to Nebrask@ Online.

State Agencies—Public Records

Criminal Records

Nebraska Highway Patrol, CID, PO Box 94907, Lincoln, NE 68509-4907, Main Telephone: 402-479-4924, Alternate Telephone: 402-479-4978, 402-471-4545, Hours: 8AM-4PM. Access by: mail, visit. Arrest records will not be released unless disposition is provided, except if an arrest without disposition is less than one year old.

Corporation Records
Limited Liability Company Records
Limited Partnerships
Trade Names
Trademarks/Servicemarks

Secretary of State, Corporation Commission, 1301 State Capitol Bldg, Lincoln, NE 68509, Main Telephone: 402-471-4079, Fax: 402-471-3666, Hours: 8AM-5PM. Access by: mail, phone, fax, visit, PC.

Uniform Commercial Code
Federal Tax Liens
State Tax Liens

UCC Division, Secretary of State, PO Box 95104, Lincoln, NE 68509, Main Telephone: 402-471-4080, Fax: 402-471-4429, Hours: 7:30AM-5PM. Access by: mail, phone, fax, visit, PC.

Sales Tax Registrations

Revenue Department, Revenue Operations Division, PO Box 94818, Lincoln, NE 68509-4818, Main Telephone: 402-471-5695, Fax: 402-471-5608, Hours: 8AM-5PM. Access by: mail, phone.

Birth Certificates

NE Health & Human Services System, Vital Statistics Section, PO Box 95065, Lincoln, NE 68509, Main Telephone: 402-471-2871, Hours: 8AM-5PM. Access by: mail, phone, visit. If the birth certificate is more than 50 years old, a release form is not required.

Death Records

PO Box 95065, Lincoln, NE 68509-5065, Main Telephone: 402-471-2871, Fax: 402-471-0383, Hours: 8AM-5PM. Access by: mail, phone, visit. If a certificate is more than 50 years in the past, release form is not required.

Marriage Certificates

PO Box 95065, Lincoln, NE 68509-5065, Main Telephone: 402-471-2871, Fax: 402-471-0383, Hours: 8AM-5PM. Access by: mail, phone, visit. If a certificate is more than 50 years old, a release is not required.

Divorce Records

PO Box 95065, Lincoln, NE 68509-5065, Main Telephone: 402-471-2871, Fax: 402-471-0383, Hours: 8AM-5PM. Access by: mail, phone, visit. If a certificate is more than 50 years, a release is not required.

Workers' Compensation Records

Workers' Compensation Court, PO Box 98908, Lincoln, NE 68509-8908, Main Telephone: 402-471-6468, Fax: 402-471-2700, Hours: 8AM-5PM. Access by: mail, phone, visit, PC.

Driver Records

Department of Motor Vehicles, Driver's Records, PO Box 94789, Lincoln, NE 68509-4789, Main Telephone: 402-471-4343, Hours: 8AM-5PM. Access by: mail, visit, PC. It is suggested you obtain copies of tickets at the local courts.

Vehicle Ownership
Vehicle Identification

Department of Motor Vehicles, Titles and Registration Section, PO Box 94789, Lincoln, NE 68509-4789, Main Telephone: 402-471-3910, Alternate Telephone: 402-471-3918, Hours: 8AM-5PM. Access by: mail, visit.

Accident Reports

Department of Roads, Accident Records Bureau, Box 94669, Lincoln, NE 68509, Main Telephone: 402-479-4645, Fax: 402-479-4325, Hours: 8AM-5PM. Access by: mail, phone, visit.

Hunting License Information
Fishing License Information

Game & Parks Commission, PO Box 30370, Lincoln, NE 68503, Main Telephone: 402-471-0641, Hours: 8AM-5PM. Access by: mail, phone, visit. Only permits for deer, antelope and turkey are available.

County Courts and Recording Offices

What You Need to Know...

About the Courts

Administration

Court Administrator	402-471-2643
PO Box 98910	Fax: 402-471-2197
Lincoln, NE 68509-8910	

Court Structure

The number of judicial districts went from 21 to the current **12** in July 1992.

County courts have juvenile jurisdiction in all but 3 counties (Douglas, Lancaster, and Sarpy), which have separate Juvenile Courts. Probate is handled by County Courts. Many have records on microfiche back to the mid/late 1800s.

Searching Hints

Many courts prefer in person searches and will only respond to very limited written search requests. The State Attorney General has recommended that courts not perform searches because of the time involved and possible legal liability.

Online Access

There is remote no online computer access in NE; however, there is a move to computerization underway.

About the Recorder's Office

Organization

93 counties, 109 filing offices. The recording officers are County Clerk (UCC and some state tax liens) and Register of Deeds (real estate and most tax liens). Most counties have a combined Clerk/Register office, which are designated "County Clerk" in this section. **Sixteen counties have separate offices for County Clerk and for Register of Deeds**—Adams, Cass, Dakota, Dawson, Dodge, Douglas, Gage, Hall, Lancaster, Lincoln, Madison, Otoe, Platte, Sarpy, Saunders, and Scotts Bluff. In combined offices, the Register of Deeds is frequently a different person from the County Clerk. 74 counties are in the Central Time Zone (CST) and 19 are in the Mountain Time Zone (MST).

UCC Records

Financing statements are filed at the state level, except for consumer goods and farm related collateral, which are filed with the County Clerk, and real estate related collateral, which are filed with the County Clerk. All non-real estate UCC filings are entered into a **statewide database** that is accessible from any county office. All but five counties will perform UCC searches. Use search request form UCC-11. The UCC statute allows for telephone searching. Search fees are usually $3.00 per debtor name. Copy fees vary.

Lien Records

All federal and some state tax liens are filed with the County Register of Deeds. Some state tax liens on personal property are filed with the County Clerk. Most counties will perform tax lien searches, some as part of a UCC search, and others for a separate fee, usually $3.00 per name in each index. Copy fees vary. Other liens include mechanics, artisans, judgment, motor vehicle, and agricultural.

Real Estate Records

Many counties will perform real estate searches, including owner of record from the legal description of the property. Address search requests and make checks payable to the Register of Deeds, **not** the County Clerk. Fees vary.

County Courts and Recording Offices

Adams County

Real Estate Recording—Adams County Register of Deeds, 500 W. 4th, Room 100, Hastings, NE 68901. 402-461-7148.

Felony, Civil Actions Over $15,000—District Court, PO Box 9, Hastings, NE 68902. 402-461-7264. Fax: 402-461-7269. 8:30AM-5PM (CST). Access by: In person only.

Misdemeanor, Civil Actions Under $15,000, Eviction, Small Claims, Probate—Adams County Court, PO Box 95, Hastings, NE 68902-0095. 402-461-7143. Fax: 402-461-7144. 8AM-5PM (CST). Access by: In person only.

Antelope County

Real Estate Recording—Register of Deeds, Courthouse, 501 Main St., Neligh, NE 68756. 402-887-4410. Fax: 402-887-4719. 8:30AM-5PM (CST).

Felony, Civil Actions Over $15,000—District Court, PO Box 45, Neligh, NE 68756. 402-887-4508. Fax: 402-887-4160. 8:30AM-5PM (CST). Access by: In person only.

Misdemeanor, Civil Actions Under $15,000, Eviction, Small Claims, Probate—Antelope County Court, 501 Main, Neligh, NE 68756. 402-887-4650. Fax: 402-887-3160. 8:30AM-5PM (CST). Access by: Fax, mail, in person.

Arthur County

Real Estate Recording—Register of Deeds, Main Street, Courthouse, Arthur, NE 69121. 308-764-2203. Fax: 308-764-2216. 8AM-4PM (MST).

Felony, Misdemeanor, Civil, Eviction, Small Claims, Probate—District and County Court, PO Box 126, Arthur, NE 69121. 308-764-2203. Fax: 308-764-2216. 8AM-4PM (MST). Access by: Phone, mail, in person.

Banner County

Real Estate Recording—Register of Deeds, State Street, Courthouse, Harrisburg, NE 69345. 308-436-5265. Fax: 308-436-4180. 8AM-12, 1-5PM (MST).

Felony, Civil Actions Over $15,000—District Court, PO Box 67, Harrisburg, NE 69345. 308-436-5265. Fax: 308-436-4180. 8AM-5PM (MST). Access by: Fax, mail, in person.

Misdemeanor, Civil Actions Under $15,000, Eviction, Small Claims, Probate—Banner County Court, PO Box 67, Harrisburg, NE 69345. 308-436-5268. Fax: 308-436-4180. 8AM-Noon, 1-5PM (MST). Access by: Fax, mail, in person.

Blaine County

Real Estate Recording—Register of Deeds, Lincoln Avenue, Courthouse, Brewster, NE 68821. 308-547-2222. Fax: 308-547-2228. 8AM-Noon, 1-4PM (CST).

Felony, Civil Actions Over $15,000—District Court, Lincoln Ave, Box 136, Brewster, NE 68821. 308-547-2222. Fax: 308-547-2228. 8AM-4PM (CST). Access by: Fax, mail, in person.

Misdemeanor, Civil Actions Under $15,000, Eviction, Small Claims, Probate—Blaine County Court, Lincoln Ave, Box 123, Brewster, NE 68821. 308-547-2225. Fax: 308-547-2228. 8AM-4PM (CST). Access by: Phone, fax, mail, in person.

Boone County

Real Estate Recording—Register of Deeds, 222 South 4th Street, Albion, NE 68620. 402-395-2055. Fax: 402-395-6592. 8:30AM-5PM (CST).

Felony, Civil Actions Over $15,000—District Court, 222 Fourth St, Albion, NE 68620. 402-395-2057. Fax: 402-395-6592. 8:30AM-5PM (CST). Access by: Phone, fax, mail, in person.

Misdemeanor, Civil Actions Under $15,000, Eviction, Small Claims, Probate—Boone County Court, 222 S 4th St, Albion, NE 68620. 402-395-6184. Fax: 402-395-6592. 8AM-5PM (CST). Access by: Fax, mail, in person.

Box Butte County

Real Estate Recording—Register of Deeds, 5th Box Butte, Courthouse, Suite 203, Alliance, NE 69301. 308-762-6565. Fax: 308-762-2867. 9AM-5PM (MST).

Felony, Civil Actions Over $15,000—District Court, 515 Box Butte Suite 300, Alliance, NE 69301. 308-762-6293. 9AM-5PM (MST). Access by: In person only.

Misdemeanor, Civil Actions Under $15,000, Eviction, Small Claims, Probate—Box Butte County Court, PO Box 613, Alliance, NE 69301. 308-762-6800. Fax: 308-762-6802. 8:30AM-5PM (MST). Access by: Phone, fax, mail, in person.

Boyd County

Real Estate Recording—Register of Deeds, Thayer Street, Courthouse, Butte, NE 68722. 402-775-2391. Fax: 402-775-2146. 8:15AM-12, 1-5PM (CST).

Felony, Civil Actions Over $15,000—District Court, PO Box 26, Butte, NE 68722. 402-775-2391. Fax: 402-775-2146. 8:45AM-5PM (CST). Access by: Mail, in person.

Misdemeanor, Civil Actions Under $15,000, Eviction, Small Claims, Probate—Boyd County Court, PO Box 396,

Butte, NE 68722. 402-775-2211. Fax: 402-775-2146. 8AM-5PM W,Th (CST). Access by: Phone, fax, mail, in person.

Brown County

Real Estate Recording—Register of Deeds, Courthouse, 148 W. 4th St., Ainsworth, NE 69210. 402-387-2705. Fax: 402-387-0918. 8AM-5PM (CST).

Felony, Civil Actions Over $15,000—District Court, 148 W Fourth St, Ainsworth, NE 69210. 402-387-2705. Fax: 402-387-0918. 8AM-5PM (CST). Access by: Phone, fax, mail, in person.

Misdemeanor, Civil Actions Under $15,000, Eviction, Small Claims, Probate—Brown County Court, 148 W Fourth St, Ainsworth, NE 69210. 402-387-2864. Fax: 402-387-0918. 8AM-5PM (CST). Access by: In person only.

Buffalo County

Real Estate Recording—Register of Deeds, 16th & Central Avenue, Kearney, NE 68847. 308-236-1239. Fax: 308-236-1291. 8AM-5PM (CST).

Felony, Civil Actions Over $15,000—District Court, PO Box 520, Kearney, NE 68848. 308-236-1246. Fax: 308-236-1243. 8AM-5PM (CST). Access by: In person only.

Misdemeanor, Civil Actions Under $15,000, Eviction, Small Claims, Probate—Buffalo County Court, PO Box 520, Kearney, NE 68848. 308-236-1228. Fax: 308-236-1243. 8AM-5PM (CST). Access by: In person only.

Burt County

Real Estate Recording—Register of Deeds, Courthouse, 111 N. 13th St., Tekamah, NE 68061. 402-374-1955. Fax: 402-374-1955. 8AM-4:30PM (CST).

Felony, Civil Actions Over $15,000—District Court, 111 N 13th St, Tekamah, NE 68061. 402-374-2605. Fax: 402-374-2746. 8AM-4:30PM (CST). Access by: In person only.

Misdemeanor, Civil Actions Under $15,000, Eviction, Small Claims, Probate—Burt County Court, 111 N 13th St, PO Box 87, Tekamah, NE 68061. 402-374-2000. Fax: 402-374-2746. 8AM-4:30PM (CST). Access by: In person only.

Butler County

Real Estate Recording—Register of Deeds, 451 5th Street, David City, NE 68632. 402-367-7430. Fax: 402-367-3329. 8:30AM-5PM (CST).

Felony, Civil Actions Over $15,000—District Court, 451 5th St, David City, NE 68632-1666. 402-367-7460. Fax: 402-367-3329. 8:30AM-5PM (CST). Access by: Phone, fax, mail, in person.

Misdemeanor, Civil Actions Under $15,000, Eviction, Small Claims, Probate—Butler County Court, 451 5th St, David City, NE 68632-1666. 402-367-7480. Fax: 402-367-3329. 8AM-Noon, 1-5PM (CST). Access by: Fax, mail, in person.

Cass County

Real Estate Recording—Cass County Register of Deeds, County Courthouse, 346 Main St., Plattsmouth, NE 68048. 402-296-9330. Fax: 402-296-9327.

Felony, Civil Actions Over $15,000—District Court, Cass County Courthouse, Plattsmouth, NE 68048. 402-296-9339. Fax: 402-296-9345. 8AM-5PM (CST). Access by: In person only.

Misdemeanor, Civil Actions Under $15,000, Eviction, Small Claims, Probate—Cass County Court, Cass County Courthouse, Plattsmouth, NE 68048. 402-296-9334. 8AM-5PM (CST). Access by: Mail, in person.

Cedar County

Real Estate Recording—Register of Deeds, Courthouse, Hartington, NE 68739. 402-254-7411. Fax: 402-254-7410. 8AM-5PM (CST).

Felony, Civil Actions Over $15,000—District Court, 101 S Broadway Ave, PO Box 456, Hartington, NE 68739. 402-254-6957. Fax: 402-254-6954. 8AM-5PM (CST). Access by: In person only.

Misdemeanor, Civil Actions Under $15,000, Eviction, Small Claims, Probate—Cedar County Court, 101 S

Broadway Ave, Hartington, NE 68739. 402-254-7441. Fax: 402-254-6954. 8AM-5PM (CST). Access by: Mail, in person.

Chase County

Real Estate Recording—Register of Deeds, 921 Broadway, Courthouse, Imperial, NE 69033. 308-882-5266. 8AM-4PM (MST).

Felony, Civil Actions Over $15,000—District Court, PO Box 1299, Imperial, NE 69033. 308-882-5266. 8AM-4PM (MST). Access by: Phone, mail, in person.

Misdemeanor, Civil Actions Under $15,000, Eviction, Small Claims, Probate—Chase County Court, PO Box 1299, Imperial, NE 69033. 308-882-4690. Fax: 308-882-5679. 7:30AM-4:30PM (MST). Access by: Phone, mail, in person.

Cherry County

Real Estate Recording—Register of Deeds, 365 North Main, Valentine, NE 69201. 402-376-2771. Fax: 402-376-3095. 8:30AM-4:30PM (MST).

Felony, Civil Actions Over $15,000—District Court, 365 N Main St, Valentine, NE 69201. 402-376-1840. Fax: 402-376-3830. 8:30AM-4:30PM (MST). Access by: Fax, mail, in person.

Misdemeanor, Civil Actions Under $15,000, Eviction, Small Claims, Probate—Cherry County Court, 365 N Main St, Valentine, NE 69201. 402-376-2590. Fax: 402-376-3830. 8AM-5PM (MST). Access by: Fax, mail, in person.

Cheyenne County

Real Estate Recording—Register of Deeds, 1000 10th Avenue, Sidney, NE 69162. 308-254-2141. Fax: 308-254-4293. 8AM-5PM (MST).

Felony, Civil Actions Over $15,000—District Court, PO Box 217, Sidney, NE 69162. 308-254-2814. Fax: 308-254-4293. 8AM-Noon,1-5PM (MST). Access by: Phone, mail, in person.

Misdemeanor, Civil Actions Under $15,000, Eviction, Small Claims, Probate—Cheyenne County Court, 1000 10th Ave, Sidney, NE 69162. 308-254-2929. Fax: 308-254-4641. 8AM-5PM (MST). Access by: Mail, in person.

Clay County

Real Estate Recording—Register of Deeds, 111 West Fairfield Street, Clay Center, NE 68933. 402-762-3463. Fax: 402-762-3250. 8:30AM-5PM (CST).

Felony, Civil Actions Over $15,000—111 W Fairfield St, Clay Center, NE 68933. 402-762-3595. Fax: 402-762-3250. 8:30AM-5PM (CST). Access by: In person only.

Misdemeanor, Civil Actions Under $15,000, Eviction, Small Claims, Probate—Clay County Court, 111 W Fairfield St, Clay Center, NE 68933. 402-762-3651. Fax: 402-762-3250. 8:30AM-5PM (CST). Access by: In person only.

Colfax County

Real Estate Recording—Register of Deeds, 411 East 11th Street, Schuyler, NE 68661. 402-352-3434. Fax: 402-352-3287. 8:30AM-5PM (CST).

Felony, Civil Actions Over $15,000—District Court, 411 E 11th St, PO Box 429, Schuyler, NE 68661. 402-352-2205. Fax: 402-352-2847. 8:30AM-5PM (CST). Access by: Fax, mail, in person.

Misdemeanor, Civil Actions Under $15,000, Eviction, Small Claims, Probate—Colfax County Court, 411 E 11th St, Schuyler, NE 68661. 402-352-3322. Fax: 402-352-2847. 8AM-5PM (CST). Access by: In person only.

Cuming County

Real Estate Recording—Register of Deeds, Courthouse, 200 S. Lincoln, West Point, NE 68788. 402-372-6002. Fax: 402-372-6017. (CST).

Felony, Civil Actions Over $15,000—District Court, 200 S Lincoln, Rm 200, West Point, NE 68788. 402-372-6004. Fax: 402-372-6017. 8:30AM-4:30PM (CST). Access by: In person only.

Misdemeanor, Civil Actions Under $15,000, Eviction, Small Claims, Probate—Cuming County Court, 200 S Lin-

coln, West Point, NE 68788. 402-372-6003. Fax: 402-372-6017. 8:30AM-4:30PM (CST). Access by: In person only.

Custer County

Real Estate Recording—Register of Deeds, 431 South 10th, Broken Bow, NE 68822. 308-872-5701. 9AM-5PM (CST).

Felony, Civil Actions Over $15,000—District Court, 431 S 10th Ave, Broken Bow, NE 68822. 308-872-2121. Fax: 308-872-6052. 9AM-5PM (CST). Access by: Phone, fax, mail, in person.

Misdemeanor, Civil Actions Under $15,000, Eviction, Small Claims, Probate—Custer County Court, 431 South 10th Ave, Broken Bow, NE 68822. 308-872-5761. Fax: 308-872-6052. 8AM-5PM (CST). Access by: Phone, fax, mail, in person.

Dakota County

Real Estate Recording—Dakota County Register of Deeds, 1601 Broadway, Courthouse Square, Dakota City, NE 68731. 402-987-2166.

Felony, Civil Actions Over $15,000—District Court, PO Box 66, Dakota City, NE 68731. 402-987-2114. Fax: 402-987-2117. 8AM-4:30PM (CST). Access by: In person only.

Misdemeanor, Civil Actions Under $15,000, Eviction, Small Claims, Probate—Dakota County Court, PO Box 385, Dakota City, NE 68731. 402-987-2145. Fax: 402-987-2185. 8AM-4:30PM (CST). Access by: In person only.

Dawes County

Real Estate Recording—Register of Deeds, 451 Main Street, Courthouse, Chadron, NE 69337. 308-432-0100. Fax: 308-432-0115. 8:30AM-4:30PM (MST).

Felony, Civil Actions Over $15,000—District Court, PO Box 630, Chadron, NE 69337. 308-432-0109. Fax: 308-432-0110. 8:30AM-4:30PM (MST). Access by: Phone, mail, in person.

Misdemeanor, Civil Actions Under $15,000, Eviction, Small Claims, Probate—Dawes County Court, PO Box 806, Chadron, NE 69337. 308-432-0116. Fax: 308-432-0110. 7:30AM-4:30PM (MST). Access by: Fax, mail, in person.

Dawson County

Real Estate Recording—Dawson County Register of Deeds, County Courthouse, Lexington, NE 68850. 308-324-4271.

Felony, Civil Actions Over $15,000—District Court, PO Box 429, Lexington, NE 68850. 308-324-4261. Fax: 308-324-3374. 8AM-5PM (CST). Access by: Fax, mail, in person.

Misdemeanor, Civil Actions Under $15,000, Eviction, Small Claims, Probate—Dawson County Court, 700 N Washington St, Lexington, NE 68850. 308-324-5606. 8AM-5PM (CST). Access by: In person only.

Deuel County

Real Estate Recording—Register of Deeds, 3rd & Vincent, Chappell, NE 69129. 308-874-3308. Fax: 308-874-2944. 8AM-4PM (MST).

Felony, Civil Actions Over $15,000—District Court, PO Box 327, Chappell, NE 69129. 308-874-3308. Fax: 308-874-3472. 8AM-4PM (MST). Access by: Fax, mail, in person.

Misdemeanor, Civil Actions Under $15,000, Eviction, Small Claims, Probate—Deuel County Court, PO Box 327, Chappell, NE 69129. 308-874-2909. Fax: 308-874-2994. 8AM-4PM (MST). Access by: Mail, in person.

Dixon County

Real Estate Recording—Register of Deeds, Courthouse, 302 Third St., Ponca, NE 68770. 402-755-2208. Fax: 402-755-4276. 8AM-4:30PM (CST).

Felony, Civil Actions Over $15,000—District Court, PO Box 395, Ponca, NE 68770. 402-755-2881. Fax: 402-755-2632. 8AM-Noon, 1-5PM (CST). Access by: In person only.

Misdemeanor, Civil Actions Under $15,000, Eviction, Small Claims, Probate—Dixon County Court, PO Box 497, Ponca, NE 68770. 402-755-2355. Fax: 402-755-2632. 8AM-4:30PM (CST). Access by: In person only.

Dodge County

Real Estate Recording—Dodge County Register of Deeds, 435 North Park, Courthouse, Fremont, NE 68025. 402-727-2735.

Felony, Civil Actions Over $15,000—District Court, PO Box 1237, Fremont, NE 68026. 402-727-2780. Fax: 402-727-2773. 8:30AM-4:30PM (CST). Access by: Mail, in person.

Misdemeanor, Civil Actions Under $15,000, Eviction, Small Claims, Probate—Dodge County Court, 428 N Broad St, Fremont, NE 68025. 402-727-2755. Fax: 402-727-2762. 8AM-5PM (CST). Access by: Fax, mail, in person.

Douglas County

Real Estate Recording—Douglas County Register of Deeds, 1819 Farnam, Room H09, Omaha, NE 68183. 402-444-7194. Fax: 402-444-6693.

Felony, Civil Actions Over $15,000—District Court, 1819 Farnam, Omaha, NE 68183. 402-444-7018. 8:30AM-4:30PM (CST). Access by: Mail, in person.

Misdemeanor, Civil Actions Under $15,000, Eviction, Small Claims, Probate—Douglas County Court, 1819 Farnam, 2nd Fl, Omaha, NE 68183. 402-444-5425. 8AM-4:30PM (CST). Access by: In person only.

Dundy County

Real Estate Recording—Register of Deeds, Courthouse, Benkelman, NE 69021. 308-423-2058. 8AM-5PM (MST).

Felony, Civil Actions Over $15,000—District Court, PO Box 506, Benkelman, NE 69021. 308-423-2058. 8AM-5PM (MST). Access by: Phone, mail, in person.

Misdemeanor, Civil Actions Under $15,000, Eviction, Small Claims, Probate—Dundy County Court, PO Box 377, Benkelman, NE 69021. 308-423-2374. 8AM-4:30PM (MST). Access by: Phone, mail, in person.

Fillmore County

Real Estate Recording—Register of Deeds, Courthouse, 900 G st., Geneva, NE 68361. 402-759-4931. Fax: 402-759-4429. 8AM-5PM (CST).

Felony, Civil Actions Over $15,000—District Court, PO Box 147, Geneva, NE 68361. 402-759-3811. Fax: 402-759-4440. 8AM-Noon, 1-5PM (CST). Access by: Phone, fax, mail, in person.

Misdemeanor, Civil Actions Under $15,000, Eviction, Small Claims, Probate—Fillmore County Court, PO Box 66, Geneva, NE 68361. 402-759-3514. Fax: 402-759-4440. 8AM-5PM (CST). Access by: Fax, mail, in person.

Franklin County

Real Estate Recording—Register of Deeds, 405 15th Avenue, Franklin, NE 68939. 308-425-6202. Fax: 402-425-6289. 8:30AM-4:30PM (CST).

Felony, Civil Actions Over $15,000—District Court, PO Box 146, Franklin, NE 68939. 308-425-6202. Fax: 308-425-6289. 8:30AM-4:30PM (CST). Access by: In person only.

Misdemeanor, Civil Actions Under $15,000, Eviction, Small Claims, Probate—Franklin County Court, PO Box 174, Franklin, NE 68939. 308-425-6288. Fax: 308-425-6289. 8:30AM-4:30PM M-F (CST). Access by: Mail, in person.

Frontier County

Real Estate Recording—Frontier County Clerk, 1 Wellington Street, Stockville, NE 69042. 308-367-8641. Fax: 308-367-8730. 8:30AM-Noon, 1-5PM (CST).

Felony, Civil Actions Over $15,000—District Court, PO Box 40, Stockville, NE 69042. 308-367-8641. Fax: 308-367-8730. 9AM-4:30PM (CST). Access by: Mail, in person.

Misdemeanor, Civil Actions Under $15,000, Eviction, Small Claims, Probate—Frontier County Court, PO Box 38, Stockville, NE 69042. 308-367-8629. Fax: 308-367-8730. 9AM-4:30PM (CST). Access by: Mail, in person.

Furnas County

Real Estate Recording—Register of Deeds, Courthouse, 912 R Street, Beaver City, NE 68926. 308-268-4145. 8AM-4PM (CST).

Felony, Civil Actions Over $15,000—District Court, PO Box 413, Beaver City, NE 68926. 308-268-4015. Fax: 308-268-2345. 10AM-Noon, 1-3PM (CST). Access by: Fax, mail, in person.

Misdemeanor, Civil Actions Under $15,000, Eviction, Small Claims, Probate—Furnas County Court, 912 R St (PO Box 373), Beaver City, NE 68926. 308-268-4025. Fax: 308-268-2345. 8AM-4PM (CST). Access by: Phone, fax, mail, in person.

Gage County

Real Estate Recording—Gage County Register of Deeds, 612 Grant St., Beatrice, NE 68310. 402-223-1361.

Felony, Civil Actions Over $15,000—District Court, PO Box 845, Beatrice, NE 68310. 402-223-1332. 8AM-5PM (CST). Access by: Mail, in person.

Misdemeanor, Civil Actions Under $15,000, Eviction, Small Claims, Probate—Gage County Court, PO Box 219, Beatrice, NE 68310. 402-223-1323. Fax: 402-223-1326. 8AM-5PM (CST). Access by: Fax, mail, in person.

Garden County

Real Estate Recording—Register of Deeds, 611 Main Street, Courthouse, Oshkosh, NE 69154. 308-772-3924. Fax: 308-772-4143. 8AM-4PM (MST).

Felony, Civil Actions Over $15,000—District Court, PO Box 486, Oshkosh, NE 69154. 308-772-3924. Fax: 308-772-4143. 8AM-4PM (MST). Access by: Fax, mail, in person.

Misdemeanor, Civil Actions Under $15,000, Eviction, Small Claims, Probate—Garden County Court, PO Box 465, Oshkosh, NE 69154. 308-772-3696. 8AM-4PM (MST). Access by: In person only.

Garfield County

Real Estate Recording—Register of Deeds, 250 South 8th Street, Burwell, NE 68823. 308-346-4161. 9AM-Noon, 1-5PM (CST).

Felony, Civil Actions Over $15,000—District Court, PO Box 218, Burwell, NE 68823. 308-346-4161. 9AM-5PM (CST). Access by: Mail, in person.

Misdemeanor, Civil Actions Under $15,000, Eviction, Small Claims, Probate—Garfield County Court, PO Box 431, Burwell, NE 68823. 308-346-4123. Fax: 308-346-5064. 9AM-4PM (CST). Access by: Mail, in person.

Gosper County

Real Estate Recording—Register of Deeds, Courthouse, 507 Smith Ave., Elwood, NE 68937. 308-785-2611. 8:30AM-4:30PM (CST).

Felony, Civil Actions Over $15,000—District Court, PO Box 136, Elwood, NE 68937. 308-785-2611. 8:30AM-4:30PM (CST). Access by: In person only.

Misdemeanor, Civil Actions Under $15,000, Eviction, Small Claims, Probate—Gosper County Court, PO Box 55, Elwood, NE 68937. 308-785-2531. Fax: 308-785-2036. 8:30AM-4:30PM (CST). Access by: Fax, mail, in person.

Grant County

Real Estate Recording—Register of Deeds, Harrison Avenue, Courthouse, Hyannis, NE 69350. 308-458-2488. Fax: 308-458-2485. 8AM-Noon,1-4PM (MST).

Felony, Civil Actions Over $15,000—District Court, PO Box 139, Hyannis, NE 69350. 308-458-2488. Fax: 308-458-2485. 8AM-4PM (MST). Access by: Fax, mail, in person.

Misdemeanor, Civil Actions Under $15,000, Eviction, Small Claims, Probate—Grant County Court, PO Box 97, Hyannis, NE 69350. 308-458-2433. Fax: 308-458-2283. 8AM-4PM (MST). Access by: Phone, mail, in person.

Greeley County

Real Estate Recording—Register of Deeds, Courthouse, Greeley, NE 68842. 308-428-3625. (CST).

Felony, Civil Actions Over $15,000—District Court, PO Box 287, Greeley, NE 68842. 308-428-3625. Fax: 308-428-6500. 8AM-4PM (CST). Access by: Mail, in person.

Misdemeanor, Civil Actions Under $15,000, Eviction, Small Claims, Probate—Greeley County Court, PO Box 302, Greeley, NE 68842. 308-428-2705. Fax: 308-428-6500. 8AM-5PM (CST). Access by: In person only.

Hall County

Real Estate Recording—Hall County Register of Deeds, 121 South Pine, Grand Island, NE 68801. 308-385-5040.

Felony, Civil Actions Over $15,000—District Court, PO Box 1926, Grand Island, NE 68802. 308-385-5144. Fax: 308-385-5110. 8AM-5PM (CST). Access by: Phone, mail, in person.

Misdemeanor, Civil Actions Under $15,000, Eviction, Small Claims, Probate—Hall County Court, 111 W 1st Suite 1, Grand Island, NE 68801. 308-385-5135. 8:30AM-5PM (CST). Access by: In person only.

Hamilton County

Real Estate Recording—Register of Deeds, Courthouse, 1111 13th St. - Suite 1, Aurora, NE 68818. 402-694-3443. Fax: 402-694-2250. 8AM-5PM (CST).

Felony, Civil Actions Over $15,000—District Court, PO Box 973, Aurora, NE 68818-0201. 402-694-3533. Fax: 402-694-2250. 8AM-5PM (CST). Access by: Fax, mail, in person.

Misdemeanor, Civil Actions Under $15,000, Eviction, Small Claims, Probate—Hamilton County Court, PO Box 323, Aurora, NE 68818. 402-694-6188. Fax: 402-694-2250. (CST). Access by: In person only.

Harlan County

Real Estate Recording—Harlan County Clerk, 706 West 2nd Street, Alma, NE 68920. 308-928-2173. Fax: 308-928-2592. 8:30AM-4:30PM (CST).

Felony, Civil Actions Over $15,000—District Court, PO Box 379, Alma, NE 68920. 308-928-2173. Fax: 308-928-2170. 8:30AM-4:30PM (CST). Access by: Phone, mail, in person.

Misdemeanor, Civil Actions Under $15,000, Eviction, Small Claims, Probate—Harlan County Court, PO Box 379, Alma, NE 68920. 308-928-2179. Fax: 308-928-2170. 8:30AM-4:30PM (CST). Access by: Fax, mail, in person.

Hayes County

Real Estate Recording—Register of Deeds, Troth Street, Courthouse, Hayes Center, NE 69032. 308-286-3413. 8AM-4PM (CST).

Felony, Civil Actions Over $15,000—District Court, PO Box 370, Hayes Center, NE 69032. 308-286-3413. Fax: 308-286-3208. 8AM-4PM (CST). Access by: Fax, mail, in person.

Misdemeanor, Civil Actions Under $15,000, Eviction, Small Claims, Probate—Hayes County Court, PO Box 370, Hayes Center, NE 69032. 308-286-3315. 9AM-Noon, 1-4PM T (Clerk's hours) (CST). Access by: Mail, in person.

Hitchcock County

Real Estate Recording—Register of Deeds, 229 East D, Trenton, NE 69044. 308-334-5646. Fax: 308-334-5351. 8:30AM-4PM (CST).

Felony, Civil Actions Over $15,000—District Court, PO Box 248, Trenton, NE 69044. 308-334-5646. Fax: 308-334-5351. 8:30AM-4PM (CST). Access by: Phone, fax, mail, in person.

Misdemeanor, Civil Actions Under $15,000, Eviction, Small Claims, Probate—Hitchcock County Court, PO Box 366, Trenton, NE 69044. 308-334-5383. 8:30AM-4PM (CST). Access by: Phone, mail, in person.

Holt County

Real Estate Recording—Register of Deeds, 204 North 4th, O'Neill, NE 68763. 402-336-1762. Fax: 402-336-2885. 8AM-4:30PM (CST).

Felony, Civil Actions Over $15,000—District Court, PO Box 755, O'Neill, NE 68763. 402-336-2840. Fax: 402-336-3601. 8AM-5PM (CST). Access by: Phone, fax, mail, in person.

Misdemeanor, Civil Actions Under $15,000, Eviction, Small Claims, Probate—Holt County Court, 204 N 4th St,

O'Neill, NE 68763. 402-336-1662. Fax: 402-336-3601. 8AM-5PM (CST). Access by: Mail, in person.

Hooker County

Real Estate Recording—Register of Deeds, 303 NW 1st, Courthouse, Mullen, NE 69152. 308-546-2244. 8:30AM-Noon, 1-4:30PM (MST).

Felony, Civil Actions Over $15,000—District Court, PO Box 184, Mullen, NE 69152. 308-546-2244. 8:30AM-4:30PM (MST). Access by: Phone, mail, in person.

Misdemeanor, Civil Actions Under $15,000, Eviction, Small Claims, Probate—Hooker County Court, PO Box 263, Mullen, NE 69152. 308-546-2249. Fax: 308-546-2490. 8:30AM-4:30PM (MST). Access by: Fax, mail, in person.

Howard County

Real Estate Recording—Register of Deeds, 612 Indian Street, St. Paul, NE 68873. 308-754-4343. Fax: 308-754-4727. 8AM-5PM (CST).

Felony, Civil Actions Over $15,000—District Court, PO Box 25, St Paul, NE 68873. 308-754-4343. Fax: 308-754-4727. 8AM-5PM (CST). Access by: Mail, in person.

Misdemeanor, Civil Actions Under $15,000, Eviction, Small Claims, Probate—Howard County Court, 612 Indian St Suite #6, St Paul, NE 68873. 308-754-4192. 8AM-5PM (CST). Access by: In person only.

Jefferson County

Real Estate Recording—Jefferson County Clerk, 411 4th, Courthouse, Fairbury, NE 68352. 402-729-5201. Fax: 402-729-2016. 9AM-5PM UCC; 9AM-Noon, 1-5PM Real Property (CST).

Felony, Civil Actions Over $15,000—District Court, 411 Fourth St, Fairbury, NE 68352. 402-729-2019. Fax: 402-729-2016. 9AM-5PM (CST). Access by: Fax, mail, in person.

Misdemeanor, Civil Actions Under $15,000, Eviction, Small Claims, Probate—Jefferson County Court, 411 Fourth St, Fairbury, NE 68352. 402-729-2312. Fax: 402-729-2016. 8AM-Noon, 1-5PM (CST). Access by: Mail, in person.

Johnson County

Real Estate Recording—Register of Deeds, Courthouse, Tecumseh, NE 68450. 402-335-3246. Fax: 402-335-3975. 8AM-12:30PM, 1-4:30PM (CST).

Felony, Civil Actions Over $15,000—District Court, PO Box 416, Tecumseh, NE 68450. 402-335-2871. Fax: 402-335-3975. 8AM-Noon, 1-4:30PM (CST). Access by: Phone, fax, mail, in person.

Misdemeanor, Civil Actions Under $15,000, Eviction, Small Claims, Probate—Johnson County Court, PO Box 285, Tecumseh, NE 68450. 402-335-3050. 8AM-4:30PM (CST). Access by: In person only.

Kearney County

Real Estate Recording—Register of Deeds, 424 North Colorado, Minden, NE 68959. 308-832-2723. Fax: 308-832-1748. 8:30AM-5PM (CST).

Felony, Civil Actions Over $15,000—District Court, PO Box 208, Minden, NE 68959. 308-832-1742. Fax: 308-832-0636. 8:30AM-5PM (CST). Access by: In person only.

Misdemeanor, Civil Actions Under $15,000, Eviction, Small Claims, Probate—Kearney County Court, PO Box 377, Minden, NE 68959. 308-832-2723. Fax: 308-832-0636. 8:30AM-5PM (CST). Access by: In person only.

Keith County

Real Estate Recording—Register of Deeds, 511 North Spruce, Ogallala, NE 69153. 308-284-4726. Fax: 308-284-6277. 8AM-4PM (MST).

Felony, Civil Actions Over $15,000—District Court, PO Box 686, Ogallala, NE 69153. 308-284-3849. Fax: 308-284-3978. 8AM-4PM (MST). Access by: Fax, mail, in person.

Misdemeanor, Civil Actions Under $15,000, Eviction, Small Claims, Probate—Keith County Court, PO Box 358, Ogallala, NE 69153. 308-284-3693. Fax: 308-284-6825.

8AM-5PM M-Th; 7AM-4PM F (MST). Access by: In person only.

Keya Paha County

Real Estate Recording—Register of Deeds, Courthouse, Springview, NE 68778. 402-497-3791. Fax: 402-497-3799. 8AM-Noon,1-5PM (CST).

Felony, Civil Actions Over $15,000—District Court, PO Box 349, Springview, NE 68778. 402-497-3791. Fax: 402-497-3799. 8AM-5PM (CST). Access by: Mail, in person.

Misdemeanor, Civil Actions Under $15,000, Eviction, Small Claims, Probate—Keya Paha County Court, PO Box 311, Springview, NE 68778. 402-497-3021. 8AM-5PM Th,F (CST). Access by: Phone, fax, mail, in person.

Kimball County

Real Estate Recording—Register of Deeds, 114 East Third Street, Kimball, NE 69145. 308-235-2241. 8AM-5PM M,T,W,Th; 8AM-4PM F (MST).

Felony, Civil Actions Over $15,000—District Court, 114 E 3rd St, Kimball, NE 69145. 308-235-3591. 8AM-5PM M-Th, 8AM-4PM F (MST). Access by: Mail, in person.

Misdemeanor, Civil Actions Under $15,000, Eviction, Small Claims, Probate—Kimball County Court, 114 E 3rd St, Kimball, NE 69145. 308-235-2831. 8AM-5PM (MST). Access by: Mail, in person.

Knox County

Real Estate Recording—Knox County Clerk (ex-officio Register of Deeds), Main Street, Courthouse, Center, NE 68724. 402-288-4424. Fax: 402-288-4424. 8:30AM-4:30PM (CST).

Felony, Civil Actions Over $15,000—District Court, PO Box 126, Center, NE 68724. 402-288-4484. Fax: 402-288-4275. 8:30AM-4:30PM (CST). Access by: In person only.

Misdemeanor, Civil Actions Under $15,000, Eviction, Small Claims, Probate—Knox County Court, PO Box 125, Center, NE 68724. 402-288-4277. Fax: 402-288-4275. 8:30AM-4:30PM (CST). Access by: In person only.

Lancaster County

Real Estate Recording—Lancaster County Register of Deeds, 555 South 10th Street, Lincoln, NE 68508. 402-441-7577. Fax: 402-441-7012.

Felony, Civil Actions Over $15,000—District Court, 555 S Tenth St, Lincoln, NE 68508. 402-441-7328. Fax: 402-441-6190. 8AM-4:30PM (CST). Access by: Phone, mail, in person.

Misdemeanor, Civil Actions Under $15,000, Eviction, Small Claims, Probate—Lancaster County Court, 555 S Tenth St, Lincoln, NE 68508. 402-441-7295. 8AM-4:30PM (CST). Access by: In person only.

Lincoln County

Real Estate Recording—Lincoln County Reister of Deeds, 301 N. Jeffers, Room 103, North Platte, NE 69101. 308-534-4350. Fax: 308-534-5287.

Felony, Civil Actions Over $15,000—District Court, 301 N Jeffers (PO Box 1616), North Platte, NE 69101. 308-534-4350. 8AM-5PM (CST). Access by: In person only.

Misdemeanor, Civil Actions Under $15,000, Eviction, Small Claims, Probate—Lincoln County Court, PO Box 519, North Platte, NE 69103. 308-534-4350. Fax: 308-534-1757. 8AM-5PM (CST). Access by: Phone, mail, in person.

Logan County

Real Estate Recording—Register of Deeds, Courthouse, Stapleton, NE 69163. 308-636-2311. 8:30AM-4:30PM M,T,W,Th; 8:30AM-4PM F (CST).

Felony, Civil Actions Over $15,000—District Court, PO Box 8, Stapleton, NE 69163. 308-636-2311. 8:30AM-4:30PM M-Th; 8:30AM-4PM F (CST). Access by: Mail, in person.

Misdemeanor, Civil Actions Under $15,000, Eviction, Small Claims, Probate—Logan County Court, PO Box 202, Stapleton, NE 69163. 308-636-2677. 8AM-Noon, 1-4:30PM M-Th; 8:30AM-Noon, 1-4PM F (CST). Access by: Phone, fax, mail, in person.

Loup County

Real Estate Recording—Register of Deeds, Courthouse, Taylor, NE 68879. 308-942-3135. Fax: 308-942-6015. 8:30AM-Noon, 1-5PM M,T,W,Th; 8:30AM-Noon F (CST).

Felony, Civil Actions Over $15,000—District Court, PO Box 146, Taylor, NE 68879. 308-942-6035. Fax: 308-942-6015. 8:30AM-4:30PM M-Th, 8:30AM-Noon F (CST). Access by: In person only.

Misdemeanor, Civil Actions Under $15,000, Eviction, Small Claims, Probate—Loup County Court, PO Box 146, Taylor, NE 68879. 308-942-6035. Fax: 308-942-6015. 8:30AM-4:30PM M-Th, 8:30AM-Noon F (CST). Access by: In person only.

Madison County

Real Estate Recording—Madison County Register of Deeds, Clara Davis Drive, Courthouse, Madison, NE 68748. 402-454-3311.

Felony, Civil Actions Over $15,000—District Court, PO Box 249, Madison, NE 68748. 402-454-3311. Fax: 402-454-6528. 8AM-5PM (CST). Access by: In person only.

Misdemeanor, Civil Actions Under $15,000, Eviction, Small Claims, Probate—Madison County Court, PO Box 230, Madison, NE 68748. 402-454-3311. Fax: 402-454-3438. 8:30AM-5PM (CST). Access by: Mail, in person.

McPherson County

Real Estate Recording—Register of Deeds, 5th & Anderson, Courthouse, Tryon, NE 69167. 308-587-2363. Fax: 308-587-2363. 8:30AM-Noon, 1-4:30PM (CST).

Felony, Civil Actions Over $15,000—District Court, PO Box 122, Tryon, NE 69167. 308-587-2363. Fax: 308-587-2363. 8:30AM-4:30PM (CST). Access by: Fax, mail, in person.

Misdemeanor, Civil Actions Under $15,000, Eviction, Small Claims, Probate—McPherson County Court, PO Box 122, Tryon, NE 69167. 308-587-2363. Fax: 308-587-2363. 8:30AM-Noon, 1-4:30PM (CST). Access by: Fax, mail, in person.

Merrick County

Real Estate Recording—Register of Deeds, Courthouse, Central City, NE 68826. 308-946-2881. Fax: 308-946-2332. 8AM-5PM (CST).

Felony, Civil Actions Over $15,000—District Court, PO Box 27, Central City, NE 68826. 308-946-2461. Fax: 308-946-3692. 8AM-5PM (CST). Access by: In person only.

Misdemeanor, Civil Actions Under $15,000, Eviction, Small Claims, Probate—Merrick County Court, County Courthouse, PO Box 27, Central City, NE 68826. 308-946-2812. 8AM-5PM (CST). Access by: In person only.

Morrill County

Real Estate Recording—Register of Deeds, 6th & Main Street, Courthouse, Bridgeport, NE 69336. 308-262-0860. Fax: 308-262-0352. 8AM-4:30PM (MST).

Felony, Civil Actions Over $15,000—District Court, PO Box 824, Bridgeport, NE 69336. 308-262-1261. 8AM-Noon, 1-4:30PM (MST). Access by: Phone, mail, in person.

Misdemeanor, Civil Actions Under $15,000, Eviction, Small Claims, Probate—Morrill County Court, PO Box 418, Bridgeport, NE 69336. 308-262-0812. 8AM-4:30PM (MST). Access by: In person only.

Nance County

Real Estate Recording—Register of Deeds, 209 Esther Street, Fullerton, NE 68638. 308-536-2331. Fax: 308-536-2742. 8AM-5PM (CST).

Felony, Civil Actions Over $15,000—District Court, PO Box 338, Fullerton, NE 68638. 308-536-2365. Fax: 308-536-2742. 8AM-5PM (CST). Access by: Phone, fax, mail, in person.

Misdemeanor, Civil Actions Under $15,000, Eviction, Small Claims, Probate—Nance County Court, PO Box 837, Fullerton, NE 68638. 308-536-2675. Fax: 308-536-2742. 8AM-5PM (CST). Access by: Fax, mail, in person.

Nemaha County

Real Estate Recording—Register of Deeds, 1824 N Street, Courthouse, Auburn, NE 68305. 402-274-4213. Fax: 402-274-4478. 8AM-5PM (CST).

Felony, Civil Actions Over $15,000—District Court, 1824 N St, Auburn, NE 68305. 402-274-3616. Fax: 402-274-4478. 8AM-5PM (CST). Access by: In person only.

Misdemeanor, Civil Actions Under $15,000, Eviction, Small Claims, Probate—Nemaha County Court, 1824 N St, Auburn, NE 68305. 402-274-3008. Fax: 402-274-4605. 8AM-5PM, Closed 12-1 (CST). Access by: In person only.

Nuckolls County

Real Estate Recording—Register of Deeds, 150 South Main, Courthouse, Nelson, NE 68961. 402-225-4361. 8:30AM-4:30PM (CST).

Felony, Civil Actions Over $15,000—District Court, PO Box 366, Nelson, NE 68961. 402-225-4341. 8:30AM-5PM (CST). Access by: In person only.

Misdemeanor, Civil Actions Under $15,000, Eviction, Small Claims, Probate—Nuckolls County Court, PO Box 372, Nelson, NE 68961. 402-225-2371. Fax: 402-225-2371. 8AM-5PM (CST). Access by: Mail, in person.

Otoe County

Real Estate Recording—Otoe County Register of Deeds, 1021 Central Ave., Room 203, Nebraska City, NE 68410. 402-873-6439. Fax: 402-873-6130.

Felony, Civil Actions Over $15,000—District Court, 1021 Central Ave, Rm 973, Nebraska City, NE 68410. 402-873-6440. 8AM-Noon, 1-5PM (CST). Access by: In person only.

Misdemeanor, Civil Actions Under $15,000, Eviction, Small Claims, Probate—Otoe County Court, 1021 Central Ave, Rm 109, PO Box 487, Nebraska City, NE 68410. 402-873-5588. Fax: 402-873-6130. 8AM-5PM (CST). Access by: Fax, mail, in person.

Pawnee County

Real Estate Recording—Register of Deeds, 625 6th Street, Pawnee City, NE 68420. 402-852-2962. Fax: 402-852-2963. 8AM-4PM (CST).

Felony, Civil Actions Over $15,000—District Court, PO Box 431, Pawnee City, NE 68420. 402-852-2963. 8AM-4PM (CST). Access by: Phone, mail, in person.

Misdemeanor, Civil Actions Under $15,000, Eviction, Small Claims, Probate—Pawnee County Court, PO Box 471, Pawnee City, NE 68420. 402-852-2388. Fax: 402-852-2388. 8AM-4:30PM (CST). Access by: In person only.

Perkins County

Real Estate Recording—Register of Deeds, 200 Lincoln Avenue, Grant, NE 69140. 308-352-4643. Fax: 308-352-2455. 8AM-4PM (MST).

Felony, Civil Actions Over $15,000—District Court, PO Box 156, Grant, NE 69140. 308-352-4643. Fax: 308-352-4368. 8AM-4PM (MST). Access by: Fax, mail, in person.

Misdemeanor, Civil Actions Under $15,000, Eviction, Small Claims, Probate—Perkins County Court, PO Box 222, Grant, NE 69140. 308-352-4415. Fax: 308-352-2455. 8AM-4PM (MST). Access by: Mail, in person.

Phelps County

Real Estate Recording—Register of Deeds, Courthouse, Holdrege, NE 68949. 308-995-4469. Fax: 308-995-4368. 9AM-5PM (CST).

Felony, Civil Actions Over $15,000—District Court, PO Box 462, Holdrege, NE 68949. 308-995-2281. 9AM-5PM (CST). Access by: Phone, fax, mail, in person.

Misdemeanor, Civil Actions Under $15,000, Eviction, Small Claims, Probate—Phelps County Court, PO Box 255, Holdrege, NE 68949. 308-995-6561. Fax: 308-995-6562. 8AM-5PM (CST). Access by: Mail, in person.

Pierce County

Real Estate Recording—Register of Deeds, 111 West Court, Courthouse - Room 1, Pierce, NE 68767. 402-329-4225. Fax: 402-329-6439. 9AM-5PM (CST).

Felony, Civil Actions Over $15,000—District Court, 111 W Court St, Rm 12, Pierce, NE 68767. 402-329-4335. Fax: 402-329-6412. 9AM-5PM (CST). Access by: In person only.

Misdemeanor, Civil Actions Under $15,000, Eviction, Small Claims, Probate—Pierce County Court, 111 W Court St, Rm 11, Pierce, NE 68767. 402-329-6245. Fax: 402-329-6412. 8:30AM-5PM (CST). Access by: Mail, in person.

Platte County

Real Estate Recording—Platte County Register of Deeds, 2610 14th Street, Columbus, NE 68601. 402-563-4911.

Felony, Civil Actions Over $15,000—District Court, PO Box 1188, Columbus, NE 68602-1188. 402-563-4906. Fax: 402-562-6718. 8:30AM-5PM (CST). Access by: In person only.

Misdemeanor, Civil Actions Under $15,000, Eviction, Small Claims, Probate—Platte County Court, PO Box 538, Columbus, NE 68602-0538. 402-563-4937. Fax: 402-562-6718. 8AM-5PM (CST). Access by: In person only.

Polk County

Real Estate Recording—Register of Deeds, Courthouse Square, Osceola, NE 68651. 402-747-5431. 8AM-5PM (CST).

Felony, Civil Actions Over $15,000—District Court, PO Box 447, Osceola, NE 68651. 402-747-3487. Fax: 402-747-8299. 8AM-Noon,1-5PM (CST). Access by: Mail, in person.

Misdemeanor, Civil Actions Under $15,000, Eviction, Small Claims, Probate—Polk County Court, PO Box 506, Osceola, NE 68651. 402-747-5371. Fax: 402-747-8299. 8AM-5PM (CST). Access by: In person only.

Red Willow County

Real Estate Recording—Register of Deeds, 502 Norris Avenue, McCook, NE 69001. 308-345-1552. Fax: 308-345-1503. 8AM-4PM (CST).

Felony, Civil Actions Over $15,000—District Court, 520 Norris Ave (PO Box 847), McCook, NE 69001. 308-345-4583. Fax: 308-345-7907. 8AM-4PM (CST). Access by: Phone, fax, mail, in person.

Misdemeanor, Civil Actions Under $15,000, Eviction, Small Claims, Probate—Red Willow County Court, 520 Norris Ave, McCook, NE 69001. 308-345-1904. Fax: 308-345-1503. 8AM-4PM (CST). Access by: Mail, in person.

Richardson County

Real Estate Recording—Richardson County Clerk, Courthouse, 1700 Stone, Falls City, NE 68355. 402-245-2911. Fax: 402-245-3725. 8:30AM-5PM (CST).

Felony, Civil Actions Over $15,000—District Court, 1700 Stone St, Falls City, NE 68355. 402-245-2023. Fax: 402-245-3725. 8:30AM-5PM (CST). Access by: Fax, mail, in person.

Misdemeanor, Civil Actions Under $15,000, Eviction, Small Claims, Probate—Richardson County Court, 1700 Stone St Room 205, Falls City, NE 68355. 402-245-2812. Fax: 402-245-3352. 8AM-5PM (CST). Access by: In person only.

Rock County

Real Estate Recording—Register of Deeds, 400 State Street, Bassett, NE 68714. 402-684-3933. 9AM-Noon, 1-5PM (CST).

Felony, Civil Actions Over $15,000—District Court, PO Box 367, Bassett, NE 68714. 402-684-3933. 9AM-5PM (CST). Access by: Mail, in person.

Misdemeanor, Civil Actions Under $15,000, Eviction, Small Claims, Probate—Rock County Court, PO Box 249, Bassett, NE 68714. 402-684-3601. Fax: 402-684-2741. 8AM-4:30PM (CST). Access by: Mail, in person.

Saline County

Real Estate Recording—Register of Deeds, 215 South Court, Wilber, NE 68465. 402-821-2374. Fax: 402-821-3381. 8AM-5PM (CST).

Felony, Civil Actions Over $15,000—District Court, 215 S Court St, Wilber, NE 68465. 402-821-2823. Fax: 402-821-2132. 8AM-5PM (CST). Access by: In person only.

Misdemeanor, Civil Actions Under $15,000, Eviction, Small Claims, Probate—Saline County Court, 215 S Court St, Wilber, NE 68465. 402-821-2131. Fax: 402-821-2132. 8AM-5PM (CST). Access by: Fax, mail, in person.

Sarpy County

Real Estate Recording—Sarpy County Register of Deeds, 1210 Golden Gate Drive #1109, Papillion, NE 68046. 402-593-2186. Fax: 402-593-2338.

Felony, Civil Actions Over $15,000—District Court, 1210 Golden Gate Dr, Ste 3131, Papillion, NE 68046. 402-593-2267. Fax: 402-593-4403. 8AM-4:45PM (CST). Access by: Phone, mail, in person.

Misdemeanor, Civil Actions Under $15,000, Eviction, Small Claims, Probate—Sarpy County Court, 1210 Golden Gate Dr, Ste 3142, Papillion, NE 68046. 402-593-2248. 8AM-4:45PM (CST). Access by: Mail, in person.

Saunders County

Real Estate Recording—Saunders County Register of Deeds, 5th & Chestnut, Courthouse, Wahoo, NE 68066. 402-443-8111. Fax: 402-443-5010.

Felony, Civil Actions Over $15,000—District Court, County Courthouse, Wahoo, NE 68066. 402-443-8113. Fax: 402-443-5010. 8AM-5PM (CST). Access by: In person only.

Misdemeanor, Civil Actions Under $15,000, Eviction, Small Claims, Probate—Saunders County Court, 433 N Chestnut, Wahoo, NE 68066. 402-443-8119. Fax: 402-443-5010. 8AM-5PM (CST). Access by: Fax, mail, in person.

Scotts Bluff County

Real Estate Recording—Scotts Bluff County Register of Deeds, 1825 10th Street, Administration Office Building, Gering, NE 69341. 308-436-6607.

Felony, Civil Actions Over $15,000—District Court, 1725 10th St, PO Box 47, Gering, NE 69341-0047. 308-436-6641. Fax: 308-436-6759. 8AM-4:30PM (MST). Access by: Mail, in person.

Misdemeanor, Civil Actions Under $15,000, Eviction, Small Claims, Probate—Scotts Bluff County Court, 1725 10th St, Gering, NE 69341. 308-436-6648. 8AM-5PM (MST). Access by: In person only.

Seward County

Real Estate Recording—Seward County Clerk, 529 Seward Street, Seward, NE 68434. 402-643-2883. Fax: 402-643-4614. 8AM-5PM (CST).

Felony, Civil Actions Over $15,000—District Court, PO Box 36, Seward, NE 68434. 402-643-4895. 8AM-5PM (CST). Access by: In person only.

Misdemeanor, Civil Actions Under $15,000, Eviction, Small Claims, Probate—Seward County Court, PO Box 37, Seward, NE 68434. 402-643-3341. Fax: 402-643-2950. 8AM-5PM (CST). Access by: In person only.

Sheridan County

Real Estate Recording—Register of Deeds, 301 East 2nd Street, Rushville, NE 69360. 308-327-2633. 8:30AM-4:30PM (MST).

Felony, Civil Actions Over $15,000—District Court, PO Box 581, Rushville, NE 69360. 308-327-2123. Fax: 308-327-2712. 8:30AM-4:30PM (MST). Access by: Mail, in person.

Misdemeanor, Civil Actions Under $15,000, Eviction, Small Claims, Probate—Sheridan County Court, PO Box 430, Rushville, NE 69360. 308-327-2692. Fax: 308-327-2936. 8AM-4:30PM (MST). Access by: Fax, mail, in person.

Sherman County

Real Estate Recording—Sherman County Clerk, Courthouse, 630 "O" Street, Loup City, NE 68853. 308-745-1513. Fax: 308-745-1820. 8:30AM-4:30PM (CST).

Felony, Civil Actions Over $15,000—District Court, 630 O St, Loup City, NE 68853. 308-745-1513. Fax: 308-745-1820. 8:30AM-4:30PM (CST). Access by: Mail, in person.

Misdemeanor, Civil Actions Under $15,000, Eviction, Small Claims, Probate—Sherman County Court, 630 O St, Loup City, NE 68853. 308-745-1510. 8:30AM-4:30PM (CST). Access by: Mail, in person.

Sioux County

Real Estate Recording—Register of Deeds, Courthouse, Harrison, NE 69346. 308-668-2443. Fax: 308-668-2443. 8AM-5PM (MST).

Felony, Civil Actions Over $15,000—District Court, PO Box 158, Harrison, NE 69346. 308-668-2443. Fax: 308-668-2443. 8AM-5PM (MST). Access by: Mail, in person.

Misdemeanor, Civil Actions Under $15,000, Eviction, Small Claims, Probate—Sioux County Court, PO Box 477, Harrison, NE 69346. 308-668-2475. 8AM-12 (MST). Access by: Phone, mail, in person.

Stanton County

Real Estate Recording—Register of Deeds, 804 Ivy Street, Stanton, NE 68779. 402-439-2222. Fax: 402-439-2229. 8:30AM-4:30PM (CST).

Felony, Civil Actions Over $15,000—District Court, PO Box 347, Stanton, NE 68779. 402-439-2222. Fax: 402-439-2229. 8:30AM-4:30PM (CST). Access by: Fax, mail, in person.

Misdemeanor, Civil Actions Under $15,000, Eviction, Small Claims, Probate—Stanton County Court, 804 Ivey St, PO Box 536, Stanton, NE 68779. 402-439-2221. Fax: 402-439-2229. (CST). Access by: Mail, in person.

Thayer County

Real Estate Recording—Register of Deeds, 225 N. 4th, Hebron, NE 68370. 402-768-6126. 8AM-Noon,1-5PM (CST).

Felony, Civil Actions Over $15,000—District Court, PO Box 297, Hebron, NE 68370. 402-768-6116. Fax: 402-768-7232. 8AM-Noon, 1-5PM (CST). Access by: Fax, mail, in person.

Misdemeanor, Civil Actions Under $15,000, Eviction, Small Claims, Probate—Thayer County Court, PO Box 94, Hebron, NE 68370. 402-768-6325. Fax: 402-768-7232. 8AM-5PM (CST). Access by: Mail, in person.

Thomas County

Real Estate Recording—Thomas County Clerk, 503 Main Street, Thedford, NE 69166. 308-645-2261. Fax: 308-645-2623. 8AM-Noon, 1-4PM M-Th; 8AM-Noon, 1-3PM F (CST).

Felony, Civil Actions Over $15,000—District Court, PO Box 226, Thedford, NE 69166. 308-645-2261. Fax: 308-645-2623. 8:30AM-Noon,1-4:30PM (CST). Access by: Phone, mail, in person.

Misdemeanor, Civil Actions Under $15,000, Eviction, Small Claims, Probate—Thomas County Court, PO Box 233, Thedford, NE 69166. 308-645-2266. Fax: 308-645-2623. 8AM-4:30PM (CST). Access by: Mail, in person.

Thurston County

Real Estate Recording—Register of Deeds, 106 South 5th Street, Pender, NE 68047. 402-385-2343. Fax: 402-385-2343. 8:30AM-5PM (CST).

Felony, Civil Actions Over $15,000—District Court, PO Box 216, Pender, NE 68047. 402-385-3318. Fax: 402-385-2762. 8:30AM-5PM (CST). Access by: In person only.

Misdemeanor, Civil Actions Under $15,000, Eviction, Small Claims, Probate—Thurston County Court, County Courthouse, PO Box 129, Pender, NE 68047. 402-385-3136. Fax: 402-385-2762. 8:30AM-Noon,1-5PM (CST). Access by: In person only.

Valley County

Real Estate Recording—Register of Deeds, 125 South 15th, Ord, NE 68862. 308-728-3700. 8AM-5PM (CST).

Felony, Civil Actions Over $15,000—District Court, 125 S 15th St, Ord, NE 68862. 308-728-3700. Fax: 308-728-7725. 8AM-5PM (CST). Access by: Fax, mail, in person.

Misdemeanor, Civil Actions Under $15,000, Eviction, Small Claims, Probate—Valley County Court, 125 S 15th St, Ord, NE 68862. 308-728-3831. Fax: 308-728-7725. 8AM-5PM (CST). Access by: Phone, fax, mail, in person.

Washington County

Real Estate Recording—Register of Deeds, 1555 Colfax Street, Blair, NE 68008. 402-426-6822. Fax: 402-426-6825. 8AM-4:30PM (CST).

Felony, Civil Actions Over $15,000—District Court, PO Box 431, Blair, NE 68008. 402-426-6899. Fax: 402-426-6821. 8AM-4:30PM (CST). Access by: In person only.

Misdemeanor, Civil Actions Under $15,000, Eviction, Small Claims, Probate—Washington County Court, 1555 Colfax St, Blair, NE 68008. 402-426-6833. Fax: 402-426-6840. 8AM-4:30PM (CST). Access by: In person only.

Wayne County

Real Estate Recording—Register of Deeds, 510 Pearl Street, Wayne, NE 68787. 402-375-2288. Fax: 402-375-3702. 8:30AM-5PM (CST).

Felony, Civil Actions Over $15,000—District Court, 510 Pearl St, Wayne, NE 68787. 402-375-2260. 8:30AM-5PM (CST). Access by: Mail, in person.

Misdemeanor, Civil Actions Under $15,000, Eviction, Small Claims, Probate—Wayne County Court, 510 Pearl St, Wayne, NE 68787. 402-375-1622. Fax: 402-375-1622. 8:30AM-5PM (CST). Access by: In person only.

Webster County

Real Estate Recording—Webster County Clerk, 621 North Cedar, Court House, Red Cloud, NE 68970. 402-746-2716. Fax: 402-746-2710. 8AM-4:30PM (CST).

Felony, Civil Actions Over $15,000—District Court, 621 N Cedar, Red Cloud, NE 68970. 402-746-2716. Fax: 402-746-2710. 8:30AM-4:30PM (CST). Access by: Phone, fax, mail, in person.

Misdemeanor, Civil Actions Under $15,000, Eviction, Small Claims, Probate—Webster County Court, 621 N Cedar, Red Cloud, NE 68970. 402-746-2777. Fax: 402-746-2771. 8:30AM-4:30PM (CST). Access by: Fax, mail, in person.

Wheeler County

Real Estate Recording—Register of Deeds, Courthouse, Bartlett, NE 68622. 308-654-3235. Fax: 308-654-3442. 9AM-Noon, 1-5PM (CST).

Felony, Civil Actions Over $15,000—District Court, PO Box 127, Bartlett, NE 68622. 308-654-3235. Fax: 308-654-3442. 9AM-5PM (CST). Access by: Mail, in person.

Misdemeanor, Civil Actions Under $15,000, Eviction, Small Claims, Probate—Wheeler County Court, PO Box 127, Bartlett, NE 68622. 308-654-3376. Fax: 308-654-3442. 9AM-5PM (CST). Access by: Mail, in person.

York County

Real Estate Recording—Register of Deeds, Courthouse, 510 Lincoln Ave., York, NE 68467. 402-362-7759. Fax: 402-362-2651. 8:30AM-5PM (CST).

Felony, Civil Actions Over $15,000—District Court, 510 Lincoln Ave, York, NE 68467. 402-362-4038. Fax: 402-362-2577. 8:30AM-5PM (CST). Access by: In person only.

Misdemeanor, Civil Actions Under $15,000, Eviction, Small Claims, Probate—York County Court, 510 Lincoln Ave, York, NE 68467. 402-362-4925. Fax: 402-362-2577. 8AM-5PM (CST). Access by: In person only.

Federal Courts

US District Court
District of Nebraska

Lincoln Division, US District Court PO Box 83468, Lincoln, NE 68501. 402-437-5225. Counties: Nebraska cases may be filed in any of the three courts at the option of an attorney, but only during trial sessions in the case of North Platte

North Platte Division, US District Court c/o Lincoln Division, PO Box 83468, Lincoln, NE 68501. 402-221-4761. Counties: Nebraska cases may be filed in any of the three court locations at the option of an attorney, except that filings in North Platte must be during trial session

Omaha Division, US District Court PO Box 129, DTS, Omaha, NE 68101. 402-221-4761. Counties: Nebraska cases may be filed in any of the three courts at the option of an attorney, except that filings in North Platte must be during the trial session

US Bankruptcy Court
District of Nebraska

Lincoln Division, US Bankruptcy Court, 460 Federal Bldg, 100 Centennial Mall N, Lincoln, NE 68508. 402-437-5100. Voice Case Information System: 402-221-3757. Counties: Adams, Antelope, Boone, Boyd, Buffalo, Butler, Cass, Clay, Colfax, Fillmore, Franklin, Gage, Greeley, Hall, Hamilton, Harlan, Holt, Howard, Jefferson, Johnson, Kearney, Lancaster, Madison, Merrick, Nance, Nemaha, Nuckolls, Otoe, Pawnee, Phelps, Platte, Polk, Richardson, Saline, Saunders, Seward, Sherman, Thayer, Webster, Wheeler, York. Cases from the North Platte Division may also be assigned here

North Platte Division, US Bankruptcy Court, c/o Omaha Division, PO Box 129, DTS, Omaha, NE 68101. 402-221-4687. Voice Case Information System: 402-221-3757. Counties: Arthur, Banner, Blaine, Box Butte, Brown, Chase, Cherry, Cheyenne, Custer, Dawes, Dawson, Deuel, Dundy, Frontier, Furnas, Garden, Garfield, Gosper, Grant, Hayes, Hitchcock, Hooker, Keith, Keya Paha, Kimball, Lincoln, Logan, Loup, McPherson, Morrill, Perkins, Red Willow, Rock, Scotts Bluff, Sheridan, Sioux, Thomas, Valley. Cases may be randomly allocated to Omaha or Lincoln

Omaha Division, US Bankruptcy Court, PO Box 428, DTS, Omaha, NE 68101-4281. 402-221-4687. Voice Case Information System: 402-221-3757. Counties: Burt, Cedar, Cuming, Dakota, Dixon, Dodge, Douglas, Knox, Pierce, Sarpy, Stanton, Thurston, Washington, Wayne

Nevada

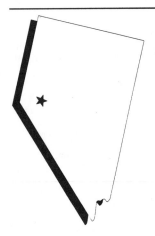

Capitol: Carson City (Carson City County)	
Number of Counties: 17	**Population:** 1,530,108
County Court Locations:	**Federal Court Locations:**
•District Courts: 17/9 Districts	•District Courts: 2
•Justice Courts: 47/56 Towns	•Bankruptcy Courts: 2
Municipal Courts: 19/ 19 Incorporated Cities/Towns	**State Agencies:** 19

State Agencies—Summary

General Help Numbers:

State Archives

State Library & Archives	702-687-5160
100 Stewart St	Fax: 702-687-8311
Carson City, NV 89701-4285	8AM-5PM
Historical Society:	702-688-1191
Reference Librarian:	702-687-5160

Governor's Office

Governor's Office	702-687-5670
Executive Chambers,	
Capitol Complex	Fax: 702-687-4486
Carson City, NV 89710	8AM-5PM

Attorney General's Office

Attorney General's Office	702-687-3510
Capitol Complex	Fax: 702-687-5798
Carson City, NV 89710	8AM-5PM

State Legislation

Nevada Legislature	702-687-6825
401 S Carson St	
Carson City, NV 89710	
Main Number:	702-687-6800
Publications:	702-687-6835

Important State Internet Sites:

🌐 Webscape		
File **Edit** **View**		**Help**

State of Nevada World Wide Web

www.state.nv.us/

This home page includes a welcome from the Governor and links to the Governor, state agencies and other sites.

The Governor's Office

www.state.nv.us/gov/gov.htm

This site includes information about the Governor's press releases, speeches, biography, and the Governor's different telephone and fax numbers.

State Legislature

www.leg.state.nv.us/

Available at this site are links the members of the State Legislature and their Committees, along with bills and resolutions.

Secretary of State

jvm.com/sos

This page is currently under construction, but will contain links to corporations, limited partnerships and other business entities. This site will also link to UCC information.

U.S. House and Senate Information

www.state.nv.us/executive/executive.htm#3

This site lists the NV members of the U.S. Congress and links to their e-mail addresses and their web pages.

State Agencies—Public Records

Criminal Records

Nevada Highway Patrol, Record & ID Services, 555 Wright Way, Carson City, NV 89711-0585, Main Telephone: 702-687-5713, Hours: 8AM-5PM. Access by: mail, visit.

Corporation Records
Limited Partnerships
Limited Liability Company Records
Limited Partnership Records

Secretary of State, Status Division, Capitol Annex, Capitol Bldg, Carson City, NV 89710, Main Telephone: 702-687-5203, Status Division: 702-687-5105, Copies Division: 702-687-3199, Fax: 702-687-3471, Hours: 8AM-5PM. Access by: mail, phone, visit, PC. Actual file copies are here, but records can be looked up on computer at the Las Vegas office. Fictitious Names and Assumed Names are found at the county level.

Trademarks/Servicemarks

Secretary of State, Corporate Expedite Office, 555 E. Washington Ave, #2900, Las Vegas, NV 89101, Main Telephone: 702-486-2880, Trademarks: 702-486-2885, Fax: 702-486-2888, Hours: 8AM-5PM. Access by: mail, phone, visit. Trademark files are kept here; however, they are on the same computer system as the Carson City office. They can do all of the same searches on corporate records as Carson City, except for making copies of actual documents in files.

Uniform Commercial Code
Federal Tax Liens
State Tax Liens

UCC Department, Secretary of State, Capitol Complex, Carson City, NV 89710, Main Telephone: 702-687-5298, Fax: 702-687-5071, Hours: 8AM-5PM. Access by: mail, fax, visit, PC.

Sales Tax Registrations

State does not impose sales tax.

Birth Certificates

Nevada Department of Health, Office of Vital Statistics, 505 E King St, Rm 102, Carson City, NV 89710, Main Telephone: 702-687-4481, Message Phone: 702-687-4480, Fax: 702-687-6151, Hours: 9AM-4PM. Access by: mail, visit.

Death Records

Nevada Department of Health, Office of Vital Statistics, 505 E King St, Rm 102, Carson City, NV 89710, Main Telephone: 702-687-4481, Message Phone: 702-687-4480, Fax: 702-687-6151, Hours: 9AM-4PM. Access by: mail, visit.

Marriage Certificates
Divorce Records

Records not available from state agency.

Workers' Compensation Records

State Industrial Insurance System, Workers Compensation Division, 515 E Musser St, Carson City, NV 89714, Main Telephone: 702-687-5220, Fax: 702-687-5786, Hours: 8AM-5PM. Access by: mail, visit.

Driver Records

Department of Motor Vehicles and Public Safety, Records Section, 555 Wright Way, Carson City, NV 89711-0250, Main Telephone: 702-687-5505, Fax: 702-687-3693, Hours: 8AM-5PM. Access by: mail, phone, visit. Copies of tickets may be obtained at the same address. There is no fee when requesting your own ticket, otherwise the fee is $8.

Vehicle Ownership
Vehicle Identification

Department of Motor Vehicles and Public Safety, Motor Vehicle Record Section, 555 Wright Way, Carson City, NV 89711-0250, Main Telephone: 702-687-5505, Fax: 702-687-3693, Hours: 8AM-5PM. Access by: mail, phone, visit.

Accident Reports

Department of Motor Vehicles, Highway Patrol Division, 555 Wright Way, Carson City, NV 89711, Main Telephone: 702-687-5300, Fax: 702-687-3564, Hours: 8AM-5PM. Access by: mail, fax, visit.

Hunting License Information
Fishing License Information

Division of Wildlife, PO Box 10678, Reno, NV 89520, Main Telephone: 702-688-1500, Fax: 702-688-1595, Hours: 8AM-12; 1PM-5PM. Access by: mail, phone.

County Courts and Recording Offices

What You Need to Know...

About the Courts

Administration

Nevada Supreme Court	702-687-5075
Administrative Office of the Courts	Fax: 702-687-5079
Capitol Complex, 201 S Carson St	9AM-5PM
Carson City, NV 89710	

Court Structure

The 56 Justice Courts are named for the township of jurisdiction. Probate is handled by the District Courts.

County courts have juvenile jurisdiction in all but 3 counties (Douglas, Lancaster, and Sarpy), which have separate Juvenile Courts. Probate is handled by County Courts. Many have records on microfiche back to the mid/late 1800s.

Searching Hints

Many of the Justice Courts are small, have very few records, the hours of operation vary widely, and contact is difficult. Recommend requesters call ahead for information prior to submitting a written request or attempting an in-person retrieval.

Online Access

There are some internal online computer systems, but none have external access nor is such access planned in the near future.

About the Recorder's Office

Organization

16 counties and **one independent city**, 17 filing offices. The recording officer is County Recorder. **Carson City has a separate filing office.** The entire state is in the Pacific Time Zone (PST).

UCC Records

Financing statements are filed at the state level, except for consumer goods, crops and real estate related collateral, which are filed only with the County Recorder. All filing offices will perform UCC searches. Search fees are $15.00 per debtor name using the approved UCC-3 request form and $20.00 using a non-Nevada. Copies cost $1.00 per page.

Lien Records

Federal tax liens on personal property of businesses are filed with the Secretary of State. Federal tax liens on personal property of individuals are filed with the County Recorder. Although **not** called state tax liens, employment withholding judgments have the same effect and are filed with the County Recorder. Most counties will provide tax lien searches for a fee of $15.00 per name—$20.00 if the standard UCC request form is not used. Other liens include mechanics.

Real Estate Records

Most counties will **not** provide real estate searches. Copies cost $1.00 per page and certification fees are usually $3.00 per document.

County Courts and Recording Offices

Carson City

Real Estate Recording—Carson City Recorder, 198 North Carson Street, Carson City, NV 89701. 702-887-2260. 8AM-5PM (PST).

Felony, Misdemeanor, Civil Actions Over $7,500, Probate—1st Judicial District Court, 198 N Carson St, Carson City, NV 89701. 702-887-2082. Fax: 702-887-2177. 9AM-5PM (PST). Access by: Mail, in person.

Civil Actions Under $7,500, Eviction, Small Claims—Justice Court Dept II, 111 W. Telegraph St, Suite 100, Carson City, NV 89701. 702-887-2275. Fax: 702-887-2297. 8:30AM-4:30PM (PST). Access by: Phone, fax, mail, in person.

Misdemeanor—Justice Court Dept I, 320 N Carson St, Carson City, NV 89701. 702-887-2121. Fax: 702-887-2297. 9AM-4PM M-W/9AM-5PM Th/9AM-3:30PM F (PST). Access by: Phone, fax, mail, in person.

Churchill County

Real Estate Recording—Churchill County Recorder, 10 West Williams Avenue, Fallon, NV 89406. 702-423-6001. Fax: 702-423-7069. 8AM-5PM (PST).

Felony, Misdemeanor, Civil Actions Over $7,500, Probate—3rd Judicial District Court, 73 N Maine St, Fallon, NV 89406. 702-423-6080. Fax: 702-423-8578. 8AM-Noon, 1-5PM (PST). Access by: Mail, in person.

Misdemeanor, Civil Actions Under $7,500, Eviction, Small Claims—Justice Court, 73 N Maine St, Fallon, NV 89406. 702-423-2845. Fax: 702-423-8578. 8AM-Noon, 1-5PM (PST). Access by: Mail, in person.

Clark County

Real Estate Recording—Clark County Recorder, 500 S. Grand Central Parkway, 2nd Floor, Las Vegas, NV 89106. 702-455-4336. Fax: 702-455-5644. 8AM-5PM (PST).

Felony, Misdemeanor, Civil Actions Over $7,500, Probate—8th Judicial District Court, 200 S 3rd (PO Box 551601), Las Vegas, NV 89155. 702-455-3156. Fax: 702-455-4929. 8AM-4PM (PST). Access by: Mail, in person.

Misdemeanor, Civil Actions Under $7,500, Eviction, Small Claims—Boulder Township Justice Court, 505 Avenue G, Boulder City, NV 89005. 702-455-8000. Fax: 702-455-8003. 7:30AM-5PM (PST). Access by: Fax, mail, in person.

Bunkerville Township Justice, 1st West & 1st North (PO Box 7185), Bunkerville, NV 89007. 702-346-5711. Fax: 702-346-7212. 8:30AM-11AM, 1:30-5PM M,W,Th; 2-5PM T (PST). Access by: Phone, mail, in person.

Henderson Township Justice, 241 Water St, Henderson, NV 89015. 702-455-7951. Fax: 702-455-7935. 7AM-6PM M-Th (PST). Access by: Mail, in person.

Goodsprings Township Jean Justice Court, 1 Main St (PO Box 19155), Jean, NV 89019. 702-874-1405. Fax: 702-874-1612. 8AM-4PM (PST). Access by: Fax, in person.

Las Vegas Township Justice, 200 S 3rd, 2nd Fl, PO Box 552511, Las Vegas, NV 89155-2511. 702-455-4435. Fax: 702-455-4529. 8AM-5PM (PST). Access by: Phone, fax, mail, in person.

Misdemeanor, Civil Actions Under $3,500, Eviction, Small Claims—Laughlin Township Justice Court, PO Box 2305, Laughlin, NV 89029. 702-298-4622. Fax: 702-298-7508. 8AM-5PM (PST). Access by: Fax, mail, in person.

Misdemeanor, Civil Actions Under $7,500, Eviction, Small Claims—Mesquite Township Justice Court, PO Box 1209, Mesquite, NV 89024. 702-346-5298. Fax: 702-346-7319. 8:30AM-5PM M,T; 8:30AM-1PM W (PST). Access by: Mail, in person.

Moapa Township Justice Court, 1340 E Com Hwy, PO Box 280, Moapa, NV 89025. 702-864-2333. Fax: 702-864-2585. 8AM-5PM M-Th (PST). Access by: Mail, in person.

North Las Vegas Township Justice, 1916 N Bruce, N Las Vegas, NV 89030. 702-455-7802. Civil: 702-455-7801. Fax: 702-399-3099. 8:30AM-4:45 PM (PST). Access by: Phone, mail, in person.

Moapa Valley Township Justice, 320 N Moapa Valley Blvd, PO Box 337, Overton, NV 89040. 702-397-2840. Fax: 702-397-2842. 7AM-4PM M-Th (PST). Access by: Mail, in person.

Searchlight Township Justice, PO Box 815, Searchlight, NV 89046. 702-297-1252. Fax: 702-297-1263. 7AM-5:30PM M-Th (PST). Access by: Fax, mail, in person.

Douglas County

Real Estate Recording—Douglas County Recorder, 1616 8th Street, Minden, NV 89423. 702-782-9026. 9AM-5PM (PST).

Felony, Civil Actions Over $7,500, Probate—9th Judicial District Court, Box 218, Minden, NV 89423. 702-782-9820. Fax: 702-782-9964. 8AM-5PM (PST). Access by: Mail, in person.

Misdemeanor, Civil Actions Under $7,500, Eviction, Small Claims—E Fork Justice Court, PO Box 218, Minden, NV 89423. 702-782-9955. Fax: 702-782-9964. 8AM-5PM (PST). Access by: Mail, in person.

Tahoe Justice Court, PO Box 7169, Stateline, NV 89449. 702-588-8100. Fax: 702-588-6844. 9AM-5PM (PST). Access by: Mail, in person.

Elko County

Real Estate Recording—Elko County Recorder, 571 Idaho St., Room 103, Elko, NV 89801. 702-738-6526. Fax: 702-738-3299. 9AM-5PM (PST).

Felony, Misdemeanor, Civil Actions Over $7,500, Probate—4th Judicial District Court, 571 Idaho St, 3rd Flr, Elko, NV 89801. 702-753-4600. Fax: 702-753-4610. 9AM-5PM (PST). Access by: Phone, fax, mail, in person.

Misdemeanor, Civil Actions Under $7,500, Eviction, Small Claims—Carlin Justice Court, PO Box 789, Carlin, NV 89822. 702-754-6321. Fax: 702-754-6893. 8AM-5PM (PST). Access by: Mail, in person.

Elko Justice Court, PO Box 176, Elko, NV 89803. 702-738-8403. Fax: 702-738-8416. 9AM-5PM (PST). Access by: Mail, in person.

Jackpot Justice Court, PO Box 229, Jackpot, NV 89825. 702-755-2456. Fax: 702-755-2727. 9AM-Noon, 1-5PM (PST). Access by: Phone, fax, mail, in person.

Jarbidge Justice Court, PO Box 26001, Jarbidge, NV 89826-2001. 702-488-2331. (PST). Access by: In person only.

Mountain City Justice Court, Courthouse, Mountain City, NV 89831. 702-763-6686. (PST). Access by: Mail, in person.

Wells Justice Municipal Court, PO Box 297, Wells, NV 89835. 702-752-3726. Fax: 702-752-3363. 9AM-Noon,1-5PM (PST). Access by: Mail, in person.

Eastline Justice Court, PO Box 2300, Wendover, NV 89883. 702-664-2305. Fax: 702-664-2979. 9AM-4PM (PST). Access by: Mail, in person.

Esmeralda County

Real Estate Recording—Esmeralda County Recorder, 458 Crook Street, Courthouse, Goldfield, NV 89013. 702-485-6337. Fax: 702-485-3524. 8AM-Noon,1-5PM (PST).

Felony, Misdemeanor, Civil Actions Over $7,500, Probate—5th Judicial District Court, PO Box 547, Goldfield, NV 89013. 702-485-6367. Fax: 702-485-3524. 8AM-5PM (PST). Access by: Fax, mail, in person.

Misdemeanor, Civil Actions Under $7,500, Eviction, Small Claims—Esmeralda Justice Court, PO Box 370, Goldfield, NV 89013. 702-485-6359. Fax: 702-485-3524. 8AM-5PM (PST). Access by: Phone, fax, mail, in person.

Eureka County

Real Estate Recording—Eureka County Recorder, 701 S. Main Street, Eureka, NV 89316. 702-237-5263. Fax: 702-237-5614. 8AM-Noon, 1-5PM (PST).

Felony, Misdemeanor, Civil Actions Over $7,500, Probate—7th Judicial District Court, PO Box 677, Eureka, NV 89316. 702-237-5262. Fax: 702-237-6015. 8AM-Noon, 1-5PM (PST). Access by: Phone, fax, mail, in person.

Misdemeanor, Civil Actions Under $7,500, Eviction, Small Claims—Beowawe Justice Court, PO Box 211065A, Beowawe Valley, NV 89821. 702-468-0244. Fax: 702-468-0323. 8AM-5PM (PST). Access by: Mail, in person.

Eureka Justice Court, PO Box 496, Eureka, NV 89316. 702-237-5540. Fax: 702-237-6016. 8AM-Noon,1-5PM (PST). Access by: Phone, fax, mail, in person.

Humboldt County

Real Estate Recording—Humboldt County Recorder, 25 West 4th Street, Winnemucca, NV 89445. 702-623-6413. 8AM-5PM (PST).

Felony, Misdemeanor, Civil Actions Over $7,500, Probate—6th Judicial District Court, 50 W Fifth St, Winnemucca, NV 89445. 702-623-6343. Fax: 702-623-6302. 8AM-5PM (PST). Access by: Phone, fax, mail, in person.

Misdemeanor, Civil Actions Under $7,500, Eviction, Small Claims—Union Justice Court, PO Box 1218, Winnemucca, NV 89446. 702-623-6377. Fax: 702-623-6439. 7AM-5PM (PST). Access by: Fax, mail, in person.

Lander County

Real Estate Recording—Lander County Recorder, 315 South Humboldt, Battle Mountain, NV 89820. 702-635-5173. Fax: 702-635-8272. 8AM-5PM (PST).

Felony, Misdemeanor, Civil Actions Over $7,500, Probate—6th Judicial District Court, 315 S Humboldt, Battle Mountain, NV 89820. 702-635-5738. Fax: 702-635-5761. 8AM-5PM (PST). Access by: Phone, fax, mail, in person.

Misdemeanor, Civil Actions Under $7,500, Eviction, Small Claims—Austin Justice Court, PO Box 100, Austin, NV 89310. 702-964-2380. Fax: 702-964-2327. 8AM-5PM M, 8AM-Noon T-Th (PST). Access by: Mail, in person.

Argenta Justice Court, 315 S Humboldt, Battle Mountain, NV 89820. 702-635-5151. Fax: 702-635-0604. 8AM-5PM (PST). Access by: Phone, fax, mail, in person.

Lincoln County

Real Estate Recording—Lincoln County Recorder, 1 Main Street, Courthouse, Pioche, NV 89043. 702-962-5495. Fax: 702-962-5180. 9AM-5PM (PST).

Felony, Misdemeanor, Civil Actions Over $7,500, Probate—7th Judicial District Court, PO Box 90, Pioche, NV 89043. 702-962-5390. Fax: 702-962-5180. 9AM-5PM (PST). Access by: Mail, in person.

Misdemeanor, Civil Actions Under $7,500, Eviction, Small Claims—Pahranagat Valley Justice Court, PO Box 449, Alamo, NV 89001. 702-725-3357. Fax: 702-725-3566. 9AM-5PM (PST). Access by: Mail, in person.

Meadow Valley Justice Court, PO Box 36, Pioche, NV 89043. 702-962-5140. Fax: 702-962-5877. 9AM-5PM (PST). Access by: Fax, mail, in person.

Lyon County

Real Estate Recording—Lyon County Recorder, 31 South Main Street, Yerington, NV 89447. 702-463-6581. Fax: 702-463-6585. 8AM-5PM (PST).

Felony, Misdemeanor, Civil Actions Over $7,500, Probate—3rd Judicial District Court, PO Box 816, Yerington, NV 89447. 702-463-6503. Fax: 702-463-6575. 8AM-5PM (PST). Access by: Phone, mail, in person.

Misdemeanor, Civil Actions Under $7,500, Eviction, Small Claims—Dayton Township Justice Court, PO Box 490, Dayton, NV 89403. 702-246-6233. Fax: 702-246-6236. 8AM-5PM (PST). Access by: Fax, mail, in person.

Canal Justice Court, PO Box 497, Fernley, NV 89408. 702-575-3355. Fax: 702-575-3359. 8AM-5PM (PST). Access by: Phone, fax, mail, in person.

Smith Valley Justice Court, PO Box 141, Smith, NV 89430. 702-465-2313. 8AM-Noon Fri or by appointment (PST). Access by: Phone, mail, in person.

Mason Valley Justice Court, 30 Nevin Way, Yerington, NV 89447. 702-463-6639. Fax: 702-463-6610. 8AM-5PM (PST). Access by: Phone, mail, in person.

Mineral County

Real Estate Recording—Mineral County Recorder, 105 South A Street, P.O. Box 1447, Hawthorne, NV 89415. 702-945-3676. Fax: 702-945-0706. 8AM-5PM (PST).

Felony, Misdemeanor, Civil Actions Over $7,500, Probate—5th Judicial District Court, PO Box 1450, Hawthorne, NV 89415. 702-945-2446. Fax: 702-945-0706. 8AM-5PM (PST). Access by: Phone, fax, mail, in person.

Misdemeanor, Civil Actions Under $7,500, Eviction, Small Claims—Hawthorne Justice Court, PO Box 1660, Hawthorne, NV 89415. 702-945-3859. Fax: 702-945-0700. 8AM-5PM (PST). Access by: Phone, fax, mail, in person.

Mina Justice Court, PO Box 415, Mina, NV 89422. 702-573-2547. Fax: 702-573-2244. 9AM-Noon, 2-4PM (PST). Access by: Mail, in person.

Schurz Justice Court, PO Box 220, Schurz, NV 89427. 702-773-2241. Fax: 702-773-2030. (PST). Access by: Fax, mail, in person.

Nye County

Real Estate Recording—Nye County Recorder, 101 Radar Rd., Tonopah, NV 89049. 702-482-8116. Fax: 702-482-8111. 8AM-Noon, 1-5PM (PST).

Felony, Misdemeanor, Civil Actions Over $7,500, Probate—5th Judicial District Court, PO Box 1031, Tonopah, NV 89049. 702-482-8131. Fax: 702-482-8133. 8AM-5PM (PST). Access by: Phone, fax, mail, in person.

Misdemeanor, Civil Actions Under $7,500, Eviction, Small Claims—Beatty Justice Court, PO Box 805, Beatty, NV 89003. 702-553-2951. Fax: 702-553-2136. 8AM-5PM (PST). Access by: Phone, mail, in person.

Gabbs Justice Court, PO Box 533, Gabbs, NV 89409. 702-285-2379. Fax: 702-285-4263. 9AM-4PM M-Th (PST). Access by: Phone, mail, in person.

Tonopah Justice Court, PO Box 1151, Tonopah, NV 89049. 702-482-8153. 8AM-5PM (PST). Access by: Phone, mail, in person.

Pershing County

Real Estate Recording—Pershing County Recorder, Courthouse, 400 Main Street, Lovelock, NV 89419. 702-273-2408. Fax: 702-273-7058. 8AM-5PM (PST).

Felony, Civil Actions Over $7,500, Probate—6th Judicial District Court, PO Box 820, Lovelock, NV 89419. 702-273-2208. Fax: 702-273-7058. 9AM-5PM (PST). Access by: Phone, fax, mail, in person.

Misdemeanor, Civil Actions Under $7,500, Eviction, Small Claims—Lake Township Justice Court, PO Box 8, Lovelock, NV 89419. 702-273-2753. Fax: 702-273-0416. 8AM-5PM (PST). Access by: Phone, mail, in person.

Storey County

Real Estate Recording—Storey County Recorder, B Street, Courthouse, Virginia City, NV 89440. 702-847-0967. Fax: 702-847-0949. 9AM-5PM (PST).

Felony, Misdemeanor, Civil Actions Over $7,500, Probate—1st Judicial District Court, PO Drawer D, Virginia City, NV 89440. 702-847-0969. Fax: 702-847-0949. 9AM-5PM (PST). Access by: Phone, fax, mail, in person.

Misdemeanor, Civil Actions Under $7,500, Eviction, Small Claims—Virginia City Justice Court, PO Box 674, Virginia City, NV 89440. 702-847-0962. Fax: 702-847-0915. 9AM-5PM (PST). Access by: Phone, fax, mail, in person.

Washoe County

Real Estate Recording—Washoe County Recorder, 1001 East 9th Street, Reno, NV 89512. 702-328-3661. 8AM-5PM (PST).

Felony, Misdemeanor, Civil Actions Over $7,500, Probate—2nd Judicial District Court, PO Box 11130, Reno, NV 89520. 702-328-3110. Fax: 702-328-3515. 8AM-5PM (PST). Access by: Phone, mail, in person.

Misdemeanor, Civil Actions Under $7,500, Eviction, Small Claims—Reno Justice Court, PO Box 11130, Reno, NV 89520. 702-325-6500. Fax: 702-325-6510. 8AM-5PM (PST). Access by: Phone, mail, in person.

Sparks Justice Court, 630 Greenbrae Dr, Sparks, NV 89431. 702-352-3000. 8AM-5PM (PST). Access by: Mail, in person.

White Pine County

Real Estate Recording—White Pine County Recorder, Courthouse Plaza, Ely, NV 89301. 702-289-4567. Fax: 702-289-1541. 9AM-5PM (PST).

Felony, Misdemeanor, Civil Actions Over $7,500, Probate—7th Judicial District Court, PO Box 659, Ely, NV 89301. 702-289-2341. Fax: 702-289-2544. 9AM-5PM (PST). Access by: Phone, fax, mail, in person.

Misdemeanor, Civil Actions Under $7,500, Eviction, Small Claims—Ely Justice Court, PO Box 396, Ely, NV 89301. 702-289-2678. Fax: 702-289-3392. 9AM-5PM (PST). Access by: Phone, fax, mail, in person.

Lund Justice Court, PO Box 86, Lund, NV 89317. 702-238-5400. Fax: 702-238-5400. 10AM-2:30PM M,T,Th,F (PST). Access by: Fax, mail, in person.

Federal Courts

US District Court
District of Nevada

Las Vegas Division, US District Court Room 4426, 300 Las Vegas Blvd S, Las Vegas, NV 89101. 702-388-6351. Counties: Clark, Esmeralda, Lincoln, Nye

Reno Division, US District Court Room 301, 400 S Virginia St, Reno, NV 89501. 702-686-5800. Counties: Carson City, Churchill, Douglas, Elko, Eureka, Humboldt, Lander, Lyon, Mineral, Pershing, Storey, Washoe, White Pine

US Bankruptcy Court
District of Nevada

Las Vegas Division, US Bankruptcy Court, Room 2130, 300 Las Vegas Blvd S, Las Vegas, NV 89101. 702-388-6257. Voice Case Information System: 702-388-6708. Counties: Clark, Esmeralda, Lincoln, Nye

Reno-Northern Division, US Bankruptcy Court, Room 1109, 300 Booth St, Reno, NV 89509. 702-784-5559. Voice Case Information System: 702-388-6708. Counties: Carson City, Churchill, Douglas, Elko, Eureka, Humboldt, Lander, Lyon, Mineral, Pershing, Storey, Washoe, White Pine

New Hampshire

Capitol: Concord (Merrimack County)	
Number of Counties: 10	**Population:** 1,148,253
County Court Locations:	**Federal Court Locations:**
•Superior Courts: 11/ 10 Counties	•District Courts: 1
•District Courts: 36/40 Districts	•Bankruptcy Courts: 1
•Municipal Courts: 2/2 Cities	**State Agencies:** 20
•Probate Courts: 10/10 Counties	
•Family Court: 8	

State Agencies—Summary

General Help Numbers:

State Archives

Department of State	603-271-2236
Records Management & Archives	Fax: 603-271-2272
71 S Fruit St	8AM-4:30PM
Concord, NH 03301	
Reference Librarian:	603-271-2397
Reference Librarian FAX:	603-271-2205

Governor's Office

Governor's Office	603-271-2121
State House	Fax: 603-271-2130
107 N Main St, Rm 208	8:30AM-5PM
Concord, NH 03301	

Attorney General's Office

Attorney General's Office	603-271-3658
33 Capitol St	Fax: 603-271-2110
Concord, NH 03301-6397	8AM-5PM
Alternate Telephone:	603-271-3655

State Legislation

New Hampshire State Library	603-271-2239
20 Part St	Fax: 603-271-2205
Concord, NH 03301	8AM-4:30PM

A dial-up system is available at a $100 setup cost plus $.75 per minute after the first month. Information includes bill status, text of bills, calendars, and other legislative data. Wang emulation software is required. Call 603-271-2021 or see their Internet site at www.state.nh.us for more information.

Important State Internet Sites:

> **⊘ Webscape**
> **File Edit View   Help**

State of New Hampshire World Wide Web
www.state.nh.us/

Links to major locations in the Maryland State Government, state libraries, education, employment and many other sites.

The Governor's Office
www.state.nh.us/governor/index.html

This site includes information about the Governor, his State of the State address, his press releases, speeches and biography.

New Hampshire General Court
www.state.nh.us/gencourt/gencourt.htm

The General Court home page links to 1996 House and Senate Bills and Resolutions, the members of the House and Senate and the state constitution.

Abandoned Property
www.state.nh.us/treasury/appage.html

You can now search by name, online for abandoned property. Any necessary forms are available online.

U.S. House and Senate Information
www.state.nh.us/nhcong/nhcong.html

This site lists the NH members of the U.S. Congress and links to their addresses, phone numbers, and you can send them e-mail.

State Agencies—Public Records

Criminal Records

State Police Headquarters, Criminal Records, James H. Hayes Bldg, 10 Hazen Dr, Concord, NH 03305, Main Telephone: 603-271-2538, Hours: 8:15AM-4:15PM. Access by: mail, visit.

Corporation Records
Limited Partnership Records
Limited Liability Company Records
Trademarks/Servicemarks
Trade Names
Limited Liability Partnerships

Secretary of State, Corporation Division, State House, Room 204, Concord, NH 03301, Main Telephone: 603-271-3244, Fax for expedited service: 603-271-3247, Hours: 8AM-4:30PM. Access by: mail, fax, phone, visit.

Uniform Commercial Code
Federal Tax Liens
State Tax Liens

UCC Division, Secretary of State, 25 Capitol St, State House Annex, 3rd Floor, Concord, NH 03301, Main Telephone: 603-271-3276, Hours: 9AM-3:30PM (searches). Access by: mail, visit.

Sales Tax Registrations

State does not impose sales tax.

Birth Certificates

Office of Health Management, Bureau of Vital Records, 6 Hazen Dr, Concord, NH 03301-6527, Main Telephone: 603-271-4650, Fax: 603-271-3447, Hours: 8:30AM-4PM. Access by: mail, phone, visit. For genealogical purposes, birth records prior to 1901 may be released without restriction.

Death Records

Division of Public Health Services, Bureau of Vital Records, 6 Hazen Dr, Concord, NH 03301-6527, Main Telephone: 603-271-4650, Fax: 603-271-3447, Hours: 8:30AM-4PM. Access by: mail, phone, visit. For genealogical purposes, death records prior to 1938 may be released without restriction.

Marriage Certificates

Office of Health Management, Bureau of Vital Records & Health Statistics, 6 Hazen Dr, Concord, NH 03301-6527, Main Telephone: 603-271-4650, Fax: 603-271-3447, Hours: 8:30AM-4PM. Access by: mail, phone, visit. For genealogical purposes, marriage records prior to 1938 may be released without restriction.

Divorce Records

Division of Public Health Services, Bureau of Vital Records, 6 Hazen Dr, Concord, NH 03301-6527, Main Telephone: 603-271-4650, Fax: 603-271-3447, Hours: 8:30AM-4PM. Access by: mail, phone, visit. For genealogical purposes, divorce records prior to 1938 may be released without restriction.

Workers' Compensation Records

Labor Department, Workers Compensation Division, State Office Park S, 95 Pleasant St, Concord, NH 03301, Main Telephone: 603-271-3174, Hours: 8AM-4:30PM. Access by: mail only.

Driver Records

Department of Motor Vehicles, Driving Records, 10 Hazen Dr, Concord, NH 03305, Main Telephone: 603-271-2322, Hours: 8:15AM-4:15PM. Access by: mail, visit. New Hampshire recommends going to the local courts for copies of tickets or Financial Responsibility.

Vehicle Identification

Department of Safety, Bureau of Title, 10 Hazen Dr, Concord, NH 03305, Main Telephone: 603-271-3111, Hours: 8:15AM-4:15PM. Access by: mail, visit.

Vehicle Ownership

Department of Safety, Registration, PO Box 327640, Montgomery, AL 36132-7640, Main Telephone: 603-271-2251, Hours: 8:15AM-4:15PM. Access by: mail, visit.

Accident Reports

Department of Safety, Accident Reproduction Section, 10 Hazen Dr, Concord, NH 03305, Main Telephone: 603-271-2128, Hours: 8:15AM-4:15PM. Access by: mail only.

Hunting License Information
Fishing License Information

Fish & Game Department, Licensing Department, Two Hazen Dr, Concord, NH 03301, Main Telephone: 603-271-3421, Fax: 603-271-1438, Hours: 8AM-4:30PM. Access by: mail, visit.

County Courts and Recording Offices

What You Need to Know...

About the Courts	About the Recorder's Office

About the Courts

Administration

Administrative Office of Courts	603-271-2521
Supreme Court Bldg, Noble Dr	Fax: 603-271-3977
Concord, NH 03301-6160	8AM-5PM

Court Structure

Felony cases include Class A misdemeanors.

The District Court upper civil limit is $25,000.

Filing a civil case in the "overlap" area between the Superior Court minimum and the District Court maximum is at the discretion of the filer.

There are only 2 Municipal Courts left in New Hampshire, Rye and Greenville, which may remain for as long as 7 years; the Hinsdale Municipal Court closed in July 1994. The courts are closed as the judge retires and the case load and records are absorbed by the nearest District Court.

Searching Hints

There is no statutory search fee; however, one is under consideration because of the large number of requests handled in some offices. All courts have gone on computer.

Online Access

There is no remote online computer access available.

About the Recorder's Office

Organization

238 cities/towns and 10 counties, 242 filing offices. The recording officers are Town/City Clerk and Register of Deeds (real estate only). Each town/city profile indicates the county in which the town/city is located. **Be careful to distinguish the following names that are identical for both a town/city and a county—**Grafton, Hillsborough, Merrimack, Strafford, and Sullivan. Many towns are so small that their mailing addresses are within another town. The following unincorporated towns do **not** have a Town Clerk, so all liens are located at the corresponding county: Cambridge (Coos), Dicksville (Coos), Green's Grant (Coos), Hale's Location (Carroll), Millsfield (Coos), and Wentworth's Location (Coos). The entire state is in the Eastern Time Zone (EST).

UCC Records

This is a **dual filing state**. Financing statements are filed at the state level and with the Town/City Clerk, except for consumer goods and farm related collateral, which are filed only with the Town/City Clerk, and real estate related collateral, which are filed with the county Register of Deeds. Most filing offices will perform UCC searches. Use search request form UCC-11. Search fees are usually $5.00 per debtor name using the standard UCC-11 request form and $7.00 using a non-standard form. Copy fees are usually $.75 per page.

Lien Records

Federal and state tax liens on personal property of businesses are filed with the Secretary of State. Other federal and state tax liens on personal property are filed with the Town/City Clerk. Federal and state tax liens on real property are filed with the county Register of Deeds. There is wide variation in indexing and searching practices among the filing offices. Where a search fee of $7.00 is indicated, it refers to a non-standard request form such as a letter. Other liens include condominium, town tax, mechanics, and welfare.

Real Estate Records

Real estate transactions are recorded at the county level, and property taxes are handled at the town/city level. Local town real estate ownership and assessment records are usually located at the Selectman's Office. Each town/city profile indicates the county in which the town/city is located. Most counties will **not** perform real estate searches. Copy fees vary. Certification fees generally are $2.00 per document.

County Courts and Recording Offices

Belknap County

Real Estate Recording—Belknap County Register of Deeds, 64 Court St., Laconia, NH 03246. 603-524-0618. Fax: 603-524-1748. 8:30AM-4PM (EST).

Felony, Civil Actions Over $1,500—Superior Court, 64 Court St, Laconia, NH 03246. 603-524-3570. 8AM-4:30PM (EST). Access by: Phone, mail, in person.

Misdemeanor, Civil Actions Under $20,000, Eviction, Small Claims—Laconia District Court, 26 Academy St, Laconia, NH 03246. 603-524-4128. 8AM-4:30PM (EST). Access by: Mail, in person.

Probate—Probate Court, 64 Court St, PO Box 1343, Laconia, NH 03247-1343. 603-524-0903. 8:30AM-4:30PM (EST). Access by: Mail, in person.

Carroll County

Real Estate Recording—Carroll County Register of Deeds, Route 171, Ossipee, NH 03864. 603-539-4872. Fax: 603-539-5239. 9AM-5PM (EST).

Felony, Civil Actions Over $1,500—Superior Court, PO Box 433, Ossipee, NH 03864. 603-539-2201. 8AM-4:30PM (EST). Access by: Mail, in person.

Misdemeanor, Civil Actions Under $25,000, Eviction, Small Claims—Northern Carroll County District Court, PO Box 940, Conway, NH 03818. 603-356-7710. 8:30AM-4:30PM (EST). Access by: Phone, mail, in person.

Southern Carroll County District Court, PO Box 421, Ossipee, NH 03864. 603-539-4561. 8AM-4PM (EST). Access by: Mail, in person.

Probate—Probate Court, PO Box 419, Ossipee, NH 03864. 603-539-4123. Fax: 603-539-4761. 8:30AM-4:30PM (phone is answered from 11:30 AM-4:30 PM (EST). Access by: Mail, in person.

Cheshire County

Real Estate Recording—Cheshire County Register of Deeds, 33 West Street, Keene, NH 03431. 603-352-0403. Fax: 603-352-7678. 8:30-4:30PM (EST).

Felony, Civil Actions Over $1,500—Superior Court, PO Box 444, Keene, NH 03431. 603-352-6902. 9AM-4:30PM (EST). Access by: Mail, in person.

Misdemeanor, Civil Actions Under $25,000, Eviction, Small Claims—Jaffrey-Peterborough District Court, 7 Knight St, PO Box 39, Jaffrey, NH 03452-0039. 603-532-8698. 8AM-4PM (EST). Access by: Mail, in person.

Keene District Court, PO Box 364, Keene, NH 03431. 603-352-2559. 8AM-4PM (EST). Access by: Mail, in person.

Probate—Probate Court, 12 Court St, Keene, NH 03431. 603-357-7786. 8AM-4:30PM (EST). Access by: Mail, in person.

Coos County

Real Estate Recording—Coos County Register of Deeds, Coos County Courthouse, 55 School St, Suite 103, Lancaster, NH 03584. 603-788-2392. Fax: 603-788-4291. 8AM-4PM (EST).

Felony, Civil Actions Over $1,500—Superior Court, PO Box 309, Lancaster, NH 03584. 603-788-4900. 8AM-4:15PM (EST). Access by: Phone, mail, in person.

Misdemeanor, Civil Actions Under $25,000, Eviction, Small Claims—Berlin District Court, 220 Main St, Berlin, NH 03570. 603-752-3160. 8AM-4PM (EST). Access by: Mail, in person.

Colebrook District Court, PO Box 5, Colebrook, NH 03576. 603-237-4229. 8AM-Noon,1-4PM (EST). Access by: Mail, in person.

Gorham District Court, PO Box 176, Gorham, NH 03581. 603-466-2454. Fax: 603-466-3631. 8AM-4PM (EST). Access by: Mail, in person.

Lancaster District Court, PO Box 485, Lancaster, NH 03584. 603-788-4485. 8:30AM-4PM (EST). Access by: Mail, in person.

Probate—Probate Court, Box 306, Lancaster, NH 03584. 603-788-2001. 8AM-4PM (EST). Access by: Mail, in person.

Grafton County

Real Estate Recording—Grafton County Register of Deeds, Route 10, North Haverhill, NH 03774. 603-787-6921. Fax: 603-787-2363. 7:30AM-4:30PM (Research); 8AM-3:45PM(Recording) (EST).

Felony, Civil Actions Over $1,500—Superior Court, RR1 Box 65, North Haverhill, NH 03774. 603-787-6961. 8AM-4:30PM (EST). Access by: Mail, in person.

Misdemeanor, Civil Actions Under $25,000, Eviction, Small Claims—Hanover District Court, 57 N Park St, PO Box 247, Lebanon, NH 03766. 603-643-5681. 8AM-4PM (EST). Access by: Mail, in person.

Littleton District Court, 134 Main St, Littleton, NH 03561. 603-444-7750. 8AM-4PM (EST). Access by: Mail, in person.

Plymouth District Court, 26 Green St, Plymouth, NH 03264. 603-536-3326. 8AM-4PM (EST). Access by: Mail, in person.

Haverhill District Court, Municipal Bldg, Court St, Woodsville, NH 03785. 603-747-3063. 8:30AM-4:30PM (EST). Access by: Mail, in person.

Probate—Probate Court, RR1 Box 65C, North Haverhill, NH 03774-9700. 603-787-6931. 8AM-4PM (EST). Access by: Phone, mail, in person.

Hillsborough County

Real Estate Recording—Hillsborough County Treasurer, 19 Temple Street, Nashua, NH 03060. 603-882-6933. Fax: 603-594-4137. 8AM-3:45PM (EST).

Felony, Civil Actions Over $1,500—Superior Court-North District, 300 Chestnut St Rm 127, Manchester, NH 03101. 603-424-9951. 8:30AM-4PM (EST). Access by: Mail, in person.

Superior Court-South District, 30 Spring St, Nashua, NH 03061. 603-883-6461. 8:30AM-4PM (EST). Access by: Mail, in person.

Misdemeanor, Civil Actions Under $25,000, Eviction, Small Claims—Milford District Court, PO Box 148, Amherst, NH 03031. 603-673-2900. 8AM-4PM (EST). Access by: Phone, mail, in person.

Goffstown District Court, PO Box 129, Goffstown, NH 03045. 603-497-2597. 8AM-4PM (EST). Access by: Mail, in person.

Hillsborough District Court, PO Box 763, Hillsborough, NH 03244. 603-464-5811. 8AM-3:30PM (EST). Access by: Mail, in person.

Manchester District Court, PO Box 456, Manchester, NH 03105. 603-624-6510. 8AM-4PM (EST). Access by: Mail, in person.

Merrimack District Court, PO Box 324, Merrimack, NH 03054-0324. 603-424-9916. 8:30AM-3PM (EST). Access by: Mail, in person.

Nashua District Court, Walnut St Oval, Nashua, NH 03060. 603-880-3333. 8AM-4:15PM (EST). Access by: Mail, in person.

Probate—Probate Court, PO Box P, Nashua, NH 03061. 603-882-1231. Fax: 603-882-1620. 8AM-4PM (EST). Access by: Mail, in person.

Merrimack County

Real Estate Recording—Merrimack County Register of Deeds, 163 North Main St., Concord, NH 03301. 603-228-0101. Fax: 603-226-0868. 8AM-4:15PM (EST).

Felony, Civil Actions Over $1,500—Superior Court, PO Box 2880, Concord, NH 03302-2880. 603-225-5501. 8:30AM-4PM (EST). Access by: Mail, in person.

Misdemeanor, Civil Actions Under $25,000, Eviction, Small Claims—Concord District Court, 32 Clinton St, PO Box 3420, Concord, NH 03302-1512. 603-271-6400. Fax: 603-271-6413. 8AM-4PM; Drive-up hours 7:30AM-4:30PM (EST). Access by: Mail, in person.

Franklin District Court, PO Box 172, Franklin, NH 03235. 603-934-3290. 8AM-4PM (EST). Access by: Mail, in person.

Henniker District Court, 2 Depot St, Henniker, NH 03242. 603-428-3214. 8AM-4PM (EST). Access by: Mail, in person.

Hooksett District Court, 101 Merrimack, Hooksett, NH 03106. 603-485-9901. 8:30AM-4PM (EST). Access by: Mail, in person.

New London District Court, PO Box 1966, New London, NH 03257. 603-526-6519. 8:30AM-4:30PM (EST). Access by: Mail, in person.

Probate—Probate Court, 163 N Main St, Concord, NH 03301. 603-224-9589. 8AM-4:30PM (EST). Access by: Mail, in person.

Rockingham County

Real Estate Recording—Rockingham County Register of Deeds, #10 Route 125, Brentwood, NH 03833. 603-642-5526. Fax: 603-642-8548. 8AM-4PM (EST).

Felony, Civil Actions Over $1,500—Superior Court, PO Box 1258, Kingston, NH 03848. 603-642-5256. 8AM-4PM (EST). Access by: In person only.

Misdemeanor, Civil Actions Under $25,000, Eviction, Small Claims—Auburn District Court, 284 Route 28 Bypass, Auburn, NH 03032. 603-624-2084. 8AM-4:30PM (EST). Access by: Phone, mail, in person.

Derry District Court, 29 W Broadway, Derry, NH 03038. 603-434-4676. 8AM-4PM (EST). Access by: Phone, mail, in person.

Hampton District Court, PO Box 10, Hampton, NH 03843-0010. 603-926-8117. 8AM-4PM (EST). Access by: Mail, in person.

Plaistow District Court, PO Box 129, Plaistow, NH 03865. 603-382-4651. Fax: 603-382-4952. 8AM-4PM (EST). Access by: Mail, in person.

Portsmouth District Court, 111 Parrott Ave, Portsmouth, NH 03801. 603-431-2192. 8AM-4PM (EST). Access by: Mail, in person.

Salem District Court, 35 Geremonty Dr, Salem, NH 03079. 603-893-4483. 8AM-4PM (EST). Access by: Mail, in person.

Probate—Probate Court, PO Box 789, Kingston, NH 03848. 603-642-7117. 8AM-4PM (EST). In person.

Strafford County

Real Estate Recording—Strafford County Register of Deeds, County Farm Road, Dover, NH 03820. 603-742-1741. Fax: 603-749-5130. 8:30AM-4:30PM (EST).

Felony, Civil Actions Over $1,500—Superior Court, PO Box 799, Dover, NH 03821-0799. 603-742-3065. 8:30AM-4:30PM (EST). Access by: Mail, in person.

Misdemeanor, Civil Actions Under $25,000, Eviction, Small Claims—Dover District Court, 25 St Thomas St, Dover, NH 03820. 603-742-7202. 8AM-4PM (EST). Access by: Mail, in person.

Durham District Court, 1 New Market Rd, Durham, NH 03824. 603-868-2323. 8AM-4:30PM (EST). Access by: Mail, in person.

Rochester District Court, 76 N Main St, Rochester, NH 03866. 603-332-3516. 8AM-4:30PM (EST). Access by: Phone, mail, in person.

Somersworth District Court, 2 Pleasant St, Somersworth, NH 03878-2543. 603-692-5967. 8AM-3PM (EST). Access by: Phone, mail, in person.

Probate—Probate Court, PO Box 799, Dover, NH 03821-0799. 603-742-2550. 8AM-4:30PM (EST). Access by: Phone, mail, in person.

Sullivan County

Real Estate Recording—Sullivan County Register of Deeds, 20 Main Street, Newport, NH 03773. 603-863-2110. Fax: 603-863-0013. 8AM-4PM (EST).

Felony, Civil Actions Over $1,500—Superior Court, 22 Main St, Newport, NH 03773. 603-863-3450. 8AM-4:30PM (EST). Access by: Mail, in person.

Misdemeanor, Civil Actions Under $25,000, Eviction, Small Claims—Claremont District Court, PO Box 313, Claremont, NH 03743. 603-542-6064. 8AM-4PM (EST). Access by: Mail, in person.

Newport District Court, PO Box 581, Newport, NH 03773. 603-863-1832. 8AM-4PM (EST). Access by: Phone, mail, in person.

Probate—Probate Court, PO Box 417, Newport, NH 03773. 603-863-3150. 8AM-4:30PM (EST). Access by: Phone, mail, in person.

Federal Courts

US District Court
District of New Hampshire

Concord Division, US District Court Warren B Rudman Courthouse, 55 Pleasant St #110, Concord, NH 03301. 603-225-1423. Counties: Belknap, Carroll, Cheshire, Coos, Grafton, Hillsborough, Merrimack, Rockingham, Strafford, Sullivan

US Bankruptcy Court
District of New Hampshire

Manchester Division, US Bankruptcy Court, Room 404, 275 Chestnut St, Manchester, NH 03101. 603-666-7532. Voice Case Information System: 603-666-7424. Counties: Belknap, Carroll, Cheshire, Coos, Grafton, Hillsborough, Merrimack, Rockingham, Strafford, Sullivan

New Jersey

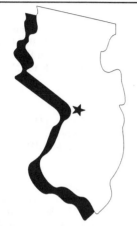

Capitol: Trenton (Mercer County)	
Number of Counties: 21	**Population:** 7,945,298
County Court Locations:	**Federal Court Locations:**
•Superior Courts: 21/ 21 Counties, 15 Vicinages	•District Courts: 3
•Special Civil Part: 21/ 21 Counties	•Bankruptcy Courts: 3
Municipal Courts: 535	**State Agencies:** 20
Tax Court: 1	

State Agencies—Summary

General Help Numbers:

State Archives

New Jersey State Archives	609-633-8334
185 W. State Street	Fax: 609-396-2454
Trenton, NJ 08625-0307	8:30AM-4:30PM TU-F
Historical Society (Newark):	201-483-3939
Records Management Admin FAX:	609-530-6121

Governor's Office

Governor's Office	609-292-6000
125 W State St, CN001	Fax: 609-292-3454
Trenton, NJ 08625	8:30AM-4:30PM

Attorney General's Office

Attorney General's Office	609-984-9574
Law & Public Safety Department	Fax: 609-292-3508
Justice Complex, CN-080	8:30AM-5PM
Trenton, NJ 08625	
Alternate Telephone:	609-292-4925

State Legislation

New Jersey State Legislature	609-292-4840
State House Annex	Fax: 609-777-2440
CN-068, Room B06	8:30AM-5PM
Trenton, NJ 08625-0068	
Copy Room:	609-292-6395

Check out the Internet site listed in the right hand column.

Important State Internet Sites:

```
Webscape
File   Edit   View                              Help
```

State of New Jersey World Wide Web
www.state.nj.us/

Links to major locations in the New Jersey Federal, State, County and Municipal Governments, state libraries, education, employment and many other sites. This page serves as the Governor's home page, e-mail can be sent to the Governor from here, and this site has a search engine.

New Jersey Legislature and Bills
www.njleg.state.nj.us/html/njleg.htm

Provides data on the state Senate and General Assembly, their committees and memberships. The site also has links to the bills of the current legislative session. Bills are searchable by number, sponsor, subject and keyword. You will need to download the ENVOY viewer (available at this site) to view the documents. Also linked to this page are the state statutes and constitution.

Uniform Commercial Code
www.state.nj.us/state/dcr/programs/ucc.html

Provides the information on performing UCC searches, included information about the required forms.

U.S. Senate Information
www.state.nj.us/senators.htm

This page links to the home pages of the two state Senators. From those pages, you can obtain their speeches, press releases, send e-mail and much more.

State Agencies—Public Records

Criminal Records
Division of State Police, Records and Identification Section, PO Box 7068, West Trenton, NJ 08628, Main Telephone: 609-882-2000, Fax: 609-530-5846, Hours: 9AM-5PM.
Restricted access.

Corporation Records
Limited Liability Company Records
Fictitious Name
Limited Partnerships
Department of State, Division of Commercial Recording, CN308, Trenton, NJ 08625, Main Telephone: 609-530-6400, Fax: 609-530-8290, Hours: 8:30AM-5:00PM. Access by: mail, phone, visit, PC.

Trademarks/Servicemarks
Department of State, Trademark Division, CN-453, Trenton, NJ 08625, Main Telephone: 609-530-6422, Hours: 8AM-5PM. Access by: mail, visit.

Uniform Commercial Code
Federal Tax Liens
State Tax Liens
UCC Division, Secretary of State, CN303, Trenton, NJ 08625, Main Telephone: 609-530-6426, Hours: 8:30AM-5PM. Access by: mail, visit.

Sales Tax Registrations
Division of Taxation, Taxpayer Services, PO Box 281, Trenton, NJ 08646-0281, Main Telephone: 609-588-2200.
Access by: mail, phone, visit. Sales tax information is considered confidential. The only way to verify if an entity has a license is to ask to look at the certificate at the place of business, per Joan Bench, Chief of Taxpayer Services Branch.

Birth Certificates
Department of Health & Senior Services, Bureau of Vital Statistics, PO Box 370, Trenton, NJ 08625-0370, Main Telephone: 609-292-4087, Credit Card Requests: 609-633-2860, Fax: 609-392-4292, Hours: 8:45AM-5PM. Access by: mail, fax, phone, visit.

Death Records
Department of Health, Bureau of Vital Statistics, PO Box 370, Trenton, NJ 08625-0370, Main Telephone: 609-292-4087, Record Check: 609-633-2860, Fax: 609-392-4292, Hours: 8:45AM-4PM. Access by: mail, fax, phone, visit.

Marriage Certificates
Department of Health & Senior Services, Bureau of Vital Statistics, PO Box 370, Trenton, NJ 08625-0370, Main Telephone: 609-292-4087, Credit Card Requests: 609-633-2860, Fax: 609-392-4292, Hours: 8:45AM-5PM. Access by: mail, fax, phone, visit.

Divorce Records
Clerk of Superior Court, Records Center, PO Box 967, Trenton, NJ 08625-0967, Main Telephone: 609-777-0092, Fax: 609-777-0094, Hours: 8:45AM-4PM. Access by: mail, fax, visit.

Workers' Compensation Records
Labor Department, Workers Compensation Division, John Fitch Plaza, CN381, Trenton, NJ 08625, Main Telephone: 609-292-6026, Hours: 8:30AM-4:30PM. Access by: mail, visit.

Driver Records
Motor Vehicle Services, Driver's Abstract Section, CN142, Trenton, NJ 08666, Main Telephone: 602-292-4558, Hours: 8AM-5PM. Access by: mail, visit, PC. Copies of tickets are not kept on file and must be obtained from the municipal courts.

Vehicle Ownership
Vehicle Identification
Motor Vehicle Services, Certified Information Unit, CN146, Trenton, NJ 08666, Main Telephone: 609-292-6500, Hours: 8AM-5PM. Access by: mail, visit, PC. Lien records must be ordered from Special Titles at CN-017 (zip is 08666-0017). Lien records are $5.00 for each lien history search and $10.50 for a complete title history.

Accident Reports
New Jersey State Police, Criminal Justice Records Bureau, PO Box 7068, West Trenton, NJ 08628-0068, Main Telephone: 609-882-2000, Hours: 8AM-5PM. Access by: mail only.

Hunting License Information
Fishing License Information
Records not available from state agency.

County Courts and Recording Offices

What You Need to Know...

About the Courts

Administration

Administrative Office of Courts	609-984-0275
RJH Justice Complex	8:30AM-4:30PM
Courts Bldg, 7th Floor, CN037	
Trenton, NJ 08625	

Court Structure

This Sourcebook contains two profiles for each Superior Court, one for the Civil Division and another for the Criminal Division because search requests should be addressed separately to each division.

The Special Civil Part of the Superior Court acts like a division of the court, and handles only the smaller civil claims. The small claims limit is **$2,000,** up from $1,500 in 1994. The Superior Court designation refers to the court where criminal cases and civil claims over $10,000 are heard. Probate is handled by Surrogates.

Searching Hints

Effective 1/1/95, all court employees became state employees and each section is responsible for its own fees.

Note that Cape May **County** offices are located in the **city** of Cape May **Court House, not** the city of Cape May.

Online Access

Online computer access is available through the ACMS, AMIS, and FACTS systems. **ACMS** (Automated Case Management System) contains data on all **active** civil cases statewide from the Law Division-Civil Part, Chancery Division-Equity Part, the Special Civil Part for 21 counties, and the Appellate Division and **AMIS** (Archival Management Information System) contains closed case information. **FACTS** (Family Automated Case Tracking System) contains information on dissolutions from all counties. The fee is $1.00 per minute of use. For further information and/or an Inquiry System Guidebook containing hardware and software requirements and an enrollment form write to: Superior Court Clerk's Office, Electronic Access, Program, 25 Market St, CN971, Trenton NJ 08625, fax 609-292-6564, or call 609-292-4987

About the Recorder's Office

Organization

21 counties, 21 filing offices. The recording officer title varies depending upon the county. It is either Register of Deeds or County Clerk. The Clerk of Circuit Court records the equivalent of some state tax liens. The entire state is in the Eastern Time Zone (EST).

UCC Records

Financing statements are filed at the state level, except for consumer goods, farm related and real estate related collateral, which are filed only with the County Clerk. Only 12 filing offices will perform UCC searches. Use search request form UCC-11. Search fees are usually $25.00 per debtor name and copy fees vary.

Lien Records

All federal tax liens are filed with the County Clerk/Register of Deeds and are indexed separately from all other liens. State tax liens comprise two categories—certificates of debt are filed with the Clerk of Superior Court (some, called docketed judgments are filed specifically with the Trenton court), and warrants of execution are filed with the County Clerk/Register of Deeds. Few counties will provide tax lien searches. Refer to *The Sourcebook of County Court Records* for information about New Jersey Superior Courts. Other liens include judgments, mechanics, and bail bond.

Real Estate Records

No counties will provide real estate searches. Copy and certification fees vary. Assessment and tax offices are at the municipal level.

County Courts and Recording Offices

Atlantic County

Real Estate Recording—Atlantic County Clerk, 5901 Main Street, Courthouse-CN 2005, Mays Landing, NJ 08330. 609-625-4011. 8:30AM-7PM M,W; 8:30AM-4:30PM T,Th,F (EST).

Civil Actions Over $10,000, Probate—Superior Court-Civil Division, Civil Courthouse, Mays Landing, NJ 08330. 609-625-7000. Fax: 609-645-5875. 8:30AM-4:30PM (EST). Access by: Mail, in person.

Felony—Superior Court-Criminal Division, Criminal Courthouse, 5909 Main St, Mays Landing, NJ 08330. 609-625-7000. Fax: 609-645-5875. 8:30AM-4:30PM (EST). Access by: Mail, in person.

Civil Actions Under $10,000, Eviction, Small Claims—Special Civil Part, 1201 Bacharach Blvd., Atlantic City, NJ 08401. 609-345-6700. Fax: 609-343-2214. 8:30AM-4:30PM (EST). Access by: Mail, in person.

Bergen County

Real Estate Recording—Bergen County Clerk, Justice Center Room 214, 10 Main St., Hackensack, NJ 07601. 973-646-2291. 9AM-4PM (EST).

Civil Actions Over $10,000, Probate—Superior Court-Civil Division, 10 Main St. Rm 119, Justice Center, Hackensack, NJ 07601. 973-646-2783. Fax: 973-752-4031. 8:30AM-5PM (EST). Access by: In person only.

Felony—Superior Court-Criminal Division, 10 Main St. Rm 132, Justice Center, Hackensack, NJ 07601. 973-646-3000. Fax: 973-342-9083. 8:30AM-4:30PM (EST). Access by: Fax, mail, in person.

Civil Actions Under $10,000, Eviction, Small Claims—Special Civil Part, 10 Main St. Rm 430, Justice Center, Hackensack, NJ 07601. 973-646-2289. 8:30AM-4:30PM (EST). Access by: Mail, in person.

Burlington County

Real Estate Recording—Burlington County Clerk, 49 Rancocas Road, Mount Holly, NJ 08060. 609-265-5122. Fax: 609-265-0696. 8AM-4:30PM (EST).

Civil Actions Over $10,000, Probate—Superior Court-Civil Division, 49 Rancocas Rd, Mount Holly, NJ 08060. 609-265-5075. 8AM-5PM (EST). Access by: Mail, in person.

Felony—Superior Court-Criminal Division, 49 Rancocas Rd, Mount Holly, NJ 08060. 609-265-5228. 8AM-5PM (EST). Access by: Mail, in person.

Civil Actions Under $10,000, Eviction, Small Claims—Special Civil Part, 49 Racocas Rd., Mount Holly, NJ 08060. 609-265-5075. 8AM-5PM (EST). Access by: Mail, in person.

Camden County

Real Estate Recording—Camden County Clerk's Office, Courthouse Room 102, 520 Market Street, Camden, NJ 08102. 609-225-5300. Fax: 609-225-5316. 9AM-4PM (EST).

Civil Actions Over $10,000, Probate—Superior Court-Civil Division, Hall of Justice, 101 S 5th St, Camden, NJ 08103. 609-225-7494. 8AM-4PM (EST). Access by: Mail, in person.

Felony—Superior Court-Criminal Division, Hall of Justice, 101 S 5th St, Camden, NJ 08103. 609-225-7452. 8AM-4PM (EST). Access by: Mail, in person.

Civil Actions Under $10,000, Eviction, Small Claims—Special Civil Part, Hall of Justice Complex, 101 S. 5th St., Camden, NJ 08103. 609-225-7433. 8:30AM-4:30PM (EST). Access by: In person only.

Cape May County

Real Estate Recording—Cape May County Clerk, 7 North Main Street, DN 109, Cape May Court House, NJ 08210. 609-465-1010. Fax: 609-465-8625. 8:30AM-4:30PM (EST).

Civil Actions Over $10,000, Probate—Superior Court-Civil Division/DN-203, 9 N Main St, Cape May Courthouse, NJ 08210. 609-463-6500. Fax: 609-463-6465. 8:30AM-4:30PM (EST). Access by: Mail, in person.

Felony—Superior Court-Criminal Division, DN-209-B 4 More Rd, Cape May Courthouse, NJ 08210. 609-463-6550. Fax: 609-463-5458. 8:30AM-4:30PM (EST). Access by: Mail, in person.

Civil Actions Under $10,000, Eviction, Small Claims—Special Civil Part, DN-203, 9 N Main St, Cape May Court House, NJ 08210. 609-463-6507. Fax: 609-463-6465. 8:30AM-4:30PM (EST). Access by: Mail, in person.

Cumberland County

Real Estate Recording—Cumberland County Clerk, 60 W. Broad St., Courthouse, Bridgeton, NJ 08302. 609-453-4864. Fax: 609-455-1410. 8:30AM-4PM (EST).

Civil Actions Over $10,000, Probate—Superior Court-Civil Division, PO Box 757, Bridgeton, NJ 08302. 609-453-4300. Fax: 609-451-7152. 8:30AM-4:30PM (EST). Access by: Mail, in person.

Felony—Superior Court-Criminal Division, PO Box 757, Bridgeton, NJ 08302. 609-453-4300. Fax: 609-451-7152. 8:30AM-4:30PM (EST). Access by: Mail, in person.

Civil Actions Under $10,000, Eviction, Small Claims—Special Civil Part, PO Box 10, Bridgeton, NJ 08302. 609-453-4350. 8:30AM-4:30PM (EST). Access by: In person only.

Essex County

Real Estate Recording—Essex County Register of Deeds, 465 Martin Luther King Boulevard, Hall of Records, Newark, NJ 07102. 973-621-4962. Fax: 973-621-6114. 9AM-4PM (EST).

Civil Actions Over $10,000, Probate—Superior Court-Civil Division, 465 Dr. Martin Luther King Nlvd Room 237, Newark, NJ 07102-1681. 973-621-4968. 8:30AM-4:30PM (EST). Access by: Fax, mail, in person.

Felony—Superior Court-Criminal Division, Rm 610, Essex County Court Bld, Newark, NJ 07102-1681. 973-621-4862. Fax: 973-621-5910. 8:30AM-4:30PM (EST). Access by: Fax, mail, in person.

Civil Actions Under $10,000, Eviction, Small Claims—Special Civil Part, 470 Martin Luther King Blvd, Newark, NJ 07102. 973-621-5368. Fax: 973-621-5914. 8:30AM-4:30PM (EST). Access by: Mail, in person.

Gloucester County

Real Estate Recording—Gloucester County Clerk, 1 North Broad Street, Corner of Broad & Delaware, Woodbury, NJ 08096. 609-853-3237. Fax: 609-853-3327. 8:30AM-4PM (EST).

Civil Actions Over $10,000, Probate—Superior Court-Civil Division, PO Box 187, Woodbury, NJ 08096. 609-853-3531. 8:30AM-4:30 PM (EST). Access by: Mail, in person.

Felony—Superior Court-Criminal Division, PO Box 187, Woodbury, NJ 08096. 609-853-3531. 8:30AM-4:30 PM (EST). Access by: Mail, in person.

Civil Actions Under $10,000, Eviction, Small Claims—Special Civil Part, Old Courthouse, 1 N Broad St., Woodbury, NJ 08096. 609-853-3392. Fax: 609-853-3429. 8:30AM-4:30PM (EST). Access by: Mail, in person.

Hudson County

Real Estate Recording—Hudson County Register of Deeds, 595 Newark Ave, Room 105, Jersey City, NJ 07306. 973-795-6571. Fax: 973-795-5179. 9AM-4PM (EST).

Civil Actions Over $10,000, Probate—Superior Court-Civil Division, 583 Newark Ave, Jersey City, NJ 07306. 973-795-6723. 8:30AM-4:30PM (EST). Access by: In person only.

Felony—Superior Court-Criminal Division, 595 Newark Ave, Jersey City, NJ 07306. 973-795-6723. 8:30AM-4:30PM (EST). Access by: In person only.

Civil Actions Under $10,000, Eviction, Small Claims—Special Civil Part, 595 Newark Ave, Jersey City, NJ 07306. 973-795-6680. 8:30AM-4:30PM (EST). Access by: In person only.

Hunterdon County

Real Estate Recording—Hunterdon County Clerk, 71 Main Street, Hall of Records, Flemington, NJ 08822. 908-788-1221. Fax: 908-782-4068. 8:30AM-4PM (EST).

Civil Actions Over $10,000, Probate—Superior Court-Civil Division, 71 Main St., Flemington, NJ 08822. 908-788-1239. 8:30AM-4:30PM (EST). Access by: Mail, in person.

Felony—Superior Court-Criminal Division, 71 Main St., Flemington, NJ 08822. 908-806-4338. 8:30AM-4:30PM (EST). Access by: Mail, in person.

Civil Actions Under $10,000, Eviction, Small Claims—Special Civil Part, 71 Main St, Hall of Records, Flemington, NJ 08822. 908-788-1216. Fax: 908-788-1285. 8:30AM-4:30PM (EST). Access by: Mail, in person.

Mercer County

Real Estate Recording—Mercer County Clerk, 209 South Broad Street, Courthouse, Room 100, Trenton, NJ 08650. 609-989-6466. Fax: 609-989-1111. 8:30AM-4PM (EST).

Civil Actions Over $10,000, Probate—Superior Court-Civil Division, 209 S. Broad, PO Box 8068, Trenton, NJ 08650-0068. 609-989-6454. Fax: 609-989-7702. 8:30AM-4:40PM (EST). Access by: Mail.

Felony—Superior Court-Criminal Division, 209 S. Broad, PO Box 8068, Trenton, NJ 08650-0068. 609-989-6452. Fax: 609-989-7702. 8:30AM-4:40PM (EST). Access by: Mail, in person.

Civil Actions Under $10,000, Eviction, Small Claims—Special Civil Part, Box 8068, Trenton, NJ 08650. 609-989-6206. Fax: 609-695-2540. 8:30AM-4:30PM (EST). Access by: Mail, in person.

Middlesex County

Real Estate Recording—Middlesex County Clerk, 1 JFK Square between Patterson & Bayard, Main Lobby in East Wing of Courthouse, New Brunswick, NJ 08903. 732-745-3204. 8:30AM-4PM (EST).

Civil Actions Over $10,000, Probate—Superior Court-Civil Division, PO Box 1110, New Brunswick, NJ 08903. 732-745-3422. 8:30AM-4:30PM (EST). Access by: Mail, in person.

Felony—Superior Court-Criminal Division, PO Box 2673, New Brunswick, NJ 08903. 732-745-3488. 8:30AM-4:30PM (EST). Access by: Mail, in person.

Civil Actions Under $10,000, Eviction, Small Claims—Special Civil Part, PO Box 1146, New Brunswick, NJ 08903. 732-745-3380. 8:30AM-4:30PM (EST). Access by: Phone, mail, in person.

Monmouth County

Real Estate Recording—Monmouth County Clerk, Hall of Records, Main Street, Room 101, Freehold, NJ 07728. 732-431-7321. 8:30AM-4:30PM (EST).

Civil Actions Over $10,000, Probate—Superior Court-Civil Division, PO Box 1255, Freehold, NJ 07728-1255. 732-431-7069. 8:30AM-4:30PM (EST). Access by: In person only.

Felony—Superior Court-Criminal Division, PO Box 1271, Rm 143, Freehold, NJ 07728-1271. 732-431-7880. Fax: 732-409-7564. 8:30AM-4:30PM (EST). Access by: In person only.

Civil Actions Under $10,000, Eviction, Small Claims—Special Civil Part, Courthouse, Courthouse and Monument St., Freehold, NJ 07728. 732-577-6749. 8:30AM-4:30PM (EST). Access by: In person only.

Morris County

Real Estate Recording—Morris County Clerk, Administration & Records Bldg., Court Street, Morristown, NJ 07960. 973-285-6135. Fax: 973-285-5231. 8:30AM-4PM (EST).

Civil Actions Over $10,000, Probate—Superior Court-Civil Division, PO Box 910, Morristown, NJ 079630-0910. 973-285-6165. Fax: 973-829-8413. 8:30AM-4:30PM (EST). Access by: In person only.

Felony—Superior Court-Criminal Division, PO Box 910, Morristown, NJ 079630-0910. 973-285-6119. Fax: 973-455-0615. 8:30AM-4:30PM (EST). Access by: In person only.

Civil Actions Under $10,000, Eviction, Small Claims—Special Civil Part, Washington and Court St, Morristown, NJ 07963. 973-285-6150. 8:30AM-4:30PM (EST). Access by: Mail, in person.

Ocean County

Real Estate Recording—Ocean County Clerk, 118 Washington Street, 1st Floor Room 108, Toms River, NJ 08753. 732-929-2110. Fax: 732-349-4336. 8:30AM-4PM (EST).

Civil Actions Over $10,000, Probate—Superior Court-Civil Division, 118 Washington, Toms River, NJ 08754. 732-929-2035. 8:30AM-4:30PM (EST). Access by: Mail, in person.

Felony—Superior Court-Criminal Division, PO Box 2192, Toms River, NJ 08754. 732-929-2009. 8:30AM-4:30PM (EST). Access by: Mail, in person.

Civil Actions Under $10,000, Eviction, Small Claims—Special Civil Part, Box 2191, Toms River, NJ 08754. 732-929-2016. Fax: 732-506-5398. 8:30AM-4:40PM (EST). Access by: Mail, in person.

Passaic County

Real Estate Recording—Passaic County Register of Deeds, 77 Hamilton Street, Courthouse, Paterson, NJ 07505. 973-881-4777. Fax: 505-434-2509. 8:30AM-4:30PM (EST).

Civil Actions Over $10,000, Probate—Superior Court-Civil Division, 77 Hamilton St., Paterson, NJ 07505-2108. 973-881-4125. 8:30AM-4:30PM (EST). Access by: Mail, in person.

Felony—Superior Court-Criminal Division, 77 Hamilton St., Paterson, NJ 07505-2108. 973-881-4126. 8:30AM-4:30PM (EST). Access by: Mail, in person.

Civil Actions Under $10,000, Eviction, Small Claims—Special Civil Part, 71 Hamilton St., Paterson, NJ 07505. 973-881-4107. 8:30AM-4:30PM (EST). Access by: In person only.

Salem County

Real Estate Recording—Salem County Clerk, 92 Market Street, Salem, NJ 08079. 609-935-7510. Fax: 609-935-8882. 8:30AM-4:30PM (EST).

Civil Actions Over $10,000, Probate—Superior Court-Civil Division, PO Box 78, Salem, NJ 08079-1913. 609-935-7510. 8:30AM-4:30PM (EST). Access by: Mail, in person.

Felony—Superior Court-Criminal Division, PO Box 78, Salem, NJ 08079-1913. 609-935-7510. 8:30AM-4:30PM (EST). Access by: Mail, in person.

Civil Actions Under $10,000, Eviction, Small Claims—Special Civil Part, 92 Market St., Salem, NJ 08079. 609-935-7510. Fax: 609-935-6551. 8:30AM-4:30PM (EST). Access by: In person only.

Somerset County

Real Estate Recording—Somerset County Clerk, 20 Grove St., Administration Building, Somerville, NJ 08876. 732-231-7006. 8:15AM-4:15PM (EST).

Civil Actions Over $10,000, Probate—Superior Court-Civil Division, PO Box 3000, Somerville, NJ 08876-1262. 732-231-7010. 8:30AM-4:30PM (EST). Access by: Mail, in person.

Felony—Superior Court-Criminal Division, PO Box 3000, Somerville, NJ 08876-1262. 732-231-7600. 8:30AM-4:30PM (EST). Access by: Mail, in person.

Civil Actions Under $10,000, Eviction, Small Claims—Special Civil Part, Courthouse, Bridge and Main St, PO Box

3000, Somerville, NJ 08876-1262. 732-231-7014. 8:30AM-4:30PM (EST). Access by: Mail, in person.

Sussex County

Real Estate Recording—Sussex County Clerk, 4 Park Place, Hall of Records, Newton, NJ 07860. 973-579-0900. Fax: 973-383-7493. 8:30AM-4:30PM (EST).

Civil Actions Over $10,000, Probate—Superior Court-Civil Division, 43-47 High St, Sussex Judicial Center, Newton, NJ 07860. 973-579-0914. 8:30AM-4:30PM (EST). Access by: Phone, mail, in person.

Felony—Superior Court-Criminal Division, 43-47 High St, Sussex Judicial Center, Newton, NJ 07860. 973-579-0933. 8:30AM-4:30PM (EST). Access by: Phone, mail, in person.

Civil Actions Under $10,000, Eviction, Small Claims—Special Civil Part, 43-47 High St., Newton, NJ 07860. 973-579-0918. 8:30AM-4:30PM (EST). Access by: Mail, in person.

Union County

Real Estate Recording—Union County Clerk, 2 Broad Street, Courthouse, Room 115, Elizabeth, NJ 07207. 732-527-4787. Fax: 732-558-2673. 8:30AM-4:30PM (EST).

Civil Actions Over $10,000, Probate—Superior Court-Civil Division, 2 Broad St, Elizabeth, NJ 07207. 732-527-4970. Fax: 732-558-2540. 8:30AM-4:30PM (EST). Access by: In person only.

Felony—Superior Court-Criminal Division, County Courthouse-New Annex,Rm 973, Elizabeth, NJ 07207. 732-527-4960. 8:30AM-4:30PM (EST). Access by: In person only.

Civil Actions Under $10,000, Eviction, Small Claims—Special Civil Part, 2 Broad St, Elizabeth, NJ 07207. 732-527-4319. 8:30AM-4:30PM (EST). Access by: Mail, in person.

Warren County

Real Estate Recording—Warren County Clerk, 413 Second Street, Courthouse, Belvidere, NJ 07823. 732-475-6211. 8:30AM-4PM (EST).

Civil Actions Over $10,000, Probate—Superior Court-Civil Division, PO Box 900, Belvidere, NJ 07823. 732-475-6140. 8:30AM-4:30PM (EST). Access by: Mail, in person.

Felony—Warren County Superior Court, Criminal Case Management Division, PO Box 900, Belvidere, NJ 07823. 732-475-6990. Fax: 732-475-6982. 8:30AM-4:30PM (EST). Access by: Mail, in person.

Civil Actions Under $10,000, Eviction, Small Claims—Special Civil Part, 314 2nd St, Belvidere, NJ 07823. 732-475-6227. 8:30AM-4:30PM (EST). Access by: Mail, in person.

Federal Courts

US District Court
District of New Jersey

Camden Division, US District Court Clerk, PO Box 2797, Camden, NJ 08101. 609-757-5021. Counties: Atlantic, Burlington, Camden, Cape May, Cumberland, Gloucester, Salem

Newark Division, US District Court ML King, Jr Federal Bldg. & US Courthouse, PO Box 419, Newark, NJ 07101-3730. 973-645-3730. Counties: Bergen, Essex, Hudson, Middlesex, Morris, Passaic, Sussex, Union

Trenton Division, US District Court Clerk, US District Court, Room 2020, 402 E State St, Trenton, NJ 08608. 609-989-2065. Counties: Hunterdon, Mercer, Monmouth, Ocean, Somerset, Warren

US Bankruptcy Court
District of New Jersey

Camden Division, US Bankruptcy Court, 15 N 7th St, Camden, NJ 08102. 609-757-5422. Voice Case Information System: 201-645-6044. Counties: Atlantic, Burlington, Camden, Cape May, Cumberland, Gloucester, Salem

Newark Division, US Bankruptcy Court, ML King Jr Federal Bldg, 50 Walnut St, Newark, NJ 07102. 201-645-2630. Voice Case Information System: 201-645-6044. Counties: Bergen, Essex, Hudson, Morris, Passaic, Sussex, Union (Elizabeth, Hillside, and Springfield only).

Trenton Division, US Bankruptcy Court, Clerk of Court, 402 E State St, Trenton, NJ 08601. 609-989-2129. Voice Case Information System: 201-645-6044. Counties: Hunterdon, Mercer, Middlesex, Monmouth, Ocean, Somerset, Union (except for Elizabeth, Hillside, and Springfield), Warren

New Mexico

Capitol: Santa Fe (Santa Fe County)	
Number of Counties: 33	**Population:** 1,685,401
County Court Locations:	**Federal Court Locations:**
•District Courts: 30/13 Districts	•District Courts: 3
•Magistrate Courts: 48/ 32 Districts	•Bankruptcy Courts: 1
•Metropolitan Court of Bernalillo County: 1	**State Agencies:** 19
Municipal Courts: 82	
• Probate 30/33 Counties	

State Agencies—Summary

General Help Numbers:

State Archives
State Records Center & Archives 505-827-7332
404 Montezuma Fax: 505-827-7331
Santa Fe, NM 87503 8AM-5PM
Reference Librarian: 505-827-7332
Historical Society: 505-827-7332

Governor's Office
Governor's Office 505-827-3000
State Capitol, Room 400 Fax: 505-827-3026
Santa Fe, NM 87503 8AM-5PM

Attorney General's Office
Attorney General's Office 505-827-6000
PO Drawer 1508 Fax: 505-827-5826
Santa Fe, NM 87504-1508 8AM-5PM

State Legislation
Legislative Council Service 505-986-4600
State Capitol Bldg 8AM-5PM
Room 311
Santa Fe, NM 87501
Bill Room (During Session Only): 505-986-4350
For bill status see the Internet site to the right.

Important State Internet Sites:

Webscape
File Edit View Help

State of New Mexico World Wide Web
www.state.nm.us/
Provides links to major locations in the New Mexico State Government, state agencies, state legislators and a link to the legislative bill locator.

The Governor's Office
www.governor.state.nm.us/
This site includes information about the Governor, his press releases, biography, and enables you to send e-mail to the Governor. There is also a link to an extensive collection of federal historical and political sites.

UCC Information
web.state.nm.us/UCC/UCCHOME.HTM
Provides complete information about state UCC search fees, UCC search companies and an online search engine.

New Mexico Legislature
www.technet.nm.org/legislature/
This site contains links to the state House and Senate, their committees and a bill finder search engine.

New Mexico Legislative Bills
www.technet.nm.org/legislature/bill_finder.html
Use to search for bills from 1996 through the current session. You can search by keywords, sponsor and bill number.

State Agencies—Public Records

Criminal Records

Department of Public Safety, Records Bureau, PO Box 1628, Santa Fe, NM 87504-1628, Main Telephone: 505-827-9181, Fax: 505-827-3396, Hours: 8AM-5PM. Access by: mail, visit.

Corporation Records
Limited Liability Company Records

State Corporation Commission, Corporate Department, PO Drawer 1269, Santa Fe, NM 87504-1269, Main Telephone: 505-827-4504, General Information: 800-947-4722, Good Standing: 505-827-4510, Copy Request: 505-827-4513, Fax: 505-827-4387, Hours: 8AM-12:00: 1PM-5PM. Access by: mail, phone, visit.

Trademarks/Servicemarks
Trade Names

Secretary of State, Tradename Division, State Capitol Bldg, Room 421, Santa Fe, NM 87503, Main Telephone: 505-827-3600, Fax: 505-827-3611, Hours: 8AM-5PM. Access by: mail, phone, visit.

Uniform Commercial Code

UCC Division, Secretary of State, State Capitol Bldg, Santa Fe, NM 87503, Main Telephone: 505-827-3600, Fax: 505-827-3634, Hours: 8AM-5PM. Access by: PC only.

Sales Tax Registrations

Taxation & Revenue Department, Tax Administistative Services Division, PO Box 630, Santa Fe, NM 87504-0630, Main Telephone: 505-827-6825, Fax 505-827-0469 Access by: mail, phone.

Birth Certificates

Department of Health, Bureau of Vital Records, PO Box 26110, Santa Fe, NM 87502, Main Telephone: 505-827-2338, Fax: 505-984-1048, Hours: 8AM-5:00PM (Counter Service: 9AM-4PM). Access by: mail, phone, visit. All requesters must sign and date the request. It is a felony to obtain a record fraudulently.

Death Records

Department of Health, Bureau of Vital Records, PO Box 26110, Santa Fe, NM 87502, Main Telephone: 505-827-2338, Fax: 505-984-1048, Hours: 8AM-5PM (Counter Service: 9AM-4PM). Access by: mail, phone, visit.

Marriage Certificates
Divorce Records

Records not available from state agency.

Workers' Compensation Records

Workers Compensation Administration, PO Box 27198, Albuquerque, NM 87125-7198, Main Telephone: 505-841-6000, Fax: 505-841-6009, Hours: 8AM-5PM.
Restricted Access.

Driver Records

Motor Vehicle Division, Driver Services Bureau, PO Box 1028, Santa Fe, NM 87504-1028, Main Telephone: 505-827-2234, Hours: 8AM-5PM. Access by: mail, visit, PC. Copies of tickets may be obtained from the same address. There is no fee.

Vehicle Ownership
Vehicle Identification

Department of Motor Vehicles, Vehicle Services Bureau, PO Box 1028, Santa Fe, NM 87504-1028, Main Telephone: 505-827-2290, Hours: 8AM-5PM. Access by: mail, visit, PC.

Accident Reports

Department of Public Safety, Records, PO Box 1628, Santa Fe, NM 87504-1628, Main Telephone: 505-827-9300, Fax: 505-827-3396, Hours: 8AM-5PM. Access by: mail, visit.

Hunting License Information
Fishing License Information

Game & Fish Department, PO Box 25112, Santa Fe, NM 87504, Main Telephone: 505-827-7911, Fax: 505-827-7915, Hours: 8AM-12PM; 1PM-5PM. Access by: visit only. Searching is only available in person.

County Courts and Recording Offices

What You Need to Know...

About the Courts

About the Recorder's Office

Administration

Administrative Office of the Courts   505-827-4800
Supreme Court Bldg, Room 25   Fax: 505-827-4824
Santa Fe, NM 87503

Court Structure

Magistrate Courts and the Bernallilo Metropolitan Court have jurisdiction in cases up to $5,000. Probate Courts handle "informal" (uncontested) probate cases and the District Courts handle "formal" (contested) probate cases.

Searching Hints

There are some "shared" courts in New Mexico, with one county handling cases arising in another. Records are held at the location(s) indicated in the text.

Online Access

Online computer access is available for the Bernilillo courts through New Mexico Technet. There is a $50.00 set up fee, a $.50 per minute connect time fee, and other fees based on type of search. The system is available 24 hours a day. Call 505-345-6555 for more information.

Organization

33 counties, 33 filing offices. The recording officer is County Clerk. Most counties maintain a grantor/grantee index and a miscellaneous index. The entire state is in the Mountain Time Zone (MST).

UCC Records

Financing statements are filed at the state level, except for consumer goods, farm related and real estate related collateral, which are filed only with the County Clerk. Only a few filing offices will perform UCC searches. Use search request form UCC-11. Search and copy fees vary.

Lien Records

All federal and state tax liens are filed with the County Clerk. Most counties will **not** provide tax lien searches. Other liens include judgments, mechanics, lis pendens, contractors, and hospital.

Real Estate Records

Most counties will **not** perform real estate searches. Copy and certification fees vary.

County Courts and Recording Offices

Bernalillo County

Real Estate Recording—Bernalillo County Clerk, 1 Civic Plaza NW, Level 6, Albuquerque, NM 87102. 505-768-4268. Fax: 505-768-4631. 8AM-4:30PM (MST).

Felony, Civil, Probate—2nd Judicial District Court, PO Box 488, Albuquerque, NM 87103. 505-841-7425. Civil: 505-841-7437. Criminal: 505-841-7459. Probate: 505-841-7404. Fax: 505-841-7446. 8AM-5PM (MST). Access by: Mail, remote online, in person.

Misdemeanor, Civil Actions Under $5,000, Eviction, Small Claims—Metropolitan Court, 401 Roma NW, Albuquerque, NM 87102. 505-841-8110. Fax: 505-841-8192. 8AM-5PM (MST). Access by: Phone, fax, mail, remote online, in person.

Probate—County Clerk, #1 Civic Plaza NW, Albuquerque, NM 87102. 505-768-4247. 8AM-4:30PM (MST). Access by: Phone, mail, in person.

Catron County

Real Estate Recording—Catron County Clerk, Main Street, Reserve, NM 87830. 505-533-6400. Fax: 505-533-6400. 8AM-4:30PM (MST).

Felony, Civil, Probate—7th Judicial District Court, PO Drawer 1129, Socorro, NM 87801. 505-835-0050. Fax: 505-835-0050. 8AM-4PM (MST). Access by: Phone, mail, in person.

Misdemeanor, Civil Actions Under $5,000, Eviction, Small Claims—Quemado Magistrate Court, PO Box 283, Quemado, NM 87829. 505-773-4604. Fax: 505-773-4688. 8AM-5PM (MST). Access by: Phone, fax, mail, in person.

Reserve Magistrate Court, PO Box 447, Reserve, NM 87830. 505-533-6474. Fax: 505-533-6623. 8AM-5PM (MST). Access by: Mail, in person.

Probate—County Clerk, PO Box I, Socorro, NM 87801. 505-835-0423. Fax: 505-835-1043. 8AM-5PM (MST). Access by: Phone, mail, in person.

Chaves County

Real Estate Recording—Chaves County Clerk, 401 North Main, Courthouse, Roswell, NM 88201. 505-624-6614. Fax: 505-624-6523. 7AM-5PM (MST).

Felony, Civil, Probate—5th Judicial District Court, Box 1776, Roswell, NM 88202. 505-622-2212. Fax: 505-624-9506. 8AM-Noon,1-5PM (MST). Access by: Mail, in person.

Misdemeanor, Civil Actions Under $5,000, Eviction, Small Claims—Magistrate Court, 200 E 4th St, Roswell, NM 88201. 505-624-6088. Fax: 505-624-6092. 8AM-4PM (MST). Access by: Mail, in person.

Cibola County

Real Estate Recording—Cibola County Clerk, 515 West High Street, Grants, NM 87020. 505-287-9431. Fax: 505-285-5434. 8AM-5PM (MST).

Felony, Civil, Probate—13th Judicial District Court, Box 758, Grants, NM 87020. 505-287-8831. Fax: 505-287-5755. 8AM-4PM (MST). Access by: Mail, in person.

Misdemeanor, Civil Actions Under $5,000, Eviction, Small Claims—Magistrate Court, 600 W Santa Fe, PO Box 130, Grants, NM 87020. 505-287-7927. 8AM-4PM (MST). Access by: Mail, in person.

Probate—County Clerk, 515 W. High, PO Box 19, Grants, NM 87020. 505-287-8107. Fax: 505-285-5434. 8AM-5PM (MST). Access by: Mail.

Colfax County

Real Estate Recording—Colfax County Clerk, Third Street & Savage Avenue, Courthouse, Raton, NM 87740. 505-445-5551. Fax: 505-445-4031. 8AM-Noon, 1-5PM (MST).

Felony, Civil, Probate—8th Judicial District Court, Box 160, Raton, NM 87740. 505-445-5585. Fax: 505-445-2626. 8AM-Noon, 1-5PM (MST). Access by: Phone, mail, in person.

Misdemeanor, Civil Actions Under $5,000, Eviction, Small Claims—Cimarron Magistrate Court, PO Drawer 367, Highway 21, Cimarron, NM 87714. 505-376-2634. (MST). Access by: In person only.

Raton Magistrate Court, 122 S Third, Raton, NM 87740. 505-445-2220. Fax: 505-445-8955. 8AM-5PM (MST). Access by: Fax, mail, in person.

Springer Magistrate Court, 300 Colbert Ave. PO Box 778, Springer, NM 87747. 505-483-2417. Fax: 505-483-0127. 8AM-Noon, 1-5PM (MST). Access by: Fax, mail, in person.

Probate—County Clerk, PO Box 159, Raton, NM 87740. 505-445-5551. Fax: 505-445-4031. 8AM-5PM (MST). Access by: Mail, in person.

Curry County

Real Estate Recording—Curry County Clerk, 700 Main Street, Clovis, NM 88101. 505-763-5591. Fax: 505-763-4232. 8AM-Noon, 1-5PM (MST).

Felony, Civil, Probate—9th Judicial District Court, Curry County Courthouse, Clovis, NM 88101. 505-763-9148. Fax: 505-763-5160. 8AM-4PM (MST). Access by: In person only.

Misdemeanor, Civil Actions Under $5,000, Eviction, Small Claims—Magistrate Court, 900 Main St, Clovis, NM 88101. 505-762-3766. Fax: 505-769-1437. 8AM-4PM (MST). Access by: Fax, mail, in person.

Probate—County Clerk, Curry County Courthouse, 700 N Main, Clovis, NM 88101. 505-762-9148. Fax: 505-763-5160. 8AM-4PM (MST). Access by: In person only.

De Baca County

Real Estate Recording—De Baca County Clerk, 514 Ave. C, Courthouse Square, Fort Sumner, NM 88119. 505-355-2601. Fax: 505-355-2441. 8AM-Noon, 1-4:30PM (MST).

Felony, Civil, Probate—10th Judicial District Court, Box 910, Ft. Sumner, NM 88119. 505-355-2896. Fax: 505-355-2896. 8AM-4:30PM (MST). Access by: Phone, mail, in person.

Misdemeanor, Civil Actions Under $5,000, Eviction, Small Claims—Magistrate Court, Box 24, Ft Sumner, NM 88119. 505-355-7371. Fax: 505-355-7149. 8AM-5PM (MST). Access by: Phone, mail, in person.

Probate—County Clerk, 514 Ave C, Box 347, Ft. Sumner, NM 88119. 505-355-2601. Fax: 505-355-2441. 8AM-Noon, 1-4:30PM (MST). Access by: Mail, in person.

Dona Ana County

Real Estate Recording—Dona Ana County Clerk, 251 West Amador, Room 103, Las Cruces, NM 88005. 505-647-7421. 8AM-5PM (MST).

Felony, Civil, Probate—3rd Judicial District Court, 201 W Puecho, Suite A, Las Cruces, NM 88005. 505-523-8200. Fax: 505-523-8290. 8AM-Noon, 1-5PM (MST). Access by: Mail, in person.

Misdemeanor, Civil Actions Under $5,000, Eviction, Small Claims—Anthony Magistrate Court, PO Box 1259, Anthony, NM 88021. 505-233-3147. 8AM-Noon, 1-5PM (MST). Access by: Phone, in person.

Las Cruces Magistrate Court, 125 S Downtown Mall, Las Cruces, NM 88005. 505-524-2814. Fax: 505-525-2951. 8AM-Noon, 1-5PM (MST). Access by: Phone, fax, mail, in person.

Eddy County

Real Estate Recording—Eddy County Clerk, 202 West Mermod, Room 204, Carlsbad, NM 88220. 505-885-3383. Fax: 505-887-1039. 8AM-5PM (MST).

Felony, Civil, Probate—5th Judicial District Court, Box 1838, Carlsbad, NM 88221. 505-885-4740. Fax: 505-887-7095. 8AM-Noon, 1-5PM (MST). Access by: Phone, mail, in person.

Misdemeanor, Civil Actions Under $5,000, Eviction, Small Claims—Artesia Magistrate Court, 611 Mahone Dr Ste A, Artesia, NM 88210. 505-746-2481. Fax: 505-746-6763. 8AM-Noon, 1-5PM (MST). Access by: Phone, fax, mail, in person.

Carlsbad Magistrate Court, 302 N Main St, Carlsbad, NM 88220. 505-887-7119. 8AM-Noon, 1-5PM (MST). Access by: Mail, in person.

Probate—County Clerk, Eddy County Probate Judge, Rm 100, Carlsbad, NM 88220. 505-885-4008. Fax: 505-887-1039. 8AM-5PM (MST). Access by: Mail, in person.

Grant County

Real Estate Recording—Grant County Clerk, 201 North Cooper, Silver City, NM 88061. 505-538-2979. Fax: 505-538-8926. 8:30AM-5PM (MST).

Felony, Civil, Probate—6th Judicial District Court, Box 2339, Silver City, NM 88062. 505-538-3250. Fax: 505-588-5439. 8AM-5PM (MST). Access by: Phone, mail, in person.

Misdemeanor, Civil Actions Under $5,000, Eviction, Small Claims—Bayard Magistrate Court, PO Box 125, Bayard, NM 88023. 505-537-3402. Fax: 505-537-7365. 8AM-5PM (MST). Access by: Mail, in person.

Silver City Magistrate Court, Box 1089, Silver City, NM 88062. 505-538-3811. Fax: 505-538-8079. 8AM-5PM; Public hours 9AM-5PM (MST). Access by: Mail, in person.

Probate—County Clerk, Box 898, Silver City, NM 88062. 505-538-2979. Fax: 505-538-8926. 8AM-5PM (MST). Access by: Phone, mail.

Guadalupe County

Real Estate Recording—Guadalupe County Clerk, 420 Parker Avenue, Courthouse-Suite 1, Santa Rosa, NM 88435. 505-472-3791. Fax: 505-472-3735. 8AM-5PM (MST).

Felony, Civil, Probate—4th Judicial District Court, 420 Parker Ave Suite #5, Guadalupe County Courthouse, Santa Rosa, NM 88435. 505-472-3888. Fax: 505-472-3888. 8AM-5PM (MST). Access by: Phone, mail, in person.

Misdemeanor, Civil Actions Under $5,000, Eviction, Small Claims—Santa Rosa Magistrate Court, 421 Corona Ave, Santa Rosa, NM 88435. 505-472-3237. 8AM-Noon, 1-5PM (MST). Access by: Mail, in person.

Vaughn Magistrate Court, PO Box 246, Vaughn, NM 88353. 505-584-2345. 8AM-Noon, 1-5PM (MST). Access by: Mail, in person.

Probate—County Clerk, 4200 Parker Ave Courthouse, Santa Rosa, NM 88435. 505-472-3791. Fax: 505-472-3735. 8AM-5PM (MST). Access by: Mail, in person.

Harding County

Real Estate Recording—Harding County Clerk, Third & Pine, Mosquero, NM 87733. 505-673-2301. Fax: 505-673-2922. 8AM-4PM (MST).

Felony, Civil, Probate—10th Judicial District Court, Box 1002, Mosquero, NM 87733. 505-673-2252. Fax: 505-673-2252. 9AM-3PM M-W,F (MST). Access by: Phone, mail, in person.

Misdemeanor, Civil Actions Under $5,000, Eviction, Small Claims—Magistrate Court, Box 9, Roy, NM 87743. 505-485-2549. Fax: 505-485-2407. 8AM-4:30PM (MST). Access by: Phone, fax, mail, in person.

Probate—County Clerk, County Clerk, Box 1002, Mosquero, NM 87733. 505-673-2301. Fax: 505-673-2922. 8AM-5PM (MST). Access by: Mail, in person.

Hidalgo County

Real Estate Recording—Hidalgo County Clerk, 300 Shakespeare Street, Lordsburg, NM 88045. 505-542-9213. 9AM-5PM (MST).

Felony, Civil, Probate—6th Judicial District Court, PO 608, Lordsburg, NM 88045. 505-542-3411. Fax: 505-542-3481. 8AM-Noon, 1-5PM (MST). Access by: Phone, mail, in person.

Misdemeanor, Civil Actions Under $5,000, Eviction, Small Claims—Magistrate Court, 420 Wabash Ave, Lordsburg, NM 88045. 505-542-3582. 8AM-5PM (MST). Access by: Mail, in person.

Probate—County Clerk, 300 Shakespeare, Lordsburg, NM 88045. 505-542-9512. Fax: 505-542-3414. 9AM-5PM (MST). Access by: Phone, mail, in person.

Lea County

Real Estate Recording—Lea County Clerk, 100 Main Street, Courthouse, Lovington, NM 88260. 505-396-8531. Fax: 505-396-5684. 8AM-5PM (MST).

Felony, Civil, Probate—5th Judicial District Court, 100 N. Main, Box 6C, Lovington, NM 88260. 505-396-8571. Fax: 505-396-2428. 8AM-5PM (MST). Access by: In person only.

Misdemeanor, Civil Actions Under $5,000, Eviction, Small Claims—Eunice Magistrate Court, PO Box 240, Eunice, NM 88231. 505-394-3368. Fax: 505-394-3335. (MST). Access by: Mail, in person.

Hobbs Magistrate Court, 114 E Taylor St, Hobbs, NM 88240. 505-397-3621. 8AM-4PM (MST). Access by: Mail, in person.

Lovington Magistrate Court, 100 W Central, Suite D, Lovington, NM 88260. 505-396-6677. Fax: 505-396-6163. 8AM-Noon,1-5PM (MST). Access by: Mail, in person.

Tatum Magistrate Court, 10 N Ave A, Tatum, NM 88267. 505-398-5300. Fax: 505-398-5310. 8AM-5PM (MST). Access by: Phone, fax, mail, remote online, in person.

Probate—County Clerk, Box 1507, Lovington, NM 88260. 505-396-8531. Fax: 505-396-5684. 8AM-5PM (MST). Access by: In person only.

Lincoln County

Real Estate Recording—Lincoln County Clerk, 300 Central Avenue, Carrizozo, NM 88301. 505-648-2394. Fax: 505-648-2576. 8AM-5PM (MST).

Felony, Civil, Probate—12th Judicial District Court, Box 725, Carrizozo, NM 88301. 505-648-2432. Fax: 505-648-2581. 8AM-Noon, 1-5PM (MST). Access by: Phone, mail, in person.

Misdemeanor, Civil Actions Under $5,000, Eviction, Small Claims—Ruidoso Magistrate court, PO Box 2426, Ruidoso, NM 88345. 505-378-7022. Fax: 505-378-8508. 8AM-4PM (MST). Access by: Mail, in person.

Probate—County Clerk, Box 338, Carrizozo, NM 88301. 505-648-2394. Fax: 505-648-2576. 8AM-5PM (MST). Access by: Mail, in person.

Los Alamos County

Real Estate Recording—Los Alamos County Clerk, 2300 Trinity Drive, Room 100, Los Alamos, NM 87544. 505-662-8010. Fax: 505-662-8008. 8AM-5PM (MST).

Felony, Misdemeanor, Civil, Eviction, Small Claims, Probate—1st Judicial District Court, All civil and criminal cases handled by Santa Fe District Court.

Misdemeanor, Civil Actions Under $5,000, Eviction, Small Claims—Magistrate Court, 1319 Trinity Dr, Los Alamos, NM 87544. 505-662-2727. Fax: 505-661-6258. 8AM-5PM (MST). Access by: Mail, in person.

Probate—County Clerk, Box 30, Los Alamos, NM 87544. 505-662-8010. Fax: 505-662-8008. 8AM-5PM (MST). Access by: Mail.

Luna County

Real Estate Recording—Luna County Clerk, 700 South Silver, Courthouse, Deming, NM 88030. 505-546-0491. Fax: 505-546-4708. 8AM-5PM (MST).

Felony, Civil, Probate—6th Judicial District Court, Luna County Courthouse Room 40, Deming, NM 88030. 505-546-9611. Fax: 505-546-2994. 8AM-Noon, 1-5PM (MST). Access by: Phone, fax, mail, in person.

Misdemeanor, Civil Actions Under $5,000, Eviction, Small Claims—Magistrate Court, 912 S Silver St, Deming, NM 88030. 505-546-9321. 8AM-Noon, 1-5PM (MST). Access by: Mail, in person.

Probate—County Clerk, PO Box 1838, Deming, NM 88030. 505-546-0491. Fax: 505-546-4708. 8AM-5PM (MST). Access by: Mail, in person.

McKinley County

Real Estate Recording—McKinley County Clerk, 201 West Hill Avenue, Courthouse, Gallup, NM 87301. 505-863-6866. 8AM-5PM (MST).

Felony, Civil, Probate—11th Judicial District Court, 201 W. Hill, Room 4, Gallup, NM 87301. 505-863-6816. Fax: 505-722-9172. 8AM-Noon, 1-5PM (MST). Access by: Phone, mail, in person.

Misdemeanor, Civil Actions Under $5,000, Eviction, Small Claims—Magistrate Court, 451 State Rd 564, Gallup, NM 87301. 505-722-6636. 8AM-4PM (MST). Access by: Mail, in person.

Probate—County Clerk, 201 W. Hill, Room 21, Gallup, NM 87301. 505-863-6866. Fax: 505-863-1419. 8AM-5PM (MST). Access by: Mail, in person.

Mora County

Real Estate Recording—Mora County Clerk, Main Street, Mora, NM 87732. 505-387-2448. Fax: 505-387-9022. 8AM-5PM (MST).

Felony, Civil, Probate—4th Judicial District Court, PO Box 1540, Las Vegas, NM 87701. 505-425-7281. Fax: 505-425-6307. 8AM-Noon, 1-5PM (MST). Access by: Mail, in person.

Misdemeanor, Civil Actions Under $5,000, Eviction, Small Claims—Magistrate Court, 1900 Hot Springs Blvd, Las Vegas, NM 87701. 505-425-5204. 8AM-4PM (MST). Access by: Mail, in person.

Probate—County Clerk, Box 360, Mora, NM 87732. 505-387-2448. Fax: 505-387-9022. 8AM-5PM (MST). Access by: Mail, in person.

Otero County

Real Estate Recording—Otero County Clerk, 1000 New York Avenue, Room 108, Alamogordo, NM 88310. 505-437-4942. 7:30AM-6PM (MST).

Felony, Civil, Probate—12th Judicial District Court, 1000 New York Ave, Rm 209, Alamogordo, NM 88310-6940. 505-437-7310. Fax: 505-434-8886. 8AM-4PM (MST). Access by: Phone, mail, in person.

Misdemeanor, Civil Actions Under $5,000, Eviction, Small Claims—Magistrate Court, 1106 New York Ave, Alamogordo, NM 88310. 505-437-9000. 8AM-4PM (MST). Access by: Mail, in person.

Probate—County Clerk, 1000 New York Ave, Rm 108, Alamogordo, NM 88310. 505-437-4942. Fax: 505-434-2509. 7:30AM-6PM (MST). Access by: Mail, in person.

Quay County

Real Estate Recording—Quay County Clerk, 301 South Third Street, Tucumcari, NM 88401. 505-461-0510. Fax: 505-461-0513. 8AM-Noon,1-5PM (MST).

Felony, Civil, Probate—10th Judicial District Court, Box 1067, Tucumcari, NM 88401. 505-461-2764. Fax: 505-461-4498. 8AM-5PM (MST). Access by: Phone, fax, mail, in person.

Misdemeanor, Civil Actions Under $5,000, Eviction, Small Claims—San Jon Magistrate Court, PO Box 35, San Jon, NM 88434. 505-576-2591. Fax: 505-576-2773. 8AM-Noon,1-5PM (MST). Access by: Mail, in person.

Tucumcari Magistrate Court, PO Box 1301, Tucumcari, NM 88401. 505-461-1700. Fax: 505-461-4522. 8AM-Noon, 1-5PM (MST). Access by: Phone, fax, mail, in person.

Probate—County Clerk, Box 1225, Tucumcari, NM 88401. 505-461-0510. Fax: 505-461-0513. 8AM-5PM (MST). Access by: Mail, in person.

Rio Arriba County

Real Estate Recording—Rio Arriba County Clerk, Courthouse, Tierra Amarilla, NM 87575. 505-588-7724. 8AM-4:30PM (MST).

Felony, Civil, Probate—1st Judicial District Court, All civil and criminal cases handled by Santa Fe District Court.

Misdemeanor, Civil Actions Under $5,000, Eviction, Small Claims—Rio Arriba Magistrate Court-Division 1, PO Box 538, Chama, NM 87520. 505-756-2278. 8AM-Noon, 1-5PM (MST). Access by: Mail, in person.

Rio Arriba Magistrate Court-Division 2, 410 Paseo de Onate, Espanola, NM 87532. 505-753-2532. 8AM-4PM (MST). Access by: Mail, in person.

Roosevelt County

Real Estate Recording—Roosevelt County Clerk, 101 West First, Portales, NM 88130. 505-356-8562. 8AM-5PM (MST).

Felony, Civil, Probate—9th Judicial District Court, 109 West 1st St, Suite 207, Portales, NM 88130. 505-356-4463. Fax: 505-356-5168. 8AM-4PM (MST). Access by: In person only.

Misdemeanor, Civil Actions Under $5,000, Eviction, Small Claims—Magistrate Court, 1700 N Boston, Portales, NM 88130. 505-356-8560. Fax: 505-359-6883. 8AM-4:30PM (MST). Access by: Mail, in person.

Probate—County Clerk, Roosevelt County Courthouse, Portales, NM 88130. 505-356-8562. Fax: 505-356-3560. 8AM-5PM (MST). Access by: Mail, in person.

San Juan County

Real Estate Recording—San Juan County Clerk, 112 South Mesa Verde, Aztec, NM 87410. 505-334-9471. Fax: 505-334-3635. 7:30AM-5:30PM (MST).

Felony, Civil, Probate—11th Judicial District Court, 103 S. Oliver, Aztec, NM 87410. 505-334-6151. Fax: 505-334-1940. 8AM-Noon, 1-5PM (MST). Access by: Phone, fax, mail, in person.

Misdemeanor, Civil Actions Under $5,000, Eviction, Small Claims—Aztec Magistrate Court, 101 S Oliver Dr Ste 1, Aztec, NM 87410. 505-334-9479. 8AM-Noon, 1-5PM (MST). Access by: Mail, in person.

Farmington Magistrate Court, 920 Municipal Dr, Suite 1, Farmington, NM 87401. 505-326-4338. Fax: 505-325-2618. 7AM-6PM (MST). Access by: Mail, in person.

Probate—County Clerk, Box 550, Aztec, NM 87410. 505-334-9471. Fax: 505-334-3635. 7:30AM-5:30PM (MST). Access by: Mail, in person.

San Miguel County

Real Estate Recording—San Miguel County Clerk, Courthouse, Las Vegas, NM 87701. 505-425-9331. Fax: 505-425-7019. 8AM-Noon, 1-5PM (MST).

Felony, Civil, Probate—4th Judicial District Court, PO Box 1540, Las Vegas, NM 87701. 505-425-7281. Fax: 505-425-6307. 8AM-Noon, 1-5PM (MST). Access by: Phone, mail, in person.

Misdemeanor, Civil Actions Under $5,000, Eviction, Small Claims—Magistrate Court, 1900 Hot Springs Blvd, Las Vegas, NM 87701. 505-425-5204. Fax: 505-425-0422. 8AM-4PM (MST). Access by: Mail, in person.

Probate—County Clerk, San Miguel County Clerk, Las Vegas, NM 87701. 505-425-9331. Fax: 505-454-7199. 8AM-Noon, 1-5PM (MST). Access by: Mail, in person.

Sandoval County

Real Estate Recording—Sandoval County Clerk, 711 Camino Del Pueblo, Courthouse, 2nd Floor, Bernalillo, NM 87004. 505-867-7527. 8AM-5PM (MST).

Felony, Civil, Probate—13th Judicial District Court, PO Box 130, Bernalillo, NM 87004. 505-867-2376. 8AM-Noon, 1-5PM (MST). Access by: Phone, mail, in person. Phone access limited to 1 search.

Misdemeanor, Civil Actions Under $5,000, Eviction, Small Claims—Bernalillo Magistrate Court, PO Box 818, Bernalillo, NM 87004. 505-867-5202. 8AM-4PM (MST). Access by: Mail, in person.

Cuba Magistrate Court, 16B Cordova St, Cuba, NM 87013. 505-289-3519. 8AM-Noon, 1-5PM (MST). Access by: In person only.

Probate—County Clerk, Box 40, Bernalillo, NM 87004. 505-867-2704. Fax: 505-828-2862. 8AM-5PM (MST). Access by: Phone, fax, mail, in person.

Santa Fe County

Real Estate Recording—Santa Fe County Clerk, 102 Grant Avenue, Santa Fe, NM 87504. 505-986-6280. 8AM-5PM (MST).

Felony, Civil, Probate—1st Judicial District Court, Box 2268, Santa Fe, NM 87504. 505-827-5035. 8AM-4PM (MST). Access by: Phone, mail, in person.

Misdemeanor, Civil Actions Under $5,000, Eviction, Small Claims—Magistrate Court, Rte 11, Box 21M, Pojoaque, NM 87501. 505-455-7938. Fax: 505-455-3053. 8AM-Noon, 1-5PM (MST). Access by: Phone, mail, in person.

Probate—County Clerk, Box 276, Santa Fe, NM 87501. 505-986-6279. Fax: 505-986-6362. 8AM-5PM (MST). Access by: Mail, in person.

Sierra County

Real Estate Recording—Sierra County Clerk, 311 Date Street, Truth or Consequences, NM 87901. 505-894-2840. Fax: 505-894-2516. 8AM-5PM (MST).

Felony, Civil, Probate—7th Judicial District Court, 311 N Date, Truth or Consequences, NM 87901. 505-894-7167. Fax: 505-894-7168. 8AM-4PM (MST). Access by: Phone, mail, in person.

Misdemeanor, Civil Actions Under $5,000, Eviction, Small Claims—Magistrate Court, 100 Date St, Truth or Consequences, NM 87901. 505-894-3051. Fax: 505-894-0476. 8AM-Noon,1-5PM (MST). Access by: Mail, in person.

Probate—County Clerk, 311 Date St., Truth or Consequences, NM 87901. 505-894-2840. Fax: 505-894-2516. 8AM-5PM (MST). Access by: Mail, in person.

Socorro County

Real Estate Recording—Socorro County Clerk, 200 Church Street, Socorro, NM 87801. 505-835-3263. Fax: 505-835-1043. 8AM-5PM (MST).

Felony, Civil, Probate—7th Judicial District Court, All civil and criminal cases are handled by Catron District Court.

Misdemeanor, Civil Actions Under $5,000, Eviction, Small Claims—Magistrate Court, 404 Park St, Socorro, NM 87801. 505-835-2500. 8AM-Noon, 1-5PM (MST). Access by: Phone, mail, in person.

Taos County

Real Estate Recording—Taos County Clerk, 105 Albright Street, Suite D, Taos, NM 87571. 505-758-8836. Fax: 505-758-3391. 8AM-Noon, 1-5PM (MST).

Felony, Civil, Probate—8th Judicial District Court, 105 Albright St Ste H, Taos, NM 87571. 505-758-3173. Fax: 505-758-1281. 8AM-5PM (MST). Access by: Phone, fax, mail, in person.

Misdemeanor, Civil Actions Under $5,000, Eviction, Small Claims—Questa Magistrate Court, PO Box 586, Questa, NM 87556. 505-586-0761. Fax: 505-586-0428. 8AM-Noon,1-5PM (MST). Access by: Phone, fax, mail, in person.

Taos Magistrate Court, Box 1121, Taos, NM 87571. 505-758-4030. Fax: 505-751-0983. 8AM-4PM (MST). Access by: Mail, in person.

Probate—County Clerk, 105 Albright, Suite D, Taos, NM 87571. 505-758-8836. Fax: 505-751-3391. 8AM-5PM (MST). Access by: Mail, in person.

Torrance County

Real Estate Recording—Torrance County Clerk, 9th & Allen Streets, Estancia, NM 87016. 505-384-2221. Fax: 505-384-5294. 8AM-5PM (MST).

Felony, Civil, Probate—7th Judicial District Court, County Courthouse, Box 78, Estancia, NM 87016. 505-384-2974. Fax: 505-384-2229. 8AM-5PM (MST). Access by: Phone, mail, in person.

Misdemeanor, Civil Actions Under $5,000, Eviction, Small Claims—Moriarty Magistrate Court, PO Box 1968, Moriarty, NM 87035. 505-832-4476. Fax: 505-832-1563. 8AM-4PM (MST). Access by: Mail, in person.

Probate—County Clerk, Box 48, Estancia, NM 87016. 505-384-2221. Fax: 505-384-4080. 8AM-Noon, 1-5PM (MST). Access by: Mail, in person.

Union County

Real Estate Recording—Union County Clerk, 200 Court Street, Courthouse, Clayton, NM 88415. 505-374-9491. Fax: 505-374-2763. 9AM-5PM (MST).

Felony, Civil, Probate—8th Judicial District Court, Box 310, Clayton, NM 88415. 505-374-9577. Fax: 505-374-2089. 8AM-5PM (MST). Access by: Mail, in person.

Misdemeanor, Civil Actions Under $5,000, Eviction, Small Claims—Magistrate Court, 118 Walnut St, Clayton, NM 88415. 505-374-9472. Fax: 505-374-9368. 8AM-Noon, 1-5PM (MST). Access by: Phone, fax, mail, in person.

Probate—County Clerk, PO Box 430, Clayton, NM 88415. 505-374-9491. Fax: 505-374-2763. 9AM-Noon, 1-5PM (MST). Access by: Mail, in person.

Valencia County

Real Estate Recording—Valencia County Clerk, 444 Luna Avenue, Los Lunas, NM 87031. 505-866-2073. Fax: 505-866-2023. 8AM-4:30PM (MST).

Felony, Civil, Probate—13th Judicial District Court, Box 1089, Los Lunas, NM 87031. 505-865-4291. Fax: 505-865-8801. 8AM-5PM (MST). Access by: Mail, in person.

Misdemeanor, Civil Actions Under $5,000, Eviction, Small Claims—Belen Magistrate Court, 237 N Main St, Belen, NM 87002. 505-864-7509. Fax: 505-864-9532. 8AM-Noon,1-5PM (MST). Access by: Mail, in person.

Los Lunas Magistrate Court, 121 Don Diego, Los Lunas, NM 87031. 505-865-4637. 8AM-4PM (MST). Access by: Fax, mail, in person.

Probate—County Clerk, Box 969, Los Lunas, NM 87031. 505-866-2073. Fax: 505-866-2023. 8AM-4:30PM (MST). Access by: Phone, mail, in person.

Federal Courts

US District Court

District of New Mexico

Albuquerque Division, US District Court PO Box 689, Albuquerque, NM 87103. 505-766-2851. Counties: All counties in New Mexico. Cases may be assigned to any of the three divisions

Las Cruces Division, US District Court 200 E Griggs, Room C-242, Las Cruces, NM 88001. 505-527-6800. Counties: All counties in New Mexico. Cases may be assigned to any of the three divisions

Santa Fe Division, US District Court PO Box 2384, Santa Fe, NM 87504-2384. 505-988-6481. Counties: All counties in New Mexico. Cases may be assigned to any of the three divisions

US Bankruptcy Court

District of New Mexico

Albuquerque Division, US Bankruptcy Court, PO Box 546, Albuquerque, NM 87103. 505-248-6500. Voice Case Information System: 505-248-6536. Counties: All counties in New Mexico

New York

Capitol: Albany (Albany County)	
Number of Counties: 62	**Population:** 18,136,081
County Court Locations:	**Federal Court Locations:**
•Supreme Courts: 11/ 12 Districts	•District Courts: 11
•County Courts: 2/57 Counties	•Bankruptcy Courts: 10
•Combined Courts: 57	**State Agencies:** 24
•City Courts: 61/61 Cities	
•District Courts: 10	
Other Local Courts:	
City/Criminal Courts of New York City: 6	•Surrogates' Courts: 62
Town and Village Justice Courts: 1487	Court of Claims: 1
	Family Courts: 62

State Agencies—Summary

General Help Numbers:

State Archives

State Archives & Records Administration	518-474-8955
11D40 Cultural Education Center	Fax: 518-473-9985
Albany, NY 12230	9AM-5PM
Reference Librarian:	518-474-5930
Historical Society:	212-783-3400
Historical Association:	607-547-2509

Governor's Office

Governor's Office	518-474-8390
Executive Chamber, State Capitol	Fax: 518-474-8390
Albany, NY 12224	9AM-5PM

Attorney General's Office

Attorney General's Office	518-474-1778
Room C49	Fax: 518-474-0714
State Capitol	8:30AM-5PM
Albany, NY 12224	

State Legislation

NY Senate Document Room	518-455-7545
State Capitol	9AM-5PM
Room 317, State & Washington Sts	
Albany, NY 12247	
Senate Document Room:	518-455-2312
Calls Without Bill Numbers:	518-455-3216

Important State Internet Sites:

```
🌐 Webscape
File  Edit  View                                    Help
```

State of New York World Wide Web
www.state.ny.us/

This state home page links to the Governor, state government, tourism and state development.

The Governor's Office
www.state.ny.us/governor

This site includes information about the Governor, his press releases, strategic programs, results, and the 1997-1998 budget.

Unclaimed Property
www.osc.state.ny.us/cgi-bin/db2www/ouffrm.d2w/input

Online searching by name, for unclaimed property, is available at this site.

New York Legislature
unix2.nysed.gov/ils/legislature/legis.html

This page provided links to the New York State Assembly and Senate.

State Agencies—Public Records

Criminal Records
Division of Criminal Justice Services, 4 Tower Place, Albany, NY 12203, Main Telephone: 518-457-6043, Fax: 518-457-6550, Hours: 8AM-5PM.
Restricted access.

Corporation Records
Limited Partnership Records
Limited Liability Company Records
Limited Liability Partnerships
Division of Corporations, Department of State, 41 State St, Albany, NY 12231, Main Telephone: 518-473-2492, Corporate Searches: 900-835-2677, Fax: 518-474-5173, Hours: 8AM-4:30PM. Access by: mail, phone, visit. In addition to the certificates, records include date of incorporation, subsequent filings, status, reserved names, principle business location, registered agent, number and type of stock shares entitled to issue, and biennial statements w/addresses.

Trademarks/Servicemarks
Department of State, Miscellaneous Records, 41 State St, Albany, NY 12231, Main Telephone: 518-474-4770, Fax: 518-473-0730, Hours: 8:30AM-4:30PM. Access by: mail, fax, phone, visit.

Uniform Commercial Code
Federal Tax Liens
State Tax Liens
UCC Division, Department of State, 41 State Street, Albany, NY 12231, Main Telephone: 518-474-4763, Hours: 8AM-4:30PM. Access by: mail, visit.

Sales Tax Registrations
Sales Tax Registration Bureau, WA Harriman Campus, Building 8, Rm 408, Albany, NY 12227, Main Telephone: 518-457-0259, Fax 518-457-8218 Access by: mail, phone, visit.

Birth Certificates
State Department of Health, Vital Records Section, Empire State Plaza, Corning Tower, Albany, NY 12237-0023, Main Telephone: 518-474-3038, Message number: 518-474-3077, Hours: 8:30AM-4:30PM. Access by: mail, phone, visit. For New York City information, see the separate entry below.

Death Records
State Department of Health, Vital Records Section, Empire State Plaza, Corning Tower, Albany, NY 12237-0023, Main Telephone: 518-474-3038, Message number: 518-474-3077, Hours: 8:30AM-4:30PM. Access by: mail, visit. For New York City, see the separate entry below.

Marriage Certificates
State Department of Health, Vital Records Section, Empire State Plaza, Corning Tower, Albany, NY 12237-0023, Main Telephone: 518-474-3038, Message number: 518-474-3077, Hours: 8:30AM-4:30PM. Access by: mail, visit. For New York City information, see the separate entry below.

Divorce Records
State Department of Health, Vital Records Section, Empire State Plaza, Corning Tower, Albany, NY 12237-0023, Main Telephone: 518-474-3038, Message number: 518-474-3077, Hours: 8:30AM-4:30PM. Access by: mail, visit. For New York City information, see the separate entry below.

Birth Certificate-New York City
Death Records-New York City
Department of Health, Bureau of Vital Statistics, PO Box 3776, Church St Station, New York, NY 10013, Main Telephone: 212-788-4504, Hours: 9AM-4PM. Access by: mail, visit.

Marriage Certificate-New York City
City Clerk's Office, Department of Records & Information Services, 1 Centre Street, Rm 252, New York, NY 10007, Main Telephone: 212-669-8898, Hours: 9AM-4:30PM M-TH; 9AM-1PM F.

Divorce Records-New York City
City Clerk's Office, Division of Old Records, 60 Centre Street, Rm 161, New York City, NY 10007, Main Telephone: 212-374-4376.

Workers' Compensation Records
NY Workers' Compensation Board, Director of Claims Office, 180 Livingston St, Room 416, Brooklyn, NY 11248, Main Telephone: 718-802-6621, Fax: 718-834-2116, Hours: 9AM-5PM. Access by: mail, phone, visit. File copies of records are not released for employment purposes, even with a signed release.

Driver Records
Department of Motor Vehicles, Data Preparation & Control, Empire State Plaza, Albany, NY 12228, Main Telephone: 518-474-0695, Hours: 8AM-5PM. Access by: mail, phone, visit, PC. Copies of tickets may be purchased from the same address for a fee of $6.00 per ticket.

Vehicle Ownership
Vehicle Identification
Department of Motor Vehicles, Certified Document Center, Empire State Plaza, Swan St Bldg, Room 232, Albany, NY 12228, Main Telephone: 518-474-0710, Hours: 8AM-5PM. Access by: mail, visit, PC.

Accident Reports
DMV Certified Document Center, Accident Report Section, Empire State Plaza, Swan St Bldg, Albany, NY 12228, Main Telephone: 518-474-0710, Hours: 8AM-4:30PM. Access by: mail, visit.

Hunting License Information
Fishing License Information
Records not available from state agency.

County Courts and Recording Offices

What You Need to Know...

About the Courts

Administration

NY State Office of Court Administration   212-417-2004
New York City Office   Fax: 212-417-2013
270 Broadway, Room 1400   9AM-5PM
New York, NY 10007

Office of Court Administrators   518-473-1196
Empire State Plaza, Agency Bldg #4, Suite 2001
Albany, NY 12223

Court Structure

"Supreme" Courts are the highest trial courts in the state, equivalent to Circuit or District Courts in other states; they are not appeals courts. Many NYC courts are indexed by plaintiff **only**. See the book *Public Records Online* by this publisher for information concerning proprietary databases of this information indexed by defendant.

Records for Supreme and County Courts are maintained by County Clerks. In most counties, the address for the clerk is the same as for the court. Exceptions are noted in the court profiles.

There is an **OCA central index of criminal cases** from courts in the counties and boroughs of Bronx, Dutchess, Erie, Kings, Nassau, New York, Orange, Putnam, Queens, Richmond, Rockland, Suffolk, and Westchester. A special application form is required for each county to be searched. The request **must** include complete name and date of birth. Include two (2) self addressed stamped return envelopes with mail requests. The fee, payable by check, is $16.00 per name per county. Mail and in person requests go to one location, and hand pick up of results are available at another:

Applications to OCA	Pick Up
Office of Administration	Office of Administration
Court Operational Services	Criminal Disposition
Criminal Records Program	Reporting Unit
80 Centre St.. Room 500D	270 Broadway Room 821
New York, NY 10013	New York, NY
	212-417-2263

You may obtain a copy of the actual disposition of a case from the specific county.

Searching Hints

Supreme and County Court records are generally maintained in the County Clerk's Office, which outside of NYC may index civil cases by defendant, whereas the court itself maintains only a plaintiff index.

Fees for Supreme and County Courts are generally as follows: $5.00 per 2 year search per name for a manual search and $16.00 per name for a computer or OCA search; $.50 per page (minimum $1.00) for copies; and $4.00 for certification. City Courts charge $5.00 for certification. Effective 4-1-95, **no** New York court accepts credit cards for **any** transaction.

Online Access

Online access is available from Rockland County. Automated courts will access their internal computer indexes, usually at a fee of $16.00 per name.

About the Recorder's Office

Organization

62 counties, 62 filing offices. The recording officers are County Clerk (New York City Register in the counties of Bronx, Kings, New York, and Queens). The entire state is in the Eastern Time Zone (EST).

UCC Records

This is a **dual filing state**. Financing statements are filed both at the state level and with the County Clerk, except for consumer goods, cooperatives (as in cooperative apartments), farm related and real estate related collateral, which are filed only with the County Clerk. All counties will perform UCC searches. Use search request form UCC-11. Search fees are usually $4.50 per debtor name using the approved UCC-11 request form and $7.50 using a non-New York form. Copies usually cost $1.50 per page.

Lien Records

Federal tax liens on personal property of businesses are filed with the Secretary of State. Other federal tax liens are filed with the County Clerk. State tax liens are filed with the County Clerk, with a master list—called **state tax warrants**—available at the Secretary of State's office. Federal tax liens are usually indexed with UCC Records. State tax liens are usually indexed with other miscellaneous liens and judgments. Some counties include **federal** tax liens as part of a UCC search, and others will search tax liens for a separate fee. Search fees and copy fees vary. Other liens include judgments, mechanics, welfare, hospital, matrimonial, wage assignment, and lis pendens.

Real Estate Records

Some counties will perform real estate searches. Certified copy fees are usually $1.00 per page with a $4.00 minimum. Tax records are located at the Treasurer's Office.

County Courts and Recording Offices

Albany County

Real Estate Recording—Albany County Clerk, County Courthouse, Room 128, Albany, NY 12207. 518-487-5100. 9AM-5PM (EST).

Felony, Civil—Supreme and County Court, Courthouse Rm 128, 16 Eagle St, Albany, NY 12207. 518-487-5118. Fax: 518-487-5099. 9AM-5PM (EST). Access by: Mail, in person. Search requests must be in writing.

Civil Actions Under $15,000, Eviction, Small Claims—Albany City Court-Civil Part, City Hall Rm 209, Albany, NY 12207. 518-434-5115. Fax: 518-434-5034. 8:30AM-5PM (EST). Access by: Mail, in person.

Misdemeanor—Albany City Court-Misdemeanors, Morton & Broad St, Albany, NY 12202. 518-449-7109. Criminal: 518-449-7109. Fax: 518-462-8074. 8AM-4PM (EST). Access by: Phone, mail, in person.

Misdemeanor, Civil Actions Under $15,000, Eviction, Small Claims—Cohoes City Court, 97 Mohawk St, PO Box 678, Cohoes, NY 12047-0678. Civil: 518-233-2133. Criminal: 518-233-2134. 8AM-4PM (EST). Access by: Mail, in person.

Watervliet City Court, 15th & Broadway, Watervliet, NY 12189. 518-270-3803. Fax: 518-270-3812. 8AM-3PM (EST). Access by: Mail, in person.

Probate—Surrogate Court, Courthouse, Albany, NY 12207. 518-487-5393. 9AM-5PM (EST).

Allegany County

Real Estate Recording—Allegany County Clerk, Court Street, Courthouse, Belmont, NY 14813. 716-268-9270. Fax: 716-268-9659. 9AM-5PM (June-August 8:30AM-4PM) (EST).

Felony, Civil—Supreme and County Court, Courthouse, Belmont, NY 14813. 716-268-5813. Fax: 716-268-7090. 9AM-5PM (EST). Access by: Phone, fax, mail, in person.

Probate—Surrogate Court, Courthouse, Belmont, NY 14813. 716-268-5815. Fax: 716-268-7090. 9AM-5PM Sept-May; 8:30AM-4PM June-Aug (EST). Access by: Mail, in person.

Bronx County

Real Estate Recording—Bronx City Register, 1932 Arthur Avenue, Bronx, NY 10457. 718-579-6828. 9AM-4PM (EST).

Civil Actions Over $25,000—Supreme Court-Civil Division, 851 Grand Concourse, Bronx, NY 10451. 718-590-3641. Fax: 718-590-8122. 9AM-5PM (EST). Access by: Mail, in person.

Felony—Supreme Court-Criminal Division, 80 Centre St, Rm 500D, New York, NY 10013. 212-417-3149. 9:30AM-4:30PM, Closed 12-2 (EST). Access by: Mail, in person.

Civil Actions Under $25,000, Eviction, Small Claims—Civil Court of the City of New York-Bronx Branch, 851 Grand Concourse, Bronx, NY 10451. 718-590-3601. Fax: 718-590-7294. 9AM-5PM (EST). Access by: In person only.

Probate—Surrogate Court, 851 Grand Concourse, Bronx, NY 10451. 718-590-3611. Fax: 718-590-3575. 9AM-5PM (EST).

Broome County

Real Estate Recording—Broome County Clerk, 44 Hawley Street, Binghamton, NY 13901. 607-778-2451. Fax: 607-778-2243. 9AM-5PM (EST).

Felony, Civil—Supreme and County Court, PO Box 2062, Binghamton, NY 13902. 607-778-2448. Fax: 607-778-6426. 9AM-5PM (EST). Access by: Mail, in person.

Misdemeanor, Civil Actions Under $15,000, Eviction, Small Claims—Binghamton City Court, Governmental Plaza, Binghamton, NY 13901. 607-772-7006. Fax: 607-772-7041. 9AM-5PM (EST). Access by: Mail, in person.

Probate—Surrogate Court, Courthouse Rm 109, Binghamton, NY 13901. 607-778-2111. Fax: 607-778-2308. 9AM-5PM (EST).

Cattaraugus County

Real Estate Recording—Cattaraugus County Clerk, 303 Court Street, Little Valley, NY 14755. 716-938-9111. Fax: 716-938-6009. 9AM-5PM (EST).

Felony, Civil—Supreme and County Court, 303 Court St, Little Valley, NY 14755. 716-938-9111. Fax: 716-938-6413. 9AM-5PM (EST). Access by: Mail, in person.

Misdemeanor, Civil Actions Under $15,000, Eviction, Small Claims—Olean City Court, PO Box 631, Olean, NY 14760. 716-376-5620. Fax: 716-376-5620. 8:30AM-4:30PM (EST). Access by: Mail, in person.

Salamanca City Court, Municipal Center, 225 Wildwood, Salamanca, NY 14779. 716-945-4153. 8AM-4PM (EST). Access by: Mail, in person.

Probate—Surrogate Court, 303 Court St, Little Valley, NY 14755. 716-938-9111. Fax: 716-938-6983. 8:30AM-5PM (EST). Access by: Mail, in person.

Cayuga County

Real Estate Recording—Cayuga County Clerk, 160 Genesee Street, Auburn, NY 13021. 315-253-1271. Fax: 315-253-1006. 9AM-5PM (July-Aug 8AM-4PM) (EST).

Felony, Civil—Supreme and County Court, 160 Genesee St, Auburn, NY 13021-3424. 315-253-1271. Fax: 315-253-1586. 9AM-5PM Sept-June; 8AM-4PM July-Aug (EST). Access by: Mail, in person.

Misdemeanor, Civil Actions Under $15,000, Eviction, Small Claims—Auburn City Court, 153 Genesee St, Auburn, NY 13021-3434. 315-253-1570. Fax: 315-253-1085. 8AM-4PM (EST). Access by: Mail, in person.

Probate—Surrogate Court, Courthouse, Auburn, NY 13021-3471. 315-255-4316. Fax: 315-255-4322. 1-4PM T, 9AM-Noon Th; Summer hours 1-3:30PM T, 9AM-Noon Th (EST). Access by: Mail, in person.

Chautauqua County

Real Estate Recording—Chautauqua County Clerk, Corner of North Erie and E. Chautauqua, Courthouse, Mayville, NY 14757. 716-753-4331. Fax: 716-753-4310. 9AM-5PM (EST).

Civil—Supreme and County Court-Civil Records, PO Box 170, Mayville, NY 14757. 716-753-4331. 9AM-5PM/Summer 8:30AM-4:30PM (EST). Access by: Mail, in person.

Felony—Supreme and County Court-Criminal Records, Courthouse, Mayville, NY 14757. 716-753-4266. Fax: 716-753-4993. 9AM-5PM/Summer 8:30AM-4:30PM (EST). Access by: Mail, in person.

Misdemeanor, Civil Actions Under $15,000, Eviction, Small Claims—Dunkirk City Court, City Hall, 342 Central Ave, Dunkirk, NY 14048. 716-366-2055. Fax: 716-366-3622. 9AM-5PM (EST). Access by: Mail, in person.

Jamestown City Court, City Hall, Jamestown, NY 14701. 716-483-7561. Fax: 716-483-7519. 9AM-5PM (EST). Access by: Mail, in person.

Probate—Surrogate Court, Gerace Office Bldg, Rm 231 (PO Box C), Mayville, NY 14757-0299. 716-753-4339. Fax: 716-753-4600. 9AM-5PM (EST).

Chemung County

Real Estate Recording—Chemung County Clerk, 210 Lake Street, Elmira, NY 14902. 607-737-2920. Fax: 607-737-2897. 8:30AM-4:30PM (EST).

Civil—Supreme and County Court-Civil Records, 210 Lake St, Elmira, NY 14901. 607-737-2920. Fax: 607-737-2897. 8:30AM-4:30PM (EST). Access by: Mail, in person.

Felony—Supreme and County Court-Criminal Records, 203 Lake St, Elmira, NY 14901-0588. 607-737-2844. 8:30AM-4:30PM (EST). Access by: Phone, mail, in person.

Misdemeanor, Civil Actions Under $15,000, Eviction, Small Claims—Elmira City Court, 317 E Church St, Elmira, NY 14901. 607-737-5681. Fax: 607-737-5820. 8AM-4PM (EST). Access by: Mail, in person.

Probate—Surrogate Court, 224 Lake St (PO Box 588), Elmira, NY 14902. 607-737-2946. Fax: 607-737-2874. 9AM-5PM (EST). Access by: Mail, in person.

Chenango County

Real Estate Recording—Chenango County Clerk, 5 Court Street, Norwich, NY 13815. 607-337-1450. 8:30AM-5PM (EST).

Felony, Civil—Supreme and County Court, County Office Bldg, Norwich, NY 13815-1676. 607-337-1450. 8:30AM-5PM (EST). Access by: Mail, in person.

Misdemeanor, Civil Actions Under $15,000, Eviction, Small Claims—Norwich City Court, 45 Broad St, Norwich, NY 13815-0430. 607-334-1224. Fax: 607-334-8494. 8:30AM-4:30PM (EST). Access by: Fax, mail, in person.

Probate—Surrogate Court, County Office Bldg, 5 Court St, Norwich, NY 13815. 607-337-1822. Fax: 607-337-1834. 9AM-Noon, 1-5PM (EST). Access by: Mail, in person.

Clinton County

Real Estate Recording—Clinton County Clerk, 137 Margaret Street, Government Center, Plattsburgh, NY 12901. 518-565-4700. Fax: 518-565-4780. 8AM-5PM (EST).

Felony, Civil—Supreme and County Court, County Government Center, 137 Margaret St, Plattsburgh, NY 12901. 518-565-4715. Fax: 518-565-4708. 9AM-5PM (EST). Access by: Mail, in person.

Misdemeanor, Civil Actions Under $15,000, Eviction, Small Claims—Plattsburg City Court, 41 City Hall Pl, Plattsburgh, NY 12901. 518-563-7870. Fax: 518-563-3124. 8AM-4PM (EST). Access by: Mail, in person.

Columbia County

Real Estate Recording—Columbia County Clerk, 401 Union St., Hudson, NY 12534. 518-828-3339. Fax: 518-828-5299. 9AM-5PM (EST).

Felony, Civil—Supreme and County Court, Courthouse, Hudson, NY 12534. 518-828-3339. Fax: 518-825-5299. 9AM-5PM (EST). Access by: Mail, in person.

Misdemeanor, Civil Actions Under $15,000, Eviction, Small Claims—Hudson City Court, 429 Warren St, Hudson, NY 12534. 518-828-3100. Fax: 518-828-3628. 8AM-4PM (EST). Access by: Fax, mail, in person.

Probate—Surrogate Court, Courthouse, 401 Union St, Hudson, NY 12534. 518-828-0414. Fax: 518-828-2101. 9AM-5PM (EST). Access by: Mail, in person.

Cortland County

Real Estate Recording—Cortland County Clerk, Courthouse, 46 Greenbush St., Cortland, NY 13045. 607-753-5021. Fax: 607-758-5500. 9AM-5PM (EST).

Felony, Civil—Supreme and County Court, 46 Greenbush St, Ste 301, Cortland, NY 13045. 607-753-5010. Civil: 607-753-5021. Criminal: 607-753-5010. Fax: 607-756-3409. 9AM-5PM (EST). Access by: Mail, in person.

Misdemeanor, Civil Actions Under $15,000, Eviction, Small Claims—Cortland City Court, 25 Court St, Cortland, NY 13045. 607-753-1811. Fax: 607-753-9932. 8:30AM-4:30PM (EST). Access by: Mail, in person.

Probate—Surrogate Court, 46 Greenbush St, Ste 301, Cortland, NY 13045. 607-753-5355. Fax: 607-756-3409. 9AM-5PM (EST).

Delaware County

Real Estate Recording—Delaware County Clerk, Court House Square, Delhi, NY 13753. 607-746-2123. Fax: 607-746-6924. 9AM-5PM (EST).

Felony, Civil—Supreme and County Court, 3 Court St, Delhi, NY 13753. 607-746-2131. Fax: 607-746-3253. 9AM-5PM (EST). Access by: Mail, in person.

Probate—Surrogate Court, 3 Court St, Delhi, NY 13753. 607-746-2126. Fax: 607-746-3253. (EST).

Dutchess County

Real Estate Recording—Dutchess County Clerk, 22 Market Street, Poughkeepsie, NY 12601. 914-486-2120. 9AM-4:45PM (EST).

Felony, Civil—Supreme and County Court, 10 Market St, Poughkeepsie, NY 12601-3203. 914-486-2125. Fax: 914-486-2138. 9AM-5PM (EST). Access by: Mail, in person.

Misdemeanor, Civil Actions Under $15,000, Eviction, Small Claims—Beacon City Court, One Municiapl Plaza, Beacon, NY 12508. 914-838-5030. Fax: 914-838-5041. 8AM-4PM (EST). Access by: Mail, in person.

Poughkeepsie City Court, Civic Center Plaza, Poughkeepsie, NY 12601. 914-451-4091. Fax: 914-451-4094. 8AM-4PM (EST). Access by: Mail, in person.

Probate—Surrogate Court, 10 Market St, Poughkeepsie, NY 12601. 914-486-2235. Fax: 914-486-2234. 9AM-5PM (EST). Access by: Mail, in person.

Erie County

Real Estate Recording—Erie County Clerk, 25 Delaware Avenue, County Hall, Buffalo, NY 14202. 716-858-6425. Fax: 716-858-6550. 9AM-5PM (EST).

Felony, Civil—Supreme and County Court, 25 Delaware Ave, Buffalo, NY 14202. 716-858-7766. Civil: 716-858-7766. Criminal: 716-858-7877. Fax: 716-858-6550. 9AM-5PM (EST). Access by: Mail, in person.

Misdemeanor, Civil Actions Under $15,000, Eviction, Small Claims—Buffalo City Court, 50 Delaware Ave, Buffalo, NY 14202. 716-847-8200. Fax: 716-847-8257. 9AM-5PM (EST). Access by: Mail, in person.

Lackawanna City Court, 714 Ridge Rd, Rm 225, Lackawanna, NY 14218. 716-827-6486. Fax: 716-827-1874. 8:30AM-4:30PM (EST). Access by: Mail, in person.

Tonawanda City Court, 200 Niagara St, Tonawanda, NY 14150. 716-693-3484. Fax: 716-693-1612. 9AM-5PM (EST). Access by: Mail, in person.

Probate—Surrogate Court, 92 Franklin St, Buffalo, NY 14202. 716-854-7867. Fax: 716-853-3741. 9AM-5PM (EST). Access by: Mail, in person.

Essex County

Real Estate Recording—Essex County Clerk, 100 Court Street, Elizabethtown, NY 12932. 518-873-3600. Fax: 518-873-3548. 8AM-5PM (EST).

Felony, Civil—Supreme and County Courts, Essex County Government Center, Court St, PO Box 217, Elizabethtown, NY 12932. 518-873-3370. Civil: 518-873-3600. Criminal: 518-873-3370. Fax: 518-873-3376. 8:30AM-5PM (EST). Access by: Mail, in person.

Probate—Surrogate Court, County Government Center, Court St, PO Box 505, Elizabethtown, NY 12932. 518-873-3384. 9AM-5PM (EST).

Franklin County

Real Estate Recording—Franklin County Clerk, 63 West Main Street, Malone, NY 12953. 518-483-1684. Fax: 518-483-9143. 9AM-5PM Jan-May; & Sept-Dec; 8AM-4PM June-Aug (EST).

Felony, Civil—Supreme and County Court, 63 W Main St, Malone, NY 12953-1817. 518-481-1748. 9AM-5PM (EST). Access by: Mail, in person.

Probate—Surrogate Court, Courthouse, 63 W Main St, Malone, NY 12953-1817. 518-483-6767. 9AM-5PM Sept-May; 8AM-4PM June-Aug (EST). Access by: Mail, in person.

Fulton County

Real Estate Recording—Fulton County Clerk, 223 West Main Street, Johnstown, NY 12095. 518-762-0555. Fax: 518-762-3839. 9AM-5PM (July-August 9AM-4PM) (EST).

Felony, Civil—Supreme and County Court, County Bldg, West Main St, Johnstown, NY 12095. 518-762-0539. Fax: 518-762-5078. 9AM-5PM (EST). Access by: Phone, mail, in person.

Misdemeanor, Civil Actions Under $15,000, Eviction, Small Claims—Gloversville City Court, City Hall, Frontage Rd, Gloversville, NY 12078. 518-773-4527. 8AM-4PM (EST). Access by: Mail, in person.

Johnstown City Court, City Hall, Johnstown, NY 12095. 518-762-0007. Fax: 518-762-2720. 8AM-4PM (EST). Access by: Mail, in person.

Genesee County

Real Estate Recording—Genesee County Clerk, Main & Court Streets, Batavia, NY 14020. 716-344-2550. Fax: 716-344-8521. 8:30AM-5PM (EST).

Felony, Civil—Supreme and County Court, Courthouse, Batavia, NY 14021-0462. 716-344-2550. Fax: 716-344-8521. 8:30AM-5PM (EST). Access by: Mail, in person.

Misdemeanor, Civil Actions Under $15,000, Eviction, Small Claims—Batavia City Court, 1 W Main St, PO Box 385, Batavia, NY 14021. 716-343-8180. Fax: 716-343-9221. 9AM-5PM (EST). Access by: Fax, mail, in person.

Probate—Surrogate Court, Genessee County #1, PO Box 462, Batavia, NY 14021-0462. 716-344-2550. Fax: 716-344-8517. 9AM-5PM (EST).

Greene County

Real Estate Recording—Greene County Clerk, 320 Main Street, Catskill, NY 12414. 518-943-2050. Fax: 518-943-2146. 9AM-5PM (June-August 8:30AM-4:30PM) (EST).

Felony, Civil—Supreme and County Court, Courthouse, Catskill, NY 12414. 518-943-2230. Fax: 518-943-7763. 9AM-5PM (EST). Access by: Fax, mail, in person.

Probate—Surrogate Court, Courthouse, 320 Main St, Catskill, NY 12414. 518-943-2484. Fax: 518-943-4372. 9AM-5PM (EST).

Hamilton County

Real Estate Recording—Hamilton County Clerk, County Clerk's Office Bldg., Rte. 8, Lake Pleasant, NY 12108. 518-548-7111. 9AM-5PM (9AM-4PM July-Aug) (EST).

Felony, Civil—Supreme and County Court, Courthouse, Rout 8, Lake Pleasant, NY 12108. 518-548-7111. 9AM-5PM Sept-June; 9AM-4PM July & Aug (EST). Access by: Mail, in person. Request must be in writing.

Probate—Surrogate Court, PO Box 780, Indian Lake, NY 12842. 518-648-5411. Fax: 518-648-6286. 9AM-Noon, 1-5PM (EST). Access by: Mail, in person.

Herkimer County

Real Estate Recording—Herkimer County Clerk, 109-111 Mary Street, County Office Building, Herkimer, NY 13350. 315-867-1134. Fax: 315-866-4396. 9AM-5PM (June-August 8:30AM-4PM) (EST).

Felony, Civil—Supreme and County Court, 109-111 Mary St, PO Box 111, Herkimer, NY 13350-0111. 315-867-1137. Fax: 315-866-4396. 9AM-5PM Sept-May; 8:30AM-4PM June-Aug (EST). Access by: Phone, mail, in person.

Misdemeanor, Civil Actions Under $15,000, Eviction, Small Claims—Little Falls City Court, 659 E Main St, Little Falls, NY 13365. 315-823-1690. Fax: 315-823-1623. 8:30AM-4:30PM (EST). Access by: Mail, in person.

Probate—Surrogate Court, 320 N Main St (PO Box 550), Herkimer, NY 13350-0749. 315-867-1170. Fax: 315-866-1722. 9AM-5PM Sept-May; 8:30AM-4PM June-Aug (EST). Access by: Mail, in person.

Jefferson County

Real Estate Recording—Jefferson County Clerk, 175 Arsenal Street, Watertown, NY 13601. 315-785-3081. Fax: 315-785-5048. 9AM-5PM (8:30AM-4PM July-Aug) (EST).

Felony, Civil—Supreme & County Courts, Jefferson County Clerk's Office, 175 Arsenal St, County Building, Watertown, NY 13601-3783. 315-785-3200. Fax: 315-785-5048. 9AM-5PM Sept-June; 8:30AM-4PM July-Aug (EST). Access by: Mail, in person.

Misdemeanor, Civil Actions Under $15,000, Eviction, Small Claims—Watertown City Court, Municipal Bldg, 245 Washington St, Watertown, NY 13601. 315-785-7785. Fax: 315-785-7818. 9AM-5PM (EST). Access by: Mail, in person.

Probate—Surrogate Court, County Office Bldg, 7th Flr, 175 Arsenal St, Watertown, NY 13601-2562. 315-785-3019. Fax: 315-785-5194. 9AM-5PM Sept-May; 8:30AM-4PM June-Aug (EST). Access by: Mail, in person.

Kings County

Real Estate Recording—Kings City Register, Municipal Building, 1st Floor, Room 2, 210 Joralemon Street, Brooklyn, NY 11201. 718-802-3589. Fax: 718-802-3745. (EST).

Civil Actions Over $25,000—Supreme Court-Civil Division, 360 Adams St, Brooklyn, NY 11201. 718-643-5894. Fax: 718-643-8187. 9AM-5PM (EST). Access by: In person only.

Felony, Misdemeanor—Court of the City of New York-Criminal Division, 80 Centre St, Rm 500D, New York, NY 10013. 212-417-3149. Fax: 212-417-5856. 9:30AM-4:30PM (EST). Access by: Mail, in person.

Civil Actions Under $25,000, Eviction, Small Claims—Civil Court of the City of New York-Kings Branch, 141 Livingston St, Brooklyn, NY 11201. 718-643-5069. 9AM-5PM (EST). Access by: In person only.

Probate—Surrogate Court, 2 Johnson St, Brooklyn, NY 11201. 718-643-5262. Fax: 718-643-6237. 9AM-5PM (EST).

Lewis County

Real Estate Recording—Lewis County Clerk, 7660 State Street, Courthouse Building, Lowville, NY 13367. 315-376-5333. 8:30AM-4:30PM (EST).

Felony, Civil—Supreme and County Court, Courthouse, PO Box 232, Lowville, NY 13367. 315-376-5333. Fax: 315-376-3768. 8:30AM-4:30PM (EST). Access by: Mail, in person.

Probate—Surrogate Court, Courthouse, 7660 State St, Lowville, NY 13367-1396. 315-376-5344. Fax: 315-376-4145. 8:30AM-4:30PM (EST).

Livingston County

Real Estate Recording—Livingston County Clerk, Government Center, 6 Court St., Room 201, Geneseo, NY 14454. 716-243-7010. 8:30AM-4:30PM Oct 1-May 30; 8AM-4PM June 1-Sept 30 (EST).

Felony, Civil—Supreme and County Court, 6 Court St, Rm 201, Geneseo, NY 14454. 716-243-7010. 8:30AM-4:30PM Oct-May; 8AM-4PM June-Sept (EST). Access by: Mail, in person.

Probate—Surrogate Court, 2 Court St, Geneseo, NY 14454. 716-243-7095. 9AM-5PM (EST).

Madison County

Real Estate Recording—Madison County Clerk, North Court Street, County Office Building, Wampsville, NY 13163. 315-366-2261. Fax: 315-366-2615. 9AM-5PM (EST).

Felony, Civil—Supreme and County Court, County Office Bldg, Wampsville, NY 13163. 315-366-2261. Fax: 315-366-2615. 9AM-5PM (EST). Access by: Mail, in person.

Misdemeanor, Civil Actions Under $15,000, Eviction, Small Claims—Oneida City Court, 109 N Main St, Oneida, NY 13421. 315-363-1310. Fax: 315-363-3230. 8:30AM-4:30PM (EST). Access by: Mail, in person.

Probate—Surrogate Court, Courthouse, PO Box 607, Wampsville, NY 13163. 315-366-2392. Fax: 315-366-2539. 9AM-5PM (EST). Access by: Mail, in person.

Monroe County

Real Estate Recording—Monroe County Clerk, 39 West Main Street, Rochester, NY 14614. 716-428-5151. Fax: 716-428-5447. 9AM-5PM (EST).

Felony, Civil—Supreme and County Court, 39 W Main St, Rochester, NY 14614. 716-428-5888. Fax: 716-428-5447. 9AM-5PM (EST). Access by: Mail, in person.

Misdemeanor, Civil Actions Under $15,000, Eviction, Small Claims—Rochester City Court, Hall of Justice, Rochester, NY 14614. Civil: 716-428-2444. Criminal: 716-428-2447. Fax: 716-428-2588. 9AM-5PM (EST). Access by: Phone, fax, mail, in person. Only certificate of disposition available.

Probate—Surrogate Court, Hall of Justice, Rm 304, Rochester, NY 14614-2185. 716-428-5200. Fax: 716-428-2650. 9AM-4PM (EST). Access by: Mail, in person.

Montgomery County

Real Estate Recording—Montgomery County Clerk, County Office Building, Fonda, NY 12068. 518-853-8115. 8:30AM-4PM (EST).

Felony, Civil—Supreme and County Court, Courthouse, Fonda, NY 12068. Civil: 518-853-8113. Criminal: 518-853-4516. Fax: 518-853-3596. 9AM-5PM; 8:30AM-4PM (civil) (EST). Access by: Phone, mail, in person.

Misdemeanor, Civil Actions Under $15,000, Eviction, Small Claims—Amsterdam City Court, Public Safety Bldg, Rm 208, Amsterdam, NY 12010. 518-842-9510. Fax: 518-843-8474. 8AM-4PM (EST). Access by: Mail, in person.

Probate—Surrogate Court, PO Box 1500, Fonda, NY 12068-1500. 518-853-8108. Fax: 518-853-8148. 9AM-5PM (EST). Access by: Mail, in person.

Nassau County

Real Estate Recording—Nassau County Clerk, 240 Old Country Road, Mineola, NY 11501. 516-571-2663. Fax: 516-742-4099. 9AM-4:45PM (EST).

Felony, Civil Actions Over $25,000—Supreme Court, Supreme Court Bldg, Supreme Court Dr, Mineola, NY 11501. 516-571-3250. Civil: 516-571-2664. 9AM-5PM (EST). Access by: In person only.

Misdemeanor, Civil Actions Under $15,000, Eviction, Small Claims—3rd District Court, 435 Middle Neck, Great Neck, NY 11023. 516-571-8400. Fax: 516-571-8403. 9AM-5PM (EST). Access by: Mail, in person.

Glen Cove City Court, 13 Glen St, Glen Cove, NY 11542-2704. 516-676-0109. 9AM-5PM (EST). Access by: In person only.

Felony, Misdemeanor, Civil Actions Under $15,000, Eviction, Small Claims—Nassau District Court, 99 Main St, Hempstead, NY 11550. 516-572-2201. Civil: 516-572-2266. Criminal: 516-572-2355. 9AM-5PM (EST). Access by: Mail, in person. Signed release required for some searches.

Civil Actions Under $15,000, Eviction, Small Claims—4th District Court, 87 Bethpage Rd, Hicksville, NY 11801. 516-571-7090. 9AM-5PM (EST). Access by: Mail, in person.

Misdemeanor, Civil Actions Under $15,000, Eviction, Small Claims—Long Beach City Court, 1 West Chester St, Long Beach, NY 11561. 516-431-1000. Fax: 516-431-4372. 9AM-5PM (EST). Access by: In person only.

Felony, Civil Actions Under $25,000—County Court, 262 Old Country Rd, Mineola, NY 11501. 516-571-2720. Fax: 516-571-2160. 9AM-5PM (EST). Access by: Mail, in person.

Probate—Surrogate Court, 262 Old County Rd, Mineola, NY 11501. 516-571-2082. Fax: 516-571-3864. 9AM-5PM (EST).

New York County

Real Estate Recording—New York City Register, 31 Chambers Street, Room 202, New York, NY 10007. 212-788-8529. Fax: 212-788-8521. 9AM-4PM (EST).

Civil Actions Over $25,000—Supreme Court-Civil Division, County Clerk, 60 Centre St, Room 103, New York City, NY 10007. 212-374-4704. 9AM-3PM (EST). Access by: Mail, in person.

Felony, Misdemeanor—Supreme Court-Criminal Division, 80 Center St, Rm 500D, New York, NY 10013. 212-417-3149. 9:30AM-12:30PM 2-4:30PM (EST). Access by: Mail, in person.

Civil Actions Under $25,000, Eviction, Small Claims—Civil Court of the City of New York, 111 Centre St, New York, NY 10013. 212-374-7915. Fax: 212-374-5709. 9AM-5PM (EST). Access by: In person only.

Probate—Surrogate Court, 31 Chambers St, New York City, NY 10007. 212-374-8233. 9AM-5PM (EST). Access by: Mail, in person.

Niagara County

Real Estate Recording—Niagara County Clerk, 175 Hawley Street, Lockport, NY 14094. 716-439-7022. Fax: 716-439-7066. 9AM-5PM (Summer 8:30AM-4:30PM) (EST).

Felony, Civil Actions Over $25,000—Supreme Court, 775 3rd St, Niagara Falls, NY 14302. 716-278-1800. Fax: 716-439-7066. 9AM-5PM (EST). Access by: Mail, in person.

Felony, Civil Actions Under $25,000—County Court, Courthouse, 175 Hawley St, PO Box 461, Lockport, NY 14095. 716-439-7022. Fax: 716-439-4023. 9AM-5PM (EST). Access by: Mail, in person.

Misdemeanor, Civil Actions Under $15,000, Eviction, Small Claims—Lockport City Court, Municipal Bldg, One Locks Plaza, Lockport, NY 14094. Civil: 716-439-6660. Criminal: 716-439-6671. Fax: 716-439-6684. 8AM-4:30PM (EST). Access by: Phone, fax, mail, in person.

Niagara Falls City Court, PO Box 1586, Niagara Falls, NY 14302-2725. Civil: 716-286-4505. Criminal: 716-286-4504. Fax: 716-286-4509. 8:30AM-4:30PM (EST). Access by: Mail, in person.

North Tonawanda City Court, City Hall, North Tonawanda, NY 14120-5446. 716-693-1010. Fax: 716-743-1754. 8AM-5PM (EST). Access by: Mail, in person.

Probate—Niagara County Surrogate's Court, Niagara County Courthouse, 175 Hawley St, Lockport, NY 14094. 716-439-7130. Fax: 716-439-7157. 9AM-5PM (EST).

Oneida County

Real Estate Recording—Oneida County Clerk, 800 Park Avenue, Utica, NY 13501. 315-798-5794. Fax: 315-798-6440. 8:30AM-5PM (EST).

Felony, Civil—Supreme and County Court, 800 Park Ave, Utica, NY 13501. 315-798-5790. 9AM-5PM (EST). Access by: Mail, in person.

Misdemeanor, Civil Actions Under $15,000, Eviction, Small Claims—Rome City Court, 301 James St, Rome, NY 13440. 315-337-6440. (EST). Access by: Mail, in person.

Sherrill City Court, 601 Sherrill Rd, Sherrill, NY 13461. 315-363-0996. 8AM-4PM (EST). Access by: Mail, in person.

Utica City Court, 411 Oriskany St West, Utica, NY 13502. Civil: 315-724-8157. Criminal: 315-724-8227. Fax: 315-724-0762. 9AM-5PM (EST). Access by: Mail, in person.

Probate—Surrogate Court, Oneida County Courthouse, 1st Flr, Elizabeth St, Utica, NY 13501. 315-798-5866. Fax: 315-798-6438. 9AM-5PM Sept-May; 8:30AM-4PM June-Aug (EST).

Onondaga County

Real Estate Recording—Onondaga County Clerk, 401 Montgomery Street, Syracuse, NY 13202. 315-435-2226. Fax: 315-435-3455. 8AM-5PM (EST).

Felony, Civil—Supreme and County Court, 401 Montgomery St Room 200, Syracuse, NY 13202. 315-435-2226. 8AM-5PM (EST). Access by: Mail, in person.

Misdemeanor, Civil Actions Under $15,000, Eviction, Small Claims—Syracuse City Court, 511 State St, Syracuse, NY 13202-2179. 315-477-2778. Fax: 315-474-2601. 9AM-5PM (EST). Access by: Fax, mail, in person.

Probate—Surrogate Court, Onondaga Courthouse, Rm 209, 401 Montgomery St, Syracuse, NY 13202. 315-435-2101. Fax: 315-435-2113. 8:30AM-5PM (EST). Access by: Mail, in person.

Ontario County

Real Estate Recording—Ontario County Clerk, 25 Pleasant Street, Canandaigua, NY 14424. 716-396-4200. Fax: 716-396-4245. 8:30AM-5PM (EST).

Felony, Civil—Supreme and County Court, 27 N Main St, Rm 130, Canandaigua, NY 14424-1447. 716-396-4239. Fax: 716-396-4576. 9AM-5PM (EST). Access by: Mail, in person.

Misdemeanor, Civil Actions Under $15,000, Eviction, Small Claims—Canandaigua City Court, 2 N Main St, Canandaigua, NY 14424-1448. 716-396-5011. Fax: 716-396-5012. 8AM-4PM (EST). Access by: Mail, in person.

Geneva City Court, Castle St, City Hall, Geneva, NY 14456. 315-789-6560. Fax: 315-781-2802. 8AM-4PM (EST). Access by: Phone, mail, in person.

Probate—Surrogate's Court, 27 N Main St, Canandaigua, NY 14424-1447. 716-396-4055. Fax: 716-396-4576. 9AM-5PM (EST). Access by: In person only.

Orange County

Real Estate Recording—Orange County Clerk, 255-275 Main Street, Goshen, NY 10924. 914-291-2690. Fax: 914-294-3171. 9AM-5PM (EST).

Felony, Civil—Supreme and County Court, 255 Main St, Goshen, NY 10924. 914-291-3080. Fax: 914-291-2691. 9AM-5PM (EST). Access by: Phone, mail, in person.

Middletown City Court, 2 James St, Middletown, NY 10940. 914-346-4050. Fax: 914-343-5737. 8AM-4PM (EST). Access by: Mail, in person.

Newburgh City Court, 57 Broadway, Newburgh, NY 12550. 914-565-3208. 8:30AM-4:30PM (EST). Access by: Mail, in person.

Port Jervis City Court, 14-18 Hammond St, Port Jervis, NY 12771-2495. 914-858-4034. Fax: 914-856-2767. 9AM-5PM (EST). Access by: Mail, in person.

Probate—Surrogate Court, Park Place, PO Box 329, Goshen, NY 10924. 914-291-2193. Fax: 914-294-2049. 9AM-5PM (EST). Access by: Mail, in person.

Orleans County

Real Estate Recording—Orleans County Clerk, 3 South Main Street, Courthouse Square, Albion, NY 14411. 716-589-5334. Fax: 716-589-1618. 9AM-5PM (July-August 8:30AM-4PM) (EST).

Felony, Civil—Supreme and County Court, Courthouse, Albion, NY 14411-9998. Civil: 716-589-5334. Criminal: 716-589-4457. Fax: 716-589-1618. 9AM-5PM (EST). Access by: Phone, mail, in person.

Probate—Surrogate Court, Courthouse Sq, Albion, NY 14411-9998. 716-589-4457. Fax: 716-589-0632. 9AM-5PM (EST). Access by: Mail, in person.

Oswego County

Real Estate Recording—Oswego County Clerk, 46 East Bridge Street, Oswego, NY 13126. 315-349-8385. Fax: 315-343-8383. 9AM-5PM (EST).

Felony, Civil—Supreme and County Court, 46 E Bridge St, Oswego, NY 13126. 315-349-8391. Fax: 315-349-8383. 9AM-5PM (EST). Access by: Mail, in person.

Misdemeanor, Civil Actions Under $15,000, Eviction, Small Claims—Fulton City Court, 141 S 1st St, Fulton, NY 13069. 315-593-8400. Fax: 315-592-3415. 8:30AM-4:30PM/Summer 8:30AM-4PM (EST). Access by: Mail, in person.

Oswego City Court, Conway Municipal Building, 20 West Oneida St, Oswego, NY 13126. 315-343-0415. Fax: 315-343-0415. 8:30AM-5PM (EST). Access by: Mail, in person.

Probate—Surrogate Court, Courthouse, East Oneida St, Oswego, NY 13126-2693. 315-349-3295. Fax: 315-349-8514. 9AM-5PM Sept-May; 8:30AM-3:30 PM June-Aug (EST). Access by: Mail, in person.

Otsego County

Real Estate Recording—Otsego County Clerk, 197 Main Street, Cooperstown, NY 13326. 607-547-4278. Fax: 607-547-7544. 9AM-5PM (July-August 9AM-4PM) (EST).

Felony, Civil—Supreme and County Court, 197 Main St, Cooperstown, NY 13326. 607-547-4276. Fax: 607-547-7544. 9AM-5PM; 9AM-4PM July-Aug (EST). Access by: Mail, in person.

Misdemeanor, Civil Actions Under $15,000, Eviction, Small Claims—Otsego City Court, Oneonta City Hall, 81 Main St, Oneonta, NY 13820. 607-432-4480. 8:30AM-4:30PM (EST). Access by: Mail, in person.

Probate—Surrogate Court, Otsego County Office Bldg, 197 Main St, Cooperstown, NY 13326. 607-547-4338. Fax: 607-547-7566. 9AM-5PM (EST). Access by: Mail, in person.

Putnam County

Real Estate Recording—Putnam County Clerk, 40 Gleneida Ave., Carmel, NY 10512. 914-225-3641. Fax: 914-228-0231. 9AM-5PM (Summer 8AM-4PM) (EST).

Felony, Civil—Supreme and County Court, 40 Gleneida Ave, Carmel, NY 10512. 914-225-3641. Fax: 914-228-0231. 9AM-5PM (EST). Access by: Mail, in person.

Probate—Surrogate Court, 1 County Center, Carmel, NY 10512. 914-225-3641. Fax: 914-228-5761. 9AM-5PM (EST). Access by: Mail, in person.

Queens County

Real Estate Recording—Queens City Register, 90-27 Sutphin Blvd., Jamaica, NY 11435. 718-658-4600. 9AM-4PM (EST).

Civil Actions Over $25,000—Supreme Court-Civil Division, 88-11 Sutphin Blvd, Jamaica, NY 11435. 718-520-3136. Fax: 718-520-4731. 9AM-5PM, no cashier transactions after 4:45PM (EST). Access by: Mail, in person.

Felony, Misdemeanor—Supreme Court-Criminal Division, 80 Center St, Rm 500D, New York, NY 10013. 212-417-3149. 9:30AM-4:30PM (EST). Access by: Mail, in person.

Civil Actions Under $25,000, Eviction, Small Claims—Civil Court of the City of New York-Queens Branch, 120-55 Queens Blvd, Kew Gardens, NY 11424. 718-520-3610. Fax: 718-520-4733. 9AM-5PM (EST). Access by: Mail, in person.

Probate—Surrogate Court, 88-11 Sutphin Blvd, Jamaica, NY 11435. 718-520-3132. 9AM-5PM (EST).

Rensselaer County

Real Estate Recording—Rensselaer County Clerk, Courthouse, Congress & 2nd Street, Troy, NY 12180. 518-270-4080. 8:30AM-5PM (EST).

Felony, Civil—Supreme and County Court, Congress & 2nd Sts, Troy, NY 12180. 518-270-4080. Fax: 518-271-7998. 9AM-5PM (EST). Access by: Mail, in person.

Misdemeanor, Civil Actions Under $15,000, Eviction, Small Claims—Rensselaer City Court, City Hall, Rensselaer, NY 12144. 518-462-6751. Fax: 518-462-3307. 8AM-3:30PM (EST). Access by: Fax, mail, in person.

Troy City Court, 51 State St, Troy, NY 12180. 518-271-1602. Fax: 518-274-2816. 9AM-3:30PM (EST). Access by: Mail, in person.

Probate—Surrogate Court, Courthouse, Troy, NY 12180. 518-270-3724. Fax: 518-272-5452. 9AM-5PM (EST).

Richmond County

Real Estate Recording—Richmond County Clerk, 18 Richmond Terrace, County Courthouse, Staten Island, NY 10301. 718-390-5386. Fax: 718-390-5269. 9AM-5PM (EST).

Civil Actions Over $25,000—Supreme Court-Civil Division, 18 Richmond Terrace, Staten Island, NY 10301. 718-390-5389. Civil: 718-390-5352. 9AM-5PM (EST). Access by: In person only.

Felony, Misdemeanor—Supreme Court-Criminal Division, 80 Center St, Rm 500D, New York, NY 10013. 212-41731493. 9:30AM-4:30PM, Closed 12-2 (EST). Access by: Mail, in person.

Civil Actions Under $25,000, Eviction, Small Claims—Civil Court of the City of New York-Richmond Branch, 927 Castleton Ave, Staten Island, NY 10310. 718-390-5417. 8AM-4:30PM (EST). Access by: Mail, in person.

Probate—Surrogate Court, 18 Richmond Terrace, Rm 201, Staten Island, NY 10301. 718-390-5400. 9AM-5PM (EST).

Rockland County

Real Estate Recording—Rockland County Clerk, 27 New Hempstead Road, New City, NY 10956. 914-638-5354. Fax: 914-638-5647. 7AM-7PM M-Th; 7AM-6PM F (EST). Access by: Mail, in person, online.

Felony, Civil—Supreme and County Court, 27 New Hempstead Rd, New City, NY 10956. 914-638-5070. Fax: 914-638-5647. 7AM-6PM (EST). Access by: Mail, in person, online.

Probate—Surrogate Court, 1 S Main St, New City, NY 10956. 914-638-5330. Fax: 914-638-5632. 9AM-5PM (EST). Access by: Mail, in person, online.

Saratoga County

Real Estate Recording—Saratoga County Clerk, 40 McMaster Street, Ballston Spa, NY 12020. 518-885-2213. Fax: 518-884-4726. Search hours: 9AM-5PM; Recording & Filing hours: 9AM-4:15PM (EST).

Felony, Civil—Supreme and County Court, 40 McMaster St, Ballston Spa, NY 12020. 518-885-2213. Fax: 518-884-4726. 9AM-5PM (EST). Access by: In person only.

Misdemeanor, Civil Actions Under $15,000, Eviction, Small Claims—Mechanicville City Court, 36 N Main St, Mechanicville, NY 12118. 518-664-9876. Fax: 518-664-8606. 8AM-4PM (EST). Access by: Mail, in person.

Saratoga Springs City Court, City Hall, 474 Broadway, Saratoga Springs, NY 12866. 518-587-3550. 9AM-5PM (EST). Access by: Mail, in person.

Probate—Surrogate Court, 30 McMaster St, Ballston Spa, NY 12020. 518-884-4722. 9AM-5PM (EST).

Schenectady County

Real Estate Recording—Schenectady County Clerk, 620 State Street, Schenectady, NY 12305. 518-388-4220. Fax: 518-388-4224. 9AM-5PM (EST).

Felony, Civil—Supreme and County Court, 612 State St, Schenectady, NY 12305. Civil: 518-388-4220. Criminal: 518-388-4322. Fax: 518-388-4224. 9AM-5PM (EST). Access by: Mail, in person.

Schenectady City Court-Civil Part, Jay St, City Hall, Schenectady, NY 12305. 518-382-5077. Fax: 518-382-5080. 8AM-4PM (EST). Access by: Mail, in person.

Probate—Surrogate Court, 612 State St, Schenectady, NY 12305. 518-388-4293. Fax: 518-377-6378. 9AM-5PM (EST).

Schoharie County

Real Estate Recording—Schoharie County Clerk, 300 Main Street, County Office Building, Schoharie, NY 12157. 518-295-8316. Fax: 518-295-8338. 8:30AM-5PM (EST).

Felony, Civil—Supreme and County Court, PO Box 549, Schoharie, NY 12157. 518-295-8316. Fax: 518-295-8338. 8:30AM-5PM (EST). Access by: Mail, in person.

Probate—Surrogate Court, Courthouse, 300 Main St, PO Box 669, Schoharie, NY 12157-0669. 518-295-8383. Fax: 518-295-8451. 9AM-5PM (EST). Access by: Mail, in person.

Schuyler County

Real Estate Recording—Schuyler County Clerk, 105 Ninth Street Box 8, County Office Building, Watkins Glen, NY 14891. 607-535-8133. 9AM-5PM (EST).

Felony, Civil—Supreme and County Court, Courthouse, Watkins Glen, NY 14891. 607-535-7760. Fax: 607-535-4918. 9AM-5PM (EST). Access by: Mail, in person.

Probate—Surrogate Court, County Courthouse, 105 Ninth St, Watkins Glen, NY 14891. 607-535-7144. Fax: 607-535-4918. 9AM-5PM (EST). Access by: Mail, in person.

Seneca County

Real Estate Recording—Seneca County Clerk, 1 DiProniro Drive, Waterloo, NY 13165. 315-539-5655. Fax: 315-539-9479. 8:30AM-5PM (EST).

Felony, Civil—Seneca County, 1 DiPronio Dr, Waterloo, NY 13165-1396. 315-539-5655. Fax: 315-539-9479. 8:30AM-5PM (EST). Access by: Fax, mail, in person.

Probate—Surrogate Court, 48 W Williams St, Waterloo, NY 13165-1393. 315-539-7531. Fax: 315-539-7929. 9AM-5PM (EST).

St. Lawrence County

Real Estate Recording—St. Lawrence County Clerk, 48 Court Street, Canton, NY 13617. 315-379-2237. Fax: 315-379-2302. 8:30AM-4:30PM (EST).

Felony, Civil—Supreme and County Court, 48 Court St, Canton, NY 13617-1199. 315-379-2237. Fax: 315-379-2302. 8:30AM-4:30PM (EST). Access by: Fax, mail, in person.

Misdemeanor, Civil Actions Under $15,000, Eviction, Small Claims—Ogdensburg City Court, 330 Ford St, Ogdensburg, NY 13669. 315-393-3941. Fax: 315-393-6839. 8AM-4PM (EST). Access by: Mail, in person.

Probate—Surrogate Court, 48 Court St, Canton, NY 13617. 315-379-2217. Fax: 315-379-2372. 9AM-5PM Sept-June; 8AM-4PM July-Aug (EST). Access by: Mail, in person.

Steuben County

Real Estate Recording—Steuben County Clerk, 3 East Pulteney Square, County Office Building, Bath, NY 14810. 607-776-9631. Fax: 607-776-9631. 8:30AM-5PM (July-August 8:30AM-4:30PM) (EST).

Felony, Civil—Supreme and County Court, Pulteney Square, Bath, NY 14810-1575. 607-776-9631. (EST). Access by: Phone, mail, in person.

Misdemeanor, Civil Actions Under $15,000, Eviction, Small Claims—Corning City Court, 12 Civic Center Plaza, Corning, NY 14830-2884. 607-936-4111. Fax: 607-936-0519. 8AM-4PM (EST). Access by: Mail, in person.

Hornell City Court, 108 Broadway, Hornell, NY 14843-0627. 607-324-7531. Fax: 607-324-6325. 8AM-4PM (EST). Access by: Fax, mail, in person.

Probate—Surrogate Court, 13 E Pulteney Square, Bath, NY 14810-1598. 607-776-9631. Fax: 607-776-4987. 9AM-5PM (EST). Access by: Mail, in person.

Suffolk County

Real Estate Recording—Suffolk County Clerk, 310 Center Drive, Riverhead, NY 11901. 516-852-2043. Fax: 516-852-2004. 9AM-5PM (EST).

Felony, Civil—Suffolk County Court, 310 Centre Dr, Attn: Court Actions, Riverhead, NY 11901. 516-852-2016. Fax: 516-852-2004. 9AM-5PM (EST). Access by: Mail, in person.

Misdemeanor, Civil Actions Under $15,000, Eviction, Small Claims—Suffolk District Court, 400 Carleton Ave, Central Islip, NY 11722. 516-853-7500. Civil: 516-853-5400. Criminal: 516-853-5357. Fax: 516-853-4505. 9AM-5PM (EST). Access by: Mail, in person.

2nd District Court, 375 Cormac Rd, Deer Park, NY 11702. 516-669-6100. Fax: 516-669-6173. 9AM-5PM; closed 1-2PM (EST). Access by: Mail, in person.

3rd District Court, 1850 New York Ave, Huntington Station, NY 11746. 516-854-4545. 9AM-4:30PM (EST). Access by: Mail, in person.

4th District Court, North County Complex Bldg C158, Hauppauge, NY 11787. Civil: 516-853-5400. Criminal: 516-853-5357. 9AM-5PM (EST). Access by: Mail, in person.

5th District Court, 400 Carlton Ave, Central Islip, NY 11722. 516-853-7626. 9AM-5PM (EST). Access by: Mail, in person.

6th District Court, 150 W Main St, Patchogue, NY 11772. 516-854-1440. 9AM-5PM (EST). Access by: Mail, in person.

Probate—Surrogate Court, 320 Centre Dr, Riverhead, NY 11901. 516-852-1745. Fax: 516-852-1777. 9AM-5PM (EST).

Sullivan County

Real Estate Recording—Sullivan County Clerk, 100 North Street, Government Center, Monticello, NY 12701. 914-794-3000. 9AM-5PM (EST).

Felony, Civil—Supreme and County Court, Courthouse, Monticello, NY 12701. 914-794-4066. 9AM-5PM (EST). Access by: Mail, in person.

Probate—Surrogate Court, The Government Center, 100 N St, PO Box 5012, Monticello, NY 12701. 914-794-3000. Fax: 914-794-0310. 9AM-5PM (EST). Access by: Mail, in person.

Tioga County

Real Estate Recording—Tioga County Clerk, 16 Court Street, Owego, NY 13827. 607-687-8660. Fax: 607-687-4612. 9AM-5PM (EST).

Felony, Civil—Supreme and County Court, PO Box 307, Owego, NY 13827. 607-687-0544. Fax: 607-687-3240. 9AM-5PM (EST). Access by: Mail, in person.

Probate—Surrogate Court, PO Box 10, Owego, NY 13827. 607-687-1303. Fax: 607-687-3240. 9AM-5PM (EST).

Tompkins County

Real Estate Recording—Tompkins County Clerk, 320 North Tioga Street, Ithaca, NY 14850. 607-274-5432. 9AM-5PM (EST).

Felony, Civil—Supreme and County Court, 320 N Tioga St, Ithaca, NY 14850. 607-274-5431. 9AM-5PM (EST). Access by: Mail, in person.

Misdemeanor, Civil Actions Under $15,000, Eviction, Small Claims—Ithaca City Court, 120 E Clinton St, Ithaca, NY 14850. 607-274-6594. 9AM-5PM (EST). Access by: Mail, in person.

Probate—Surrogate Court, PO Box 70, Ithaca, NY 14851. 607-277-0622. Fax: 607-277-5027. 9AM-5PM (EST). Access by: Mail, in person.

Ulster County

Real Estate Recording—Ulster County Clerk, 240-244 Fair Street, County Office Building, Kingston, NY 12401. 914-340-3000. Fax: 914-331-0754. 9AM-5PM (EST).

Felony, Civil—Supreme and County Court, PO Box 1800, Kingston, NY 12401. 914-340-3288. Fax: 914-340-3299. 9AM-5PM (EST). Access by: Mail, remote online, in person.

Misdemeanor, Civil Actions Under $15,000, Eviction, Small Claims—Kingston City Court, 1 Garraghan Dr, Kingston, NY 12401. 914-338-2974. 8AM-4PM (EST). Access by: Mail, in person.

Probate—Surrogate Court, PO Box 1800, Kingston, NY 12402-1800. 914-340-3000. Fax: 914-340-3352. 9AM-5PM (EST). Access by: Mail, in person.

Warren County

Real Estate Recording—Warren County Clerk, Municipal Center, 1340 State Route 9, Lake George, NY 12845. 518-761-6426. Fax: 518-761-6551. 9AM-5PM (EST).

Felony, Civil—Supreme and County Court, Rt US 9, Lake George, NY 12845. 518-761-6430. Fax: 518-761-6253. 9AM-5PM (EST). Access by: Fax, mail, in person.

Misdemeanor, Civil Actions Under $15,000, Eviction, Small Claims—Glens Falls City Court, 42 Ridge St, Glens Falls, NY 12801. 518-798-4714. Fax: 518-798-0137. 8:30AM-4:30PM (EST). Access by: Fax, mail, in person.

Probate—Surrogate Court, Municipal Center, 1340 Rt US 9, Lake George, NY 12845. 518-761-6514. Fax: 518-761-6465. 9AM-5PM (EST). Access by: In person only.

Washington County

Real Estate Recording—Washington County Clerk, 383 Broadway, Bldg A, Fort Edward, NY 12828. 518-746-2170. Fax: 518-746-2166. 8:30AM-4:30PM (EST).

Felony, Civil—Supreme and County Court, 383 Broadway, Fort Edward, NY 12828. Civil: 518-746-2170. Criminal: 518-746-2520. 8:30AM-4:30PM (EST). Access by: Mail, in person.

Probate—Surrogate Court, 383 Broadway, Fort Edward, NY 12828. 518-746-2546. Fax: 518-746-2547. 8:30AM-4:30PM (EST). Access by: Mail, in person.

Wayne County

Real Estate Recording—Wayne County Clerk, 9 Pearl Street, Lyons, NY 14489. 315-946-5870. Fax: 315-946-5978. 9AM-5PM (EST).

Felony, Civil—Supreme & County Courts, 9 Pearl St, PO Box 608, Lyons, NY 14489-1134. 315-946-5870. Fax: 315-946-5870. 9AM-5PM (EST). Access by: Fax, mail, in person.

Probate—Surrogate Court, 54 Broad St, Lyons, NY 14489-1134. 315-946-5430. Fax: 315-946-5433. 9AM-4PM (EST).

Westchester County

Real Estate Recording—Westchester County Clerk, 110 Grove St., Room 345, White Plains, NY 10601. 914-285-3096. Fax: 914-285-3172. 8AM-5:45PM (EST).

Felony, Civil—Supreme and County Court, 111 Grove St, White Plains, NY 10601. 914-285-3070. Fax: 914-285-3172. 8AM-5:45PM (EST). Access by: Mail, in person.

Misdemeanor, Civil Actions Under $15,000, Eviction, Small Claims—Mt Vernon City Court, Municipal Bldg, Mt Vernon, NY 10550-2019. 914-665-2400. Fax: 914-699-1230. 8:30AM-4:30PM (EST). Access by: Mail, in person.

Peekskill City Court, 2 Nelson Ave, Peekskill, NY 10566. 914-737-3405. 9AM-5PM (EST). Access by: Mail, in person.

Rye City Court, 21 Third St, Rye, NY 10580. 914-967-1599. Fax: 914-967-3308. 8:30AM-5PM (EST). Access by: Mail, in person.

White Plains City Court, 77 S Lexington Ave, White Plains, NY 10601. 914-422-6050. Fax: 914-422-6058. 8:30AM-4:30PM (EST). Access by: Mail, in person.

Yonkers City Court, 100 S Broadway, Yonkers, NY 10701. 914-377-6352. Fax: 914-377-6395. 9AM-5PM (EST). Access by: Mail, in person.

Probate—Surrogate Court, 140 Grand St, White Plains, NY 10601. 914-285-3712. Fax: 914-285-3728. 9AM-5PM (EST). Access by: Mail, in person.

Wyoming County

Real Estate Recording—Wyoming County Clerk, 143 North Main Street, Warsaw, NY 14569. 716-786-8810. Fax: 716-786-3703. 9AM-5PM (EST).

Felony, Civil—Supreme and County Court, 143 N Main St, Warsaw, NY 14569. 716-786-3148. Fax: 716-786-3800. 9AM-5PM (EST). Access by: Mail, in person.

Probate—Surrogate Court, 143 N Main St, Warsaw, NY 14569. 716-786-3148. Fax: 716-786-3800. 9AM-5PM (EST). Access by: Mail, in person.

Yates County

Real Estate Recording—Yates County Clerk, 110 Court Street, Penn Yan, NY 14527. 315-536-5120. Fax: 315-536-5545. 9AM-5PM (EST).

Felony, Civil—Supreme and County Court, 110 Court St, Penn Yan, NY 14527-1191. 315-536-5120. Fax: 315-536-5545. 8:30AM-5PM (EST). Access by: Mail, in person.

Probate—Surrogate Court, 108 Court St, Penn Yan, NY 14527. 315-536-5130. Fax: 315-536-5190. (EST).

Federal Courts

US District Court

Eastern District of New York

Brooklyn Division, US District Court Brooklyn Courthouse, 225 Cadman Plaza E, Room 130, Brooklyn, NY 11201. 718-260-2600. Counties: Kings, Queens, Richmond. Cases from Nassau and Suffolk may also be heard here

Hauppauge Division, US District Court 300 Rabro Dr, Hauppauge, NY 11788. 516-582-1100. Counties: Suffolk

Uniondale Division, US District Court 2 Uniondale Ave, Room 303, Uniondale, NY 11553. 516-485-6500. Counties: Nassau

Northern District of New York

Albany Division, US District Court 445 Broadway, Room 222, Albany, NY 12207-2924. 518-431-0279. Counties: Albany, Clinton, Columbia, Essex, Greene, Rensselaer, Saratoga, Schenectady, Schoharie, Ulster, Warren, Washington

Binghamton Division, US District Court 15 Henry St, Binghamton, NY 13901. 607-773-2893. Counties: Broome, Chenango, Delaware, Franklin, Jefferson, Lewis, Otsego, St. Lawrence, Tioga

Syracuse Division, US District Court PO Box 7367, Syracuse, NY 13261-7367. 315-448-0507. Counties: Cayuga, Cortland, Fulton, Hamilton, Herkimer, Madison, Montgomery, Onondaga, Oswego, Tompkins

Utica Division, US District Court Alexander Pirnie Bldg, 10 Broad St, Utica, NY 13501. 315-793-8151. Counties: Oneida

Southern District of New York

New York City Division, US District Court 500 Pearl St, New York, NY 10007. 212-805-0136. Counties: Bronx, New York. Some cases from the counties in the White Plains Division are also assigned to the New York Division

White Plains Division, US District Court 300 Quarropas St, White Plains, NY 10601. 914-390-4000. Counties: Dutchess, Orange, Putnam, Rockland, Sullivan, Westchester. Some cases may be assigned to New York Division

Western District of New York

Buffalo Division, US District Court Room 304, 68 Court St, Buffalo, NY 14202. 716-551-4211. Counties: Allegany, Cattaraugus, Chautauqua, Erie, Genesee, Niagara, Orleans, Wyoming. Prior to 1982, this division included what is now the Rochester Division

Rochester Division, US District Court Room 2120, 100 State St, Rochester, NY 14614. 716-263-6263. Counties: Chemung, Livingston, Monroe, Ontario, Schuyler, Seneca, Steuben, Wayne, Yates

US Bankruptcy Court

Eastern District of New York

Brooklyn Division, US Bankruptcy Court, 75 Clinton St, Brooklyn, NY 11201. 718-330-2188. Voice Case Information System: 718-852-5726. Counties: Kings, Queens, Richmond. Kings and Queens County Chapter 11 cases may also be assigned to Westbury. Other Queens County cases may also be assigned to Westbury Division. Nassau County Chapter 11 cases may be assigned here

Hauppauge Division, US Bankruptcy Court, 601 Veterans Memorial Hwy, Hauppauge, NY 11788. 516-361-8038. Voice Case Information System: 718-852-5726. Counties: Suffolk. Suffolk County Chapter 11 cases may also be assigned to Westbury Division. Nassau County Chapter 11 cases may be assigned here. Other cases for western Suffolk County may also be assigned to Westbury Division

Westbury Division, US Bankruptcy Court, 1635 Privado Rd, Westbury, NY 11590. 516-832-8801. Voice Case Information System: 718-852-5726. Counties: Nassau. Chapter 11 cases for Nassau County may also be assigned to the Brooklyn or Hauppauge divisions. Kings and Suffolk County Chapter 11 cases may be assigned here. Any Queens County cases may be assigned here. Non-Chapter 11 cases from western Suffolk County may also be assigned here

Northern District of New York

Albany Division, US Bankruptcy Court, James T Foley Courthouse, 445 Broadway, Albany, NY 12207. 518-431-0188. Counties: Albany, Clinton, Essex, Franklin, Fulton, Jefferson, Montgomery, Rensselaer, Saratoga, Schenectady, Schoharie, St. Lawrence, Warren, Washington

Utica Division, US Bankruptcy Court, Room 230, 10 Broad St, Utica, NY 13501. 315-793-8101. Counties: Broome, Cayuga, Chenago, Cortland, Delaware, Hamilton, Herkimer, Lewis, Madison, Oneida, Onondaga, Ostego, Oswego, Tioga, Tompkins

Southern District of New York

New York Division, US Bankruptcy Court, Room 511, 1 Bowling Green, New York, NY 10004-1408. 212-668-2870. Voice Case Information System: 212-668-2772. Counties: Bronx, New York

Poughkeepsie Division, US Bankruptcy Court, 176 Church St, Poughkeepsie, NY 12601. 914-551-4200. Voice Case Information System: 212-668-2772. Counties: Columbia, Dutchess, Greene, Orange, Putnam, Sullivan, Ulster

White Plains Division, US Bankruptcy Court, 300 Quarropas St, White Plains, NY 10601. 914-390-4060. Voice Case Information System: 212-668-2772. Counties: Rockland, Westchester

Western District of New York

Buffalo Division, US Bankruptcy Court, 310 US Courthouse, 68 Court St, Buffalo, NY 14202. 716-551-4130. Voice Case Information System: 716-551-5311. Counties: Allegany, Cattaraugus, Chautauqua, Erie, Genesee, Niagara, Orleans, Wyoming

Rochester Division, US Bankruptcy Court, Room 1220, 100 State St, Rochester, NY 14614. 716-263-3148. Voice Case Information System: 716-551-5311. Counties: Chemung, Livingston, Monroe, Ontario, Schuyler, Seneca, Steuben, Wayne, Yates

North Carolina

Capitol: Raleigh (Wake County)	
Number of Counties: 100	**Population:** 7,195,138
County Court Locations:	**Federal Court Locations:**
•Superior Courts: 0/34 Districts	•District Courts: 14
• District Courts: 0/34 Districts	•Bankruptcy Courts: 5
•Combined Courts: 100	**State Agencies:** 19

State Agencies—Summary

General Help Numbers:

State Archives

Cultural Resources Department	919-733-3952
Archives & History Division	Fax: 919-733-1354
109 E Jones St	8AM-5:30PM TU-F, 9-5 SA
Raleigh, NC 27601-2807	
Reference Librarian:	919-733-2570

Governor's Office

Office of the Governor	919-733-4240
State Capitol	Fax: 919-733-2120
Capitol Square, 116 W Jones St	8AM-6PM
Raleigh, NC 27603-8001	

Attorney General's Office

Attorney General's Office	919-716-6400
Justice Department	Fax: 919-716-6750
PO Box 629	8AM-5PM
Raleigh, NC 27602	

State Legislation

North Carolina General Assembly	919-733-7779
State Legislative Bldg	8:30AM-5:30PM
16 W. Jones Street, 1st Fl	
Raleigh, NC 27603	
Archives:	919-733-3270
Order Desk:	919-733-5648

Important State Internet Sites:

```
Webscape
File   Edit   View                                    Help
```

State of North Carolina World Wide Web

www.state.nc.us/

This is the home page for the state and contains links to public and business information, North Carolina employees, education, the top 10 links for North Carolina and a search engine.

State General Assembly

www.ncga.state.nc.us

This site provides links to the Senate and House and bills of the General Assembly

Bills of the General Assembly

www.ncga.state.nc.us/.html/bills.html

Bill information is available by searching by county and by members. It also includes a bill status report and a voting history.

Archives and History

www.ah.dcr.state.nc.us

This is the home page of the Division of Archives and History. From here you can link to the archives and records section. Online searches are not available.

Unclaimed Property

www.treasurer.state.nc.us/Treasurer/
escheats/escheat.htm

Provided at this site is information about the unclaimed property process in North Carolina. This service is through the State Treasury Department. No online searching is available.

Uniform Commercial Code

www.secstate.state.nc.us/secstate/ucc.htm

Limited UCC searching information is available here.

State Agencies—Public Records

Criminal Records
State Bureau of Investigation, Identification Section, 407 N Blount St, Raleigh, NC 27601-1009, Main Telephone: 919-662-4500, Fax: 919-662-4380, Hours: 7:30AM-5PM.
Restricted access.

Corporation Records
Limited Partnerships
Limited Liability Company Records
Trademarks/Servicemarks
Secretary of State, Corporations Section, 300 N Salisbury St, Raleigh, NC 27603-5909, Main Telephone: 919-733-4201, Fax: 919-733-1837, Hours: 8AM-5PM. Access by: mail, fax, phone, visit, PC. Fictitious Names and Assumed Name records are found at the county levels.

Uniform Commercial Code
Federal Tax Liens
State Tax Liens
UCC Division, Secretary of State, 300 North Salisbury St, Raleigh, NC 27603-5909, Main Telephone: 919-733-4205, Hours: 7:30AM-5PM. Access by: mail, fax, visit, PC.

Sales Tax Registrations
Revenue Department, Sales & Use Tax Division, PO Box 25000, Raleigh, NC 27604,
This agency refuses to release any information about registrants, but will validate a number if presented with one.

Birth Certificates
Dept of Environment, Health & Natural Resources, Vital Records Section, PO Box 29537, Raleigh, NC 27626-0537, Main Telephone: 919-733-3526, Fax: 919-733-1511, Hours: 8AM-4PM. Access by: mail, phone, visit.

Death Records
Dept of Environment, Health & Natural Resources, Vital Records Section, PO Box 29537, Raleigh, NC 27626-0537, Main Telephone: 919-733-3526, Fax: 919-733-1511, Hours: 8AM-4PM. Access by: mail, phone, visit.

Marriage Certificates
Dept of Environment, Health & Natural Resources, Vital Records Section, PO Box 29537, Raleigh, NC 27626-0537, Main Telephone: 919-733-3526, Fax: 919-733-1511, Hours: 8AM-4PM. Access by: mail, phone, visit.

Divorce Records
Dept of Environment, Health & Natural Resources, Vital Records Section, PO Box 29537, Raleigh, NC 27626-0537, Main Telephone: 919-733-3526, Fax: 919-733-1511, Hours: 8AM-4PM. Access by: mail, phone, visit.

Workers' Compensation Records
NC Industrial Commission, Dobbs Bldg, 430 N Salisbury-6th floor, Raleigh, NC 27611, Main Telephone: 919-733-1989, Hours: 8AM-5PM. Access by: mail, visit.

Driver Records
Division of Motor Vehicles, Driver's License Section, 1100 New Bern Ave, Raleigh, NC 27697, Main Telephone: 919-715-7000, Hours: 8AM-5PM. Access by: mail, visit, PC. Copies of tickets may be purchased from the same address for a fee of $5.00 per ticket.

Vehicle Ownership
Vehicle Identification
Division of Motor Vehicles, Registration/Correspondence Unit, 1100 New Bern Ave, Raleigh, NC 27697, Main Telephone: 919-715-7000, Hours: 8AM-5PM. Access by: mail, visit.

Accident Reports
Division of Motor Vehicles, Collision Reports Section, 1100 New Bern Ave, Room 101, Raleigh, NC 27697, Main Telephone: 919-733-7250, Fax: 919-733-9605, Hours: 8AM-5PM. Access by: mail, visit.

Hunting License Information
Fishing License Information
Records not available from state agency.

County Courts and Recording Offices

What You Need to Know...

About the Courts

About the Recorder's Office

Administration

Administrative Office of Courts	919-733-7107
2 E Morgan St	Fax: 919-715-5779
Justice Bldg, 4th Floor	
Raleigh, NC 27602	

Court Structure

Probate is handled by County Clerks.

Searching Hints

Most courts recommend that civil searches be done in person or by a retriever and that only criminal searches be requested in writing (for a $5.00 search fee). Many courts have archived records prior to 1968 in the Raleigh State Archives, 919-733-5722.

Online Access

There is an **internal** online computer system which links all civil and criminal courts. There is no **external** access.

Organization

100 counties, 100 filing offices. The recording officers are Register of Deeds and Clerk of Superior Court (tax liens). The entire state is in the Eastern Time Zone (EST).

UCC Records

This is a **dual filing state**. Financing statements are filed both at the state level and with the Register of Deeds, except for consumer goods, farm related and real estate related collateral. All counties will perform UCC searches. Use search request form UCC-11. Search fees are usually $8.00 per debtor name. Copies usually cost $1.00 per page.

Lien Records

Federal tax liens on personal property of businesses are filed with the Secretary of State. Other federal and all state tax liens are filed with the county Clerk of Superior Court, **not** with the Register of Deeds. (Oddly, even tax liens on real property are also filed with the Clerk of Superior Court, **not** with the Register of Deeds.) Refer to BRB Publications' *The Sourcebook of County Court Records* for information about North Carolina Superior Courts. Other liens include judgments, and mechanics (all at Clerk of Superior Court).

Real Estate Records

Counties will **not** perform real estate searches. Copy fees are usually $1.00 per page. Certification usually costs $3.00 for the first page and $1.00 for each additional page of a document.

County Courts and Recording Offices

Alamance County

Real Estate Recording—Alamance County Register of Deeds, 118 West Harden Street, Graham, NC 27253. 910-570-6565. 8AM-5PM (EST).

Felony, Misdemeanor, Civil, Eviction, Small Claims, Probate—Superior-District Court, 212 West Elm St, Suite 105, Graham, NC 27253. Civil: 910-570-6865. Criminal: 910-570-6867. 8AM-5PM (EST). Access by: Mail, in person.

Alexander County

Real Estate Recording—Alexander County Register of Deeds, 201 First Street SW, Suite 1, Taylorsville, NC 28681. 704-632-3152. 8AM-5PM (EST).

Felony, Misdemeanor, Civil, Eviction, Small Claims, Probate—Superior-District Court, PO Box 100, Taylorsville, NC 28681. 704-632-2215. Fax: 704-632-3550. 8AM-5PM (EST). Access by: Mail, in person.

Alleghany County

Real Estate Recording—Alleghany County Register of Deeds, 12 N. Main Street, Sparta, NC 28675. 910-372-4342. Fax: 910-372-2061. 8AM-5PM (EST).

Felony, Misdemeanor, Civil, Eviction, Small Claims, Probate—Superior-District Court, PO Box 61, Sparta, NC 28675. 910-372-8949. Fax: 910-372-4899. 8AM-5PM (EST). Access by: Fax, mail, in person.

Anson County

Real Estate Recording—Anson County Register of Deeds, Green Street Courthouse, Wadesboro, NC 28170. 704-694-3212. 8:30AM-5PM (EST).

Felony, Misdemeanor, Civil, Eviction, Small Claims, Probate—Superior-District Court, PO Box 1064, Wadesboro, NC 28170. 704-694-2314. Fax: 704-695-1161. 8AM-5PM (EST). Access by: Mail, in person.

Ashe County

Real Estate Recording—Ashe County Register of Deeds, East Main Street, Courthouse, Jefferson, NC 28640. 910-246-9338. 8AM-5PM (EST).

Felony, Misdemeanor, Civil, Eviction, Small Claims, Probate—Superior-District Court, PO Box 95, Jefferson, NC 28640. 910-246-5641. Fax: 910-246-4276. 8AM-5PM (EST). Access by: Phone, fax, mail, in person.

Avery County

Real Estate Recording—Avery County Register of Deeds, Avery Square, Courthouse - Room 101, Newland, NC 28657. 704-733-8260. 8AM-4:30PM (EST).

Felony, Misdemeanor, Civil, Eviction, Small Claims, Probate—Superior-District Court, PO Box 115, Newland, NC 28657. 704-733-2900. Fax: 704-733-8410. 8AM-4:30PM (EST). Access by: Mail, in person.

Beaufort County

Real Estate Recording—Beaufort County Register of Deeds, 112 West Second Street, Courthouse, Washington, NC 27889. 919-946-2323. 8:30AM-5PM (EST).

Felony, Misdemeanor, Civil, Eviction, Small Claims, Probate—Superior-District Court, PO Box 1403, Washington, NC 27889. 919-946-5184. 8:30AM-5:30PM (EST). Access by: Mail, in person.

Bertie County

Real Estate Recording—Bertie County Register of Deeds, Corner of King & Dundee, Windsor, NC 27983. 919-794-5309. Fax: 919-794-5327. 8:30AM-5PM (EST).

Felony, Misdemeanor, Civil, Eviction, Small Claims, Probate—Superior-District Court, PO Box 370, Windsor, NC 27983. 919-794-3039. Fax: 919-794-2482. 8AM-5PM (EST). Access by: Fax, mail, in person.

Bladen County

Real Estate Recording—Bladen County Register of Deeds, Courthouse Drive, Elizabethtown, NC 28337. 910-862-6710. Fax: 910-862-6767. 8:30AM-5PM (EST).

Felony, Misdemeanor, Civil, Eviction, Small Claims, Probate—Superior-District Court, PO Box 547, Elizabethtown, NC 28337. 910-862-2143. 8:30AM-5:00PM (EST). Access by: Mail, in person.

Brunswick County

Real Estate Recording—Brunswick County Register of Deeds, Government Complex, Highway 17-Business, Bolivia, NC 28422. 910-253-4371. Fax: 910-253-7022. 8:30AM-5PM (EST).

Felony, Misdemeanor, Civil, Eviction, Small Claims, Probate—Superior-District Court, PO Box 127, Bolivia, NC 28422. 910-253-8502. Fax: 910-253-7652. 8:30AM-5:00PM (EST). Access by: Mail, in person.

Buncombe County

Real Estate Recording—Buncombe County Register of Deeds, 60 Court Plaza, Asheville, NC 28801. 704-255-5541. Fax: 704-255-5829. 8:30AM-5PM (EST).

Felony, Misdemeanor, Civil, Eviction, Small Claims, Probate—Superior-District Court, 60 Court Plaza, Asheville, NC 28801-3519. 704-255-4702. Fax: 704-251-6257. 8:30AM-5PM (EST). Access by: Mail, in person.

Burke County

Real Estate Recording—Burke County Register of Deeds, 201 South Green Street, Courthouse, Morganton, NC 28655. 704-438-5450. Fax: 704-438-5463. 8AM-5PM (EST).

Felony, Misdemeanor, Civil, Eviction, Small Claims, Probate—Superior-District Court, PO Box 796, Morganton, NC 28655. 704-432-2800. Fax: 704-438-5460. 8AM-5PM (EST). Access by: Fax, mail, in person.

Cabarrus County

Real Estate Recording—Cabarrus County Register of Deeds, 65 Church Street S.E., Concord, NC 28025. 704-788-8112. Fax: 704-788-9898. 8AM-5PM (EST).

Felony, Misdemeanor, Civil, Eviction, Small Claims, Probate—Superior-District Court, PO Box 70, Concord, NC 28026-0070. 704-786-4137. Civil: 704-786-4201. Criminal: 704-786-4211. 8:30AM-5PM (EST). Access by: Mail, in person.

Caldwell County

Real Estate Recording—Caldwell County Register of Deeds, 905 West Avenue N.W., County Office Building, Lenoir, NC 28645. 704-757-1310. Fax: 704-757-1294. 8AM-5PM (EST).

Felony, Misdemeanor, Civil, Eviction, Small Claims, Probate—Superior-District Court, PO Box 1376, Lenoir, NC 28645. 704-757-1375. Fax: 704-757-1479. 8AM-5PM (EST). Access by: Fax, mail, in person.

Camden County

Real Estate Recording—Camden County Register of Deeds, County Courthouse, 117 North 343, Camden, NC 27921. 919-335-4077. 8AM-5PM (EST).

Felony, Misdemeanor, Civil, Eviction, Small Claims, Probate—Superior-District Court, PO Box 219, Camden, NC 27921. 919-335-7942. Fax: 919-331-4827. 8:00AM-5:00PM (EST). Access by: Mail, in person.

Carteret County

Real Estate Recording—Carteret County Register of Deeds, Courthouse Square, Beaufort, NC 28516. 919-728-8474. 8AM-5PM (EST).

Felony, Misdemeanor, Civil, Eviction, Small Claims, Probate—Superior-District Court, Courthouse Square,

Beaufort, NC 28516. 919-728-8500. Fax: 919-728-6502. 8AM-5PM (EST). Access by: Phone, fax, mail, in person. Call first.

Caswell County

Real Estate Recording—Caswell County Register of Deeds, 139 E. Church St., Courthouse, Yanceyville, NC 27379. 910-694-4193. 8AM-5PM (EST).

Felony, Misdemeanor, Civil, Eviction, Small Claims, Probate—Superior-District Court, PO Drawer 790, Yanceyville, NC 27379. 910-694-4171. Fax: 910-694-7338. 8AM-5PM (EST). Access by: Mail, in person.

Catawba County

Real Estate Recording—Catawba County Register of Deeds, Catawba County Justice Center, Highway 321/ 100 Justice Place, Newton, NC 28658. 704-465-1573. 8AM-5PM (EST).

Felony, Misdemeanor, Civil, Eviction, Small Claims, Probate—Superior-District Court, PO Box 790, Newton, NC 28658. 704-464-5216. 8AM-5PM (EST). Access by: Mail, in person.

Chatham County

Real Estate Recording—Chatham County Register of Deeds, Courthouse Circle, Pittsboro, NC 27312. 919-542-8235. 8AM-4:30PM (EST).

Felony, Misdemeanor, Civil, Eviction, Small Claims, Probate—Superior-District Court, PO Box 368, Pittsboro, NC 27312. 919-542-3240. 8AM-5PM (EST). Access by: Mail, in person.

Cherokee County

Real Estate Recording—Cherokee County Register of Deeds, Courthouse, Murphy, NC 28906. 704-837-2613. Fax: 704-837-9684. 8AM-5PM (EST).

Felony, Misdemeanor, Civil, Eviction, Small Claims, Probate—Superior-District Court, 201 Peachtree St, Murphy, NC 28906. 704-837-2522. 9AM-5PM (EST). Access by: Mail, in person.

Chowan County

Real Estate Recording—Chowan County Register of Deeds, 101 South Broad Street, Courthouse, Edenton, NC 27932. 919-482-2619. 8AM-5PM (EST).

Felony, Misdemeanor, Civil, Eviction, Small Claims, Probate—Superior-District Court, N.C. Courier Box 106319, PO Box 588, Edenton, NC 27932. 919-482-4150. Fax: 919-482-2190. 9AM-5PM (EST). Access by: Mail, in person.

Clay County

Real Estate Recording—Clay County Register of Deeds, Main Street, Hayesville, NC 28904. 704-389-0087. Fax: 704-389-9749. 8AM-5PM (EST).

Felony, Misdemeanor, Civil, Eviction, Small Claims, Probate—Superior-District Court, PO Box 506, Hayesville, NC 28904. 704-389-8334. Fax: 704-389-3329. 8AM-5PM (EST). Access by: Fax, mail, in person.

Cleveland County

Real Estate Recording—Cleveland County Register of Deeds, 311 East Marion St., Room 101, Shelby, NC 28150. 704-484-4834. Fax: 704-484-4909. 8AM-5PM (EST).

Felony, Misdemeanor, Civil, Eviction, Small Claims, Probate—Superior-District Court, 100 Justice Place, Shelby, NC 28150. 704-484-4851. Fax: 704-480-5487. 8AM-5PM (EST). Access by: Fax, mail, in person.

Columbus County

Real Estate Recording—Columbus County Register of Deeds, Courthouse, Whiteville, NC 28472. 910-640-6625. Fax: 910-640-2547. 8:30AM-5PM (EST).

Felony, Misdemeanor, Civil, Eviction, Small Claims, Probate—Superior-District Court, PO Box 1587, Whiteville, NC 28472. 910-641-3000. Fax: 910-641-3027. 8:30AM-5PM (EST). Access by: Phone, fax, mail, in person.

Craven County

Real Estate Recording—Craven County Register of Deeds, 406 Craven Street, New Bern, NC 28560. 919-636-6617. 8AM-5PM (EST).

Felony, Misdemeanor, Civil, Eviction, Small Claims, Probate—Superior-District Court, PO Box 1187, New Bern, NC 28563. 919-514-4774. Fax: 919-514-4891. 8AM-5PM (EST). Access by: Mail, in person.

Cumberland County

Real Estate Recording—Cumberland County Register of Deeds, 117 Dick Street, Room 114, Fayetteville, NC 28302. 910-678-7775. Fax: 910-323-1456. 8AM-5PM (EST).

Felony, Misdemeanor, Civil, Eviction, Small Claims, Probate—Superior-District Court, PO Box 363, Fayetteville, NC 28302. Civil: 910-678-2909. Criminal: 910-678-2906. 8:30AM-5PM (EST). Access by: Mail, in person.

Currituck County

Real Estate Recording—Currituck County Register of Deeds, 101 Courthouse Road, Currituck, NC 27929. 919-232-3297. 8AM-5PM (EST).

Felony, Misdemeanor, Civil, Eviction, Small Claims, Probate—Superior-District Court, PO Box 175, Currituck, NC 27929. 919-232-2010. Fax: 919-232-3722. 8AM-5PM (EST). Access by: Fax, mail, in person.

Dare County

Real Estate Recording—Dare County Register of Deeds, 300 Queen Elizabeth Avenue, Courthouse, PO Box 70, Manteo, NC 27954. 919-473-3438. 8:30AM-5PM (EST).

Felony, Misdemeanor, Civil, Eviction, Small Claims, Probate—Superior-District Court, PO Box 1849, Manteo, NC 27954. 919-473-2950. 8:30AM-5PM (EST). Access by: Mail, in person.

Davidson County

Real Estate Recording—Davidson County Register of Deeds, 110 West Center Street, Court House, Lexington, NC 27292. 910-242-2150. 8AM-5PM (EST).

Felony, Misdemeanor, Civil, Eviction, Small Claims, Probate—Superior-District Court, PO Box 1064, Lexington, NC 27293-1064. Civil: 910-249-0351. Criminal: 910-249-0351. Fax: 910-249-6951. 8AM-5PM (EST). Access by: Mail, in person.

Davie County

Real Estate Recording—Davie County Register of Deeds, 123 South Main Street, Mocksville, NC 27028. 704-634-2513. 8:30AM-5PM (EST).

Felony, Misdemeanor, Civil, Eviction, Small Claims, Probate—Superior-District Court, 140 S Main St, Mocksville, NC 27028. Civil: 704-634-3507. Criminal: 704-634-3508. Fax: 704-634-4720. 8:30AM-5PM (EST). Access by: Mail, in person.

Duplin County

Real Estate Recording—Duplin County Register of Deeds, Courthouse, Kenansville, NC 28349. 910-296-2108. Fax: 910-296-2344. 8AM-5PM (EST).

Felony, Misdemeanor, Civil, Eviction, Small Claims, Probate—Superior-District Court, PO Box 189, Kenansville, NC 28349. 910-296-1686. Civil: 910-296-1686. Criminal: 910-296-0110. Fax: 910-296-2310. 8AM-5PM (EST). Access by: Mail, in person.

Durham County

Real Estate Recording—Durham County Register of Deeds, 200 East Main Street, Ground Floor, Durham, NC 27701. 919-560-0480. Fax: 919-560-0497. 8:30-5PM (EST).

Felony, Misdemeanor, Civil, Eviction, Small Claims, Probate—Superior-District Court, PO Box 1772, Durham, NC 27702. Civil: 919-560-6823. Criminal: 919-560-6821. 8:30AM-5PM (EST). Access by: Mail, in person.

Edgecombe County

Real Estate Recording—Edgecombe County Register of Deeds, 301 St. Andrews Street, Courthouse, Tarboro, NC 27886. 919-641-7924. Fax: 919-641-1771. 8AM-5PM (EST).

Felony, Misdemeanor, Civil, Eviction, Small Claims, Probate—Superior-District Court, PO Drawer 9, Tarboro, NC 27886. Civil: 919-823-6161. Criminal: 919-823-2056. 8AM-5PM (EST). Access by: Mail, in person.

Forsyth County

Real Estate Recording—Forsyth County Register of Deeds, 200 North Main, Room 208, Winston-Salem, NC 27101. 910-727-2903. Fax: 910-727-2341. 8AM-5PM (EST).

Felony, Misdemeanor, Civil, Eviction, Small Claims, Probate—Superior-District Court, PO Box 20099, Winston Salem, NC 27120-0099. 910-761-2250. Civil: 910-761-2340. Criminal: 910-761-2366. Fax: 910-761-2018. 8AM-5PM (EST). Access by: Mail, in person.

Franklin County

Real Estate Recording—Franklin County Register of Deeds, 113 South Main Street, Louisburg, NC 27549. 919-496-3500. 8AM-5PM (EST).

Felony, Misdemeanor, Civil, Eviction, Small Claims, Probate—Superior-District Court, 102 S Main St, Louisburg, NC 27549. 919-496-5104. Fax: 919-496-0407. 8:30AM-5PM (EST). Access by: Fax, mail, in person.

Gaston County

Real Estate Recording—Gaston County Register of Deeds, 151 South Street, Gastonia, NC 28052. 704-866-3181. Fax: 704-852-6019. 8:30AM-5PM (EST).

Felony, Misdemeanor, Civil, Eviction, Small Claims, Probate—Superior-District Court, PO Box 340, Gastonia, NC 28053. 704-868-5801. 8AM-5PM (EST). Access by: Mail, in person.

Gates County

Real Estate Recording—Gates County Register of Deeds, Court Street, Gatesville, NC 27938. 919-357-0850. Fax: 919-357-0073. 9AM-5PM (EST).

Felony, Misdemeanor, Civil, Eviction, Small Claims, Probate—Superior-District Court, PO Box 31, Gatesville, NC 27938. 919-357-1365. 8AM-5PM (EST). Access by: Mail, in person.

Graham County

Real Estate Recording—Graham County Register of Deeds, Main Street, Courthouse, Robbinsville, NC 28771. 704-479-7971. Fax: 704-479-7988. 8:30AM-4:30PM (EST).

Felony, Misdemeanor, Civil, Eviction, Small Claims, Probate—Superior-District Court, PO Box 1179, Robbinsville, NC 28771. 704-479-7986. Civil: 704-479-7986 X7974. Criminal: 704-479-7986 X7975. Fax: 704-479-6417. 8AM-5PM M-Th; 8AM-4:30PM Fri (EST). Access by: Mail, in person.

Granville County

Real Estate Recording—Granville County Register of Deeds, 101 Main Street, Courthouse, Oxford, NC 27565. 919-693-6314. Fax: 919-603-1345. 8:30AM-5PM (EST).

Felony, Misdemeanor, Civil, Eviction, Small Claims, Probate—Superior-District Court, Courthouse, 101 Main Street, Oxford, NC 27565. 919-693-2649. Fax: 919-693-8944. (EST). Access by: Phone, mail, in person.

Greene County

Real Estate Recording—Greene County Register of Deeds, Greene Street, Courthouse, Snow Hill, NC 28580. 919-747-3620. 8AM-5PM (EST).

Felony, Misdemeanor, Civil, Eviction, Small Claims, Probate—Superior-District Court, PO Box 675, Snow Hill, NC 28580. 919-747-3505. 8AM-5PM (EST). Access by: Mail, in person.

Guilford County

Real Estate Recording—Guilford County Register of Deeds, Guilford County Courthouse, 201 S. Eugene St., Room LG53, Greensboro, NC 27401. 910-373-7556. 8AM-5PM (EST).

Felony, Misdemeanor, Civil, Eviction, Small Claims, Probate—Superior-District Court, 201 S Eugene, PO Box 3008, Greensboro, NC 27402. 910-574-4305. Civil: 910-574-4305. Criminal: 910-574-4307. 8AM-5PM (EST). Access by: Mail, in person.

Halifax County

Real Estate Recording—Halifax County Register of Deeds, Ferrell Lane, Halifax, NC 27839. 919-583-2101. Fax: 919-583-1273. 8:30AM-5PM (EST).

Felony, Misdemeanor, Civil, Eviction, Small Claims, Probate—Superior-District Court, PO Box 66, Halifax, NC 27839. 919-583-5061. 8:30AM-5PM (EST). Access by: Mail, in person.

Harnett County

Real Estate Recording—Harnett County Register of Deeds, Courthouse, 729 Main Street, Lillington, NC 27546. 910-893-7540. Fax: 910-814-3841. 8AM-5PM (EST).

Felony, Misdemeanor, Civil, Eviction, Small Claims, Probate—Superior-District Court, PO Box 849, Lillington, NC 27546. 910-893-5164. Fax: 910-893-3683. 8:15AM-5:15PM (EST). Access by: Mail, in person.

Haywood County

Real Estate Recording—Haywood County Register of Deeds, Courthouse, 215 N. Main St., Waynesville, NC 28786. 704-452-6635. Fax: 704-452-6762. 8AM-5PM (EST).

Felony, Misdemeanor, Civil, Eviction, Small Claims, Probate—Superior-District Court, 420 N. Main, Waynesville, NC 28786. 704-456-3540. 8:30AM-5PM (EST). Access by: Mail, in person.

Henderson County

Real Estate Recording—Henderson County Register of Deeds, Suite 129, 200 N. Grove St., Hendersonville, NC 28792. 704-697-4901. 8:30AM-5PM (EST).

Felony, Misdemeanor, Civil, Eviction, Small Claims, Probate—Superior-District Court, PO Box 965, Hendersonville, NC 28793. Civil: 704-697-4851. Criminal: 704-697-4860. 8AM-5PM (EST). Access by: Mail, in person.

Hertford County

Real Estate Recording—Hertford County Register of Deeds, Courthouse, Winton, NC 27986. 919-358-7850. Fax: 919-358-7806. 8:30AM-5PM (EST).

Felony, Misdemeanor, Civil, Eviction, Small Claims, Probate—Superior-District Court, PO Box 86, Winton, NC 27986. 919-358-7845. 8AM-5PM (EST). Access by: Mail, in person.

Hoke County

Real Estate Recording—Hoke County Register of Deeds, 036103, 304 N. Main St., Raeford, NC 28376. 910-875-2035. 8AM-5PM (EST).

Felony, Misdemeanor, Civil, Eviction, Small Claims, Probate—Superior-District Court, PO Drawer 410, Raeford, NC 28376. 910-875-3728. Fax: 910-904-1708. 8:30AM-5PM (EST). Access by: Mail, in person.

Hyde County

Real Estate Recording—Hyde County Register of Deeds, Courthouse Square, Swanquarter, NC 27885. 919-926-3011. Fax: 919-926-3082. 8AM-5PM (EST).

Felony, Misdemeanor, Civil, Eviction, Small Claims, Probate—Superior-District Court, PO Box 337, Swanquarter, NC 27885. 919-926-4101. Fax: 919-926-1002. 8:30AM-5:30PM (EST). Access by: Phone, mail, in person.

Iredell County

Real Estate Recording—Iredell County Register of Deeds, 201 Water Street, Statesville, NC 28677. 704-872-7468. Fax: 704-878-3055. 8AM-5PM (EST).

Felony, Misdemeanor, Civil, Eviction, Small Claims, Probate—Superior-District Court, PO Box 186, Statesville, NC 28677. 704-878-4204. Fax: 704-878-3261. 8AM-5PM (EST). Access by: Phone, mail, in person.

Jackson County

Real Estate Recording—Jackson County Register of Deeds, 401 Grindstaff Cove Rd., Sylva, NC 28779. 704-586-4055. Fax: 704-586-6879. 8:30AM-5PM (EST).

Felony, Misdemeanor, Civil, Eviction, Small Claims, Probate—Superior-District Court, 401 Grind Staff Cove Rd, Sylva, NC 28779. 704-586-4312. Fax: 704-586-9009. 8:30AM-5PM (EST). Access by: Mail, in person.

Johnston County

Real Estate Recording—Johnston County Register of Deeds, Market Street, Courthouse Square, Smithfield, NC 27577. 919-989-5164. 8AM-5PM (EST).

Felony, Misdemeanor, Civil, Eviction, Small Claims, Probate—Superior-District Court, PO Box 297, Smithfield, NC 27577. 919-934-3192. Fax: 919-934-5857. 8AM-5PM (EST). Access by: Mail, in person.

Jones County

Real Estate Recording—Jones County Register of Deeds, 101 Market St., Trenton, NC 28585. 919-448-2551. Fax: 919-448-1357. 8AM-5PM (EST).

Felony, Misdemeanor, Civil, Eviction, Small Claims, Probate—Superior-District Court, PO Box 280, Trenton, NC 28585. 919-448-7351. Fax: 919-448-1608. 8AM-5PM (EST). Access by: Phone, mail, in person.

Lee County

Real Estate Recording—Lee County Register of Deeds, 1408 South Horner Blvd., Sanford, NC 27331. 919-774-4821. Fax: 919-774-5063. 8AM-5PM (EST).

Felony, Misdemeanor, Civil, Eviction, Small Claims, Probate—Superior-District Court, PO Box 4209, Sanford, NC 27331. 919-708-4400. Fax: 919-775-3483. 8AM-5PM (EST). Access by: Mail, in person.

Lenoir County

Real Estate Recording—Lenoir County Register of Deeds, County Courthouse, 130 S. Queen St., Kinston, NC 28501. 919-523-2390. Fax: 919-523-6139. 8:30AM-5PM (EST).

Felony, Misdemeanor, Civil, Eviction, Small Claims, Probate—Superior-District Court, PO Box 68, Kinston, NC 28502-0068. 919-527-6231. Fax: 919-527-9154. 8AM-5PM (EST). Access by: Mail, in person.

Lincoln County

Real Estate Recording—Lincoln County Register of Deeds, Courthouse, Lincolnton, NC 28092. 704-736-8530. 8AM-5PM (EST).

Felony, Misdemeanor, Civil, Eviction, Small Claims, Probate—Superior-District Court, PO Box 8, Lincolnton, NC 28093. 704-736-8566. Fax: 704-736-8718. 8AM-5PM (EST). Access by: Mail, in person.

Macon County

Real Estate Recording—Macon County Register of Deeds, 5 West Main Street, Franklin, NC 28734. 704-349-2095. Fax: 704-369-6382. 8AM-5PM (EST).

Felony, Misdemeanor, Civil, Eviction, Small Claims, Probate—Superior-District Court, PO Box 288, Franklin, NC 28734. 704-349-2000. 8:30AM-5PM (EST). Access by: Mail, in person.

Madison County

Real Estate Recording—Madison County Register of Deeds, Courthouse, Marshall, NC 28753. 704-649-3131. 8:30AM-5PM (EST).

Felony, Misdemeanor, Civil, Eviction, Small Claims, Probate—Superior-District Court, PO Box 217, Marshall, NC 28753. 704-649-2531. 8AM-5PM (EST). Access by: Mail, in person.

Martin County

Real Estate Recording—Martin County Register of Deeds, 305 East Main Street, Williamston, NC 27892. 919-792-1683. Fax: 919-792-7477. 8AM-5PM (EST).

Felony, Misdemeanor, Civil, Eviction, Small Claims, Probate—Superior-District Court, PO Box 807, Williamston, NC 27892. 919-792-2515. Fax: 919-792-6668. 8AM-5PM (EST). Access by: Mail, in person.

McDowell County

Real Estate Recording—McDowell County Register of Deeds, 1 South Main Street, Courthouse, Marion, NC 28752. 704-652-4727. Fax: 704-659-3484. 8:30AM-5PM (EST).

Felony, Misdemeanor, Civil, Eviction, Small Claims, Probate—Superior-District Court, PO Drawer 729, Marion, NC 28752. 704-652-7717. 8:30AM-5PM (EST). Access by: Mail, in person.

Mecklenburg County

Real Estate Recording—Mecklenburg County Register of Deeds, 720 East 4th Street, Ste. 100, Charlotte, NC 28202. 704-336-2443. Fax: 704-336-7699. (EST).

Felony, Misdemeanor, Civil, Eviction, Small Claims, Probate—Superior-District Court, 800 E 4th St, Charlotte, NC 28202. Civil: 704-347-7814. Criminal: 704-347-7809. 8AM-5PM (EST). Access by: Mail, in person.

Mitchell County

Real Estate Recording—Mitchell County Register of Deeds, Crimson Laurel Way, Administrative Building, Bakersville, NC 28705. 704-688-2139. Fax: 704-688-3666. 8AM-5PM (EST).

Felony, Misdemeanor, Civil, Eviction, Small Claims, Probate—Superior-District Court, PO Box 402, Bakersville, NC 28705. 704-688-2161. Fax: 704-688-2168. 8:30AM-5PM (EST). Access by: Fax, mail, in person.

Montgomery County

Real Estate Recording—Montgomery County Register of Deeds, 102 East Spring St., Troy, NC 27371. 910-576-4271. Fax: 910-576-2209. 8AM-5PM (EST).

Felony, Misdemeanor, Civil, Eviction, Small Claims, Probate—Superior-District Court, PO Box 182, Troy, NC 27371. 910-576-4211. 8AM-5PM (EST). Access by: Fax, mail, in person.

Moore County

Real Estate Recording—Moore County Register of Deeds, 100 Dowd Street, Carthage, NC 28327. 910-947-6370. Fax: 910-947-6396. 8AM-5PM (EST).

Felony, Misdemeanor, Civil, Eviction, Small Claims, Probate—Superior-District Court, PO Box 936, Carthage, NC 28327. 910-947-2396. Fax: 910-947-1444. 8AM-5PM (EST). Access by: Mail, in person.

Nash County

Real Estate Recording—Nash County Register of Deeds, Washington Street, Nashville, NC 27856. 919-459-9836. Fax: 919-459-9889. 8AM-5PM (EST).

Felony, Misdemeanor, Civil, Eviction, Small Claims, Probate—Superior-District Court, PO Box 759, Nashville, NC 27856. 919-459-4081. Civil: 919-459-4081. Criminal: 919-459-4085. Fax: 919-459-6050. 8AM-5PM (EST). Access by: Mail, in person.

New Hanover County

Real Estate Recording—New Hanover County Register of Deeds, 316 Princess Street, Room 216, Wilmington, NC 28401. 910-341-4530. Fax: 910-341-4323. 8:30AM-4:45PM (EST).

Felony, Misdemeanor, Civil, Eviction, Small Claims, Probate—Superior-District Court, PO Box 2023, Wilmington, NC 28402. 910-341-4430. Fax: 910-251-2676. 8AM-5PM (EST). Access by: Mail, in person.

Northampton County

Real Estate Recording—Northampton County Register of Deeds, Courthouse, Jackson, NC 27845. 919-534-2511. 8AM-5PM (EST).

Felony, Misdemeanor, Civil, Eviction, Small Claims, Probate—Superior-District Court, PO Box 217, Jackson, NC 27845. 919-534-1631. 8:30AM-5PM (EST). Access by: Mail, in person.

Onslow County

Real Estate Recording—Onslow County Register of Deeds, 109 Old Bridge St., Room 107, Jacksonville, NC 28540. 910-347-3451. 8AM-5PM (EST).

Felony, Misdemeanor, Civil, Eviction, Small Claims, Probate—Superior-District Court, 625 Court St, Jacksonville, NC 28540. 910-455-4458. 8AM-5PM (EST). Access by: Mail, in person.

Orange County

Real Estate Recording—Orange County Register of Deeds, 200 South Cameron Street, Hillsborough, NC 27278. 919-732-8181. Fax: 919-644-3015. 8AM-5PM (EST).

Felony, Misdemeanor, Civil, Eviction, Small Claims, Probate—Superior-District Court, 106 E Margaret Lane, Hillsborough, NC 27278. 919-732-8181. Fax: 919-644-3043. 8AM-5PM (EST). Access by: Mail, in person.

Pamlico County

Real Estate Recording—Pamlico County Register of Deeds, Courthouse, Bayboro, NC 28515. 919-745-4421. 8AM-5PM (EST).

Felony, Misdemeanor, Civil, Eviction, Small Claims, Probate—Superior-District Court, PO Box 38, Bayboro, NC 28515. 919-745-3881. Fax: 919-745-3399. 8AM-5PM (EST). Access by: Mail, in person.

Pasquotank County

Real Estate Recording—Pasquotank County Register of Deeds, 206 East Main Street, Elizabeth City, NC 27909. 919-335-4367. 8AM-5PM (EST).

Felony, Misdemeanor, Civil, Eviction, Small Claims, Probate—Superior-District Court, PO Box 449, Elizabeth City, NC 27909. 919-331-4751. 8AM-5PM (EST). Access by: Mail, in person.

Pender County

Real Estate Recording—Pender County Register of Deeds, 102 Wright Street, Courthouse, Burgaw, NC 28425. 910-259-1225. Fax: 910-259-1299. 8AM-5PM (Recording 8AM-4:30PM) (EST).

Felony, Misdemeanor, Civil, Eviction, Small Claims, Probate—Superior-District Court, PO Box 308, Burgaw, NC 28425. 910-259-1229. 8AM-5PM (EST). Access by: Mail, in person.

Perquimans County

Real Estate Recording—Perquimans County Register of Deeds, 128 North Church Street, Hertford, NC 27944. 919-426-5660. Fax: 919-426-4034. 8:30AM-5PM (EST).

Felony, Misdemeanor, Civil, Eviction, Small Claims, Probate—Superior-District Court, PO Box 33, Hertford, NC 27944. 919-426-1505. 8:00AM-5:00PM (EST). Access by: Mail, in person.

Person County

Real Estate Recording—Person County Register of Deeds, Courthouse Square, Roxboro, NC 27573. 910-597-1733. 8:30AM-5PM (EST).

Felony, Misdemeanor, Civil, Eviction, Small Claims, Probate—Superior-District Court, Main St, Roxboro, NC 27573. 910-597-0554. Civil: 910-597-0554. Criminal: 910-597-0556. Fax: 910-597-0568. 8:30AM-5PM (EST). Access by: Mail, in person.

Pitt County

Real Estate Recording—Pitt County Register of Deeds, 3rd & Evans Streets, Courthouse, Greenville, NC 27834. 919-830-4128. 8AM-5PM (EST).

Felony, Misdemeanor, Civil, Eviction, Small Claims, Probate—Superior-District Court, PO Box 6067, Greenville, NC 27834. 919-830-6400. Civil: 919-830-6420. Criminal: 919-830-6419. Fax: 919-830-3144. 8AM-5PM (EST). Access by: Mail, in person.

Polk County

Real Estate Recording—Polk County Register of Deeds, 102 Courthouse Street, Columbus, NC 28722. 704-894-8450. Fax: 704-894-5781. 8:30AM-5PM (EST).

Felony, Misdemeanor, Civil, Eviction, Small Claims, Probate—Superior-District Court, PO Box 38, Columbus, NC 28722. 704-894-8231. Fax: 704-894-5752. 8AM-5PM (EST). Access by: Mail, in person.

Randolph County

Real Estate Recording—Randolph County Register of Deeds, 158 Worth Street, Asheboro, NC 27203. 910-318-6960. 8AM-5PM (EST).

Felony, Misdemeanor, Civil, Eviction, Small Claims, Probate—Superior-District Court, PO Box 1925, Asheboro, NC 27204-1925. Civil: 910-318-6750. Criminal: 910-318-6710. Fax: 910-318-6709. 8AM-5PM (EST). Access by: Mail, in person.

Richmond County

Real Estate Recording—Richmond County Register of Deeds, 114 E Franklin St., Suite 101, Rockingham, NC 28379. 910-997-8250. Fax: 910-997-8499. 8AM-5PM (EST).

Felony, Misdemeanor, Civil, Eviction, Small Claims, Probate—Superior-District Court, PO Box 724, Rockingham, NC 28379. Civil: 910-997-9100. Criminal: 910-997-9102. 8AM-5PM (EST). Access by: Mail, in person.

Robeson County

Real Estate Recording—Robeson County Register of Deeds, 500 North Elm Street, Courthouse - Room 102, Lumberton, NC 28358. 910-671-3043. 8:15AM-5:15PM (EST).

Felony, Misdemeanor, Civil, Eviction, Small Claims, Probate—Superior-District Court, PO Box 1084, Lumberton, NC 28358. Civil: 910-671-3372. Criminal: 910-671-3395. Fax: 910-618-5598. 8:30AM-5PM (EST). Access by: Mail, in person.

Rockingham County

Real Estate Recording—Rockingham County Register of Deeds, County Courthouse, Suite 99, 1086 NC 65, Wentworth, NC 27375. 910-342-8820. 8AM-5PM (EST).

Felony, Misdemeanor, Civil, Eviction, Small Claims, Probate—Superior-District Court, PO Box 127, Wentworth, NC 27375. 910-342-8700. 8AM-5PM (EST). Access by: Mail, in person.

Rowan County

Real Estate Recording—Rowan County Register of Deeds, 402 North Main Street, County Office Building, Salisbury, NC 28144. 704-638-3102. 8AM-5PM (EST).

Felony, Misdemeanor, Civil, Eviction, Small Claims, Probate—Superior-District Court, PO Box 4599, 210 N Main St, Salisbury, NC 28144. 704-639-7505. 8AM-5PM (EST). Access by: Mail, in person.

Rutherford County

Real Estate Recording—Rutherford County Register of Deeds, Main Street, Rutherfordton, NC 28139. 704-287-6155. Fax: 704-287-6470. 8:30AM-5PM (EST).

Felony, Misdemeanor, Civil, Eviction, Small Claims, Probate—Superior-District Court, PO Box 630, Rutherfordton, NC 28139. Civil: 704-286-9136. Criminal: 704-286-3243. 8:30AM-5PM (EST). Access by: Mail, in person.

Sampson County

Real Estate Recording—Sampson County Register of Deeds, Main Street, Courthouse, Clinton, NC 28328. 910-592-8026. 8AM-5:15PM (EST).

Felony, Misdemeanor, Civil, Eviction, Small Claims, Probate—Superior-District Court, Courthouse, Clinton, NC 28328. 910-592-5191. Civil: 910-592-5192. Criminal: 910-592-6891. Fax: 910-592-5502. 8AM-5PM (EST). Access by: Phone, mail, in person.

Scotland County

Real Estate Recording—Scotland County Register of Deeds, 212 Biggs Street, Courthouse, Room 250, Laurinburg, NC 28352. 910-277-2575. Fax: 910-277-3133. 8AM-5PM (EST).

Felony, Misdemeanor, Civil, Eviction, Small Claims, Probate—Superior-District Court, PO Box 769, Laurinburg, NC 28352. 910-277-3240. (EST). Access by: Mail, in person.

Stanly County

Real Estate Recording—Stanly County Register of Deeds, 201 South Second Street, Albemarle, NC 28001. 704-983-7235. 8:30AM-5PM (EST).

Felony, Misdemeanor, Civil, Eviction, Small Claims, Probate—Superior-District Court, PO Box 668, Albemarle, NC 28002-0668. 704-982-2161. Fax: 704-982-8107. 8:30AM-5PM (EST). Access by: Mail, in person.

Stokes County

Real Estate Recording—Stokes County Register of Deeds, Main Street, Government Center, Danbury, NC 27016. 910-593-2811. Fax: 910-593-9360. 8:30AM-5PM (EST).

Felony, Misdemeanor, Civil, Eviction, Small Claims, Probate—Superior-District Court, PO Box 256, Danbury, NC 27016. 910-593-2416. 8AM-5PM (EST). Access by: Mail, in person.

Surry County

Real Estate Recording—Surry County Register of Deeds, 114 W. Atkins St., Courthouse, Dobson, NC 27017. 910-401-8150. Fax: 910-401-8151. 8:15AM-5PM (EST).

Felony, Misdemeanor, Civil, Eviction, Small Claims, Probate—Superior-District Court, PO Box 345, Dobson, NC 27017. 910-386-8131. Fax: 910-386-9879. 8AM-5PM (EST). Access by: Mail, in person.

Swain County

Real Estate Recording—Swain County Register of Deeds, 101 Mitchell Street, Bryson City, NC 28713. 704-488-9273. Fax: 704-488-2754. 8:30AM-4:30PM (EST).

Felony, Misdemeanor, Civil, Eviction, Small Claims, Probate—Superior-District Court, PO Box 1397, Bryson City, NC 28713. 704-488-2288. Fax: 704-488-9360. 8:30AM-5PM (EST). Access by: Mail, in person.

Transylvania County

Real Estate Recording—Transylvania County Register of Deeds, 12 East Main Street, Courthouse, Brevard, NC 28712. 704-884-3162. 8:30AM-5PM (EST).

Felony, Misdemeanor, Civil, Eviction, Small Claims, Probate—Superior-District Court, 12 E Main St, Brevard, NC 28712. 704-884-3120. Fax: 704-883-2161. 8AM-5PM (EST). Access by: Mail, in person.

Tyrrell County

Real Estate Recording—Tyrrell County Register of Deeds, 403 Main Street, Columbia, NC 27925. 919-796-2901. Fax: 919-796-0148. 9AM-5PM (EST).

Felony, Misdemeanor, Civil, Eviction, Small Claims, Probate—Superior-District Court, PO Box 406, Columbia, NC 27925. 919-796-6281. 8:30AM-5PM (EST). Access by: Mail, in person.

Union County

Real Estate Recording—Union County Register of Deeds, 500 North Main Street, Room 205, Monroe, NC 28112. 704-283-3727. Fax: 704-283-3569. 9AM-5PM (EST).

Felony, Misdemeanor, Civil, Eviction, Small Claims, Probate—Superior-District Court, PO Box 5038, Monroe, NC 28111. 704-283-4313. 8AM-5PM (EST). Access by: Mail, in person.

Vance County

Real Estate Recording—Vance County Register of Deeds, 122 Young Street, Courthouse, Suite F, Henderson, NC 27536. 919-438-4155. 8:30AM-5PM (EST).

Felony, Misdemeanor, Civil, Eviction, Small Claims, Probate—Superior-District Court, 122 Young St, Henderson, NC 27536. 919-492-0031. 8AM-5PM (EST). Access by: Mail, in person.

Wake County

Real Estate Recording—Wake County Register of Deeds, 300 S. Salisbury St., Room 104, Raleigh, NC 27601. 919-856-5460. 8:30AM-5:15PM (EST).

Felony, Misdemeanor, Civil, Eviction, Small Claims, Probate—Superior-District Court, PO Box 351, Raleigh, NC 27602. 919-755-4105. Civil: 919-755-4108. Criminal: 919-755-4110. 8:30AM-5:00PM (EST). Access by: Mail, in person.

Warren County

Real Estate Recording—Warren County Register of Deeds, Main Street, Courthouse, Warrenton, NC 27589. 919-257-3265. Fax: 919-257-1524. 8:30AM-5PM (EST).

Felony, Misdemeanor, Civil, Eviction, Small Claims, Probate—Superior-District Court, PO Box 709, Warrenton, NC 27589. 919-257-3261. Fax: 919-257-5529. 8:30AM-5PM (EST). Access by: Mail, in person.

Washington County

Real Estate Recording—Washington County Register of Deeds, 120 Adams Street, Courthouse, Plymouth, NC 27962. 919-793-2325. 8:30AM-5PM (EST).

Felony, Misdemeanor, Civil, Eviction, Small Claims, Probate—Superior-District Court, PO Box 901, Plymouth, NC 27962. 919-793-3013. Fax: 919-793-1081. 8AM-5PM (EST). Access by: Mail, in person.

Watauga County

Real Estate Recording—Watauga County Register of Deeds, Courthouse, Room 119, Boone, NC 28607. 704-265-8052. Fax: 704-265-8018. 8AM-5PM (EST).

Felony, Misdemeanor, Civil, Eviction, Small Claims, Probate—Superior-District Court, Courthouse Suite 13, 842 West King St, Boone, NC 28607-3525. 704-265-5364. Fax: 704-262-5753. 8AM-5PM (EST). Access by: Mail, in person.

Wayne County

Real Estate Recording—Wayne County Register of Deeds, William Street, Courthouse, Goldsboro, NC 27530. 919-731-1449. 8AM-5PM (EST).

Felony, Misdemeanor, Civil, Eviction, Small Claims, Probate—Superior-District Court, PO Box 267, Goldsboro, NC 27530. 919-731-7910. Fax: 919-731-2037. 8AM-5PM (EST). Access by: Mail, in person.

Wilkes County

Real Estate Recording—Wilkes County Register of Deeds, Main Street, Courthouse, Wilkesboro, NC 28697. 910-838-2052. 8:30AM-5PM (EST).

Felony, Misdemeanor, Civil, Eviction, Small Claims, Probate—Superior-District Court, Main St., PO Box 58, Wilkesboro, NC 28697. Civil: 910-667-1201. Criminal: 910-667-5266. Fax: 910-667-1985. 8AM-5PM (EST). Access by: Mail, in person.

Wilson County

Real Estate Recording—Wilson County Register of Deeds, 125 East Nash Street, Wilson, NC 27893. 919-399-2935. 8AM-5PM (EST).

Felony, Misdemeanor, Civil, Eviction, Small Claims, Probate—Superior-District Court, PO Box 1608, Wilson, NC 27893. Civil: 919-291-7502. Criminal: 919-291-7500. Fax: 919-291-8049. 9AM-5PM (EST). Access by: Mail, in person.

Yadkin County

Real Estate Recording—Yadkin County Register of Deeds, Courthouse, Yadkinville, NC 27055. 910-679-4225. Fax: 910-679-2703. 8AM-5PM (EST).

Felony, Misdemeanor, Civil, Eviction, Small Claims, Probate—Superior-District Court, PO Box 95, Yadkinville, NC 27055. 910-679-8838. Fax: 910-679-4378. 8AM-5PM (EST). Access by: Mail, in person.

Yancey County

Real Estate Recording—Yancey County Register of Deeds, Courthouse, Room #4, Burnsville, NC 28714. 704-682-2174. Fax: 704-682-4520. 9AM-5PM (EST).

Felony, Misdemeanor, Civil, Eviction, Small Claims, Probate—Superior-District Court, 110 Town Square, Burnsville, NC 28714. 704-682-2122. 8:30AM-5PM (EST). Access by: Mail, in person.

Federal Courts

US District Court

Eastern District of North Carolina

Elizabeth City Division, US District Court c/o Raleigh Division, PO Box 25670, Raleigh, NC 27611. 919-856-4370. Counties: Bertie, Camden, Chowan, Currituck, Dare, Gates, Hertford, Northampton, Pasquotank, Perquimans, Tyrrell, Washington

Greenville-Eastern Division, US District Court Room 214, 215 Evans St, Greenville, NC 27858-1133. 919-830-6009. Counties: Beaufort, Carteret, Craven, Edgecombe, Greene, Halifax, Hyde, Jones, Lenoir, Martin, Pamlico, Pitt

Raleigh Division, US District Court Clerk's Office, PO Box 25670, Raleigh, NC 27611. 919-856-4370. Counties: Cumberland, Franklin, Granville, Harnett, Johnston, Nash, Vance, Wake, Warren, Wayne, Wilson

Wilmington Division, US District Court PO Box 338, Wilmington, NC 28402. 910-815-4663. Counties: Bladen, Brunswick, Columbus, Duplin, New Hanover, Onslow, Pender, Robeson, Sampson

Middle District of North Carolina

Durham Division, US District Court c/o Greensboro Division, PO Box 2708, Greensboro, NC 27402-6100. 910-332-6000. Counties: Chatham, Durham, Lee, Orange, Person

Greensboro Division, US District Court Clerk's Office, PO Box 2708, Greensboro, NC 27402. 910-332-6000. Counties: Alamance, Caswell, Guilford, Randolph, Rockingham

Rockingham Division, US District Court c/o Greensboro Division, PO Box 2708, Greensboro, NC 27402-6100. 910-332-6000. Counties: Hoke, Montgomery, Moore, Richmond, Scotland

Salisbury Division, US District Court c/o Greensboro Division, PO Box 2708, Greensboro, NC 27402-6100. 910-332-6000. Counties: Cabarrus, Davidson, Davie, Rowan, Stanly

Winston-Salem Division, US District Court c/o Greensboro Division, PO Box 2708, Greensboro, NC 27402-6100. 910-332-6000. Counties: Forsyth, Stokes, Surry, Yadkin

Western District of North Carolina

Asheville Division, US District Court Clerk of the Court, Room 309, US Courthouse, 100 Otis St, Asheville, NC 28801-2611. 704-271-4648. Counties: Avery, Buncombe, Haywood, Henderson, Madison, Mitchell, Transylvania, Yancey

Bryson City Division, US District Court c/o Asheville Division, Clerk of the Court, Room 309, US Courthouse, 100 Otis St, Asheville, NC 28801-2611. 704-271-4648. Counties: Cherokee, Clay, Graham, Jackson, Macon, Swain

Charlotte Division, US District Court Clerk, Room 210, 401 W Trade St, Charlotte, NC 28202. 704-350-7400. Counties: Anson, Gaston, Mecklenburg, Union

Shelby Division, US District Court c/o Asheville Division, Clerk of the Court, Room 309, US Courthouse, 100 Otis St, Asheville, NC 28801-2611. 704-271-4648. Counties: Burke, Cleveland, McDowell, Polk, Rutherford

Statesville Division, US District Court PO Box 466, Statesville, NC 28687. 704-873-7112. Counties: Alexander, Alleghany, Ashe, Caldwell, Catawba, Iredell, Lincoln, Watauga, Wilkes

US Bankruptcy Court

Eastern District of North Carolina

Raleigh Division, US Bankruptcy Court, PO Box 1441, Raleigh, NC 27602. 919-856-4752. Voice Case Information System: 919-234-7655. Counties: Franklin, Granville, Harnett, Johnston, Vance, Wake, Warren

Wilson Division, US Bankruptcy Court, PO Drawer 2807, Wilson, NC 27894-2807. 919-237-0248. Voice Case Information System: 919-234-7655. Counties: Beaufort, Bertie, Bladen, Brunswick, Camden, Carteret, Chowan, Columbus, Craven, Cumberland, Currituck, Dare, Duplin, Edgecombe, Gates, Greene, Halifax, Hertford, Hyde, Jones, Lenoir, Martin, Nash, New Hanover, Northampton, Onslow, Pamlico, Pasquotank, Pender, Perquimans, Pitt, Robeson, Sampson, Tyrrell, Washington, Wayne, Wilson

Middle District of North Carolina

Greensboro Division, US Bankruptcy Court, PO Box 26100, Greensboro, NC 27420-6100. 910-333-5647. Voice Case Information System: 910-333-5532. Counties: Alamance, Cabarrus, Caswell, Chatham, Davidson, Davie, Durham, Guilford, Hoke, Lee, Montgomery, Moore, Orange, Person, Randolph, Richmond, Rockingham, Rowan, Scotland, Stanly

Winston-Salem Division, US Bankruptcy Court, 226 S Liberty St, Winston-Salem, NC 27101. 910-631-5340. Voice Case Information System: 910-333-5532. Counties: Davidson, Forsyth, Stokes, Surry, Yadkin

Western District of North Carolina

Charlotte Division, US Bankruptcy Court, 401 W Trade St, Charlotte, NC 28202. 704-344-6103. Voice Case Information System: 704-350-7500. Counties: Alexander, Alleghany, Anson, Ashe, Avery, Buncombe, Burke, Caldwell, Catawba, Cherokee, Clay, Cleveland, Gaston, Graham, Haywood, Henderson, Iredell, Jackson, Lincoln, Macon, Madison, McDowell, Mecklenburg, Mitchell, Polk, Rutherford, Swain, Transylvania, Union, Watauga, Wilkes, Yancey

North Dakota

Capitol: Bismark (Burleigh County)	
Number of Counties: 53	**Population:** 641,367
County Court Locations:	**Federal Court Locations:**
•District Courts: 53/7 Districts	•District Courts: 4
Municipal Courts: 112/ 112 Cities	•Bankruptcy Courts: 1
	State Agencies: 19

State Agencies—Summary

General Help Numbers:

State Archives

Historical Society	701-328-2666
State Archives & Historical Research Library	Fax: 701-328-3710
N Dakota Heritage Center, 612 E Boulevard Ave	8AM-5PM
Bismarck, ND 58505-0830	
Alternate Telephone:	701-328-2668
Reference Librarian:	701-328-2091

Governor's Office

Governor's Office	701-328-2200
State Capitol, 1st Floor	Fax: 701-328-2205
600 E Boulevard Ave	8AM-5PM
Bismarck, ND 58505-0001	

Attorney General's Office

Attorney General's Office	701-328-2210
State Capitol	Fax: 701-328-2226
1st Floor, 600 E Boulevard Ave	8AM-5PM
Bismarck, ND 58505-0040	

State Legislation

North Dakota Legislative Council	701-328-2916
State Capitol	8AM-5PM
600 E Boulevard Ave	
Bismarck, ND 58505	
Secretary of State:	701-328-2900
Bismarck, ND 58505-0530	

See right hand column for Internet site information.

Important State Internet Sites:

State of North Dakota World Wide Web

www.state.nd.us/

The homepage includes links to all branches of government, and other general information and services.

The Governor's Office

www ehs.health.state.nd.us/gov/index.htm

This site includes information about the Governor's press releases, speeches, and enables you to send e-mail to the Governor.

State Legislative Assembly

www.state.nd.us/lr/

This site links to both houses of the Assembly and a link of how to contact a legislator.

Archives and History

www.state.nd.us/hist/

This site links to the state archives and historical research library. Access to these holdings is primarily through the North Dakota Heritage Center in Bismark.

Bills and Resolutions

www.state.nd.us/lr/access.html

Provides access to a bills status report, the text of journals, bills and amendments and more.

Unclaimed Property

www.land.state.nd.us/main/abp/htm

Contains information about unclaimed property. No online searching is available.

State Agencies—Public Records

Criminal Records

Bureau of Criminal Investigation, PO Box 1054, Bismarck, ND 58502-1054, Main Telephone: 701-328-5500, Fax: 701-328-5510, Hours: 8AM-5PM. Access by: mail, visit.

Corporation Records
Limited Liability Company Records
Limited Partnership Records
Trademarks/Servicemarks
Fictitious Name
Assumed Name

Secretary of State, Corporation Division, 600 E Boulevard Ave, 1st Floor, Bismarck, ND 58505-0500, Main Telephone: 701-328-4284, Fax: 701-328-2992, Hours: 8AM-5PM. Access by: mail, phone, visit.

Uniform Commercial Code
Federal Tax Liens
State Tax Liens

UCC Division, Secretary of State, 600 E Boulevard Ave, Bismarck, ND 58505-0500, Main Telephone: 701-328-3662, Fax: 701-328-4214, Hours: 7AM-5PM. Access by: mail, phone, fax, visit. This office holds all federal and state tax liens on businesses. For tax liens on individuals, you must go to the county.

Sales Tax Registrations

State Tax Commission, Sales & Special Tax Division, State Capitol, 600 E Boulevard Ave, Bismarck, ND 58505-0599, Main Telephone: 701-328-3470, Fax: 701-328-3700, Hours: 8AM-5PM. Access by: mail, fax, phone.

Birth Certificates

ND Department of Health, Vital Records, State Capitol, 600 E Blvd, 1st Floor, Bismarck, ND 58505-0200, Main Telephone: 701-328-2360, Fax: 701-328-1850, Hours: 7:30AM-5PM. Access by: mail, phone, fax, visit.

Death Records

ND Department of Health, Vital Records, State Capitol, 600 E Blvd, 1st Floor, Bismarck, ND 58505-0200, Main Telephone: 701-328-2360, Fax: 701-328-1850, Hours: 7:30AM-5PM. Access by: mail, phone, fax, visit.

Marriage Certificates

ND Department of Health, Vital Records, State Capitol, 600 E Blvd, 1st Floor, Bismarck, ND 58505-0200, Main Telephone: 701-328-2360, Fax: 701-328-1850, Hours: 7:30AM-5PM. Access by: mail, phone, fax, visit.

Divorce Records

Records not available from state agency.

Workers' Compensation Records

Workers Compensation Bureau, 500 E Front Ave, Bismarck, ND 58504-5685, Main Telephone: 701-328-3800, Fax: 701-328-3820, Hours: 8AM-5PM. Access by: mail only.

Driver Records

Department of Transportation, Driver License & Traffic Safety Division, 608 E Boulevard Ave, Bismarck, ND 58505-0700, Main Telephone: 701-328-2603, Fax: 701-328-2435, Hours: 8AM-5PM. Access by: mail, fax, visit. Copies of tickets are no longer available from this address and must be obtained from the local courts.

Vehicle Ownership
Vehicle Identification

Department of Transportation, Records Section/Motor Vehicle Div., 608 E Boulevard Ave, Bismarck, ND 58505-0780, Main Telephone: 701-328-2725, Fax: 701-328-3500, Hours: 8AM-4:50PM. Access by: mail, visit. Records on mobile homes are also maintained by this agency.

Accident Reports

Driver License & Traffic Safety Division, Accident Report Section, 608 E Boulevard Ave, Bismarck, ND 58505-0700, Main Telephone: 701-328-2553, Fax: 701-328-2435, Hours: 8AM-5PM. Access by: mail, visit.

Hunting License Information
Fishing License Information

Game & Fish Department, 100 N Bismarck Expressway, Bismarck, ND 58501, Main Telephone: 701-328-6300, Fax: 701-328-6352, Hours: 8AM-5PM. Access by: mail, visit.

County Courts and Recording Offices

What You Need to Know...

About the Courts

Administration

Court Administrator   701-328-4216
North Dakota Supreme Court   Fax: 701-328-4480
1st Floor Judicial Wing, 600 E Blvd   8AM-5PM
Bismarck, ND 58505-0530

Court Structure

Small claims are handled by the District Courts effective 1/1/95. Probate is handled by the District Court; it was, formerly, a County Court function.

Effective 1/1/95, the County Courts were merged with the District Courts across the entire state. Prior County Court records are maintained by the District Courts and may be requested from them. We recommend stating "include County Court cases" in search requests.

Online Access

Online computer access is not currently available. A statewide computer system is under development with a policy governing its operation due by early 1998. It will not have public access initially; however, the plan calls for some level of public access in the future (2-4 years).

About the Recorder's Office

Organization

53 counties, 53 filing offices. The recording officer is Register of Deeds. The entire state is in the Central Time Zone (CST).

UCC Records

Financing statements may be filed either at the state level or with any Register of Deeds, except for real estate related collateral, which are filed only with the Register of Deeds. All counties access a **statewide computer database** of filings and will perform UCC searches. Use search request form UCC-11. Various search options are available, including by federal tax identification number or Social Security number The search with copies costs $7.00 per debtor name, including three pages of copies and $1.00 per additional page. Copies may be faxed for an additional fee of $3.00.

Lien Records

Federal tax liens on personal property of businesses are filed with the Secretary of State. Other federal and all state tax liens are filed with the county Register of Deeds. All counties will perform tax lien searches. Some counties automatically include business federal tax liens as part of a UCC search because they appear on the statewide database. (**Be careful**—federal tax liens on **individuals** may only be in the county lien books, not on the statewide system.) Separate searches are usually available at $5.00-7.00 per name. Copy fees vary. Copies may be faxed. Other liens include mechanics, judgments, hospital, repair, and egg cutter.

Real Estate Records

Some counties will perform real estate searches by name or by legal description. Copy fees are usually $1.00 per page. Certified copies usually cost $5.00 for the first page and $2.00 for each additional page. Copies may be faxed.

County Courts and Recording Offices

Adams County

Real Estate Recording—Adams County Register of Deeds, 602 Adams Avenue, Courthouse, Hettinger, ND 58639. 701-567-2460. Fax: 701-567-2910. 8:30AM-Noon, 1-5PM (MST).

Felony, Misdemeanor, Civil, Eviction, Probate—Southwest Judicial District Court, 602 Adams Ave, PO Box 469, Hettinger, ND 58639. 701-567-2460. Fax: 701-567-2910. 8:30AM-5PM (MST). Access by: Phone, fax, mail, in person.

Barnes County

Real Estate Recording—Barnes County Register of Deeds, 231 NE Third Street, Valley City, ND 58072. 701-845-8506. Fax: 701-845-8538. 8AM-5PM (CST).

Felony, Misdemeanor, Civil, Eviction, Probate—Southeast Judicial District Court, PO Box 774, Valley City, ND 58072. 701-845-1341. Fax: 701-845-8543. 8AM-5PM (CST). Access by: Phone, fax, mail, in person.

Benson County

Real Estate Recording—Benson County Register of Deeds, Courthouse, Minnewaukan, ND 58351. 701-473-5332. Fax: 701-473-5571. 8:30AM-Noon, 12:30-4:30PM (CST).

Felony, Misdemeanor, Civil, Eviction, Probate—Northeast Judicial District Court, PO Box 213, Minnewaukan, ND 58351. 701-473-5345. Fax: 701-473-5571. 8:30AM-4:30PM (CST). Access by: Phone, fax, mail, in person. Signed release required for juvenile cases.

Billings County

Real Estate Recording—Billings County Register of Deeds, Courthouse, 4th & Pacific, Medora, ND 58645. 701-623-4491. Fax: 701-623-4896. 9AM-Noon, 1-5PM (MST).

Felony, Misdemeanor, Civil, Eviction, Probate—Southwest Judicial District Court, PO Box 138, Medora, ND 58645. 701-623-4492. Fax: 701-623-4896. 9AM-Noon, 1-5PM (MST). Access by: Fax, mail, in person.

Bottineau County

Real Estate Recording—Bottineau County Register of Deeds, 314 West 5th Street, Bottineau, ND 58318. 701-228-2786. Fax: 701-228-3658. 8:30AM-5PM (CST).

Felony, Misdemeanor, Civil, Eviction, Probate—Northeast Judicial District Court, 314 W 5th St, Bottineau, ND 58318. 701-228-3983. Fax: 701-228-2336. (CST). Access by: Phone, fax, mail, in person.

Bowman County

Real Estate Recording—Bowman County Register of Deeds, 104 West 1st Street, Courthouse, Bowman, ND 58623. 701-523-3450. Fax: 701-523-5443. 8:30AM-5PM (MST).

Felony, Misdemeanor, Civil, Eviction, Probate—Southwest Judicial District Court, PO Box 379, Bowman, ND 58623. 701-523-3450. Fax: 701-523-5443. 8:30AM-Noon, 1-5PM (MST). Access by: Phone, fax, mail, in person.

Burke County

Real Estate Recording—Burke County Register of Deeds, Main Street, Courthouse, Bowbells, ND 58721. 701-377-2818. Fax: 701-377-2020. 8:30AM-Noon, 1-5PM (CST).

Felony, Misdemeanor, Civil, Eviction, Probate—Northwest Judicial District Court, PO Box 219, Bowbells, ND 58721. 701-377-2718. Fax: 701-377-2020. 8:30AM-Noon, 1-5 PM (CST). Access by: Phone, fax, mail, in person.

Burleigh County

Real Estate Recording—Burleigh County Register of Deeds, 221 North 5th Street, Bismarck, ND 58501. 701-222-6749. Fax: 701-222-6717. 8AM-5PM (CST).

Felony, Misdemeanor, Civil, Eviction, Probate—South Central Judicial District Court, PO Box 1055, Bismarck, ND 58502. 701-222-6690. Fax: 701-222-6689. 8AM-5PM (CST). Access by: Phone, fax, mail, in person.

Cass County

Real Estate Recording—Cass County Register of Deeds, 211 Ninth Street South, Fargo, ND 58103. 701-241-5620. Fax: 701-241-5621. 8AM-5PM (CST).

Felony, Misdemeanor, Civil, Eviction, Probate—East Central Judicial District Court, 211 South 9th St, Fargo, ND 58108. 701-241-5645. Fax: 701-241-5636. 8AM-5PM (CST). Access by: Mail, in person.

Cavalier County

Real Estate Recording—Cavalier County Register of Deeds, 901 3rd Street, Langdon, ND 58249. 701-256-2136. Fax: 701-256-2566. 8:30AM-4:30PM (CST).

Felony, Misdemeanor, Civil, Eviction, Probate—Northeast Judicial District Court, 901 Third St, Langdon, ND 58249. 701-256-2124. Fax: 701-256-2124. 8:30AM-4:30PM (CST). Access by: Phone, fax, mail, in person.

Dickey County

Real Estate Recording—Dickey County Register of Deeds, 309 North 2nd, Courthouse, Ellendale, ND 58436. 701-349-3029. Fax: 701-349-4639. 8:30AM-5PM (CST).

Felony, Misdemeanor, Civil, Eviction, Probate—Southeast Judicial District Court, PO Box 336, Ellendale, ND 58436. 701-349-3013. 9AM-5PM, Closed 12-1 (CST). Access by: Phone, mail, in person.

Divide County

Real Estate Recording—Divide County Register of Deeds, Courthouse, 300 2nd Ave. North, Crosby, ND 58730. 701-965-6661. Fax: 701-965-6943. 8:30AM-Noon, 1-5PM (CST).

Felony, Misdemeanor, Civil, Eviction, Probate—Northwest Judicial District Court, PO Box 68, Crosby, ND 58730. 701-965-6831. Fax: 701-965-6943. 8:30AM-Noon, 1-5PM (CST). Access by: Phone, fax, mail, in person.

Dunn County

Real Estate Recording—Dunn County Register of Deeds, Courthouse, 101 Owens, Manning, ND 58642. 701-573-4443. Fax: 701-573-4444. 8AM-Noon, 12:30-4:30PM (MST).

Felony, Misdemeanor, Civil, Eviction, Probate—Southwest Judicial District Court, PO Box 136, Manning, ND 58642-0136. 701-573-4447. 8AM-Noon,12:30-4:30PM (MST). Access by: Phone, fax, mail, in person.

Eddy County

Real Estate Recording—Eddy County Register of Deeds, 524 Central Avenue, New Rockford, ND 58356. 701-947-2813. Fax: 701-947-2067. 8AM-Noon, 12:30-4PM (CST).

Felony, Misdemeanor, Civil, Eviction, Probate—Southeast Judicial District Court, 524 Central Ave, New Rockford, ND 58356. 701-947-2813. Fax: 701-947-2067. 8AM-4PM (CST). Access by: Phone, fax, mail, in person.

Emmons County

Real Estate Recording—Emmons County Register of Deeds, Courthouse, Linton, ND 58552. 701-254-4812. Fax: 701-254-4012. 8:30AM-Noon, 1-5PM (CST).

Felony, Misdemeanor, Civil, Eviction, Probate—South Central Judicial District Court, PO Box 905, Linton, ND 58552. 701-254-4812. Fax: 701-254-4012. 8:30AM-Noon, 1-5PM (CST). Access by: Fax, mail, in person.

Foster County

Real Estate Recording—Foster County Register of Deeds, 1000 Central Avenue, Carrington, ND 58421. 701-

652-2491. Fax: 701-652-2173. 9AM-5PM (8AM-4PM Summer Hours) (CST).

Felony, Misdemeanor, Civil, Eviction, Probate—Southeast Judicial District Court, PO Box 257, Carrington, ND 58421. 701-652-1001. Fax: 701-652-2173. 8AM-4PM (summer) 9AM-5PM (winter) (CST). Access by: Phone, fax, mail, in person.

Golden Valley County

Real Estate Recording—Golden Valley County Register of Deeds, 150 1st Avenue S.E., Courthouse, Beach, ND 58621. 701-872-4352. Fax: 701-872-4383. 8AM-Noon, 1-4PM (MST).

Felony, Misdemeanor, Civil, Eviction, Probate—Southwest Judicial District Court, PO Box 9, Beach, ND 58621-0009. 701-872-4352. Fax: 701-872-4383. 8AM-4PM (MST). Access by: Phone, fax, mail, in person.

Grand Forks County

Real Estate Recording—Grand Forks County Register of Deeds, County Office Bldg., 201 South 4th St., Grand Forks, ND 58201. 701-780-8261. Fax: 701-780-8212. 8AM-5PM (CST).

Felony, Misdemeanor, Civil, Eviction, Probate—Northeast Central Judicial District Court, PO Box 5939, Grand Forks, ND 58206-5939. 701-780-8214. 8AM-5PM (CST). Access by: Mail, in person.

Grant County

Real Estate Recording—Grant County Register of Deeds, Courthouse, Carson, ND 58529. 701-622-3544. Fax: 701-622-3717. 8AM-4PM (MST).

Felony, Misdemeanor, Civil, Eviction, Probate—South Central Judicial District Court, PO Box 258, Carson, ND 58529. 701-622-3615. Fax: 701-622-3717. 8AM-Noon, 12:30-4PM (MST). Access by: Phone, fax, mail, in person.

Griggs County

Real Estate Recording—Griggs County Register of Deeds, Courthouse, 45th & Rollins, Cooperstown, ND 58425. 701-797-2771. Fax: 701-797-3587. 8AM-12, 1-4:30PM (CST).

Felony, Misdemeanor, Civil, Eviction, Probate—Northeast Central Judicial District Court, PO Box 326, Cooperstown, ND 58425. 701-797-2772. Fax: 701-797-3170. 8AM-4:30PM (CST). Access by: Phone, fax, mail, in person.

Hettinger County

Real Estate Recording—Hettinger County Register of Deeds, Courthouse, 336 Pacific Ave., Mott, ND 58646. 701-824-2545. Fax: 701-824-2717. 8AM-4:30PM (MST).

Felony, Misdemeanor, Civil, Eviction, Probate—Southwest Judicial District Court, PO Box 668, Mott, ND 58646. 701-824-2645. Fax: 701-824-2717. 8AM-4:30PM (MST). Access by: Phone, fax, mail, in person.

Kidder County

Real Estate Recording—Kidder County Register of Deeds, Courthouse on Broadway, Steele, ND 58482. 701-475-2651. Fax: 701-475-2202. 9AM-5PM (CST).

Felony, Misdemeanor, Civil, Eviction, Small Claims, Probate—PO Box 66, Steele, ND 58482. 701-475-2651. Fax: 701-475-2202. 9AM-5PM (CST). Access by: Phone, fax, mail, in person.

La Moure County

Real Estate Recording—La Moure County Register of Deeds, Courthouse, 202 4th Ave. N.E., La Moure, ND 58458. 701-883-5304. Fax: 701-883-5304. 9AM-5PM (CST).

Felony, Misdemeanor, Civil, Eviction, Probate—Southeast Judicial District Court, PO Box 5, LaMoure, ND 58458. 701-883-5193. Fax: 701-883-5304. 9AM-Noon, 1-5PM (CST). Access by: Phone, fax, mail, in person.

Logan County

Real Estate Recording—Logan County Register of Deeds, Highway 3, Courthouse, Napoleon, ND 58561. 701-754-2751. Fax: 701-754-2270. 8:30AM-Noon, 1-4:30PM (CST).

Felony, Misdemeanor, Civil, Eviction, Probate—South Central Judicial District Court, PO Box 6, Napoleon, ND 58561. 701-754-2751. Fax: 701-754-2270. 8:30AM-5PM (CST). Access by: Fax, mail, in person.

McHenry County

Real Estate Recording—McHenry County Register of Deeds, South Main, Courthouse, Towner, ND 58788. 701-537-5634. Fax: 701-537-5969. 8AM-Noon, 1-4:30PM (CST).

Felony, Misdemeanor, Civil, Eviction, Probate—Northeast Judicial District Court, PO Box 117, Towner, ND 58788. 701-537-5729. Fax: 701-537-5969. 8AM-4:30PM (CST). Access by: Phone, fax, mail, in person.

McIntosh County

Real Estate Recording—McIntosh County Register of Deeds, 112 North East 1st, Ashley, ND 58413. 701-288-3589. Fax: 701-288-3671. 8AM-4:30PM (CST).

Felony, Misdemeanor, Civil, Eviction, Probate—South Central Judicial District Court, PO Box 179, Ashley, ND 58413. 701-288-3450. Fax: 701-288-3671. 8AM-4:30PM (CST). Access by: Mail, in person.

McKenzie County

Real Estate Recording—McKenzie County Register of Deeds, 201 West 5th Street, Watford City, ND 58854. 701-842-3453. Fax: 701-842-3902. 8:30AM-Noon, 1-5PM (CST).

Felony, Misdemeanor, Civil, Eviction, Probate—Northwest District Court, PO Box 524, Watford City, ND 58854. 701-842-3452. Fax: 701-842-3916. 8:30AM-Noon,1-5PM (CST). Access by: Fax, mail, in person.

McLean County

Real Estate Recording—McLean County Register of Deeds, 712 5th Avenue, Courthouse, Washburn, ND 58577. 701-462-8541. Fax: 701-462-3633. 8AM-Noon, 12:30-4:30PM (CST).

Felony, Misdemeanor, Civil, Eviction, Probate—South Central Judicial District Court, PO Box 1108, Washburn, ND 58577. 701-462-8541. Fax: 701-462-3441. 8AM-Noon, 12:30-4:30PM (CST). Access by: Mail, in person.

Mercer County

Real Estate Recording—Mercer County Register of Deeds, 1021 Arthur Street, Stanton, ND 58571. 701-745-3272. Fax: 701-745-3364. 8AM-4PM (MST).

Felony, Misdemeanor, Civil, Eviction, Probate—South Central Judicial District Court, PO Box 39, Stanton, ND 58571. 701-745-3262. Fax: 701-745-3364. 8AM-4PM (MST). Access by: Fax, mail, in person.

Morton County

Real Estate Recording—Morton County Register of Deeds, 210 2nd Avenue, Mandan, ND 58554. 701-667-3305. Fax: 701-667-3453. 8AM-Noon, 1-5PM (MST).

Felony, Misdemeanor, Civil, Eviction, Probate—South Central Judicial District Court, 210 2nd Ave NW, Mandan, ND 58554. 701-667-3358. 8AM-5PM (MST). Access by: Mail, in person.

Mountrail County

Real Estate Recording—Mountrail County Register of Deeds, North Main, Courthouse, Stanley, ND 58784. 701-628-2945. Fax: 701-628-2276. 8:30AM-Noon, 1-4:30PM (CST).

Felony, Misdemeanor, Civil, Eviction, Probate—Northwest Judicial District Court, PO Box 69, Stanley, ND 58784. 701-628-2915. Fax: 701-628-3975. 8:30AM-4:30PM (CST). Access by: Phone, fax, mail, in person.

Nelson County

Real Estate Recording—Nelson County Register of Deeds, Courthouse, 210 W. B Ave., Lakota, ND 58344. 701-247-2433. Fax: 701-247-2412. 8:30AM-Noon, 1-5PM (CST).

Felony, Misdemeanor, Civil, Eviction, Probate—Northeast Central Judicial District Court, PO Box 565, Lakota, ND 58344. 701-247-2462. Fax: 701-247-2412. 8:30AM-5PM (CST). Access by: Phone, fax, mail, in person.

Oliver County

Real Estate Recording—Oliver County Register of Deeds, Courthouse, Center, ND 58530. 701-794-8777. Fax: 701-794-3476. 8AM-Noon, 1-4PM (CST).

Felony, Misdemeanor, Civil, Eviction, Probate—South Central Judicial District Court, Box 125, Center, ND 58530. 701-794-8777. Fax: 701-794-3476. 8AM-4PM (CST). Access by: Phone, fax, mail, in person.

Pembina County

Real Estate Recording—Pembina County Register of Deeds, 301 Dakota Street W. 10, Cavalier, ND 58220. 701-265-4373. Fax: 701-265-4876. 8:30AM-5PM (CST).

Felony, Misdemeanor, Civil, Eviction, Probate—Pembina County District Court, 301 Dakota St West #6, Cavalier, ND 58220-4100. 701-265-4275. Fax: 701-265-4876. 8:30AM-5PM (CST). Access by: Phone, mail, in person.

Pierce County

Real Estate Recording—Pierce County Register of Deeds, 240 S.E. 2nd Street, Rugby, ND 58368. 701-776-5206. Fax: 701-776-5707. 9AM-Noon, 1PM-5PM (CST).

Felony, Misdemeanor, Civil, Eviction, Probate—Northeast Judicial District Court, 240 SE 2nd St, Rugby, ND 58368. 701-776-6161. Fax: 701-776-5707. 9AM-5PM (CST). Access by: Phone, fax, mail, in person.

Ramsey County

Real Estate Recording—Ramsey County Register of Deeds, 524 4th Avenue #30, Devils Lake, ND 58301. 701-662-7018. Fax: 701-662-7093. 8AM-Noon,1-5PM (CST).

Felony, Misdemeanor, Civil, Eviction, Probate—Northeast Judicial District Court, 524 4th Ave #4, Devils Lake, ND 58301. 701-662-7066. Fax: 701-662-7049. 8AM-5PM (CST). Access by: Fax, mail, in person.

Ransom County

Real Estate Recording—Ransom County Register of Deeds, Courthouse, Lisbon, ND 58054. 701-683-5823. Fax: 701-683-5827. 8:30AM-Noon, 1-4:30PM (CST).

Felony, Misdemeanor, Civil, Eviction, Probate—Southeast Judicial District Court, PO Box 626, Lisbon, ND 58054. 701-683-5823. Fax: 701-683-5827. 8:30AM-4:30PM (CST). Access by: Phone, fax, mail, in person.

Renville County

Real Estate Recording—Renville County Register of Deeds, 205 Main Street East, Mohall, ND 58761. 701-756-6398. Fax: 701-756-6398. 9AM-4:30PM (CST).

Felony, Misdemeanor, Civil, Eviction, Probate—Northeast Judicial District Court, PO Box 68, Mohall, ND 58761. 701-756-6398. Fax: 701-756-6398. 9AM-4:30PM (CST). Access by: Fax, mail, in person.

Richland County

Real Estate Recording—Richland County Register of Deeds, 418 2nd Avenue North, Courthouse, Wahpeton, ND 58075. 701-642-7800. Fax: 701-642-7820. 8AM-5PM (CST).

Felony, Misdemeanor, Civil, Eviction, Probate—Southeast Judicial District Court, 418 2nd Ave North, Wahpeton, ND 58074. 701-642-7818. Fax: 701-671-1512. 8AM-5PM (CST). Access by: Mail, in person.

Rolette County

Real Estate Recording—Rolette County Register of Deeds, 102 NE 2nd, Rolla, ND 58367. 701-477-3166. Fax: 701-477-5770. 8:30AM-12:30PM, 1-4:30PM (CST).

Felony, Misdemeanor, Civil, Eviction, Probate—Northeast Judicial District Court, PO Box 460, Rolla, ND 58367. 701-477-3816. Fax: 701-477-5770. 8:30AM-4:30PM (CST). Access by: Phone, mail, in person.

Sargent County

Real Estate Recording—Sargent County Register of Deeds, 645 Main Street, Forman, ND 58032. 701-724-6241. Fax: 701-724-6244. 9AM-Noon, 12:30-4:30PM (CST).

Felony, Misdemeanor, Civil, Eviction, Probate—Southeast Judicial District Court, 355 Main St (PO Box 176), Forman, ND 58032. 701-724-6241. Fax: 701-724-6244. 9AM-Noon, 12:30-4:30PM (CST). Access by: Phone, fax, mail, in person.

Sheridan County

Real Estate Recording—Sheridan County Register of Deeds, 215 2nd Street, Courthouse, McClusky, ND 58463. 701-363-2207. Fax: 701-363-2953. 9AM-Noon,1-5PM (CST).

Felony, Misdemeanor, Civil, Eviction, Probate—South Central Judicial District Court, PO Box 668, McClusky, ND 58463. 701-363-2207. Fax: 701-363-2953. 9AM-Noon, 1-5PM (CST). Access by: Mail, in person.

Sioux County

Real Estate Recording—Sioux County Register of Deeds, Courthouse, Fort Yates, ND 58538. 701-854-3853. Fax: 701-854-3854. 9AM-5PM (MST).

Felony, Misdemeanor, Civil, Eviction, Probate—South Central Judicial District Court, Box L, Fort Yates, ND 58538. 701-854-3853. Fax: 701-854-3854. 9AM-5PM (MST). Access by: Phone, fax, mail, in person.

Slope County

Real Estate Recording—Slope County Register of Deeds, Courthouse, Amidon, ND 58620. 701-879-6275. Fax: 701-879-6278. 9AM-Noon, 1-5PM (MST).

Felony, Misdemeanor, Civil, Eviction, Probate—Southwest Judicial District Court, PO Box JJ, Amidon, ND 58620. 701-879-6275. Fax: 701-879-6278. 9AM-5PM (MST). Access by: Phone, fax, mail, in person.

Stark County

Real Estate Recording—Stark County Register of Deeds, Sims & 3rd Avenue, Courthouse, Dickinson, ND 58601. 701-264-7645. Fax: 701-264-7628. 8AM-5PM (MST).

Felony, Misdemeanor, Civil, Eviction, Probate—District Court, PO Box 130, Dickinson, ND 58602. Civil: 701-264-7636. Criminal: 701-264-7637. Fax: 701-264-7640. 7AM-5PM (MST). Access by: Mail, in person.

Steele County

Real Estate Recording—Steele County Register of Deeds, Washington Street, Courthouse, Finley, ND 58230. 701-524-2152. Fax: 701-524-1325. (CST).

Felony, Misdemeanor, Civil, Eviction, Probate—East Central Judicial District Court, PO Box 296, Finley, ND 58230. 701-524-2152. 8AM-4:30PM (CST). Access by: Mail, in person.

Stutsman County

Real Estate Recording—Stutsman County Register of Deeds, 511 2nd Avenue S.E., Courthouse, Jamestown, ND 58401. 701-252-9034. Fax: 701-251-1603. 8AM-Noon; 1-5PM (CST).

Felony, Misdemeanor, Civil, Eviction, Probate—Southeast Judicial District Court, 511 2nd Ave SE, Jamestown, ND 58401. 701-252-9042. Fax: 701-251-1006. 8AM-5PM (CST). Access by: Mail, in person.

Towner County

Real Estate Recording—Towner County Register of Deeds, Courthouse, 315 2nd Street, Cando, ND 58324. 701-968-4343. Fax: 701-968-4344. 8:30AM-Noon, 1-5PM (CST).

Felony, Misdemeanor, Civil, Eviction, Probate—Northeast Judicial District Court, Box 517, Cando, ND 58324. 701-968-4345. Fax: 701-968-4344. 8:30AM-5PM (CST). Access by: Phone, fax, mail, in person.

Traill County

Real Estate Recording—Traill County Register of Deeds, 13 1st Street N.W., Courthouse, Hillsboro, ND 58045. 701-436-4457. Fax: 701-436-4457. 8AM-Noon, 12:30PM-4:30PM (CST).

Felony, Misdemeanor, Civil, Eviction, Probate—East Central Judicial District Court, PO Box 805, Hillsboro, ND

58045. 701-436-4454. Fax: 701-436-4457. 8AM-4:30PM (CST). Access by: Phone, fax, mail, in person.

Walsh County

Real Estate Recording—Walsh County Register of Deeds, 600 Cooper Avenue, Courthouse, Grafton, ND 58237. 701-352-2380. Fax: 701-352-3340. 8:30-Noon, 12:30-5PM (CST).

Felony, Misdemeanor, Civil, Eviction, Probate—Northeast Judicial District Court, 600 Cooper Ave, Grafton, ND 58237. 701-352-0350. Fax: 701-352-1104. 8:30AM-5PM (CST). Access by: Phone, fax, mail, in person.

Ward County

Real Estate Recording—Ward County Register of Deeds, 315 S.E. Third Street, Courthouse, Minot, ND 58705. 701-857-6410. Fax: 701-857-6414. 8AM-4:30PM (CST).

Felony, Misdemeanor, Civil, Eviction, Probate—Northwest Judicial District Court, PO Box 5005, Minot, ND 58702-5005. 701-857-6460. Fax: 701-857-6469. 8AM-4:30PM (CST). Access by: Mail, in person.

Wells County

Real Estate Recording—Wells County Register of Deeds, Court Street, Courthouse, P.O. Box 125, Fessenden, ND 58438. 701-547-3141. Fax: 701-547-3719. 8AM-Noon, 1-4:30PM (CST).

Felony, Misdemeanor, Civil, Eviction, Probate—Southeast Judicial District Court, PO Box 596, Fessenden, ND 58438. 701-547-3122. Fax: 701-547-3719. 8AM-4:30PM (CST). Access by: Mail, in person.

Williams County

Real Estate Recording—Williams County Treasurer/Recorder, 205 East Broadway, Williston, ND 58801. 701-572-1740. Fax: 701-572-1759. 9AM-5PM (CST).

Felony, Misdemeanor, Civil, Eviction, Probate—Northwest Judicial District Court, PO Box 2047, Williston, ND 58802. 701-572-1720. Fax: 701-572-1760. 9AM-5PM (CST). Access by: Mail, in person.

Federal Courts

US District Court
District of North Dakota

Bismarck-Southwestern Division, US District Court PO Box 1193, Bismarck, ND 58502. 701-250-4295. Counties: Adams, Billings, Bowman, Burleigh, Dunn, Emmons, Golden Valley, Grant, Hettinger, Kidder, Logan, McIntosh, McLean, Mercer, Morton, Oliver, Sioux, Slope, Stark

Fargo-Southeastern Division, US District Court PO Box 870, Fargo, ND 58107. 701-239-5377. Counties: Barnes, Cass, Dickey, Eddy, Foster, Griggs, La Moure, Ransom, Richland, Sargent, Steele, Stutsman

Grand Forks-Northeastern Division, US District Court c/o Fargo-Southeastern Division, PO Box 870, Fargo, ND 58107. 701-239-5377. Counties: Benson, Cavalier, Grand Forks, Nelson, Pembina, Ramsey, Towner, Traill, Walsh. Case records prior to 1995 for Rolette County may be located in Fargo

Minot-Northwestern Division, US District Court c/o Bismarck Division, PO Box 1193, Bismarck, ND 58502. 701-250-4295. Counties: Bottineau, Burke, Divide, McHenry, McKenzie, Mountrail, Pierce, Renville, Rolette, Sheridan, Ward, Wells, Williams. Case records from Rolette County prior to 1995 may be located in Fargo

US Bankruptcy Court
District of North Dakota

Fargo Division, US Bankruptcy Court, PO Box 1110, Fargo, ND 58107. 701-239-5129. Voice Case Information System: 701-239-5641. Counties: All counties in North Dakota

Ohio

Capitol: Columbus (Franklin County)	
Number of Counties: 88	**Population:** 11,150,506
County Court Locations:	**Federal Court Locations:**
•Court of Common Pleas: 89	•District Courts: 7
•County Courts: 44	•Bankruptcy Courts: 8
•Municipal Courts: 83	**State Agencies:** 18
•Combined Municipal/County Courts: 18	
Mayors Courts: 441	
Court of Claims: 1	

State Agencies—Summary

General Help Numbers:

State Archives

Historical Society	614-297-2510
Archives/Library	Fax: 614-297-2546
1982 Velma Ave	9AM-5PM TH-SA
Columbus, OH 43211-2497	
Reference Librarian:	614-297-2510

Governor's Office

Governor's Office	614-466-3555
77 S High St, 30th Floor,	
Vern Riffe Center	Fax: 614-466-9354
Columbus, OH 43266-0601	8AM-5PM

Attorney General's Office

Attorney General's Office	614-466-4320
30 E Broad St, 17th Floor	Fax: 614-466-5087
Columbus, OH 43266-0410	8AM-5PM
Alternate Telephone:	614-466-3376

State Legislation

Ohio General Assembly	614-466-8842
State House	
Columbus, OH 43215	
Copies:	614-466-9745

Important State Internet Sites:

```
Webscape
File   Edit   View                              Help
```

State of Ohio World Wide Web
www.state.oh.us/

The home page includes links to all branches of government, a state directory and other general information and services.

The Governor's Office
www.state.oh.us/gov/

This site includes information about the Governor's cabinet, speeches, and enables you to send e-mail to the Governor.

Ohio State Legislature
www.odn.ohio.gov/ohio/index-le.htmlx

This site links to members directories for both the House and the Senate. The directories include addresses and phone numbers.

Uniform Commercial Code
www.state.oh.us/sos/ucc.html

A very thorough web page about UCC searching. No online searching is available

Unclaimed Funds
www.state.oh.us/com/ucf/

This site provides all the information about searching for unclaimed funds, which can be accomplished online.

State Agencies—Public Records

Criminal Records
Ohio Bureau of Investigation, Identification Division, PO Box 365, London, OH 43140, Main Telephone: 614-466-8204, Hours: 8:00AM-5:45PM. Access by: mail only.

Corporation Records
Fictitious Name
Limited Partnership Records
Assumed Name
Trademarks/Servicemarks
Limited Liability Company Records
Secretary of State, Attn: Certification Desk, 30 E Broad St, 14th Floor, Columbus, OH 43266-0418, Main Telephone: 614-466-3910, Fax: 614-466-2892, Hours: 8AM-5PM. Access by: mail, phone, visit. Information regarding officers is available from the Department of Taxation at 614-438-5339.

Uniform Commercial Code
Federal Tax Liens
State Tax Liens
UCC Division, Secretary of State, 30 E Broad St, State Office Tower, Columbus, OH 43266-0418, Main Telephone: 614-466-3623, Fax: 614-466-2892, Hours: 8AM-5PM. Access by: mail, phone, visit.

Sales Tax Registrations
Taxation Department, Sale & Use Tax Division, 30 E Broad St, 20th Floor, Columbus, OH 43215, Main Telephone: 614-466-7350, Fax: 614-466-4977, Hours: 8AM-5PM M-F.
Restricted access.

Birth Certificates
Ohio Department of Health, Bureau of Vital Statistics, PO Box 15098, Columbus, OH 43215-0098, Main Telephone: 614-466-2531, Hours: 7:45AM-4:30PM. Access by: mail, fax, visit.

Death Records
Ohio Department of Health, Bureau of Vital Statistics, PO Box 15098, Columbus, OH 43215-0098, Main Telephone: 614-466-2531, Hours: 7:45AM-4:30PM. Access by: mail, fax, visit.

Marriage Certificates
Divorce Records
Records not available from state agency.

Workers' Compensation Records
Bureau of Workers Compensation, Customer Assistance, 30 W Spring St, Fl 10, Columbus, OH 43215-2241, Main Telephone: 800-644-6292, Fax: 614-752-4732, Hours: 7:30AM-5:30PM. Access by: mail, phone, fax, visit.

Driver Records
Department of Public Safety, Bureau of Motor Vehicles, 4300 Kimberly Pkwy, Columbus, OH 43232, Main Telephone: 614-752-7600, Hours: 8AM-5:30PM M-T-W; 8AM-4:30PM TH-F. Access by: mail, fax, visit, PC. Copies of tickets are available from the Bureau of Motor Vehicles, Transcript Records, PO Box 16520, Columbus 43266-0020. The fee is $1.00 per page.

Vehicle Ownership
Vehicle Identification
Bureau of Motor Vehicles, Motor Vehicle Title Records, 4300 Kimberly Pkwy, Columbus, OH 43232, Main Telephone: 614-752-7671, Hours: 8AM-5:30PM M-T-W; 8AM-4:30PM TH-F. Access by: mail, phone, visit, PC.

Accident Reports
Department of Public Safety, Traffic Crash Records Section, PO Box 7167, Columbus, OH 43266-0563, Main Telephone: 614-752-1575, Fax: 614-752-1363, Hours: 7AM-4:15PM. Access by: mail, visit.

Hunting License Information
Fishing License Information
Records not available from state agency.

County Courts and Recording Offices

What You Need to Know...

About the Courts

Administration

Administrative Director	614-466-2653
Supreme Court of Ohio	8AM-4:30PM
39 E Broad St, 3rd Floor	
Columbus, OH 43266-0419	

Court Structure

The lower limit for civil claims in Common Pleas Court differs depending upon whether the county has a County Court (limit $3,000) or a Municipal Court ($10,000).

Probate courts are separate from the Court of Common Pleas, but the probate court phone numbers are given with that court in each county.

Online Access

There is no statewide computer system. Each court sets the level of access to court records.

About the Recorder's Office

Organization

88 counties, 88 filing offices. The recording officer is County Recorder and Clerk of Common Pleas Court (state tax liens). The entire state is in the Eastern Time Zone (EST).

UCC Records

This is a **dual filing state**. Financing statements are filed both at the state level and with the County Recorder, except for consumer goods, farm related and real estate related collateral, which are filed only with the County Recorder. All counties will perform UCC searches. Use search request form UCC-11. Search fees are usually $9.00 per debtor name. Copies usually cost $1.00 per page.

Lien Records

All federal tax liens are filed with the County Recorder. All state tax liens are filed with the Clerk of Common Pleas Court. Refer to BRB Publications' *The Sourcebook of County Court Records* for information about Ohio courts. Federal tax liens are filed in the "Official Records" of each county. Most counties will **not** perform a federal tax lien search. Other liens include mechanics, workers compensation, and judgments.

Real Estate Records

Counties will **not** perform real estate searches. Copy fees are usually $1.00 per page. Certification usually costs $50 per document. Tax records are located at the Auditor's Office.

County Courts and Recording Offices

Adams County

Real Estate Recording—Adams County Recorder, 110 West Main, Courthouse, West Union, OH 45693. 937-544-5051. 8AM-4PM (EST).

Felony, Civil Actions Over $3,000, Probate—Common Pleas Court, 110 W Main, West Union, OH 45693. 937-544-2344. Probate: 937-544-2368. Fax: 937-544-8911. 8:30AM-4PM (EST). Access by: Mail, in person.

Misdemeanor, Civil Actions Under $15,000, Small Claims—County Court, 110 W Main, Rm 202, West Union, OH 45693. 937-544-2011. Fax: 937-544-8911. 8AM-4PM (EST). Access by: Mail, in person.

Allen County

Real Estate Recording—Allen County Recorder, 301 North Main Street, Lima, OH 45801. 419-223-8517. 8AM-4:30PM (EST).

Felony, Civil Actions Over $10,000, Probate—Common Pleas Court, PO Box 1243, Lima, OH 45802. 419-228-3700. Fax: 419-222-8427. 8AM-4:30PM (EST). Access by: In person only.

Misdemeanor, Civil Actions Under $15,000, Eviction, Small Claims—Lima Municipal Court, 109 N Union St (PO Box 1529), Lima, OH 45802. 419-221-5275. Fax: 419-228-2305. 8AM-5PM (EST). Access by: Phone, fax, mail, in person.

Ashland County

Real Estate Recording—Ashland County Recorder, 2nd Street, Courthouse, Ashland, OH 44805. 419-282-4238. Fax: 419-281-5715. 8AM-4PM (EST).

Felony, Civil Actions Over $10,000, Probate—Common Pleas Court, PO Box 365, Ashland, OH 44805. 419-289-0000. 8AM-4PM (EST). Access by: Mail, in person.

Misdemeanor, Civil Actions Under $15,000, Eviction, Small Claims—Ashland Municipal Court, PO Box 354, Ashland, OH 44805. 419-289-8137. Fax: 419-289-8545. 8AM-5PM (EST). Access by: Mail, in person.

Ashtabula County

Real Estate Recording—Ashtabula County Recorder, 25 West Jefferson Street, Jefferson, OH 44047. 440-576-3762. Fax: 440-576-3231. 8AM-4:30PM (EST).

Felony, Civil Actions Over $10,000, Probate—Common Pleas Court, 25 W Jefferson St, Jefferson, OH 44047. 440-576-3637. Probate: 440-576-3637. Fax: 440-576-2819. 8AM-4:30PM (EST). Access by: Fax, mail, in person.

Misdemeanor, Civil Actions Under $15,000, Small Claims—County Court Western Division, 185 Water St, Geneva, OH 44041. 440-466-1184. Fax: 440-466-7171. 8AM-4:30PM (EST). Access by: In person only.

County Court Eastern Division, 25 W Jefferson St, Jefferson, OH 44047. 440-576-3617. 8AM-4:30PM (EST). Access by: Mail, in person.

Ashtabula Municipal Court, 110 W 44th St, Ashtabula, OH 44004. 440-992-7110. Fax: 440-998-5786. 8AM-4:30PM (EST). Access by: In person only.

Athens County

Real Estate Recording—Athens County Recorder, Room 236, 15 South Court, Athens, OH 45701. 740-592-3228. 8AM-4PM (EST).

Felony, Civil Actions Over $10,000, Probate—Common Pleas Court, PO Box 290, Athens, OH 45701-0290. 740-592-3236. Probate: 740-592-3251. 8AM-4PM (EST). Access by: In person only.

Misdemeanor, Civil Actions Under $15,000, Eviction, Small Claims—Athens Municipal Court, Washington St, Athens, OH 45701. 740-592-3228. Fax: 740-592-3331. 8AM-4PM (EST). Access by: Phone, fax, mail, in person.

Auglaize County

Real Estate Recording—Auglaize County Recorder, Courthouse, Suite 101, 201 S. Willipie St., Wapakoneta, OH 45895. 419-738-4318. Fax: 419-738-4115. 8AM-4:30PM (EST).

Felony, Civil Actions Over $10,000, Probate—Common Pleas Court, PO Box 409, Wapakoneta, OH 45895. 419-738-4219. Probate: 419-738-7710. 8AM-4:30PM (EST). Access by: In person only.

Misdemeanor, Civil Actions Under $15,000, Eviction, Small Claims—Auglaize County Municipal Court, PO Box 409, Wapakoneta, OH 45895. 419-738-2923. 8AM-4:30PM (EST). Access by: In person only.

Belmont County

Real Estate Recording—Belmont County Recorder, 100 Main Street, Courthouse, Room 105, St. Clairsville, OH 43950. 740-695-2121. 8:30AM-4:30PM (EST).

Felony, Civil Actions Over $3,000, Probate—Common Pleas Court, Main St, Courthouse, St Clairsville, OH 43950. 740-695-2121. Probate: 740-695-2121 X202. 8:30AM-4:30PM (EST). Access by: Mail, in person.

Misdemeanor, Civil Actions Under $15,000, Small Claims—County Court Eastern Division, 400 W 26th St, Bellaire, OH 43906. 740-676-4490. 8AM-4PM (EST). Access by: Mail, in person.

County Court Northern Division, 101 S 4th St, Martins Ferry, OH 43935. 740-633-3147. Fax: 740-633-6631. 8AM-4PM (EST). Access by: Mail, in person.

County Court Western Division, 147 W Main St, St Clairsville, OH 43950. 740-695-2875. Fax: 740-695-7285. 8AM-4PM (EST). Access by: Mail, in person.

Brown County

Real Estate Recording—Brown County Recorder, Administration Building, 800 Mt. Orab Pike, Georgetown, OH 45121. 937-378-6478. Fax: 937-378-2848. 8AM-4PM (EST).

Felony, Civil Actions Over $3,000, Probate—Common Pleas Court, 101 S Main, Georgetown, OH 45121. 937-378-3100. Probate: 937-378-6549. 8AM-4PM (EST). Access by: Mail, in person.

Misdemeanor, Civil Actions Under $15,000, Small Claims—County Court, 770 Mount Orab Pike, Georgetown, OH 45121. 937-378-6358. Fax: 937-378-2462. 8AM-4PM (EST). Access by: In person only.

Butler County

Real Estate Recording—Butler County Recorder, 130 High Street, Hamilton, OH 45011. 513-887-3192. Fax: 513-887-3198. 8:30AM-4:30PM; 8:30AM-4PM(Recording) (EST).

Felony, Civil Actions Over $3,000, Probate—Common Pleas Court, 130 High St, Hamilton, OH 45011. 513-887-3996. Probate: 513-887-3089. 8:30AM-4:30PM (EST). Access by: Fax, remote online, in person.

Misdemeanor, Civil Actions Under $15,000, Small Claims—County Court Area #2, 130 High St, Hamilton, OH 45011. 513-887-3462. 8:30AM-4:30PM (EST). Access by: In person only.

County Court Area #1, 118 West High, Oxford, OH 45056. 513-523-4748. Fax: 513-523-4737. 8:30AM-4:30PM (EST). Access by: Phone, mail, in person.

County Court Area #3, 9113 Cincinnati, Dayton Rd, West Chester, OH 45069. 513-867-5070. Fax: 513-777-0558. 8:30AM-4:30PM (EST). Access by: Mail, in person.

Carroll County

Real Estate Recording—Carroll County Recorder, Courthouse, 119 Public Square, Carrollton, OH 44615. 330-627-4545. Fax: 330-627-4295. 8AM-4PM (EST).

Felony, Civil Actions Over $3,000, Probate—Common Pleas Court, PO Box 367, Carrollton, OH 44615. 330-627-

4886. Probate: 216-627-2323. 8AM-4PM (EST). Access by: Mail, in person.

Misdemeanor, Civil Actions Under $15,000, Small Claims—County Court, Courthouse, 3rd Fl, Carrollton, OH 44615. 330-627-5049. Fax: 330-627-6656. 8AM-4PM (EST). Access by: In person only.

Champaign County

Real Estate Recording—Champaign County Recorder, 200 North Main Street, Urbana, OH 43078. 937-652-2263. Fax: 937-652-1515. 8AM-4PM (EST).

Felony, Civil Actions Over $10,000, Probate—Common Pleas Court, 200 N Main St, Urbana, OH 43078. 937-653-2746. Probate: 937-652-2108. 8AM-4PM (EST). Access by: In person only.

Misdemeanor, Civil Actions Under $15,000, Eviction, Small Claims—Champaign County Municipal Court, PO Box 85, Urbana, OH 43078. 937-653-7376. 8AM-4PM (EST). Access by: Mail, in person.

Clark County

Real Estate Recording—Clark County Recorder, 31 North Limestone Street, Springfield, OH 45502. 937-328-2445. Fax: 937-328-4620. 8AM-4:30PM (EST).

Felony, Civil Actions Over $10,000, Probate—Common Pleas Court, 101 N Limestone St, Springfield, OH 45502. 937-328-2458. Fax: 937-328-2436. 8AM-4:30PM (EST). Access by: In person only.

Misdemeanor, Civil Actions Under $15,000, Eviction, Small Claims—Clark County Municipal Court, 50 E Columbia St, Springfield, OH 45502. 937-328-3700. 8AM-5PM (EST). Access by: Mail, in person.

Clermont County

Real Estate Recording—Clermont County Recorder, 101 E. Main Street, Batavia, OH 45103. 513-732-7236. Fax: 513-732-7891. 8:30AM-6PM (EST).

Felony, Civil Actions Over $10,000, Probate—Common Pleas Court, 270 Main St, Batavia, OH 45103. 513-732-7130. Probate: 513-732-7243. Fax: 513-732-7050. 8:30AM-4:30PM (EST). Access by: In person only.

Misdemeanor, Civil Actions Under $15,000, Eviction, Small Claims—Clermont County Municipal Court, 289 Main St, Batavia, OH 45103. Civil: 513-732-7292. Criminal: 513-732-7294. 8:30AM-4:30PM (EST). Access by: In person only.

Clinton County

Real Estate Recording—Clinton County Recorder, 46 S. South Street, Courthouse, Wilmington, OH 45177. 937-382-2067. 8AM-4PM (EST).

Felony, Civil Actions Over $3,000, Probate—Common Pleas Court, 46 S South St, Wilmington, OH 45177. 937-382-2316. Probate: 937-382-2280. Fax: 937-383-3455. 7:30AM-4:30PM (EST). Access by: Fax, mail, in person.

Misdemeanor, Civil Actions Under $15,000, Eviction, Small Claims—Clinton County Municipal Court, 69 N South St, Wilmington, OH 45177. 937-382-8985. Fax: 937-383-0130. 8AM-3:30PM (EST). Access by: Phone, mail, in person.

Columbiana County

Real Estate Recording—Columbiana County Recorder, County Courthouse, 105 South Market St., Lisbon, OH 44432. 330-424-9511. 8AM-4PM (EST).

Felony, Civil Actions Over $10,000, Probate—Common Pleas Court, 105 S Market St, Lisbon, OH 44432. 330-424-9511. Probate: 216-424-9511 X290. 8AM-4:30PM (EST). Access by: In person only.

Misdemeanor, Civil Actions Under $15,000, Small Claims—County Court East Area, 31 North Market St, East Palestine, OH 44413. 330-426-3774. Fax: 330-426-6328. 8AM-4PM (EST). Access by: Mail, in person.

County Court Southwest Area, 41 N Park Ave, Lisbon, OH 44432. 330-424-5326. Fax: 330-424-6658. 8AM-4PM (EST). Access by: In person only.

County Court Northwest Area, 130 Penn Ave, Salem, OH 44460. 330-332-0297. 8AM-4PM (EST). Access by: Mail, in person.

Misdemeanor, Civil Actions Under $15,000, Eviction, Small Claims—East Liverpool Municipal Court, 126 W 6th St, East Liverpool, OH 43920. 330-385-5151. Fax: 330-385-1566. 8AM-4PM (EST). Access by: Phone, mail, in person.

Coshocton County

Real Estate Recording—Coshocton County Recorder, 349 Main Street, Courthouse Annex, Coshocton, OH 43812. 740-622-2817. 8AM-4PM (EST).

Felony, Civil Actions Over $10,000, Probate—Common Pleas Court, 318 Main St, Coshocton, OH 43812. 740-622-1456. Probate: 740-622-1837. 8AM-4PM (EST). Access by: Mail, in person.

Misdemeanor, Civil Actions Under $15,000, Eviction, Small Claims—Coshocton Municipal Court, 760 Chesnut St, Coshocton, OH 43812. 740-622-2871. Fax: 740-623-5928. 8AM-4:30PM M-W,F; 8AM-Noon Th (EST). Access by: Phone, fax, mail, in person.

Crawford County

Real Estate Recording—Crawford County Recorder, 112 East Mansfield Street, Bucyrus, OH 44820. 419-562-6961. 8:30AM-4:30PM (EST).

Felony, Civil Actions Over $3,000, Probate—Common Pleas Court, PO Box 470, Bucyrus, OH 44820. 419-562-2766. Probate: 419-562-8891. Fax: 419-562-8011. 8:30AM-4:30PM (EST). Access by: Mail, in person.

Misdemeanor, Civil Actions Under $15,000, Eviction, Small Claims—Crawford County Municipal Court, PO Box 550, Bucyrus, OH 44820. 419-562-2731. 8:30AM-4:30PM (EST). Access by: Mail, in person.

Galion Municipal Court Branch Office, 301 Harding Way East, Galion, OH 44833. 419-468-6819. 8:30AM-4:30PM (EST). Access by: Mail, in person.

Cuyahoga County

Real Estate Recording—Cuyahoga County Recorder, 1219 Ontario Street, Room 220, Cleveland, OH 44113. 216-443-8194. Fax: 216-443-8193. 8:30AM-4:30PM (EST).

Felony, Civil Actions Over $10,000, Probate—Common Pleas Court, 1200 Ontario St, Cleveland, OH 44113. 216-443-8560. Civil: 216-443-7966. Criminal: 216-443-7985. Probate: 216-443-8764. 8:30AM-4:30PM (EST). Access by: Mail, in person.

Civil Actions Under $15,000, Eviction, Small Claims—Cleveland Municipal Court-Civil Division, 1200 Ontario St, Cleveland, OH 44113. 216-664-4870. Fax: 216-664-4065. 8AM-3:50PM (EST). Access by: Mail, in person.

Misdemeanor—Cleveland Municipal Court-Criminal Division, 1200 Ontario St, Cleveland, OH 44113. 216-664-4790. 8AM-3:50PM (EST). Access by: Mail, in person.

Misdemeanor, Civil Actions Under $15,000, Eviction, Small Claims—Bedford Municipal Court, 65 Columbus Rd, Bedford, OH 44146. 216-232-3420. Fax: 216-232-2510. 8:30AM-4:30PM (EST). Access by: Fax, mail, in person.

Berea Municipal Court, 11 Berea Commons, Berea, OH 44017. 216-826-5860. Fax: 216-891-3387. 8AM-5PM (EST). Access by: Phone, fax, mail, in person.

Cleveland Heights Municipal Court, 40 Severence Circle, Cleveland Heights, OH 44118. 216-291-4901. Fax: 216-291-2459. 8AM-5PM (EST). Access by: In person only.

East Cleveland Municipal Court, 14340 Euclid Ave, East Cleveland, OH 44112. 216-681-5020. 8AM-4:30PM (EST). Access by: Mail, in person.

Euclid Municipal Court, 555 E 222 St, Euclid, OH 44123. 216-289-2888. 8:30AM-4:30PM (EST). Access by: Mail, in person.

Garfield Heights Municipal Court, 5555 Turney Rd, Garfield Heights, OH 44125. 216-475-1900. 8:30AM-4:30PM (EST). Access by: Phone, mail, in person.

Lakewood Municipal Court, 12650 Detroit Ave, Lakewood, OH 44107. 216-529-6700. Fax: 216-529-7687. 8AM-5PM (EST). Access by: Fax, mail, in person.

Lyndhurst Municipal Court, 5301 Mayfield Rd, Lyndhurst, OH 44124. 216-461-6500. 8:30AM-5PM (EST). Access by: Mail, in person.

Parma Municipal Court, 5750 W 54th St, Parma, OH 44129. 216-884-4000. 8:30AM-4:30PM (EST). Access by: In person only.

Rocky River Municipal Court, 21012 Hilliard Blvd, Rocky River, OH 44116. 216-333-0066. Fax: 216-356-5613. 8:30AM-4:30PM (EST). Access by: In person only.

Shaker Heights Municipal Court, 3355 Lee Rd, Shaker Heights, OH 44120. 216-491-1300. Fax: 216-491-1314. 8:30AM-5PM (EST). Access by: Phone, mail, in person. Phone access limited to gov't agencies.

South Euclid Municipal Court, 1349 S Green Rd, South Euclid, OH 44121. 216-381-0400. Fax: 216-381-1195. 8:30AM-5PM (EST). Access by: Mail, in person.

Darke County

Real Estate Recording—Darke County Recorder, 504 Broadway, Courthouse, Greenville, OH 45331. 937-547-7390. 8:30AM-4:30PM (EST).

Felony, Civil Actions Over $3,000, Probate—Common Pleas Court, Courthouse, Greenville, OH 45331. 937-547-7335. Probate: 937-547-7335. Fax: 937-547-7305. 8:30AM-4:30PM (EST). Access by: Mail, in person.

Misdemeanor, Civil Actions Under $15,000, Small Claims—County Court, Courthouse, Greenville, OH 45331. 937-547-7340. Fax: 937-547-7378. 8:30AM-4:30PM (EST). Access by: Mail, in person.

Defiance County

Real Estate Recording—Defiance County Recorder, 221 Clinton Street, Courthouse, Defiance, OH 43512. 419-782-4741. Fax: 419-784-2761. 8:30AM-4:30PM (EST).

Felony, Civil Actions Over $10,000, Probate—Common Pleas Court, PO Box 716, Defiance, OH 43512. 419-782-1936. 8:30AM-4:30PM (EST). Access by: In person only.

Misdemeanor, Civil Actions Under $15,000, Eviction, Small Claims—Defiance Municipal Court, 324 Perry St, Defiance, OH 43512. 419-782-5756. Fax: 419-782-2018. 8AM-5PM (EST). Access by: Mail, in person.

Delaware County

Real Estate Recording—Delaware County Recorder, 91 North Sandusky Street, Courthouse, Delaware, OH 43015. 614-368-1835. 8:30AM-4:30PM (EST).

Felony, Civil Actions Over $10,000, Probate—Common Pleas Court, 91 N Sandusky, Delaware, OH 43015. 614-368-1850. Probate: 614-368-1880. Fax: 614-368-1849. 8:30AM-4:30PM (EST). Access by: Fax, mail, in person.

Misdemeanor, Civil Actions Under $15,000, Eviction, Small Claims—Delaware Municipal Court, 70 N Union St, Delaware, OH 43015. 614-363-1296. Fax: 614-368-1583. 8AM-5PM (EST). Access by: Phone, mail, in person.

Erie County

Real Estate Recording—Erie County Recorder, Erie County Office Bldg, Room 225, 247 Columbus Ave., Sandusky, OH 44870. 419-627-7686. 8AM-4PM; 8AM-5PM F (EST).

Felony, Civil Actions Over $10,000, Probate—Common Pleas Court, 323 Columbus Ave, Sandusky, OH 44870. 419-627-7705. Fax: 419-627-6873. 8AM-4PM M-Th/8AM-5PM F (EST). Access by: Fax, mail, in person.

Misdemeanor, Civil Actions Under $15,000, Small Claims—County Court, 150 W Mason Rd, Milan, OH 44846. 419-499-4689. 8AM-4PM (EST). Access by: Phone, mail, in person.

Sandusky Municipal Court, 222 Meigs St, Sandusky, OH 44870. 419-627-5917. Fax: 419-627-5950. 7AM-4PM (EST). Access by: Phone, fax, mail, in person.

Vermilion Municipal Court, PO Box 258, Vermilion, OH 44089. 440-967-6543. Fax: 440-967-1467. 8AM-4PM (EST). Access by: Fax, mail, in person.

Fairfield County

Real Estate Recording—Fairfield County Recorder, 210 East Main Street, Courthouse, Lancaster, OH 43130. 740-687-7100. Fax: 740-687-7104. 8AM-4PM (EST).

Felony, Civil Actions Over $10,000, Probate—Common Pleas Court, 224 E Main (PO Box 370), 2nd Flr, Lancaster, OH 43130-0370. 740-687-7030. Probate: 740-687-7093. 8AM-4PM (EST). Access by: Phone, mail, in person.

Misdemeanor, Civil Actions Under $15,000, Eviction, Small Claims—Lancaster Municipal Court, PO Box 2390, Lancaster, OH 43130. 740-687-6621. 8AM-4PM (EST). Access by: Mail, in person.

Fayette County

Real Estate Recording—Fayette County Recorder, 110 East Court Street, Courthouse Building, Washington Court House, OH 43160. 614-335-1770. 9AM-4PM (EST).

Felony, Civil Actions Over $10,000, Probate—Common Pleas Court, 110 E Court St, Washington Court House, OH 43160. 614-335-6371. Probate: 614-335-0640. 9AM-4PM (EST). Access by: Mail, in person.

Misdemeanor, Civil Actions Under $15,000, Eviction, Small Claims—Municipal Court, Washington Courthouse, 119 N Main St, Washington Court House, OH 43160. 614-636-2350. Fax: 614-636-2359. 8AM-4PM (EST). Access by: Mail, in person.

Franklin County

Real Estate Recording—Franklin County Recorder, 373 S. High Street, 18th Floor, Columbus, OH 43215. 614-462-3930. Fax: 614-462-4312. 8AM-5PM (EST).

Felony, Civil Actions Over $10,000, Probate—Common Pleas Court, 373 S High St, Columbus, OH 43215-6311. 614-462-3894. Probate: 614-462-3894. 8AM-5PM (EST). Access by: Mail, in person.

Civil Actions Under $15,000, Eviction, Small Claims—Franklin County Municipal Court, Civil Division, 375 S High St, 3rd Flr, Columbus, OH 43215. 614-645-7220. 8AM-5PM Civil; Criminal open 24hrs (EST). Access by: Mail, in person.

Misdemeanor—Franklin County Municipal Court, Criminal Division, 375 S High St, 2nd Flr, Columbus, OH 43215. 614-645-8161. Open 24 hours a day (EST). Access by: Mail, in person.

Fulton County

Real Estate Recording—Fulton County Recorder, Courthouse, 210 S. Fulton St., Wauseon, OH 43567. 419-337-9232. Fax: 419-337-9282. 8:30AM-4:30PM (EST).

Felony, Civil Actions Over $3,000, Probate—Common Pleas Court, 210 S Fulton, Wauseon, OH 43567. 419-337-9230. Probate: 419-337-9242. 8:30AM-4:30PM (EST). Access by: In person only.

Misdemeanor, Civil Actions Under $15,000, Small Claims—County Court Eastern District, 128 N Main St, Swanton, OH 43558. 419-826-5636. Fax: 419-825-3324. 8:30AM-4:30PM (EST). Access by: Mail, in person.

County Court Western District, 224 S Fulton St, Wauseon, OH 43567. 419-337-9212. Fax: 419-337-9286. 8:30AM-4:30PM (EST). Access by: Phone, mail, in person.

Gallia County

Real Estate Recording—Gallia County Recorder, 18 Locust Street, Room 1265, Gallipolis, OH 45631. 614-446-4612. Fax: 614-446-4804. 8AM-4PM (EST).

Felony, Civil Actions Over $10,000, Probate—Common Pleas Court-Gallia County Courthouse, 18 Locust St, Rm 1290, Gallipolis, OH 45631-1290. 614-446-4612. Probate: 614-446-4612. 8AM-4PM (EST). Access by: In person only.

Misdemeanor, Civil Actions Under $15,000, Eviction, Small Claims—Gallipolis Municipal Court, 518 2nd Ave, Gallipolis, OH 45631. 614-446-9400. Fax: 614-446-2070. 9AM-4:30PM (EST). Access by: Phone, mail, in person.

Geauga County

Real Estate Recording—Geauga County Recorder, 231 Main Street, Courthouse Annex, Chardon, OH 44024. 440-285-2222. 8AM-4:30PM (EST).

Felony, Civil Actions Over $10,000, Probate—Common Pleas Court, 100 Short Court, Chardon, OH 44024. 440-285-2222. Probate: 440-285-2222. Fax: 440-285-2063. 8AM-4:30PM (EST). Access by: Mail, in person.

Misdemeanor, Civil Actions Under $15,000, Eviction, Small Claims—Chardon Municipal Court, 108 S Hambden (PO Box 339), Chardon, OH 44024-0339. 440-286-2670. Fax: 440-286-2679. 8AM-4:30PM (EST). Access by: Mail, in person.

Greene County

Real Estate Recording—Greene County Recorder, 69 Greene Street, 3rd Floor, Xenia, OH 45385. 937-376-5270. Fax: 937-376-5386. 8AM-4:30PM (EST).

Felony, Civil Actions Over $10,000, Probate—Common Pleas Court, 45 N Detroit St (PO Box 156), Xenia, OH 45385. 937-376-5292. Probate: 937-376-5280. Fax: 937-376-5309. 8AM-4PM (EST). Access by: Mail, in person.

Misdemeanor, Civil Actions Under $15,000, Eviction, Small Claims—Fairborn Municipal Court, 44 W Hebble Ave, Fairborn, OH 45324. Civil: 937-754-3044. Criminal: 937-754-1735. 7:30AM-4:30PM (EST). Access by: Mail, in person.

Xenia Municipal Court, 101 N Detroit, Xenia, OH 45385. 937-376-7298. Fax: 937-376-7288. 8AM-4:30PM (EST). Access by: Fax, mail, in person.

Guernsey County

Real Estate Recording—Guernsey County Recorder, Courthouse D-202, Wheeling Avenue, Cambridge, OH 43725. 740-432-9275. 8AM-4PM (EST).

Felony, Civil Actions Over $10,000, Probate—Common Pleas Court, 801 E Wheeling Ave D-300, Cambridge, OH 43725. 740-432-9230. Probate: 740-432-9262. Fax: 740-432-7807. 8:30AM-4PM (EST). Access by: In person only.

Misdemeanor, Civil Actions Under $15,000, Eviction, Small Claims—Cambridge Municipal Court, 134 Southgate Parkway, Cambridge, OH 43725. 740-439-5585. Fax: 740-439-5666. 8:30AM-4:30PM (EST). Access by: In person only.

Hamilton County

Real Estate Recording—Hamilton County Recorder, Room 205, 138 East Court Street, Cincinnati, OH 45202. 513-632-8677. Fax: 513-632-6617. 8AM-4PM (EST).

Felony, Civil Actions Over $10,000, Probate—Common Pleas Court, 1000 Main St, Room 315, Cincinnati, OH 45202. 513-632-8283. Civil: 513-632-8247. Criminal: 513-632-8245. Probate: 513-632-8277. Fax: 513-763-4860. 8AM-4PM (EST). Access by: Fax, mail, remote online, in person.

Misdemeanor, Civil Actions Under $15,000, Eviction, Small Claims—Hamilton County Municipal Court, 1000 Main St, Cincinnati, OH 45202. Civil: 513-632-8891. Criminal: 513-632-8255. Fax: 513-763-4860. 8AM-4PM (EST). Access by: Fax, mail, in person.

Hancock County

Real Estate Recording—Hancock County Recorder, 300 South Main Street, Courthouse, Findlay, OH 45840. 419-424-7091. Fax: 419-424-7828. 8:30AM-4:30PM (EST).

Felony, Civil Actions Over $10,000, Probate—Common Pleas Court, 300 S Main St, Findlay, OH 45840. 419-424-7037. Probate: 419-424-7141. 8:30AM-4:30PM (EST). Access by: Mail, in person.

Misdemeanor, Civil Actions Under $15,000, Eviction, Small Claims—Findlay Municipal Court, PO Box 826, Findlay, OH 45839. 419-424-7141. Fax: 419-424-7803. 8AM-5PM (EST). Access by: Mail, in person.

Hardin County

Real Estate Recording—Hardin County Recorder, One Courthouse Square, Suite 220, Kenton, OH 43326. 419-674-2250. Fax: 419-675-2802. 8:30AM-4PM; 8:30AM-6PM F (EST).

Felony, Civil Actions Over $10,000, Probate—Common Pleas Court, Courthouse, Ste 310, Kenton, OH 43326. 419-674-2278. Probate: 419-674-2230. Fax: 419-674-2273. 8:30AM-4PM M-Th; 8:30AM-6PM F (EST). Access by: Mail, in person.

Misdemeanor, Civil Actions Under $15,000, Eviction, Small Claims—Hardin County Municipal Court, PO Box 250, Kenton, OH 43326. 419-674-4362. Fax: 419-674-4096. 8:30AM-4PM (EST). Access by: Fax, mail, in person.

Harrison County

Real Estate Recording—Harrison County Recorder, 100 West Market Street, Courthouse, Cadiz, OH 43907. 740-942-8869. 8:30AM-4:30PM (EST).

Felony, Civil Actions Over $3,000, Probate—Common Pleas Court, 100 W Market, Cadiz, OH 43907. 740-942-8863. 8:30AM-4:30PM (EST). Access by: Mail, in person.

Misdemeanor, Civil Actions Under $15,000, Small Claims—County Court, 100 W Market St, Cadiz, OH 43907. 740-942-8861. Fax: 740-942-4693. 8:30AM-4:30PM (EST). Access by: In person only.

Henry County

Real Estate Recording—Henry County Recorder, 660 North Perry Street, Courthouse, Napoleon, OH 43545. 419-592-1766. Fax: 419-592-1652. 8:30AM-4:30PM (EST).

Felony, Civil Actions Over $10,000, Probate—Common Pleas Court, PO Box 71, Napoleon, OH 43545. 419-592-5886. Probate: 419-592-7771. Fax: 419-599-0803. 8:30AM-4:30PM (EST). Access by: Mail, in person.

Misdemeanor, Civil Actions Under $15,000, Eviction, Small Claims—Napoleon Municipal Court, PO Box 502, Napoleon, OH 43545. 419-592-2851. Fax: 419-592-1805. 8AM-5PM (EST). Access by: Phone, fax, mail, in person.

Highland County

Real Estate Recording—Highland County Recorder, 119 Governor Foraker, County Administration Building, Hillsboro, OH 45133. 937-393-9954. Fax: 937-393-5855. 8:30AM-4PM (EST).

Felony, Civil Actions Over $10,000, Probate—Common Pleas Court, PO Box 821, Hillsboro, OH 45133. 937-393-9957. 8AM-4PM (EST). Access by: Mail, in person.

Misdemeanor, Civil Actions Under $15,000, Eviction, Small Claims—Hillsboro County Municipal Court, 108 Governor Trimble Pl, Hillsboro, OH 45133. 937-393-3022. 7AM-3:30PM M,T,Th,F; 7AM-Noon W (EST). Access by: Mail, in person.

Hocking County

Real Estate Recording—Hocking County Recorder, 1 East Main Street, Courthouse, Logan, OH 43138. 740-385-2031. Fax: 740-385-0377. 8:30AM-4PM (EST).

Felony, Civil Actions Over $10,000, Probate—Common Pleas Court, PO Box 108, Logan, OH 43138. 740-385-2616. Probate: 740-385-3022. Fax: 740-385-1822. 8:30AM-4PM (EST). Access by: Phone, fax, mail, in person.

Misdemeanor, Civil Actions Under $15,000, Eviction, Small Claims—Hocking County Municipal Court, 1 E Main St (PO Box 950), Logan, OH 43138-1278. 740-385-2250. 8:30AM-4:30PM (EST). Access by: Mail, in person.

Holmes County

Real Estate Recording—Holmes County Recorder, Courthouse - Suite 202, 1 East Jackson St., Millersburg, OH 44654. 330-674-5916. 8:30AM-4:30PM (EST).

Felony, Civil Actions Over $10,000, Probate—Common Pleas Court, 1 E Jackson St #306, Millersburg, OH 44654. 330-674-1876. Probate: 330-674-5881. Fax: 330-674-0289. 8:30AM-4:30PM (EST). Access by: Fax, mail, in person.

Misdemeanor, Civil Actions Under $15,000, Small Claims—County Court, 1 E Jackson St, Ste 101, Millersburg, OH 44654. 330-674-4901. Fax: 330-674-5514. 8:30AM-4:30PM (EST). Access by: Fax, in person.

Huron County

Real Estate Recording—Huron County Recorder, 2 East Main Street, Norwalk, OH 44857. 419-668-1916. Fax: 419-663-4052. 8AM-4:30PM (EST).

Felony, Civil Actions Over $10,000, Probate—Common Pleas Court, 2 E Main St, Norwalk, OH 44857. 419-668-5113. Probate: 419-668-4383. Fax: 419-663-4048. 8AM-4:30PM (EST). Access by: Fax, mail, in person.

Misdemeanor, Civil Actions Under $15,000, Eviction, Small Claims—Bellevue Municipal Court, 117 N Sandusky, PO Box 305, Bellevue, OH 44811. 419-483-5880. Fax: 419-483-9701. 8:30AM-4:30PM (EST). Access by: Phone, mail, in person.

Norwalk Municipal Court, 45 N Linwood, Norwalk, OH 44857. 419-663-6750. Fax: 419-663-6749. 8:30AM-4:30PM (EST). Access by: Fax, mail, in person.

Jackson County

Real Estate Recording—Jackson County Recorder, 226 E. Main St., Courthouse, Suite 1, Jackson, OH 45640. 740-286-1919. 8AM-4PM (EST).

Felony, Civil Actions Over $10,000, Probate—Common Pleas Court, 226 Main St, Jackson, OH 45640. 740-286-2006. Probate: 740-286-1401. Fax: 740-286-4061. 8AM-4PM (EST). Access by: Mail, in person.

Misdemeanor, Civil Actions Under $15,000, Eviction, Small Claims—Jackson County Municipal Court, 226 Main St, Jackson, OH 45640-2006. 740-286-2718. Fax: 740-286-4061. 8AM-4PM (EST). Access by: In person only.

Jefferson County

Real Estate Recording—Jefferson County Recorder, 3rd & Market Street, Courthouse, Steubenville, OH 43952. 740-283-8566. 8:30AM-4:30PM (EST).

Felony, Civil Actions Over $10,000, Probate—Common Pleas Court, 301 Market St (PO Box 1326), Steubenville, OH 43952. 740-283-8583. Probate: 740-283-8554. 8:30AM-4:30PM (EST). Access by: Mail, in person.

Misdemeanor, Civil Actions Under $15,000, Small Claims—County Court #3, PO Box 495, Dillonvale, OH 43917. 740-769-2903. 8:30AM-4PM (EST). Access by: Mail, in person.

County Court #1, 1007 Franklin Ave, Toronto, OH 43964. 740-537-2020. 9AM-4PM (EST). Access by: Mail, in person.

County Court #2, PO Box 2207, Wintersville, OH 43952. 740-264-7644. 8:30AM-4PM (EST). Access by: Mail, in person.

Steubenville Municipal Court, 123 S 3rd St, Steubenville, OH 43952. 740-283-6020. Fax: 740-283-6167. 8:30AM-4PM (EST). Access by: Fax, mail, in person.

Knox County

Real Estate Recording—Knox County Recorder, 106 East High Street, Mount Vernon, OH 43050. 740-393-6755. 8AM-4PM (EST).

Felony, Civil Actions Over $10,000, Probate—Common Pleas Court, 111 E High St, Mt Vernon, OH 43050. 740-393-6788. Probate: 740-393-6797. 8AM-4PM, til 6PM on Wed (EST). Access by: In person only.

Misdemeanor, Civil Actions Under $15,000, Eviction, Small Claims—Mount Vernon Municipal Court, 5 North Gay St, Mount Vernon, OH 43050. 740-393-9510. Fax: 740-393-5349. 8AM-4PM (EST). Access by: Phone, mail, in person.

Lake County

Real Estate Recording—Lake County Recorder, 105 Main Street, Painesville, OH 44077. 440-350-2510. Fax: 440-350-5940. 8AM-4:30PM (EST).

Felony, Civil Actions Over $10,000, Probate—Common Pleas Court, PO Box 490, Painesville, OH 44077. 440-350-2658. Probate: 440-350-2624. 8AM-4:30PM (EST). Access by: In person only.

Misdemeanor, Civil Actions Under $15,000, Eviction, Small Claims—Painesville Municipal Court, 7 Richmond St (PO Box 601), Painesville, OH 44077. 440-352-9301. Fax: 440-352-0028. 8AM-4:30PM (EST). Access by: Fax, mail, in person.

Lawrence County

Real Estate Recording—Lawrence County Recorder, 111 South 4th Street, Courthouse, Ironton, OH 45638. 740-533-4314. Fax: 740-533-4411. 8AM-4PM (EST).

Felony, Civil Actions Over $10,000, Probate—Common Pleas Court, PO Box 208, Ironton, OH 45638. 740-533-4355. Probate: 740-533-4340. 8:30AM-4PM (EST). Access by: Mail, in person.

Misdemeanor, Civil Actions Under $15,000, Eviction, Small Claims—Lawrence County Municipal Court, PO Box 126, Chesapeake, OH 45619. 740-867-3128. Fax: 740-867-3547. 8:30AM-4PM (EST). Access by: Phone, fax, mail, in person.

Ironton Municipal Court, PO Box 237, Ironton, OH 45638. 740-532-3062. Fax: 740-533-6088. 8:30AM-4PM (EST). Access by: Fax, mail, in person.

Licking County

Real Estate Recording—Licking County Recorder, 20 South Second Street, Third Floor, Newark, OH 43055. 740-349-6061. Fax: 740-349-1415. 8:30AM-4:30PM (EST).

Felony, Civil Actions Over $10,000, Probate—Common Pleas Court, PO Box 4370, Newark, OH 43058-4370. 740-349-6171. Probate: 740-349-6141. 8AM-4:30PM (EST). Access by: Mail, in person.

Misdemeanor, Civil Actions Under $15,000, Eviction, Small Claims—Licking County Municipal Court, 40 W Main St, Newark, OH 43055. 740-349-6627. 8AM-4:30PM (EST). Access by: In person only.

Logan County

Real Estate Recording—Logan County Recorder, 100 South Madriver, Suite A, Bellefontaine, OH 43311. 937-599-7201. Fax: 937-599-7287. 8:30AM-4:30PM (EST).

Felony, Civil Actions Over $10,000, Probate—Common Pleas Court, 101 S Main St Rm 12, Bellefontaine, OH 43311-2055. 513-599-7275. 8AM-4:30PM (EST). Access by: Mail, in person.

Misdemeanor, Civil Actions Under $15,000, Eviction, Small Claims—Bellefontaine Municipal Court, 226 W Columbus Ave, Bellefontaine, OH 43311. 513-599-6127. 8AM-4:30PM (EST). Access by: In person only.

Lorain County

Real Estate Recording—Lorain County Recorder, 226 Middle Avenue, Elyria, OH 44035. 440-329-5148. Fax: 440-329-5199. 8AM-4:30PM (EST).

Felony, Civil Actions Over $10,000, Probate—Common Pleas Court, 226 Middle Ave, Elyria, OH 44035. 440-329-5536. Probate: 440-329-5175. Fax: 440-329-5404. 8AM-4:30PM (EST). Access by: Mail, in person.

Misdemeanor, Civil Actions Under $15,000, Eviction, Small Claims—Avon Lake Municipal Court, 150 Avon Beldon Rd, Avon Lake, OH 44012. 440-930-4103. 8:30AM-4:30PM (EST). Access by: Phone, mail, in person.

Elyria Municipal Court, 328 Broad St (PO Box 1498), Elyria, OH 44036. 440-323-5743. Fax: 440-323-8095. 8AM-4:25PM (EST). Access by: Fax, mail, in person.

Lorain Municipal Court, 100 W Erie Ave, Lorain, OH 44052. 440-244-2286. 8:30AM-4:30PM (EST). Access by: In person only.

Oberlin Municipal Court, 85 S Main St, Oberlin, OH 44074. 440-775-7229. Fax: 440-775-0619. 8AM-4PM (EST). Access by: In person only.

Vermilion Municipal Court, PO Box 258, Vermilion, OH 44089. 440-967-6543. Fax: 440-967-1467. 8AM-4PM (EST). Access by: Fax, mail, in person.

Lucas County

Real Estate Recording—Lucas County Recorder, 1 Government Center, Jackson Street, Toledo, OH 43604. 419-245-4400. Fax: 419-245-4284. 8AM-5PM (EST).

Felony, Civil Actions Over $10,000, Probate—Common Pleas Court, 700 Adams, Courthouse, Toledo, OH 43624. 419-245-4483. Probate: 419-245-4775. Fax: 419-245-4487. 8AM-4:45PM (EST). Access by: Mail, in person.

Misdemeanor, Civil Actions Under $15,000, Eviction, Small Claims—Toledo Municipal Court, 555 N Erie St, Toledo, OH 43624. 419-245-1926. Civil: 419-245-1927. Criminal: 419-245-1776. Fax: 419-245-1801. 8AM-4:30PM civil; 8AM-5:45PM M-F, 8-11:30AM Sat crim & traffic (EST). Access by: Mail, in person.

Madison County

Real Estate Recording—Madison County Recorder, High & Main Streets, Courthouse, Room 40, London, OH 43140. 614-852-1854. 8AM-4PM (EST).

Felony, Civil Actions Over $10,000, Probate—Common Pleas Court, PO Box 227, London, OH 43140. 614-852-9776. Probate: 614-852-0756. 8AM-4PM (EST). Access by: In person only.

Misdemeanor, Civil Actions Under $15,000, Eviction, Small Claims—Madison County Municipal Court, Main & High St, PO Box 646, London, OH 43140. 614-852-1669. Fax: 614-852-0812. 8AM-4PM (EST). Access by: Phone, fax, mail, in person.

Mahoning County

Real Estate Recording—Mahoning County Recorder, 120 Market Street, Youngstown, OH 44503. 330-740-2345. Fax: 330-740-2006. 8AM-4:30PM (EST).

Felony, Civil Actions Over $10,000, Probate—Common Pleas Court, 120 Market St, Youngstown, OH 44503. 330-740-2104. Probate: 330-740-2312. Fax: 330-740-2105. 8AM-4PM (EST). Access by: In person only.

Misdemeanor, Civil Actions Under $15,000, Small Claims—County Court #2, 127 Boardman Canfield Rd, Boardman, OH 44512. 330-726-5546. Fax: 330-740-2035. 8:30AM-4PM (EST). Access by: Mail, in person.

County Court #5, 72 N Broad St, Canfield, OH 44406. 330-533-3643. Fax: 330-740-2034. 8:30AM-4PM (EST). Access by: Mail, in person.

County Court #3, 605 E Ohio Ave, Sebring, OH 44672. 330-938-9873. Fax: 330-938-6518. 8:30AM-4PM (EST). Access by: Mail, in person.

County Court #4, 6000 Mahoning Ave, Youngstown, OH 44515. 330-740-2001. Fax: 330-740-2036. 8:30AM-4PM (EST). Access by: Phone, fax, mail, in person.

Civil Actions Under $15,000, Eviction, Small Claims—Youngstown Municipal Court-Civil Records, PO Box 6047, Youngstown, OH 44501-6047. 330-742-8863. Fax: 330-742-8786. 8AM-4PM (EST). Access by: Mail, in person.

Misdemeanor—Youngstown Municipal Court-Criminal Records, 25 S Phelphs St, Youngstown, OH 44503. 330-742-8900. Fax: 330-742-8786. 8AM-4PM (EST). Access by: Fax, mail, in person.

Misdemeanor, Civil Actions Under $15,000, Eviction, Small Claims—Campbell Municipal Court, 351 Tenney Ave, Campbell, OH 44405. 330-755-2165. Fax: 330-755-3058. 8AM-4PM (EST). Access by: Fax, mail, in person.

Struthers Municipal Court, 6 Elm St, Struthers, OH 44471. 330-755-1800. Fax: 330-755-2790. 8AM-4PM; Public access only on Tuesday and Thursday (EST). Access by: Mail, in person.

Marion County

Real Estate Recording—Marion County Recorder, 100 North Main Street, Courthouse Square, Marion, OH 43302. 614-387-4521. Fax: 614-383-1190. 8:30AM-4:30PM (EST).

Felony, Civil Actions Over $10,000, Probate—Common Pleas Court, 100 N Main St, Marion, OH 43302. 614-387-8128. Probate: 614-387-7614. Fax: 614-383-1190. 8:30AM-4:30PM (EST). Access by: Mail, in person.

Misdemeanor, Civil Actions Under $15,000, Eviction, Small Claims—Marion Municipal Court, 233 W Center St, Marion, OH 43302-0326. 614-387-2020. Fax: 614-382-5274. 8:30AM-4:30PM (EST). Access by: Mail, in person.

Medina County

Real Estate Recording—Medina County Recorder, County Administration Bldg, 144 N. Broadway, Medina, OH 44256. 330-725-9782. 8AM-4:30PM (EST).

Felony, Civil Actions Over $10,000, Probate—Common Pleas Court, 93 Public Square, Medina, OH 44256. 330-723-3641. Probate: 330-725-9703. 8AM-4:30PM (EST). Access by: Mail, in person.

Misdemeanor, Civil Actions Under $15,000, Eviction, Small Claims—Medina Municipal Court, 135 N Elmwood, Medina, OH 44256. 330-723-3287. Fax: 330-225-1108. 8AM-4:30PM (EST). Access by: In person only.

Wadsworth Municipal Court, 120 Maple St, Wadsworth, OH 44281-1825. 330-335-1596. Fax: 330-335-2723. 8AM-4PM (EST). Access by: Fax, mail, in person.

Meigs County

Real Estate Recording—Meigs County Recorder, 100 East Second Street, Courthouse, Pomeroy, OH 45769. 740-992-3806. Fax: 740-992-2867. 8:30AM-4:30PM (EST).

Felony, Civil Actions Over $3,000, Probate—Common Pleas Court, PO Box 151, Pomeroy, OH 45769. 740-992-5290. Probate: 740-992-3096. Fax: 740-992-2270. 8:30AM-4:30PM (EST). Access by: In person only.

Misdemeanor, Civil Actions Under $15,000, Small Claims—Meigs County Court, Courthouse, Pomeroy, OH 45769. 740-992-2279. Fax: 740-992-2270. 8:30AM-4:30PM (EST). Access by: Mail, in person.

Mercer County

Real Estate Recording—Mercer County Recorder, 101 North Main Street, Courthouse Square-Room 203, Celina, OH 45822. 419-586-4232. Fax: 419-586-3541. 8:30AM-4PM (M-open until 5PM) (EST).

Felony, Civil Actions Over $10,000, Probate—Common Pleas Court, 101 N Main St, Rm 306, PO Box 28, Celina, OH 45822. 419-586-6461. Probate: 419-586-2418. Fax: 419-586-5826. 8:30AM-4PM (EST). Access by: In person only.

Misdemeanor, Civil Actions Under $15,000, Eviction, Small Claims—Celina Municipal Court, PO Box 362, Celina, OH 45822. 419-586-6491. 8AM-5PM (EST). Access by: Mail, in person.

Miami County

Real Estate Recording—Miami County Recorder, 201 West Main Street, Troy, OH 45373. 937-332-6912. Fax: 937-332-6806. 8AM-4PM (EST).

Felony, Civil Actions Over $10,000, Probate—Common Pleas Court & Court of Appeals, Safety Bldg, 201 West Main St, 3rd Flr, Troy, OH 45373. 937-332-6855. Probate: 937-332-6832. Fax: 937-332-7069. 8AM-4PM (EST). Access by: Mail, in person.

Misdemeanor, Civil Actions Under $15,000, Eviction, Small Claims—Miami County Municipal Court, 201 West Main St, Troy, OH 45373. 937-332-6920. Fax: 937-332-6932. 8AM-4PM (EST). Access by: Mail, in person.

Monroe County

Real Estate Recording—Monroe County Recorder, 101 North Main Street, Courthouse, Room 20, Woodsfield, OH 43793. 614-472-5264. 8AM-4PM (EST).

Felony, Civil Actions Over $3,000, Probate—Common Pleas Court, 101 N Main St Rm 39, Woodsfield, OH 43793. 614-472-0761. Probate: 614-472-1654. 8:30AM-4:30PM (EST). Access by: Mail, in person.

Misdemeanor, Civil Actions Under $15,000, Small Claims—County Court, 101 N Main St, Woodsfield, OH 43793. 614-472-5181. 9AM-4:30PM (EST). Access by: Mail, in person.

Montgomery County

Real Estate Recording—Montgomery County Recorder, 451 West Third Street, 5th Floor, County Administration Building, Dayton, OH 45402. 937-225-4282. Fax: 937-225-5980. 8AM-4PM (EST).

Felony, Civil Actions Over $10,000, Probate—Common Pleas Court, 41 N Perry St, Dayton, OH 45422. 937-225-4512. Criminal: 937-225-4536. Probate: 937-225-4640. Fax: 937-496-7389. 8AM-4:30PM (EST). Access by: In person only.

Misdemeanor, Civil Actions Under $15,000, Small Claims—County Court-District #2, 7525 Brandt Pike, Huber Heights, OH 45424. 937-496-7231. Fax: 937-496-7236. 8AM-4PM M-W (EST). Access by: Phone, fax, mail, in person.

County Court-District #1, 3100 Shiloh Springs Rd, Trotwood, OH 45426. 937-837-3351. Fax: 937-837-0948. 8AM-4PM (EST). Access by: Mail, in person.

Civil Actions Under $15,000, Eviction, Small Claims—Dayton Municipal Court-Civil Division, 301 W 3rd St, PO Box 968, Dayton, OH 45402-0968. 937-443-4480. 8AM-4:30PM (EST). Access by: Mail, in person.

Misdemeanor—Dayton Municipal Court-Criminal Division, 301 W 3rd St, Rm 331, Dayton, OH 45402. 937-443-4315. Fax: 937-443-4490. 8AM-4:30PM (EST). Access by: In person only.

Dayton Municipal Court-Traffic Division, 301 W 3rd St, PO Box 968, Dayton, OH 45402. 937-443-4313. 8AM-4:30PM (EST). Access by: Phone, mail, in person.

Misdemeanor, Civil Actions Under $15,000, Eviction, Small Claims—Kettering Municipal Court, 3600 Shroyer Rd, Dayton, OH 45429. 937-296-2461. Fax: 937-296-3284. 8:30AM-4:30PM (EST). Access by: Mail, in person.

Oakwood Municipal Court, 30 Park Ave, Dayton, OH 45429. 937-293-3058. 8AM-4PM (EST). Access by: Mail, in person.

Miamisburg Municipal Court, 10 N First St, Miamisburg, OH 45342. 937-866-2203. Fax: 937-866-0135. 8AM-4PM (EST). Access by: Mail, in person.

Vandalia Municipal Court, Bohanan Drive, Vandalia, OH 45377. 937-898-3996. Fax: 937-898-6648. 8AM-4PM (EST). Access by: Mail, in person.

Morgan County

Real Estate Recording—Morgan County Recorder, 19 East Main Street, McConnelsville, OH 43756. 740-962-4051. Fax: 740-962-3364. 8AM-4PM (EST).

Felony, Civil Actions Over $3,000, Probate—Common Pleas Court, 19 E Main St, McConnelsville, OH 43756. 740-962-4752. Probate: 740-962-2861. Fax: 740-962-4589. 8AM-4PM M-Th; 8AM-5PM F (EST). Access by: Mail, in person.

Misdemeanor, Civil Actions Under $15,000, Small Claims—Morgan County Court, 37 E Main St, McConnelsville, OH 43756. 740-962-4031. Fax: 740-962-4035. 8AM-4PM (EST). Access by: Phone, fax, mail, in person.

Morrow County

Real Estate Recording—Morrow County Recorder, 48 East High Street, Mount Gilead, OH 43338. 419-947-3060. Fax: 419-947-3709. 8:30AM-4PM (EST).

Felony, Civil Actions Over $3,000, Probate—Common Pleas Court, 48 E High St, Mount Gilead, OH 43338. 419-947-2085. Probate: 419-947-5575. Fax: 419-947-5421. 8AM-4PM (EST). Access by: Phone, fax, mail, in person.

Misdemeanor, Civil Actions Under $15,000, Small Claims—County Court, 48 E High St, Mount Gilead, OH 43338. 419-947-5045. Fax: 419-947-1860. 8:30AM-4PM (EST). Access by: In person only.

Muskingum County

Real Estate Recording—Muskingum County Recorder, Corner 4th & Main, Courthouse, Zanesville, OH 43701. 740-455-7107. Fax: 740-455-7943. 8:30AM-4:30PM (EST).

Felony, Civil Actions Over $10,000, Probate—Common Pleas Court, PO Box 268, Zanesville, OH 43702-0268. 740-455-7104. Probate: 740-455-7113. 8:30AM-4:30PM (EST). Access by: Mail, in person.

Misdemeanor, Civil Actions Under $15,000, Small Claims—County Court, 27 N 5th St, Zanesville, OH 43701. 740-455-7138. Fax: 740-455-7157. 8:30AM-4PM (EST). Access by: Fax, mail, in person.

Zanesville Municipal Court, PO Box 566, Zanesville, OH 43702. 740-454-3269. Fax: 740-455-0739. 9AM-4:30PM (EST). Access by: Mail, in person.

Noble County

Real Estate Recording—Noble County Recorder, 260 Courthouse, Caldwell, OH 43724. 740-732-4319. 8AM-4PM M-W; 8AM-11:30AM Th; 8AM-7PM F (EST).

Felony, Civil Actions Over $3,000, Probate—Common Pleas Court, 350 Courthouse, Caldwell, OH 43724. 740-732-4408. Probate: 740-732-5047. Fax: 740-732-5702. 8-11:30AM,12:30-4PM M-W; 8-11:30AM Th; 8-11:30AM, 12:30-7PM F (EST). Access by: Phone, fax, mail, in person.

Misdemeanor, Civil Actions Under $15,000, Small Claims—County Court, 100 Courthouse, Caldwell, OH 43724. 740-732-5795. 8:30AM-4PM M-W,F; 8:30-11:30AM Th (EST). Access by: Mail, in person.

Ottawa County

Real Estate Recording—Ottawa County Recorder, 315 Madison Street, Room 204, Port Clinton, OH 43452. 419-734-6730. Fax: 419-734-6851. 8:30AM-4:30PM (EST).

Felony, Civil Actions Over $10,000, Probate—Common Pleas Court, 315 Madison St, Port Clinton, OH 43452. 419-734-6755. Probate: 419-734-6830. 8:30AM-4:30PM (EST). Access by: In person only.

Misdemeanor, Civil Actions Under $15,000, Eviction, Small Claims—Ottawa County Municipal Court, 1860 East Perry St, Port Clinton, OH 43452. 419-734-4143. Fax: 419-732-2862. 8:30AM-4:30PM (EST). Access by: In person only.

Paulding County

Real Estate Recording—Paulding County Recorder, Courthouse, 115 N. Williams St., Paulding, OH 45879. 419-399-8275. Fax: 419-399-2862. 8AM-4PM (EST).

Felony, Civil Actions Over $3,000, Probate—Common Pleas Court, 115 N Williams St, Paulding, OH 45879. 419-399-8210. Probate: 419-339-8256. Fax: 419-399-8248. 8AM-4PM (EST). Access by: Fax, mail, in person.

Misdemeanor, Civil Actions Under $15,000, Small Claims—County Court, 103B East Perry, Paulding, OH 45879. 419-399-8235. Fax: 419-399-8299. 8AM-4PM (EST). Access by: Fax, mail, in person.

Perry County

Real Estate Recording—Perry County Recorder, 105 Main Street, Courthouse, New Lexington, OH 43764. 740-342-2494. 8:30AM-4:30PM (EST).

Felony, Civil Actions Over $3,000, Probate—Common Pleas Court, PO Box 67, New Lexington, OH 43764. 740-342-1022. Probate: 740-342-1493. 8AM-4PM (EST). Access by: In person only.

Misdemeanor, Civil Actions Under $15,000, Small Claims—Perry County Court, PO Box 207, New Lexington, OH 43764-0207. 740-342-3156. Fax: 740-342-2189. 8:30AM-4:30PM (EST). Access by: In person only.

Pickaway County

Real Estate Recording—Pickaway County Recorder, 207 South Court Street, Circleville, OH 43113. 740-474-5826. Fax: 740-477-6361. 8AM-4PM (EST).

Felony, Civil Actions Over $10,000, Probate—Common Pleas Court, County Courthouse, 207 Court Street PO Box 270, Circleville, OH 43113. 740-474-5231. Probate: 740-474-3950. 8AM-4PM (EST). Access by: Mail, in person.

Misdemeanor, Civil Actions Under $15,000, Eviction, Small Claims—Circleville Municipal Court, PO Box 128, Circleville, OH 43113. 740-474-3171. Fax: 740-477-8291. 8AM-4PM (EST). Access by: Mail, in person.

Pike County

Real Estate Recording—Pike County Recorder, Courthouse, 100 E. 2nd St., Waverly, OH 45690. 740-947-2622. Fax: 740-947-7997. 8:30AM-4PM (EST).

Felony, Civil Actions Over $3,000, Probate—Common Pleas Court, 100 East 2nd St, Waverly, OH 45690. 740-947-

2715. Probate: 740-947-2560. Fax: 740-947-5065. 8:30AM-4PM (EST). Access by: In person only.

Misdemeanor, Civil Actions Under $15,000, Small Claims—Pike County Court, 106 N Market St, Waverly, OH 45690. 740-947-4003. 8:30AM-4:30PM (EST). Access by: Mail, in person.

Portage County

Real Estate Recording—Portage County Recorder, 449 South Meridian Street, Ravenna, OH 44266. 330-297-3553. Fax: 330-297-7349. 8AM-4:30PM (EST).

Felony, Civil Actions Over $10,000, Probate—Common Pleas Court, PO Box 1035, Ravenna, OH 44266. 330-297-3644. Probate: 216-297-3870. Fax: 330-297-4554. 8AM-4PM (EST). Access by: In person only.

Misdemeanor, Civil Actions Under $15,000, Eviction, Small Claims—Kent Municipal Court, 214 S Water, Kent, OH 44240. 330-678-9170. Fax: 330-677-9944. 8AM-4PM (EST). Access by: Mail, in person.

Portage County Municipal Court, PO Box 958, Ravenna, OH 44266. 330-297-3636. Fax: 330-297-3526. 8AM-4PM (EST). Access by: In person only.

Preble County

Real Estate Recording—Preble County Recorder, Courthouse, 101 East Main St., Eaton, OH 45320. 937-456-8173. 8AM-4:30PM (EST).

Felony, Civil Actions Over $10,000, Probate—Common Pleas Court, 100 E Main, 3rd Fl, Eaton, OH 45320. 937-456-8160. Probate: 937-456-8138. 8AM-4:30PM (EST). Access by: Mail, in person.

Misdemeanor, Civil Actions Under $15,000, Eviction, Small Claims—Eaton Municipal Court, PO Box 65, Eaton, OH 45320. 937-456-4941. Fax: 937-456-4685. 8AM-Noon, 1-4:30PM (EST). Access by: Mail, in person.

Putnam County

Real Estate Recording—Putnam County Recorder, 245 East Main Street, Courthouse - Suite 202, Ottawa, OH 45875. 419-523-6490. Fax: 419-523-4403. 8:30AM-4:30PM (EST).

Felony, Civil Actions Over $3,000, Probate—Common Pleas Court, 245 E Main, Rm 303, Ottawa, OH 45875. 419-523-3110. Probate: 419-523-3012. Fax: 419-523-5284. 8:30AM-4:30PM (EST). Access by: Fax, mail, in person.

Misdemeanor, Civil Actions Under $15,000, Small Claims—Putnam County Court, 245 E Main, Rm 301, Ottawa, OH 45875. 419-523-3110. Fax: 419-523-5284. 8:30AM-4:30PM (EST). Access by: Mail, in person.

Richland County

Real Estate Recording—Richland County Recorder, 50 Park Avenue East, Mansfield, OH 44902. 419-774-5599. Fax: 419-774-5603. 8AM-4PM (EST).

Felony, Civil Actions Over $10,000, Probate—Common Pleas Court, PO Box 127, Mansfield, OH 44901. 419-774-5690. Probate: 419-755-5583. 8AM-4PM (EST). Access by: In person only.

Misdemeanor, Civil Actions Under $15,000, Eviction, Small Claims—Mansfield Municipal Court, PO Box 1228, Mansfield, OH 44901. 419-755-9600. Fax: 419-755-9647. 8AM-4PM (EST). Access by: Mail, in person.

Ross County

Real Estate Recording—Ross County Recorder, 2 North Paint Street, Courthouse, Chillicothe, OH 45601. 740-702-3000. Fax: 740-702-3006. 8:30AM-4:30PM (EST).

Felony, Civil Actions Over $10,000, Probate—Common Pleas Court, County Courthouse, 2 N Paint St, Ste A, Chillicothe, OH 45601. 740-773-2330. Probate: 740-774-1179. Fax: 740-773-2334. 8AM-4PM (EST). Access by: In person only.

Misdemeanor, Civil Actions Under $15,000, Eviction, Small Claims—Chillicothe Municipal Court, 26 S Paint St, Chillicothe, OH 45601. 740-773-3515. Fax: 740-774-1101. 7:30AM-4:30PM (EST). Access by: Mail, in person.

Sandusky County

Real Estate Recording—Sandusky County Recorder, 100 N. Park Ave., Courthouse, Fremont, OH 43420. 419-334-6226. 8AM-4:30PM (EST).

Felony, Civil Actions Over $3,000, Probate—Common Pleas Court, 100 N Park Ave, Fremont, OH 43420. 419-334-6161. Probate: 419-334-6217. Fax: 419-334-6164. 8AM-4:30PM (EST). Access by: Phone, fax, mail, in person.

Misdemeanor, Civil Actions Under $15,000, Small Claims—County Court #1, 123 W Buckeye St, Clyde, OH 43410. 419-547-0915. Fax: 419-547-9198. 8AM-4:30PM (EST). Access by: Mail, in person.

County Court #2, 128 E Main St, Woodville, OH 43469. 419-849-3961. Fax: 419-849-3932. 8AM-4:30PM (EST). Access by: Phone, fax, mail, in person.

Scioto County

Real Estate Recording—Scioto County Recorder, 602 7th Street, Room 110, Portsmouth, OH 45662. 740-355-8304. Fax: 740-353-7358. 8AM-4:30PM (EST).

Felony, Civil Actions Over $10,000, Probate—Common Pleas Court, 602 7th St, Portsmouth, OH 45662. 740-355-8226. Probate: 740-355-8243. 8AM-4:30PM (EST). Access by: In person only.

Misdemeanor, Civil Actions Under $15,000, Eviction, Small Claims—Portsmouth Municipal Court, 728 2nd St, Portsmouth, OH 45662. 740-354-3283. Fax: 740-353-6645. 8AM-4PM (EST). Access by: Mail, in person.

Seneca County

Real Estate Recording—Seneca County Recorder, 103 South Washington Street, Room 7, Tiffin, OH 44883. 419-447-4434. 8:30AM-4:30PM (EST).

Felony, Civil Actions Over $10,000, Probate—Common Pleas Court, 103 S Washington St, Tiffin, OH 44883. 419-447-0671. Probate: 419-447-3121. Fax: 419-443-7919. 8:30AM-4:30PM (EST). Access by: Mail, in person.

Misdemeanor, Civil Actions Under $15,000, Eviction, Small Claims—Tiffin Municipal Court, PO Box 694, Tiffin, OH 44883. Civil: 419-448-5418. Criminal: 419-448-5411. Fax: 419-448-5419. 8:30AM-4:30PM (EST). Access by: Mail, in person.

Shelby County

Real Estate Recording—Shelby County Recorder, 129 East Court Street, Shelby County Annex, Sidney, OH 45365. 513-498-7270. Fax: 513-498-7272. 7:30AM-4PM (F open until 6PM) (EST).

Felony, Civil Actions Over $10,000, Probate—Common Pleas Court, PO Box 809, Sidney, OH 45365. 513-498-7221. Fax: 513-498-7824. 8:30AM-4:30PM M-Th; 8:30AM-6PM F (EST). Access by: In person only.

Misdemeanor, Civil Actions Under $15,000, Eviction, Small Claims—Sidney Municipal Court, 201 W Poplar, Sidney, OH 45365. 513-498-8109. Fax: 513-498-8179. 8AM-4:30PM (EST). Access by: Phone, fax, mail, in person.

Stark County

Real Estate Recording—Stark County Recorder, 110 Central Plaza South, Suite 170, Canton, OH 44702. 330-438-0443. Fax: 330-438-0394. 8:30AM-4:30PM (Recording: 8:30AM-4PM) (EST).

Felony, Civil Actions Over $10,000, Probate—Common Pleas Court-Civil Division, PO Box 21160, Canton, OH 44701. 330-438-0795. Fax: 330-438-0853. 8:30AM-4:30PM (EST). Access by: Mail, in person.

Felony—Common Pleas Court-Criminal Division, PO Box 21160, Canton, OH 44701-1160. 330-438-0929. Fax: 330-438-0853. 8:30AM-4:30PM (EST). Access by: Phone, mail, in person.

Misdemeanor, Civil Actions Under $15,000, Eviction, Small Claims—Canton Municipal Court, 218 Cleveland Ave SW (PO Box 24218), Canton, OH 44702-4218. 330-489-3203. Fax: 330-489-3075. 8AM-4:30PM (EST). Access by: Phone, fax, mail, in person.

Summit County

Real Estate Recording—Summit County Recorder, 175 South Main Street, Akron, OH 44308. 330-643-2717. Fax: 330-643-8755. 7:30AM-4PM (EST).

Felony, Civil Actions Over $10,000, Probate—Summit County Clerk of Common Pleas Court, 53 University Ave, County Safety Bldg, 2nd Flr, Akron, OH 44308. 330-643-2217. Probate: 216-643-2350. 7:30AM-4PM; Probate hours 8AM-4PM (EST). Access by: Mail, in person.

Misdemeanor, Civil Actions Under $15,000, Eviction, Small Claims—Akron Municipal Court, 217 S High St, Rm 837, Akron, OH 44308. Civil: 330-375-2920. Criminal: 330-375-2570. Fax: 330-375-2427. 8AM-4:30PM (EST). Access by: Mail, in person.

Trumbull County

Real Estate Recording—Trumbull County Recorder, 160 High Street N.W., Warren, OH 44481. 330-675-2401. Fax: 330-675-2404. 8:30AM-4:30PM (EST).

Felony, Civil Actions Over $10,000, Probate—Common Pleas Court, 160 High St, Warren, OH 44481. 330-675-2557. Probate: 216-675-2521. Fax: 330-675-2563. 8:30AM-4:30PM (EST). Access by: Mail, in person.

Misdemeanor, Civil Actions Under $15,000, Eviction, Small Claims—Warren Municipal Court, 141 South St SE (PO Box 1550), Warren, OH 44482. Civil: 330-841-2527. Criminal: 330-841-2666. 8AM-4:30PM (EST). Access by: Mail, in person.

Tuscarawas County

Real Estate Recording—Tuscarawas County Recorder, 125 East High Avenue, New Philadelphia, OH 44663. 330-364-8811. 8AM-4:30PM (EST).

Felony, Civil Actions Over $10,000, Probate—Common Pleas Court, 125 E High (PO Box 628), New Philadelphia, OH 44663. 330-364-8811. Fax: 330-343-4682. 8AM-4:30PM (EST). Access by: In person only.

Misdemeanor, Civil Actions Under $15,000, Small Claims—County Court, 220 E 3rd, Uhrichsville, OH 44683. 614-922-4795. Fax: 614-922-7020. 8AM-4:30PM (EST). Access by: Fax, mail, in person.

New Philadelphia Municipal Court, 166 E High Ave, New Philadelphia, OH 44663. 330-364-4491. Fax: 330-364-6885. 8AM-4PM (EST). Access by: Mail, in person.

Union County

Real Estate Recording—Union County Recorder, 233 West Sixth St., Marysville, OH 43040. 937-645-3032. 8:30AM-4PM (EST).

Felony, Civil Actions Over $10,000, Probate—Common Pleas Court, County Courthouse, 215 W 5th, PO Box 605, Marysville, OH 43040. 937-645-3006. Fax: 937-645-3162. 8:30AM-4PM (EST). Access by: In person only.

Misdemeanor, Civil Actions Under $15,000, Eviction, Small Claims—Marysville Municipal Court, PO Box 322, Marysville, OH 43040. 937-644-9102. 8AM-4PM (EST). Access by: Phone, fax, mail, in person.

Van Wert County

Real Estate Recording—Van Wert County Recorder, 121 East Main Street, Courthouse - Room 206, Van Wert, OH 45891. 419-238-2558. Fax: 419-238-5410. 8:30AM-4PM (M-open until 5PM) (EST).

Felony, Civil Actions Over $10,000, Probate—Common Pleas Court, PO Box 366, Van Wert, OH 45891. 419-238-1022. Probate: 419-238-0027. Fax: 419-238-1022. 8AM-4PM (EST). Access by: In person only.

Misdemeanor, Civil Actions Under $15,000, Eviction, Small Claims—Van Wert Municipal Court, 124 S Market, Van Wert, OH 45891. 419-238-5767. 8AM-4PM (EST). Access by: Mail, in person.

Vinton County

Real Estate Recording—Vinton County Recorder, East Main Street, Courthouse, McArthur, OH 45651. 740-596-4314. 8:30-11:30AM, 12:30-3:30PM M,T,W,F; 8:30AM-11:30AM Th (EST).

Felony, Civil Actions Over $3,000, Probate—Common Pleas Court, County Courthouse, 100 E Main St, McArthur, OH 45651. 740-596-3001. Probate: 740-596-5480. Fax: 740-596-3438. 8:30AM-4PM M-F (EST). Access by: Mail, in person.

Misdemeanor, Civil Actions Under $15,000, Small Claims—Vinton County Court, County Courthouse, McArthur, OH 45651. 740-596-5000. Fax: 740-596-4702. 8:30AM-4PM (EST). Access by: Phone, mail, in person.

Warren County

Real Estate Recording—Warren County Recorder, 320 East Silver Street, Lebanon, OH 45036. 513-933-1382. Fax: 513-933-2949. 8:30AM-4:30PM (EST).

Felony, Civil Actions Over $3,000, Probate—Common Pleas Court, PO Box 238, Lebanon, OH 45036. 513-933-1120. Probate: 513-933-1180. Fax: 513-933-2965. 8:30AM-4:30PM (EST). Access by: Phone, mail, in person.

Misdemeanor, Civil Actions Under $15,000, Small Claims—County Court, 550 Justice Dr, Lebanon, OH 45036. 513-933-1370. 8AM-4:30PM (EST). Access by: Mail, in person.

Washington County

Real Estate Recording—Washington County Recorder, 205 Putnam Street, Courthouse, Marietta, OH 45750. 740-373-6623. Fax: 740-373-9643. 8AM-5PM (EST).

Felony, Civil Actions Over $10,000, Probate—Common Pleas Court, 205 Putname St, Marietta, OH 45750. 740-373-6623. Probate: 740-373-6623. 8AM-4:15PM (EST). Access by: In person only.

Misdemeanor, Civil Actions Under $15,000, Eviction, Small Claims—Marietta Municipal Court, PO Box 615, Marietta, OH 45750. 740-373-4474. Fax: 740-373-2547. 8AM-5PM (EST). Access by: Phone, mail, in person.

Wayne County

Real Estate Recording—Wayne County Recorder, 428 West Liberty Street, Wooster, OH 44691. 330-287-5460. Fax: 330-287-5685. 8AM-4:30PM (EST).

Felony, Civil Actions Over $10,000, Probate—Common Pleas Court, PO Box 507, Wooster, OH 44691. 330-287-5590. Probate: 330-287-5575. 8AM-4:30PM (EST). Access by: Phone, mail, in person.

Misdemeanor, Civil Actions Under $15,000, Eviction, Small Claims—Wayne County Municipal Court, 538 N Market St, Wooster, OH 44691. 330-287-5650. Fax: 330-263-4043. 8AM-4:30PM (EST). Access by: In person only.

Williams County

Real Estate Recording—Williams County Recorder, 1 Courthouse Square, Bryan, OH 43506. 419-636-3259. 8:30AM-4:30PM (EST).

Felony, Civil Actions Over $10,000, Probate—Common Pleas Court, 1 Courthouse Square, Bryan, OH 43506. 419-636-1551. Probate: 419-636-1548. Fax: 419-636-7877. 8:30AM-4:30PM (EST). Access by: In person only.

Misdemeanor, Civil Actions Under $15,000, Eviction, Small Claims—Bryan Municipal Court, 516 E High, PO Box 546, Bryan, OH 43506. 419-636-6939. Fax: 419-636-3417. 8:30AM-4:30PM (EST). Access by: Mail, in person.

Wood County

Real Estate Recording—Wood County Recorder, 1 Courthouse Square, Bowling Green, OH 43402. 419-354-9140. 8:30AM-4:30PM (EST).

Felony, Civil Actions Over $10,000, Probate—Common Pleas Court, Courthouse Square, Bowling Green, OH 43402. 419-354-9280. Probate: 419-354-9230. Fax: 419-354-9241. 8:30AM-4:30PM (EST). Access by: Phone, mail, in person.

Misdemeanor, Civil Actions Under $15,000, Eviction, Small Claims—Bowling Green Municipal Court, PO Box 326, Bowling Green, OH 43402. 419-352-5263. Fax: 419-

352-9407. 8:30AM-4:30PM (EST). Access by: Phone, fax, mail, in person.

Perrysburg Municipal Court, 300 Walnut, Perrysburg, OH 43551. 419-872-7900. Fax: 419-872-7905. 8AM-4:30PM (EST). Access by: Phone, fax, mail, remote online, in person.

Wyandot County

Real Estate Recording—Wyandot County Recorder, Courthouse, 109 S. Sandusky Ave., Upper Sandusky, OH 43351. 419-294-1442. 8:30AM-4:30PM (EST).

Felony, Civil Actions Over $10,000, Probate—Common Pleas Court, 109 S Sandusky Ave, Upper Sandusky, OH 43351. 419-294-1432. Probate: 419-294-2302. 8:30AM-4:30PM (EST). Access by: Mail, in person.

Misdemeanor, Civil Actions Under $15,000, Eviction, Small Claims—Upper Sandusky Municipal Court, 119 N 7th St, Upper Sandusky, OH 43351. 419-294-3354. Fax: 419-294-6767. 8AM-4:30PM (EST). Access by: Mail, in person.

Federal Courts

US District Court

Northern District of Ohio

Akron Division, US District Court 568 Federal Bldg, 2 S Main St, Akron, OH 44308. 330-375-5407. Counties: Carroll, Holmes, Portage, Stark, Summit, Tuscarawas, Wayne

Cleveland Division, US District Court 201 Superior Ave, NE, Cleveland, OH 44114. 330-522-4355. Counties: Ashland, Ashtabula, Crawford, Cuyahoga, Geauga, Lake, Lorain, Medina, Richland. Cases prior to July 1995 for the counties of Ashland, Crawford, Medina and Richland are located in the Akron Division

Toledo Division, US District Court 114 US Courthouse, 1716 Spielbusch, Toledo, OH 43624. 419-259-6412. Counties: Allen, Auglaize, Defiance, Erie, Fulton, Hancock, Hardin, Henry, Huron, Lucas, Marion, Mercer, Ottawa, Paulding, Putnam, Sandusky, Seneca, Van Wert, Williams, Wood, Wyandot

Youngstown Division, US District Court 337 Federal Bldg, 125 Market St, Youngstown, OH 44503-1787. 330-746-1726. Counties: Columbiana, Mahoning, Trumbull. This division was reactivated in the middle of 1995. Older cases will be found in Akron or Cleveland

Southern District of Ohio

Cincinnati Division, US District Court Clerk, US District Court, 324 Courthouse Bldg, 100 E 5th St, Cincinnati, OH 45202. 513-564-7500. Counties: Adams, Brown, Butler, Clermont, Clinton, Hamilton, Highland, Lawrence, Scioto, Warren

Columbus Division, US District Court Office of the Clerk, Room 260, 85 Marconi Blvd, Columbus, OH 43215. 614-469-5442. Counties: Athens, Belmont, Coshocton, Delaware, Fairfield, Fayette, Franklin, Gallia, Guernsey, Harrison, Hocking, Jackson, Jefferson, Knox, Licking, Logan, Madison, Meigs, Monroe, Morgan, Morrow, Muskingum, Noble, Perry, Pickaway, Pike, Ross, Union, Vinton, Washington

Dayton Division, US District Court Federal Bldg, 200 W 2nd, Room 712, Dayton, OH 45402. 513-225-2896. Counties: Champaign, Clark, Darke, Greene, Miami, Montgomery, Preble, Shelby

US Bankruptcy Court

Northern District of Ohio

Akron Division, US Bankruptcy Court, 455 Federal Bldg, 2 S Main, Akron, OH 44308. 330-375-5840. Voice Case Information System: 330-489-4731. Counties: Medina, Portage, Summit

Canton Division, US Bankruptcy Court, Frank T Bow Federal Bldg, 201 Cleveland Ave SW, Canton, OH 44702. 330-489-4426. Voice Case Information System: 330-489-4731. Counties: Ashland, Carroll, Crawford, Holmes, Richland, Stark, Tuscarawas, Wayne

Cleveland Division, US Bankruptcy Court, 127 Public Square, Key Tower, 31st Floor, Cleveland, OH 44114. 216-522-4373. Voice Case Information System: 330-489-4731. Counties: Cuyahoga, Geauga, Lake, Lorain

Toledo Division, US Bankruptcy Court, Room 411, 1716 Spielbusch Ave, Toledo, OH 43624. 419-259-6440. Voice Case Information System: 330-489-4731. Counties: Allen, Auglaize, Defiance, Erie, Fulton, Hancock, Hardin, Henry, Huron, Lucas, Marion, Mercer, Ottawa, Paulding, Putnam, Sandusky, Seneca, Van Wert, Williams, Wood, Wyandot

Youngstown Division, US Bankruptcy Court, PO Box 147, Youngstown, OH 44501. 330-746-7027. Voice Case Information System: 330-489-4731. Counties: Ashtabula, Columbiana, Mahoning, Trumbull

Southern District of Ohio

Cincinnati Division, US Bankruptcy Court, Atrium Two, 221 E Fourth St, Suite 800, Cincinnati, OH 45202. 513-684-2572. Voice Case Information System: 513-225-2544. Counties: Adams, Brown, Clermont, Hamilton, Highland, Lawrence, Scioto. They also some cases from Butler.

Columbus Division, US Bankruptcy Court, 170 N High St, Columbus, OH 43215. 614-469-6638. Voice Case Information System: 513-225-2562. Counties: Athens, Belmont, Coshocton, Delaware, Fairfield, Fayette, Franklin, Gallia, Guernsey, Harrison, Hocking, Jackson, Jefferson, Knox, Licking, Logan, Madison, Meigs, Monroe, Morgan, Morrow, Muskingum, Noble, Perry, Pickaway, Pike, Ross, Union, Vinton, Washington

Dayton Division, US Bankruptcy Court, 120 W 3rd St, Dayton, OH 45402. 937-225-2516. Voice Case Information System: 513-225-2544. Counties: Butler, Champaign, Clark, Clinton, Darke, Greene, Miami, Montgomery, Preble, Shelby, Warren

Oklahoma

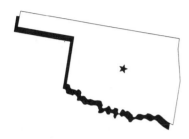

Capitol: Oklahoma City (Oklahoma County)	
Number of Counties: 77	**Population:** 3,277,687
County Court Locations:	**Federal Court Locations:**
•District Courts: 80/26 Districts	•District Courts: 3
Municipal Courts of Record: 2	•Bankruptcy Courts: 3
Municipal Courts Not of Record: 340	**State Agencies:** 18
Workers' Compensation Courts: 1	

State Agencies—Summary

General Help Numbers:

State Archives

Libraries Department	405-521-2502
Archives & Records Office	Fax: 405-525-7804
200 NE 18th St	8AM-5PM
Oklahoma City, OK 73105-3298	
Reference Librarian:	405-521-2502

Governor's Office

Office of the Governor	405-521-2342
State Capitol, Suite 212	Fax: 405-521-3353
Oklahoma City, OK 73105	8AM-5PM

Attorney General's Office

Attorney General's Office	405-521-3921
112 State Capitol	Fax: 405-521-6246
Oklahoma City, OK 73105	8:30AM-5PM

State Legislation

Oklahoma Legislature	405-521-5642
State Capitol	8:30PM-4:30PM
Status Info-Room 309, Copies-Room 310	
Oklahoma City, OK 73105	
Alternate Telephone:	405-524-0126

Important State Internet Sites:

> 🌐 **Webscape**
>
> **File   Edit   View**   **Help**

State of Oklahoma World Wide Web

www.state.ok.us/

Extensive web site with links to arts & culture, business, science and technology, education, environment, events, State Government and politics, health and human services and e-mail addresses.

Oklahoma Legislature

www.lsb.state.ok.us/

This site contains links to the state House and Senate home pages, and a link to bill information.

Oklahoma Legislative Bills

www.lsb.state.ok.us/docs/billtext.html

This site provides the information necessary to obtain the full text of bills. No bills are available online.

U.S. Senate and House Information

www.state.ok.us/osfdocs/ussen.html
www.state.ok.us/osfdocs/usreps.html

This site links to the members of the U.S. Senate and House in Oklahoma. Different information is available at the site of each member.

Unclaimed Property

www.kocotv.com/5oys/fortune.html

This site allows you to search online for unclaimed property.

State Agencies—Public Records

Criminal Records
State Bureau of Investigation, Criminal History Information, PO Box 11497, Oklahoma City, OK 73136, Main Telephone: 405-848-6724, Hours: 8AM-5PM. Access by: mail, visit.

Corporation Records
Limited Liability Company Records
Limited Partnerships
Trademarks/Servicemarks
Secretary of State, 2300 N Lincoln Blvd, Oklahoma City, OK 73105-4897, Main Telephone: 405-521-3911, Corporate Records: 900-825-2424, Fax: 405-521-3771, Hours: 8AM-5PM. Access by: mail, fax, phone, visit.

Uniform Commercial Code
Federal Tax Liens
State Tax Liens
UCC Recorder, Oklahoma County Clerk, 320 R.S. Kerr Ave, County Office Bldg, Rm 105, Oklahoma City, OK 73102, Main Telephone: 405-278-1521, Hours: 8AM-5PM. Access by: mail, visit.

Sales Tax Registrations
Taxpayer Assistance, Business Tax Division, 2501 N Lincoln Blvd, Oklahoma City, OK 73194, Main Telephone: 405-521-3160, Fax: 405-522-0576, Hours: 7:30AM-4:30PM. Access by: mail, phone.

Birth Certificates
State Department of Health, Vital Records Section, PO Box 53551, Oklahoma City, OK 73152, Main Telephone: 405-271-4040, Hours: 8:30AM-4PM. Access by: mail, visit.

Death Records
State Department of Health, Vital Records Section, PO Box 53551, Oklahoma City, OK 73152, Main Telephone: 405-271-4040, Hours: 8:30AM-4PM. Access by: mail, visit.

Marriage Certificates
Divorce Records
Records not available from state agency.

Workers' Compensation Records
Workers Compensation, 1915 W Stiles, Oklahoma City, OK 73105-4918, Main Telephone: 405-557-7600, Fax: 405-557-7647, Hours: 8AM-5PM. Access by: mail, visit.

Driver Records
Department of Public Safety, Driver's Record Services, PO Box 11415, Oklahoma City, OK 73136, Main Telephone: 405-425-2226, Hours: 8AM-4:45PM. Access by: mail, visit. Copies of tickets may be obtained for $3.00 per page from the address listed above. Most tickets are two pages.

Vehicle Ownership
Vehicle Identification
Oklahoma Tax Commission, Motor Vehicle Division, Attn: Research, 2501 N Lincoln Blvd, Oklahoma City, OK 73194, Main Telephone: 405-521-3221, Hours: 7:30AM-4:30PM. Access by: mail, visit.

Accident Reports
Department of Public Safety, Accident Reports Section, PO Box 11415, Oklahoma City, OK 73136, Main Telephone: 405-425-2192, Fax: 405-425-2046, Hours: 8AM-4:45PM. Access by: mail, phone, visit.

Hunting License Information
Fishing License Information
Records not available from state agency.

County Courts and Recording Offices

What You Need to Know...

About the Courts

About the Recorder's Office

Administration

Administrative Director of Courts   405-521-2450
1915 N Stiles, #305
Oklahoma City, OK 73105

Court Structure

Cities with populations in excess of 200,000 (Oklahoma City and Tulsa) have municipal criminal courts of record; those with less than 200,000 do not have such courts.

Online Access

Online computer access for **internal** use **only**, is available through the Case Processing System(**CPS**) for 9 counties with a goal of 18 counties at a time in the future to be determined. Access is available only through a "state" terminal. CPS will be expanded to include the entire state in "the distant future," at which time external access may be considered.

Case information is available in bulk for download to computer. For information, call the Administrative Director of Courts, 405-521-2450.

Organization

77 counties, 77 filing offices. The recording officer is County Clerk. The entire state is in the Central Time Zone (CST).

UCC Records

Financing statements are filed centrally with the County Clerk of Oklahoma County, except for consumer goods, which are dual filed, and farm related and real estate related collateral, which are filed with the County Clerk. All counties will perform UCC searches. Use search request form UCC-4. Search fees are usually $5.00 per debtor name for a written request and $3.00 per name by telephone. Copies usually cost $1.00 per page.

Lien Records

Federal tax liens on personal property of businesses are filed with the County Clerk of Oklahoma County, which is the central filing office for the state. Other federal and all state tax liens are filed with the County Clerk. Usually state and federal tax liens on personal property are filed in separate indexes. Some counties will perform tax lien searches. Search fees vary. Other liens include judgments, mechanics, physicians, and hospital.

Real Estate Records

Many counties will perform real estate searches by legal description. Copy fees are usually $1.00 per page. Certification usually costs $1.00 per document.

County Courts and Recording Offices

Adair County

Real Estate Recording—Adair County Clerk, Division Street & Highway 59, Stilwell, OK 74960. 918-696-7198. Fax: 918-696-2603. 8AM-4:30PM (CST).

Felony, Misdemeanor, Civil, Eviction, Small Claims, Probate—15th Judicial District Court, PO Box 426 (220 W Division), Stilwell, OK 74960. 918-696-7633. 8AM-4PM (CST). Access by: Mail, in person.

Alfalfa County

Real Estate Recording—Alfalfa County Clerk, 300 South Grand, Cherokee, OK 73728. 405-596-3158. 8:30AM-4:30PM (CST).

Felony, Misdemeanor, Civil, Eviction, Small Claims, Probate—4th Judicial District Court, County Courthouse, Cherokee, OK 73728. 405-596-3523. 8:30AM-4:30PM (CST). Access by: Phone, mail, in person.

Atoka County

Real Estate Recording—Atoka County Clerk, 200 East Court Street, Atoka, OK 74525. 405-889-5157. Fax: 405-889-5063. 8:30AM-4:30PM (CST).

Felony, Misdemeanor, Civil, Eviction, Small Claims, Probate—25th Judicial District Court, 200 E. Court St, Atoka, OK 74525. 405-889-3565. 8:30AM-4:30PM (CST). Access by: Mail, in person.

Beaver County

Real Estate Recording—Beaver County Clerk, 111 West Second Street, Beaver, OK 73932. 405-625-3141. Fax: 405-625-3430. 9AM-5PM (CST).

Felony, Misdemeanor, Civil, Eviction, Small Claims, Probate—1st Judicial District Court, PO Box 237, Beaver, OK 73932. 405-625-3191. 9AM-Noon, 1-5PM (CST). Access by: Mail, in person.

Beckham County

Real Estate Recording—Beckham County Clerk, Courthouse, 302 E. Main St., Sayre, OK 73662. 405-928-3383. 9AM-5PM (CST).

Felony, Misdemeanor, Civil, Eviction, Small Claims, Probate—2nd Judicial District Court, PO Box 520, Sayre, OK 73662. 405-928-3330. 9:00AM-5:00PM (CST). Access by: Mail, in person.

Blaine County

Real Estate Recording—Blaine County Clerk, 212 North Weigel, Watonga, OK 73772. 405-623-5890. Fax: 405-623-5009. 8AM-4PM (CST).

Felony, Misdemeanor, Civil, Eviction, Small Claims, Probate—4th Judicial District Court, 212 N. Weigle, Watonga, OK 73772. 405-623-5970. 8:00AM-4:00PM (CST). Access by: Mail, in person.

Bryan County

Real Estate Recording—Bryan County Clerk, 402 West Evergreen, Durant, OK 74701. 405-924-2202. Fax: 405-924-3094. 8AM-Noon, 1-5PM (CST).

Felony, Misdemeanor, Civil, Eviction, Small Claims, Probate—19th Judicial District Court, Courthouse 3rd Fl, Durant, OK 74701. 405-924-1446. 8:00AM-12:00PM, 1:00PM-5:00PM (CST). Access by: Mail, in person.

Caddo County

Real Estate Recording—Caddo County Clerk, Southwest Second & Oklahoma, Anadarko, OK 73005. 405-247-6609. Fax: 405-247-6510. 8:30AM-4:30PM (CST).

Felony, Misdemeanor, Civil, Eviction, Small Claims, Probate—6th Judicial District Court, PO Box 10, Anadarko, OK 73005. 405-247-3393. 8:30AM-4:30PM (CST). Access by: Mail, in person.

Canadian County

Real Estate Recording—Canadian County Clerk, 201 North Choctaw, El Reno, OK 73036. 405-262-1070. Fax: 405-422-2411. 8AM-4:30PM (CST).

Felony, Misdemeanor, Civil, Eviction, Small Claims, Probate—26th Judicial District Court, PO Box 730, El Reno, OK 73036. 405-262-1070. 8AM-4:30PM (CST). Access by: Mail, in person.

Carter County

Real Estate Recording—Carter County Clerk, 1st & B SW, Ardmore, OK 73401. 405-223-8162. 8AM-5PM (CST).

Felony, Misdemeanor, Civil, Eviction, Small Claims, Probate—20th Judicial District Court, PO Box 37, Ardmore, OK 73402. 405-223-5253. 8AM-NOON, 1PM-5PM (CST). Access by: Mail, in person.

Cherokee County

Real Estate Recording—Cherokee County Clerk, 213 West Delaware, Room 200, Tahlequah, OK 74464. 918-456-3171. 8AM-4:30PM (Recording hours 8AM-4PM) (CST).

Felony, Misdemeanor, Civil, Eviction, Small Claims, Probate—15th Judicial District Court, 213 W. Delaware, Tahlequah, OK 74464. 918-456-0691. Fax: 918-458-6587. 8:00AM-4:30PM (CST). Access by: Phone, mail, in person.

Choctaw County

Real Estate Recording—Choctaw County Clerk, Courthouse, 300 E. Duke, Hugo, OK 74743. 405-326-3778. Fax: 405-326-6787. 8:30AM-4:30PM (CST).

Felony, Misdemeanor, Civil, Eviction, Small Claims, Probate—17th Judicial District Court, 300 E. Duke, Hugo, OK 74743. 405-326-7555. 8AM-4PM (CST). Access by: Mail, in person.

Cimarron County

Real Estate Recording—Cimarron County Clerk, Courthouse Square, Boise City, OK 73933. 405-544-2251. Fax: 405-544-3420. 8AM-Noon, 1-5PM (CST).

Felony, Misdemeanor, Civil, Eviction, Small Claims, Probate—1st Judicial District Court, PO Box 788, Boise City, OK 73933. 405-544-2221. 9AM-Noon, 1-5PM (CST). Access by: Phone, mail, in person.

Cleveland County

Real Estate Recording—Cleveland County Clerk, 201 South Jones, Room 204, Norman, OK 73069. 405-366-0240. 8:30AM-4:30PM (CST).

Civil, Eviction, Small Claims, Probate—21st Judicial District Court-Civil Branch, 200 S. Peters, Norman, OK 73069. 405-321-6402. 8:00AM-5:00PM (CST). Access by: Mail, in person.

Felony, Misdemeanor—21st Judicial District Court-Criminal, 200 S. Peters, Norman, OK 73069. 405-321-6402. 8:00AM-5:00PM (CST). Access by: Mail, in person.

Coal County

Real Estate Recording—Coal County Clerk, 4 North Main, Suite 1, Coalgate, OK 74538. 405-927-2103. Fax: 405-927-4003. 8AM-5PM (CST).

Felony, Misdemeanor, Civil, Eviction, Small Claims, Probate—25th Judicial District Court, 4 N Main #9, Coalgate, OK 74538. 405-927-2281. 8AM-5PM (CST). Access by: Mail, in person.

Comanche County

Real Estate Recording—Comanche County Clerk, 315 SW 5th, Room 304, Lawton, OK 73501. 405-355-5214. 8:30AM-5PM (CST).

Felony, Misdemeanor, Civil, Eviction, Small Claims, Probate—5th Judicial District Court, 315 SW 5th Street,

Rm 504, Lawton, OK 73501-4390. 405-355-4017. 8AM-5PM (CST). Access by: Mail, in person.

Cotton County

Real Estate Recording—Cotton County Clerk, 301 North Broadway, Walters, OK 73572. 405-875-3026. Fax: 405-875-3756. 8AM-4:30PM (CST).

Felony, Misdemeanor, Civil, Eviction, Small Claims, Probate—5th Judicial District Court, 301 N. Broadway, Walters, OK 73572. 405-875-3029. 8:00AM-4:30PM (CST). Access by: Phone, mail, in person.

Craig County

Real Estate Recording—Craig County Clerk, Courthouse, Vinita, OK 74301. 918-256-2507. Fax: 918-256-3617. 8:30AM-4:30PM (CST).

Felony, Misdemeanor, Civil, Eviction, Small Claims, Probate—12th Judicial District Court, 301 W. Canadian, Vinita, OK 74301. 918-256-6451. 8:30AM-4:30PM (CST). Access by: Mail, in person.

Creek County

Real Estate Recording—Creek County Clerk, 317 E. Lee, First Floor, Sapulpa, OK 74066. 918-224-4084. 8AM-5PM (CST).

Felony, Misdemeanor, Civil, Eviction, Small Claims, Probate—24th Judicial District Court, PO Box 1410, Sapulpa, OK 74067. 918-227-2525. Fax: 918-227-5030. 8AM-5PM (CST). Access by: In person only.

Custer County

Real Estate Recording—Custer County Clerk, 675 West "B" Street, Arapaho, OK 73620. 405-323-1221. Fax: 405-323-4421. 8AM-4PM (CST).

Felony, Misdemeanor, Civil, Eviction, Small Claims, Probate—2nd Judicial District Court, Box D, Arapaho, OK 73620. 405-323-3233. Fax: 405-331-1121. 8AM-4PM (CST). Access by: Mail, in person.

Delaware County

Real Estate Recording—Delaware County Clerk, 327 5th Street, Jay, OK 74346. 918-253-4520. 8AM-4:30PM (CST).

Felony, Misdemeanor, Civil, Eviction, Small Claims, Probate—13th Judicial District Court, Box 407, Jay, OK 74346. 918-253-4420. 8:30AM-4:30PM (CST). Access by: Mail, in person.

Dewey County

Real Estate Recording—Dewey County Clerk, Corner of Broadway & Ruble, Taloga, OK 73667. 405-328-5361. 8AM-4PM (CST).

Felony, Misdemeanor, Civil, Eviction, Small Claims, Probate—4th Judicial District Court, Box 278, Taloga, OK 73667. 405-328-5521. 8AM-4PM (CST). Access by: Phone, mail, in person.

Ellis County

Real Estate Recording—Ellis County Clerk, 100 Courthouse Square, Arnett, OK 73832. 405-885-7301. Fax: 405-885-7258. 8:30AM-4:30PM (CST).

Felony, Misdemeanor, Civil, Eviction, Small Claims, Probate—2nd Judicial District Court, Box 217, Arnett, OK 73832. 405-885-7255. 8:30AM-4:30PM (CST). Access by: Phone, mail, in person.

Garfield County

Real Estate Recording—Garfield County Clerk, 114 West Broadway, Enid, OK 73701. 405-237-0226. Fax: 405-249-5951. 8AM-4PM (CST).

Felony, Misdemeanor, Civil, Eviction, Small Claims, Probate—4th Judicial District Court, 114 W Broadway, Enid, OK 73701-4024. 405-237-0232. 8:00AM-4:30PM (CST). Access by: Mail, in person.

Garvin County

Real Estate Recording—Garvin County Clerk, 201 West Grant, Pauls Valley, OK 73075. 405-238-2772. Fax: 405-238-6283. 8:30AM-4:30PM (CST).

Felony, Misdemeanor, Civil, Eviction, Small Claims, Probate—21st Judicial District Court, PO Box 239, Pauls Valley, OK 73075. 405-238-5596. 8:30AM-4:30PM (CST). Access by: Mail, in person.

Grady County

Real Estate Recording—Grady County Clerk, 4th & Choctaw, Chickasha, OK 73018. 405-224-7388. Fax: 405-222-4506. 8AM-4:30PM (CST).

Felony, Misdemeanor, Civil, Eviction, Small Claims, Probate—6th Judicial District Court, PO Box 605, 328 Choctaw St, Chickasha, OK 73023. 405-224-7446. 8:00AM-4:30PM (CST). Access by: Mail, in person.

Grant County

Real Estate Recording—Grant County Clerk, 112 East Guthrie, Medford, OK 73759. 405-395-2274. 8AM-4:30PM (CST).

Felony, Misdemeanor, Civil, Eviction, Small Claims, Probate—4th Judicial District Court, 100 E Guthrie, Medford, OK 73759. 405-395-2828. 8AM-4:30PM (CST). Access by: Mail, in person.

Greer County

Real Estate Recording—Greer County Clerk, Courthouse Square, Mangum, OK 73554. 405-782-3664. Fax: 405-782-3803. 9AM-Noon,1-5PM (CST).

Felony, Misdemeanor, Civil, Eviction, Small Claims, Probate—2nd Judicial District Court, PO Box 216, Mangum, OK 73554. 405-782-3665. 8:30AM-4:30PM (CST). Access by: Mail, in person.

Harmon County

Real Estate Recording—Harmon County Clerk, Courthouse, Hollis, OK 73550. 405-688-3658. (CST).

Felony, Misdemeanor, Civil, Eviction, Small Claims, Probate—2nd Judicial District Court, 114 W. Hollis, Hollis, OK 73550. 405-688-3617. 8:00AM-5:00PM (CST). Access by: Phone, mail, in person.

Harper County

Real Estate Recording—Harper County Clerk, 311 SE First Street, Buffalo, OK 73834. 405-735-2012. 9AM-5PM (CST).

Felony, Misdemeanor, Civil, Eviction, Small Claims, Probate—1st Judicial District Court, Box 347, Buffalo, OK 73834. 405-735-2010. 9:00AM-5:00PM (CST). Access by: Phone, mail, in person.

Haskell County

Real Estate Recording—Haskell County Clerk, 202 East Main, Courthouse, Stigler, OK 74462. 918-967-2884. Fax: 918-967-2885. 8AM-4:30PM (CST).

Felony, Misdemeanor, Civil, Eviction, Small Claims, Probate—16th Judicial District Court, 202 E. Main, Stigler, OK 74462. 918-967-3323. Fax: 918-967-2443. 8:00AM-4:30PM (CST). Access by: Phone, fax, mail, in person.

Hughes County

Real Estate Recording—Hughes County Clerk, 200 North Broadway ST. #5, Holdenville, OK 74848. 405-379-5487. 8AM-4:30PM (CST).

Felony, Misdemeanor, Civil, Eviction, Small Claims, Probate—22nd Judicial District Court, Box 32, Holdenville, OK 74848. 405-379-3384. 8AM-4:30PM (CST). Access by: Mail, in person.

Jackson County

Real Estate Recording—Jackson County Clerk, Main & Broadway, Courthouse-Room 203, Altus, OK 73522. 405-482-4070. 9AM-5PM (CST).

Felony, Misdemeanor, Civil, Eviction, Small Claims, Probate—3rd Judicial District Court, 101 N. Main, Rm. 303, Altus, OK 73521. 405-482-0448. 9:00AM-5:00PM (CST). Access by: Mail, in person.

Jefferson County

Real Estate Recording—Jefferson County Clerk, 220 North Main, Courthouse - Room 103, Waurika, OK 73573. 405-228-2029. Fax: 405-228-3418. 8AM-4PM (CST).

Felony, Misdemeanor, Civil, Eviction, Small Claims, Probate—5th Judicial District Court, 220 N. Main, Waurika, OK 73573. 405-228-2961. 8:00AM-4:00PM (CST). Access by: Mail, in person.

Johnston County

Real Estate Recording—Johnston County Clerk, 414 West Main, Room 101, Tishomingo, OK 73460. 405-371-3184. 8:30AM-4:30PM (CST).

Felony, Misdemeanor, Civil, Eviction, Small Claims, Probate—20th Judicial District Court, 414 W. 9th Suite 201, Tishomingo, OK 73460. 405-371-3281. 8:30AM-4:30PM (CST). Access by: Phone, mail, in person.

Kay County

Real Estate Recording—Kay County Clerk, Courthouse, 201 S. Main, Newkirk, OK 74647. 405-362-2537. Fax: 405-362-3300. 8AM-4:30PM (CST).

Felony, Misdemeanor, Civil, Eviction, Small Claims, Probate—8th Judicial District Court, Box 428, Newkirk, OK 74647. 405-362-2350. 8:00AM-4:30PM (CST). Access by: Mail, in person.

Kingfisher County

Real Estate Recording—Kingfisher County Clerk, 101 South Main, Room #3, Kingfisher, OK 73750. 405-375-3887. Fax: 405-375-6033. 8AM-4:30PM (CST).

Felony, Misdemeanor, Civil, Eviction, Small Claims, Probate—4th Judicial District Court, Box 328, Kingfisher, OK 73750. 405-375-3813. 8:30AM-4:30PM (CST). Access by: Mail, in person.

Kiowa County

Real Estate Recording—Kiowa County Clerk, 316 South Main, Hobart, OK 73651. 405-726-5286. Fax: 405-726-6033. 9AM-5PM (CST).

Felony, Misdemeanor, Civil, Eviction, Small Claims, Probate—3rd Judicial District Court, Box 854, Hobart, OK 73651. 405-726-5125. 9:00AM-5:00PM (CST). Access by: Phone, mail, in person.

Latimer County

Real Estate Recording—Latimer County Clerk, 109 North Central, Room 103, Wilburton, OK 74578. 918-465-3543. Fax: 918-465-4001. 8AM-4:30PM (CST).

Felony, Misdemeanor, Civil, Eviction, Small Claims, Probate—16th Judicial District Court, 109 N. Central, Rm 200, Wilburton, OK 74578. 918-465-2011. 8AM-4:30PM (CST). Access by: Phone, mail, in person.

Le Flore County

Real Estate Recording—Le Flore County Clerk, 100 South Broadway, Poteau, OK 74953. 918-647-5738. Fax: 918-647-8930. 8AM-5PM (CST).

Felony, Misdemeanor, Civil, Eviction, Small Claims, Probate—16th Judicial District Court, PO Box 688, Poteau, OK 74953. 918-647-3181. 8AM-4:30PM (CST). Access by: Mail, in person.

Lincoln County

Real Estate Recording—Lincoln County Clerk, Courthouse, 800 Manvel Ave., Chandler, OK 74834. 405-258-1264. 8:30AM-4:30PM (CST).

Felony, Misdemeanor, Civil, Eviction, Small Claims, Probate—23rd Judicial District Court, PO Box 307, Chandler, OK 74834. 405-258-1309. 8:00AM-4:30PM (CST). Access by: Mail, in person.

Logan County

Real Estate Recording—Logan County Clerk, 301 East Harrison, Suite 102, Guthrie, OK 73044. 405-282-0266. 8:30AM-4:30PM (CST).

Felony, Misdemeanor, Civil, Eviction, Small Claims, Probate—9th Judicial District Court, 301 E. Harrison, Guthrie, OK 73044. 405-282-0123. 8:30AM-4:30PM (CST). Access by: Mail, in person.

Love County

Real Estate Recording—Love County Clerk, 405 West Main, Room 203, Marietta, OK 73448. 405-276-3059. 8AM-Noon, 12:30-4:30PM (CST).

Felony, Misdemeanor, Civil, Eviction, Small Claims, Probate—20th Judicial District Court, 405 W. Main, Marietta, OK 73448. 405-276-2235. 8AM-4:30PM (CST). Access by: Mail, in person.

Major County

Real Estate Recording—Major County Clerk, 9th & Broadway, Fairview, OK 73737. 405-227-4732. Fax: 405-227-2736. 8:30AM-4:30PM (CST).

Felony, Misdemeanor, Civil, Eviction, Small Claims, Probate—4th Judicial District Court, 500 E Broadway, Fairview, OK 73737. 405-227-4690. 8:30AM-4:30PM (CST). Access by: Phone, mail, in person.

Marshall County

Real Estate Recording—Marshall County Clerk, Marshall County Courthouse, Room 101, Madill, OK 73446. 405-795-3220. 8:30AM-Noon, 12:30-5PM (CST).

Felony, Misdemeanor, Civil, Eviction, Small Claims, Probate—20th Judicial District Court, Box 58, Madill, OK 73446. 405-795-3278. 8:30AM-5:00PM (CST). Access by: Phone, mail, in person.

Mayes County

Real Estate Recording—Mayes County Clerk, Northeast 1st Street, Pryor, OK 74361. 918-825-2426. Fax: 918-825-2913. 9AM-5PM (CST).

Felony, Misdemeanor, Civil, Eviction, Small Claims, Probate—12th Judicial District Court, Box 867, Pryor, OK 74362. 918-825-2185. 9AM-5PM (CST). Access by: Phone, mail, in person.

McClain County

Real Estate Recording—McClain County Clerk, 2nd & Washington, Purcell, OK 73080. 405-527-3360. 8AM-4:30PM (CST).

Felony, Misdemeanor, Civil, Eviction, Small Claims, Probate—21st Judicial District Court, 121 N. 2nd Rm 231, Purcell, OK 73080. 405-527-3221. 8:00AM-4:30PM (CST). Access by: Mail, in person.

McCurtain County

Real Estate Recording—McCurtain County Clerk, 108 North Central, Idabel, OK 74745. 405-286-2370. 8AM-4PM (CST).

Felony, Misdemeanor, Civil, Eviction, Small Claims, Probate—17th Judicial District Court, Box 1378, Idabel, OK 74745. 405-286-3693. Fax: 405-286-7095. 8:00AM-4:00PM (CST). Access by: Mail, in person.

McIntosh County

Real Estate Recording—McIntosh County Clerk, 110 North 1st Street, Eufaula, OK 74432. 918-689-2741. Fax: 918-689-3385. 8AM-4PM (CST).

Felony, Misdemeanor, Civil, Eviction, Small Claims, Probate—18th Judicial District Court, Box 426, Eufaula, OK 74432. 918-689-2282. 8:00AM-4:00PM (CST). Access by: Phone, mail, in person.

Murray County

Real Estate Recording—Murray County Clerk, 10th & Wyandotte, Sulphur, OK 73086. 405-622-3920. Fax: 405-622-6209. 7:30AM-Noon, 1-4:30PM (CST).

Felony, Misdemeanor, Civil, Eviction, Small Claims, Probate—20th Judicial District Court, Box 578, Sulphur, OK 73086. 405-622-3223. 8AM-4:30PM, closed for lunch (CST). Access by: Phone, mail, in person.

Muskogee County

Real Estate Recording—Muskogee County Clerk, Corner of State & Court Streets, Muskogee, OK 74401. 918-682-7781. 8AM-4:30PM (CST).

Felony, Misdemeanor, Civil, Eviction, Small Claims, Probate—15th Judicial District Court, Box 1350, Muskogee, OK 74402. 918-682-7873. 8AM-4:30PM (CST). Access by: Mail, in person.

Noble County

Real Estate Recording—Noble County Clerk, 300 Courthouse Dr., Courthouse, Box 11, Perry, OK 73077. 405-336-2141. Fax: 405-336-2481. 8AM-4PM (CST).

Felony, Misdemeanor, Civil, Eviction, Small Claims, Probate—8th Judicial District Court, 300 Courthouse Dr, Box 14, Perry, OK 73077. 405-336-5187. 8AM-4:30PM (CST). Access by: Mail, in person.

Nowata County

Real Estate Recording—Nowata County Clerk, 229 North Maple, Nowata, OK 74048. 918-273-2480. Fax: 918-273-2481. 8AM-4:30PM (CST).

Felony, Misdemeanor, Civil, Eviction, Small Claims, Probate—11th Judicial District Court, 229 N. Maple, Nowata, OK 74048. 918-273-0127. 8:00AM-4:30PM (CST). Access by: Mail, in person.

Okfuskee County

Real Estate Recording—Okfuskee County Clerk, 3rd & Atlanta, Okfuskee County Courthouse, Okemah, OK 74859. 918-623-1724. Fax: 918-623-0739. 8AM-4PM (CST).

Felony, Misdemeanor, Civil, Eviction, Small Claims, Probate—24th Judicial District Court, Box 30, Okemah, OK 74859. 918-623-0525. 8:30AM-4:30PM (CST). Access by: Phone, mail, in person.

Oklahoma County

Real Estate Recording—Oklahoma County Clerk, 320 Robert S. Kerr Avenue, Room 203, Oklahoma City, OK 73102. 405-278-1521. 8AM-5PM (CST).

Felony, Misdemeanor, Civil, Eviction, Small Claims, Probate—7th Judicial District Court, 320 Robert S. Kerr St, Oklahoma City, OK 73102. 405-236-2727. 8AM-5PM (CST). Access by: Mail, in person.

Okmulgee County

Real Estate Recording—Okmulgee County Clerk, 7th & Seminole, Courthouse, Okmulgee, OK 74447. 918-756-0788. Fax: 918-758-1202. 8AM-4:30PM (CST).

Felony, Misdemeanor, Civil, Eviction, Small Claims, Probate—24th Judicial District Court-Henryetta Branch, 114 S 4th, Henryetta, OK 74437. 918-652-7142. 8:30AM-4:30PM (CST). Access by: Phone, mail, in person.

24th Judicial District Court-Okmulgee Branch, 314 W 7th, Okmulgee, OK 74447. 918-756-3042. 8AM-4:30PM (CST). Access by: Phone, mail, in person.

Osage County

Real Estate Recording—Osage County Clerk, 6th & Grandview, Courthouse, Pawhuska, OK 74056. 918-287-3136. 8:30AM-5PM (CST).

Felony, Misdemeanor, Civil, Eviction, Small Claims, Probate—10th Judicial District Court, County Courthouse, 600 Grandview, Pawhuska, OK 74056. 918-287-4104. 9:00AM-5:00PM (CST). Access by: Mail, in person.

Ottawa County

Real Estate Recording—Ottawa County Clerk, 102 E. Central, Suite 203, Miami, OK 74354. 918-542-3332. 9AM-Noon,1-5PM (CST).

Felony, Misdemeanor, Civil, Eviction, Small Claims, Probate—13th Judicial District Court, 102 E Central Ave, Suite 300, Miami, OK 74354. 918-542-2801. 9:00AM-5:00PM (CST). Access by: Phone, mail, in person.

Pawnee County

Real Estate Recording—Pawnee County Clerk, Courthouse, Room 202, 500 Harrison St., Pawnee, OK 74058. 918-762-2732. 8AM-4:30PM (CST).

Felony, Misdemeanor, Civil, Eviction, Small Claims, Probate—14th Judicial District Court, Courthouse, 500 Harrison St, Pawnee, OK 74058. 918-762-2547. 8AM-4:30PM (CST). Access by: Mail, in person.

Payne County

Real Estate Recording—Payne County Clerk, 606 South Husband St, Room 210, Stillwater, OK 74074. 405-747-8347. 8AM-5PM (CST).

Felony, Misdemeanor, Civil, Eviction, Small Claims, Probate—9th Judicial District Court, 606 S. Husband Rm 308, Stillwater, OK 74074. 405-372-4774. 8:00AM-5:00PM (CST). Access by: Mail, in person.

Pittsburg County

Real Estate Recording—Pittsburg County Clerk, 115 East Carl Albert Parkway, McAlester, OK 74501. 918-423-6865. Fax: 918-423-7321. 8AM-5PM (CST).

Felony, Misdemeanor, Civil, Eviction, Small Claims, Probate—18th Judicial District Court, Box 460, McAlester, OK 74502. 918-423-4859. 8:30AM-5PM (CST). Access by: Mail, in person.

Pontotoc County

Real Estate Recording—Pontotoc County Clerk, 13th & Broadway, Ada, OK 74820. 405-332-1425. Fax: 405-332-9509. 8AM-5PM (CST).

Felony, Misdemeanor, Civil, Eviction, Small Claims, Probate—22nd Judicial District Court, Box 427, Ada, OK 74820. 405-332-5763. Fax: 405-436-5613. 8:00AM-5:00PM (CST). Access by: Phone, mail, in person.

Pottawatomie County

Real Estate Recording—Pottawatomie County Clerk, 325 North Broadway, Shawnee, OK 74801. 405-273-8222. Fax: 405-275-6898. 8:30AM-5PM (CST).

Felony, Misdemeanor, Civil, Eviction, Small Claims, Probate—23rd Judicial District Court, 325 N. Broadway, Shawnee, OK 74801. 405-273-3624. 8:30AM-Noon (CST). Access by: Mail, in person.

Pushmataha County

Real Estate Recording—Pushmataha County Clerk, 302 SW 'B', Antlers, OK 74523. 405-298-3626. 8AM-4:30PM (CST).

Felony, Misdemeanor, Civil, Eviction, Small Claims, Probate—17th Judicial District Court, Push County Courthouse, Antlers, OK 74523. 405-298-2274. 8AM-4:30PM (CST). Access by: Mail, in person.

Roger Mills County

Real Estate Recording—Roger Mills County Clerk, Broadway & L.L. Males Avenue, Cheyenne, OK 73628. 405-497-3395. Fax: 405-497-3488. 9AM-4:30PM (CST).

Felony, Misdemeanor, Civil, Eviction, Small Claims, Probate—2nd Judicial District Court, Box 409, Cheyenne, OK 73628. 405-497-3361. 8:00AM-12:00PM, 1:00AM-4:30PM (CST). Access by: Phone, mail, in person.

Rogers County

Real Estate Recording—Rogers County Clerk, 219 South Missouri, Claremore, OK 74017. 918-341-1860. 8AM-5PM (CST).

Felony, Misdemeanor, Civil, Eviction, Small Claims, Probate—12th Judicial District Court, Box 839, Claremore, OK 74018. 918-341-5711. 8:00AM-4:30PM (CST). Access by: Phone, mail, in person.

Seminole County

Real Estate Recording—Seminole County Clerk, 100 South Wewoka, Courthouse, Wewoka, OK 74884. 405-257-2501. Fax: 405-257-6422. 8AM-4PM (CST).

Felony, Misdemeanor, Civil, Eviction, Small Claims, Probate—22nd Judicial District Court-Seminole Branch, Box 1320, 401 Main St, Seminole, OK 74868. 405-382-3424. 8AM-Noon, 1-4PM (CST). Access by: Phone, mail, in person. No criminal records here since 1978.

22nd Judicial District Court-Wewoka Branch, Box 130, Wewoka, OK 74884. 405-257-6236. 8:00AM-4:00PM (CST). Access by: Mail, in person.

Sequoyah County

Real Estate Recording—Sequoyah County Clerk, 120 East Chickasaw, Sallisaw, OK 74955. 918-775-4516. 8AM-4PM (CST).

Felony, Misdemeanor, Civil, Eviction, Small Claims, Probate—15th Judicial District Court, 120 E Chickasaw, Sallisaw, OK 74955. 918-775-4411. 8AM-4PM (CST). Access by: Phone, mail, in person.

Stephens County

Real Estate Recording—Stephens County Clerk, 101 S. 11th St., Room 203, Duncan, OK 73533. 405-255-0977. Fax: 405-255-0991. 8:30AM-4:30PM (CST).

Felony, Misdemeanor, Civil, Eviction, Small Claims, Probate—5th Judicial District Court, 101 S 11th Rm 301, Duncan, OK 73533. 405-255-8460. 8:30AM-4:30PM (CST). Access by: Phone, mail, in person.

Texas County

Real Estate Recording—Texas County Clerk, 319 North Main, Guymon, OK 73942. 405-338-3141. 9AM-5PM (CST).

Felony, Misdemeanor, Civil, Eviction, Small Claims, Probate—1st Judicial District Court, Box 1081, Guymon, OK 73942. 405-338-3003. 9AM-5PM (CST). Access by: Mail, in person.

Tillman County

Real Estate Recording—Tillman County Clerk, 10th & Gladstone, Courthouse, Frederick, OK 73542. 405-335-3421. Fax: 405-335-3795. 8:30AM-Noon, 1-5PM (CST).

Felony, Misdemeanor, Civil, Eviction, Small Claims, Probate—3rd Judicial District Court, Box 116, Frederick, OK 73542. 405-335-3023. 9AM-5PM (CST). Access by: Phone, mail, in person.

Tulsa County

Real Estate Recording—Tulsa County Clerk, County Admin. Bldg, Room 120, 500 South Denver St., Tulsa, OK 74103. 918-596-5801. Fax: 918-596-5819. 8:30AM-5PM (CST).

Felony, Misdemeanor, Civil, Eviction, Small Claims, Probate—14th Judicial District Court, 500 S. Denver, Tulsa, OK 74103-3832. 918-596-5000. Fax: 918-596-5216. 8:30AM-5:00PM (CST). Access by: Mail, in person.

Wagoner County

Real Estate Recording—Wagoner County Clerk, 307 East Cherokee, Wagoner, OK 74467. 918-485-2216. Fax: 918-485-8677. 8AM-4:30PM (CST).

Felony, Misdemeanor, Civil, Eviction, Small Claims, Probate—15th Judicial District Court, Box 249, Wagoner, OK 74477. 918-485-4508. 8:00AM-4:30PM (CST). Access by: Mail, in person.

Washington County

Real Estate Recording—Washington County Clerk, 420 South Johnstone, Room 102, Bartlesville, OK 74003. 918-337-2840. Fax: 918-337-2894. 8AM-5PM (CST).

Felony, Misdemeanor, Civil, Eviction, Small Claims, Probate—11th Judicial District Court, 420 S Johnstone Rm 212, Bartlesville, OK 74003. 918-337-2870. Fax: 918-337-2897. 8AM-5PM (CST). Access by: Phone, fax, mail, in person.

Washita County

Real Estate Recording—Washita County Clerk, 100 East Main, Cordell, OK 73632. 405-832-3548. 8AM-4PM (CST).

Felony, Misdemeanor, Civil, Eviction, Small Claims, Probate—3rd Judicial District Court, Box 397, Cordell, OK 73632,. 405-832-3836. 8:00AM-4:00PM (CST). Access by: Mail, in person.

Woods County

Real Estate Recording—Woods County Clerk, Courthouse, 407 Government Street, Alva, OK 73717. 405-327-0998. Fax: 405-327-0998. 9AM-5PM (CST).

Felony, Misdemeanor, Civil, Eviction, Small Claims, Probate—4th Judicial District Court, Box 924, Alva, OK 73717. 405-327-3119. 9:00AM-5:00PM (CST). Access by: Mail, in person.

Woodward County

Real Estate Recording—Woodward County Clerk, 1600 Main Street, Woodward, OK 73801. 405-254-6800. 9AM-5PM (CST).

Felony, Misdemeanor, Civil, Eviction, Small Claims, Probate—4th Judicial District Court, 1600 Main, Woodward, OK 73801. 405-256-3413. 9AM-5PM (CST). Access by: Phone, mail, in person.

Federal Courts

US District Court
Eastern District of Oklahoma

Muskogee Division, US District Court Clerk, PO Box 607, Muskogee, OK 74401. 918-687-2471. Counties: Adair, Atoka, Bryan, Carter, Cherokee, Choctaw, Coal, Haskell, Hughes, Johnston, Latimer, Le Flore, Love, McCurtain, McIntosh, Marshall, Murray, Muskogee, Okfuskee, Pittsburg, Pontotoc, Pushmataha, Seminole, Sequoyah, Wagoner

Northern District of Oklahoma

Tulsa Division, US District Court 411 US Courthouse, 333 W 4th St, Tulsa, OK 74103. 918-699-4700. Counties: Craig, Creek, Delaware, Mayes, Nowata, Okmulgee, Osage, Ottawa, Pawnee, Rogers, Tulsa, Washington

Western District of Oklahoma

Oklahoma City Division, US District Court Clerk, Room 1210, 200 NW 4th St, Oklahoma City, OK 73102. 405-231-4792. Counties: Alfalfa, Beaver, Beckham, Blaine, Caddo, Canadian, Cimarron, Cleveland, Comanche, Cotton, Custer, Dewey, Ellis, Garfield, Garvin, Grady, Grant, Greer, Harmon, Harper, Jackson, Jefferson, Kay, Kingfisher, Kiowa, Lincoln, Logan, McClain, Major, Noble, Oklahoma, Payne, Pottawatomie, Roger Mills, Stephens, Texas, Tillman, Washita, Woods, Woodward

US Bankruptcy Court
Eastern District of Oklahoma

Okmulgee Division, US Bankruptcy Court, PO Box 1347, Okmulgee, OK 74447. 918-758-0126. Voice Case Information System: 918-756-8617. Counties: Adair, Atoka, Bryan, Carter, Cherokee, Choctaw, Coal, Haskell, Hughes, Johnston, Latimer, Le Flore, Love, Marshall, McCurtain, McIntosh, Murray, Muskogee, Okfuskee, Okmulgee, Pittsburg, Pontotoc, Pushmataha, Seminole, Sequoyah, Wagoner

Northern District of Oklahoma

Tulsa Division, US Bankruptcy Court, 224 S. Boulder, Tulsa, OK 74103. 918-581-7181. Counties: Craig, Creek, Delaware, Mayes, Nowata, Osage, Ottawa, Pawnee, Rogers, Tulsa, Washington

Western District of Oklahoma

Oklahoma City Division, US Bankruptcy Court, 1st Floor, Old Post Office Bldg, 215 Dean A McGee Ave, Oklahoma City, OK 73102. 405-231-5141. Voice Case Information System: 405-231-4768. Counties: Alfalfa, Beaver, Beckham, Blaine, Caddo, Canadian, Cimarron, Cleveland, Comanche, Cotton, Custer, Dewey, Ellis, Garfield, Garvin, Grady, Grant, Greer, Harmon, Harper, Jackson, Jefferson, Kay, Kingfisher, Kiowa, Lincoln, Logan, Major, McClain, Noble, Oklahoma, Payne, Pottawatomie, Roger Mills, Stephens, Texas, Tillman, Washita, Woods, Woodward

Oregon

Capitol: Salem (Marion County)	
Number of Counties: 36	**Population:** 3,140,585
County Court Locations:	**Federal Court Locations:**
•Circuit Courts: 8, 22 Districts	•District Courts: 3
•District Courts: 2, 30 Counties	•Bankruptcy Courts: 2
•Combined Courts: 28	**State Agencies:** 19
•County Courts: 6, 6 Counties	
•Justice Courts: 35	
•Municipal Courts: 112	
•Tax Court: 1	

State Agencies

General Help Numbers:

State Archives

Secretary of State	503-373-0701
Archives Division	Fax: 503-373-0953
800 Summer St NE	8AM-4:45PM
Salem, OR 97310	
Reference Librarian:	502-373-0701
Historical Society:	503-306-5200

Governor's Office

Office of the Governor	503-378-3111
254 State Capitol	Fax: 503-378-8970
Salem, OR 97310-0370	8AM-5PM

Attorney General's Office

Attorney General's Office	503-378-4400
Justice Department	Fax: 503-378-4017
1162 Court St NE	8AM-5PM
Salem, OR 97310	
Alternate Telephone:	503-378-6002

State Legislation

Oregon Legislative Assembly	503-986-1180
State Capitol-Information Services	8AM-5PM
State Capitol, Rm 49	
Salem, OR 97310	
Archives:	503-373-0701

Important State Internet Sites:

❖ Webscape

File Edit View   Help

State of Oregon World Wide Web
www.state.or.us/

This home page links to government, community, commerce and education.

Oregon Legislature
www.leg.state.or.us/

This site contains links to the state House and Senate home pages, and links to bill information.

Oregon Bills and Laws
www.leg.state.or.us/bills.html

This page links to legislative measures, the Revised Statutes, the State and U.S. Constitution and has two search engines.

Archives and History
arcweb.sos.state.or.us/

This is the home page for the state archives. This site has a search engine.

UCC Information
www.sos.state.or.us/corporation/ucc/ucc.htm

This site has excellent information. You can download the needed forms, and there is a search engine to search for active filings.

State Agencies—Public Records

Criminal Records
Oregon State Police, Identification Services Section, PO Box 430034, Salem, OR 97208, Main Telephone: 503-378-3070, Fax: 503-378-2121, Hours: 8AM-5PM. Access by: mail, PC.

Corporation Records
Limited Partnership Records
Trademarks/Servicemarks
Fictitious Name
Assumed Name
Limited Liability Company Records
Corporation Division, Public Service Building, 255 Capital St NE, #151, Salem, OR 97310-1327, Main Telephone: 503-986-2200, Hours: 8AM-5PM. Access by: mail, fax, phone, visit, PC.

Uniform Commercial Code
Federal Tax Liens
State Tax Liens
UCC Division, Secretary of State, 255 Capitol St NE, Suite 151, Salem, OR 97310-1327, Main Telephone: 503-986-2200, Fax: 503-373-1166, Hours: 8AM-5PM. Access by: mail, fax, phone, visit, PC.

Sales Tax Registrations
State does not impose sales tax.

Birth Certificates
Oregon State Health Division, Vital Records, PO Box 14050, Portland, OR 97293-0050, Main Telephone: 503-731-4095, Alternate Telephone: 503-731-4108, Fax: 503-234-8417, Hours: 8AM-4:30PM. Access by: mail, phone, fax, visit.

Death Records
Oregon State Health Division, Vital Records, PO Box 14050, Portland, OR 97293-0050, Main Telephone: 503-731-4095, Alternate Telephone: 503-731-4108, Fax: 503-234-8417, Hours: 8AM-4:30PM. Access by: mail, phone, fax, visit, PC.

Marriage Certificates
Oregon State Health Division, Vital Records, PO Box 14050, Portland, OR 97293-0050, Main Telephone: 503-731-4095, Alternate Telephone: 503-731-4108, Fax: 503-234-8417, Hours: 8AM-4:30PM. Access by: mail, phone, fax, visit, PC.

Divorce Records
Oregon State Health Division, Vital Records, Suite 205, PO Box 14050, Portland, OR 97293-0050, Main Telephone: 503-731-4095, Alternate Telephone: 502-731-4108, Fax: 503-234-8417, Hours: 8AM-4:30PM. Access by: mail, phone, fax, visit, PC.

Workers' Compensation Records
Department of Consumer & Business Srvs, Workers Compensation Division, 350 Winter Street NE, Salem, OR 97310, Main Telephone: 503-945-7881, Fax: 503-945-7630, Hours: 8AM-5PM. Access by: mail, visit.

Driver Records
Driver and Motor Vehicle Services, Record Services, 1905 Lana Ave, NE, Salem, OR 97314, Main Telephone: 503-945-5000, Hours: 8AM-5PM. Access by: mail, phone, visit.

Vehicle Ownership
Vehicle Identification
Driver and Motor Vehicle Services, Record Services Unit, 1905 Lana Ave, NE, Salem, OR 97314, Main Telephone: 503-945-5000, Fax: 503-945-5425, Hours: 8AM-5PM. Access by: mail, phone, visit.

Accident Reports
Motor Vehicle Division, Accident Reports & Information, 1905 Lana Ave, NE, Salem, OR 97314, Main Telephone: 503-945-5098, Fax: 503-945-5267, Hours: 8AM-5PM (until 8:30PM W). Access by: mail, fax, visit.

Hunting License Information
Fishing License Information
Fish & Wildlife Department, Licensing Division, PO Box 59, Portland, OR 97207, Main Telephone: 503-872-5275, Fax: 503-872-5261, Hours: 8AM-5PM. Access by: mail, phone.

County Courts and Recording Offices

What You Need to Know...

About the Courts

About the Recorder's Office

Administration

Court Administrator	503-986-5500
Supreme Court Bldg, 1163 State St	Fax: 503-986-5880
Salem, OR 97310	8AM-5PM

Court Structure

Seven counties (Grant, Gilliam, Harney, Malheur, Morrow, Sherman, and Wheeler) do **not** have District Courts and District Court actions in those counties are handled by the Circuit Courts.

Probate is handled by the Circuit Court except in 6 counties (Gilliam, Grant, Harney, Malheir, Sherman, and Wheeler) where Probate in handled by County Courts.

Searching Hints

Many courts indicated that **in person** searches would markedly improve request turnaround time as the offices are understaffed or spread very thin. Most Circuit & District Courts which have records on computer do have a public access terminal which will speed-up in person or retriever searches. Most record offices close from Noon to 1PM Oregon time for lunch and **no staff** is available during that period.

Online Access

Online computer access is available through the Oregon Judicial Information Network (**OJIN**). OJIN contains almost all cases filed in the Oregon state courts; however, it does **not** contain any records from municipal nor county courts. Generally, the OJIN database contains criminal, civil, small claims, probate, and some, but not all, juvenile records. There is an annual fee of $100 to cover setup, documentation, and PC communications software. Further, there is a monthly usage charge based on transaction type, type of job, shift, and number of units/pages. For further information and/or a registration packet, write to: Oregon Judicial System, Information Systems Division, ATTN: Technical Support, 1163 State Street, Salem OR 97310, 503-378-4049.

Organization

36 counties, 36 filing offices. The recording officer is County Clerk. 35 counties are in the Pacific Time Zone (PST) and one is in the Mountain Time Zone (MST).

UCC Records

Financing statements are filed at the state level, except for real estate related collateral. All counties will perform UCC searches. Use search request form UCC-11. Search fees are usually $3.75 or $5.00, and copy fees vary.

Lien Records

All federal tax liens on personal property are filed with the Secretary of State. Other federal tax liens and all state tax liens are filed with the County Clerk. Most counties will perform tax lien searches and include both with a UCC search for an extra $7.50 per name. Search fees vary widely. Other liens include county tax, public utility, construction, judgment, and hospital.

Real Estate Records

Some counties will **not** perform real estate searches. Search fees vary. Many counties will search all liens together for $12.50 per name. Copy fees are usually $.25 per page. Certification usually costs $3.75 per document. The Assessor keeps tax and ownership records.

County Courts and Recording Offices

Baker County

Real Estate Recording—Baker County Clerk, 1995 Third Street, Baker, OR 97814. 541-523-8207. Fax: 541-523-8240. 8AM-Noon,1-5PM (PST).

Felony, Civil Actions Over $2,500, Probate—Circuit Court, 1995 3rd St., Baker City, OR 97814. 541-523-6305. Fax: 541-523-9738. 8AM-Noon, 1-5PM (PST). Access by: Phone, mail, remote online, in person.

Benton County

Real Estate Recording—Benton County Recorder, 120 NW 4th Street, Corvallis, OR 97330. 541-757-6831. Fax: 541-754-2870. 8AM-Noon, 1-5PM (Recording Hours: 9AM-Noon, 1-4PM) (PST).

Felony, Misdemeanor, Civil Actions Over $2,500, Eviction, Small Claims, Probate—Circuit & District Court, Box 1870, Corvallis, OR 97339. 541-757-6828. Fax: 541-754-1615. 8AM-Noon,1-5PM (PST). Access by: Phone, mail, remote online, in person.

Clackamas County

Real Estate Recording—Clackamas County Clerk, 807 Main Street, Room 104, Oregon City, OR 97045. 503-655-8551. 8:30AM-5PM M,W,Th,F; 9:30AM-5PM T (PST).

Felony, Misdemeanor, Civil Actions Over $2,500, Eviction, Small Claims, Probate—Circuit & District Court, 807 Main St., Oregon City, OR 97045. 503-655-8447. 8:30AM-5PM (PST). Access by: Mail, remote online, in person.

Clatsop County

Real Estate Recording—Clatsop County Clerk, 749 Commercial, Astoria, OR 97103. 503-325-8511. Fax: 503-325-9307. 8:30AM-5PM (PST).

Felony, Civil Actions Over $10,000, Probate—Circuit Court, Box 835, Astoria, OR 97103. 503-325-8583. Fax: 503-325-9300. 8AM-Noon, 1-5PM (PST). Access by: Phone, mail, remote online, in person.

Misdemeanor, Civil Actions Under $10,000, Eviction, Small Claims—District Court, Box 659, Astoria, OR 97103. 503-325-8536. Fax: 503-325-9300. 8AM-5PM (PST). Access by: Mail, remote online, in person.

Columbia County

Real Estate Recording—Columbia County Clerk, Courthouse, St. Helens, OR 97051. 503-397-3796. Fax: 503-397-7266. 8:30AM-5PM (Recording 9AM-4PM) (PST).

Felony, Civil Actions Over $2,500, Eviction, Small Claims, Probate—Circuit & District Court, Columbia County Courthouse, St. Helens, OR 97051. 503-397-2327. Fax: 503-397-3226. 8AM-Noon, 1-5PM (PST). Access by: Mail, remote online, in person.

Coos County

Real Estate Recording—Coos County Clerk, Courthouse, 2nd and Baxter, Coquille, OR 97423. 541-396-3121. Fax: 541-396-4861. 8AM-5PM (PST).

Felony, Misdemeanor, Civil Actions Over $2,500, Eviction, Small Claims, Probate—Circuit & District Court, Courthouse, Coquille, OR 97423. 541-396-3121. Fax: 541-396-3456. 8AM-Noon,1-5PM (PST). Access by: Phone, mail, remote online, in person.

Crook County

Real Estate Recording—Crook County Clerk, 300 East Third, Prineville, OR 97754. 541-447-6553. Fax: 541-447-1051. 8:30AM-5PM (PST).

Felony, Misdemeanor, Civil Actions Over $2,500, Eviction, Small Claims, Probate—Circuit & District Court, Courthouse, Prineville, OR 97754. 541-447-6541. 8AM-5PM (PST). Access by: Phone, mail, remote online, in person.

Curry County

Real Estate Recording—Curry County Clerk, 28821 Ellensburg Ave., Gold Beach, OR 97444. 541-247-7011. Fax: 541-247-2718. 8:30AM-Noon, 1-5PM (PST).

Felony, Misdemeanor, Civil Actions Over $2,500, Eviction, Small Claims, Probate—Circuit & District Court, Box H, Gold Beach, OR 97444. 541-247-4511. 8AM-5PM (PST). Access by: Phone, mail, remote online, in person.

Deschutes County

Real Estate Recording—Deschutes County Clerk, 1340 NW Wall St., Bend, OR 97701. 541-388-6549. Fax: 541-389-6830. 8AM-5PM (PST).

Felony, Misdemeanor, Civil Actions Over $2,500, Eviction, Small Claims, Probate—Circuit & District Court, 1164 NW Bond, Bend, OR 97701. 541-388-5300. 8AM-5PM (PST). Access by: Phone, mail, remote online, in person.

Douglas County

Real Estate Recording—Douglas County Clerk, 1036 SE Douglas, Room 221, Roseburg, OR 97470. 541-440-4322. Fax: 541-440-4408. 8AM-4PM (PST).

Felony, Misdemeanor, Civil Actions Over $2,500, Eviction, Small Claims, Probate—Circuit & District Court, 1036 S E Douglas Rm 202, Roseburg, OR 97470. 541-957-2470. Fax: 541-957-2461. 8AM-5PM (PST). Access by: Phone, mail, remote online, in person.

Gilliam County

Real Estate Recording—Gilliam County Clerk, 221 South Oregon Street, Condon, OR 97823. 541-384-2311. Fax: 541-384-2166. 8:30AM-Noon, 1-5PM (PST).

Felony, Misdemeanor, Civil Actions Over $2,500—Circuit Court, Box 622, Condon, OR 97823. 541-384-3572. Fax: 541-384-2166. 1-5PM (PST). Access by: Phone, mail, remote online, in person.

Probate—County Court, 221 S Oregon, PO Box 427, Condon, OR 97823. 541-384-2311. Fax: 541-384-2166. 8:30AM-Noon, 1-5PM (PST).

Grant County

Real Estate Recording—Grant County Clerk, 200 South Humbolt, Canyon City, OR 97820. 541-575-1675. Fax: 541-575-2248. 8AM-5PM (PST).

Felony, Civil Actions Over $2,500—Circuit Court, Box 159, Canyon City, OR 97820. 541-575-1438. Fax: 541-575-2165. 8AM-Noon, 1-5PM (PST). Access by: Mail, remote online, in person.

Probate—County Court, PO Box 39, Canyon City, OR 97820. 541-575-1675. Fax: 541-575-2248. 8AM-5PM (PST).

Harney County

Real Estate Recording—Harney County Clerk, 450 North Buena Vista, Burns, OR 97720. 541-573-6641. Fax: 541-573-8387. 8:30AM-Noon, 1-5PM (PST).

Felony, Misdemeanor, Civil Actions Over $2,500—Circuit Court, 450 N. Buena Vista, Burns, OR 97720. 541-573-5207. Fax: 541-573-5715. 8AM-5PM (PST). Access by: Phone, mail, remote online, in person.

Probate—County Court, PO Box 699, Burns, OR 97720. 541-573-6641. Fax: 541-573-8387. 8:30AM-Noon, 1-5PM (PST).

Hood River County

Real Estate Recording—Hood River County Recorder, 309 State Street, Hood River, OR 97031. 541-386-1442. Fax: 541-386-9392. 8AM-5PM (Recording 9AM-4PM) (PST).

Felony, Misdemeanor, Civil Actions Over $2,500, Eviction, Small Claims, Probate—Circuit & District Court, 309 State St., Hood River, OR 97031. 541-386-1862. Fax: 541-

386-3465. 8AM-Noon, 1-5PM (PST). Access by: Mail, remote online, in person.

Jackson County

Real Estate Recording—Jackson County Clerk, 10 South Oakdale, Medford, OR 97501. 541-776-7258. 8AM-5PM (PST).

Felony, Misdemeanor, Civil Actions Over $2,500, Eviction, Small Claims, Probate—Circuit & District Court, 100 S. Oakdale, Medford, OR 97501. 541-776-7243. Fax: 541-776-7057. 8AM-5PM (PST). Access by: Mail, remote online, in person.

Jefferson County

Real Estate Recording—Jefferson County Clerk, 75 S.E. C Street, Madras, OR 97741. 541-475-4451. Fax: 541-475-4454. 8:30AM-5PM (PST).

Felony, Misdemeanor, Civil Actions Over $2,500, Eviction, Small Claims, Probate—Circuit & District Court, 75 SE C St., Madras, OR 97741-1750. 541-475-3317. Fax: 541-475-3421. 8AM-5PM (PST). Access by: Mail, remote online, in person.

Josephine County

Real Estate Recording—Josephine County Clerk, Courthouse, 6 & C Streets, Grants Pass, OR 97526. 541-474-5240. Fax: 541-476-5246. 9AM-4PM (PST).

Felony, Misdemeanor, Civil Actions Over $2,500, Eviction, Small Claims, Probate—Circuit & District Court, Josephine County Courthouse, Rm 254, Grants Pass, OR 97526. 541-476-2309. Fax: 541-471-2079. 8AM-5PM (PST). Access by: Fax, mail, remote online, in person.

Klamath County

Real Estate Recording—Klamath County Clerk, 507 Main St., Klamath Falls, OR 97601. 541-883-5134. 8:30AM-5PM; Recording Hours 9AM-Noon, 1-4PM (PST).

Felony, Misdemeanor, Civil Actions Over $2,500, Eviction, Small Claims, Probate—Circuit & District Court, 317 S 7th St, 2nd Fl, Klamath Falls, OR 97601. 541-883-5504. Fax: 541-882-6109. 8:30AM-5PM (PST). Access by: Mail, remote online, in person.

Lake County

Real Estate Recording—Lake County Clerk, 513 Center Street, Lakeview, OR 97630. 541-947-6006. Fax: 541-947-6015. 8AM-5PM (PST).

Felony, Misdemeanor, Civil Actions Over $2,500, Eviction, Small Claims, Probate—Circuit & District Court, 513 Center St., Lakeview, OR 97630. 541-947-6051. Fax: 541-947-3724. 8AM-5PM (PST). Access by: Mail, remote online, in person.

Lane County

Real Estate Recording—Deeds & Records, 125 East 8th Avenue, Eugene, OR 97401. 541-682-3654. 8AM-5PM; Recording 9AM-4PM (PST).

Felony, Misdemeanor, Civil Actions Over $2,500, Eviction, Small Claims, Probate—Circuit & District Court, 125 E. 8th Ave., Eugene, OR 97401. 541-687-4020. 8AM-5PM (PST). Access by: Phone, remote online, in person.

Lincoln County

Real Estate Recording—Lincoln County Clerk, 225 West Olive Street, Room 201, Newport, OR 97365. 541-265-4121. Fax: 541-265-4950. 8:30AM-5PM (PST).

Felony, Misdemeanor, Civil Actions Over $2,500, Eviction, Small Claims, Probate—Circuit & District Court, PO Box 100, Newport, OR 97365. 541-265-4236. Fax: 541-265-7561. 8AM-5PM (PST). Access by: Mail, remote online, in person.

Linn County

Real Estate Recording—Linn County Recorder, 300 SW 4th St., Courthouse Room 207, Albany, OR 97321. 541-967-3829. Fax: 541-926-5109. 8:30AM-5PM (Recording ends at 4PM) (PST).

Felony, Misdemeanor, Civil Actions Over $2,500, Eviction, Small Claims, Probate—Circuit & District Court, PO Box 1749, Albany, OR 97321. 541-967-3845. 8AM-5PM (PST). Access by: Mail, remote online, in person.

Malheur County

Real Estate Recording—Malheur County Clerk, 251 B Street West, Vale, OR 97918. 541-473-5151. Fax: 541-473-5168. 8:30AM-5PM (MST).

Felony, Misdemeanor, Civil Actions Over $2,500, Eviction, Small Claims—Circuit & District Court, 251 B St West Box 3, Vale, OR 97918. 541-473-5171. Fax: 541-473-2213. 8AM-5PM; 9AM-Noon, 1-4PM (Record Inquiry) (MST). Access by: Mail, remote online, in person.

Probate—County Court, 251 B St W #5, Vale, OR 97918. 541-473-5123. Fax: 541-473-5168. 8AM-Noon, 1-4:30PM (MST).

Marion County

Real Estate Recording—Marion County Clerk, 100 High Street NE, Room 1331, Salem, OR 97301. 503-588-5225. Fax: 503-588-5237. 8:30AM-5PM (PST).

Felony, Misdemeanor, Civil Actions Over $2,500, Eviction, Small Claims, Probate—Circuit & District Court, 100 High St NE, 1st Floor, Salem, OR 97301. 503-588-5101. Fax: 503-373-4360. 8AM-5PM (PST). Access by: Mail, remote online, in person.

Morrow County

Real Estate Recording—Morrow County Clerk, 100 Court Street, Heppner, OR 97836. 541-676-9061. Fax: 541-676-9876. 8AM-5PM (PST).

Felony, Misdemeanor, Civil Actions Over $2,500, Eviction, Small Claims, Probate—Circuit & District Court, PO Box 609, Heppner, OR 97836. 541-676-5264. Fax: 541-676-9902. 8AM-Noon, 1-4:45PM (PST). Access by: Mail, remote online, in person.

Multnomah County

Real Estate Recording—Multnomah County Recorder, Room 308, 421 SW 6th Ave., Portland, OR 97204. 503-248-3034. 8AM-5PM; Phone hours: 9AM-4:30PM (PST).

Felony, Misdemeanor, Civil Actions Over $10,000, Probate—Circuit Court, 1021 SW 4th Ave, Rm 131, Portland, OR 97204. 503-248-3003. 8AM-5PM (PST). Access by: Mail, remote online, in person.

Misdemeanor, Civil Actions Under $10,000, Eviction, Small Claims—District Court, 1021 SW 4th Ave, Rm 210, Portland, OR 97204. Civil: 503-248-3022. Criminal: 503-248-3235. 8:30AM-5PM (PST). Access by: Mail, remote online, in person.

Polk County

Real Estate Recording—Polk County Clerk, Courthouse, 850 Main St., Dallas, OR 97338. 503-623-9217. Fax: 503-623-0717. 8AM-5PM (PST).

Felony, Misdemeanor, Civil Actions Over $2,500, Eviction, Small Claims, Probate—Circuit & District Court, Polk County Courthouse, Rm 301, Dallas, OR 97338. 503-623-3154. Fax: 503-623-6614. 8AM-Noon, 1-5PM (PST). Access by: Phone, fax, mail, remote online, in person.

Sherman County

Real Estate Recording—Sherman County Clerk, 500 Court Street, Moro, OR 97039. 541-565-3606. Fax: 541-565-3312. 8AM-5PM (PST).

Felony, Misdemeanor, Civil Actions Over $2,500—Circuit & District Court, PO Box 402, Moro, OR 97039. 541-565-3650. 1-5PM (PST). Access by: Mail, remote online, in person.

Probate—County Court, PO Box 365, Moro, OR 97039. 541-565-3606. Fax: 541-565-3312. 8AM-5PM (PST). Access by: Mail, in person.

Tillamook County

Real Estate Recording—Tillamook County Clerk, 201 Laurel Avenue, Tillamook, OR 97141. 503-842-3402. Fax: 503-842-2721. 9AM-4PM (PST).

Felony, Misdemeanor, Civil Actions Over $2,500, Eviction, Small Claims, Probate—Circuit & District Court, 201 Laurel Ave, Tillamook, OR 97141. 503-842-8014. Fax: 503-842-2597. 8AM-5PM (PST). Access by: Mail, remote online, in person.

Umatilla County

Real Estate Recording—Umatilla County, 216 SE 4th Street, Room 108, Pendleton, OR 97801. 541-278-6236. Fax: 541-278-5463. 8AM-5PM; Recording Hours 9AM-4PM (PST).

Felony, Misdemeanor, Civil Actions Over $2,500, Eviction, Small Claims, Probate—Circuit & District Court, PO Box 1307, Pendleton, OR 97801. 541-278-0341. Fax: 541-278-2071. 8AM-5PM (PST). Access by: Mail, remote online, in person.

Union County

Real Estate Recording—Union County Clerk, 1001 4th St., Suite "D", La Grande, OR 97850. 541-963-1006. Fax: 541-963-1013. 8:30AM-5PM (Recording ends at 4:30PM) (PST).

Felony, Misdemeanor, Civil Actions Over $2,500, Eviction, Small Claims, Probate—Circuit & District Court, 1008 K Ave, La Grande, OR 97850. 541-962-9500. Fax: 541-963-0444. 8AM-Noon, 1-5PM (PST). Access by: Mail, remote online, in person.

Wallowa County

Real Estate Recording—Wallowa County Clerk, 101 South River, Room 100 Door16, Enterprise, OR 97828. 541-426-4543. Fax: 541-426-5901. 8:30AM-5PM (PST).

Felony, Misdemeanor, Civil Actions Over $2,500, Eviction, Small Claims, Probate—Circuit & District Court, 101 S River St, Rm 204, Enterprise, OR 97828. 541-426-4991. Fax: 541-426-4992. 8AM-5PM (PST). Access by: Phone, mail, remote online, in person.

Wasco County

Real Estate Recording—Wasco County Clerk, 511 Washington St., Courthouse, The Dalles, OR 97058. 541-296-6159. Fax: 541-298-3607. 10AM-4PM (PST).

Felony, Misdemeanor, Civil Actions Over $2,500, Eviction, Small Claims, Probate—Circuit & District Court, PO Box 821, The Dalles, OR 97058. 541-296-3196. Probate: 541-296-3196. Fax: 541-298-5611. 8AM-Noon,1-5PM (PST). Access by: Mail, remote online, in person.

Washington County

Real Estate Recording—Washington County Clerk, Public Services Building, 155 North First Avenue Suite 130, Hillsboro, OR 97124. 503-648-8752. 8:30AM-4:30PM (PST).

Felony, Misdemeanor, Civil Actions Over $2,500, Eviction, Small Claims, Probate—Circuit & District Court, 150 N 1st, Hillsboro, OR 97124. Civil: 503-648-8888. Probate: 503-648-8891. Fax: 503-693-4971. 8AM-5PM (PST). Access by: Mail, remote online, in person.

Wheeler County

Real Estate Recording—Wheeler County Clerk, 701 Adams Street, Room204, Fossil, OR 97830. 541-763-2400. Fax: 541-763-4771. 8:30AM-Noon, 1-5PM (PST).

Felony, Misdemeanor, Civil Actions Over $2,500—Circuit Court, PO Box 308, Fossil, OR 97830. 541-763-2541. 8:30AM-11:30AM (PST). Access by: Mail, remote online, in person.

Probate—County Court, PO Box 327, Fossil, OR 97830. 541-763-2911. Fax: 541-763-4771. 9-5PM (PST). Access by: Mail, in person.

Yamhill County

Real Estate Recording—Yamhill County Clerk, 535 NE 5th Street, Room 119, McMinnville, OR 97128. 503-434-7518. Fax: 503-434-7520. 9AM-5PM (PST).

Felony, Misdemeanor, Civil Actions Over $2,500, Eviction, Small Claims, Probate—Circuit & District Court, 5th & Evans St, McMinnville, OR 97128. 503-472-9371. 8AM-Noon, 1-5PM (PST). Access by: Mail, remote online, in person.

Federal Courts

US District Court
District of Oregon

Eugene Division, US District Court 100 Federal Bldg, 211 E 7th Ave, Eugene, OR 97401. 541-465-6423. Counties: Benton, Coos, Deschutes, Douglas, Lane, Lincoln, Linn, Marion

Medford Division, US District Court 201 James A Redden US Courthouse, 310 W 6th St, Medford, OR 97501. 541-776-3926. Counties: Curry, Jackson, Josephine, Klamath, Lake. Court set up in April 1994; prior cases were tried in Eugene

Portland Division, US District Court Clerk, 531 Gus J Solomon US Courthouse, 620 SW Main, Portland, OR 97205. 503-326-5412. Counties: Baker, Clackamas, Clatsop, Columbia, Crook, Gilliam, Grant, Harney, Hood River, Jefferson, Malheur, Morrow, Multnomah, Polk, Sherman, Tillamook, Umatilla, Union, Wallowa, Wasco, Washington, Wheeler, Yamhill.

US Bankruptcy Court
District of Oregon

Eugene Division, US Bankruptcy Court, PO Box 1335, Eugene, OR 97440. 541-465-6448. Voice Case Information System: 503-326-2249. Counties: Benton, Coos, Curry, Deschutes, Douglas, Jackson, Josephine, Klamath, Lake, Lane, Lincoln, Linn, Marion

Portland Division, US Bankruptcy Court, Suite 700, 1001 SW 5th Ave, Portland, OR 97204. 503-326-2231. Voice Case Information System: 503-326-2249. Counties: Baker, Clackamas, Clatsop, Columbia, Crook, Gilliam, Grant, Harney, Hood River, Jefferson, Malheur, Morrow, Multnomah, Polk, Sherman, Tillamook, Umatilla, Union, Wallowa, Wasco, Washington, Wheeler, Yamhill

Pennsylvania

Capitol: Harrisburg (Dauphin County)	
Number of Counties: 67	**Population:** 12,071,842
County Court Locations:	**Federal Court Locations:**
•Court of Common Pleas : 103/ 60 Districts	•District Courts: 8
Philadelphia Municipal Court: 1/ 1st District	•Bankruptcy Courts: 6
Philadelphia Traffic Court: 1/ 1st District	**State Agencies:** 19
Pittsburgh Magistrates Courts: 1/5th District	
•Register in Wills: 59	
•District Justice Courts: 538	

State Agencies—Summary

General Help Numbers:

State Archives

Historical & Museum Commission	717-787-3362
Archives & History Division	Fax: 717-787-4822
Box 1026	9AM-5PM TU-SU
Harrisburg, PA 17108-1026	
Alternate Telephone:	717-787-3051
Historical Society:	717-732-6900

Governor's Office

Governor's Office	717-787-2500
225 Main Capitol Bldg	Fax: 717-772-8284
Harrisburg, PA 17120	8:30AM-5PM

Attorney General's Office

Attorney General's Office	717-787-3391
Strawberry Square, 16th Floor	Fax: 717-787-8242
Harrisburg, PA 17120	8:30AM-5PM

State Legislation

Pennsylvania General Assembly	717-787-2342
Main Capitol Bldg	
House-8:30AM-4:30PM/Senate-8:30AM-5PM	
Room 641	
Harrisburg, PA 17120	
House Bills:	717-787-5320
Senate Bills:	717-787-6732

Important State Internet Sites:

Webscape
File Edit View   Help

State of Pennsylvania World Wide Web
www.state.pa.us/

Provides links to a directory for the Commonwealth.

Pennsylvania Legislature
www.pasen.gov/Welcome.html

This site contains links to both the State and Federal government.

Archives and Records Management
www.state.pa.us/PA_Exec/Historical_Museum/DARMS/overview.htm

This page provides information about the management of the archives and links to the state archives. It also links to state and local government records programs.

Unclaimed Property
www.libertynet.org/~patreas/Unclaimed.html

Provided at this site is information about the unclaimed property process in Pennsylvania. This service is through the State Treasury Department. No online searching is available, but an inquiry form can be sent online.

State Agencies—Public Records

Criminal Records

State Police Central Repository, 1800 Elmerton Ave, Harrisburg, PA 17110-9758, Main Telephone: 717-783-5592, Fax: 717-772-3681, Hours: 8:15AM-4:15PM. Access by: mail, visit.

Corporation Records
Limited Partnership Records
Trademarks/Servicemarks
Fictitious Name
Assumed Name
Limited Liability Company Records

Corporation Bureau, Department of State, PO Box 8722, Harrisburg, PA 17105-8722, Main Telephone: 717-787-1057, Fax: 717-783-2244, Hours: 8AM-5PM. Access by: mail, phone, fax, visit.

Uniform Commercial Code
Federal Tax Liens
State Tax Liens

UCC Division, Department of State, PO Box 8721, Harrisburg, PA 17105-8721, Main Telephone: 717-787-1057, Fax: 717-783-2244, Hours: 8:30AM-4:30PM. Access by: mail, fax, visit.

Sales Tax Registrations

Revenue Department, Sales Tax Division, Dept 280905, Harrisburg, PA 17128-0905, Main Telephone: 717-783-9360, Fax: 717-787-3990, Hours: 7:30AM-5PM. Access by: mail, phone.

Birth Certificates

Department of Health, Division of Vital Records, PO Box 1528, New Castle, PA 16103-1528, Main Telephone: 412-656-3100, Fax: 412-652-8951, Hours: 8AM-4PM. Access by: mail, phone, fax, visit.

Death Records

Department of Health, Division of Vital Records, PO Box 1528, New Castle, PA 16103-1528, Main Telephone: 412-656-3100, Fax: 412-652-8951, Hours: 8AM-4PM. Access by: mail, phone, fax, visit.

Marriage Certificates
Divorce Records

Records not available from state agency.

Workers' Compensation Records

Bureau of Workers' Compensation, 1171 S Cameron St, Rm 103, Harrisburg, PA 17104-2501, Main Telephone: 717-772-4447, Hours: 8AM-5PM. Access by: mail only. Address all record requests to Karen Mark.

Driver Records

Department of Transportation, Driver Record Services, PO Box 68695, Harrisburg, PA 17106-8695, Main Telephone: 717-391-6190, In-state only: 800-932-4600, Hours: 7:30AM-4:30PM. Access by: mail, visit. Copies of tickets may be purchased from this location for a fee of $5.00 each.

Vehicle Ownership
Vehicle Identification

Department of Transportation, Vehicle Record Services, PO Box 68695, Harrisburg, PA 17106-8695, Main Telephone: 717-391-6190, In-state: 800-932-6000, TDD: 717-391-6191, Hours: 7:30AM-4:30PM. Access by: mail only. This agency also holds records for unattached mobile homes.

Accident Reports

State Police Headquarters, Accident Records Unit, 1800 Elmerton Ave, Harrisburg, PA 17110, Main Telephone: 717-783-5516, Hours: 8AM-5PM. Access by: mail, visit.

Fishing License Information

Fish & Boat Commission, Fishing License Division, PO Box 67000, Harrisburg, PA 17106, Main Telephone: 717-657-4518, Hunting License Division: 717-787-2084, Fax: 717-657-4549, Hours: 8AM-4PM. Access by: mail, visit. The address above is the division for fishing license information only. They do not have a database for their records. They have all hand written records which are public records. Hunting license information is at another agency and is not released.

Hunting License Information

Records not available from state agency.

County Courts and Recording Offices

What You Need to Know...

About the Courts

Administration

Administrative Office of Courts	717-795-2000
PO Box 719	Fax: 717-795-2084
Mechanicsburg, PA 17055-0719	8AM-4:30PM

Court Structure

The civil records section of the Court of Common Pleas is called the Prothonotary.

Small claims cases are, usually, handled by the District Justice Courts/Magistrates. However, all small claims actions are recorded through the Prothonotary Section (civil) of the Court of Common Pleas and, then, holds the records. It is not necessary to check with each District Justice Court, but rather with the Prothonotary. Small claims limits have changed to $8,000 in many cases. The limit is still $4,000 in Allegany, Beaver, Indiana, Luzerne, Monroe, and Washington counties and has changed to $5,000 in Philadelphia county and $9,000 in Somerset County.

Probate is handled in the Prothonotary by the Register in Wills.

Searching Hints

Fees vary widely across jurisdictions. Many courts will not conduct searches due to a lack of personnel or, if they do search, turnaround time may be excessive. Many courts have public access terminals for in person searches.

Online Access

There is an online computer system which is for only internal access for criminal cases. Some courts provide remote online access systems.

About the Recorder's Office

Organization

67 counties, 134 filing offices. Each county has two different filing offices: the Prothonotary—their term for Clerk—accepts UCC and tax lien filings, and the Recorder of Deeds maintains real estate records. The entire state is in the Eastern Time Zone (EST).

UCC Records

This is a **dual filing state**. Financing statements are filed both at the state level and with the Prothonotary, except for real estate related collateral, which are filed with the Recorder of Deeds. Some county offices will **not** perform UCC searches. Use search request form UCC-11. Search fees are usually $49.50 per debtor name. Copies usually cost $.50-$2.00 per page. Counties also charge $4.50 per financing statement found on a search.

Lien Records

All federal and state tax liens on personal property and on real property are filed with the Prothonotary. Usually, tax liens on personal property are filed in the judgment index of the Prothonotary. Some Prothonotaries will perform tax lien searches. Search fees are usually $5.00 per name. Other liens include judgments, municipal, and mechanics.

Real Estate Records

County Recorders of Deeds will **not** perform real estate searches. Copy fees and certification fees vary.

County Courts and Recording Offices

Adams County

Real Estate Recording—Adams County Recorder of Deeds, 111-117 Baltimore Street, County Courthouse Room 102, Gettysburg, PA 17325. 717-334-6781. 8AM-4:30PM (EST).

Civil, Eviction—Court of Common Pleas-Civil, 111-117 Baltimore St Rm 104, Gettysburg, PA 17325. 717-334-6781. 8AM-4:30PM (EST). Access by: Mail, in person.

Felony, Misdemeanor—Court of Common Pleas-Criminal, 111-117 Baltimore St, Gettysburg, PA 17325. 717-334-6781. 8AM-4:30PM (EST). Access by: Mail, in person.

Probate—Register of Wills, 111-117 Baltimore St Rm 102, Gettysburg, PA 17325. 717-334-6781. 8AM-4:30PM (EST).

Allegheny County

Real Estate Recording—Allegheny County Recorder of Deeds, 101 County Office Building, 542 Forbes Avenue, Pittsburgh, PA 15219. 412-350-4226. Fax: 412-350-6877. 8:30AM-4:30PM (EST).

Civil, Eviction—Court of Common Pleas-Civil, City County Bldg, 414 Grant St, Pittsburgh, PA 15219. 412-350-4213. Fax: 412-350-5260. 8:30AM-4:30PM (EST). Access by: Mail, in person.

Felony, Misdemeanor—Court of Common Pleas-Criminal, Grant St, Rm 114 Courthouse, Pittsburgh, PA 15219. 412-355-5378. 8:30AM-4:30PM (EST). Access by: Mail, in person.

Probate—Register of Wills, 414 Grant St, City County Bldg, PIttsburgh, PA 15219. 412-350-4180. 8:30AM-4:25PM (EST). Access by: Mail, in person.

Armstrong County

Real Estate Recording—Armstrong County Recorder of Deeds, County Courthouse, 500 Market St., Kittanning, PA 16201. 412-548-3256. Fax: 412-548-3236. 8:30AM-4PM (EST).

Civil, Eviction—Court of Common Pleas-Civil, 500 Market St, Kittanning, PA 16201. 412-548-3251. 8:30AM-4PM M,T,Th,F; 8AM-6PM W (EST). Access by: In person only.

Felony, Misdemeanor—Court of Common Pleas-Criminal, 500 Market St, Kittanning, PA 16201. 412-548-3252. 8:30AM-4PM (EST). Access by: Mail, in person.

Beaver County

Real Estate Recording—Beaver County Recorder of Deeds, 3rd Street, County Courthouse, Beaver, PA 15009. 412-728-5700. Fax: 412-728-3630. 8:30AM-4:30PM (EST).

Civil, Eviction—Court of Common Pleas-Civil, Beaver County Courthouse, 3rd St, Beaver, PA 15009. 412-728-5700. 8:30AM-4:30PM (EST). Access by: In person only.

Felony, Misdemeanor—Court of Common Pleas-Criminal, Beaver County Courthouse, 3rd St, Beaver, PA 15009. 412-728-5700. Fax: 412-728-8853. 8:30AM-4:30PM (EST). Access by: Mail, in person.

Probate—Register of Wills, Beaver County Courthouse, 3rd St, Beaver, PA 15009. 412-728-5700. Fax: 412-728-9810. 8:30AM-4:30PM (EST). Access by: Mail, in person.

Bedford County

Real Estate Recording—Bedford County Recorder of Deeds, 200 South Juliana Street, County Courthouse, Bedford, PA 15522. 814-623-4836. 8:30AM-4:30PM (EST).

Felony, Misdemeanor, Civil, Eviction—Court of Common Pleas-Criminal/Civil, Bedford County Courthouse, Bedford, PA 15522. 814-623-4833. Fax: 814-622-0991. 8:30AM-4:30PM (EST). Access by: Mail, in person.

Berks County

Real Estate Recording—Berks County Recorder of Deeds, 633 Court St., 3rd Floor, Reading, PA 19601. 610-478-3380. Fax: 610-478-3359. 8AM-5PM (EST).

Civil, Eviction—Court of Common Pleas-Civil, 2nd Floor, 633 Court St, Reading, PA 19601. 610-478-6970. Fax: 610-478-6969. 8AM-4PM (EST). Access by: In person only.

Felony, Misdemeanor—Court of Common Pleas-Criminal, 4th Floor, 633 Court St, Reading, PA 19601. 610-478-6550. Fax: 610-478-6570. 8AM-5PM (EST). Access by: In person only.

Probate—Register of Wills, 633 Court St 2nd Floor, Reading, PA 19601. 610-478-6600. 8AM-5PM (EST). Access by: Mail, in person.

Blair County

Real Estate Recording—Blair County Recorder of Deeds, 423 Allegheny Street, Hollidaysburg, PA 16648. 814-693-3096. 8AM-4PM (EST).

Felony, Misdemeanor, Civil, Eviction—Court of Common Pleas-Criminal/Civil, PO Box 719, Hollidaysburg, PA 16648. 814-693-3080. 8AM-4:30PM (EST). Access by: Mail, in person.

Bradford County

Real Estate Recording—Bradford County Recorder of Deeds, 301 Main Street, Courthouse, Towanda, PA 18848. 717-265-1702. Fax: 717-265-1721. 8AM-5PM (EST).

Felony, Misdemeanor, Civil, Eviction—Court of Common Pleas-Criminal/Civil, Courthouse, 301 Main St, Towanda, PA 18848. 717-265-1705. 9AM-5PM (EST). Access by: Mail, in person.

Probate—Register of Wills, 301 Main St., Towanda, PA 18848. 717-265-1702. 9AM-5PM (EST). Access by: Mail, in person.

Bucks County

Real Estate Recording—Bucks County Recorder of Deeds, Courthouse, 55 E. Court St., Doylestown, PA 18901. 215-348-6209. 8:15AM-4:15PM (Recording Hours 8:15AM-4PM) (EST).

Civil, Eviction—Court of Common Pleas-Civil, 55 E Court St, Doylestown, PA 18901. 215-348-6191. 8:15AM-4:15PM (EST). Access by: In person only.

Felony, Misdemeanor—Court of Common Pleas-Criminal, Bucks County Courthouse, Doylestown, PA 18901. 215-348-6389. Fax: 215-348-6379. 8AM-4:30PM (EST). Access by: Mail, remote online, in person. Contact Jack Morris at 215-348-6579 for information about remote access. Fees include $24 annual subscription and $.60 per minute. Available daily..

Probate—Register of Wills, Bucks County Courthouse, Doylestown, PA 18901. 215-348-6285. Fax: 215-348-6156. 8:15AM-4:15PM M-F; 8:15AM-7:30PM 1st & 3rd Wed of month (EST). Access by: Mail, in person.

Butler County

Real Estate Recording—Butler County Recorder of Deeds, 124 West Diamond St., County Government Bldg., Butler, PA 16001. 412-284-5340. Fax: 412-285-9099. 8:30AM-4:30PM (EST).

Civil, Eviction—Court of Common Pleas-Civil, Butler County Courthouse, PO Box 1208, Butler, PA 16001-1208. 412-284-5214. 8:30AM-4:30PM (EST). Access by: In person only.

Felony, Misdemeanor—Court of Common Pleas-Criminal, Butler County Courthouse, PO Box 1208, Butler, PA 16003-1208. 412-284-5233. Fax: 412-284-5244. 8:30AM-4:30PM (EST). Access by: Mail, in person.

Probate—Register of Wills, Butler County Coutrhouse, PO Box 1208, Butler, PA 16003-1208. 412-284-5348. Fax:

412-285-9099. 8:30AM-4:30PM (EST). Access by: Mail, in person.

Cambria County

Real Estate Recording—Cambria County Recorder of Deeds, S. Center Street, Courthouse, Ebensburg, PA 15931. 814-472-5440. 9AM-4PM (EST).

Civil, Eviction—Court of Common Pleas-Civil, PO Box 208, Ebensburg, PA 15931. 814-472-1636. Fax: 814-472-2353. 9AM-4PM (EST). Access by: In person only.

Felony, Misdemeanor—Court of Common Pleas-Criminal, Cambria County Courthouse S Center St, Ebensburg, PA 15931. 814-472-1543. 9AM-4PM (EST). Access by: Mail, in person.

Probate—Register of Wills, PO Box 298, Ebensburg, PA 15931. 814-472-5440. 9AM-4PM (EST).

Cameron County

Real Estate Recording—Cameron County Recorder of Deeds, 20 E. 5th Street, Emporium, PA 15834. 814-486-3349. Fax: 814-486-0464. 8:30AM-4PM (EST).

Civil, Eviction—Court of Common Pleas-Civil, Cameron County Courthouse, East 5th St, Emporium, PA 15834. 814-486-3355. Fax: 814-468-0464. 8:30AM-4:30PM (EST). Access by: Phone, fax, mail, in person.

Felony, Misdemeanor—Court of Common Pleas-Criminal, 20 East 5th St, Emporium, PA 15834. 814-486-3349. Fax: 814-486-0464. 8:30AM-4PM (EST). Access by: Phone, fax, mail, in person.

Probate—Register of Wills, Cameron County Coutrhouse, East 5th St., Emporium, PA 15834. 814-486-3355. Fax: 814-486-0464. 8:30AM-4PM (EST). Access by: In person only.

Carbon County

Real Estate Recording—Carbon County Recorder of Deeds, Courthouse Annexe, Rte. 209 & Hazard Square, Jim Thorpe, PA 18229. 717-325-2651. 8:30AM-4:30PM (EST).

Civil, Eviction—Court of Common Pleas-Civil, PO Box 127, Courthouse, Jim Thorpe, PA 18229. 717-325-2481. Fax: 717-325-8047. 8:30AM-4:30PM (EST). Access by: Mail, in person.

Felony, Misdemeanor—Court of Common Pleas-Criminal, County Courthouse, Jim Thorpe, PA 18229. 717-325-3637. Fax: 717-325-3525. 8:30AM-4:30PM (EST). Access by: Phone, mail, in person.

Centre County

Real Estate Recording—Centre County Recorder of Deeds, Room 105, County Courthouse, Bellefonte, PA 16823. 814-355-6801. 8:30AM-5PM (EST).

Felony, Misdemeanor, Civil, Eviction—Court of Common Pleas-Criminal/Civil, Centre County Courthouse, Bellefonte, PA 16823. 814-355-6796. 8:30AM-5PM (EST). Access by: Phone, mail, in person.

Probate—Register of Wills, Centre County Courthouse, Bellefonte, PA 16823. 814-355-6760. 8:30AM-5PM (EST).

Chester County

Real Estate Recording—Chester County Recorder of Deeds, Suite 100, 235 West Market St., West Chester, PA 19382. 610-344-6330. Fax: 610-344-6408. 8:30AM-4:30PM (EST).

Civil, Eviction—Court of Common Pleas-Civil, 2 North High St, Ste 130, West Chester, PA 19380. 610-344-6300. 8:30AM-4:30PM (EST). Access by: In person only.

Felony, Misdemeanor—Court of Common Pleas-Criminal, 2 North High St, West Chester, PA 19380. 610-344-6135. 8:30AM-4:30PM (EST). Access by: Mail, remote online, in person. Contact Gail Galliger aat 610-344-6884 for information about remote access.

Probate—Register of Wills, 2 North High St, Suite 109, West Chester, PA 19380-3073. 610-344-6335. Fax: 610-344-6218. 8:30AM-4:30PM (EST). Access by: Mail, in person.

Clarion County

Real Estate Recording—Clarion County Recorder of Deeds, Courthouse, Corner of 5th Ave. & Main St., Clarion, PA 16214. 814-226-4000. Fax: 814-226-8069. 8:30AM-4:30PM (EST).

Civil, Eviction—Court of Common Pleas-Civil, Clarion County Courthouse, Main St, Clarion, PA 16214. 814-226-1119. Fax: 814-226-8069. 8:30AM-4:30PM (EST). Access by: Mail, in person.

Felony, Misdemeanor—Court of Common Pleas-Criminal, Clarion County Courthouse, Main St, Clarion, PA 16214. 814-226-4000. Fax: 814-226-8069. 8AM-4:30PM (EST). Access by: Phone, fax, mail, in person.

Probate—Register of Wills, Clarion County Courthouse, Corner of 5th & Main, Clarion, PA 16214. 814-226-4000. Fax: 814-226-8069. 8:30AM-4:30PM (EST). Access by: Mail, in person.

Clearfield County

Real Estate Recording—Clearfield County Recorder of Deeds, Corner of 2nd & Market Streets, Clearfield, PA 16830. 814-765-2641. Fax: 814-765-6089. 8:30AM-4PM (EST).

Felony, Misdemeanor, Civil, Eviction—Court of Common Pleas-Criminal/Civil, 1 N 2nd St, Clearfield, PA 16830. 814-765-2641. Fax: 814-765-6089. 8:30AM-4PM (EST). Access by: Mail, in person.

Probate—Register of Wills & Clerk of Orphans Court, PO Box 361, Clearfield, PA 16830. 814-765-2641. Fax: 814-765-6089. 8:30AM-4PM (EST). Access by: Mail, in person.

Clinton County

Real Estate Recording—Clinton County Recorder of Deeds, Corner of Water & Jay Streets, Courthouse, Lock Haven, PA 17745. 717-893-4010. 8:30AM-5PM (EST).

Felony, Misdemeanor, Civil, Eviction—Court of Common Pleas-Criminal/Civil, 230 E Water St, Lock Haven, PA 17745. 717-893-4007. 8:30AM-5PM (EST). Access by: In person only.

Probate—Register of Wills, PO Box 943, Lock Haven, PA 17745. 717-893-4010. 8:30AM-5PM (EST). Access by: Mail, in person.

Columbia County

Real Estate Recording—Columbia County Recorder of Deeds, Main Street, Court House, Bloomsburg, PA 17815. 717-389-5632. Fax: 717-784-0257. 8AM-4:30PM (EST).

Felony, Misdemeanor, Civil, Eviction—Court of Common Pleas-Criminal/Civil, PO Box 380, Bloomsburg, PA 17815. 717-389-5600. 8AM-4:30PM (EST). Access by: Mail, in person.

Probate—Register of Wills, Columbia County Courthouse, PO Box 380, Bloomsburg, PA 17815. 717-389-5632. Fax: 717-784-0257. 8AM-4:30PM (EST). Access by: Mail, in person.

Crawford County

Real Estate Recording—Crawford County Recorder of Deeds, Courthouse, 903 Diamond Park, Meadville, PA 16335. 813-333-7338. Fax: 814-337-5296. 8:30AM-4:30PM (EST).

Civil, Eviction—Court of Common Pleas-Civil, Crawford County Courthouse, Meadville, PA 16335. 814-425-2541. 8:30AM-4:30PM (EST). Access by: Mail, in person.

Felony, Misdemeanor—Court of Common Pleas-Criminal, Crawford County Courthouse, Meadville, PA 16335. 814-336-1151. Fax: 814-337-0457. 8:30AM-4:30PM (EST). Access by: Mail, in person.

Probate—Register of Wills, 903 Diamond Park, Meadville, PA 16335. 814-336-1151. 8:30AM-4:30PM (EST). Access by: Mail, in person.

Cumberland County

Real Estate Recording—Cumberland County Recorder of Deeds, County Courthouse, 1 Courthouse Square, Carlisle,

PA 17013. 717-240-6370. Fax: 717-240-6490. 8AM-4:30PM (EST).

Civil, Eviction—Court of Common Pleas-Civil, Cumberland County Courthouse, Rm 100, One Courthouse Square, Carlisle, PA 17013-3387. 717-240-6195. Fax: 717-240-6573. 8AM-4:30PM (EST). Access by: In person only.

Felony, Misdemeanor—Court of Common Pleas-Criminal, Cumberland County Courthouse, East Wing, 1 Courthouse Sq, Carlisle, PA 17013-3387. 717-240-6250. Fax: 717-240-6571. 8AM-4:30PM (EST). Access by: Mail, in person.

Probate—Register of Wills, Cumberland County Courthouse, Rm 102, 1 Courthouse Sq, Carlisle, PA 17013. 717-240-6345. Fax: 717-240-6490. 8AM-4:30PM (EST). Access by: Mail, in person.

Dauphin County

Real Estate Recording—Dauphin County Recorder of Deeds, Front & Market Streets, Courthouse, Harrisburg, PA 17101. 717-255-2802. Fax: 717-257-1521. 8:30AM-4:30PM M-Th; (F 8:30AM-4PM) (EST).

Civil, Eviction—Court of Common Pleas-Civil, PO Box 945, Harrisburg, PA 17108. 717-255-2698. 8:30AM-4:30PM M-Th, 8:30AM-4PM F (EST). Access by: Mail, in person.

Felony, Misdemeanor—Court of Common Pleas-Criminal, Front & Market St, Harrisburg, PA 17101. 717-255-2692. Fax: 717-255-2694. 8:30AM-4:30PM (EST). Access by: Mail, in person.

Probate—Register of Wills, PO Box 1295, Harrisburg, PA 17101. 717-255-2656. Fax: 717-257-1604. 8:30AM-4:30PM M-Th, 8:30AM-4PM F (EST). Access by: In person only.

Delaware County

Real Estate Recording—Delaware County Recorder of Deeds, 201 W. Front Street, Room 107, Government Center Building, Media, PA 19063. 610-891-4156. 8:30AM-4:30PM (EST).

Felony, Misdemeanor, Civil, Eviction—Court of Common Pleas-Criminal/Civil, Veteran's Square Courthouse, PO Box 1057, Media, PA 19063. 610-891-5399. 8:30AM-4:30PM (EST). Access by: Mail, in person.

Probate—Register of Wills, Delaware County Courthouse, 201 W Front St, Media, PA 19063. 610-891-4400. 8:30AM-4:30PM (EST). Access by: In person only.

Elk County

Real Estate Recording—Elk County Recorder of Deeds, Main Street, Courthouse, Ridgway, PA 15853. 814-776-5349. Fax: 814-776-5379. 8:30AM-4PM (EST).

Felony, Misdemeanor, Civil, Eviction—Court of Common Pleas-Criminal/Civil, PO Box 237, Ridgway, PA 15853. 814-776-5344. Fax: 814-776-5379. 8:30AM-4PM (EST). Access by: Phone, mail, in person.

Probate—Register of Wills, PO Box 314, Ridgway, PA 15853. 814-776-5349. Fax: 814-776-5379. 8:30AM-4PM (EST). Access by: Mail, in person.

Erie County

Real Estate Recording—Erie County Recorder of Deeds, 140 West 6th Street, Erie, PA 16501. 814-451-6246. Fax: 814-451-6213. 8:30AM-4:30PM (EST).

Civil, Eviction—Court of Common Pleas-Civil, Erie County Courthouse, 140 West 6th St., Erie, PA 16501. 814-451-6076. 8:30AM-4:30PM (EST). Access by: In person only.

Felony, Misdemeanor—Court of Common Pleas-Criminal, Erie County Courthouse, 140 West 6th St, Erie, PA 16501. 814-451-6229. Fax: 814-451-6420. 8:30AM-4:30PM (EST). Access by: Mail, in person.

Probate—Register of Wills, Erie County Courthouse 140 W 6th St, Erie, PA 16501. 814-451-6260. 8:30AM-4:30PM (EST). Access by: Mail.

Fayette County

Real Estate Recording—Fayette County Recorder of Deeds, 61 East Main Street, Courthouse, Uniontown, PA 15401. 412-430-1238. 8AM-4:30PM (EST).

Civil, Eviction—Court of Common Pleas-Civil, 61 East Main St, Uniontown, PA 15401. 412-430-1272. Fax: 412-430-1265. 8AM-4:30PM (EST). Access by: Mail, in person.

Felony, Misdemeanor—Court of Common Pleas-Criminal, 61 East Main St, Uniontown, PA 15401. 412-430-1253. Fax: 412-438-8410. 8AM-4:30PM (EST). Access by: Fax, mail, in person.

Probate—Register of Wills, 61 East Main St, Uniontown, PA 15401. 412-430-1206. 8AM-4:30PM (EST). Access by: Mail, in person.

Forest County

Real Estate Recording—Forest County Recorder of Deeds, 526 Elm Street, Courthouse P.O. Box 423, Tionesta, PA 16353. 814-755-3526. Fax: 814-755-8837. 9AM-4PM (EST).

Felony, Misdemeanor, Civil, Eviction—Court of Common Pleas-Criminal/Civil, Forest County Courthouse, PO Box 423, Tionesta, PA 16353. 814-755-3526. Fax: 814-755-8837. 9AM-4PM (EST). Access by: Mail, in person.

Franklin County

Real Estate Recording—Franklin County Recorder of Deeds, 157 Lincoln Way East, Chambersburg, PA 17201. 717-261-3872. Fax: 717-267-3438. 8:30AM-4:30PM (EST).

Civil, Eviction—Court of Common Pleas-Civil, 157 Lincoln Way East, Chambersburg, PA 17201. 717-261-3858. Fax: 717-267-3438. 8:30AM-4:30PM (EST). Access by: In person only.

Felony, Misdemeanor—Court of Common Pleas-Criminal, 157 Lincoln Way East, Chambersburg, PA 17201. 717-261-3805. Fax: 717-267-3438. 8:30AM-4:30PM (EST). Access by: Mail, in person.

Probate—Register of Wills, 157 Lincoln Way East, Chambersburg, PA 17201. 717-261-3872. Fax: 717-267-3438. 8:30AM-4:30PM (EST). Access by: Mail, in person.

Fulton County

Real Estate Recording—Fulton County Recorder of Deeds, 201 North Second Street, Fulton County Courthouse, McConnellsburg, PA 17233. 717-485-4212. 8:30AM-4:30PM (EST).

Felony, Misdemeanor, Civil, Eviction—Court of Common Pleas-Criminal/Civil, Fulton County Courthouse, 201 N 2nd St, McConnellsburg, PA 17233. 717-485-4212. Fax: 717-485-9411. 8:30AM-4:30PM (EST). Access by: In person only.

Greene County

Real Estate Recording—Greene County Recorder of Deeds, Courthouse, Waynesburg, PA 15370. 412-852-5283. 8:30AM-4:30PM (EST).

Civil, Eviction—Fort Jackson County Bldg, Waynesburg, PA 15370. 412-852-5289. 8:30AM-4:30PM (EST). Access by: Mail, in person.

Felony, Misdemeanor—Court of Common Pleas-Criminal, Greene County Courthouse, Waynesburg, PA 15370. 412-852-5281. Fax: 412-627-4716. 8:30AM-4:30PM (EST). Access by: Fax, mail, in person.

Probate—Register of Wills, Greene County Courthouse, 2 E High St, Waynesburg, PA 15370. 412-852-5283. 8:30AM-4PM (EST). Access by: Mail, in person.

Huntingdon County

Real Estate Recording—Huntingdon County Recorder of Deeds, 223 Penn Street, Courthouse, Huntingdon, PA 16652. 814-643-2740. 8:30AM-4:30PM (EST).

Felony, Misdemeanor, Civil, Eviction—Court of Common Pleas-Criminal/Civil, PO Box 39, Courthouse, Huntingdon, PA 16652. 814-643-1610. Fax: 814-643-8152. 8:30AM-4:30PM (EST). Access by: Phone, mail, in person.

Probate—Register of Wills, 223 Penn St, Huntingdon, PA 16652. 814-643-2740. 8:30AM-4:30PM (EST). Access by: Mail, in person.

Indiana County

Real Estate Recording—Indiana County Recorder of Deeds, 825 Philadelphia Street, Courthouse, Indiana, PA

15701. 412-465-3860. Fax: 412-465-3863. 8AM-4:30PM (EST).

Felony, Misdemeanor, Civil, Eviction—Court of Common Pleas-Criminal/Civil, County Courthouse, 825 Philadelphia St, Indiana, PA 15701. 412-465-3855. Fax: 412-465-3968. 8AM-4:30PM (EST). Access by: Fax, mail, in person.

Probate—Register of Wills, County Courthouse, 825 Philadelphia St, Indiana, PA 15701. 412-465-3860. Fax: 412-465-3863. 8AM-4:30PM (EST). Access by: Mail, in person.

Jefferson County

Real Estate Recording—Jefferson County Recorder of Deeds, 200 Main Street, Courthouse, Brookville, PA 15825. 814-849-1610. Fax: 814-849-1612. 8:30AM-4:30PM (EST).

Felony, Misdemeanor, Civil, Eviction—Court of Common Pleas-Criminal/Civil, 200 Main St, Brookville, PA 15825. 814-849-8031. Fax: 814-849-1649. 8:30AM-4:30PM (EST). Access by: Mail, in person.

Probate—Register of Wills, Jefferson County Courthouse, 200 Main St, Brookville, PA 15825. 814-849-1610. Fax: 814-849-1612. 8:30AM-4:30PM (EST). Access by: Mail, In person.

Juniata County

Real Estate Recording—Juniata County Recorder of Deeds, Courthouse, Mifflintown, PA 17059. 717-436-8991. Fax: 717-436-5543. 8AM-4:30PM (EST).

Felony, Misdemeanor, Civil, Eviction—Court of Common Pleas-Criminal/Civil, Juniata County Courthouse, Mifflintown, PA 17059. 717-436-7715. Fax: 717-436-7734. 8AM-4:30PM (EST). Access by: Phone, mail, in person.

Probate—Register of Wills, Juniata County Courthouse, PO Box 68, Mifflintown, PA 17059. 717-436-8991. Fax: 717-436-7756. 8AM-4:30PM M-F, 8AM-12PM Wed (June-Sept) (EST). Access by: Mail, in person.

Lackawanna County

Real Estate Recording—Lackawanna County Recorder of Deeds, 200 North Washington, Courthouse, Scranton, PA 18503. 717-963-6775. 9AM-4PM (EST).

Civil, Eviction—Court of Common Pleas-Civil, Clerk of Judicial Records, PO Box 133, Scranton, PA 18503. 717-963-6724. Civil: 717-963-6723. 9AM-4PM (EST). Access by: In person only.

Felony, Misdemeanor—Court of Common Pleas-Criminal, Lackawanna County Courthouse, Scranton, PA 18503. 717-963-6759. Fax: 717-963-6459. 9AM-4PM (EST). Access by: Mail, in person.

Probate—Register of Wills, Registrar of Wills, County Courthouse, 200 N Washington Ave, Scranton, PA 18503. 717-963-6708. 9AM-4PM (EST). Access by: Mail, in person.

Lancaster County

Real Estate Recording—Lancaster County Recorder of Deeds, 50 North Duke Street, Lancaster, PA 17602. 717-299-8238. 8:30AM-4:30PM (for recording); 8:30AM-5PM (for the public) (EST).

Civil, Eviction—Court of Common Pleas-Civil, 50 N Duke St, PO Box 83480, Lancaster, PA 17608-3480. 717-299-8282. Fax: 717-293-7210. 8:30AM-5PM (EST). Access by: Mail, in person.

Felony, Misdemeanor—Court of Common Pleas-Criminal, 50 North Duke St, Lancaster, PA 17602. 717-299-8275. 8:30AM-5PM (EST). Access by: Mail, in person.

Probate—Register of Wills, 50 N. Duke St., Lancaster, PA 17602. 717-299-8243. 8:30AM-5PM (EST). Access by: Phone, Mail, In person.

Lawrence County

Real Estate Recording—Lawrence County Recorder of Deeds, 430 Court Street, Government Center, New Castle, PA 16101. 412-656-2127. Fax: 412-656-1966. 8AM-4PM (EST).

Felony, Misdemeanor, Civil, Eviction—Court of Common Pleas-Criminal/Civil, 430 Court St, New Castle, PA 16101-

3593. 412-656-2143. Fax: 412-656-1988. 8AM-4PM (EST). Access by: Mail, in person.

Probate—Register of Wills, 430 Court St., New Castle, PA 16101-3593. 412-656-2128. Fax: 412-656-1966. 8AM-4PM (EST). Access by: Mail, in person.

Lebanon County

Real Estate Recording—Lebanon County Recorder of Deeds, 400 South 8th Street, Room 107, Lebanon, PA 17042. 717-274-2801. Recording Hours 8:30AM-4PM (EST).

Civil, Eviction—Court of Common Pleas-Civil & Criminal, Municipal Bldg, Rm 104, 400 S 8th St, Lebanon, PA 17042. 717-274-2801. 8:30AM-4:30PM (EST). Access by: In person only.

Felony, Misdemeanor—Court of Common Pleas-Criminal, Municipal Bldg, Rm 106, 400 S 8th St, Lebanon, PA 17042. 717-274-2801. 8:30AM-4:30PM (EST). Access by: Phone, in person. Action number required for phone access.

Probate—Register of Wills, Municipal Bldg, Rm 105, 400 S 8th St, Lebanon, PA 17042. 717-274-2801. Fax: 717-274-8094. 8:30AM-4:30PM (EST). Access by: Mail, in person.

Lehigh County

Real Estate Recording—Lehigh County Recorder of Deeds, 455 Hamilton Street, Allentown, PA 18101. 610-820-3162. Fax: 610-820-2039. 8AM-4PM (EST).

Civil, Eviction—Court of Common Pleas-Civil, Civil Division, PO Box 1548, Allentown, PA 18105. 610-820-3148. 8AM-4PM (EST). Access by: In person only.

Felony, Misdemeanor—Court of Common Pleas-Criminal, PO Box 1548, Allentown, PA 18105-1548. 610-820-3077. 8:30AM-4:30PM (EST). Access by: Mail, remote online, in person. All types of county records, including civil cases and real estate are available remotely online. Call 610-820-3627 for more information.

Probate—Register of Wills, Box 1548, Allentown, PA 18105. 610-820-3170. Fax: 610-820-3439. 8AM-4PM (EST). Access by: Mail, in person.

Luzerne County

Real Estate Recording—Luzerne County Recorder of Deeds, 200 North River Street, Courthouse, Wilkes-Barre, PA 18711. 717-825-1641. 9AM-4:30PM (EST).

Civil, Eviction—Court of Common Pleas-Civil, 200 N River St, Wilkes Barre, PA 18711. 717-825-1745. 9AM-4:30PM (EST). Access by: Mail, in person.

Felony, Misdemeanor—Court of Common Pleas-Criminal, 200 N River St, Wilkes Barre, PA 18711. 717-825-1585. Fax: 717-825-1843. 9AM-4:30PM (EST). Access by: Phone, fax, mail, in person.

Probate—Register of Wills, 200 N River St, Wilkes Barre, PA 18711. 717-825-1672. 9AM-4:30PM (EST). Access by: Mail, in person.

Lycoming County

Real Estate Recording—Lycoming County Recorder of Deeds, 48 West Third Street, Williamsport, PA 17701. 717-327-2263. Fax: 717-327-2511. 8:30AM-5PM (EST).

Felony, Misdemeanor, Civil, Eviction—Court of Common Pleas-Criminal/Civil, 48 W 3rd St, Williamsport, PA 17701. 717-327-2200. 8:30AM-5PM (EST). Access by: Mail, in person.

Probate—Register of Wills, Lycoming Co Courthouse, 48 W 3rd St, Williamsport, PA 17701. 717-327-2258. 8:30AM-5PM (EST). Access by: Mail, in person.

McKean County

Real Estate Recording—McKean County Recorder of Deeds, Main Street, Courthouse, Smethport, PA 16749. 814-887-5571. 8:30AM-4:30PM (EST).

Felony, Misdemeanor, Civil, Eviction—Court of Common Pleas-Criminal and Civil, PO Box 273, Smethport, PA 16749. 814-887-5571. Fax: 814-887-2242. 8:30AM-4:30PM (EST). Access by: Mail, in person.

Probate—Register of Wills, PO Box 202, Smethport, PA 16749-0202. 814-887-5571. Fax: 814-887-2712. 8:30AM-4:30PM (EST). Access by: Mail, in person.

Mercer County

Real Estate Recording—Mercer County Recorder of Deeds, North Diamond Street, Courthouse Room 109, Mercer, PA 16137. 412-662-3800. Fax: 412-662-2096. 8:30AM-4:30PM (EST).

Civil, Eviction—Court of Common Pleas-Civil, 105 Mercer County Courthouse, Mercer, PA 16137. 412-662-3800. 8:30AM-4:30PM (EST). Access by: Mail, in person.

Felony, Misdemeanor—Court of Common Pleas-Criminal, 112 Mercer County Courthouse, Mercer, PA 16137. 412-662-3800. 8:30AM-4:30PM (EST). Access by: Mail, in person.

Probate—Register of Wills, 112 Mercer County Courthouse, Mercer, PA 16137. 412-662-3800. Fax: 412-662-1530. 8:30AM-4:30PM (EST). Access by: In person only.

Mifflin County

Real Estate Recording—Mifflin County Recorder of Deeds, 20 North Wayne Street, Lewistown, PA 17044. 717-242-1449. 8AM-4:30PM (EST).

Felony, Misdemeanor, Civil, Eviction—Court of Common Pleas-Criminal and Civil, 20 N Wayne St, Lewistown, PA 17044. 717-248-8146. 8AM-4:30PM (EST). Access by: In person only.

Probate—Register of Wills, 20 N. Wayne St., Lewistown, PA 17044. 717-242-1449. 8AM-4:30PM M-F, 8:30AM-4:30PM Wed (June-Sept) (EST). Access by: Mail, in person.

Monroe County

Real Estate Recording—Monroe County Recorder of Deeds, 7th & Monroe Street, Courthouse, Stroudsburg, PA 18360. 717-420-3530. Fax: 717-420-3537. 8:30AM-4:30PM (EST).

Civil, Eviction—Court of Common Pleas-Civil, Monroe County Courthouse, Stroudsburg, PA 18360. 717-420-3570. 8:30AM-4:30PM (EST). Access by: Mail, in person.

Felony, Misdemeanor—Court of Common Pleas-Criminal, Monroe County Courthouse, Stroudsburg, PA 18360-2190. 717-420-3710. 8:30AM-4:30PM (EST). Access by: Mail, in person.

Probate—Register of Wills, Monroe County Courthouse, Stroudsburg, PA 18360. 717-420-3540. 8:30AM-4:30PM (EST). Access by: Mail, in person.

Montgomery County

Real Estate Recording—Montgomery County Recorder of Deeds, One Montgomery Plaza, Suite 303, Swede & Airy Sts., Norristown, PA 19404. 610-278-3289. Fax: 610-278-3869. 8:30AM-4:15PM (EST).

Civil, Eviction—Court of Common Pleas-Civil, PO Box 311, Airy & Swede St, Norristown, PA 19404-0311. 610-278-3360. 8:30AM-4:15PM (EST). Access by: Mail, in person.

Felony, Misdemeanor—Court of Common Pleas-Criminal, PO Box 311, Airy & Swede St, Norristown, PA 19404. 610-278-3346. Fax: 610-278-5188. 8:30AM-4:15PM (EST). Access by: Phone, fax, mail, remote online, in person. For information abour remote access, call 800-360-8989, extension 5. There is a $10 registration fee plus $.15 per minute of usage. Index goes back 10 years.

Probate—Montgomery County Register in Wills, Clerk of Orphan's Court, Airy & Swede St, PO Box 311, Norristown, PA 19404. 610-278-3400. Fax: 610-278-3240. 8:30AM-4:10PM (EST). Access by: Mail, in person.

Montour County

Real Estate Recording—Montour County Recorder of Deeds, 29 Mill Street, Courthouse, Danville, PA 17821. 717-271-3012. Fax: 717-271-3088. 9AM-4PM (EST).

Felony, Misdemeanor, Civil, Eviction—Court of Common Pleas-Criminal and Civil, Montour County Courthouse, 29 Mill St, Danville, PA 17821. 717-271-3010. Fax: 717-271-3088. 9AM-4PM (EST). Access by: Phone, mail, in person.

Probate—Register of Wills, 29 Mill St, Danville, PA 17821. 717-271-3012. Fax: 717-271-3088. 9AM-4PM (EST). Access by: Mail, in person.

Northampton County

Real Estate Recording—Northampton County Recorder of Deeds, 669 Washington Streets, Government Center, Easton, PA 18042. 610-559-3077. Fax: 610-559-3103. 8:30AM-4:30PM (EST).

Civil, Eviction—Court of Common Pleas-Civil, Gov't Center, 669 Washington St Rm 207, Easton, PA 18042-7498. 610-559-3060. 8:30AM-4:30PM (EST). Access by: Mail, in person.

Felony, Misdemeanor—Court of Common Pleas-Criminal, 669 Washington St, Easton, PA 18042-7494. 610-559-3000. Fax: 610-262-4391. 8:30AM-4:30PM (EST). Access by: Phone, mail, in person.

Probate—Register of Wills, Governnment Center, 669 Washington St, Easton, PA 18042. 610-559-3092. Fax: 610-559-3735. 8:30AM-4:30PM (EST). Access by: Mail, in person.

Northumberland County

Real Estate Recording—Northumberland County Recorder of Deeds, 2nd & Market Streets, Court House, Sunbury, PA 17801. 717-988-4141. 9AM-4:30PM (EST).

Civil, Eviction—Court of Common Pleas-Civil, County Courthouse, 2nd & Market St, Sunbury, PA 17801. 717-988-4151. 9AM-5PM M; 9AM-4:30PM T-F (EST). Access by: Mail, in person.

Felony, Misdemeanor—Court of Common Pleas-Criminal, County Courthouse, 201 Market St, Rm 7, Sunbury, PA 17801-3468. 717-988-4148. Fax: 717-988-4445. 9AM-5PM M; 9AM-4:30PM T-F (EST). Access by: Mail, in person.

Probate—Register of Wills, County Courthouse, 201 Market St, Sunbury, PA 17801. 717-988-4143. 9AM-4:30PM (EST). Access by: Mail, in person.

Perry County

Real Estate Recording—Perry County Recorder of Deeds, Courthouse, New Bloomfield, PA 17068. 717-582-2131. 8AM-4PM (EST).

Felony, Misdemeanor, Civil, Eviction—Court of Common Pleas-Criminal and Civil, PO Box 325, New Bloomfield, PA 17068. 717-582-2131. 8AM-4PM (EST). Access by: Phone, mail, in person.

Probate—Register of Wills, PO Box 223, New Bloomfield, PA 17068. 717-582-2131. Fax: 717-582-8570. 8AM-4PM (EST). Access by: Phone, mail, in person.

Philadelphia County

Real Estate Recording—Philadelphia County Recorder of Deeds, Broad & Market Streets, City Hall Room 156, Philadelphia, PA 19107. 215-686-2260. (EST).

Civil, Eviction—Court of Common Pleas-Civil, First Judicial District of PA, Room 284, City Hall, Philadelphia, PA 19107. 215-686-8859. Fax: 215-567-7380. 9AM-5PM (EST). Access by: Mail, in person.

Felony, Misdemeanor—Clerk of Quarter Session, 1301 Filbert St Ste 10, Philadelphia, PA 19107. 215-686-7700. 8AM-5PM (EST). Access by: Mail, in person.

Felony, Misdemeanor, Civil Actions Under $15,000, Eviction—Municipal Court, 34 S 11th St, 5th floor, Philadelphia, PA 19107. 215-686-7997. 9AM-5PM (EST). Access by: Mail, in person.

Probate—Register of Wills, City Hall Rm 180, Philadelphia, PA 19107. 215-686-6250. Fax: 215-686-6293. 8:30AM-4:30PM (EST). Access by: Mail, in person.

Pike County

Real Estate Recording—Pike County Recorder of Deeds, 506 Broad Street, Milford, PA 18337. 717-296-3508. 8:30AM-4:30PM (EST).

Felony, Misdemeanor, Civil, Eviction—Court of Common Pleas-Criminal and Civil, 412 Broad St, Milford, PA 18337.

717-296-7231. 8:30AM-4:30PM (EST). Access by: Mail, in person.

Potter County

Real Estate Recording—Potter County Recorder of Deeds, Courthouse, Room 20, Coudersport, PA 16915. 814-274-8370. 8:30AM-4:30PM (EST).

Felony, Misdemeanor, Civil, Eviction—Court of Common Pleas-Criminal and Civil, 1 E 2nd St Rm 23, Coudersport, PA 16915. 814-274-9740. Fax: 814-174-0584. 8:30AM-4:30PM (EST). Access by: Phone, mail, in person.

Probate—Register of Wills, 1 E 2nd St, Coudersport, PA 16915. 814-274-8370. 8:30AM-4:30PM (EST).

Schuylkill County

Real Estate Recording—Schuylkill County Recorder of Deeds, 401 N. Second St., Pottsville, PA 17901. 717-628-1480. 9AM-4PM (EST).

Civil, Eviction—Court of Common Pleas-Civil, 401 N 2nd St, Pottsville, PA 17901-2528. 717-628-1270. Fax: 717-628-1108. 9AM-4PM (EST). Access by: Mail, in person.

Felony, Misdemeanor—Court of Common Pleas-Criminal, 410 N 2nd St, Pottsville, PA 17901. 717-622-5570. Fax: 717-628-1108. 9AM-4PM (EST). Access by: Fax, mail, in person.

Probate—Register of Wills, Courthouse 401 N 2nd St, Pottsville, PA 17901-2520. 717-628-1377. Fax: 717-628-1108. 9AM-4PM (EST). Access by: Mail, in person.

Snyder County

Real Estate Recording—Snyder County Recorder of Deeds, 9-11 West Market Street, Courthouse, Middleburg, PA 17842. 717-837-4225. Fax: 717-837-4225. 8:30AM-4PM (EST).

Felony, Misdemeanor, Civil, Eviction—Court of Common Pleas-Criminal and Civil, Snyder County Courthouse, PO Box 217, Middleburg, PA 17842. 717-837-4202. 8:30AM-4PM (EST). Access by: Mail, in person.

Probate—Register of Wills, County Courthouse, PO Box 217, Middleburg, PA 17842. 717-837-4224. 8:30AM-4PM (EST). Access by: Mail, in person.

Somerset County

Real Estate Recording—Somerset County Recorder of Deeds, 111 E. Main St., Suite 140, Somerset, PA 15501. 814-445-2160. 8:30AM-4PM (EST).

Civil, Eviction—Court of Common Pleas-Civil, 111 E Union St Suite 190, Somerset, PA 15501-0586. 814-445-2186. Fax: 814-445-7991. 8:30AM-4PM (EST). Access by: Fax, mail, in person.

Felony, Misdemeanor—Court of Common Pleas-Criminal, 111 E Union St Suite 180, Somerset, PA 15501. 814-445-5154. 8:30AM-4PM (EST). Access by: Phone, mail, in person.

Probate—Register of Wills, 111 E Union St Suite 170, Somerset, PA 15501-0586. 814-445-2096. Fax: 814-445-7991. 8:30AM-4PM (EST). Access by: Mail, in person.

Sullivan County

Real Estate Recording—Sullivan County Recorder of Deeds, Main Street, Courthouse, Laporte, PA 18626. 717-946-7351. 8:30AM-4PM (EST).

Felony, Misdemeanor, Civil, Eviction—Court of Common Pleas-Criminal and Civil, Main Street, Laporte, PA 18626. 717-946-7351. 8:30AM-4PM (EST). Access by: Mail, in person.

Susquehanna County

Real Estate Recording—Susquehanna County Recorder of Deeds, Courthouse, Montrose, PA 18801. 717-278-4600. Fax: 717-278-9268. 9AM-4:30PM (EST).

Civil, Eviction—Court of Common Pleas-Civil, Susquehanna Courthouse, PO Box 218, Montrose, PA 18801. 717-278-4600. 8:30AM-4:30PM (EST). Access by: Mail, in person.

Felony, Misdemeanor—Court of Common Pleas-Criminal, Susquehanna Courthouse, PO Box 218, Montrose, PA 18801. 717-278-4600. 8:30AM-4:30PM (EST). Access by: Mail, in person.

Probate—Register of Wills, Susquehanna County Courthouse, PO Box 218, Montrose, PA 18801. 717-278-4600. Fax: 717-278-9268. 9AM-4:30PM (EST). Access by: Mail, in person.

Tioga County

Real Estate Recording—Tioga County Recorder of Deeds, 116 Main Street, Courthouse, Wellsboro, PA 16901. 717-724-9260. 9AM-4:30PM (EST).

Felony, Misdemeanor, Civil, Eviction—Court of Common Pleas-Criminal and Civil, 116 Main St, Wellsboro, PA 16901. 717-724-9281. 9AM-4:30PM (EST). Access by: Mail, in person.

Probate—Register of Wills, 116 Main St, Wellsboro, PA 16901. 717-724-9260. 9AM-4:30PM (EST).

Union County

Real Estate Recording—Union County Recorder of Deeds, 103 South 2nd Street, Courthouse, Lewisburg, PA 17837. 717-524-8761. 8:30AM-4:30PM (EST).

Felony, Misdemeanor, Civil, Eviction—Court of Common Pleas-Criminal and Civil, 103 S 2nd St, Lewisburg, PA 17837. 717-524-8751. 8:30AM-4:30PM (EST). Access by: Phone, mail, in person.

Probate—Register of Wills, 103 S 2nd St, Lewisburg, PA 17837. 717-524-8761. 8:30AM-4:30PM (EST). Access by: In person only.

Venango County

Real Estate Recording—Venango County Recorder of Deeds, Courthouse, Franklin, PA 16323. 814-432-9539. Fax: 814-432-9569. 8:30AM-4:30PM (EST).

Felony, Misdemeanor, Civil, Eviction—Court of Common Pleas-Criminal and Civil, Venango County Courthouse, Franklin, PA 16323. 814-432-9577. Fax: 814-432-9569. 8:30AM-4:30PM (EST). Access by: Mail, in person.

Probate—Register of Wills/Recorder of Deeds, 1168 Liberty St, Franklin, PA 16323. 814-432-9539. Fax: 814-432-9569. 8:30AM-4:30PM (EST). Access by: Phone, mail, in person.

Warren County

Real Estate Recording—Warren County Recorder of Deeds, 4th & Market Streets, Courthouse, Warren, PA 16365. 814-723-7550. 8:30AM-3:30PM (EST).

Felony, Misdemeanor, Civil, Eviction—Court of Common Pleas-Criminal and Civil, 4th & Market St, Warren, PA 16365. 814-723-7550. Fax: 814-723-8115. 8:30AM-4:30PM (EST). Access by: Mail, in person.

Probate—Register of Wills, Courthouse, 204 4th Ave, Warren, PA 16365. 814-723-7550. Fax: 814-723-8115. 8:30AM-4:30PM (EST). Access by: Mail, in person.

Washington County

Real Estate Recording—Washington County Recorder of Deeds, Washington County Courthouse, 1 South Main St., Room 1006, Washington, PA 15301. 412-228-6806. Fax: 412-228-6737. 9AM-4:30PM (EST).

Civil, Eviction—Court of Common Pleas-Civil, 1 S Main St Suite 1001, Washington, PA 15301. 412-228-6770. 9AM-4:30PM (EST). Access by: In person only.

Felony, Misdemeanor—Court of Common Pleas-Criminal, Courthouse Ste 1005, 1 S Main St, Washington, PA 15301. 412-228-6787. Fax: 412-228-6890. 9AM-4:30PM (EST). Access by: Mail, in person.

Probate—Register of Wills, Courthouse, 1 S Main St Suite 1002, Washington, PA 15301. 412-228-6775. 9AM-4:30PM (EST). Access by: Mail, in person.

Wayne County

Real Estate Recording—Wayne County Recorder of Deeds, 925 Court Street, Honesdale, PA 18431. 717-253-5970. 8:30AM-4:30PM (EST).

Felony, Misdemeanor, Civil, Eviction—Court of Common Pleas-Criminal and Civil, 925 Court St, Honesdale, PA 18431. 717-253-5970. 8:30AM-4:30PM (EST). Access by: In person only.

Probate—Register of Wills, 925 Court St, Honesdale, PA 18431. 717-253-5970. 8:30AM-4:30PM (EST). Access by: Phone, mail, in person.

Westmoreland County

Real Estate Recording—Westmoreland County Recorder of Deeds, Main Street, Courthouse Square Room 503, Greensburg, PA 15601. 412-830-3526. Fax: 412-832-8757. 8:30AM-4PM (EST).

Civil, Eviction—Court of Common Pleas-Civil, Courthouse Sq, Rm 501, Greensburg, PA 15601-1168. 412-830-3500. 8:30AM-4PM (EST). Access by: In person only.

Felony, Misdemeanor—Court of Common Pleas-Criminal, Criminal Division, 203 Courthouse Square, Greensburg, PA 15601-1168. 412-830-3734. Fax: 412-830-3472. 8:30AM-4PM (EST). Access by: Fax, mail, remote online, in person.

Probate—Register of Wills, Registrar of Wills, 301 Courthouse Sq, Greensburg, PA 15601. 412-830-3177. Fax: 412-850-3976. 8:30AM-4PM (EST). Access by: Mail, in person.

Wyoming County

Real Estate Recording—Wyoming County Recorder of Deeds, 1 Courthouse Square, Tunkhannock, PA 18657. 717-836-3200. 8:30AM-4PM (EST).

Felony, Misdemeanor, Civil, Eviction—Court of Common Pleas-Criminal and Civil, Wyoming County Courthouse, Tunkhannock, PA 18657. 717-836-3200. 8:30AM-4PM (EST). Access by: In person only.

Probate—Register of Wills, County Courthouse, 1 Courthouse Sq, Tunkhannock, PA 18657. 717-836-3200. 8:30AM-4PM (EST). Access by: Mail, in person.

York County

Real Estate Recording—York County Recorder of Deeds, 28 East Market Street, York, PA 17401. 717-771-9608. 8:30AM-4:30PM (EST).

Civil, Eviction—Court of Common Pleas-Civil, York County Courthouse, 28E Market St, York, PA 17401. 717-771-9611. 8:30AM-4:30PM (EST). Access by: In person only.

Felony, Misdemeanor—Court of Common Pleas-Criminal, York County Courthouse 28 E Market St, York, PA 17401. 717-771-9612. Fax: 717-771-9096. 8:30AM-4:30PM (EST). Access by: Mail, in person.

Probate—Register of Wills, York County Courthouse 28 E Market St, York, PA 17401. 717-771-9263. Fax: 717-771-4678. 8:30AM-4:15PM (EST). Access by: Mail, in person.

Federal Courts

US District Court

Eastern District of Pennsylvania

Allentown/Reading Division, US District Court c/o 504 Hamilton St, Suite 1601, Allentown, PA 18101-5600. 610-434-3896. Counties: Berks, Lancaster, Lehigh, Northampton, Schuylkill

Philadelphia Division, US District Court Room 2609, US Courthouse, 601 Market St, Philadelphia, PA 19106-1797. 215-597-7704. Counties: Bucks, Chester, Delaware, Montgomery, Philadelphia

Middle District of Pennsylvania

Harrisburg Division, US District Court PO Box 983, Harrisburg, PA 17108-0983. 717-221-3920. Counties: Adams, Cumberland, Dauphin, Franklin, Fulton, Huntingdon, Juniata, Lebanon, Mifflin, York

Scranton Division, US District Court Clerk's Office, PO Box 1148, Scranton, PA 18501. 717-347-0205. Counties: Bradford, Carbon, Lackawanna, Luzerne, Monroe, Pike, Susquehanna, Wayne, Wyoming

Williamsport Division, US District Court PO Box 608, Williamsport, PA 17703. 717-323-6380. Counties: Cameron, Centre, Clinton, Columbia, Lycoming, Montour, Northumberland, Perry, Potter, Snyder, Sullivan, Tioga, Union

Western District of Pennsylvania

Erie Division, US District Court 102 US Courthouse, 617 State St, Erie, PA 16501. 814-453-4829. Counties: Crawford, Elk, Erie, Forest, McKean, Venango, Warren

Johnstown Division, US District Court Penn Traffic Bldg, Room 208, 319 Washington St, Johnstown, PA 15901. 814-533-4504. Counties: Bedford, Blair, Cambria, Clearfield, Somerset

Pittsburgh Division, US District Court US Post Office & Courthouse, Room 829, 7th Ave & Grant St, Pittsburgh, PA 15219. 412-644-3527. Counties: Allegheny, Armstrong, Beaver, Butler, Clarion, Fayette, Greene, Indiana, Jefferson, Lawrence, Mercer, Washington, Westmoreland

US Bankruptcy Court

Eastern District of Pennsylvania

Philadelphia Division, US Bankruptcy Court, 900 Market St, 4th Floor, Philadelphia, PA 19107. 215-408-2800. Voice Case Information System: 215-597-2244. Counties: Bucks, Chester, Delaware, Montgomery, Philadelphia

Reading Division, US Bankruptcy Court, Suite 300, The Madison, 400 Washington St, Reading, PA 19601. 610-320-5255. Voice Case Information System: 215-597-2244. Counties: Berks, Lancaster, Lehigh, Northampton, Schuylkill

Middle District of Pennsylvania

Harrisburg Division, US Bankruptcy Court, PO Box 908, Harrisburg, PA 17108. 717-782-2260. Counties: Adams, Centre, Cumberland, Dauphin, Franklin, Fulton, Huntingdon, Juniata, Lebanon, Mifflin, Montour, Northumberland, Perry, Snyder, Union, York

Wilkes-Barre Division, US Bankruptcy Court, Room 217, 197 S Main St, Wilkes-Barre, PA 18701. 717-826-6450. Counties: Bradford, Cameron, Carbon, Clinton, Columbia, Lackawanna, Luzerne, Lycoming, Monroe, Pike, Potter, Sullivan, Susquehanna, Tioga, Wayne, Wyoming

Western District of Pennsylvania

Erie Division, US Bankruptcy Court, 717 State St, #501, Erie, PA 16501. 814-453-7580. Voice Case Information System: 412-355-3210. Counties: Clarion, Crawford, Elk, Erie, Forest, Jefferson, McKean, Mercer, Venango, Warren

Pittsburgh Division, US Bankruptcy Court, 1602 Federal Bldg, 1000 Liberty Ave, Pittsburgh, PA 15219. 412-644-2700. Voice Case Information System: 412-355-3210. Counties: Allegheny, Armstrong, Beaver, Bedford, Blair, Butler, Cambria, Clearfield, Fayette, Greene, Indiana, Lawrence, Somerset, Washington, Westmoreland

Rhode Island

Capitol: Providence (Providence County)	
Number of Counties: 5	**Population:** 989,794
County Court Locations:	**Federal Court Locations:**
•Superior Courts: 4/4 Divisions	•District Courts: 1
•District Courts: 4/4 Divisions	•Bankruptcy Courts: 1
•Combined Courts: 1	**State Agencies:** 20
Municipal Courts: 14	
•Probate Courts: 39/ 39 Cities/Towns	
Family Courts: 4 Divisions	
Workers' Compensation Courts: 1	

State Agencies—Summary

General Help Numbers:

State Archives

Secretary of State	401-277-2353
Archives & Public Record Admin	Fax: 401-277-3199
337 Westminster St	8:30AM-4:30PM M-SA
Providence, RI 02903	
Historical Society:	401-331-8575

Governor's Office

Governor's Office	401-277-2080
State House, Room 143	Fax: 401-861-5894
Providence, RI 02903	8:30AM-4:30PM

Attorney General's Office

Attorney General's Office	401-274-4400
150 S. Main St	Fax: 401-277-1302
Providence, RI 02903-2856	8:30AM-4:30PM

State Legislation

Rhode Island General Assembly	401-277-3580
State House	8:30AM-4:30PM
Document Room (Basement)	
Providence, RI 02903	
State Library:	401-277-2473

Important State Internet Sites:

🌐 Webscape	
File Edit View	Help

State of Rhode Island World Wide Web
www.state.ri.us/

The home page includes links to all branches of government, business, history and other state links.

Rhode Island Bills and Laws
www.state.ri.us/submenus/leglink.htm

This site links to information about House and Senate bills, bills by subject, bills by sponsor and the action taken on these bills.

State Archives
gopher://archives.state.ri.us

Home page of the state archives. The archives holds records back to 1638. Many items are available online from this site.

Unclaimed Property
www.state.ri.us/treas/moneylst.htm

This page provides you with all the information necessary to search for unclaimed property, such as checking and savings accounts, payroll, wages, insurance, refunds and much more. You can search online at this site.

State Agencies—Public Records

Criminal Records
Department of Attorney General, Bureau of Criminal Identification, 72 Pine St, Providence, RI 02903, Main Telephone: 401-274-2238, Hours: 8AM-5PM. Access by: mail, visit.

Corporation Records
Fictitious Name
Limited Partnerships
Limited Liability Company Records
Limited Liability Partnerships
Secretary of State, Corporations Division, 100 N Main St, Providence, RI 02903, Main Telephone: 401-277-3040, Fax: 401-277-1309, Hours: 8:30AM-4:30PM. Access by: mail, phone, visit, PC.

Trademarks/Servicemarks
Secretary of State, Trademark Division, 100 N Main St, Providence, RI 02903, Main Telephone: 401-277-1487, Hours: 8:30AM-4:30PM. Access by: mail, phone, visit.

Uniform Commercial Code
Federal Tax Liens
State Tax Liens
UCC Division, Secretary of State, 100 North Main St, Providence, RI 02903, Main Telephone: 401-277-2249, Hours: 8:30AM-4:30PM. Access by: mail, phone, visit.

Sales Tax Registrations
Taxation Division, Sales & Use Tax Office, One Capitol Hill, Providence, RI 02908-5890, Main Telephone: 401-277-2937, Fax: 401-277-6006, Hours: 8:30AM-4PM. Access by: mail, phone, visit.

Birth Certificates
State Department of Health, Division of Vital Records, 3 Capitol Hill, Room 101, Providence, RI 02908-5097, Main Telephone: 401-277-2812, Message Phone: 401-277-2811, Hours: 8:30AM-4:30PM. Access by: mail, visit.

Death Records
State Department of Health, Division of Vital Records, 3 Capitol Hill, Room 101, Providence, RI 02908-5097, Main Telephone: 401-277-2812, Message Phone: 401-277-2811, Hours: 8:30AM-4:30PM;. Access by: mail, visit.

Marriage Certificates
State Department of Health, Division of Vital Records, 3 Capitol Hill, Room 101, Providence, RI 02908-5097, Main Telephone: 401-277-2812, Message Phone: 401-277-2811, Hours: 8:30AM-4:30PM M-F;. Access by: mail, visit.

Divorce Records
Records not available from state agency.

Workers' Compensation Records
Department of Labor & Training, Division of Workers' Compensation, PO Box 3500, Providence, RI 02909-0500, Main Telephone: 401-457-1800, Fax: 401-277-2127, Hours: 8AM-4:30PM. Access by: mail, visit.

Driver Records
Division of Motor Vehicles, Driving Record Clerk, Operator Control, 345 Harris Ave, Providence, RI 02909, Main Telephone: 401-277-2994, Hours: 8:30AM-4:30PM. Access by: mail, visit. Copies of tickets may be obtained without fee by writing to the Division of Adjudication at the address listed above.

Vehicle Ownership
Vehicle Identification
Registry of Motor Vehicles, c/o Registration Files, 286 Main Street, Pawtucket, RI 02860, Main Telephone: 401-277-2970, Hours: 8:30AM-3:30PM. Access by: mail, visit.

Accident Reports
Rhode Island State Police, Accident Record Division, 311 Danielson Pike, North Scituate, RI 02857, Main Telephone: 401-444-1143, Fax: 401-444-1133, Hours: 10AM-3:30PM M,T,TH,F. Access by: mail, visit.

Hunting License Information
Fishing License Information
Natural Resources, Fish, Wildlife and Esturian Resources Division, 22 Hayes St, Providence, RI 02908, Main Telephone: 401-277-3576, Hours: 8:30AM-4:30PM. Access by: phone, visit. This agency will only confirm, by phone, that an individual has a current hunting or salt water or commercial fishing license. They will provide no other information.

County Courts and Recording Offices

What You Need to Know...

About the Courts	About the Recorder's Office

About the Courts

Administration

Court Administrator	401-277-3272
Supreme Court	Fax: 401-277-3599
250 Benefit St	8:30AM-4:30PM
Providence, RI 02903	

Court Structure

RI has 5 counties but only 4 Superior/District Court Locations (2nd. 3rd, 4th, and 6th Districts). Bristol and Providence counties are completely merged at the Providence location. Civil claims between $5,000 and $10,000 may be filed in either Superior or District Court at the discretion of the filer. Probate is handled by the Town Clerk at the 39 cities and towns across RI.

Online Access

Online computer access is **not** available in Rhode Island

About the Recorder's Office

Organization

5 counties and 39 towns, 39 filing offices. The recording officer is Town/City Clerk (Recorder of Deeds). The Town/City Clerk usually also serves as Recorder of Deeds. **There is no county administration in Rhode Island.** The entire state is in the Eastern Time Zone (EST).

UCC Records

Financing statements are filed at the state level, except for farm related and real estate related collateral, which are filed with the Town/City Clerk. Most filing offices will **not** perform UCC searches. Use search request form UCC-11. Copy fees are usually $1.50 per page.

Lien Records

All federal and state tax liens on personal property and on real property are filed with the Recorder of Deeds. Towns will **not** perform tax lien searches. Other liens include mechanics, municipal, and lis pendens.

Real Estate Records

Towns will **not** perform real estate searches. Copy fees are usually $1.50 per page. Certification usually costs $3.00 per document.

County Courts and Recording Offices

Barrington Town

Real Estate Recording—Barrington Town Clerk, 283 County Road, Town Hall, Barrington, RI 02806. 401-247-1900. 8:30AM-4:30PM (EST).

Bristol County

Real Estate Recording—There is no real estate recording at the county level in Rhode Island. You must determine the city or town where the property is located.

Felony, Misdemeanor, Civil, Eviction, Small Claims—Superior and District Courts, Handled by Providence County courts.

Probate—Barrington Town Hall, 283 County Road, Barrington, RI 02806. 401-247-1900. Fax: Call first. 8:30AM-4:30PM (EST).

Bristol Town Hall, 10 Court Street, Bristol, RI 02809. 401-253-7000. Fax: 401-253-3080. 8:30AM-4PM (EST). Access by: Mail, in person.

Warren Town Hall, 514 Main Street, Warren, RI 02885. 401-245-7340. Fax: 401-245-7421. 9AM-4PM (EST).

Bristol Town

Real Estate Recording—Bristol Town Clerk, 10 Court Street, Town Hall, Bristol, RI 02809. 401-253-7000. 8:30AM-4PM (EST).

Burrillville Town

Real Estate Recording—Burrillville Town Clerk, 105 Harrisville Main Street, Town Hall, Harrisville, RI 02830. 401-568-4300. Fax: 401-568-0490. 8:30AM-4:30PM (Recording until 4PM) (EST).

Central Falls City

Real Estate Recording—Central Falls City Clerk, 580 Broad Street, City Hall, Central Falls, RI 02863. 401-727-7400. Fax: 401-727-7476. 8:30AM-4:30PM (EST).

Charlestown Town

Real Estate Recording—Charlestown Town Clerk, 4540 South County Trail, Charlestown, RI 02813. 401-364-1200. Fax: 401-364-1238. 8:30AM-4:30PM (Recording until 4PM) (EST).

Coventry Town

Real Estate Recording—Coventry Town Clerk, 1670 Flat River Road, Town Hall, Coventry, RI 02816. 401-822-9174. Fax: 401-822-9132. 8:30AM-4:30PM (EST).

Cranston City

Real Estate Recording—Cranston City Clerk, 869 Park Avenue, City Hall, Cranston, RI 02910. 401-461-1000. 8:30AM-4:30PM (EST).

Cumberland Town

Real Estate Recording—Cumberland Town Clerk, 45 Broad Street, Town Hall, Cumberland, RI 02864. 401-728-2400. Fax: 401-724-3311. 8:30AM-4:30PM (EST).

East Greenwich Town

Real Estate Recording—East Greenwich Town Clerk, Town Hall, 125 Main St., East Greenwich, RI 02818. 401-886-8603. Fax: 401-886-8625. 8:30AM-4:30PM (EST).

East Providence City

Real Estate Recording—East Providence City Clerk, 145 Taunton Avenue, City Hall, East Providence, RI 02914. 401-435-7500. Fax: 401-438-1719. 8AM-4PM (EST).

Exeter Town

Real Estate Recording—Exeter Town Clerk, 675 Ten Rod Road, Town Hall, Exeter, RI 02822. 401-294-3891. Fax: 401-295-1248. 9AM-4PM (EST).

Foster Town

Real Estate Recording—Foster Town Clerk, 181 Howard Hill Road, Town Hall, Foster, RI 02825. 401-392-9200. Fax: 401-397-9736. 9AM-3:30PM (EST).

Glocester Town

Real Estate Recording—Glocester Town Clerk, 1145 Putnam Pike, Town Hall, Glocester/ Chepachet, RI 02814. 401-568-6206. Fax: 401-568-5850. 8AM-4:30PM (EST).

Hopkinton Town

Real Estate Recording—Hopkinton Town Clerk, 1 Town House Road, Town Hall, Hopkinton, RI 02833. 401-377-7777. Fax: 401-377-7788. 8:30AM-4:30PM (EST).

Jamestown Town

Real Estate Recording—Jamestown Town Clerk, 93 Narragansett Avenue, Town Hall, Jamestown, RI 02835. 401-423-7200. Fax: 401-423-7229. 8AM-4:30PM (EST).

Johnston Town

Real Estate Recording—Johnston Town Clerk, 1385 Hartford Avenue, Town Hall, Johnston, RI 02919. 401-351-6618. Fax: 401-331-4271. 9AM-4:30PM (EST).

Kent County

Real Estate Recording—There is no real estate recording at the county level in Rhode Island. You must determine the town or city where the property is located.

Felony, Civil Actions Over $10,000—Superior Court, 222 Quaker Lane, Warwick, RI 02886-0107. 401-822-1311. 8:30AM-4:30PM (EST). Access by: In person only.

Misdemeanor, Civil Actions Under $10,000, Eviction, Small Claims—3rd Division District Court, 222 Quaker Lane, Warwick, RI 02886-0107. 401-822-1771. 8:30AM-4:30PM (EST). Access by: In person only.

Probate—Coventry Town Hall, 1670 Flat River Road, Coventry, RI 02816. 401-822-9174. Fax: 401-822-9132. 8:30AM-4:30PM (EST). Access by: Mail, in person.

East Greenwich Town Hall, 111 Peirce Street, East Greenwich, RI 02818. 401-886-8603. Fax: 401-886-8625. 8:30AM-4:30PM (EST).

Warwick City Hall, 3275 Post Road, Warwick, RI 02886. 401-738-2000. Fax: 401-738-6639. 8:30AM-4:30PM (EST). Access by: Mail, in person.

West Greenwich Town Hall, 280 Victory Highway, West Greenwich, RI 02817. 401-397-5016. Fax: 401-392-3805. 9AM-4PM M,T,Th,F; 9AM-4PM, 7-9PM W (EST). Access by: Mail, in person.

West Warwick Town Hall, 1170 Main Street, West Warwick, RI 02893. 401-822-9200. Fax: 401-822-9266. 8:30AM-4:30PM; 8:30AM-4PM June 1st-Labor Day (EST).

Lincoln Town

Real Estate Recording—Lincoln Town Clerk, 100 Old River Road, Town Hall, Lincoln, RI 02865. 401-333-1100. Fax: 401-333-3648. 9AM-4:30PM (EST).

Little Compton Town

Real Estate Recording—Little Compton Town Clerk, 40 Commons, Town Hall, Little Compton, RI 02837. 401-635-4400. Fax: 401-635-2470. 8AM-4PM (EST).

Middletown Town

Real Estate Recording—Middletown Town Clerk, 350 East Main Road, Town Hall, Middletown, RI 02842. 401-847-0009. Fax: 401-848-0500. 9AM-5PM (EST).

Narragansett Town

Real Estate Recording—Narragansett Town Clerk, 25 Fifth Avenue, Town Hall, Narragansett, RI 02882. 401-789-1044. Fax: 401-783-9637. 8:30AM-4:30PM (EST).

New Shoreham Town

Real Estate Recording—New Shoreham Town Clerk, Old Town Road, Town Hall, Block Island, RI 02807. 401-466-3200. Fax: 401-466-3219. 9AM-3PM; 9AM-1PM Sat (EST).

Newport City

Real Estate Recording—Newport City Clerk, 43 Broadway, Town Hall, Newport, RI 02840. 401-846-9600. 9AM-5PM (Recording Hours 9AM-4PM) (EST).

Newport County

Real Estate Recording—There is no real estate recording at the county level in Rhode Island. You must determine the town or city where the property is located.

Felony, Civil Actions Over $10,000—Superior Court, Florence K Murray Judicial Complex, 45 Washington Sq, Newport, RI 02840. 401-841-8330. 8:30AM-4:30PM (July and August till 4PM) (EST). Access by: Mail, in person.

Civil Actions Under $10,000, Eviction, Small Claims—2nd Division District Court, Eisenhower Square, Newport, RI 02840. 401-841-8350. Fax: 401-841-8394. 8:30AM-4:30PM (4PM-summer months) (EST). Access by: Phone, mail, in person.

Probate—Jamestown Town Hall, 93 Narragansett Avenue, Jamestown, RI 02835. 401-423-7200. Fax: 401-423-7230. 8AM-4:30PM (EST). Access by: Mail, in person.

Little Compton Town Hall, 40 Commons, PO Box 523, Little Compton, RI 02837. 401-635-4400. Fax: 401-635-2470. 8AM-4PM (EST).

Middletown Town Hall, 350 East Main Road, Middletown, RI 02842. 401-847-0009. Fax: 401-845-0400. 9AM-5PM (EST).

Newport City Hall, 43 Broadway, Newport, RI 02840. 401-846-9600. Fax: 401-848-5750. 8:45AM-5PM (EST).

Portsmouth Town Hall, 2200 East Main Road, PO Box 155, Portsmouth, RI 02871. 401-683-2101. 9AM-4PM (EST).

Tiverton Town Hall, 343 Highland Road, Tiverton, RI 02878. 401-625-6700. Fax: 401-624-8640. 8:30AM-4PM (EST).

North Kingstown Town

Real Estate Recording—North Kingstown Town Clerk, 80 Boston Neck Road, Town Hall, North Kingstown, RI 02852. 401-294-3331. Fax: 401-885-7373. 8:30AM-4:30PM (EST).

North Providence Town

Real Estate Recording—North Providence Town Clerk, 2000 Smith Street, Town Hall, North Providence, RI 02911. 401-232-0900. Fax: 401-233-1409. 8:30AM-4:30PM (Summer hours 8:30 AM-4PM) (EST).

North Smithfield Town

Real Estate Recording—North Smithfield Town Clerk, 1 Main Street, Town Hall, Slatersville, RI 02876. 401-767-2200. Fax: 401-766-0016. 8AM-4PM (Recording until 3:30PM) (EST).

Pawtucket City

Real Estate Recording—Pawtucket City Clerk, 137 Roosevelt Avenue, City Hall, Pawtucket, RI 02860. 401-728-0500. Fax: 401-728-8932. 8:30AM-4:30PM; Recording until 3:30PM (EST).

Portsmouth Town

Real Estate Recording—Portsmouth Town Clerk, 2200 East Main Road, Town Hall, Portsmouth, RI 02871. 401-683-2101. Recording Hours 9AM-3:45PM (EST).

Providence City

Real Estate Recording—Providence City Recorder of Deeds, 25 Dorrance Street, City Hall, Providence, RI 02903. 401-421-7740. 8:30AM-4:30PM (Recording Hours 8:30AM-4PM) (EST).

Providence County

Real Estate Recording—There is no real estate recording at the county level in Rhode Island. You must determine the proper town or city based on property location.

Felony, Civil Actions Over $10,000—Providence/Bristol Superior Court, 250 Benefit St, Providence, RI 02903. 401-277-3250. 8:30AM-4:30PM (EST). Access by: Mail, in person.

Misdemeanor, Civil Actions Under $10,000, Eviction, Small Claims—6th Division District Court, 1 Dorrance Plaza 2nd Floor, Providence, RI 02903. 401-277-6710. 8:30AM-4:30PM (EST). Access by: Phone, mail, in person. Phone requests limited to one name.

Probate—Central Falls City Hall, 580 Broad Street, Central Falls, RI 02863. 401-727-7400. Fax: 401-727-7476. 8:30AM-4:30PM (EST). Access by: In person only.

Cranston City Hall, 869 Park Avenue, Cranston, RI 02910. 401-461-1000. Fax: 401-461-9650. 8:30AM-4:30PM (EST).

Cumberland Town Hall, 45 Broad Street, PO Box 7, Cumberland, RI 02864. 401-728-2400. Fax: 401-724-3311. 8:30AM-4:30PM (EST).

East Providence City Hall, 145 Taunton Avenue, East Providence, RI 02914. 401-435-7500. Fax: 401-438-1719. 8AM-4PM (EST).

Smithfield Town Hall, 64 Farnum Pike, Esmond, RI 02917. 401-233-1000. Fax: 401-232-7244. 9AM-4PM (EST). Access by: Mail, in person.

Foster Town Hall, 181 Howard Hill Road, Foster, RI 02825. 401-392-9200. Fax: 401-397-9736. 9AM-4PM (EST).

Glocester Town Hall, 1145 Putnam Pike, Glocester/Chepachet, RI 02814. 401-568-6206. Fax: 401-568-5850. 8AM-4:30PM (EST). Access by: Mail, in person.

Burrillville Town Hall, 105 Harrisville Main Street, Harrisville, RI 02830. 401-568-4300. Fax: 401-568-0490. 8:30AM-4:30PM (EST).

Johnston Town Hall, 1385 Hartford Avenue, Johnston, RI 02919. 401-351-6618. Fax: 401-553-8835. 9AM-4:30PM (EST). Access by: In person only.

Lincoln Town Hall, 100 Old River Road, Lincoln, RI 02865. 401-333-1100. Fax: 401-333-3648. 9AM-4:30PM (EST).

North Providence Town Hall, 2000 Smith Street, North Providence, RI 02911. 401-232-0900. Fax: 401-233-1409. 8:30AM-4:30PM (EST).

Scituate Town Hall, 195 Danielson Pike, PO Box 328, North Scituate, RI 02857. 401-647-7466. Fax: Call first. 9AM-4PM (EST).

Pawtucket City Hall, 137 Roosevelt Avenue, Pawtucket, RI 02860. 401-728-0500. Fax: 401-728-8932. 8:30AM-4:30PM (EST).

Providence City Hall, 25 Dorrance Street, Providence, RI 02903. 401-421-7740. Fax: 401-861-6208. 8:45AM-4:15PM (EST). Access by: Mail, in person.

North Smithfield Town Hall, 1 Main Street, Slatersville, RI 02876. 401-767-2200. Fax: 401-766-0016. 8AM-4PM (EST).

Woonsocket City Hall, 169 Main Street, Woonsocket, RI 02895. 401-762-6400. Fax: 401-765-4569. 8:30AM-4PM (EST).

Richmond Town

Real Estate Recording—Richmond Town Clerk, 5 Richmond Townhouse Rd., Town Hall, Wyoming, RI 02898. 401-539-2497. Fax: 401-539-1089. 9AM-4PM (6-7:30PM M) (EST).

Scituate Town

Real Estate Recording—Scituate Town Clerk, 195 Danielson Pike, Town Hall, North Scituate, RI 02857. 401-647-2822. 9AM-4PM (EST).

Smithfield Town

Real Estate Recording—Smithfield Town Clerk, 64 Farnum Pike, Town Hall, Esmond, RI 02917. 401-233-1000. Fax: 401-232-7244. 9AM-4PM (EST).

South Kingstown Town

Real Estate Recording—South Kingstown Town Clerk, 180 High Street, Town Hall, Wakefield, RI 02879. 401-789-9331. 8:30AM-4:30PM (EST).

Tiverton Town

Real Estate Recording—Tiverton Town Clerk, 343 Highland Road, Town Hall, Tiverton, RI 02878. 401-625-6700. Fax: 401-624-8640. 8:30AM-4PM (EST).

Warren Town

Real Estate Recording—Warren Town Clerk, 514 Main Street, Town Hall, Warren, RI 02885. 401-245-7340. Fax: 401-245-7421. 9AM-4PM (EST).

Warwick City

Real Estate Recording—Warwick City Clerk, 3275 Post Road, City Hall, Warwick, RI 02886. 401-738-2000. 8:30AM-4:30PM (Recording 8:30AM-4PM) (EST).

Washington County

Real Estate Recording—There is no real estate recording at the county level in Rhode Island. You must determine the town or city where the property is located.

Felony, Civil Actions Over $10,000—Superior Court, 4800 Towerhill Rd, Wakefield, RI 02879. 401-782-4121. 8:30AM-4:30PM (Sept-June) 8:30AM-4PM (July & Aug) (EST). Access by: Mail, in person.

Misdemeanor, Civil Actions Under $10,000, Eviction, Small Claims—4th District Court, 4800 Towerhill Rd, Wakefield, RI 02879. 401-782-4131. 8:30AM-4:30PM (EST). Access by: In person only.

Probate—New Shoreham Town Hall, Old Town Road, PO Drawer 220, Block Island, RI 02807. 401-466-3200. Fax: 401-466-3219. 9AM-3PM (EST).

Charlestown Town Hall, 4540 South County Trail, Charlestown, RI 02813. 401-364-1200. Fax: 401-364-1238. 8:30AM-4:30PM (EST).

Exeter Town Hall, 675 Ten Rod Road, Exeter, RI 02822. 401-294-3891. Fax: 401-295-1248. 9AM-4PM (EST).

Hopkinton Town Hall, 1 Town House Road, Hopkinton, RI 02833. 401-377-7777. Fax: 401-377-7788. 10AM-3PM or by appointment (EST). Access by: Mail, in person.

Narragansett Town Hall, 25 Fifth Avenue, Narragansett, RI 02882. 401-789-1044. Fax: 401-783-9637. 8:30AM-4:30PM (EST).

North Kingstown Town Hall, 80 Boston Neck Road, North Kingstown, RI 02852. 401-294-3331. Fax: 401-885-7373. 8:30AM-4:30PM (EST).

South Kingstown Town Hall, 180 High Street, Wakefield, RI 02879. 401-789-9331. Fax: 401-789-5280. 8:30AM-4:30PM (EST). Access by: Mail, in person.

Westerly Town Hall, 45 Broad Street, Westerly, RI 02891. 401-348-2500. Fax: 401-348-2571. 8:30AM-4:30PM (EST). Access by: In person only.

Richmond Town Hall, 5 Richmond Townhouse Rd., Wyoming, RI 02898. 401-539-2497. Fax: 401-539-1089. 9AM-4PM, 6-7:30PM M; 9AM-4PM T-F (EST).

West Greenwich Town

Real Estate Recording—West Greenwich Town Clerk, 280 Victory Highway, Town Hall, West Greenwich, RI 02817. 401-397-5016. Fax: 401-392-3805. (EST).

West Warwick Town

Real Estate Recording—West Warwick Town Clerk, 1170 Main Street, Town Hall, West Warwick, RI 02893. 401-822-9200. Fax: 401-822-9266. 8:30AM-4:30PM (June-August 8:30AM-4PM) (EST).

Westerly Town

Real Estate Recording—Westerly Town Clerk, 45 Broad Street, Town Hall, Westerly, RI 02891. 401-348-2500. Fax: 401-348-2571. 8:30AM-4:30PM (EST).

Woonsocket City

Real Estate Recording—Woonsocket City Clerk, 169 Main Street, City Hall, Woonsocket, RI 02895. 401-762-6400. Fax: 401-765-4569. 8:30-4PM (EST).

Federal Courts

US District Court
District of Rhode Island

Providence Division, US District Court Clerk's Office, One Exchange Terrace, Federal Bldg, Providence, RI 02903. 401-528-5100. Counties: All counties in Rhode Island

US Bankruptcy Court
District of Rhode Island

Providence Division, US Bankruptcy Court, 6th Floor, 380 Westminster Mall, Providence, RI 02903. 401-528-4477. Voice Case Information System: 401-528-4476. Counties: All counties in Rhode Island

South Carolina

Capitol: Columbia (Richland County)	
Number of Counties: 46	**Population:** 3,673,287
County Court Locations:	**Federal Court Locations:**
•Circuit Courts: 46/16 Circuits	•District Courts: 8
•Magistrate Courts: 258	•Bankruptcy Courts: 1
Municipal Courts: 175	**State Agencies:** 20
•Probate Courts: 46	
Family Courts: 46/16 Circuits	

State Agencies—Summary

General Help Numbers:

State Archives

Archives & History Department	803-734-8577
PO Box 11669	Fax: 803-734-8820
Columbia, SC 29211 9AM-9PM TU-FR, 9-6 SA, 1-6 SU	
Reference Librarian:	803-734-8596
Historical Society:	803-723-3225

Governor's Office

Governor's Office	803-734-9818
PO Box 11369	Fax: 803-734-1598
Columbia, SC 29211	8:30AM-5:30PM

Attorney General's Office

Attorney General's Office	803-734-3970
PO Box 11549	Fax: 803-734-4323
Columbia, SC 29211	8:30AM-5:30PM

State Legislation

South Carolina Legislature	803-734-2060
937 Assembly Street, Rm 220	
Columbia, SC 29261	
Legislative Research(Older Bills):	803-734-2145

Important State Internet Sites:

```
Webscape
File  Edit  View                                Help
```

State of South Carolina World Wide Web

www.state.sc.us/

This site links to such sites as education, government, history, tourism and includes a welcome message from the Governor.

State General Assembly

www.lpitr.state.sc.us/

This is an extensive site with links to the State House, address and e-mail lists, the State Constitution, bills and resolutions and much more.

Bills and Resolution Information

www.lpitr.state.sc.us/legbe4.htm

This site includes bill information that dates back to 1991 a daily update schedule, new laws this session and the 1997-98 budget.

State Archives

129.252.216.12/homepage.htm

This site includes a history of the archives, what's new, and their policies and procedures. No online searches are available.

Bills and Resolutions

www.leginfo.state.sc.us/

This site links to bills and resolutions for the General Assembly, committees, sponsors, actions, past legislation and more.

State Agencies—Public Records

Criminal Records

South Carolina Law Enforcement Division (SLED), Criminal Records Section, PO Box 21398, Columbia, SC 29221, Main Telephone: 803-737-9000, Alternate Telephone: 803-737-4205, Fax: 803-896-7022, Hours: 8:30AM-5PM. Access by: mail, visit.

Corporation Records
Trademarks/Servicemarks
Limited Partnerships
Limited Liability Company Records

Corporation Division, Capitol Complex, PO Box 11350, Columbia, SC 29211, Main Telephone: 803-734-2158, Fax: 803-734-2164, Hours: 8:30PM-5PM. Access by: mail, phone, visit, PC. Trademarks and service marks are not on the computer but are in this department. Trade names, fictitious and assumed names are at the county level.

Annual Reports, Directors and Officers

Department of Revenue, Annual Reports Division, 301 Gervias St, Columbia, SC 29201, Main Telephone: 803-737-4866, Fax: 803-737-4898, Hours: 8:30AM-5PM. Access by: mail, phone, visit.

Uniform Commercial Code
Federal Tax Liens
State Tax Liens

UCC Division, Secretary of State, PO Box 11350, Columbia, SC 29211, Main Telephone: 803-734-2175, Fax: 803-734-2164, Hours: 8:30AM-5PM. Access by: mail, visit, PC.

Sales Tax Registrations

Revenue Department, Sales Tax Registration Section, PO Box 125, Columbia, SC 29214, Main Telephone: 803-737-4872, Fax: 803-737-4981, Hours: 9AM-5PM. Access by: mail, phone.

Birth Certificates

South Carolina DHEC, Vital Records, 2600 Bull St, Columbia, SC 29201, Main Telephone: 803-734-4830, Fax: 803-799-0301, Hours: 8:30AM-4:30PM. Access by: mail, phone, visit. A "short form" wallet size birth certificate can be obtained from the county of issue. This form will not show parent names.

Death Records

South Carolina DHEC, Vital Records, 2600 Bull St, Columbia, SC 29201, Main Telephone: 803-734-4830,

Fax: 803-799-0301, Hours: 8:30AM-4:30PM. Access by: mail, phone, visit.

Marriage Certificates

South Carolina DHEC, Vital Records, 2600 Bull St, Columbia, SC 29201, Main Telephone: 803-734-4830, Fax: 803-799-0301, Hours: 8:30AM-4:30PM. Access by: mail, phone, visit. Copies may also be obtained from the Probate Judge in the county where license was issued.

Divorce Records

South Carolina DHEC, Vital Records, 2600 Bull St, Columbia, SC 29201, Main Telephone: 803-734-4830, Fax: 803-799-0301, Hours: 8:30AM-4:30PM. Access by: mail, phone, visit.

Workers' Compensation Records

Workers Compensation Commission, PO Box 1715, Columbia, SC 29202, Main Telephone: 803-737-5700, Fax: 803-737-5768, Hours: 8:30AM-5PM. Access by: mail, visit.

Driver License Information
Driver Records

Division of Motor Vehicles, Driver Records Section, PO Box 100178, Columbia, SC 29202-3178, Main Telephone: 803-737-2940, Fax: 803-737-1077, Hours: 8:30AM-5PM. Access by: mail, visit, PC. Copies of tickets are available from this department for a fee of $2.00 per record.

Vehicle Ownership
Vehicle Identification

Division of Motor Vehicles, Title and Registration Records Section, PO Box 1498, Columbia, SC 29216, Main Telephone: 803-251-2950, Registrations: 803-251-2960, Hours: 8:30AM-5PM. Access by: mail, phone, visit. For the PO Box address, use ZIP 29216-0022 for Registration and ZIP 29216-0024 for Titles.

Accident Reports

Accident Reports, PO Box 100178, Columbia, SC 29202-3178, Main Telephone: 803-251-2969, Fax: 803-737-1578, Hours: 8:30AM-5PM. Access by: mail, phone, visit.

Hunting License Information
Fishing License Information

Records not available from state agency.

County Courts and Recording Offices

What You Need to Know...

About the Courts

About the Recorder's Office

Administration

Court Administration	803-734-1800
1015 Sumter St, 2nd Floor	Fax: 803-734-1821
Columbia, SC 29250	8:30AM-5PM

Court Structure

Magistrate and Municipal Courts only handle misdemeanor cases involving 30 days maximum jail time.

The maximum civil claim level for the Magistrate Courts increased to **$5,000** from the $2,500 on 1/1/96.

Searching Hints

The Clerk of the Circuit Court maintains the records of both divisions of the Circuit Court, Court of General Sessions and Court of Common Pleas as well as for the Family Court. General Sessions and Common Pleas are co-located in every county. If requesting a record in writing, it is recommended that the words *"request that general session, common pleas, and family court records be searched"* be included in the request.

Most courts will **not** conduct searches. However, if a **name and case number** are provided, many will pull and copy the record. Search fees vary widely as they are set by each county.

Online Access

There is no online public access available in SC.

Organization

46 counties, 46 filing offices. The recording officer is Register of Mesne Conveyances or Clerk of Court (varies by county). The entire state is in the Eastern Time Zone (EST).

UCC Records

Financing statements are filed at the state level, except for consumer goods, farm related and real estate related collateral, which are filed with the Register. All filing offices will perform UCC searches. Use search request form UCC-4. Searches fees are usually $5.00 per debtor name. Copy fees are usually $1.00 per page.

Lien Records

All federal and state tax liens on personal property and on real property are filed with the Register of Mesne Conveyances (Clerk of Court). Some counties will perform tax lien searches. Search fees and copy fees vary.

Real Estate Records

Most counties will **not** perform real estate searches. Copy and certification fees vary. The Assessor keeps tax records.

County Courts and Recording Offices

Abbeville County

Real Estate Recording—Abbeville Clerk of Court, Court Square, Abbeville, SC 29620. 864-459-5074. 9AM-5PM (EST).

Felony, Misdemeanor, Civil Actions Over $5,000—Circuit Court, PO Box 99, Abbeville, SC 29620. 864-459-5074. 9AM-5PM (EST). Access by: Mail, in person.

Civil Actions Under $5,000, Eviction, Small Claims—Abbeville Magistrate Court, 111 Pinckney St (PO Drawer 1156), Abbeville, SC 29620. 864-459-2080. Fax: 864-459-4982. 9AM-5PM (EST). Access by: Mail, in person.

Probate—Probate Court, PO Box 70, Abbeville, SC 29620. 864-459-4626. Fax: 864-459-4982. 9AM-5PM (EST). Access by: Phone, fax, mail, in person.

Aiken County

Real Estate Recording—Aiken County Register of Mesne Conveyances, 828 Richland Avenue West, Aiken, SC 29801. 803-642-2072. 8:30AM-5PM (EST).

Felony, Misdemeanor, Civil Actions Over $5,000—Circuit Court, PO Box 583, Aiken, SC 29802. 803-642-2099. Fax: 803-642-1718. 8:30AM-5PM (EST). Access by: In person only.

Civil Actions Under $5,000, Eviction, Small Claims—Aiken Magistrate Court, 1680 Richland Ave W, Ste 70, Aiken, SC 29801. 803-642-1744. (EST). Access by: Mail, in person.

Graniteville Magistrate Court, 14 Masonic Shopping Ctr, Graniteville, SC 29829. 803-663-6634. Fax: 803-663-6635. 9AM-4:30PM (EST). Access by: Mail, in person.

Langley Magistrate Court, PO Box 769, Langley, SC 29834. 803-593-5171. Fax: 803-593-8402. (EST). Access by: Mail, in person.

Monetta Magistrate Court, 5697 Columbia Hwy N (PO Box 190), Monetta, SC 29105. 803-685-7125. (EST). Access by: Mail, in person.

New Ellenton Magistrate Court, PO Box 40, New Ellenton, SC 29809. 803-652-3609. Fax: 803-652-2653. 9AM-4:30PM, Closed 1-2 (EST). Access by: In person only.

North Augusta Magistrate Court, PO Box 6493, North Augusta, SC 29861. 803-202-3580. (EST). Access by: Mail, in person.

Salley Magistrate Court, PO Box 422, Salley, SC 29137. 803-258-3118. (EST). Access by: Mail, in person.

Probate—Probate Court, 109 Park Ave, PO Box 1576, Aiken, SC 29802. 803-642-2001. Fax: 803-642-2007. 8:30AM-5PM (EST).

Allendale County

Real Estate Recording—Allendale Clerk of Court, Pine Street, Courthouse, Allendale, SC 29810. 803-584-2737. Fax: 803-584-7058. (EST).

Felony, Misdemeanor, Civil Actions Over $5,000—Circuit Court, PO Box 126, Allendale, SC 29810. 803-584-2737. Fax: 803-584-7058. 9AM-5PM (EST). Access by: Phone, mail, in person.

Civil Actions Under $5,000, Eviction, Small Claims—Allendale Magistrate Court, 205 N Main St, Allendale, SC 29810. 803-584-3755. 9AM-5PM (EST). Access by: Phone, mail, in person.

Fairfax Magistrate Court, 115 N Hampton Ave (PO Box 421), Fairfax, SC 29827. 803-632-3871. (EST). Access by: Mail, in person.

Probate—Probate Court, PO Box 737, Allendale, SC 29810. 803-584-3157. 9AM-5PM (EST). Access by: Mail, in person.

Anderson County

Real Estate Recording—Anderson County RMC Office, 100 South Main Street, Courthouse, Anderson, SC 29624. 864-260-4054. Fax: 864-260-4443. 8:30AM-5PM (EST).

Felony, Misdemeanor, Civil Actions Over $5,000—Circuit Court, PO Box 8002, Anderson, SC 29622. 864-260-4053. Fax: 864-260-4715. 8:30AM-5PM (EST). Access by: In person only.

Civil Actions Under $5,000, Eviction, Small Claims—Anderson Magistrate Court, PO Box 8002, Anderson, SC 29622. 864-260-4156. (EST). Access by: Mail, in person.

Honea Path Magistrate Court, PO Box 214, Honea Path, SC 29654. 864-369-0015. (EST). Access by: Mail, in person.

Iva Magistrate Court, 626 E Front St (PO Box 1163), Iva, SC 29655. 864-348-3456. (EST). Access by: Mail, in person.

Pelzer Magistrate Court, PO Box 731, Pelzer, SC 29669. 864-947-1700. (EST). Access by: Mail, in person.

Pendleton Magistrate Court, 100 E Queen St (PO Box 181), Pendleton, SC 29670. 864-646-6701. (EST). Access by: Mail, in person.

Piedmont Magistrate Court, 1903 Hwy 86, Piedmont, SC 29673. 864-845-7620. 9AM-5PM (EST). Access by: Mail, in person.

Starr Magistrate Court, 7626 Hwy 81, PO Box 247, Starr, SC 29684. 864-352-3157. (EST). Access by: Mail, in person.

Townville Magistrate Court, 105 Conneross Rd (PO Box 99), Townville, SC 29689. 864-287-0550. (EST). Access by: Mail, in person.

Williamston Magistrate Court, 12 W Main St (PO Box 175), Williamston, SC 29697. 864-847-7280. (EST). Access by: Mail, in person.

Probate—Probate Court, PO Box 4046, Anderson, SC 29622. 864-260-4049. Fax: 864-260-4811. 8AM-5PM (EST). Access by: In person only.

Bamberg County

Real Estate Recording—Bamberg Clerk of Court, 110 North Main Street, Bamberg, SC 29003. 803-245-3025. Fax: 803-245-3027. 9AM-5PM (EST).

Felony, Misdemeanor, Civil Actions Over $5,000—Circuit Court, PO Box 150, Bamberg, SC 29003. 803-245-3025. Fax: 803-245-3027. 9AM-5PM (EST). Access by: Mail, in person.

Civil Actions Under $5,000, Eviction, Small Claims—Bamberg Magistrate Court, PO Box 187, Bamberg, SC 29003. 803-245-3016. (EST). Access by: Mail, in person.

Olar Magistrate Court, PO Box 108, Olar, SC 29843. 803-368-2162. (EST). Access by: Mail, in person.

Probate—Probate Court, PO Box 180, Bamberg, SC 29003. 803-245-3008. Fax: 803-245-3027. 9AM-5PM (EST).

Barnwell County

Real Estate Recording—Barnwell Clerk of Court, Courthouse Building, Room 114, Barnwell, SC 29812. 803-541-1020. Fax: 803-541-1025. 9AM-5PM (EST).

Felony, Misdemeanor, Civil Actions Over $5,000—Circuit Court, PO Box 723, Barnwell, SC 29812. 803-541-1020. Fax: 803-541-1025. 9AM-5PM (EST). Access by: Mail, in person.

Civil Actions Under $5,000, Eviction, Small Claims—Barnwell Magistrate Court, PO Box 1205, Barnwell, SC 29812. 803-541-1035. 9AM-Noon, 1-5PM (EST). Access by: Mail, in person.

Blackville Magistrate Court, 213 N Lartique St, Blackville, SC 29817. 803-284-2765. (EST). Access by: Mail, in person.

Williston Magistrate Court, PO Box 485, Williston, SC 29853. 803-266-3700. Fax: 803-266-5496. 9AM-5PM (EST). Access by: Mail, in person.

Probate—Probate Court, Room 112, County Courthouse, Barnwell, SC 29812. 803-541-1031. Fax: 803-541-1025. 9AM-5PM (EST).

Beaufort County

Real Estate Recording—Beaufort County Register of Mesne Conveyances, 100 Ribaut Rd., Administration Bldg. Rm 205, Beaufort, SC 29902. 703-525-7300. Fax: 803-525-7297. 8AM-5PM (EST).

Felony, Misdemeanor, Civil Actions Over $5,000—Circuit Court, PO Drawer 1128, Beaufort, SC 29901. 803-525-7306. 8AM-5PM (EST). Access by: Mail, in person.

Civil Actions Under $5,000, Eviction, Small Claims—Beaufort Magistrate Court, PO Box 2207, Beaufort, SC 29901-2207. 803-525-7402. (EST). Access by: Mail, in person.

Bluffton Magistrate Court, PO Box 840, Bluffton, SC 29910. 803-757-1500. (EST). Access by: Mail, in person.

Hilton Head Magistrate Court, PO Box 22895, Hilton Head, SC 29925. 803-681-4690. (EST). Access by: Mail, in person.

Lobeco Magistrate Court, PO Box 845, Lobeco, SC 29931-0845. 864-846-3902. (EST). Access by: Mail, in person.

St Helena Island Magistrate Court, PO Box 126, St Helena Island, SC 29920. 803-838-3212. (EST). Access by: Mail, in person.

Probate—Probate Court, PO Box 1083, Beaufort, SC 29901-1083. 803-525-7440. Fax: 803-525-7475. 8AM-5PM (EST). Access by: Mail, in person.

Berkeley County

Real Estate Recording—Berkeley County Register of Mesne Conveyances, 223 North Live Oak Drive, Moncks Corner, SC 29461. 803-761-6900. 9AM-5PM (EST).

Felony, Misdemeanor, Civil Actions Over $5,000—Circuit Court, PO Box 219, Moncks Corner, SC 29461. 803-761-6900. 9AM-5PM (EST). Access by: In person only.

Civil Actions Under $5,000, Eviction, Small Claims—Alvin Magistrate Court, Rt 2 Box 735, Alvin, SC 29479. 803-257-2122. (EST). Access by: Mail, in person.

Goose Creek Magistrate Court, 225 Red Bank Rd (PO Box 98), Goose Creek, SC 29445. 803-553-7080. 11AM-7PM M-TH, 11AM-5PM F (EST). Access by: Phone, mail, in person.

Moncks Corner Magistrate Court, 103 Gulledge St, PO Box 875, Moncks Corner, SC 29461. 803-761-8180. (EST). Access by: Mail, in person.

St Stephen Magistrate Court, PO Box 1433, St Stephen, SC 29479. 803-567-7400. (EST). Access by: Mail, in person.

Summerville Magistrate Court, Box 10212, Deming Way, Summerville, SC 29483. 803-832-0370. (EST). Access by: Mail, in person.

Probate—Probate Court, 300 B California Ave, Moncks Corner, SC 29461. 803-761-6900. Fax: 803-761-4359. 9AM-5PM (EST). Access by: In person only.

Calhoun County

Real Estate Recording—Calhoun Clerk of Court, 302 F.R. Huff Drive, Courthouse, St. Matthews, SC 29135. 803-874-3524. Fax: 803-874-1942. 9AM-5PM (EST).

Felony, Misdemeanor, Civil Actions Over $5,000—Circuit Court, 302 S Huff Dr, St Matthews, SC 29135. 803-874-3524. Fax: 803-874-1942. 9AM-5PM (EST). Access by: Mail, in person.

Civil Actions Under $5,000, Eviction, Small Claims—Cameron Magistrate Court, Rt 1 Box 541, Cameron, SC 29030. 803-826-6000. (EST). Access by: Mail, in person.

Cameron Magistrate Court, PO Box 663, Cameron, SC 29030. 803-823-2266. 4-7PM M & Th (EST). Access by: Mail, in person.

St Matthews Magistrate Court, 112 W Bridge St (PO Box 191), St Matthews, SC 29135. 803-874-1112. (EST). Access by: Mail, in person.

Probate—Probate Court, 302 S Huff Dr, St Matthews, SC 29135. 803-874-3514. Fax: 803-874-4575. (EST). Access by: Mail, in person.

Charleston County

Real Estate Recording—Charleston County Register of Mesne Conveyances, 2 Courthouse Square, Room 201, Meeting Street, Charleston, SC 29401. 803-723-6780. Fax: 803-720-2210. 8AM-5PM (EST).

Felony, Misdemeanor, Civil Actions Over $5,000—Circuit Court, PO Box 70219, Charleston, SC 29415. 803-740-5700. (EST). Access by: Mail, in person.

Civil Actions Under $5,000, Eviction, Small Claims—Charleston Magistrate Court, PO Box 941, Charleston, SC 29402. 803-724-6719. (EST). Access by: Mail, in person.

Charleston Magistrate Court, 995 Morrison Dr, Charleston, SC 29403-4237. 803-724-6720. Fax: 803-724-6785. (EST). Access by: Mail, in person.

Charleston Magistrate Court, 4050 Bridgeview, Charleston, SC 29405. 803-745-2217. Fax: 803-745-2317. 8:30AM-4:30PM (EST). Access by: Mail, in person.

Charleston Magistrate Court, PO Box 32412, Charleston, SC 29405. 803-745-2223. Fax: 803-745-2339. 9AM-5PM (EST). Access by: Mail, in person.

Charleston Magistrate Court, PO Box 12226, Charleston, SC 29412. 803-795-1140. 8:30AM-5PM (EST). Access by: Mail, in person.

Charleston Magistrate Court, PO Box 31861, Charleston, SC 29417. 803-766-6531. Fax: 803-571-4751. (EST). Access by: Mail, in person.

Esidto Island Magistrate Court, 8070 Indigo Hill Rd (PO Box 216), Edisto Island, SC 29438. 803-869-2909. (EST). Access by: Mail, in person.

Johns Island Magistrate Court, 1527 Main Rd, Johns Island, SC 29455. 803-559-1218. (EST). Access by: Mail, in person.

McClellanville Magistrate Court, 9888 Randall Rd (PO Box 7), McClellanville, SC 29458. 803-887-3334. Fax: 803-887-3901. 9AM-Noon, 1Pm-4PM M,W (EST). Access by: In person only.

Mt Pleasant Magistrate Court, 1189 Iron Bridge Rd, Ste 300, Mt Pleasant, SC 29464. 803-856-1206. Fax: 803-856-1204. 8:30AM-5PM (EST). Access by: Mail, in person.

North Charleston Magistrate Court, 2036 Cherokee St, North Charleston, SC 29405. 803-745-2216. (EST). Access by: Mail, in person.

North Charleston Magistrate Court, 2144 Melbourne St, North Charleston, SC 29405. 803-740-5873. (EST). Access by: Mail, in person.

North Charleston Magistrate Court, 7272 Cross County Rd (PO Box 61870), North Charleston, SC 29419. 803-767-2743. (EST). Access by: Mail, in person.

Ravenel Magistrate Court, 5962 Hwy 165, Ravenel, SC 29470. 803-889-8332. (EST). Access by: Mail, in person.

Probate—Probate Court, 2144 Melbourne Ave, Charleston, SC 29415. 803-740-5889. Fax: 803-740-5897. 8:30AM-5PM (EST). Access by: In person only.

Cherokee County

Real Estate Recording—Cherokee Clerk of Court, Floyd Baker Blvd, Gaffney, SC 29340. 864-487-2571. Fax: 864-487-2754. 9AM-5PM (EST).

Felony, Misdemeanor, Civil Actions Over $5,000—Circuit Court, PO Drawer 2289, Gaffney, SC 29342. 864-487-2571. Fax: 864-487-2751. 9AM-5PM (EST). Access by: In person only.

Civil Actions Under $5,000, Eviction, Small Claims—Blacksburg Magistrate Court, 303 W Pine St, PO Box 427, Blacksburg, SC 29702. 864-839-2492. (EST). Access by: Mail, in person.

Gaffney Magistrate Court, PO Box 336, Gaffney, SC 29342. 864-487-2533. Fax: 864-487-2754. 9AM-5PM (EST). Access by: Mail, in person.

Probate—Probate Court, PO Box 22, Gaffney, SC 29342. 864-487-2583. Fax: 864-902-8426. 9AM-5PM (EST).

Chester County

Real Estate Recording—Chester Clerk of Court, 140 Main Street, Chester, SC 29706. 803-385-2605. Fax: 803-581-7975. 8:30AM-5PM (EST).

Felony, Misdemeanor, Civil Actions Over $5,000—Circuit Court, PO Drawer 580, Chester, SC 29706. 803-385-2605. Fax: 803-385-2022. 8:30AM-5PM (EST). Access by: Mail, in person.

Civil Actions Under $5,000, Eviction, Small Claims—Chester Magistrate Court, 2811 Cassels Rd, Chester, SC 29706. 803-789-5010. (EST). Access by: Mail, in person.

Chester Magistrate Court-1st District, 2740 Dawson Dr, PO Box 727, Chester, SC 29706. 803-581-5136. Fax: 803-581-5552. 8:30AM-5PM (EST). Access by: Mail, in person.

Richburg Magistrate Court, PO Box 148, Richburg, SC 29729. 803-789-5010. (EST). Access by: Mail, in person.

Probate—Probate Court, PO Drawer 580, Chester, SC 29706. 803-385-2604. Fax: 803-581-5180. 8:30AM-5PM (EST). Access by: Mail, in person.

Chesterfield County

Real Estate Recording—Chesterfield Clerk of Court, 200 West Main Street, Chesterfield, SC 29709. 803-623-2574. Fax: 803-623-3945. 8:30AM-5PM (EST).

Felony, Misdemeanor, Civil Actions Over $5,000—Circuit Court, PO Box 529, Chesterfield, SC 29709. 803-623-2574. 8:30AM-5PM (EST). Access by: Mail, in person.

Civil Actions Under $5,000, Eviction, Small Claims—Cheraw Magistrate Court, PO Box 681, Cheraw, SC 29520. 803-498-6701. (EST). Access by: Mail, in person.

Cheraw Magistrate Court, 258 2nd St, Cheraw, SC 29520. 803-537-7139. (EST). Access by: Mail, in person.

Cheraw Magistrate Court, Rt 1 Box 366-A, Hinson Hill Rd, Cheraw, SC 29520. 803-623-2955. (EST). Access by: Mail, in person.

Cheraw Magistrate Court, 309 Clyde Ave (PO Box 749), Cheraw, SC 29520. 803-537-7292. (EST). Access by: Mail, in person.

Chesterfield Magistrate Court, Rt 1 Box 40, Chesterfield, SC 29709. 803-623-7929. (EST). Access by: Mail, in person.

Chesterfield Magistrate Court, Rte 1 Box 40, Chesterfield, SC 29709. 803-623-7929. (EST). Access by: Mail, in person.

Jefferson Magistrate Court, 167 S Main St (PO Box 396), Jefferson, SC 29718. 803-658-7180. (EST). Access by: Mail, in person.

McBee Magistrate Court, Rt 1 Box 455, McBee, SC 29101. 803-335-8467. (EST). Access by: Mail, in person.

Pageland Magistrate Court, 126 N Pearl St, Pageland, SC 29728. 803-672-6914. (EST). Access by: Mail, in person.

Patrick Magistrate Court, Rt 1 Box 385, Patrick, SC 29584. 803-498-6640. (EST). Access by: Mail, in person.

Ruby Magistrate Court, PO Box 131, Ruby, SC 29741. 803-634-6597. (EST). Access by: Mail, in person.

Probate—Probate Court, County Courthouse, 200 W Main St, Chesterfield, SC 29709. 803-623-2376. Fax: 803-623-3945. 8:30AM-5PM (EST).

Clarendon County

Real Estate Recording—Clarendon County RMC Department, Boyce Street, Courthouse, Manning, SC 29102. 803-435-4444. Fax: 803-435-4844. 8:30AM-5PM (EST).

Felony, Misdemeanor, Civil Actions Over $5,000—Circuit Court, PO Drawer E, Manning, SC 29102. 803-435-4444. 8:30AM-5PM (EST). Access by: Mail, in person.

Civil Actions Under $5,000, Eviction, Small Claims—Lake City Magistrate Court, Rt 1 Box 617, Lake City, SC 29560. 803-389-2484. By Appointment (EST). Access by: Mail, in person.

Manning Magistrate Court, PO Box 371, Manning, SC 29102. 803-435-2670. 8:30AM-5PM (EST). Access by: Mail, in person.

Summerton Magistrate Court, 102 Main St (PO Box 277), Summerton, SC 29148. 803-435-2855. Fax: 803-485-2855. (EST). Access by: Mail, in person.

Probate—Probate Court, PO Box 307, Manning, SC 29102. 803-435-8774. 8:30AM-5PM (EST). Access by: Mail, in person.

Colleton County

Real Estate Recording—Colleton Clerk of Court, No. 1 Washington Street, Courthouse, Walterboro, SC 29488. 803-549-5791. Fax: 803-549-2875. 8:30AM-5PM (EST).

Felony, Misdemeanor, Civil Actions Over $5,000—Circuit Court, PO Box 620, Walterboro, SC 29488. 803-549-5791. 8:30AM-5PM (EST). Access by: Mail, in person.

Civil Actions Under $5,000, Eviction, Small Claims—Green Pond Magistrate Court, Rt 2 Box 131, Green Pond, SC 29446. 803-844-2594. 9AM-5PM (EST). Access by: Mail, in person.

Walterboro Magistrate Court, PO Box 1732, Walterboro, SC 29488. 803-549-1122. Fax: 803-549-2875. 8:30AM-5PM (EST). Access by: Mail, in person.

Walterboro Magistrate Court, Rt 7 Box 239-C, Walterboro, SC 29488. 803-538-3637. 8:30AM-5PM (EST). Access by: Mail, in person.

Walterboro Magistrate Court, 1201 Green Pond Hwy, Walterboro, SC 29488. 803-549-1522. (EST). Access by: Mail, in person.

Probate—Probate Court, PO Box 1036, Walterboro, SC 29488. 803-549-7216. Fax: 803-549-5571. 8:30AM-5PM (EST). Access by: Mail, in person.

Darlington County

Real Estate Recording—Darlington Clerk of Court, Courthouse, Darlington, SC 29532. 803-398-4330. Fax: 803-398-4172. 8:30AM-5PM (EST).

Felony, Misdemeanor, Civil Actions Over $5,000—Circuit Court, PO Box 498, Darlington, SC 29532. 803-398-4339. 8:30AM-5PM (EST). Access by: Mail, in person.

Civil Actions Under $5,000, Eviction, Small Claims—Darlington Magistrate Court, 115 Camp Rd, Darlington, SC 29532. 803-398-4341. 8AM-5PM (EST). Access by: Mail, in person.

Florence Magistrate Court, 4522 Blitsgel Dr, Florence, SC 29501. (EST). Access by: Mail, in person.

Hartsville Magistrate Court, PO Box 1765, 404 S 4th St, Hartsville, SC 29550. 8AM-5PM (EST).

Lamar Magistrate Court, Town Hall, 117 Main St, Lamar, SC 29069. 803-326-5441. (EST). Access by: Mail, in person.

Society Hill Magistrate Court, Rt 2 Box 297, Society Hill, SC 29593. 803-378-4601. (EST). Access by: Mail, in person.

Probate—Probate Court, Courthouse #1 Public Sq Rm 208, Darlington, SC 29532. 803-398-4310. Fax: 803-398-4172. 8:30AM-5PM (EST). Access by: Mail, in person.

Dillon County

Real Estate Recording—Dillon Clerk of Court, 401 West Main Street, City-County Complex, Suite 201, Dillon, SC 29536. 803-774-1425. Fax: 803-774-1443. 8:30AM-5PM (EST).

Felony, Misdemeanor, Civil Actions Over $5,000—Circuit Court, PO Drawer 1220, Dillon, SC 29536. 803-774-1425. 8:30AM-5PM (EST). Access by: Mail, in person.

Civil Actions Under $5,000, Eviction, Small Claims—Dillon Magistrate Court, 200 S 5th Ave (PO Box 1016), Dillon, SC 29536. 803-774-1407. 7PM-9PM (EST). Access by: Mail, in person.

Dillon Magistrate Court, PO Box 1281, Dillon, SC 29536. 803-774-5330. (EST). Access by: Mail, in person.

Hamer Magistrate Court, 101 Lee Blvd (PO Box 1), Hamer, SC 29547. 803-774-2041. (EST). Access by: Mail, in person.

Lake View Magistrate Court, PO Box 272, Lake View, SC 29563. (EST). Access by: Mail, in person.

Probate—Probate Court, PO Box 189, Dillon, SC 29536. 803-774-1423. 8:30AM-5PM (EST).

Dorchester County

Real Estate Recording—Dorchester County Register of Mesne Conveyances, 101 Ridge Street, St. George, SC 29477. 803-563-0184. 8:30AM-5PM (Recording 8:30AM-4:30PM) (EST).

Felony, Misdemeanor, Civil Actions Over $5,000—Circuit Court, PO Box 158, St George, SC 29477. 803-563-0160. 8:30AM-5PM (EST). Access by: In person only.

Civil Actions Under $5,000, Eviction, Small Claims—Dorchester County Court, 102 Sears St, St George, SC 29477. 803-563-4854. 8AM-5PM (EST). Access by: Mail, in person.

Summerville Magistrate Court, 133 E 1st North St, Summerville, SC 29483. 803-873-0781. (EST). Access by: Mail, in person.

Summerville Magistrate Court, 212 Deming Way Box 10, Summerville, SC 29483. 803-873-0781. 8AM-5PM (EST). Access by: Mail, in person.

Summerville Magistrate Court, PO Box 1372, Summerville, SC 29485. 803-871-1000. (EST). Access by: Mail, in person.

Probate—Probate Court, 101 Ridge St, St George, SC 29477. 803-563-0105. Fax: 803-832-0187. 8:30AM-5PM (EST).

Edgefield County

Real Estate Recording—Edgefield Clerk of Court, 129 Courthouse Square, Edgefield, SC 29824. 803-637-4080. Fax: 803-637-4117. 8:30AM-5PM (EST).

Felony, Misdemeanor, Civil Actions Over $5,000—Circuit Court, PO Box 34, Edgefield, SC 29824. 803-637-4082. 8:30AM-5PM (EST). Access by: Mail, in person.

Civil Actions Under $5,000, Eviction, Small Claims—Edgefield Magistrate Court, PO Box 664, Edgefield, SC 29824. 803-637-4090. Fax: 803-637-4101. 8:30AM-4:30PM (EST). Access by: Mail, in person.

Probate—Probate Court, 127 Courthouse Square, Edgefield, SC 29824. 803-637-4076. 8:30AM-5PM (EST). Access by: Mail, in person.

Fairfield County

Real Estate Recording—Fairfield Clerk of Court, Congress Street, Courthouse, Winnsboro, SC 29180. 803-635-1411. 9AM-5PM (EST).

Felony, Misdemeanor, Civil Actions Over $5,000—Circuit Court, PO Drawer 299, Winnsboro, SC 29180. 803-635-1411. 9AM-5PM (EST). Access by: In person only.

Civil Actions Under $5,000, Eviction, Small Claims—Great Falls Magistrate Court, Rt 1 Box 1064, Great Falls, SC 29055. 803-482-2283. 8AM-5PM (EST). Access by: Mail, in person.

Jenkinsville Magistrate Court, Rt 1 Box 148, Jenkinsville, SC 29065. 803-345-4635. (EST). Access by: Mail, in person.

Winnsboro Magistrate Court, PO Box 423, Winnsboro, SC 29180. 803-635-4525. 9AM-5PM (EST). Access by: Mail, in person.

Probate—Probate Court, PO Box 385, Winnsboro, SC 29180. 803-635-1411. Fax: 803-635-2767. 9AM-5PM (EST). Access by: Mail, in person.

Florence County

Real Estate Recording—Florence Clerk of Court, 180 North Irby, Courthouse, Florence, SC 29501. 803-665-3031. 8:30AM-5PM (EST).

Felony, Misdemeanor, Civil Actions Over $5,000—Circuit Court, Drawer E, City County Complex, Florence, SC 29501. 803-665-3031. 8:30AM-5PM (EST). Access by: Mail, in person.

Civil Actions Under $5,000, Eviction, Small Claims—Florence Magistrate Court, 180 N Irby St, Florence, SC 29501. 803-665-0031. 8:30-5PM (EST). Access by: Mail, in person.

Johnsonville Magistrate Court, 119 Broadway St (PO Box 186), Johnsonville, SC 29555. 803-386-3422. 9:30AM-5:30PM M,TH,F (EST). Access by: Mail, in person.

Lake City Magistrate Court, 345 S Ron McNair Blvd (PO Box 39), Lake City, SC 29560. 803-394-5461. 8:30AM-5PM (EST). Access by: Mail, in person.

Olanta Magistrate Court, PO Box 277, Olanta, SC 29114. 803-396-4798. (EST). Access by: Mail, in person.

Pamplico Magistrate Court, 136 E 3rd Ave, Pamplico, SC 29583. 803-493-0072. 8:30AM-5PM T-F (EST). Access by: Mail, in person.

Timmonsville Magistrate Court, 307 Smith St (PO Box 190), Timmonsville, SC 29161. 803-346-7472. 8:30-5PM (EST). Access by: Mail, in person.

Probate—Probate Court, 180 N Irby, MSC-L, Florence, SC 29501. 803-665-3085. Fax: 803-665-3068. 8:30AM-5PM (EST). Access by: Phone, mail, in person.

Georgetown County

Real Estate Recording—Georgetown County RMC, 715 Prince Street, Georgetown, SC 29440. 803-527-6315. Fax: 803-546-2144. 8:30AM-5PM (EST).

Felony, Misdemeanor, Civil Actions Over $5,000—Circuit Court, PO Box 1270, Georgetown, SC 29442. 803-546-5011. Civil: 803-527-6388. Criminal: 803-527-6314. Fax: 803-546-2144. 8:30AM-5PM (EST). Access by: Mail, in person.

Civil Actions Under $5,000, Eviction, Small Claims—Andrews Magistrate Court, 408 E Main, Andrews, SC 29510. 803-264-8811. 8AM-5PM (EST). Access by: Mail, in person.

Georgetown Magistrate Court, PO Box 807, Georgetown, SC 29442. 803-546-4650. 8AM-5PM (EST). Access by: Mail, in person.

Georgetown Magistrate Court, PO Box 1838, 333 Clelend St, Georgetown, SC 29442. 803-527-8980. (EST). Access by: Mail, in person.

Hemingway Magistrate Court, Rt 3 Box 46, Hemingway, SC 29564. 803-546-4650. (EST). Access by: Mail, in person.

Murrells Inlet Magistrate Court, PO Box 859, Murrells Inlet, SC 29576. 803-651-6292. 8AM-5PM (EST). Access by: Mail, in person.

Pawleys Island Magistrate Court, PO Box 1830, Pawleys Island, SC 29585. 803-237-8995. 8AM-5PM (EST). Access by: Mail, in person.

Probate—Probate Court, PO Box 1270, Georgetown, SC 29442. 803-527-6325. Fax: 803-546-4730. 8:30AM-5PM (EST). Access by: Mail, in person.

Greenville County

Real Estate Recording—Greenville County Register of Mesne Conveyances, 301 University Ridge, County Square Suite 1300, Greenville, SC 29601. 864-467-7240. Fax: 864-467-7107. 8:30AM-5PM (EST).

Felony, Misdemeanor, Civil Actions Over $5,000—Circuit Court, 305 E. North St, Greenville, SC 29601. 864-467-8551. Fax: 864-467-8540. 8:30AM-5PM (EST). Access by: In person only.

Civil Actions Under $5,000, Eviction, Small Claims—Greenville Magistrate Court, Law Enforcement Ctr-116A, 4 McGee St, Greenville, SC 29601. 864-467-5312. Fax: 864-467-5361. 8:30AM-5PM (EST). Access by: Mail, in person.

Greenville Magistrate Court, 12 Howe St, Greenville, SC 29601. 864-467-5295. (EST). Access by: Mail, in person.

Greenville Magistrate Court, 720 S Washington Ave, Greenville, SC 29611. 864-269-0991. (EST). Access by: Mail, in person.

Greenville Magistrate Court, 6247 White Horse Rd, Greenville, SC 29611. 864-294-4810. 8:30AM-5PM (EST). Access by: Mail, in person.

Greer Magistrate Court, 1306 W Poinsett St #A, Greer, SC 29650-1250. 864-877-7464. (EST). Access by: Mail, in person.

Landrum Magistrate Court, 2015 Hwy 11, Landrum, SC 29356. 864-895-0478. Fax: 864-895-3437. 9AM-1PM1PM (EST). Access by: Mail, in person.

Marietta Magistrate Court, #3208 Geer Hwy (PO Box 506), Marietta, SC 29661. 864-836-3671. 8:30-Noon, 1PM-5PM (EST). Access by: Mail, in person.

Piedmont Magistrate Court, 8150 August Rd, Piedmont, SC 29673. 864-277-9555. (EST). Access by: Mail, in person.

Simpsonville Magistrate Court, 116 S Main St, Simpsonville, SC 29681. 864-963-3457. (EST). Access by: Mail, in person.

Taylors Magistrate Court, 2801 Wade Hampton Blvd, Taylors, SC 29687. 864-244-2922. Fax: 864-268-1333. 8:30AM-5PM (EST). Access by: Phone, fax, mail, in person.

Travelers Rest Magistrate Court, 114 N Poinsett Hwy, Travelers Rest, SC 29690. 864-834-6910. Fax: 864-834-6911. 9AM-4PM (EST). Access by: Phone, mail, in person.

Probate—Probate Court, 301 University Ridge, Ste 1200, Greenville, SC 29601. 864-467-7170. Fax: 864-467-7082. 8:30AM-5PM (EST). Access by: Phone, fax, mail, in person.

Greenwood County

Real Estate Recording—Greenwood Clerk of Court, Courthouse, 528 Monument St., Greenwood, SC 29646. 864-942-8551. 8:30AM-5PM (EST).

Felony, Misdemeanor, Civil Actions Over $5,000—Circuit Court, Courthouse, Rm 114, 528 Monument St, Greenwood, SC 29646. 864-942-8612. Fax: 864-943-8620. 8:30AM-5PM (EST). Access by: Mail, in person.

Civil Actions Under $5,000, Eviction, Small Claims—Greenwood Magistrate Court, Greenood County Courthouse, Rm 106, Greenwood, SC 29646. 864-942-8655. (EST). Access by: Mail, in person.

Probate—Probate Court, PO Box 1210, Greenwood, SC 29648. 864-942-8625. Fax: 864-942-8620. 8:30AM-5PM (EST). Access by: Fax, in person.

Hampton County

Real Estate Recording—Hampton Clerk of Court, Courthouse Square, Elm Street, Hampton, SC 29924. 803-943-7510. Fax: 803-943-7596. 8AM-5PM (EST).

Felony, Misdemeanor, Civil Actions Over $5,000—Circuit Court, PO Box 7, Hampton, SC 29924. 803-943-7500. 8AM-5PM (EST). Access by: Mail, in person.

Civil Actions Under $5,000, Eviction, Small Claims—Estill Magistrate Court, PO Box 969, Estill, SC 29918. 803-625-3232. (EST). Access by: Mail, in person.

Hampton Magistrate Court, PO Box 314, Hampton, SC 29924. 803-943-7511. (EST). Access by: Mail, in person.

Probate—Probate Court, PO Box 601, Hampton, SC 29924. 803-943-7512. Fax: 803-943-7596. 8AM-5PM (EST). Access by: Mail, in person.

Horry County

Real Estate Recording—Horry County Register of Mesne Conveyances, 101-A Beaty Street, Conway, SC 29526. 803-248-1252. Fax: 803-248-1566. 8AM-5PM (EST).

Felony, Misdemeanor, Civil Actions Over $5,000—Circuit Court, PO Box 677, Conway, SC 29526. 803-248-1270. Fax: 803-248-1341. 8AM-5PM (EST). Access by: Phone, mail, in person.

Civil Actions Under $5,000, Eviction, Small Claims—Aynor Magistrate Court, PO Box 115, Aynor, SC 29511. 803-358-6320. Fax: 803-358-0704. 8AM-5PM (EST). Access by: Mail, in person.

Conway Magistrate Court, 1316 1st Ave (PO Box 544), Conway, SC 29526. 803-248-6356. (EST). Access by: Mail, in person.

Conway Magistrate Court, PO Box 1236, Conway, SC 29528. 803-248-1373. (EST). Access by: Mail, in person.

Conway Magistrate Court, 4152 J Reuben Long Ave (PO Box 2115), Conway, SC 29528. 803-248-1373. (EST). Access by: Mail, in person.

Green Sea Magistrate Court, 5527 Hwy #9 (PO Box 153), Green Sea, SC 29545. 803-756-5250. (EST). Access by: Mail, in person.

Loris Magistrate Court, 3817 Walnut St, Loris, SC 29569. 803-756-7918. (EST). Access by: Mail, in person.

Myrtle Beach Magistrate Court, 1201 21st North Ave, Myrtle Beach, SC 29577. 803-448-7810. (EST). Access by: Mail, in person.

N Myrtle Beach Magistrate Court, PO Box 33, N Myrtle Beach, SC 29597-0033. 803-249-2411. Fax: 803-399-6792. 8AM-5PM (EST). Access by: Mail, in person.

Surfside Beach Magistrate Court, 1106 Glenns Bay Rd, Surfside Beach, SC 29575. 803-238-3277. 8AM-5PM (EST). Access by: Mail, in person.

Probate—Probate Court, PO Box 288, Conway, SC 29528. 803-248-1294. Fax: 803-248-1298. 8AM-5PM (EST). Access by: In person only.

Jasper County

Real Estate Recording—Jasper Clerk of Court, 305 Russell Street, Ridgeland, SC 29936. 803-726-7710. Fax: 803-726-7782. 9AM-5PM (EST).

Felony, Misdemeanor, Civil Actions Over $5,000—Circuit Court, PO Box 248, Ridgeland, SC 29936. 803-726-7710. 8:30AM-5PM (EST). Access by: Mail, in person.

Civil Actions Under $5,000, Eviction, Small Claims—Hardeeville Magistrate Court, PO Box 1169, Hardeeville, SC 29927. 803-784-2131. (EST). Access by: Mail, in person.

Ridgeland Magistrate Court, PO Box 1281, Ridgeland, SC 29936. 803-726-8590. (EST). Access by: Mail, in person.

Ridgeland Magistrate Court, PO Box 665, Ridgeland, SC 29936. 803-726-7737. (EST). Access by: Mail, in person.

Probate—Probate Court, PO Box 1739, Ridgeland, SC 29936. 803-726-7719. Fax: 803-726-7782. 9AM-5PM (EST). Access by: Mail, in person.

Kershaw County

Real Estate Recording—Kershaw Clerk of Court, Courthouse - Room 313, 1121 Broad St., Camden, SC 29020. 803-425-1527. Fax: 803-425-1505. 9AM-5PM (EST).

Felony, Misdemeanor, Civil Actions Over $5,000—Circuit Court, County Courthouse, Rm 313, PO Box 1557, Camden, SC 29020. 803-425-1527. 9AM-5PM (EST). Access by: Mail, in person.

Civil Actions Under $5,000, Eviction, Small Claims—Bethune Magistrate Court, PO Box 1528, Bethune, SC 29020. 803-334-8450. (EST). Access by: Mail, in person.

Probate—Probate Court, 1121 Broad St, Rm 302, Camden, SC 29020. 803-425-1500. Fax: 803-425-1526. 9AM-5PM (EST). Access by: Mail, in person.

Lancaster County

Real Estate Recording—Lancaster Clerk of Court, Corner of Cawtaba & Dunlap Streets, Lancaster, SC 29720. 803-285-1581. 8:30AM-5PM (EST).

Felony, Misdemeanor, Civil Actions Over $5,000—Circuit Court, PO Box 1809, Lancaster, SC 29720. 803-285-1581. 8:30AM-5PM (EST). Access by: In person only.

Civil Actions Under $5,000, Eviction, Small Claims—Fort Mill Magistrate Court, 8097 Charlotte Hwy, Fort Mill, SC 29715. 803-547-5332. (EST). Access by: Mail, in person.

Kershaw Magistrate Court, Rt 2 Box 174, Kershaw, SC 29067. 803-475-6643. (EST). Access by: Mail, in person.

Lancaster Magistrate Court, 4141 Bessie Hudson Rd, Lancaster, SC 29720. 803-285-1048. (EST). Access by: Mail, in person.

Lancaster Magistrate Court, PO Box 1809, Lancaster, SC 29720. 803-283-3983. (EST). Access by: Mail, in person.

Lancaster Magistrate Court, 2055 Lynwood Dr, Lancaster, SC 29720. 803-285-1587. (EST). Access by: Mail, in person.

Probate—Probate Court, PO Box 1809, Lancaster, SC 29721. 803-283-3379. Fax: 803-283-3370. 8:30AM-5PM (EST). Access by: Phone, mail, in person.

Laurens County

Real Estate Recording—Laurens Clerk of Court, Public Square, Laurens, SC 29360. 864-984-3538. 9AM-5PM (EST).

Felony, Misdemeanor, Civil Actions Over $5,000—Circuit Court, PO Box 287, Laurens, SC 29360. 864-984-3538. 9AM-5PM (EST). Access by: Mail, in person.

Civil Actions Under $5,000, Eviction, Small Claims—Clinton Magistrate Court, 102 N Broad St, Clinton, SC 29325. 864-833-5879. (EST). Access by: Mail, in person.

Gray Court Magistrate Court, Rt 3 Box 152, Gray Court, SC 29645. 803-876-3533. (EST). Access by: Mail, in person.

Laurens Magistrate Court, PO Box 925, Laurens, SC 29360. 864-683-4485. (EST). Access by: Mail, in person.

Probate—Probate Court, PO Box 194, Laurens, SC 29360. 864-984-3538. 9AM-5PM (EST). Access by: Phone, mail, in person.

Lee County

Real Estate Recording—Lee Clerk of Court, 123 South Main Street, Courthouse, Bishopville, SC 29010. 803-484-5341. Fax: 803-484-5043. 9AM-5PM (EST).

Felony, Misdemeanor, Civil Actions Over $5,000—Circuit Court, PO Box 281, Bishopville, SC 29010. 803-484-5341. Fax: 803-484-6512. 9AM-5PM (EST). Access by: Mail, in person.

Civil Actions Under $5,000, Eviction, Small Claims—Dalzell Magistrate Court, Rt 1 Box 108-A, Dalzell, SC 29040. 803-484-5341. (EST). Access by: Mail, in person.

Mayesville Magistrate Court, Rt 1 Box 191, Mayesville, SC 29104. 803-428-6762. (EST). Access by: Mail, in person.

Probate—Probate Court, PO Box 24, Bishopville, SC 29010. 803-484-5341. Fax: 803-484-6512. 9AM-5PM (EST). Access by: In person only.

Lexington County

Real Estate Recording—Lexington County Register of Deeds, 212 South Lake Drive, Lexington, SC 29072. 803-359-8168. Fax: 803-359-0023. 8AM-5PM (EST).

Felony, Misdemeanor, Civil Actions Over $5,000—Circuit Court, Lexington County Courthouse, Rm 107, 139 East Main St, Lexington, SC 29072-33494. 803-359-8212. Fax: 803-359-8314. 8AM-5PM (EST). Access by: Mail, in person.

Civil Actions Under $5,000, Eviction, Small Claims—Batesburg Leesville Magistrate Court, 231 W Church St, Batesburg, SC 29006. 803-359-8330. Fax: 803-532-0357. (EST). Access by: Mail, in person.

Cayce Magistrate Court, 650 Knox Abbott Dr, Cayce, SC 29033. 803-796-7100. Fax: 803-796-7635. (EST). Access by: Mail, in person.

Columbia Magistrate Court, 108 Harbison Blvd, Columbia, SC 29212. 803-781-7584. (EST). Access by: Mail, in person.

Lexington Magistrate Court, 304 S Lakeshore Dr, Lexington, SC 29072. 803-359-8221. (EST). Access by: Mail, in person.

Swansea Magistrate Court, 500 Charlie Rast Rd (PO Box 457), Swansea, SC 29160. 803-568-3616. Fax: 803-568-4078. (EST). Access by: Mail, in person.

Probate—Probate Court, County Courthouse, Rm 110, 139 E Main St, Lexington, SC 29072-3448. 803-359-8324. 8AM-5PM (EST). Access by: Mail, in person.

Marion County

Real Estate Recording—Marion Clerk of Court, West Court Street, Marion, SC 29571. 803-423-8240. Fax: 803-423-8306. 8:30AM-5PM (EST).

Felony, Misdemeanor, Civil Actions Over $5,000—Circuit Court, PO Box 295, Marion, SC 29571. 803-423-8240. 8:30AM-5PM (EST). Access by: Mail, in person.

Civil Actions Under $5,000, Eviction, Small Claims—Gresham Magistrate Court, PO Box 35, Gresham, SC 29546. 803-362-0180. 8:30AM-5PM (EST). Access by: Mail, in person.

Marion Magistrate Court, PO Box 847, Marion, SC 29571. 803-423-8208. Fax: 803-423-8306. 8:30AM-4PM (EST). Access by: Mail, in person.

Mullins Magistrate Court, 151 N East Front St (PO Box 612), Mullins, SC 29574. 803-464-6027. 8:30AM-12:30PM, 1:30PM-5PM (EST). Access by: Mail.

Probate—Probate Court, PO Box 583, Marion, SC 29571. 803-423-8244. Fax: 803-423-8224. 8:30AM-5PM (EST). Access by: Mail, in person.

Marlboro County

Real Estate Recording—Marlboro Clerk of Court, Main Street, Courthouse, Bennettsville, SC 29512. 803-479-5613. Fax: 803-479-5640. 8:30AM-5PM (EST).

Felony, Misdemeanor, Civil Actions Over $5,000—Circuit Court, PO Drawer 996, Bennettsville, SC 29512. 803-479-5613. 8:30AM-5PM (EST). Access by: Mail, in person.

Civil Actions Under $5,000, Eviction, Small Claims—Marlboro County Magistrate Court, PO Box 418, Bennettsville, SC 29512. 803-479-5620. Fax: 803-479-5646. 8:30AM-4:30PM (EST). Access by: Mail, in person.

McColl Magistrate Court, PO Box 502, McColl, SC 29570. 803-479-5646. 10AM-5PM M-Th (EST). Access by: Mail, in person.

Probate—Probate Court, PO Box 455, Bennettsville, SC 29512. 803-479-5610. 8:30AM-5PM (EST). Access by: Mail, in person.

McCormick County

Real Estate Recording—McCormick Clerk of Court, 133 South Mine Street, Courthouse, Room 102, McCormick, SC 29835. 864-465-0071. 9AM-5PM (EST).

Felony, Misdemeanor, Civil Actions Over $5,000—Circuit Court, 133 Mine St, McCormick, SC 29835. 864-465-2195. 9AM-5PM (EST). Access by: Mail, in person.

Civil Actions Under $5,000, Eviction, Small Claims—McCormick Magistrate Court, 109 Augusta St (PO Box 1116), McCormick, SC 29835. 864-465-2316. Fax: 864-465-2582. 9AM-5PM (EST). Access by: Mail, in person.

Probate—Probate Court, 133 S Mine St, McCormick, SC 29835. 864-465-2630. Fax: 864-465-0071. 9AM-5PM (EST). Access by: Phone, mail, in person.

Newberry County

Real Estate Recording—Newberry Clerk of Court, College Street, Courthouse Room 5, Newberry, SC 29108. 803-321-2110. Fax: 803-321-2102. 8:30AM-5PM (EST).

Felony, Misdemeanor, Civil Actions Over $5,000—Circuit Court, PO Box 278, Newberry, SC 29108. 803-321-2110. Fax: 803-321-2102. 8:30AM-5PM (EST). Access by: In person only.

Civil Actions Under $5,000, Eviction, Small Claims—Little Mountain Magistrate Court, PO Box 9511, Little Mountain, SC 29075. 803-321-2144. (EST). Access by: Mail, in person.

Newberry Magistrate Court, 3239 Louis Rich Rd, Newberry, SC 29108. 803-321-2144. 8:30-5PM (EST) Access by: Mail, in person.

Peak Magistrate Court, 6 River St (PO Box 198), Peak, SC 29122. 803-945-7455. (EST). Access by: Mail, in person.

Whitmire Magistrate Court, PO Box 62, Whitmire, SC 29178. 803-694-4927. 1PM-5PM T,TH (EST). Access by: Mail, in person.

Probate—Probate Court, PO Box 442, Newberry, SC 29108. 803-321-2118. Fax: 803-321-2119. 8:30AM-5PM (EST). Access by: Mail, in person.

Oconee County

Real Estate Recording—Oconee Clerk of Court, 211 W. Main St., Walhalla, SC 29691. 864-638-4280. 8:30AM-5PM (EST).

Felony, Misdemeanor, Civil Actions Over $5,000—
Circuit Court, PO Box 678, Walhalla, SC 29691. 864-638-4280. 8:30AM-5PM (EST). Access by: Mail, in person.

Civil Actions Under $5,000, Eviction, Small Claims—
Seneca Magistrate Court, 312 W North 1st St, Seneca, SC 29678. 864-882-7321. Fax: 864-882-0058. (EST). Access by: Mail, in person.

Walhalla Magistrate Court, 300 S Church St, Walhalla, SC 29691. 864-638-4125. 8:30AM-5PM (EST). Access by: Mail, in person.

Probate—Probate Court, PO Box 471, Walhalla, SC 29691. 864-638-4275. Fax: 864-638-4278. 8:30AM-5PM (EST). Access by: In person only.

Orangeburg County

Real Estate Recording—Orangeburg County Register Mesne Conveyance, 190 Gibson St., Room 108, Orangeburg, SC 29115. 803-533-6236. Fax: 803-534-3848. 8:30AM-5PM (EST).

Felony, Misdemeanor, Civil Actions Over $5,000—
Circuit Court, PO Box 9000, Orangeburg, SC 29116. 803-533-6243. Fax: 803-534-3848. 8:30AM-5PM (EST). Access by: In person only.

Civil Actions Under $5,000, Eviction, Small Claims—
Bowman Magistrate Court, Main St (PO Box 365), Bowman, SC 29018. 803-829-2831. (EST). Access by: Mail, in person.

Branchville Magistrate Court, PO Box 85, Rt 1 Box 71-AA, Branchville, SC 29432. 803-274-8820. Fax: 803-274-8760. (EST). Access by: Mail, in person.

Elloree Magistrate Court, PO Box 646, Elloree, SC 29047. 803-897-1064. (EST). Access by: Mail, in person.

Eutawville Magistrate Court, Hwy #6, Rt 1 Box 467 (PO Box 188), Eutawville, SC 29048. 803-492-3697. (EST). Access by: Mail, in person.

Holly Hill Magistrate Court, PO Box 957, Holly Hill, SC 29059. 803-496-9533. (EST). Access by: Mail, in person.

North Magistrate Court, PO Box 399, North, SC 29112. 803-642-1530. (EST). Access by: Mail, in person.

Norway Magistrate Court, Pinehurst St (PO Box 437), Norway, SC 29113. 803-263-4433. (EST). Access by: Mail, in person.

Orangeburg Magistrate Court, 2345 Norway Rd, Orangeburg, SC 29115. 803-534-8933. (EST). Access by: Mail, in person.

Orangeburg County Magistrate Court, PO Box 9000, Orangeburg, SC 29116. 803-533-5847. Fax: 803-533-5929. 8:30AM-5PM (EST). Access by: Mail, in person.

Springfield Magistrate Court, 705 Railroad Ave (PO Box 355), Springfield, SC 29146. 803-258-3315. Fax: 803-258-3951. 9AM-5PM (EST). Access by: Mail, in person.

Probate—Probate Court, PO Drawer 9000, Orangeburg, SC 29116-9000. 803-533-6280. Fax: 803-532-6279. 8:30AM-5PM (EST). Access by: Mail, in person.

Pickens County

Real Estate Recording—Pickens Register of Mesne Conveyance, 222 McDaniel Ave. B-5, Pickens, SC 29671. 864-898-5868. Fax: 864-898-5924. 8:30AM-5PM (EST).

Felony, Misdemeanor, Civil Actions Over $5,000—
Circuit Court, PO Box 215, Pickens, SC 29671. 864-898-5866. Fax: 864-898-5863. 8:30AM-5PM (EST). Access by: Mail, in person.

Civil Actions Under $5,000, Eviction, Small Claims—
Clemson Magistrate Court, 139 Anderson Hwy #170, Clemson, SC 29631. 864-654-3338. 8:30AM-5PM (EST). Access by: In person only.

Easley Magistrate Court, 135 Folger Ave, West End Hall, Easley, SC 29640. 864-850-7076. (EST). Access by: Mail, in person.

Liberty Magistrate Court, 431 E Main St, Liberty, SC 29657. 864-850-3500. Fax: 864-850-3501. 8:30AM-5PM (EST). Access by: Mail, in person.

Pickens Magistrate Court, 216-Ste A, LEC Rd, Pickens, SC 29671. 864-898-5551. Fax: 864-898-5531. 8:30AM-5PM (EST). Access by: Fax, mail, in person.

Probate—Probate Court, 222 McDaniel Ave B-16, Pickens, SC 29671. 864-898-5903. Fax: 864-898-5924. 8:30AM-5PM (EST). Access by: Mail, in person.

Richland County

Real Estate Recording—Richland County Register of Mesne Conveyances, 1701 Main Street, Columbia, SC 29201. 803-748-4800. 8:45AM-5PM (EST).

Felony, Misdemeanor, Civil Actions Over $5,000—
Circuit Court, PO Box 1781, Columbia, SC 29202. 803-748-4684. 8:45AM-5PM (EST). Access by: Mail, in person.

Civil Actions Under $5,000, Eviction, Small Claims—
Columbia Magistrate Court, 1328 Huger St, Columbia, SC 29201. 803-776-3962. (EST). Access by: Mail, in person.

Columbia Magistrate Court, 1215 1/2 Rosewood Dr, Columbia, SC 29201. 803-799-1779. (EST). Access by: Mail, in person.

Columbia Magistrate Court, PO Box 192, Columbia, SC 29202. 803-748-4741. (EST). Access by: Mail, in person.

Columbia Magistrate Court, 4919 Rhett St, Columbia, SC 29203. 803-754-2250. (EST). Access by: Mail, in person.

Columbia Magistrate Court, 6941 A North Trenholm Rd, Columbia, SC 29206. 803-782-2807. (EST). Access by: Mail, in person.

Columbia Magistrate Court, 5205 Trenholm Rd #201, Columbia, SC 29206. 803-738-9019. (EST). Access by: Mail, in person.

Dutch Fork Magistrate Court, 1223 St Andrews Rd, Columbia, SC 29210. 803-772-6464. Fax: 803-798-6144. 9AM-Noon; 1:30PM-5PM (EST). Access by: Mail, in person.

Lykesland Magistrate Court, PO Box 9523, Columbia, SC 29290. 803-776-0454. Fax: 803-783-2667. 9AM-5PM (EST). Access by: Mail, in person.

Elgin Magistrate Court, 10535 Two Notch Rd, Elgin, SC 29045. 803-788-8232. (EST). Access by: Mail, in person.

Hopkins Magistrate Court, 135 American Ave, Hopkins, SC 29209. 803-783-2424. Fax: 803-783-2425. 8:45AM-5PM (EST). Access by: Mail, in person.

Probate—Probate Court, PO Box 192, Columbia, SC 29202. 803-748-4705. Fax: 803-748-4814. 8:45AM-5PM (EST). Access by: Mail, in person.

Saluda County

Real Estate Recording—Saluda Clerk of Court, Courthouse, Saluda, SC 29138. 864-445-3303. Fax: 864-445-3772. 8:30AM-5PM (EST).

Felony, Misdemeanor, Civil Actions Over $5,000—
Circuit Court, County Courthouse, Saluda, SC 29138. 864-445-3303. Fax: 864-445-9726. 8:30AM-5PM (EST). Access by: Fax, mail, in person. Request must be in writing.

Probate—Probate Court, County Courthouse, Saluda, SC 29138. 864-445-7110. Fax: 864-445-9726. 8:30AM-5PM (EST). Access by: Mail, in person.

Spartanburg County

Real Estate Recording—Spartanburg County Register of Mesne Conveyances, 366 North Church Street, County Administrative Offices, Spartanburg, SC 29303. 864-596-2514. 8:30AM-5PM (EST).

Felony, Misdemeanor, Civil—Circuit Court, County Courthouse, 180 Magnolia St, Spartanburg, SC 29306. 864-596-2591. Fax: 864-596-2239. 8:30AM-5PM (EST). Access by: In person only.

Civil Actions Under $5,000, Eviction, Small Claims—
Inman Magistrate Court, PO Box 642, Inman, SC 29349. 864-472-4447. (EST). Access by: Mail, in person.

Landrum Magistrate Court, 100 N Bomar Ave, Landrum, SC 29356. 864-457-7245. (EST). Access by: Mail, in person.

Landrum Magistrate Court, PO Box 128, Landrum, SC 29356. 864-596-2564. (EST). Access by: Mail, in person.

Pacolet Magistrate Court, PO Box 416, Pacolet, SC 29372. 864-474-9504. (EST). Access by: Mail, in person.

Reidville Magistrate Court, PO Box 37, Reidville, SC 29375. 864-949-5023. (EST). Access by: Mail, in person.

Spartanburg Magistrate Court, County Courthouse, Rm 134, Spartanburg, SC 29301. 864-596-2564. (EST). Access by: Mail, in person.

Spartanburg Magistrate Court, 767 California Ave, Spartanburg, SC 29303. 864-461-3402. (EST). Access by: Mail, in person.

Spartanburg Magistrate Court, PO Box 16243, Spartanburg, SC 29316. 803-578-6319. (EST). Access by: Mail, in person.

Probate—Probate Court, 180 Magnolia St, Spartanburg, SC 29306-2392. 864-596-2556. Fax: 864-596-2011. 8:30AM-5PM (EST). Access by: Mail, in person.

Sumter County

Real Estate Recording—Sumter County Register of Mesne Conveyances, Courthouse, Room 202, 141 N. Main St., Sumter, SC 29150. 803-436-2177. 8:30AM-5PM (EST).

Felony, Misdemeanor, Civil Actions Over $5,000—Circuit Court, 141 N Main, Sumter, SC 29150. 803-436-2227. 8:30AM-5PM (EST). Access by: Mail, in person.

Civil Actions Under $5,000, Eviction, Small Claims—Mayesville Magistrate Court, PO Box 461, Mayesville, SC 29104. 803-453-5919. (EST). Access by: Mail, in person.

Pinewood Magistrate Court, PO Box 236, Pinewood, SC 29125. 803-452-5878. (EST). Access by: Mail, in person.

Sumter Magistrate Court, 115 N Harvin St (PO Box 1394, 29151), Sumter, SC 29150. 803-436-2280. (EST). Access by: Mail, in person.

Probate—Probate Court, 141 N Main, Rm 111, Sumter, SC 29150. 803-436-2166. Fax: 803-436-2407. 8:30AM-5PM (EST). Access by: Mail, in person.

Union County

Real Estate Recording—Union Clerk of Court, 210 West Main Street, Union, SC 29379. 864-429-1630. Fax: 864-429-4454. 9AM-5PM (EST).

Felony, Misdemeanor, Civil Actions Over $5,000—Circuit Court, PO Box 200, Union, SC 29379. 864-429-1630. Fax: 864-429-4454. 9AM-5PM (EST). Access by: Mail, in person.

Civil Actions Under $5,000, Eviction, Small Claims—Carlisle Magistrate Court, PO Box 35, Carlisle, SC 29031. 864-427-6987. (EST). Access by: Mail, in person.

Jonesville Magistrate Court, PO Box 33, Jonesville, SC 29353. 864-674-5102. (EST). Access by: Mail, in person.

Lockhart Magistrate Court, 319 Mount Tabor Church Rd, Union, SC 29379. 864-545-2338. (EST). Access by: Mail, in person.

Union Magistrate Court, Union County Courthouse, PO Box 200, Union, SC 29379. 864-429-1648. (EST). Access by: Mail, in person.

Probate—Probate Court, PO Box 447, Union, SC 29379. 864-429-1625. Fax: 864-429-1603. 9AM-5PM (EST). Access by: Mail, in person.

Williamsburg County

Real Estate Recording—Williamsburg Clerk of Court, 125 West Main Street, Courthouse Square, Kingstree, SC 29556. 803-354-6855. Fax: 803-354-2106. 9AM-5PM (EST).

Felony, Misdemeanor, Civil Actions Over $5,000—Circuit Court, PO Box 86, Kingstree, SC 29556. 803-354-6855. Fax: 803-354-2106. 9AM-5PM (EST). Access by: Mail, in person.

Civil Actions Under $5,000, Eviction, Small Claims—Andrews Magistrate Court, Rt 4 Box 87, Andrews, SC 29510. 803-221-5438. (EST). Access by: Mail, in person.

Cades Magistrate Court, Rt 1 Box 146, Cades, SC 29568. 803-389-4494. (EST). Access by: Mail, in person.

Greeleyville Magistrate Court, Town Hall, Rt 2 Box 19-A, Greeleyville, SC 29056. 803-426-2945. (EST). Access by: Mail, in person.

Hemingway Magistrate Court, PO Box 416, 206 E Broad St, Hemingway, SC 29554. 803-558-2116. (EST). Access by: Mail, in person.

Kingstree Magistrate Court, Rt 4 Box 200, Kingstree, SC 29556. 803-382-9723. (EST). Access by: Mail, in person.

Kingstree Magistrate Court, Rt 1 Box 216-A (PO Box 956), Kingstree, SC 29556. 803-382-2181. (EST). Access by: Mail, in person.

Kingstree Magistrate Court, 10 Courthouse Sq (PO Box 673), Kingstree, SC 29556. 803-354-9602. (EST). Access by: Mail, in person.

Lake city Magistrate Court, Rt 2 Box 253-D, Lake city, SC 29560. 803-389-4787. (EST). Access by: Mail, in person.

Lane Magistrate Court, Rt 2 Box 94-A, Lane, SC 29564. 803-387-5726. (EST). Access by: Mail, in person.

Nesmith Magistrate Court, Rt 1 Box 297, Nesmith, SC 29580. 803-382-2249. (EST). Access by: Mail, in person.

Probate—Probate Court, PO Box 1005, Kingstree, SC 29556. 803-354-6655. Fax: 803-354-2106. 8:30AM-5PM (EST). Access by: Mail, in person.

York County

Real Estate Recording—York Clerk of Court, 2 South Congress, York, SC 29745. 803-684-8510. 8AM-5PM (EST).

Felony, Misdemeanor, Civil Actions Over $5,000—Circuit Court, PO Box 649, York, SC 29745. 803-688-8506. 8AM-5PM (EST). Access by: Mail, in person.

Civil Actions Under $5,000, Eviction, Small Claims—Clover Magistrate Court, 201 S Main St (PO Box 165), Clover, SC 29710. 803-222-9404. (EST). Access by: Mail, in person.

Fort Mill Magistrate Court, 114 Springs St, Fort Mill, SC 29715. 803-547-5572. (EST). Access by: Mail, in person.

Hickoy Grove Magistrate Court, PO Box 37, Hickory Grove, SC 29717. 803-925-2815. (EST). Access by: Mail, in person.

Rock Hill Magistrate Court, 529 S Cherry Rd (PO Box 11166), Rock Hill, SC 29731. 803-328-1866. (EST). Access by: Mail, in person.

Rock Hill Magistrate Court, 2211 Zinker Rd, Rock Hill, SC 29732. 803-328-1866. (EST). Access by: Mail, in person.

York Magistrate Court, 1675-1D York Hwy, York, SC 29745. 803-628-3029. (EST). Access by: Mail, in person.

Probate—Probate Court, PO Box 219, York, SC 29745. 803-684-8513. 8AM-5PM (EST). Access by: Mail, in person.

Federal Courts

US District Court

District of South Carolina

Anderson Division, US District Court c/o Greenville Division, PO Box 10768, Greenville, SC 29603. 864-233-2781. Counties: Abbeville, Anderson, Edgefield, Greenwood, McCormick, Newberry, Oconee, Pickens, Saluda

Beaufort Division, US District Court c/o Charleston Division, Hollings Judicial Center, 83 Broad St., Charleston, SC 29401. 803-727-4688. Counties: Beaufort, Hampton, Jasper

Charleston Division, US District Court 83 Broad St, Hollings Judicial Center, Charleston, SC 29401. 803-727-4688. Counties: Berkeley, Charleston, Clarendon, Colleton, Dorchester, Georgetown

Columbia Division, US District Court 1845 Assembly St, Columbia, SC 29201. 803-765-5816. Counties: Kershaw, Lee, Lexington, Richland, Sumter

Florence Division, US District Court PO Box 2317, Florence, SC 29503. 803-676-3820. Counties: Chesterfield, Darlington, Dillon, Florence, Horry, Marion, Marlboro, Williamsburg

Greenville Division, US District Court PO Box 10768, Greenville, SC 29603. 864-241-2700. Counties: Greenville, Laurens

Greenwood Division, US District Court c/o Greenville Division, PO Box 10768, Greenville, SC 29603. 864-233-2781. Counties: Aiken, Allendale, Bamberg, Barnwell, Calhoun, Fairfield, Lancaster, Orangeburg

Spartanburg Division, US District Court c/o Greenville Division, PO Box 10768, Greenville, SC 29603. 864-233-2781. Counties: Cherokee, Chester, Spartanburg, Union, York

US Bankruptcy Court
District of South Carolina

Columbia Division, US Bankruptcy Court, PO Box 1448, Columbia, SC 29202. 803-765-5436. Voice Case Information System: 803-765-5211. Counties: All counties in South Carolina

South Dakota

Capitol: Pierre (Hughs County)	
Number of Counties: 66	**Population:** 729,034
	Federal Court Locations:
County Court Locations:	•District Courts: 4
•Circuit Courts: 66/8 Circuits	•Bankruptcy Courts: 2
	State Agencies: 19

State Agencies—Summary

General Help Numbers:

State Archives
State Historical Society	605-773-3804
Cultural Heritage Center/	
State Archives	Fax: 605-773-6041
900 Governors Dr	9AM-4:30PM
Pierre, SD 57501-2217	
Reference Librarian:	605-733-3804

Governor's Office
Governor's Office	605-773-3212
State Capitol, 500 E Capitol Ave	Fax: 605-773-5844
Pierre, SD 57501-5070	8AM-5PM

Attorney General's Office
Attorney General's Office	605-773-3215
State Capitol, 500 E Capitol Ave	Fax: 605-773-4106
Pierre, SD 57501-5070	8AM-5PM

State Legislation
South Dakota Legislature	605-773-3835
Capitol Bldg – Legislative Docs	Fax: 605-773-4576
500 E Capitol Ave	8AM-5PM
Pierre, SD 57501	

Important State Internet Sites:

🌐 **Webscape**	
File Edit View	**Help**

State of South Dakota World Wide Web
www.state.sd.us/

This is the home page for the state and contains links to government, public and business information, fish and game, tourism and a search engine.

The Governor's Office
www.state.sd.us/state/executive/governor/governor .htm

This site includes information about the Governor's mission statement, State of the State address, press releases and e-mail can be sent to the Governor from this site.

Legislative Research Counsel
www.state.sd.us/state/legis/lrc.htm

This site leads to the members of both the Senate and House, their committees and current legislation information.

Unclaimed Property
www.state.sd.us/state/executive/treasurer/prop.htm

This site only provides limited information about unclaimed property, but does provide an e-mail address to make inquiries.

State Archives
www.state.sd.us/state/executive/deca/cultural/archi ves.htm

Site of the Archives home page. General information is available at this site.

State Agencies—Public Records

Criminal Records

Division of Criminal Investigation, Office of Attorney General, 500 E Capitol, Pierre, SD 57501-5070, Main Telephone: 605-773-3331, Fax: 605-773-4629, Hours: 8AM-5PM. Access by: mail only. Each request (other than criminal justice agencies) must include a signed authorization using the state form and a fingerprint card.

Corporation Records
Limited Partnerships
Limited Liability Company Records
Trademarks/Servicemarks

Corporation Division, Secretary of State, 500 E Capitol Ave, Suite B-05, Pierre, SD 57501-5070, Main Telephone: 605-773-4845, Fax: 605-773-4550, Hours: 8AM-5PM. Access by: mail, phone, visit. Fictitious and assumed names are found at the county levels.

Uniform Commercial Code
Federal Tax Liens
State Tax Liens

UCC Division, Secretary of State, 500 East Capitol, Pierre, SD 57501-5077, Main Telephone: 605-773-4422, Fax: 605-773-4550, Hours: 8AM-5PM. Access by: mail, phone, fax, visit, PC.

Sales Tax Registrations

Revenue Department, Business Tax Division, 700 Governors Dr, Pierre, SD 57501-2291, Main Telephone: 605-773-3311, Fax: 605-773-5129, Hours: 8AM-5PM. Access by: mail, phone.

Birth Certificates

South Dakota Department of Health, Vital Records, 600 E Capitol, c/o 500 E. Capitol, Pierre, SD 57501-5070, Main Telephone: 605-773-4961, Message Phone: 605-773-3355, Hours: 8AM-5PM. Access by: mail, phone, visit.

Death Records

South Dakota Department of Health, Vital Records, 600 E Capitol, c/o 500 E. Capitol, Pierre, SD 57501-5070, Main Telephone: 605-773-4961, Message Phone: 605-773-3355, Hours: 8AM-5PM. Access by: mail, phone, visit.

Marriage Certificates

South Dakota Department of Health, Vital Records, 600 E Capitol, c/o 500 E. Capitol, Pierre, SD 57501-5070, Main Telephone: 605-773-4961, Message Phone: 605-773-3355, Hours: 8AM-5PM. Access by: mail, phone, visit.

Divorce Records

South Dakota Department of Health, Vital Records, 600 E Capitol, c/o 500 E. Capitol, Pierre, SD 57501-5070, Main Telephone: 605-773-4961, Message Phone: 605-773-3355, Hours: 8AM-5PM. Access by: mail, phone, visit.

Workers' Compensation Records

Labor Department, Workers Compensation Division, 700 Governors Dr, Pierre, SD 57501, Main Telephone: 605-773-3681, Fax: 605-773-4211, Hours: 8AM-5PM. Access by: mail, visit.

Driver Records

Dept of Commerce & Regulation, Office of Driver Licensing, 118 W Capitol, Pierre, SD 57501, Main Telephone: 605-773-6883, Fax: 605-773-3018, Hours: 8AM-5PM. Access by: mail, phone, visit, PC. Ticket information is maintained at the local courts, not at the state.

Vehicle Ownership
Vehicle Identification

Division of Motor Vehicles, Information Section, 445 E Capitol Ave, Pierre, SD 57501-3185, Main Telephone: 605-773-3541, Fax: 605-773-4117, Hours: 8AM-5PM. Access by: mail, visit. An opt out provision was instituted 7/97 for vehicle owners who do not wish their information released for marketing purposes.

Accident Reports

Department of Transportation, Accident Records, 700 E. Broadway, Pierre, SD 57501-2586, Main Telephone: 605-773-3868, Fax: 605-773-3921, Hours: 8AM-5PM. Access by: mail, visit.

Hunting License Information
Fishing License Information

Records not available from state agency.

County Courts and Recording Offices

What You Need to Know...

About the Courts

About the Recorder's Office

Administration

State Court Administrator	605-773-3474
State Capitol Bldg	Fax: 605-773-6128
500 E Capitol Ave	8AM-5PM
Pierre, SD 57501	

Searching Hints

The Unified Judicial System for the state issued guidelines in December 1995 recommending procedures for counties to follow in conducting searches. As a result, most counties do not allow the public to perform searches, but rather require the court clerk to do them for a fee of $5.00 per name. Searches will be returned with a disclaimer stating that the clerk is not responsible for the completeness of the search. Clerks are **not** required to respond to telephone nor fax requests. Many courts are not open all day so they prefer written requests.

Online Access

There is no statewide online access computer system currently available to the public. Some of the larger courts are now being placed on computer at a rate of 4 to 5 courts per year. Smaller courts are putting their information on computer cards which are sent to Pierre for input by the state office.

Organization

66 counties, 66 filing offices. The recording officer is Register of Deeds. 48 counties are in the Central Time Zone (CST) and 18 are in the Mountain Time Zone (MST).

UCC Records

Financing statements are filed at the state level, except for real estate related collateral, which are filed with the Register of Deeds. All filing offices will perform UCC searches. All counties have access to a statewide database of UCC filings Use search request form UCC-11. Searches fees are usually $4.00 per debtor name. Copy fees are usually $.50 per page.

Lien Records

Federal and state tax liens on personal property of businesses are filed with the Secretary of State. Other federal and state tax liens are filed with the county Register of Deeds. Most counties will perform tax lien searches. Search fees and copy fees vary. Other liens include mechanics, motor vehicle, and materials.

Real Estate Records

Many counties will perform real estate searches. Search fees and copy fees vary. Certification usually costs $2.00 per document.

County Courts and Recording Offices

Aurora County

Real Estate Recording—Aurora County Register of Deeds, Main Street, Courthouse, Plankinton, SD 57368. 605-942-7161. Fax: 605-942-7751. 8AM-Noon,1-5PM (CST).

Felony, Misdemeanor, Civil, Eviction, Small Claims, Probate—Circuit Court, PO Box 366, Plankinton, SD 57368. 605-942-7165. Fax: 605-942-7751. 8AM-Noon, 1-5PM (CST). Access by: Mail, in person.

Beadle County

Real Estate Recording—Beadle County Register of Deeds, 450-3rd St. SW, Huron, SD 57350. 605-352-3168. Fax: 605-352-1328. 8AM-5PM (CST).

Felony, Misdemeanor, Civil, Eviction, Small Claims, Probate—Circuit Court, PO Box 1358, Huron, SD 57350. 605-353-7165. 8AM-5PM (CST). Access by: Mail, in person.

Bennett County

Real Estate Recording—Bennett County Register of Deeds, 202 Main Street, Courthouse, Martin, SD 57551. 605-685-6054. Fax: 605-685-6311. 8AM-Noon, 12:30-4:30PM (MST).

Felony, Misdemeanor, Civil, Eviction, Small Claims, Probate—Circuit Court, PO Box 281, Martin, SD 57551. 605-685-6969. 8AM-4:30PM (MST). Access by: Mail, in person.

Bon Homme County

Real Estate Recording—Bon Homme County Register of Deeds, Cherry Street, Courthouse, Tyndall, SD 57066. 605-589-4217. (CST).

Felony, Misdemeanor, Civil, Eviction, Small Claims, Probate—Circuit Court, PO Box 6, Tyndall, SD 57066. 605-589-4215. Fax: 605-589-4209. 8AM-4:30PM (CST). Access by: Mail, in person.

Brookings County

Real Estate Recording—Brookings County Register of Deeds, 314 6th Avenue, Courthouse, Brookings, SD 57006. 605-692-2724. 8AM-5PM (CST).

Felony, Misdemeanor, Civil, Eviction, Small Claims, Probate—Circuit Court, 314 6th Ave, Brookings, SD 57006. 605-688-4200. Fax: 605-688-4952. 8AM-5PM (CST). Access by: Mail, in person.

Brown County

Real Estate Recording—Brown County Register of Deeds, 25 Market Street, Aberdeen, SD 57402. 605-626-7140. Fax: 605-626-4010. 8AM-5PM (CST).

Felony, Misdemeanor, Civil, Eviction, Small Claims, Probate—Circuit Court, 101 1st Ave SE, Aberdeen, SD 57401. 605-626-2451. Fax: 605-626-2491. 8AM-5PM (CST). Access by: Mail, in person.

Brule County

Real Estate Recording—Brule County Register of Deeds, 300 South Courtland, Suite 110, Chamberlain, SD 57325. 605-734-5310. 8AM-Noon,1-5PM (CST).

Felony, Misdemeanor, Civil, Eviction, Small Claims, Probate—Circuit Court, 300 S Courtland #111, Chamberlain, SD 57325-1599. 605-734-5443. Fax: 605-734-4151. 8AM-Noon, 1-5PM (CST). Access by: Fax, mail, in person.

Buffalo County

Real Estate Recording—Buffalo County Register of Deeds, Main Street, Courthouse, Gannvalley, SD 57341. 605-293-3239. Fax: 605-293-3240. 9AM-5PM (CST).

Felony, Misdemeanor, Civil, Eviction, Small Claims, Probate—Circuit Court, PO Box 148, Gann Valley, SD 57341. 605-293-3234. Fax: 605-293-3240. 9AM-Noon (CST). Access by: Mail, in person.

Butte County

Real Estate Recording—Butte County Register of Deeds, 839 Fifth Avenue, Belle Fourche, SD 57717. 605-892-2912. 8AM-5PM (MST).

Felony, Misdemeanor, Civil, Eviction, Small Claims, Probate—Circuit Court, PO Box 237, Belle Fourche, SD 57717. 605-892-2516. Fax: 605-892-2836. 8AM-Noon, 1-5PM (MST). Access by: Mail, in person.

Campbell County

Real Estate Recording—Campbell County Register of Deeds, 2nd and Main Street, Courthouse, Mound City, SD 57646. 605-955-3505. Fax: 605-955-3308. 8AM-Noon,1-5PM (CST).

Felony, Misdemeanor, Civil, Eviction, Small Claims, Probate—Circuit Court, PO Box 146, Mound City, SD 57646. 605-955-3536. Fax: 605-955-3308. 8AM-Noon (CST). Access by: Mail, in person.

Charles Mix County

Real Estate Recording—Charles Mix County Register of Deeds, Courthouse, Main Street, Lake Andes, SD 57356. 605-487-7141. Fax: 605-487-7221. 8AM-4:30PM (CST).

Felony, Misdemeanor, Civil, Eviction, Small Claims, Probate—Circuit Court, PO Box 640, Lake Andes, SD 57356. 605-487-7511. Fax: 605-487-7221. 8AM-4:30PM (CST). Access by: Fax, mail, in person.

Clark County

Real Estate Recording—Clark County Register of Deeds, 202 N. Commercial St., Clark, SD 57225. 605-532-5363. Fax: 605-532-5931. 8AM-5PM (CST).

Felony, Misdemeanor, Civil, Eviction, Small Claims, Probate—Circuit Court, PO Box 294, Clark, SD 57225. 605-532-5851. 8AM-Noon, 1-5PM (CST). Access by: Mail, in person.

Clay County

Real Estate Recording—Clay County Register of Deeds, 211 West Main Street, Courthouse, Vermillion, SD 57069. 605-677-7130. 8AM-5PM (CST).

Felony, Misdemeanor, Civil, Eviction, Small Claims, Probate—Circuit Court, PO Box 377, Vermillion, SD 57069. 605-677-6755. Fax: 605-677-7105. 8AM-5PM (CST). Access by: Mail, in person.

Codington County

Real Estate Recording—Codington County Register of Deeds, 14 1st Avenue S.E., Watertown, SD 57201. 605-886-4719. 8AM-5PM (CST).

Felony, Misdemeanor, Civil, Eviction, Small Claims, Probate—Circuit Court, PO Box 1054, Watertown, SD 57201. 605-882-5095. Fax: 605-882-5106. 8AM-5PM (CST). Access by: Mail, in person.

Corson County

Real Estate Recording—Corson County Register of Deeds, Courthouse, McIntosh, SD 57641. 605-273-4395. 8AM-Noon,1-5PM (MST).

Felony, Misdemeanor, Civil, Eviction, Small Claims, Probate—Circuit Court, PO Box 175, McIntosh, SD 57641. 605-273-4201. Fax: 605-273-4533. 8AM-Noon, 1-3PM (MST). Access by: Mail, in person.

Custer County

Real Estate Recording—Custer County Register of Deeds, 420 Mount Rushmore Road, Custer, SD 57730. 605-673-2784. Fax: 605-673-3439. 8AM-5PM (MST).

Felony, Misdemeanor, Civil, Eviction, Small Claims, Probate—Circuit Court, 420 Mt Rushmore Rd, Custer, SD 57730. 605-673-4816. Fax: 605-673-3416. 8AM-5PM (MST). Access by: Mail, in person.

Davison County

Real Estate Recording—Davison County Register of Deeds, 200 East 4th, Courthouse, Mitchell, SD 57301. 605-996-2209. 8AM-5PM (CST).

Felony, Misdemeanor, Civil, Eviction, Small Claims, Probate—Circuit Court, PO Box 927, Mitchell, SD 57301. 605-995-4705. Fax: 605-995-3134. 8AM-5PM (CST). Access by: Mail, in person.

Day County

Real Estate Recording—Day County Register of Deeds, 710 West First Street, Webster, SD 57274. 605-345-4162. Fax: 605-345-4162. 8AM-5PM (CST).

Felony, Misdemeanor, Civil, Eviction, Small Claims, Probate—Circuit Court, 710 W 1st St, Webster, SD 57274. 605-345-3771. Fax: 605-345-3818. 8AM-5PM (CST). Access by: Mail, in person.

Deuel County

Real Estate Recording—Deuel County Register of Deeds, Courthouse, Clear Lake, SD 57226. 605-874-2268. Fax: 605-874-2916. 8AM-5PM (CST).

Felony, Misdemeanor, Civil, Eviction, Small Claims, Probate—Circuit Court, PO Box 308, Clear Lake, SD 57226. 605-874-2120. 8AM-5PM (CST). Access by: Mail, in person.

Dewey County

Real Estate Recording—Dewey County Register of Deeds, C Street, Courthouse, Timber Lake, SD 57656. 605-865-3661. Fax: 605-865-3691. 8AM-Noon,1-5PM (MST).

Felony, Misdemeanor, Civil, Eviction, Small Claims, Probate—Circuit Court, PO Box 96, Timber Lake, SD 57656. 605-865-3566. 9:30AM-Noon, 1-2:30PM (MST). Access by: Mail, in person.

Douglas County

Real Estate Recording—Douglas County Register of Deeds, Courthouse, 1st & Braddock (Hwy 281), Armour, SD 57313. 605-724-2204. Fax: 605-724-2204. 8AM-Noon,1-5PM (CST).

Felony, Misdemeanor, Civil, Eviction, Small Claims, Probate—Circuit Court, PO Box 36, Armour, SD 57313. 605-724-2585. Fax: 605-724-2204. 8AM-Noon, 1-5PM (CST). Access by: Phone, mail, in person.

Edmunds County

Real Estate Recording—Edmunds County Register of Deeds, Courthouse, Ipswich, SD 57451. 605-426-6431. Fax: 605-426-6257. 8AM-Noon,1-5PM (CST).

Felony, Misdemeanor, Civil, Eviction, Small Claims, Probate—Circuit Court, PO Box 384, Ipswich, SD 57451. 605-426-6671. Fax: 605-426-6164. 8AM-Noon, 1-5PM (CST). Access by: Mail, in person.

Fall River County

Real Estate Recording—Fall River County Register of Deeds, 906 North River Street, Hot Springs, SD 57747. 605-745-5139. Fax: 605-745-3855. 8AM-5PM (MST).

Felony, Misdemeanor, Civil, Eviction, Small Claims, Probate—Circuit Court, 906 N River St, Hot Springs, SD 57747. 605-745-5131. 8AM-5PM (MST). Access by: Mail, in person.

Faulk County

Real Estate Recording—Faulk County Register of Deeds, Courthouse, Faulkton, SD 57438. 605-598-6228. Fax: 605-598-6680. 8AM-Noon,1-5PM (CST).

Felony, Misdemeanor, Civil, Eviction, Small Claims, Probate—Circuit Court, PO Box 357, Faulkton, SD 57438. 605-598-6223. 9AM-3PM (CST). Access by: Mail, in person.

Grant County

Real Estate Recording—Grant County Register of Deeds, 210 East Fifth Avenue, Milbank, SD 57252. 605-432-4752. 8AM-5PM (CST).

Felony, Misdemeanor, Civil, Eviction, Small Claims, Probate—Circuit Court, PO Box 509, Milbank, SD 57252. 605-432-5482. 8AM-Noon, 1-5PM (CST). Access by: Mail, in person.

Gregory County

Real Estate Recording—Gregory County Register of Deeds, Courthouse, Burke, SD 57523. 605-775-2624. Fax: 605-775-2596. 8AM-Noon,1-5PM (CST).

Felony, Misdemeanor, Civil, Eviction, Small Claims, Probate—Circuit Court, PO Box 430, Burke, SD 57523. 605-775-2665. 8AM-Noon, 1-5PM (CST). Access by: Mail, in person.

Haakon County

Real Estate Recording—Haakon County Register of Deeds, 130 South Howard, Courthouse, Philip, SD 57567. 605-859-2785. 8AM-Noon,1-5PM (MST).

Felony, Misdemeanor, Civil, Eviction, Small Claims, Probate—Circuit Court, PO Box 70, Philip, SD 57567. 605-859-2627. 1-5PM (MST). Access by: Phone, mail, in person.

Hamlin County

Real Estate Recording—Hamlin County Register of Deeds, Main Street, Courthouse, Hayti, SD 57241. 605-783-3206. 8AM-12, 1PM-5PM (CST).

Felony, Misdemeanor, Civil, Eviction, Small Claims, Probate—Circuit Court, PO Box 256, Hayti, SD 57241. 605-783-3751. Fax: 605-783-3201. 8AM-Noon, 1-5PM (CST). Access by: Mail, in person.

Hand County

Real Estate Recording—Hand County Register of Deeds, 415 West 1st Avenue, Miller, SD 57362. 605-853-3512. Fax: 605-853-2769. 8AM-5PM (CST).

Felony, Misdemeanor, Civil, Eviction, Small Claims, Probate—Circuit Court, PO Box 122, Miller, SD 57362. 605-853-3337. Fax: 605-853-2769. 8AM-5PM (CST). Access by: Mail, in person.

Hanson County

Real Estate Recording—Hanson County Register of Deeds, Courthouse, 720 5th Street, Alexandria, SD 57311. 605-239-4512. Fax: 605-239-4296. 8AM-Noon,1-5PM (CST).

Felony, Misdemeanor, Civil, Eviction, Small Claims, Probate—Circuit Court, PO Box 127, Alexandria, SD 57311. 605-239-4446. 8AM-5PM (CST). Access by: Mail, in person.

Harding County

Real Estate Recording—Harding County Register of Deeds, Courthouse, Buffalo, SD 57720. 605-375-3321. 8AM-12, 1PM-5PM (MST).

Felony, Misdemeanor, Civil, Eviction, Small Claims, Probate—Circuit Court, PO Box 534, Buffalo, SD 57720. 605-375-3351. 9:30AM-Noon, 1-2:30PM (MST). Access by: Mail, in person.

Hughes County

Real Estate Recording—Hughes County Register of Deeds, 104 East Capital, Pierre, SD 57501. 605-773-7495. 8AM-5PM (CST).

Felony, Misdemeanor, Civil, Eviction, Small Claims, Probate—Circuit Court, 104 E Capital, Pierre, SD 57501. 605-773-3713. 8AM-5PM (CST). Access by: Mail, in person.

Hutchinson County

Real Estate Recording—Hutchinson County Register of Deeds, 140 Euclid Street, Room 37, Olivet, SD 57052. 605-387-4217. Fax: 605-387-4209. 8AM-Noon, 1-5PM (CST).

Felony, Misdemeanor, Civil, Eviction, Small Claims, Probate—Circuit Court, 140 Euclid Rm 36, Olivet, SD 57052-2103. 605-387-4215. Fax: 605-387-4209. 8AM-Noon, 1-5PM (CST). Access by: Mail, in person.

Hyde County

Real Estate Recording—Hyde County Register of Deeds, 412 Commercial S.E., Courthouse, Highmore, SD 57345. 605-852-2517. (CST).

Felony, Misdemeanor, Civil, Eviction, Small Claims, Probate—Circuit Court, PO Box 306, Highmore, SD 57345. 605-852-2512. Fax: 605-852-2171. 10AM-2PM (CST). Access by: Fax, mail, in person.

Jackson County

Real Estate Recording—Jackson County Register of Deeds, Main Street, Courthouse, Kadoka, SD 57453. 605-837-2420. 8AM-5PM (MST).

Felony, Misdemeanor, Civil, Eviction, Small Claims, Probate—Circuit Court, PO Box 128, Kadoka, SD 57543. 605-837-2121. 8AM-5PM (MST). Access by: Phone, mail, in person.

Jerauld County

Real Estate Recording—Jerauld County Register of Deeds, Courthouse, 205 So. Wallace, Wessington Springs, SD 57382. 605-539-1221. 8AM-12, 1PM-5PM (CST).

Felony, Misdemeanor, Civil, Eviction, Small Claims, Probate—Circuit Court, PO Box 435, Wessington Springs, SD 57382. 605-539-1202. 8AM-5PM (CST). Access by: Mail, in person.

Jones County

Real Estate Recording—Jones County Register of Deeds, 310 Main Street, Courthouse, Murdo, SD 57559. 605-669-2132. 8AM-5PM (CST).

Felony, Misdemeanor, Civil, Eviction, Small Claims, Probate—Circuit Court, PO Box 448, Murdo, SD 57559. 605-669-2361. 8AM-5PM (CST). Access by: Mail, in person.

Kingsbury County

Real Estate Recording—Kingsbury County Register of Deeds, Courthouse, 101 2nd St. SE, De Smet, SD 57231. 605-854-3591. Fax: 605-854-3833. 8AM-Noon,1-5PM (CST).

Felony, Misdemeanor, Civil, Eviction, Small Claims, Probate—Circuit Court, PO Box 176, De Smet, SD 57231-0176. 605-854-3811. Fax: 605-854-3833. 8AM-Noon, 1-5PM (CST). Access by: Mail, in person.

Lake County

Real Estate Recording—Lake County Register of Deeds, 200 East Center, Courthouse, Madison, SD 57042. 605-256-7614. Fax: 605-256-7622. 8AM-12, 1PM-5PM (CST).

Felony, Misdemeanor, Civil, Eviction, Small Claims, Probate—Circuit Court, 200 E Center St, Madison, SD 57042. 605-256-5644. 8AM-Noon, 1-5PM (CST). Access by: Mail, in person.

Lawrence County

Real Estate Recording—Lawrence County Register of Deeds, 90 Sherman Street, Deadwood, SD 57732. 605-578-3930. 8AM-5PM (MST).

Felony, Misdemeanor, Civil, Eviction, Small Claims, Probate—Circuit Court, PO Box 626, Deadwood, SD 57732. 605-578-2040. 8AM-5PM (MST). Access by: Mail, in person.

Lincoln County

Real Estate Recording—Lincoln County Register of Deeds, 100 East 5th, Canton, SD 57013. 605-987-5661. Fax: 605-987-5932. 8AM-5PM (CST).

Felony, Misdemeanor, Civil, Eviction, Small Claims, Probate—Circuit Court, 100 E 5th St, Canton, SD 57013. 605-987-5891. 8AM-5PM (CST). Access by: Mail, in person.

Lyman County

Real Estate Recording—Lyman County Register of Deeds, 100 Main Street, Courthouse, Kennebec, SD 57544. 605-869-2297. Fax: 605-869-2203. 8AM-Noon,1-5PM (CST).

Felony, Misdemeanor, Civil, Eviction, Small Claims, Probate—Circuit Court, PO Box 235, Kennebec, SD 57544. 605-869-2277. 8AM-5PM (CST). Access by: Mail, in person.

Marshall County

Real Estate Recording—Marshall County Register of Deeds, Vander Horck Avenue, Courthouse, Britton, SD 57430. 605-448-2352. 8AM-Noon,1-5PM (CST).

Felony, Misdemeanor, Civil, Eviction, Small Claims, Probate—Circuit Court, PO Box 130, Britton, SD 57430. 605-448-5213. 8AM-5PM (CST). Access by: Phone, mail, in person.

McCook County

Real Estate Recording—McCook County Register of Deeds, 130 West Essex Street, Salem, SD 57058. 605-425-2701. Fax: 605-425-2791. 8:30AM-4:30PM (CST).

Felony, Misdemeanor, Civil, Eviction, Small Claims, Probate—Circuit Court, PO Box 504, Salem, SD 57058. 605-425-2781. Fax: 605-425-2781. 8AM-5PM (CST). Access by: Fax, mail, in person.

McPherson County

Real Estate Recording—McPherson County Register of Deeds, Main Street, Courthouse, Leola, SD 57456. 605-439-3151. Fax: 605-439-3394. 8AM-12, 1PM-5PM (CST).

Felony, Misdemeanor, Civil, Eviction, Small Claims, Probate—Circuit Court, PO Box 248, Leola, SD 57456. 605-439-3361. Fax: 605-439-3394. 8AM-Noon (CST). Access by: Phone, mail, in person.

Meade County

Real Estate Recording—Meade County Register of Deeds, 1425 Sherman Street, Sturgis, SD 57785. 605-347-2356. Fax: 605-347-5925. 8AM-5PM (MST).

Felony, Misdemeanor, Civil, Eviction, Small Claims, Probate—Circuit Court, PO Box 939, Sturgis, SD 57785. 605-347-4411. Fax: 605-347-3526. 8AM-Noon, 1-5PM (MST). Access by: Mail, in person.

Mellette County

Real Estate Recording—Mellette County Register of Deeds, Courthouse, White River, SD 57579. 605-259-3371. 8AM-Noon,1-5PM (MST).

Felony, Misdemeanor, Civil, Eviction, Small Claims, Probate—Circuit Court, PO Box 257, White River, SD 57579. 605-259-3230. Fax: 605-259-3194. 8AM-Noon (MST). Access by: Phone, mail, in person.

Miner County

Real Estate Recording—Miner County Register of Deeds, Main Street, Courthouse, Howard, SD 57349. 605-772-5621. Fax: 605-772-4148. 8AM-Noon,1-5PM (CST).

Felony, Misdemeanor, Civil, Eviction, Small Claims, Probate—Circuit Court, PO Box 265, Howard, SD 57349. 605-772-4612. Fax: 605-772-1148. 8AM-5PM (CST). Access by: Mail, in person.

Minnehaha County

Real Estate Recording—Minnehaha County Register of Deeds, 415 North Dakota Avenue, Sioux Falls, SD 57104. 605-367-4223. Fax: 605-367-8314. 8AM-5PM (CST).

Felony, Misdemeanor, Civil, Eviction, Small Claims, Probate—Circuit Court, 425 N Dakota Ave, Sioux Falls, SD 57104. 605-367-5900. Fax: 605-335-2877. 8AM-5PM (CST). Access by: Mail, in person.

Moody County

Real Estate Recording—Moody County Register of Deeds, Pipestone Avenue, Courthouse, Flandreau, SD 57028. 605-997-3151. 8AM-5PM (CST).

Felony, Misdemeanor, Civil, Eviction, Small Claims, Probate—Circuit Court, 101 E Pipestone, Flandreau, SD 57028. 605-997-3181. 8AM-5PM (CST). Access by: Mail, in person.

Pennington County

Real Estate Recording—Pennington County Register of Deeds, 315 St. Joe Street, Rapid City, SD 57701. 605-394-2177. 8AM-5PM (MST).

Felony, Misdemeanor, Civil, Eviction, Small Claims, Probate—Circuit Court, PO Box 230, Rapid City, SD 57709. 605-394-2575. 8AM-5PM (MST). Access by: Mail, in person.

Perkins County

Real Estate Recording—Perkins County Register of Deeds, Main Street, Courthouse, Bison, SD 57620. 605-244-5620. Fax: 605-244-7110. 8AM-Noon,1-5PM (MST).

Felony, Misdemeanor, Civil, Eviction, Small Claims, Probate—Circuit Court, PO Box 426, Bison, SD 57620-0426. 605-244-5626. Fax: 605-244-7110. 8AM-Noon, 1-5PM (MST). Access by: Mail, in person.

Potter County

Real Estate Recording—Potter County Register of Deeds, 201 South Exene, Gettysburg, SD 57442. 605-765-9467. Fax: 605-765-2412. 8AM-Noon, 1PM-5PM (CST).

Felony, Misdemeanor, Civil, Eviction, Small Claims, Probate—Circuit Court, 201 S Exene, Gettysburg, SD 57442. 605-765-9472. 8AM-Noon, 1-5PM (CST). Access by: Mail, in person.

Roberts County

Real Estate Recording—Roberts County Register of Deeds, 411 East 2nd Avenue, Sisseton, SD 57262. 605-698-7152. 8AM-5PM (CST).

Felony, Misdemeanor, Civil, Eviction, Small Claims, Probate—Circuit Court, 411 2nd Ave E, Sisseton, SD 57262. 605-698-3395. Fax: 605-698-7894. 8AM-5PM (CST). Access by: Mail, in person.

Sanborn County

Real Estate Recording—Sanborn County Register of Deeds, Courthouse, Woonsocket, SD 57385. 605-796-4516. (CST).

Felony, Misdemeanor, Civil, Eviction, Small Claims, Probate—Circuit Court, PO Box 56, Woonsocket, SD 57385. 605-796-4515. Fax: 605-796-4509. 8AM-5PM (CST). Access by: Mail, in person.

Shannon County

Real Estate Recording—Shannon County Register of Deeds, 906 North River Street, Hot Springs, SD 57747. 605-745-5139. Fax: 605-745-3855. 8AM-5PM (MST).

Felony, Misdemeanor, Civil, Eviction, Small Claims, Probate—Circuit Court, 906 N River St, Hot Springs, SD 57747. 605-745-5131. 8AM-5PM (MST). Access by: Mail, in person.

Spink County

Real Estate Recording—Spink County Register of Deeds, 210 East 7th Avenue, Redfield, SD 57469. 605-472-0150. Fax: 605-472-2301. 8AM-5PM (CST).

Felony, Misdemeanor, Civil, Eviction, Small Claims, Probate—Circuit Court, 210 E 7th Ave, Redfield, SD 57469. 605-472-1922. Fax: 605-472-2301. 8AM-5PM (CST). Access by: Phone, fax, mail, in person.

Stanley County

Real Estate Recording—Stanley County Register of Deeds, 8 East 2nd Avenue, Courthouse, Fort Pierre, SD 57532. 605-223-2610. Fax: 605-223-9948. 8AM-Noon,1-5PM (CST).

Felony, Misdemeanor, Civil, Eviction, Small Claims, Probate—Circuit Court, PO Box 758, Fort Pierre, SD 57532. 605-773-3992. 8AM-5PM (CST). Access by: Mail, in person.

Sully County

Real Estate Recording—Sully County Register of Deeds, 700 Ash Avenue, Courthouse, Onida, SD 57564. 605-258-2331. Fax: 605-258-2382. 8AM-Noon,1-5PM (CST).

Felony, Misdemeanor, Civil, Eviction, Small Claims, Probate—Circuit Court, PO Box 188, Onida, SD 57564. 605-258-2535. Fax: 605-258-2382. 8AM-Noon (CST). Access by: Mail, in person.

Todd County

Real Estate Recording—Todd County Register of Deeds, Courthouse, 200 E. 3rd St., Winner, SD 57580. 605-842-2208. Fax: 605-842-2224. 8AM-5PM (MST).

Felony, Misdemeanor, Civil, Eviction, Small Claims, Probate—Circuit Court, 200 E 3rd St, Winner, SD 57580. 605-842-2266. 8AM-5PM (MST). Access by: Mail, in person.

Tripp County

Real Estate Recording—Tripp County Register of Deeds, Courthouse, 200 E. 3rd St., Winner, SD 57580. 605-842-2208. Fax: 605-842-2224. 8AM-5PM (CST).

Felony, Misdemeanor, Civil, Eviction, Small Claims, Probate—Circuit Court, 200 E 3rd St, Winner, SD 57580. 605-842-2266. 8AM-5PM (CST). Access by: Mail, in person.

Turner County

Real Estate Recording—Turner County Register of Deeds, 400 South Main Street, Courthouse, Parker, SD 57053. 605-297-3443. Fax: 605-297-5556. 8:30AM-5PM (CST).

Felony, Misdemeanor, Civil, Eviction, Small Claims, Probate—Circuit Court, PO Box 446, Parker, SD 57053. 605-297-3115. Fax: 605-297-3871. 8AM-5PM (CST). Access by: Mail, in person.

Union County

Real Estate Recording—Union County Register of Deeds, Courthouse, 200 E. Main, Elk Point, SD 57025. 605-356-2191. Fax: 605-356-3047. 8:30AM-5PM (CST).

Felony, Misdemeanor, Civil, Eviction, Small Claims, Probate—Circuit Court, PO Box 757, Elk Point, SD 57025. 605-356-2132. 8:30AM-5PM (CST). Access by: Mail, in person.

Walworth County

Real Estate Recording—Walworth County Register of Deeds, Courthouse, Selby, SD 57472. 605-649-7057. Fax: 605-649-7867. 8AM-Noon,1-5PM (CST).

Felony, Misdemeanor, Civil, Eviction, Small Claims, Probate—Circuit Court, PO Box 328, Selby, SD 57472. 605-649-7311. Fax: 605-649-7624. 8AM-5PM (CST). Access by: Mail, in person.

Yankton County

Real Estate Recording—Yankton County Register of Deeds, 3rd & Broadway, Courthouse, Yankton, SD 57078. 605-665-2422. 9AM-5PM (CST).

Felony, Misdemeanor, Civil, Eviction, Small Claims, Probate—Circuit Court, PO Box 155, Yankton, SD 57078. 605-668-3080. 8AM-5PM (CST). Access by: Mail, in person.

Ziebach County

Real Estate Recording—Ziebach County Register of Deeds, Courthouse, Dupree, SD 57623. 605-365-5165. 8AM-5PM (MST).

Felony, Misdemeanor, Civil, Eviction, Small Claims, Probate—Circuit Court, PO Box 306, Dupree, SD 57623. 605-365-5159. 9:30AM-Noon, 1-2:30PM (MST). Access by: Mail, in person.

Federal Courts

US District Court
District of South Dakota

Aberdeen Division, US District Court c/o Pierre Division, Federal Bldg & Courthouse, 225 S Pierre St, Room 405, Pierre, SD 57501. 605-342-3066. Counties: Brown, Butte, Campbell, Clark, Codington, Corson, Day, Deuel, Edmunds, Grant, Hamlin, McPherson, Marshall, Roberts, Spink, Walworth. Judge Battey's closed case records are located at the Rapid City Division

Pierre Division, US District Court Federal Bldg & Courthouse, Room 405, 225 S Pierre St, Pierre, SD 57501. 605-224-5849. Counties: Buffalo, Dewey, Faulk, Gregory, Haakon, Hand, Hughes, Hyde, Jackson, Jerauld, Jones, Lyman, Mellette, Potter, Stanley, Sully, Todd, Tripp, Ziebach

Rapid City Division, US District Court Clerk's Office, Room 302, 515 9th St, Rapid City, SD 57701. 605-342-3066. Counties: Bennett, Custer, Fall River, Harding, Lawrence, Meade, Pennington, Perkins, Shannon

Sioux Falls Division, US District Court Room 220, US Courthouse, 400 S Phillips Ave, Sioux Falls, SD 57102. 605-330-4447. Counties: Aurora, Beadle, Bon Homme, Brookings, Brule, Charles Mix, Clay, Davison, Douglas, Hanson, Hutchinson, Kingsbury, Lake, Lincoln, McCook, Miner, Minnehaha, Moody, Sanborn, Turner, Union, Yankton

US Bankruptcy Court
District of South Dakota

Pierre Division, US Bankruptcy Court, Clerk, Room 203, Federal Bldg, 225 S Pierre St, Pierre, SD 57501. 605-224-6013. Voice Case Information System: 605-330-4559. Counties: Bennett, Brown, Buffalo, Butte, Campbell, Clark, Codington, Corson, Custer, Day, Deuel, Dewey, Edmunds, Fall River, Faulk, Grant, Gregory, Haakon, Hamlin, Hand, Harding, Hughes, Hyde, Jackson, Jerauld, Jones, Lawrence, Lyman, Marshall, McPherson, Meade, Mellette, Pennington, Perkins, Potter, Roberts, Shannon, Spink, Stanley, Sully, Todd, Tripp, Walworth, Ziebach

Sioux Falls Division, US Bankruptcy Court, PO Box 5060, Sioux Falls, SD 57117-5060. 605-330-4541. Voice Case Information System: 605-330-4559. Counties: Aurora, Beadle, Bon Homme, Brookings, Brule, Charles Mix, Clay, Davison, Douglas, Hanson, Hutchinson, Kingsbury, Lake, Lincoln, McCook, Miner, Minnehaha, Moody, Sanborn, Turner, Union, Yankton

Tennessee

Capitol: Nashville (Davidson County)	
Number of Counties: 95	**Population:** 5,256,051
County Court Locations:	**Federal Court Locations:**
•Circuit Courts: 15/31 Districts	•District Courts: 9
•Criminal Courts: 0/31 Districts	•Bankruptcy Courts: 5
• Chancery Courts: 89 31 Districts	**State Agencies:** 20
•General Sessions Courts: 16	
•Combined Circuit/General Courts: 87	
Municipal Courts: 300	
•Probate Courts: 2	
Juvenile Courts: 98	

State Agencies—Summary

General Help Numbers:

State Archives

Secretary of State	615-741-7996
State Library & Archives Division	Fax: 615-741-6471
403 7th Ave N	8AM-6PM M-SA
Nashville, TN 37243-0312	
Reference Librarian:	615-741-7996
Historical Society:	615-741-8934

Governor's Office

Governor's Office	615-741-2001
State Capitol, 1st Floor	Fax: 615-532-9711
Nashville, TN 37243-0001	7AM-5PM

Attorney General's Office

Attorney General's Office	615-741-3491
500 Charlotte Ave	Fax: 615-741-2009
Nashville, TN 37243-0497	8AM-4:30PM

State Legislation

Tennessee General Assembly	615-741-3511
Office of Legislative Information Services	8AM-4:30PM
Rachel Jackson Bldg, 1st Floor	
Nashville, TN 37243	

Important State Internet Sites:

Webscape
File Edit View   Help

State of Tennessee World Wide Web
www.state.tn.us/governor/

Links to all three branches of State Government. E-mail can be sent to the Governor, as well as being able to do searches from this site.

State Library and Archives
www.state.tn.us/sos/statelib/tslahome.htm

Provides a information about the archives, the Tennessee regional library system, registers of manuscripts, historical and genealogical resources.

Tennessee Government Phone Numbers
www.state.tn.us/sos/phone.htm

Contains phone numbers for different State agencies.

General Assembly
www.legislature.state.tn.us

Links to the Senate,House, and legislative information.

Unclaimed Property
www.state.tn.us/treasury/unclaim.htm

Provides information needed to search in writing for unclaimed property.

State Agencies—Public Records

Criminal Records
Tennessee Bureau of Investigation, Records and Identification Unit, 1144 Foster Ave, Menzler-Nix Bldg, Nashville, TN 37210, Main Telephone: 615-741-0430, Hours: 8AM-5PM.
Restricted access.

Corporation Records
Limited Partnership Records
Fictitious Name
Assumed Name
Limited Liability Company Records
Corporation Section, Secretary of State, James K Polk Bldg, Suite 1800, Nashville, TN 37243-0306, Main Telephone: 615-741-0537, Fax: 615-741-7310, Hours: 8AM-4:30PM. Access by: mail, phone, visit.

Trademarks/Servicemarks
Trade Names
Secretary of State, Trademarks/Tradenames Division, James K. Polk Bldg, Nashville, TN 37243-0306, Main Telephone: 615-741-0531, Fax: 615-741-7310, Hours: 8AM-4:30PM. Access by: mail, phone, visit.

Uniform Commercial Code
Federal Tax Liens
State Tax Liens
UCC Division, Secretary of State, James K Polk Bldg, Suite 1800, Nashville, TN 37243-0306, Main Telephone: 615-741-3276, Hours: 8AM-4:30PM. Access by: mail, visit.

Sales Tax Registrations
Revenue Department, Tax Enforcement Division, Andrew Jackson Bldg, 500 Deaderick St, Nashville, TN 37242-0100, Main Telephone: 615-741-7071, Hours: 8AM-4:30PM.
Restricted access.

Birth Certificates
Tennessee Department of Health, Office of Vital Records, 421 5th Ave North, 1st floor, Nashville, TN 37247-0450, Main Telephone: 615-741-1763, Credit card order:: 615-741-0778, Fax: 615-726-2559, Hours: 8AM-4PM. Access by: mail, fax, phone, visit.

Death Records
Tennessee Department of Health, Office of Vital Records, 421 5th Ave North, 1st floor, Nashville, TN 37247-0450, Main Telephone: 615-741-1763, Credit card order:: 615-741-0778, Fax: 615-726-2559, Hours: 8AM-4PM. Access by: mail, fax, phone, visit.

Marriage Certificates
Tennessee Department of Health, Office of Vital Records, 421 5th Ave North, 1st floor, Nashville, TN 37247-0450, Main Telephone: 615-741-1763, Credit card order:: 615-741-0778, Fax: 615-726-2559, Hours: 8AM-4PM. Access by: mail, fax, phone, visit.

Divorce Records
Tennessee Department of Health, Office of Vital Records, 421 5th Ave North, 1st floor, Nashville, TN 37247-0450, Main Telephone: 615-741-1763, Credit card order:: 615-741-0778, Fax: 615-726-2559, Hours: 8AM-4PM. Access by: mail, fax, phone, visit.

Workers' Compensation Records
Tennessee Department of Labor, Workers Compensation Division, 710 James Robertson Pwy, 2nd Floor, Nashville, TN 37243-0661, Main Telephone: 615-741-2395, Fax: 615-532-1468, Hours: 8AM-4:30PM. Access by: mail only.

Driver Records
Dept. of Safety, Financial Responsibility Section, Attn: Driving Records, 1150 Foster Ave, Nashville, TN 37249-4000, Main Telephone: 615-741-3954, Hours: 8AM-4:30PM. Access by: mail, visit. Tickets are available from this office for a $5.00 fee per record.

Vehicle Ownership
Vehicle Identification
Titling and Registration Division, Information Unit, 44 Vantage Way #160, Nashville, TN 37243-8050, Main Telephone: 615-741-3101, Fax: 615-401-6782, Hours: 8AM-4:30PM. Access by: mail, visit.

Accident Reports
Financial Responsibility Section, Accident Reports/Records Unit, 1150 Foster Avenue, Nashville, TN 37249, Main Telephone: 615-741-3954, Hours: 8AM-4:30PM. Access by: mail, visit. Also, you can obtain accident reports from the investigating agency.

Hunting License Information
Fishing License Information
Records not available from state agency.

County Courts and Recording Offices

What You Need to Know...

About the Courts	About the Recorder's Office

Administration

Administrative Office of the Courts	615-741-2687
600 Nashville City Center	Fax: 615-741-6285
511 Union St	8AM-4PM
Nashville, TN 37243-0607	

Court Structure

Some larger metropolitan General Sessions Courts have raised the civil to **$15,000** from $10,000. The Chancery Courts, in addition to handling probate, also hear certain types of equitable civil cases.

Criminal cases are handled by the Circuit Courts and General Sessions Courts, which we have included with the Circuit Courts in this Sourcebook. Combined courts vary by county, and the counties of Davidson, Hamilton, Knox, and Shelby have separate Criminal Courts.

Probate is handled in the Chancery or County Courts, except in Shelby and Davidson Counties where it is handled by the Probate Court.

Online Access

There is currently **no** statewide, online computer system available, internal or external. The AOC has provided computers and CD-ROM readers to state judges, and a project named TnCIS is under way to implement statewide court automation.

Organization

95 counties, 96 filing offices. The recording officer is Register of Deeds. **Sullivan County has two offices.** 66 counties are in the Central Time Zone (CST) and 29 are in the Eastern Time Zone (EST).

UCC Records

Financing statements are filed at the state level, except for consumer goods, farm and real estate related collateral, which are filed with the Register of Deeds. Most filing offices will **not** perform UCC searches. Use search request form UCC-11. Search fees and copy fees vary.

Lien Records

All federal tax liens are filed with the county Register of Deeds. State tax liens are filed with the Secretary of State or the Register of Deeds. Counties will **not** perform tax lien searches. Other liens include judgment, materialman, mechanics, and trustee.

Real Estate Records

Counties will **not** perform real estate searches. Copy fees and certification fees vary. Tax records are kept at the Assessor's Office.

County Courts and Recording Offices

Anderson County

Real Estate Recording—Anderson County Register of Deeds, 100 North Main Street, Courthouse, Room 205, Clinton, TN 37716. 423-457-5400. Fax: 423-457-1638. 8:30AM-4:30PM (EST).

Felony, Misdemeanor, Civil, Eviction, Small Claims—7th District Circuit Court and General Sessions, 100 Main St, Rm 301, Clinton, TN 37716. 423-457-5400. 8AM-4:30PM (EST). Access by: In person only.

Civil, Probate—Chancery Court, Anderson County Courthouse, Clinton, TN 37717. 423-457-5400. Fax: 423-457-4828. 8:30AM-4:30PM (EST). Access by: Mail, in person.

Bedford County

Real Estate Recording—Bedford County Register of Deeds, 108 Northside Square, Shelbyville, TN 37160. 931-684-5719. Fax: 931-685-2086. 8AM-4PM M,T,Th,F; 8AM-4PM W; 8AM-Noon Sat (CST).

Felony, Misdemeanor, Civil, Eviction, Small Claims—17th District Circuit Court and General Sessions, 1 Public Sq, Suite 200, Shelbyville, TN 37160. 931-684-3223. 8AM-4PM M-Th, 8AM-5PM Fri (CST). Access by: Mail, in person.

Civil, Probate—Chancery Court, Chancery Court, 1 Public Sq, Suite 302, Shelbyville, TN 37160. 931-684-1672. 8AM-4PM M-Th, 8AM-5PM Fri (CST). Access by: Mail, in person.

Benton County

Real Estate Recording—Benton County Register of Deeds, 1 E. Court Sq., Suite 105, Camden, TN 38320. 901-584-6661. 8AM-4PM; 8AM-5PM F (CST).

Felony, Misdemeanor, Civil, Eviction, Small Claims—24th District Circuit Court, General Sessions and Juvenile, 1 East Court Sq Rm 207, Camden, TN 38320. 901-584-6711. Fax: 901-584-0475. 8AM-4PM (CST). Access by: Mail, in person.

Civil, Probate—Chancery Court, 1 E Court Sq, Courthouse Rm 206, Camden, TN 38320. 901-584-4435. Fax: 901-584-5956. 8AM-4PM M-Th; 8AM-5PM F (CST). Access by: In person only.

Bledsoe County

Real Estate Recording—Bledsoe County Register of Deeds, Main Street, Courthouse, Pikeville, TN 37367. 423-447-2020. 8AM-4PM M-W,F; 8AM-Noon Sat (CST).

Felony, Misdemeanor, Civil, Eviction, Small Claims—12th District Circuit Court and General Sessions, PO Box 455, Pikeville, TN 37367. 423-447-6488. Fax: 423-447-6856. 8AM-4PM (CST). Access by: In person only.

Civil, Probate—Chancery Court, Chancery Court, PO Box 413, Pikeville, TN 37367. 423-447-2484. Fax: 423-447-6865. 8AM-4PM (CST). Access by: Phone, mail, in person.

Blount County

Real Estate Recording—Blount County Register of Deeds, 349 Court Street, Maryville, TN 37804. 423-982-5741. Fax: 423-681-2455. 8AM-4:30PM (EST).

Felony, Misdemeanor, Civil, Eviction, Small Claims—5th District Circuit Court and General Sessions, 391 Court St, Maryville, TN 37804-5906. 423-982-3762. Fax: 423-681-2457. 8AM-4:30PM (EST). Access by: Mail, in person.

Misdemeanor, Civil—County Court, 301 Court St, Maryville, TN 37804. 423-982-3762. Probate: 423-982-4391. 8AM-4:30PM (EST). Access by: Mail, in person.

Probate—Probate Court, 345 Court St, Maryville, TN 37804-5906. 423-982-4391. 9AM-5PM M-F, 9AM-12PM Sat (EST). Access by: Mail, in person.

Bradley County

Real Estate Recording—Bradley County Register of Deeds, 155 North Ocoee, Courthouse, Room 102, Cleveland, TN 37311. 615-476-0514. Fax: 423-478-8888. 8:30AM-4:30PM M-Th; 8:30AM-5PM F (EST).

Felony, Misdemeanor, Civil, Eviction, Small Claims—10th District Criminal, Circuit, and General Sessions Court, PO Box 1167, Cleveland, TN 37311. 423-476-0544. Fax: 423-476-0488. 8:30AM-4:30PM M-Th, 8:30AM-5PM Fri (EST). Access by: Mail, in person.

Civil, Probate—Chancery Court, Chancery Court, 155 N. Ocoee St, Cleveland, TN 37311. 423-476-0526. 8:30AM-4:30PM M-Th, 8:30AM-5PM Fri (EST). Access by: Mail, in person.

Campbell County

Real Estate Recording—Campbell County Register of Deeds, Courthouse, Suite 102, 570 Main Street, Jacksboro, TN 37757. 423-562-3864. 8AM-4:30PM (EST).

Felony, Misdemeanor, Civil, Eviction, Small Claims—8th District Criminal, Circuit, and General Sessions Court, PO Box 26, Jacksboro, TN 37757. 423-562-2624. 8AM-4:30PM (EST). Access by: In person only.

Civil, Probate—Chancery Court, PO Box 182, Jacksboro, TN 37757. 423-562-3496. 8AM-4:30PM (EST). Access by: Mail, in person.

Cannon County

Real Estate Recording—Cannon County Register of Deeds, Courthouse, Woodbury, TN 37190. 615-563-2041. Fax: 615-563-5696. 8AM-4PM M,T,Th,F; 8AM-Noon Sat (CST).

Felony, Misdemeanor, Civil, Eviction, Small Claims—16th District Circuit Court and General Sessions, County Courthouse Public Sq, Woodbury, TN 37190. 615-563-4461. Fax: 615-563-6391. 8AM-4:30PM M,T,Th,F; 8AM-Noon Wed (CST). Access by: Mail, in person.

Probate—County Court, Public Sq, Woodbury, TN 37190. 615-563-4278. Fax: 615-563-5696. 8AM-4PM M,T,Th,F; 8AM-Noon Sat (CST). Access by: Mail.

Carroll County

Real Estate Recording—Carroll County Register of Deeds, Court Square, Courthouse, Huntingdon, TN 38344. 901-986-1952. Fax: 901-986-1955. 8AM-4PM; 8AM-Noon Sat (CST).

Felony, Misdemeanor, Civil, Eviction, Small Claims—24th District Circuit Court and General Sessions, PO Box 487, Huntingdon, TN 38344. 901-986-1931. 8AM-4PM (CST). Access by: In person only.

Civil, Probate—Chancery Court, PO Box 186, Huntingdon, TN 38344. 901-986-1920. 8AM-4PM (CST). Access by: Mail, in person.

Carter County

Real Estate Recording—Carter County Register of Deeds, 801 East Elk Avenue, Elizabethton, TN 37643. 423-542-1830. 8:30AM-5PM (EST).

Felony, Misdemeanor, Civil, Eviction, Small Claims—1st District Criminal, Circuit, and General Sessions Court, Carter County Justice Center, 900 E Elk Ave, Elizabethton, TN 37643. 423-542-1835. Fax: 423-542-3742. 8AM-5PM (EST). Access by: In person only.

Probate—County Court, Old Courthouse, Main St, Elizabethton, TN 37643. 423-542-1812. 8AM-5PM (EST). Access by: Mail, in person.

Cheatham County

Real Estate Recording—Cheatham County Register of Deeds, 100 Public Square, Suite 117, Ashland City, TN 37015. 615-792-4317. Fax: 615-792-2039. 8AM-4PM (CST).

Felony, Misdemeanor, Civil, Eviction, Small Claims— 23rd District Circuit Court and General Sessions, 100 Public Sq, Ashland City, TN 37015. 615-792-3272. 8AM-4PM (CST). Access by: Phone, mail, in person.

Civil, Probate—Chancery Court, Clerk & Master, Suite 106, Ashland City, TN 37015. 615-792-4620. 8AM-4PM (CST). Access by: Phone, mail, in person.

Chester County

Real Estate Recording—Chester County Register of Deeds, Main Street, Courthouse, Henderson, TN 38340. 901-989-4991. 8AM-4PM (CST).

Felony, Misdemeanor, Civil, Eviction, Small Claims— 26th District Circuit Court and General Sessions, PO Box 133, Henderson, TN 38340. 901-989-2454. 8AM-4PM (CST). Access by: Phone, mail, in person.

Civil, Probate—Chancery Court, Clerk & Master, PO Box 262, Henderson, TN 38340. 901-989-7171. Fax: 901-989-7176. 8AM-4PM (CST). Access by: Mail, in person.

Claiborne County

Real Estate Recording—Claiborne County Register of Deeds, Main Street, Courthouse, Tazewell, TN 37879. 423-626-3325. 8:30AM-4PM (EST).

Felony, Misdemeanor, Civil, Eviction, Small Claims—8th District Criminal, Circuit, and General Sessions Court, Box 34, Tazewell, TN 37879. 423-626-3334. 8:30AM-4PM M-F, 8:30AM-Noon Sat (EST). Access by: Mail, in person.

Civil, Probate—Chancery Court, PO Drawer G, Tazewell, TN 37879. 423-626-3284. 8:30AM-4PM (EST). Access by: Mail.

Clay County

Real Estate Recording—Clay County Register of Deeds, East Lake Avenue, Celina, TN 38551. 931-243-3298. 8AM-4PM M,T,Th,F; 8AM-Noon Sat (CST).

Felony, Misdemeanor, Civil, Eviction, Small Claims— 13th District Criminal, Circuit, and General Sessions Court, PO Box 749, Celina, TN 38551. 931-243-2557. 8AM-4PM (CST). Access by: Mail, in person.

Civil, Probate—Chancery Court, PO Box 332, Celina, TN 38551. 931-243-3145. 8AM-4PM (CST). Access by: Mail, in person.

Cocke County

Real Estate Recording—Cocke County Register of Deeds, 111 Court Ave., Room 102, Courthouse, Newport, TN 37821. 423-623-7540. 8AM-4PM M,T,Th,F; 8AM-Noon W,Sat (EST).

Felony, Misdemeanor, Civil Actions Over $15,000—4th District Circuit Court, 111 Court Ave Rm 201, Newport, TN 37821. 423-623-6124. Fax: 423-625-3889. 8:30AM-5PM (EST). Access by: Phone, mail, in person.

Misdemeanor, Civil Actions Under $15,000, Eviction, Small Claims—General Sessions, 111 Court Ave, Newport, TN 37821. 423-623-8619. Fax: 423-623-9808. 8AM-4PM (EST). Access by: Phone, mail, in person.

Civil, Probate—Chancery Court, Chancery Court, Clerk & Master, Newport, TN 37821. 423-623-3321. Fax: 423-625-3642. 8AM-4:30PM (EST). Access by: Phone, mail, in person.

Coffee County

Real Estate Recording—Coffee County Register of Deeds, 1341 McArthur St., Ste 2, Manchester, TN 37355. 931-723-5130. Fax: 931-723-8232. 8AM-4:30PM (CST).

Felony, Misdemeanor, Civil, Eviction, Small Claims— 14th District Circuit Court and General Sessions, PO Box 629, Manchester, TN 37355. 931-723-5110. 8AM-4:30PM (CST). Access by: Mail, in person.

Civil, Probate—Chancery Court, 101 W. Fort St, Box 5, Manchester, TN 37355. 931-723-5132. 8AM-4:30PM (CST). Access by: Mail, in person.

Crockett County

Real Estate Recording—Crockett County Register of Deeds, Courthouse, Alamo, TN 38001. 901-696-5455. 8AM-4PM (CST).

Felony, Misdemeanor, Civil, Eviction, Small Claims— Circuit Court and General Sessions, 1 South Bell St, Ste 6 Courthouse, Alamo, TN 38001. 901-696-5462. Fax: 901-696-4101. 8AM-4PM (CST). Access by: Mail, in person.

Civil, Probate—Chancery Court, 1 South Bells St, Suite 5, Alamo, TN 38001. 901-696-5458. Fax: 901-696-4101. 8AM-4PM (CST). Access by: Mail, in person.

Cumberland County

Real Estate Recording—Cumberland County Register of Deeds, 2 North Main St., Suite 204, Crossville, TN 38555. 931-484-5559. 8AM-4PM (CST).

Felony, Misdemeanor, Civil, Eviction, Small Claims— 13th District Criminal, Circuit, and General Sessions Court, 2 N Main St, Suite 302, Crossville, TN 38555. 931-484-6647. Fax: 931-484-1931. 8AM-4PM (CST). Access by: In person only.

Civil, Probate—Chancery Court, 2 N Main St, Suite 101, Crossville, TN 38555-4583. 931-484-4731. 8AM-4PM (CST). Access by: Mail, in person.

Davidson County

Real Estate Recording—Davidson County Register of Deeds, 103 Courthouse, Nashville, TN 37201. 615-862-6790. 8AM-4:25PM (CST).

Misdemeanor, Civil Actions Under $10,000, Eviction, Small Claims—General Sessions Court, 100 James Robinson Parkway, Ben West Bldg Room 2, Nashville, TN 37201. 615-862-5195. Fax: 615-862-5924. 8AM-4:30PM (CST). Access by: In person only.

Civil Actions Over $15,000—Circuit Court, 303 Metro Courthouse, Nashville, TN 37201. 615-862-5181. 8AM-4:30PM (CST). Access by: Mail, in person.

Felony, Misdemeanor—20th District Criminal Court, Room 309 Metro Courthouse, Nashville, TN 37201. 615-862-5600. Fax: 615-862-5676. 8AM-4PM (CST). Access by: Mail, in person.

De Kalb County

Real Estate Recording—De Kalb County Register of Deeds, 201 Courthouse, Smithville, TN 37166. 615-597-4153. Fax: 615-597-7420. 8AM-4:30PM M-Th; 8AM-5PM F (CST).

Felony, Misdemeanor, Civil, Eviction, Small Claims— 13th District Criminal, Circuit, and General Sessions Court, Public Sq, Smithville, TN 37166. 615-597-5711. 8AM-4:30PM MTWTh, 8AM-5PM Fri (CST). Access by: Mail, in person.

Civil, Probate—Chancery Court, De Kalb County Courthouse Rm 302, Smithville, TN 37166. 615-597-4360. 8AM-4PM (CST). Access by: In person only.

Decatur County

Real Estate Recording—Decatur County Register of Deeds, Main Street, Courthouse, Decaturville, TN 38329. 901-852-3712. 8AM-4PM M,T,Th,F; 8AM-Noon W,Sat (CST).

Felony, Misdemeanor, Civil, Eviction, Small Claims— 24th District Circuit Court and General Sessions, PO Box 488, Decaturville, TN 38329. 901-852-3125. Fax: 901-852-2130. 8AM-4PM (CST). Access by: In person only.

Civil, Probate—Chancery Court, Clerk & Master, Decaturville, TN 38329. 901-852-3422. Fax: 901-852-2130. 8:30AM-4PM M,T,Th,F; 9AM-Noon Sat (CST). Access by: Phone, mail, in person.

Dickson County

Real Estate Recording—Dickson County Register of Deeds, Court Square, Courthouse, Charlotte, TN 37036. 615-789-4171. Fax: 615-789-3893. 8AM-4PM (CST).

Felony, Misdemeanor, Civil Actions Over $15,000—23rd District Circuit Court, Court Square, PO Box 220, Charlotte, TN 37036. 615-789-7010. Fax: 615-789-7018. 8AM-4PM (CST). Access by: Phone, fax, mail, in person.

Civil Actions Under $10,000, Eviction, Small Claims—General Sessions, PO Box 217, Charlotte, TN 37036. 615-789-5414. Fax: 615-789-3456. 8AM-4PM (CST). Access by: Phone, fax, mail, in person.

Probate—County Court, Court Square, PO Box 220, Charlotte, TN 37036. 615-789-5093. 8AM-4PM MTWF, 8AM-Noon Th & Sat (CST). Access by: Mail, in person.

Dyer County

Real Estate Recording—Dyer County Register of Deeds, Courthouse, Veteran's Square, Dyersburg, TN 38024. 901-286-7806. Fax: 901-286-3584. 8:30AM-4:30PM; 8:30AM-5PM F (CST).

Felony, Misdemeanor, Civil, Eviction, Small Claims—29th District Circuit Court and General Sessions, PO Box 1360, Dyersburg, TN 38024. 901-286-7809. Fax: 901-286-3580. 8:30AM-4:30PM M-Th, 8:30AM-5PM F (CST). Access by: Mail, in person.

Civil, Probate—Chancery Court, PO Box 1360, Dyersburg, TN 38024. 901-286-7818. Fax: 901-286-7812. 8:30AM-4:30PM M-Th, 8:30AM-5PM Fri (CST). Access by: Mail, in person.

Fayette County

Real Estate Recording—Fayette County Register of Deeds, 1 Court Square, Courthouse, Somerville, TN 38068. 901-465-5251. 9AM-5PM (CST).

Felony, Misdemeanor, Civil, Eviction, Small Claims—25th District Circuit Court and General Sessions, PO Box 670, Somerville, TN 38068. 901-465-5205. Fax: 901-465-5215. 9AM-5PM (CST). Access by: Mail, in person.

Civil, Probate—Chancery Court, PO Drawer 220, Somerville, TN 38068. 901-465-5220. Fax: 901-465-5215. 9AM-5PM (CST). Access by: In person only.

Fentress County

Real Estate Recording—Fentress County Register of Deeds, Courthouse, Jamestown, TN 38556. 931-879-7818. 8AM-4PM (CST).

Felony, Misdemeanor, Civil, Eviction, Small Claims—8th District Criminal, Circuit and General Sessions Court, PO Box 699, Jamestown, TN 38556. 931-879-7919. 8AM-4PM M-F; 8AM-Noon Sat (CST). Access by: Mail, in person.

Civil, Probate—Chancery Court, PO Box 151, Jamestown, TN 38556. 931-879-8931. Fax: 931-879-1575. 9AM-5PM M,T,Th,F; 9AM-Noon Wed (CST). Access by: Mail, in person.

Franklin County

Real Estate Recording—Franklin County Register of Deeds, Public Square, Winchester, TN 37398. 931-967-2840. 8AM-4:30PM; 8AM-Noon Sat (CST).

Felony, Misdemeanor, Civil, Eviction, Small Claims—12th District Circuit Court and General Sessions, 1 South Jefferson St, Winchester, TN 37398. 931-967-2923. Fax: 931-962-1479. 8AM-4:30PM (CST). Access by: Mail, in person.

Probate—County Court, 1 South Jefferson St, Winchester, TN 37398. 931-967-2541. Fax: 931-962-1473. 8AM-4:30PM M-F, 8AM-Noon Sat (CST). Access by: Mail, in person.

Gibson County

Real Estate Recording—Gibson County Register of Deeds, Courthouse, Trenton, TN 38382. 901-855-7628. Fax: 901-855-7650. 8AM-4:30PM; 8AM-Noon Sat (CST).

Felony, Misdemeanor, Civil, Eviction, Small Claims—28th District Circuit Court and General Sessions, 295 N College, PO Box 147, Trenton, TN 38382. 901-855-7615. Fax: 901-855-7676. 8AM-4:30PM (CST). Access by: Phone, fax, mail, in person.

Civil, Probate—Chancery Court, Clerk & Master, PO Box 290, Trenton, TN 38382. 901-855-7639. Fax: 901-855-7846. 8AM-4:30PM (CST). Access by: Mail, in person.

Giles County

Real Estate Recording—Giles County Register of Deeds, Courthouse, Pulaski, TN 38478. 931-363-5137. Fax: 931-424-6101. 8AM-4PM; 8AM-5PM M (CST).

Felony, Misdemeanor, Civil, Eviction, Small Claims—22nd District Circuit Court and General Sessions, PO Box 678, Pulaski, TN 38478. 931-363-5311. Fax: 931-424-6101. 8AM-4:30PM (CST). Access by: Mail, in person.

Probate—County Court, PO Box 678, Pulaski, TN 38478. 931-363-1509. Fax: 931-424-6101. 8AM-4PM M-F (CST). Access by: Mail, in person.

Grainger County

Real Estate Recording—Grainger County Register of Deeds, Main Street, Highway 11W, Rutledge, TN 37861. 423-828-3523. Fax: 423-828-4284. 8:30AM-4:30PM M,T,Th,F; 8:30AM-Noon W,Sat (EST).

Felony, Misdemeanor, Civil, Eviction, Small Claims—4th District Circuit Court and General Sessions, PO Box 157, Rutledge, TN 37861. 423-828-3605. Fax: 423-828-3339. 8:30AM-4:30PM (EST). Access by: Phone, mail, in person.

Civil, Probate—Chancery Court, Clerk & Master, Rutledge, TN 37861. 423-828-4436. Fax: 423-828-4284. 8:30AM-4:30PM M,T,Th,F, 8:30AM-Noon Wed (EST). Access by: Mail, in person.

Greene County

Real Estate Recording—Greene County Register of Deeds, Courthouse, 101 S. Main St. Suite 201, Greeneville, TN 37743. 423-639-0196. 8AM-4:30PM (EST).

Felony, Misdemeanor, Civil, Eviction, Small Claims—3rd District Criminal, Circuit and General Sessions Court, 101 S Main, Geene County Courthouse, Greeneville, TN 37743. 423-638-4332. Fax: 423-638-7160. 8AM-4:30PM (EST). Access by: Mail, in person.

Probate—County Court, 101 S Main St., Greeneville, TN 37743. 423-638-4332. Fax: 423-638-7160. 8AM-4:30PM (EST). Access by: Mail, in person.

Grundy County

Real Estate Recording—Grundy County Register of Deeds, Highway 56 & 108, City Hall, Altamont, TN 37301. 931-692-3621. Fax: 931-692-3627. 8AM-4PM M,T,Th,F; 8AM-Noon W,Sat (CST).

Felony, Misdemeanor, Civil, Eviction, Small Claims—12th District Circuit Court and General Sessions, PO Box 161, Altamont, TN 37301. 931-692-3368. Fax: 931-692-2414. 8AM-4:30PM (CST). Access by: Fax, mail, in person.

Civil, Probate—Chancery Court, PO Box 174, Altamont, TN 37301. 931-692-3455. Fax: 931-692-3627. 8AM-4PM M,T,Th,F; 8AM-Noon Wed & Sat (CST). Access by: Mail, in person.

Hamblen County

Real Estate Recording—Hamblen County Register of Deeds, 511 West 2nd North Street, Morristown, TN 37814. 423-586-6551. Fax: 423-587-9798. 8AM-4:30PM M-F; 9AM-Noon Sat (CST).

Felony, Misdemeanor, Civil, Eviction, Small Claims—3rd District, Criminal, Circuit and General Sessions Court, 510 Allison St, Morristown, TN 37814. 423-586-5640. Fax: 423-585-2764. 8AM-4PM M-Th, 8AM-5PM Fri, 9-11:30AM Sat (CST). Access by: Mail, in person.

Civil—County Court, 511 West 2nd North St, Morristown, TN 37814. 423-586-9112. 8AM-4PM M-Th; 8AM-4:30PM F (CST). Access by: In person only.

Hamilton County

Real Estate Recording—Hamilton County Register of Deeds, 625 Georgia Ave., Room 400, Chattanooga, TN 37402. 423-209-6560. Fax: 423-209-6561. 7:30AM-5PM (EST).

Civil Actions Over $15,000—11th District Circuit Court, 6th & Walnut St. Room 500, Chattanooga, TN 37402. 423-209-6700. 8AM-4PM (EST). Access by: In person only.

Civil Actions Under $15,000, Eviction, Small Claims—
11th District General Sessions, Civil Division, 600 Market St, Room 111, Chattanooga, TN 37402. 423-209-7631. Fax: 423-209-7631. 7AM-4PM (EST). Access by: Phone, mail, in person.

Felony, Misdemeanor—11th District Criminal Court, 600 Market St, Room 102, Chattanooga, TN 37402. 423-209-7500. Fax: 423-209-7501. 8AM-4PM (EST). Access by: Mail, in person.

Civil, Probate—Chancery Court, Chancery Court, Clerk & Master, Room 300, Chattanooga, TN 37402. 423-209-6615. Fax: 423-209-6601. 8AM-4PM (EST). Access by: Phone, fax, mail.

Hancock County

Real Estate Recording—Hancock County Register of Deeds, Courthouse, Sneedville, TN 37869. 423-733-4545. 9AM-4PM; 9AM-Noon W,Sat (EST).

Felony, Misdemeanor, Civil, Eviction, Small Claims—3rd District, Criminal, Circuit and General Sessions Court, PO Box 347, Sneedville, TN 37869. 423-733-2954. Fax: 423-733-2119. 8AM-4PM (EST). Access by: Fax, mail, in person.

Civil, Probate—Chancery Court, PO Box 277, Sneedville, TN 37869. 423-733-4524. Fax: 423-733-2762. 9AM-4PM (EST). Access by: Mail, in person.

Hardeman County

Real Estate Recording—Hardeman County Register of Deeds, Courthouse, Bolivar, TN 38008. 901-658-3476. 8:30AM-4:30PM; 8:30AM-5PM F (CST).

Felony, Misdemeanor, Civil, Eviction, Small Claims—25th District Circuit Court and General Sessions, Courthouse, 100 N Main, Bolivar, TN 38008. 901-658-6524. Fax: 901-658-4584. 8:30AM-4:30PM M-Th, 8AM-5PM Fri (CST). Access by: Phone, mail, in person.

Civil, Probate—Chancery Court, PO Box 45, Bolivar, TN 38008. 901-658-3142. Fax: 901-658-4580. 8:30AM-4:30PM M-Th, 8:30AM-5PM Fri (CST). Access by: Mail, in person.

Hardin County

Real Estate Recording—Hardin County Register of Deeds, Courthouse, Savannah, TN 38372. 901-925-4936. 8AM-5PM M,T,Th,F; 8AM-Noon W (CST).

Felony, Misdemeanor, Civil, Eviction, Small Claims—24th District Circuit Court and General Sessions, 601 Main St, Savannah, TN 38372. 901-925-3583. Fax: 901-926-2955. 8AM-4:30PM M,T,Th,F, 8AM-Noon Wed (CST). Access by: In person only.

Probate—County Court, 601 Main St, Savannah, TN 38372. 901-925-3921. 8AM-4:30PM MTTF, 8AM-12PM Wed & Sat (CST). Access by: Mail, in person.

Hawkins County

Real Estate Recording—Hawkins County Register of Deeds, 100 E. Main Street, Courthouse - Room 101, Rogersville, TN 37857. 423-272-8304. 8AM-4PM; 8AM-Noon W,Sat (EST).

Felony, Misdemeanor, Civil, Eviction, Small Claims—3rd District Criminal, Circuit and General Sessions Court, PO Box 9, Rogersville, TN 37857. 423-272-3397. Fax: 423-272-9646. 8AM-4PM (EST). Access by: In person only.

Civil, Probate—Chancery Court, Clerk & Master, Rogersville, TN 37857. 423-272-8150. 8AM-4PM (EST). Access by: In person only.

Haywood County

Real Estate Recording—Haywood County Register of Deeds, 1 North Washington, Courthouse, Brownsville, TN 38012. 901-772-0332. 8:30AM-5PM (CST).

Felony, Misdemeanor, Civil, Eviction, Small Claims—28th District Circuit Court and General Sessions, 1 N Washington, Brownsville, TN 38012. 901-772-1112. Fax: 901-772-3864. 8:30AM-5PM (CST). Access by: Phone, mail, in person.

Civil, Probate—Chancery Court, 1 N Washington, Brownsville, TN 38012. 901-772-0122. Fax: 901-772-3864. 8:30AM-5PM (CST). Access by: Mail, in person.

Henderson County

Real Estate Recording—Henderson County Register of Deeds, Courthouse, Lexington, TN 38351. 901-968-2941. 8AM-4:30PM M,T,Th,F; 8AM-Noon Sat (CST).

Felony, Misdemeanor, Civil, Eviction, Small Claims—26th District Circuit Court and General Sessions, Henderson County Courthouse, Lexington, TN 38351. Civil: 901-968-9441. Fax: 901-967-9441. 8AM-4:30PM M,T,Th,F (CST). Access by: Phone, mail, in person.

Civil, Probate—Chancery Court, PO Box 67, Lexington, TN 38351. 901-968-2801. 8AM-4:30PM M,T,Th,F; 8AM-Noon Sat (CST). Access by: Phone, mail, in person.

Henry County

Real Estate Recording—Henry County Register of Deeds, 101 West Washington St., Paris, TN 38242. 901-642-4081. 8:30AM-4:30PM (CST).

Felony, Misdemeanor, Civil, Eviction, Small Claims—24th District Circuit Court and General Sessions, PO Box 429, Paris, TN 38242. 901-642-0461. 8AM-4:30PM (CST). Access by: Mail, in person.

Probate—County Court, PO Box 24, Paris, TN 38242. 901-642-2412. Fax: 901-642-6531. 8AM-4:30PM (CST). Access by: Mail, in person.

Hickman County

Real Estate Recording—Hickman County Register of Deeds, #1 Courthouse, Centerville, TN 37033. 931-729-4882. 7:30AM-4PM; 8AM-Noon Sat (CST).

Felony, Misdemeanor, Civil, Eviction, Small Claims—21st District Circuit Court and General Sessions, #9 Courthouse, Centerville, TN 37033. 931-729-2211. Fax: 931-729-6141. 7:30AM-5PM (CST). Access by: In person only.

Civil, Probate—Chancery Court, #10, Centerville, TN 37033. 931-729-2522. Fax: 931-729-6141. 8AM-4PM M-F; 8:30AM-Noon Sat (CST). Access by: Mail, in person.

Houston County

Real Estate Recording—Houston County Register of Deeds, Main Street, Court Square, Erin, TN 37061. 931-289-3510. Fax: 931-289-4240. 8AM-4:30PM; 8AM-Noon Sat (CST).

Felony, Misdemeanor, Civil, Eviction, Small Claims—23rd District Circuit Court and General Sessions, PO Box 403, Erin, TN 37061. 931-289-4673. Fax: 931-289-4240. 8AM-4:30PM (CST). Access by: Phone, mail, in person.

Civil, Probate—Chancery Court, PO Box 332, Erin, TN 37061. 931-289-3870. 8AM-4PM (CST). Access by: Mail, in person.

Humphreys County

Real Estate Recording—Humphreys County Register of Deeds, 102 Thompson Street, Courthouse Annex, Room 3, Waverly, TN 37185. 931-296-7681. 8AM-4:30PM (CST).

Felony, Misdemeanor, Civil, Eviction, Small Claims—23rd District Circuit Court and General Sessions, Room 106, Waverly, TN 37185. 931-296-2461. 8AM-4:30PM (CST). Access by: Phone, mail, in person.

Probate—County Court, Clerk, Room 2 Courthouse Annex, Waverly, TN 37185. 931-296-7671. Fax: 931-296-5011. 8AM-4:30PM (CST). Access by: Mail, in person.

Jackson County

Real Estate Recording—Jackson County Register of Deeds, Main Street, Courthouse, Gainesboro, TN 38562. 931-268-9012. 8AM-4PM M,T,Th,F; 8AM-3PM W; 8AM-12 Sat (CST).

Felony, Misdemeanor, Civil, Eviction, Small Claims—15th District Criminal, Circuit and General Sessions Court, PO Box 205, Gainesboro, TN 38562. 931-268-9314. Fax: 931-268-9060. 8AM-4:00PM, 8AM-3PM S (CST). Access by: Phone, fax, mail, in person.

Probate—County Court, PO Box 346, Gainesboro, TN 38562. 931-268-9212. 8AM-4PM M,T,Th,F; 8AM-2PM Sat (CST). Access by: Mail, in person.

Jefferson County

Real Estate Recording—Jefferson County Register of Deeds, 202 Main Street, Courthouse, Dandridge, TN 37725. 423-397-2918. 8AM-4PM; 8-11AM Sat (EST).

Felony, Misdemeanor, Civil, Eviction, Small Claims—4th District Circuit Court and General Sessions, PO Box 671, Dandridge, TN 37725. 423-397-2786. Fax: 423-397-4894. 8AM-4PM M-F; 8-11AM Sat (EST). Access by: Mail, in person.

Probate—County Court, PO Box 710, Dandridge, TN 37725. 423-397-2935. Fax: 423-397-3839. 8AM-4PM M-F, 8AM-11PM Sat (EST). Access by: Phone, fax, mail, in person.

Johnson County

Real Estate Recording—Johnson County Register of Deeds, 222 Main Street, Mountain City, TN 37683. 423-727-7841. Fax: 423-727-7047. 8:30AM-5PM M,T,Th,F; 8:30AM-Noon W,Sat (EST).

Felony, Misdemeanor, Civil, Eviction, Small Claims—1st District Criminal, Circuit and General Sessions Court, PO Box 73, Mountain City, TN 37683. 423-727-9012. Fax: 423-727-7047. 8:30AM-5PM (EST). Access by: Phone, mail, in person.

Civil, Probate—Chancery Court, PO Box 196, Mountain City, TN 37683. 423-727-7853. Fax: 423-727-7047. 8:30AM-5PM (EST). Access by: Mail, in person.

Knox County

Real Estate Recording—Knox County Register of Deeds, 400 W. Main Avenue, Room 224, Knoxville, TN 37902. 423-215-2330. Fax: 423-215-2332. 8AM-4:30PM (EST).

Civil Actions Over $10,000—Circuit Court, 400 Main Ave, Room M-30 or PO Box 379, Knoxville, TN 37901. 423-215-2400. Fax: 423-521-4251. 8AM-4:30PM (EST). Access by: Phone, fax, mail, in person.

Civil Actions Under $15,000, Eviction, Small Claims—General Sessions, 400 Main Ave, Knoxville, TN 37902. Civil: 423-215-2518. Criminal: 423-215-2375. 8AM-4:30PM (EST). Access by: In person only.

Felony, Misdemeanor—6th District Criminal Court, 400 Main Ave, Room 149, Knoxville, TN 37902. 423-215-2492. Fax: 423-521-4291. 8AM-5PM M-Th; 8AM-4:30PM F (EST). Access by: Phone, fax, mail, in person.

Civil, Probate—Chancery Court, 400 Main Ave, Knoxville, TN 37902. 423-215-2555. Probate: 615-521-2389. Fax: 423-215-2920. 8AM-4:30PM (EST). Access by: Mail, in person.

Lake County

Real Estate Recording—Lake County Register of Deeds, 229 Church St., Box 5, Courthouse, Tiptonville, TN 38079. 901-253-7462. Fax: 901-253-6815. 9AM-4PM M,T,W,F; 8AM-Noon Th (CST).

Felony, Misdemeanor, Civil, Eviction, Small Claims—29th District Circuit Court and General Sessions, 227 Church St, PO Box 11, Tiptonville, TN 38079. 901-253-7137. Fax: 901-253-9815. 9AM-4PM M-W & F; 8AM-Noon Th (CST). Access by: Phone, mail, in person.

Civil, Probate—Chancery Court, PO Box 12, Tiptonville, TN 38079. 901-253-8926. 9AM-4PM MTWF, 8AM-12PM Th (CST). Access by: Mail.

Lauderdale County

Real Estate Recording—Lauderdale County Register of Deeds, Courthouse, Ripley, TN 38063. 901-635-2171. Fax: 901-635-9682. 8AM-4:30PM M,T,Th,F; 8AM-Noon W,Sat (CST).

Felony, Misdemeanor, Civil Actions Over $15,000—25th District Circuit Court, Lauderdale County Justice Center, 675 Hwy 51 S, PO Box 509, Ripley, TN 38063. 901-635-0101. Fax: 901-635-0583. 8AM-4:30PM (CST). Access by: Mail, in person.

Civil Actions Under $15,000, Eviction, Small Claims—General Sessions Court, PO Box 509, Ripley, TN 38063.

901-635-2572. Fax: 901-635-9682. 8AM-4:30PM (CST). Access by: Mail, in person.

Probate—County Court, Courthouse, 100 Court Sq, Ripley, TN 38063. 901-635-2561. 8AM-4:30PM M,T,Th,F; 8AM-Noon W & Sat (CST). Access by: Mail.

Lawrence County

Real Estate Recording—Lawrence County Register of Deeds, 240 West Gaines Street, N.B.U. #18, Lawrenceburg, TN 38464. 931-766-4100. Fax: 931-766-4100. 8AM-4:30PM (CST).

Felony, Misdemeanor, Civil, Eviction, Small Claims—22nd District Circuit Court and General Sessions, NBU #12 240 W Gaines, Lawrenceburg, TN 38464. 931-762-4398. Fax: 931-766-2219. 8AM-4:30PM (CST). Access by: In person only.

Civil, Probate—County Court, 240 Gaines St, NBU #2, Lawrenceburg, TN 38464. 931-762-7700. 8AM-4:30PM (CST). Access by: In person only.

Lewis County

Real Estate Recording—Lewis County Register of Deeds, Courthouse, Hohenwald, TN 38462. 931-796-2255. 8AM-4:30PM (CST).

Felony, Misdemeanor, Civil, Eviction, Small Claims—21st Judicial District Circuit Court and General Sessions, Courthouse 110 Park Avenue N, Hohenwald, TN 38462. 931-796-3724. Fax: 931-796-6010. 8AM-4:30PM (CST). Access by: Phone, mail, in person.

Civil, Probate—Chancery Court, Chancery Court, Clerk & Master, Hohenwald, TN 38462. 931-796-3734. 8AM-4:30PM (CST). Access by: Mail, in person.

Lincoln County

Real Estate Recording—Lincoln County Register of Deeds, Courthouse, Room 104, Fayetteville, TN 37334. 931-433-5366. 8AM-4PM (CST).

Felony, Misdemeanor, Civil, Eviction, Small Claims—17th Judicial District Circuit Court and General Sessions, PO Box 578, Fayetteville, TN 37334. 931-433-2334. Fax: 931-438-1577. 8AM-4PM (CST). Access by: Phone, fax, mail, in person.

Civil, Probate—Chancery Court, PO Box 57, Fayetteville, TN 37334. 931-433-1482. Fax: 931-433-9979. 8AM-4PM (CST). Access by: Mail, in person.

Loudon County

Real Estate Recording—Loudon County Register of Deeds, 101 Mulberry St., Loudon, TN 37774. 423-458-2605. 8AM-4:30PM (M-open until 5:30PM) (EST).

Felony, Misdemeanor, Civil, Eviction, Small Claims—9th District Criminal & Circuit Court, PO Box 160, Loudon, TN 37774. 423-458-2042. Fax: 423-458-2043. 8AM-5:30PM Mon, 8AM-4:30PM T-F; 8AM-8PM(General Session Juv) (EST). Access by: Mail, in person.

Probate—County Court, 101 Mulberry St #200, Loudon, TN 37774. 423-458-2726. Fax: 423-458-9891. 8AM-5:30PM Mon, 8AM-4:30PM T-F (EST). Access by: Mail, in person.

Macon County

Real Estate Recording—Macon County Register of Deeds, Courthouse, Room 102, Lafayette, TN 37083. 615-666-2353. Fax: 615-666-5323. 8AM-4:30PM (CST).

Felony, Misdemeanor, Civil, Eviction, Small Claims—15th District Criminal, Circuit, and General Sessions Court, Room 202, Lafayette, TN 37083. 615-666-2354. Fax: 615-666-3001. 8AM-4:30PM M-Th; 8AM-5PM F (CST). Access by: In person only.

Probate—County Court, County Court Clerk, Rm 104, Lafayette, TN 37083. 615-666-2333. Fax: 615-666-5323. 8AM-4:30PM M-W, Closed Thu, 8AM-5PM Fri, 8AM-1:30PM Sat (CST). Access by: Mail, in person.

Madison County

Real Estate Recording—Madison County Register of Deeds, Courthouse, Room 109, 100 Main St., Jackson, TN 38301. 901-423-6028. Fax: 901-422-1171. 9AM-5PM (CST).

Felony, Misdemeanor, Civil Actions Over $15,000—26th District Circuit Court, 100 E Main St Rm 203, Jackson, TN 38301. 901-423-6035. 9AM-5PM (CST). Access by: In person only.

Civil Actions Under $15,000, Eviction, Small Claims—General Sessions, 100 E. Main St, Jackson, TN 38301. 901-423-6041. 9AM-5PM (CST). Access by: In person only.

Probate—General Sessions Division II, Probate Division, 100 Main St, Room 104, Jackson, TN 38301. 901-423-6023. Fax: 901-422-1171. 9AM-5PM (CST). Access by: Phone, mail, in person.

Marion County

Real Estate Recording—Marion County Register of Deeds, Highway 41, Courthouse, Jasper, TN 37347. 423-942-2573. 8AM-4PM M-F; 8AM-Noon Sat (CST).

Felony, Misdemeanor, Civil, Eviction, Small Claims—12th District Circuit Court and General Sessions, PO Box 789, Courthouse Sq, Jasper, TN 37347. 423-942-2134. Fax: 423-942-4160. 8AM-4PM (CST). Access by: Phone, mail, in person.

Civil, Probate—Chancery Court, PO Box 789, Jasper, TN 37347. 423-942-2601. Fax: 423-942-1327. 8AM-4PM (CST). Access by: Mail, in person.

Marshall County

Real Estate Recording—Marshall County Register of Deeds, 205 Marshall County Courthouse, Lewisburg, TN 37091. 931-359-4933. 8AM-4PM (CST).

Felony, Misdemeanor, Civil, Eviction, Small Claims—17th District Circuit Court and General Sessions, Courthouse, Lewisburg, TN 37091. 931-359-1312. Fax: 931-359-0543. (CST). Access by: Mail, in person.

Probate—County Court, 207 Marshall County Courthouse, Lewisburg, TN 37091. 931-359-1072. Fax: 931-359-0543. 8AM-4PM (CST). Access by: Mail, in person.

Maury County

Real Estate Recording—Maury County Register of Deeds, #1 Public Square, Columbia, TN 38401. 423-381-3690. 8AM-4PM (CST).

Felony, Misdemeanor, Civil, Eviction, Small Claims—22nd Circuit Court and General Sessions, Public Square, Room 202, Columbia, TN 38401. 423-745-1923. 8:00AM-5:00PM (CST). Access by: In person only.

McMinn County

Real Estate Recording—McMinn County Register of Deeds, Washington Avenue, Courthouse, Athens, TN 37303. 423-745-1232. Fax: 423-745-0095. 8:30AM-4PM (EST).

Felony, Misdemeanor, Civil, Eviction, Small Claims—10th District Criminal, Circuit and General Sessions Court, PO Box 506, Athens, TN 37303. 423-745-1923. Fax: 423-745-0095. 8:30AM-4PM (EST). Access by: Phone, mail, in person.

McNairy County

Real Estate Recording—McNairy County Register of Deeds, Court Avenue, Courthouse, Selmer, TN 38375. 901-645-3656. Fax: 901-645-3656. 8AM-4:30PM M,T,Th,F; 8AM-Noon Sat (CST).

Felony, Misdemeanor, Civil, Eviction, Small Claims—25th District Circuit Court and General Sessions, 300 Industrial Park, Selmer, TN 38375. 901-645-1015. 8AM-4:30PM M,T,Th,F; 8AM Noon Sat (CST). Access by: Mail, in person.

Civil, Probate—Chancery Court, Chancery Court, Clerk & Master, Selmer, TN 38375. 901-645-5446. Fax: 901-645-3656. 8AM-4:30PM (CST). Access by: Mail, in person.

Meigs County

Real Estate Recording—Meigs County Register of Deeds, Courthouse, Decatur, TN 37322. 423-334-5228. 8AM-5PM M,T,Th,F; 8AM-Noon W & Sat (EST).

Felony, Misdemeanor, Civil, Eviction, Small Claims—9th District Criminal, Circuit and General Sessions Court, PO Box 205, Decatur, TN 37322. 423-334-5821. Fax: 423-334-4819. 8AM-5PM M,T,Th,F; 8AM-12PM Sat (EST). Access by: Mail, in person.

Civil, Probate—Chancery Court, PO Box 5, Decatur, TN 37322. 423-334-5243. 8AM-5PM M,T,Th,F; 8:30AM-Noon Wed (EST). Access by: Mail, in person.

Monroe County

Real Estate Recording—Monroe County Register of Deeds, 103 College Street - Suite 4, Madisonville, TN 37354. 423-442-2440. 8:30AM-4:30PM M,T,Th,F; 8:30AM-Noon W & Sat (EST).

Felony, Misdemeanor, Civil, Eviction, Small Claims—10th District Criminal, Circuit and General Sessions Court, 105 College St, Madisonville, TN 37354. 423-442-2396. Fax: 423-442-9538. 8AM-4:30PM (EST). Access by: Mail, in person.

Civil, Probate—Chancery Court, PO Box 56, Madisonville, TN 37354. 423-442-2644. Fax: 423-442-6791. 8:30AM-4:30PM (EST). Access by: Mail, in person.

Montgomery County

Real Estate Recording—Montgomery County Register of Deeds, 214 Franklin St., 2nd Floor, # 202, Clarksville, TN 37040. 931-648-5713. Fax: 931-553-5157. 8AM-4:30PM (CST).

Felony, Civil Actions Over $10,000—19th District Circuit Court, PO Box 384, Clarksville, TN 37041-0384. 931-648-5700. 8:30AM-4:30PM (CST). Access by: In person only.

Misdemeanor, Civil Actions Under $10,000, Eviction, Small Claims—General Sessions, 120 Commerce St, Clarksville, TN 37040. Civil: 931-648-5769. Criminal: 931-648-5771. 8:30AM-4:30PM (CST). Access by: Mail, in person.

Civil, Probate—Chancery Court, Chancery Court, Clerk & Master, Clarksville, TN 37040. 931-648-5703. 8AM-4:30PM (CST). Access by: Mail, in person.

Moore County

Real Estate Recording—Moore County Register of Deeds, Courthouse, Lynchburg, TN 37352. 931-759-7913. 8AM-4:30PM; Closed Th; 8AM-Noon Sat (CST).

Felony, Misdemeanor, Civil, Eviction, Small Claims—17th District Circuit Court and General Sessions, Courthouse, PO Box 206, Lynchburg, TN 37352. 931-759-7208. Fax: 931-759-7028. 8AM-4:30PM MTWF; 8AM-12PM Sat (CST). Access by: Mail, in person.

Civil, Probate—Chancery Court, PO Box 206, Lynchburg, TN 37352. 931-759-7028. 8AM-4:30PM M-W,F; 8AM-Noon Sat (CST). Access by: Mail, in person.

Morgan County

Real Estate Recording—Morgan County Register of Deeds, Courthouse Square, Room 102, Wartburg, TN 37887. 423-346-3105. 8AM-4PM (EST).

Felony, Misdemeanor, Civil, Eviction, Small Claims—9th District Criminal, Circuit and General Sessions Court, PO Box 163, Wartburg, TN 37887. 423-346-3503. 8AM-4PM (EST). Access by: Mail, in person.

Civil, Probate—Chancery Court, PO Box 789, Wartburg, TN 37887. 423-346-3881. 8AM-4PM (EST). Access by: Phone, mail, in person.

Obion County

Real Estate Recording—Obion County Register of Deeds, 5 Bill Burnch Circle, Union City, TN 38261. 901-885-9351. Fax: 901-885-7515. 8AM-4:30PM (CST).

Felony, Misdemeanor, Civil Actions Over $10,000—27th District Circuit Court, 7 Bill Burnett Circle, Union City, TN 38261. 901-885-1372. Fax: 901-885-7515. 8:30AM-4:30PM (CST). Access by: Phone, mail, in person.

Civil Actions Under $15,000, Eviction, Small Claims—General Sessions, PO Box 236, Union City, TN 38281-0236. 901-885-1811. Fax: 901-885-7515. 9AM-4PM (CST). Access by: Mail, in person.

Civil, Probate—Chancery Court, PO Box 187, Union City, TN 38281. 901-885-2562. 8:30AM-4:30PM (CST). Access by: Mail, in person.

Overton County

Real Estate Recording—Overton County Register of Deeds, 317 East University St., Livingston, TN 38570. 931-823-4011. 8AM-4:30PM (CST).

Felony, Misdemeanor, Civil, Eviction, Small Claims—13th District Criminal, Circuit and General Sessions Court, Overton County Courthouse, Livingston, TN 38570. 931-823-2312. Fax: 931-823-9728. 8AM-4:30PM MTTF, 8AM-12PM Wed and Sat (CST). Access by: Mail, in person.

Probate—County Court, Courthouse Annex, University St, Livingston, TN 38570. 931-823-2631. 8AM-4:30PM M,T,Th,F; 8AM-Noon W & Sat (CST). Access by: Mail, in person.

Perry County

Real Estate Recording—Perry County Register of Deeds, Main Street, Courthouse, Linden, TN 37096. 931-589-2210. 8AM-4PM M,T,Th,F; Closed Wed; 8-11AM Sat (CST).

Felony, Misdemeanor, Civil, Eviction, Small Claims—21st District Circuit Court and General Sessions, PO Box 91, Linden, TN 37096. 931-589-2218. 8AM-4PM (CST). Access by: Mail, in person.

Civil, Probate—Chancery Court, PO Box 251, Linden, TN 37096. 931-589-2217. Fax: 931-589-2350. 8AM-4PM (CST). Access by: Mail, in person.

Pickett County

Real Estate Recording—Pickett County Register of Deeds, Main Street, Courthouse, Byrdstown, TN 38549. 931-864-3316. Fax: 931-864-6931. 8AM-4PM (CST).

Felony, Misdemeanor, Civil, Eviction, Small Claims—13th District, Criminal, Circuit and General Sessions Court, PO Box 5, Byrdstown, TN 38549. 931-864-3958. Fax: 931-864-6885. 8AM-4PM (CST). Access by: Mail, in person.

Probate—County Court, PO Box 5 Courthoue Square, Byrdstown, TN 38549. 931-864-3879. 8AM-4PM M,T,Th,F, 8AM-Noon W & Sat (CST). Access by: Mail, in person.

Polk County

Real Estate Recording—Polk County Register of Deeds, 411 Highway, Courthouse, Benton, TN 37307. 423-338-4537. 9AM-4:30PM; Closed Th; 9AM-Noon Sat (EST).

Felony, Misdemeanor, Civil, Eviction, Small Claims—10th District Criminal, Circuit and General Sessions Court, PO Box 256, Benton, TN 37307. 423-338-4524. Fax: 423-338-4558. 8:30AM-4:30PM M-F; 9AM-Noon Sat (EST). Access by: Phone, mail, in person.

Civil, Probate—Chancery Court, PO Drawer L, Benton, TN 37307. 423-338-4522. 8:30AM-4:30PM M-F, 8:30AM-Noon Sat (EST). Access by: Mail, in person.

Putnam County

Real Estate Recording—Putnam County Register of Deeds, 300 East Spring Street, Courthouse - Room 3, Cookeville, TN 38501. 931-526-7101. 8AM-4PM (CST).

Felony, Misdemeanor, Civil, Eviction, Small Claims—13th District Criminal, Circuit and General Sessions Court, 421 E Spring St, 1C-49A, Cookeville, TN 38501. 931-528-1508. 8Am-4PM (CST). Access by: Mail, in person.

Probate—County Court, 29 N Washington, Cookeville, TN 38501. 931-526-7106. Fax: 931-372-8201. 8AM-4:30PM (CST). Access by: Mail, in person.

Rhea County

Real Estate Recording—Rhea County Register of Deeds, 1475 Market Street, Dayton, TN 37321. 423-775-7841. 8AM-4PM (EST).

Felony, Misdemeanor, Civil, Eviction, Small Claims—12th District Circuit Court and General Sessions, 1475 Market St Rm 200, Dayton, TN 37321. 423-775-7805. Fax: 423-775-5553. 8AM-4PM M-Th; 8AM-5:30PM F (EST). Access by: In person only.

Probate—County Court, 1475 Market St, Rm 105, Dayton, TN 37321. 423-775-7808. Fax: 423-775-5553. 8AM-4PM M-Th; 8AM-5:30PM F (EST). Access by: Mail, in person.

Roane County

Real Estate Recording—Roane County Register of Deeds, 200 Race Street, Courthouse, Kingston, TN 37763. 423-376-4673. 8:30AM-6PM M; 8:30AM-4:30PM T-F (EST).

Felony, Misdemeanor, Civil, Eviction, Small Claims—9th District Criminal, Circuit, and General Sessions Court, PO Box 73, Kingston, TN 37763. 423-376-2390. Fax: 423-376-4458. 8:30AM-6PM Mon; 8:30AM-4:30PM T-F (EST). Access by: Mail, in person.

Civil, Probate—Chancery Court, PO Box 402, Kingston, TN 37763. 423-376-2487. Fax: 423-376-4318. 8:30AM-6PM Mon, 8:30AM-4:30PM T-F (EST). Access by: Phone, mail, in person.

Robertson County

Real Estate Recording—Robertson County Register of Deeds, 525 S. Brown St., Springfield, TN 37172. 615-384-3772. 8AM-4:30PM (CST).

Felony, Misdemeanor, Civil, Eviction, Small Claims—19th District Circuit Court and General Sessions, Room 200, Springfield, TN 37172. 615-382-2324. Fax: 615-384-8246. 8AM-4:30PM (CST). Access by: Phone, fax, mail, in person. No long distance outgoing faxing.

Civil, Probate—Chancery Court, 207 Robertson, County Courthouse, Springfield, TN 37172. 615-384-5650. 8:30AM-4:30PM (CST). Access by: Mail, in person.

Rutherford County

Real Estate Recording—Rutherford County Register of Deeds, Judicial Building Room 501, Public Square, Murfreesboro, TN 37133. 615-898-7870. 8AM-4PM (CST).

Felony, Misdemeanor, Civil Actions Over $15,000—16th District Circuit Court, Room 201, Murfreesboro, TN 37130. Civil: 615-898-7820. Criminal: 615-898-7812. Fax: 615-849-9553. 8AM-4:15PM (CST). Access by: In person only.

Civil Actions Under $10,000, Eviction, Small Claims—General Sessions, Room 101, Murfreesboro, TN 37130. 615-898-7831. Fax: 615-898-7835. 8AM-4:15PM (CST). Access by: In person only.

Probate—County Court, 319 N Maple St, Murfreesboro, TN 37130. 615-898-7798. Fax: 615-898-7830. 8AM-4PM M-Th; 8AM-5PM F (CST). Access by: Mail, in person.

Scott County

Real Estate Recording—Scott County Register of Deeds, 3 Courthouse Square, Huntsville, TN 37756. 423-663-2417. 8AM-4:30PM (EST).

Felony, Misdemeanor, Civil, Eviction, Small Claims—8th District Criminal, Circuit, and General Sessions Court, PO Box 73, Huntsville, TN 37756. 423-663-2440. Fax: 423-663-3803. 8AM-4:30PM (EST). Access by: Phone, fax, mail, in person.

Sequatchie County

Real Estate Recording—Sequatchie County Register of Deeds, Cherry Street, Courthouse - 307E, Dunlap, TN 37327. 423-949-2512. Fax: 423-949-6554. 8AM-4PM; Closed Th; 8AM-Noon Sat (CST).

Felony, Misdemeanor, Civil, Eviction, Small Claims—12th District Circuit Court and General Sessions, PO Box 551, Dunlap, TN 37327. 423-949-2618. Fax: 423-949-2902. 8AM-4PM MTWF; 8AM-Noon Sat (CST). Access by: Phone, mail, in person.

Civil, Probate—Chancery Court, PO Box 1651, Dunlap, TN 37327. 423-949-3670. Fax: 423-949-2579. 8AM-4PM (CST). Access by: Mail.

Sevier County

Real Estate Recording—Sevier County Register of Deeds, 125 Court Avenue, Courthouse Suite 209W, Sevierville, TN 37862. 423-453-2758. 8AM-4:30PM M-Th; 8AM-6PM F (EST).

Felony, Misdemeanor, Civil, Eviction, Small Claims—4th District Circuit Court and General Sessions, 125 Court Ave 204 E, Sevierville, TN 37862. 423-453-5536. 8AM-4:30PM M-T, 8AM-6PM Fri (EST). Access by: Phone, mail, in person.

Probate—County Court, 125 Court Ave, Suite 202, Sevierville, TN 37862. 423-453-5502. Fax: 423-453-6830. 8AM-4:30PM (EST). Access by: Mail, in person.

Shelby County

Real Estate Recording—Shelby County Register of Deeds, 160 North Mid America Mall, Room 519, Memphis, TN 38103. 901-576-4366. Fax: 901-576-3837. 8AM-4:30PM (CST).

Civil Actions Over $15,000—Circuit Court, 140 Adams, Memphis, TN 38103. 901-576-4006. Fax: 901-576-4372. 8AM-4:30PM (CST). Access by: Fax, mail, in person.

Felony—30th District Criminal Court, 201 Poplar, Room 401, Memphis, TN 38103. 901-576-5001. Fax: 901-576-3679. 8AM-4:30PM (CST). Access by: Fax, mail, in person.

Civil Actions Under $15,000, Eviction, Small Claims—General Sessions-Civil, 140 Adams, Room 106, Memphis, TN 38103. 901-576-4031. Fax: 901-576-3451. 8AM-4:30PM (CST). Access by: Fax, mail, in person.

Misdemeanor—General Sessions-Criminal, 201 Poplar, Room 81, Memphis, TN 38103. 901-576-5098. Fax: 901-576-3655. 8AM-4:30PM (CST). Access by: Mail, in person.

Probate—Probate Court, 140 Adams, Room 124, Memphis, TN 38103. 901-576-4040. Fax: 901-576-4746. 8AM-4:30PM (CST). Access by: Phone, fax, mail.

Smith County

Real Estate Recording—Smith County Register of Deeds, 211 N. Main St., Carthage, TN 37030. 615-735-1760. 8AM-4PM (CST).

Felony, Misdemeanor, Civil, Eviction, Small Claims—15th District Criminal, Circuit, and General Sessions Court, 211 Main St, Carthage, TN 37030. 615-735-0500. 8AM-4PM M-F; 8AM-Noon Sat (CST). Access by: Phone, mail, in person.

Civil, Probate—Chancery Court, 211 N Main St, Carthage, TN 37030. 615-735-2092. 8AM-4PM (CST). Access by: Mail, in person.

Stewart County

Real Estate Recording—Stewart County Register of Deeds, Courthouse, 225 Donelson Parkway, Dover, TN 37058. 931-232-5990. 8AM-4:30PM (CST).

Felony, Misdemeanor, Civil, Eviction, Small Claims—23rd District Circuit Court and General Sessions, PO Box 193, Dover, TN 37058. 931-232-7042. Fax: 931-232-3111. 8AM-4:30PM (CST). Access by: Mail, in person.

Civil, Probate—Chancery Court, PO Box 102, Dover, TN 37058. 931-232-5665. Fax: 931-232-3111. 8AM-4:30PM (CST). Access by: Mail, in person.

Sullivan County

Real Estate Recording—Sullivan County Register of Deeds, Blountville Office, 3411 Highway 126, Courthouse, Blountville, TN 37617. 423-323-6420. 8AM-5PM (EST).

Sullivan County Register of Deeds, Bristol Office, 801 Broad St., Bristol, TN 37620. 423-989-4370.

Civil—Bristol Circuit Court-Civil Division, Room 211 Courthouse, Bristol, TN 37620. 423-989-4354. 8AM-5PM (EST). Access by: Mail, in person.

Civil Actions Over $15,000—Kingsport Circuit Court-Civil Division, 225 W Center St, Kingsport, TN 37660. 423-224-1724. 8AM-5PM (EST). Access by: Phone, mail, in person.

Felony, Misdemeanor—2nd District Circuit Court, 140 Blockville ByPass, PO Box 585, Blountville, TN 37617. 423-323-5158. 8AM-5PM (EST). Access by: In person only.

Misdemeanor, Civil Actions Under $10,000, Eviction, Small Claims—Bristol General Sessions, 801 Broad St Rm 211 Courthouse, Bristol, TN 37620. 423-989-4352. 8AM-5PM (EST). Access by: Phone, mail, in person.

Misdemeanor, Civil Actions Under $15,000, Eviction, Small Claims—Kingsport General Sessions, 200 Shelby St, Kingsport, TN 37660. 423-279-2752. 8AM-5PM (EST). Access by: Phone, mail, in person.

Civil, Probate—Chancery Court, PO Box 327, Blountville, TN 37617. 423-323-6483. 8AM-5PM (EST). Access by: Mail, in person.

Sumner County

Real Estate Recording—Sumner County Register of Deeds, 355 N. Belvedere Dr., S.C. Admin. Bldg, Rm 201, Gallatin, TN 37066. 615-452-3892. 8AM-4:30PM (CST).

Felony, Misdemeanor, Civil, Eviction, Small Claims—18th District Criminal, Circuit, and General Sessions Court, Public Sq, PO Box 549, Gallatin, TN 37066. 615-452-4367. Fax: 615-451-6027. 8AM-4:30PM (CST). Access by: In person only.

Civil, Probate—Chancery Court, Room 300, Sumner County Courthouse, Gallatin, TN 37066. 615-452-4282. Fax: 615-451-6031. 8AM-4:30PM (CST). Access by: Mail, in person.

Tipton County

Real Estate Recording—Tipton County Register of Deeds, Court Square, Courthouse, Room 105, Covington, TN 38019. 901-476-0204. Fax: 901-476-0227. 8AM-5PM (CST).

Felony, Misdemeanor, Civil, Eviction, Small Claims—25th District Circuit Court and General Sessions, PO Box 1008, Covington, TN 38019. 901-476-0216. 8:30AM-4:30PM M-Th; 8AM-5PM F (CST). Access by: Mail, in person.

Civil, Probate—Chancery Court, Tipton County Courthouse, Court Sq, PO Box 87, Covington, TN 38019. 901-476-0209. Fax: 901-476-0227. 8AM-5PM (CST). Access by: Phone, mail.

Trousdale County

Real Estate Recording—Trousdale County Register of Deeds, 200 E. Main St. #8, Hartsville, TN 37074. 615-374-2921. Fax: 615-374-1100. 8AM-4:30PM (CST).

Felony, Misdemeanor, Civil, Eviction, Small Claims—15th District Criminal, Circuit, and General Sessions Court, 200 East Main St, Rm 5, Hartsville, TN 37074. 615-374-3411. Fax: 615-374-1100. 8AM-4:30PM (CST). Access by: In person only.

Civil, Probate—Chancery Court, PO Box 74, Hartsville, TN 37074. 615-374-2996. Fax: 615-374-1100. 8AM-4:30PM (CST). Access by: Mail, in person.

Unicoi County

Real Estate Recording—Unicoi County Register of Deeds, Main Street, Courthouse, Erwin, TN 37650. 423-743-6104. 9AM-5PM; 9AM-Noon Sat (EST).

Felony, Misdemeanor, Civil, Eviction, Small Claims—1st District Criminal, Circuit, and General Sessions Court, PO Box 376, Erwin, TN 37650. 423-743-3541. 8AM-5PM (EST). Access by: Mail, in person.

Probate—Probate Court, PO Box 340, Erwin, TN 37650. 423-743-3381. Fax: 423-743-7115. 9AM-5PM M-F, 9AM-Noon Sat (EST). Access by: Mail, in person.

Union County

Real Estate Recording—Union County Register of Deeds, Main Street, Maynardville, TN 37807. 423-992-8024. 8AM-4PM M,T,Th.F; 8AM-Noon W,Sat (EST).

Felony, Misdemeanor, Civil, Eviction, Small Claims—8th District Criminal, Circuit, and General Sessions Court, PO Box 306, Maynardville, TN 37807. 423-992-5493. 8AM-4PM M,T,Th,F; 8AM-Noon W & Sat (EST). Access by: Mail, in person.

Civil, Probate—Chancery Court, PO Box 224, Maynardville, TN 37807. 423-992-5942. 8AM-4PM M,T,Th,F, 8AM-Noon Wed & Sat (EST). Access by: Phone, mail, in person.

Van Buren County

Real Estate Recording—Van Buren County Register of Deeds, Courthouse Square, Spencer, TN 38585. 931-946-2263. Fax: 931-946-2388. 8AM-5PM (CST).

Felony, Misdemeanor, Civil, Eviction, Small Claims—31st District Circuit Court and General Sessions, PO Box 126, Spencer, TN 38585. 931-946-2153. Fax: 931-946-2388. 8AM-4PM M,T,Th,F; 8AM-Noon W & Sat (CST). Access by: Phone, mail, in person.

Probate—County Court, PO Box 126, Spencer, TN 38585. 931-946-2121. Fax: 931-946-2388. 8AM-4PM M,T,Th,F, 8AM-Noon Wed & Sat (CST). Access by: Mail, in person.

Warren County

Real Estate Recording—Warren County Register of Deeds, 111 S. Court Square, McMinnville, TN 37110. 931-473-2926. 8AM-4:30PM M-Th; 8AM-5PM F (CST).

Felony, Misdemeanor, Civil, Eviction, Small Claims—31st District Circuit Court and General Sessions, 111 Court Sq, PO Box 639, McMinnville, TN 37111. 931-473-2373. Fax: 931-473-3726. 8AM-4:30PM M-Th; 8AM-5PM F (CST). Access by: Mail, in person.

Civil, Probate—Chancery Court, PO Box 639, McMinnville, TN 37110. 931-473-2364. Fax: 931-473-3726. 8AM-4:30PM M-Th, 8AM-5PM F (CST). Access by: Mail, in person.

Washington County

Real Estate Recording—Washington County Register of Deeds, Main Street, Courthouse, Jonesboro, TN 37659. 423-753-1644. Fax: 423-753-1743. 8AM-4:30PM (EST).

Felony, Misdemeanor, Civil, Eviction, Small Claims—1st District Circuit Court and General Sessions, PO Box 356, Jonesborough, TN 37659. 423-753-1611. Fax: 423-753-1809. 8AM-5PM (EST). Access by: Mail, in person.

Civil Actions Under $10,000, Eviction, Small Claims—General Sessions, 101 E Market St, Johnson City, TN 37604. 423-461-1412. Fax: 423-926-4862. 8AM-5PM (EST). Access by: Mail, in person.

Civil Actions Over $10,000—Johnson City Law Court-Civil, 101 E Market St, Johnson City, TN 37604. 423-461-1475. Fax: 423-926-4862. 8AM-5PM (EST). Access by: Mail, in person.

Probate—County Court, PO Box 218, Jonesborough, TN 37659. 423-753-1623. Fax: 423-753-4716. 8AM-5PM (EST). Access by: Mail, in person.

Wayne County

Real Estate Recording—Wayne County Register of Deeds, Court Square, Waynesboro, TN 38485. 931-722-5518. Fax: 931-722-5994. 8AM-4PM M,T,Th,F; 8AM-Noon W,Sat (CST).

Felony, Misdemeanor, Civil, Eviction, Small Claims—22nd District Circuit Court and General Sessions, PO Box 869, Waynesboro, TN 38485. 931-722-5519. Fax: 931-722-5994. 8AM-4PM M,T,Th,F, 8AM-Noon W & Sat (CST). Access by: Phone, fax, mail, in person.

Civil, Probate—Chancery Court, PO Box 101, Waynesboro, TN 38485. 931-722-5517. Fax: 931-722-5994. 8AM-4PM (CST). Access by: Mail, in person.

Weakley County

Real Estate Recording—Weakley County Register of Deeds, Courthouse, Room 102, Dresden, TN 38225. 901-364-3646. Fax: 901-364-5389. 8AM-4:30PM (CST).

Felony, Misdemeanor, Civil, Eviction, Small Claims—27th District Circuit Court and General Sessions, PO Box 28, Dresden, TN 38225. 901-364-3455. Fax: 901-364-6765. 8AM-4:30PM (CST). Access by: Fax, mail, in person.

Civil, Probate—Chancery Court, PO Box 197, Dresden, TN 38225. 901-364-3454. Fax: 901-364-5247. 8AM-4:30PM (CST). Access by: Mail, in person.

White County

Real Estate Recording—White County Register of Deeds, Courthouse Rm 118, 1 East Bockman Way, Sparta, TN 38583. 615-836-2817. Fax: 615-836-8418. 8AM-5PM (CST).

Felony, Misdemeanor, Civil, Eviction, Small Claims—13th District Criminal, Circuit, and General Sessions Court, Room 304, Sparta, TN 38583. 615-836-3205. Fax: 615-836-3526. 8AM-5PM M,T,Th,F; 8AM-Noon W & Sat (CST). Access by: In person only.

Civil, Probate—Chancery Court, Clerk & Master, Sparta, TN 38583. 615-836-3787. 8AM-4:30PM (CST). Access by: Mail, in person.

Williamson County

Real Estate Recording—Williamson County Register of Deeds, 1320 West Main Street, Room 201, Franklin, TN 37064. 615-790-5706. 8AM-4:30PM (CST).

Felony, Misdemeanor, Civil, Eviction, Small Claims—21st District Circuit Court and General Sessions, Room 107, Franklin, TN 37064. 615-790-5454. Fax: 615-790-5432. 8AM-4:30PM (CST). Access by: Mail, in person.

Civil, Probate—Chancery Court, Clerk & Master, Franklin, TN 37064. 615-790-5428. Fax: 615-790-5626. 8AM-4:30PM (CST). Access by: Phone, mail, in person.

Wilson County

Real Estate Recording—Wilson County Register of Deeds, Wilson County Register, 228 East Main St., Lebanon, TN 37087. 615-443-2611. Fax: 615-443-3288. 8AM-4PM; 8AM-5PM F (CST).

Felony, Misdemeanor, Civil, Eviction, Small Claims—15th District Criminal, Circuit, and General Sessions Court, PO Box 518, Lebanon, TN 37088-0518. 615-444-2042. Fax: 615-449-3420. 8AM-4PM M-Th, 8AM-5PM F (CST). Access by: In person only.

Probate—County Court, PO Box 918, Lebanon, TN 37088-0918. 615-443-2627. Fax: 615-443-2628. 8AM-4:30PM M-Th, 8AM-5PM Fri (CST). Access by: Phone, mail, in person.

Federal Courts

US District Court
Eastern District of Tennessee

Chattanooga Division, US District Court Clerk's Office, PO Box 591, Chattanooga, TN 37401. 423-752-5200. Counties: Bledsoe, Bradley, Hamilton, McMinn, Marion, Meigs, Polk, Rhea, Sequatchie

Greenville Division, US District Court 101 Summer St W, Greenville, TN 37743. 423-639-3105. Counties: Carter, Cocke, Greene, Hamblen, Hancock, Hawkins, Johnson, Sullivan, Unicoi, Washington

Knoxville Division, US District Court Clerk's Office, PO Box 2348, Knoxville, TN 37901. 423-545-4228. Counties: Anderson, Blount, Campbell, Claiborne, Grainger, Jefferson, Knox, Loudon, Monroe, Morgan, Roane, Scott, Sevier, Union

Winchester Division, US District Court c/o Chattanooga Division, PO Box 591, Chattanooga, TN 37401. 423-752-5200. Counties: Bedford, Coffee, Franklin, Grundy, Lincoln, Moore, Van Buren, Warren

Middle District of Tennessee

Columbia Division, US District Court c/o Nashville Division, US Courthouse Room 800, 801 Broadway, Nashville, TN 37203. 615-736-5498. Counties: Giles, Hickman, Lawrence, Lewis, Marshall, Maury, Wayne

Cookeville Division, US District Court PO Box 806, Cookeville, TN 38503. 931-526-3269. Counties: Clay, Cumberland, De Kalb, Fentress, Jackson, Macon, Overton, Pickett, Putnam, Smith, White

Nashville Division, US District Court US Courthouse Room 800, 801 Broadway, Nashville, TN 37203. 615-736-5498. Counties: Cannon, Cheatham, Davidson, Dickson, Houston, Humphreys, Montgomery, Robertson, Rutherford, Stewart, Sumner, Trousdale, Williamson, Wilson

Western District of Tennessee

Jackson Division, US District Court Federal Bldg, Room 101, 109 S Highland Ave, Jackson, TN 38301. 901-427-6586. Counties: Benton, Carroll, Chester, Crockett, Decatur, Gibson, Hardeman, Hardin, Haywood, Henderson, Henry, Lake, McNairy, Madison, Obion, Perry, Weakley

Memphis Division, US District Court Federal Bldg, Room 242, 167 N Main, Memphis, TN 38103. 901-495-1200. Counties: Dyer, Fayette, Lauderdale, Shelby, Tipton

US Bankruptcy Court
Eastern District of Tennessee

Chattanooga Division, US Bankruptcy Court, Historic US Courthouse, 31 E 11th St, Chattanooga, TN 37402. 423-752-5163. Voice Case Information System: 423-752-5272. Counties: Bedford, Bledsoe, Bradley, Coffee, Franklin, Grundy, Hamilton, Lincoln, Marion, McMinn, Meigs, Moore, Polk, Rhea, Sequatchie, Van Buren, Warren

Knoxville Division, US Bankruptcy Court, Suite 1501, 1st Tennessee Plaza, Knoxville, TN 37929. 423-545-4279. Voice Case Information System: 423-752-5272. Counties: Anderson, Blount, Campbell, Carter, Claiborne, Cocke, Grainger, Greene, Hamblen, Hancock, Hawkins, Jefferson, Johnson, Knox, Loudon, Monroe, Morgan, Roane, Scott, Sevier, Sullivan, Unicoi, Union, Washington

Middle District of Tennessee

Nashville Division, US Bankruptcy Court, 701 Broadway, Nashville, TN 37203. 615-736-5584. Voice Case Information System: 423-752-5272. Counties: Cannon, Cheatham, Clay, Cumberland, Davidson, De Kalb, Dickson, Fentress, Giles, Hickman, Houston, Humphreys, Jackson, Lawrence, Lewis, Macon, Marshall, Maury, Montgomery, Overton, Perry, Pickett, Putnam, Robertson, Rutherford, Smith, Stewart, Sumner, Trousdale, Wayne, White, Williamson, Wilson

Western District of Tennessee

Jackson Division, US Bankruptcy Court, Room 312, 109 S Highland Ave, Jackson, TN 38301. 901-424-9751. Voice Case Information System: 901-544-4325. Counties: Benton, Carroll, Chester, Crockett, Decatur, Gibson, Hardeman, Hardin, Haywood, Henderson, Henry, Lake, Madison, McNairy, Obion, Weakley

Memphis Division, US Bankruptcy Court, Suite 413, 200 Jefferson Ave, Memphis, TN 38103. 901-544-3202. Voice Case Information System: 901-544-4325. Counties: Dyer, Fayette, Lauderdale, Shelby, Tipton

Texas

Capitol: Austin (Travis County)	
Number of Counties: 254	**Population:** 18,723,991
County Court Locations:	**Federal Court Locations:**
•District Courts: 187	•District Courts: 26
•County Courts: 181	•Bankruptcy Courts: 18
•Combined Courts: 72	**State Agencies:** 19
•Justice of the Peace Courts: 842	
• Municipal Courts: 853	
•Probate Courts: 8	

State Agencies—Summary

General Help Numbers:

State Archives
Library & Archives Commission	512-463-5455
PO Box 12927	Fax: 512-463-5436
Austin, TX 78711	8AM-5PM, Genealogy 8-5 TU-SA
Texas Historical Foundation:	512-453-2154
State Historical Assn:	512-471-1525

Governor's Office
Governor's Office	512-463-2000
PO Box 12428	Fax: 512-463-1849
Austin, TX 78711	7:30AM-5:30PM

Attorney General's Office
Attorney General's Office	512-463-2100
PO Box 12548	Fax: 512-463-2063
Austin, TX 78711-2548	8AM-5PM

State Legislation
Legislature Reference Library	512-463-1252
State Capitol	
(Senate or House Copy Section)	Fax: 512-475-4626
PO Box 12488	8AM-5PM
Austin, TX 78711-2488	
Senate Bill Copies:	512-463-0252
House Bill Copies:	512-463-1144

Important State Internet Sites:

🌐 Webscape	
File Edit View	Help

State of Texas World Wide Web
www.state.tx.us/

Provides links to all levels of government.

The Governor's Office
www.governor.state.tx.us/

Includes information about the Governor's cabinet, press releases, and speeches. No option to send e-mail.

Texas Legislative and Legislation Site
www.capitol.state.tx.us/

Links to the members of the House and Senate, the Texas Constitution and the 75th session legislation.

State Library and Archives
www.tsl.state.tx.us/

Links to the electronic library which features online access to the state collections, other state agencies libraries, the state law library and more.

UCC Information
www.sos.state.tx.us/function/ucc/cover.htm

Contains information on UCC searches and filings. Complete information is provided through the "Table of Contents" link. Electronic filing is available.

Unclaimed Property
www.window.state.tx.us/comptorl/unclprop/unclprop.html

Provides information on searching and filing for unclaimed property. Searches can be accomplished online.

State Agencies—Public Records

Criminal Records

Crime Records Service, Correspondence Section, PO Box 15999, Austin, TX 78761-5999, Main Telephone: 512-424-2079, Hours: 8AM-5PM. Access by: mail, visit.

Corporation Records
Fictitious Name
Limited Partnership Records
Limited Liability Company Records
Assumed Name
Trademarks/Servicemarks

Secretary of State, Corporation Section, PO Box 13697, Austin, TX 78711-3697, Main Telephone: 512-463-5555, Copies: 512-463-5578, Fax: 512-463-5709, Hours: 8AM-5PM. Access by: mail, phone, fax, visit, PC.

Uniform Commercial Code
Federal Tax Liens
State Tax Liens

UCC Section, Secretary of State, PO Box 13193, Austin, TX 78711-3193, Main Telephone: 512-475-2705, Fax: 512-475-2812, Hours: 8AM-5PM. Access by: mail, phone, fax, visit, PC.

Sales Tax Registrations

Controller of Public Accounts, LBJ Office Bldg, 111 E 17th St, Austin, TX 78774, Main Telephone: 512-463-4600, Fax: 512-475-1610, Hours: 8AM-5PM. Access by: mail, phone, visit.

Birth Certificates

Texas Department of Health, Bureau of Vital Statistics, PO Box 12040, Austin, TX 78711-2040, Main Telephone: 512-458-7111, Fax: 512-458-7711, Hours: 8AM-5PM. Access by: mail, fax, visit.

Death Records

Texas Department of Health, Bureau of Vital Statistics, PO Box 12040, Austin, TX 78711-2040, Main Telephone: 512-458-7111, Fax: 512-458-7711, Hours: 8AM-5PM. Access by: mail, fax, visit.

Marriage Certificates

Texas Department of Health, Bureau of Vital Statistics, PO Box 12040, Austin, TX 78711-2040, Main Telephone: 512-458-7111, Fax: 512-458-7711, Hours: 8AM-5PM. Access by: mail, fax, visit.

Divorce Records

Texas Department of Health, Bureau of Vital Statistics, PO Box 12040, Austin, TX 78711-2040, Main Telephone: 512-458-7111, Fax: 512-458-7711, Hours: 8AM-5PM. Access by: mail, fax, visit.

Workers' Compensation Records

Texas Workers' Compensation Commission, Southfield Building, 4000 South, IH-35, MS-92B, Austin, TX 78704-7491, Main Telephone: 512-448-7900, Reprographics Department: 512-385-5161, Fax: 512-385-5232, Hours: 8AM-5PM. Access by: mail only.

Driver Records

Department of Public Safety, Driver Records Section, PO Box 15999, Austin, TX 78761-5999, Main Telephone: 512-424-2032, Hours: 8AM-5PM. Access by: mail, visit. Tickets are only available from the court system.

Vehicle Ownership
Vehicle Identification

Department of Transportation, Production Data Control-Titles & Registration, 40th St and Jackson, Austin, TX 78779, Main Telephone: 512-465-7611, Fax: 512-465-7736, Hours: 8AM-5PM. Access by: mail, PC.

Accident Reports

Texas Department of Public Safety, Accident Reports, PO Box 15999, Austin, TX 78761-5999, Main Telephone: 512-424-2600, Hours: 8AM-5PM. Access by: mail, visit.

Hunting License Information
Fishing License Information

Parks & Wildlife Department, License Section, 4200 Smith School Rd, Austin, TX 78744, Main Telephone: 512-389-4820, Fax: 512-389-4330, Hours: 8AM-5PM. Access by: mail, fax, visit.

County Courts and Recording Offices

What You Need to Know...

About the Courts

Administration

Office of Court Administration	512-463-1625
PO Box 12066	Fax: 512-463-1648
Austin, TX 78711	8AM-5PM

Court Structure

The legal court structure for Texas takes up 30 pages in the "Texas Judicial Annual Report." We have not tried to make entire sense of all the variations in court structure throughout Texas, but rather have showed the basic configuration of courts for the purpose of accomplishing a search for relevant cases.

Generally, the District courts have general civil jurisdiction and exclusive felony jurisdiction, along with typical variations such as contested probate and divorce.

The County Court structure includes two forms of courts—"Constitutional" and "at Law"—which come in various configurations depending upon the county. We have chosen not to show civil claim upper limits for these County Courts because they vary from $5,000 to $100,000.

In addition, you should keep in mind that the Municipal Courts have, per the Texas manual, "limited civil penalties in cases involving dangerous dogs."

For civil matters up to **$5,000,** we recommend searchers start at the Constitutional County Court as they, generally, have a shorter waiting time for cases in urban areas.

In some counties the District Court or County Court handles evictions.

Only District Courts handle felonies. County Courts handle misdemeanors and general civil cases. Probate is handled in Probate Court in the 18 largest counties and in District Courts or County Courts at Law in other counties. **However,** the County Clerk is responsible for the records in every **county.**

Online Access

There is **no** statewide-online computer access available, internal or external. Dallas and Harris Counties have online access available for civil and criminal records.

About the Recorder's Office

Organization

254 counties, 254 filing offices. The recording officer is County Clerk. 252 counties are in the Central Time Zone (CST) and 2 are in the Mountain Time Zone (MST).

UCC Records

Financing statements are filed at the state level, except for real estate related collateral, which are filed with the County Clerk. All filing offices will perform UCC searches. Searches fees are usually $10.00 per debtor name using the approved UCC-11 request form, plus $15.00 for using a non-Texas form. Copy fees are usually $1.00-1.50 per page with a minimum copy fee of $5.00.

Lien Records

Federal tax liens on personal property of businesses are filed with the Secretary of State. Other federal and all state tax liens are filed with the County Clerk. All counties will perform tax lien searches. Search fees and copy fees vary. Other liens include mechanics, judgments, hospital, labor, and lis pendens.

Real Estate Records

Some counties will perform real estate searches. Copy fees are usually $1.00 per page. Certification usually costs $5.00 per document. Each county has an "Appraisal District" which is responsible for collecting taxes.

County Courts and Recording Offices

Anderson County

Real Estate Recording—Anderson County Clerk, 500 North Church Street, Palestine, TX 75801. 903-723-7402. 8AM-5PM (CST).

Felony, Civil—District Court, PO Box 1159, Palestine, TX 75802-1159. 903-723-7412. 8AM-Noon, 1-5PM (CST). Access by: Mail, in person.

Misdemeanor, Civil, Probate—County Court, 500 N Church, Palestine, TX 75801. 903-723-7432. 8AM-5PM (CST). Access by: Mail, in person.

Andrews County

Real Estate Recording—Andrews County Clerk, 215 N.W. 1st Street, Annex Building Room 121A, Andrews, TX 79714. 915-524-1426. Fax: 915-524-1473. 8AM-5PM (CST).

Felony, Civil—District Court, PO Box 328, Andrews, TX 79714. 915-524-1417. 8AM-5PM (CST). Access by: Mail, in person.

Misdemeanor, Civil, Probate—County Court, PO Box 727, Andrews, TX 79714. 915-524-1426. 8AM-5PM (CST). Access by: Mail, in person.

Angelina County

Real Estate Recording—Angelina County Clerk, 215 East Lufkin Avenue, Lufkin, TX 75901. 409-634-8339. Fax: 409-634-8460. 8AM-5PM (CST).

Felony, Civil—District Court, PO Box 908, Lufkin, TX 75902. 409-634-4312. 8AM-5PM (CST). Access by: Mail, in person.

Misdemeanor, Civil, Probate—County Court, PO Box 908, Lufkin, TX 75902. 409-634-8339. Fax: 409-634-5915. 8AM-5PM (CST). Access by: Mail, in person.

Aransas County

Real Estate Recording—Aransas County Clerk, 301 North Live Oak, Rockport, TX 78382. 512-790-0122. 8AM-5PM (CST).

Felony, Civil—District Court, 301 North Live Oak, Rockport, TX 78382. 512-790-0128. 8AM-5PM (CST). Access by: Mail, in person.

Misdemeanor, Civil, Probate—County Court, 301 N Live Oak, Rockport, TX 78382. 512-790-0122. Fax: 512-790-0125. 8AM-4:30PM (CST). Access by: Mail, in person.

Archer County

Real Estate Recording—Archer County Clerk, Center & Main, Archer City, TX 76351. 940-574-4615. 8:30AM-5PM (CST).

Felony, Misdemeanor, Civil, Eviction, Probate—District and County Court, PO Box 815, Archer City, TX 76351. 940-574-4615. 8:30AM-5PM (CST). Access by: Phone, mail, in person.

Armstrong County

Real Estate Recording—Armstrong County Clerk, Trice Street, Courthouse, Claude, TX 79019. 806-226-2081. Fax: 806-226-2030. 8AM-Noon, 1-5PM (CST).

Felony, Misdemeanor, Civil, Eviction, Probate—District and County Court, PO Box 309, Claude, TX 79019. 806-226-2081. Fax: 806-226-3221. 8AM-Noon, 1-5PM (CST). Access by: Mail, in person.

Atascosa County

Real Estate Recording—Atascosa County Clerk, Circle Drive, Room 6-1, Jourdanton, TX 78026. 830-769-2511. 8AM-5PM (CST).

Felony, Civil—District Court, #52 Courthouse Circle, Jourdanton, TX 78026. 830-769-3011. 8AM-Noon, 1-5PM (CST). Access by: Mail, in person.

Misdemeanor, Civil, Probate—County Court, Circle Dr Rm 6-1, Jourdanton, TX 78026. 830-769-2511. 8AM-5PM (CST). Access by: In person only.

Austin County

Real Estate Recording—Austin County Clerk, 1 East Main, Bellville, TX 77418. 409-865-5911. Fax: 409-865-0336. 8AM-5PM (CST).

Felony, Civil—District Court, 1 East Main, Bellville, TX 77418-1598. 409-865-5911. 8AM-5PM (CST). Access by: Mail, in person.

Misdemeanor, Civil, Probate—County Court, 1 E Main, Bellville, TX 77418. 409-865-5911. Fax: 409-865-8786. 8AM-5PM (CST). Access by: Mail, in person.

Bailey County

Real Estate Recording—Bailey County Clerk, 300 South First, Muleshoe, TX 79347. 806-272-3044. 8AM-Noon, 1-5PM (CST).

Felony, Civil—District Court, 300 S 1st St, Muleshoe, TX 79347. 806-272-3165. Fax: 806-272-3879. 8AM-5PM (CST). Access by: Phone, mail, in person.

Misdemeanor, Civil, Probate—County Court, 300 S 1st St, Muleshoe, TX 79347. 806-272-3044. 8AM-4PM (CST). Access by: Mail, in person.

Bandera County

Real Estate Recording—Bandera County Clerk, 500 Main Street, Bandera, TX 78003. 830-796-3332. Fax: 830-796-8323. 8AM-5PM (CST).

Felony, Misdemeanor, Civil, Eviction, Probate—District and County Court, PO Box 823, Bandera, TX 78003. 830-796-3332. Fax: 830-796-8323. 8AM-5PM (CST). Access by: Mail, in person.

Bastrop County

Real Estate Recording—Bastrop County Clerk, 803 Pine Street, Courthouse, Bastrop, TX 78602. 512-321-4443. 8AM-Noon, 1-5PM (CST).

Felony, Civil—District Court, PO Box 770, Bastrop, TX 78602. 512-321-2114. 8AM-5PM (CST). Access by: Mail, in person.

Misdemeanor, Probate—County Court, PO Box 577, Bastrop, TX 78602. 512-321-4443. 8AM-5PM (CST). Access by: Phone, mail, in person.

Baylor County

Real Estate Recording—Baylor County Clerk, 101 South Washington, Seymour, TX 76380. 940-888-3322. 8:30AM-5PM (CST).

Felony, Misdemeanor, Civil, Eviction, Probate—District and County Court, PO Box 689, Seymour, TX 76380. 940-888-3322. 8:30AM-5PM (CST). Access by: Phone, mail, in person.

Bee County

Real Estate Recording—Bee County Clerk, 105 West Corpus Christi Street, Room 103, Beeville, TX 78102. 512-362-3247. Fax: 512-362-3247. 8AM-Noon, 1-5PM (CST).

Felony, Civil—District Court, PO Box 666, Beeville, TX 78102-0666. 512-362-3242. Fax: 512-362-3282. 8AM-5PM (CST). Access by: Mail, in person.

Misdemeanor, Civil, Probate—County Court, 105 W Corpus Christi St Rm 103, Beeville, TX 78102. 512-362-3245. Fax: 512-362-3247. 8AM-Noon, 1-5PM (CST). Access by: Phone, fax, mail, in person.

Bell County

Real Estate Recording—Bell County Clerk, 101 E. Central, Belton, TX 76513. 817-933-5171. Fax: 254-933-5176. 8AM-5PM (CST).

Felony, Civil—District Court, 104 S Main St, PO Box 909, Belton, TX 76513. 254-933-5197. Fax: 254-933-5199. 8AM-5PM (CST). Access by: Mail, in person.

Misdemeanor, Civil, Probate—County Court, PO Box 480, Belton, TX 76513. Civil: 254-933-5174. Criminal: 254-933-5161. Fax: 254-933-5176. 8AM-5PM (CST). Access by: Mail, in person.

Bexar County

Real Estate Recording—Bexar County Clerk, Bexar County Courthouse, 100 Dolorosa, Room 108, San Antonio, TX 78205. 210-220-2581. Fax: 210-220-2813. 8AM-5PM (CST).

Felony, Civil—District Court, 100 Dolorosa, County Courthouse, San Antonio, TX 78205. 210-220-2083. 8AM-5PM (CST). Access by: Mail, in person.

Civil—County Court-Civil, 100 Dolorosa, San Antonio, TX 78205-3083. 210-220-2231. 8AM-5PM (CST). Access by: Phone, mail, in person.

Misdemeanor—County Court-Criminal, 300 Dolorosa, Suite 4101, San Antonio, TX 78205. 210-220-2220. 8AM-5PM (CST). Access by: Mail, remote online, in person.

Probate—Probate Court #2, 100 Dolorosa St, San Antonio, TX 78205. 210-220-2546. 8AM-5PM (CST). Access by: Mail, in person.

Blanco County

Real Estate Recording—Blanco County Clerk, 7th Street, Courthouse, Johnson City, TX 78636. 210-868-7357. 8AM-5PM (CST).

Felony, Misdemeanor, Civil, Eviction, Probate—District and County Court, PO Box 65, Johnson City, TX 78636. 830-868-7111. 8AM-5PM (CST). Access by: Phone, mail, in person.

Borden County

Real Estate Recording—Borden County Clerk, 101 Main, Gail, TX 79738. 806-756-4312. 8AM-Noon, 1-5PM (CST).

Felony, Misdemeanor, Civil, Eviction, Probate—District and County Court, PO Box 124, Gail, TX 79738. 806-756-4312. 8AM-5PM (CST). Access by: Mail, in person.

Bosque County

Real Estate Recording—Bosque County Clerk, 103 River Street, Meridian, TX 76665. 254-435-2201. 8AM-5PM (CST).

Felony, Civil—District Court, Main & Morgan St, Po Box 674, Meridian, TX 76665. 254-435-2334. Fax: 254-435-2152. 8AM-5PM (CST). Access by: Mail, in person.

Misdemeanor, Civil, Probate—County Court, PO Box 617, Meridian, TX 76665. 254-435-2382. 8AM-5PM (CST). Access by: Phone, mail, in person.

Bowie County

Real Estate Recording—Bowie County Clerk, 710 James Bowie Drive, New Boston, TX 75570. 903-628-6740. Fax: 903-628-6729. 8AM-5PM (CST).

Felony, Civil—District Court, 710 James Bowie Dr, PO Box 248, New Boston, TX 75570. 903-628-2571. 8AM-5PM (CST). Access by: Mail, in person.

Probate—County Court, PO Box 248, New Boston, TX 75570. 903-628-2571. 8AM-5PM (CST). Access by: Phone, mail, in person.

Brazoria County

Real Estate Recording—Brazoria County Clerk, 111 East Locust, Suite 200, Angleton, TX 77515. 409-849-5711. Fax: 409-849-3293. 8AM-5PM (CST).

Felony, Civil—District Court, 111 E Locus #400, Angleton, TX 77515-4678. 409-849-5711. 8AM-5PM (CST). Access by: Phone, mail, in person.

Misdemeanor, Civil—County Court, 111 E Locust #200, Angleton, TX 77515. 409-849-5711. Fax: 409-848-1951. 8AM-5PM (CST). Access by: Fax, mail, in person.

Probate—Probate Court, County Courthouse, 111 E Locust, Angleton, TX 77515. 409-849-5711. Fax: 409-849-3293. 8AM-5PM (CST).

Brazos County

Real Estate Recording—Brazos County Clerk, 300 East 26th Street, Suite 120, Bryan, TX 77803. 409-361-4128. 8AM-5PM (CST).

Felony, Civil—District Court, 300 E 26th St #216 (PO Box 2208), Bryan, TX 77806. 409-361-4233. Fax: 409-361-0197. 8AM-5PM (CST). Access by: Mail, in person.

Misdemeanor, Civil, Probate—County Court, 300 E 26th St #120, Bryan, TX 77803. 409-361-4128. 8AM-5PM (CST). Access by: Mail, in person.

Brewster County

Real Estate Recording—Brewster County Clerk, 201 West Avenue E, Alpine, TX 79830. 915-837-3366. Fax: 915-837-1536. 9AM-12, 1-5PM (CST).

Felony, Misdemeanor, Civil, Eviction, Probate—District and County Court, PO Box 119, Alpine, TX 79831. 915-837-3366. Fax: 915-837-1536. 9AM-5PM (CST). Access by: Mail, in person.

Briscoe County

Real Estate Recording—Briscoe County Clerk, 415 Main Street, Silverton, TX 79257. 806-823-2134. Fax: 806-823-2359. 8AM-5PM (CST).

Felony, Misdemeanor, Civil, Eviction, Probate—District and County Court, PO Box 375, Silverton, TX 79257. 806-823-2134. Fax: 806-823-2359. 8AM-5PM (CST). Access by: Fax, mail, in person.

Brooks County

Real Estate Recording—Brooks County Clerk, 110 East Miller, Falfurrias, TX 78355. 512-325-5604. 8AM-5PM (CST).

Felony, Civil—District Court, PO Box 534, Falfurrias, TX 78355. 512-325-5604. Fax: 512-325-5679. 8AM-5PM (CST). Access by: Mail, in person.

Misdemeanor, Civil, Probate—County Court, PO Box 427, Falfurrias, TX 78355. 512-325-5604. Fax: 512-325-5679. 8AM-5PM (CST). Access by: Phone, fax, mail, in person.

Brown County

Real Estate Recording—Brown County Clerk, 200 South Broadway, Courthouse, Brownwood, TX 76801. 915-643-2594. 8:30AM-5PM (CST).

Felony, Civil—District Court, 200 S Broadway, Brownwood, TX 76801. 915-646-5514. 8:30AM-5PM (CST). Access by: Mail, in person.

Misdemeanor, Civil, Probate—County Court, 200 S Broadway, Brownwood, TX 76801. 915-643-2594. 8:30AM-5PM (CST). Access by: Mail, in person.

Burleson County

Real Estate Recording—Burleson County Clerk, Buck & Main Street, Courthouse, 2nd Floor, Caldwell, TX 77836. 409-567-4326. 9AM-5PM (CST).

Felony, Civil—District Court, Courthouse Sq 3rd Flr Rm 303, PO Box 179, Caldwell, TX 77836. 409-567-4237. 8AM-5PM (CST). Access by: Mail, in person.

Misdemeanor, Civil, Probate—County Court, PO Box 57, Caldwell, TX 77836. 409-567-4326. Fax: 409-567-7407. 9AM-5PM (CST). Access by: In person only.

Burnet County

Real Estate Recording—Burnet County Clerk, 220 South Pierce Street, Burnet, TX 78611. 512-756-5406. Fax: 512-756-5410. 8AM-5PM (CST).

Felony, Civil—District Court, 220 S Pierce, Burnet, TX 78611. 512-756-5450. 8AM-5PM (CST). Access by: Mail, in person.

Misdemeanor, Civil, Probate—County Court, 220 S Pierce, Burnet, TX 78611. 512-756-5403. Fax: 512-756-5410. 8AM-5PM (CST). Access by: Fax, mail, in person.

Caldwell County

Real Estate Recording—Caldwell County Clerk, Main & Market, Courthouse, Lockhart, TX 78644. 512-398-1804. 8:30AM-Noon, 1-4:45PM (CST).

Felony, Civil—District Court, 110 S Main St, PO Box 749, Lockhart, TX 78644. 512-398-1806. 8:30AM-Noon, 1-5PM (CST). Access by: Mail, in person.

Misdemeanor, Civil, Probate—County Court, PO Box 906, Lockhart, TX 78644. 512-398-1804. 8:30AM-NOON, 1PM-4:45PM (CST). Access by: Mail, in person.

Calhoun County

Real Estate Recording—Calhoun County Clerk, 211 South Ann, Port Lavaca, TX 77979. 512-553-4411. 8AM-5PM (CST).

Felony, Civil—District Court, 211 S Ann, Port Lavaca, TX 77979. 512-553-4630. 8AM-5PM (CST). Access by: Mail, in person.

Misdemeanor, Civil, Probate—County Court, 211 S Ann, Port Lavaca, TX 77979. 512-553-4411. 8AM-5PM (CST). Access by: Phone, mail, in person.

Callahan County

Real Estate Recording—Callahan County Clerk, 100 W. 4th, Ste. 104, Courthouse, Baird, TX 79504. 915-854-1217. Fax: 915-854-1227. 8AM-5PM (CST).

Felony, Civil—District Court, 100 W 4th St Suite 300, Baird, TX 79504-5396. 915-854-1800. 8AM-5PM (CST). Access by: Mail, in person.

Misdemeanor, Civil, Probate—County Court, 400 Market St #104, Baird, TX 79504. 915-854-1217. Fax: 915-854-1227. 8AM-5PM (CST). Access by: Mail, in person.

Cameron County

Real Estate Recording—Cameron County Clerk, 964 East Harrison, Brownsville, TX 78520. 956-544-0815. Fax: 210-550-7287. 8AM-5PM (CST).

Felony, Civil—District Court, 974 E Harrison St, Brownsville, TX 78520. 956-544-0839. 8AM-12PM 1PM-5PM (CST). Access by: Mail, in person.

Misdemeanor, Civil, Probate—County Court, PO Box 2178, Brownsville, TX 78522-2178. 956-544-0848. Fax: 956-544-0894. 8AM-5PM (CST). Access by: Mail, in person.

Camp County

Real Estate Recording—Camp County Clerk, 126 Church Street, Room 102, Pittsburg, TX 75686. 903-856-2731. Fax: 903-856-0811. 8AM-Noon, 1-5PM (CST).

Felony, Civil—District Court, 126 Church St Rm 203, Pittsburg, TX 75686. 903-856-3221. 8AM-5PM (CST). Access by: Mail, in person.

Misdemeanor, Civil, Probate—County Court, 126 Church St Rm 102, Pittsburg, TX 75686. 903-856-2731. Fax: 903-856-2309. 8AM-Noon, 1-5PM (CST). Access by: Fax, mail, in person.

Carson County

Real Estate Recording—Carson County Clerk, 5th & Main Street, Courthouse, Panhandle, TX 79068. 806-537-3873. 8AM-12, 1-5PM (CST).

Felony, Misdemeanor, Civil, Eviction, Probate—District and County Court, PO Box 487, Panhandle, TX 79068. 806-537-3873. Fax: 806-537-3724. 8AM-Noon, 1PM-5PM (CST). Access by: Mail, in person.

Cass County

Real Estate Recording—Cass County Clerk, Main & Houston, Courthouse, Linden, TX 75563. 903-756-5071. 8AM-5PM (CST).

Felony, Civil—District Court, PO Box 510, Linden, TX 75563. 903-756-7514. 8AM-5PM (CST). Access by: Mail, in person.

Misdemeanor, Probate—County Court, PO Box 449, Linden, TX 75563. 903-756-5071. 8AM-5PM (CST). Access by: Mail, in person.

Castro County

Real Estate Recording—Castro County Clerk, 100 East Bedford, Dimmitt, TX 79027. 806-647-3338. 8AM-Noon, 1-5PM (CST).

Felony, Misdemeanor, Civil, Eviction, Probate—District and County Court, 100 E Bedford, Dimmitt, TX 79027. 806-647-3338. 8AM-5PM (CST). Access by: Mail, in person.

Chambers County

Real Estate Recording—Chambers County Clerk, 404 Washington Street, Anahuac, TX 77514. 409-267-8309. Fax: 409-267-4453. 8AM-5PM (CST).

Felony, Civil—District Clerk, Drawer NN, Anahuac, TX 77514. 409-267-8276. 8AM-Noon, 1-5PM (CST). Access by: Mail, in person.

Misdemeanor, Civil, Probate—County Court, PO Box 728, Anahuac, TX 77514. 409-267-8309. Fax: 409-267-4453. 8AM-5PM (CST). Access by: Mail, in person.

Cherokee County

Real Estate Recording—Cherokee County Clerk, 402 N. Main, Courthouse, Rusk, TX 75785. 903-683-2350. Fax: 903-683-2393. 8AM-5PM (CST).

Felony, Civil—District Court, Drawer C, Rusk, TX 75785. 903-683-4533. 8AM-Noon, 1-5PM (CST). Access by: Mail, in person.

Misdemeanor, Civil, Probate—County Court, Cherokee County Clerk, PO Box 420, Rusk, TX 75785. 903-683-2350. Fax: 903-683-2393. 8AM-5PM (CST). Access by: Mail, in person.

Childress County

Real Estate Recording—Childress County Clerk, 100 Avenue E NW, Childress, TX 79201. 940-937-6143. Fax: 817-937-3479. 8:30AM-Noon, 1-5PM (CST).

Felony, Misdemeanor, Civil, Eviction, Probate—District and County Court, Courthouse Box 4, Childress, TX 79201. 940-937-6143. Fax: 940-937-3479. 8:30AM-Noon, 1-5PM (CST). Access by: Mail, in person.

Clay County

Real Estate Recording—Clay County Clerk, 100 North Bridge, Henrietta, TX 76365. 940-538-4631. 8AM-5PM (CST).

Felony, Civil—District Clerk, PO Box 554, Henrietta, TX 76365. 940-538-4561. Fax: 940-538-4431. 8AM-Noon, 1-5PM (CST). Access by: Mail, in person.

Misdemeanor, Civil, Probate—County Court, PO Box 548, Henrietta, TX 76365. 940-538-4631. 8AM-5PM (CST). Access by: Mail, in person.

Cochran County

Real Estate Recording—Cochran County Clerk, 100 North Main, Courthouse, Morton, TX 79346. 806-266-5450. 8AM-5PM (CST).

Felony, Misdemeanor, Civil, Eviction, Probate—District and County Court, County Courthouse Rm 102, Morton, TX 79346. 806-266-5450. Fax: 806-266-5629. 8AM-5PM (CST). Access by: Fax, mail, in person.

Coke County

Real Estate Recording—Coke County Clerk, 13 East 7th Street, Courthouse, Robert Lee, TX 76945. 915-453-2631. Fax: 915-453-2157. 8AM-5PM (CST).

Felony, Misdemeanor, Civil, Eviction, Probate—District and County Court, PO Box 150, Robert Lee, TX 76945. 915-453-2631. 8AM-5PM (CST). Access by: Mail, in person.

Coleman County

Real Estate Recording—Coleman County Clerk, Courthouse, Coleman, TX 76834. 915-625-2889. 8AM-5PM (CST).

Felony, Civil—District Court, PO Box 512, Coleman, TX 76834. 915-625-2568. 8-11:30AM, 12:30-5PM (CST). Access by: Mail, in person.

Misdemeanor, Civil, Probate—County Court, PO Box 591, Coleman, TX 76834. 915-625-2889. 8AM-5PM (CST). Access by: Mail, in person.

Collin County

Real Estate Recording—Collin County Clerk, 200 South McDonald, Annex "A", Suite 120, McKinney, TX 75069. 214-548-4152. 8AM-5PM (8AM-4PM Land Recording) (CST).

Felony, Civil—District Clerk, PO Box 578, McKinney, TX 75069. 214-548-4365. 8AM-5PM (CST). Access by: Mail, remote online, in person.

Misdemeanor, Civil, Probate—County Court, 210 S McDonald St Rm 542, McKinney, TX 75069. 214-548-4529. Fax: 214-542-1014. 8AM-5PM (CST). Access by: Fax, mail, in person.

Collingsworth County

Real Estate Recording—Collingsworth County Clerk, Courthouse, Room 3, 800 West Ave., Wellington, TX 79095. 806-447-2408. Fax: 806-447-5418. 9AM-5PM (CST).

Felony, Misdemeanor, Civil, Eviction, Probate—District and County Court, County Courthouse, Rm 3, 1800 West Ave 1st Fl, Wellington, TX 79095. 806-447-2408. Fax: 806-447-5418. 9AM-5PM (CST). Access by: Mail, in person.

Colorado County

Real Estate Recording—Colorado County Clerk, 400 Spring Street, Courthouse, Columbus, TX 78934. 409-732-2155. Fax: 409-732-8852. 8AM-5PM (CST).

Felony, Civil—District Court, 400 Spring, County Courthouse, Columbus, TX 78934. 409-732-2536. 8AM-Noon, 1-5PM (CST). Access by: Mail, in person.

Misdemeanor, Civil, Probate—County Court, PO Box 68, County Courthouse, Columbus, TX 78934. 409-732-2155. 8AM-5PM (CST). Access by: Mail, in person.

Comal County

Real Estate Recording—Comal County Clerk, 100 Main Plaza, Suite 104, New Braunfels, TX 78130. 830-620-5513. Fax: 830-620-3410. 8AM-4:30PM (CST).

Felony, Civil—District Court, 150 N Seguin Ste 317, New Braunfels, TX 78130-5161. 830-620-5562. Fax: 830-628-2006. 8AM-5PM (CST). Access by: Fax, mail, in person.

Misdemeanor, Civil, Probate—County Court at Law, 100 Main Plaza, Ste 303, New Braunfels, TX 78130. 830-620-5582. Fax: 830-608-2021. 8AM-4:30PM (CST). Access by: Phone, fax, mail, in person.

Comanche County

Real Estate Recording—Comanche County Clerk, Courthouse, Comanche, TX 76442. 915-356-2655. 8:30-5PM (CST).

Felony, Civil—District Court, County Courthouse, Comanche, TX 76442. 915-356-2342. 8:30AM-Noon, 1-5PM (CST). Access by: Mail, in person.

Misdemeanor, Civil, Probate—County Court, County Courthouse, Comanche, TX 76442. 915-356-2655. 8:30AM-5PM (CST). Access by: Mail, in person.

Concho County

Real Estate Recording—Concho County Clerk, Highway 83, Courthouse, Paint Rock, TX 76866. 915-732-4322. Fax: 915-732-4307. 8:30AM-5PM (CST).

Felony, Misdemeanor, Civil, Eviction, Probate—District and County Court, PO Box 98, Paint Rock, TX 76866. 915-732-4322. Fax: 915-732-4307. 8:30AM-5PM (CST). Access by: Mail, in person.

Cooke County

Real Estate Recording—Cooke County Clerk, Courthouse, Gainesville, TX 76240. 940-668-5420. Fax: 940-668-5440. 8AM-5PM (CST).

Felony, Civil—District Court, County Courthouse, Gainesville, TX 76240. 940-668-5450. 8AM-5PM (CST). Access by: Mail, in person.

Misdemeanor, Civil, Probate—County Court, County Courthouse, Gainesville, TX 76240. 940-668-5422. 8AM-5PM (CST). Access by: Mail, in person.

Coryell County

Real Estate Recording—Coryell County Clerk, Courthouse, Gatesville, TX 76528. 254-865-5016. Fax: 254-865-8631. 8AM-5PM (CST).

Felony, Civil—District Court, PO Box 4, Gatesville, TX 76528. 254-865-5911. Fax: 254-865-5064. 8AM-5PM (CST). Access by: Fax, mail, in person.

Misdemeanor, Civil, Probate—County Court, PO Box 237, Gatesville, TX 76528. 254-865-5016. Fax: 254-865-8631. 8AM-Noon, 1PM-5PM (CST). Access by: In person only.

Cottle County

Real Estate Recording—Cottle County Clerk, Courthouse, 9th & Richards, Paducah, TX 79248. 806-492-3823. (CST).

Felony, Misdemeanor, Civil, Eviction, Probate—District and County Court, PO Box 717, Paducah, TX 79248. 806-492-3823. 9AM-12PM 1PM-5PM (CST). Access by: Mail, in person.

Crane County

Real Estate Recording—Crane County Clerk, 6th East Alford Street, Courthouse, Crane, TX 79731. 915-558-3581. 9AM-12, 1-5PM (CST).

Felony, Misdemeanor, Civil, Eviction, Probate—District and County Court, PO Box 578, Crane, TX 79731. 915-558-3581. 9AM-5PM (CST). Access by: Mail, in person.

Crockett County

Real Estate Recording—Crockett County Clerk, 907 Avenue D, Ozona, TX 76943. 915-392-2022. Fax: 915-392-2675. 8AM-5PM M-Th; 8AM-4PM F (CST).

Felony, Misdemeanor, Civil, Eviction, Probate—District and County Court, PO Drawer C, Ozona, TX 76943. 915-392-2022. 8AM-5PM (CST). Access by: Mail, in person.

Crosby County

Real Estate Recording—Crosby County Clerk, Aspen & Berkshire Streets, Courthouse, Crosbyton, TX 79322. 806-675-2334. 8AM-12, 1-5PM (CST).

Felony, Civil—District Court, PO Box 495, Crosbyton, TX 79322. 806-675-2071. Fax: 806-675-2804. 8AM-5PM (CST). Access by: Phone, mail, in person.

Misdemeanor, Civil, Probate—County Court, PO Box 218, Crosbyton, TX 79322. 806-675-2334. 8AM-5PM (CST). Access by: Mail, in person.

Culberson County

Real Estate Recording—Culberson County Clerk, 301 La Caverna, Courthouse, Van Horn, TX 79855. 915-283-2058. Fax: 915-283-9234. 8AM-Noon,1-5PM (CST).

Felony, Misdemeanor, Civil, Eviction, Probate—District and County Court, PO Box 158, Van Horn, TX 79855. 915-283-2058. 8AM-5PM (CST). Access by: Phone, mail, in person.

Dallam County

Real Estate Recording—Dallam County Clerk, 101 East 5th, Dalhart, TX 79022. 806-249-4751. Fax: 806-249-2252. 9AM-5PM (CST).

Felony, Misdemeanor, Civil, Eviction, Probate—District and County Court, PO Box 1352, Dalhart, TX 79022. 806-249-4751. Fax: 806-249-2252. 9AM-5PM (CST). Access by: Fax, mail, in person.

Dallas County

Real Estate Recording—Dallas County Clerk's Office, Records Bldg, 2nd Floor, 509 Main St., Dallas, TX 75202. 214-653-7275. 8AM-4:30PM (CST).

Civil—District Court-Civil, 600 Commerce, Dallas, TX 75202-4606. 214-653-7421. 8AM-4:30PM (CST). Access by: Mail, in person, online.

Felony—District Court-Criminal, 133 N Industrial Blvd, Dallas, TX 75202-4313. 214-653-5950. 8AM-4:30PM (CST). Access by: Mail, remote online, in person. The Public Access System makes felony and other records available remotely at a cost of $1.00 per minute, billed on your telephone bill. Access number is 900-263-INFO. Call the Public Access Administrator at 214-653-7717.

Criminal District Courts 1-5, 133 N Industrial Blvd, Dallas, TX 75207. 214-653-7421. 8:00AM-4:30PM M-F (CST). Access by: Mail, in person.

Misdemeanor—District Court-Misdemeanor, 133 N Industrial Blvd, Dallas, TX 75207-4313. 214-653-5740. 8AM-4:30PM (CST). Access by: Mail, remote online, in person. Public Access System allows remote access billed to your telephone bill at $1.00 per minute. Access number is 900-263-INFO. ProComm Plus is recommended. Call the Public Access Administrator at 214-653-7717 for more information.

Civil—County Court-Civil, 509 W Main 3rd Floor, Dallas, TX 75202. 214-653-7131. 8AM-4:30PM (CST). Access by: Mail, in person.

Probate—Probate Court #3, Records Bldg, 2nd Floor, Dallas, TX 75202. 214-653-6166. 8AM-4:30PM (CST).

Dawson County

Real Estate Recording—Dawson County Clerk, North 1st & Main Street, Courthouse, Lamesa, TX 79331. 806-872-3778. Fax: 806-872-3395. 8:30AM-5PM (CST).

Felony, Civil—District Court, Drawer 1268, Lamesa, TX 79331. 806-872-7373. Fax: 806-872-9513. 8:30AM-5PM (CST). Access by: In person only.

Misdemeanor, Civil, Probate—County Court, Drawer 1268, Lamesa, TX 79331. 806-872-3778. Fax: 806-872-2473. 8:30AM-5PM (CST). Access by: Mail, in person.

De Witt County

Real Estate Recording—De Witt County Clerk, 307 North Gonzales, Courthouse, Cuero, TX 77954. 512-275-3724. Fax: 512-275-8994. 8AM-Noon, 1-5PM (CST).

Felony, Civil—District Court, PO Box 224, Cuero, TX 77954. 512-275-2221. 8AM-5PM (CST). Access by: Mail, in person.

Misdemeanor, Probate—District Court, 307 N Gonzales, Cuero, TX 77954. 512-275-3724. 8AM-5PM (CST). Access by: Mail, in person.

Deaf Smith County

Real Estate Recording—Deaf Smith County Clerk, 235 East 3rd, Room 203, Hereford, TX 79045. 806-363-7077. Fax: 806-364-8830. 8AM-5PM (CST).

Felony, Civil—District Court, 235 E Third St Rm 304, Hereford, TX 79045. 806-364-3901. Fax: 806-364-8830. 8AM-5PM (CST). Access by: Phone, fax, mail, in person.

Misdemeanor, Civil, Probate—County Court, Deaf Smith Courthouse, 235 E Third, Room 203, Hereford, TX 79045. 806-363-7077. 8AM-5PM (CST). Access by: Mail, in person.

Delta County

Real Estate Recording—Delta County Clerk, 200 West Dallas Avenue, Cooper, TX 75432. 903-395-4110. Fax: 903-395-2178. 8AM-5PM (CST).

Felony, Misdemeanor, Civil, Eviction, Probate—District and County Court, PO Box 455, Cooper, TX 75432. 903-395-4110. Fax: 903-395-2211. 8AM-5PM (CST). Access by: Mail, in person.

Denton County

Real Estate Recording—Denton County Clerk, 401 West Hickory, Denton, TX 76201. 940-565-8501. 8AM-4:30PM (CST).

Felony, Civil—District Court, PO Box 2146, Denton, TX 76202. 940-565-8528. Fax: 940-565-8607. 8AM-4:30PM (CST). Access by: Mail, in person.

Misdemeanor, Civil, Probate—County Court, PO Box 2187, Denton, TX 76202. 940-565-8518. 8AM-4:30PM (CST). Access by: Mail, in person.

Dickens County

Real Estate Recording—Dickens County Clerk, Montgomery St. & Hwy 82, Dickens, TX 79229. 806-623-5531. Fax: 806-623-5319. 8AM-12, 1-5PM (CST).

Felony, Misdemeanor, Civil, Eviction, Probate—District and County Court, PO Box 120, Dickens, TX 79229. 806-623-5531. Fax: 806-623-5319. 8AM-5PM (CST). Access by: Mail, in person.

Dimmit County

Real Estate Recording—Dimmit County Clerk, 103 North 5th Street, Carrizo Springs, TX 78834. 830-876-3569. Fax: 830-876-5036. 8AM-Noon, 1-5PM (CST).

Felony, Civil—District Court, 103 N 5th, Carrizo Springs, TX 78834. 830-876-2321. Fax: 830-876-5036. 8AM-5PM (CST). Access by: Fax, mail, in person.

Misdemeanor, Civil, Probate—County Court, 103 N 5th, Carrizo Springs, TX 78834. 830-876-3569. Fax: 210-876-5036. 8AM-5PM (CST). Access by: Mail, in person.

Donley County

Real Estate Recording—Donley County Clerk, 300 South Sully, Clarendon, TX 79226. 806-874-3436. 8AM-Noon,1-5PM (CST).

Felony, Misdemeanor, Civil, Eviction, Probate—District and County Court, PO Drawer U, Clarendon, TX 79226. 806-874-3436. Fax: 806-874-5146. 8AM-Noon, 1-5PM (CST). Access by: Mail, in person.

Duval County

Real Estate Recording—Duval County Clerk, 400 East Gravis on Highway 44, San Diego, TX 78384. 512-279-3322. 8AM-Noon, 1-5PM (CST).

Felony, Civil—District Court, PO Drawer 428, San Diego, TX 78384. 512-279-3322. 8AM-5PM (CST). Access by: Phone, mail, in person.

Misdemeanor, Civil, Probate—County Court, PO Box 248, San Diego, TX 78384. 512-279-3322. 8AM-NOON, 1PM-5PM (CST). Access by: Mail, in person.

Eastland County

Real Estate Recording—Eastland County Clerk, 100 West Main, Courthouse, Eastland, TX 76448. 254-629-1583. Fax: 254-629-8125. 8AM-5PM (CST).

Felony, Civil—District Court, PO Box 670, Eastland, TX 76448. 254-629-2664. Fax: 254-629-1558. 8AM-5PM (CST). Access by: Phone, fax, mail, in person.

Misdemeanor, Probate—County Court, PO Box 110, Eastland, TX 76448. 254-629-1583. 8AM-5PM (CST). Access by: Mail, in person.

Ector County

Real Estate Recording—Ector County Clerk, 300 Grant Avenue, Courthouse, Room 111, Odessa, TX 79761. 915-335-3045. 8AM-5PM (CST).

Felony, Civil—District Court, County Courthouse, 300 N Grant, Rm 301, Odessa, TX 79761. 915-335-3144. Fax: 915-335-3112. 8AM-5PM (CST). Access by: Phone, mail, in person.

Misdemeanor, Civil, Probate—County Court, PO Box 707, Odessa, TX 79760. 915-335-3045. 8AM-5PM (CST). Access by: Mail, in person.

Edwards County

Real Estate Recording—Edwards County Clerk, 400 Main, Rocksprings, TX 78880. 830-683-2235. Fax: 830-683-5376. 8AM-5PM (CST).

Felony, Misdemeanor, Civil, Eviction, Probate—District and County Court, PO Box 184, Rocksprings, TX 78880. 830-683-2235. Fax: 830-683-5376. 8AM-Noon, 1-5PM (CST). Access by: Fax, mail, in person.

El Paso County

Real Estate Recording—El Paso County Clerk, 501 East Overland Street, Room 105, El Paso, TX 79901. 915-546-2074. 8AM-4:45PM (MST).

Felony, Civil—District Court, 500 East San Antonio Rm 103, El Paso, TX 79901. 915-546-2021. 8AM-4:45PM (MST). Access by: Mail, in person.

Misdemeanor, Civil—County Court, 500 E San Antonio St Rm 105, El Paso, TX 79901. 915-546-2071. 8AM-4:45PM (MST). Access by: Mail, in person.

Probate—Probate Court, 500 E San Antonio, Rm 1201 A, El Paso, TX 79901. 915-546-2161. Fax: 915-533-4448. 8AM-5PM (MST). Access by: Mail, in person.

Ellis County

Real Estate Recording—Ellis County Clerk, Records Building, 117 W. Franklin, Waxahachie, TX 75165. 972-923-5070. 8AM-4:45PM (CST).

Felony, Civil—District Court, 101 W Main St County Courthouse, Waxahachie, TX 75165. 972-923-5000. 8AM-5PM (CST). Access by: Mail, in person.

Misdemeanor, Civil, Probate—County Court, PO Box 250, Waxahachie, TX 75165. 972-923-5070. 8AM-4:30PM (CST). Access by: Mail, in person.

Erath County

Real Estate Recording—Erath County Clerk, Courthouse, 100 W. Washington St., Stephenville, TX 76401. 254-965-1482. 8AM-12, 1-5PM (CST).

Felony, Civil—District Court, 112 W College, Courthouse Annex, Stephenville, TX 76401. 254-965-1431. 8AM-5PM (CST). Access by: Mail, in person.

Misdemeanor, Civil, Probate—County Court, County Courthouse, Stephenville, TX 76401. 254-965-1482. 8AM-NOON, 1PM-5PM (CST). Access by: Mail, in person.

Falls County

Real Estate Recording—Falls County Clerk, Corner of Business Hwy 6 and Hwy 7, Courthouse, Marlin, TX 76661. 254-883-1408. 8AM-Noon, 1-5PM (CST).

Felony, Civil—District Court, PO Box 229, Marlin, TX 76661. 254-883-3181. 8AM-Noon, 1-5PM (CST). Access by: Mail, in person.

Misdemeanor, Civil, Probate—County Court, PO Box 458, Marlin, TX 76661. 254-883-2061. 8AM-5PM (CST). Access by: Phone, mail, in person.

Fannin County

Real Estate Recording—Fannin County Clerk, Courthouse, Suite 102, 101 E. Sam Rayburn Dr., Bonham, TX 75418. 903-583-7486. Fax: 903-583-7811. 8AM-5PM (CST).

Felony, Civil—District Court, Fannin County Courthouse Ste 201, Bonham, TX 75418. 903-583-7459. Fax: 903-583-7811. 8AM-Noon, 1-5PM (CST). Access by: Mail, in person.

Misdemeanor, Civil, Probate—County Court, County Courthouse, 101 E Sam Rayburn Ste 102, Bonham, TX 75418. 903-583-7486. Fax: 903-583-7811. 8AM-5PM (CST). Access by: Phone, mail, in person. Phone search limited to 1 year.

Fayette County

Real Estate Recording—Fayette County Clerk, 151 North Washington, Courthouse, La Grange, TX 78945. 409-968-3251. 8AM-Noon, 1-5PM (CST).

Felony, Civil—District Court, Fayette County Courthouse, 151 N Washington, La Grange, TX 78945. 409-968-3548. Fax: 409-968-8621. 8AM-5PM (CST). Access by: Mail, in person.

Misdemeanor, Civil, Probate—County Court, PO Box 59, La Grange, TX 78945. 409-968-3251. 8AM-5PM (CST). Access by: Phone, mail, in person.

Fisher County

Real Estate Recording—Fisher County Clerk, Corner of US Highway 180 & 70, Courthouse, Roby, TX 79543. 915-776-2401. Fax: 915-776-2815. 8AM-12, 1-5PM (CST).

Felony, Civil—District Court, PO Box 88, Roby, TX 79543. 915-776-2279. Fax: 915-776-2815. 8AM-5PM (CST). Access by: Mail, in person.

Misdemeanor, Civil, Probate—County Court, County Courthouse Box 368, Roby, TX 79543. 915-776-2401. 8AM-5PM (CST). Access by: Mail, in person.

Floyd County

Real Estate Recording—Floyd County Clerk, 100 Main Street, Courthouse, Floydada, TX 79235. 806-983-4900. 8:30AM-12, 1-5PM (CST).

Felony, Civil—District Court, PO Box 67, Floydada, TX 79235. 806-983-4923. 8:30AM-Noon, 1-5PM (CST). Access by: Mail, in person.

Misdemeanor, Civil, Probate—County Court, PO Box 476, Floydada, TX 79235. 806-983-4900. 8:30AM-Noon, 1-5PM (CST). Access by: Phone, mail, in person.

Foard County

Real Estate Recording—Foard County Clerk, 100 Main and Commerce, Crowell, TX 79227. 940-684-1365. Fax: 940-684-1947. 9AM-11:45AM, 1-4:30PM (CST).

Felony, Misdemeanor, Civil, Eviction, Probate—District and County Court, PO Box 539, Crowell, TX 79227. 940-684-1365. 9AM-4:30PM (CST). Access by: Mail, in person.

Fort Bend County

Real Estate Recording—Fort Bend County Clerk, 301 Jackson, Richmond, TX 77469. 713-341-8650. Fax: 713-341-8669. 8AM-4PM (CST).

Felony, Civil—District Court, 3101 Jackson, Richmond, TX 77469. 713-342-3411. 8AM-5PM (CST). Access by: Mail, in person.

Misdemeanor, Civil, Probate—County Court, 301 Jackson St, Richmond, TX 77469. 713-342-3411. Fax: 713-341-4520. 8AM-4PM (CST). Access by: Mail, in person.

Franklin County

Real Estate Recording—Franklin County Clerk, Corner of Dallas & Kaufman Streets, Courthouse, Mount Vernon, TX 75457. 903-537-4252. Fax: 903-537-2418. 8AM-5PM (CST).

Felony, Civil—District Court, PO Box 68, Mount Vernon, TX 75457. 903-537-4786. 8AM-5PM (CST). Access by: Mail, in person.

Misdemeanor, Civil, Probate—County Court, PO Box 68, Mount Vernon, TX 75457. 903-537-4252. Fax: 903-537-2418. 8AM-5PM (CST). Access by: Mail, in person.

Freestone County

Real Estate Recording—Freestone County Clerk, Corner of Main & Mount Streets, Courthouse Annex, Fairfield, TX 75840. 903-389-2635. 8AM-5PM (CST).

Felony, Civil—District Court, PO Box 722, Fairfield, TX 75840. 903-389-2534. 8AM-5PM (CST). Access by: Mail, in person.

Misdemeanor, Civil, Probate—County Court, PO Box 1017, Fairfield, TX 75840. 903-389-2635. 8AM-5PM (CST). Access by: Mail, in person.

Frio County

Real Estate Recording—Frio County Clerk, 500 E San Antonio Street, # 6, Pearsall, TX 78061. 830-334-2214. Fax: 830-334-4881. 8AM-12, 1-5PM (CST).

Felony, Civil—District Court, 500 E San Antonio Box 8, Pearsall, TX 78061. 830-334-8073. Fax: 830-334-2845. 8AM-5PM (CST). Access by: Mail, in person.

Misdemeanor, Civil, Probate—County Court, 500 E San Antonio St #6, Pearsall, TX 78061. 830-334-3200. Fax: 830-334-4881. 8AM-NOON, 1PM-5PM (CST). Access by: Mail, in person.

Gaines County

Real Estate Recording—Gaines County Clerk, 101 S. Main, Room 107, Seminole, TX 79360. 915-758-4003. 8AM-5PM (CST).

Felony, Civil—District Court, 101 S Main Rm 213, Seminole, TX 79360. 915-758-4013. Fax: 915-758-4036. 8AM-NOON, 1PM-5PM (CST). Access by: Phone, mail, in person.

Misdemeanor, Civil, Probate—County Court, 101 S Main Rm 107, Seminole, TX 79360. 915-758-4003. 8AM-5PM (CST). Access by: Phone, mail, in person.

Galveston County

Real Estate Recording—Galveston County Clerk, 722 Moody Avenue, Galveston, TX 77550. 409-766-2208. 8AM-5PM (CST).

Felony, Civil—District Court, 722 Moody St Rm 404, Galveston, TX 77550. 409-766-2424. Fax: 409-766-2292. 8AM-5PM (CST). Access by: Fax, mail, in person.

Misdemeanor, Civil—County Court, PO Box 2450, Galveston, TX 77553-2450. Civil: 409-766-2203. Criminal: 409-766-2206. 8AM-5PM (CST). Access by: Mail, in person.

Probate—Probate Court, PO Box 2450, Galveston, TX 77553-2450. 409-766-2202. 8AM-5PM (CST). Access by: Mail, in person.

Garza County

Real Estate Recording—Garza County Clerk, 300 W. Main, Post, TX 79356. 806-495-4430. Fax: 806-495-4431. 8AM-Noon, 1-5PM (CST).

Felony, Misdemeanor, Civil, Eviction, Probate—District and County Court, PO Box 366, Post, TX 79356. 806-495-4430. Fax: 806-495-4431. 8AM-Noon,1-5PM (CST). Access by: Mail, in person.

Gillespie County

Real Estate Recording—Gillespie County Clerk, 101 West Main, Room 109, Unit #13, Fredericksburg, TX 78624. 830-997-6515. Fax: 830-997-9958. 8AM-4PM (CST).

Felony, Civil—District Court, 101 W Main Rm 204, Fredericksburg, TX 78624. 830-997-6517. Public hours 8AM-Noon, 1-4PM (CST). Access by: Mail, in person.

Misdemeanor, Civil, Probate—County Court, 101 W Main Unit #13, Fredericksburg, TX 78624. 830-997-6515. Fax: 830-997-9958. 8AM-4PM (CST). Access by: Mail, in person.

Glasscock County

Real Estate Recording—Glasscock County Clerk, Courthouse, Highway 158, Garden City, TX 79739. 915-354-2371. 8AM-4PM (CST).

Felony, Misdemeanor, Civil, Eviction, Probate—District and County Court, PO Box 190, 117 E Currie, Garden City, TX 79739. 915-354-2371. 8AM-4PM (CST). Access by: Mail, in person.

Goliad County

Real Estate Recording—Goliad County Clerk, 127 N. Courthouse Square, Goliad, TX 77963. 512-645-3294. Fax: 512-645-3858. 8AM-5PM (CST).

Felony, Misdemeanor, Civil, Eviction, Probate—District and County Court, PO Box 5, Goliad, TX 77963. 512-645-2443. Fax: 512-645-3858. 8AM-5PM (CST). Access by: Mail, in person.

Gonzales County

Real Estate Recording—Gonzales County Clerk, 1709 Sarah DeWitt Dr., Courthouse, Gonzales, TX 78629. 830-672-2801. Fax: 830-672-2636. 8AM-5PM (CST).

Felony, Civil—District Court, PO Box 34, Gonzales, TX 78629-0034. 830-672-2326. Fax: 830-672-9313. 8AM-Noon 1-5PM (CST). Access by: Phone, fax, mail, in person.

Misdemeanor, Civil, Probate—County Court, PO Box 77, Gonzales, TX 78629. 830-672-2801. Fax: 830-672-2636. 8AM-5PM (CST). Access by: Phone, fax, mail, in person.

Gray County

Real Estate Recording—Gray County Clerk, 205 North Russell, Courthouse, Pampa, TX 79065. 806-669-8004. Fax: 806-669-8054. 8:30AM-12, 1-5PM (CST).

Felony, Civil—District Court, PO Box 1139, Pampa, TX 79066-1139. 806-669-8010. Fax: 806-669-8053. 8:30AM-5PM (CST). Access by: Phone, fax, mail, in person.

Misdemeanor, Civil, Probate—PO Box 1902, Pampa, TX 79066-1902. 806-669-8004. Fax: 806-669-8054. 8:30AM-5PM (CST). Access by: Phone, fax, mail, in person.

Grayson County

Real Estate Recording—Grayson County Clerk, 100 West Houston #17, Sherman, TX 75090. 903-813-4242. Fax: 903-870-0829. 8AM-5PM (CST).

Felony, Civil—District Court, 200 S Crockett Rm 120-A, Sherman, TX 75090-7167. 903-813-4352. 8AM-5PM (CST). Access by: Mail, in person.

Misdemeanor, Civil, Probate—County Court, 200 S Crockett, Sherman, TX 75090. 903-813-4336. Fax: 903-892-8300. 8AM-5PM (CST). Access by: Mail, in person.

Gregg County

Real Estate Recording—Gregg County Clerk, 100 East Methvin, Suite 200, Longview, TX 75601. 903-236-8430. Fax: 903-237-2574. 8AM-5PM (CST).

Felony, Civil—District Court, PO Box 711, Longview, TX 75606. 903-758-6181. 8AM-5PM (CST). Access by: Mail, in person.

Misdemeanor, Civil, Probate—County Court, PO Box 3049, Longview, TX 75606. 903-236-8430. 8AM-5PM (CST). Access by: Phone, mail, in person.

Grimes County

Real Estate Recording—Grimes County Clerk, Courthouse, 100 Main St., Anderson, TX 77830. 409-873-2111. 8AM-Noon, 1-4:45PM (CST).

Felony, Civil—District Court, PO Box 234, Anderson, TX 77830. 409-873-2111. Fax: 409-873-2415. 8AM-4:45PM (CST). Access by: Phone, fax, mail, in person.

Misdemeanor, Civil, Probate—County Court, PO Box 209, Anderson, TX 77830. 409-873-2662. 8AM-4:45PM (CST). Access by: Mail, in person.

Guadalupe County

Real Estate Recording—Guadalupe County Clerk, 101 East Court Street, Rm 209, Seguin, TX 78155. 830-303-4188. 8AM-4:30PM (CST).

Felony, Civil—District Court, 101 E Court St, Seguin, TX 78155. 830-303-4188. Fax: 830-379-1843. 8AM-5PM (CST). Access by: In person only.

Misdemeanor, Civil, Probate—County Court, 101 E Court St, Seguin, TX 78155. 830-303-4188. Fax: 830-401-0300. 8AM-4:30PM (CST). Access by: Mail, in person.

Hale County

Real Estate Recording—Hale County Clerk, 500 Broadway #140, Plainview, TX 79072. 806-291-5261. Fax: 806-296-7786. 8AM-Noon,1-5PM (CST).

Felony, Civil—District Court, 500 Broadway #200, Plainview, TX 79072. 806-291-5226. 8AM-5PM (CST). Access by: Phone, mail, in person.

Misdemeanor, Civil, Probate—County Court, 500 Broadway #140, Plainview, TX 79072-8030. 806-291-5261. Fax: 806-296-7786. 8AM-Noon, 1-5PM (CST). Access by: Mail, in person.

Hall County

Real Estate Recording—Hall County Clerk, Courthouse, Box 8, Memphis, TX 79245. 806-259-2627. 8:30AM-5PM (CST).

Felony, Misdemeanor, Civil, Eviction, Probate—District and County Court, County Courthouse, Memphis, TX 79245. 806-259-2627. 8:30AM-5PM (CST). Access by: Phone, mail, in person.

Hamilton County

Real Estate Recording—Hamilton County Clerk, Main Street, Courthouse, Hamilton, TX 76531. 254-386-3518. Fax: 254-386-8727. 8AM-5PM (CST).

Felony, Civil—District Court, County Courthouse, Hamilton, TX 76531. 254-386-3417. Fax: 254-386-8727. 8AM-5PM M-Th; 8AM-4:30PM F (CST). Access by: Fax, mail, in person.

Misdemeanor, Civil, Probate—County Court, County Courthouse, Hamilton, TX 76531. 254-386-3518. 8AM-NOON, 1PM-5PM (CST). Access by: Mail, in person.

Hansford County

Real Estate Recording—Hansford County Clerk, Hansford Co. Clerk, 1 N.W. Court, Spearman, TX 79081. 806-659-4110. Fax: 806-659-2025. 8:30AM-5PM (CST).

Felony, Misdemeanor, Civil, Eviction, Probate—District and County Court, PO Box 397, Spearman, TX 79081. 940-659-2666. Fax: 806-659-2025. 8:30AM-5PM (CST). Access by: Phone, fax, mail, in person.

Hardeman County

Real Estate Recording—Hardeman County Clerk, 300 Main Street, Quanah, TX 79252. 817-663-2901. 8:30AM-5PM (CST).

Felony, Misdemeanor, Civil, Eviction, Probate—District and County Court, PO Box 30, Quanah, TX 79252. 940-663-2901. 8:30AM-5PM (CST). Access by: Mail, in person.

Hardin County

Real Estate Recording—Hardin County Clerk, Courthouse Square, Highway 326, Kountze, TX 77625. 409-246-5185. 8AM-5PM (CST).

Felony, Civil—District Court, PO Box 2997, Kountze, TX 77625. 409-246-5150. 8AM-4PM (CST). Access by: Phone, mail, in person.

Misdemeanor, Civil, Probate—County Court, PO Box 38, Kountze, TX 77625. 409-246-5185. 8AM-5PM (CST). Access by: Mail, in person.

Harris County

Real Estate Recording—Harris County Clerk, 1001 Preston, 4th Floor-Receptionist, Houston, TX 77002. 713-755-6439. Fax: 713-755-8839. 8AM-4:30PM (CST).

Felony, Civil—District Court, PO Box 4651, Houston, TX 77210. 713-755-5711. 8AM-5PM (CST). Access by: Phone, mail, in person, online.

Civil—County Court, PO Box 1525, Houston, TX 77251-1525. 713-755-6421. 8AM-4:30PM (CST). Access by: Mail, in person, online.

Probate—Probate Court, 1115 Congress, 6th Floor, Houston, TX 77002. 713-755-6084. Fax: 713-755-4349. 6AM-5PM (CST).

Harrison County

Real Estate Recording—Harrison County Clerk, Corner of W. Houston & S. Wellington, Courthouse, Marshall, TX 75670. 903-935-4858. 8AM-5PM (CST).

Felony, Civil—District Court, County Courthouse, 200 W Houston, Marshall, TX 75670. 903-935-4845. 8AM-5PM (CST). Access by: Phone, mail, in person.

Misdemeanor, Civil, Probate—County Court, PO Box 1365, Marshall, TX 75671. 903-935-4858. 8AM-5PM (CST). Access by: Mail, in person.

Hartley County

Real Estate Recording—Hartley County Clerk, 9th & Railroad, Channing, TX 79018. 806-235-3582. Fax: 806-235-2316. 8:30AM-Noon, 1-5PM (CST).

Felony, Misdemeanor, Civil, Eviction, Probate—District and County Court, PO Box Q, Channing, TX 79018. 806-235-3582. Fax: 806-235-2316. 8:30AM-Noon, 1-5PM (CST). Access by: Mail, in person.

Haskell County

Real Estate Recording—Haskell County Clerk, Courthouse, 1 Ave. D, Haskell, TX 79521. 940-864-2451. Fax: 940-864-6164. 8AM-5PM (CST).

Felony, Civil—District Court, PO Box 27, Haskell, TX 79521. 940-864-2030. 8AM-Noon, 1-5PM M-Th; 8AM-4:30PM F (CST). Access by: Mail, in person.

Misdemeanor, Civil, Probate—County Court, PO Box 725, Haskell, TX 79521. 940-864-2451. 8AM-Noon, 1PM-5PM (CST). Access by: Phone, mail, in person.

Hays County

Real Estate Recording—Hays County Clerk, 137 N. Guadalupe, Hays County Records Building, San Marcos, TX 78666. 512-396-2601. Fax: 512-392-4225. 8AM-5PM (CST).

Felony, Civil—110 E Martin Luther King, Suite 123, San Marcos, TX 78666. 512-393-7660. Fax: 512-393-7674. 8AM-5PM (CST). Access by: Phone, mail, in person.

Misdemeanor, Civil, Probate—County Court, Justice Center, 110 E Martin L King Dr, San Marcos, TX 78666. 512-393-7738. Fax: 512-393-7735. 8AM-5PM (CST). Access by: Mail, in person.

Hemphill County

Real Estate Recording—Hemphill County Clerk, 400 Main Street, Courthouse, Canadian, TX 79014. 806-323-6212. 8AM-5PM (CST).

Felony, Misdemeanor, Civil, Eviction, Probate—District and County Court, PO Box 867, Canadian, TX 79014. 806-323-6212. 8AM-5PM (CST). Access by: Mail, in person.

Henderson County

Real Estate Recording—Henderson County Clerk, Courthouse Square, South Side, First Floor, Athens, TX 75751. 903-675-6140. 8AM-5PM (CST).

Felony, Civil—District Court, Henderson County Courthouse, Athens, TX 75751. 903-675-6115. 8AM-5PM (CST). Access by: Phone, mail, in person.

Misdemeanor, Civil, Probate—County Court, PO Box 632, Athens, TX 75751. 903-675-6140. 8AM-5PM (CST). Access by: Mail, in person.

Hidalgo County

Real Estate Recording—Hidalgo County Clerk, 100 North Closner, Courthouse, Edinburg, TX 78539. 956-318-2100. 8:30AM-5:30PM (CST).

Felony, Civil—District Court, 100 N Closner, Box 87, Edinburg, TX 78540. 956-318-2200. 8AM-5PM (CST). Access by: Phone, mail, in person.

Misdemeanor, Civil, Probate—County Court, PO Box 58, Edinburg, TX 78540. 956-318-2100. 8AM-5PM (CST). Access by: Mail, in person.

Hill County

Real Estate Recording—Hill County Clerk, Courthouse, 126 S. Covington, Hillsboro, TX 76645. 254-582-2161. 8AM-5PM (CST).

Felony, Misdemeanor, Civil—District Court, PO Box 634, Hillsboro, TX 76645. 254-582-3512. 8AM-5PM (CST). Access by: Mail, in person.

Probate—County Court, PO Box 398, Hillsboro, TX 76645. 254-582-2161. 8AM-5PM (CST). Access by: Mail, in person.

Hockley County

Real Estate Recording—Hockley County Clerk, 800 Houston St., Ste 213, Levelland, TX 79336. 806-894-3185. 9AM-5PM (CST).

Felony, Civil—District Court, 802 Houston St, Ste 316, Levelland, TX 79336. 806-894-8527. 9AM-5PM (CST). Access by: Phone, mail, in person.

Misdemeanor, Civil, Probate—County Court, County Courthouse, 802 Houston St Ste 213, Levelland, TX 79336. 806-894-3185. 9AM-5PM (CST). Access by: Phone, mail, in person.

Hood County

Real Estate Recording—Hood County Clerk, Courthouse, 100 E Pearl, Granbury, TX 76048. 817-579-3222. Fax: 817-579-3227. 8AM-5PM (CST).

Felony, Civil—District Court, County Courthouse, Granbury, TX 76048. 817-579-3236. Fax: 817-579-3239. 8AM-5PM (CST). Access by: Fax, mail, in person.

Misdemeanor, Civil, Probate—County Court, PO Box 339, Granbury, TX 76048. 817-579-3222. Fax: 817-579-3227. 8AM-5PM (CST). Access by: Mail, in person.

Hopkins County

Real Estate Recording—Hopkins County Clerk, 118 Church Street, Courthouse, Sulphur Springs, TX 75482. 903-885-3929. Fax: 903-885-2487. 8AM-5PM (CST).

Felony, Civil—District Court, PO Box 391, Sulphur Springs, TX 75482. 903-885-2656. 8AM-5PM (CST). Access by: Mail, in person.

Misdemeanor, Civil, Probate—County Court, PO Box 288, Sulphur Springs, TX 75483. 903-885-3929. 8AM-5PM (CST). Access by: Mail, in person.

Houston County

Real Estate Recording—Houston County Clerk, Courthouse Square, 401 E. Houston, Crockett, TX 75835. 409-544-3255. Fax: 409-544-8053. 8AM-4:30PM (CST).

Felony, Civil—District Court, County Courthouse, 410 E Houston, PO Box 1186, Crockett, TX 75835. 409-544-3255. Fax: 409-544-8053. 8AM-5PM (CST). Access by: Fax, mail, in person.

Misdemeanor, Civil, Probate—County Court, PO Box 370, Crockett, TX 75835. 409-544-3255. Fax: 409-544-8053. 8AM-4:30 (CST). Access by: Mail, in person.

Howard County

Real Estate Recording—Howard County Clerk, 300 Main, Courthouse, Big Spring, TX 79720. 915-264-2213. Fax: 915-264-2215. 8AM-5PM (CST).

Felony, Civil—District Court, PO Box 2138, Big Spring, TX 79721. 915-264-2223. Fax: 915-264-2256. 8AM-5PM (CST). Access by: Mail, in person.

Misdemeanor, Civil, Probate—County Court, PO Box 1468, Big Spring, TX 79721. 915-264-2213. Fax: 915-264-2215. 8AM-5PM (CST). Access by: Phone, mail, in person.

Hudspeth County

Real Estate Recording—Hudspeth County Clerk, FM 1111, Courthouse Square, Sierra Blanca, TX 79851. 915-369-2301. Fax: 915-369-2361. 8AM-5PM (MST).

Felony, Misdemeanor, Civil, Eviction, Probate—District and County Court, PO Drawer A, Sierra Blanca, TX 79851. 915-369-2301. Fax: 915-369-2361. 8AM-5PM (MST). Access by: Phone, fax, mail, in person.

Hunt County

Real Estate Recording—Hunt County Clerk, 2500 Lee Street, Courthouse, 2nd Fl., East End, Greenville, TX 75401. 903-408-4130. 8AM-5PM (CST).

Felony, Civil—District Court, PO Box 1437, Greenville, TX 75403. 903-408-4172. 8AM-5PM (CST). Access by: Mail, in person.

Misdemeanor, Civil, Probate—County Court, PO Box 1316, Greenville, TX 75403-1316. 903-408-4130. 8AM-5PM (CST). Access by: Mail, in person.

Hutchinson County

Real Estate Recording—Hutchinson County Clerk, 6th & Main, Courthouse, Stinnett, TX 79083. 806-878-4002. 9AM-5PM (CST).

Felony, Civil—District Court, PO Box 580, Stinnett, TX 79083. 806-878-4017. Fax: 806-878-4023. 9AM-5PM (CST). Access by: Mail, in person.

Misdemeanor, Civil, Probate—County Court, PO Drawer 1186, Stinnett, TX 79083. 806-878-4002. 9AM-5PM (CST). Access by: Mail, in person.

Irion County

Real Estate Recording—Irion County Clerk, 209 N. Parkview, Mertzon, TX 76941. 915-835-2421. Fax: 915-835-2008. 8AM-4PM (CST).

Felony, Misdemeanor, Civil, Eviction, Probate—District and County Court, PO Box 736, Mertzon, TX 76941. 915-835-2421. Fax: 915-835-2008. 8AM-5PM (CST). Access by: Phone, mail, in person.

Jack County

Real Estate Recording—Jack County Clerk, 100 Main Street, Jacksboro, TX 76458. 940-567-2111. 8AM-Noon, 1-5PM (CST).

Felony, Civil—District Court, 100 Main, County Courthouse, Jacksboro, TX 76458. 940-567-2141. Fax: 940-567-5029. 8AM-5PM (CST). Access by: Phone, mail, in person.

Misdemeanor, Civil, Probate—County Court, 100 Main, Jacksboro, TX 76458. 940-567-2111. 8AM-NOON, 1PM-5PM (CST). Access by: Phone, mail, in person.

Jackson County

Real Estate Recording—Jackson County Clerk, 115 West Main, Room 101, Edna, TX 77957. 512-782-3563. 8AM-5PM (CST).

Felony, Civil—District Court, 115 W Main Rm 203, Edna, TX 77957. 512-782-3812. 8AM-5PM (CST). Access by: Phone, mail, in person.

Misdemeanor, Civil, Probate—County Court, 115 W Main Rm101, Edna, TX 77957. 512-782-3563. 8AM-5PM (CST). Access by: Phone, mail, in person.

Jasper County

Real Estate Recording—Jasper County Clerk, Courthouse, Room 103, Main at Lamar St., Jasper, TX 75951. 409-384-2632. 8AM-5PM (CST).

Felony, Civil—District Court, County Courthouse #202, PO Box 2088, Jasper, TX 75951. 409-384-2721. 8AM-Noon, 1-5PM (CST). Access by: Mail, in person.

Misdemeanor, Civil, Probate—County Court, Rm 103, Courthouse, Main at Lamar, PO Box 2070, Jasper, TX 75951. 409-384-9481. Fax: 409-384-9745. 8AM-5PM (CST). Access by: Mail, in person.

Jeff Davis County

Real Estate Recording—Jeff Davis County Clerk, Main Street, Fort Davis, TX 79734. 915-426-3251. Fax: 915-426-3760. 9AM-Noon, 1-5PM (CST).

Felony, Misdemeanor, Civil, Eviction, Probate—District and County Court, PO Box 398, Fort Davis, TX 79734. 915-426-3251. Fax: 915-426-3760. 9AM-Noon, 1-5PM (CST). Access by: Mail, in person.

Jefferson County

Real Estate Recording—Jefferson County Clerk, 1149 Pearl Street, Beaumont, TX 77701. 409-835-8475. Fax: 409-839-2394. 8AM-5PM (CST).

Felony, Civil—District Court, PO Box 3707, Beaumont, TX 77704. Civil: 409-835-8580. Criminal: 409-835-8431. Fax: 409-835-8527. 8AM-5PM (CST). Access by: Mail, in person.

Misdemeanor, Civil, Probate—County Court, PO Box 1151, Beaumont, TX 77704. 409-835-8479. Fax: 409-839-2394. 8AM-5PM (CST). Access by: Mail, in person.

Jim Hogg County

Real Estate Recording—Jim Hogg County Clerk, 102 East Tilley, Hebbronville, TX 78361. 512-527-4031. Fax: 512-527-5843. 9AM-5PM (CST).

Felony, Misdemeanor, Civil, Eviction, Probate—District and County Court, PO Box 870, Hebbronville, TX 78361. 512-527-4031. Fax: 512-527-5843. 9AM-5PM (CST). Access by: Mail, in person.

Jim Wells County

Real Estate Recording—Jim Wells County Clerk, 200 North Almond Street, Alice, TX 78332. 512-668-5702. 8:30AM-Noon, 1-5PM (CST).

Felony, Civil—District Court, PO Drawer 2219, Alice, TX 78333. 512-668-5717. Fax: 512-664-6855. 8AM-Noon, 1-5PM (CST). Access by: Mail, in person.

Misdemeanor, Civil, Probate—County Court, PO Box 1459, 200 N Almond, Alice, TX 78333. 512-668-5702. 8:30AM-NOON, 1PM-5PM (CST). Access by: Phone, mail, in person.

Johnson County

Real Estate Recording—Johnson County Clerk, 2 North Main, Room 101, Cleburne, TX 76031. 817-556-6310. Fax: 817-556-6326. 8AM-4:30PM (CST).

Felony, Civil—District Court, PO Box 495, Cleburne, TX 76033-0495. 817-556-6300. Fax: 817-556-6210. 8AM-5PM (CST). Access by: Fax, mail, in person.

Misdemeanor, Civil, Probate—County Court, PO Box 662, Cleburne, TX 76033-0662. 817-556-6300. 8AM-NOON, 1PM-4:30PM (CST). Access by: Mail, in person.

Jones County

Real Estate Recording—Jones County Clerk, 12th & Commercial, Courthouse, Anson, TX 79501. 915-823-3762. Fax: 915-823-4223. 8AM-5PM (CST).

Felony, Civil—District Court, PO Box 308, Anson, TX 79501. 915-823-3731. Fax: 915-823-3513. 8AM-5PM (CST). Access by: Mail, in person.

Karnes County

Real Estate Recording—Karnes County Clerk, 101 North Panna Maria Ave., Courthouse - Suite 9, Karnes City, TX 78118. 830-780-3938. Fax: 830-780-4538. 8AM-5PM (CST).

Felony, Civil—District Court, County Courthouse, 101 N Panna Maria, Karnes City, TX 78118. 830-780-2562. Fax: 830-780-3227. 8AM-5PM (CST). Access by: Mail, in person.

Misdemeanor, Civil, Probate—County Court, 101 N Panna Maria Ave #9 Courthouse, Karnes City, TX 78118-2929. 830-780-3938. 8AM-5PM (CST). Access by: Mail, in person.

Kaufman County

Real Estate Recording—Kaufman County Clerk, Courthouse, Kaufman, TX 75142. 972-932-4331. Fax: 972-932-7628. 8AM-5PM (CST).

Felony, Civil—District Court, County Courthouse, Kaufman, TX 75142. 972-932-4331. 8AM-5PM (CST). Access by: Phone, mail, in person.

Misdemeanor, Civil, Probate—County Court, County Courthouse, Kaufman, TX 75142. 972-932-4331. 8AM-5PM (CST). Access by: Mail, in person.

Kendall County

Real Estate Recording—Kendall County Clerk, 204 East San Antonio, Suite 2, Boerne, TX 78006. 830-249-9343. Fax: 830-249-3472. 8:30AM-Noon, 1-5PM (CST).

Felony, Civil—District Court, 204 E San Antonio #3, Boerne, TX 78006. 830-249-9343. 8:30AM-Noon, 1-5PM (CST). Access by: Mail, in person.

Misdemeanor, Civil, Probate—County Court, 204 E San Antonio #2, Boerne, TX 78006. 830-249-9343. 8:30AM-5PM (CST). Access by: Mail, in person.

Kenedy County

Real Estate Recording—Kenedy County Clerk, 101 Mallory Street, Sarita, TX 78385. 512-294-5220. Fax: 512-294-5218. 8:30AM-11:30AM, 1:30-4:30PM (CST).

Felony, Misdemeanor, Civil, Eviction, Probate—District and County Court, PO Box 1519, Sarita, TX 78385. 512-294-5220. Fax: 512-294-5218. 8:30AM-11:30AM 1:30PM-4:30PM (CST). Access by: Mail, in person.

Kent County

Real Estate Recording—Kent County Clerk, Courthouse, Jayton, TX 79528. 806-237-3881. Fax: 806-237-2632. 8:30AM-Noon, 1-5PM (CST).

Felony, Misdemeanor, Civil, Eviction, Probate—District and County Court, PO Box 9, Jayton, TX 79528. 806-237-3881. Fax: 806-237-2632. 8:30AM-Noon, 1-5PM (CST). Access by: Mail, in person.

Kerr County

Real Estate Recording—Kerr County Clerk, Courthouse, Room 122, 700 Main, Kerrville, TX 78028. 830-792-2255. Fax: 830-792-2274. 9AM-5PM (CST).

Felony, Civil—District Court, 700 Main, County Courthouse, Kerrville, TX 78028. 830-792-2281. 8AM-5PM (CST). Access by: Mail, in person.

Misdemeanor, Civil, Probate—County Court & County Court at Law, 700 Main St, County Courthouse, Kerrville, TX 78028-5389. 830-792-2255. Fax: 830-792-2274. 8AM-5PM (CST). Access by: Mail, in person.

Kimble County

Real Estate Recording—Kimble County Clerk, 501 Main Street, Junction, TX 76849. 915-446-3353. Fax: 915-446-4361. 8AM-Noon, 1-5PM (CST).

Felony, Misdemeanor, Civil, Eviction, Probate—District and County Court, 501 Main St, Junction, TX 76849. 915-446-3353. Fax: 915-446-4361. 8AM-12PM 1PM-5PM (CST). Access by: Mail, in person.

King County

Real Estate Recording—King County Clerk, Courthouse, Highway 82, Guthrie, TX 79236. 806-596-4412. Fax: 806-596-4664. 9AM-Noon, 1-5PM (CST).

Felony, Misdemeanor, Civil, Eviction, Probate—District and County Court, PO Box 135, Guthrie, TX 79236. 806-596-4412. 9AM-NOON, 1PM-5PM (CST). Access by: Mail, in person.

Kinney County

Real Estate Recording—Kinney County Clerk, 501 Ann Street, Brackettville, TX 78832. 830-563-2521. Fax: 830-563-2644. 8AM-12, 1-5PM (CST).

Felony, Misdemeanor, Civil, Eviction, Probate—District and County Court, PO Drawer 9, Brackettville, TX 78832. 830-563-2521. 8AM-5PM (CST). Access by: Mail, in person.

Kleberg County

Real Estate Recording—Kleberg County Clerk, 700 East Kleberg Street, First Floor, East Wing, Kingsville, TX 78363. 512-595-8548. 8AM-12, 1-5PM (CST).

Felony, Misdemeanor, Civil, Eviction, Probate—District and County Court, PO Box 312, Kingsville, TX 78364-0312. 512-595-8561. Fax: 512-595-8525. 8AM-5PM (CST). Access by: Phone, fax, mail, in person.

Misdemeanor—County Court-Criminal, PO Box 1327, Kingsville, TX 78364. 512-595-8548. 8AM-5PM (CST). Access by: Mail, in person.

Knox County

Real Estate Recording—Knox County Clerk, Corner of Highway 6 & 82, Benjamin, TX 79505. 940-454-2441. Fax: 940-454-2022. 8AM-12, 1-5PM (CST).

Felony, Misdemeanor, Civil, Eviction, Probate—District and County Court, PO Box 196, Benjamin, TX 79505. 940-454-2441. 8AM-Noon, 1-5PM (CST). Access by: Mail, in person.

La Salle County

Real Estate Recording—La Salle County Clerk, 101 Courthouse Square, Cotulla, TX 78014. 830-879-2117. Fax: 210-879-2933. 8AM-Noon, 1-5PM (CST).

Felony, Civil—District Court, PO Box 340, Cotulla, TX 78014. 830-879-2421. 8AM-5PM (CST). Access by: Mail, in person.

Misdemeanor, Civil, Eviction, Probate—District and County Courts, PO Box 340, Cotulla, TX 78014. 830-879-2117. 8AM-5PM (CST). Access by: Mail, in person.

Lamar County

Real Estate Recording—Lamar County Clerk, Courthouse, 119 N. Main #109, Paris, TX 75460. 903-737-2420. 8AM-5PM (CST).

Felony, Civil—District Court, 119 N Main Rm 306, Paris, TX 75460. 903-737-2427. 8AM-5PM (CST). Access by: Mail, in person.

Misdemeanor, Civil, Probate—County Court, 119 N Main, Paris, TX 75460. 903-737-2420. 8AM-5PM (CST). Access by: Phone, fax, mail, in person.

Lamb County

Real Estate Recording—Lamb County Clerk, 100 6th Street, Room 103 Box 3, Littlefield, TX 79339. 806-385-4222. Fax: 806-385-6485. 8:30AM-5PM (CST).

Felony, Civil—District Court, 100 6th Rm 212, Courthouse, Littlefield, TX 79339. 806-385-4222. 8:30AM-Noon, 1-5PM (CST). Access by: Mail, in person.

Misdemeanor, Civil, Probate—County Court, County Courthouse Rm 103, Littlefield, TX 79339-3366. 806-385-4222. Fax: 806-385-6485. 8AM-5PM (CST). Access by: Mail, in person.

Lampasas County

Real Estate Recording—Lampasas County Clerk, 400 Live Oak Street, Lampasas, TX 76550. 512-556-8271. 8AM-5PM (CST).

Felony, Civil—District Court, PO Box 327, Lampasas, TX 76550. 512-556-8271. Fax: 512-556-8270. 8AM-5PM (CST). Access by: Mail, in person.

Misdemeanor, Civil, Probate—County Court, PO Box 347, Lampasas, TX 76550. 512-556-8271. 8AM-5PM (CST). Access by: Mail, in person.

Lavaca County

Real Estate Recording—Lavaca County Clerk, 201 North LaGrange Street, Courthouse, Hallettsville, TX 77964. 512-798-3612. 8AM-5PM (CST).

Felony, Civil—District Court, PO Box 306, Hallettsville, TX 77964. 512-798-2351. 8AM-Noon, 1-5PM (CST). Access by: Mail, in person.

Misdemeanor, Civil, Probate—County Court, PO Box 326, Hallettsville, TX 77964. 512-798-3612. 8AM-5PM (CST). Access by: Phone, mail, in person.

Lee County

Real Estate Recording—Lee County Clerk, Hempstead & Main, Courthouse, Giddings, TX 78942. 409-542-3684. Fax: 409-542-2623. 8AM-5PM (CST).

Felony, Civil—District Court, PO Box 176, Giddings, TX 78942. 409-542-2947. 8AM-5PM (CST). Access by: Mail, in person.

Misdemeanor, Civil, Probate—County Court, PO Box 419, Giddings, TX 78942. 409-542-3684. Fax: 409-542-2623. 8AM-5PM (CST). Access by: Mail, in person.

Leon County

Real Estate Recording—Leon County Clerk, Corner Cass and St. Mary Street, Courthouse Square, Centerville, TX 75833. 903-536-2352. Fax: 903-536-2431. 8AM-5PM (CST).

Felony, Civil—District Court, PO Box 39, Centerville, TX 75833. 903-536-2227. 8AM-5PM (CST). Access by: Mail, in person.

Misdemeanor, Civil, Probate—County Court, PO Box 98, Centerville, TX 75833. 903-536-2352. 8AM-5PM (CST). Access by: Mail, in person.

Liberty County

Real Estate Recording—Liberty County Clerk, 1923 Sam Houston, Room 209, Liberty, TX 77575. 409-336-4673. 8AM-5PM (CST).

Felony, Civil—District Court, 1923 Sam Houston Rm 303, Liberty, TX 77575. 409-336-4600. 8AM-Noon, 1-5PM (CST). Access by: Mail, in person.

Misdemeanor, Civil, Probate—County Court, PO Box 369, Liberty, TX 77575. 409-336-4670. 8AM-5PM (CST). Access by: Mail, in person.

Limestone County

Real Estate Recording—Limestone County Clerk, 200 West State Street, Groesbeck, TX 76642. 817-729-5504. Fax: 817-729-2951. 8AM-5PM (CST).

Felony, Civil—District Court, PO Box 230, Groesbeck, TX 76642. 254-729-3206. Civil: 817-729-3206. Criminal: 817-729-2953. Fax: 254-729-2960. 8AM-Noon, 1-5PM (CST). Access by: Phone, mail, in person.

Misdemeanor, Civil, Probate—County Court, PO Box 350, Groesbeck, TX 76642. 254-729-5504. Fax: 254-729-2951. 8AM-5PM (CST). Access by: Mail, in person.

Lipscomb County

Real Estate Recording—Lipscomb County Clerk, Main Street, Courthouse, Lipscomb, TX 79056. 806-862-3091. Fax: 806-862-2603. 8:30AM-5PM (CST).

Felony, Misdemeanor, Civil, Eviction, Probate—District and County Court, PO Box 70, Lipscomb, TX 79056. 806-862-3091. Fax: 806-862-2603. 8:30AM-NOON, 1PM-5PM (CST). Access by: Fax, mail, in person.

Live Oak County

Real Estate Recording—Live Oak County Clerk, 301 Houston, George West, TX 78022. 512-449-2733. 8AM-Noon, 1-5PM (CST).

Felony, Civil—District Court, PO Drawer O, George West, TX 78022. 512-449-2733. 8AM-5PM (CST). Access by: Mail, in person.

Misdemeanor, Civil, Probate—County Court, PO Box 280, George West, TX 78022. 512-449-2733. 8AM-5PM (CST). Access by: Mail, in person.

Llano County

Real Estate Recording—Llano County Clerk, 107 W. Sandstone, Llano, TX 78643. 915-247-4455. 8AM-5PM (CST).

Felony, Civil—District Clerk, PO Box 877, Llano, TX 78643-0877. 915-247-5036. 8AM-5PM (CST). Access by: Mail, in person.

Misdemeanor, Civil, Probate—County Court, 107 W Sandstone, Llano, TX 78643. 915-247-4455. 8AM-4:30PM (CST). Access by: Mail, in person.

Loving County

Real Estate Recording—Loving County Clerk, Courthouse, 100 Bell St., Mentone, TX 79754. 915-377-2441. 9AM-Noon, 1-5PM (CST).

Felony, Misdemeanor, Civil, Eviction, Probate—District and County Court, PO Box 194, Mentone, TX 79754. 915-377-2441. 9AM-NOON, 1PM-5PM (CST). Access by: Mail, in person.

Lubbock County

Real Estate Recording—Lubbock County Clerk, 904 Broadway, 2nd Floor Rm.207, Lubbock, TX 79401. 806-767-1056. Fax: 806-767-1381. 8:30-5PM (CST).

Felony, Civil—District Court, PO Box 10536, Lubbock, TX 79408-3536. 806-767-1311. 8AM-5PM (CST). Access by: Mail, in person.

Misdemeanor, Civil, Probate—County Court, PO Box 10536, Lubbock, TX 79408. 806-767-1051. 8:30AM-5PM (CST). Access by: Mail, in person.

Lynn County

Real Estate Recording—Lynn County Clerk, Courthouse, Tahoka, TX 79373. 806-998-4750. Fax: 806-998-4151. 8:30AM-5PM (CST).

Felony, Civil—District Court, PO Box 939, Tahoka, TX 79373. 806-998-4274. Fax: 806-998-4151. 8:30AM-5PM (CST). Access by: Fax, mail, in person.

Misdemeanor, Civil, Probate—County Court, PO Box 937, Tahoka, TX 79373. 806-998-4750. Fax: 806-998-4151. 8:30AM-5PM (CST). Access by: Mail, in person.

Madison County

Real Estate Recording—Madison County Clerk, 101 West Main, Room 102, Madisonville, TX 77864. 409-348-2638. Fax: 409-348-5858. 8AM-5PM (CST).

Felony, Civil—District Court, 101 W Main Rm 226, Madisonville, TX 77864. 409-348-9203. 8AM-Noon, 1-5PM (CST). Access by: Mail, in person.

Misdemeanor, Civil, Probate—County Court, 101 W Main Rm 102, Madisonville, TX 77864. 409-348-2638. Fax: 409-348-5858. 8AM-5PM (CST). Access by: Mail, in person.

Marion County

Real Estate Recording—Marion County Clerk, 102 West Austin, Room 206, Jefferson, TX 75657. 903-665-3971. 8AM-Noon, 1-5PM (CST).

Felony, Civil—District Court, PO Box 628, Jefferson, TX 75657. 903-665-2441. 8AM-5PM (CST). Access by: Mail, in person.

Misdemeanor, Probate—County Court, PO Drawer F, Jefferson, TX 75657. 903-665-3971. 8AM-Noon, 1-5PM (CST). Access by: Mail, in person.

Martin County

Real Estate Recording—Martin County Clerk, 301 North St. Peter Street, Stanton, TX 79782. 915-756-3412. Fax: 915-756-2992. 8AM-5PM (CST).

Felony, Misdemeanor, Civil, Eviction, Probate—District and County Court, PO Box 906, Stanton, TX 79782. 915-756-3412. Fax: 915-756-2992. 8AM-NOON, 1PM-5PM (CST). Access by: Mail, in person.

Mason County

Real Estate Recording—Mason County Clerk, 201 Ft. McKavitt, Mason, TX 76856. 915-347-5253. 8AM-Noon,1-5PM (CST).

Felony, Misdemeanor, Civil, Eviction, Probate—District and County Court, PO Box 702, Mason, TX 76856. 915-347-5253. 8AM-Noon, 1-5PM (CST). Access by: Mail, in person.

Matagorda County

Real Estate Recording—Matagorda County Clerk, 1700 7th Street, Room 202, Bay City, TX 77404. 409-244-7680. Fax: 409-244-7688. 8AM-5PM (CST).

Felony, Civil—District Court, 1700 7th St Rm 307, Bay City, TX 77414-5092. 409-244-7621. 8AM-Noon, 1-5PM (CST). Access by: Mail, in person.

Misdemeanor, Civil, Probate—County Court, 1700 7th St Rm 202, Bay City, TX 77414-5094. 409-244-7680. Fax: 409-244-7688. 8AM-5PM (CST). Access by: Mail, in person.

Maverick County

Real Estate Recording—Maverick County Clerk, 500 Quarry Street, Eagle Pass, TX 78852. 830-773-2829. 8AM-12, 1-5PM (CST).

Felony, Civil—District Court, PO Box 3659, Eagle Pass, TX 78853. 830-773-2629. 8AM-5PM (CST). Access by: Mail, in person.

Misdemeanor, Civil, Probate—County Court, PO Box 4050, Eagle Pass, TX 78853. 830-773-2829. (CST). Access by: Mail, in person.

McCulloch County

Real Estate Recording—McCulloch County Clerk, Courthouse, Brady, TX 76825. 915-597-0733. Fax: 915-597-1731. 8AM-5PM (CST).

Felony, Civil—District Court, County Courthouse Rm 205, Brady, TX 76825. 915-597-0733. Fax: 915-597-0606. 8:30AM-5PM (CST). Access by: Mail, in person.

Misdemeanor, Civil, Probate—County Court, County Courthouse, Brady, TX 76825. 915-597-0733. 8AM-5PM (CST). Access by: Mail, in person.

McLennan County

Real Estate Recording—McLennan County Clerk, 215 North 5th, Waco, TX 76701. 254-757-5078. 8AM-5PM (CST).

Felony, Civil—PO Box 2451, Waco, TX 76703. 254-757-5054. Civil: 254-757-5057. Criminal: 254-757-5054. Fax: 254-757-5060. 8AM-Noon, 1-5PM (CST). Access by: Fax, mail, in person.

Misdemeanor, Civil, Probate—County Court, PO Box 1727, Waco, TX 76703. 254-757-5185. 8AM-5PM (CST). Access by: Mail, in person.

McMullen County

Real Estate Recording—McMullen County Clerk, River Street & Elm, Courthouse, Tilden, TX 78072. 512-274-3215. Fax: 512-274-3618. 8AM-4PM (CST).

Felony, Misdemeanor, Civil, Eviction, Probate—District and County Court, PO Box 235, Tilden, TX 78072. 512-274-3215. Fax: 512-274-3618. 8AM-4PM (CST). Access by: Mail, in person.

Medina County

Real Estate Recording—Medina County Clerk, Courthouse, Room 109, Hondo, TX 78861. 830-741-6041. Fax: 830-741-6015. 8AM-12, 1-5PM (CST).

Felony, Civil—District Court, County Courthouse Rm 209, Hondo, TX 78861. 830-741-6000. 8AM-Noon, 1-5PM (CST). Access by: Mail, in person.

Misdemeanor, Civil, Probate—County Courthouse Rm 109, Hondo, TX 78861. 830-741-6000. 8AM-Noon, 1-5PM (CST). Access by: Mail, in person.

Menard County

Real Estate Recording—Menard County Clerk, 210 East San Saba, Menard, TX 76859. 915-396-4682. Fax: 915-396-2047. 8AM-12, 1PM-5PM (CST).

Felony, Misdemeanor, Civil, Eviction, Probate—District and County Court, PO Box 1028, Menard, TX 76859. 915-396-4682. Fax: 915-396-2047. 8AM-NOON, 1PM-5PM (CST). Access by: Mail, in person.

Midland County

Real Estate Recording—Midland County Clerk, 200 West Wall Street, Suite 105, Midland, TX 79701. 915-688-1075. Fax: 915-688-8973. 8AM-5PM (CST).

Felony, Civil—District Court, 200 W Wall #301, Midland, TX 79701. 915-688-1107. 8AM-5PM (CST). Access by: Mail, in person.

Misdemeanor, Civil, Probate—County Court, PO Box 211, Midland, TX 79702. 915-688-1070. Fax: 915-688-8973. 8AM-5PM (CST). Access by: Mail, in person.

Milam County

Real Estate Recording—Milam County Clerk, 100 South Fannin, Cameron, TX 76520. 254-697-6596. Fax: 254-697-4433. 8AM-5PM (CST).

Felony, Civil—District Court, PO Box 999, Cameron, TX 76520. 254-697-3952. 8AM-5PM (CST). Access by: Mail, in person.

Misdemeanor, Civil, Probate—County Court, PO Box 191, Cameron, TX 76520. 254-697-6596. Fax: 254-697-4433. 8AM-5PM (CST). Access by: Mail, in person.

Mills County

Real Estate Recording—Mills County Clerk, 1011 4th Street, Goldthwaite, TX 76844. 915-648-2711. 8AM-Noon, 1-5PM (CST).

Felony, Misdemeanor, Civil, Eviction, Probate—District and County Court, PO Box 646, Goldthwaite, TX 76844. 915-648-2711. Fax: 915-648-2806. 8AM-Noon, 1-5PM (CST). Access by: Mail, in person.

Mitchell County

Real Estate Recording—Mitchell County Clerk, 349 Oak St. #103, Colorado City, TX 79512. 915-728-3481. 8AM-Noon, 1-5PM M,T,Th,F; 8AM-5PM W (CST).

Felony, Civil—District Court, County Courthouse, Colorado City, TX 79512. 915-728-5918. 8AM-5PM (CST). Access by: Mail, in person.

Misdemeanor, Civil, Probate—County Court, 349 Oak St Rm 103, Colorado City, TX 79512. 915-728-3481. Fax: 915-728-8697. 8AM-Noon, 1-5PM (CST). Access by: Mail, in person.

Montague County

Real Estate Recording—Montague County Clerk, Rush & Washington, Courthouse, Montague, TX 76251. 940-894-2461. Fax: 940-894-3110. 8AM-5PM (CST).

Felony, Civil—District Court, PO Box 155, Montague, TX 76251. 940-894-2571. 8AM-5PM (CST). Access by: Mail, in person.

Misdemeanor, Civil, Probate—County Court, PO Box 77, Montague, TX 76251. 940-894-2461. 8AM-5PM (CST). Access by: Mail, in person.

Montgomery County

Real Estate Recording—Montgomery County Clerk, 300 North Main, Room 111, Conroe, TX 77301. 409-539-7885. Fax: 409-760-6990. 8:30AM-4:30PM (CST).

Felony, Civil—District Court, PO Box 2985, Conroe, TX 77305. 409-539-7949. 8AM-5PM (CST). Access by: Mail, in person.

Misdemeanor, Civil, Probate—County Court, PO Box 959, Conroe, TX 77305. 409-539-7885. Fax: 409-760-6990. 8AM-5PM (CST). Access by: Mail, in person.

Moore County

Real Estate Recording—Moore County Clerk, 715 Dumas Ave., Rm. 105, Dumas, TX 79029. 806-935-2009. Fax: 806-935-9004. 8:30AM-5PM (CST).

Felony, Civil—District Court, 715 Dumas Ave #109, Dumas, TX 79029. 806-935-4218. Fax: 806-935-5102. 8:30AM-5PM (CST). Access by: Mail, in person.

Misdemeanor, Civil, Probate—County Court, 715 Dumas Ave Rm 105, Dumas, TX 79029. 806-935-6164. 8:30AM-5PM (CST). Access by: Mail, in person.

Morris County

Real Estate Recording—Morris County Clerk, 500 Broadnax Street, Daingerfield, TX 75638. 903-645-3911. 8AM-5PM (CST).

Felony, Civil—District Court, 500 Brodnax, Daingerfield, TX 75638. 903-645-2321. 8AM-5PM (CST). Access by: Mail, in person.

Misdemeanor, Probate—County Court, 500 Brodnax, Daingerfield, TX 75638. 903-645-3911. 8AM-5PM (CST). Access by: Mail, in person.

Motley County

Real Estate Recording—Motley County Clerk, Main & Dundee, Courthouse, Matador, TX 79244. 806-347-2621. Fax: 806-347-2220. 9AM-5PM (CST).

Felony, Misdemeanor, Civil, Eviction, Probate—District and County Court, PO Box 66, Matador, TX 79244. 806-347-2621. Fax: 806-347-2220. 9AM-Noon, 1-5PM (CST). Access by: Mail, in person.

Nacogdoches County

Real Estate Recording—Nacogdoches County Clerk, 101 West Main, Nacogdoches, TX 75961. 409-560-7733. 8AM-5PM (CST).

Felony, Civil—District Court, 101 W Main, Nacogdoches, TX 75961. 409-560-7730. 8AM-5PM (CST). Access by: Mail, in person.

Misdemeanor, Civil, Probate—County Court, 101 W Main, Nacogdoches, TX 75961. 409-560-7733. 8AM-5PM (CST). Access by: Mail, in person.

Navarro County

Real Estate Recording—Navarro County Clerk, 300 West Third Avenue, Courthouse - Suite 101, Corsicana, TX 75110. 903-654-3035. 8AM-5PM (CST).

Felony, Civil—District Court, PO Box 1439, Corsicana, TX 75151. 903-654-3040. Fax: 903-654-3088. 8AM-5PM (CST). Access by: Phone, fax, mail, in person.

Misdemeanor, Civil, Probate—County Court, PO Box 423, Corsicana, TX 75151. 903-654-3035. 8AM-5PM (CST). Access by: Mail, in person.

Newton County

Real Estate Recording—Newton County Clerk, Courthouse Square, Newton, TX 75966. 409-379-5341. Fax: 409-565-9049. 8AM-4:30PM (CST).

Felony, Civil—District Court, PO Box 535, Newton, TX 75966. 409-379-3951. 8AM-4:30PM (CST). Access by: Mail, in person.

Misdemeanor, Civil, Probate—County Court, PO Box 484, Newton, TX 75966. 409-379-5341. 8AM-4:30PM (CST). Access by: Mail, in person.

Nolan County

Real Estate Recording—Nolan County Clerk, 100 East 3rd, East Wing - Room 100-A, Sweetwater, TX 79556. 915-235-2462. 8:30AM-Noon, 1-5PM (CST).

Felony, Civil—PO Box 1236, Sweetwater, TX 79556. 915-235-2111. 8:30AM-Noon, 1-5PM (CST). Access by: Mail, in person.

Misdemeanor, Civil, Probate—County Clerk, PO Drawer 98, Sweetwater, TX 79556. 915-235-2462. 8:30AM-Noon, 1-5PM (CST). Access by: Mail, in person.

Nueces County

Real Estate Recording—Recording Section, 901 Leopard St., Rm.201, Courthouse, Corpus Christi, TX 78401. 512-888-0611. Fax: 512-888-0329. 8AM-5PM (CST).

Felony, Civil—District Court, PO Box 2987, Corpus Christi, TX 78403. 512-888-0719. 8AM-5PM (CST). Access by: Mail, in person.

Misdemeanor, Civil, Probate—County Court, PO Box 2627, Corpus Christi, TX 78403. 512-888-0422. Civil: 512-888-0422. Criminal: 512-888-0757. Probate: 512-888-0365. Fax: 512-888-0FAX. 8AM-5PM (CST). Access by: Mail, in person.

Ochiltree County

Real Estate Recording—Ochiltree County Clerk, 511 South Main, Perryton, TX 79070. 806-435-8105. Fax: 806-435-2081. 8:30AM-12, 1-5PM (CST).

Felony, Civil—District Court, 511 S Main, Perryton, TX 79070. 806-435-8160. Fax: 806-435-4341. 8:30AM-5PM (CST). Access by: Mail, in person.

Misdemeanor, Civil, Probate—County Court, 511 S Main St, Perryton, TX 79070. 806-435-8105. Fax: 806-435-2081. 8:30AM-NOON, 1PM-5PM (CST). Access by: Fax, mail, in person.

Oldham County

Real Estate Recording—Oldham County Clerk, Highway 385 & Main Street, Courthouse, Vega, TX 79092. 806-267-2667. 8:30AM-5PM (CST).

Felony, Misdemeanor, Civil, Eviction, Probate—District and County Court, PO Box 360, Vega, TX 79092. 806-267-2667. 8:30AM-NOON, 1PM-5PM (CST). Access by: Mail, in person.

Orange County

Real Estate Recording—Orange County Clerk, 801 Division, Courthouse, Orange, TX 77630. 409-882-7055. Fax: 409-882-0379. 8:30AM-5PM (CST).

Felony, Civil—District Court, PO Box 427, Orange, TX 77630. 409-883-7740. 8AM-5PM (CST). Access by: Mail, in person.

Misdemeanor, Civil, Probate—County Court, PO Box 1536, Orange, TX 77631-1536. 409-882-7055. Fax: 409-882-0379. 8:30AM-5PM (CST). Access by: Phone, mail, in person.

Palo Pinto County

Real Estate Recording—Palo Pinto County Clerk, 520 Oak St., Courthouse, Palo Pinto, TX 76484. 940-659-1277. 8:30AM-4:30PM (CST).

Felony, Civil—District Court, PO Box 189, Palo Pinto, TX 76484-0189. 940-659-1279. 8:30AM-4:30PM (CST). Access by: Mail, in person.

Misdemeanor, Civil, Probate—County Court, PO Box 219, Palo Pinto, TX 76484. 940-659-1277. Fax: 940-659-2590. 8:30AM-4:30PM (CST). Access by: Mail, in person.

Panola County

Real Estate Recording—Panola County Clerk, Sabine & Sycamore, Courthouse Bldg., Room 201, Carthage, TX 75633. 903-693-0302. 8AM-5PM (CST).

Felony, Civil—District Court, County Courthouse Rm 227, Carthage, TX 75633. 903-693-0306. 8AM-5PM (CST). Access by: Mail, in person.

Misdemeanor, Civil, Probate—County Court, County Courthouse Rm 201, Carthage, TX 75633. 903-693-0302. 8AM-5PM (CST). Access by: Mail, in person.

Parker County

Real Estate Recording—Parker County Clerk, 1112 Santa Fe Drive, Weatherford, TX 76086. 817-599-6591. Fax: 817-594-7461. 8AM-5PM (CST).

Felony, Civil—District Court, PO Box 340, Weatherford, TX 76086-0340. 817-599-6591. 8AM-5PM (CST). Access by: Mail, in person.

Misdemeanor, Civil, Probate—County Court, PO Box 819, Weatherford, TX 76086-0819. 817-599-6591. 8AM-NOON, 1PM-5PM (CST). Access by: Mail, in person.

Parmer County

Real Estate Recording—Parmer County Clerk, 400 Third Street, Farwell, TX 79325. 806-481-3691. 8:30AM-5PM (CST).

Felony, Civil—District Court, PO Box 195, Farwell, TX 79325. 806-481-3419. Fax: 806-481-9416. 8:30AM-Noon, 1-5PM (CST). Access by: Fax, mail, in person.

Misdemeanor, Civil, Probate—County Court, PO Box 356, Farwell, TX 79325. 806-481-3691. 8:30AM-5PM (CST). Access by: Mail, in person.

Pecos County

Real Estate Recording—Pecos County Clerk, 103 West Callaghan Street, Fort Stockton, TX 79735. 915-336-7555. Fax: 915-336-7557. 8AM-5PM (CST).

Felony, Civil—District Court, 400 S Nelson, Fort Stockton, TX 79735. 915-336-3503. Fax: 915-336-6437. 8AM-5PM (CST). Access by: Mail, in person.

Misdemeanor, Civil, Probate—County Court, 103 W Callaghan, Fort Stockton, TX 79735. 915-336-7555. Fax: 915-336-7575. 8AM-5PM (CST). Access by: Mail, in person.

Polk County

Real Estate Recording—Polk County Clerk, 101 West Church Street, Livingston, TX 77351. 409-327-6804. 8AM-5PM (CST).

Felony, Civil—District Court, 101 W Church, Livingston, TX 77351. 409-327-6814. 8AM-5PM (CST). Access by: Mail, in person.

Misdemeanor, Civil, Probate—County Court, PO Drawer 2119, Livingston, TX 77351. 409-327-6804. 8AM-5PM (CST). Access by: Mail, in person.

Potter County

Real Estate Recording—Potter County Clerk, 500 S. Fillmore, Room 205, Amarillo, TX 79101. 806-379-2275. Fax: 806-379-2296. 8AM-5PM (CST).

Felony, Civil—District Court, PO Box 9570, Amarillo, TX 79105-9570. 806-379-2300. 7:30AM-5:30PM (CST). Access by: Mail, in person.

Misdemeanor, Civil, Probate—County Court & County Courts at Law 1 & 2, PO Box 9638, Amarillo, TX 79105. 806-379-2275. Fax: 806-379-2296. 8AM-5PM (CST). Access by: Mail, in person.

Presidio County

Real Estate Recording—Presidio County Clerk, Courthouse, 320 N. Highland, Marfa, TX 79843. 915-729-4812. Fax: 915-729-4313. 8AM-12, 1-5PM (CST).

Felony, Misdemeanor, Civil, Eviction, Probate—District and County Court, PO Box 789, Marfa, TX 79843. 915-729-4812. Fax: 915-729-4313. 8AM-Noon, 1PM-5PM (CST). Access by: Mail, in person.

Rains County

Real Estate Recording—Rains County Clerk, 100 Quitman Street, Emory, TX 75440. 903-473-2461. 8AM-5PM (CST).

Felony, Misdemeanor, Civil, Eviction, Probate—District and County Court, PO Box 187, Emory, TX 75440. 903-473-2461. 8AM-5PM (CST). Access by: Mail, in person.

Randall County

Real Estate Recording—Randall County Clerk, 401 15th Street, Canyon, TX 79015. 806-655-6330. 8AM-5PM (On Weekends by Appointment) (CST).

Felony, Civil—District Courts, PO Box 1096, Canyon, TX 79015. 806-655-6200. Fax: 806-655-6205. 8AM-5PM (CST). Access by: Fax, mail, in person.

Misdemeanor, Civil, Probate—County Court, PO Box 660, Canyon, TX 79015. 806-655-6330. 8AM-5PM (CST). Access by: Mail, in person.

Reagan County

Real Estate Recording—Reagan County Clerk, 3rd at Plaza, Courthouse, Big Lake, TX 76932. 915-884-2442. 8:30AM-5PM (CST).

Felony, Misdemeanor, Civil, Eviction, Probate—District and County Court, PO Box 100, Big Lake, TX 76932. 915-884-2442. 8:30AM-5PM (CST). Access by: Mail, in person.

Real County

Real Estate Recording—Real County Clerk, Courthouse Square, Leakey, TX 78873. 830-232-5202. Fax: 830-232-6040. 8AM-5PM (CST).

Felony, Misdemeanor, Civil, Eviction, Probate—District and County Court, PO Box 656, Leakey, TX 78873. 830-232-5202. Fax: 830-232-6040. 8AM-5PM (CST). Access by: Mail, in person.

Red River County

Real Estate Recording—Red River County Clerk, 200 North Walnut, Courthouse Annex, Clarksville, TX 75426. 903-427-2401. 8:30AM-12:00, 1:00PM-5PM (CST).

Felony, Civil—District Court, 400 N Walnut, Clarksville, TX 75426. 903-427-3761. 8:30AM-Noon, 1-5PM (CST). Access by: Mail, in person.

Misdemeanor, Probate—County Court, 200 N Walnut, Clarksville, TX 75426. 903-427-2401. 8:30AM-5PM (CST). Access by: Phone, mail, in person.

Reeves County

Real Estate Recording—Reeves County Clerk, 100 East 4th Street, Room 101, Pecos, TX 79772. 915-445-5467. 8AM-5PM (CST).

Felony, Civil—District Court, PO Box 848, Pecos, TX 79772. 915-445-2714. Fax: 915-445-7455. 8AM-5PM (CST). Access by: Mail, in person.

Misdemeanor, Civil, Probate—County Court, PO Box 867, Pecos, TX 79772. 915-445-5467. 8AM-5PM (CST). Access by: Mail, in person.

Refugio County

Real Estate Recording—Refugio County Clerk, 808 Commerce, Rm.112, Courthouse, Refugio, TX 78377. 512-526-2233. 8AM-5PM (CST).

Felony, Civil—District Court, PO Box 736, Refugio, TX 78377. 512-526-2721. 8AM-5PM (CST). Access by: Mail, in person.

Misdemeanor, Civil, Probate—County Court, PO Box 704, Refugio, TX 78377. 512-526-2233. 8AM-5PM (CST). Access by: Mail, in person.

Roberts County

Real Estate Recording—Roberts County Clerk, Highway 60 & Kiowa Street, Courthouse, Miami, TX 79059. 806-868-2341. Fax: 806-868-3381. 8AM-Noon, 1-5PM (CST).

Felony, Misdemeanor, Civil, Eviction, Probate—District and County Court, PO Box 477, Miami, TX 79059. 806-868-

2341. 8AM-NOON, 1PM-5PM (CST). Access by: Phone, mail, in person.

Robertson County

Real Estate Recording—Robertson County Clerk, Courthouse Square on Center Street, Room 104, Franklin, TX 77856. 409-828-4130. 8AM-5PM (CST).

Felony, Civil—District Court, PO Box 250, Franklin, TX 77856. 409-828-3636. 8AM-5PM (CST). Access by: Mail, in person.

Misdemeanor, Civil, Probate—County Court, PO Box 1029, Franklin, TX 77856. 409-828-4130. 8AM-5PM (CST). Access by: Mail, in person.

Rockwall County

Real Estate Recording—Rockwall County Clerk, 1101 Ridge Rd., S-101, Rockwall, TX 75087. 972-771-5141. 8AM-5PM (CST).

Felony, Civil—District Court, 1101 Ridge Rd #209, Rockwall, TX 75087. 972-722-3382. 8AM-5PM (CST). Access by: Mail, in person.

Misdemeanor, Civil, Probate—County Court, 1101 Ridge Rd, Rockwall, TX 75087. 972-771-5141. Fax: 972-722-1854. 8AM-5PM (CST). Access by: Mail, in person.

Runnels County

Real Estate Recording—County Clerk, Runnels County, Broadway & Hutchings, 600 Courthouse Square, Ballinger, TX 76821. 915-365-2720. 8:30AM-Noon, 1-5PM (CST).

Felony, Civil—District Court, PO Box 166, Ballinger, TX 76821. 915-365-2638. Fax: 915-365-3408. 8:30AM-5PM (CST). Access by: Phone, mail, in person.

Misdemeanor, Civil, Probate—County Court, PO Box 189, Ballinger, TX 76821. 915-365-2720. 8:30AM-Noon, 1-5PM (CST). Access by: Phone, mail, in person.

Rusk County

Real Estate Recording—Rusk County Clerk, 115 North Main, Courthouse, Henderson, TX 75652. 903-657-0330. 8AM-5PM (CST).

Felony, Civil—District Court, PO Box 1687, Henderson, TX 75653. 903-657-0353. 8AM-5PM (CST). Access by: Mail, in person.

Misdemeanor, Civil, Probate—County Court at Law, PO Box 1687, Henderson, TX 75653-1687. 903-657-0348. 8AM-5PM (CST). Access by: Mail, in person.

Sabine County

Real Estate Recording—Sabine County Clerk, Corner of Oak & Main, Courthouse, Hemphill, TX 75948. 409-787-3786. Fax: 409-787-2044. 8AM-4PM (CST).

Felony, Civil—District Court, PO Box 850, Hemphill, TX 75948. 409-787-2912. 8AM-4PM (CST). Access by: Mail, in person.

Misdemeanor, Probate—County Court, PO Drawer 580, Hemphill, TX 75948-0580. 409-787-3786. 8AM-4PM (CST). Access by: Mail, in person.

San Augustine County

Real Estate Recording—San Augustine County Clerk, 106 Courthouse, 100 W. Columbia, San Augustine, TX 75972. 409-275-2452. 8AM-11:45AM, 1-4:45PM (CST).

Felony, Civil—District Court, County Courthouse Rm 202, San Augustine, TX 75972. 409-275-2231. 8AM-4:15PM (CST). Access by: Phone, mail, in person.

Misdemeanor, Civil, Probate—County Court, County Courthouse Rm 106, San Augustine, TX 75972. 409-275-2452. 8-11:45AM, 1-4:45PM (CST). Access by: Mail, in person.

San Jacinto County

Real Estate Recording—San Jacinto County Clerk, Corner of Church & Byrd, Courthouse, Coldspring, TX 77331. 409-653-2324. 8AM-4:30PM (CST).

Felony, Civil—District Court, PO Box 369, Coldspring, TX 77331. 409-653-2909. 8AM-Noon, 1-5PM (CST). Access by: Mail, in person.

Misdemeanor, Civil, Probate—County Court, PO Box 669, Coldspring, TX 77331. 409-653-2324. 8AM-4:30PM (CST). Access by: Mail, in person.

San Patricio County

Real Estate Recording—San Patricio County Clerk, 400 West Sinton Street, Sinton, TX 78387. 512-364-6296. Fax: 512-364-3825. 8AM-5PM (CST).

Felony, Civil—District Court, PO Box 1084, Sinton, TX 78387. 512-364-6225. 8AM-5PM (CST). Access by: Mail, in person.

Misdemeanor, Civil, Probate—County Court, PO Box 578, Sinton, TX 78387. 512-364-6290. 8AM-5PM (CST). Access by: Mail, in person.

San Saba County

Real Estate Recording—San Saba County Clerk, 500 East Wallace, San Saba, TX 76877. 915-372-3614. Fax: 915-372-5746. 8AM-12, 1-5PM (CST).

Felony, Misdemeanor, Civil, Eviction, Probate—District and County Court, County Courthouse, San Saba, TX 76877. 915-372-3375. 8AM-NOON, 1PM-5PM (CST). Access by: Mail, in person.

Schleicher County

Real Estate Recording—Schleicher County Clerk, Highway 277, Courthouse, Eldorado, TX 76936. 915-853-2833. Fax: 915-853-2603. 9AM-5PM (CST).

Felony, Misdemeanor, Civil, Eviction, Probate—District and County Court, PO Drawer 580, Eldorado, TX 76936. 915-853-2833. Fax: 915-853-2603. 9AM-NOON, 1PM-5PM (CST). Access by: Mail, in person.

Scurry County

Real Estate Recording—Scurry County Clerk, 1806 25th Street, Suite 300, Snyder, TX 79549. 915-573-5332. 8:30AM-5PM (CST).

Felony, Civil—District Court, 1806 25th St #402, Snyder, TX 79549. 915-573-5641. 8AM-5PM (CST). Access by: Mail, in person.

Misdemeanor, Civil, Probate—County Court, County Courthouse, 1806 25th St Ste 300, Snyder, TX 79549. 915-573-5332. 8:30AM-5PM (CST). Access by: Mail, in person. Written request always required.

Shackelford County

Real Estate Recording—Shackelford County Clerk, 225 S. Main, Albany, TX 76430. 915-762-2232. 8:30AM-Noon, 1-5PM (CST).

Felony, Misdemeanor, Civil, Probate—District and County Court, PO Box 247, Albany, TX 76430. 915-762-2232. 8:30AM-12PM 1PM-5PM (CST). Access by: Mail, in person.

Shelby County

Real Estate Recording—Shelby County Clerk, 200 San Augustine St., Suite A, Center, TX 75935. 409-598-6361. 8AM-4:30PM (CST).

Felony, Civil—District Court, PO Drawer 1953, Center, TX 75935. 409-598-4164. 8AM-4:30PM (CST). Access by: Mail, in person.

Misdemeanor, Civil, Probate—County Court, PO Box 1987, Center, TX 75935. 409-598-6361. Fax: 409-598-3701. 8AM-4:30PM (CST). Access by: Mail, in person. In person request must be accompanied by written request.

Sherman County

Real Estate Recording—Sherman County Clerk, 701 North 3rd Street, Stratford, TX 79084. 806-396-2371. Fax: 806-396-5670. 8AM-Noon,1-5PM (CST).

Felony, Misdemeanor, Civil, Eviction, Probate—District and County Court, PO Box 270, Stratford, TX 79084. 806-396-2371. 8AM-NOON, 1PM-5PM (CST). Access by: Mail, in person.

Smith County

Real Estate Recording—Smith County Clerk, Courthouse, 100 Broadway, Rm.104, Tyler, TX 75702. 903-535-0641. Fax: 903-535-0684. 8AM-5PM (CST).

Felony, Civil—District Court, PO Box 1077, Tyler, TX 75710. 903-535-0666. Fax: 903-535-0683. 8AM-5PM (CST). Access by: Mail, in person.

Misdemeanor, Civil, Probate—County Court, PO Box 1018, Tyler, TX 75710. 903-535-0634. Fax: 903-535-0684. 8AM-5PM (CST). Access by: Phone, fax, mail, in person.

Somervell County

Real Estate Recording—Somervell County Clerk, 107 N.E. Vernon St., Glen Rose, TX 76043. 254-897-4427. 8AM-5PM (CST).

Felony, Misdemeanor, Civil, Eviction, Probate—District and County Court, PO Box 1098, Glen Rose, TX 76043. 254-897-4427. Fax: 254-897-3233. 8AM-5PM (CST). Access by: Mail, in person.

Starr County

Real Estate Recording—Starr County Clerk, Courthouse, Rio Grande City, TX 78582. 210-487-2954. Fax: 956-487-6227. 8AM-5PM (CST).

Felony, Misdemeanor, Civil, Eviction, Probate—County Court at Law, Starr County Courthouse, Room 201, Rio Grande City, TX 78582. 956-487-2101. Fax: 956-487-6227. 8AM-5PM (CST). Access by: Mail, in person.

District and County Court, Starr County Courthouse, Room 304, Rio Grande City, TX 78582. 956-487-2610. Fax: 956-487-4885. 8AM-5PM (CST). Access by: Mail, in person.

Stephens County

Real Estate Recording—Stephens County Clerk, Courthouse, Breckenridge, TX 76424. 254-559-3700. 8AM-5PM (CST).

Felony, Civil—District and County Court, 200 W Walker, Breckenridge, TX 76424. 254-559-3151. Fax: 254-559-8127. 8:30AM-5PM (CST). Access by: Fax, mail, in person.

Sterling County

Real Estate Recording—Sterling County Clerk, 609 4th Street, Courthouse, Sterling City, TX 76951. 915-378-5191. 8:30AM-Noon, 1-5PM (CST).

Felony, Misdemeanor, Civil, Eviction, Probate—District and County Court, PO Box 55, Sterling City, TX 76951. 915-378-5191. 8:30AM-12PM 1PM-5PM (CST). Access by: Mail, in person.

Stonewall County

Real Estate Recording—Stonewall County Clerk, 510 South Broadway, Aspermont, TX 79502. 940-989-2272. 8AM-4:30PM (CST).

Felony, Misdemeanor, Civil, Eviction, Probate—District and County Court, PO Drawer P, Aspermont, TX 79502. 940-989-2272. 8AM-Noon, 1-4:30PM (CST). Access by: Phone, mail, in person.

Sutton County

Real Estate Recording—Sutton County Clerk, Sutton County Annex, 300 E. Oak, Suite 3, Sonora, TX 76950. 915-387-3815. 8:30AM-4:30PM (CST).

Felony, Misdemeanor, Civil, Eviction, Probate—District and County Court, 300 E Oak, Ste 3, Sonora, TX 76950. 915-387-3815. 8:30AM-4:30PM (CST). Access by: Mail, in person.

Swisher County

Real Estate Recording—Swisher County Clerk, Courthouse, Tulia, TX 79088. 806-995-3294. Fax: 806-995-2214. 8AM-5PM (CST).

Felony, Misdemeanor, Civil, Eviction, Probate—District and County Court, County Courthouse, Tulia, TX 79088. 806-995-4396. Fax: 806-995-2214. 8AM-5PM (CST). Access by: Mail, in person.

Tarrant County

Real Estate Recording—Tarrant County Clerk, 100 West Weatherford, Courthouse, Room 180, Ft. Worth, TX 76196. 817-884-1060. 8AM-4:30PM (CST).

Felony, Civil—District Court, 401 W Belknap, Fort Worth, TX 76196-0402. 817-884-1574. Civil: 817-884-1240. Criminal: 817-884-1342. Fax: 817-884-1484. 8AM-5PM (CST). Access by: Mail, remote online, in person.

Misdemeanor, Civil—County Court, 100 W Weatherford Rm 250, Fort Worth, TX 76196. 817-884-1076. 7:30AM-4:30PM (CST). Access by: Mail, in person.

Probate—Probate Court, County Courthouse, 100 W Weatherford St, Probate Court #1 Rm 260A, Fort Worth, TX 76196. 817-884-1200. Fax: 817-884-3178. 8AM-4:30PM (CST). Access by: Mail, in person.

Taylor County

Real Estate Recording—Taylor County Clerk, 300 Oak, Courthouse, Abilene, TX 79602. 915-674-1202. Fax: 915-674-1279. 8AM-5PM (CST).

Felony, Civil—District Court, 300 Oak St, Abilene, TX 79602. 915-674-1316. Fax: 915-674-1307. 8AM-Noon, 1-5PM (CST). Access by: Fax, mail, in person.

Misdemeanor, Civil, Probate—County Court, PO Box 5497, Abilene, TX 79608. 915-674-1202. Fax: 915-674-1279. 8AM-5PM (CST). Access by: Mail, in person.

Terrell County

Real Estate Recording—Terrell County Clerk, Courthouse Square, 108 Hackberry, Sanderson, TX 79848. 915-345-2391. Fax: 915-345-2653. 9AM-5PM (CST).

Felony, Misdemeanor, Civil, Eviction, Probate—District and County Court, PO Drawer 410, Sanderson, TX 79848. 915-345-2391. Fax: 915-345-2653. 9AM-5PM (CST). Access by: Mail, in person.

Terry County

Real Estate Recording—Terry County Clerk, 500 West Main, Room 105, Brownfield, TX 79316. 806-637-8551. Fax: 806-637-4874. 8:30AM-5PM (CST).

Felony, Civil—District Court, 500 W Main Rm 209E, Brownfield, TX 79316. 806-637-4202. 8:30AM-5PM (CST). Access by: Mail, in person.

Misdemeanor, Civil, Probate—County Court, 500 W Main Rm 105, Brownfield, TX 79316-4398. 806-637-8551. Fax: 806-637-4874. 8:30AM-5PM (CST). Access by: Mail, in person.

Throckmorton County

Real Estate Recording—Throckmorton County Clerk, 105 Minter Street, Courthouse, Throckmorton, TX 76483. 940-849-2501. Fax: 940-849-3220. 8AM-5PM (CST).

Felony, Misdemeanor, Civil, Eviction, Probate—District and County Court, PO Box 309, Throckmorton, TX 76483. 940-849-2501. 8AM-Noon, 1-5PM (CST). Access by: Mail, in person.

Titus County

Real Estate Recording—Titus County Clerk, 100 W. 1 St., 2nd Floor, Suite 204, Mount Pleasant, TX 75455. 903-577-6796. Fax: 903-577-6793. 8AM-5PM (CST).

Felony, Civil—District Court, 105 W 1st St, Mount Pleasant, TX 75455. 903-577-6721. 8AM-5PM (CST). Access by: Mail, in person.

Misdemeanor, Civil, Probate—County Court, 100 W 1st St #204, Mount Pleasant, TX 75455. 903-577-6796. Fax: 903-577-6793. 8AM-5PM (CST). Access by: Mail, in person.

Tom Green County

Real Estate Recording—Tom Green County Clerk, 124 West Beauregard, San Angelo, TX 76903. 915-659-6552. 8AM-Noon, 1-4:30PM (CST).

Felony, Civil—District Court, County Courthouse, 112 W Beauregard, San Angelo, TX 76903. 915-659-6579. Fax: 915-658-6703. 8AM-5PM (CST). Access by: Mail, in person.

Misdemeanor, Civil, Probate—County Court, 124 W Beauregard, San Angelo, TX 76903. 915-659-6555. 8AM-5PM (CST). Access by: Mail, in person.

Travis County

Real Estate Recording—Travis County Clerk, 1000 Guadalupe, Room 222, Austin, TX 78701. 512-473-9188. Fax: 512-473-9075. 8AM-5PM (CST).

Felony, Civil—District Court, PO Box 1748, Austin, TX 78767. Civil: 512-473-9547. Criminal: 512-473-9420. Fax: 512-473-9549. 8AM-5PM (CST). Access by: Phone, fax, mail, in person.

Misdemeanor, Civil—County Court, PO Box 1748, Austin, TX 78767-1748. Civil: 512-473-9595/9090. Criminal: 512-473-9440. Probate: 512-473-9595/9090. Fax: 512-473-9075. 8AM-5PM (CST). Access by: Phone, mail, in person.

Probate—Civil/Probate Division, PO Box 1748, Austin, TX 78767. 512-473-9258. Fax: 512-473-9595. 8AM-5PM (CST). Access by: Phone, mail, in person.

Trinity County

Real Estate Recording—Trinity County Clerk, First Street, Courthouse, Groveton, TX 75845. 409-642-1208. 8AM-5PM (CST).

Felony, Civil—District Court, PO Box 548, Groveton, TX 75845. 409-642-1118. 8AM-5PM (CST). Access by: Mail, in person.

Misdemeanor, Civil, Probate—County Court, PO Box 456, Groveton, TX 75845. 409-642-1208. 8AM-5PM (CST). Access by: Mail, in person.

Tyler County

Real Estate Recording—Tyler County Clerk, 110 Courthouse, Woodville, TX 75979. 409-283-2281. 8AM-4:30PM (CST).

Felony, Civil—District Court, 203 Courthouse, Woodville, TX 75979. 409-283-2162. 8AM-4:30PM (CST). Access by: Mail, in person.

Misdemeanor, Civil, Probate—County Court, County Courthouse Rm 110, Woodville, TX 75979. 409-283-2281. Fax: 409-283-7296. 8AM-4:30PM (CST). Access by: Phone, mail, in person.

Upshur County

Real Estate Recording—Upshur County Clerk, Highway 154, Courthouse, Gilmer, TX 75644. 903-843-4015. 8AM-5PM (CST).

Felony, Misdemeanor, Civil, Probate—District and County Court, PO Box 730, Gilmer, TX 75644. 903-843-4015. 8AM-5PM (CST). Access by: Mail, in person.

Upton County

Real Estate Recording—Upton County Clerk, 205 East 10th Street, Rankin, TX 79778. 915-693-2861. Fax: 915-693-2129. 8AM-5PM (CST).

Felony, Misdemeanor, Civil, Eviction, Probate—District and County Court, PO Box 465, Rankin, TX 79778. 915-693-2861. Fax: 915-693-2243. 8AM-5PM (CST). Access by: Mail, in person.

Uvalde County

Real Estate Recording—Uvalde County Clerk, Main & Getty, Courthouse, Uvalde, TX 78801. 830-278-6614. 8AM-5PM (CST).

Felony, Civil—District Court, County Courthouse Suite #15, Uvalde, TX 78801. 830-278-3918. 8AM-5PM (CST). Access by: Mail, in person.

Misdemeanor, Civil, Probate—County Court, PO Box 284, Uvalde, TX 78802. 830-278-6614. 8AM-5PM (CST). Access by: Mail, in person.

Val Verde County

Real Estate Recording—Val Verde County Clerk, 100 Broadway St., Del Rio, TX 78840. 830-774-7564. 8AM-4:30PM (CST).

Felony, Civil—District Court, PO Box 1544, Del Rio, TX 78841. 830-774-7538. 8AM-4:30PM (CST). Access by: Mail, in person.

Misdemeanor, Probate—County Court, PO Box 1267, Del Rio, TX 78841-1267. 830-774-7564. 8AM-4:30PM (CST). Access by: Mail, in person.

Van Zandt County

Real Estate Recording—Van Zandt County Clerk, 121 East Dallas St, Courthouse - Room 202, Canton, TX 75103. 903-567-6503. Fax: 903-567-6996. 8AM-5PM (CST).

Felony, Civil—District Court, 121 E Dallas St Rm 302, Canton, TX 75103. 903-567-6576. Fax: 903-567-4700. 8AM-5PM (CST). Access by: Phone, mail, in person.

Misdemeanor, Civil, Probate—County Court, 121 E Dallas St #202, Canton, TX 75103. 903-567-6503. Fax: 903-567-6722. 8AM-5PM (CST). Access by: Mail, in person.

Victoria County

Real Estate Recording—Victoria County Clerk, 115 North Bridge Street #103, Victoria, TX 77901. 512-575-1478. Fax: 512-575-6276. 8AM-5PM (CST).

Felony, Civil—District Court, PO Box 2238, Victoria, TX 77902. 512-575-0581. Fax: 512-572-5682. 8AM-5PM (CST). Access by: Mail, in person.

Misdemeanor, Civil, Probate—County Court, PO Box 2410, Victoria, TX 77902. 512-575-1478. Fax: 512-575-6276. 8AM-5PM (CST). Access by: Phone, mail, in person.

Walker County

Real Estate Recording—Walker County Clerk, 1100 University Avenue, Huntsville, TX 77340. 409-436-4922. Fax: 409-436-4930. 8AM-5PM (CST).

Felony, Civil—District Court, 1100 University Ave Rm 301, Huntsville, TX 77340. 409-436-4972. 8AM-Noon, 1-4:30PM (CST). Access by: Mail, in person.

Misdemeanor, Civil, Probate—County Court, PO Box 210, Huntsville, TX 77342-0210. 409-291-9500. 8AM-4:30PM (CST). Access by: Mail, in person.

Waller County

Real Estate Recording—Waller County Clerk, 836 Austin Street, Room 217, Hempstead, TX 77445. 409-826-3357. 8AM-Noon, 1-5PM (CST).

Felony, Civil—District Court, 836 Austin St Rm 318, Hempstead, TX 77445. 409-826-3357. 8AM-12PM 1PM-5PM (CST). Access by: Mail, in person.

Misdemeanor, Civil, Probate—County Court, 836 Austin St, Rm 217, Hempstead, TX 77445. 409-826-3357. 8AM-Noon, 1-5PM (CST). Access by: Mail, in person.

Ward County

Real Estate Recording—Ward County Clerk, Courthouse, 400 S. Allen St., Monahans, TX 79756. 915-943-3294. Fax: 915-942-6054. 8AM-5PM (CST).

Felony, Civil—District Court, PO Box 440, Monahans, TX 79756. 915-943-2751. Fax: 915-943-3810. 8AM-5PM (CST). Access by: Fax, mail, in person.

Misdemeanor, Civil, Probate—County Court, County Courthouse, Monahans, TX 79756. 915-943-3294. Fax: 915-943-6054. 8AM-5PM (CST). Access by: Mail, in person.

Washington County

Real Estate Recording—Washington County Clerk, 100 East Main, Suite 102, Brenham, TX 77833. 409-277-6200. Fax: 409-277-6278. 8AM-5PM (CST).

Felony, Civil—District Court, 100 E Main #304, Brenham, TX 77833-3753. 409-277-6200. 8AM-5PM (CST). Access by: Mail, in person.

Misdemeanor, Civil, Probate—County Court, 100 E Main #102, Brenham, TX 77833. 409-277-6200. Fax: 409-277-6278. 8AM-5PM (CST). Access by: Mail, in person.

Webb County

Real Estate Recording—Webb County Clerk, 1110 Victoria Street, Suite 201, Laredo, TX 78040. 956-721-2640. Fax: 956-721-2288. (CST).

Felony, Civil—District Court, PO Box 667, Laredo, TX 78042-0667. 956-721-2455. Fax: 956-721-2458. 8AM-5PM (CST). Access by: Mail, in person.

Misdemeanor, Civil Under $5,000, Probate—County Court, PO Box 29, Laredo, TX 78042. 210-721-2640. Civil: 210-721-2653. Criminal: 210-721-2651. Probate: 210-721-2656. Fax: 956-721-2288. 8AM-5PM (CST). Access by: Mail, in person.

Wharton County

Real Estate Recording—Wharton County Clerk, 100 East Milam, Wharton, TX 77488. 409-532-2381. 8AM-5PM (CST).

Felony, Civil—District Court, PO Drawer 391, Wharton, TX 77488. 409-532-5542. 8AM-NOON, 1PM-5PM (CST). Access by: Mail, in person.

Misdemeanor, Civil, Probate—County Court, PO Box 69, Wharton, TX 77488. 409-532-2381. 8AM-5PM (CST). Access by: Mail, in person.

Wheeler County

Real Estate Recording—Wheeler County Clerk, 400 Main Street, Courthouse, Wheeler, TX 79096. 806-826-5544. Fax: 806-826-3282. 8AM-5PM (CST).

Felony, Civil—District Court, PO Box 528, Wheeler, TX 79096. 806-826-5931. Fax: 806-826-3282. 8AM-5PM (CST). Access by: Phone, mail, in person.

Misdemeanor, Civil, Probate—County Court, PO Box 465, Wheeler, TX 79096. 806-826-5544. Fax: 806-826-3282. 8AM-5PM (CST). Access by: Phone, mail, in person.

Wichita County

Real Estate Recording—Wichita County Clerk, 900 7th Street, Room 250, Wichita Falls, TX 76301. 940-766-8175. 8AM-5PM (CST).

Felony, Civil—District Court, PO Box 718, Wichita Falls, TX 76307. 940-766-8100. 8AM-5PM (CST). Access by: Phone, mail, in person.

Misdemeanor, Probate—County Court, PO Box 1679, Wichita Falls, TX 76307. 940-766-8100. Criminal: 940-766-8173. Probate: 940-766-8172. 8AM-5PM (CST). Access by: Phone, mail, in person.

Wilbarger County

Real Estate Recording—Wilbarger County Clerk, Courthouse, 1700 Main St. #15, Vernon, TX 76384. 940-552-5486. 8AM-5PM (CST).

Felony, Civil—District Court, 1700 Wilbarger Rm 33, Vernon, TX 76384. 940-553-3411. 8AM-5PM (CST). Access by: Mail, in person.

Misdemeanor, Civil, Probate—County Court, 1700 Wilbarger Rm 15, Vernon, TX 76384. 940-552-5486. 8AM-5PM (CST). Access by: Mail, in person.

Willacy County

Real Estate Recording—Willacy County Clerk, 540 West Hidalgo Avenue, Courthouse Building, First Floor, Raymondville, TX 78580. 956-689-2710. 8AM-Noon, 1-5PM (CST).

Felony, Civil—District Court, County Courthouse, Raymondville, TX 78580. 956-689-2532. 8AM-5PM (CST). Access by: Mail, in person.

Misdemeanor, Civil, Probate—County Court, 540 W Hidalgo, Raymondville, TX 78580. 956-689-2710. 8AM-Noon, 1PM-5PM (CST). Access by: Mail, in person.

Williamson County

Real Estate Recording—Williamson County Clerk, 8th & Austin Avenue, Courthouse, Georgetown, TX 78626. 512-930-4315. Fax: 512-930-4461. 8AM-5PM (CST).

Felony, Civil—District Court, PO Box 24, Georgetown, TX 78627. 512-930-4426. 8AM-5PM (CST). Access by: Mail, in person.

Misdemeanor, Civil, Probate—County Court, PO Box 18, (405 MLK St, 78626), Georgetown, TX 78627. Civil: 512-930-4310. Criminal: 512-930-4375. Probate: 512-930-4310.

Fax: 512-930-3245. 8AM-5PM M,T,Th,F (CST). Access by: Mail, in person.

Wilson County

Real Estate Recording—Wilson County Clerk, 1420 3rd Street, Floresville, TX 78114. 830-393-7308. 8AM-5PM (CST).

Felony, Civil—District Court, PO Box 812, Floresville, TX 78114. 830-393-7322. Fax: 830-393-7319. 8AM-Noon, 1-5PM (CST). Access by: Fax, mail, in person.

Misdemeanor, Civil, Probate—County Court, PO Box 27, Floresville, TX 78114. 830-393-7307. 8AM-5PM (CST). Access by: Mail, in person.

Winkler County

Real Estate Recording—Winkler County Clerk, 100 East Winkler Street, Courthouse, Kermit, TX 79745. 915-586-3401. 8AM-5PM (CST).

Felony, Civil—District Court, PO Box 1065, Kermit, TX 79745. 915-586-3359. 8:30AM-5PM (CST). Access by: Mail, in person.

Misdemeanor, Civil, Probate—County Court, PO Box 1007, Kermit, TX 79745. 915-586-3401. 8AM-5PM (CST). Access by: Mail, in person.

Wise County

Real Estate Recording—Wise County Clerk, 200 North Trinity, Records Bldg., Decatur, TX 76234. 940-627-3351. 8AM-5PM (CST).

Felony, Civil—District Court, PO Box 308, Decatur, TX 76234. 940-627-5535. 8AM-5PM (CST). Access by: Mail, in person.

Misdemeanor, Civil, Probate—County Court, PO Box 359, Decatur, TX 76234. 940-627-3351. Fax: 940-627-2138. 8AM-5PM (CST). Access by: Mail, in person.

Wood County

Real Estate Recording—Wood County Clerk, 1 Main Street, Courthouse, Quitman, TX 75783. 903-763-2711. Fax: 903-763-2902. 8AM-5PM (CST).

Felony, Civil—District Court, PO Box 488, Quitman, TX 75783. 903-763-2361. 8AM-12PM 1PM-5PM (CST). Access by: Mail, in person.

Misdemeanor, Civil, Probate—County Court, PO Box 338, Quitman, TX 75783. 903-763-2711. Fax: 903-763-2902. 8AM-5PM (CST). Access by: Mail, in person.

Yoakum County

Real Estate Recording—Yoakum County Clerk, Courthouse, Cowboy Way & Avenue G, Plains, TX 79335. 806-456-2721. Fax: 806-456-6175. 8AM-5PM (CST).

Felony, Civil—District Court, PO Box 899, Plains, TX 79355. 806-456-7453. Fax: 806-456-6175. 8AM-5PM (CST). Access by: Phone, fax, mail, in person.

Misdemeanor, Civil, Probate—County Court, PO Box 309, Plains, TX 79355. 806-456-2721. Fax: 806-456-6175. 8AM-5PM (CST). Access by: Mail, in person.

Young County

Real Estate Recording—Young County Clerk, Young County Courthouse, 516 Fourth St., Room 104, Graham, TX 76450. 940-549-8432. 8:30AM-5PM (CST).

Felony, Civil—District Court, 516 4th St Rm 201, Courthouse, Graham, TX 76450. 940-549-0029. Fax: 940-549-4874. 8:30AM-Noon, 1-5PM (CST). Access by: Fax, mail, in person.

Misdemeanor, Civil, Probate—County Court, 516 4th St Rm 104, Graham, TX 76450. 940-549-8432. 8:30AM-12PM 1PM-5PM (CST). Access by: Phone, fax, mail, in person.

Zapata County

Real Estate Recording—Zapata County Clerk, 7th Avenue & Hidalgo Street, Zapata, TX 78076. 956-765-9915. Fax: 956-765-9933. 8AM-5PM (CST).

Felony, Civil—District Court, PO Box 788, Zapata, TX 78076. 956-765-9930. Fax: 956-765-9931. 8AM-NOON, 1PM-5PM (CST). Access by: Fax, mail, in person.

Misdemeanor, Civil, Probate—County Court, PO Box 789, Zapata, TX 78076. 956-765-9915. Fax: 956-765-9933. 8AM-12PM 1PM-5PM (CST). Access by: Mail, in person.

Zavala County

Real Estate Recording—Zavala County Clerk, Zavala Courthouse, Crystal City, TX 78839. 830-374-2331. Fax: 830-374-5955. 8AM-5PM (CST).

Felony, Civil—District Court, PO Box 704, Crystal City, TX 78839. 830-374-3456. 8AM-12PM 1PM-5PM (CST). Access by: Phone, mail, in person.

Misdemeanor, Civil, Probate—County Court, Zavala County Courthouse, Crystal City, TX 78839. 830-374-2331. Fax: 830-374-5955. 8AM-5PM (CST). Access by: Mail, in person.

Federal Courts

US District Court
Eastern District of Texas

Beaumont Division, US District Court PO Box 3507, Beaumont, TX 77704. 409-654-7000. Counties: Hardin, Jasper, Jefferson, Liberty, Newton, Orange

Marshall Division, US District Court PO Box 1499, Marshall, TX 75671-1499. 903-935-2912. Counties: Camp, Cass, Harrison, Marion, Morris, Upshur

Sherman Division, US District Court 101 E Pecan St, Sherman, TX 75090. 903-892-2921. Counties: Collin, Cooke, Delta, Denton, Fannin, Grayson, Hopkins, Lamar, Red River

Texarkana Division, US District Court Clerk's Office, 500 State Line Ave #302, Texarkana, TX 75501. 903-794-8561. Counties: Angelina, Bowie, Franklin, Houston, Nacogdoches, Polk, Sabine, San Augustine, Shelby, Titus, Trinity, Tyler

Tyler Division, US District Court Clerk, Room 106, 211 W Ferguson, Tyler, TX 75702. 903-592-8195. Counties: Anderson, Cherokee, Gregg, Henderson, Panola, Rains, Rusk, Smith, Van Zandt, Wood

Northern District of Texas

Abilene Division, US District Court PO Box 1218, Abilene, TX 79604. 915-677-6311. Counties: Callahan, Eastland, Fisher, Haskell, Howard, Jones, Mitchell, Nolan, Shackelford, Stephens, Stonewall, Taylor, Throckmorton

Amarillo Division, US District Court 205 E 5th St, Amarillo, TX 79101. 806-324-2352. Counties: Armstrong, Briscoe, Carson, Castro, Childress, Collingsworth, Dallam, Deaf Smith, Donley, Gray, Hall, Hansford, Hartley, Hemphill, Hutchinson, Lipscomb, Moore, Ochiltree, Oldham, Parmer, Potter, Randall, Roberts, Sherman, Swisher, Wheeler

Dallas Division, US District Court Room 14A20, 1100 Commerce St, Dallas, TX 75242. 214-767-0787. Counties: Dallas, Ellis, Hunt, Johnson, Kaufman, Navarro, Rockwall

Fort Worth Division, US District Court Clerk's Office, 310 US Courthouse, 501 W 10th St, Fort Worth, TX 76102. 817-978-3132. Counties: Comanche, Erath, Hood, Jack, Palo Pinto, Parker, Tarrant, Wise

Lubbock Division, US District Court Clerk, Room C-105, 904 Broadway, Lubbock, TX 79401. 806-767-1317. Counties: Bailey, Borden, Cochran, Crosby, Dawson, Dickens, Floyd, Gaines, Garza, Hale, Hockley, Kent, Lamb, Lubbock, Lynn, Motley, Scurry, Terry, Yoakum

San Angelo Division, US District Court Clerk's Office, Room 202, 33 E Twohig, San Angelo, TX 76903. 915-655-4506. Counties: Brown, Coke, Coleman, Concho, Crockett, Glasscock, Irion, Menard, Mills, Reagan, Runnels, Schleicher, Sterling, Sutton, Tom Green

Wichita Falls Division, US District Court PO Box 1234, Wichita Falls, TX 76307. 940-767-1902. Counties: Archer, Baylor, Clay, Cottle, Foard, Hardeman, King, Knox, Montague, Wichita, Wilbarger, Young

Southern District of Texas

Brownsville Division, US District Court PO Box 2299, Brownsville, TX 78522. 956-548-2500. Counties: Cameron, Willacy

Corpus Christi Division, US District Court Clerk's Office, 521 Starr St, Corpus Christi, TX 78401. 512-888-3142. Counties: Aransas, Bee, Brooks, Duval, Jim Wells, Kenedy, Kleberg, Live Oak, Nueces, San Patricio

Galveston Division, US District Court Clerk's Office, PO Drawer 2300, Galveston, TX 77553. 409-766-3530. Counties: Brazoria, Chambers, Galveston, Matagorda

Houston Division, US District Court PO Box 61010, Houston, TX 77208. 713-250-5500. Counties: Austin, Brazos, Colorado, Fayette, Fort Bend, Grimes, Harris, Madison, Montgomery, San Jacinto, Walker, Waller, Wharton

Laredo Division, US District Court PO Box 597, Laredo, TX 78042-0597. 956-723-3542. Counties: Jim Hogg, La Salle, McMullen, Webb, Zapata

McAllen Division, US District Court Suite 1011, 1701 W Business Hwy 83, McAllen, TX 78501. 956-618-8065. Counties: Hidalgo, Starr

Victoria Division, US District Court Clerk US District Court, PO Box 1541, Victoria, TX 77902. 512-788-5000. Counties: Calhoun, De Witt, Goliad, Jackson, Lavaca, Refugio, Victoria

Western District of Texas

Austin Division, US District Court Room 308, 200 W 8th St, Austin, TX 78701. 512-916-5896. Counties: Bastrop, Blanco, Burleson, Burnet, Caldwell, Gillespie, Hays, Kimble, Lampasas, Lee, Llano, McCulloch, Mason, San Saba, Travis, Washington, Williamson

Del Rio Division, US District Court Room L100, 111 E Broadway, Del Rio, TX 78840. 830-703-2054. Counties: Edwards, Kinney, Maverick, Terrell, Uvalde, Val Verde, Zavala

El Paso Division, US District Court US District Clerk's Office, Room 350, 511 E San Antonio, El Paso, TX 79901. 915-534-6725. Counties: El Paso

Midland Division, US District Court Clerk, US District Court, 200 E Wall St, Room 310, Midland, TX 79701. 915-686-4001. Counties: Andrews, Crane, Ector, Martin, Midland, Upton

Pecos Division, US District Court US Courthouse, 410 S Cedar St, Pecos, TX 79772. 915-445-4228. Counties: Brewster, Culberson, Hudspeth, Jeff Davis, Loving, Pecos, Presidio, Reeves, Ward, Winkler

San Antonio Division, US District Court US Clerk's Office, 655 E Durango, Suite G-65, San Antonio, TX 78206. 210-472-6550. Counties: Atascosa, Bandera, Bexar, Comal, Dimmit, Frio, Gonzales, Guadalupe, Karnes, Kendall, Kerr, Medina, Real, Wilson

Waco Division, US District Court Clerk, PO Box 608, Waco, TX 76703. 254-750-1501. Counties: Bell, Bosque, Coryell, Falls, Freestone, Hamilton, Hill, Leon, Limestone, McLennan, Milam, Robertson, Somervell

US Bankruptcy Court
Eastern District of Texas

Beaumont Division, US Bankruptcy Court, Suite 100, 300 Willow, Beaumont, TX 77701. 409-839-2617. Voice Case Information System: 903-592-6119. Counties: Angelina, Hardin, Houston, Jasper, Jefferson, Liberty, Nacogdoches, Newton, Orange, Polk, Sabine, San Augustine, Shelby, Trinity, Tyler

Marshall Division, US Bankruptcy Court, c/o Tyler Division, 200 E Ferguson, Tyler, TX 75702. 903-592-1212. Voice Case Information System: 903-592-6119. Counties: Camp, Cass, Harrison, Marion, Morris, Upshur

Plano Division, US Bankruptcy Court, Suite 300B, 660 N Central Expressway, Plano, TX 75074. 972-509-1240. Voice Case Information System: 903-592-6119. Counties: Bowie, Collin, Cooke, Delta, Denton, Fannin, Franklin, Grayson, Hopkins, Lamar, Red River, Titus.

Texarkana Division, US Bankruptcy Court, c/o Plano Division, 660 N Central Expressway, #300B, Plano, TX 75074. 972-509-1240. Voice Case Information System: 903-592-6119. Counties: Bowie, Franklin, Titus

Tyler Division, US Bankruptcy Court, 200 E Ferguson, Tyler, TX 75702. 903-592-1212. Voice Case Information System: 903-592-6119. Counties: Anderson, Cherokee, Gregg, Henderson, Panola, Rains, Rusk, Smith, Van Zandt, Wood

Northern District of Texas

Amarillo Division, US Bankruptcy Court, PO Box 15960, Amarillo, TX 79105-0960. 806-324-2302. Voice Case Information System: 214-767-8092. Counties: Armstrong, Briscoe, Carson, Castro, Childress, Collingsworth, Dallam, Deaf Smith, Donley, Gray, Hall, Hansford, Hartley, Hemphill, Hutchinson, Lipscomb, Moore, Ochiltree, Oldham, Parmer, Potter, Randall, Roberts, Sherman, Swisher, Wheeler

Dallas Division, US Bankruptcy Court, 1100 Commerce St, Suite 12A24, Dallas, TX 75242. 214-767-0814. Voice Case Information System: 214-767-8092. Counties: Dallas, Ellis, Hunt, Johnson, Kaufman, Navarro, Rockwall

Fort Worth Division, US Bankruptcy Court, 501 W 10th, Suite 147, Fort Worth, TX 76102. 817-978-3802. Voice Case Information System: 214-767-8092. Counties: Comanche, Erath, Hood, Jack, Palo Pinto, Parker, Tarrant, Wise

Lubbock Division, US Bankruptcy Court, 102 Federal Bldg, 1205 Texas Ave, Lubbock, TX 79401. 806-472-7336. Voice Case Information System: 214-767-8092. Counties: Bailey, Borden, Brown, Callahan, Cochran, Cooke, Coleman, Concho, Crockett, Crosby, Dawson, Dickens, Eastland, Fisher, Floyd, Gaines, Garza, Glasscock, Hale, Haskell, Hockley, Howard, Irion, Jones, Kent, Lamb, Lubbock, Lynn, Menard, Mills, Mitchell, Motley, Nolan, Reagan, Runnels, Schleicher, Scurry, Shackelford, Stephens, Sterling, Stonewall, Sutton, Taylor, Terry, Throckmorton, Tom Green, Yoakum

Wichita Falls Division, US Bankruptcy Court, c/o Dallas Division, Suite 12A24, 1100 Commerce St, Dallas, TX 75242. 214-767-0814. Voice Case Information System: 214-

767-8092. Counties: Archer, Baylor, Clay, Cottle, Foard, Hardeman, King, Knox, Montague, Wichita, Wilbarger, Young

Southern District of Texas

Corpus Christi Division, US Bankruptcy Court, Room 113, 615 Leopard St, Corpus Christi, TX 78476. 512-888-3484. Voice Case Information System: 713-250-5049. Counties: Aransas, Bee, Brooks, Calhoun, Cameron, DeWitt, Duval, Goliad, Hidalgo, Jackson, Jim Wells, Kenedy, Kleberg, Lavaea, Live Oak, Nueces, Refugio, San Patricio, Starr, Willacy. Files from Brownsville, Corpus Christi and McAllen Divisions are maintained here

Houston Division, US Bankruptcy Court, Room 1217, 515 Rusk Ave, Houston, TX 77002. 713-250-5500. Voice Case Information System: 713-250-5049. Counties: Austin, Brazoria, Brazos, Chambers, Colorado, Fayette, Fort Bend, Galveston, Grimes, Harris, Jim Hogg, Laredo, La Salle, Madison, Matagorda, McMullen, Montgomery, San Jacinto, Victoria, Walker, Waller, Web, Wharton, Zapata

Western District of Texas

Austin Division, US Bankruptcy Court, Homer Thornberry Judicial Bldg, 903 San Jacinto Blvd, Room 326, Austin, TX 78701-2450. 512-916-5237. Voice Case Information System: 210-472-4023. Counties: Bastrop, Blanco, Burleson, Burnet, Caldwell, Gillespie, Hays, Kimble, Lampasas, Lee, Llano, Mason, McCulloch, San Saba, Travis, Washington, Williamson

El Paso Division, US Bankruptcy Court, 8515 Lockheed, El Paso, TX 79925. 915-779-7362. Voice Case Information System: 210-472-4023. Counties: El Paso

Midland/Odessa Division, US Bankruptcy Court, US Post Office Annex, Room P-163, 100 E Wall St, Midland, TX 79701. 915-683-1650. Voice Case Information System: 210-472-4023. Counties: Andrews, Crane, Ector, Martin, Midland, Upton

Pecos Division, US Bankruptcy Court, 410 S. Cedar, Pecos, TX 79772. 915-445-4228. Voice Case Information System: 210-472-4023. Counties: Brewster, Culberson, Hudspeth, Jeff Davis, Loving, Pecos, Presidio, Reeves, Ward, Winkler

San Antonio Division, US Bankruptcy Court, PO Box 1439, San Antonio, TX 78295. 210-472-6720. Voice Case Information System: 210-472-4023. Counties: Atascosa, Bandera, Bexar, Comal, Dimmit, Edwards, Frio, Gonzales, Guadalupe, Karnes, Kendall, Kerr, Kinney, Maverick, Medina, Real, Terrell, Uvalde, Val Verde, Wilson, Zavala

Waco Division, US Bankruptcy Court, PO Box 687, Waco, TX 76703. 254-754-1481. Voice Case Information System: 210-472-4023. Counties: Bell, Bosque, Coryell, Falls, Freestone, Hamilton, Hill, Leon, Limestone, McLennan, Milam, Robertson, Somervell

Utah

Capitol: Salt Lake City (Salt Lake County)	
Number of Counties: 29	**Population:** 1,951,408
County Court Locations:	**Federal Court Locations:**
•District Courts: 41/8 Districts	•District Courts: 1
Justice Courts: 171/ 171 Cities/Counties	•Bankruptcy Courts: 1
Juvenile Courts: 8 Juvenile Districts	**State Agencies:** 19

State Agencies—Summary

General Help Numbers:

State Archives

Administrative Services Department	801-538-3012
Archives Division	Fax: 801-538-3354
State Archives Bldg	8AM-5PM
Salt Lake City, UT 84114	
Historical Society-LDS:	801-240-2331
Historical Society-State:	801-533-3537

Governor's Office

Governor's Office	801-538-1000
210 State Capitol	Fax: 801-538-1528
Salt Lake City, UT 84114	8AM-5PM

Attorney General's Office

Attorney General's Office	801-538-1015
236 State Capitol	Fax: 801-538-1121
Salt Lake City, UT 84114	8AM-5:30PM

State Legislation

Utah Legislature	801-538-1022
Research and General Counsel	8AM-5PM
436 State Capitol	
Salt Lake City, UT 84114	
Bill Room:	801-538-1588
Older Passed Bills:	801-538-1032

Important State Internet Sites:

🌑 *Webscape*	
File **Edit** **View**	**Help**

State of Utah World Wide Web
www.state.ut.us/

This site links to such sites as education, government, tourism, the court system, government news, travel information, and includes a search engine.

Utah Legislature
www.le.state.ut.us/welcome.htm

This site contains links to the state House and Senate home pages, the members home pages, contains the Utah Code and a link to bill information.

State Archives
www.archives.state.ut.us/

This is the home page for the state archives agency. Linked to this site are the archives division, the state archives and vital records. At the archives site you can request a search through e-mail.

Unclaimed Property
www.treasurer.state.ut.us/

This site provides limited information about unclaimed property and an e-mail address to make inquiries.

Legislation
www.le.state.ut.us/years.htm

Listed at this site are the bills for the last 2 years. There are many different ways to search for a specific bill.

State Agencies—Public Records

Criminal Records

Bureau of Criminal Identification, 4501 S 2700 W, Salt Lake City, UT 84119, Main Telephone: 801-965-4561, Fax: 801-965-4749, Hours: 8AM-5PM. Restricted access.

Corporation Records
Limited Liability Company Records
Fictitious Name
Limited Partnership Records
Assumed Name
Trademarks/Servicemarks

Commerce Department, Corporate Division, PO Box 146705, Salt Lake City, UT 84114-6705, Main Telephone: 801-530-4849, Certified Records: 801-530-6205, Non-Certified: 801-530-6034, Good Standing: 801-530-6363, Fax: 801-530-6111, Hours: 8AM-5PM. Access by: mail, phone, fax, visit, PC. This agency also has records of non-profit corporations. Please note the different phone numbers for the type of record needed. These are order lines which record your order.

Uniform Commercial Code
Federal Tax Liens
State Tax Liens

Division of Corporations and Commercial Code, State of Utah, PO Box 146705, Salt Lake City, UT 84114-6705, Main Telephone: 801-530-6025, Fax: 801-530-6438, Hours: 8AM-5PM. Access by: mail, phone, fax, visit, PC.

Sales Tax Registrations

Tax Commission, Taxpayer Services, 210 N 1950 W, Salt Lake City, UT 84134, Main Telephone: 801-297-2200, Fax: 801-297-7697, Hours: 8AM-5PM. Access by: mail, phone, visit, PC. General forms and tax law information can be downloaded from their web site at tax.ex.state.ut.us.

Birth Certificates

Department of Health, Bureau of Vital Records, Box 142855, Salt Lake City, UT 84114-2855, Main Telephone: 801-538-6105, Hours: 9AM-5PM. Access by: mail, visit.

Death Records

Department of Health, Bureau of Vital Records, Box 142855, Salt Lake City, UT 84114-2855, Main Telephone: 801-538-6380, Hours: 9AM-5PM. Access by: mail, visit.

Marriage Certificates

Records not available from state agency.

Divorce Records

Records not available from state agency.

Workers' Compensation Records

Industrial Commission, Industrial Accidents Division, PO Box 146610, Salt Lake City, UT 84114-6610, Main Telephone: 801-530-6800, Fax: 801-530-6804, Hours: 8AM-4:30PM. Access by: mail, visit.

Driver Records

Department of Public Safety, Driver's License & Driving Records Section, PO Box 30560, Salt Lake City, UT 84130-0560, Main Telephone: 801-965-4437, Fax: 801-965-4496, Hours: 8AM-5PM. Access by: mail, visit. Copies of tickets can be purchased for $5.00 per record. However, if the ticket information came to the state via magnetic tape, the state will refer the requester to the court.

Vehicle Ownership
Vehicle Identification

State Tax Commission, Motor Vehicle Records Section, 210 North 1950 West, Salt Lake City, UT 84134, Main Telephone: 801-297-3507, Fax: 801-297-3578, Hours: 8AM-5PM. Access by: mail, phone, visit.

Accident Reports

Driver's License Division, Accident Reports Section, PO Box 30560, Salt Lake City, UT 84130-0560, Main Telephone: 801-965-4428, Hours: 8AM-5PM. Access by: mail, fax, visit.

Hunting License Information
Fishing License Information

Utah Division of Wildlife Resources, PO Box 146301, Salt Lake City, UT 84114-6301, Main Telephone: 801-538-4700, Fax: 801-538-4709, Hours: 8AM-5PM. Access by: mail only.

County Courts and Recording Offices

What You Need to Know...

<table>
<tr><td>

About the Courts

</td><td>

About the Recorder's Office

</td></tr>
</table>

About the Courts

Administration

Court Administrator	801-578-3800
230 S 500 E, #300	Fax: 801-578-3843
Salt Lake City, UT 84102	8AM-5PM

Court Structure

Effective 7/1/96 all remaining Circuit Courts (the lower court) have been combined with the District Courts (the higher court) in each county. It is reported that branch courts in larger counties such as Salt Lake which were formerly Circuit Courts have been elevated to District Courts, with full jurisdiction over felony as well as misdemeanor cases. Therefore, it may be necessary to search for felony records at more courts than previously necessary. Since this change is so recent, we recommend including a statement in written requests to District Courts to "include Circuit Court cases in your search" to assure that index records from the former court are checked.

Searching Hints

Personal checks are generally accepted across the state. SASE are, generally, required across the state. Fees are set by statute as follows: Search Fee $10.00 per hour, Certification Fee $2.00 per document plus $.50 per page, Copy Fee $.25 per page.

Online Access

There is an online public access computer bulletin board called the Utah Courts Information **XChange** available for a $25.00 one-time registration fee and $30.00 per month usage fee for unlimited use. Records on **XChange** go back to varying dates 7 years for both civil and criminal dockets and some judgments (full case documentation is **not** available). Counties representing approximately 93% of cases filed in the state are included on **XChange** as of the end of 1996. This is **not** a "common" database; thus, a search of **each court** must be performed separately. **Be aware that in some counties only some courts are on the system.** There are plans to have a "warehouse" type database which will open the entire state to one search. For additional information and/or registration, contact: The Office of the Courts, Director of Information Services, 230 S 500 East, #380, Salt Lake City UT 84102, 801-238-7804

About the Recorder's Office

Organization

29 counties 29 filing offices. The recording officers are County Recorder and Clerk of District Court (state tax liens). The entire state is in the Mountain Time Zone (MST).

UCC Records

Financing statements are filed at the state level, except for real estate related collateral, which are filed with the Register of Deeds (and at the state level in certain cases). Filing offices will **not** perform UCC searches. Copy fees vary.

Lien Records

All federal tax liens are filed with the County Recorder. They do **not** per form searches. All state tax liens are filed with Clerk of District Court, many of which have on-line access. Refer to *The Sourcebook of County Court Records* for information about Utah District Courts.

Real Estate Records

County Recorders will **not** perform real estate searches. Copy fees vary, and certification fees are usually $2.00 per document.

County Courts and Recording Offices

Beaver County

Real Estate Recording—Beaver County Recorder, 105 East Center, Beaver, UT 84713. 435-438-6480. Fax: 435-438-6481. 9AM-5PM (MST).

Felony, Misdemeanor, Civil, Eviction, Small Claims, Probate—5th District Court, PO Box 392, Beaver, UT 84713. 435-438-6463. Fax: 435-438-5305. 9AM-NOON, 1PM-5PM (MST). Access by: Mail, in person.

Box Elder County

Real Estate Recording—Box Elder County Recorder, 1 South Main, Courthouse, Brigham City, UT 84302. 435-734-2031. Fax: 435-734-2038. 8AM-5PM (MST).

Felony, Misdemeanor, Civil, Eviction, Small Claims, Probate—1st District Court, 43 N Main, PO Box 873, Brigham City, UT 84302. 435-734-4600. Fax: 435-734-4610. 8AM-5PM (MST). Access by: Mail, remote online, in person.

Cache County

Real Estate Recording—Cache County Recorder, 179 North Main Street, Logan, UT 84321. 435-752-5561. Fax: 435-753-7120. 8AM-5PM (MST).

Felony, Misdemeanor, Civil, Eviction, Small Claims, Probate—1st District Court, 140 N. 100 W., Logan, UT 84321. 435-752-6893. Fax: 435-753-0372. 8AM-5PM (MST). Access by: Phone, mail, remote online, in person.

Carbon County

Real Estate Recording—Carbon County Recorder, Courthouse Building, 120 East Main, Price, UT 84501. 435-637-4700. Fax: 435-637-6757. 9AM-5PM (MST).

Felony, Misdemeanor, Civil, Eviction, Small Claims, Probate—7th District Court, 149 E. 100 South, Price, UT 84501. 435-637-2150. Fax: 435-637-7349. 8AM-5PM (MST). Access by: Phone, mail, in person.

Daggett County

Real Estate Recording—Daggett County Recorder, 95 North 1st West, Manila, UT 84046. 435-784-3210. Fax: 435-784-3335. 9AM-Noon,1-5PM (MST).

Felony, Misdemeanor, Civil, Eviction, Small Claims, Probate—8th District Court, PO Box 219, Manila, UT 84046. 435-784-3154. Fax: 435-784-3335. 9AM-5PM (MST). Access by: Mail, in person.

Davis County

Real Estate Recording—Davis County Recorder, 28 East State, Farmington, UT 84025. 801-451-3224. Fax: 801-451-3111. 8:30AM-5PM (MST).

Felony, Misdemeanor, Civil, Eviction, Small Claims, Probate—2nd District Court, PO Box 769, Farmington, UT 84025. 801-451-4400. Fax: 801-451-4470. 8AM-5PM (MST). Access by: Phone, mail, remote online, in person.

2nd District Court-Bountiful Department, 745 South Main, Bountiful, UT 84010. 801-298-6152. Fax: 801-397-7010. 8AM-5PM (MST). Access by: Phone, fax, mail, remote online, in person.

2nd District Court-Layton Department, 425 Wasatch Dr, Layton, UT 84041. 801-546-2484. Fax: 801-546-8224. 8AM-5PM (MST). Access by: Mail, remote online, in person.

Duchesne County

Real Estate Recording—Duchesne County Recorder, 100 South 50 East, Duchesne, UT 84021. 435-738-2435. Fax: 435-738-5522. 8:30AM-5PM (MST).

Felony, Misdemeanor, Civil, Eviction, Small Claims, Probate—8th District Court, PO Box 990, Duchesne, UT 84021. 435-738-2753. Fax: 435-738-2754. 8AM-5PM (MST). Access by: Mail, in person.

8th District Court-Roosevelt Department, PO Box 1286, Roosevelt, UT 84066. 435-722-0235. 8AM-5PM (MST). Access by: Mail, in person.

Emery County

Real Estate Recording—Emery County Recorder, 95 East Main, Castle Dale, UT 84513. 435-381-2414. Fax: 435-381-5529. 8AM-5PM (MST).

Felony, Misdemeanor, Civil, Eviction, Small Claims, Probate—7th District Court, PO Box 907, Castle Dale, UT 84513. 435-381-2465. Fax: 435-381-5183. 8:30AM-5PM (MST). Access by: Mail, in person.

Garfield County

Real Estate Recording—Garfield County Recorder, 55 South Main, Panguitch, UT 84759. 435-676-8826. Fax: 435-676-8239. 9AM-Noon, 1-5PM (MST).

Felony, Misdemeanor, Civil, Eviction, Small Claims, Probate—6th District Court, PO Box 77, Panguitch, UT 84759. 435-676-8826. Fax: 435-676-8239. 9AM-5PM (MST). Access by: Fax, mail, in person.

Grand County

Real Estate Recording—Grand County Recorder, 125 East Center St., Moab, UT 84532. 435-259-1331. Fax: 435-259-2959. 8AM-5PM (MST).

Felony, Misdemeanor, Civil, Eviction, Small Claims, Probate—7th District Court, 125 E. Center, Moab, UT 84532. 435-259-1349. Fax: 435-259-4081. 8AM-5PM (MST). Access by: Phone, mail, in person.

Iron County

Real Estate Recording—Iron County Recorder, 68 South 100 East, Parowan, UT 84761. 435-477-8350. 8:30AM-5PM (MST).

Felony, Misdemeanor, Civil, Eviction, Small Claims, Probate—5th District Court, 40 North 100 East, Cedar City, UT 84720. 435-586-7440. Fax: 435-586-4801. 8AM-5PM (MST). Access by: Mail, in person.

Juab County

Real Estate Recording—Juab County Recorder, 160 North Main, Nephi, UT 84648. 435-623-1480. 8:30AM-5PM (MST).

Felony, Misdemeanor, Civil, Eviction, Small Claims, Probate—4th District Court, 160 N. Main, PO Box 249, Nephi, UT 84648. 435-623-0901. Fax: 435-623-0922. 8AM-5PM (MST). Access by: Phone, mail, remote online, in person.

Kane County

Real Estate Recording—Kane County Recorder, 76 North Main #14, Kanab, UT 84741. 435-644-2360. 8AM-Noon, 1-5PM (MST).

Felony, Misdemeanor, Civil, Eviction, Small Claims, Probate—6th District Court, 76 North Main, Kanab, UT 84741. 435-644-2458. Fax: 435-644-2052. 8AM-5PM (MST). Access by: Phone, mail, in person.

Millard County

Real Estate Recording—Millard County Recorder, 50 South Main, Fillmore, UT 84631. 435-743-6210. Fax: 435-743-4221. 8AM-5PM (MST).

Felony, Misdemeanor, Civil, Eviction, Small Claims, Probate—4th District Court, Star Rt Box 55, Fillmore, UT 84631. 435-743-6223. Fax: 435-743-6923. 8AM-5PM (MST). Access by: Phone, mail, remote online, in person.

Morgan County

Real Estate Recording—Morgan County Recorder, 48 West Young Street, Morgan, UT 84050. 801-829-3277. Fax: 801-829-6176. 8AM-5PM (MST).

Felony, Misdemeanor, Civil, Eviction, Small Claims, Probate—2nd District Court, PO Box 886, Morgan, UT 84050. 801-829-6811. Fax: 801-829-6176. 8AM-5PM (MST). Access by: Phone, mail, remote online, in person.

Piute County

Real Estate Recording—Piute County Recorder, Courthouse, Junction, UT 84740. 435-577-2505. Fax: 435-577-2433. 9AM-5PM (MST).

Felony, Misdemeanor, Civil, Eviction, Small Claims, Probate—6th District Court, PO Box 99, Junction, UT 84740. 435-577-2840. Fax: 435-577-2433. 9AM-5PM (MST). Access by: Mail, in person.

Rich County

Real Estate Recording—Rich County Recorder, 20 South Main, Randolph, UT 84064. 435-793-2005. 9AM-Noon,1-5PM (MST).

Felony, Misdemeanor, Civil, Eviction, Small Claims, Probate—1st District Court, PO Box 218, Randolph, UT 84064. 435-793-2415. Fax: 435-793-2410. 9AM-5PM (MST). Access by: Phone, fax, mail, in person.

Salt Lake County

Real Estate Recording—Salt Lake County Recorder, 2001 South State Street, Room N-1600, Salt Lake City, UT 84190. 801-468-3391. 8AM-5PM (MST).

Felony, Misdemeanor, Civil, Eviction, Small Claims, Probate—3rd District Court, 240 East 400 South, Salt Lake City, UT 84111. 801-535-5581. Fax: 801-535-5957. 8AM-5PM (MST). Access by: Phone, mail, remote online, in person.

3rd District Court-Murray Department, 5022 S. State St, Murray, UT 84107. 801-261-0677. Fax: 801-263-8901. 8AM-5PM (MST). Access by: Mail, remote online, in person.

3rd District Court-Salt Lake City, 451 South 2nd East, Salt Lake City, UT 84111. 801-238-7480. Fax: 801-238-7396. 8AM-5PM (MST). Access by: Mail, remote online, in person.

3rd District Court-Sandy Department, 210 West 10,000 South, Sandy, UT 84070-3282. 801-565-5714. Fax: 801-565-5703. 8AM-5PM (MST). Access by: Phone, mail, remote online, in person.

3rd District Court-West Valley Department, 3636 S. Constitution Blvd, West Valley, UT 84119. 801-963-8181. Fax: 801-967-9857. 8AM-5PM (MST). Access by: Mail, remote online, in person.

San Juan County

Real Estate Recording—San Juan County Recorder, 117 South Main, Room 103, Monticello, UT 84535. 435-587-3228. Fax: 435-587-2425. 8AM-5PM (MST).

Felony, Misdemeanor, Civil, Eviction, Small Claims, Probate—7th District Court, PO Box 68, Monticello, UT 84535. 435-587-2122. Fax: 435-587-2372. 8AM-5PM (MST). Access by: Mail, in person.

Sanpete County

Real Estate Recording—Sanpete County Recorder, 160 North Main, Manti, UT 84642. 435-835-2181. Fax: 435-835-2143. 8:30AM-5PM (MST).

Felony, Misdemeanor, Civil, Eviction, Small Claims, Probate—6th District Court, 160 N. Main, Manti, UT 84642. 435-835-2131. Fax: 435-835-2135. 8:30AM-5PM (MST). Access by: Phone, mail, in person.

Sevier County

Real Estate Recording—Sevier County Recorder, 250 North Main, Richfield, UT 84701. 435-896-9262. Fax: 435-896-8888. 8:30AM-5PM (MST).

Felony, Misdemeanor, Civil, Eviction, Small Claims, Probate—6th District Court, 895 E 300 N, Richfield, UT 84701-2345. 435-896-9256. Fax: 435-896-8047. 8AM-5PM (MST). Access by: Mail, in person.

Summit County

Real Estate Recording—Summit County Recorder, 54 North Main, Coalville, UT 84017. 435-336-4451. Fax: 435-336-4450. 8AM-5PM (MST).

Felony, Misdemeanor, Civil, Eviction, Small Claims, Probate—3rd District Court, PO Box 128, Coalville, UT 84017. 435-336-4451. Fax: 435-336-4450. 8AM-5PM (MST). Access by: Mail, remote online, in person.

3rd District Court-Park City Deprtment, PO Box 1480, 455 Marsac Ave, Park City, UT 84060. 435-645-5070. 8AM-5PM (MST). Access by: Mail, remote online, in person.

Tooele County

Real Estate Recording—Tooele County Recorder, 47 South Main Street, Courthouse, Tooele, UT 84074. 435-843-3180. Fax: 435-882-7317. 8:30AM-5PM (MST).

Felony, Misdemeanor, Civil, Eviction, Small Claims, Probate—3rd District Court, 47 S. Main, Tooele, UT 84074. 435-882-9210. Fax: 435-885-8524. 8AM-5PM (MST). Access by: Fax, mail, remote online, in person.

Uintah County

Real Estate Recording—Uintah County Recorder, 147 East Main St., County Building, Vernal, UT 84078. 435-781-5461. Fax: 435-781-5319. 8AM-5PM (MST).

Felony, Misdemeanor, Civil, Eviction, Small Claims, Probate—8th District Court, PO Box 1015, Vernal, UT 84078. 435-789-7534. Fax: 435-789-0564. 8AM-5PM (MST). Access by: Mail, in person.

Utah County

Real Estate Recording—Utah County Recorder, County Administration Bldg.-Room 1300, 100 East Center, Provo, UT 84606. 801-370-8179. Fax: 801-370-8181. 8:30AM-5PM (MST).

Felony, Misdemeanor, Civil, Eviction, Small Claims, Probate—4th District Court, 125 North, 100 West, Provo, UT 84603. 801-429-1039. 8AM-5PM (MST). Access by: Mail, remote online, in person.

4th District Court-American Fork Department, 98 N Center St, American Fork, UT 84003. 801-756-9654. Fax: 801-763-0153. 8AM-5PM (MST). Access by: Mail, remote online, in person.

4th District Court-Orem Department, 97 E Center, Orem, UT 84057. 801-764-5870. Fax: 801-226-5244. 8AM-5PM (MST). Access by: Mail, remote online, in person.

4th District Court-Spanish Forks Department, 40 S Main St, Spanish Forks, UT 84660. 801-798-8674. Fax: 801-798-1377. 8AM-5PM (MST). Access by: Mail, remote online, in person.

Wasatch County

Real Estate Recording—Wasatch County Recorder, 25 North Main, Heber, UT 84032. 435-654-3211. 8AM-5PM (MST).

Felony, Misdemeanor, Civil, Eviction, Small Claims, Probate—4th District Court, PO Box 730, Heber City, UT 84032. 435-654-4676. Fax: 435-654-5281. 8AM-5PM (MST). Access by: Phone, mail, remote online, in person.

Washington County

Real Estate Recording—Washington County Recorder, 197 East Tabernacle, St. George, UT 84770. 435-634-5709. Fax: 435-634-5718. 8AM-5PM (MST).

Felony, Misdemeanor, Civil, Eviction, Small Claims, Probate—5th District Court, 220 North 200 East, St. George, UT 84770. 435-673-7225. Fax: 435-628-7870. 8AM-5PM (MST). Access by: Mail, in person.

Wayne County

Real Estate Recording—Wayne County Recorder, 88 South Main, Loa, UT 84747. 435-836-2765. Fax: 435-836-2479. 8:30AM-5PM (MST).

Felony, Misdemeanor, Civil, Eviction, Small Claims, Probate—6th District Court, PO Box 189, Loa, UT 84747.

435-836-2731. Fax: 435-836-2479. 9AM-5PM (MST). Access by: Mail, in person.

Weber County

Real Estate Recording—Weber County Recorder, 2380 Washington Blvd, Ogden, UT 84401. 801-399-8441. 8AM-5PM (MST).

Felony, Misdemeanor, Civil, Eviction, Small Claims, Probate—2nd District Court, 2549 Washington Blvd., Ogden, UT 84401. 801-399-8481. Fax: 801-399-8313. 8AM-5PM (MST). Access by: Phone, mail, remote online, in person.

2nd District Court-Roy Department, 5051 South 1900 West, Roy, UT 84067. 801-774-1060. 8AM-5PM (MST). Access by: Mail, in person.

Federal Courts

US District Court
District of Utah
Division, US District Court Clerk's Office, Room 150, 350 S Main St, Salt Lake City, UT 84101. 801-524-6100. Counties: All counties in Utah. Although all cases are heard here, the district is divided into Northern and Central Divisions. The Northern Division includes the counties of Box Elder, Cache, Rich, Davis, Morgan and Weber, and the Central Division includes all other counties

US Bankruptcy Court
District of Utah
Division, US Bankruptcy Court, Clerk of Court, Frank E Moss Courthouse, 350 S Main St, Room 301, Salt Lake City, UT 84101. 801-524-5157. Voice Case Information System: 801-524-3107. Counties: All counties in Utah. Although all cases are handled here, the court divides itself into two divisions. The Northern Division includes the counties of Box Elder, Cache, Rich, Davis, Morgan and Weber, and the Central Division includes the remaining counties

Vermont

Capitol: Montpelier (Washington County)	
Number of Counties: 14	**Population:** 584,771
County Court Locations:	**Federal Court Locations:**
•Superior Courts: 11/ 14 Counties	•District Courts: 2
•District Courts: 11/4 Circuits	•Bankruptcy Courts: 1
•Combined Courts: 3	**State Agencies:** 18
Probate Courts: 18	
Family Courts: 14/14 Counties	
•Environmental Court: 1	

State Agencies—Summary

General Help Numbers:

State Archives

Secretary of State	802-828-2308
State Papers Archives Division	Fax: 802-828-2496
109 State St	7:45AM-4:30PM
Montpelier, VT 05609-1103	
Reference Librarian:	802-828-2369
Historical Society:	802-828-2291

Governor's Office

Governor's Office	802-828-3333
Pavillion Office Bldg	Fax: 802-828-3339
5th Floor, 109 State St	7:45AM-4:30PM
Montpelier, VT 05609	

Attorney General's Office

Attorney General's Office	802-828-3171
109 State St	Fax: 802-828-2154
Montpelier, VT 05609-1001	7:45AM-4:30PM

State Legislation

Vermont General Assembly	802-828-2231
State House-Legislative Council	Fax: 802-828-2424
PO Drawer 33	8AM-4:30PM
Montpelier, VT 05633	

Important State Internet Sites:

> 🏠 **Webscape**
> **File   Edit   View**   **Help**

State of Vermont World Wide Web

www.state.vt.us/

Provides links to such sites as education, State and Federal Government, tourism, state agencies, the court system, libraries, and includes a search engine.

Vermont Legislature

www.leg.state.vt.us/

This site links to information about the members of the legislature, the bill tracking system, bills, acts and resolutions and the Vermont Constitution and Statutes.

Bill Tracking System

www.leg.state.vt.us/database/database.htm

This site links to legislation back to the 1987-88 session. You can search bills by sponsor or keyword.

Uniform Commercial Code

www.sec.state.vt.us/seek/UCC_SEEK.HTM

UCC searches are available online from this site.

Unclaimed Property

www.state.vt.us/treasurer/abanprop.htm

This is the site for unclaimed/abandoned property. You can download a searchable file, or search by name, online. The information is also available in printed form or on a disk.

State Agencies—Public Records

Criminal Records
State Repository, Vermont Criminal Information Center, 103 S. Main St., Waterbury, VT 05671-2101, Main Telephone: 802-244-8727, Fax: 802-244-1106, Hours: 8AM-4:30PM.
Restricted access.

Corporation Records
Secretary of State, Corporation Division, 109 State St, Montpelier, VT 05609-1104, Main Telephone: 802-828-2386, Fax: 802-828-2853, Hours: 7:45AM-4:30PM. Access by: mail, phone, visit, PC.

Uniform Commercial Code
Federal Tax Liens
State Tax Liens
UCC Division, Secretary of State, 109 State St, Montpelier, VT 05609-1104, Main Telephone: 802-828-2386, Fax: 802-828-2853, Hours: 7:45AM-4:30PM. Access by: mail, visit, PC.

Sales Tax Registrations
Administrative Agency/Tax Department, Business Tax Division, 109 State St, Montpelier, VT 05609-1401, Main Telephone: 802-828-2551, Fax: 802-828-2428, Hours: 7:45AM-4:30PM.
Access by: mail, phone.

Birth Certificates
Vermont Department of Health, Vital Records Section, PO Box 70, Burlington, VT 05402, Main Telephone: 802-863-7275, Hours: 8AM-4:15PM. Access by: mail, visit.

Death Records
Vermont Department of Health, Vital Records Section, PO Box 70, Burlington, VT 05402, Main Telephone: 802-863-7275, Hours: 8AM-4:15PM. Access by: mail, visit.

Marriage Certificates
Vermont Department of Health, Vital Records Section, PO Box 70, Burlington, VT 05402, Main Telephone: 802-863-7275, Hours: 8AM-4:15PM. Access by: mail, visit.

Divorce Records
Vermont Department of Health, Vital Records Section, PO Box 70, Burlington, VT 05402, Main Telephone: 802-863-7275, Hours: 8AM-4:15PM. Access by: mail, visit.

Workers' Compensation Records
Labor and Industry, Workers Compensation Division, Drawer 20, Montpelier, VT 05620-3401, Main Telephone: 802-828-2286, Fax: 802-828-2195, Hours: 7:45AM-4:30PM. Access by: mail, phone, visit.

Driver Records
Driver License Information
Department of Motor Vehicles, Driver Improvement Information, 120 State St, Montpelier, VT 05603, Main Telephone: 802-828-2050, Fax: 802-828-2098, Hours: 7:45AM-4:30PM. Access by: mail, visit, PC. This office is closed on Wed. mornings. Ticket information is available from the Vermont Traffic and Municipal Ordinance Bureau, PO Box 607, White River Junction, VT 05001, 802-295-8869. There is no charge, but no information is given over the phone.

Vehicle Ownership
Vehicle Identification
Department of Motor Vehicles, Registration & License Information/Records, 120 State St, Montpelier, VT 05603, Main Telephone: 802-828-2000, Hours: 7:45AM-4:30PM. Access by: mail, visit.

Accident Reports
Department of Motor Vehicles, Accident Report Section, 120 State St, Montpelier, VT 05603, Main Telephone: 802-828-2050, Hours: 7:45AM-4PM. Access by: mail only. The office is closed Wednesday mornings.

Hunting License Information
Fishing License Information
Records not available from state agency.

County Courts and Recording Offices

What You Need to Know...

About the Courts

Administration

Court Administrator	802-828-3278
Administrative Office of Courts	Fax: 802-828-3278
109 State St	8AM-4:30PM
Montpelier, VT 05609-0701	

Court Structure

Bennington District Court has a diversion program in which 1st offenders go through a program which includes a letter of apology, community service, etc. and, after 2 years, the record is expunged. These records are **never** released.

There is one Probate Court per county except in the five southern counties (Bennington, Orange, Rutland, Windsor, and Wyndham), each of which has two.

The Family Courts were established in 1991.

Online Access

There is no online computer access, internal or external, but is planned for the near future.

About the Recorder's Office

Organization

14 counties and 246 towns/cities, 246 filing offices. The recording officer is Town/City Clerk. **There is no county administration in Vermont.** Many towns are so small that their mailing addresses are in different towns. Four towns/cities have the same name as counties—Barre, Newport, Rutland, and St. Albans. The entire state is in the Eastern Time Zone (EST).

UCC Records

This has been a **dual filing state** until December 31, 1994. As of January 1, 1995, only consumer goods and real estate related collateral are filed with Town/City Clerks. Most filing offices will perform UCC searches. Use search request form UCC-11. Search fees are usually $10.00 per name, and copy fees vary.

Lien Records

All federal and state tax liens on personal property and on real property are filed with the Town/City Clerk in the lien/attachment book and indexed in real estate records. Most towns/cities will **not** perform tax lien searches. Other liens include mechanics, local tax, judgments, and foreclosure.

Real Estate Records

Most towns/cities will **not** perform real estate searches. Copy fees and certification fees vary. Certified copies are generally very expensive at $6.00 per page total. Deed copies usually cost $2.00 flat.

County Courts and Recording Offices

Addison County

Real Estate Recording—There is no real estate recording at the county level in Vermont. Determine the town or city in which the property is located.

Civil, Eviction—Superior Court, 7 Mahady Ct, Middlebury, VT 05753. 802-388-7741. 8:30AM-4:30PM (EST). Access by: Mail, in person.

Felony, Misdemeanor, Small Claims—District Court, 7 Mahady Ct, Middlebury, VT 05753. 802-388-4237. 8AM-4:30PM (EST). Access by: Phone, in person.

Probate—Probate Court, 7 Mahady Court, Middlebury, VT 05753. 802-388-2612. 8AM-4:30PM (EST).

Addison Town

Real Estate Recording—Addison Town Clerk, RD 1, Route 17 West, Addison, VT 05491. 802-759-2020. Fax: 802-759-2233. 8:30AM-4:30PM (EST).

Albany Town

Real Estate Recording—Albany Town Clerk, Rt 14, Albany, VT 05820. 802-755-6100. 9AM-4PM T,Th; 9AM-7PM W (EST).

Alburg Town

Real Estate Recording—Alburg Town Clerk, Main Street, Alburg, VT 05440. 802-796-3468. Fax: 802-796-3939. 9AM-Noon,1-5PM (EST).

Andover Town

Real Estate Recording—Andover Town Clerk, Route 1, Box 179, Weston-Andover Rd., Andover, VT 05143. 802-875-2765. Fax: 802-875-2765. 9AM-1PM (EST).

Arlington Town

Real Estate Recording—Arlington Town Clerk, Main Street, Town Hall, Arlington, VT 05250. 802-375-2332. Fax: 802-375-6474. 9AM-2PM (EST).

Athens Town

Real Estate Recording—Athens Town Clerk, RD 3, Box 214, Athens, VT 05143. 802-869-3370. By Appointment (EST).

Bakersfield Town

Real Estate Recording—Bakersfield Town Clerk, Town Road 3, Bakersfield, VT 05441. 802-827-4495. 9AM-Noon (EST).

Baltimore Town

Real Estate Recording—Baltimore Town Clerk, RD 4, Box 365, Baltimore, VT 05143. 802-263-5419. By Appointmment Evenings M-F; 10AM-Noon Sat (EST).

Barnard Town

Real Estate Recording—Barnard Town Clerk, North Rd., Barnard, VT 05031. 802-234-9211. 8AM-3:30PM M,T,Th (EST).

Barnet Town

Real Estate Recording—Barnet Town Clerk, US Route 5, Main Street, Barnet, VT 05821. 802-633-2256. Fax: 802-633-2256. 9AM-Noon, 1-4:30PM (EST).

Barre City

Real Estate Recording—Barre City Clerk, 12 North Main Street, Barre, VT 05641. 802-476-0242. Fax: 802-476-0264. 8:30AM-5PM (EST).

Barre Town

Real Estate Recording—Barre Town Clerk, Municipal Building, 149 Websterville Road, Websterville, VT 05678. 802-479-9391. Fax: 802-479-9332. 8AM-Noon, 1-4:30PM (EST).

Barton Town

Real Estate Recording—Barton Town Clerk, Main Street, Howard Bank Building, Barton, VT 05822. 802-525-6222. 8:30AM-5PM (EST).

Belvidere Town

Real Estate Recording—Belvidere Town Clerk, RR 1, Box 1062, Belvidere Center, VT 05492. 802-644-2498. (EST).

Bennington County

Real Estate Recording—There is no real estate recording at the county level in Vermont. Determine the town or city in which the property is located.

Civil, Eviction—Superior Court, 207 South St, Bennington, VT 05201. 802-447-2700. Fax: 802-447-2703. 8AM-4:30PM (EST). Access by: Phone, mail, in person.

Felony, Misdemeanor, Small Claims—District Court, 1 Veterans Memorial Dr, Bennington, VT 05201. 802-447-2727. Fax: 802-447-2750. 7:45AM-4:30PM (EST). Access by: Phone, mail, in person.

Probate—Probate Court-Bennington District, 207 South St, PO Box 65, Bennington, VT 05201. 802-447-2705. Fax: 802-447-2703. 9AM-Noon, 1:30-4PM (EST). Access by: Mail, in person.

Probate Court-Manchester District, PO Box 446, Manchester, VT 05254. 802-362-1410. 8AM-Noon, 1-4:20PM (EST). Access by: Mail, in person.

Bennington Town

Real Estate Recording—Bennington Town Clerk, 205 South Street, Bennington, VT 05201. 802-442-1043. Fax: 802-442-1068. 8AM-5PM (EST).

Benson Town

Real Estate Recording—Benson Town Clerk, Stage Street, Benson, VT 05731. 802-537-2611. 9AM-4:30PM M-W & F (EST).

Berkshire Town

Real Estate Recording—Berkshire Town Clerk, RFD 1, Box 2560, Enosburg Falls, VT 05450. 802-933-2335. 9AM-Noon, 1-4PM M,T,Th,F; 9AM-Noon W (EST).

Berlin Town

Real Estate Recording—Berlin Town Clerk, Shed Road, Berlin Municipal Building, Berlin, VT 05602. 802-229-9298. 8:30AM-Noon,1-4:30PM (July-August 8:30AM-Noon, 1-3:30PM) (EST).

Bethel Town

Real Estate Recording—Bethel Town Clerk, South Main Street, Town Office, Bethel, VT 05032. 802-234-9722. Fax: 802-234-6840. 8AM-Noon T,F; 8AM-12:30, 1-4PM M,Th (EST).

Bloomfield Town

Real Estate Recording—Bloomfield Town Clerk, RFD 1 Box 900 Rte 102, Guildhall, VT 05905. 802-962-5191. Fax: 802-962-5548. 9AM-3PM T or by appointment (EST).

Bolton Town

Real Estate Recording—Bolton Town Clerk, Route 2 Town Hall, Bolton, VT 05676. 802-434-3064. Fax: 802-434-6404. 7AM-3PM M-Th; 7AM-Noon F (EST).

Bradford Town

Real Estate Recording—Bradford Town Clerk, Main Street, Bradford, VT 05033. 802-222-4727. Fax: 802-222-4728. 8:30AM-4:30PM (EST).

Braintree Town

Real Estate Recording—Braintree Town Clerk, Route 12A, Braintree, VT 05060. 802-728-9787. T 9AM-12AM, 1:30PM-4:30; W 1:30PM-4:30PM; Th 9AM-12, 1:30PM-4:30PM (EST).

Brandon Town

Real Estate Recording—Brandon Town Clerk, 49 Center Street, Brandon, VT 05733. 802-247-5721. Fax: 802-247-5481. 8:30AM-4PM (EST).

Brattleboro Town

Real Estate Recording—Brattleboro Town Clerk, 230 Main Street, Brattleboro, VT 05301. 802-254-4541. Fax: 802-257-2322. 8:30AM-5PM (EST).

Bridgewater Town

Real Estate Recording—Bridgewater Town Clerk, Route 4, Clerk's Office, Bridgewater, VT 05034. 802-672-3334. Fax: 802-672-3833. 8:30AM-1:30PM (EST).

Bridport Town

Real Estate Recording—Bridport Town Clerk, Town Hall, Bridport, VT 05734. 802-758-2483. 8AM-4PM M-W,F; 8AM-Noon Th; Treasurer 9AM-4PM F (EST).

Brighton Town

Real Estate Recording—Brighton Town Clerk, Main Street, Town Hall, Island Pond, VT 05846. 802-723-4405. Fax: 802-723-4405. 8AM-3:30PM M,T,W,F; 8AM-6PM Th (EST).

Bristol Town

Real Estate Recording—Bristol Town Clerk, 1 South Street, Bristol, VT 05443. 802-843-3180. Fax: 802-843-3127. 8:30AM-4PM (EST).

Brookfield Town

Real Estate Recording—Brookfield Town Clerk, Ralph Rd., Brookfield, VT 05036. 802-276-3352. Fax: 802-276-3926. 9AM-4PM M,T,F (EST).

Brookline Town

Real Estate Recording—Brookline Town Clerk, PO Box 403, Brookline, VT 05345. 802-365-4648. 9AM-Noon Th (EST).

Brownington Town

Real Estate Recording—Brownington Town Clerk, RFD 2, Box 158, Orleans, VT 05860. 802-754-8401. 1PM-3:30PM W; 9AM-Noon Th (EST).

Brunswick Town

Real Estate Recording—Brunswick Town Clerk, Route 102, RFD 1, Box 470, Guildhall, VT 05905. 802-962-5283. M-Sat by appointment (EST).

Burke Town

Real Estate Recording—Burke Town Clerk, Town Office, School St., West Burke, VT 05871. 802-467-3717. Fax: 802-467-8623. 8AM-5PM M; 8AM-4PM T-F (EST).

Burlington City

Real Estate Recording—Burlington City Clerk, City Hall, Room 20, 149 Church St., Burlington, VT 05401. 815-865-7133. Fax: 802-865-7024. 8AM-7:30PM M; 8AM-4:30PM T-F (EST).

Cabot Town

Real Estate Recording—Cabot Town Clerk, Main Street, Town Hall, Cabot, VT 05647. 802-563-2279. M 9-6; Tu 9-5; W 12-5; Th 9-5; F 9-1 (EST).

Calais Town

Real Estate Recording—Calais Town Clerk, RR 1, Box 35, West County Rd., Calais, VT 05648. 802-223-5952. 8AM-5PM M,T,Th; 8AM-Noon Sat (EST).

Caledonia County

Real Estate Recording—There is no real estate recording at the county level in Vermont. Determine the town or city in which the property is located.

Civil, Eviction—Superior Court, Box 4129, St Johnsbury, VT 05819. 802-748-6600. Fax: 802-748-6603. 8AM-4:30PM (EST). Access by: Phone, mail, in person.

Felony, Misdemeanor, Small Claims—District Court, 27 Main St, St Johnsbury, VT 05819. 802-748-6610. Fax: 802-748-6603. 8AM-4:30PM (EST). Access by: Fax, mail, in person.

Probate—Probate Court, 27 Main St, PO Box 406, St Johnsbury, VT 05819. 802-748-6605. Fax: 802-748-6603. 8AM-4:30PM (EST). Access by: Mail, in person.

Cambridge Town

Real Estate Recording—Cambridge Town Clerk, Clerk's Office, Jeffersonville, VT 05464. 802-644-2251. 8AM-Noon,1-4PM (EST).

Canaan Town

Real Estate Recording—Canaan Town Clerk, Route 253, Town Hall, Canaan, VT 05903. 802-266-3370. Fax: 802-266-7085. 9AM-3PM (EST).

Castleton Town

Real Estate Recording—Castleton Town Clerk, Main Street, Town Hall, Castleton, VT 05735. 802-468-2212. Fax: 802-468-5482. 8:30AM-Noon, 1-4PM (EST).

Cavendish Town

Real Estate Recording—Cavendish Town Clerk, High Street, Town Hall, Cavendish, VT 05142. 802-226-7292. Fax: 802-226-7291. 9AM-Noon, 1-4:30PM (EST).

Charleston Town

Real Estate Recording—Charleston Town Clerk, Route 105, Town Hall, West Charleston, VT 05872. 802-895-2814. 8AM-3PM M,T,Th,F (EST).

Charlotte Town

Real Estate Recording—Charlotte Town Clerk, 159 Ferry Road, Charlotte, VT 05445. 802-425-3071. Fax: 802-425-4241. 8AM-4PM (EST).

Chelsea Town

Real Estate Recording—Chelsea Town Clerk, Main Street, Town Hall, Chelsea, VT 05038. 802-685-4460. 8AM-Noon, 1-4PM (EST).

Chester Town

Real Estate Recording—Chester Town Clerk, Town Hall, 556 Elm St., Chester, VT 05143. 802-875-2173. Fax: 802-875-2237. 8AM-5PM (EST).

Chittenden

Real Estate Recording—There is no real estate recording at the county level in Vermont. Determine the proper town/city in which to record based upon property location.

Chittenden County

Civil, Eviction—Superior Court, 175 Main St.(PO Box 187), Burlington, VT 05402. 802-863-3467. 8AM-4:30PM (EST). Access by: Phone, mail, in person.

Felony, Misdemeanor, Small Claims—District Court, 32 Cherry St #300, Burlington, VT 05401. 802-651-1800. 8AM-4:30PM (EST). Access by: Mail, in person.

Probate—Probate Court, PO Box 511, Burlington, VT 05402. 802-651-1518. 8AM-4:30PM (EST). Access by: Mail, in person.

Chittenden Town

Real Estate Recording—Chittenden Town Clerk, Holden Road, Town Hall, Chittenden, VT 05737. 802-483-6647. 10AM-2PM (EST).

Clarendon Town

Real Estate Recording—Clarendon Town Clerk, Middle Road, North Clarendon, VT 05759. 802-775-4274. Fax: 802-775-4274. 10AM-4PM M,T; 10AM-3PM W,F (EST).

Colchester Town

Real Estate Recording—Colchester Town Clerk, 172 Blakely Road, Colchester, VT 05446. 802-654-0812. Fax: 802-654-0757. 8AM-4PM (EST).

Concord Town

Real Estate Recording—Concord Town Clerk, Main St., Concord, VT 05824. 802-695-2220. 9AM-Noon,1-4PM (Closed Th); 1-7PM 1st & 3rd M (EST).

Corinth Town

Real Estate Recording—Corinth Town Clerk, Cookeville Road, Town Hall, Corinth, VT 05039. 802-439-5850. 8:30AM-Noon, 1-4PM M,T,Th,F (EST).

Cornwall Town

Real Estate Recording—Cornwall Town Clerk, Town Hall, Jct. Rts 30 & 74, Town of Cornwall, Middlebury, VT 05753. 802-462-2775. Fax: 802-462-2606. 12:30PM-4:30PM T,W,Th,F (EST).

Coventry Town

Real Estate Recording—Coventry Town Clerk, Coventry Community Center, Coventry, VT 05825. 802-754-2288. 9:30AM-4PM M,Th (EST).

Craftsbury Town

Real Estate Recording—Craftsbury Town Clerk, Main Street, Town Hall, Craftsbury, VT 05826. 802-586-2823. Fax: 802-586-2823. 8:30AM-4PM T-F (EST).

Danby Town

Real Estate Recording—Danby Town Clerk, Brook Road, Danby, VT 05739. 802-293-5136. 9AM-Noon, 1-4PM (Closed F) (EST).

Danville Town

Real Estate Recording—Danville Town Clerk, Main Street, Town Hall, Danville, VT 05828. 802-684-3352. Fax: 802-684-9606. 8AM-4:30PM (EST).

Derby Town

Real Estate Recording—Derby Town Clerk, Main Street, Town Hall, Derby, VT 05829. 802-766-4906. 8AM-4PM (EST).

Dorset Town

Real Estate Recording—Dorset Town Clerk, Mad Tom Road, Town Hall, East Dorset, VT 05253. 802-362-1178. Fax: 802-362-5156. 9AM-2PM (& by appointment) (EST).

Dover Town

Real Estate Recording—Dover Town Clerk, Route 100 North, Town Clerk's Office, Dover, VT 05356. 802-464-5100. Fax: 802-464-8721. 9AM-5PM (EST).

Dummerston Town

Real Estate Recording—Dummerston Town Clerk, Middle Road, Town Hall, Dummerston, VT 05346. 802-257-1496. Fax: 802-257-4671. 9AM-3PM M,T,Th,F; 11AM-5PM W (EST).

Duxbury Town

Real Estate Recording—Duxbury Town Clerk, Route 100 Crossett Hill, Waterbury, VT 05676. 802-244-6660. 8AM-5PM M-Th (EST).

East Haven Town

Real Estate Recording—East Haven Town Clerk, 19 Maple St., East Haven, VT 05837. 802-467-3772. 4-7PM T; 8AM-Noon Th (EST).

East Montpelier Town

Real Estate Recording—East Montpelier Town Clerk, Kelton Road, Town Municipal Building, East Montpelier, VT 05651. 802-223-3313. 9AM-5PM M-Th; 9AM-Noon F (EST).

Eden Town

Real Estate Recording—Eden Town Clerk, Route 100, Town Office Building, Eden Mills, VT 05653. 802-635-2528. Fax: 802-635-2528. 8AM-4PM M-Th (EST).

Elmore Town

Real Estate Recording—Elmore Town Clerk, Town Hall, Towm Clerk's Office, Lake Elmore, VT 05657. 802-888-2637. 9AM-3PM T,W,Th (EST).

Enosburg Town

Real Estate Recording—Enosburg Town Clerk, 95 Main Street, Enosburg Falls, VT 05450. 802-933-4421. 9AM-Noon,1-4PM (EST).

Essex County

Real Estate Recording—There is no real estate recording at the county level in Vermont. Determine the proper town/city in which to record based on property location.

Felony, Misdemeanor, Civil, Eviction, Small Claims—District and Superior Court, Box 75, Guildhall, VT 05905. 802-676-3910. Fax: 802-676-3463. 8AM-4:30PM (EST). Access by: Phone, mail, in person.

Probate—Probate Court, PO Box 426, Island Pond, VT 05846. 802-723-4770. 8:30AM-Noon, 1-3:30PM (EST).

Essex Town

Real Estate Recording—Essex Town Clerk, 81 Main Street, Essex Junction, VT 05452. 802-879-0413. Fax: 802-878-1353. 8AM-4:30PM (EST).

Fair Haven Town

Real Estate Recording—Fair Haven Town Clerk, 3 North Park Place, Fair Haven, VT 05743. 802-265-3610. Fax: 802-265-2158. 8AM-Noon, 1PM-4PM (EST).

Fairfax Town

Real Estate Recording—Fairfax Town Clerk, Town Office, 67 Hunt St., Fairfax, VT 05454. 802-849-6111. 9AM-4PM (EST).

Fairfield Town

Real Estate Recording—Fairfield Town Clerk, Town Hall, Fairfield, VT 05455. 802-827-3261. 10AM-2PM (EST).

Fairlee Town

Real Estate Recording—Fairlee Town Clerk, Main Street, Fairlee, VT 05045. 802-333-4363. Fax: 802-333-4363. 9AM-2PM M,T,Th,F; 1PM-6PM W (EST).

Fayston Town

Real Estate Recording—Fayston Town Clerk, North Fayston Road, Town Hall, Moretown, VT 05660. 802-496-2454. 9AM-4PM M,T,Th; 1-5PM W; 9AM-1PM F (EST).

Ferrisburgh Town

Real Estate Recording—Ferrisburgh Town Clerk, Route 7, Town Hall, Ferrisburgh, VT 05456. 802-877-3429. Fax: 802-877-3429. 8AM-4PM (EST).

Fletcher Town

Real Estate Recording—Fletcher Town Clerk, Town Hall, Fletcher, VT 05444. 802-849-6616. 9AM-3:30PM M,T,Th,F; 9AM-Noon W (EST).

Franklin County

Real Estate Recording—There is no real estate recording at the county level in Vermont. Determine the proper town/city in which to record based on property location.

Civil, Eviction—Superior Court, Box 808 Church St, St Albans, VT 05478. 802-524-3863. Fax: 802-524-7996. 8AM-4:30PM (EST). Access by: Phone, mail, in person.

Felony, Misdemeanor, Small Claims—District Court, 36 Lake St, St Albans, VT 05478. 802-524-7997. Fax: 802-524-7946. 8AM-4:30PM (EST). Access by: Phone, fax, mail, in person.

Probate—Franklin Probate Court, 17 Church St, St Albans, VT 05478. 802-524-4112. 8AM-Noon, 1-4:30PM (EST). Access by: In person only.

Franklin Town

Real Estate Recording—Franklin Town Clerk, Haston Library, Franklin, VT 05457. 802-285-2101. 9AM-4PM M,T,F; 9AM-7PM Th; 9AM-Noon W (EST).

Georgia Town

Real Estate Recording—Georgia Town Clerk, Route 7, Town Hall, St. Albans, VT 05478. 802-524-3524. Fax: 802-524-9794. 11AM-5PM, 7-9PM M; 8AM-4PMT,Th,F; Closed to public Wed (EST).

Glover Town

Real Estate Recording—Glover Town Clerk, Municipal Building, Glover, VT 05839. 802-525-6227. 8AM-4PM (EST).

Goshen Town

Real Estate Recording—Goshen Town Clerk, RR 3, Box 3384, Goshen, VT 05733. 802-247-6455. 12:30-2:30PM T & Th (EST).

Grafton Town

Real Estate Recording—Grafton Town Clerk, Main Street, Grafton, VT 05146. 802-843-2419. 9AM-12, 1PM-5PM M,T,Th,F (EST).

Granby Town

Real Estate Recording—Granby Town Clerk, Granby Road, Granby, VT 05840. 802-328-3611. Fax: 802-328-3611. By appointment (EST).

Grand Isle County

Real Estate Recording—There is no real estate recording at the county level in Vermont. Determine the proper town/city in which to record based on property location.

Felony, Misdemeanor, Civil, Eviction, Small Claims—District and Superior Court, PO Box 7, North Hero, VT 05474. 802-372-8350. Fax: 802-372-3221. 8AM-4:30PM (EST). Access by: Phone, mail, in person.

Probate—Probate Court, PO Box 7, North Hero, VT 05474. 802-372-8350. Fax: 802-372-3221. 8AM-4:30PM (EST). Access by: Mail, in person.

Grand Isle Town

Real Estate Recording—Grand Isle Town Clerk, 9 Hyde Road, Grand Isle, VT 05458. 802-372-8830. Fax: 802-372-8815. 8:30AM-Noon, 1-4:30PM (EST).

Granville Town

Real Estate Recording—Granville Town Clerk, Route 100, Granville, VT 05747. 802-767-4403. 9AM-3PM M-Th (Closed F) (EST).

Greensboro Town

Real Estate Recording—Greensboro Town Clerk, Town Hall, Greensboro, VT 05841. 802-533-2911. M 8AM-Noon; T-F 8AM-Noon,1-4PM (EST).

Groton Town

Real Estate Recording—Groton Town Clerk, Route 302, 314 Scott Highway, Groton, VT 05046. 802-584-3276. Fax: 802-584-3276. 8AM-Noon, 1-3:30PM M-Th; 8AM-Noon, 1-3PM F (EST).

Guildhall Town

Real Estate Recording—Guildhall Town Clerk, Route 102, Guildhall, VT 05905. 802-676-3797. Fax: 802-676-3518. 1-3PM T,Th (EST).

Guilford Town

Real Estate Recording—Guilford Town Clerk, RR 3, Box 255, School Rd., Guilford, VT 05301. 802-254-6857. Fax: 802-257-5764. 9AM-4PM M,T,Th,F; 9AM-Noon, 6:30PM-8:30PM W (EST).

Halifax Town

Real Estate Recording—Halifax Town Clerk, Branch Brook Rd., West Halifax, VT 05358. 802-368-7390. 9AM-4PM M,T,F; 9AM-Noon Sat (EST).

Hancock Town

Real Estate Recording—Hancock Town Clerk, Rt 125, Hancock, VT 05748. 802-767-3660. 8:30AM-3:30PM M,W,Th; 11AM-5PM F (EST).

Hardwick Town

Real Estate Recording—Hardwick Town Clerk, 2 Church Street, Hardwick, VT 05843. 802-472-5971. Fax: 802-472-6865. 9AM-4PM T-F (EST).

Hartford Town

Real Estate Recording—Hartford Town Clerk, 15 Bridge Street, White River Junction, VT 05001. 802-295-2785. 9AM-Noon, 1-4PM (EST).

Hartland Town

Real Estate Recording—Hartland Town Clerk, Damon Hall, Hartland, VT 05048. 802-436-2444. Fax: 802-436-2444. 9AM-4PM (EST).

Highgate Town

Real Estate Recording—Highgate Town Clerk, Municipal Building, Route 78, Highgate Center, VT 05459. 802-868-4697. 8:30AM-12, 1PM-4:30PM (EST).

Hinesburg Town

Real Estate Recording—Hinesburg Town Clerk, Main Street, Town Hall, Hinesburg, VT 05461. 802-482-2281. Fax: 802-482-2096. Noon-8PM M; 8AM-5PM T-F (EST).

Holland Town

Real Estate Recording—Holland Town Clerk, RFD 1, Box 37, Derby Line, Holland, VT 05830. 802-895-4440. Fax: 802-895-4440. 9AM-2PM M,T,Th,F (EST).

Hubbardton Town

Real Estate Recording—Hubbardton Town Clerk, RR 1, Box 2828, Fair Haven, VT 05743. 802-273-2951. 9AM-2PM M,W,F (EST).

Huntington Town

Real Estate Recording—Huntington Town Clerk, 4930 Main Rd., Huntington, VT 05462. 802-434-2032. 9AM-4PM M,T,W,Th; 8:30AM-2PM F (EST).

Hyde Park Town

Real Estate Recording—Hyde Park Town Clerk, Route 15, Hyde Park Town Clerk's Office, Hyde Park, VT 05655. 802-888-2300. Fax: 802-888-2113. 8AM-4PM (EST).

Ira Town

Real Estate Recording—Ira Town Clerk, RFD 1, Box 3420, West Rutland, VT 05777. 802-235-2745. By Appointment (EST).

Irasburg Town

Real Estate Recording—Irasburg Town Clerk, Route 58, Irasburg, VT 05845. 802-754-2242. 9AM-4PM M,T,Th (EST).

Isle La Motte Town

Real Estate Recording—Isle La Motte Town Clerk, Rt 129, Town Hall, Isle La Motte, VT 05463. 802-928-3434. Fax: 802-928-3002. 9AM-3PM T,Th; 9AM-Noon Sat (EST).

Jamaica Town

Real Estate Recording—Jamaica Town Clerk, White Building behind J.A.Muzzy, in center of Jamaica Village,

Jamaica, VT 05343. 802-874-4681. 9AM-Noon, 1-4PM T,W,Th,F (EST).

Jay Town

Real Estate Recording—Jay Town Clerk, RFD 2, Box 136, Jay, VT 05859. 802-988-2996. 7AM-4PM (Closed M) (EST).

Jericho Town

Real Estate Recording—Jericho Town Clerk, Route 15, Jericho, VT 05465. 802-899-4936. Fax: 802-899-4786. 8AM-5PM M-Th; 8AM-3PM F (EST).

Johnson Town

Real Estate Recording—Johnson Town Clerk, Pearl Street, Johnson, VT 05656. 802-635-2611. Fax: 802-635-9523. 7:30AM-4PM (EST).

Kirby Town

Real Estate Recording—Kirby Town Clerk, Town of Kirby, TH#29-Kirby, Lyndonville, VT 05851. 802-626-9386. Fax: 802-626-9386. 8AM-3PM T,Th (EST).

Lamoille County

Real Estate Recording—There is no real estate recording at the county level in Vermont. Determine the proper town/city in which to record based on property location.

Civil, Eviction—Superior Court, Box 490, Hyde Park, VT 05655. 802-888-2207. 8AM-4:30PM (EST). Access by: Mail, in person.

Felony, Misdemeanor, Small Claims—District Court, PO Box 489, Hyde Park, VT 05655-0489. 802-888-3887. Fax: 802-888-2531. 8AM-4:30PM (EST). Access by: Fax, mail, in person.

Probate—Probate Court, PO Box 102, Hyde Park, VT 05655-0102. 802-888-3306. Fax: 802-888-2531. 8AM-Noon, 1-4:30PM (EST). Access by: Mail, in person.

Landgrove Town

Real Estate Recording—Landgrove Town Clerk, Casey Henson, Red Pine Dr.-End of Landgrove Hollow Rd, Landgrove, VT 05148. 802-824-3716. Fax: 802-824-3716. 9AM-Noon Th (EST).

Leicester Town

Real Estate Recording—Leicester Town Clerk, RR 2, Box 2117-1, Brandon, VT 05733. 802-247-5961. 1-4PM M-W; 9AM-1PM Th,F (EST).

Lemington Town

Real Estate Recording—Lemington Town Clerk, RR 1, Box 183, Canaan, VT 05903. 802-277-4814. Noon-3PM W (EST).

Lincoln Town

Real Estate Recording—Lincoln Town Clerk, RD 1, Box 1830, Bristol, VT 05443. 802-453-2980. Fax: 802-453-2980. 9AM-4PM M,T,Th,F; 10AM-Noon Sat (EST).

Londonderry Town

Real Estate Recording—Londonderry Town Clerk, Old School St., South Londonderry, VT 05155. 802-824-3356. 9AM-3PM T-F; 9AM-12 Sat (EST).

Lowell Town

Real Estate Recording—Lowell Town Clerk, 58 West, Lowell, VT 05847. 802-744-6559. 9AM-2:30PM M & Th (EST).

Ludlow Town

Real Estate Recording—Ludlow Town Clerk, 37 Depot Street, Ludlow, VT 05149. 802-228-3232. Fax: 802-228-2813. 8:30AM-4:30PM (EST).

Lunenburg Town

Real Estate Recording—Lunenburg Town Clerk, Box 54 Main St., Lunenburg, VT 05906. 802-892-5959. 8:30AM-Noon, 1PM-4PM (EST).

Lyndon Town

Real Estate Recording—Lyndon Town Clerk, 20 Park Avenue, Lyndonville, VT 05851. 802-626-5785. Fax: 802-626-1265. 7:30AM-4:30PM (EST).

Maidstone Town

Real Estate Recording—Maidstone Town Clerk, RR 1 Box 67, Susan Irwin, Guildhall, VT 05905. 802-676-3210. 9-11AM M & Th (EST).

Manchester Town

Real Estate Recording—Manchester Town Clerk, Route 7A North, Manchester Center, VT 05255. 802-362-1315. Fax: 802-362-1314. 8:30AM-4:30PM M-Th; 8:30AM-6PM F (EST).

Marlboro Town

Real Estate Recording—Marlboro Town Clerk, Town Office, Marlboro, VT 05344. 802-254-2181. 9AM-2PM M,W,Th (EST).

Marshfield Town

Real Estate Recording—Marshfield Town Clerk, Depot Street, Marshfield, VT 05658. 802-426-3305. Fax: 802-426-3305. 8:30AM-Noon, 12:30-4:30PM T-F (EST).

Mendon Town

Real Estate Recording—Mendon Town Clerk, 34 US Route 4, Mendon, VT 05701. 802-775-1662. 9AM-3PM (EST).

Middlebury Town

Real Estate Recording—Middlebury Town Clerk, Municipal Building, 94 Main St., Middlebury, VT 05753. 802-388-4041. 8:30AM-5PM (EST).

Middlesex Town

Real Estate Recording—Middlesex Town Clerk, RR 3, Box 4600, Montpelier, VT 05602. 802-223-5915. Fax: 802-223-0569. 8:30AM-Noon, 1PM-4:30PM (EST).

Middletown Springs Town

Real Estate Recording—Middletown Springs Town Clerk, 10 Park Street, Middletown Springs, VT 05757. 802-235-2220. 1-4PM M,T,F; 9AM-Noon Sat (EST).

Milton Town

Real Estate Recording—Milton Town Clerk, 43 Bombardier Rd., Milton, VT 05468. 802-893-4111. Fax: 802-893-1005. 8AM-5PM (EST).

Monkton Town

Real Estate Recording—Monkton Town Clerk, RR 1, Box 2015, North Ferrisburg, VT 05473. 802-453-3800. 8AM-2PM M,T,Th,F; 8:30AM-Noon Sat (EST).

Montgomery Town

Real Estate Recording—Montgomery Town Clerk, 3 Main Street, Montgomery Center, VT 05471. 802-326-4719. Fax: 802-326-4939. 9AM-Noon, 1-4PM M,T,Th,F; 9AM-Noon W (EST).

Montpelier City

Real Estate Recording—Montpelier City Clerk, 39 Main Street, City Hall, Montpelier, VT 05602. 802-223-9500. Fax: 802-223-9518. 8AM-4:30PM (EST).

Moretown Town

Real Estate Recording—Moretown Town Clerk, Route 100B, Moretown, VT 05660. 802-496-3645. 9AM-4:30PM (EST).

Morgan Town

Real Estate Recording—Morgan Town Clerk, Town Clerk Rd., Morgan, VT 05853. 802-895-2927. 9AM-Noon, 1-4PM M,T,Th,F (EST).

Morristown Town

Real Estate Recording—Morristown Town Clerk, 16 Main St., Morrisville, VT 05661. 802-888-6370. Fax: 802-888-6375. 8:30AM-4:30PM M,T,Th,F; 8:30AM-12:30PM W (EST).

Mount Holly Town

Real Estate Recording—Mount Holly Town Clerk, School Street, Mount Holly, VT 05758. 802-259-2391. Fax: 802-259-2391. 8AM-4PM M,T,Th,F (EST).

Mount Tabor Town

Real Estate Recording—Mount Tabor Town Clerk, Brooklyn Rd., Town Office, Mt. Tabor, VT 05739. 802-293-5282. 8AM-Noon, 1-4:30PM T; 8AM-Noon, 1-5PM W (EST).

New Haven Town

Real Estate Recording—New Haven Town Clerk, RD 1, Box 4, North St., New Haven, VT 05472. 802-453-3516. 9AM-3PM M,T,Th,F; Closed W (EST).

Newark Town

Real Estate Recording—Newark Town Clerk, RFD 1, Box 50C, West Burke, VT 05871. 802-467-3336. 9AM-4PM M,W,Th (EST).

Newbury Town

Real Estate Recording—Newbury Town Clerk, Main St., Newbury, VT 05051. 802-866-5521. 7AM-1PM (EST).

Newfane Town

Real Estate Recording—Newfane Town Clerk, Rt 30, Main St., Newfane, VT 05345. 802-365-7772. 9AM-1PM M; 9AM-3PM T-F; 9AM-Noon Sat (EST).

Newport City

Real Estate Recording—Newport City Clerk, 74 Main Street, Newport, VT 05855. 802-334-2112. Fax: 802-334-2818. 8AM-4:30PM (EST).

Newport Town

Real Estate Recording—Newport Town Clerk, Vance Hill, Newport Center, VT 05857. 802-334-6442. Fax: 802-334-6442. 9AM-5PM M,T,Th,F; 9AM-Noon W (EST).

North Hero Town

Real Estate Recording—North Hero Town Clerk, Route 2, Town Offices, North Hero, VT 05474. 802-372-6926. 9AM-3PM M,T,Th,F; Sat 9-Noon (EST).

Northfield Town

Real Estate Recording—Northfield Town Clerk, 26 South Main Street, Northfield, VT 05663. 802-485-5421. Fax: 802-485-8426. 8AM-4:30PM (EST).

Norton Town

Real Estate Recording—Norton Town Clerk, Nelson Store, Norton, VT 05907. 802-822-5513. 9AM-5PM M,T,Th; 9AM-Noon F,Sat (EST).

Norwich Town

Real Estate Recording—Norwich Town Clerk, 300 Main St., Norwich, VT 05055. 802-649-1419. 8:30AM-4:30PM M-F; 10AM-Noon Sat (EST).

Orange County

Real Estate Recording—There is no real estate recording at the county level in Vermont. Determine the proper town/city in which to record based on property location.

Felony, Misdemeanor, Civil, Eviction, Small Claims—District and Superior Court, RR1, Box 30, Chelsea, VT 05038-9746. 802-685-4870. Fax: 802-685-3246. 8AM-4:30PM (EST). Access by: Phone, mail, in person.

Probate—Probate Court-Orange District, South Common, RR1 Box 30, Chelsea, VT 05038-9746. 802-685-4610. Fax: 802-685-3246. 8AM-Noon, 1-4:30PM (EST). Access by: Mail, in person.

Orange Town

Real Estate Recording—Orange Town Clerk, US Rte 302, (3 miles east of East Barre), East Barre, VT 05649. 802-479-2673. 8AM-Noon, 1PM-3PM M,W; 8AM-Noon F (EST).

Orleans County

Real Estate Recording—There is no real estate recording at the county level in Vermont. Determine the proper town/city in which to record based upon property location.

Civil, Eviction—Superior Court, 83 Main St, Newport, VT 05855. 802-334-3344. Fax: 802-334-3385. 8AM-4:30PM (EST). Access by: Phone, mail, in person.

Felony, Misdemeanor, Small Claims—District Court, 81 Main St, Newport, VT 05855. 802-334-3325. 8AM-4:30PM (EST). Access by: Phone, mail, in person.

Probate—Probate Court, 83 Main St, Newport, VT 05855. 802-334-3366. 8AM-Noon, 1-4:30PM (EST). Access by: Mail, in person.

Orwell Town

Real Estate Recording—Orwell Town Clerk, Main St., Orwell, VT 05760. 802-948-2032. 9:30AM-Noon, 1-3:30PM (EST).

Panton Town

Real Estate Recording—Panton Town Clerk, RFD 3, Panton Corners, Panton, VT 05491. 802-475-2333. 9AM-4:30PM M,T (EST).

Pawlet Town

Real Estate Recording—Pawlet Town Clerk, Town Hall, School Street, Pawlet, VT 05761. 802-325-3309. Fax: 802-325-6109. 9AM-3PM T,W,Th; 9AM-Noon F (EST).

Peacham Town

Real Estate Recording—Peacham Town Clerk, Church St., Peacham, VT 05862. 802-592-3218. 8AM-Noon M,T,Th,F; 1-4PM Th; 4PM-7PM W (EST).

Peru Town

Real Estate Recording—Peru Town Clerk, Main St., Peru, VT 05152. 802-824-3065. 9AM-3PM T,W,Th (EST).

Pittsfield Town

Real Estate Recording—Pittsfield Town Clerk, Park Drive, Pittsfield, VT 05762. 802-746-8170. Noon-6PM T; 9AM-3PM W,Th (EST).

Pittsford Town

Real Estate Recording—Pittsford Town Clerk, P.O. Box 10, Pittsford, VT 05763. 802-483-2931. Fax: 802-483-6612. 8AM-4:30PM (EST).

Plainfield Town

Real Estate Recording—Plainfield Town Clerk, P.O. Box 217, Plainfield, VT 05667. 802-454-8461. 8AM-Noon, 1-5PM (EST).

Plymouth Town

Real Estate Recording—Plymouth Town Clerk, Rt 100, Plymouth Union, Plymouth, VT 05056. 802-672-3655. Fax: 802-672-5466. 8:30-11:30AM, 12:30-3:30PM (EST).

Pomfret Town

Real Estate Recording—Pomfret Town Clerk, Main St., Town Clerk, North Pomfret, VT 05053. 802-457-3861. 8AM-2:30PM M,W,F (EST).

Poultney Town

Real Estate Recording—Poultney Town Clerk, 86-88 Main Street, Poultney, VT 05764. 802-287-5761. 8:30AM-12:30, 1:30-4PM (EST).

Pownal Town

Real Estate Recording—Pownal Town Clerk, Center St., Pownal, VT 05261. 802-823-7757. Fax: 802-823-0116. 9AM-2PM M,W,Th,F; 9AM-4PM T (EST).

Proctor Town

Real Estate Recording—Proctor Town Clerk, 45 Main Street, Proctor, VT 05765. 802-459-3333. 8AM-4PM (EST).

Putney Town

Real Estate Recording—Putney Town Clerk, Town Hall, Main Street, Putney, VT 05346. 802-387-5862. 9AM-2PM M, Th, F; 9AM-2PM, 7-9PM W; 9AM-12 Sat (EST).

Randolph Town

Real Estate Recording—Randolph Town Clerk, 7 Summer Street, Randolph, VT 05060. 802-728-5682. 8AM-4:30PM (EST).

Reading Town

Real Estate Recording—Reading Town Clerk, Rt 106, Robinson Hall, Reading, VT 05062. 802-484-7250. 9AM-Noon, 1-4PM, M,W,F (EST).

Readsboro Town

Real Estate Recording—Readsboro Town Clerk, School Rd., Readsboro, VT 05350. 802-423-5405. Fax: 802-423-5423. 9AM-3PM (EST).

Richford Town

Real Estate Recording—Richford Town Clerk, Main St., Town Hall, Richford, VT 05476. 802-848-7751. Fax: 802-848-7752. 8:30AM-4PM (F open until 5PM) (EST).

Richmond Town

Real Estate Recording—Richmond Town Clerk, Bridge St./Town Center, Richmond, VT 05477. 802-434-2221. Fax: 802-434-5570. 8AM-7PM M; 8AM-4PM T-Th; 8AM-1PM F (EST).

Ripton Town

Real Estate Recording—Ripton Town Clerk, Rte 125, Ripton, VT 05766. 802-388-2266. 2PM-6PM M; 9AM-1PM T,W,Th,F (EST).

Rochester Town

Real Estate Recording—Rochester Town Clerk, School St., Rochester, VT 05767. 802-767-3631. 8AM-4PM T-F (EST).

Rockingham Town

Real Estate Recording—Rockingham Town Clerk, Municipal in the Square, Bellows Falls, VT 05101. 802-463-4336. Fax: 802-463-1228. 8:30AM-4:30PM (EST).

Roxbury Town

Real Estate Recording—Roxbury Town Clerk, Rt 12A, Roxbury, VT 05669. 802-485-7840. Fax: 802-485-7860. 9AM-Noon, 1-4PM T-F (EST).

Royalton Town

Real Estate Recording—Royalton Town Clerk, Basement - Royalton Memorial Library, Safford Street, South Royalton, VT 05068. 802-763-7207. Fax: 802-763-7967. 9AM-1PM, 2-5PM T-Th (EST).

Rupert Town

Real Estate Recording—Rupert Town Clerk, Route 153, Sherman's Store Complex, West Rupert, VT 05776. 802-394-7728. 10AM-4PM (EST).

Rutland City

Real Estate Recording—Rutland City Clerk, 1 Strongs Avenue, City Hall, Rutland, VT 05701. 802-773-1801. 9AM-Noon, 1-4:45PM (EST).

Rutland County

Real Estate Recording—There is no real estate recording at the county level in Vermont. Determine the town/city in which to record based upon property location.

Civil, Eviction—Superior Court, 83 Center St, Rutland, VT 05702. 802-775-4394. Fax: 802-775-2291. 8AM-4:30PM (EST). Access by: Mail, in person.

Felony, Misdemeanor, Small Claims—District Court, 92 State St, Rutland, VT 05701. 802-786-5880. 8AM-4:30PM (EST). Access by: Phone, mail, in person.

Probate—Probate Court-Fair Haven District, North Park Place, Fair Haven, VT 05743. 802-265-3380. 8AM-4PM (EST).

Probate Court-Rutland District, 83 Center St, Rutland, VT 05702. 802-775-0114. 8AM-4:30PM (EST). Access by: Mail, in person.

Rutland Town

Real Estate Recording—Rutland Town Clerk, Route 4 West, Center Rutland, VT 05736. 802-773-2528. Fax: 802-773-7295. 8AM-4:30PM (EST).

Ryegate Town

Real Estate Recording—Ryegate Town Clerk, Town Highway #1, Bayley-Hazen Road, Ryegate, VT 05042. 802-584-3880. 1-5PM M-W; 9AM-1PM F (EST).

Salisbury Town

Real Estate Recording—Salisbury Town Clerk, Maple St., Salisbury, VT 05769. 802-352-4228. Fax: 802-352-4228. 2PM-6PM M; 9AM-Noon T & F; 9AM-Noon, 1-4PM W & Th (EST).

Sandgate Town

Real Estate Recording—Sandgate Town Clerk, RR 1,, Box 2466, Sandgate, VT 05250. 802-375-9075. 9AM-3PM T,W (EST).

Searsburg Town

Real Estate Recording—Searsburg Town Clerk, Route 9, Searsburg, VT 05363. 802-464-8081. 8AM-Noon M,T,F (EST).

Shaftsbury Town

Real Estate Recording—Shaftsbury Town Clerk, East St., Shaftsbury, VT 05262. 802-442-4038. Fax: 802-442-4043. 8AM-4PM M; 9AM-2PM T-F (EST).

Sharon Town

Real Estate Recording—Sharon Town Clerk, Rt 132, Sharon, VT 05065. 802-763-8268. 7:30AM-12:30PM, 1:30-6PM T & Th; 7:30AM-12:30PM W (EST).

Sheffield Town

Real Estate Recording—Sheffield Town Clerk, Town Highway #32, Sheffield, VT 05866. 802-626-8862. 9AM-2PM (EST).

Shelburne Town

Real Estate Recording—Shelburne Town Clerk, Town Hall, 2135 Shelburne Rd., Shelburne, VT 05482. 802-985-5116. Fax: 802-985-9550. 8:30AM-4:30PM (EST).

Sheldon Town

Real Estate Recording—Sheldon Town Clerk, Main St., Sheldon, VT 05483. 802-933-2524. 8AM-3PM (EST).

Sherburne Town

Real Estate Recording—Sherburne Town Clerk, River Road, Killington, VT 05751. 802-422-3243. Fax: 802-422-3030. 9AM-3PM (EST).

Shoreham Town

Real Estate Recording—Shoreham Town Clerk, Main Street, Shoreham, VT 05770. 802-897-5841. 9AM-4PM M-W & F (EST).

Shrewsbury Town

Real Estate Recording—Shrewsbury Town Clerk, RR 1, Box 301, Cuttingsville, VT 05738. 802-492-3511. Fax: 802-492-3511. 10AM-2PM M,T,Th,F (EST).

South Burlington City

Real Estate Recording—South Burlington City Clerk, 575 Dorset Street, City Hall, South Burlington, VT 05403. 802-658-7952. Fax: 802-658-4748. 8AM-4:30PM (EST).

South Hero Town

Real Estate Recording—South Hero Town Clerk, 333 Rt.2, South Hero, VT 05486. 802-372-5552. 8:30AM-Noon, 1-4:30PM M-W; 8:30AM-Noon,1:30-6PM Th (EST).

Springfield Town

Real Estate Recording—Springfield Town Clerk, 96 Main Street, Springfield, VT 05156. 802-885-2104. 8AM-4:30PM (EST).

St. Albans City

Real Estate Recording—St. Albans City Clerk, 100 N. Main, St. Albans, VT 05478. 802-524-1501. 7:30AM-4PM (EST).

St. Albans Town

Real Estate Recording—St. Albans Town Clerk, Lake Road, St. Albans Bay, VT 05481. 802-524-2415. Fax: 802-524-9609. 9AM-5PM M,T,Th,F; 9AM-Noon W (EST).

St. George Town

Real Estate Recording—St. George Town Clerk, RR 2, Box 455, Williston, VT 05495. 802-482-5272. 8AM-Noon (EST).

St. Johnsbury Town

Real Estate Recording—St. Johnsbury Town Clerk, 34 Main Street, St. Johnsbury, VT 05819. 802-748-4331. Fax: 802-748-1268. 8AM-5PM (May-September 7AM-4PM) (EST).

Stamford Town

Real Estate Recording—Stamford Town Clerk, RR 1, Box 718, Main Rd., Stamford, VT 05352. 802-694-1361. 11AM-4PM T & W; Noon-4PM, 7-9pm Th; Noon-4pm F (EST).

Stannard Town

Real Estate Recording—Stannard Town Clerk, AN ADDRESS IS NOT AVAILABLE FOR, COURIER DELIVERY, 802-533-2577. 8AM-Noon W (EST).

Starksboro Town

Real Estate Recording—Starksboro Town Clerk, Rt 116, Starksboro, VT 05487. 802-453-2639. 9AM-5PM M,T,Th,F (EST).

Stockbridge Town

Real Estate Recording—Stockbridge Town Clerk, Blackmer Blvd., Stockbridge, VT 05772. 802-234-9371. Fax: 802-234-9371. 9AM-3PM T,Th; 9AM-Noon W,F (EST).

Stowe Town

Real Estate Recording—Stowe Town Clerk, 67 Main St., Stowe, VT 05672. 802-253-6133. Fax: 802-253-6137. 8AM-4:30PM (EST).

Strafford Town

Real Estate Recording—Strafford Town Clerk, Justin Morrill Highway, Strafford, VT 05072. 802-765-4411. (EST).

Stratton Town

Real Estate Recording—Stratton Town Clerk, West Jamaica Rd., West Wardsboro, VT 05360. 802-896-6184. Fax: 802-896-6630. 9AM-3PM M-Th (EST).

Sudbury Town

Real Estate Recording—Sudbury Town Clerk, RR 1, Box 1238, Sudbury, VT 05733. 802-623-7296. 9AM-4PM M; 9AM-1PM W,F (EST).

Sunderland Town

Real Estate Recording—Sunderland Town Clerk, South Rd., Sunderland, VT 05252. 802-375-6106. 8AM-2PM M,T,Th,F; 8AM-Noon, 6-8PM W (EST).

Sutton Town

Real Estate Recording—Sutton Town Clerk, State Aid #1, Sutton, VT 05867. 802-467-3377. 9AM-5PM M,T,Th,F; 9AM-Noon W (EST).

Swanton Town

Real Estate Recording—Swanton Town Clerk, Academy Street, Swanton, VT 05488. 802-868-4421. 8AM-4PM (EST).

Thetford Town

Real Estate Recording—Thetford Town Clerk, Rt. 113, Thetford Center, VT 05075. 802-785-4927. Fax: 802-785-2031. 7PM-9PM M; 8AM-3PM T-F (EST).

Tinmouth Town

Real Estate Recording—Tinmouth Town Clerk, RR 1, Box 551, Wallingford, VT 05773. 802-446-2498. 8AM-Noon, 1-4PM M & Th (EST).

Topsham Town

Real Estate Recording—Topsham Town Clerk, RR# 1, West Topsham, VT 05086. 802-439-5505. 10AM-2PM M,T (EST).

Townshend Town

Real Estate Recording—Townshend Town Clerk, Rte 30, Town Hall, Townshend, VT 05353. 802-365-7300. 9AM-4PM M-W & F (EST).

Troy Town

Real Estate Recording—Troy Town Clerk, Main Street, North Troy, VT 05859. 802-988-2663. 8AM-Noon, 1-4PM (EST).

Tunbridge Town

Real Estate Recording—Tunbridge Town Clerk, Main St., Tunbridge, VT 05077. 802-889-5521. Fax: 802-889-3744. 9:30AM-Noon, 1-4PM (EST).

Underhill Town

Real Estate Recording—Underhill Town Clerk, 12 Pleasant Valley Rd., Underhill, VT 05489. 802-899-4434. Fax: 802-899-2137. 8AM-4PM M,T,Th,F; 8AM-7PM W (EST).

Vergennes City

Real Estate Recording—Vergennes City Clerk, 120 Main St., Vergennes, VT 05491. 802-877-2841. Fax: 802-877-1157. 8AM-4:30PM (EST).

Vernon Town

Real Estate Recording—Vernon Town Clerk, RR2 Box 525, Vernon, VT 05354. 802-257-0292. Fax: 802-254-3561. 8:30AM-4PM M-W; 8:30AM-6:30PM Th; 8:30AM-4PM F (EST).

Vershire Town

Real Estate Recording—Vershire Town Clerk, RR 1, Box 66C, Vershire, VT 05079. 802-685-2227. 8:30AM-3PM T-Th (EST).

Victory Town

Real Estate Recording—Victory Town Clerk, E. Finkle - River Rd., North Concord, VT 05858. 802-328-3907. By Appointment (EST).

Waitsfield Town

Real Estate Recording—Waitsfield Town Clerk, RD, Box 390, Bridge Street, Waitsfield, VT 05673. 802-496-2218. 9AM-Noon,1-4PM (EST).

Walden Town

Real Estate Recording—Walden Town Clerk, RR 1, Box 57, West Danville, VT 05873. 802-563-2220. 9:30AM-4PM M,T,Th,F (EST).

Wallingford Town

Real Estate Recording—Wallingford Town Clerk, School St., Wallingford, VT 05773. 802-446-2336. 8AM-Noon, 1-4:30PM M-Th; 8AM-Noon F (EST).

Waltham Town

Real Estate Recording—Waltham Town Clerk, Maple Street Ext., Waltham, VT 05491. 802-877-3641. 9-Noon T; 9AM-Noon, 4-6PM Th (EST).

Wardsboro Town

Real Estate Recording—Wardsboro Town Clerk, Main St., Wardsboro, VT 05355. 802-896-6055. 9AM-Noon, 1-4:30PM (Closed F) (EST).

Warren Town

Real Estate Recording—Warren Town Clerk, Main St., Town Clerk, Warren, VT 05674. 802-496-2709. 9AM-4:30PM (EST).

Washington County

Real Estate Recording—There is no real estate recording at the county level in Vermont. Determine the proper town/city in which to record based upon property location.

Civil, Eviction—Superior Court, Box 426, Montpelier, VT 05602. 802-828-2091. 8AM-4:30PM (EST). Access by: Phone, mail, in person.

Felony, Misdemeanor, Small Claims—District Court, 255 N Main, Barre, VT 05641. 802-479-4252. 8AM-4:30PM (EST). Access by: Phone, mail, in person.

Probate—Probate Court, PO Box 15, Montpelier, VT 05601. 802-828-3405. 8AM-Noon, 1-4:30PM M-Th; 8AM-Noon, 1-4PM F (EST). Access by: Mail, in person.

Washington Town

Real Estate Recording—Washington Town Clerk, Clerk's Office, Washington, VT 05675. 802-883-2218. 8:30AM-2PM M,T (EST).

Waterbury Town

Real Estate Recording—Waterbury Town Clerk, 51 South Main Street, Waterbury, VT 05676. 802-244-8447. Fax: 802-244-1014. 8AM-4:30PM (EST).

Waterford Town

Real Estate Recording—Waterford Town Clerk, State Aid #2, Lower Waterford, VT 05848. 802-748-2122. Fax: 802-748-8196. 8:30AM-3:30PM M,Th,F; Noon-6PM T (EST).

Waterville Town

Real Estate Recording—Waterville Town Clerk, 102 Main St., Waterville, VT 05492. 802-644-8865. (EST).

Weathersfield Town

Real Estate Recording—Weathersfield Town Clerk, Rt. 5, Ascutney Village at Martin Memorial Hall, Weathersfield, VT 05030. 802-674-2626. 9AM-4PM M-W; 9AM-5PM Th (EST).

Wells Town

Real Estate Recording—Wells Town Clerk, Rt.30, Wells, VT 05774. 802-645-0486. 9AM-1PM (EST).

West Fairlee Town

Real Estate Recording—West Fairlee Town Clerk, Rt 113, Town Clerk, West Fairlee, VT 05083. 802-333-9696. 10AM-4PM M,W,F (EST).

West Haven Town

Real Estate Recording—West Haven Town Clerk, RD1, Box 3895, Fair Haven, VT 05743. 802-265-4880. 1-3:30PM M & W (EST).

West Rutland Town

Real Estate Recording—West Rutland Town Clerk, Corner of Main and Marble, West Rutland, VT 05777. 802-438-2204. Fax: 802-438-5133. 9AM-Noon, 1-3PM M-Th; Fri by appointment (EST).

West Windsor Town

Real Estate Recording—West Windsor Town Clerk, Rt. 44 & Hartland-Brownsville Rd., Brownsville, VT 05037. 802-484-7212. Fax: 802-484-7212. 9AM-Noon, 1:30-4:30PM Mon-Th; 9AM-Noon Fri (EST).

Westfield Town

Real Estate Recording—Westfield Town Clerk, RR 1 Box 171, Westfield, VT 05874. 802-744-2484. 8AM-Noon, 1PM-5PM M-Th (EST).

Westford Town

Real Estate Recording—Westford Town Clerk, 1713 Vermont Route 128, Westford, VT 05494. 802-878-4587. Fax: 802-879-6503. 8:30AM-4:30PM (EST).

Westminster Town

Real Estate Recording—Westminster Town Clerk, Rt. 5, Town Hall, Westminster, VT 05158. 802-722-4091. Fax: 802-722-4255. 9AM-4PM (EST).

Westmore Town

Real Estate Recording—Westmore Town Clerk, RFD 2, Box 854, Orleans, VT 05860. 802-525-3007. Fax: 802-525-3007. 9AM-Noon, 1PM-4PM M-Th (EST).

Weston Town

Real Estate Recording—Weston Town Clerk, 12 Lawrence Hill Rd., Weston, VT 05161. 802-824-6645. Fax: 802-824-4121. 9AM-1PM (EST).

Weybridge Town

Real Estate Recording—Weybridge Town Clerk, 1727 Quaker Village Rd., Weybridge, VT 05753. 802-545-2450. Fax: 802-545-2450. 9AM-2PM M,T,Th,F (EST).

Wheelock Town

Real Estate Recording—Wheelock Town Clerk, Rt.122, Wheelock, VT 05851. 802-626-9094. Fax: 802-626-9094. 9AM-3:30PM T,Th,F (EST).

Whiting Town

Real Estate Recording—Whiting Town Clerk, 29 S. Main St., Whiting, VT 05778. 802-623-7813. 9AM-Noon M,W,F (EST).

Whitingham Town

Real Estate Recording—Whitingham Town Clerk, Municipal Center, Jacksonville, VT 05342. 802-368-7887. Fax: 802-368-7519. 9AM-2PM (5:30-7:30PM W); 1st Sat of month 9AM-2PM (EST).

Williamstown Town

Real Estate Recording—Williamstown Town Clerk, Main Street, Williamstown, VT 05679. 802-433-5455. 8AM-Noon,12:30-4:30PM M,T,Th,F;8AM-Noon,1-5:30PM W (EST).

Williston Town

Real Estate Recording—Williston Town Clerk, 722 Williston Rd., Williston, VT 05495. 802-878-5121. 8AM-4:30PM (EST).

Wilmington Town

Real Estate Recording—Wilmington Town Clerk, Main Street, Wilmington, VT 05363. 802-464-5836. Fax: 802-464-8477. 8AM-Noon, 1PM-4PM (EST).

Windham County

Real Estate Recording—There is no real estate recording at the county level in Vermont. Determine the proper town/city in which to record based upon property location.

Civil, Eviction—Superior Court, Box 207, Newfane, VT 05345. 802-365-7979. Fax: 802-365-4360. 9AM-4PM (EST). Access by: Phone, mail, in person.

Felony, Misdemeanor, Small Claims—District Court, 6 Putney Rd, Brattleboro, VT 05301. 802-257-2800. Fax: 802-257-2853. 8AM-4:30PM (EST). Access by: Phone, mail, in person.

Probate—Probate Court-Westminster District, PO Box 47, Bellows Falls, VT 05101. 802-463-3019. 8AM-Noon,1-4:30PM (EST). Access by: Mail, in person.

Probate Court-Marlboro District, PO Box 523, Brattleboro, VT 05302. 802-257-2898. 8AM-Noon, 1-4:30PM (EST). Access by: Mail, in person.

Windham Town

Real Estate Recording—Windham Town Clerk, RR 1, Box 109, West Townshend, VT 05359. 802-874-4211. 10AM-3PM T,Th,F (EST).

Windsor County

Real Estate Recording—There is no real estate recording at the county level in Vermont. Determine the proper town/city in which to record based on property location.

Civil, Eviction—Superior Court, Box 458, Woodstock, VT 05091. 802-457-2121. Fax: 802-457-3446. 8AM-4:30PM (EST). Access by: Phone, mail, in person.

Felony, Misdemeanor, Small Claims—District Court, Windsor Circuit Unit 1, PO Box 425, White River Junction, VT 05001. 802-295-8865. 8AM-4:30PM (EST). Access by: Phone, mail, in person.

Probate—Probate Court-Windsor District, PO Box 402, North Springfield, VT 05150. 802-886-2284. Fax: 802-886-2285. 8AM-Noon, 1-4:30PM (EST). Access by: Mail, in person.

Probate Court-Hartford District, PO Box 275, Woodstock, VT 05091. 802-457-1503. Fax: 802-457-3446. 8AM-Noon, 1-4:30PM (EST). Access by: Mail, in person.

Windsor Town

Real Estate Recording—Windsor Town Clerk, 147 Main Street, Windsor, VT 05089. 802-674-5610. Fax: 802-674-5610. 8AM-4PM (F open until 3:30PM) (EST).

Winhall Town

Real Estate Recording—Winhall Town Clerk, River Rd., Bondville, VT 05340. 802-297-2122. 9AM-Noon (Closed Th) (EST).

Winooski City

Real Estate Recording—Winooski City Clerk, 27 West Allen Street, Winooski, VT 05404. 802-655-6419. Fax: 802-655-6414. 8AM-5PM (EST).

Wolcott Town

Real Estate Recording—Wolcott Town Clerk, Main Street, Wolcott, VT 05680. 802-888-2746. Fax: 802-888-2746. 8AM-3PM T-F; 6-8PM Tue (EST).

Woodbury Town

Real Estate Recording—Woodbury Town Clerk, Rt 14, Town Clerk, Woodbury, VT 05681. 802-456-7051. 8:30AM-1PM T-Th; 6-8PM Th evening (EST).

Woodford Town

Real Estate Recording—Woodford Town Clerk, HRC 65 Box 600, Bennington, VT 05201. 802-442-4895. Fax: 802-442-4895. 8:30AM-Noon M-Th (EST).

Woodstock Town

Real Estate Recording—Woodstock Town Clerk, 31 The Green, Woodstock, VT 05091. 802-457-3611. Fax: 802-457-2329. 8:30AM-Noon, 1-3:30PM (EST).

Worcester Town

Real Estate Recording—Worcester Town Clerk, 20 Worcester Village Rd., Worcester, VT 05682. 802-223-6942. 8AM-Noon, 1-3PM M,T,Th; 8AM-1PM F; 8-10AM Sat (EST).

Federal Courts

US District Court

District of Vermont

Burlington Division, US District Court Clerk's Office, PO Box 945, Burlington, VT 05402-0945. 802-951-6301. Counties: Caledonia, Chittenden, Essex, Frankin, Grand Isle, Lamoille, Orleans, Washington. However, cases from all counties in the state are assigned randomly to either Burlington or Brattleboro

Rutland Division, US District Court PO Box 607, Rutland, VT 05702-0607. 802-773-0245. Counties: Addison, Bennington, Orange, Rutland, Windsor, Windham. However, cases from all counties in the state are randomly assigned to either Burlington or Brattleboro

US Bankruptcy Court

District of Vermont

Rutland Division, US Bankruptcy Court, PO Box 6648, Rutland, VT 05702. 802-747-7625. Voice Case Information System: 802-747-7627. Counties: All counties in Vermont

Virginia

Capitol: Richmond (Richmond City County)	
Number of Counties: 95	**Population:** 6,618,358
County Court Locations:	**Federal Court Locations:**
•Circuit Courts: 117/31 Circuits	•District Courts: 11
•District Courts: 122	•Bankruptcy Courts: 7
•Combined Courts: 5	**State Agencies:** 20

State Agencies—Summary

General Help Numbers:

State Archives
The Library of Vitginia	804-692-3500
800 E. Broad St	9AM-5PM
Richmond, VA 23219-1905	
Historical Society:	804-358-4901

Governor's Office
Governor's Office	804-786-2211
Capitol Bldg, 3rd Floor	Fax: 804-371-6351
Richmond, VA 23219	8AM-5:30PM

Attorney General's Office
Attorney General's Office	804-786-2071
900 E Main St	Fax: 804-786-1991
Richmond, VA 23219	8:30AM-5PM

State Legislation
House of Delegates	804-786-6530
Legislative Information	Fax: 804-786-3215
PO Box 406	8AM-5PM
Richmond, VA 23218	

In addition to the Internet site listed to the right, a dial up system is also available at a cost of $1200 for setup and $20 per hour. The dial-up system allows you to create lists of legislation to follow automatically. Contact Barbara Lee at 804-786-3215 for subscription information.

Important State Internet Sites:

🌐 Webscape		
File Edit View		Help

State of Virginia World Wide Web
www.state.va.us/

This site links to such sites as education, government, travel, weather information, and what's new.

State General Assembly
legis.state.va.us/

Linked to this site are the state legislature, the legislative information system, legislative agencies and links to other states.

Legislative Information System
leg1.state.va.us

This site includes bill information that dates back to 1994. There are numerous ways to search for bills from this site. The Code of Virginia is also available to be searched.

Judicial System
www.courts.state.va.us/

This site links to all of the courts in the state.

UCC Information
www.state.va.us/scc/division/clk/index.htm

Limited information is provided about UCC filings. The information is obtained through the Office of the Clerk, through the State Corporation Commission.

State Library and Archives
leo.vsla.edu/

This site contains links to the archives and records management systems and many more useful sites.

State Agencies—Public Records

Criminal Records

Virginia State Police, CCRE, PO Box C-85076, Richmond, VA 23261-5076, Main Telephone: 804-674-2084, Fax: 804-674-2277, Hours: 8AM-5PM. Access by: mail only.

Corporation Records
Limited Liability Company Records
Fictitious Name
Limited Partnership Records
Assumed Name

State Corporation Commission, Clerks Office, PO Box 1197, Richmond, VA 23218-1197, Main Telephone: 804-371-9733, Other fax: 804-371-9133, Fax: 804-371-9118, Hours: 8:15AM-5PM. Access by: mail, phone, fax, visit, PC.

Trademarks/Servicemarks

State Corporation Commission, Division of Security & Retail Franchises, 900 E Main St, Richmond, VA 23219, Main Telephone: 804-371-9051, Fax: 804-371-9911, Hours: 8:15AM-5PM. Access by: mail, phone, visit.

Uniform Commercial Code
Federal Tax Liens
State Tax Liens

UCC Division, State Corporation Commission, PO Box 1197, Richmond, VA 23218-1197, Main Telephone: 804-371-9189, Fax: 804-371-9118, Hours: 8:15AM-5PM. Access by: mail, fax, visit, PC. The agency now accepts filing using EDI. For more information contact Wanda at 804 371-9380.

Sales Tax Registrations

Taxation Department, Sales - Taxpayer Assistance, PO Box 1880, Richmond, VA 23218-1880, Main Telephone: 804-367-8037, Fax: 804-367-0971, Hours: 8:30AM-4:30PM. Access by: mail, phone. Registration information of businesses is available from the Corporation Commission.

Birth Certificates

State Health Department, Division of Vital Records, PO Box 1000, Richmond, VA 23218-1000, Main Telephone: 804-786-6228, Fax: 804-644-2550, Hours: 8AM-5:30PM M-W,F; 8-6 Th. Access by: mail, phone, visit.

Death Records

State Health Department, Division of Vital Records, PO Box 1000, Richmond, VA 23218-1000, Main Telephone: 804-786-6228, Message Phone: 804-786-6228, Fax: 804-644-2550, Hours: 8AM-5:30PM M-F, 8-6 Th. Access by: mail, phone, visit.

Marriage Certificates

State Health Department, Division of Vital Records, PO Box 1000, Richmond, VA 23218-1000, Main Telephone: 804-786-6228, Message Phone: 804-786-6228, Fax: 804-644-2550, Hours: 8AM-5:30PM M-W,F; 8-6 Th. Access by: mail, phone, visit.

Divorce Records

State Health Department, Division of Vital Records, PO Box 1000, Richmond, VA 23218-1000, Main Telephone: 804-786-6228, Fax: 804-644-2550, Hours: 8AM-5:30PM M-W,F; 8-6 Th. Access by: mail, phone, visit.

Workers' Compensation Records

Workers' Compensation Commission, 1000 DMV Dr, Richmond, VA 23220, Main Telephone: 804-367-8633, Fax: 804-367-9740, Hours: 8:15AM-5PM. Access by: mail, visit.

Driver Records

Department of Motor Vehicles, Motorist Records Services, PO Box 27412, Richmond, VA 23269, Main Telephone: 804-367-0538, Hours: 8:30AM-5:30PM M-F; 8:30AM-12:30PM S. Access by: mail, visit, PC. Copies of tickets from non-computerized courts are available at this address for $5.00 per record only to driver or driver's authorized representative. Ticket information from computerized courts must be obtained from each court.

Vehicle Ownership
Vehicle Identification

Motorist Records Services, Customer Records Request Section, PO Box 27412, Richmond, VA 23269, Main Telephone: 804-367-6729, Hours: 8:30AM-5:30PM M-F; 8:30AM-12:30PM S. Access by: mail, phone, visit, PC. Lien information is only released to lending institutions and collection agencies.

Accident Reports

Department of Motor Vehicles, Customer Record Requests, Rm 517, Main Telephone: 804-367-0538, Fax: 804-367-0390, Hours: 8:30AM-5:30PM M-F; 8:30AM-12:30PM S. Access by: mail, fax, visit.

Hunting License Information
Fishing License Information

Records not available from state agency.

County/City Courts and Recording Offices

What You Need to Know...

<table>
<tr><td colspan="2">

About the Courts

</td><td colspan="2">

About the Recorder's Office

</td></tr>
</table>

About the Courts

Administration

Executive Secretary	804-786-6455
Administrative Office of Courts	Fax: 804-786-4542
100 N 9th St, 3rd Floor	9AM-5PM
Richmond, VA 23219	

Court Structure

Records of civil action from $1,000 to $10,000 can be at either the Circuit or District Court as either can have jurisdiction. It is necessary to check both record locations as there is no concurrent database nor index.

Searching Hints

In most jurisdictions, the Certification Fee is $2.00 per document plus copy fee and the Copy Fee is $.50 per page.

Online Access

An online, statewide public access computer system is available, called Law Office Public Access System (LOPAS). **The system allows remote access to the court case indexes and abstracts from most of the state's courts.** In order to determine which courts are on LOPAS, you must obtain and ID and password (instructions below), and search on the system; a summary list is not available. Searching is by specific court; there is no combined index.

The system contains information from the Supreme and Appellate courts, as well as criminal and civil case information from the Circuit and District courts. The number of years of information provided varies widely from court to court, depending on when the particular court went on LOPAS.

The preferred communication software is PROCOM+. There are no sign-up or other fees to use LOPAS. Access is granted on a request-by-request basis. Anyone wishing to establish an account or receive information on LOPAS must contact: Ken Mittendorf, Director of MIS, Supreme Court of Virginia, at the address above or by phone at 804-786-6455 or by fax at 804-786-4542.

About the Recorder's Office

Organization

95 counties and 41 independent cities, 123 filing offices. The recording officer is Clerk of Circuit Court. **Fourteen independent cities share the Clerk of Circuit Court with the county**—Bedford, Emporia (Greenville County), Fairfax, Falls Church (Arlington or Fairfax County), Franklin (Southhampton County), Galax (Carroll County), Harrisonburg (Rockingham County), Lexington (Rockbridge County), Manassas and Manassas Park (Prince William County), Norton (Wise County), Poquoson (York County), South Boston (Halifax County), and Williamsburg (James City County. **Charles City and James City are counties, not cities. The City of Franklin is not in Franklin County, the City of Richmond is not in Richmond County, and the City of Roanoke is not in Roanoke County.** The entire state is in the Eastern Time Zone (EST).

UCC Records

This is a **dual filing state**. Financing statements are filed at the state level and with the Clerk of Circuit Court, except for consumer goods, farm and real estate related collateral, which are filed only with the Clerk of Circuit Court. Many filing offices will perform UCC searches. Use search request form UCC-11. Searches fees and copy fees vary.

Lien Records

Federal tax liens on personal property of businesses are filed with the State Corporation Commission. Other federal and all state tax liens are filed with the county Clerk of Circuit Court. They are usually filed in a "Judgment Lien Book." Most counties will **not** perform tax lien searches. Other liens include judgments, mechanics, hospital and lis pendens.

Real Estate Records

Only a few Clerks of Circuit Court will perform real estate searches. Copy fees and certification fees vary. The independent cities may have separate Assessor Offices.

County/City Courts and Recording Offices

Accomack County

Real Estate Recording—Accomack County Clerk of the Circuit Court, 23316 Courthouse Avenue, Accomac, VA 23301. 757-787-5776. Fax: 757-787-1849. 9AM-5PM (EST).

Felony, Civil Actions Over $10,000, Probate—2nd Circuit Court, PO Box 126, Accomac, VA 23301. 757-787-5776. Fax: 757-787-1849. 9AM-5PM (EST). Access by: Fax, mail, in person.

Misdemeanor, Civil Actions Under $10,000, Eviction, Small Claims—2A General District Court, PO Box 276, Accomac, VA 23301. 757-787-5785. 9AM-5PM (EST). Access by: Phone, mail, in person.

Albemarle County

Real Estate Recording—Albemarle County Clerk of the Circuit Court, 501 E. Jefferson St., Room 225, Charlottesville, VA 22902. 804-972-4083. Fax: 804-972-4071. 8:30AM-4:30PM (EST).

Felony, Misdemeanor, Civil, Eviction, Probate—16th Circuit and District Court, 501 E Jefferson St, Charlottesville, VA 22902. 804-972-4084. 8:30AM-4:30PM (EST). Access by: Mail, in person.

Alexandria City

Real Estate Recording—Alexandria City Clerk of the Circuit Court, 520 King Street, Room 307, Alexandria, VA 22314. 703-838-4066. 9AM-5PM (EST).

Felony, Civil Actions Over $10,000, Probate—10th Circuit Court, 520 King St. #307, Alexandria, VA 22314. 703-838-4044. 9AM-5PM. Access by: In person only.

Misdemeanor, Civil Actions Under $10,000, Eviction, Small Claims—18th Judicial District Court, 520 King St #201, PO Box 20206, Alexandria, VA 22314. 703-838-4010. Civil: 703-838-4021. Criminal: 703-838-4030. 8AM-4PM. Access by: In person only.

Alleghany County

Real Estate Recording—Alleghany County Clerk of the Circuit Court, 266 West Main Street, Covington, VA 24426. 540-965-1730. Fax: 540-965-1732. 9AM-5PM; 9AM-Noon Sat (EST).

Felony, Civil Actions Over $10,000, Probate—Circuit Court of Alleghany County, PO Box 670, Covington, VA 24426. 540-965-1730. Fax: 540-965-1732. 9AM-5PM M-F; 9AM-Noon Sat (EST). Access by: In person only.

Misdemeanor, Civil Actions Under $10,000, Eviction, Small Claims—25th General District Court, PO Box 139, Covington, VA 24426. 540-965-1720. Fax: 540-965-1722. 9AM-5PM (EST). Access by: Mail, in person.

Amelia County

Real Estate Recording—Amelia County Clerk of the Circuit Court, 16441 Court St., Courthouse, Amelia Court House, VA 23002. 804-561-2128. 8:30AM-4:30PM (EST).

Felony, Civil Actions Over $10,000, Probate—11th Circuit Court, 16441 Court St, PO Box 237, Amelia, VA 23002. 804-561-2128. 8:30AM-4:30PM (EST). Access by: Mail, in person.

Misdemeanor, Civil Actions Under $10,000, Eviction, Small Claims—11th General District Court, PO Box 24, Amelia, VA 23002. 804-561-2456. 8:15AM-4:15PM (EST). Access by: Mail, in person.

Amherst County

Real Estate Recording—Amherst County Clerk of the Circuit Court, 100 East Court Street, Courthouse, Amherst, VA 24521. 804-946-9321. 8AM-5PM (EST).

Felony, Civil Actions Over $10,000, Probate—24th Circuit Court, PO Box 462, Amherst, VA 24521. 804-929-9321. 8AM-5PM (EST). Access by: In person only.

Misdemeanor, Civil Actions Under $10,000, Eviction, Small Claims—24th General District Court, PO Box 513, Amherst, VA 24521. 804-946-9351. Fax: 804-946-9359. 8AM-4:30PM (EST). Access by: Fax, mail, in person.

Appomattox County

Real Estate Recording—Appomattox County Clerk of the Circuit Court, Courthouse Square, Court Street, Appomattox, VA 24522. 804-352-5275. Fax: 804-352-2781. 8:30AM-4:30PM (EST).

Felony, Civil Actions Over $10,000, Probate—10th Circuit Court, PO Box 672, Appomattox, VA 24522. 804-352-5275. 8:30AM-4:30PM (EST). Access by: In person only.

Misdemeanor, Civil Actions Under $10,000, Eviction, Small Claims—10th General District Court, PO Box 187, Appomattox, VA 24522. 804-352-5540. 8:30AM-4:30PM (EST). Access by: Mail, in person.

Arlington County

Real Estate Recording—Arlington County Clerk of the Circuit Court, 1425 N. Courthouse Rd., #6200, Arlington, VA 22201. 703-358-4369. 8AM-5PM (EST).

Felony, Civil Actions Over $10,000, Probate—17th Circuit Court, 1425 N Courthouse Rd, Arlington, VA 22201. 703-358-7010. 8AM-5PM (EST). Access by: Mail, in person.

Misdemeanor, Civil Actions Under $10,000, Eviction, Small Claims—17th General District Court, 1425 N Courthouse Rd, Arlington, VA 22201. 703-358-4590. 8AM-4PM (EST). Access by: Mail, in person.

Augusta County

Real Estate Recording—Augusta County Clerk of the Circuit Court, 1 East Johnson Street, Courthouse, Staunton, VA 24401. 540-245-5321. Fax: 540-245-5318. 8AM-5PM (EST).

Felony, Civil Actions Over $10,000, Probate—25th Circuit Court, PO Box 689, Staunton, VA 24402-0689. 540-245-5321. 8AM-5PM (EST). Access by: Phone, mail, in person.

Misdemeanor, Civil Actions Under $10,000, Eviction, Small Claims—25th General District Court, 6 E Johnson St, 2nd Floor, Staunton, VA 24401. 540-245-5300. Fax: 540-839-7222. 8:30AM-4:30PM (EST). Access by: Mail, in person.

Bath County

Real Estate Recording—Bath County Clerk of the Circuit Court, Courthouse, Room 101, Warm Springs, VA 24484. 540-839-7226. 8:30AM-4:30PM (EST).

Felony, Civil Actions Over $10,000, Probate—25th Circuit Court, PO Box 180, Warm Springs, VA 24484. 540-839-7226. 8:30AM-4:30PM (EST). Access by: In person only.

Misdemeanor, Civil Actions Under $10,000, Eviction, Small Claims—25th General District Court, PO Box 96, Warm Springs, VA 24484. 540-839-7241. Fax: 540-839-7222. 8:30AM-4:30PM (EST). Access by: Phone, mail, in person.

Bedford City

Real Estate Recording—Bedford County handles real estate recording for this city.

Felony, Misdemeanor, Civil, Eviction, Small Claims, Probate—Circuit and District Courts. Handled by Bedford County courts.

Bedford County

Real Estate Recording—Bedford County Clerk of the Circuit Court, Courthouse, Corner Court & Main Streets, Bedford, VA 24523. 540-586-7632. 8:30AM-5PM (EST).

Felony, Civil Actions Over $10,000, Probate—24th Circuit Court, PO Box 235, Bedford, VA 24523. 540-586-7632. 8:30AM-5PM (EST). Access by: In person only.

Misdemeanor, Civil Actions Under $10,000, Eviction, Small Claims—Bedford General District Court, 123 E Main St, Rm 204, Bedford, VA 24523. 540-586-7637. 8AM-4PM (EST). Access by: Mail, in person.

Bland County

Real Estate Recording—Bland County Clerk of the Circuit Court, #1 Courthouse Square, Bland, VA 24315. 540-688-4562. Fax: 540-688-4562. 8AM-6PM (EST).

Felony, Civil Actions Over $10,000, Probate—27th Circuit Court, PO Box 295, Bland, VA 24315. 540-688-4562. Fax: 540-688-4562. 8AM-6PM (EST). Access by: Mail, in person.

Misdemeanor, Civil Actions Under $10,000, Eviction, Small Claims—27th General District Court, PO Box 157, Bland, VA 24315. 540-688-4433. Fax: 540-688-4622. 8AM-5PM (EST). Access by: Phone, mail, in person.

Botetourt County

Real Estate Recording—Botetourt County Clerk of the Circuit Court, Main St. and Roanoke St., Courthouse, Fincastle, VA 24090. 540-473-8274. 8:30AM-4:30PM (EST).

Felony, Civil Actions Over $10,000, Probate—25th Circuit Court, PO Box 219, Fincastle, VA 24090. 540-473-8274. Fax: 540-473-8276. 8:30AM-4:30PM (EST). Access by: Mail, in person.

Misdemeanor, Civil Actions Under $10,000, Eviction, Small Claims—25th General District Court, PO Box 205, Fincastle, VA 24090. 540-473-8244. Fax: 540-473-8344. 8AM-4PM (EST). Access by: Mail, in person.

Bristol City

Real Estate Recording—Bristol City Clerk of the Circuit Court, 497 Cumberland Street, Room 210, Bristol, VA 24201. 540-645-7321. 9AM-5PM (EST).

Felony, Civil Actions Over $10,000, Probate—28th Circuit Court, 497 Cumberland St, Bristol, VA 24201. 540-466-2221. Fax: 540-645-7321. 9AM-5PM. Access by: In person only.

Misdemeanor, Civil Actions Under $10,000, Eviction, Small Claims—28th General District Court, 497 Cumberland St, Bristol, VA 24201. 540-645-7341. Fax: 540-645-7345. 8:30AM-5PM. Access by: Mail, in person.

Brunswick County

Real Estate Recording—Brunswick County Circuit Court, 216 N. Main St., Lawrenceville, VA 23868. 804-848-2215. Fax: 804-848-4307. 8:30AM-5PM (EST).

Felony, Civil, Probate—6th Circuit Court, 216 N Main St, Lawrenceville, VA 23868. 804-848-2215. Fax: 804-848-4307. 8:30AM-5PM (EST). Access by: In person only.

Misdemeanor, Civil Actions Under $10,000, Eviction, Small Claims—6th General District Court, PO Box 66, 228 Main St, Lawrenceville, VA 23868. 804-848-2315. 8:30AM-4:30PM (EST). Access by: Mail, in person.

Buchanan County

Real Estate Recording—Buchanan County Clerk of the Circuit Court, Courthouse, 2nd Floor, Grundy, VA 24614. 540-935-6567. 8:30AM-5PM (EST).

Felony, Misdemeanor, Civil, Eviction, Probate—29th Circuit and District Court, PO Box 929, Grundy, VA 24614. 540-935-6575. 8:30AM-5PM (EST). Access by: Phone, mail, in person.

Buckingham County

Real Estate Recording—Buckingham County Clerk of the Circuit Court, Highway 60, Courthouse, Buckingham, VA 23921. 804-969-4734. Fax: 804-959-2043. 8:30AM-4:30PM (EST).

Felony, Civil Actions Over $10,000, Probate—10th Circuit Court, Route 60, PO Box 107, Buckingham, VA 23921. 804-969-4734. Fax: 804-969-2043. 8:30AM-4:30PM (EST). Access by: In person only.

Misdemeanor, Civil Actions Under $10,000, Eviction, Small Claims—Buckingham General District Court, PO Box 127, Buckingham, VA 23921. 804-969-4755. 8:30AM-4:30PM (EST). Access by: Mail, in person.

Buena Vista City

Real Estate Recording—Clerk of Circuit Court, 2039 Sycamore Ave., Buena Vista, VA 24416. 540-261-8627. Fax: 540-261-2142.

Felony, Misdemeanor, Civil, Eviction, Probate—25th Circuit and District Court, 2039 Sycamore Ave, Buena Vista, VA 24416. 540-261-6121. Fax: 540-261-2142. 8:30AM-5PM. Access by: Mail, in person.

Campbell County

Real Estate Recording—Campbell County Clerk of the Circuit Court, Main Street, New Courthouse, Rustburg, VA 24588. 804-592-9517. 8:30AM-4:30PM (EST).

Felony, Civil Actions Over $10,000, Probate—24th Circuit Court, State RD 501 Village Hwy, PO Box 7, Rustburg, VA 24588. 804-332-5161. 8:30AM-4:30PM (EST). Access by: In person only.

Misdemeanor, Civil Actions Under $10,000, Eviction, Small Claims—24th General District Court, Campbell County Courthouse, New Courthouse Bldg, PO Box 7, Rustburg, VA 24588. 804-332-5161. 8:30AM-4:30PM (EST). Access by: In person only.

Caroline County

Real Estate Recording—Caroline County Clerk of the Circuit Court, Main St. & Courthouse Lane, Bowling Green, VA 22427. 804-633-5800. 8:30AM-5PM (Recording Hours 8:30AM-4:30PM) (EST).

Felony, Civil Actions Over $10,000, Probate—15th Circuit Court, Main St & Courthouse Ln, PO Box 309, Bowling Green, VA 22427. 804-633-5800. 9AM-5PM (EST). Access by: In person only.

Misdemeanor, Civil Actions Under $10,000, Eviction, Small Claims—15th General District Court, PO Box 511, Bowling Green, VA 22427. 804-633-5720. 8AM-4PM (EST). Access by: Mail, in person.

Carroll County

Real Estate Recording—Carroll County Clerk of the Circuit Court, 515 North Main Street, Courthouse, Hillsville, VA 24343. 540-728-3117. Fax: 540-728-0255. 8AM-5PM (EST).

Felony, Civil Actions Over $10,000, Probate—27th Circuit Court, PO Box 218, Hillsville, VA 24343. 540-728-3117. 8AM-5PM (EST). Access by: Mail, in person.

Misdemeanor, Civil Actions Under $10,000, Eviction, Small Claims—27th General District Court, PO Box 698, Hillsville, VA 24343. 540-728-7751. Fax: 540-728-2582. 8AM-4:30PM (EST). Access by: In person only.

Charles City County

Real Estate Recording—Charles City County Clerk of the Circuit Court, 10700 Courthouse Road, Intersection of Rts 5 and 155, Charles City, VA 23030. 804-829-9212. Fax: 804-829-5647. 8:30AM-4:30PM (EST).

Felony, Civil Actions Over $10,000, Probate—9th Circuit Court, 10700 Courthouse Rd, PO Box 86, Charles City, VA 23030-0086. 804-829-9212. Fax: 804-829-5647. 8:30AM-4:30PM (EST). Access by: Mail, in person.

Misdemeanor, Civil Actions Under $10,000, Eviction, Small Claims—9th General District Court, Charles City Courthouse, 10700 Courthouse Rd, Charles City, VA 23030. 757-829-9224. 8:30AM-4:30PM (EST). Access by: Mail, in person.

Charlotte County

Real Estate Recording—Charlotte County Clerk of the Circuit Court, Courthouse, Charlotte Court House, VA 23923. 804-542-5147. Fax: 804-542-4336. 8:30AM-4:30PM (EST).

Felony, Civil Actions Over $10,000, Probate—10th Circuit Court, #8 LeGrande Ave PO Box 38, Charlotte Court, VA 23923. 804-542-5147. 8:30AM-4:30PM (EST). Access by: In person only.

Misdemeanor, Civil Actions Under $10,000, Eviction, Small Claims—Charlotte General District Court, PO Box 127, Charlotte Courthouse, VA 23923. 804-542-5600. Fax: 804-542-5902. 8:30AM-4:30PM (EST). Access by: In person only.

Charlottesville City

Real Estate Recording—Charlottesville City Clerk of the Circuit Court, 315 East High Street, Charlottesville, VA 22901. 804-295-3182. 8:30AM-4:30PM (EST).

Felony, Civil Actions Over $10,000, Probate—16th Circuit Court, 315 E High St, Charlottesville, VA 22902. 804-295-3182. 8:30AM-4:30PM. Access by: In person only.

Misdemeanor, Civil Actions Under $10,000, Eviction, Small Claims—Charlottesville General District Court, 606 E Market St, PO Box 2677, Charlottesville, VA 22902. 804-971-3385. Fax: 804-971-3387. 8:30AM-4:30PM. Access by: Mail, in person.

Chesapeake City

Real Estate Recording—Chesapeake Clerk of the Circuit Court, 300 Cedar Road, Chesapeake, VA 23320. 757-382-6513. Fax: 757-382-8750. 8:30AM-5PM (EST).

Felony, Civil Actions Over $10,000, Probate—1st Circuit Court, PO Box 15205, Chesapeake, VA 23328. 757-547-6111. 8:30AM-5PM. Access by: In person only.

Misdemeanor, Civil Actions Under $10,000, Eviction, Small Claims—1st General District Court, 308 Shed Dr, Chesapeake, VA 23320. 757-382-6396. 8AM-4PM. Access by: Mail, in person.

Chesterfield County

Real Estate Recording—Chesterfield County Clerk of the Circuit Court, 9500 Courthouse Road, Chesterfield, VA 23832. 804-748-1285. Fax: 804-796-5625. 8:30AM-5PM (Recording hours: 8:30AM-4PM M-Th; 8:30AM-3PM F) (EST).

Felony, Civil Actions Over $10,000, Probate—12th Circuit Court, 9500 Courthouse Rd, PO Box 125, Chesterfield, VA 23832. 804-748-1241. Fax: 804-796-5625. 8:30AM-5PM (EST). Access by: Mail, in person.

Misdemeanor, Civil Actions Under $10,000, Eviction, Small Claims—12th General District Court, PO Box 144, Chesterfield, VA 23832. 804-748-1231. 8AM-4PM (EST). Access by: Mail, in person.

Clarke County

Real Estate Recording—Clarke County Clerk of the Circuit Court, 102 North Church Street, Courthouse, Berryville, VA 22611. 540-955-5116. 9AM-5PM (EST).

Felony, Civil Actions Over $10,000, Probate—26th Circuit Court, PO Box 189, Berryville, VA 22611. 540-955-5116. 9AM-5PM (EST). Access by: In person only.

Misdemeanor, Civil Actions Under $10,000, Eviction, Small Claims—26th General District Court, 104 N Church St (PO Box 612), Berryville, VA 22611. 540-955-5128. Fax: 540-955-1195. 8:30AM-4:30PM (EST). Access by: Mail, in person.

Clifton Forge City

Real Estate Recording—Clifton Forge City Clerk of the Circuit Court, 547 Main St., Clifton Forge, VA 24422. 540-863-2508.

Felony, Civil Actions Over $10,000, Probate—25th Circuit Court, 547 Main St, PO Box 27, Clifton Forge, VA 24422. 540-863-8536. 9AM-5PM. Access by: Mail, in person.

Misdemeanor, Civil Actions Under $10,000, Eviction, Small Claims—25th General District Court, 547 Main St, Clifton Forge, VA 24422. 540-863-2510. 9AM-5PM. Access by: Mail, in person.

Colonial Heights City

Real Estate Recording—Clerk, Colonial Heights Circuit Court, 401 Temple Avenue, Courthouse, Colonial Heights, VA 23834. 804-520-9364. 8:30AM-5PM (EST).

Felony, Civil Actions Over $10,000, Probate—12th Circuit Court, 401 Temple Ave, PO Box 3401, Colonial Heights, VA 23834. 804-520-9364. 8:30AM-5PM. Access by: Mail, in person.

Misdemeanor, Civil Actions Under $10,000, Eviction, Small Claims—12th General District Court, 401 Temple Ave, PO Box 279, Colonial Heights, VA 23834. 804-520-9346. 8:30AM-4:30PM. Access by: In person only.

Covington City

Real Estate Recording—Alleghany County handles real estate recording for this city.

Felony, Misdemeanor, Civil, Eviction, Small Claims, Probate—Circuit and District Courts. Handled by Alleghany County courts.

Craig County

Real Estate Recording—Craig County Clerk of the Circuit Court, 303 Main Street, Courthouse, New Castle, VA 24127. 540-864-6141. 9AM-5PM (EST).

Felony, Civil Actions Over $10,000, Probate—25th Circuit Court, PO Box 185, New Castle, VA 24127. 540-864-6141. 9AM-5PM (EST). Access by: In person only.

Misdemeanor, Civil Actions Under $10,000, Eviction, Small Claims—25th General District Court, PO Box 232, New Castle, VA 24127. 540-864-5989. 8:15AM-4:45PM (EST). Access by: Mail, in person.

Culpeper County

Real Estate Recording—Culpeper County Clerk of the Circuit Court, 135 West Cameron Street, Culpeper, VA 22701. 540-825-8086. 8:30AM-4:30PM (EST).

Felony, Civil Actions Over $10,000, Probate—16th Circuit Court, 135 W Cameron St, Culpeper, VA 22701. 540-825-8086. 8:30AM-4:30PM (EST). Access by: Mail, in person.

Misdemeanor, Civil Actions Under $10,000, Eviction, Small Claims—16th General District Court, 135 W Cameron St, Culpeper, VA 22701. 540-825-0065. 8:30AM-4:30PM (EST). Access by: Mail, in person.

Cumberland County

Real Estate Recording—Cumberland County Clerk of the Circuit Court, County Office Building, Cumberland, VA 23040. 804-492-4442. Fax: 804-492-4876. 8:30AM-4:30PM (EST).

Felony, Civil Actions Over $10,000, Probate—10th Circuit Court, PO Box 8, Cumberland, VA 23040. 804-492-4442. 8:30AM-4:30PM (EST). Access by: Phone, mail, in person.

Misdemeanor, Civil Actions Under $10,000, Eviction, Small Claims—10th General District Court, PO Box 24, Cumberland, VA 23040. 804-492-4848. Fax: 804-492-9455. 8:30AM-4:30PM (EST). Access by: Phone, fax, mail, in person.

Danville City

Real Estate Recording—Danville City Clerk of the Circuit Court, 212 Lynn Street, Danville, VA 24541. 804-799-5168. Fax: 804-799-6502. 8:30AM-5PM (EST).

Felony, Civil Actions Over $10,000, Probate—22nd Circuit Court, PO Box 3300, Danville, VA 24543. 804-799-5168. Fax: 804-799-6502. 8:30AM-5PM. Access by: In person only.

Misdemeanor, Civil Actions Under $10,000, Eviction, Small Claims—22nd General District Court, PO Box 3300, Danville, VA 24543. 804-799-5179. Fax: 804-797-8814. 8:30AM-4:30PM. Access by: In person only.

Dickenson County

Real Estate Recording—Dickenson County Clerk of the Circuit Court, Main Street, Courthouse, Clintwood, VA 24228. 540-926-1616. Fax: 540-926-1649. 8:30AM-4:30PM (EST).

Felony, Civil Actions Over $10,000, Probate—29th Circuit Court, PO Box 190, Clintwood, VA 24228. 540-926-1616. Fax: 540-926-1649. 8:30AM-4:30PM (EST). Access by: Phone, mail, in person.

Misdemeanor, Civil Actions Under $10,000, Eviction, Small Claims—29th General District Court, PO Box 128, Clintwood, VA 24228. 540-926-1630. Fax: 540-926-1649. 8:30AM-4:30PM (EST). Access by: Phone, mail, in person.

Dinwiddie County

Real Estate Recording—Dinwiddie County Clerk of the Circuit Court, Courthouse, Dinwiddie, VA 23841. 804-469-4540. 9AM-5PM (EST).

Felony, Civil Actions Over $10,000, Probate—11th Circuit Court, PO Box 63, Dinwiddie, VA 23841. 804-469-4540. 9AM-5PM (EST). Access by: Mail, in person.

Misdemeanor, Civil Actions Under $10,000, Eviction, Small Claims—11th General District Court, PO Box 280, Dinwiddie, VA 23841. 804-469-4533. Fax: 804-469-4412. 8:30AM-4:30PM (EST). Access by: Mail, in person.

Emporia City

Real Estate Recording—Greenville County handles real estate recording for this city.

Misdemeanor, Civil Actions Under $10,000, Eviction, Small Claims—6th General District Court, PO Box 511, 201 S Main, Emporia, VA 23847. 804-634-5400. 8:30AM-4:30PM. Access by: Mail, in person.

Essex County

Real Estate Recording—Essex County Clerk of the Circuit Court, 305 Prince Street, Tappahannock, VA 22560. 804-443-3541. 9AM-5PM (EST).

Felony, Civil Actions Over $10,000, Probate—15th Circuit Court, PO Box 445, Tappahannock, VA 22560. 804-443-3541. 9AM-5PM (EST). Access by: In person only.

Misdemeanor, Civil Actions Under $10,000, Eviction, Small Claims—15th General District Court, PO Box 66, Tappahannock, VA 22560. 804-443-3744. 8:30AM-12:30PM, 1-4:30PM (EST). Access by: In person only.

Fairfax City

Real Estate Recording—Fairfax County handles real estate recoridng for this city.

Misdemeanor—19th General District Court, 10455 Armstrong St #304, Fairfax, VA 22030. 703-385-7866. Fax: 703-352-3195. 8:30AM-4:30PM. Access by: Mail, in person.

Fairfax County

Real Estate Recording—Fairfax County Clerk of the Circuit Court, 4110 Chain Bridge Road, 3rd Floor, Fairfax, VA 22030. 703-246-4100. 8AM-4PM (EST).

Felony, Civil Actions Over $10,000, Probate—19th Circuit Court, 4110 Chain Bridge Rd, Fairfax, VA 22030. Civil: 703-591-8507. Criminal: 703-246-2228. 8AM-4PM (EST). Access by: In person only.

Misdemeanor, Civil Actions Under $10,000, Eviction, Small Claims—19th General District Court, 4110 Chain Bridge Rd, Fairfax, VA 22030. Civil: 703-246-3012. Criminal: 703-246-3305. 8AM-4PM (EST). Access by: Phone, in person.

Falls Church City

Real Estate Recording—Real estate documents for this city should be submitted to Arlington County or Fairfax County, depending on ZIP Code.

Misdemeanor, Civil Actions Under $10,000, Eviction, Small Claims—17th District Courts Combined, 300 Park Ave, Falls Church, VA 22046-3305. 703-241-5096. Fax: 703-241-1407. 8AM-4PM. Access by: Fax, mail, in person.

Fauquier County

Real Estate Recording—Fauquier County Clerk of the Circuit Court, First Floor, 40 CulpeperSt., Warrenton, VA 20186. 540-347-8606. 8AM-4:30PM (EST).

Felony, Civil Actions Over $10,000, Probate—20th Circuit Court, 40 Culpepper St, Warrenton, VA 20186. 540-347-8610. 8AM-4:30PM (EST). Access by: In person only.

Misdemeanor, Civil Actions Under $10,000, Eviction, Small Claims—20th General District Court, 6 Court St,

Warrenton, VA 22086. 540-347-8676. Fax: 540-347-5756. 8:30AM-4:30PM (EST). Access by: In person only.

Floyd County

Real Estate Recording—Floyd County Clerk of the Circuit Court, 100 East Main Street, Room 200, Floyd, VA 24091. 540-745-9330. 8:30AM-4:30PM; 8:30AM-Noon Sat (Closed Sat if holiday weekend) (EST).

Felony, Civil Actions Over $10,000, Probate—27th Circuit Court, 100 East Main St, #200, Floyd, VA 24091. 540-745-9330. 8:30AM-4:30PM M-F, 8:30AM-Noon Sat (EST). Access by: In person only.

Misdemeanor, Civil Actions Under $10,000, Eviction, Small Claims—27th General District Court, 100 East Main St, Floyd, VA 24091. 540-745-9327. 8AM-4:30PM (EST). Access by: Mail, in person.

Fluvanna County

Real Estate Recording—Fluvanna County Clerk of the Circuit Court, Clerk's Office Bldg., Court Green & Rt. 15, Palmyra, VA 22963. 804-589-8011. Fax: 804-589-6004. 8AM-4:30PM (EST).

Felony, Civil Actions Over $10,000, Probate—16th Circuit Court, PO Box 299, Palmyra, VA 22963. 804-589-8011. Fax: 804-589-6004. 8:30AM-4:30PM (EST). Access by: Fax, mail, in person.

Misdemeanor, Civil Actions Under $10,000, Eviction, Small Claims—16th General District Court, Fluvanna County Courthouse, PO Box 417, Palmyra, VA 22963. 804-589-8022. Fax: 804-589-6934. 8:30AM-4:30PM (EST). Access by: In person only.

Franklin City

Real Estate Recording—Southampton County handles real estate recording for this city.

Misdemeanor, Civil Actions Under $10,000, Eviction, Small Claims—22nd General District Court, PO Box 569, Rocky Mount, VA 24151. 540-483-3060. Fax: 540-483-3036. 8:30AM-4:30PM. Access by: Mail, in person.

Franklin County

Real Estate Recording—Franklin County Clerk of the Circuit Court, Courthouse Building, Rocky Mount, VA 24151. 540-483-3065. Fax: 540-483-3042. 8:30AM-5PM (EST).

Felony, Civil Actions Over $10,000, Probate—22nd Circuit Court, PO Box 190, Courtland, VA 23837. 540-653-2200. 8:30AM-5PM (EST). Access by: Mail, in person.

Frederick County

Real Estate Recording—Frederick County Clerk of the Circuit Court, 5 North Kent Street, Winchester, VA 22601. 540-667-5770. 9AM-5PM (EST).

Felony, Misdemeanor, Civil, Eviction, Probate—26th Circuit and District Court, 5 North Kent St, Winchester, VA 22601. 540-667-5770. 9AM-5PM (EST). Access by: In person only.

Fredericksburg City

Real Estate Recording—Fredericksburg City Clerk of the Circuit Court, 815 Princess Anne Street, Fredericksburg, VA 22401. 540-372-1066. 8AM-4PM (EST).

Felony, Civil Actions Over $10,000, Probate—Fredericksburg Circuit Court, 815 Princess Anne St, PO Box 359, Fredericksburg, VA 22404-0359. 540-372-1066. 8AM-4PM. Access by: In person only.

Misdemeanor, Civil Actions Under $10,000, Eviction, Small Claims—15th General District Court, PO Box 180, Fredericksburg, VA 22404. 540-372-1044. 8AM-4PM. Access by: Mail, in person.

Galax City

Real Estate Recording—Carroll County handles real estate recording for this city.

Misdemeanor, Civil Actions Under $10,000, Eviction, Small Claims—27th General District Court, 353 N Main St,

PO Box 214, Galax, VA 24333. 540-236-8731. Fax: 540-236-2754. 8:30AM-5PM. Access by: Mail, in person.

Giles County

Real Estate Recording—Giles County Clerk of the Circuit Court, 501 Wenonah Avenue, Pearisburg, VA 24134. 540-921-1722. Fax: 540-921-3825. 9AM-5PM (EST).

Felony, Civil Actions Over $10,000, Probate—27th Circuit Court, 501 Wenonah Ave, Pearisburg, VA 24134. 540-921-1722. 9AM-5PM (EST). Access by: Mail, in person.

Misdemeanor, Civil Actions Under $10,000, Eviction, Small Claims—27th General District Court, Giles County Courthouse, Pearisburg, VA 24134. 540-921-3533. Fax: 540-921-2752. 8:30AM-4:30PM (EST). Access by: Fax, mail, in person.

Gloucester County

Real Estate Recording—Gloucester County Clerk of the Circuit Court, Courts & Office Bldg, Room 207, 6489 Main Street, Gloucester, VA 23061. 804-693-2502. Fax: 804-693-2186. 8AM-4:30PM (EST).

Felony, Civil Actions Over $10,000, Probate—9th Circuit Court, Box N, Gloucester, VA 23061. 804-693-2502. Fax: 804-693-2186. 8AM-4:30PM (EST). Access by: In person only.

Misdemeanor, Civil Actions Under $10,000, Eviction, Small Claims—9th General District Court, PO Box 873, Gloucester, VA 23061. 804-693-4860. Fax: 804-693-6669. 8:30AM-4:30PM (EST). Access by: Mail, in person.

Goochland County

Real Estate Recording—Goochland County Clerk of the Circuit Court, 2938 River Road West, Goochland, VA 23063. 804-556-5353. 8:30AM-5PM (EST).

Felony, Civil Actions Over $10,000, Probate—16th Circuit Court, PO Box 196, Goochland, VA 23063. 804-556-5353. 8:30AM-5PM (EST). Access by: In person only.

Misdemeanor, Civil Actions Under $10,000, Eviction, Small Claims—General District Court, PO Box 47, Goochland, VA 23063. 804-556-5309. 8:30AM-4:30PM (EST). Access by: In person only.

Grayson County

Real Estate Recording—Grayson County Clerk of the Circuit Court, 129 Davis Street, Independence, VA 24348. 540-773-2231. Fax: 540-773-3338. 8AM-5PM (EST).

Felony, Civil Actions Over $10,000, Probate—27th Circuit Court, PO Box 130, Independence, VA 24348. 540-773-2231. Fax: 540-773-3338. 8AM-5PM (EST). Access by: Mail, in person.

Misdemeanor, Civil Actions Under $10,000, Eviction, Small Claims—27th General District Court, PO Box 280, Independence, VA 24348. 540-773-2011. 8AM-4:30PM (EST). Access by: Mail, in person.

Greene County

Real Estate Recording—Greene County Clerk of the Circuit Court, Courthouse, Court Square, Stanardsville, VA 22973. 804-985-5208. 8:15AM-4:30PM (EST).

Felony, Civil Actions Over $10,000, Probate—16th Circuit Court, PO Box 386, Stanardsville, VA 22973. 804-985-5208. 8:30AM-4:30PM; Recording until 4:15 PM (EST). Access by: Mail, in person.

Misdemeanor, Civil Actions Under $10,000, Eviction, Small Claims—16th General District Court, Greene County Courthouse (PO Box 245), Stanardsville, VA 22973. 804-985-5224. 8AM-4:30PM (EST). Access by: Mail, in person.

Greensville County

Real Estate Recording—Greensville County Clerk of the Circuit Court, 308 South Main Street, Emporia, VA 23847. 804-348-4215. Fax: 804-348-4020. 9AM-5PM (EST).

Felony, Civil Actions Over $10,000, Probate—6th Circuit Court, PO Box 631, Emporia, VA 23847. 804-348-4215. 9AM-5PM (EST). Access by: In person only.

Misdemeanor, Civil Actions Under $10,000, Eviction, Small Claims—6th General District Court, Greensville

County Courthouse, 301 S Main St, Emporia, VA 23847. 804-348-4266. 8:30AM-4:30PM (EST). Access by: In person only.

Halifax County

Real Estate Recording—Halifax County Clerk of the Circuit Court, Courthouse Square, Halifax, VA 24558. 804-476-6211. (EST).

Felony, Civil Actions Over $10,000, Probate—10th Circuit Court, PO Box 729, Halifax, VA 24558. 804-476-6211. 8:30AM-5PM (EST). Access by: Mail, in person.

Misdemeanor, Civil Actions Under $10,000, Eviction, Small Claims—10th General District Court, Halifax County Courthouse, PO Box 450, Halifax, VA 24558. 804-476-6217. 8:30AM-4:30PM (EST). Access by: In person only.

Hampton City

Real Estate Recording—Hampton Clerk of the Circuit Court, 101 Kingsway Mall, Hampton, VA 23669. 757-727-6896. 8:30AM-5PM (EST).

Felony, Civil Actions Over $10,000, Probate—8th Circuit Court, 101 King's Way, PO Box 40, Hampton, VA 23669. 804-727-6105. 8:30AM-5PM. Access by: Mail, in person.

Misdemeanor, Civil Actions Under $10,000, Eviction, Small Claims—8th General District Court, Courthouse, Po Box 70, Hampton, VA 23669. Civil: 804-727-6480. Criminal: 804-727-6260/6262. 8AM-4PM. Access by: Mail, in person.

Hanover County

Real Estate Recording—Hanover County Clerk of the Circuit Court, 7507 Library Dr., 2nd Floor, Hanover, VA 23069. 804-537-6151. 8:30AM-4:30PM (EST).

Felony, Civil Actions Over $10,000, Probate—15th Circuit Court, PO Box 39, Hanover, VA 23069. 804-537-6143. 8:30AM-4:30PM (EST). Access by: In person only.

Misdemeanor, Civil Actions Under $10,000, Eviction, Small Claims—15th General District Court, Hanover County Courthouse, PO Box 176, Hanover, VA 23069. 804-537-6000. 8AM-4PM (EST). Access by: In person only.

Harrisonburg City

Real Estate Recording—Rockingham County handles real estate recording for this city.

Felony, Misdemeanor, Civil, Eviction, Small Claims, Probate—Circuit and District Courts. Handled by Rockingham County courts.

Henrico County

Real Estate Recording—Henrico Circuit Court Clerk, 4301 East Parham Road, Richmond, VA 23228. 804-672-4249. 8AM-4:30PM; (Recording Hours 8AM-3:30PM) (EST).

Felony, Civil Actions Over $10,000, Probate—14th Circuit Court, PO Box 27032, Richmond, VA 23273-7032. 804-672-4203. Criminal: 804-672-4764. 8AM-4:30PM (EST). Access by: Mail, in person.

Misdemeanor, Civil Actions Under $10,000, Eviction, Small Claims—14th General District Court, PO Box 27032, Richmond, VA 23273. 804-672-4723. Civil: 804-672-4721. Criminal: 804-672-4723. Fax: 804-672-4141. 8AM-4PM (EST). Access by: In person only.

Henry County

Real Estate Recording—Henry County Clerk of the Circuit Court, 3160 Kings Mountain Rd. #B, Martinsville, VA 24112. 540-634-4880. 9AM-5PM (EST).

Felony, Civil Actions Over $10,000, Probate—21st Circuit Court, 3160 King's Mountain Rd Suite B, Martinsville, VA 24114. 540-634-4880. 9AM-5PM (EST). Access by: In person only.

Misdemeanor, Civil Actions Under $10,000, Eviction, Small Claims—21st General District Court, 3160 King's Mountain Rd Ste A, Martinsville, VA 24112. 540-638-7531. Fax: 540-638-1148. 9AM-5PM (EST). Access by: Fax, mail, in person.

Highland County

Real Estate Recording—Highland County Clerk of the Circuit Court, Spruce Street, Courthouse, Monterey, VA 24465. 540-468-2447. Fax: 540-468-3447. 8:45AM-4:30PM (EST).

Felony, Civil Actions Over $10,000, Probate—25th Circuit Court, PO Box 190, Monterey, VA 24465. 540-468-2447. 8:45AM-4:30PM (EST). Access by: Mail, in person.

Misdemeanor, Civil Actions Under $10,000, Eviction, Small Claims—25th General District Court, Highland County Courthouse, PO Box 88, Monterey, VA 24465. 540-468-2445. Fax: 540-468-3447. 8:30AM-4:30PM (EST). Access by: Fax, mail, in person.

Hopewell City

Real Estate Recording—Hopewell City Clerk of the Circuit Court, 100 E. Broadway, Room 251, Hopewell, VA 23860. 804-541-2239. 8:30AM-4:30PM (EST).

Felony, Civil Actions Over $10,000, Probate—6th Circuit Court, 100 E Broadway, PO Box 354, Hopewell, VA 23860. 804-541-2239. 8:30AM-4:30PM. Access by: In person only.

Misdemeanor, Civil Actions Under $10,000, Eviction, Small Claims—Hopewell District Court, 100 E Broadway, Hopewell, VA 23860. 804-541-2257. Fax: 804-541-2364. 8:30AM-4:30PM. Access by: In person only.

Isle of Wight County

Real Estate Recording—Isle of Wight County Clerk of the Circuit Court, 17122 Monument Circle, Hwy 258, Courthouse, Isle of Wight, VA 23397. 757-357-3191. 9AM-5PM (EST).

Felony, Civil Actions Over $10,000, Probate—5th Circuit Court, 17122 Monument Circle, PO Box 110, Isle of Wight, VA 23397. 757-357-3191. 9AM-5PM (EST). Access by: In person only.

Misdemeanor, Civil Actions Under $10,000, Eviction, Small Claims—5th General District Court, Isle of Wight Courthouse, PO Box 122, Isle of Wight, VA 23397. 757-357-3191. 8:30AM-5PM (EST). Access by: In person only.

James City County

Real Estate Recording—Williamsburg-James City County Clerk of the Circuit Court, 321-45 Court Street West, Room 28, Williamsburg, VA 23185. 757-229-2552. 8:30AM-4:30PM (EST).

Felony, Civil Actions Over $10,000, Probate—9th Circuit Court, PO Box 3045, Williamsburg, VA 23187-3045. 757-229-2552. 8:30AM-4:30PM (EST). Access by: Mail, in person.

Misdemeanor, Civil Actions Under $10,000, Eviction, Small Claims—9th General District Court, James City County Courthouse, PO Box 3005, Williamsburg, VA 23187. 757-229-2228. Fax: 757-220-8360. 7:30AM-4PM (EST). Access by: Fax, mail, in person.

King George County

Real Estate Recording—King George County Clerk of the Circuit Court, 9483 Kings Highway, Courthouse, King George, VA 22485. 540-775-3322. 8:30AM-4:30PM (EST).

Felony, Civil Actions Over $10,000, Probate—15th Circuit Court, PO Box 105, King George, VA 22485. 540-775-3322. 8:30AM-4:30PM (EST). Access by: Mail, in person.

Misdemeanor, Civil Actions Under $10,000, Eviction, Small Claims—15th Judicial District King George Combined Court, County Courthouse PO Box 279, King George, VA 22485. 540-775-3573. 8AM-4:30PM (EST). Access by: Mail, in person.

King William County

Real Estate Recording—King William County Clerk of the Circuit Court, Route 619, King William, VA 23086. 804-769-2311. 8:30AM-4:30PM (EST).

Felony, Civil Actions Over $10,000, Probate—9th Circuit Court, PO Box 216, King William, VA 23086. 804-769-4938. 8:30AM-4:30PM (EST). Access by: In person only.

Misdemeanor, Civil Actions Under $10,000, Eviction, Small Claims—King & Queen General District Court, PO Box 5, King William, VA 23086. 804-769-4971. Fax: 804-769-4971. 8:30AM-4:30PM (EST). Access by: Fax, mail, in person.

King and Queen County

Real Estate Recording—King and Queen County Clerk of the Circuit Court, Route 681, Courthouse, King and Queen Court House, VA 23085. 804-785-2460. Fax: 804-785-2928. 9AM-5PM (EST).

Felony, Civil Actions Over $10,000, Probate—9th Circuit Court, PO Box 67, King & Queen Court House, VA 23085. 804-785-2460. 9AM-5PM (EST). Access by: In person only.

Misdemeanor, Civil Actions Under $10,000, Eviction, Small Claims—King & Queen General District Court, PO Box 5, King William, VA 23086. 804-769-4947. Fax: 804-769-4971. 8:30AM-4:30PM (EST). Access by: Fax, mail, in person.

Lancaster County

Real Estate Recording—Lancaster County Clerk of the Circuit Court, Courthouse, Route 3, Lancaster, VA 22503. 804-462-5611. 9AM-5PM (EST).

Felony, Civil Actions Over $10,000, Probate—15th Circuit Court, Courthouse Building, PO Box 125, Lancaster, VA 22503. 804-462-5611. 9AM-5PM (EST). Access by: In person only.

Misdemeanor, Civil Actions Under $10,000, Eviction, Small Claims—15th General District Court, PO 129, Lancaster, VA 22503. 804-462-0012. 8:30AM-4:30PM (EST). Access by: Mail, in person.

Lee County

Real Estate Recording—Lee County Clerk of the Circuit Court, Main Street, Courthouse, Jonesville, VA 24263. 540-346-7763. 8:30AM-5PM; 9AM-Noon Sat (EST).

Felony, Civil Actions Over $10,000, Probate—30th Circuit Court, PO Box 326, Jonesville, VA 24263. 540-346-7763. 8:30AM-5PM M-F, 9AM-Noon Sat (EST). Access by: Mail, in person.

Misdemeanor, Civil Actions Under $10,000, Eviction, Small Claims—30th General District Court, Lee County Courthouse, PO Box 306, Jonesville, VA 24263. 540-346-7729. 8:30AM-4:30PM (EST). Access by: Mail, in person.

Lexington City

Real Estate Recording—Rockbridge County handles real estate recording for this city.

Felony, Misdemeanor, Civil, Eviction, Small Claims, Probate—Circuit and District Courts. Handled Rockbridge County courts.

Loudoun County

Real Estate Recording—Loudoun County Clerk of the Circuit Court, 18 North King Street, Leesburg, VA 20176. 703-777-0270. 9AM-4:30PM (EST).

Felony, Civil Actions Over $10,000, Probate—20th Circuit Court, 18 N King St, PO Box 550, Leesburg, VA 20178. 703-777-0270. 9AM-5PM (EST). Access by: Mail, in person. Mail access for deeds & wills only.

Misdemeanor, Civil Actions Under $10,000, Eviction, Small Claims—20th General District Court, 18 E Market St, Leesburg, VA 20178. 703-777-0312. Fax: 703-777-0311. 8:30AM-4:30PM (EST). Access by: Mail, in person.

Louisa County

Real Estate Recording—Louisa County Clerk of the Circuit Court, 102 Main Street, Courthouse, Louisa, VA 23093. 540-967-3444. 8:30AM-5PM (Stop Recording 4:15PM) (EST).

Felony, Civil Actions Over $10,000, Probate—16th Circuit Court, Box 37, Louisa, VA 23093. 540-967-5314. 8:30AM-5PM (EST). Access by: Mail, in person.

Misdemeanor, Civil Actions Under $10,000, Eviction, Small Claims—16th General District Court, PO Box 452,

Louisa, VA 23093. 540-967-5330. 8:30AM-4:30PM (EST). Access by: In person only.

Lunenburg County

Real Estate Recording—Lunenburg County Clerk of the Circuit Court, Courthouse, Lunenburg, VA 23952. 804-696-2230. 8:30AM-4:30PM (EST).

Felony, Civil Actions Over $10,000, Probate—10th Circuit Court, Courthouse, Lunenburg, VA 23952. 804-696-2230. 8:30AM-4:30PM (EST). Access by: In person only.

Misdemeanor, Civil Actions Under $10,000, Eviction, Small Claims—10th General District Court, Courthouse, Lunenburg, VA 23952. 804-696-5508. Fax: 804-696-3665. 8:30AM-5PM (EST). Access by: Mail, in person.

Lynchburg City

Real Estate Recording—Lynchburg City Clerk of the Circuit Court, 900 Court Street, Lynchburg, VA 24504. 804-847-1590. Fax: 804-847-1864. 8:30AM-4:45PM (EST).

Felony, Civil Actions Over $10,000, Probate—24th Circuit Court, 900 Court St, PO Box 4, Lynchburg, VA 24505-0004. 804-847-1590. 8:30AM-4:45PM. Access by: Mail, in person.

Civil Actions Under $10,000, Eviction, Small Claims—24th General District Court-Civil Division, 901 Church St 3rd Flr, PO Box 60, Lynchburg, VA 24505. 804-847-1639. 8:30AM-4:30PM. Access by: In person only.

Misdemeanor—24th General District Court-Criminal Division, 905 Court St, Lynchburg, VA 24505. 804-847-1560. 8:30AM-4:30PM. Access by: In person only.

Madison County

Real Estate Recording—Madison County Clerk of the Circuit Court, 100 Court Square, Madison, VA 22727. 540-948-6888. Fax: 540-948-3759. 8:30AM-4:30PM (EST).

Felony, Civil Actions Over $10,000, Probate—16th Circuit Court, PO Box 220, Madison, VA 22727. 540-948-6888. Fax: 540-948-3759. 8:30AM-4:30PM (EST). Access by: Mail, in person.

Misdemeanor, Civil Actions Under $10,000, Eviction, Small Claims—16th General District Court, Madison County Courthouse, Madison, VA 22727. 540-948-4657. 8:30AM-4:30PM (EST). Access by: Mail, in person.

Manassas City

Real Estate Recording—Prince William County handles real estate recording for this city.

Felony, Misdemeanor, Civil, Eviction, Small Claims, Probate—Circuit and District Courts. Handled by Prince William County courts.

Manassas Park City

Real Estate Recording—Prince William County handles real estate recording for this city.

Felony, Misdemeanor, Civil, Eviction, Small Claims, Probate—Circuit and District Courts. Handled by Prince William County courts.

Martinsville City

Real Estate Recording—Martinsville City Clerk of the Circuit Court, 55 West Church Street, Martinsville, VA 24112. 540-656-5106. 9AM-5PM (EST).

Felony, Civil Actions Over $10,000, Probate—Henry County Circuit Court ST 10, 3160 Kings Mountain Rd #8, Martinsville, VA 24112-3956. 540-638-3961. 9AM-5PM. Access by: In person only.

Misdemeanor, Civil Actions Under $10,000, Eviction, Small Claims—21st General District Court, 3160 King's Mountain Rd Suite A, PO Box 1402, Martinsville, VA 24112. 540-638-7531. Fax: 540-638-8584. 8AM-5PM. Access by: Mail, in person.

Mathews County

Real Estate Recording—Mathews County Clerk of the Circuit Court, Courthouse Square, Mathews, VA 23109. 804-725-2550. 8AM-4PM (EST).

Felony, Civil Actions Over $10,000, Probate—9th Circuit Court, PO Box 463, Mathews, VA 23109. 804-725-2550. 8AM-4PM (EST). Access by: Mail, in person.

Misdemeanor, Civil Actions Under $10,000, Eviction, Small Claims—9th General District Court, PO Box 169, Saluda, VA 23149. 804-758-4312. 8:30AM-4:30PM (EST). Access by: Mail, in person.

Mecklenburg County

Real Estate Recording—Mecklenburg County Clerk of the Circuit Court, 393 Washington Street, Boydton, VA 23917. 804-738-6191. Fax: 804-738-6191. 8:30AM-5PM (EST).

Felony, Civil Actions Over $10,000, Probate—10th Circuit Court, PO Box 530, Boydton, VA 23917. 804-738-6191. 8:30AM-4:30PM (EST). Access by: In person only.

Misdemeanor, Civil Actions Under $10,000, Eviction, Small Claims—10th General District Court, 1294 Jefferson Street (PO Box 306), Boydton, VA 23917. 804-738-6191. 8:30AM-4:30PM (EST). Access by: Mail, in person.

Middlesex County

Real Estate Recording—Middlesex County Clerk of the Circuit Court, Route 17 Courthouse, Saluda, VA 23149. 804-758-5317. 8:30AM-4:30PM (EST).

Felony, Civil Actions Over $10,000, Probate—9th Circuit Court, PO Box 158, Saluda, VA 23149. 804-758-5317. 8:30AM-4:30PM (EST). Access by: In person only.

Misdemeanor, Civil Actions Under $10,000, Eviction, Small Claims—9th General District Court, PO Box 169, Saluda, VA 23149. 804-758-4312. 8:30AM-4:30PM (EST). Access by: Mail, in person.

Montgomery County

Real Estate Recording—Clerk of the Circuit Court, 1 East Main Street, Suite B5, Christiansburg, VA 24073. 540-382-5760. 8:30AM-4:30PM (EST).

Felony, Civil Actions Over $10,000, Probate—27th Circuit Court, PO Box 209, Christiansburg, VA 24073. 540-382-5760. 8:30AM-4:30PM (EST). Access by: In person only.

Misdemeanor, Civil Actions Under $10,000, Eviction, Small Claims—27th General District Court, Montgomery County Courthouse, PO Box 336, Christiansburg, VA 24073. 540-382-5735. 8:30AM-4:30PM (EST). Access by: Mail, in person.

Nelson County

Real Estate Recording—Nelson County Clerk of the Circuit Court, 84 Courthouse Square, Lovingston, VA 22949. 804-263-4069. Fax: 804-263-8313. 9AM-5PM (EST).

Felony, Civil Actions Over $10,000, Probate—24th Circuit Court, PO Box 10, Lovingston, VA 22949. 804-263-4069. Fax: 804-263-8313. 9AM-5PM (EST). Access by: In person only.

Misdemeanor, Civil Actions Under $10,000, Eviction, Small Claims—24th General District Court, Nelson County Courthouse, 84 Courthouse St, PO Box 55, Lovingston, VA 22949. 804-263-4245. Fax: 804-263-4264. 8AM-4:30PM (EST). Access by: Fax, mail, in person.

New Kent County

Real Estate Recording—New Kent County Clerk of the Circuit Court, 12001 Courthouse Circle, Courthouse, New Kent, VA 23124. 804-966-9520. 8:30AM-4:30PM (EST).

Felony, Civil Actions Over $10,000, Probate—9th Circuit Court, PO Box 98, New Kent, VA 23124. 804-966-9520. Fax: 804-966-9528. 8:30AM-4:30PM (EST). Access by: In person only.

Misdemeanor, Civil Actions Under $10,000, Eviction, Small Claims—9th General District Court, PO Box 127, New Kent, VA 23124. 804-966-9530. Fax: 804-966-9534. 8:30AM-4:30PM (EST). Access by: Mail, in person.

Newport News City

Real Estate Recording—Newport News Clerk of the Circuit Court, 2500 Washington Avenue, Courthouse, Newport

News, VA 23607. 757-247-8561. Fax: 757-247-8531. 8AM-4:45PM (EST).

Felony, Civil Actions Over $10,000, Probate—7th Circuit Court, 2500 Washington Ave, Newport News, VA 23607. 804-247-8691. Fax: 804-247-8531. 8AM-4:45PM. Access by: In person only.

Misdemeanor, Civil Actions Under $10,000, Eviction, Small Claims—7th General District Court, 2500 Washington Ave, Newport News, VA 23607. 804-247-8811. Civil: 804-247-2439. Criminal: 804-247-8111. 7:30AM-4PM. Access by: Mail, in person.

Norfolk City

Real Estate Recording—Norfolk City Clerk of the Circuit Court, 100 St. Paul's Blvd., Norfolk, VA 23510. 757-664-4380. 9AM-5PM (EST).

Felony, Civil Actions Over $10,000, Probate—4th Circuit Court, 100 St Paul's Blvd, Norfolk, VA 23510. 757-664-4380. 9AM-5PM. Access by: In person only.

Misdemeanor, Civil Actions Under $10,000, Eviction, Small Claims—4th General District Court, 811 E City Hall Ave, Norfolk, VA 23510. 757-664-4900. Criminal: 757-664-4916. 8AM-4PM. Access by: Mail, in person.

Northampton County

Real Estate Recording—Northampton County Clerk of the Circuit Court, 16404 Courthouse Rd., Courthouse, Eastville, VA 23347. 757-678-0465. Fax: 757-678-5410. 9AM-5PM (EST).

Felony, Civil Actions Over $10,000, Probate—2nd Circuit Court, PO Box 36, Eastville, VA 23347. 757-678-0465. 9AM-5PM (EST). Access by: Phone, mail, in person.

Misdemeanor, Civil Actions Under $10,000, Eviction, Small Claims—2nd General District Court, PO Box 125, Eastville, VA 23347. 757-678-0466. 8AM-5PM (EST). Access by: Mail, in person.

Northumberland County

Real Estate Recording—Northumberland County Clerk of the Circuit Court, Highway 360, Courthouse, Heathsville, VA 22473. 804-580-3700. 9AM-5PM (EST).

Felony, Civil Actions Over $10,000, Probate—15th Circuit Court, PO Box 217, Heathsville, VA 22473. 804-580-3700. 9AM-5PM (EST). Access by: Mail, in person.

Misdemeanor, Civil Actions Under $10,000, Eviction, Small Claims—15th General District Court, Northumberland Courthouse, PO Box 114, Heathsville, VA 22473. 804-580-4323. 8AM-4:30PM (EST). Access by: In person only.

Norton City

Real Estate Recording—Wise County handles real estate recording for this city.

Felony, Misdemeanor, Civil, Eviction, Small Claims, Probate—Circuit and District Courts. Handled by Wise County courts.

Nottoway County

Real Estate Recording—Nottoway County Clerk of the Circuit Court, State Route 625, Courthouse, Nottoway, VA 23955. 804-645-9043. Fax: 804-645-2144. 8:30AM-4:30PM (EST).

Felony, Civil Actions Over $10,000, Probate—11th Circuit Court, Courthouse, PO Box 25, Nottoway, VA 23955. 804-645-9043. 8:30AM-4:30PM (EST). Access by: Mail, in person.

Misdemeanor, Civil Actions Under $10,000, Eviction, Small Claims—11th General District Court, Courthouse, Nottoway, VA 23955. 804-645-9312. 8AM-4:15PM (EST). Access by: In person only.

Orange County

Real Estate Recording—Orange County Clerk of the Circuit Court, 109 West Main Street, Orange, VA 22960. 540-672-4030. Fax: 540-672-2939. 8:30AM-4:30PM (EST).

Felony, Civil Actions Over $10,000, Probate—16th Circuit Court, PO Box 230, Orange, VA 22960. 540-672-4030. 8:30AM-4:30PM (EST). Access by: In person only.

Misdemeanor, Civil Actions Under $10,000, Eviction, Small Claims—16th General District Court, Orange County Courthouse, PO Box 821, Orange, VA 22960. 540-672-3150. 8:30AM-4:30PM (EST). Access by: Mail, in person.

Page County

Real Estate Recording—Page County Clerk of the Circuit Court, 116 South Court Street, Suite A, Luray, VA 22835. 540-743-4064. 9AM-5PM (EST).

Felony, Civil Actions Over $10,000, Probate—26th Circuit Court, 116 S Court St, Luray, VA 22835. 540-743-4064. 9AM-5PM (EST). Access by: In person only.

Misdemeanor, Civil Actions Under $10,000, Eviction, Small Claims—26th General District Court, 101 S Court St, Luray, VA 22835. 540-743-5705. 8AM-4:30PM (EST). Access by: Mail, in person.

Patrick County

Real Estate Recording—Patrick County Clerk of the Circuit Court, Courthouse, Blue Ridge & Main Streets, Stuart, VA 24171. 540-694-7213. Fax: 540-694-6943. 9AM-5PM (EST).

Felony, Civil Actions Over $10,000, Probate—21st Circuit Court, PO Box 148, Stuart, VA 24171. 540-694-7213. 9AM-5PM (EST). Access by: In person only.

Misdemeanor, Civil Actions Under $10,000, Eviction, Small Claims—21st General District Court, PO Box 149, Stuart, VA 24171. 540-694-7258. Fax: 540-694-5614. 8:30AM-5PM (EST). Access by: Mail, in person.

Petersburg City

Real Estate Recording—Petersburg City Clerk of the Circuit Court, 7 Courthouse Ave., Petersburg, VA 23803. 804-733-2367. Fax: 804-732-5548. 8AM-4:30PM (Recording until 4PM) (EST).

Felony, Civil Actions Over $10,000, Probate—11th Circuit Court, 7 Courthouse Ave, Petersburg, VA 23803. 804-733-2367. 8AM-4:30PM. Access by: In person only.

Misdemeanor, Civil Actions Under $10,000, Eviction, Small Claims—11th General District Court, 35 E Tabb St, Petersburg, VA 23803. 804-733-2374. Fax: 804-862-9120. 8AM-4PM. Access by: In person only.

Pittsylvania County

Real Estate Recording—Pittsylvania County Clerk of the Circuit Court, 1 North Main Street, Courthouse, Chatham, VA 24531. 804-432-2041. 8:30AM-5PM (EST).

Felony, Civil Actions Over $10,000, Probate—22nd Circuit Court, PO Drawer 31, Chatham, VA 24531. 804-432-2041. 8:30AM-5PM (EST). Access by: In person only.

Misdemeanor, Civil Actions Under $10,000, Eviction, Small Claims—22nd General District Court, Pittsylvania Courthouse Annex 2nd Flr, PO Box 695, Chatham, VA 24531. 804-432-2041. Fax: 804-432-1418. 8:30AM-4:30PM (EST). Access by: Mail, in person.

Poquoson City

Real Estate Recording—York County handles real estate recording for this city.

Felony, Misdemeanor, Civil, Eviction, Small Claims, Probate—Circuit and District Courts. Handled by York County courts.

Portsmouth City

Real Estate Recording—Portsmouth City Clerk of the Circuit Court, 601 Crawford Street, Portsmouth, VA 23704. 804-393-8671. 9AM-5PM (EST).

Felony, Civil Actions Over $10,000, Probate—3rd Circuit Court, PO Drawer 1217, Portsmouth, VA 23705. 804-393-8671. Fax: 804-399-4826. 9AM-5PM. Access by: Mail, in person.

Misdemeanor, Civil Actions Under $10,000, Eviction, Small Claims—3rd General District Court, PO Box 129, Portsmouth, VA 23705. Civil: 804-393-8624. Criminal: 804-393-8681. Fax: 804-353-8634. 8:30AM-4:30PM. Access by: Mail, in person.

Powhatan County

Real Estate Recording—Powhatan County Clerk of the Circuit Court, 3880 Old Buckingham Road, Powhatan, VA 23139. 804-598-5660. 8:30AM-5PM (EST).

Felony, Civil Actions Over $10,000, Probate—11th Circuit Court, PO Box 37, Powhatan, VA 23139. 804-598-5660. 8:30AM-5PM (EST). Access by: Mail, in person.

Misdemeanor, Civil Actions Under $10,000, Eviction, Small Claims—11th General District Court, Courthouse, PO Box 113, Powhatan, VA 23139. 804-598-5665. 8:30AM-5PM (EST). Access by: Mail, in person.

Prince Edward County

Real Estate Recording—Prince Edward County Clerk of the Circuit Court, 124 North Main Street, Courthouse, Farmville, VA 23901. 804-392-5145. 9AM-4:30PM (EST).

Felony, Civil Actions Over $10,000, Probate—10th Circuit Court, PO Box 304, Farmville, VA 23901. 804-392-5145. 8:30AM-4:30PM (EST). Access by: In person only.

Misdemeanor, Civil Actions Under $10,000, Eviction, Small Claims—General District Court, PO Box 41, Farmville, VA 23901-0041. 804-392-4024. Fax: 804-392-3800. 8:30AM-4:30PM (EST). Access by: Mail, in person.

Prince George County

Real Estate Recording—Prince George County Clerk of the Circuit Court, 6601 Courts Dr., Prince George, VA 23875. 804-733-2640. Recording Hours 8:30AM-4:30PM (EST).

Felony, Civil Actions Over $10,000, Probate—6th Circuit Court, PO Box 98, Prince George, VA 23875. 804-733-2640. 8:30AM-5PM (EST). Access by: Mail, in person.

Misdemeanor, Civil Actions Under $10,000, Eviction, Small Claims—6th General District Court, P.C. Courthouse, PO Box 187, Prince George, VA 23875. 804-733-2783. 8:30AM-4:30PM (EST). Access by: Mail, in person.

Prince William County

Real Estate Recording—Prince William County Clerk of the Circuit Court, 9311 Lee Avenue, Room 300, Manassas, VA 20110. 703-792-6035. Fax: 703-792-4721. 8:30AM-4PM (Actual Recording); 8:30AM-5PM (General Information) (EST).

Felony, Civil Actions Over $10,000, Probate—31st Circuit Court, 9311 Lee Ave, Manassas, VA 20110. 703-792-6015. 8:30AM-5PM (EST). Access by: Mail, in person.

Misdemeanor, Civil Actions Under $10,000, Eviction, Small Claims—31st General District Court, 9311 Lee Ave, Manassas, VA 20110. Civil: 703-792-6149. Criminal: 703-792-6141. 8:30AM-4:30PM (EST). Access by: Mail, in person.

Pulaski County

Real Estate Recording—Pulaski County Clerk of the Circuit Court, Suite 101, 45 3rd St. NW, Pulaski, VA 24301. 540-980-7825. Fax: 540-980-7835. 8:30AM-4:30PM (EST).

Felony, Civil Actions Over $10,000, Probate—27th Circuit Court, 45 3rd St NW Suite 101, Pulaski, VA 24301. 540-980-7825. Fax: 540-980-7829. 8:30AM-4:30PM (EST). Access by: Mail, in person.

Misdemeanor, Civil Actions Under $10,000, Eviction, Small Claims—27th General District Court, 45 3rd St NW Ste 102, Pulaski, VA 24301. 540-980-7470. Fax: 540-980-7792. 8:30AM-4:30PM (EST). Access by: In person only.

Radford City

Real Estate Recording—Radford City Clerk of the Circuit Court, 619 Second Street, Courthouse, Radford, VA 24141. 540-731-3610. Fax: 540-731-3689. 8:30AM-5PM (No machine receipts after 4:30PM) (EST).

Felony, Civil Actions Over $10,000, Probate—27th Circuit Court, 619 2nd St, Radford, VA 24141. 540-731-3610. Fax: 540-731-3689. 8:30AM-5PM. Access by: Mail, in person.

Misdemeanor, Civil Actions Under $10,000, Eviction, Small Claims—Radford General District Court, 27th Judicial District, 619 2nd St, Radford, VA 24141. 540-731-3609. Fax: 540-731-3692. 8:30AM-4:30PM. Access by: Fax, mail, in person.

Rappahannock County

Real Estate Recording—Clerk of the Circuit Court, 238 Gay Street, Clerk's Office, Washington, VA 22747. 540-675-3621. 8:30AM-4:30PM (EST).

Felony, Civil Actions Over $10,000, Probate—20th Circuit Court, 238 Gay Street (PO Box 517), Washington, VA 22747. 540-675-3621. 8:30AM-4:30PM (EST). Access by: Mail, in person.

Misdemeanor, Civil Actions Under $10,000, Eviction, Small Claims—20th General District Court, Gay Street Courthouse (PO Box 206), Washington, VA 22747. 540-675-3518. 8:30AM-4:30PM (EST). Access by: Mail, in person.

Richmond City

Real Estate Recording—Richmond City Clerk of the Circuit Court, 400 N. 9th St., Richmond, VA 23219. 804-780-6520. 9AM-3:30PM (EST).

Felony, Civil Actions Over $10,000, Probate—13th Circuit Court-Division I, John Marshall Courts Building, 400 N 9th St, Richmond, VA 23219. 804-780-6536. 9AM-4:45PM. Access by: In person only.

13th Circuit Court-Division II, Manchester Courthouse, 10th and Hull St, Richmond, VA 23224-0129. 804-780-5370. 8:45AM-4:45PM. Access by: Mail, in person.

Civil Actions Under $10,000, Eviction, Small Claims—13th General District Court, Division I, 400 N 9th St Rm 203, Richmond, VA 23219. 804-780-6461. 8AM-4PM. Access by: Phone, mail, in person.

Misdemeanor—13th General District Court, Division II, 905 Decatur St, Richmond, VA 23224. 804-780-5390. Fax: 804-232-7862. 8AM-4:30PM. Access by: Mail, in person.

Richmond County

Real Estate Recording—Richmond County Clerk of the Circuit Court, 10 Court Circle, Warsaw, VA 22572. 804-333-3781. 9AM-5PM (EST).

Felony, Civil Actions Over $10,000, Probate—15th Circuit Court, 101 Court Circle, PO Box 1000, Warsaw, VA 22572. 804-333-3781. 9AM-5PM (EST). Access by: Mail, in person.

Misdemeanor, Civil Actions Under $10,000, Eviction, Small Claims—15th General District Court, Richmond County Courthouse, PO Box 1000, Warsaw, VA 22572. 804-333-4616. 8AM-4:30PM (EST). Access by: Mail, in person.

Roanoke City

Real Estate Recording—Roanoke City Clerk of the Circuit Court, 315 Church Ave S.W., Room 357, Roanoke, VA 24016. 540-853-6701. 8:30AM-4:30PM (EST).

Felony, Civil Actions Over $10,000, Probate—23rd Circuit Court, PO Box 2610, Roanoke, VA 24010. Civil: 540-853-6702. Criminal: 540-853-6723. 8:30AM-4:20PM. Access by: In person only.

Misdemeanor, Civil Actions Under $10,000, Eviction, Small Claims—23rd General District Court, 315 W Church Ave, Roanoke, VA 24016-5007. Civil: 540-981-2364. Criminal: 540-981-2361. 8AM-4PM. Access by: In person only.

Roanoke County

Real Estate Recording—Roanoke County Clerk of the Circuit Court, 305 East Main Street, Salem, VA 24153. 540-387-6205. Fax: 540-387-6145. 8:30AM-4:30PM (EST).

Felony, Civil Actions Over $10,000, Probate—23rd Circuit Court, PO Box 1126, Salem, VA 24153, Attn. 540-387-6261. 8:30AM-4:30PM (EST). Access by: In person only.

Misdemeanor, Civil Actions Under $10,000, Eviction, Small Claims—23rd General District Court, PO Box 997, Salem, VA 24153. 540-387-6168. Fax: 540-387-6066. 8:30AM-4:30PM (EST). Access by: Mail, in person.

Rockbridge County

Real Estate Recording—Rockbridge County Clerk of the Circuit Court, 2 South Main Street, Court House, Lexington, VA 24450. 540-463-2232. Fax: 540-463-3850. 8:30AM-4:30PM (EST).

Felony, Civil Actions Over $10,000, Probate—25th Circuit Court, Courthouse Square, 2 S Main St, Lexington, VA 24450. 540-463-2232. 8:30AM-4:30PM (EST). Access by: In person only.

Misdemeanor, Civil Actions Under $10,000, Eviction, Small Claims—25th General District Court, 150 S Main St, Lexington, VA 24450. 540-463-3631. 8:30AM-4:30PM (EST). Access by: Mail, in person.

Rockingham County

Real Estate Recording—Rockingham County Clerk of the Circuit Court, Courthouse, Harrisonburg, VA 22801. 540-564-3126. Fax: 540-564-3127. 9AM-5PM; Th-until 6PM (EST).

Felony, Civil Actions Over $10,000, Probate—26th Circuit Court, Courthouse, Harrisonburg, VA 22801. Civil: 540-564-3114. Criminal: 540-564-3118. 9AM-5PM (EST). Access by: In person only.

Misdemeanor, Civil Actions Under $10,000, Eviction, Small Claims—26th General District Court, 53 Court Square, Harrisonburg, VA 22801. Civil: 540-564-3135. Criminal: 540-564-3130. Fax: 540-564-3372. 8AM-4PM (EST). Access by: Phone, mail, in person.

Russell County

Real Estate Recording—Russell County Clerk of the Circuit Court, Main Street, Courthouse, Lebanon, VA 24266. 540-889-8023. Fax: 540-889-8011. 8:30AM-4:30PM (EST).

Felony, Civil Actions Over $10,000, Probate—29th Circuit Court, PO Box 435, Lebanon, VA 24266. 540-889-8023. 8:30AM-4:30PM (EST). Access by: In person only.

Misdemeanor, Civil Actions Under $10,000, Eviction, Small Claims—29th General District Court, Russell County Courthouse, Lebanon, VA 24266. 540-889-8051. Fax: 540-889-8091. 8:30AM-4:30PM (EST). Access by: Mail, in person.

Salem City

Real Estate Recording—Salem City Clerk of the Circuit Court, 2 East Calhoun Street, Salem, VA 24153. 540-375-3067. Fax: 540-375-4039. 8:30AM-5PM (EST).

Felony, Civil Actions Over $10,000, Probate—23rd Circuit Court, 2 E Calhoun St, PO Box 891, Salem, VA 24153. 540-375-3067. 8:30AM-5PM. Access by: In person only.

Misdemeanor, Civil Actions Under $10,000, Eviction, Small Claims—23rd General District Court, 2 E Calhoun St, Salem, VA 24153. 540-375-3044. Fax: 540-375-4024. 8AM-4PM. Access by: Mail, in person.

Scott County

Real Estate Recording—Scott County Clerk of the Circuit Court, 104 East Jackson Street, Courthouse, Suite 2, Gate City, VA 24251. 540-386-3801. 8AM-Noon,1-5PM (EST).

Felony, Civil Actions Over $10,000, Probate—30th Circuit Court, 104 E Jackson St, Suite 2, Gate City, VA 24251. 540-386-3801. 8AM-Noon, 1-5PM (EST). Access by: Phone, mail, in person.

Misdemeanor, Civil Actions Under $10,000, Eviction, Small Claims—30th General District Court, 104 E Jackson St, Suite 9, Gate City, VA 24251. 540-386-7341. 8AM-4PM (EST). Access by: Mail, in person.

Shenandoah County

Real Estate Recording—Shenandoah County Clerk of the Circuit Court, 112 South Main Street, Woodstock, VA 22664. 540-459-6150. Fax: 540-459-6155. 9AM-5PM (EST).

Felony, Civil Actions Over $10,000, Probate—26th Circuit Court, 112 S Main St, PO Box 406, Woodstock, VA 22664. 540-459-3791. Fax: 540-459-6154. 9AM-5PM (EST). Access by: In person only.

Misdemeanor, Civil Actions Under $10,000, Eviction, Small Claims—26th General District Court, W Court St, PO Box 189, Woodstock, VA 22664. 540-459-6130. Fax: 540-459-6139. 8:30AM-4:30PM (EST). Access by: Mail, in person.

Smyth County

Real Estate Recording—Smyth County Clerk of the Circuit Court, Courthouse, Room 144, 109 West Main, Marion, VA 24354. 540-783-7186. Fax: 540-783-4430. 9AM-5PM (EST).

Felony, Civil Actions Over $10,000, Probate—28th Circuit Court, PO Box 1025, Marion, VA 24354. 540-783-7186. 9AM-5PM (EST). Access by: Mail, in person.

Misdemeanor, Civil Actions Under $10,000, Eviction, Small Claims—28th General District Court, Smythe County Courthouse, Rm 231, 109 W Main St, Marion, VA 24354. 540-783-5021. 8:30AM-4:30PM (EST). Access by: Phone, mail, in person.

South Boston City

Real Estate Recording—Halifax County handles real estate recording for this city.

Felony, Misdemeanor, Civil, Eviction, Small Claims, Probate—Circuit and District Courts. Handled by Halifax County courts.

Southampton County

Real Estate Recording—Southampton County Clerk of the Circuit Court, 22350 Main Street, Courthouse - Room 106, Courtland, VA 23837. 757-653-9245. 8:30AM-5PM (EST).

Felony, Civil Actions Over $10,000, Probate—5th Circuit Court, PO Box 190, Courtland, VA 23837. 757-653-2200. 8:30AM-5PM (EST). Access by: Mail, in person.

Misdemeanor, Civil Actions Under $10,000, Eviction, Small Claims—5th General District Court, PO Box 347, Courtland, VA 23837. 757-653-2673. 8:30AM-5PM (EST). Access by: Mail, in person.

Spotsylvania County

Real Estate Recording—Spotsylvania County Clerk of the Circuit Court, 91130 Courthouse Rd, Spotsylvania, VA 22553. 540-582-7090. Fax: 540-582-2169. 8AM-4:30PM (Recording Real Property 3:30PM) (EST).

Felony, Civil Actions Over $10,000, Probate—15th Circuit Court, 9113 Coutrhouse Rd, PO Box 96, Spotsylvania, VA 22553. 540-582-7090. 8AM-4:30PM (EST). Access by: In person only.

Misdemeanor, Civil Actions Under $10,000, Eviction, Small Claims—15th General District Court, 9111 Courthouse Rd, PO Box 114, Spotsylvania, VA 22553. 540-582-7110. 8AM-4PM (EST). Access by: In person only.

Stafford County

Real Estate Recording—Stafford County Clerk of the Circuit Court, 1300 Courthouse Rd., Stafford, VA 22554. 540-659-8752. 8AM-4PM (EST).

Felony, Civil Actions Over $10,000, Probate—15th Circuit Court, PO Box 69, Stafford, VA 22555. 540-659-8750. 8:30AM-4PM (EST). Access by: Mail, in person.

Misdemeanor, Civil Actions Under $10,000, Eviction, Small Claims—15th General District Court, 1300 Courthouse Rd, Stafford, VA 22554. 540-659-8763. Fax: 540-720-4834. 8:AM-4PM (EST). Access by: Phone, fax, mail, in person.

Staunton City

Real Estate Recording—Staunton City Clerk of the Circuit Court, 113 East Beverly Street, Staunton, VA 24401. 540-332-3874. Fax: 540-332-3970. 8:30AM-5PM (EST).

Felony, Civil Actions Over $10,000, Probate—25th Circuit Court, PO Box 1286, Staunton, VA 24402-1286. 540-332-3874. Fax: 540-332-3970. 8:30AM-5PM. Access by: In person only.

Misdemeanor, Civil Actions Under $10,000, Eviction, Small Claims—25th General District Court, 113 E Beverly St, Staunton, VA 24401. 540-332-3878. Fax: 540-332-3985. 8:30AM-4:30PM. Access by: Mail, in person.

Suffolk City

Real Estate Recording—Suffolk City Clerk of the Circuit Court, 441 Market Street, Municipal Building, Suffolk, VA 23434. 804-925-6450. 8:30AM-5PM (EST).

Felony, Civil Actions Over $10,000, Probate—5th Circuit Court, PO Box 1604, Suffolk, VA 23439-1604. 804-925-6450. 8:30AM-5PM. Access by: In person only.

Misdemeanor, Civil Actions Under $10,000, Eviction, Small Claims—5th General District Court, 524 N Main St, PO Box 1648, Suffolk, VA 23434. 804-539-1531. 8AM-4PM. Access by: In person only.

Surry County

Real Estate Recording—Surry County Clerk of the Circuit Court, 28 Colonial Trail East, Courthouse, Surry, VA 23883. 804-294-3161. 9AM-5PM (EST).

Felony, Civil Actions Over $10,000, Probate—6th Circuit Court, Rt 10 and School St, Po Box 332, Surry, VA 23883. 804-294-5201. 8:30AM-4:30PM (EST). Access by: In person only.

Misdemeanor, Civil Actions Under $10,000, Eviction, Small Claims—6th General District Court, Hwy 10 and School St, PO Box 332, Surry, VA 23883. 804-294-5201. 8:30AM-4:30PM (EST). Access by: In person only.

Sussex County

Real Estate Recording—Sussex County Clerk of the Circuit Court, Route 735, 15088 Courthouse Road, Sussex, VA 23884. 757-246-5511. 9AM-5PM (EST).

Felony, Civil Actions Over $10,000, Probate—6th Circuit Court, PO Box 1337, Sussex, VA 23884. 757-246-5511. 9AM-5PM (EST). Access by: Phone, mail, in person.

Misdemeanor, Civil Actions Under $10,000, Eviction, Small Claims—6th General District Court, Sussex County Courthouse 15098 Courthouse Rd Rt 73, PO Box 1315, Sussex, VA 23884. 757-246-5511. 8:30AM-4:30PM (EST). Access by: Phone, mail, in person.

Tazewell County

Real Estate Recording—Tazewell County Clerk of the Circuit Court, 101 Main Street, Tazewell, VA 24651. 540-988-7541. Fax: 540-988-7501. 8AM-4:30PM (EST).

Felony, Civil Actions Over $10,000, Probate—29th Circuit Court, PO Box 968, Tazewell, VA 24651. 540-988-7541. Fax: 540-988-7501. 8AM-4:30PM (EST). Access by: Mail, in person.

Misdemeanor, Civil Actions Under $10,000, Eviction, Small Claims—29th General District Court, PO Box 566, Tazewell, VA 24651. 540-988-9057. Fax: 540-988-6202. 8AM-4:30PM (EST). Access by: Mail, in person.

Virginia Beach City

Real Estate Recording—Virginia Beach Clerk of the Circuit Court, Judicial Center, 2305 Judicial Blvd., Virginia Beach, VA 23456. 757-427-8821. Fax: 757-426-5686. 8:30AM-5PM (EST).

Felony, Civil Actions Over $15,000, Probate—2nd Circuit Court, 2305 Judicial Blvd, Virginia Beach, VA 23456. 757-427-4181. Fax: 757-426-5686. 8:30AM-5PM. Access by: In person only.

Misdemeanor, Civil Actions Under $10,000, Eviction, Small Claims—2nd General District Court, 2305 Judicial Blvd, Judicial Center, Virginia Beach, VA 23456. Civil: 757-427-4277. Criminal: 757-427-4707. 8:30AM-4PM. Access by: Mail, in person.

Warren County

Real Estate Recording—Warren County Clerk of the Circuit Court, 1 East Main Street, Front Royal, VA 22630. 540-635-2435. Fax: 540-636-3274. 9AM-5PM (EST).

Felony, Civil Actions Over $10,000, Probate—26th Circuit Court, 1 East Main St, Front Royal, VA 22630. 540-635-2435. 9AM-5PM (EST). Access by: Phone, mail, in person.

Misdemeanor, Civil Actions Under $10,000, Eviction, Small Claims—26th General District Court, 1 East Main St, Front Royal, VA 22630. 540-635-2335. Fax: 540-636-8233. 8AM-4:30PM (EST). Access by: Mail, in person.

Washington County

Real Estate Recording—Washington County Clerk of the Circuit Court, 189 E. Main St., Abingdon, VA 24210. 540-676-6226. 7:30AM-5PM (EST).

Felony, Civil Actions Over $10,000, Probate—Circuit Court of Washington County, PO Box 289, Abingdon, VA 24212-0289. 540-676-6224. 7:30AM-5PM (EST). Access by: In person only.

Misdemeanor, Civil Actions Under $10,000, Eviction, Small Claims—28th General District Court, 191 E Main St, Abingdon, VA 24210. 540-676-6279. Fax: 540-676-6293. 8:30AM-5PM (EST). Access by: Mail, in person.

Waynesboro City

Real Estate Recording—Waynesboro City Clerk of the Circuit Court, 250 South Wayne Avenue, Waynesboro, VA 22980. 540-942-6616. 8:30AM-5PM (EST).

Felony, Civil Actions Over $10,000, Probate—25th Circuit Court, 250 S Wayne Ave, PO Box 910, Waynesboro, VA 22980. 540-942-6616. 8:30AM-5PM. Access by: In person only.

Misdemeanor, Civil Actions Under $10,000, Eviction, Small Claims—25th General District Court-Waynesboro, 250 S Wayne and PO Box 1028, Waynesboro, VA 22980. 540-942-6636. 8:30AM-4:30PM. Access by: Mail, in person.

Westmoreland County

Real Estate Recording—Westmoreland County Clerk of the Circuit Court, Courthouse, Rte. 3 and Polk St., Montross, VA 22520. 804-493-0108. 9AM-5PM (EST).

Felony, Civil Actions Over $10,000, Probate—15th Circuit Court, PO Box 307, Montross, VA 22520. 804-493-0108. 9AM-5PM (EST). Access by: In person only.

Misdemeanor, Civil Actions Under $10,000, Eviction, Small Claims—15th General District Court, PO Box 688, Montross, VA 22520. 804-493-0105. 8AM-4:30PM (EST). Access by: In person only.

Williamsburg City

Real Estate Recording—James City County handles real estate recording for this city.

Felony, Misdemeanor, Civil, Eviction, Small Claims, Probate—Circuit and District Courts. Handled by James City County courts.

Winchester City

Real Estate Recording—Winchester City Clerk of the Circuit Court, 5 N. Kent Street, Winchester, VA 22601. 540-667-5770. 9AM-5PM (EST).

Felony, Civil Actions Over $10,000, Probate—Circuit Court, 5 N Kent St, Winchester, VA 22601. 540-667-5770. Fax: 540-667-6638. 9AM-5PM. Access by: Mail, in person.

Misdemeanor, Civil Actions Under $10,000, Eviction, Small Claims—26th General District Court, 5 N Kent St, PO Box 526, Winchester, VA 22604. 540-667-5770. 8AM-4PM. Access by: Mail, in person.

Wise County

Real Estate Recording—Wise County/City of Norton Clerk of the Circuit Court, 125 Main Street, Courthouse, Wise, VA 24293. 540-328-6111. Fax: 540-328-0039. 8:30PM-5PM (EST).

Felony, Civil Actions Over $10,000, Probate—30th Circuit Court, PO Box 1248, Wise, VA 24293. 540-328-6111. 8:30AM-5PM (EST). Access by: Mail, in person.

Misdemeanor, Civil Actions Under $10,000, Eviction, Small Claims—30th General District Court, Wise County Courthouse, PO Box 829, Wise, VA 24293. 540-328-3426. 8AM-4PM (EST). Access by: Mail, in person.

Wythe County

Real Estate Recording—Wythe County Clerk of the Circuit Court, 225 South Fourth Street, Room 105, Wytheville,

VA 24382. 540-223-6050. Fax: 540-223-6057. 8:30AM-5PM (EST).

Felony, Civil Actions Over $10,000, Probate—27th Circuit Court, 225 S Fourth St, Rm 105, Wytheville, VA 24382. 540-223-6050. Fax: 540-223-6057. 8:30AM-5PM (EST). Access by: Mail, in person.

Misdemeanor, Civil Actions Under $10,000, Eviction, Small Claims—27th General District Court, 225 S. Fourth St., Rm 203, Wytheville, VA 24382. 540-223-6075. Fax: 540-223-6087. 8AM-4:30PM (EST). Access by: Fax, mail, in person.

York County

Real Estate Recording—York County Clerk of the Circuit Court, 301 Main Street, Yorktown, VA 23690. 757-890-3350. Fax: 757-890-3364. 8:30AM-5PM (EST).

Felony, Civil Actions Over $10,000, Probate—9th Circuit Court, PO Box 371, Yorktown, VA 23690. 757-890-3350. Fax: 757-890-3364. 8:30AM-5PM (EST). Access by: Mail, in person.

Misdemeanor, Civil Actions Under $10,000, Eviction, Small Claims—9th Judicial District Court, York County GDC, PO Box 316, Yorktown, VA 23690. 757-890-3450. Fax: 757-890-3459. 8:30AM-4:30PM (EST). Access by: Fax, mail, in person.

Federal Courts

US District Court
Eastern District of Virginia

Alexandria Division, US District Court 401 Courthouse Square, Alexandria, VA 22314-5798. 703-299-2100. Counties: Arlington, Fairfax, Fauquier, Loudoun, Prince William, Stafford, City of Alexandria, City of Fairfax, City of Falls Church, City of Manassas, City of Manassas Park

Newport News Division, US District Court Clerk's Office, PO Box 494, Newport News, VA 23607. 757-244-0539. Counties: Gloucester, James City, Mathews, York, City of Hampton, City of Newport News, City of Poquoson, City of Williamsburg

Norfolk Division, US District Court US Courthouse, Room 193, 600 Granby St, Norfolk, VA 23510. 804-441-3250. Counties: Accomack, City of Chesapeake, City of Franklin, Isle of Wight, City of Norfolk, Northampton, City of Portsmouth, City of Suffolk, Southampton, City of Virginia Beach

Richmond Division, US District Court Lewis F Powell, Jr Courthouse Bldg, 1000 E Main St, Room 307, Richmond, VA 23219-3525. 804-771-2612. Counties: Amelia, Brunswick, Caroline, Charles City, Chesterfield, Dinwiddie, Essex, Goochland, Greensville, Hanover, Henrico, King and Queen, King George, King William, Lancaster, Lunenburg, Mecklenburg, Middlesex, New Kent, Northumberland, Nottoway, City of Petersburg, Powhatan, Prince Edward, Prince George, Richmond, City of Richmond, Spotsylvania, Surry, Sussex, Westmoreland, City of Colonial Heights, City of Emporia, City of Fredericksburg, City of Hopewell

Western District of Virginia

Abingdon Division, US District Court Clerk's Office, PO Box 398, Abingdon, VA 24212. 540-628-5116. Counties: Buchanan, City of Bristol, Russell, Smyth, Tazewell, Washington

Big Stone Gap Division, US District Court PO Box 490, Big Stone Gap, VA 24219. 540-523-3557. Counties: Dickenson, Lee, Scott, Wise, City of Norton

Charlottesville Division, US District Court Clerk, Room 304, 255 W Main St, Charlottesville, VA 22902. 804-296-9284. Counties: Albemarle, Culpeper, Fluvanna, Greene, Louisa, Madison, Nelson, Orange, Rappahannock, City of Charlottesville

Danville Division, US District Court PO Box 52, Danville, VA 24543-0053. 804-793-7147. Counties: Charlotte, Halifax, Henry, Patrick, Pittsylvania, City of Danville, City of Martinsville, City of South Boston

Harrisonburg Division, US District Court Clerk, PO Box 1207, Harrisonburg, VA 22801. 540-434-3181. Counties: Augusta, Bath, Clarke, Frederick, Highland, Page, Rockingham, Shenandoah, Warren, City of Harrisonburg, City of Staunton, City of Waynesboro, City of Winchester

Lynchburg Division, US District Court Clerk, PO Box 744, Lynchburg, VA 24505. 804-847-5722. Counties: Amherst, Appomattox, Bedford, Buckingham, Campbell, Cumberland, Rockbridge, City of Bedford, City of Buena Vista, City of Lexington, City of Lynchburg

Roanoke Division, US District Court Clerk, PO Box 1234, Roanoke, VA 24006. 540-857-2224. Counties: Alleghany, Bland, Botetourt, Carroll, Craig, Floyd, Franklin, Giles, Grayson, Montgomery, Pulaski, Roanoke, Wythe, City of Covington, City of Clifton Forge, City of Galax, City of Radford, City of Roanoke, City of Salem

US Bankruptcy Court
Eastern District of Virginia

Alexandria Division, US Bankruptcy Court, PO Box 19247, Alexandria, VA 22320-0247. 703-557-1716. Voice Case Information System: 804-771-2736. Counties: City of Alexandria, Arlington, Fairfax, City of Fairfax, City of Falls Church, Fauquier, Loudoun, City of Manassas, City of Manassas Park, Prince William, Stafford

Newport News Division, US Bankruptcy Court, Suite 201, 825 Diligence Dr, Newport News, VA 23606. 757-595-9805. Voice Case Information System: 804-771-2736. Counties: Gloucester, City of Hampton, James City, Mathews, City of Newport News, City of Poquoson, City of Williamsburg, York

Norfolk Division, US Bankruptcy Court, PO Box 1938, Norfolk, VA 23501-1938. 757-441-6651. Voice Case Information System: 804-771-2736. Counties: Accomack, City of Cape Charles, City of Chesapeake, City of Franklin, Isle of Wight, City of Norfolk, Northampton, City of Portsmouth, Southampton, City of Suffolk, City of Virginia Beach

Richmond Division, US Bankruptcy Court, Office of the Clerk, 1100 E Main St, Suite 310, Richmond, VA 23219. 804-771-2878. Voice Case Information System: 804-771-2736. Counties: Amelia, Brunswick, Caroline, Charles City, Chesterfield, City of Colonial Heights, Dinwiddie, City of Emporia, Essex, City of Fredericksburg, Goochland, Greensville, Hanover, Henrico, City of Hopewell, King and Queen, King George, King William, Lancaster, Lunenburg, Mecklenburg, Middlesex, New Kent, Northumberland, Nottoway, City of Petersburg, Powhatan, Prince Edward, Prince George, Richmond, City of Richmond, Spotsylvania, Surry, Sussex, Westmoreland

Western District of Virginia

Harrisonburg Division, US Bankruptcy Court, PO Box 1407, Harrisonburg, VA 22801. 540-434-8327. Counties: Alleghany, Augusta, Bath, City of Buena Vista, Clarke, City of Clifton Forge, City of Covington, Frederick, City of Harrisonburg, Highland, City of Lexington, Page, Rappahannock, Rockbridge, Rockingham, Shenandoah, City of Staunton, Warren, City of Waynesboro, City of Winchester

Lynchburg Division, US Bankruptcy Court, PO Box 6400, Lynchburg, VA 24505. 804-845-0317. Counties: Albemarle, Amherst, Appomattox, Bedford, City of Bedford, Buckingham, Campbell, Charlotte, City of Charlottesville, Culpeper, Cumberland, City of Danville, Fluvanna, Greene,

Halifax, Henry, Louisa, City of Lynchburg, Madison, City of Martinsville, Nelson, Orange, Patrick, Pittsylvania, City of South Boston

Roanoke Division, US Bankruptcy Court, PO Box 2390, Roanoke, VA 24010. 540-857-2391. Counties: Bland, Botetourt, City of Bristol, Buchanan, Carroll, Craig, Dickenson, Floyd, Franklin, City of Galax, Giles, Grayson, Lee, Montgomery, City of Norton, Pulaski, City of Radford, Roanoke, City of Roanoke, Russell, City of Salem, Scott, Smyth, Tazewell, Washington, Wise, Wythe

Washington

Capitol: Olympia (Thurston County)	
Number of Counties: 39	**Population:** 5,430,940
County Court Locations:	**Federal Court Locations:**
•Superior Courts: 39/ 30 Districts	•District Courts: 4
•District Courts: 65/39 Counties	•Bankruptcy Courts: 3
Municipal Courts: 131/ 131 Cities	**State Agencies:** 20

State Agencies—Summary

General Help Numbers:

State Archives

Secretary of State	360-753-5485
State Archives	Fax: 360-664-8814
1120 Washington ST SE	8:30AM-4:30PM
Olympia, WA 98504-0238	
Reference Librarian:	360-753-5485
Historical Society:	206-798-5903

Governor's Office

Office of the Governor	360-753-6780
PO Box 40002	Fax: 360-753-4110
Olympia, WA 98504-0002	7:30AM-5PM

Attorney General's Office

Attorney General's Office	360-753-6200
PO Box 40100	Fax: 360-664-0228
Olympia, WA 98504-0100	8AM-5PM
Alternate Telephone:	360-664-8564

State Legislation

Washington Legislature	360-753-5000
State Capitol	9AM-12PM; 1PM-5PM
Room 120, 1st Floor	
Olympia, WA 98504-0600	
Information-Local:	800-562-6000
Bill Room:	360-786-7573

Important State Internet Sites:

> **Webscape**
> **File Edit View**   **Help**

State of Washington World Wide Web
www.wa.gov/

This site links to such sites as education, government, employment, and what's new. Also linked to this site is a search engine.

Washington Legislature
leginfo.leg.wa.gov/

This site contains links to the state House and Senate home pages, legislative information, legislative agencies and other information.

Bills Information
leginfo.leg.wa.gov/www/bills.htm

This site links to bill information, has a bill search engine, provides legislative calendars and contains the Revised Code of Washington.

UCC Information
www.wa.gov/dol/bpd/uccfront.htm

Information is provided for the filing process for UCC, crop liens, federal tax liens, and processor and prepared liens.

Unclaimed Property
www.wa.gov/dor/unclaim/unchome.htm

This page provides you with all the information necessary to search for unclaimed property, such as, checking and savings accounts, payroll, wages, insurance, refunds and much more.

State Agencies—Public Records

Criminal Records
Washington State Patrol, Identification Section, PO Box 42633, Olympia, WA 98504-2633, Main Telephone: 360-705-5100, Fax: 360-664-9461, Hours: 8AM-5PM. Access by: mail, PC.

Corporation Records
Trademarks/Servicemarks
Limited Partnerships
Limited Liability Company Records
Secretary of State, Corporations Division, PO Box 40234, Olympia, WA 98504-0234, Main Telephone: 360-753-7115, Fax: 360-664-8781, Hours: 8AM-4PM. Access by: mail, phone, visit, PC.

Trade Names
Department of Licensing, Business & Professional Div, PO Box 9034, Olympia, WA 98507-9034, Main Telephone: 360-753-4401, Tradename Search: 900-463-6000, Fax: 360-753-9668, Hours: 8AM-5PM. Access by: mail, phone, fax, visit, PC.

Uniform Commercial Code
Federal Tax Liens
State Tax Liens
UCC Division, Department of Licensing, PO Box 9660, Olympia, WA 98507-9660, Main Telephone: 360-753-2523, Fax: 360-586-1404, Hours: 8AM-5PM. Access by: mail, fax, phone, PC.

Sales Tax Registrations
Revenue Department, Taxpayer Account Administration, PO Box 47476, Olympia, WA 98504-7476, Main Telephone: 360-902-7180, Fax: 360-586-5543, Hours: 8AM-5PM. Access by: mail, fax, phone.

Birth Certificates
Department of Health, Center for Health Statistics, PO Box 9709, Olympia, WA 98507-9709, Main Telephone: 360-753-5936, Credit Card Ordering: 360-753-4379, Fax: 360-352-2586, Hours: 8 AM - 4:30 PM. Access by: mail, phone, visit.

Death Records
Department of Health, Vital Records, PO Box 9709, Olympia, WA 98507-9709, Main Telephone: 360-753-5936, Fax: 360-352-2586, Hours: 8 AM - 4:30 PM. Access by: mail, phone, visit.

Marriage Certificates
Department of Health, Vital Records, PO Box 9709, Olympia, WA 98507-9709, Main Telephone: 360-753-5936, Fax: 360-352-2586, Hours: 8 AM - 4:30 PM. Access by: mail, phone, visit.

Divorce Records
Department of Health, Vital Records, PO Box 9709, Olympia, WA 98507-9709, Main Telephone: 360-753-5936, Fax: 360-352-2586, Hours: 8 AM - 4:30 PM. Access by: mail, phone, visit.

Workers' Compensation Records
Labor and Industries, Workers Compensation Division, PO Box 4100, Olympia, WA 98504-4100, Main Telephone: 360-902-4937, Fax: 360-902-5798, Hours: 8AM-5PM. Access by: mail only.

Driver Records
Department of Licensing, Driver Services Division, PO Box 9030, Olympia, WA 98507-9030, Main Telephone: 360-902-3921, Fax: 360-586-9044, Hours: 8AM-4:30PM. Access by: mail, visit. Copies of tickets may be requested by the driver or driver's authorized representative. The fee is $.75 per ticket; the first 4 are free.

Vehicle Ownership
Vehicle Identification
Department of Licensing, Vehicles Services, PO Box 9038, Mail Stop MS48001, Olympia, WA 98507-9038, Main Telephone: 360-902-4000, Fax: 360-664-0831, Hours: 8AM-5PM. Access by: mail, phone, visit. It is recommended that on-going, high volume users enter into a disclosure agreement with this agency.

Accident Reports
Department of Licensing, Accident Reports, PO Box 9030, Olympia, WA 98507-9030, Main Telephone: 360-902-3900, Hours: 8AM-4:30PM. Access by: mail, visit. Only the person who filed the accident report may receive a copy of the report. An outside party, such as a lawyer or insurance agent, may receive a copy with written permission of the filer.

Hunting License Information
Fishing License Information
Records not available from state agency.

County Courts and Recording Offices

What You Need to Know...

<table>
<tr><td>

About the Courts

</td><td>

About the Recorder's Office

</td></tr>
<tr><td>

Administration

Court Administrator	360-357-2121
Temple of Justice	8:30AM-4:30PM
PO Box 41174	
Olympia, WA 98504-1174	

Court Structure

District Courts retain civil records for 10 years from date of final disposition and then the records are destroyed. District Courts retain criminal records for 10 years from date of final disposition and then the records are destroyed.

There is a mandatory arbitration requirement for civil disputes for $35,000 or less; however, either party may request a trial in Superior Court if dissatisfied with the arbitrator's decision.

Searching Hints

SASE is required in every jurisdiction which responds to written search requests.

Online Access

Appellate, Superior and District Court records are available through the Superior Court Management Information System (**SCOMIS**), the Appellate Records System (ACORDS) and the District/Municipal Court Information System (**DISCIS**), on the Judicial Information System's **JIS-Link**. Case records available through JIS-Link from 1977 include criminal, civil, domestic, probate, and judgments. JIS-Link is, generally, available Monday through Friday from 6:30AM to Midnight WA time. Equipment requirements are a PC running Windows or MS-DOS (3.3 or higher) and a Hayes-compatible modem (9600, 2400, or 1200 baud). There is a one-time installation fee of $125.00 per site and a connect time charge of $25.00 per hour (approximately $.42 per minute). For additional information and/or a registration packet, contact: JISLink Coordinator, Office of the Administrator for the Courts, 1206 S Quince St., PO Box 41170, Olympia WA 98504-1170, 360-357-2407.

</td><td>

Organization

39 counties, 39 filing offices. The recording officer is County Auditor. County records are usually combined in a Grantor/Grantee index. The entire state is in the Pacific Time Zone (PST).

UCC Records

Financing statements are filed at the state level, except for real estate related collateral, which are filed with the County Auditor. Most filing offices will perform UCC searches. Use search request form UCC-11R. Searches fees and copy fees vary.

Lien Records

All federal tax liens on personal property are filed with the Department of Licensing. Other federal and all state tax liens are filed with the County Auditor. Most counties will perform tax lien searches. Search fees are usually $8.00 per hour.

Real Estate Records

Many County Auditors will perform real estate searches, including record owner. Search fees and copy fees vary. Copies usually cost $1.00 per page and $2.00 for certification per document. If the Auditor does **not** provide searches, contact the Assessor for record owner information. Contact the Treasurer (Finance Department in King County) for information about unpaid real estate taxes.

</td></tr>
</table>

County Courts and Recording Offices

Adams County

Real Estate Recording—Adams County Auditor, 210 West Broadway, Ritzville, WA 99169. 509-659-0090. Fax: 509-659-0118. 8:30AM-4:30PM (PST).

Felony, Civil Actions Over $25,000, Eviction, Probate—Superior Court, 210 W Broadway (PO Box 187), Ritzville, WA 99169-0187. 509-659-0090. Fax: 509-659-0118. 8:30AM-Noon, 1-4:30PM (PST). Access by: Phone, fax, mail, remote online, in person.

Misdemeanor, Civil Actions Under $25,000, Small Claims—Othello District Court, 165 N 1st, Othello, WA 99344. 509-659-0090. Fax: 509-488-5406. 8:30AM-4:30PM (PST). Access by: Phone, fax, mail, remote online, in person.

Ritzville District Court, 210 W Broadway, Ritzville, WA 99169. 509-659-1002. Fax: 509-659-0118. 8:30AM-4:30PM (PST). Access by: Fax, mail, remote online, in person.

Asotin County

Real Estate Recording—Asotin County Auditor, 135 2nd Street, Asotin, WA 99402. 509-243-2084. Fax: 509-243-2087. 9AM-5PM (PST).

Felony, Civil Actions Over $25,000, Eviction, Probate—Superior Court, PO Box 159, Asotin, WA 99402-0159. 509-243-2081. Fax: 509-243-4978. 9AM-5PM (PST). Access by: Phone, fax, mail, remote online, in person.

Misdemeanor, Civil Actions Under $25,000, Small Claims—District Court, PO Box 429, Asotin, WA 99402-0429. 509-243-2027. Fax: 509-243-4978. 8AM-5PM (PST). Access by: Fax, mail, remote online, in person.

Benton County

Real Estate Recording—Benton County Auditor, 620 Market Street, Courthouse, Prosser, WA 99350. 509-786-5616. Fax: 509-786-5528. 8AM-5PM (PST).

Felony, Civil Actions Over $25,000, Eviction, Probate—Superior Court, 7320 W Quinault, Kennewick, WA 99336-7690. 509-735-8388. 8AM-4PM (PST). Access by: Phone, fax, mail, remote online, in person.

Misdemeanor, Civil Actions Under $25,000, Small Claims—District Court, 7320 W Quinault, Kennewick, WA 99336. 509-735-8476. Fax: 509-736-3069. 7:30AM-Noon, 1-4:30PM (PST). Access by: Mail, remote online, in person.

Chelan County

Real Estate Recording—Chelan County Auditor, 350 Orondo, Courthouse, Wenatchee, WA 98801. 509-664-5432. Fax: 509-664-5246. 8:30AM-5PM (PST).

Felony, Civil Actions Over $25,000, Eviction, Probate—Superior Court, 401 Washington (PO Box 3025), Wenatchee, WA 98807-3025. 509-664-5380. Fax: 509-664-2611. 8:30AM-5PM (PST). Access by: Phone, fax, mail, remote online, in person.

Misdemeanor, Civil Actions Under $25,000, Small Claims—Chelan County District Court, PO Box 2182, Courthouse 4th Fl, Wenatchee, WA 98807. 509-664-5393. Fax: 509-664-5456. 8:30AM-5PM (PST). Access by: Fax, mail, remote online, in person.

Clallam County

Real Estate Recording—Clallam County Auditor, 223 East Fourth Street, Port Angeles, WA 98362. 360-417-2220. Fax: 360-417-2517. 8AM-4:30PM (PST).

Felony, Civil Actions Over $25,000, Eviction, Probate—Superior Court, 223 E Fourth St, Port Angeles, WA 98362-3098. 360-417-2333. Fax: 360-417-2495. 8AM-5PM (PST). Access by: Phone, fax, mail, remote online, in person.

Misdemeanor, Civil Actions Under $25,000, Small Claims—District Court Two, PO Box 1937, Forks, WA 98331. 360-374-6383. Fax: 360-374-2100. 8AM-5PM (PST). Access by: Mail, remote online, in person.

District Court One, 223 E 4th St, Port Angeles, WA 98362. 360-417-2285. Fax: 360-417-2470. 8AM-5PM (PST). Access by: Mail, remote online, in person.

Clark County

Real Estate Recording—Clark County Auditor, 12th & Franklin, Vancouver, WA 98660. 360-699-2208. Fax: 360-737-6007. 8AM-5PM (PST).

Felony, Civil Actions Over $25,000, Eviction, Probate—Superior Court, 1200 Franklin St, PO Box 5000, Vancouver, WA 98668. 360-699-2295. 8:30AM-4:30PM (PST). Access by: Phone, mail, remote online, in person.

Misdemeanor, Civil Actions Under $25,000, Small Claims—District Court, PO Box 5000, Vancouver, WA 98666-5000. Civil: 360-699-2411. Criminal: 360-699-2424. Fax: 360-737-6044. 8:30AM-4:30PM (PST). Access by: Phone, fax, mail, remote online, in person.

Columbia County

Real Estate Recording—Columbia County Auditor, 341 East Main St., Dayton, WA 99328. 509-382-4541. Fax: 509-382-4830. 8:30AM-4:30PM (PST).

Felony, Civil Actions Over $25,000, Eviction, Probate—Superior Court, 341 E Main St, Dayton, WA 99328. 509-382-4321. Fax: 509-382-4830. 8:30AM-Noon, 1-4:30PM (PST). Access by: Phone, fax, mail, remote online, in person.

Misdemeanor, Civil Actions Under $25,000, Small Claims—District Court, 341 E Main St, Dayton, WA 99328-1361. 509-382-4812. Fax: 509-382-4830. 8:30AM-4:30PM (PST). Access by: Mail, remote online, in person.

Cowlitz County

Real Estate Recording—Cowlitz County Auditor, 207 Fourth Avenue North, Kelso, WA 98626. 360-577-3006. Fax: 360-414-5552. 8AM-5PM (PST).

Felony, Civil Actions Over $25,000, Eviction, Probate—Superior Court, 312 SW First Ave, Kelso, WA 98626-1724. 360-577-3016. Fax: 360-577-2323. 8:30-11:30AM, 12:30-4:30PM (PST). Access by: Phone, fax, mail, remote online, in person.

Misdemeanor, Civil Actions Under $25,000, Small Claims—District Court, 312 SW First Ave, Kelso, WA 98626-1724. 360-577-3073. 8:30AM-5PM (PST). Access by: Mail, remote online, in person.

Douglas County

Real Estate Recording—Douglas County Auditor, 213 South Rainier, Waterville, WA 98858. 509-884-9422. Fax: 509-884-9468. 8AM-5PM; (Recording hours: 8AM-4PM) (PST).

Felony, Civil Actions Over $25,000, Eviction, Probate—Superior Court, PO Box 516, Waterville, WA 98858-0516. 509-745-8529. Fax: 509-745-8027. 8AM-5PM (PST). Access by: Phone, fax, mail, remote online, in person.

Misdemeanor, Civil Actions Under $25,000, Small Claims—District Court-Bridgeport, 1206 Columbia Ave (PO Box 730), Bridgeport, WA 98813-0730. 509-686-2034. Fax: 509-686-4671. 8:30AM-4:30PM (PST). Access by: Fax, mail, remote online, in person.

District Court-East Wenatchee, 110 3rd St NE, East Wenatchee, WA 98802. 509-884-3536. Fax: 509-884-5973. 8:30AM-4:30PM (PST). Access by: Fax, mail, remote online, in person.

Ferry County

Real Estate Recording—Ferry County Auditor, 350 East Delaware, Republic, WA 99166. 509-775-5208. Fax: 509-775-2492. 8AM-4PM (PST).

Felony, Civil Actions Over $25,000, Eviction, Probate—Superior Court, 350 E Delaware, Republic, WA 99166. 509-775-5245. 8AM-4PM (PST). Access by: Phone, mail, remote online, in person.

Misdemeanor, Civil Actions Under $25,000, Small Claims—District Court, PO Box 214, Republic, WA 99166-0214. 509-775-5244. Fax: 509-775-5221. 8AM-4PM (PST). Access by: Remote online, in person.

Franklin County

Real Estate Recording—Franklin County Auditor, 1016 North Fourth Street, Pasco, WA 99301. 509-545-3536. Fax: 509-545-2142. 8:30AM-5PM (PST).

Felony, Civil Actions Over $25,000, Eviction, Probate—Superior Court, 1016 N 4th St, Pasco, WA 99301. 509-545-3525. 8:30AM-5PM (PST). Access by: Mail, remote online, in person.

Misdemeanor, Civil Actions Under $25,000, Small Claims—District Court, 1016 N 4th St, Pasco, WA 99301. 509-545-3593. Fax: 509-545-3588. 8:30AM-Noon, 1-5PM (PST). Access by: Mail, remote online, in person.

Garfield County

Real Estate Recording—Garfield County Auditor, Corner of 8th & Main, Pomeroy, WA 99347. 509-843-1411. Fax: 509-843-1224. 8:30AM-5PM (PST).

Felony, Civil Actions Over $25,000, Eviction, Probate—Superior Court, PO Box 915, Pomeroy, WA 99347-0915. 509-843-3731. Fax: 509-843-1224. 8:30AM-Noon, 1-5PM (PST). Access by: Phone, fax, mail, in person.

Misdemeanor, Civil Actions Under $25,000, Small Claims—District Court, PO Box 817, Pomeroy, WA 99347-0817. 509-843-1002. 8:30AM-5PM (PST). Access by: Mail, remote online, in person.

Grant County

Real Estate Recording—Grant County Auditor, 1st & C Street NW, Ephrata, WA 98823. 509-754-2011. 8AM-5PM (PST).

Felony, Civil Actions Over $25,000, Eviction, Probate—Superior Court, PO Box 37, Ephrata, WA 98823-0037. 509-754-2011. Fax: 509-754-5638. 8AM-5PM (PST). Access by: Phone, fax, mail, remote online, in person.

Misdemeanor, Civil Actions Under $25,000, Small Claims—District Court, PO Box 37, Ephrata, WA 98823-0037. 509-754-2011. 8AM-5PM (PST). Access by: Mail, remote online, in person.

Grays Harbor County

Real Estate Recording—Grays Harbor County Auditor, 101 W. Broadway, Montesano, WA 98563. 360-249-4232. Fax: 360-249-3330. 8AM-5PM (PST).

Felony, Civil Actions Over $25,000, Eviction, Probate—Superior Court, 102 W Broadway, PO Box 711, Montesano, WA 98563-0711. 360-249-3842. Fax: 360-249-6381. 8AM-5PM (PST). Access by: Phone, fax, mail, remote online, in person.

Misdemeanor, Civil Actions Under $25,000, Small Claims—District Court No 2, PO Box 142, Aberdeen, WA 98520-0035. 360-532-7061. Fax: 360-532-7704. 8AM-5PM (PST). Access by: Fax, mail, remote online, in person.

District Court No 1, 102 W Broadway, Rm 202, Montesano, WA 98563-0647. 360-249-3441. Fax: 360-249-6382. 8AM-Noon, 1-5PM (PST). Access by: Phone, fax, mail, remote online, in person.

Island County

Real Estate Recording—Island County Auditor, 6th & Main, Coupeville, WA 98239. 360-679-7366. Fax: 360-240-5553. 8AM-4:30PM (PST).

Felony, Civil Actions Over $25,000, Eviction, Probate—Superior Court, PO Box 5000, Coupeville, WA 98239-5000. 360-679-7359. 8AM-4:30PM (PST). Access by: Phone, mail, remote online, in person.

Misdemeanor, Civil Actions Under $25,000, Small Claims—District Court, 800 S 8th Ave, Oak Harbor, WA 98277. 360-675-5988. Fax: 360-675-8231. 8AM-4:30PM (PST). Access by: Fax, mail, remote online, in person.

Jefferson County

Real Estate Recording—Jefferson County Auditor, 1820 Jefferson Street, Port Townsend, WA 98368. 360-385-9116. Fax: 360-385-9228. 9AM-5PM (PST).

Felony, Civil Actions Over $25,000, Eviction, Probate—Superior Court, PO BOX 1220, Port Townsend, WA 98368-0920. 360-385-9125. 9AM-5PM (PST). Access by: Phone, mail, remote online, in person.

Misdemeanor, Civil Actions Under $25,000, Small Claims—District Court, PO Box 1220, Port Townsend, WA 98368-0920. 360-385-9135. Fax: 360-385-9367. 9AM-5PM (PST). Access by: Phone, fax, mail, remote online, in person.

King County

Real Estate Recording—King County Records, 500 4th Avenue, Administration Building, Room 311, Seattle, WA 98104. 206-296-1570. Fax: 206-296-1535. 8:30AM-4:30PM; Recording Hours 8:30AM-3:30PM (PST).

Felony, Misdemeanor, Civil Actions Over $25,000, Eviction, Probate—Superior Court, 516 Third Ave, E-609 Courthouse, Seattle, WA 98104-2386. 206-296-9300. Fax: 206-296-0906. 8:30AM-4:30AM (PST). Access by: Mail, remote online, in person.

Misdemeanor, Civil Actions Under $25,000, Small Claims—District Court (Bellevue Div), 585 112th Ave SE, Bellevue, WA 98004. 206-296-3650. Fax: 206-296-0589. 8:30AM-4:30PM (PST). Access by: Mail, remote online, in person.

District Court (Federal Way Div), 33506 10th Pl South, Federal Way, WA 98003-6396. 206-296-7784. Fax: 206-296-0590. 8:30AM-4:30PM (PST). Access by: Phone, mail, remote online, in person.

District Court (Issaquah Div), 640 NW Gilman Blvd, Issaquah, WA 98027-2448. 206-296-7688. Fax: 206-296-0591. 8:30AM-4:30PM (PST). Access by: Mail, remote online, in person.

District Court (Aukeen Div), 1210 S Central, Kent, WA 98032-7426. 206-296-7740. 8:30AM-4:30PM (PST). Access by: Mail, remote online, in person.

District Court (Northeast Div), 8601 160th Ave NE 85th (PO Box 425), Redmond, WA 98073-0425. 206-296-3667. 8:30AM-4:30PM (PST). Access by: Mail, remote online, in person.

District Court (Renton Div), 3407 NE 2nd St, Renton, WA 98056-4193. 206-296-3532. Fax: 206-796-0593. 8:30AM-4:30PM (PST). Access by: Phone, fax, mail, remote online, in person.

District Court (Seattle Div), 516 Third Ave E-327 Courthouse, Seattle, WA 98104-3273. 206-296-3565. 8:30AM-4:30PM (PST). Access by: Mail, remote online, in person.

District Court (Shoreline Div), 18050 Meridian Ave N, Seattle, WA 98133-4642. 206-296-3679. Fax: 206-296-0594. 8:30AM-4:30PM (PST). Access by: Phone, fax, mail, remote online, in person.

District Court (Southwest Division-Seattle), 601 SW 149th St, Seattle, WA 98166. 206-296-0133. Fax: 206-296-0585. 8:30AM-4:30PM (PST). Access by: Mail, remote online, in person.

District Court (Southwest Div-Vashon), 19021 99th SW (PO Box 111), Vashon, WA 98070-0111. 206-296-3664. Fax: 206-296-0578. 8:30AM-Noon, 1:15-4:30PM M,W,F (PST). Access by: Phone, fax, mail, remote online, in person.

Kitsap County

Real Estate Recording—Kitsap County Auditor, 614 Division Street, Room 106 /MS 31, Port Orchard, WA 98366. 360-876-7133. Fax: 360-895-3945. 8AM-4:30PM (PST).

Felony, Civil Actions Over $25,000, Eviction, Probate—Superior Court, 614 Division St, Port Orchard, WA 98366-4699. 360-876-7164. 8AM-4:30PM (PST). Access by: Mail, remote online, in person.

Misdemeanor, Civil Actions Under $25,000, Small Claims—District Court South, 614 Division St, MS 25, Port Orchard, WA 98366. 360-876-7033. Fax: 360-895-4865.

8:30AM-4:30PM (PST). Access by: Phone, fax, mail, remote online, in person.

District Court North, 19050 Jensen Way NE, Poulsbo, WA 98370-0910. 360-779-5600. 8:30AM-4:30PM, closed 12:15-1:15PM (PST). Access by: Mail, remote online, in person.

Kittitas County

Real Estate Recording—Kittitas County Auditor, 205 West 5th, Room 105, Ellensburg, WA 98926. 509-962-7504. Fax: 509-962-7650. 9AM-5PM (PST).

Felony, Misdemeanor, Civil Actions Over $25,000, Eviction, Probate—Superior Court, 205 W 5th Rm 210, Ellensburg, WA 98926. 509-962-7531. Fax: 509-962-7667. 9AM-Noon, 1-5PM (PST). Access by: Phone, fax, mail, remote online, in person.

Misdemeanor, Civil Actions Under $25,000, Small Claims—District Court Upper Kittitas, 618 E First, Cle Elum, WA 98922. 509-674-5533. Fax: 509-674-4209. 8AM-5PM (PST). Access by: Mail, remote online, in person.

District Court Lower Kittitas, 5th and Main, Rm 180, Ellensburg, WA 98926. 509-962-7511. 9AM-5PM (PST). Access by: Mail, remote online, in person.

Klickitat County

Real Estate Recording—Klickitat County Auditor, 205 S. Columbus Avenue, MS-CH-2, Goldendale, WA 98620. 509-773-4001. Fax: 509-773-4244. 9AM-5PM (PST).

Felony, Civil Actions Over $25,000, Eviction, Probate—Superior Court, 205 S Columbus, Rm 204, Goldendale, WA 98620. 509-773-5744. 9AM-5PM (PST). Access by: Phone, mail, remote online, in person.

Misdemeanor, Civil Actions Under $25,000, Small Claims—East District Court, 205 S Columbus, Rm 107, Goldendale, WA 98620-9290. 509-773-4670. 8AM-5PM (PST). Access by: Phone, mail, remote online, in person.

West District Court, PO Box 435, White Salmon, WA 98672-0435. 509-493-1190. Fax: 509-493-4469. 8AM-5PM (PST). Access by: Mail, remote online, in person.

Lewis County

Real Estate Recording—Lewis County Auditor, 351 NW North Street, Chehalis, WA 98532. 360-740-1163. Fax: 360-740-1421. 8AM-5PM (PST).

Felony, Misdemeanor, Civil Actions Over $25,000, Eviction, Probate—Superior Court, 360 NW North St, MS:CLK 01, Chehalis, WA 98532-1900. 360-740-1433. 8AM-5PM (PST). Access by: Phone, mail, remote online, in person.

Misdemeanor, Civil Actions Under $25,000, Small Claims—District Court, PO Box 336, Chehalis, WA 98532-0336. 360-740-1203. Fax: 360-740-2779. 8AM-5PM (PST). Access by: Mail, remote online, in person.

Lincoln County

Real Estate Recording—Lincoln County Auditor, 450 Logan, Davenport, WA 99122. 509-725-4971. Fax: 509-725-0820. 8:30AM-4:30PM (PST).

Felony, Misdemeanor, Civil Actions Over $25,000, Eviction, Probate—Superior Court, Box 369, Davenport, WA 99122-0396. 509-725-1401. Fax: 509-725-1150. 8AM-5PM (PST). Access by: Phone, mail, remote online, in person.

Misdemeanor, Civil Actions Under $25,000, Small Claims—District Court, PO Box 118, Davenport, WA 99122-0118. 509-725-2281. 8:30AM-5PM (PST). Access by: Mail, remote online, in person.

Mason County

Real Estate Recording—Mason County Auditor, 411 North 5th Street, Shelton, WA 98584. 360-427-9670. Fax: 360-427-8425. 8:30AM-5PM (PST).

Felony, Misdemeanor, Civil Actions Over $25,000, Eviction, Probate—Superior Court, PO Box 340, Shelton, WA 98584. 360-427-9670. 8:30AM-5PM (PST). Access by: Phone, mail, remote online, in person.

Misdemeanor, Civil Actions Under $25,000, Small Claims—District Court, PO Box "O", Shelton, WA 98584-

0090. 360-427-9670. Fax: 360-427-8425. 8:30AM-5PM (PST). Access by: Mail, remote online, in person.

Okanogan County

Real Estate Recording—Okanogan County Auditor, Courthouse, 149 North 3rd, Okanogan, WA 98840. 509-422-7240. 8:30AM-5PM (PST).

Felony, Misdemeanor, Civil Actions Over $25,000, Eviction, Probate—Superior Court, PO Box 72, Okanogan, WA 98840. 509-422-7275. Fax: 509-826-7295. 8AM-5PM (PST). Access by: Phone, fax, mail, remote online, in person.

Misdemeanor, Civil Actions Under $25,000, Small Claims—District Court, PO Box 980, Okanogan, WA 98840-0980. 509-422-7170. Fax: 509-422-7174. 8AM-5PM (PST). Access by: Phone, mail, remote online, in person.

Pacific County

Real Estate Recording—Pacific County Auditor, 300 Memorial Drive, South Bend, WA 98586. 360-875-9318. Fax: 360-875-9333. 8AM-5PM (PST).

Felony, Civil Actions Over $25,000, Eviction, Probate—Superior Court, PO Box 67, South Bend, WA 98586. 360-875-9320. Fax: 360-875-9321. 8AM-5PM (PST). Access by: Phone, fax, mail, remote online, in person.

Misdemeanor, Civil Actions Under $25,000, Small Claims—District Court South, PO Box 794, Ilwaco, WA 98624. 360-642-9417. Fax: 360-642-9417. 8AM-Noon, 1-5PM (PST). Access by: Phone, fax, mail, remote online, in person.

District Court North, Box 134, South Bend, WA 98586-0134. 360-875-9354. Fax: 360-875-9362. 8:30AM-5PM (PST). Access by: Phone, fax, mail, remote online, in person.

Pend Oreille County

Real Estate Recording—Pend Oreille County Auditor, West 625 4th Street, Newport, WA 99156. 509-447-3185. Fax: 509-447-3475. 8AM-4:30PM (PST).

Felony, Civil Actions Over $25,000, Eviction, Probate—Superior Court, 229 S Garden Ave (PO Box 5020), Newport, WA 99156-5020. 509-447-2435. Fax: 509-447-2734. 8AM-Noon, 1-4:30PM (PST). Access by: Phone, mail, remote online, in person.

Misdemeanor, Civil Actions Under $25,000, Small Claims—District Court, PO Box 5030, Newport, WA 99156-5030. 509-447-4110. Fax: 509-447-5724. 8AM-4:30PM (PST). Access by: Fax, mail, remote online, in person.

Pierce County

Real Estate Recording—Pierce County Auditor, 2401 South 35th Street, Room 200, Tacoma, WA 98409. 253-591-7440. Fax: 253-596-2761. 8:30AM-4:30PM (PST).

Felony, Civil Actions Over $25,000, Eviction, Probate—Superior Court, 930 Tacoma Ave South, Rm 110, Tacoma, WA 98402. 253-591-7455. Fax: 253-597-3428. 8:30AM-4:30PM (PST). Access by: Mail, remote online, in person.

Misdemeanor, Civil Actions Under $25,000, Small Claims—District Court #4, PO Box 110, Buckley, WA 98321-0110. 360-829-0411. 9AM-4PM (PST). Access by: Phone, mail, remote online, in person.

District Court #3, PO Box 105, Eatonville, WA 98328-0105. 360-832-6000. 8AM-4:30PM (PST). Access by: Mail, remote online, in person.

District Court #2, 6659 Kimball Dr, Suite E-503, Gig Harbor, WA 98335-1229. 253-851-5131. Fax: 253-858-2184. 8:30AM-4:30PM (PST). Access by: Phone, fax, mail, remote online, in person.

District Court #1, 930 Tacoma Ave S, Rm 601, Tacoma, WA 98402-2175. 253-591-7474. 8:30AM-4:30PM (PST). Access by: Mail, remote online, in person.

San Juan County

Real Estate Recording—San Juan County Auditor, 350 Court Street, Friday Harbor, WA 98250. 360-378-2161. Fax: 360-378-6256. 8AM-4:30PM (PST).

Felony, Misdemeanor, Civil Actions Over $25,000, Eviction, Probate—Superior Court, 350 Court St, #7, Friday

Harbor, WA 98250. 360-378-2163. Fax: 360-378-3967. 8AM-4:30PM (PST). Access by: Phone, fax, mail, remote online, in person.

Misdemeanor, Civil Actions Under $25,000, Small Claims—District Court, PO Box 127, Friday Harbor, WA 98250-0127. 360-378-4017. Fax: 360-378-4099. 8AM-5PM (PST). Access by: Mail, remote online, in person.

Skagit County

Real Estate Recording—Skagit County Auditor, 700 So. 2nd St., 2nd Floor, Admin. Bldg., Mount Vernon, WA 98273. 360-336-9420. Fax: 360-336-9429. 8:30AM-4:30PM (PST).

Felony, Misdemeanor, Civil Actions Over $25,000, Eviction, Probate—Superior Court, PO Box 837, Mount Vernon, WA 98273-0837. 360-336-9440. 8:30AM-4:30PM (PST). Access by: Mail, remote online, in person.

Misdemeanor, Civil Actions Under $25,000, Small Claims—District Court, 600 S 3rd, Mount Vernon, WA 98273. 360-336-9319. Fax: 360-336-9318. 8:30AM-4:30PM (PST). Access by: Fax, mail, remote online, in person.

Skamania County

Real Estate Recording—Skamania County Auditor, 240 Vancouver Avenue, Stevenson, WA 98648. 509-427-9420. Fax: 509-427-4165. 8:30AM-5PM (PST).

Felony, Misdemeanor, Civil Actions Over $25,000, Eviction, Probate—Superior Court, PO Box 790, Stevenson, WA 98648. 509-427-9431. Fax: 509-427-7386. 8:30AM-5PM (PST). Access by: Phone, mail, remote online, in person.

Misdemeanor, Civil Actions Under $25,000, Small Claims—District Court, PO Box 790, Stevenson, WA 98648. 509-427-9430. Fax: 509-427-7386. 8:30AM-5PM (PST). Access by: Phone, fax, mail, remote online, in person.

Snohomish County

Real Estate Recording—Snohomish County Auditor, Dept. R., M/S # 204, 3000 Rockefeller Avenue, Everett, WA 98201. 425-388-3483. Fax: 425-259-2777. 9AM-5PM (PST).

Felony, Civil Actions Over $25,000, Eviction, Probate—Superior Court, Mission Bldg #246, 3000 Rockefeller, Everett, WA 98201. 425-388-3466. 9AM-5PM (PST). Access by: Phone, mail, remote online, in person.

Misdemeanor, Civil Actions Under $25,000, Small Claims—Cascade District Court, 415 E Burke, Arlington, WA 98223. 360-652-9552. Fax: 360-435-0873. 9AM-5PM (PST). Access by: Phone, fax, mail, remote online, in person.

Everett District Court, 3000 Rockefeller Ave MS 508, Everett, WA 98201. 425-388-3331. Fax: 425-388-3565. 8AM-5PM (PST). Access by: Phone, fax, mail, remote online, in person.

South District Court, 20520 68th Ave W, Lynnwood, WA 98036-7457. 425-774-8803. Fax: 425-744-6820. 8:30AM-5PM (PST). Access by: Mail, remote online, in person.

Evergreen District Court, 14414 179th Ave SE, PO Box 625, Monroe, WA 98272-0625. 360-568-8572. Fax: 360-794-6644. 8AM-Noon, 1-5PM (PST). Access by: Phone, mail, remote online, in person.

Spokane County

Real Estate Recording—Spokane County Auditor, West 1116 Broadway, Spokane, WA 99260. 509-456-2270. 8:30AM-5PM (PST).

Felony, Civil Actions Over $25,000, Eviction, Probate—Superior Court, W 1116 Broadway, Spokane, WA 99260. 509-456-2211. 8:30AM-5PM (PST). Access by: Phone, mail, remote online, in person.

Misdemeanor, Civil Actions Under $25,000, Small Claims—District Court, Public Safety Bldg, W 1100 Mallon, Spokane, WA 99260. Civil: 509-456-2230. Criminal: 509-456-4770. 8:30AM-5PM (PST). Access by: Mail, remote online, in person.

Stevens County

Real Estate Recording—Stevens County Auditor, 215 South Oak St., Colville, WA 99114. 509-684-7512. Fax: 509-684-8310. 8:30AM-4:30PM (PST).

Felony, Civil Actions Over $25,000, Eviction, Probate—Superior Court, 215 S Oak Rm 206, Colville, WA 99114. 509-684-7520. 8AM-Noon, 1-4:30PM (PST). Access by: Mail, remote online, in person.

Misdemeanor, Civil Actions Under $25,000, Small Claims—District Court, PO Box 163, Colville, WA 99114-0163. 509-684-5249. 8AM-Noon, 1-4:30PM (PST). Access by: Phone, mail, remote online, in person.

Thurston County

Real Estate Recording—Thurston County Auditor, 2000 Lakeridge Drive SW, Olympia, WA 98502. 360-786-5405. Fax: 360-786-5223. 8AM-5PM (PST).

Felony, Misdemeanor, Civil Actions Over $25,000, Eviction, Probate—Superior Court, 2000 Lakeridge Dr SW, Bldg 2, Olympia, WA 98502. 360-786-5430. 8AM-5PM (PST). Access by: Mail, remote online, in person.

Misdemeanor, Civil Actions Under $25,000, Small Claims—District Court, 2000 Lakeridge Dr SW, Bldg 3, Olympia, WA 98502. 360-786-6483. Fax: 360-754-3359. 9AM-5PM (PST). Access by: Phone, fax, mail, remote online, in person.

Wahkiakum County

Real Estate Recording—Wahkiakum County Auditor, 64 Main Street, Cathlamet, WA 98612. 360-795-3219. Fax: 360-795-0824. 8AM-4PM (PST).

Felony, Misdemeanor, Civil Actions Over $25,000, Eviction, Probate—Superior Court, PO Box 116, Cathlamet, WA 98612. 360-795-3558. Fax: 360-795-8813. 8AM-4PM (PST). Access by: Mail, remote online, in person.

Misdemeanor, Civil Actions Under $25,000, Small Claims—District Court, PO Box 144, Cathlamet, WA 98612. 360-795-3461. Fax: 360-795-6506. 8AM-4PM (PST). Access by: Phone, fax, mail, remote online, in person.

Walla Walla County

Real Estate Recording—Walla Walla County Auditor, 315 West Main Street, Walla Walla, WA 99362. 509-527-3204. Fax: 509-527-3214. 9AM-5PM (PST).

Felony, Civil Actions Over $25,000, Eviction, Probate—Superior Court, PO Box 836, Walla Walla, WA 99362. 509-527-3221. Fax: 509-527-3214. 9AM-4PM (PST). Access by: Phone, mail, remote online, in person.

Misdemeanor, Civil Actions Under $25,000, Small Claims—District Court, 328 W Poplar, Walla Walla, WA 99362. 509-527-3236. 9AM-4PM (PST). Access by: Mail, remote online, in person.

Whatcom County

Real Estate Recording—Whatcom County Auditor, 311 Grand Avenue, Bellingham, WA 98225. 360-676-6740. Fax: 360-738-4556. 8:30AM-4:30PM (PST).

Felony, Civil Actions Over $25,000, Eviction, Probate—Superior Court, PO Box 1144, Bellingham, WA 98227. 360-676-6777. Fax: 360-676-7727. 8:30AM-Noon, 1-4:30PM (PST). Access by: Phone, fax, mail, remote online, in person.

Misdemeanor, Civil Actions Under $25,000, Small Claims—District Court, 311 Grand Ave, Bellingham, WA 98225. 360-676-6770. Fax: 360-738-2452. 8AM-4:30PM (PST). Access by: Remote online, in person.

Whitman County

Real Estate Recording—Whitman County Auditor, North 404 Main, 2nd Floor, Colfax, WA 99111. 509-397-6270. Fax: 509-397-6351. 8AM-5PM (Recording Until 2:30PM) (PST).

Felony, Civil Actions Over $25,000, Eviction, Probate—Superior Court, Box 390, Colfax, WA 99111. 509-397-6244. Fax: 509-397-3546. 8AM-5PM (PST). Access by: Phone, fax, mail, remote online, in person.

Misdemeanor, Civil Actions Under $25,000, Small Claims—District Court, N 404 Main St, Colfax, WA 99111. 509-397-6260. Fax: 509-397-5584. 8AM-5PM (PST). Access by: Phone, fax, mail, remote online, in person.

District Court, PO Box 249, Pullman, WA 99163. 509-332-2065. Fax: 509-332-5740. 8AM-5PM (PST). Access by: Fax, mail, remote online, in person.

Yakima County

Real Estate Recording—Yakima County Auditor, 128 N. 2nd St., #117, Yakima, WA 98901. 509-574-1330. Fax: 509-574-1341. 9AM-4:30PM (PST).

Felony, Civil Actions Over $25,000, Eviction, Probate—Superior Court, 128 N 2nd St, Rm 323, Yakima, WA 98901. 509-574-1430. 8:30AM-4:30PM (PST). Access by: Phone, mail, remote online, in person.

Misdemeanor, Civil Actions Under $25,000, Small Claims—District Court, 505 S 7th St, Sunnyside, WA 98944. 509-837-3713. Fax: 509-837-2125. 8:30AM-4:30PM (PST). Access by: Phone, fax, mail, remote online, in person.

District Court, PO Box 446, Toppenish, WA 98948. 509-574-1800. 8:30AM-5PM (PST). Access by: Mail, remote online, in person.

District Court, 128 N 2nd St, Rm 225, Yakima, WA 98901-2631. 509-574-1800. Fax: 509-574-1801. 8:30AM-4:30PM (PST). Access by: Phone, fax, mail, remote online, in person.

Federal Courts

US District Court

Eastern District of Washington

Spokane Division, US District Court PO Box 1493, Spokane, WA 99210-1493. 509-353-2150. Counties: Adams, Asotin, Benton, Chelan, Columbia, Douglas, Ferry, Franklin, Garfield, Grant, Lincoln, Okanogan, Pend Oreille, Spokane, Stevens, Walla Walla, Whitman

Yakima Division, US District Court PO Box 2706, Yakima, WA 98907. 509-575-5838. Counties: Kittitas, Klickitat, Yakima. Cases assigned primarily to Judge McDonald are here

Western District of Washington

Seattle Division, US District Court Clerk of Court, 215 US Courthouse, 1010 5th Ave, Seattle, WA 98104. 206-553-5598. Counties: Island, King, San Juan, Skagit, Snohomish, Whatcom

Tacoma Division, US District Court Clerk's Office, Room 3100, 1717 Pacific Ave, Tacoma, WA 98402-3200. 253-593-6313. Counties: Clallam, Clark, Cowlitz, Grays Harbor, Jefferson, Kitsap, Lewis, Mason, Pierce, Skamania, Thurston, Wahkiakum

US Bankruptcy Court

Eastern District of Washington

Spokane Division, US Bankruptcy Court, PO Box 2164, Spokane, WA 99210-2164. 509-353-2404. Voice Case Information System: 509-353-2404. Counties: Adams, Asotin, Benton, Chelan, Columbia, Douglas, Ferry, Franklin, Garfield, Grant, Kittitas, Klickitat, Lincoln, Okanogan, Pend Oreille, Spokane, Stevens, Walla Walla, Whitman, Yakima

Western District of Washington

Seattle Division, US Bankruptcy Court, Clerk of Court, 315 Park Place Bldg, 1200 6th Ave, Seattle, WA 98101. 206-553-7545. Voice Case Information System: 206-553-8543. Counties: Clallam, Island, Jefferson, King, Kitsap, San Juan, Skagit, Snohomish, Whatcom

Tacoma Division, US Bankruptcy Court, Suite 2100, 1717 Pacific Ave, Tacoma, WA 98402-3233. 206-593-6310. Voice Case Information System: 206-553-8543. Counties: Clark, Cowlitz, Grays Harbor, Lewis, Mason, Pacific, Pierce, Skamania, Thurston, Wahkiakum

West Virginia

Capitol: Charleston (Kanawha County)	
Number of Counties: 55	**Population:** 1,828,140
County Court Locations:	**Federal Court Locations:**
•Circuit Courts: 55/31 Circuits	•District Courts: 9
•Magistrate Courts: 54/ 55 Counties	•Bankruptcy Courts: 2
Municipal Courts: 122	**State Agencies:** 19

State Agencies—Summary

General Help Numbers:

State Archives

Division of Culture & History	304-558-0220
Archives & History Section	Fax: 304-558-2779
Cultural Center,	
State Capitol Complex	9AM-5PM M-F, 1-5 SA
Charleston, WV 25305-0300	
Reference Librarian:	304-558-0230

Governor's Office

Governor's Office	304-558-2000
Office of the Governor	Fax: 304-342-7025
State Capitol,	
1900 Kanawha Blvd E	8AM-6PM M-TH; 8AM-5PM F
Charleston, WV 25305-0370	

Attorney General's Office

Attorney General's Office	304-558-2021
State Capitol, Room 26, E Wing	Fax: 304-558-0140
Charleston, WV 25305-0220	8:30AM-5PM

State Legislation

West Virginia State Legislature	304-347-4830
State Capitol	800-642-8650
Documents	8:30AM-4:30PM
Charleston, WV 25305	

State Court Administrator

Administrative Office	304-558-0145
State Court of Appeals	Fax: 304-558-1212
1900 Kanawha Blvd, Bldg 1 E 400	9AM-4PM
Charleston, WV 25305-0830	

Important State Internet Sites:

Webscape
File Edit View   Help

State of West Virginia World Wide Web
www.state.wv.us/

This site links to such sites as news and current events, government highlights, departments and a Governor's message.

The Governor's Office
www.state.wv.us/governor

Located here are the Governors speeches and press releases. You can also send the Governor e-mail.

Legislators
www.wvlc.wvnet.edu/legisinfo/legishp.html

This site links to the members of the state Senate and the House of Delegates and their committies. It also lists the members of the US House and Senate. This site links to Bill information. E-mail can be sent to all legislators.

State Archives and Historical Records
www.wvlc.wvnet.edu/history/historyw.html

Linked to this site are the state archives and historical records and societies. The archives site lists information about what is available in the archives.

West Virginia Online
www.wvon-line.com/

Provided at this site are links to arts and entertainment, cities and counties, education, media, real estate, travel and West Virginia University.

State Agencies—Public Records

Criminal Records
State Police, Criminal Identification Bureau, Records Section, 725 Jefferson Rd, South Charleston, WV 25309, Main Telephone: 304-746-2277, Fax: 304-746-2402, Hours: 8AM-5PM. Access by: mail only.

Corporation Records
Limited Liability Company Records
Limited Partnerships
Trademarks/Servicemarks
Secretary of State, Corporation Division, State Capitol Bldg, Room W139, Charleston, WV 25305-0776, Main Telephone: 304-558-8000, Fax: 304-558-0900, Hours: 8:30AM-4:30PM. Access by: mail, phone, visit. Members of the Bar Association have online access, call Tom Tinder at 304-558-2456 for details.

Uniform Commercial Code
Federal Tax Liens
State Tax Liens
UCC Division, Secretary of State, State Capitol Bldg, Rm W131, Charleston, WV 25305, Main Telephone: 304-345-4000, Fax: 304-558-0900, Hours: 8:30AM-4:30PM. Access by: mail, phone, visit.

Sales Tax Registrations
Tax Administration Department, Revenue Division, PO Box 2389, Charleston, WV 25330, Main Telephone: 304-558-8500, Fax: 304-558-8733, Hours: 8AM-4PM. Access by: mail, phone, visit.

Birth Certificates
Bureau of Public Health, Vital Records, State Capitol Complex Bldg 3-Rm 516, Charleston, WV 25305, Main Telephone: 304-558-2931, Hours: 8AM-4PM. Access by: mail, phone, visit.

Death Records
Bureau of Public Health, Vital Records, State Capitol Complex Bldg 3-Rm 516, Charleston, WV 25305, Main Telephone: 304-558-2931, Hours: 8AM-4PM. Access by: mail, phone, visit.

Marriage Certificates
Bureau of Public Health, Vital Records, State Capitol Complex Bldg 3-Rm 516, Charleston, WV 25305, Main Telephone: 304-558-2931, Hours: 8AM-4PM. Access by: mail, phone, visit.

Divorce Records
Records not available from state agency.

Workers' Compensation Records
Bureau of Employment Programs, Workers Compensation Division, 4700 McCorkle Ave, Charleston, WV 25304, Main Telephone: 304-558-5587, Hours: 8AM-5PM. Access by: mail, visit.

Driver License Information
Driver Records
Division of Motor Vehicles, Driver Improvement Unit, Building 3, State Capitol Complex, Charleston, WV 25317, Main Telephone: 304-558-0238, Fax: 304-558-0037, Hours: 8:30AM-4:30PM. Access by: mail, visit, PC. Ticket information is available from this office for the convictee only (no fee). Others must request ticket information from the court system.

Vehicle Ownership
Vehicle Identification
Division of Motor Vehicles, Titles and Registration Division, 1606 Washington St East, Charleston, WV 25317, Main Telephone: 304-558-0282, Fax: 302-558-1012, Hours: 8:30AM-4:30PM. Access by: mail, visit. This agency maintains records for unattached mobile homes and boats.

Accident Reports
Department of Public Safety, Traffic Records Section, 725 Jefferson Rd, South Charleston, WV 25309-1698, Main Telephone: 304-746-2128, Fax: 304-746-2245, Hours: 8:30AM-4:30PM. Access by: mail, fax, visit. It is suggested to send a letter explaining purpose of request and state if involved in some manner.

Hunting License Information
Fishing License Information
Natural Resources Department, Licensing Division, 1900 Kanawha Blvd E, Bldg 3, Room 658, Charleston, WV 25305, Main Telephone: 304-558-2758, Fax: 304-558-3147, Hours: 8:30AM-4:30PM. Access by: mail only.

County Courts and Recording Offices

What You Need to Know...

About the Courts

Administration

Administrative Office	304-558-0145
State Court of Appeals	Fax: 304-558-1212
1900 Kanawha Blvd, Bldg 1 E 400	9AM-4PM
Charleston, WV 25305-0830	

Court Structure

The upper limit for civil claims in the Magistrate Courts is $5000. Probate is handled by the Circuit Court. Records are held at the County Commissioner's Office.

Searching Hints

There is a statewide requirement that search turn-around time not exceed 10 days; however, most courts do far better than that limit. There is a discrepancy in what courts will and will not release with the choice resting with the judges and clerks in the various jurisdictions.

Online Access

There is no statewide online computer system, internal or external. Most courts with a computer system use FORTUNE software; however, there is **no** external access permitted.

About the Recorder's Office

Organization

55 counties, 55 filing offices. The recording officer is County Clerk. The entire state is in the Eastern Time Zone (EST).

UCC Records

Financing statements are filed at the state level, except for real estate related collateral, which are filed only with the Register of Deeds, and consumer goods, which are filed in both places. Many filing offices will perform UCC searches. Use search request form UCC-11. Searches fees and copy fees vary.

Lien Records

All federal and state tax liens are filed with the County Clerk. Most counties will **not** perform tax lien searches. Other liens include judgments, mechanics, and lis pendens.

Real Estate Records

Most County Clerks will **not** perform real estate searches. Copy fees are usually $1.50 up to two pages and $1.00 for each additional page. Certification usually costs $1.00 per document.

County Courts and Recording Offices

Barbour County

Real Estate Recording—Barbour County Clerk, 8 North Main Street, Courthouse, Philippi, WV 26416. 304-457-2232. 8:30AM-4:30PM (EST).

Felony, Civil Actions Over $5,000, Probate—Circuit Court, 8 N Main St, Philippi, WV 26416. 304-457-3454. 8:30AM-4:30PM (EST). Access by: Phone, mail, in person.

Misdemeanor, Civil Actions Under $5,000, Eviction, Small Claims—Magistrate Court, PO Box 541, Philippi, WV 26416. 304-457-3676. 8:30AM-4:30PM (EST). Access by: In person only.

Berkeley County

Real Estate Recording—Berkeley County Clerk, 100 West King Street, Martinsburg, WV 25401. 304-264-1927. Fax: 304-267-1794. 9AM-5PM (EST).

Felony, Civil Actions Over $5,000, Probate—Circuit Court, 110 W King St, Martinsburg, WV 25401-3210. 304-264-1918. 9AM-5PM (EST). Access by: Phone, in person. Phone# 304-746-2177.

Misdemeanor, Civil Actions Under $5,000, Eviction, Small Claims—Magistrate Court, 120 W John St, Martinsburg, WV 25401. 304-264-1956. Fax: 304-263-9154. 9AM-5PM (EST). Access by: In person only.

Boone County

Real Estate Recording—Boone County Clerk, 200 State Street, Madison, WV 25130. 304-369-7337. Fax: 304-369-7329. 8AM-4PM (EST).

Felony, Civil Actions Over $5,000, Probate—Circuit Court, 200 State St, Madison, WV 25130. 304-369-3925. Fax: 304-369-7326. 8AM-4PM (EST). Access by: Phone, fax, mail, in person.

Misdemeanor, Civil Actions Under $5,000, Eviction, Small Claims—Magistrate Court, 200 State St., Madison, WV 25130. 304-369-7300. Fax: 304-369-1932. 8AM-4PM (EST). Access by: Mail, in person.

Braxton County

Real Estate Recording—Braxton County Clerk, 300 Main Street, Sutton, WV 26601. 304-765-2833. Fax: 304-765-2093. 8AM-4PM (EST).

Felony, Civil Actions Over $5,000, Probate—Circuit Court, 300 Main St, Sutton, WV 26601. 304-765-2837. Fax: 304-765-2093. 8AM-4PM (EST). Access by: Fax, mail, in person.

Misdemeanor, Civil Actions Under $5,000, Eviction, Small Claims—Magistrate Court, 307 Main St, Sutton, WV 26601. 304-765-5678. Fax: 304-765-7368. 8:30AM-4:30PM (EST). Access by: Mail, in person.

Brooke County

Real Estate Recording—Brooke County Clerk, 632 Main Street, Courthouse, Wellsburg, WV 26070. 304-737-3661. Fax: 304-737-3668. 9AM-5PM; Sat 9AM-Noon (EST).

Felony, Civil Actions Over $5,000, Probate—Circuit Court, Brooke County Courthouse, Wellsburg, WV 26070. 304-737-3662. 9AM-5PM (EST). Access by: Mail, in person.

Misdemeanor, Civil Actions Under $5,000, Eviction, Small Claims—Magistrate Court, 632 Main St, Wellsburg, WV 26070. 304-737-1321. Fax: 304-737-1509. 9AM-4PM (EST). Access by: In person only.

Cabell County

Real Estate Recording—Cabell County Clerk, Cabell County Courthouse, 750 Fifth Ave., Room 108, Huntington, WV 25701. 304-526-8625. Fax: 304-526-8632. 8:30AM-4:30PM (EST).

Felony, Civil Actions Over $5,000, Probate—Circuit Court, PO Box 0545, Huntington, WV 25710-0545. 304-526-8622. Fax: 304-526-8699. 8:30AM-4:30PM (EST). Access by: Mail, in person.

Misdemeanor, Civil Actions Under $5,000, Eviction, Small Claims—Magistrate Court, 750 5th Ave, Basement, Huntington, WV 25701. 304-526-8642. 8:30AM-4:30PM (EST). Access by: In person only.

Calhoun County

Real Estate Recording—Calhoun County Clerk, Main Street, Courthouse, Grantsville, WV 26147. 304-354-6725. 9AM-4:30PM (EST).

Felony, Civil Actions Over $5,000, Probate—Circuit Court, PO Box 266, Grantsville, WV 26147. 304-354-6910. Fax: 304-354-6910. 9AM-4:30PM, 9AM-Noon 1st Sat ea month (EST). Access by: Phone, fax, mail, in person.

Misdemeanor, Civil Actions Under $5,000, Eviction, Small Claims—Magistrate Court, PO Box 186, Grantsville, WV 26147. 304-354-6698. Fax: 304-354-6698. 9AM-4:30PM (EST). Access by: Mail, in person.

Clay County

Real Estate Recording—Clay County Clerk, Courthouse, 207 Main St., Clay, WV 25043. 304-587-4259. Fax: 304-587-7329. 8AM-4PM (EST).

Felony, Civil Actions Over $5,000, Probate—Circuit Court, PO Box 129, Clay, WV 25043. 304-587-4256. Fax: 304-587-4346. 8AM-4PM (EST). Access by: Phone, fax, mail, in person.

Misdemeanor, Civil Actions Under $5,000, Eviction, Small Claims—Magistrate Court, PO Box 393, Clay, WV 25043. 304-587-2131. Fax: 304-587-2727. 8:30AM-4:30PM (EST). Access by: Phone, mail, in person.

Doddridge County

Real Estate Recording—Doddridge County Clerk, 118 East Court Street, Room 102, West Union, WV 26456. 304-873-2631. 8:30AM-4PM (EST).

Felony, Civil Actions Over $5,000, Probate—Circuit Court, 118 E. Court St, West Union, WV 26456. 304-873-2331. 8:30AM-4PM (EST). Access by: Phone, mail, in person.

Misdemeanor, Civil Actions Under $5,000, Eviction, Small Claims—Magistrate Court, PO Box 207, West Union, WV 26456. 304-873-2694. Fax: 304-873-2643. 8AM-4PM (EST). Access by: Fax, mail, in person.

Fayette County

Real Estate Recording—Fayette County Clerk, Courthouse, Fayetteville, WV 25840. 304-574-1200. 8AM-4PM (EST).

Felony, Civil Actions Over $5,000, Probate—Circuit Court, 100 Court St, Fayetteville, WV 25840. 304-574-1200. 8AM-4PM (EST). Access by: Mail, in person.

Misdemeanor, Civil Actions Under $5,000, Eviction, Small Claims—Magistrate Court, 100 Court St, Fayetteville, WV 25840. 304-574-1200. Fax: 304-574-2458. 9AM-9PM M-F, 9AM-Noon Sat (EST). Access by: In person only.

Gilmer County

Real Estate Recording—Gilmer County Clerk, 10 Howard Street, Courthouse, Glenville, WV 26351. 304-462-7641. Fax: 304-462-5134. 8AM-4PM (EST).

Felony, Civil Actions Over $5,000, Probate—Circuit Court, Gilmer County Courthouse, Glenville, WV 26351. 304-462-7241. Fax: 304-462-5134. 8AM-4PM (EST). Access by: Phone, mail, in person.

Misdemeanor, Civil Actions Under $5,000, Eviction, Small Claims—Magistrate Court, Courthouse Annex, Glenville, WV 26351. 304-462-7812. Fax: 304-462-8582. 8:30AM-4PM (EST). Access by: Phone, fax, mail, in person.

Grant County

Real Estate Recording—Grant County Clerk, 5 Highland Avenue, Petersburg, WV 26847. 304-257-4550. Fax: 304-257-2593. 9AM-4PM (EST).

Felony, Civil Actions Over $5,000, Probate—Circuit Court, 5 Highland Ave, Petersburg, WV 26847. 304-257-4545. Fax: 304-257-2593. 8:30AM-4:30PM (EST). Access by: Phone, fax, mail, in person.

Misdemeanor, Civil Actions Under $5,000, Eviction, Small Claims—Magistrate Court, 5 Highland Ave (PO Box 216), Petersburg, WV 26847. 304-257-4637. Fax: 304-257-2593. 9AM-4PM (EST). Access by: Phone, fax, mail, in person.

Greenbrier County

Real Estate Recording—Greenbrier County Clerk, 200 North Court Street, Lewisburg, WV 24901. 304-647-6602. Fax: 304-647-6666. 8:30AM-4:30PM (EST).

Felony, Civil Actions Over $5,000, Probate—Circuit Court, PO Drawer 751, Lewisburg, WV 24901. 304-647-6626. Fax: 304-647-6666. 8:30AM-4:30PM (EST). Access by: Phone, fax, mail, in person.

Misdemeanor, Civil Actions Under $5,000, Eviction, Small Claims—Magistrate Court, 200 North Court St, Lewisburg, WV 24901. 304-647-6632. Fax: 304-647-3612. 8:30AM-4:30PM (EST). Access by: Phone, fax, mail, in person.

Hampshire County

Real Estate Recording—Hampshire County Clerk, Main Street, Courthouse, Romney, WV 26757. 304-822-5112. Fax: 304-822-4039. 9AM-4PM (F open until 8PM) (EST).

Felony, Civil Actions Over $5,000, Probate—Circuit Court, PO Box 343, Romney, WV 26757. 304-822-5022. 9AM-4PM M-F 5PM-8PM Friday evening (EST). Access by: Phone, mail, in person.

Misdemeanor, Civil Actions Under $5,000, Eviction, Small Claims—Magistrate Court, 239 W Birch Ln, PO Box 881, Romney, WV 26757. 304-822-4311. Fax: 304-822-3981. 8:30AM-4PM (EST). Access by: Phone, mail, in person.

Hancock County

Real Estate Recording—Hancock County Clerk, 102 Court Street, New Cumberland, WV 26047. 304-564-3311. Fax: 304-564-5941. 8:30AM-4:30PM (EST).

Felony, Civil Actions Over $5,000, Probate—Circuit Court, PO Box 428, New Cumberland, WV 26047. 304-564-3311. Fax: 304-564-5014. 8:30AM-4:30PM (EST). Access by: Fax, mail, in person.

Misdemeanor, Civil Actions Under $5,000, Eviction, Small Claims—Magistrate Court, 106 Court St, New Cumberland, WV 26047. 304-564-3355. Fax: 304-564-3852. 8AM-4PM M-W, F; 8AM-9PM Th (EST). Access by: Phone, fax, mail, in person.

Hardy County

Real Estate Recording—Hardy County Clerk, 204 Washington Street, Courthouse - Room 111, Moorefield, WV 26836. 304-538-2929. Fax: 304-538-6832. 9AM-4PM; Sat 9AM-Noon (EST).

Felony, Civil Actions Over $5,000, Probate—Circuit Court, 204 Washington St, RM 237, Moorefield, WV 26836. 304-538-7869. Fax: 304-538-6197. 9AM-4PM (EST). Access by: Phone, fax, mail, in person.

Misdemeanor, Civil Actions Under $5,000, Eviction, Small Claims—Magistrate Court, 204 Washington St, Moorefield, WV 26836. 304-538-6836. Fax: 304-538-2072. 9AM-4PM (EST). Access by: Phone, fax, mail, in person.

Harrison County

Real Estate Recording—Harrison County Clerk, 301 West Main Street, Courthouse, Clarksburg, WV 26301. 304-624-8612. Fax: 304-624-8673. 8:30AM-4PM (EST).

Felony, Civil Actions Over $5,000, Probate—Circuit Court, 301 W. Main, Suite 301, Clarksburg, WV 26301-2967. 304-624-8640. Fax: 304-624-8710. 8:30AM-4PM (EST). Access by: In person only.

Misdemeanor, Civil Actions Under $5,000, Eviction, Small Claims—Magistrate Court, 301 W. Main, Rm 203, Clarksburg, WV 26301. 304-624-8645. Fax: 304-624-8697. 8AM-4PM (EST). Access by: Phone, fax, mail, in person.

Jackson County

Real Estate Recording—Jackson County Clerk, Court & Main Streets, P.O. Box 800, Ripley, WV 25271. 304-372-2011. Fax: 304-372-5259. 9AM-4PM; 9AM-Noon Sat (EST).

Felony, Civil Actions Over $5,000, Probate—Circuit Court, PO Box 427, Ripley, WV 25271. 304-372-2011. Fax: 304-372-5259. 9AM-4PM M-F, 9AM-Noon Sat (EST). Access by: Phone, mail, in person.

Misdemeanor, Civil Actions Under $5,000, Eviction, Small Claims—Magistrate Court, PO Box 368, Ripley, WV 25271. 304-372-2011. 9AM-4PM (EST). Access by: Phone, mail, in person.

Jefferson County

Real Estate Recording—Jefferson County Clerk, 100 East Washington Street, Courthouse, Charles Town, WV 25414. 304-728-3216. Fax: 304-728-1957. 9AM-5PM (F open until 7PM) (EST).

Felony, Civil Actions Over $5,000, Probate—Circuit Court, PO Box 584, Charles Town, WV 25414. 304-725-9761. Fax: 304-725-7916. 9AM-5PM (EST). Access by: In person only.

Misdemeanor, Civil Actions Under $5,000, Eviction, Small Claims—Magistrate Court, PO Box 607, Charles Town, WV 25414. 304-725-0471. Fax: 304-728-3235. 7:30AM-4:30PM (EST). Access by: Phone, fax, mail, in person.

Kanawha County

Real Estate Recording—Kanawha County Clerk, 409 Virginia Street East, Charleston, WV 25301. 304-357-0130. 8AM-4PM M,T,W,F; 8AM-7PM Th (EST).

Felony, Civil Actions Over $5,000, Probate—Circuit Court, PO Box 2351, Charleston, WV 25328. 304-357-0440. Fax: 304-357-0473. 8AM-5PM (EST). Access by: In person only.

Misdemeanor, Civil Actions Under $5,000, Eviction, Small Claims—Magistrate Court, 111 Court St, Charleston, WV 25333. 304-357-0400. Fax: 304-357-0205. 8:30AM-4:30PM (EST). Access by: Mail, in person.

Lewis County

Real Estate Recording—Lewis County Clerk, 110 Center Avenue, Courthouse, Weston, WV 26452. 304-269-8215. Fax: 304-269-8202. 8:30AM-4:30PM (EST).

Felony, Civil Actions Over $5,000, Probate—Circuit Court, PO Box 69, Weston, WV 26452. 304-269-8210. Fax: 304-269-8202. 8:30AM-4:30PM (EST). Access by: Phone, fax, mail, in person.

Misdemeanor, Civil Actions Under $5,000, Eviction, Small Claims—Magistrate Court, 111 Court St, PO Box 260, Weston, WV 26452. 304-269-8230. Fax: 304-269-8253. 8:30AM-Noon, 1-4:30PM (EST). Access by: Phone, fax, mail, in person.

Lincoln County

Real Estate Recording—Lincoln County Clerk, 8000 Court Avenue, Hamlin, WV 25523. 304-824-3336. Fax: 304-824-7972. 9AM-4:30PM (EST).

Felony, Civil Actions Over $5,000, Probate—Circuit Court, PO Box 338, Hamlin, WV 25523. 304-824-7887. Fax: 304-824-7909. 9AM-4:30PM (EST). Access by: Phone, fax, mail, in person.

Misdemeanor, Civil Actions Under $5,000, Eviction, Small Claims—Magistrate Court, PO Box 573, Hamlin, WV 25523. 304-824-5001. Fax: 304-824-5280. 8AM-4:30PM (EST). Access by: Phone, fax, mail, in person.

Logan County

Real Estate Recording—Logan County Clerk, Stratton & Main Street, Courthouse, Room 101, Logan, WV 25601. 304-792-8600. Fax: 304-792-8621. 8:30AM-4:30PM (EST).

Felony, Civil Actions Over $5,000, Probate—Circuit Court, Logan County Courthouse, Rm 311, Logan, WV 25601. 304-792-8550. Fax: 304-792-8555. 8:30AM-4:30PM (EST). Access by: Mail, in person.

Misdemeanor, Civil Actions Under $5,000, Eviction, Small Claims—Magistrate Court, Logan County Courthouse, Logan, WV 25601. 304-792-8651. Fax: 304-752-0790. 8:30AM-4:30PM (EST). Access by: Mail, in person.

Marion County

Real Estate Recording—Marion County Clerk, 217 Adams Street, Courthouse, Fairmont, WV 26554. 304-367-5440. Fax: 304-367-5448. 8:30AM-4:30PM (EST).

Felony, Civil Actions Over $5,000, Probate—Circuit Court, PO Box 1269, Fairmont, WV 26554. 304-367-5360. Fax: 304-367-5374. 8:30AM-4:30PM (EST). Access by: In person only.

Misdemeanor, Civil Actions Under $5,000, Eviction, Small Claims—Magistrate Court, 200 Jackson St, Fairmont, WV 26554. 304-367-5330. 8:30AM-4:30PM M-W, F; 8:30AM-9PM Th (EST). Access by: Phone, mail, in person.

Marshall County

Real Estate Recording—Marshall County Clerk, 7th Street & Tomlinson Avenue, Moundsville, WV 26041. 304-845-1220. Fax: 304-845-5891. 8:30AM-4:30PM (F open until 5:30PM) (EST).

Felony, Civil Actions Over $5,000, Probate—Circuit Court, Marshall County Courthouse, 7th St, Moundsville, WV 26041. 304-845-2130. Fax: 304-845-3948. 8:30AM-4:30PM (EST). Access by: Phone, fax, mail, in person.

Mason County

Real Estate Recording—Mason County Clerk, 200 6th Street, Point Pleasant, WV 25550. 304-675-1997. Fax: 304-675-2521. 8:30AM-4:30PM (EST).

Felony, Civil Actions Over $5,000, Probate—Circuit Court, PO Box 402, Point Pleasant, WV 25550. 304-675-4400. Fax: 304-675-7419. 8:30AM-4:30PM (EST). Access by: Phone, fax, mail, in person.

Misdemeanor, Civil Actions Under $5,000, Eviction, Small Claims—Magistrate Court, Cor. of 6th St and Viand, Point Pleasant, WV 25550. 304-675-6840. 8:30AM-4:30PM (EST). Access by: Phone, mail, in person.

McDowell County

Real Estate Recording—McDowell County Clerk, 90 Wyoming Street, Suite 109, Welch, WV 24801. 304-436-8544. 9AM-5PM (EST).

Felony, Civil Actions Over $5,000, Probate—Circuit Court, PO Box 400, Welch, WV 24801. 304-436-8535. 9AM-5PM (EST). Access by: Phone, mail, in person.

Misdemeanor, Civil Actions Under $5,000, Eviction, Small Claims—Magistrate Court, PO Box 447, Welch, WV 24801. 304-436-8587. Fax: 304-436-8503. 9AM-5PM (EST). Access by: Phone, fax, mail, in person.

Mercer County

Real Estate Recording—Mercer County Clerk, Courthouse Square, Princeton, WV 24740. 304-487-8312. Fax: 304-487-8351. 8:30AM-4PM (EST).

Felony, Civil Actions Over $5,000, Probate—Circuit Court, 1501 W. Main St, Princeton, WV 24740. 304-487-8369. Fax: 304-487-8351. 8:30AM-4:30PM (EST). Access by: Phone, mail, in person.

Misdemeanor, Civil Actions Under $5,000, Eviction, Small Claims—Magistrate Court, 701 Mercer St, Princeton, WV 24740. 304-425-7952. 8:30AM-4:30PM (EST). Access by: In person only.

Mineral County

Real Estate Recording—Mineral County Clerk, 150 Armstrong Street, Keyser, WV 26726. 304-788-3924. Fax: 304-788-4109. 8:30AM-5PM (EST).

Felony, Civil Actions Over $5,000, Probate—Circuit Court, 150 Armstrong St, Keyser, WV 26726. 304-788-1562. Fax: 304-788-4109. 8:30AM-5PM (EST). Access by: Fax, mail, in person.

Misdemeanor, Civil Actions Under $5,000, Eviction, Small Claims—Magistrate Court, 105 West St, Keyser, WV 26726. 304-788-2625. Fax: 304-788-9835. 8:30AM-4:30PM (EST). Access by: Phone, mail, in person.

Mingo County

Real Estate Recording—Mingo County Clerk, 75 E. 2nd Ave., Williamson, WV 25661. 304-235-0330. Fax: 304-235-0565. 8:30AM-4:30PM (EST).

Felony, Civil Actions Over $5,000, Probate—Circuit Court, PO Box 435, Williamson, WV 25661. 304-235-0320. 8:30AM-4:30PM M-W,F, 8:30AM-6:30PM Th (EST). Access by: Mail, in person.

Misdemeanor, Civil Actions Under $5,000, Eviction, Small Claims—Magistrate Court, PO Box 986, Williamson, WV 25661. 304-235-2445. 8:30AM-4:30PM (EST). Access by: Phone, mail, in person.

Monongalia County

Real Estate Recording—Monongalia County Clerk, 243 High Street, Courthouse - Room 123, Morgantown, WV 26505. 304-291-7230. Fax: 304-291-7233. 9AM-7PM M; 9AM-5PM T-F (EST).

Felony, Civil Actions Over $5,000, Probate—Circuit Court, County Courthouse, 243 High St Rm 110, Morgantown, WV 26505. 304-291-7240. Fax: 304-291-7273. 9AM-7PM M; 9AM-5PM T-F (EST). Access by: Phone, fax, mail, in person.

Misdemeanor, Civil Actions Under $5,000, Eviction, Small Claims—Magistrate Court, 265 Spruce St, Morgantown, WV 26505. 304-291-7296. Fax: 304-284-7313. 8AM-7PM (EST). Access by: Fax, mail, in person.

Monroe County

Real Estate Recording—Monroe County Clerk, Main Street, Union, WV 24983. 304-772-3096. 8:30AM-4:30PM (EST).

Felony, Civil Actions Over $5,000, Probate—Circuit Court, PO Box 350, Union, WV 24983. 304-772-3017. Fax: 304-772-5051. 8AM-4PM (EST). Access by: Phone, mail, in person.

Misdemeanor, Civil Actions Under $5,000, Eviction, Small Claims—Magistrate Court, PO Box 4, Union, WV 24983. 304-772-3321. Fax: 304-772-4357. 8:30AM-4:30PM (EST). Access by: Fax, mail, in person.

Morgan County

Real Estate Recording—Morgan County Clerk of County Commission, 202 Fairfax Street, Suite 100, Berkeley Springs, WV 25411. 304-258-8547. 9AM-5PM M,T,Th; 9AM-1PM W; 9AM-7PM F (EST).

Felony, Civil Actions Over $5,000, Probate—Circuit Court, 202 Fairfax St, Ste 101, Berkeley Springs, WV 25411-1501. 304-258-8554. Fax: 304-258-8630. 9AM-5PM MTTh, 9AM-1PM Wed, 9AM-7PM Fri (EST). Access by: In person only.

Misdemeanor, Civil Actions Under $5,000, Eviction, Small Claims—Magistrate Court, 202 Fairfax St, Ste 202, Berkeley Springs, WV 25411. 304-258-8631. Fax: 304-258-8639. 9AM-4:30PM (EST). Access by: Phone, fax, mail, in person.

Nicholas County

Real Estate Recording—Nicholas County Clerk, 700 Main Street, Suite 2, Summersville, WV 26651. 304-872-3630. Fax: 304-872-1425. 8:30AM-4:30PM (EST).

Felony, Civil Actions Over $5,000, Probate—Circuit Court, 700 Main St, Summersville, WV 26651. 304-872-3630. 8:30AM-4:30PM (EST). Access by: In person only.

Misdemeanor, Civil Actions Under $5,000, Eviction, Small Claims—Magistrate Court, 511 Church St, Summersville, WV 26651. 304-872-3630. Fax: 304-872-5450. 8:30AM-4:30PM (EST). Access by: In person only.

Ohio County

Real Estate Recording—Ohio County Clerk, 205 City County Building, Wheeling, WV 26003. 304-234-3656. Fax: 304-234-3829. 8:30AM-5PM (EST).

Felony, Civil Actions Over $5,000, Probate—Circuit Court, 1500 Chapline St, City & County Bldg Rm 403, Wheeling, WV 26003. 304-234-3611. Fax: 304-232-0550. 8:30AM-5PM (EST). Access by: In person only.

Misdemeanor, Civil Actions Under $5,000, Eviction, Small Claims—Magistrate Court, Courthouse Annex, 46 15th St, Wheeling, WV 26003. 304-234-3709. Fax: 304-234-3898. 8AM-4PM (EST). Access by: Phone, fax, mail, in person.

Pendleton County

Real Estate Recording—Pendleton County Clerk, Main Street, Courthouse, Franklin, WV 26807. 304-358-2505. Fax: 304-358-2473. 8:30AM-4PM; Sat 8:30AM-Noon (EST).

Felony, Civil Actions Over $5,000, Probate—Circuit Court, PO Box 846, Franklin, WV 26807. 304-358-7067. Fax: 304-358-2473. 8:30AM-4PM (EST). Access by: Phone, fax, mail, in person.

Misdemeanor, Civil Actions Under $5,000, Eviction, Small Claims—Magistrate Court, PO Box 637, Franklin, WV 26807. 304-358-2343. Fax: 304-358-2473. 9AM-4PM (EST). Access by: Phone, fax, mail, in person.

Pleasants County

Real Estate Recording—Pleasants County Clerk, Courthouse, 301 Court Lane, Room 101, St. Marys, WV 26170. 304-684-3542. Fax: 304-684-9315. 8:30AM-4:30PM (EST).

Felony, Civil Actions Over $5,000, Probate—Circuit Court, 301 Court Lane, Rm 201, St. Mary's, WV 26170. 304-684-3513. Fax: 304-684-9315. 8:30AM-4:30PM (EST). Access by: In person only.

Misdemeanor, Civil Actions Under $5,000, Eviction, Small Claims—Magistrate Court, 301 Court Lane, Rm B-6, St Mary's, WV 26170. 304-684-7197. 8:30AM-4:30PM (EST). Access by: Phone, mail, in person.

Pocahontas County

Real Estate Recording—Pocahontas County Clerk, 900C 10th Avenue, Marlinton, WV 24954. 304-799-4549. 9AM-4:30PM (EST).

Felony, Civil Actions Over $5,000, Probate—Circuit Court, 900-D 10th Ave, Marlinton, WV 24954. 304-799-4604. 9AM-4:30PM (EST). Access by: Mail, in person.

Misdemeanor, Civil Actions Under $5,000, Eviction, Small Claims—Magistrate Court, 900 10th Ave, Marlinton, WV 24954. 304-799-6603. Fax: 304-799-6331. 9AM-4:30PM (EST). Access by: Phone, fax, mail, in person.

Preston County

Real Estate Recording—Preston County Clerk, 101 West Main Street, Room 201, Kingwood, WV 26537. 304-329-0070. 9AM-5PM (F open until 7PM) (EST).

Felony, Civil Actions Over $5,000, Probate—Circuit Court, 101 W. Main St, Rm 301, Kingwood, WV 26537. 304-329-0047. Fax: 304-329-0372. 9AM-5PM M-Th, 9AM-7PM Fri (EST). Access by: Phone, fax, mail, in person.

Misdemeanor, Civil Actions Under $5,000, Eviction, Small Claims—Magistrate Court, 328 Tunnelton, Kingwood, WV 26537. 304-329-2764. Fax: 304-329-0855. 8:30AM-4:30PM (EST). Access by: Mail, in person.

Putnam County

Real Estate Recording—Putnam County Clerk, 3389 Winfield Rd., Winfield, WV 25213. 304-586-0202. Fax: 304-586-0200. 8AM-4PM (EST).

Felony, Civil Actions Over $5,000, Probate—Circuit Court, 3389 Winfield Rd, Winfield, WV 25213. 304-586-0203. Fax: 304-586-0221. 8AM-4PM MTWF, 8AM-7PM Th (EST). Access by: Phone, fax, mail, in person.

Misdemeanor, Civil Actions Under $5,000, Eviction, Small Claims—Magistrate Court, PO Box 507, Winfield, WV 25213. 304-755-7234. 8:30AM-4:30PM (EST). Access by: Mail, in person.

Raleigh County

Real Estate Recording—Raleigh County Clerk, 215 Main Street, Courthouse, Beckley, WV 25801. 304-255-9123. Fax: 304-255-9352. 8:30AM-4PM (EST).

Felony, Civil Actions Over $5,000, Probate—Circuit Court, 215 Main St, Beckley, WV 25801. 304-255-9135. Fax: 304-255-9353. 8:30AM-4:30PM (EST). Access by: Phone, fax, mail, in person.

Misdemeanor, Civil Actions Under $5,000, Eviction, Small Claims—Magistrate Court, 115 W Prince St, Suite A, Beckley, WV 25801. 304-255-9197. Fax: 304-255-9354. 8AM-4PM (EST). Access by: Phone, fax, mail, in person.

Randolph County

Real Estate Recording—Randolph County Clerk, 4 Randolph Avenue, Elkins, WV 26241. 304-636-0543. (EST).

Felony, Civil Actions Over $5,000, Probate—Circuit Court, Courthouse, Elkins, WV 26241. 304-636-2765. Fax: 304-636-5989. 8AM-4:30PM (EST). Access by: In person only.

Misdemeanor, Civil Actions Under $5,000, Eviction, Small Claims—Magistrate Court, #2 Randolph Ave, Elkins, WV 26241. 304-636-5885. Fax: 304-636-5989. 8AM-4:30PM (EST). Access by: Phone, fax, mail, in person.

Ritchie County

Real Estate Recording—Ritchie County Clerk, 115 East Main Street, Courthouse - Room 201, Harrisville, WV 26362. 304-643-2164. 8AM-4PM (EST).

Felony, Civil Actions Over $5,000, Probate—Circuit Court, 115 E. Main St, Harrisville, WV 26362. 304-643-2163. 8AM-4PM (EST). Access by: Mail, in person.

Misdemeanor, Civil Actions Under $5,000, Eviction, Small Claims—Magistrate Court, 319 E. Main St, Harrisville, WV 26362. 304-643-4409. Fax: 304-643-2098. 8:30AM-4:30PM (EST). Access by: Phone, fax, mail, in person.

Roane County

Real Estate Recording—Roane County Clerk, 200 Main Street, Spencer, WV 25276. 304-927-2860. Fax: 304-927-4165. 9AM-4PM; 9AM-Noon 1st Sat of the month (EST).

Felony, Civil Actions Over $5,000, Probate—Circuit Court, PO Box 122, Spencer, WV 25276. 304-927-2750. Fax: 304-927-4165. 9AM-Noon, 1-4PM M-F; 9AM-Noon Sat (EST). Access by: Phone, fax, mail, in person.

Misdemeanor, Civil Actions Under $5,000, Eviction, Small Claims—Magistrate Court, PO Box 663, Spencer, WV 25276. 304-927-4750. Fax: 304-927-2754. 9AM-4PM (EST). Access by: In person only.

Summers County

Real Estate Recording—Summers County Clerk, 120 Ballengee Street, Courthouse, Hinton, WV 25951. 304-466-7104. 8:30AM-4:30PM (EST).

Felony, Civil Actions Over $5,000, Probate—Circuit Court, PO Box 1058, Hinton, WV 25951. 304-466-7103. Fax: 304-466-7124. 8:30AM-4:30PM (EST). Access by: Phone, fax, mail, in person.

Misdemeanor, Civil Actions Under $5,000, Eviction, Small Claims—Magistrate Court, PO Box 1059, Hinton, WV 25951. 304-466-7129. Fax: 304-466-4912. 8:30AM-4:30PM (EST). Access by: Phone, fax, mail, in person.

Taylor County

Real Estate Recording—Taylor County Clerk, 214 West Main Street, Room 101, Courthouse, Grafton, WV 26354. 304-265-1401. Fax: 304-265-3016. (EST).

Felony, Civil Actions Over $5,000, Probate—Circuit Court, 214 W. Main St, Rm 104, Grafton, WV 26354. 304-265-2480. 8:30AM-Noon, 1-4:30PM (EST). Access by: Phone, mail, in person.

Misdemeanor, Civil Actions Under $5,000, Eviction, Small Claims—Magistrate Court, 214 W. Main St, Grafton, WV 26354. 304-265-1322. Fax: 304-265-3016. 8:30AM-4:30PM (EST). Access by: Phone, fax, mail, in person.

Tucker County

Real Estate Recording—Tucker County Clerk, Courthouse, 215 First St., Parsons, WV 26287. 304-478-2414. Fax: 304-478-4464. 8AM-4PM (EST).

Felony, Civil Actions Over $5,000, Probate—Circuit Court, PO Box 267, Parsons, WV 26287. 304-478-2606. Fax: 304-478-4464. 8AM-4PM (EST). Access by: In person only.

Misdemeanor, Civil Actions Under $5,000, Eviction, Small Claims—Magistrate Court, 201 Walnut St, Parsons, WV 26287. 304-478-2665. Fax: 304-478-4836. 8:30AM-4:30PM (EST). Access by: Mail, in person.

Tyler County

Real Estate Recording—Tyler County Clerk, Corner of Main & Court Street, Middlebourne, WV 26149. 304-758-2102. Fax: 304-758-2126. 8AM-4PM (EST).

Felony, Civil Actions Over $5,000, Probate—Circuit Court, PO Box 8, Middlebourne, WV 26149. 304-758-4811. 8AM-4PM (EST). Access by: Phone, mail, in person.

Misdemeanor, Civil Actions Under $5,000, Eviction, Small Claims—Magistrate Court, PO Box 127, Middlebourne, WV 26149. 304-758-2137. 9AM-4PM (EST). Access by: Mail, in person.

Upshur County

Real Estate Recording—Upshur County Clerk, 40 W. Main Street, Courthouse - Room 101, Buckhannon, WV 26201. 304-472-1068. Fax: 304-472-1029. 8AM-4:30PM (EST).

Felony, Civil Actions Over $5,000, Probate—Circuit Court, 40 W. Main St, Rm 102, Buckhannon, WV 26201. 304-472-2370. Fax: 304-472-2168. 8AM-4:30PM (EST). Access by: Fax, mail, in person.

Misdemeanor, Civil Actions Under $5,000, Eviction, Small Claims—Magistrate Court, 69 W. Main St, Buckhannon, WV 26201. 304-472-2053. 8:30AM-4:30PM (EST). Access by: Phone, mail, in person.

Wayne County

Real Estate Recording—Wayne County Clerk, Courthouse, Room 108, 700 Hendricks Street, Wayne, WV 25570. 304-272-6372. Fax: 304-272-5318. 8AM-4PM M-W, F; 8AM-8PM Th (EST).

Felony, Civil Actions Over $5,000, Probate—Circuit Court, PO Box 38, Wayne, WV 25570. 304-272-6359. 8AM-4PM M,T,W,F; 8AM-8PM Th (EST). Access by: Phone, mail, in person.

Misdemeanor, Civil Actions Under $5,000, Eviction, Small Claims—Magistrate Court, PO Box 667, Wayne, WV 25570. 304-272-5648. 8AM-4PM (EST). Access by: Phone, mail, in person.

Webster County

Real Estate Recording—Webster County Clerk, Courthouse - Room G-1, 2 Court Square, Webster Springs, WV

26288. 304-847-2508. Fax: 304-847-7671. 8:30AM-4PM (EST).

Felony, Civil Actions Over $5,000, Probate—Circuit Court, 2 Court Square, Rm G-4, Webster Springs, WV 26288. 304-847-2421. Fax: 304-847-7671. 8:30AM-4PM (EST). Access by: Phone, fax, mail, in person.

Misdemeanor, Civil Actions Under $5,000, Eviction, Small Claims—Magistrate Court, 2 Court Square, Rm B-1, Webster Springs, WV 26288. 304-847-2613. Fax: 304-847-7747. 8:30AM-4PM (EST). Access by: Mail, in person.

Wetzel County

Real Estate Recording—Wetzel County Clerk, Main Street, Courthouse, New Martinsville, WV 26155. 304-455-8224. Fax: 304-455-3256. 9AM-4:30PM M,T,W,F; 9AM-4PM Th; 9AM-Noon Sat (EST).

Felony, Civil Actions Over $5,000, Probate—Circuit Court, PO Box 263, New Martinsville, WV 26155. 304-455-8219. Fax: 304-455-5256. 9AM-4:30PM (EST). Access by: Phone, fax, mail, in person.

Misdemeanor, Civil Actions Under $5,000, Eviction, Small Claims—Magistrate Court, PO Box 147, New Martinsville, WV 26155. 304-455-5040. Fax: 304-455-2859. 8:30AM-4:30PM (EST). Access by: Phone, mail, in person.

Wirt County

Real Estate Recording—Wirt County Clerk, Courthouse Square, Elizabeth, WV 26143. 304-275-4271. 8:30AM-4PM (EST).

Felony, Civil Actions Over $5,000, Probate—Circuit Court, PO Box 465, Elizabeth, WV 26143. 304-275-6597. Fax: 304-275-3418. 8:30AM-4PM (EST). Access by: Phone, fax, mail, in person.

Misdemeanor, Civil Actions Under $5,000, Eviction, Small Claims—Magistrate Court, PO Box 249, Elizabeth, WV 26143. 304-275-3641. 8:30AM-4PM (EST). Access by: Mail, in person.

Wood County

Real Estate Recording—Wood County Clerk, #1 Court Square, Room 201, Parkersburg, WV 26102. 304-424-1850. 8:30AM-4:30PM (EST).

Felony, Civil Actions Over $5,000, Probate—Circuit Court, Wood County Judicial, #2 Government Sq, Parkersburg, WV 26101-5353. 304-424-1700. 8:30AM-4:30PM (EST). Access by: Mail, in person.

Misdemeanor, Civil Actions Under $5,000, Eviction, Small Claims—Magistrate Court, 208 Avery St, Parkersburg, WV 26101. 304-422-3444. Fax: 304-422-5013. 8:30AM-4:30PM (EST). Access by: Phone, fax, mail, in person.

Wyoming County

Real Estate Recording—Wyoming County Clerk, Main Street, Courthouse, Pineville, WV 24874. 304-732-8000. Fax: 304-732-9659. 8AM-4PM (EST).

Felony, Civil Actions Over $5,000, Probate—Circuit Court, PO Box 190, Pineville, WV 24874. 304-732-8000. 9AM-4PM (EST). Access by: Phone, mail, in person.

Misdemeanor, Civil Actions Under $5,000, Eviction, Small Claims—Magistrate Court, PO Box 598, Pineville, WV 24874. 304-732-8000. Fax: 304-732-7247. 9AM-4PM M-Th, 9AM-6PM Fri (EST). Access by: Phone, mail, in person. Court will search for criminal cases up to 8/95.

Federal Courts

US District Court
Northern District of West Virginia

Clarksburg Division, US District Court PO Box 2857, Clarksburg, WV 26302-2857. 304-622-8513. Counties: Braxton, Calhoun, Doddridge, Gilmer, Harrison, Lewis, Marion, Monongalia, Pleasants, Ritchie, Taylor, Tyler

Elkins Division, US District Court PO Box 1518, Elkins, WV 26241. 304-636-1445. Counties: Barbour, Grant, Hardy, Mineral, Pendleton, Pocahontas, Preston, Randolph, Tucker, Upshur, Webster

Martinsburg Division, US District Court Room 207, 217 W King St, Martinsburg, WV 25401. 304-267-8225. Counties: Berkeley, Hampshire, Jefferson, Morgan

Wheeling Division, US District Court Clerk, PO Box 471, Wheeling, WV 26003. 304-232-0011. Counties: Brooke, Hancock, Marshall, Ohio, Wetzel

Southern District of West Virginia

Beckley Division, US District Court PO Drawer 5009, Beckley, WV 25801. 304-253-7481. Counties: Fayette, Greenbrier, Nicholas, Raleigh, Wyoming

Bluefield Division, US District Court Clerk's Office, PO Box 4128, Bluefield, WV 24701. 304-327-9798. Counties: McDowell, Mercer, Monroe, Summers

Charleston Division, US District Court PO Box 3924, Charleston, WV 25339-3924. 304-347-5114. Counties: Boone, Clay, Kanawha, Logan, Putnam, Roane

Huntington Division, US District Court Clerk of Court, PO Box 1570, Huntington, WV 25716. 304-529-5588. Counties: Cabell, Lincoln, Mason, Mingo, Wayne

Parkersburg Division, US District Court Clerk of Court, PO Box 1526, Parkersburg, WV 26102. 304-420-6490. Counties: Jackson, Wirt, Wood

US Bankruptcy Court
Northern District of West Virginia

Wheeling Division, US Bankruptcy Court, PO Box 70, Wheeling, WV 26003. 304-233-1655. Voice Case Information System: 304-233-7318. Counties: Barbour, Berkeley, Braxton, Brooke, Calhoun, Doddridge, Gilmer, Grant, Hampshire, Hancock, Hardy, Harrison, Jefferson, Lewis, Marion, Marshall, Mineral, Monongalia, Morgan, Ohio, Pendleton, Pleasants, Pocahontas, Preston, Randolph, Ritchie, Taylor, Tucker, Tyler, Upshur, Webster, Wetzel

Southern District of West Virginia

Charleston Division, US Bankruptcy Court, PO Box 3924, Charleston, WV 25339. 304-347-5114. Voice Case Information System: 304-347-5337. Counties: Boone, Cabell, Clay, Fayette, Greenbrier, Jackson, Kanawha, Lincoln, Logan, Mason, McDowell, Mercer, Mingo, Monroe, Nicholas, Putnam, Raleigh, Roane, Summers, Wayne, Wirt, Wood, Wyoming

Wisconsin

Capitol: Madison (Dane County)	
Number of Counties: 72	**Population:** 5,122,871
County Court Locations:	**Federal Court Locations:**
•Circuit Courts: 74/69 Circuits	•District Courts: 2
Municipal Courts: 205	•Bankruptcy Courts: 3
•Probate Courts: 72	**State Agencies:** 20

State Agencies—Summary

General Help Numbers:

State Archives

Historical Society	608-264-6450
Archives Division	Fax: 608-264-6472
816 State St	8AM-5PM M-F, 9-4 SA
Madison, WI 53706	
Archives Reference:	608-264-6460

Governor's Office

Governor's Office	608-266-1212
PO Box 7863	Fax: 608-267-8983
Madison, WI 53707-7863	8AM-5PM

Attorney General's Office

Attorney General's Office	608-266-1221
Justice Department	Fax: 608-267-2779
PO Box 7857	8AM-5PM
Madison, WI 53707-7857	

State Legislation

Wisconsin Legislative	608-266-0341
Reference Bureau	7:45AM-4:30PM
PO Box 2037	
Madison, WI 53701-2037	
Bill Status:	800-362-9472
See Internet site noted in right hand column.	

Important State Internet Sites:

> ⊗ *Webscape*
> **File   Edit   View**   **Help**

State of Wisconsin World Wide Web
www.state.wi.us/

This site links to such sites as government, state agencies, directory information and tourism.

Wisconsin Legislature
www.legis.state.wi.us/

This site contains links to the state Assembly and Senate home pages, legislative information, legislative agencies, Wisconsin Statutes and bill tracking.

Acts and Proposals
www.legis.state.wi.us/billtrack.html

This site contains links to such information as a subject index of acts, 1997-98 acts, and a subject index of legislative proposals.

UCC and Corporation Information
badger.state.wi.us/agencies/dfi/corp/corp.htm

While this site is still under construction, it does provide many of the forms necessary for filings. Orders can be placed by fax.

Unclaimed Property
bucky.state.wi.us/agencies/ost/html/
unclaim.html

This page has an online search engine to search for unclaimed property, such as, checking and savings accounts, payroll, wages, insurance, refunds and much more.

State Agencies—Public Records

Criminal Records

Wisconsin Department of Justice, Crime Information Bureau, Record Check Unit, PO Box 2688, Madison, WI 53701-2688, Main Telephone: 608-266-7314, Hours: 8AM-4:30PM. Access by: mail, visit.

Corporation Records
Limited Partnership Records
Limited Liability Company Records

Department of Financial Institutions, Division of Corporate & Consumer Services, PO Box 7846, Madison, WI 53707-7846, Main Telephone: 608-261-9555, Fax: 608-267-6813, Hours: 7:45AM-4:30PM. Access by: mail, phone, fax, visit.

Trademarks/Servicemarks
Trade Names

Secretary of State, Tradenames/Trademarks Division, PO Box 7848, Madison, WI 53707-7848, Main Telephone: 608-266-5653, Fax: 608-266-3159, Hours: 7:45AM-4:30PM. Access by: mail, phone, fax, visit.

Uniform Commercial Code
Federal Tax Liens
State Tax Liens

Department of Financial Institutions, CCS/UCC, PO Box 7847, Madison, WI 53707-7847, Main Telephone: 608-261-9555, Fax: 608-264-7965, Hours: 7:45AM-4:30PM. Access by: mail, phone, visit, PC.

Sales Tax Registrations

Revenue Department, Income, Sales, & Excise Tax Division, PO Box 8933, Madison, WI 53708-8933, Main Telephone: 608-266-1911, Fax: 608-266-5718, Hours: 7:45AM-4:30PM. Access by: mail, phone, visit.

Birth Certificates

The Center of Health Statistics, Vital Records, PO Box 309, Madison, WI 53701, Main Telephone: 608-266-1372, Message Phone: 608-266-1371, Hours: 8AM-4:15PM. Access by: mail, phone, visit.

Death Records

The Center of Health Statistics, Vital Records, PO Box 309, Madison, WI 53701, Main Telephone: 608-266-1372, Hours: 8AM-4:15PM. Access by: mail, phone, visit.

Marriage Certificates

The Center of Health Statistics, Vital Records, PO Box 309, Madison, WI 53701, Main Telephone: 608-266-1372, Hours: 8AM-4:15PM. Access by: mail, phone, visit.

Divorce Records

The Center of Health Statistics, Vital Records, PO Box 309, Madison, WI 53701, Main Telephone: 608-266-1372, Hours: 8AM-4:15PM. Access by: mail, phone, visit.

Workers' Compensation Records

Dept of Industry, Labor and Human Relations, Workers Compensation Division, PO Box 7901, Madison, WI 53707-7901, Main Telephone: 608-266-1340, Hours: 7:45AM-4:30PM. Access by: mail, visit.

Driver Records

Division of Motor Vehicles, Records & Licensing Section, PO Box 7995, Madison, WI 53707-7995, Main Telephone: 608-264-7060, Alternate Telephone: 608-264-7069, Fax: 608-267-3636, Hours: 7:30AM-4:30PM. Access by: mail, phone, visit. Copies of tickets may be obtained from this address for $3.50 per citation.

Vehicle Ownership
Vehicle Identification

Department of Transportation, Vehicle Records Section, PO Box 7911, Madison, WI 53707-7911, Main Telephone: 608-266-3666, Registration Laws: 608-266-1466, Fax: 608-267-6966, Hours: 7:30AM-4:30PM. Access by: mail, visit.

Accident Reports

Division of Motor Vehicles, Traffic Accident Section, PO Box 7919, Madison, WI 53707-7919, Main Telephone: 608-266-8753, Fax: 608-267-0606, Hours: 7:30AM-4:30PM. Access by: mail, phone, visit.

Hunting License Information
Fishing License Information

Records not available from state agency.

County Courts and Recording Offices

What You Need to Know...

<table>
<tr><th>About the Courts</th><th>About the Recorder's Office</th></tr>
</table>

About the Courts

Administration

Director of State Courts	608-266-6828
Supreme Court	Fax: 608-267-0980
PO Box 1688	8AM-4:30PM
Madison, WI 53701-1688	

Court Structure

The Small Claims limit was raised to $5000 in mid-1995.

Probate filing is a function of the Circuit Court; however, each county has a Register in Probate who maintains and manages the probate records. The Register in Probate, also, maintains juvenile, adoption, guardianship, mental health, and termination of parental rights records, most of which are sealed but may be **opened for cause** with a court order. The fee schedule is: Search Fee — $4.00 per name, Certification Fee — $3.00 per document plus copy fee, Copy Fee — $1.00 per page.

Most Registers in Probate are putting pre-1950 records on microfilm and destroying the hard copies; however, this is done as "time and load permits," so it is not uniform across the state.

Searching Hints

Most courts, and particularly Registers in Probate, close for lunch from Noon to 1PM WI time. The statutory fee schedule for the Circuit Courts is: Search Fee—$5.00 per name, Copy Fee—$1.25 per page; Certification Fee—$5.00. In about half the Circuit Courts, no search fee is charged if the case number is provided. There is.k normally no search fee charged for in person searches.

Online Access

The Circuit Court Automation Program (**CCAP**) is in place in all but two counties. Public access terminals are planned to be available at each court by mid 1998. Remote online access may be provided in the future.

About the Recorder's Office

Organization

72 counties, 72 filing offices. The recording officers are Register of Deeds and Clerk of Court (state tax liens). The entire state is in the Central Time Zone (CST).

UCC Records

Financing statements are filed at the state level, except for consumer goods, farm and real estate related collateral, which are filed only with the Register of Deeds. All filing offices will perform UCC searches, and many will accept a search by phone. Use search request form UCC-11 for mail-in searches; use of a non-Wisconsin form may cost $10.00 extra. Searches fees are usually $10.00 per debtor name. Copy fees are usually $1.00 per page.

Lien Records

Federal tax liens on personal property of businesses are filed with the Secretary of State. Other federal tax liens are filed with the county Register of Deeds. State tax liens are filed with the Clerk of Court. Refer to *The Sourcebook of County Court Records* for information about Wisconsin courts. Many Registers will perform federal tax lien searches. Search fees and copy fees vary. Other liens include judgments, mechanics, and breeders.

Real Estate Records

Registers will **not** perform real estate searches. Copy fees and certification fees vary. Assessor telephone numbers are for local municipalities or for property listing agencies. Counties do not have assessors. Copies usually cost $2.00 for the first page and $1.00 for each additional page. Certification usually costs $.25 per document. The Treasurer maintains property tax records.

County Courts and Recording Offices

Adams County

Real Estate Recording—Adams County Register of Deeds, 402 Main Street, Friendship, WI 53934. 608-339-4206. 8AM-4:30PM (CST).

Felony, Misdemeanor, Civil, Eviction, Small Claims—Circuit Court, PO Box 220, Friendship, WI 53934. 608-339-4208. Fax: 608-339-6414. 8AM-4:30PM (CST). Access by: Phone, mail, in person.

Probate—Register in Probate, PO Box 200, Friendship, WI 53934. 608-339-4213. Fax: 608-339-6414. 8AM-4:30PM (CST). Access by: Mail, in person.

Ashland County

Real Estate Recording—Ashland County Register of Deeds, 201 West Main Street, Ashland, WI 54806. 715-682-7008. Fax: 715-682-7035. 8AM-Noon, 1-4PM (CST).

Felony, Misdemeanor, Civil, Eviction, Small Claims—Circuit Court, Courthouse 210 W Main St Rm 307, Ashland, WI 54806. 715-682-7016. Fax: 715-682-7919. 8AM-Noon, 1-4PM (CST). Access by: Mail, in person.

Probate—Register in Probate, Courthouse Rm 203, Ashland, WI 54806. 715-682-7009. 8AM-Noon, 1-4PM (CST). Access by: Mail, in person.

Barron County

Real Estate Recording—Barron County Register of Deeds, 330 East LaSalle, Room 201, Barron, WI 54812. 715-537-6210. Fax: 715-537-6277. 8AM-4PM (CST).

Felony, Misdemeanor, Civil, Eviction, Small Claims—Circuit Court, Barron County Courthouse, 330 E LaSalle Ave, Barron, WI 54812. 715-537-6265. Fax: 715-537-6269. 8AM-4PM (CST). Access by: In person only.

Probate—Register in Probate, Courthouse Rm 218, Barron, WI 54812. 715-537-6261. Fax: 715-537-6277. 8AM-4PM (CST). Access by: Mail, in person.

Bayfield County

Real Estate Recording—Bayfield County Register of Deeds, 117 East 5th, Washburn, WI 54891. 715-373-6119. 8AM-4PM (CST).

Felony, Misdemeanor, Civil, Eviction, Small Claims—Circuit Court, 117 E 5th, Washburn, WI 54891. 715-373-6108. Fax: 715-373-6153. 8AM-4PM (CST). Access by: Mail, in person.

Probate—Register in Probate, 117 E 5th, PO Box 536, Washburn, WI 54891. 715-373-6108. Fax: 715-373-6153. 8AM-4PM (CST). Access by: Mail, in person.

Brown County

Real Estate Recording—Brown County Register of Deeds, 305 E. Walnut, Room 260, Green Bay, WI 54301. 920-448-4470. Fax: 920-448-4449. 8AM-4:30PM (CST).

Felony, Misdemeanor, Civil, Eviction, Small Claims—Circuit Court, PO Box 23600, Green Bay, WI 54305-3600. 920-448-4161. Fax: 920-448-4156. 8AM-4:30PM (CST). Access by: Mail, in person.

Probate—Register in Probate, PO Box 23600, Green Bay, WI 54305-3600. 920-448-4275. 8AM-Noon, 1-4:30PM (CST). Access by: Mail, in person.

Buffalo County

Real Estate Recording—Buffalo County Register of Deeds, 407 Second Street, Alma, WI 54610. 608-685-6230. Fax: 608-685-6213. 8AM-4:30PM (CST).

Felony, Misdemeanor, Civil, Eviction, Small Claims—Circuit Court, 407 S 2nd, PO Box 68, Alma, WI 54610. 608-685-6212. Fax: 608-685-6213. 8AM-4:30PM (CST). Access by: Mail, in person.

Probate—Register in Probate, 407 S 2nd, PO Box 68, Alma, WI 54610. 608-685-6202. Fax: 608-685-6213. 8AM-4:30PM (CST). Access by: Phone, mail, in person.

Burnett County

Real Estate Recording—Burnett County Register of Deeds, 7410 County Road K #103, Siren, WI 54872. 715-349-2183. 8:30AM-4:30PM (CST).

Felony, Misdemeanor, Civil, Eviction, Small Claims—Circuit Court, 7410 County Road K #115, Siren, WI 54872. 715-349-2147. 8:30AM-4:30PM (CST). Access by: Mail, in person.

Probate—Register in Probate, 7410 County Road K #110, Siren, WI 54872. 715-349-2177. Fax: 715-349-2102. 8:30AM-4:30PM (CST). Access by: Mail, in person.

Calumet County

Real Estate Recording—Calumet County Register of Deeds, 206 Court Street, Chilton, WI 53014. 920-849-1441. Fax: 920-849-1469. 8AM-Noon, 1-4:30PM (CST).

Felony, Misdemeanor, Civil, Eviction, Small Claims—Circuit Court, 206 Court St, Chilton, WI 53014. 920-849-1414. Fax: 920-849-1431. 8AM-4:30PM (CST). Access by: Mail, in person.

Probate—Register in Probate, 206 Court St, Chilton, WI 53014-1198. 920-849-1455. Fax: 920-849-1464. 8AM-Noon, 1-4:30PM (CST). Access by: Mail, in person.

Chippewa County

Real Estate Recording—Chippewa County Register of Deeds, 711 North Bridge Street, Chippewa Falls, WI 54729. 715-726-7994. Fax: 715-726-7987. 8AM-4:30PM (CST).

Felony, Misdemeanor, Civil, Eviction, Small Claims—Circuit Court, 711 N Bridge St, Chippewa Falls, WI 54729-1879. 715-726-7758. Fax: 715-726-7786. 8AM-4:30PM (CST). Access by: Mail, in person.

Probate—Register in Probate, 711 N Bridge St, Chippewa Falls, WI 54729. 715-726-7737. Fax: 715-726-7786. 8AM-4:30PM (CST). Access by: Mail, in person.

Clark County

Real Estate Recording—Clark County Register of Deeds, 517 Court Street, Room 303, Neillsville, WI 54456. 715-743-5162. Fax: 715-743-5154. 8AM-Noon, 12:30-5PM (CST).

Felony, Misdemeanor, Civil, Eviction, Small Claims—Circuit Court, 517 Court St, Neillsville, WI 54456. 715-743-5181. Fax: 715-743-5154. 8AM-5PM (CST). Access by: Mail, in person.

Probate—Register in Probate, 517 Court St, Rm 403, Neillsville, WI 54456. 715-743-5172. Fax: 715-743-4350. 8AM-5PM (CST). Access by: Mail, in person.

Columbia County

Real Estate Recording—Columbia County Register of Deeds, 400 DeWitt Street, Portage, WI 53901. 608-742-9677. Fax: 608-742-9602. 8AM-4:30PM (CST).

Felony, Misdemeanor, Civil, Eviction, Small Claims—Circuit Court, PO Box 587, Portage, WI 53901. 608-742-2191. Fax: 608-742-9601. 8AM-4:30PM (CST). Access by: Mail, in person.

Probate—Register in Probate, 400 DeWitt, PO Box 221, Portage, WI 53901. 608-742-2191. Fax: 608-742-9601. 8AM-4:30PM (CST). Access by: Mail, in person.

Crawford County

Real Estate Recording—Crawford County Register of Deeds, 220 North Beaumont Road, Prairie du Chien, WI 53821. 608-326-0219. Fax: 608-326-0220. 8AM-4:30PM (CST).

Felony, Misdemeanor, Civil, Eviction, Small Claims—Circuit Court, 220 N Beaumont Rd, Prairie Du Chien, WI 53821. 608-326-0211. 8AM-4:30PM (CST). Access by: Mail, in person.

Probate—Register in Probate, 220 N Beaumont Rd, Prairie Du Chien, WI 53821. 608-326-0206. Fax: 608-326-0288. 8AM-4:30PM (CST). Access by: Phone, mail, in person.

Dane County

Real Estate Recording—Dane County Register of Deeds, 210 Martin Luther King Jr. Blvd., Room 110, Madison, WI 53709. 608-266-4141. Fax: 608-267-3110. 7:45AM-4PM (CST).

Felony, Misdemeanor, Civil, Eviction, Small Claims—Circuit Court, 210 Martin Luther King Jr Blvd, Rm GR10, Madison, WI 53709. 608-266-4311. Fax: 608-266-9286. 7:45AM-4:30PM (CST). Access by: Mail, in person.

Probate—Register in Probate, 210 Martin Luther King Jr Blvd, Rm 305, Madison, WI 53709. 608-266-4331. 7:45AM-4:30PM (CST). Access by: Mail, in person.

Dodge County

Real Estate Recording—Dodge County Register of Deeds, 127 East Oak Street, Administration Building, Juneau, WI 53039. 920-386-3720. Fax: 920-386-3902. 8AM-Noon, 12:30-4:30PM (CST).

Felony, Misdemeanor, Civil, Eviction, Small Claims—Circuit Court, 105 N Main, Juneau, WI 53039. 920-386-4411. Fax: 920-386-3587. 8AM-4:30PM (CST). Access by: Mail, in person.

Probate—Register in Probate, 105 N Main St, Juneau, WI 53039-1056. 920-386-3550. Fax: 920-386-3587. 8AM-4:30PM (CST). Access by: Mail, in person.

Door County

Real Estate Recording—Door County Register of Deeds, 421 Nebraska Street, Sturgeon Bay, WI 54235. 920-746-2270. Fax: 920-746-2330. 8AM-4:30PM (CST).

Felony, Misdemeanor, Civil, Eviction, Small Claims—Circuit Court, PO Box 670, Sturgeon Bay, WI 54235. 920-746-2205. Fax: 920-746-2381. 8AM-4:30PM (CST). Access by: Mail, in person.

Probate—Register in Probate, PO Box 670, Sturgeon Bay, WI 54235. 920-746-2280. Fax: 920-746-2320. 8AM-4:30PM (CST). Access by: Fax, mail, in person.

Douglas County

Real Estate Recording—Douglas County Register of Deeds, Courthouse Room 108, 1313 Belknap St., Superior, WI 54880. 715-395-1359. Fax: 715-395-1421. 8AM-4:30PM (CST).

Felony, Misdemeanor, Civil, Eviction, Small Claims—Circuit Court, 1313 Belknap, Superior, WI 54880. 715-395-1240. Fax: 715-395-1421. 8AM-4:30PM (CST). Access by: Mail, in person.

Probate—Register in Probate, 1313 Belknap, Superior, WI 54880. 715-395-1229. Fax: 715-395-1421. 8AM-4:30PM (CST). Access by: Mail, in person.

Dunn County

Real Estate Recording—Dunn County Register of Deeds, 800 Wilson Avenue, Menomonie, WI 54751. 715-232-1228. Fax: 715-232-1324. 8AM-4:30PM (CST).

Felony, Misdemeanor, Civil, Eviction, Small Claims—Circuit Court, 800 Wilson Ave, Menomonie, WI 54751. 715-232-2611. 8AM-4:30PM (CST). Access by: Mail, in person.

Probate—Register in Probate, 800 Wilson Ave, Menomonie, WI 54751. 715-232-1449. Fax: 715-232-1324. 8AM-4:30PM (CST). Access by: Mail, in person.

Eau Claire County

Real Estate Recording—Eau Claire County Register of Deeds, 721 Oxford Avenue, Courthouse, Room 1310, Eau Claire, WI 54703. 715-839-4745. 8AM-5PM (CST).

Felony, Misdemeanor, Civil, Eviction, Small Claims—Circuit Court, 721 Oxford Ave, Eau Claire, WI 54703. 715-839-4816. Fax: 715-839-4817. 8AM-5PM (CST). Access by: Mail, in person.

Probate—Register in Probate, 721 Oxford Ave, Eau Claire, WI 54703. 715-839-4823. 8AM-5PM (CST). Access by: Mail, in person.

Florence County

Real Estate Recording—Florence County Register of Deeds, 501 Lake Avenue, Florence, WI 54121. 715-528-4252. Fax: 715-528-5470. 8:30AM-Noon, 12:30-4PM (CST).

Felony, Misdemeanor, Civil, Eviction, Small Claims—Circuit Court, PO Box 410, Florence, WI 54121. 715-528-3205. Fax: 715-528-5470. 8:30AM-4PM (CST). Access by: Mail, in person.

Probate—Register in Probate, PO Box 410, Florence, WI 54121. 715-528-3205. Fax: 715-528-5470. 8:30AM-Noon, 1-4PM (CST). Access by: Mail.

Fond du Lac County

Real Estate Recording—Fond du Lac County Register of Deeds, 160 South Macy Street, Fond du Lac, WI 54935. 920-929-3018. (CST).

Felony, Misdemeanor, Civil, Eviction, Small Claims—Circuit Court, PO Box 1355, Fond Du Lac, WI 54936-1355. 920-929-3041. Fax: 920-929-3933. 8AM-4:30PM (CST). Access by: Mail, in person.

Probate—Register in Probate, PO Box 1355, Fond Du Lac, WI 54936-1355. 920-929-3084. Fax: 920-929-7058. 8AM-Noon, 1-4:30PM (CST). Access by: Mail, in person.

Forest County

Real Estate Recording—Forest County Register of Deeds, 200 E. Madison Street, Crandon, WI 54520. 715-478-3823. (CST).

Felony, Misdemeanor, Civil, Eviction, Small Claims—Circuit Court, 200 E Madison St, Crandon, WI 54520. 715-478-3323. Fax: 715-478-2430. 8:30AM-4:30PM (CST). Access by: Mail, in person.

Probate—Register in Probate, 200 E Madison St, Crandon, WI 54520. 715-478-2418. Fax: 715-478-2430. 8:30AM-4:30PM (CST). Access by: Mail, in person.

Grant County

Real Estate Recording—Grant County Register of Deeds, 130 West Maple, Lancaster, WI 53813. 608-723-2727. Fax: 608-723-7370. 8AM-4:30PM (CST).

Felony, Misdemeanor, Civil, Eviction, Small Claims—Circuit Court, PO Box 110, Lancaster, WI 53813. 608-723-2752. Fax: 608-723-7370. 8AM-4:30PM (CST). Access by: Mail, in person.

Probate—Register in Probate, 130 W Maple St, Lancaster, WI 53813. 608-723-2697. Fax: 608-723-7370. 8AM-4:30PM (CST). Access by: Mail, in person.

Green County

Real Estate Recording—Green County Register of Deeds, 1016 16th Avenue, Courthouse, Monroe, WI 53566. 608-328-9439. Fax: 608-328-2835. 8AM-5PM (CST).

Felony, Misdemeanor, Civil, Eviction, Small Claims—Circuit Court, 1016 16th Ave, Monroe, WI 53566. 608-328-9433. Fax: 608-328-2835. 8AM-5PM (CST). Access by: Mail, in person.

Probate—Register in Probate, 1016 16th Ave, Monroe, WI 53566. 608-328-9430. Fax: 608-328-2835. 8AM-5PM (CST). Access by: Mail, in person.

Green Lake County

Real Estate Recording—Green Lake County Register of Deeds, 492 Hill Street, Green Lake, WI 54941. 920-294-4021. Fax: 920-294-4009. 8:30AM-4:30PM (CST).

Felony, Misdemeanor, Civil, Eviction, Small Claims—Circuit Court, 492 Hill St, PO Box 3188, Green Lake, WI 54941. 920-294-4142. Fax: 920-294-4150. 8:30AM-4:30PM (CST). Access by: Mail, in person.

Probate—Register in Probate, 492 Hill St, Green Lake, WI 54941. 920-294-4044. Fax: 920-294-4150. 8:30AM-4:30PM (CST). Access by: Mail, in person.

Iowa County

Real Estate Recording—Iowa County Register of Deeds, 222 North Iowa Street, Dodgeville, WI 53533. 608-935-0396. Fax: 608-935-3024. 8:30AM-4:30PM (CST).

Felony, Misdemeanor, Civil, Eviction, Small Claims— Circuit Court, 222 N Iowa St, Dodgeville, WI 53533. 608-935-5052. Fax: 608-935-3024. 8:30AM-4:30PM (CST). Access by: Mail, in person.

Probate—Register in Probate, 222 N Iowa St, Dodgeville, WI 53533. 608-935-5812. Fax: 608-935-3024. 8:30AM-Noon, 1-4:30PM (CST). Access by: Fax, mail, in person.

Iron County

Real Estate Recording—Iron County Register of Deeds, 300 Taconite Street, Hurley, WI 54534. 715-561-2945. Fax: 715-561-2128. 8AM-4PM (CST).

Felony, Misdemeanor, Civil, Eviction, Small Claims— Circuit Court, 300 Taconite St, Hurley, WI 54534. 715-561-4084. Fax: 715-561-4054. 8AM-4PM (CST). Access by: Mail, in person.

Probate—Register in Probate, 300 Taconite St, Hurley, WI 54534. 715-561-3434. Fax: 715-561-4054. 8AM-4PM (CST). Access by: Mail, in person.

Jackson County

Real Estate Recording—Jackson County Register of Deeds, 307 Main, Black River Falls, WI 54615. 715-284-0204. Fax: 715-284-0261. 8AM-4:30PM (CST).

Felony, Misdemeanor, Civil, Eviction, Small Claims— Circuit Court, 307 Main St, PO Box 517, Black River Falls, WI 54615. 715-284-0208. Fax: 715-284-0270. 8AM-4:30PM (CST). Access by: Mail, in person.

Probate—Register in Probate, 307 Main St, Black River Falls, WI 54615. 715-284-0213. Fax: 715-284-0277. 8AM-4:30PM (CST). Access by: Mail, in person.

Jefferson County

Real Estate Recording—Jefferson County Register of Deeds, 320 South Main Street, Courthouse, Room 106, Jefferson, WI 53549. 920-674-7235. 8AM-4:30PM (CST).

Felony, Misdemeanor, Civil, Eviction, Small Claims— Circuit Court, 320 S Main St, Jefferson, WI 53549. 920-674-7150. 8AM-4:30PM (CST). Access by: Mail, in person.

Probate—Register in Probate, 320 S Main St, Jefferson, WI 53549. 920-674-7245. Fax: 920-674-7127. 8AM-4:30PM (CST). Access by: Mail, in person.

Juneau County

Real Estate Recording—Juneau County Register of Deeds, Courthouse, 220 E. State St., Mauston, WI 53948. 608-847-9325. Fax: 608-849-9369. 8AM-Noon, 12:30-4:30PM (CST).

Felony, Misdemeanor, Civil, Eviction, Small Claims— Circuit Court, 220 E State St, Mauston, WI 53948. 608-847-9356. Fax: 608-847-9360. 8AM-Noon, 12:30-4:30PM (CST). Access by: Mail, in person.

Probate—Register in Probate, 220 E State St Rm 205, Mauston, WI 53948. 608-847-9346. Fax: 608-847-9360. 8AM-4:30PM (CST). Access by: Mail, in person.

Kenosha County

Real Estate Recording—Kenosha County Register of Deeds, 1010 56 St., Kenosha, WI 53140. 414-653-2414. Fax: 414-653-2564. 8AM-5PM (CST).

Felony, Misdemeanor, Civil, Eviction, Small Claims— Circuit Court, 912 56th St, Kenosha, WI 53140. 414-653-2664. Fax: 414-653-2435. (CST). Access by: Mail, in person.

Probate—Register in Probate, Courthouse Rm 302, 912 56th St, Kenosha, WI 53140. 414-653-6678. Fax: 414-653-2435. 8AM-5PM (CST). Access by: Mail, in person.

Kewaunee County

Real Estate Recording—Kewaunee County Register of Deeds, 613 Dodge Street, Kewaunee, WI 54216. 920-388-4410. Fax: 920-388-4410. 8AM-4:30PM (CST).

Felony, Misdemeanor, Civil, Eviction, Small Claims— Circuit Court, 613 Dodge St, Kewaunee, WI 54216. 920-388-4410. Fax: 920-388-3139. 8AM-4:30PM (CST). Access by: Phone, mail, in person.

Probate—Register in Probate, 613 Dodge St, Kewaunee, WI 54216. 920-388-4410. Fax: 920-388-4410. 8AM-4:30PM (CST). Access by: Mail, in person.

La Crosse County

Real Estate Recording—La Crosse County Register of Deeds, Administrative Center, Room 106, 400 North 4th St., La Crosse, WI 54601. 608-785-9645. 8:30AM-5PM (CST).

Felony, Misdemeanor, Civil, Eviction, Small Claims— Circuit Court, 400 N 4th St, La Crosse, WI 54601. 608-785-9590. Fax: 608-789-7821. 8:30AM-5PM (CST). Access by: Phone, mail, in person.

Probate—Register in Probate, 400 N 4th St Rm 312, La Crosse, WI 54601. 608-785-9882. 8:30AM-5PM (CST). Access by: Mail, in person.

Lafayette County

Real Estate Recording—Lafayette County Register of Deeds, 626 Main Street, Darlington, WI 53530. 608-776-4838. 8AM-4:30PM (CST).

Felony, Misdemeanor, Civil, Eviction, Small Claims— Circuit Court, 626 Main St, Darlington, WI 53530. 608-776-4832. 8AM-4:30PM (CST). Access by: Mail, in person.

Probate—Register in Probate, 626 Main St, Darlington, WI 53530. 608-776-4811. 8AM-4:30PM (CST). Access by: Mail, in person.

Langlade County

Real Estate Recording—Langlade County Register of Deeds, 800 Clermont Street, Antigo, WI 54409. 715-627-6209. Fax: 715-627-6303. 8:30AM-4:30PM (CST).

Felony, Misdemeanor, Civil, Eviction, Small Claims— Circuit Court, 800 Clairmont St, Antigo, WI 54409. 715-627-6215. 8:30AM-4:30PM (CST). Access by: Mail, in person.

Probate—Register in Probate, 800 Clermont St, Antigo, WI 54409. 715-627-6213. Fax: 715-627-6303. 8:30AM-4:30PM (CST). Access by: Mail, in person.

Lincoln County

Real Estate Recording—Lincoln County Register of Deeds, 1110 East Main, Courthouse, Merrill, WI 54452. 715-536-0318. Fax: 715-536-0360. 8:15AM-4:30PM (CST).

Felony, Misdemeanor, Civil, Eviction, Small Claims— Circuit Court, 1110 E Main St, Merrill, WI 54452. 715-536-0320. Fax: 715-536-6528. 8:15AM-4:30PM (CST). Access by: Mail, in person.

Probate—Register in Probate, 1110 E Main St, Merrill, WI 54452. 715-536-0342. Fax: 715-536-5230. 8:15AM-Noon, 1-4:30PM (CST). Access by: Mail, in person.

Manitowoc County

Real Estate Recording—Manitowoc County Register of Deeds, 1010 South 8th Street, Courthouse, Manitowoc, WI 54220. 920-683-4011. 8:30AM-5PM M; 8:30AM-4:30PM T-F (CST).

Felony, Misdemeanor, Civil, Eviction, Small Claims— Circuit Court, PO Box 2000, Manitowoc, WI 54221-2000. 920-683-4030. 8:30AM-5PM M; 8:30AM-4:30PM T-F (CST). Access by: Phone, mail, in person.

Probate—Register in Probate, 1010 S 8th St Rm 116, Manitowoc, WI 54220. 920-683-4015. Fax: 920-683-4499. 8:30AM-5PM (CST). Access by: Mail, in person.

Marathon County

Real Estate Recording—Marathon County Register of Deeds, 500 Forest Street, Courthouse, Wausau, WI 54403. 715-847-5214. Fax: 715-848-9210. 8AM-5PM (CST).

Felony, Misdemeanor, Civil, Eviction, Small Claims— Circuit Court, 500 Forest St, Wausau, WI 54403. 715-847-5495. Civil: 715-847-5493. Fax: 715-848-3962. 8AM-5PM (Summer hours 8AM-4:30PM Memorial-Labor Day) (CST). Access by: Mail, in person.

Probate—Register in Probate, 500 Forest St, Wausau, WI 54403. 715-847-5218. Fax: 715-847-5200. 8AM-5PM (CST). Access by: Mail, in person.

Marinette County

Real Estate Recording—Marinette County Register of Deeds, 1926 Hall Avenue, Courthouse, Marinette, WI 54143. 715-732-7550. Fax: 715-732-7532. 8:30AM-4:30PM (CST).

Felony, Misdemeanor, Civil, Eviction, Small Claims—Circuit Court, PO Box 320, Marinette, WI 54143-0320. 715-732-7450. 8:30AM-4:30PM (CST). Access by: Mail, in person.

Probate—Register in Probate, PO Box 320, Marinette, WI 54143-0320. 715-732-7475. Fax: 715-732-7496. 8:30AM-Noon, 1-4:30PM (CST). Access by: Mail, in person.

Marquette County

Real Estate Recording—Marquette County Register of Deeds, 77 West Park, Montello, WI 53949. 608-297-9132. Fax: 608-297-7606. 8AM-Noon, 12:30-4:30PM (CST).

Felony, Misdemeanor, Civil, Eviction, Small Claims—Circuit Court, PO Box 187, Montello, WI 53949. 608-297-9102. Fax: 608-297-7606. 8AM-Noon, 12:30-4:30PM (CST). Access by: Mail, in person.

Probate—Register in Probate, 77 W Park St, PO Box 749, Montello, WI 53949. 608-297-9105. Fax: 608-297-7606. 8AM-4:30PM (CST).

Menominee County

Real Estate Recording—Menominee County Register of Deeds, Courthouse Lane, Keshena, WI 54135. 715-799-3312. Fax: 715-799-1322. 8AM-Noon, 1-4:30PM (CST).

Felony, Misdemeanor, Civil, Eviction, Small Claims—Circuit Court, PO Box 279, Keshena, WI 54135. 715-799-3313. Fax: 715-799-1322. 8AM-4:30PM (CST). Access by: Mail, in person.

Probate—Register in Probate, 311 N Main St, Shawano, WI 54166. 715-526-9352. Fax: 715-526-4915. (CST). Access by: Mail, in person.

Milwaukee County

Real Estate Recording—Milwaukee County Register of Deeds, 901 North 9th Street, Milwaukee, WI 53233. 414-278-4005. Fax: 414-223-1257. 8AM-4:30PM (CST).

Civil, Eviction, Small Claims—Circuit Court-Civil, 901 9th St Rm G-9, Milwaukee, WI 53233. 414-278-4128. Fax: 414-223-1256. 8AM-NOON, 2PM-4PM (CST).

Felony, Misdemeanor—Circuit Court-Criminal, 821 W State St, Milwaukee, WI 53233. 414-278-4588. 8AM-4PM, Closed 12-1 (CST). Access by: In person only.

Probate—Register in Probate, 901 N 9th St Rm 207, Milwaukee, WI 53233. 414-278-4444. Fax: 414-223-1814. 8AM-5PM (CST). Access by: Mail, in person.

Monroe County

Real Estate Recording—Monroe County Register of Deeds, Administrative Center, 202 S. "K" St., Sparta, WI 54656. 608-269-8716. 8AM-4:30PM (CST).

Felony, Misdemeanor, Civil, Eviction, Small Claims—Circuit Court, PO Box 186, Sparta, WI 54656. 608-269-8745. 8AM-4:30PM (CST). Access by: Mail, in person.

Probate—Register in Probate, PO Box 165, Sparta, WI 54656. 608-269-8701. Fax: 608-269-8950. 8AM-4:30PM (CST). Access by: Phone, mail, in person.

Oconto County

Real Estate Recording—Oconto County Register of Deeds, 301 Washington Street, Oconto, WI 54153. 920-834-6807. 8AM-4PM (CST).

Felony, Misdemeanor, Civil, Eviction, Small Claims—Circuit Court, 301 Washington St, Oconto, WI 54153. 920-834-6855. Fax: 920-834-6867. 8AM-4PM (CST). Access by: Mail, in person.

Probate—Register in Probate, 301 Washington St, Oconto, WI 54153. 920-834-6839. Fax: 920-834-6867. 8AM-4PM (CST). Access by: Mail, in person.

Oneida County

Real Estate Recording—Oneida County Register of Deeds, Oneida Avenue, Courthouse, Rhinelander, WI 54501. 715-369-6150. Fax: 715-369-6222. 8AM-4:30PM (CST).

Felony, Misdemeanor, Civil, Eviction, Small Claims—Circuit Court, PO Box 400, Rhinelander, WI 54501. 715-369-6120. 8AM-4:30PM (CST). Access by: Mail, in person.

Probate—Register in Probate, PO Box 400, Rhinelander, WI 54501. 715-369-6159. 8AM-4:30PM (CST). Access by: Mail, in person.

Outagamie County

Real Estate Recording—Outagamie County Register of Deeds, 410 South Walnut Street, Appleton, WI 54911. 920-832-5095. 8:30AM-5PM (CST).

Felony, Misdemeanor, Civil, Eviction, Small Claims—Circuit Court, 320 S Walnut St, Appleton, WI 54911. 920-832-5130. 8:30AM-5PM (CST). Access by: Mail, in person.

Probate—Register in Probate, 320 S Walnut St, Appleton, WI 54911. 920-832-5601. Fax: 920-832-5115. 8:30AM-Noon, 1-5PM (CST). Access by: Mail, in person.

Ozaukee County

Real Estate Recording—Ozaukee County Register of Deeds, 121 West Main Street, Port Washington, WI 53074. 414-284-8260. Fax: 414-284-8100. 8:30AM-5PM (CST).

Felony, Misdemeanor, Civil, Eviction, Small Claims—Circuit Court, 1201 S Spring St, Port Washington, WI 53074. 414-284-8409. Fax: 414-284-8491. 8:30AM-5PM (CST). Access by: Mail, in person.

Probate—Register in Probate, PO Box 994, Port Washington, WI 53074. 414-284-8370. Fax: 414-284-8491. 8:30AM-5PM (CST). Access by: Mail, in person.

Pepin County

Real Estate Recording—Pepin County Register of Deeds, 740 7th Avenue West, County Government Center, Durand, WI 54736. 715-672-8856. Fax: 715-672-8677. 8:30AM-Noon, 12:30PM-4:30PM (CST).

Felony, Misdemeanor, Civil, Eviction, Small Claims—Circuit Court, PO Box 39, Durand, WI 54736. 715-672-8861. 8:30AM-Noon, 12:30-4:30PM (CST). Access by: Mail, in person.

Probate—Register in Probate, PO Box 39, Durand, WI 54736. 715-672-8859. Fax: 715-672-8753. 8:30AM-Noon, 1-4:30PM (CST). Access by: Mail, in person.

Pierce County

Real Estate Recording—Pierce County Register of Deeds, 414 West Main Street, Ellsworth, WI 54011. 715-273-3531. Fax: 715-273-6861. 8AM-5PM (CST).

Felony, Misdemeanor, Civil, Eviction, Small Claims—Circuit Court, PO Box 129, Ellsworth, WI 54011. 715-273-3531. 8:30AM-4:30PM (CST). Access by: Mail, in person.

Probate—Register in Probate, PO Box 97, Ellsworth, WI 54011. 715-273-3531. Fax: 715-273-6855. 8AM-5PM (CST). Access by: Mail, in person.

Polk County

Real Estate Recording—Polk County Register of Deeds, 100 Polk County Plaza, Suite 160, Balsam Lake, WI 54810. 715-485-9249. Fax: 715-485-9202. 8:30AM-4:30PM (CST).

Felony, Misdemeanor, Civil, Eviction, Small Claims—Circuit Court, 100 Polk Plaza, Balsam Lake, WI 54810. 715-485-3161. Fax: 715-485-3099. 8:30AM-4:30PM (CST). Access by: In person only.

Probate—Register in Probate, 100 Polk Plaza, Suite 230, Balsam Lake, WI 54810. 715-485-9238. Fax: 715-485-9275. 8:30AM-4:30PM (CST). Access by: Mail, in person.

Portage County

Real Estate Recording—Portage County Register of Deeds, 1516 Church Street, County-City Building, Stevens Point, WI 54481. 715-346-1430. Fax: 715-345-5361. 7:30AM-4:30PM (CST).

Felony, Misdemeanor, Civil, Eviction, Small Claims— Circuit Court (Branches 1, 2 & 3), 1516 Church St, Stevens Point, WI 54481. 715-346-1351. Fax: 715-346-1236. 7:30AM-4:30PM (CST). Access by: Mail, in person.

Probate—Register in Probate, 1516 Church St, Stevens Point, WI 54481. 715-346-1362. Fax: 715-346-1486. 7:30AM-4:30PM (CST). Access by: Phone, mail, in person.

Price County

Real Estate Recording—Price County Register of Deeds, 126 Cherry, Phillips, WI 54555. 715-339-2515. 8AM-Noon, 1-4:30PM (CST).

Felony, Misdemeanor, Civil, Eviction, Small Claims— Circuit Court, Courthouse, Phillips, WI 54555. 715-339-2353. Fax: 715-339-3089. 8AM-Noon, 1-4:30PM (CST). Access by: Phone, mail, in person.

Probate—Register in Probate, Courthouse, 126 Cherry St, Phillips, WI 54555. 715-339-3078. Fax: 715-339-3089. 8AM-4:30PM (CST). Access by: Mail, in person.

Racine County

Real Estate Recording—Racine County Register of Deeds, 730 Wisconsin Avenue, Racine, WI 53403. 414-636-3208. Fax: 414-636-3851. 8AM-5PM (CST).

Felony, Misdemeanor, Civil, Eviction, Small Claims, Probate—Circuit Court, 730 Wisconsin Ave, Racine, WI 53403. 414-636-3333. Fax: 414-636-3341. 8AM-5PM (CST). Access by: Mail, in person.

Probate—Register in Probate, 730 Wisconsin Ave, Racine, WI 53403. 414-636-3137. Fax: 414-636-3341. 8AM-5PM (CST). Access by: Mail, in person.

Richland County

Real Estate Recording—Richland County Register of Deeds, Seminary Street, Courthouse, Richland Center, WI 53581. 608-647-3011. 8:30AM-4:30PM (CST).

Felony, Misdemeanor, Civil, Eviction, Small Claims— Circuit Court, PO Box 655, Richland Center, WI 53581. 608-647-3956. Fax: 608-647-2624. 8:30AM-4:30PM (CST). Access by: Mail, in person.

Probate—Register in Probate, PO Box 427, Richland Center, WI 53581. 608-647-2626. Fax: 608-647-6134. 8:30AM-Noon, 1-4:30PM (CST). Access by: Mail, in person.

Rock County

Real Estate Recording—Rock County Register of Deeds, 51 South Main Street, Janesville, WI 53545. 608-757-5657. 8AM-5PM (CST).

Felony, Misdemeanor, Civil, Eviction, Small Claims— Circuit Court-South, 250 Garden Ln, Beloit, WI 53511. 608-364-2010. 8AM-5PM (CST). Access by: Mail, in person.

Circuit Court-North, 51 S Main, Janesville, WI 53545. 608-757-5556. Fax: 608-757-5584. 8AM-5PM (CST). Access by: Mail, in person.

Probate—Register in Probate, 51 S Main, Janesville, WI 53545. 608-757-5635. 8AM-5PM (CST). Access by: Mail, in person.

Rusk County

Real Estate Recording—Rusk County Register of Deeds, 311 Miner Avenue, Ladysmith, WI 54848. 715-532-2139. Fax: 715-532-2237. 8AM-4:30PM (CST).

Felony, Misdemeanor, Civil, Eviction, Small Claims— Circuit Court, 311 Miner Ave East, Ladysmith, WI 54848. 715-532-2108. 8AM-4:30PM (CST). Access by: Mail, in person.

Probate—Register in Probate, 311 E Miner Ave, Ladysmith, WI 54848. 715-532-2147. Fax: 715-532-2175. 8AM-4:30PM (CST). Access by: Mail, in person.

Sauk County

Real Estate Recording—Sauk County Register of Deeds, 505 Broadway St., Baraboo, WI 53913. 608-355-3288. Fax: 608-355-3292. 8AM-4:30PM (CST).

Felony, Misdemeanor, Civil, Eviction, Small Claims— Circuit Court, PO Box 449, Baraboo, WI 53913. 608-356-

5581. Fax: 608-355-3292. 8AM-4:30PM (CST). Access by: Mail, in person.

Probate—Register in Probate, 515 Oak St, Baraboo, WI 53913. 608-355-3226. 8AM-4:30PM (CST). Access by: Mail, in person.

Sawyer County

Real Estate Recording—Sawyer County Register of Deeds, 406 Main, Hayward, WI 54843. 715-634-4867. 8AM-4PM (CST).

Felony, Misdemeanor, Civil, Eviction, Small Claims— Circuit Court, PO Box 508, Hayward, WI 54843. 715-634-4887. 8AM-4PM (CST). Access by: Mail, in person.

Probate—Register in Probate, PO Box 447, Hayward, WI 54843. 715-634-4886. 8AM-4PM (CST). Access by: Mail, in person.

Shawano County

Real Estate Recording—Shawano County Register of Deeds, 311 North Main, Shawano, WI 54166. 715-524-2129. Fax: 715-524-5157. 8AM-4:30PM (CST).

Felony, Misdemeanor, Civil, Eviction, Small Claims— Circuit Court, 311 N Main Rm 206, Shawano, WI 54166. 715-526-9347. Fax: 715-526-4915. 8AM-4:30PM (CST). Access by: Mail, in person.

Probate—Register in Probate, 311 N Main, Shawano, WI 54166. 715-526-9352. Fax: 715-526-4915. 8AM-4:30PM (CST). Access by: Mail, in person.

Sheboygan County

Real Estate Recording—Sheboygan County Register of Deeds, 615 North 6th Street, Courthouse - Room 106, Sheboygan, WI 53081. 920-459-3023. 8AM-5PM (CST).

Felony, Misdemeanor, Civil, Eviction, Small Claims— Circuit Court, 615 N 6th St, Sheboygan, WI 53081. 920-459-3068. Fax: 920-459-3921. 8AM-5PM (CST). Access by: Mail, in person.

Probate—Register in Probate, 615 N 6th St, Sheboygan, WI 53081. 920-459-3068. Fax: 920-459-3921. 8AM-5PM (CST). Access by: Mail, in person.

St. Croix County

Real Estate Recording—St. Croix County Register of Deeds, 1101 Carmichael Rd., Hudson, WI 54016. 715-386-4652. Fax: 715-386-4687. 8AM-5PM (CST).

Felony, Misdemeanor, Civil, Eviction, Small Claims— Circuit Court, 1101 Carmichael Rd, Hudson, WI 54016. 715-386-4629. Fax: 715-381-4396. 8AM-5PM (CST). Access by: Mail, in person.

Probate—Register in Probate, 1101 Carmichael Rd, Rm 2242, Hudson, WI 54016. 715-386-4618. Fax: 715-381-4401. 8AM-5PM (CST). Access by: Phone, mail, in person.

Taylor County

Real Estate Recording—Taylor County Register of Deeds, 224 South 2nd Street, Medford, WI 54451. 715-748-1483. 8:30AM-4:30PM (CST).

Felony, Misdemeanor, Civil, Eviction, Small Claims— Circuit Court, PO Box 97, Medford, WI 54451. 715-748-1425. Fax: 715-748-2465. 8:30AM-4:30PM (CST). Access by: Mail, in person.

Probate—Register in Probate, 224 S 2nd, Medford, WI 54451. 715-748-1435. Fax: 715-748-2465. 8:30AM-4:30PM (CST). Access by: Mail, in person.

Trempealeau County

Real Estate Recording—Trempealeau County Register of Deeds, Courthouse, 36245 Main St., Whitehall, WI 54773. 715-538-2311. 8AM-4:30PM (CST).

Felony, Misdemeanor, Civil, Eviction, Small Claims— Circuit Court, 36245 Main St, Whitehall, WI 54773. 715-538-2311. 8AM-4:30PM (CST). Access by: Mail, in person.

Probate—Register in Probate, 36245 Main St, PO Box 67, Whitehall, WI 54773. 715-538-2311. Fax: 715-538-4400. 8AM-4:30PM (CST). Access by: Mail, in person.

Vernon County

Real Estate Recording—Vernon County Register of Deeds, 400 Court House Square St., Court House Annex, Viroqua, WI 54665. 608-637-3568. Fax: 608-637-7976. 8:30AM-4:30PM (CST).

Felony, Misdemeanor, Civil, Eviction, Small Claims—Circuit Court, PO Box 426, Viroqua, WI 54665. 608-637-3220. Fax: 608-637-8772. 8:30AM-4:30PM (CST). Access by: Phone, mail, in person.

Probate—Register in Probate, PO Box 448, Viroqua, WI 54665. 608-637-3872. Fax: 608-637-8772. 8:30AM-4:30PM (CST). Access by: Mail, in person.

Vilas County

Real Estate Recording—Vilas County Register of Deeds, 330 Court St., Eagle River, WI 54521. 715-479-3660. Fax: 715-479-3605. 8AM-4PM (CST).

Felony, Misdemeanor, Civil, Eviction, Small Claims—Circuit Court, PO Box 369, Eagle River, WI 54521. 715-479-3632. Fax: 715-479-3605. 8AM-4PM (CST). Access by: Mail, in person.

Probate—Register in Probate, PO Box 369, Eagle River, WI 54521. 715-479-3642. Fax: 715-479-3605. 8AM-4PM (CST). Access by: Mail, in person.

Walworth County

Real Estate Recording—Walworth County Register of Deeds, Courthouse - Room 102, 100 W. Walworth St., Elkhorn, WI 53121. 414-741-4236. 8AM-5PM (UCC 8AM-4:30PM) (CST).

Felony, Misdemeanor, Civil, Eviction, Small Claims—Circuit Court, PO Box 1001, Elkhorn, WI 53121. 414-741-4224. Fax: 414-741-4379. 8AM-5PM (CST). Access by: Mail, in person.

Probate—Register in Probate, PO Box 1001, Elkhorn, WI 53121. 414-741-4256. Fax: 414-741-4379. 8AM-5PM (CST). Access by: Phone, fax, mail, in person.

Washburn County

Real Estate Recording—Washburn County Register of Deeds, 10 4th Avenue, Shell Lake, WI 54871. 715-468-7421. Fax: 715-468-7836. 8AM-4:30PM (CST).

Felony, Misdemeanor, Civil, Eviction, Small Claims—Circuit Court, PO Box 339, Shell Lake, WI 54871. 715-468-7468. Fax: 715-468-7836. 8AM-4:30PM (CST). Access by: Mail, in person.

Probate—Register in Probate, PO Box 316, Shell Lake, WI 54871. 715-468-2960. Fax: 715-468-7836. 8AM-4:30PM (CST). Access by: Mail, in person.

Washington County

Real Estate Recording—Washington County Register of Deeds, 432 East Washington Street, Room 2084, West Bend, WI 53095. 414-335-4318. 8AM-4:30PM (CST).

Felony, Misdemeanor, Civil, Eviction, Small Claims—Circuit Court, PO Box 1986, West Bend, WI 53095-7986. 414-335-4341. Fax: 414-335-4776. 8AM-4:30PM (CST). Access by: Mail, in person.

Probate—Register in Probate, PO Box 82, West Bend, WI 53095. 414-335-4334. Fax: 414-335-4776. 8AM-4:30PM (CST). Access by: Mail, in person.

Waukesha County

Real Estate Recording—Waukesha County Register of Deeds, 1320 Pewaukee Rd., Room 110, Waukesha, WI 53188. 414-548-7590. 8AM-4:30PM (CST).

Felony, Misdemeanor, Civil, Eviction, Small Claims—Circuit Court, 515 W Moreland Blvd, Waukesha, WI 53188. Civil: 414-548-7524. Criminal: 414-548-7484. Fax: 414-896-8228. 8AM-4:30PM M,T,Th,F; 7:30AM-5:30PM F (CST). Access by: Mail, in person.

Probate—Register in Probate, 515 W Moreland, Rm 375, Waukesha, WI 53188. 414-548-7468. 8AM-4:30PM M,T,Th,F; 7:30AM-5:30PM W (CST). Access by: Mail, in person.

Waupaca County

Real Estate Recording—Waupaca County Register of Deeds, 811 Harding Street, Waupaca, WI 54981. 715-258-6250. Fax: 715-258-6212. 8AM-4PM (CST).

Felony, Misdemeanor, Civil, Eviction, Small Claims—Circuit Court, PO Box 354, Waupaca, WI 54981. 715-258-6460. 8AM-4PM (CST). Access by: Mail, in person.

Probate—Register in Probate, 811 Harding St, Waupaca, WI 54981. 715-258-6429. Fax: 715-258-6440. 8AM-4PM (CST). Access by: Mail, in person.

Waushara County

Real Estate Recording—Waushara County Register of Deeds, 209 South St. Marie, Wautoma, WI 54982. 920-787-0444. Fax: 920-787-0425. 8AM-4PM (CST).

Felony, Misdemeanor, Civil, Eviction, Small Claims—Circuit Court, PO Box 507, Wautoma, WI 54982. 920-787-4631. 8AM-4:30PM (CST). Access by: Mail, in person.

Probate—Register in Probate, PO Box 508, Wautoma, WI 54982. 920-787-0448. 8AM-4:30PM (CST). Access by: Mail, in person.

Winnebago County

Real Estate Recording—Winnebago County Register of Deeds, 415 Jackson Street, Courthouse, Oshkosh, WI 54901. 920-236-4885. 8AM-4:30PM (CST).

Felony, Misdemeanor, Civil, Eviction, Small Claims—Circuit Court, PO Box 2808, Oshkosh, WI 54903-2808. 920-236-4848. Fax: 920-424-7780. 8AM-4:30PM (CST). Access by: Mail, in person.

Probate—Register in Probate, PO Box 2808, Oshkosh, WI 54903. 920-236-4833. Fax: 920-424-7536. 8AM-Noon, 1-4:30PM (CST). Access by: Mail, in person.

Wood County

Real Estate Recording—Wood County Register of Deeds, 400 Market Street, Wisconsin Rapids, WI 54494. 715-421-8450. 8AM-Noon, 1-4:45PM (CST).

Felony, Misdemeanor, Civil, Eviction, Small Claims—Circuit Court, 400 Market St, Po Box 8095, Wisconsin Rapids, WI 54494-958095. 715-421-8490. 8AM-Noon, 1-4:45PM (CST). Access by: Mail, in person.

Probate—Register in Probate, 400 Market St, Wisconsin Rapids, WI 54494. 715-421-8520. Fax: 715-421-8808. 8AM-4:45PM (CST). Access by: Mail, in person.

Federal Courts

US District Court
Eastern District of Wisconsin

Milwaukee Division, US District Court Clerk's Office, Room 362, 517 E Wisconsin Ave, Milwaukee, WI 53202. 414-297-3372. Counties: Brown, Calumet, Dodge, Door, Florence, Fond du Lac, Forest, Green Lake, Kenosha, Kewaunee, Langlade, Manitowoc, Marinette, Marquette, Menominee, Milwaukee, Oconto, Outagamie, Ozaukee, Racine, Shawano, Sheboygan, Walworth, Washington, Waukesha, Waupaca, Waushara, Winnebago

Western District of Wisconsin

Madison Division, US District Court PO Box 432, 120 N Henry St, Madison, WI 53701. 608-264-5156. Counties: Adams, Ashland, Barron, Bayfield, Buffalo, Burnett, Chippewa, Clark, Columbia, Crawford, Dane, Douglas, Dunn, Eau Claire, Grant, Green, Iowa, Iron, Jackson, Jefferson, Juneau, La Crosse, Lafayette, Lincoln, Marathon, Monroe, Oneida, Pepin, Pierce, Polk, Portage, Price, Richland, Rock, Rusk, Sauk, Sawyer, St. Croix, Taylor, Trempealeau, Vernon, Vilas, Washburn, Wood

US Bankruptcy Court
Eastern District of Wisconsin

Milwaukee Division, US Bankruptcy Court, Room 126, 517 E Wisconsin Ave, Milwaukee, WI 53202. 414-297-3291. Voice Case Information System: 414-297-3582. Counties: Brown, Calumet, Dodge, Door, Florence, Fond du Lac, Forest, Green Lake, Kenosha, Kewaunee, Langlade, Manitowoc, Marinette, Marquette, Menominee, Milwaukee, Oconto, Outagamie, Ozaukee, Racine, Shawano, Sheboygan, Walworth, Washington, Waukesha, Waupaca, Waushara, Winnebago

Western District of Wisconsin

Eau Claire Division, US Bankruptcy Court, PO Box 5009, Eau Claire, WI 54702-5009. 715-839-2980. Counties: Ashland, Barron, Bayfield, Buffalo, Burnett, Chippewa, Clark, Douglas, Dunn, Eau Claire, Iron, Jackson, Juneau, La Crosse, Lincoln, Marathon, Monroe, Oneida, Pepin, Pierce, Polk, Portage, Price, Rusk, Sawyer, St. Croix, Taylor, Trempealeau, Vernon, Vilas, Washburn, Wood. Division has satellite offices in LaCrosse and Wausau

Madison Division, US Bankruptcy Court, PO Box 548, Madison, WI 53701. 608-264-5178. Counties: Adams, Columbia, Crawford, Dane, Grant, Green, Iowa, Jefferson, Lafayette, Richland, Rock, Sauk

Wyoming

Capitol: Cheyenne (Laramie County)	
Number of Counties: 23	**Population:** 480,184
County Court Locations:	**Federal Court Locations:**
•District Courts: 23/9 Districts	•District Courts: 2
•County Courts: 18,/12 Counties	•Bankruptcy Courts: 1
•Justice of the Peace Courts: 9/ 11 Counties	**State Agencies:** 19
Municipal Courts: 80	

State Agencies—Summary

General Help Numbers:

State Archives

Department of Commerce	307-777-7826
Archives Division	Fax: 307-777-7044
6101 Yellowstone Rd LLr	8AM-5PM
Cheyenne, WY 82002	
Reference Librarian:	307-777-7826
Historical Society:	307-635-4881

Governor's Office

Governor's Office	307-777-7434
State Capitol Building, Room 124	Fax: 307-632-3909
Cheyenne, WY 82002-0010	8AM-5PM

Attorney General's Office

Attorney General's Office	307-777-7841
123 State Capitol	Fax: 307-777-6869
Cheyenne, WY 82002	8AM-5PM

State Legislation

Wyoming Legislature	307-777-7881
State Capitol	8AM-5PM
Room 213	
Cheyenne, WY 82002	

Important State Internet Sites:

> **Webscape**
> File Edit View   Help

State of Wyoming World Wide Web

www.state.wy.us/

This site links to such sites as the Governor's office, government, online services, business and industry and tourism.

The Governor's Office

www.state.wy.us/governor/
governor_home.html

Provides information about the Governor, his press releases, boards and commissions, and state agencies. E-mail can be sent to the Governor from here.

Legislators and Elected Officials

www.state.wy.us/state/government/
government.html

Provides links to local, state and federal government. From there you can link to members e-mail addresses, access the State Statutes and obtain session information.

Corporation Information

soswy.state.wy.us/

This is the site for information about corporations. Many necessary forms are available online.

Unclaimed Property

www.state.wy.us/~sot/index.html

The unclaimed property division is managed by the State Treasurers office. You can search online for unclaimed property at this site.

State Agencies—Public Records

Criminal Records
Division of Criminal Investigation, Criminal Record Section, 316 W 22nd St, Cheyenne, WY 82002, Main Telephone: 307-777-7523, Fax: 307-777-7252, Hours: 8:30-10:30AM; 1:30-3:30PM. Access by: mail, visit.

Corporation Records
Limited Liability Company Records
Limited Partnership Records
Fictitious Name
Trademarks/Servicemarks
Corporations Division, Secretary of State, State Capitol, Cheyenne, WY 82002, Main Telephone: 307-777-7311, Fax: 307-777-5339, Hours: 8AM-5PM. Access by: mail, phone, fax, visit, PC.

Uniform Commercial Code
Federal Tax Liens
State Tax Liens
UCC Division, Secretary of State, The Capitol, Cheyenne, WY 82002-0020, Main Telephone: 307-777-5372, Fax: 307-777-5988, Hours: 8AM-5PM. Access by: mail, fax, visit, PC.

Sales Tax Registrations
Revenue Department, Excise Tax Division, Herscher Bldg, 122 W 25th St, Cheyenne, WY 82002, Main Telephone: 307-777-5203, Fax: 307-777-7722, Hours: 8AM-5PM. Access by: mail, phone.

Birth Certificates
Wyoming Department of Health, Vital Records Service, Hathaway Bldg, Cheyenne, WY 82002, Main Telephone: 307-777-7591, Hours: 8AM-5PM. Access by: mail, visit.

Death Records
Wyoming Department of Health, Vital Records Services, Hathaway Bldg, Cheyenne, WY 82002, Main Telephone: 307-777-7591, Hours: 8AM-5PM. Access by: mail, visit.

Marriage Certificates
Wyoming Department of Health, Vital Records Services, Hathaway Bldg, Cheyenne, WY 82002, Main Telephone: 307-777-7591, Hours: 8AM-5PM. Access by: mail, visit.

Divorce Records
Wyoming Department of Health, Vital Records Services, Hathaway Bldg, Cheyenne, WY 82002, Main Telephone: 307-777-7591, Hours: 8AM-5PM. Access by: mail, visit.

Workers' Compensation Records
Employment Department, Workers Compensation Division, 122 W 25th St, Cheyenne, WY 82002, Main Telephone: 307-777-7159, Fax: 307-777-5946, Hours: 8AM-4:30PM.
Access by: mail only.

Driver License Information
Driver Records
Wyoming Department of Transportation, Driver Services, PO Box 1708, Cheyenne, WY 82003-1708, Main Telephone: 307-777-4800, Fax: 307-777-4773, Hours: 8AM-5PM. Access by: mail, visit. Tickets may be obtained from the address above for a fee of $5.00 per citation.

Vehicle Ownership
Vehicle Identification
Department of Transportation, Motor Vehicle Licensing and Titles, PO Box 1708, Cheyenne, WY 82003-1708, Main Telephone: 307-777-4709, Fax: 307-777-4772, Hours: 8AM-5PM. Access by: mail, visit.

Accident Reports
Department of Transportation, Accident Records Section, PO Box 1708, Cheyenne, WY 82003-1708, Main Telephone: 307-777-4450, Hours: 8AM-5PM. Access by: mail, visit.

Hunting License Information
Fishing License Information
Game & Fish Department, License Section, 5400 Bishop Blvd, Cheyenne, WY 82006, Main Telephone: 307-777-4600, Hours: 8AM-5PM. Access by: mail, phone, visit. They have a central database for lottery (big game, elk, deer & antelope) permits only.

County Courts and Recording Offices

What You Need to Know...

About the Courts

Administration

Court Administrator	307-777-7480
Supreme Court Bldg	Fax: 307-777-3447
2301 Capitol Ave	8AM-5PM
Cheyenne, WY 82002	

Court Structure

Some counties have County Courts and others have Justice Courts; so each county has a District Court and either a County **or** Justice Court. County Courts handle civil claims up to $2,000 while Justice Courts handle civil claims up to $3,000. The District Courts take cases over the applicable limit in each county, not just over $7,000 as indicated in some profiles. Three counties have **2** county courts each—Fremont, Park, and Sweetwater. Cases may be filed in either of the two courts in the county and records requests are referred between the two courts within the county. The Small Claims limit is $2,000.

The Park and Sublette County Justice Courts were eliminated on 1/2/95 and were replaced by **County Courts**; however, records remain in place with the new court. Probate is handled by the District Court .

Online Access

Online computer access is not available in Wyoming.

About the Recorder's Office

Organization

23 counties, 23 filing offices. The recording officer is County Clerk. The entire state is in the Mountain Time Zone (MST).

UCC Records

Financing statements are usually filed with the County Clerk. Accounts receivable and farm products require filing at the state level as well. All filing offices will perform UCC searches. Use search request form UCC-11. Searches fees are usually $10.00 per debtor name. Copy fees vary.

Lien Records

Federal tax liens on personal property of businesses are filed with the Secretary of State. Other federal and all state tax liens are filed with the County Clerk. Most counties will perform tax lien searches. Search fees are usually $10.00 per name.

Real Estate Records

County Clerks will **not** perform real estate searches. Copy fees and certification fees vary. The Assessor maintains property tax records.

County Courts and Recording Offices

Albany County

Real Estate Recording—Albany County Clerk, 525 Grand Ave. Room 202, Laramie, WY 82070. 307-721-2547. Fax: 307-721-2544. 9AM-5PM (MST).

Felony, Civil Actions Over $3,000, Probate—2nd Judicial District Court, County Courthouse, 525 Grand, Rm 305, Laramie, WY 82070. 307-721-2508. 9AM-5PM (MST). Access by: Mail, in person.

Misdemeanor, Civil Actions Under $3,000, Eviction, Small Claims—Albany County Court, County Courthouse, 525 Grand, Rm 105, Laramie, WY 82070. 307-742-5747. Fax: 307-742-5610. 8AM-5PM (MST). Access by: Mail, in person.

Big Horn County

Real Estate Recording—Big Horn County Clerk, 420 West C Street, Basin, WY 82410. 307-568-2357. Fax: 307-568-9375. 8AM-5PM (MST).

Felony, Civil Actions Over $3,000, Probate—5th Judicial District Court, PO Box 670, Basin, WY 82410. 307-568-2381. Fax: 307-568-2791. 8AM-Noon, 1-5PM (MST). Access by: Mail, in person.

Civil Actions Under $3,000, Small Claims—Justice Court, PO Box 749, Basin, WY 82410. 307-568-2367. Fax: 307-568-9375. 8AM-5PM (MST). Access by: Fax, mail, in person.

Campbell County

Real Estate Recording—Campbell County Clerk, 500 South Gillette Avenue, Suite 220, Gillette, WY 82716. 307-687-6255. Fax: 307-687-6455. 8AM-5PM (MST).

Felony, Civil Actions Over $7,000, Probate—6th Judicial District Court, PO Box 817, Gillette, WY 82717. 307-682-3424. Fax: 307-687-6209. 8AM-5PM (MST). Access by: Phone, mail, in person.

Civil Actions Under $7,000, Eviction, Small Claims—Campbell County Court, 500 S Gillette Ave #301, Gillette, WY 82716. 307-682-2190. Fax: 307-687-6214. 8AM-5PM (MST). Access by: Mail, in person.

Carbon County

Real Estate Recording—Carbon County Clerk, 415 West Pine, P.O. Box 6, Courthouse, Rawlins, WY 82301. 307-328-2677. Fax: 307-328-2690. 8AM-5PM (MST).

Felony, Civil Actions Over $3,000, Probate—2nd Judicial District Court, PO Box 67, Rawlins, WY 82301. 307-328-2628. Fax: 307-328-2629. 8AM-5PM (MST). Access by: Phone, fax, mail, in person.

Civil Actions Under $3,000, Eviction, Small Claims—County Court, Attn: Chief Clerk, Courthouse, Rawlins, WY 82301. 307-324-6655. Fax: 307-328-2669. 8AM-5PM (MST). Access by: Mail, in person.

Converse County

Real Estate Recording—Converse County Clerk, 107 North 5th Street, Suite 114, Douglas, WY 82633. 307-358-2244. Fax: 307-358-4065. 9AM-5PM (MST).

Felony, Civil Actions Over $7,000, Probate—8th Judicial District Court, Box 189, Douglas, WY 82633. 307-358-3165. Fax: 307-358-6703. 9AM-5PM (MST). Access by: Phone, fax, mail, in person.

Misdemeanor, Civil Actions Under $7,000, Eviction, Small Claims—Converse County Court, PO Box 45, Douglas, WY 82633. 307-358-2196. Fax: 307-358-2501. 8AM-5PM (MST). Access by: Fax, mail, in person.

Crook County

Real Estate Recording—Crook County Clerk, 309 Cleveland Street, P.O. Box 37, Sundance, WY 82729. 307-283-1323. Fax: 307-283-1091. 8AM-5PM (MST).

Felony, Civil Actions Over $7,000, Probate—6th Judicial District Court, Box 904, Sundance, WY 82729. 307-283-2523. Fax: 307-283-2996. 8AM-5PM (MST). Access by: Mail, in person.

Misdemeanor, Civil Actions Under $3,000, Small Claims—Justice Court, PO Box 117, Sundance, WY 82729. 307-283-2929. Fax: 307-283-1091. 8AM-5PM (MST). Access by: Mail, in person.

Fremont County

Real Estate Recording—Fremont County Clerk, 450 N. 2nd Street, Courthouse - Room 220, Lander, WY 82520. 307-332-2405. Fax: 307-332-1132. 8AM-5PM (MST).

Felony, Civil Actions Over $7,000, Probate—9th Judicial District Court, PO Box 370, Lander, WY 82520. 307-332-1134. Fax: 307-332-1143. 8AM-Noon, 1-5PM (MST). Access by: Phone, fax, mail, in person.

Misdemeanor, Civil Actions Under $7,000, Eviction, Small Claims—Dubois County Court, Box 952, Dubois, WY 82513. 307-455-2920. Fax: 307-455-2567. 8AM-Noon (MST). Access by: Mail, in person.

Fremount County Court, 450 N. 2nd Rm 230, Lander, WY 82520. 307-332-3239. Fax: 307-332-4059. 8AM-5PM (MST). Access by: Mail, in person.

Riverton County Court, 818 S Federal Blvd, Riverton, WY 82501. 307-856-7259. Fax: 307-857-3635. 8AM-5PM (MST). Access by: Fax, mail, in person.

Goshen County

Real Estate Recording—Goshen County Clerk, 2125 East A Street, Torrington, WY 82240. 307-532-4051. Fax: 307-532-7375. 8AM-4PM (MST).

Felony, Civil Actions Over $7,000, Probate—8th Judicial District Court, Clerk of District Court, PO Box 818, Torrington, WY 82240. 307-532-2155. Fax: 307-532-8608. 7:30AM-4PM (MST). Access by: Mail, in person.

Misdemeanor, Civil Actions Under $7,000, Eviction, Small Claims—Goshen County, Drawer BB, Torrington, WY 82240. 307-532-2938. Civil: 307-532-2938 X251. Criminal: 307-532-2938 X249. Fax: 307-532-5101. 7AM-4PM (MST). Access by: Mail, in person.

Hot Springs County

Real Estate Recording—Hot Springs County Clerk, 415 Arapahoe Street, Courthouse, Thermopolis, WY 82443. 307-864-3515. Fax: 307-864-5116. 8AM-5PM (MST).

Felony, Civil Actions Over $3,000, Probate—5th Judicial District Court, 415 Arapahoe St, Thermopolis, WY 82443. 307-864-3323. Fax: 307-864-5116. 8AM-5PM (MST). Access by: Mail, in person.

Misdemeanor, Civil Actions Under $3,000, Small Claims—Justice Court, 417 Arapahoe St, Thermopolis, WY 82443. 307-864-5161. Fax: 307-864-5116. 8AM-5PM (MST). Access by: Mail, in person.

Johnson County

Real Estate Recording—Johnson County Clerk, 76 North Main Street, Buffalo, WY 82834. 307-684-7272. Fax: 307-684-2708. 8AM-5PM (MST).

Felony, Civil Actions Over $7,000, Probate—4th Judicial District Court, 76 N Main, Buffalo, WY 82834. 307-684-7271. Fax: 307-684-2708. 8AM-5PM (MST). Access by: Phone, mail, in person.

Misdemeanor, Civil Actions Under $3,000, Small Claims—Justice Court, 639 Fort St., Buffalo, WY 82834. 307-684-5720. Fax: 307-684-5585. 8AM-5PM (MST). Access by: Mail, in person.

Laramie County

Real Estate Recording—Laramie County Clerk, Room 1600, 309 West 20th St., Cheyenne, WY 82001. 307-638-4350. Fax: 307-633-4240. 8:30AM-5PM (MST).

Felony, Civil Actions Over $7,000, Probate—1st Judicial District Court, PO Box 787, 309 W 20th St, Cheyenne, WY

82003. 307-633-4270. Fax: 307-633-4277. 8AM-5PM (MST). Access by: Phone, fax, mail, in person.

Misdemeanor, Civil Actions Under $7,000, Eviction, Small Claims—Laramie County Court, 309 1/2 W 20th St Rm 2300, Cheyenne, WY 82001. 307-633-4298. Fax: 307-633-4392. 8AM-5PM (MST). Access by: Fax, mail, in person.

Lincoln County

Real Estate Recording—Lincoln County Clerk, 925 Sage, Courthouse, Kemmerer, WY 83101. 307-877-9056. Fax: 307-877-3101. 8AM-5PM (MST).

Felony, Civil Actions Over $7,000, Probate—3rd Judicial District Court, PO Drawer 510, Kemmerer, WY 83101. 307-877-9056. Fax: 307-877-6263. 8AM-5PM (MST). Access by: Phone, fax, mail, in person.

Misdemeanor, Civil Actions Under $7,000, Eviction, Small Claims—County Court, PO Box 949, Kemmerer, WY 83101. 307-877-4431. Fax: 307-877-4936. 8AM-5PM (MST). Access by: Mail, in person.

Natrona County

Real Estate Recording—Natrona County Clerk, 200 North Center, Casper, WY 82601. 307-235-9206. Fax: 307-235-9367. 8AM-5PM (MST).

Felony, Civil Actions Over $7,000, Probate—7th Judicial District Court, Clerk of District Court, PO Box 3120, Casper, WY 82602. 307-235-9243. Fax: 307-235-9493. 8AM-5PM (MST). Access by: Phone, fax, mail, in person.

Misdemeanor, Civil Actions Under $7,000, Eviction, Small Claims—Natrana County Court, PO Box 1339, Casper, WY 82602. 307-235-9266. Fax: 307-235-9331. 8AM-5PM (MST). Access by: Phone, fax, mail, in person.

Niobrara County

Real Estate Recording—Niobrara County Clerk, 424 South Elm, Lusk, WY 82225. 307-334-2211. Fax: 307-334-3013. 8AM-4PM (MST).

Felony, Civil Actions Over $3,000, Probate—8th Judicial District Court, Clerk of District Court, PO Box 1318, Lusk, WY 82225. 307-334-2736. Fax: 307-334-2703. 8AM-Noon, 1-4PM (MST). Access by: Phone, fax, mail, in person.

Misdemeanor, Civil Actions Under $3,000, Small Claims—Justice Court, PO Box 209, Lusk, WY 82225. 307-334-3845. Fax: 307-334-3846. 9AM-Noon, 1-5PM (MST). Access by: Mail, in person.

Park County

Real Estate Recording—Park County Clerk, Courthouse, 1002 Sheridan Ave., Cody, WY 82414. 307-527-8600. Fax: 307-527-8626. 8AM-5PM (MST).

Felony, Civil Actions Over $7,000, Probate—5th Judicial District Court, Clerk of District Court, PO Box 1960, Cody, WY 82414. 307-587-2204. Fax: 307-587-6927. 8AM-5PM (MST). Access by: Phone, fax, mail, in person.

Misdemeanor, Civil Actions Under $7,000, Eviction, Small Claims—County Court-Cody, 1002 Sheridan Ave., Cody, WY 82414. 307-587-2204. Fax: 307-587-9788. 8AM-5PM (MST). Access by: Fax, mail, in person.

County Court-Powell, 109 W. 14th, Powell, WY 82435. 307-754-5163. 8AM-5PM (MST). Access by: Mail, in person.

Platte County

Real Estate Recording—Platte County Clerk, 800 9th Street, Wheatland, WY 82201. 307-322-2315. Fax: 307-322-5402. 8AM-5PM (MST).

Felony, Civil Actions Over $7,000, Probate—8th Judicial District Court, PO Box 158, Wheatland, WY 82201. 307-322-3857. Fax: 307-322-5402. 8AM-5PM (MST). Access by: Mail, in person.

Misdemeanor, Civil Actions Under $3,000, Small Claims—Justice Court, PO Box 306, Wheatland, WY 82201. 307-322-3441. Fax: 307-322-5402. 8AM-5PM (MST). Access by: Mail, in person.

Sheridan County

Real Estate Recording—Sheridan County Clerk, 224 South Main Street, Suite B-2, Sheridan, WY 82801. 307-674-2500. Fax: 307-674-2529. 8AM-5PM (MST).

Felony, Civil Actions Over $7,000, Probate—4th Judicial District Court, 224 S. Main, Suite B-11, Sheridan, WY 82801. 307-674-2960. Fax: 307-674-2909. 8AM-5PM (MST). Access by: Mail, in person.

Misdemeanor, Civil Actions Under $7,000, Eviction, Small Claims—County Court, 224 S. Main, Suite B-7, Sheridan, WY 82801. 307-672-9718. Fax: 307-674-2944. 8AM-5PM (MST). Access by: Mail, in person.

Sublette County

Real Estate Recording—Sublette County Clerk, 21 South Tyler Avenue, Pinedale, WY 82941. 307-367-4372. Fax: 307-367-6396. 8AM-5PM (MST).

Felony, Civil Actions Over $7,000, Probate—9th Judicial District Court, PO Box 292, Pinedale, WY 82941. 307-367-4376. Fax: 307-367-6474. 8AM-5PM (MST). Access by: Phone, fax, mail, in person.

Misdemeanor, Civil Actions Under $7,000, Eviction, Small Claims—Sublette County Court, PO Box 1796, Pinedale, WY 82941. 307-367-2556. Fax: 307-367-2658. 8AM-5PM (MST). Access by: Mail, in person.

Sweetwater County

Real Estate Recording—Sweetwater County Clerk, 80 West Flaming Gorge Way, Green River, WY 82935. 307-872-6409. Fax: 307-872-6337. 9AM-5PM (MST).

Felony, Civil Actions Over $7,000, Probate—3rd Judicial District Court, PO Box 430, Green River, WY 82935. 307-872-6440. Fax: 307-872-6439. 9AM-5PM (MST). Access by: Phone, fax, mail, in person.

Misdemeanor, Civil Actions Under $7,000, Eviction, Small Claims—Green River County Court, PO Drawer 1720, Green River, WY 82935. 307-872-6460. Fax: 307-872-6375. 8AM-5PM (MST). Access by: Fax, mail, in person.

Sweetwater County Court, PO Box 2028, Rock Springs, WY 82902. 307-352-6817. Fax: 307-352-6758. 8AM-5PM (MST). Access by: Fax, mail, in person.

Teton County

Real Estate Recording—Teton County Clerk, 200 S. Willow Ste 9, Jackson, WY 83001. 307-733-4430. Fax: 307-739-8681. 8AM-5PM (MST).

Felony, Civil Actions Over $7,000, Probate—9th Judicial District Court, PO Box 4460, Jackson, WY 83001. 307-733-2533. Fax: 307-734-1562. 8AM-5PM (MST). Access by: Phone, fax, mail, in person.

Misdemeanor, Civil Actions Under $3,000, Small Claims—Justice Court, PO Box 2906, Jackson, WY 83001. 307-733-7713. Fax: 307-733-8694. 8AM-5PM (MST). Access by: Mail, in person.

Uinta County

Real Estate Recording—Uinta County Clerk, 225 9th Street, Evanston, WY 82930. 307-783-0306. Fax: 307-783-0511. 8AM-5PM (MST).

Felony, Civil Actions Over $7,000, Probate—3rd Judicial District Court, PO Drawer 1906, Evanston, WY 82931. 307-783-0320. Fax: 307-783-0400. 8AM-5PM (MST). Access by: Phone, fax, mail, in person.

Misdemeanor, Civil Actions Under $7,000, Eviction, Small Claims—Uinta County Court, 225 9th St, 2nd Fl, Evanston, WY 82931. 307-789-2471. Fax: 307-789-5062. 8AM-5PM (MST). Access by: Mail, in person.

Washakie County

Real Estate Recording—Washakie County Clerk, 10th & Big Horn, Courthouse, Worland, WY 82401. 307-347-3131. Fax: 307-347-9366. 8AM-5PM (MST).

Felony, Civil Actions Over $7,000, Probate—5th Judicial District Court, PO Box 862, Worland, WY 82401. 307-347-4821. Fax: 307-347-9366. 8AM-5PM (MST). Access by: Phone, fax, mail, in person.

Misdemeanor, Civil Actions Under $3,000, Small Claims—Justice Court, PO Box 927, Worland, WY 82401. 307-347-2702. Fax: 307-347-9366. 8AM-5PM (MST). Access by: Mail, in person.

Weston County

Real Estate Recording—Weston County Clerk, One West Main, Newcastle, WY 82701. 307-746-4744. Fax: 307-746-9505. 8AM-5PM (MST).

Felony, Civil Actions Over $7,000, Probate—6th Judicial District Court, 1 W Main, Newcastle, WY 82701. 307-746-4778. Fax: 307-746-9505. 8AM-5PM (MST). Access by: Phone, fax, mail, in person.

Misdemeanor, Civil Actions Under $3,000, Small Claims—Justice Court, 6 W Warwick, Newcastle, WY 82701. 307-746-3547. Fax: 307-746-3558. 8:30AM-4:30PM (MST). Access by: Fax, mail, in person.

Federal Courts

US District Court
District of Wyoming

Casper Division, US District Court 111 South Wolcott, Casper, WY 82601. 307-261-5440. Counties: Cases from any county in the state may be assigned here

Cheyenne Division, US District Court PO Box 727, Cheyenne, WY 82003. 307-772-2145. Counties: All counties in Wyoming. Some criminal records are held in Casper

US Bankruptcy Court
District of Wyoming

Cheyenne Division, US Bankruptcy Court, PO Box 1107, Cheyenne, WY 82003. 307-772-2191. Counties: All counties in Wyoming

STATE AGENCY PUBLIC RECORD RESTRICTIONS TABLE

O = Open to Public
F = Special Form Needed
R = Some Access Restrictions (Requesters Screened)
S = Severe Access Restrictions (Signed Authorization, etc.)
N/A = Not Available to the Public
L = Available only at Local Level

State	Criminal Records	UCC Records	Vital Records Birth	Vital Records Death	Vital Records Marriage	Vital Records Divorce	Worker's Comp	Driver History	Vehicle (Single)	Vehicle* (Bulk)	Voter Reg.
Alabama	S	O,F	R	R	R	R	S	S	S	N/A	S
Alaska	N/A	O,F	R	S	S	S	R	S	R	R	O
Arizona	S,L	O,F	S	S	L	L	S	S	S	R	S
Arkansas	S	O,F	S	S	S	S	O	S	R	N/A	O
California	N/A,L	O,F	O	O	O	O	S	S,F	S,F	S	L
Colorado	R	O,F	R	R	L	L	S	S	R,F	S	O
Connecticut	O	O,F	N/A	O	O	L	O	R,F	R,F	R	O
Delaware	S	O,F	S	S	S	L	S	R	R	R	O
Dist. of Columbia	S	O,F	R	R	O	O	R	S	S	S	O
Florida	O	O,F	R	O	O	O	S	R	R	R	R
Georgia	S,F	L,F₁	S	S	S	L	S	S,F	S	N/A	O
Hawaii	O	O,F	S	S	S	S	S	R	N/A	N/A	S
Idaho	S,F	O,F	R	R	R	R	S	R	R	R	S
Illinois	R	O,F	N/A	O	L	L	O	S	R	R	S
Indiana	R,F	O,F	S	S	L	L	S	R	R	N/A	S
Iowa	O	O,F	S	S	S	L	O	R	R	R	S
Kansas	O	O,F	S	O	S	S	O	R	R	S	S
Kentucky	S	O,F	O	O	O	O	R	S	S	S	S
Louisiana	R	L,F₁	S	S	L	L	R	R	R	R	O
Maine	O	O,F	R	R	R	R	R	R	R	R	O
Maryland	R	O,F	S	S	S	S	O	R	R	R	S
Massachusetts	R,F	O,F	R	R	O	L	R	R	R	R	O
Michigan	O	O,F	S	O	O	O	S	R	R	R	O
Minnesota	S	O,F	R	O	L	L	R	R	R	R	S
Mississippi	N/A,L	O,F	R	R	R	L	R	R	R	R	O
Missouri	O	O,F	S	S	O,L	O,L	S	R	R	R	O

| State | Criminal Records | UCC Records | Vital Records | | | | Worker's Comp | Driver History | Vehicle (Single) | Vehicle* (Bulk) | Voter Reg. |
			Birth	Death	Marriage	Divorce					
Montana	O	O,F	R	R	L	L	S	R	R	R	R
Nebraska	O	O,F	R	R	R	R	O	R	R	R	S
Nevada	N/A,L	O,F	R	R	L	L	S	R	R	R	S
New Hampshire	S	O,F	S	S	S	S	S	R	R	R	O
New Jersey	N/A	O,F	O	O	O	O	O,F	S	S	R	R
New Mexico	S	O,F	S	S	L	L	S	S	S	S	S
New York	N/A	O,F	S	S	S	S	S	R	R	S	O
North Carolina	N/A,L	O,F	O	O	O	O	R	R	R	R	O
North Dakota	S	O,F	R	O	O	L	S	R	R	R	O
Ohio	S,F	O,F	O	O	L	L	R	R	R	S	O
Oklahoma	O	O,F	S	O	L	L	O	R	R	N/A	O
Oregon	O	O,F	S	R	O	O	S	S	S	S	S
Pennsylvania	R,F	O,F	S	S	L	L	N/A	S	S	S	S
Rhode Island	S,L	O,F	S	S	S	L	S	R	R	R	S
South Carolina	O	O,F	R	R	R	R	S	R	R	R	O
South Dakota	S,F	O,F	O	O	O	O	S	R	R	R	O
Tennessee	N/A,L	O,F	S	S	S	S	N/A	R	R	R	S
Texas	S,F	O,F	S	S	O,L	O,L	N/A	R	R	R	R
Utah	N/A,L	O,F	S	S	L	L	S	S	S	S	O
Vermont	N/A,L	O,F	O	O	O	O	S	R	R	R	O
Virginia	S	O,F	S	S	S	S	S	S	S	S	N/A
Washington	O,F	O,F	O	O	O	O	S	R	R	R	R
West Virginia	S,F	O,F	R	R	O	L	S	R	R	R	O
Wisconsin	R	O,F	S	S	S	S	S	R	R	R	O
Wyoming	S,F	O,F	S	S	S	S	S	R,F	R	R	S

1 = Georgia and Louisiana are filed locally, but a state central index is available.

* = This category refers primarily to release of data for marketing purposes. All states cooperate with the release of information for vehicle recall and statistical purposes. Alos, please note that many state DMVs are watching the outcome of DPPA litigation against the US Government and release of DMV records are subject to change in the pursuing months.

The Appeals and Regional Records Services Facility Locator

State	Circuit	Appeals Court	Regional Records Services Facility
AK	9	San Francisco, CA	Anchorage (Some temporary storage in Seattle)
AL	11	Atlanta, GA	Atlanta
AR	8	St. Louis, MO	Fort Worth
AZ	9	San Francisco, CA	Los Angeles
CA	9	San Francisco, CA	Los Angeles (Central & Southern) San Francisco (Eastern & Northern)
CO	10	Denver, CO	Denver
CT	2	New York, NY	Boston
DC		Washington, DC	Washington, DC
DE	3	Philadelphia, PA	Philadelphia
FL	11	Atlanta, GA	Atlanta
GA	11	Atlanta, GA	Atlanta
GU	9	San Francisco, CA	San Francisco
HI	9	San Francisco, CA	San Francisco
IA	8	St. Louis, MO	Kansas City, MO
ID	9	San Francisco, CA	Seattle
IL	7	Chicago, IL	Chicago
IN	7	Chicago, IL	Chicago
KS	10	Denver, CO	Kansas City, MO
KY	6	Cincinnati, OH	Atlanta
LA	5	New Orleans, LA	Fort Worth
MA	1	Boston, MA	Boston
MD	4	Richmond, VA	Philadelphia
ME	1	Boston, MA	Boston
MI	6	Cincinnati, OH	Chicago
MN	8	St. Louis, MO	Chicago
MO	8	St. Louis, MO	Kansas City, MO
MS	5	New Orleans, LA	Atlanta

State	Circuit	Appeals Court	Regional Records Services Facility
MT	9	San Francisco, CA	Denver
NC	4	Richmond, VA	Atlanta
ND	8	St. Louis, MO	Denver
NE	8	St. Louis, MO	Kansas City, MO
NH	1	Boston, MA	Boston
NJ	3	Philadelphia, PA	New York[1]
NM	10	Denver, CO	Denver
NV	9	San Francisco, CA	Los Angeles (Clark County) San Francisco (Other counties)
NY	2	New York, NY	New York[1]
OH	6	Cincinnati, OH	Chicago Dayton (Some bankruptcy)
OK	10	Denver, CO	Fort Worth
OR	9	San Francisco, CA	Seattle
PA	3	Philadelphia, PA	Philadelphia
PR	1	Boston, MA	New York[1]
RI	1	Boston, MA	Boston
SC	4	Richmond, VA	Atlanta
SD	8	St. Louis, MO	Denver
TN	6	Cincinnati, OH	Atlanta
TX	5	New Orleans, LA	Fort Worth
UT	10	Denver, CO	Denver
VA	4	Richmond, VA	Philadelphia
VI	3	Philadelphia, PA	New York[1]
VT	2	New York, NY	Boston
WA	9	San Francisco, CA	Seattle
WI	7	Chicago, IL	Chicago
WV	4	Richmond, VA	Philadelphia
WY	10	Denver, CO	Denver

[1] Court records will be transferred to Lee's Summit, MO by July 1998.

According to some odd logic, the following Regional Records Services Facilities are located somewhere else:

Atlanta—East Point, GA
Boston—Waltham, MA
Los Angeles—Laguna Niguel, CA
San Francisco—San Bruno, CA

US Appeals Courts and Regional Records Services Facility Addresses and Telephone Numbers

US Courts of Appeals

District of Columbia Circuit, US Court of Appeals, E Barrett Prettyman Courthouse, 333 Constitution Ave, NW, Washington, DC, 20001-2866. 202-216-7300

First Circuit, US Court of Appeals, 1606 John W. McCormack PO and Courthouse, Boston, MA 02109. 617-223-9057

Second Circuit, US Court of Appeals, US Courthouse, Foley Square, New York, NY 10007. 212-857-8500

Third Circuit, US Court of Appeals, 21400 US Courthouse, 601 Market St, Philadelphia, PA 19106. 215-597-2995

Fourth Circuit, US Court of Appeals, 1100 E. Main St., Rm 501, Richmond, VA 23219. 804-771-2213

Fifth Circuit, US Court of Appeals, 100 US Courthouse, 600 Camp St, New Orleans, LA 70130. 504-589-6514

Sixth Circuit, US Court of Appeals, 532 US Courthouse Building, 100 E Fifth St, Cincinnati, OH 45202. 513-564-7000

Seventh Circuit, US Court of Appeals, 219 S.Dearborn St, Chicago, IL 60604. 312-435-5850

Eighth Circuit, US Court of Appeals, 511 US Court and Custom House, 1114 Market St, St Louis, MO 63101. 314-539-3609

Ninth Circuit, US Court of Appeals, 95 7th St, San Francisco, CA 94103-1526. 415-556-9800

Tenth Circuit, US Court of Appeals, Byron White US Courthouse, 1823 Stout St, Denver, CO 80257. 303-844-3157

Eleventh Circuit, US Court of Appeals, 56 Forsyth St., NW, Atlanta, GA 30303. 404-331-6187

Federal Circuit, US Court of Appeals, 717 Madison Place, NW, Washington, DC, DC 20439. 202-633-6550

US Court of Appeals for the Armed Forces, 450 E St., NW, Washington, DC, DC 20442. 202-761-5210

US Court of Federal Claims, 717 Madison Place, NW, Washington, DC, DC 20005. 202-219-9657

US Court of International Trade, One Federal Plaza, New York, NY 10278-0001. 212-264-2814

US Tax Court, 400 Second St., NW, Washington, DC, DC 20217. 202-606-8754

Regional Records Services Facilities

Alaska, Regional Records Services Facility - Anchorage, 654 W 3rd Ave, Anchorage, AK 99501. 907-271-2441

California, Regional Records Services Facility - Los Angeles, 24000 Avila Rd., Laguna Niguel, CA 92656. 714-360-2626

California Regional Records Services Facility - San Francisco, 1000 Commodore Drive, San Bruno, CA 94066. 415-876-9001

Colorado, Regional Records Services Facility - Denver, PO Box 25307, Denver, CO 80225-0307. 303-236-0804

District of Columbia, Washington National Records Center, Washington, DC, 4205 Suitland Road, Suitland, MD, DC 20746. 301-457-7010

Georgia, Regional Records Services Facility - Atlanta, 1557 St Joseph Avenue, East Point, GA 30344. 404-763-7474

Illinois, Regional Records Services Facility - Chicago, 7358 South Pulaski Road, Chicago, IL 60629. 773-581-7816

Massachusetts, Regional Records Services Facility - Boston, 380 Trapelo Rd., Waltham, MA 02154. 781-647-8104

Missouri—Lee's Summit, Regional Records Services Facility - Lee's Summit, 200 Space Center Dr., Lee's Summit, MO 64064. 816-478-7079.

Missouri—Kansas City, Regional Records Services Facility - Kansas City, 2312 East Bannister Rd., Kansas City, MO 64131. 816-926-7272

*New Jersey, Regional Records Services Facility - New York, Building 22, Military Ocean Terminal, Bayonne, NJ 07002-5388. 201-823-7242

Ohio, Regional Records Services Facility, 3150 Springboro Rd, Dayton, OH 45439. 937-225-2852

Pennsylvania, Regional Records Services Facility - Philadelphia, 14700 Townsend Rd., Philadelphia, PA 19154. 215-671-8241

Texas, Regional Records Services Facility - Fort Worth, PO Box 6216., Fort Worth, TX 76115. 817-334-5515

Washington, Regional Records Services Facility - Seattle, 6125 Sand Point Way NE, Seattle, WA 98115. 206-526-6504

* Some records are at the Missouri—Lee's Summit location, depending on the accession number.